PROPERTY OF
LIBRARY
Tompkins-Cortland Community College
170 North St. P.O. Box 139
Dryden, N.Y. 13053-0139

D0931634

HANDBOOK
of
PSYCHOLOGY

HANDBOOK
of
PSYCHOLOGY

VOLUME 10
ASSESSMENT PSYCHOLOGY

John R. Graham
Jack A. Naglieri

Volume Editors

Irving B. Weiner

Editor-in-Chief

John Wiley & Sons, Inc.

This book is printed on acid-free paper. ♾

Copyright © 2003 by John Wiley & Sons, Inc., Hoboken, New Jersey. All rights reserved.

Published simultaneously in Canada.

No part of this publication may be reproduced, stored in a retrieval system, or transmitted in any form or by any means, electronic, mechanical, photocopying, recording, scanning, or otherwise, except as permitted under Section 107 or 108 of the 1976 United States Copyright Act, without either the prior written permission of the Publisher, or authorization through payment of the appropriate per-copy fee to the Copyright Clearance Center, Inc., 222 Rosewood Drive, Danvers, MA 01923, (978) 750-8400, fax (978) 750-4470, or on the web at www.copyright.com. Requests to the Publisher for permission should be addressed to the Permissions Department, John Wiley & Sons, Inc., 111 River Street, Hoboken, NJ 07030, (201) 748-6011, fax (201) 748-6008, e-mail: permcoordinator@wiley.com.

Limit of Liability/Disclaimer of Warranty: While the publisher and author have used their best efforts in preparing this book, they make no representations or warranties with respect to the accuracy or completeness of the contents of this book and specifically disclaim any implied warranties of merchantability or fitness for a particular purpose. No warranty may be created or extended by sales representatives or written sales materials. The advice and strategies contained herein may not be suitable for your situation. You should consult with a professional where appropriate. Neither the publisher nor author shall be liable for any loss of profit or any other commercial damages, including but not limited to special, incidental, consequential, or other damages.

This publication is designed to provide accurate and authoritative information in regard to the subject matter covered. It is sold with the understanding that the publisher is not engaged in rendering professional services. If legal, accounting, medical, psychological or any other expert assistance is required, the services of a competent professional person should be sought.

Designations used by companies to distinguish their products are often claimed as trademarks. In all instances where John Wiley & Sons, Inc. is aware of a claim, the product names appear in initial capital or all capital letters. Readers, however, should contact the appropriate companies for more complete information regarding trademarks and registration.

For general information on our other products and services please contact our Customer Care Department within the U.S. at (800) 762-2974, outside the United States at (317) 572-3993 or fax (317) 572-4002.

Wiley also publishes its books in a variety of electronic formats. Some content that appears in print may not be available in electronic books.

Library of Congress Cataloging-in-Publication Data:

Handbook of psychology / Irving B. Weiner, editor-in-chief.
     p. cm.
     Includes bibliographical references and indexes.
     Contents: v. 1. History of psychology / edited by Donald K. Freedheim — v. 2. Research methods in psychology / edited by John A. Schinka, Wayne F. Velicer — v. 3. Biological psychology / edited by Michela Gallagher, Randy J. Nelson — v. 4. Experimental psychology / edited by Alice F. Healy, Robert W. Proctor — v. 5. Personality and social psychology / edited by Theodore Millon, Melvin J. Lerner — v. 6. Developmental psychology / edited by Richard M. Lerner, M. Ann Easterbrooks, Jayanthi Mistry — v. 7. Educational psychology / edited by William M. Reynolds, Gloria E. Miller — v. 8. Clinical psychology / edited by George Stricker, Thomas A. Widiger — v. 9. Health psychology / edited by Arthur M. Nezu, Christine Maguth Nezu, Pamela A. Geller — v. 10. Assessment psychology / edited by John R. Graham, Jack A. Naglieri — v. 11. Forensic psychology / edited by Alan M. Goldstein — v. 12. Industrial and organizational psychology / edited by Walter C. Borman, Daniel R. Ilgen, Richard J. Klimoski.
     ISBN 0-471-17669-9 (set) — ISBN 0-471-38320-1 (cloth : alk. paper : v. 1)
   — ISBN 0-471-38513-1 (cloth : alk. paper : v. 2) — ISBN 0-471-38403-8 (cloth : alk. paper : v. 3)
   — ISBN 0-471-39262-6 (cloth : alk. paper : v. 4) — ISBN 0-471-38404-6 (cloth : alk. paper : v. 5)
   — ISBN 0-471-38405-4 (cloth : alk. paper : v. 6) — ISBN 0-471-38406-2 (cloth : alk. paper : v. 7)
   — ISBN 0-471-39263-4 (cloth : alk. paper : v. 8) — ISBN 0-471-38514-X (cloth : alk. paper : v. 9)
   — ISBN 0-471-38407-0 (cloth : alk. paper : v. 10) — ISBN 0-471-38321-X (cloth : alk. paper : v. 11)
   — ISBN 0-471-38408-9 (cloth : alk. paper : v. 12)
     1. Psychology. I. Weiner, Irving B.

BF121.H1955 2003
150—dc21
                                       2002066380

Printed in the United States of America.

10   9   8   7   6   5   4   3   2   1

Editorial Board

Volume 1
History of Psychology

Donald K. Freedheim, PhD
Case Western Reserve University
Cleveland, Ohio

Volume 2
Research Methods in Psychology

John A. Schinka, PhD
University of South Florida
Tampa, Florida

Wayne F. Velicer, PhD
University of Rhode Island
Kingston, Rhode Island

Volume 3
Biological Psychology

Michela Gallagher, PhD
Johns Hopkins University
Baltimore, Maryland

Randy J. Nelson, PhD
Ohio State University
Columbus, Ohio

Volume 4
Experimental Psychology

Alice F. Healy, PhD
University of Colorado
Boulder, Colorado

Robert W. Proctor, PhD
Purdue University
West Lafayette, Indiana

Volume 5
Personality and Social Psychology

Theodore Millon, PhD
Institute for Advanced Studies in
    Personology and Psychopathology
Coral Gables, Florida

Melvin J. Lerner, PhD
Florida Atlantic University
Boca Raton, Florida

Volume 6
Developmental Psychology

Richard M. Lerner, PhD
M. Ann Easterbrooks, PhD
Jayanthi Mistry, PhD

Tufts University
Medford, Massachusetts

Volume 7
Educational Psychology

William M. Reynolds, PhD
Humboldt State University
Arcata, California

Gloria E. Miller, PhD
University of Denver
Denver, Colorado

Volume 8
Clinical Psychology

George Stricker, PhD
Adelphi University
Garden City, New York

Thomas A. Widiger, PhD
University of Kentucky
Lexington, Kentucky

Volume 9
Health Psychology

Arthur M. Nezu, PhD
Christine Maguth Nezu, PhD
Pamela A. Geller, PhD

Drexel University
Philadelphia, Pennsylvania

Volume 10
Assessment Psychology

John R. Graham, PhD
Kent State University
Kent, Ohio

Jack A. Naglieri, PhD
George Mason University
Fairfax, Virginia

Volume 11
Forensic Psychology

Alan M. Goldstein, PhD
John Jay College of Criminal
    Justice–CUNY
New York, New York

Volume 12
Industrial and Organizational
Psychology

Walter C. Borman, PhD
University of South Florida
Tampa, Florida

Daniel R. Ilgen, PhD
Michigan State University
East Lansing, Michigan

Richard J. Klimoski, PhD
George Mason University
Fairfax, Virginia

Parents are powerful forces in the development of their sons and daughters. In recognition of that positive influence, we dedicate our efforts on this book to the loving memory of Craig Parris (1910–2001) and Sam Naglieri (1926–2001).

Handbook of Psychology **Preface**

Psychology at the beginning of the twenty-first century has become a highly diverse field of scientific study and applied technology. Psychologists commonly regard their discipline as the science of behavior, and the American Psychological Association has formally designated 2000 to 2010 as the "Decade of Behavior." The pursuits of behavioral scientists range from the natural sciences to the social sciences and embrace a wide variety of objects of investigation. Some psychologists have more in common with biologists than with most other psychologists, and some have more in common with sociologists than with most of their psychological colleagues. Some psychologists are interested primarily in the behavior of animals, some in the behavior of people, and others in the behavior of organizations. These and other dimensions of difference among psychological scientists are matched by equal if not greater heterogeneity among psychological practitioners, who currently apply a vast array of methods in many different settings to achieve highly varied purposes.

Psychology has been rich in comprehensive encyclopedias and in handbooks devoted to specific topics in the field. However, there has not previously been any single handbook designed to cover the broad scope of psychological science and practice. The present 12-volume *Handbook of Psychology* was conceived to occupy this place in the literature. Leading national and international scholars and practitioners have collaborated to produce 297 authoritative and detailed chapters covering all fundamental facets of the discipline, and the *Handbook* has been organized to capture the breadth and diversity of psychology and to encompass interests and concerns shared by psychologists in all branches of the field.

Two unifying threads run through the science of behavior. The first is a common history rooted in conceptual and empirical approaches to understanding the nature of behavior. The specific histories of all specialty areas in psychology trace their origins to the formulations of the classical philosophers and the methodology of the early experimentalists, and appreciation for the historical evolution of psychology in all of its variations transcends individual identities as being one kind of psychologist or another. Accordingly, Volume 1 in the *Handbook* is devoted to the history of psychology as it emerged in many areas of scientific study and applied technology.

A second unifying thread in psychology is a commitment to the development and utilization of research methods suitable for collecting and analyzing behavioral data. With attention both to specific procedures and their application in particular settings, Volume 2 addresses research methods in psychology.

Volumes 3 through 7 of the *Handbook* present the substantive content of psychological knowledge in five broad areas of study: biological psychology (Volume 3), experimental psychology (Volume 4), personality and social psychology (Volume 5), developmental psychology (Volume 6), and educational psychology (Volume 7). Volumes 8 through 12 address the application of psychological knowledge in five broad areas of professional practice: clinical psychology (Volume 8), health psychology (Volume 9), assessment psychology (Volume 10), forensic psychology (Volume 11), and industrial and organizational psychology (Volume 12). Each of these volumes reviews what is currently known in these areas of study and application and identifies pertinent sources of information in the literature. Each discusses unresolved issues and unanswered questions and proposes future directions in conceptualization, research, and practice. Each of the volumes also reflects the investment of scientific psychologists in practical applications of their findings and the attention of applied psychologists to the scientific basis of their methods.

The *Handbook of Psychology* was prepared for the purpose of educating and informing readers about the present state of psychological knowledge and about anticipated advances in behavioral science research and practice. With this purpose in mind, the individual *Handbook* volumes address the needs and interests of three groups. First, for graduate students in behavioral science, the volumes provide advanced instruction in the basic concepts and methods that define the fields they cover, together with a review of current knowledge, core literature, and likely future developments. Second, in addition to serving as graduate textbooks, the volumes offer professional psychologists an opportunity to read and contemplate the views of distinguished colleagues concerning the central thrusts of research and leading edges of practice in their respective fields. Third, for psychologists seeking to become conversant with fields outside their own specialty and for persons outside of psychology seeking information about psychological matters, the *Handbook* volumes serve as a reference source for expanding their knowledge and directing them to additional sources in the literature.

The preparation of this *Handbook* was made possible by the diligence and scholarly sophistication of the 25 volume editors and co-editors who constituted the Editorial Board. As Editor-in-Chief, I want to thank each of them for the pleasure of their collaboration in this project. I compliment them for having recruited an outstanding cast of contributors to their volumes and then working closely with these authors to achieve chapters that will stand each in their own right as valuable contributions to the literature. I would like finally to express my appreciation to the editorial staff of John Wiley and Sons for the opportunity to share in the development of this project and its pursuit to fruition, most particularly to Jennifer Simon, Senior Editor, and her two assistants, Mary Porterfield and Isabel Pratt. Without Jennifer's vision of the *Handbook* and her keen judgment and unflagging support in producing it, the occasion to write this preface would not have arrived.

IRVING B. WEINER
Tampa, Florida

Volume Preface

The title of this volume, *Assessment Psychology,* was deliberately chosen to make the point that the assessment activities of psychologists constitute a legitimate and important subdiscipline within psychology. The methods and techniques developed by assessment pioneers were central in establishing a professional role for psychologists in schools, hospitals, and other settings. Although interest in psychological assessment has waxed and waned over the years and various assessment procedures and instruments have come under attack, the premise of this volume is that assessment psychology is alive and well and continues to be of paramount importance in the professional functioning of most psychologists. In addition, assessment psychology contributes greatly to the well-being of the thousands of individuals who are assessed each year.

A primary goal of this volume is to address important issues in assessment psychology. Some of these issues have been around a long time (e.g., psychometric characteristics of assessment procedures), whereas others have come on the scene more recently (e.g., computer-based psychological assessment). The volume also has chapters devoted to the unique features of assessment in different kinds of settings (adult and child mental health, schools, medical centers, business and industry, forensic and correctional, and geriatric). Other chapters address assessment in various domains of functioning (e.g., cognitive and intellectual, interests, personality and psychopathology). Still other chapters address various approaches used in the assessment process (e.g., interviews, behavioral methods, projective approaches, and self-report inventories). The final chapter summarizes the major conclusions reached by other authors in the volume and speculates about the future of assessment psychology.

We should also state clearly what this volume does not include. Although many specific tests and procedures are described (some in greater detail than others), the volume is not intended as a practical guide for the administration and interpretation of tests and other procedures. There are other excellent interpretive handbooks already available, and many of these are referenced in the various chapters of this volume.

It is our hope that the detailed and insightful consideration of issues and problems will provide a strong foundation for all who are part of the discipline of assessment psychology, regardless of the specific techniques or instruments that they employ. We view this volume as having been successful if it raises the sensitivity of assessment psychologists to the important issues inherent in the use of assessment procedures in a wide variety of settings and to the strengths and weaknesses of the various approaches and instruments.

This volume is intended for several audiences. Graduate students in psychology, education, and related disciplines should find the chapters informative and thought provoking as they master the assessment process. Psychologists who engage in psychological assessment, either routinely or on a more limited basis, should find the various chapters to be enlightening. Finally, those who use the results of psychological assessment (e.g., medical and social work professionals, teachers, parents, clients) should become more informed consumers after reading the chapters in this volume.

We want to thank those who contributed to the completion of this volume. Of course, the most important contributors are those who wrote the individual chapters. Their efforts resulted in informative and thought-provoking chapters. The editor-in-chief of the series of which this volume is a part, Irv Weiner, deserves considerable credit for his organizational skills in making the project happen as planned and for his specific contributions to each of the chapters in this volume. We also want to thank Alice Early and Brian O'Reilly for their editorial contributions. The Department of Psychology at Kent State University and the Department of Psychology and the Center for Cognitive Development at George Mason University supported this project in various ways.

JOHN R. GRAHAM
JACK A. NAGLIERI

Contents

PART TWO
ASSESSMENT SETTINGS

PART THREE
ASSESSMENT METHODS

Contributors

R. Michael Bagby, PhD
Department of Psychiatry
University of Toronto
Toronto, Ontario, Canada

Paul Barrett, PhD
Department of Psychiatry
Henry Ford Health System
Detroit, Michigan

Yossef S. Ben-Porath, PhD
Department of Psychology
Kent State University
Kent, Ohio

Bruce A. Bracken, PhD
School of Education
College of William and Mary
Williamsburg, Virginia

Jeffery P. Braden, PhD
Department of Educational Psychology
University of Wisconsin
Madison, Wisconsin

James N. Butcher, PhD
Department of Psychology
University of Minnesota
Minneapolis, Minnesota

Andrew D. Carson, PhD
Riverside Publishing
Itasca, Illinois

Amanda Jill Clemence, BA
Department of Psychology
University of Tennessee
Knoxville, Tennessee

Robert J. Craig, PhD
West Side VA Medical Center and
    Illinois School of Professional Psychology
Chicago, Illinois

Philip A. DeFina, PhD
Department of Clinical Neuropsychology
The Fielding Institute
Santa Barbara, California

Kevin S. Douglas, LLB, PhD
Department of Mental Health Law and Policy
Louis de la Parte Florida Mental Health Institute
University of South Florida
Tampa, Florida

Barry A. Edelstein, PhD
Department of Psychology
West Virginia University
Morgantown, West Virginia

Howard N. Garb, PhD
Veterans Administration Pittsburgh
    Healthcare System and Department of Psychiatry
University of Pittsburgh
Pittsburgh, Pennsylvania

Kurt F. Geisinger, PhD
Office of Academic Affairs and
    Department of Psychology
The University of St. Thomas
Houston, Texas

Elkhonon Goldberg, PhD
Department of Neurology
New York University School of Medicine
New York, New York

John R. Graham, PhD
Department of Psychology
Kent State University
Kent, Ohio

Leonard Handler, PhD
Department of Psychology
University of Tennessee
Knoxville, Tennessee

Stephen N. Haynes, PhD
Department of Psychology
University of Hawaii Manoa
Honolulu, Hawaii

Richard J. Klimoski, PhD
Department of Psychology
George Mason University
Fairfax, Virginia

Gerald P. Koocher, PhD
Graduate School for Health Studies
Simmons College
Boston, Massachusetts

Lesley P. Koven, MA
Department of Psychology
West Virginia University
Morgantown, West Virginia

David Lachar, PhD
Department of Psychiatry and Behavioral Sciences
University of Texas Houston Health Science Center
Houston, Texas

Rodney L. Lowman, PhD
College of Organizational Studies
Alliant International University
San Diego, California

Ronald R. Martin, PhD
Department of Psychology
West Virginia University
Morgantown, West Virginia

Mark E. Maruish, PhD
United Behavioral Health
Minneapolis, Minnesota

AnneMarie McCullen, MA
Department of Psychology
University of Windsor
Windsor, Ontario, Canada

Jennifer J. McGrath, MA
Department of Psychology
Bowling Green State University
Bowling Green, Ohio

Edwin I. Megargee, PhD
Department of Psychology
Florida State University
Tallahassee, Florida

Jack A. Naglieri, PhD
Department of Psychology and
    Center for Cognitive Development
George Mason University
Fairfax, Virginia

William H. O'Brien, PhD
Department of Psychology
Bowling Green State University
Bowling Green, Ohio

James R. P. Ogloff, JD, PhD
School of Psychology, Psychiatry, and
    Psychological Medicine
Monash University and Victorian
    Institute of Forensic Mental Health
Victoria, Australia

Kenneth Podell, PhD
Department of Psychiatry
Henry Ford Health System
Detroit, Michigan

Michael C. Ramsay, PhD
Department of Educational Psychology
Texas A&M University
College Station, Texas

Celiane M. Rey-Casserly, PhD
Department of Psychiatry
Children's Hospital and Harvard Medical School
Boston, Massachusetts

Cecil R. Reynolds, PhD
Department of Educational Psychology
Texas A&M University
College Station, Texas

Bridget Rivera, MS
California School of Professional Psychology
Alliant International University
San Diego, California

Yana Suchy, PhD
Department of Psychology
Finch University of Health Sciences
Chicago Medical School
North Chicago, Illinois

Jerry J. Sweet, PhD
Evanston Northwestern Healthcare and
    Department of Psychiatry and Behavioral Sciences
Northwestern University Medical School
Chicago, Illinois

Steven M. Tovian, PhD
Evanston Northwestern Healthcare and
    Department of Psychiatry and Behavioral Sciences
Northwestern University Medical School
Chicago, Illinois

Andrea Turner, BSc
Department of Psychology
University of Windsor
Windsor, Ontario, Canada

Donald J. Viglione, PhD
California School of Professional Psychology
Alliant University
San Diego, California

John D. Wasserman, PhD
Department of Psychology and
    Center for Cognitive Development
George Mason University
Fairfax, Virginia

Irving B. Weiner, PhD
Department of Psychiatry and Behavioral Medicine
University of South Florida
Tampa, Florida

Nicole Wild, BSc
Department of Psychology
University of Windsor
Windsor, Ontario, Canada

Lori B. Zukin, PhD
Booz Allen Hamilton
McLean, Virginia

PART ONE

ASSESSMENT ISSUES

CHAPTER 1

The Assessment Process

IRVING B. WEINER

Assessment psychology is the field of behavioral science concerned with methods of identifying similarities and differences among people in their personal characteristics and capacities. As such, psychological assessment comprises a variety of procedures that are employed in diverse ways to achieve numerous purposes. Assessment has sometimes been equated with testing, but the assessment process goes beyond merely giving tests. Psychological assessment involves integrating information gleaned not only from test protocols, but also from interview responses, behavioral observations, collateral reports, and historical documents. The *Standards for Educational and Psychological Testing* (American Educational Research Association [AERA], American Psychological Association, and National Council on Measurement in Education, 1999) specify in this regard that

> the use of tests provides one method of collecting information within the larger framework of a psychological assessment of an individual. . . . A psychological assessment is a comprehensive examination undertaken to answer specific questions about a client's psychological functioning during a particular time interval or to predict a client's psychological functioning in the future. (p. 119)

The diverse ways in which assessment procedures are employed include many alternative approaches to obtaining and combining information from different sources, and the numerous purposes that assessment serves arise in response to a broad range of referral questions raised in such companion fields as clinical, educational, health, forensic, and industrial/organizational psychology. Subsequent chapters in this volume

elaborate the diversity of assessment procedures, the nature of the assessment questions that arise in various settings, and the types of assessment methods commonly employed to address these questions.

This introductory chapter sets the stage for what is to follow by conceptualizing assessment as a three-stage process comprising an initial phase of *information input,* a subsequent phase of *information evaluation,* and a final phase of *information output.* Information input involves *collecting* assessment data of appropriate kinds and in sufficient amounts to address referral questions in meaningful and useful ways. Information evaluation consists of *interpreting* assessment data in a manner that provides accurate descriptions of respondents' psychological characteristics and behavioral tendencies. Information output calls for *utilizing* descriptions of respondents to formulate conclusions and recommendations that help to answer referral questions. Each of these phases of the assessment process requires assessors to accomplish some distinctive tasks, and each involves choices and decisions that touch on critical issues in conducting psychological assessments.

COLLECTING ASSESSMENT INFORMATION

The process of collecting assessment information begins with a formulation of the purposes that the assessment is intended to serve. A clear sense of why an assessment is being conducted helps examiners select tests and other sources of information that will provide an adequate basis for arriving at useful conclusions and recommendations. Additionally helpful in planning the data collection process is attention to several examiner, respondent, and data management issues that influence the nature and utility of whatever findings are obtained.

Formulating Goals

Psychological assessments are instigated by referrals that pose questions about aspects of a person's psychological functioning or likely future behavior. When clearly stated and psychologically relevant, *referral questions* guide psychologists in determining what kinds of assessment data to collect, what considerations to address in examining these data, and what implications of their findings to emphasize in their reports. If referral questions lack clarity or psychological relevance, some reformulation is necessary to give direction to the assessment process. For example, a referral in a clinical setting that asks vaguely for personality evaluation or differential diagnosis needs to be specified in consultation with the referring person to identify why a personality evaluation is being sought or what diagnostic possibilities are at issue. Assessment in the absence of a specific referral question can result in a sterile exercise in which neither the data collection process nor the psychologist's inferences can be focused in a meaningful way.

Even when adequately specified, referral questions are not always psychological in nature. Assessors doing forensic work are frequently asked to evaluate whether criminal defendants were insane at the time of their alleged offense. *Sanity* is a legal term, however, not a psychological term. There are no assessment methods designed to identify insanity, nor are there any research studies in which being insane has been used as an independent variable. In instances of this kind, in order to help assessors plan their procedures and frame their reports, the referral must be translated into psychological terms, as in defining *insanity* as the inability to distinguish reality from fantasy.

As a further challenge in formulating assessment goals, specific and psychologically phrased referral questions may still lack clarity as a consequence of addressing complex and multidetermined patterns of behavior. In employment evaluations, for example, a referring person may want to know which of three individuals is likely to perform best in a position of leadership or executive responsibility. To address this type of question effectively, assessors must first be able to identify psychological characteristics that are likely to make a difference in the particular circumstances, as by proceeding, in this example, in the belief that being energetic, decisive, assertive, self-confident, and reasonably unflappable contribute to showing effective and responsible leadership.

Then the data collection process can be planned to measure these characteristics, and the eventual report can be focused on using them as a basis for recommending a hiring decision.

Selecting Tests

The multiple sources of assessment information previously noted include the results of formal psychological testing with standardized instruments; responses to questions asked in structured and unstructured interviews; observations of behavior in various types of contrived situations and natural settings; reports from relatives, friends, employers, and other collateral persons concerning an individual's previous life history and current characteristics and behavioral tendencies; and documents such as medical records, school records, and written reports of earlier assessments. Individual assessments vary considerably in the availability and utility of these diverse sources of information. Assessments may sometimes be based entirely on record reviews and collateral reports, because the person being assessed is unwilling to be seen directly by an examiner or is for some reason prevented from doing so. Some persons being assessed are quite forthcoming when interviewed but are reluctant to be tested; others find it difficult to talk about themselves but are quite responsive to testing procedures; and in still other cases, in which both interview and test data are ample, there may be a dearth of other information sources on which to draw.

There is little way to know before the fact which sources of information will prove most critical or valuable in an assessment process. What collateral informants say about a person in a particular instance may be more revealing and reliable than what the person says about him- or herself, and in some instances historical documents may prove more informative and dependable than either first-person or collateral reports. Behavioral observations and interview data may sometimes contribute more to an adequate assessment than standardized tests, or may even render testing superfluous; whereas in other instances formal psychological testing may reveal vital diagnostic information that would otherwise not have been uncovered.

The fact that psychological assessment can proceed effectively without psychological testing helps to distinguish between these two activities. The terms *psychological assessment* and *psychological testing* are sometimes used synonymously, as noted earlier, but psychological testing is only one among many sources of information that may be utilized in conducting a psychological assessment. Whereas *testing* refers to the administration of standardized measuring instruments, *assessment* involves multiple data collection procedures leading to the integration of information from diverse sources. Thus the data collection procedures employed in testing contribute only a portion of the information that is typically utilized in the complex decision-making process that constitutes assessment. This distinction between assessment and testing has previously been elaborated by Fernandez-Ballesteros (1997), Maloney and Ward (1976, chapter 3), and Matarazzo (1990), among others.

Nonetheless, psychological testing stands out among the data collection procedures employed in psychological assessment as the one most highly specialized, diverse, and in need of careful regulation. Psychological testing brings numerous issues to the assessment process, beginning with selection of an appropriate test battery from among an extensive array of available measuring instruments (see Conoley & Impara, 1995, and Fischer & Corcoran, 1994; see also chapters 18–24 of the present volume). The chief considerations that should determine the composition of a test battery are the psychometric adequacy of the measures being considered; the relevance of these measures to the referral questions being addressed; the likelihood that these measures will contribute incremental validity to the decision-making process; and the additive, confirmatory, and complementary functions that individual measures are likely to serve when used jointly.

Psychometric Adequacy

As elaborated by Anastasi and Urbina (1997), in the *Standards for Educational and Psychological Testing* (AERA, et al., 1999, chapters 1, 2, & 5), and in the chapter by Wasserman and Bracken in this volume, the *psychometric adequacy* of an assessment instrument consists of the extent to which it involves standardized test materials and administration procedures, can be coded with reasonably good interscorer agreement, demonstrates acceptable reliability, has generated relevant normative data, and shows valid corollaries that serve the purposes for which it is intended. Assessment psychologists may at times choose to use tests with uncertain psychometric properties, perhaps for exploratory purposes or for comparison with a previous examination using these tests. Generally speaking, however, formal testing as part of a psychological assessment should be limited to standardized, reliable, and valid instruments for which there are adequate normative data.

Relevance

The tests selected for inclusion in an assessment battery should provide information relevant to answering the questions that have been raised about the person being examined. Questions that relate to personality functions (e.g., *What kind of approach in psychotherapy is likely to be helpful to this person?*) call for personality tests. Questions that relate to

educational issues (e.g., *Does this student have a learning disability?*) call for measures of intellectual abilities and academic aptitude and achievement. Questions that relate to neuropsychological functions (e.g., *Are there indications of memory loss?*) call for measures of cognitive functioning, with special emphasis on measures of capacities for learning and recall.

These examples of relevance may seem too obvious to mention. However, they reflect an important and sometimes overlooked guiding principle that test selection should be justifiable for each measure included in an assessment battery. Insufficient attention to justifying the use of particular measures in specific instances can result in two ill-advised assessment practices: (a) conducting examinations with a fixed and unvarying battery of measures regardless of what questions are being asked in the individual case, and (b) using favorite instruments at every opportunity even when they are unlikely to serve any central or unique purpose in a particular assessment. The administration of minimally useful tests that have little relevance to the referral question is a wasteful procedure that can result in warranted criticism of assessment psychologists and the assessment process. Likewise, the propriety of charging fees for unnecessary procedures can rightfully be challenged by persons receiving or paying for services, and the competence of assessors who give tests that make little contribution to answering the questions at issue can be challenged in such public forums as the courtroom (see Weiner, 2002).

Incremental Validity

Incremental validity in psychological assessment refers to the extent to which new information increases the accuracy of a classification or prediction above and beyond the accuracy achieved by information already available. Assessors pay adequate attention to incremental validity by collecting the amount and kinds of information they need to answer a referral question, but no more than that. In theory, then, familiarity with the incremental validity of various measures when used for certain purposes, combined with test selection based on this information, minimizes redundancy in psychological assessment and satisfies both professional and scientific requirements for justifiable test selection.

In practice, however, strict adherence to incremental validity guidelines often proves difficult and even disadvantageous to implement. As already noted, it is difficult to anticipate which sources of information will prove to be most useful. Similarly, with respect to which instruments to include in a test battery, there is little way to know whether the tests administered have yielded enough data, and which tests have contributed most to understanding the person being examined, until after the data have been collected and analyzed. In most practice settings, it is reasonable to conduct an interview and review previous records as a basis for deciding whether formal testing would be likely to help answer a referral question— that is, whether it will show enough incremental validity to warrant its cost in time and money. Likewise, reviewing a set of test data can provide a basis for determining what kind of additional testing might be worthwhile. However, it is rarely appropriate to administer only one test at a time, to choose each subsequent test on the basis of the preceding one, and to schedule a further testing session for each additional test administration. For this reason, responsible psychological assessment usually consists of one or two testing sessions comprising a battery of tests selected to serve specific additive, confirmatory, and complementary functions.

Additive, Confirmatory, and Complementary Functions of Tests

Some referral questions require selection of multiple tests to identify relatively distinct and independent aspects of a person's psychological functioning. For example, students receiving low grades may be referred for an evaluation to help determine whether their poor academic performance is due primarily to limited intelligence or to personality characteristics that are fostering negative attitudes toward achieving in school. A proper test battery in such a case would include some measure of intelligence and some measure of personality functioning. These two measures would then be used in an *additive* fashion to provide separate pieces of information, both of which would contribute to answering the referral question. As this example illustrates, the additive use of tests serves generally to broaden understanding of the person being examined.

Other assessment situations may create a need for *confirmatory* evidence in support of conclusions based on test findings, in which case two or more measures of the same psychological function may have a place in the test battery. Assessors conducting a neuropsychological examination to address possible onset of Alzheimer's disease, for example, ordinarily administer several memory tests. Should each of these tests identify memory impairment consistent with Alzheimer's, then from a technical standpoint, only one of them would have been necessary and the others have shown no incremental validity. Practically speaking, however, the multiple memory measures taken together provide confirmatory evidence of memory loss. Such confirmatory use of tests strengthens understanding and helps assessors present conclusions with confidence.

The confirmatory function of a multitest battery is especially useful when tests of the same psychological function measure it in different ways. The advantages of multimethod assessment of variables have long been recognized in psychology, beginning with the work of Campbell and Fiske (1959) and continuing with contemporary reports by the American Psychological Association's (APA's) Psychological Assessment Work Group, which stress the improved validity that results when phenomena are measured from a variety of perspectives (Kubiszyn et al., 2000; Meyer et al., 2001):

> The optimal methodology to enhance the construct validity of nomothetic research consists of combining data from multiple methods and multiple operational definitions. . . . Just as effective nomothetic research recognizes how validity is maximized when variables are measured by multiple methods, particularly when the methods produce meaningful discrepancies . . . the quality of idiographic assessment can be enhanced by clinicians who integrate the data from multiple methods of assessment. (Meyer et al., p. 150)

Such confirmatory testing is exemplified in applications of the Minnesota Multiphasic Personality Inventory (MMPI, MMPI-2) and the Rorschach Inkblot Method (RIM), which are the two most widely researched and frequently used personality assessment instruments (Ackerman & Ackerman, 1997; Butcher & Rouse, 1996; Camara, Nathan, & Puente, 2000; Watkins, Campbell, Nieberding, & Hallmark, 1995). As discussed later in this chapter and in the chapters by Viglione and Rivera and by Ben-Porath in this volume, the MMPI-2 is a relatively structured self-report inventory, whereas the RIM is a relatively unstructured measure of perceptual-cognitive and associational processes (see also Exner, 2003; Graham, 2000; Greene, 2000; Weiner, 1998). Because of differences in their format, the MMPI-2 and the RIM measure normal and abnormal characteristics in different ways and at different levels of a person's ability and willingness to recognize and report them directly. Should a person display some type of disordered functioning on both the MMPI-2 and the RIM, this confirmatory finding becomes more powerful and convincing than having such information from one of these instruments but not other, even though technically in this instance no incremental validity derives from the second instrument.

Confirmatory evidence of this kind often proves helpful in professional practice, especially in forensic work. As described by Blau (1998), Heilbrun (2001), Shapiro (1991), and others, multiple sources of information pointing in the same direction bolsters courtroom testimony, whereas conclusions based on only one measure of some characteristic can result in assessors' being criticized for failing to conduct a thorough examination.

Should multiple measures of the same psychological characteristics yield different rather than confirmatory results, these results can usually serve valuable *complementary* functions in the interpretive process. At times, apparent lack of agreement between two purported measures of the same characteristic has been taken to indicate that one of the measures lacks convergent validity. This negative view of divergent test findings fails to take adequate cognizance of the complexity of the information provided by multimethod assessment and can result in misleading conclusions. To continue with the example of conjoint MMPI-2 and RIM testing, suppose that a person's responses show elevation on indices of depression on one of these measures but not the other. Inasmuch as indices on both measures have demonstrated some validity in detecting features of depression, the key question to ask is not which measure is wrong in this instance, but rather why the measures have diverged.

Perhaps, as one possible explanation, the respondent has some underlying depressive concerns that he or she does not recognize or prefers not to admit to others, in which case depressive features might be less likely to emerge in response to the self-report MMPI-2 methodology than on the more indirect Rorschach task. Or perhaps the respondent is not particularly depressed but wants very much to give the impression of being in distress and needing help, in which case the MMPI-2 might be more likely to show depression than the RIM. Or perhaps the person generally feels more relaxed and inclined to be forthcoming in relatively structured than relatively unstructured situations, and then the MMPI-2 is more likely than the RIM to reveal whether the person is depressed.

As these examples show, multiple measures of the same psychological characteristic can complement each other when they diverge, with one measure sometimes picking up the presence of a characteristic (a true positive) that is missed by the other (a false negative). Possible reasons for the false negative can contribute valuable information about the respondent's test-taking attitudes and likelihood of behaving differently in situations that differ in the amount of structure they provide. The translation of such divergence between MMPI-2 and RIM findings into clinically useful diagnostic inferences and individual treatment planning is elaborated by Finn (1996) and Ganellen (1996). Whatever measures may be involved in weighing the implications of divergent findings, this complementary use of test findings frequently serves to deepen understanding gleaned from the assessment process.

Examiner Issues

The amount and kind of data collected in psychological assessments depend in part on two issues concerning the examiners who conduct these assessments. The first issue involves the qualifications and competence of examiners to utilize the procedures they employ, and the second has to do with ways in which examiners' personal qualities can influence how different kinds of people respond to them.

Qualifications and Competence

There is general consensus that persons who conduct psychological assessments should be qualified by education and training to do so. The *Ethical Principles and Code of Conduct* promulgated by the APA (1992) offers the following general guideline in this regard: "Psychologists provide services, teach, and conduct research only within the boundaries of their competence, based on their education, training, supervised experience, or appropriate professional experience" (Ethical Code 1.04[a]). Particular kinds of knowledge and skill that are necessary for test users to conduct adequate assessments are specified further in the *Test User Qualifications* endorsed by the APA (2001). Finally of note with respect to using tests in psychological assessments, the *Standards for Educational and Psychological Testing* (AERA et al., 1999) identify who is responsible for the proper use of tests: "The ultimate responsibility for appropriate test use and interpretation lies predominantly with the test user. In assuming this responsibility, the user must become knowledgeable about a test's appropriate uses and the populations for which it is suitable" (p. 112).

Despite the clarity of these statements and the considerable detail provided in the *Test User Qualifications,* two persistent issues in contemporary assessment practice remain unresolved. First, adequate psychological testing qualifications are typically inferred for any examiners holding a graduate degree in psychology, being licensed in their state, and presenting themselves as competent to practice psychological assessment. Until such time as the criteria proposed in the *Test User Qualifications* become incorporated into formal accreditation procedures, qualification as an assessor will continue to be conferred automatically on psychologists obtaining licensure. Unfortunately, being qualified by license to use psychological tests does not ensure being competent in using them. Being *competent* in psychological testing requires familiarity with the latest revision of whatever instruments an assessor is using, with current research and the most recent normative data concerning these instruments, and with the manifold interpretive complexities they are likely to involve. Assessment competence also requires appreciation for a variety of psychometric, interpersonal, sociocultural, and contextual issues that affect not only the collection but also the interpretation and utilization of assessment information (see Sandoval, Frisby, Geisinger, & Scheuneman, 1990). The chapters that follow in this volume bear witness to the broad range of these issues and to the steady output of new or revised measures, research findings, and practice guidelines that make assessment psychology a dynamic and rapidly evolving field with a large and burgeoning literature. Only by keeping reasonably current with these developments can psychological assessors become and remain competent, and only by remaining competent can they fulfill their ethical responsibilities (Kitchener, 2000, chapter 9; Koocher & Keith-Spiegel, 1998; Weiner, 1989).

The second persistent issue concerns assessment by persons who are not psychologists and are therefore not bound by this profession's ethical principles or guidelines for practice. Nonpsychologist assessors who can obtain psychological tests are free to use them however they wish. When easily administered measures yield test scores that seem transparently interpretable, as in the case of an elevated Borderline scale on the Millon Multiaxial Clinical Inventory–III (MCMI-III; Choca, Shanley, & Van Denberg, 1997) or an elevated Acquiescence scale on the Holland Vocational Preference Inventory (VPI; Holland, 1985), unqualified examiners can draw superficial conclusions that take inadequate account of the complexity of these instruments, the interactions among their scales, and the limits of their applicability. It accordingly behooves assessment psychologists not only to maintain their own competence, but also to call attention in appropriate circumstances to assessment practices that fall short of reasonable standards of competence.

Personal Influence

Assessors can influence the information they collect by virtue of their personal qualities and by the manner in which they conduct a psychological examination. In the case of self-administered measures such as interest surveys or personality questionnaires, examiner influence may be minimal. Interviews and interactive testing procedures, on the other hand, create ample opportunity for an examiner's age, gender, ethnicity, or other characteristics to make respondents feel more or less comfortable and more or less inclined to be forthcoming. Examiners accordingly need to be alert to instances in which such personal qualities may be influencing the nature and amount of the data they are collecting.

The most important personal influence that examiners cannot modify or conceal is their language facility. Psychological assessment procedures are extensively language-based, either in their content or in the instructions that introduce nonverbal tasks, and accurate communication is therefore essential for obtaining reliable assessment information. It is widely agreed that both examiners and whomever they are interviewing or testing should be communicating either in their native language or in a second language in which they are highly proficient (AERA et al., 1999, chapter 9). The use of interpreters to circumvent language barriers in the assessment process rarely

provides a satisfactory solution to this problem. Unless an interpreter is fully conversant with idiomatic expressions and cultural referents in both languages, is familiar with standard procedures in psychological assessment, and is a stranger to the examinee (as opposed to a friend, relative, or member of the same closely knit subcultural community), the obtained results may be of questionable validity. Similarly, in the case of self-administered measures, instructions and test items must be written in a language that the respondent can be expected to understand fully. Translations of pencil-and-paper measures accordingly require close attention to the idiomatic vagaries of each new language and to culture-specific contents of individual test items, in order to ensure equivalence of measures in the cross-cultural applications of tests (Allen & Walsh, 2000; Dana, 2000a).

Unlike their fixed qualities, the manner in which examiners conduct the assessment process is within their control, and untoward examiner influence can be minimized by appropriate efforts to promote full and open response to the assessment procedures. To achieve this end, an assessment typically begins with a review of its purposes, a description of the procedures that will be followed, and efforts to establish a rapport that will help the person being evaluated feel comfortable and willing to cooperate with the assessment process. Variations in examiner behavior while introducing and conducting psychological evaluations can substantially influence how respondents perceive the assessment situation—for example, whether they see it as an authoritarian investigative process intended to ferret out defects and weaknesses, or as a mutually respectful and supportive interaction intended to provide understanding and help. Even while following closely the guidelines for a structured interview and adhering faithfully to standardized procedures for administering various tests, the examiner needs to recognize that his or her manner, tone of voice, and apparent attitude are likely to affect the perceptions and comfort level of the person being assessed and, consequently, the amount and kind of information that person provides (see Anastasi & Urbina, 1977; Masling, 1966, 1998).

Respondent Issues

Examiner influence in the assessment process inevitably interacts with the attitudes and inclinations of the person being examined. Some respondents may feel more comfortable being examined by an older person than a younger one, for example, or by a male than a female examiner, whereas other respondents may prefer a younger and female examiner. Among members of a minority group, some may prefer to be examined by a person with a cultural or ethnic background similar to theirs, whereas others are less concerned with the examiner's background than with his or her competence. Similarly, with respect to examiner style, a passive, timid, and dependent person might feel comforted by a warm, friendly, and supportive examiner approach that would make an aloof, distant, and mistrustful person feel uneasy; conversely, an interpersonally cautious and detached respondent might feel safe and secure when being examined in an impersonal and businesslike manner that would be unsettling and anxiety provoking to an interpersonally needy and dependent respondent. With such possibilities in mind, skilled examiners usually vary their behavioral style with an eye to conducting assessments in ways that will be likely to maximize each individual respondent's level of comfort and cooperation.

Two other respondent issues that influence the data collection process concern a person's right to give *informed consent* to being evaluated and his or her specific *attitudes toward being examined*. With respect to informed consent, the introductory phase of conducting an assessment must ordinarily include not only the explanation of purposes and procedures mentioned previously, which informs the respondent, but also an explicit agreement by the respondent or persons legally responsible for the respondent to undergo the evaluation. As elaborated in the *Standards for Educational and Psychological Testing* (AERA et al., 1999), informed consent can be waived only when an assessment has been mandated by law (as in a court-ordered evaluation) or when it is implicit, as when a person applies for a position or opportunity for which being assessed is a requirement (i.e., a job for which all applicants are being screened psychologically; see also Kitchener, 2000, and the chapters by Geisinger and by Koocher and Rey-Casserly in this volume). Having given their consent to be evaluated, moreover, respondents are entitled to revoke it at any time during the assessment process. Hence, the prospects for obtaining adequate assessment data depend not only on whether respondents can be helped to feel comfortable and be forthcoming, but even more basically on whether they consent in the first place to being evaluated and remain willing during the course of the evaluation.

Issues involving a respondent's specific attitudes toward being examined typically arise in relation to whether the assessment is being conducted for clinical or for administrative purposes. When assessments are being conducted for *clinical* purposes, the examiner is responsible to the person being examined, the person being examined is seeking some type of assistance, and the examination is intended to be helpful to this person and responsive to his or her needs. As common examples in clinical assessments, people concerned about their psychological well-being may seek an evaluation to learn whether they need professional mental health care, and people uncertain about their educational or vocational plans may want look

for help in determining what their abilities and interests suit them to do. In administrative assessments, by contrast, examiners are responsible not to the person being examined, but to some third party who has requested the evaluation to assist in arriving at some judgment about the person. Examiners in an administrative assessment are ethically responsible for treating the respondent fairly and with respect, but the evaluation is being conducted for the benefit of the party requesting it, and the results may or may not meet the respondent's needs or serve his or her best interests. Assessment for administrative purposes occurs commonly in forensic, educational, and organizational settings when evaluations are requested to help decide such matters as whether a prison inmate should be paroled, a student should be admitted to a special program, or a job applicant should be hired (see Monahan, 1980).

As for their attitudes, respondents being evaluated for clinical purposes are relatively likely to be motivated to reveal themselves honestly, whereas those being examined for administrative purposes are relatively likely to be intent on making a certain kind of impression. Respondents attempting to manage the impression they give are likely to show themselves not as they are, but as they think the person requesting the evaluation would view favorably. Typically such efforts at impression management take the form of denying one's limitations, minimizing one's shortcomings, attempting to put one's very best foot forward, and concealing whatever might be seen in a negative light. Exceptions to this general trend are not uncommon, however. Whereas most persons being evaluated for administrative purposes want to make the best possible impression, some may be motivated in just the opposite direction. For example, a plaintiff claiming brain damage in a personal injury lawsuit may see benefit in making the worst possible impression on a neuropsychological examination. Some persons being seen for clinical evaluations, despite having come of their own accord and recognizing that the assessment is being conducted for their benefit, may nevertheless be too anxious or embarrassed to reveal their difficulties fully. Whatever kind of impression respondents may want to make, the attitudes toward being examined that they bring with them to the assessment situation can be expected to influence the amount and kind of data they produce. These attitudes also have a bearing on the interpretation of assessment data, and the further implications of impression management for malingering and defensiveness are discussed later in the chapter.

Data Management Issues

A final set of considerations in collecting assessment information concerns appropriate ways of managing the data that are obtained. Examiners must be aware in particular of issues concerning the use of computers in data collection; the responsibility they have for safeguarding the security of their measures; and their obligation, within limits, to maintain the confidentiality of what respondents report or reveal to them.

Computerized Data Collection

Software programs are available to facilitate the data collection process for most widely used assessment methods. Programs designed for use with self-report questionnaires typically provide for online administration of test items, automated coding of item responses to produce scale scores, and quantitative manipulation of these scale scores to yield summary scores and indices. For instruments that require examiner administration and coding (e.g., a Wechsler intelligence test), software programs accept test scores entered by the examiner and translate them into the test's quantitative indices (e.g., the Wechsler IQ and Index scores). Many of these programs store the test results in files that can later be accessed or exported, and some even provide computational packages that can generate descriptive statistics for sets of test records held in storage.

These features of computerized data management bring several benefits to the process of collecting assessment information. Online administration and coding of responses help respondents avoid mechanical errors in filling out test forms manually, and they eliminate errors that examiners sometimes make in scoring these responses (see Allard & Faust, 2000). For measures that require examiner coding and data entry, the utility of the results depends on accurate coding and entry, but once the data are entered, software programs eliminate examiner error in calculating summary scores and indices from them. The data storage features of many software programs facilitate assessment research, particularly for investigators seeking to combine databases from different sources, and they can also help examiners meet requirements in most states and many agencies for keeping assessment information on file for some period of time. For such reasons, the vast majority of assessment psychologists report that they use software for test scoring and feel comfortable doing so (McMinn, Ellens, & Soref, 1999).

Computerized collection of assessment information has some potential disadvantages as well, however. When assessment measures are administered online, first of all, the reliability of the data collected can be compromised by a lack of equivalence between an automated testing procedure and the noncomputerized version on which it is based. As elaborated by Butcher, Perry, and Atlis (2000), Honaker and Fowler (1990), and Snyder (2000) and discussed in the chapter by

Butcher in the present volume, the extent of such equivalence is currently an unresolved issue. Available data suggest fairly good reliability for computerized administrations based on pencil-and-paper questionnaires, especially those used in personality assessment. With respect to the MMPI, for example, a meta-analysis by Finger and Ones (1999) of all available research comparing computerized with booklet forms of the instrument has shown them to be psychometrically equivalent. On the other hand, good congruence with the original measures has yet to be demonstrated for computerized versions of structured clinical interviews and for many measures of visual-spatial functioning used in neuropsychological assessment. Among software programs available for test administration, moreover, very few have been systematically evaluated with respect to whether they obtain exactly the same information as would emerge in a standard administration of the measure on which they are based.

A second potential disadvantage of computerized data collection derives from the ease with which it can be employed. Although frequently helpful to knowledgeable assessment professionals and thus to the persons they examine, automated procedures also simplify psychological testing for untrained and unqualified persons who lack assessment skills and would not be able to collect test data without the aid of a computer. The availability of software programs thus creates some potential for assessment methods to be misused and respondents to be poorly served. Such outcomes are not an inescapable by-product of computerized assessment procedures, however. They constitute instead an abuse of technology by uninformed and irresponsible persons.

Test Security

Test security refers to restricting the public availability of test materials and answers to test items. Such restrictions address two important considerations in psychological assessment. First, publicly circulated information about tests can undermine their validity, particularly in the case of measures comprising items with right and wrong or more or less preferable answers. Prior exposure to tests of this kind and information about correct or preferred answers can affect how persons respond to them and prevent an examiner from being able to collect a valid protocol. The validity of test findings is especially questionable when a respondent's prior exposure has included specific coaching in how to answer certain questions. As for relatively unstructured assessment procedures that have no right or wrong answers, even on these measures various kinds of responses carry particular kinds of interpretive significance. Hence, the possibility exists on relatively unstructured measures as well that persons intent on making a certain kind of impression can be helped to do so by pretest instruction concerning what various types of responses are taken to signify. However, the extent to which public dissemination of information about the inferred meaning of responses does in fact compromise the validity of relatively unstructured measures has not yet been examined empirically and is a subject for further research.

Second, along with helping to preserve the validity of obtained results, keeping assessment measures secure protects test publishers against infringement of their rights by pirated or plagiarized copies of their products. Ethical assessors respect copyright law by not making or distributing copies of published tests, and they take appropriate steps to prevent test forms, test manuals, and assessment software from falling into the hands of persons who are not qualified to use them properly or who feel under no obligation to keep them secure. Both the *Ethical Principles and Code of Conduct* (APA, 1992, Section 2.10) and the *Standards for Educational and Psychological Testing* (AERA et al., 1999, p. 117) address this professional responsibility in clear terms.

These considerations in safeguarding test security also have implications for the context in which psychological assessment data are collected. Assessment data have become increasingly likely in recent years to be applied in forensic settings, and litigious concerns sometimes result in requests to have a psychological examination videotaped or observed by a third party. These intrusions on traditional examination procedures pose a threat to the validity of the obtained data in two respects. First, there is no way to judge or measure the impact of the videotaping or the observer on what the respondent chooses to say and do. Second, the normative standards that guide test interpretation are derived from data obtained in two-person examinations, and there are no comparison data available for examinations conducted in the presence of a camera or an observer. Validity aside, exposure of test items to an observer or through a videotape poses the same threat to test security as distributing test forms or manuals to persons who are under no obligation to keep them confidential. Psychological assessors may at times decide for their own protection to audiotape or videotape assessments when they anticipate legal challenges to the adequacy of their procedures or the accuracy of their reports. They may also use recordings on occasion as an alternative to writing a long and complex test protocol verbatim. For purposes of test security, however, recordings made for other people to hear or see, like third-party observers, should be avoided.

Confidentiality

A third and related aspect of appropriate data management pertains to maintaining the confidentiality of a respondent's assessment information. Like certain aspects of safeguarding test security, confidentiality is an ethical matter in assessment psychology, not a substantive one. The key considerations in maintaining the confidentiality of assessment information, as specified in the *Ethical Principles and Code of Conduct* (APA, 1992, Section 5) and elaborated by Kitchener (2000, chapter 6) involve (a) clarifying the nature and limits of confidentiality with clients and patients prior to undertaking an evaluation; (b) communicating information about persons being evaluated only for appropriate scientific or professional purposes and only to an extent relevant to the purposes for which the evaluation was conducted; (c) disclosing information only to persons designated by respondents or other duly authorized persons or entities, except when otherwise permitted or required by law; and (d) storing and preserving respondents' records in a secure fashion. Like the matter of informed consent discussed previously, confidentiality is elaborated as an ethical issue in the chapter by Koocher and Rey-Casserly in this volume.

INTERPRETING ASSESSMENT INFORMATION

Following the collection of sufficient relevant data, the process of psychological assessment continues with a phase of evaluation in which these data are interpreted. The interpretation of assessment data consists of drawing inferences and forming impressions concerning what the findings reveal about a respondent's psychological characteristics. Accurate and adequately focused interpretations result in summary descriptions of psychological functioning that can then be utilized in the final phase of the assessment process as a foundation for formulating conclusions and recommendations that answer referral questions. Reaching this output phase requires consideration during the evaluation phase of the basis on which inferences are drawn and impressions formed, the possible effects on the findings of malingering or defensiveness, and effective ways of integrating data from diverse sources.

Basis of Inferences and Impressions

The interpretation of assessment data involves four sets of alternatives with respect to how assessors go about drawing inferences and forming impressions about what these data indicate. Interpretations can be based on either empirical or conceptual approaches to decision making; they can be guided either by statistically based decision rules or by clinical judgment; they can emphasize either nomothetic or idiographic characteristics of respondents; and they can include more or less reliance on computer-generated interpretive statements. Effective assessment usually involves informed selection among these alternatives and some tailoring of the emphasis given each of them to fit the particular context of the individual assessment situation.

Empirical and Conceptual Guidelines

The interpretation of assessment information can be approached in several ways. In what may be called an *intuitive* approach, assessment decisions stem from impressions that have no identifiable basis in the data. Instead, interpretations are justified by statements like "It's just a feeling I have about her," or "I can't say where I get it from, but I just know he's that way." In what may be called an *authoritative* approach, interpretations are based on the pronouncements of well-known or respected assessment psychologists, as in saying, "These data mean what they mean because that's what Dr. Expert says they mean." The intuition of unusually empathic assessors and reliance on authority by well-read practitioners who choose their experts advisedly may on occasion yield accurate and useful impressions. Both approaches have serious shortcomings, however. Unless intuitive assessors can identify specific features of the data that help them reach their conclusions, their diagnostic sensitivity cannot be taught to other professionals or translated into scientifically verifiable procedures. Unless authoritative assessors can explain in their own words the basis on which experts have reached the conclusions being cited, they are unlikely to impress others as being professionally knowledgeable themselves or as knowing what to think in the absence of being told by someone else what to think.

Moreover, neither intuitive nor authoritative approaches to interpreting assessment information are likely to be as consistently reliable as approaches based on empirical and conceptual guidelines. *Empirical guidelines* to decision making derive from the replicated results of methodologically sound research. When a specific assessment finding has repeatedly been found to correlate highly with the presence of a particular psychological characteristic, it is empirically sound to infer the presence of that characteristic in a respondent who displays that assessment finding. Conceptual guidelines to decision making consist of psychological constructs that provide a logical bridge between assessment findings and the inferences drawn from them. If subjectively felt distress contributes to a person's remaining in and benefiting from psychotherapy (for which there is considerable evidence; see Garfield, 1994; Greencavage & Norcross, 1990; Mohr, 1995), and if a test includes a valid index of subjectively felt distress (which many tests do), then it is reasonable to expect that a positive finding on this test index will increase the predicted likelihood of a favorable outcome in psychotherapy.

Both empirical and conceptual guidelines to interpretation bring distinct benefits to the assessment process. Empirical perspectives are valuable because they provide a foundation for achieving certainty in decision making. The adequacy of psychological assessment is enhanced by quantitative data concerning the normative distribution and other psychometric properties of measurements that reflect dimensions of psychological functioning. Lack of such data limits the confidence with which assessors can draw conclusions about the implications of their findings. Without being able to compare an individual's test responses with normative expectations, for example, or without a basis for estimating false positive and false negative possibilities in the measures they have used, assessors can only be speculative in attaching interpretive significance to their findings. Similarly, the absence of externally validated cutting scores detracts considerably from the certainty with which assessors can translate test scores into qualitative distinctions, such as whether a person is mildly, moderately, or severely depressed.

Conceptual perspectives are valuable in the assessment process because they provide some explanation of why certain findings are likely to identify certain kinds of psychological characteristics or predict certain kinds of behavior. Having such explanations in hand offers assessors the pleasure of understanding not only how their measures work but also why they work as they do; they help assessors focus their attention on aspects of their data that are relevant to the referral question to which they are responding; and they facilitate the communication of results in terms that address characteristics of the person being examined and not merely those of the data obtained. As a further benefit of conceptual formulations of assessment findings, they foster hypotheses concerning previously unknown or unexplored linkages between assessment findings and dimensions of psychological functioning and thereby help to extend the frontiers of knowledge.

Empirical guidelines are thus necessary to the scientific foundations of assessment psychology, as a basis for certainty in decision making, but they are not sufficient to bring this assessment to its full potential. Conceptual guidelines do not by themselves provide a reliable basis for drawing conclusions with certainty. However, by enriching the assessment process with explanatory hypotheses, they point the way to advances in knowledge.

For the purposes that each serves, then, both empirical and conceptual guidelines have an important place in the interpretation of assessment information. At times, concerns about preserving the scientific respectability of assessment have led to assertions that only empirical guidelines constitute an acceptable basis for decision making and that unvalidated conceptual guidelines have no place in scientific psychology. McFall and Treat (1999), for example, maintain that "the aim of clinical assessment is to gather data that allow us to reduce uncertainty concerning the probability of events" (p. 215). From their perspective, the information value of assessment data resides in scaled numerical values and conditional probabilities.

As an alternative point of view, let it be observed that the river of scientific discovery can flow through inferential leaps of deductive reasoning that suggest truths long before they are confirmed by replicated research findings. Newton grasped the reason that apples fall from trees well in advance of experiments demonstrating the laws of gravity, Einstein conceived his theory of relativity with full confidence that empirical findings would eventually prove him correct, and neither has suffered any challenges to his credentials as a scientist. Even though empirical guidelines are, on the average, more likely to produce reliable conclusions than are conceptual formulations, as already noted, logical reasoning concerning the implications of clearly formulated concepts can also generate conclusions that serve useful purposes and stand the test of time.

Accordingly, the process of arriving at conclusions in individual case assessment can involve creative as well as confirmatory aspects of scientific thinking, and the utilization of assessment to generate hypotheses and fuel speculation may in the course of scientific endeavor increase rather than decrease uncertainty in the process of identifying new alternative possibilities to pursue. This perspective is echoed by DeBruyn (1992) in the following comment: "Both scientific decision making in general, and diagnostic decision making in particular, have a repetitive side, which consists of formulas and algorithmic procedures, and a constructive side, which consists of generating hypotheses and theories to explain things or to account for unexpected findings" (p. 192).

Statistical Rules and Clinical Judgment

Empirical guidelines for decision making have customarily been operationalized by using statistical rules to arrive at conclusions concerning what assessment data signify. *Statistical rules* for interpreting assessment data comprise empirically derived formulas, or algorithms, that provide an objective, actuarial basis for deciding what these data indicate. When statistical rules are applied to the results of a psychological evaluation, the formula makes the decision concerning whether certain psychological characteristics are present (as in deciding whether a respondent has a particular trait or disorder) or whether certain kinds of actions are likely to ensue (as in predicting the likelihood of a respondent's behaving violently or performing well in some job). Statistical rules have the advantage of ensuring that examiners applying a formula correctly to the same set of data will always arrive at the same

conclusion concerning what these data mean. As a disadvantage, however, the breadth of the conclusions that can be based on statistical rules and their relevance to referral questions are limited by the composition of the database from which they have been derived.

For example, statistical rules may prove helpful in determining whether a student has a learning disability, but say nothing about the nature of this student's disability; they may predict the likelihood of a criminal defendant's behaving violently, but offer no clues to the kinds of situations that are most likely to evoke violence in this particular criminal defendant; or they may help identify the suitability of a person for one type of position in an organization, but be mute with respect to the person's suitability for other types of positions in the same organization. In each of these instances, moreover, a statistical rule derived from a group of people possessing certain demographic characteristics (e.g., age, gender, socioeconomic status, cultural background) and having been evaluated in a particular setting may lack validity generalization to persons with different demographic characteristics evaluated in some other kind of setting. Garb (2000) has similarly noted in this regard that "statistical-prediction rules are of limited value because they have typically been based on limited information that has not been demonstrated to be optimal and they have almost never been shown to be powerful" (p. 31).

In other words, then, the scope of statistical rules is restricted to findings pertaining to the particular kinds of persons, psychological characteristics, and circumstances that were anticipated in building them. For many of the varied types of people seen in actual assessment practice, and for many of the complex and specifically focused referral questions raised about these people, then, statistical rules that by themselves provide fully adequate answers may be in short supply.

As a further limitation of statistical rules, they share with all quantified assessment scales some unavoidable artificiality that accompanies translating numerical scores into qualitative descriptive categories. On the Beck Depression Inventory (BDI; Beck, Steer, & Garbin, 1988), for example, a score of 14 to 19 is taken to indicate mild depression and a score of 20 to 28 indicates moderate depression. Hence two people who have almost identical BDI scores, one with a 19 and the other with a 20, will be described much differently by the statistical rule, one as mildly depressed and the other as moderately depressed. Likewise, in measuring intelligence with the Wechsler Adult Intelligence Scale–III (WAIS-III; Kaufman, 1990) a Full Scale IQ score of 109 calls for describing a person's intelligence as average, whereas a person with almost exactly the same level of intelligence and a Full Scale IQ of 110 falls in the high average range. According to the WAIS-III formulas, a person with a Full Scale IQ of 91 and a person with a Full Scale IQ of 119 would also be labeled, respectively, as average and high average. Some assessors minimize this problem by adding some further specificity to the WAIS-III categories, as in labeling a 109 IQ as the high end of the average range and a 110 IQ as the low end of the high average range. Although additional categorical descriptions for more narrowly defined score ranges can reduce the artificiality in the use of statistical rules, there are limits to how many quantitative data points on a scale can be assigned a distinctive qualitative designation.

Conceptual guidelines for decision making have been operationalized in terms of *clinical judgment*, which consists of the cumulative wisdom that practitioners acquire from their experience. Clinical guidelines may come to represent the shared beliefs of large numbers of practitioners, but they emerge initially as impressions formed by individual practitioners. In contrast to the objective and quantitative features of statistical rules, clinical judgments constitute a subjective and qualitative basis for arriving at conclusions. When clinical judgment is applied to assessment data, decisions are made by the practitioner, not by a formula. Clinical judgments concerning the interpretive significance of a set of assessment data are consequently less uniform than actuarial decisions and less likely to be based on established fact. On the other hand, the applicability of clinical judgments is infinite, and their breadth and relevance are limited not by any database, but only by the practitioner's capacity to reason logically concerning possible relationships between psychological characteristics identified by the assessment data and psychological characteristics relevant to addressing referral questions, whatever their complexity and specificity.

The relative merit of statistical rules and clinical judgment in the assessment process has been the subject of considerable debate since this distinction was first formulated by Meehl (1954) in his book *Clinical Versus Statistical Prediction*. Subsequent publications of note concerning this important issue include articles by Grove and Meehl (1996), Grove, Zald, Lebow, Snitz, and Nelson (2000), Holt (1958, 1986), Karon (2000), Meehl (1986), and Swets, Dawes, and Monahan (2000), and a book by Garb (1998) entitled *Studying the Clinician*. Much of the literature on this topic has consisted of assertions and rebuttals concerning whether statistical methods generally produce more accurate assessment results than clinical methods. In light of the strengths and weaknesses inherent in both statistical prediction and clinical judgment, as elaborated in the chapter by Garb in this volume, such debate serves little purpose and is regrettable when it leads to disparagement of either approach to interpreting assessment data.

As testimony to the utility of both approaches, it is important to note that the creation of good statistical rules for making assessment decisions typically begins with clinically informed selection of both (a) test items, structured interview questions, and other measure components to be used as predictor variables, and (b) psychological conditions, behavioral tendencies, and other criterion variables to which the predictor variables are expected to relate. Empirical methods of scale construction and cross-validation are then employed to shape these clinically relevant assessment variables into valid actuarial measures of these clinically relevant criterion variables. Hence good statistical rules should almost always produce more accurate results than clinical judgment, because they encompass clinical wisdom plus the sharpening of this wisdom by replicated research findings. Clinical methods of assessment at their best depend on the impressions and judgment of individual practitioners, whereas statistical methods at their best constitute established fact that has been built on clinical wisdom. To rely only on clinical judgment in decision-making situations for which adequate actuarial guidelines are available is tantamount to playing cards with half a deck. Even the best judgment of the best practitioner can at times be clouded by inadvertent bias, insufficient awareness of base rates, and other sources of influence discussed in the final section of this chapter and elaborated in the chapter by Reynolds and Ramsay in this volume. When one is given a reasonable choice, then, assessment decisions are more advisedly based on established fact rather than clinical judgment.

On the other hand, the previously noted diversity of people and of the circumstances that lead to their being referred for an evaluation mean that assessment questions regularly arise for which there are no available statistical rules, and patterns of assessment data often resemble but do not quite match the parameters for which replicated research has demonstrated certain correlates. When statistical rules cannot fully answer questions being asked, what are assessors to do in the absence of fully validating data? Decisions could be deferred, on the grounds that sufficient factual basis for a decision is lacking, and recommendation could be delayed, pending greater certainty about what recommendation to make. Alternatively, assessors in a situation of uncertainty can supplement whatever empirical guidelines they do have at their disposal with logical reasoning and cumulative clinical wisdom to arrive at conclusions and recommendations that are more responsive and at least a little more likely to be helpful than saying nothing at all.

As these observations indicate, statistical rules and clinical judgment can properly be regarded as complementary components of effective decision making, rather than as competing and mutually exclusive alternatives. Each brings value to assessment psychology and has a respectable place in it. Geisinger and Carlson (2002) comment in this regard that the time has come "to move beyond both purely judgmental, speculative interpretation of test results as well as extrapolations from the general population to specific cases that do not much resemble the remainder of the population" (p. 254).

Assessment practice should accordingly be subjected to and influenced by research studies, lest it lead down blind alleys and detract from the pursuit of knowledge and the delivery of responsible professional service. Concurrently, however, lack of unequivocal documentation should not deter assessment psychologists from employing procedures and reaching conclusions that in their judgment will assist in meeting the needs of those who seek their help. Commenting on balanced use of objective and subjective contributions to assessment decision making, Swets et al. (2000) similarly note that "the appropriate role of the SPR [Statistical Prediction Rule] vis-à-vis the diagnostician will vary from one context to another" and that the most appropriate roles of each "can be determined for each diagnostic setting in accordance with the accumulated evidence about what works best" (p. 5). Putting the matter in even simpler terms, Kleinmuntz (1990) observed that "the reason why we still use our heads, flawed as they may be, instead of formulas is that for many decisions, choices and problems, there are as yet no available formulas" (p. 303).

Nomothetic and Idiographic Emphasis

Empirical guidelines and statistical rules constitute a basically nomothetic approach to interpreting assessment information, whereas conceptual guidelines and clinical judgment underlie a basically idiographic approach. *Nomothetic interpretations* address ways in which people resemble other kinds of people and share various psychological characteristics with many of them. Hence, these interpretations involve comparisons between the assessment findings for the person being examined and assessment findings typically obtained from groups of people with certain known characteristics, as in concluding that "this person's responses show a pattern often seen in people who feel uncomfortable in social situations and are inclined to withdraw from them." The manner in which nomothetic interpretations are derived and expressed is thus primarily quantitative in nature and may even specify the precise frequency with which an assessment finding occurs in particular groups of people.

Idiographic interpretations, by contrast, address ways in which people differ from most other kinds of people and show psychological characteristics that are fairly unique to them and their particular circumstances. These interpretations typically comprise statements that attribute person-specific meaning to assessment information on the basis of general notions of psychological processes, as in saying that "this person

gives many indications of being a passive and dependent individual who is more comfortable being a follower than a leader and will as a consequence probably have difficulty functioning effectively in an executive position." Deriving and expressing idiographic interpretations is thus a largely qualitative procedure in which examiners are guided by informed impressions rather than by quantitative empirical comparisons.

In the area of personality assessment, both nomothetic and idiographic approaches to interpretation have a long and distinguished tradition. Nomothetic perspectives derive from the work of Cattell (1946), for whom the essence of personality resided in traits or dimensions of functioning that all people share to some degree and on which they can be compared with each other. Idiographic perspectives in personality theory were first clearly articulated by Allport (1937), who conceived the essence of personality as residing in the uniqueness and individuality of each person, independently of comparisons to other people. Over the years, assessment psychologists have at times expressed different convictions concerning which of these two traditions should be emphasized in formulating interpretations. Practitioners typically concur with Groth-Marnat (1997) that data-oriented descriptions of people rarely address the unique problems a person may be having and that the essence of psychological assessment is an attempt "to evaluate an individual in a problem situation so that the information derived from the assessment can somehow help with the problem" (p. 32). Writing from a research perspective, however, McFall and Townsend (1998) grant that practitioners must of necessity provide idiographic solutions to people's problems, but maintain that "nomothetic knowledge is a prerequisite to valid idiographic solutions" (p. 325). In their opinion, only nomothetic variables have a proper place in the clinical science of assessment.

To temper these points of view in light of what has already been said about statistical and clinical prediction, there is no reason that clinicians seeking solutions to idiographic problem cannot or should not draw on whatever nomothetic guidelines may help them frame accurate and useful interpretations. Likewise, there is no reason that idiography cannot be managed in a scientific fashion, nor is a nomothetic-idiographic distinction between clinical science and clinical practice likely to prove constructive in the long run. Stricker (1997) argues to the contrary, for example, that science incorporates an attitude and a set of values that can characterize office practitioners as well as laboratory researchers, and that "the same theoretical matrix must generate both science and practice activities" (p. 442).

Issues of definition aside, then, there seems little to be gained by debating whether people can be described better in terms of how they differ from other people or how they resemble them. In practice, an optimally informative and useful description of an individual's psychological characteristics and functioning will encompass the person's resemblance to and differences from other people in similar circumstances about whom similar referral questions have been posed. Nomothetic and idiographic perspectives thus complement each other, and a balanced emphasis on both promotes the fullest possible understanding of a person being examined.

Computer-Generated Interpretive Statements

Most published tests include software programs that not only assist in the collection of assessment data, as already discussed, but also generate interpretive statements describing the test findings and presenting inferences based on them. Like computerized data collection, computer-based test interpretation (CBTI) brings some distinct advantages to the assessment process. By virtue of its automation, CBTI guarantees a thorough scan of the test data and thereby eliminates human error that results from overlooking items of information in a test protocol. CBTI similarly ensures that a pattern of test data will always generate the same interpretive statement, uniformly and reliably, thus eliminating examiner variability and bias as potential sources of error. CBTI can also facilitate the teaching and learning of assessment methods, by using computer-generated narratives as an exercise requiring the learner to identify the test variables likely to have given rise to particular statements. The potential benefits of computerizing test interpretations, as well as some drawbacks of doing so, are elaborated in the chapter by Butcher in this volume (see also Butcher, 2002). Four limitations of CBTI have a particular bearing on the extent to which examiners should rely on computer-generated statements in formulating and expressing their impressions.

First, although test software generates interpretive statements by means of quantitative algorithmic formulas, these computer programs are not entirely empirically based. Instead, they typically combine empirically validated correlates of test scores with clinical judgments about what various patterns of scores are likely to signify, and many algorithms involve beliefs as well as established fact concerning what these patterns mean. Different test programs, and even different programs for the same test, vary in the extent to which their interpretive statements are research based. Although CBTI generally increases the validity and utility of test interpretations, then, considerable research remains to be done to place computerized interpretation on a solid empirical basis (see Garb, 2000). In the meantime, computer-generated interpretations will embody at least some of the strengths and weaknesses of both statistical and clinical methods of decision making.

Second, the previously noted limitation of statistical rules with respect to designating quantitative score ranges with qualitative descriptors carries over into CBTI algorithms. Cutting points must be established, below which one kind or degree of descriptive statement is keyed and above which a different kind or degree of description will be generated. As a consequence, two people who show very similar scores on some index or scale may be described by a computer narrative in very different terms with respect to psychological characteristics measured by this index or scale.

Third, despite often referring specifically to the person who took the test (i.e., using the terms *he, she,* or *this person*) and thus giving the appearance of being idiographic, computer-generated interpretations do not describe the individual person who was examined. Instead, these interpretations describe test protocols, in the sense that they indicate what research findings or clinical wisdom say about people in general who show the kinds of test scores and patterns appearing in the protocol being scanned. Hence computer narratives are basically nomothetic, and most of them phrase at least some interpretive statements in terms of normative comparisons or even, as previously noted, specific frequencies with which the respondent's test patterns occur in certain groups of people. However, because no two people are exactly alike and no one person matches any comparison group perfectly, some computer-generated interpretive statements may not describe an individual respondent accurately. For this reason, well-developed test software narratives include a caveat indicating that (a) the interpretive statements to follow describe groups of people, not necessarily the person who took the test; (b) misleading and erroneous statements may occur as a reflection of psychological characteristics or environmental circumstances unique to the person being examined and not widely shared within any normative group; and (c) other sources of information and the assessor's judgment are necessary to determine which of the statements in an interpretive narrative apply to the respondent and which do not.

Fourth, the availability of computer-generated interpretive statements raises questions concerning their proper utilization in the preparation of an assessment report. Ideally, assessors should draw on computer narratives for some assistance, as for example in being sure that they have taken account of all of the relevant data, in checking for discrepancies between their own impressions and the inferences presented by the machine, and perhaps in getting some guidance on how best to organize and what to emphasize in their report. Less ideal is using CBTI not merely for supportive purposes but as a replacement for assessors' being able and willing to generate their own interpretations of the measures they are using.

Most of the assessment psychologists responding to the previously mentioned McMinn et al. (1999) survey reported that they never use CBTI as their primary resource for case formulation and would question the ethicality of doing so.

Even among ethical assessors, however, CBTI can present some temptations, because many computerized narratives present carefully crafted sentences and paragraphs that communicate clearly and lend themselves to being copied verbatim into a psychological report. Professional integrity would suggest that assessors relying on computer-generated conclusions should either express them in their own words or, if they are copying verbatim, should identify the copied material as a quotation and indicate its source. Beyond ethicality and integrity, unfortunately, the previously mentioned software accessibility that allows untrained persons to collect and score test protocols by machine also makes it possible for them to print out narrative interpretations and reproduce them fully or in part as a report, passing them off as their own work without any indication of source. Aside from representing questionable professional ethics, the verbatim inclusion of computer-generated interpretations in assessment reports is likely to be a source of confusion and error, because of the fact that these printouts are normatively rather than idiographically based and hence often include statements that are not applicable to the person being examined.

Malingering and Defensiveness

Malingering and defensiveness consist of conscious and deliberate attempts by persons being examined to falsify the information they are giving and thereby to mislead the examiner. *Malingering* involves intent to present oneself as being worse off psychologically than is actually the case and is commonly referred to as *faking bad*. *Defensiveness* involves seeking to convey an impression of being better off than one actually is and is commonly called *faking good*. Both faking bad and faking good can range in degree from slight exaggeration of problems and concerns or of assets and capabilities, to total fabrication of difficulties never experienced or accomplishments never achieved. These two types of efforts to mislead examiners arise from different kinds of motivation, but both of them can usually be detected from patterns of inconsistency that appear in the assessment data unless respondents have been carefully coached to avoid them.

Identifying Motivations to Mislead

People who fake bad during psychological assessments are usually motivated by some specific reason for wanting to appear less capable or more disturbed than they really are. In clinical settings, for example, patients who are concerned about not getting as much help or attention as they would like to receive may exaggerate or fabricate symptoms in order to convince a mental health professional that they should be taken into psychotherapy, that they should be seen more frequently if they are already in outpatient treatment, or that they should be admitted to an inpatient facility (or kept in a residential setting if they are already in one). In forensic settings, plaintiffs seeking damages in personal injury cases may malinger the extent of their neuropsychological or psychosocial impairments in hopes of increasing the amount of the settlement they receive, and defendants in criminal actions may malinger psychological disturbance in hopes of being able to minimize the penalties that will be imposed on them. In employment settings, claimants may malinger inability to function in order to begin or continue receiving disability payments or unemployment insurance.

People who fake good during psychological assessments, in an effort to appear more capable or better adjusted than they really are, also show a variety of motivations related to the setting in which they are being evaluated. Defensive patients in clinical settings may try to conceal the extent of their difficulties when they hope to be discharged from a hospital to which they were involuntarily committed, or when they would like to be told or have others told that they do not have any significant psychological problems for which they need treatment. In forensic settings, making the best possible impression can be a powerful inducement to faking good among divorced parents seeking custody of their children and among prison inmates requesting parole. In personnel settings, applicants for positions, candidates for promotion, and persons asking for reinstatement after having been found impaired have good reasons for putting their best foot forward during a psychological evaluation, even to the extent of overstating their assets and minimizing their limitations.

Detecting Malingering and Defensiveness

Attempts to mislead psychological assessors usually result in patterns of inconsistency that provide reliable clues to malingering and defensiveness. In the case of efforts to fake bad, these inconsistencies are likely to appear in three different forms. First, malingerers often produce inconsistent data within individual assessment measures. Usually referred to as *intratest scatter,* this form of inconsistency involves failing relatively easy items on intelligence or ability tests while succeeding on much more difficult items of the same kind, or responding within the normal range on some portions of a personality test but in an extremely deviant manner on other portions of the same test.

A second form of inconsistency frequently found in the assessment data of malingerers occurs between test results and the examiner's behavioral observations. In some instances, for example, people who appear calm and relaxed during an interview, talk clearly and sensibly about a variety of matters, and conduct themselves in a socially appropriate fashion then produce test protocols similar to those seen in people who are extremely anxious or emotionally upset, incapable of thinking logically and coherently, out of touch with reality, and unable to participate comfortably in interpersonal relationships. Such discrepancies between test and interview data strongly suggest the deployment of deceptive tactics to create a false impression of disturbance.

The third form of inconsistency that proves helpful in detecting malingering consists of a sharp discrepancy between the interview and test data collected by the examiner and the respondent's actual circumstances and past history as reported by collateral sources or recorded in formal documents. In these instances, the person being evaluated may talk and act strangely during an interview and give test responses strongly suggestive of serious psychological disturbance, but never previously have seen a mental health professional, received counseling or psychotherapy, been prescribed psychotropic medication, or been considered by friends, relatives, teachers, or employers to have any emotional problems. Such contrasts between serious impairments or limitations suggested by the results of an examination and a life history containing little or no evidence of these impairments or limitations provide good reason to suspect malingering.

Defensiveness in an effort to look good is similarly likely to result in inconsistencies in the assessment data that help to detect it. Most common in this regard are guarded test protocols and minimally informative interview responses that fall far short of reflecting a documented history of psychological disorder or problem behavior. Although being guarded and tight-lipped may successfully conceal difficulties, it also alerts examiners that a respondent is not being forthcoming and that the data being obtained probably do not paint a full picture of the person's psychological problems and limitations. As another possibility, fake-good respondents may, instead of being guarded and closed-mouthed, become quite talkative and expansive in an effort to impress the examiner with their admirable qualities and many capabilities, in which case the assessment information becomes noteworthy for claims of knowledge, skills, virtues, and accomplishments that far exceed reasonable likelihood. These and other guidelines for the clinical detection of efforts to mislead assessors by faking either good or bad are elaborated by Berry, Wetter, and Baer (2002), McCann (1998, chapters 3–4), and Rogers (1997a).

Most self-report inventories include validity scales that are based on inconsistent and difficult-to-believe responses that can often help to identify malingering and defensiveness. (Greene, 1997; see also the chapter by Naglieri and Graham in this volume). A variety of specific interview, self-report, and ability measures have also been developed along these lines to assist in identifying malingering, including the Structured Interview of Reported Symptoms (SIRS; Rogers, Gillis, Dickens, & Bagby, 1991; see also Rogers, 1997b), the M test for detecting efforts to malinger schizophrenia (Beaber, Marston, Michelli, & Mills, 1985; see also Smith, 1997), and the Test of Memory Malingering (TOMM; Tombaugh, 1997; see also Pankratz & Binder, 1997). Commonly used projective and other expressive measures do not include formal validity scales, but they are nevertheless quite sensitive to inconsistencies in performance that suggest malingering or defensiveness (Schretlen, 1997; see also the chapter by Ben-Porath in the present volume). Moreover, because relatively unstructured expressive measures convey much less meaning to respondents than self-report questionnaires concerning what their responses might signify, there is reason to believe that they may be less susceptible to impression management or even that the fakability of an assessment instrument is directly related to its face validity (Bornstein, Rossner, Hill, & Stepanian, 1994). This does not mean that unstructured measures like the Rorschach Inkblot Method and Thematic Apperception Test are impervious to malingering and defensiveness, which they are not, but only that efforts to mislead may be more obvious and less likely to convey a specific desired impression on these measures than on relatively structured measures.

Coaching

A companion issue to the ease or difficulty of faking assessment measures is the extent to which respondents can be taught to deceive examiners with a convincingly good-looking or bad-looking performance. Research findings indicate that even psychologically naive participants who are given some information about the nature of people with certain disorders or characteristics can shape their test behaviors to make themselves resemble a target group more closely than they would have without such instruction. Misleading results are even more likely to occur when respondents are coached specifically in how to answer certain kinds of questions and avoid elevating validity scales (Ben-Porath, 1994; Rogers, Gillis, Bagby, & Monteiro, 1991; Storm & Graham, 2000). The group findings in these research studies have not yet indicated whether a generally instructed or specifically coached respondent can totally mislead an experienced examiner in actual practice, without generating any suspicion that the obtained results may not be valid, and this remains a subject for further investigation.

With further respect to individual assessments in actual practice, however, there are reports in the literature of instances in which attorneys have coached their clients in how to answer questions on self-report inventories (e.g., Lees-Haley, 1997; Wetter & Corrigan, 1995; Youngjohn, 1995), and a Web site available on the Internet claims to provide a list of supposed good and bad responses for each of the 10 Rorschach inkblots. As previously mentioned in discussing test security, prior knowledge of test questions and answers can detract from the practical utility of psychological assessment methods that feature right and wrong answers. The confounding effect of pretest information on unstructured measures, for which correct or preferable answers are difficult to specify out of context, may be minimal, but the susceptibility of these measures to successful deception by well-coached respondents is another topic for future research. Less uncertain are the questionable ethics of persons who coach test-takers in dishonesty and thereby thwart the legitimate purposes for which these respondents are being evaluated.

Integrating Data Sources

As noted at the beginning of this chapter, psychological assessment information can be derived from administering tests, conducting interviews, observing behavior, speaking with collateral persons, and reviewing historical documents. Effective integration of data obtained from such multiple sources calls for procedures based on the previously described additive, confirmatory, and complementary functions served by a multimethod test battery. In some instances, for example, a respondent may during an interview report a problem for which there is no valid test index (e.g., having been sexually abused), and may demonstrate on testing a problem that is ordinarily not measured by interview data (e.g., poor perceptual-motor coordination). These two data sources can then be used additively to identify that the person has both a substance use disorder and a neuropsychological impairment. In another instance, a person who describes himself or herself during an interview as being a bright, well-educated individual with good leadership skills and a strong work ethic, and who then produces reliable documents attesting these same characteristics, offers assessors an opportunity for confirmatory use of these different data sources to lend certainty to a positive personnel report.

A third and somewhat more complicated set of circumstances may involve a respondent who behaves pleasantly and deferentially toward the assessor, reports being a kindly and even-tempered person, and produces limited and mostly conventional test responses that fall in the normal range. At the same time, however, the respondent is described by friends and relatives as a rageful and abusive person, and police reports show an arrest record for assault and domestic violence. Familiar to forensic psychologists consulting in the criminal justice system, this pattern of discrepant data can usually be explained by using them in a complementary fashion to infer defensiveness and a successful fake-good approach to the interviewing and testing situations. As a further example in educational settings, a student whose poor grades suggest limited intelligence but whose test performance indicates considerable intelligence gives assessors a basis for drawing in a complementary fashion on the divergent data to infer the likelihood of psychologically determined underachievement.

Because of the increased understanding of people that can accrue from integrating multiple sources of information, thorough psychological evaluation utilizes all of the available data during the interpretation phase of the assessment process. This consideration in conducting psychological assessments touches on the question of how much data should be collected in the first place. Theoretically, there can never be too much information in an assessment situation. There may be redundant information that provides more confirmatory evidence than is needed, and there may be irrelevant information that serves no additive function in answering the referral question, but examiners can choose to discard the former and ignore the latter. Moreover, all test, interview, and observational data that may be collected reflect some psychological characteristics of the person showing this behavior and therefore signify something potentially helpful to know about the person being assessed.

On the other hand, there are practical limits to how much assessment information should be collected to guide the formulation of interpretations. Above all, psychological assessors are responsible for conducting evaluations in a cost-effective manner that provides adequate responses to referral questions with the least possible expense of time and money. As noted previously, practitioners who provide and charge for services that they know will make little difference are exploiting the recipients of their services and jeopardizing their own professional respectability. Assessment psychologists may differ in the amount and kind of data they regard as sufficient to conduct a fully adequate evaluation, but they generally recognize their ethical obligations to avoid going beyond what they genuinely believe will be helpful.

With further respect to providing answers to referral questions, two additional guidelines can help assessment psychologists in drawing wisely and constructively on the assessment data at their disposal. First, by taking full account of indications of both psychological strengths and weaknesses in people they examine, assessors can present a balanced description of their assets and liabilities. Psychological assessment has often addressed mainly what is wrong with people while giving insufficient attention to their adaptive capacities, positive potentials, and admirable qualities. In keeping with contemporary trends in psychology toward emphasizing wellness, happiness, optimism, and other positive features of the human condition (see Seligman & Csikszentmihalyi, 2000), assessment psychology serves its purposes best when the interpretive process gives full measure to adaptive capacities as well as functioning limitations.

Second, by recognizing that the inferences and impressions they derive from assessment data are likely to vary in the strength of the evidence supporting them, examiners can couch their interpretive statements in language that conveys their level of confidence in what they have to say. Most respondents provide clear and convincing evidence of at least some psychological characteristic, which examiners can then appropriately report in what may be called the *language of certainty*. The language of certainty states in direct terms what people are like and how they are likely to conduct themselves, as in saying, "This student has a marked reading disability," or "Mr. A. appears to be an impulsive person with limited self-control," or "Ms. B. is an outgoing and gregarious person who seeks out and enjoys interpersonal relationships." For other characteristics of a person being evaluated, the evidence may be fragmentary or suggestive rather than compelling and conclusive, in which case impressions are properly reported in what may be called the *language of conjecture*. Conjectural language suggests or speculates about possible features of a person's nature or likely behavior, as in saying, "There is some evidence to suggest that this child may have an auditory processing deficit," or "She occasionally shows tendencies to be inflexible in her approach to solving problems, which might limit the creativity of her decision-making as an executive," or "The data provide some basis for speculating that his lack of effort represents a passive-aggressive way of dealing with underlying anger and resentment he feels toward people who have demanded a lot from him."

UTILIZING ASSESSMENT INFORMATION

The assessment process culminates in the utilization of descriptions of psychological characteristics and behavioral tendencies as a basis for formulating conclusions and recommendations. Interpretations or assessment information are now translated into their implications for various decisions,

and the overall purpose and eventual goal of assessment can accordingly be conceived as a way of facilitating decision making about classification, selection, placement, diagnosis, and treatment of people being evaluated. In this output phase, however, account must be taken of the fact that assessment data and the descriptions to which they give rise may have different implications for different kinds of people living in different circumstances. Most important in this regard are possible sources of bias, applicable base rates, value judgments calling for cutting-score adjustments, and the cultural background and social context of the person being evaluated. Good assessment decisions depend on recognizing these considerations and preventing them from exerting undue influence on conclusions and recommendations.

Bias and Base Rates

As elaborated in Reynolds and Ramsay's chapter in the present volume, *bias* occurs in the utilization of assessment information when examiners allow preconceived notions and previously held beliefs to influence how they view the implications of their data. Assessment bias may arise either inadvertently, from attitudes of which examiners are unaware, or consciously, as purposeful intent on their part. Whether inadvertent or intentional, *assessment bias* takes the form of expectations that affect the meaning assigned to a set of findings, and most of these expectations originate in turn from demographic beliefs, environmental impressions, and epidemiological notions.

As an example of demographic beliefs, an assessor who thinks that older people and males are generally likely to perform better as managers than younger people and females may advise hiring a 45-year-old man and not hiring a 30-year-old woman for a managerial position, even if their psychological assessment information would be seen by most examiners as comparable or even favoring the female candidate. Similarly, an assessor who harbors a conviction that blue-collar African Americans are generally less likely to respond to psychotherapy than white-collar Caucasians may discourage psychotherapy for the former and recommend it for the latter, even when looking at assessment information showing equivalent treatment accessibility.

Environmental impressions as a source of biased expectations refer to the setting in which assessors are conducting an evaluation. Psychologists working in an inpatient facility in which a large percentage of patients are psychotically disturbed come to expect most of they people they examine to be psychotic, at least on admission, and they may accordingly be inclined to infer psychosis from a set of assessment data that would not have led them to this conclusion had they obtained it in an outpatient clinic in which psychotic disturbance is rarely seen. Similarly, psychologists assessing prison in-mates, among whom antisocial personality disorder is com-monly found, may be more likely to expect and diagnose this disorder than they would if they were working with similar data in a university counseling center.

As for *epidemiological* notions, examiners may be con-sciously or inadvertently influenced in the conclusions they draw by how they view the nature and incidence of various conditions. Those who believe that borderline personality disorder is widespread are likely to diagnose this condition more frequently than those who think this diagnostic cate-gory lacks precision and is used too frequently. Those who believe that attention-deficit/hyperactivity disorder (ADHD) occurs mainly in boys, and adolescent anorexia mainly in girls, are relatively unlikely to diagnose ADHD in girls and anorexia in boys.

In all such instances of possible influence derived from demographic, environmental, and epidemiological expecta-tions, the challenge for assessment psychologists is to recog-nize their personal biases and prevent them as much as possible from exerting inappropriate influence on the conclu-sions and recommendations they derive from their assess-ment data. On the other hand, the previous examples were chosen to indicate that epidemiological and environmental expectations may have some basis in fact. There are more psychotic patients in hospital than in clinic populations, there are more antisocial individuals in prison than on college cam-puses, and there are substantial gender differences in the in-cidence of ADHD and anorexia. From a strictly actuarial point of view, then, being hospitalized does increase the probability of being psychotic, being incarcerated does increase the probability of being antisocial, and being male or female does increase the probability of being attention disor-dered or anorexic, respectively. Taking adequate account of such actual setting and group differences, while preventing them from resulting in biased conclusions, involves being alert to whatever base-rate information may be available in the individual case.

Base-rate information refers to the expected frequency of a characteristic or behavior in particular persons or circum-stances. Attention to applicable base rates provides a way of estimating the utility of assessment procedures, particularly with respect to their efficiency in assessing rare events. As first identified by Meehl and Rosen (1955), base rates can be-come problematic for measuring instruments when the ex-pected frequency of an event falls very far below 50%. For example, in a clinical setting in which 10% of the patients are suicidal, a valid test of suicidality that has a hit rate of 60% (i.e., is correct 60% of the time in identifying people in gen-eral as suicidal or nonsuicidal) is technically less efficient

than simply calling all of the patients nonsuicidal, which would be correct 90% of the time.

Although technically correct from a psychometric per-spective, this type of base-rate emphasis on efficiency does not always satisfy priorities in actual assessment practice. Assessment methods that are inefficient in assessing suicidal-ity, given its low base rate even in most patient populations, may nevertheless correctly identify a subgroup of patients in whom suicidal behavior is relatively likely to occur. An ex-aminer can then use this information to recommend suicide precautions for this apparently suicidal subgroup, which is preferable to overlooking the self-destructive potential of the high-risk group by exercising the technically more efficient option of calling all of the patients nonsuicidal.

The base-rate problem can also be minimized by focusing assessment efforts on restricted populations in which the ex-pected frequency of the characteristic being evaluated is less rare than in the general population. Kamphuis and Finn (2002) note in this regard that the more closely a base rate approxi-mates 50%, the better prospects a valid measure has of im-proving on the efficiency of concluding that either everyone or no one has a certain characteristic or behavioral tendency. As an example of increasing the base rate by restricting the popu-lation, efficient prediction of violent behavior among people in general is difficult to achieve, because most people are non-violent. In a population of criminal offenders, however, many of whom have a history of violence, a valid measure of vio-lence potential may prove quite efficient in identifying those at greatest risk for violent behavior in the future.

Value Judgments and Cutting Scores

Value judgments in the present context refers to the purposes for which a respondent is being evaluated in relation to the frequency of false-positive and false-negative outcomes that an assessment variable is likely to produce. *False-positive outcomes* result in decisions based on assuming that people have certain conditions and tendencies that they in fact do not, whereas *false-negative outcomes* result in inferring that people lack certain conditions and tendencies that in actuality do characterize them. When assessments are being conducted to assist in making decisions about psychological characteris-tics and their consequences that most people would regard as undesirable, like being suicidal or homicidal, false positives may be of less concern than false negatives. A false-positive decision concerning dangerousness might result in a person's being unnecessarily supervised or even restrained, which is a regrettable but not a fatal outcome. A false-negative decision, on the other hand, by failing to identify dangerousness to oneself or others, can result in loss of life.

Conversely, false-positive outcomes may be more problematic than false-negative outcomes when referral questions concern desirable characteristics and consequences, like whether a person should be given a scholarship, a job, a promotion, or a parole. False negatives in this kind of assessment situation may result in denying people opportunities for which they are qualified and deserving, which is disadvantageous and perhaps unfair to them as individuals. However, when false positives result in promotion of personnel to positions of responsibility that exceed their capacities, or the parole of felons whose criminal tendencies have not abated, then many people other than the individual are likely to suffer serious consequences.

In relation to such value judgments, then, a set of assessment data may have different implications in difference assessment circumstances and thereby call for assessors to select carefully the *cutting scores* they utilize in formulating their conclusions and recommendations. For quantifiable dimensions of assessment that correlate positively with the presence of a characteristic or behavioral tendency, moving *up* the numerical scale produces a progressively decreasing percentage of false positives, and moving *down* the scale produces a progressively decreasing percentage of false negatives; just the opposite will be the case for assessment dimensions that are inversely correlated with what they measure. As a way of deciding the implications of assessment findings in a particular circumstance, cutting scores can thus be selected to minimize the likelihood of false-positive outcomes in examinations concerned with desirable consequences and minimize false-negative outcomes in the estimation of undesirable consequences.

Culture and Context

Just as assessment information may have different implications for people examined in different settings and for different purposes, it may also vary in its significance for respondents coming from different cultures or living in different social contexts. Hence the utilization phase of the assessment process must always take account of how characteristics of individuals identified in the interpretive phase are likely to affect their psychological functioning in their particular circumstances. Attention to cross-cultural influences has a long history in assessment psychology (see, e.g., Hallowell, 1951; Lindzey, 1961) and has seen a recent resurgence of interest, as described in the chapter by Geisinger in this volume and in contributions by Dana (1993, 2000b), Kazarian and Evans (1998), Suzuki, Ponterotto, and Meller (2000), and Williams, Satterwhite, and Saiz (1998).

The distinction drawn in this overview of the assessment process between interpreting and utilizing assessment information provides some useful guidelines for a two-step process in taking account of background and situational differences among respondents. The interpretive phase of assessment provides the first step, which consists of arriving at descriptive statements that identify a respondent's psychological characteristics as they exist independently of his or her cultural context and circumstances. Having superior intelligence, being orderly and compulsive, experiencing memory loss, being emotionally reserved, having an assertive and competitive bent, and being prone to acute anxiety in unfamiliar surroundings are examples of characteristics that define the nature of the individual. As revealed by assessment data, such characteristics will be present in people regardless of where they live, from whence they come, and in what they are involved. The utilization phase of the assessment process provides the second step, which involves being sufficiently sensitive to respondents' cultural and experiential contexts to estimate accurately the implications of their psychological characteristics in their particular life circumstances. Especially important in this regard is determining whether their psychological characteristics are likely to prove adaptive or maladaptive in their everyday world and what kinds of successful or unsuccessful adaptation might result from these characteristics in their particular circumstances.

Research findings document that cultural differences can lead to cross-cultural variation in modal psychological characteristics, and that the demands and expectations people face often determine the implications and consequences of particular characteristics, especially with respect to how adaptive they are (see Kazarian & Evans, 1998). For example, a generally passive, dependent, agreeable, and acquiescent person may be prone to adjustment difficulties in a cultural context that values autonomy, self-reliance, assertiveness, and competitiveness. Conversely, a fiercely independent and highly competitive person might feel comfortable and flourish psychologically in a subculture that values assertiveness, but might feel alienated and adapt poorly in a society that subordinates individual needs and preferences to the wishes and welfare of the group, and in which a passive and acquiescent person would get along very well.

These contextual influences on the implications of psychological characteristics extend to specific circumstances in persons' lives as well as their broader sociocultural contexts. A modest level of intelligence can be a source of comfort and success to young people whose personal and family expectations are simply that they graduate from high school, but a source of failure and dismay to those for whom graduation from a prestigious college is a minimum expectation. Similarly, a person with good coping skills and abundant adaptive capacities who is carrying a heavy burden of responsibilities and confronting numerous obstacles to meeting them may be susceptible to anxiety, irritability, and other consequences of a stress overload, whereas a person with limited coping skills and few adaptive capacities who is leading a narrowly restricted life involving very few demands may be able to maintain a comfortable psychological equilibrium and experience little in the way of subjectively felt distress. Likewise, a contemplative person who values being as careful as possible in completing tasks and arriving at conclusions may perform well in a job situation that calls for accuracy and thoroughness and involves relatively little time pressure, but may perform poorly in a position involving strict deadlines or requiring quick decisions on the basis of sketchy information, and in which a more decisive and action-oriented person would function more effectively.

As illustrated by the final example and those that have preceded it in this chapter, psychological assessment is a complex process. Diverse perspectives and attention to interacting variables are necessary in assessment psychology as elsewhere in behavioral science to expand knowledge and guide its practical application, and there is little to be gained from doctrinaire pronouncements of unidimensional approaches. To collect, interpret, and utilize assessment data effectively, one must give each of the issues identified in this introduction to the assessment process its just due, and the 24 chapters that follow are designed for this purpose.

REFERENCES

Ackerman, M. J., & Ackerman, M. C. (1997). Custody evaluation practices: A survey of experienced professionals (revisited). *Professional Psychology, 28,* 137–145.

Allard, G., & Faust, D. (2000). Errors in scoring objective personality tests. *Assessment, 7,* 119–129.

Allen, J., & Walsh, J. A. (2000). A construct-based approach to equivalence: Methodologies for cross-cultural/multicultural personality assessment research. In R. H. Dana (Ed.), *Handbook of cross-cultural and multicultural personality assessment* (pp. 63–86). Mahwah, NJ: Erlbaum.

Allport, G. W. (1937). *Personality: A psychological interpretation.* New York: Holt.

American Educational Research Association, American Psychological Association, and National Council on Measurement in Education. (1999). *Standards for educational and psychological testing.* Washington, DC: American Educational Research Association.

American Psychological Association. (1992). Ethical principles of psychologists and code of conduct. *American Psychologist, 47,* 1597–1611.

American Psychological Association. (2001). APA's guidelines for test user qualifications. *American Psychologist, 56,* 1099–1113.

Anastasi, A., & Urbina, S. (1997). *Psychological testing* (7th ed.). Englewood Cliffs, NJ: Prentice-Hall.

Beaber, R. J., Marston, A., Michelli, J., & Mills, M. J. (1985). A brief test for measuring malingering in schizophrenic individuals. *American Journal of Psychiatry, 142,* 1478–1481.

Beck, A. T., Steer, R. A., & Garbin, M. A. (1988). Psychometric properties of the Beck Depression Inventory: Twenty-five years of evaluation. *Clinical Psychology Review, 8,* 177–200.

Ben-Porath, Y. S. (1994). The ethical dilemma of coached malingering research. *Psychological Assessment, 6,* 14–15.

Berry, D. T. R., Wetter, M. W., & Baer, R. A. (2002). Assessment of malingering. In J. N. Butcher (Ed.), *Clinical personality assessment* (2nd ed., pp. 269–302). New York: Guilford.

Blau, T. H. (1998). *The psychologist as expert witness* (2nd ed.). New York: Wiley.

Bornstein, R. F., Rossner, S. C., Hill, E. L., & Stepanian, M. L. (1994). Face validity and fakability of objective and projective measures of dependency. *Journal of Personality Assessment, 63,* 363–386.

Butcher, J. N. (2002). How to use computer-based reports. In J. N. Butcher (Ed.), *Clinical personality assessment* (2nd ed., pp. 109–125). New York: Oxford University Press.

Butcher, J. N., Perry, J. N., & Atlis, M. M. (2000). Validity and utility of computer-based interpretations. *Psychological Assessment, 12,* 6–18.

Butcher, J. N., & Rouse, S. V. (1996). Personality: Individual differences and clinical assessment. *Annual Review of Psychology, 47,* 87–111.

Camara, W. J., Nathan, J. S., & Puente, A. E. (2000). Psychological test usage: Implications in professional psychology. *Professional Psychology, 31,* 141–154.

Campbell, D. T., & Fiske, D. W. (1959). Convergent and discriminant validation by the multitrait-multimethod matrix. *Psychological Bulletin, 56,* 81–105.

Cattell, R. B. (1946). *Description and measurement of personality.* New York: World Book.

Choca, J. P., Shanley, L. A., & Van Denberg, E. (1997). *Interpretive guide to the Millon Clinical Multiaxial Inventory* (2nd ed.). Washington, DC: American Psychological Association.

Conoley, J. C., & Impara, J. (Eds.). (1995). *The twelfth mental measurements yearbook.* Lincoln: University of Nebraska Press.

Dana, R. H. (1993). *Multicultural assessment perspectives for professional psychology.* Boston: Allyn and Bacon.

Dana, R. H. (2000a). An assessment-intervention model for research and practice with multicultural populations. In R. H. Dana (Ed.), *Handbook of cross-cultural and multicultural personality assessment* (pp. 5–17). Mahwah, NJ: Erlbaum.

Dana, R. H. (Ed.). (2000b). *Handbook of cross-cultural and multicultural personality assessment.* Mahwah, NJ: Erlbaum.

De Bruyn, E. E. J. (1992). A normative-prescriptive view on clinical psychodiagnostic decision making. *European Journal of Psychological Assessment, 8,* 163–171.

Exner, J. E., Jr. (2003). *The Rorschach: A comprehensive system. Vol. 1. Foundations* (4th ed.). New York: Wiley.

Fernandez-Ballesteros, R. (1997). Guidelines for the assessment process (GAP). *European Psychologist, 2,* 352–355.

Finger, M. S., & Ones, D. S. (1999). Psychometric equivalence of the computer and booklet forms of the MMPI: A meta-analysis. *Psychological Assessment, 11,* 58–66.

Finn, S. E. (1996). Assessment feedback integrating MMPI-2 and Rorschach findings. *Journal of Personality Assessment, 67,* 543–557.

Fischer, J., & Corcoran, K. J. (1994). *Measures for clinical practice: A sourcebook* (2nd ed., Vols. 1–2). New York: Macmillan.

Ganellen, R. J. (1996). *Integrating the Rorschach and the MMPI in personality assessment.* Mahwah, NJ: Erlbaum.

Garb, H. N. (1998). *Studying the clinician.* Washington, DC: American Psychological Association.

Garb, H. N. (2000). Computers will become increasingly important for psychological assessment: Not that there's anything wrong with that! *Psychological Assessment, 12,* 31–39.

Garfield, S. L. (1994). Research on client variables in psychotherapy. In A. E. Bergin & S. L. Garfield (Eds.), *Handbook of psychotherapy and behavior change* (4th ed., pp. 190–228). New York: Wiley.

Geisinger, K. F., & Carlson, J. F. (2002). Standards and standardization. In J. N. Butcher (Ed.), *Clinical personality assessment* (2nd ed., pp. 243–256). New York: Guilford.

Graham, J. R. (2000). *MMPI-2: Assessing personality and psychopathology* (3rd ed.). New York: Oxford University Press.

Greencavage, L. M., & Norcross, J. C. (1990). What are the commonalities among the therapeutic factors? *Professional Psychology, 21,* 372–378.

Greene, R. L. (1997). Assessment of malingering and defensiveness by multiscale inventories. In R. Rogers (Ed.), *Clinical assessment of malingering and deception* (2nd ed., pp. 169–207). New York: Guilford.

Greene, R. L. (2000). *The MMPI-2: An interpretive manual* (2nd ed.). Boston: Allyn and Bacon.

Groth-Marnat, G. (1997). *Handbook of psychological assessment* (3rd ed.). New York: Wiley.

Grove, W. M., & Meehl, P. E. (1996). Comparative efficiency of informal (subjective, impressionistic) and formal (mechanical, algorithmic) prediction procedures: The clinical-statistical controversy. *Psychology, Public Policy, and Law, 2,* 293–323.

Grove, W. M., Zald, D. H., Lebow, B. S., Snitz, B. E., & Nelson, C. (2000). Clinical versus mechanical prediction: A meta-analysis. *Psychological Assessment, 12,* 19–30.

Hallowell, A. I. (1951). The use of projective techniques in the study of the socio-psychological aspects of acculturation. *Journal of Projective Techniques, 15,* 27–44.

Heilbrun, K. (2001). *Principles of forensic mental health assessment.* New York: Kluwer Academic/Plenum Publishers.

Holland, J. L. (1985). *Vocational Preference Inventory (VPI).* Odessa, FL: Psychological Assessment Resources.

Holt, R. R. (1958). Clinical *and* statistical prediction: A reformulation and some new data. *Journal of Abnormal and Social Psychology, 56,* 1–12.

Holt, R. R. (1986). Clinical and statistical prediction: A retrospective and would-be integrative perspective. *Journal of Personality Assessment, 50,* 376–385.

Honaker, L. M., & Fowler, R. D. (1990). Computer-assisted psychological assessment. In G. Goldstein & M. Hersen (Eds.), *Handbook of psychological assessment* (2nd ed., pp. 521–546). New York: Pergamon Press.

Kamphuis, J. H., & Finn, S. E. (2002). Incorporating base rate information in daily clinical decision making. In J. N. Butcher (Ed.), *Clinical personality assessment* (2nd ed., pp. 257–268). New York: Oxford University Press.

Karon, B. P. (2000). The clinical interpretation of the Thematic Apperception Test, Rorschach, and other clinical data: A reexamination of statistical versus clinical prediction. *Professional Psychology, 31,* 230–233.

Kaufman, A. S. (1990). *Assessing adolescent and adult intelligence.* Boston: Allyn and Bacon.

Kazarian, S., & Evans, D. R. (Eds.). (1998). *Cultural clinical psychology.* New York: Oxford University Press.

Kitchener, K. S. (2000). *Foundations of ethical practice, research, and teaching in psychology.* Mahwah, NJ: Erlbaum.

Kleinmuntz, B. (1990). Why we still use our heads instead of the formulas: Toward an integrative approach. *Psychological Bulletin, 107,* 296–310.

Koocher, G. P., & Keith-Spiegel, P. (1998). *Ethics in psychology.* New York: Oxford University Press.

Kubiszyn, T. W., Finn, S. E., Kay, G. G., Dies, R. R., Meyer, G. J., Eyde, L. D., et al. (2000). Empirical support for psychological assessment in clinical health care settings. *Professional Psychology, 31,* 119–130.

Lees-Haley, P. R. (1997). Attorneys influence expert evidence in forensic psychological and neuropsychological cases. *Assessment, 4,* 321–324.

Lindzey, G. (1961). *Projective techniques and cross-cultural research.* New York: Appleton-Century-Crofts.

Maloney, M., & Ward, M. P. (1976). *Psychological assessment: A conceptual approach.* New York: Oxford University Press.

Masling, J. M. (1966). Role-related behavior of the subject and psychologist and its effect upon psychological data. In D. Levine (Ed.), *Nebraska symposium on motivation* (pp. 67–104). Lincoln: University of Nebraska Press.

Masling, J. M. (1998). Interpersonal and actuarial dimensions of projective testing. In L. Handler & M. J. Hilsenroth (Eds.), *Teaching and learning personality assessment* (pp. 119–135). Mahwah, NJ: Erlbaum.

Matarazzo, J. D. (1990). Psychological assessment versus psychological testing. *American Psychologist, 45,* 999–1017.

McCann, J. T. (1998). *Malingering and deception in adolescents.* Washington, DC: American Psychological Association.

McFall, R. M., & Townsend, J. T. (1998). Foundations of psychological assessment: Implications for cognitive assessment in clinical science. *Psychological Assessment, 10,* 316–330.

McFall, R. M., & Treat, T. A. (1999). Quantifying the information value of clinical assessments with signal detection theory. *Annual Review of Psychology, 50,* 215–241.

McMinn, M. F., Ellens, B. M., & Soref, E. (1999). Ethical perspectives and practice behaviors involving computer-based test interpretations. *Assessment, 6,* 71–77.

Meehl, P. E. (1954). *Clinical versus statistical prediction.* Minneapolis: University of Minnesota Press.

Meehl, P. E. (1986). Causes and effects of my disturbing little book. *Journal of Personality Assessment, 50,* 370–375.

Meehl, P. E., & Rosen, A. (1955). Antecedent probability and the efficiency of psychometric signs, patterns, or cutting scores. *Psychological Bulletin, 52,* 194–216.

Meyer, G. J., Finn, S. E., Eyde, L. D., Kay, G. G., Moreland, K. L., Dies, R. R., et al. (2001). Psychological testing and psychological assessment: A review of evidence and issues. *American Psychologist, 56,* 128–165.

Mohr, D. C. (1995). Negative outcome in psychotherapy. *Clinical Psychology, 2,* 1–27.

Monahan, J. (Ed.). (1980). *Who is the client?* Washington, DC: American Psychological Association.

Pankratz, L., & Binder, L. M. (1997). Malingering on intellectual and neuropsychological measures. In R. Rogers (Ed.), *Clinical assessment of malingering and deception* (2nd ed., pp. 223–236). New York: Guilford Press.

Rogers, R. (1997a). Current status of clinical methods. In R. Rogers (Ed.), *Clinical assessment of malingering and deception* (2nd ed., pp. 373–397). New York: Guilford Press.

Rogers, R. (1997b). Structured interviews and dissimulation. In R. Rogers (Ed.), *Clinical assessment of malingering and deception* (2nd ed., pp. 301–327). New York: Guilford Press.

Rogers, R., Gillis, J. R., Bagby, R. M., & Monteiro, E. (1991). Detection of malingering on the Structured Interview of Reported Symptoms (SIRSP): A study of coached and uncoached simulators. *Psychological Assessment, 3,* 673–677.

Rogers, R., Gillis, J. R., Dickens, S. E., & Bagby, R. M. (1991). Standardized assessment of malingering: Validation of the Structure Inventory of Reported Symptoms. *Psychological Assessment, 3,* 89–96.

Sandoval, J., Frisby, C. L., Geisinger, K. F., & Scheuneman, J. D. (Eds.). (1990). *Test interpretation and diversity.* Washington, DC: American Psychological Association.

Sawyer, J. (1965). Measurement *and* prediction, clinical *and* statistical. *Psychological Bulletin, 66,* 178–200.

Schretlen, D. J. (1997). Dissimulation on the Rorschach and other projective measures. In R. Rogers (Ed.), *Clinical assessment of malingering and deception* (2nd ed., pp. 208–222). New York: Guilford Press.

Seligman, M. E. P., & Csikszentmihalyi, M. (2000). Positive psychology: An introduction. *American Psychologist, 55,* 5–14.

Shapiro, D. L. (1991). *Forensic psychological assessment.* Boston: Allyn and Bacon.

Smith, G. P. (1997). Assessment of malingering with self-report measures. In R. Rogers (Ed.), *Clinical assessment of malingering and deception* (2nd ed., pp. 351–370). New York: Guilford Press.

Snyder, D. K. (2000). Computer-assisted judgment: Defining strengths and liabilities. *Psychological Assessment, 12,* 52–60.

Storm, J., & Graham, J. R. (2000). Detection of coached malingering on the MMPI-2. *Psychological Assessment, 12,* 158–165.

Stricker, G. (1997). Are science and practice commensurable? *American Psychologist, 52,* 442–448.

Suzuki, L. A., Ponterotto, J. G., & Meller, P. J. (Eds.). (2000). *The handbook of multicultural assessment* (2nd ed.). New York: Wiley.

Swets, J. A., Dawes, R. M., & Monahan, J. (2000). Psychological science can improve diagnostic decisions. *Psychological Science in the Public Interest, 1,* 1–26.

Tombaugh, T. N. (1997). The Test of Memory Malingering (TOMM): Normative data from cognitively intact and cognitively impaired individuals. *Psychological Assessment, 9,* 260–268.

Watkins, C. E., Campbell, V. L., Nieberding, R., & Hallmark, R. (1995). Contemporary practice of psychological assessment by clinical psychologists. *Professional Psychology, 26,* 54–60.

Weiner, I. B. (1989). On competence and ethicality in psychodiagnostic assessment. *Journal of Personality Assessment, 53,* 827–831.

Weiner, I. B. (1998). *Principles of Rorschach interpretation.* Mahwah, NJ: Erlbaum.

Weiner, I. B. (2002). How to anticipate ethical and legal challenges in personality assessments. In J. N. Butcher (Ed.), *Clinical personality assessment* (2nd ed., pp. 126–134). New York: Oxford University Press.

Wetter, M. W., & Corrigan, S. K. (1995). Providing information to clients about psychological tests: A survey of attorneys' and law students' attitudes. *Professional Psychology, 26,* 474–477.

Williams, J. E., Satterwhite, R. C., & Saiz, J. L. (1998). *The importance of psychological traits: A cross-cultural study.* New York: Plenum Press.

Youngjohn, J. R. (1995). Confirmed attorney coaching prior to neuropsychological evaluation. *Assessment, 2,* 279–284.

CHAPTER 2

Clinical Judgment and Mechanical Prediction

HOWARD N. GARB

As described in other chapters in this volume, considerable effort has been made to improve the quality of assessment information (e.g., by constructing new tests). However, it is also important that advances be made in the way that assessment information is used to make judgments and decisions. Two general methods for making judgments and decisions will be described and critiqued in this chapter: clinical judgment and mechanical prediction.

Having suffered through statistics classes, students and professionals may be put off by the term *mechanical prediction*. They may even feel weak and bewildered when confronted with terms such as *actuarial prediction, automated assessment,* and *statistical prediction.* Terminology in this area is sometimes confusing, so it will behoove us to take a moment to clarify the meaning of these and other terms.

In the context of personality assessment, *clinical judgment* refers to the method by which judgments and decisions that are made by mental health professionals. *Statistical prediction* refers to the method by which judgments and decisions that are made by using mathematical equations (most often linear regression equations). These mathematical equations are usually empirically based—that is, the parameters and weights for these equations are usually derived from empirical data. However, some statistical prediction rules (e.g., unit weight linear rules) are not derived using empirical data. The terms *statistical prediction* and *actuarial prediction* are close in meaning: They can be used interchangeably to describe rules that are derived from empirical data. Statistical

and actuarial prediction can be distinguished from *automated assessment*. Automated assessment computer programs consist of a series of *if-then statements*. These statements are written by expert clinicians based on their clinical experiences and their knowledge of the research literature and clinical lore. *Computer-based test interpretation programs* are examples of automated assessment programs. They have been enormously popular—for example, for the interpretation of the Minnesota Multiphasic Personality Inventory–II (MMPI-2; Butcher, Dahlstrom, Graham, Tellegen, & Kaemmer, 1989). They will be described in detail in the chapter by Butcher in this volume. Finally, the term *mechanical prediction* also needs to be defined. As defined by Grove, Zald, Lebow, Snitz, and Nelson (2000), mechanical prediction is "statistical prediction (using explicit equations), actuarial prediction (as with insurance companies' actuarial tables), and what we may call algorithmic prediction (e.g., a computer program emulating expert judges). . . . Mechanical predictions are 100% reproducible" (p. 19). In other words, mechanical prediction is a global term that subsumes statistical prediction, actuarial prediction, and automated assessment, but not clinical judgment.

To clarify how mechanical prediction rules can be used in personality assessment, it will be helpful to describe a model study. In a study conducted at Western Psychiatric Institute and Clinic at the University of Pittsburgh (Gardner, Lidz, Mulvey, & Shaw, 1996), the judgment task was to predict whether patients would become violent in the next 6 months. Clinicians were psychiatrists, psychiatric residents, and nurse-clinicians who had seen the patients in the emergency (admissions) department and who had conferred on the cases together. Clinical and statistical predictions were made for 784 patients. To obtain outcome scores, patients and significant others were interviewed over the following 6 months. Additional information was also used to learn if a patient had become violent: commitment, hospital, and police records were searched for reports of violent incidents. Patients were said to be violent if they had "laid hands on another person with violent intent or threatened someone with a weapon" (Lidz, Mulvey, & Gardner, 1993, p. 1008). One of the strengths of the study is that the data were analyzed using receiver operating characteristics (ROC) analysis. ROC methods form an important part of signal detection theory. Using ROC methods, measures of validity are unaffected by base rates or by clinicians' biases for or against Type I or Type II errors (McFall & Treat, 1999; Mossman, 1994; Rice & Harris, 1995). For both clinical prediction and statistical prediction, the average area under the ROC curve (AUC) was reported. For this task, the AUC is equal to the probability of a randomly selected violent patient's being predicted to be violent more often than a randomly selected nonviolent patient. The greater the AUC, the greater the accuracy of predictions. A value of .5 represents the chance level of prediction. With regard to the results, the AUC for statistical prediction was .74 and the AUC for clinical prediction was only .62.

Historically, the issue of clinical versus statistical prediction has been the subject of intense debate. The issue first drew a great deal of attention in 1954 when Paul Meehl published his classic book, *Clinical versus Statistical Prediction: A Theoretical Analysis and a Review of the Evidence.* This is a book that for many years was read by nearly all graduate students in clinical and counseling psychology programs. In his book, Meehl noted that in almost every comparison between clinical and statistical prediction, the statistical method was equal or superior to informal clinical judgment. This conclusion has generally been supported in subsequent reviews (e.g., Dawes, Faust, & Meehl, 1989, 1993; Garb, 1994; Goldberg, 1991; Grove et al., 2000; Grove & Meehl, 1996; Kleinmuntz, 1990; Marchese, 1992; Meehl, 1986; Wiggins, 1981). Meehl is one of the most highly regarded psychologists in the history of clinical psychology, and late in his career he bemoaned the fact that psychologists were neglecting the research on statistical prediction. According to Meehl (1986):

> There is no controversy in social science that shows such a large body of qualitatively diverse studies coming out so uniformly in the same direction as this one. When you are pushing 90 investigations, predicting everything from the outcome of football games to the diagnosis of liver disease and when you can hardly

come up with a half dozen studies showing even a weak tendency in favor of the clinician, it is time to draw a practical conclusion, whatever theoretical differences may still be disputed. (pp. 373–374)

According to Meehl and other advocates of statistical prediction, mental health professionals should be using statistical rules to make diagnoses, descriptions of traits and symptoms, behavioral predictions, and other types of judgments and decisions. Yet, clinicians rarely do this. One is left wondering why.

The following topics will be covered in this chapter: (a) results on clinical versus mechanical prediction, (b) the strengths and limitations of clinical judgment, (c) the strengths and limitations of automated assessment, and (d) the strengths and limitations of statistical prediction. Recommendations will be made for improving the way that judgments and decisions are made in clinical practice.

CLINICAL VERSUS MECHANICAL PREDICTION

The most comprehensive and sophisticated review of studies on clinical versus mechanical prediction was conducted by Grove et al. (2000). In addition to locating more studies than anyone else, they published the only meta-analysis in this area. Their review will be described in detail.

In their search of the literature, Grove et al. (2000) included only studies in the areas of psychology and medicine. Studies were included if clinicians and mechanical procedures were used to "predict human behavior, make psychological or medical diagnoses or prognoses, or assess states and traits (including abnormal behavior and normal personality)" (p. 20). Also, studies were included only if the clinicians and the mechanical procedures had access to "the same (or almost the same) predictor variables" (p. 20). After an extensive search of the literature, 136 studies were found that qualified for inclusion.

The results reported by Grove et al. (2000) favor mechanical prediction. Mechanical prediction techniques substantially outperformed clinical prediction in 44%, or 60%, of the studies. In contrast, clinicians substantially outperformed mechanical prediction techniques in 6%, or 8%, of the studies (results were calculated from their Figure 1, p. 21). In the remaining studies, clinical predictions were roughly as accurate as mechanical predictions. On average, mechanical prediction rules were about 10% more accurate than clinicians.

Overall, the results of the meta-analysis support the general superiority of mechanical prediction. However, in light of these findings, comments made by statistical prediction advocates seem too extreme. For example, Meehl's (1986, p. 374) claim that there are only "a half dozen studies showing even a weak tendency in favor of the clinician" no longer seems accurate. As noted by Grove et al. (2000), "Our results qualify overbroad statements in the literature opining that such superiority is completely uniform" (p. 25).

Grove et al. (2000) also reported additional interesting findings. The general superiority of mechanical prediction holds across categories: "It holds in general medicine, in mental health, in personality, and in education and training settings" (p. 25). They also found that mechanical prediction was usually superior regardless of whether clinicians were "inexperienced or seasoned judges" (p. 25). With regard to a third result, one variable was notable in the eight studies in which clinical judgment outperformed mechanical prediction: In seven of those eight studies, the clinicians received more data than the mechanical prediction rules. One implication of this finding is that optimal information has not always been used as input for mechanical prediction rules. One more result will be mentioned. Mechanical prediction rules were superior to clinicians by a larger margin when interview information was available. Limitations of interview information have been described in the clinical judgment literature (Ambady & Rosenthal, 1992; Garb, 1998, pp. 18–20).

To check on the integrity of their findings, Grove et al. (2000) conducted additional analyses:

[We] examined specific study design factors that are rationally related to quality (e.g., peer-reviewed journal versus chapter or dissertation, sample size, level of training and experience for judges, cross-validated versus non-cross-validated statistical formulae). Essentially all of these study-design factors failed to significantly influence study effect sizes; no such factor produced a sizable influence on study outcomes. (p. 25)

Thus, roughly the same results were obtained in studies varying in terms of methodological quality.

The Grove et al. (2000) meta-analysis is a landmark study, but it does not address many important issues. For example, specific mechanical prediction rules that clinicians should be using are not described; nor are obstacles to developing better mechanical prediction rules. Finally, conditions under which clinical judgment should be preferred to mechanical prediction are not described. These issues and others will now be discussed.

CRITIQUE OF MECHANICAL PREDICTION

Automated Assessment

As already noted, automated assessment programs consist of a series of if-then statements. They are written by clinicians on the basis of their clinical experiences and their knowledge of the research literature and clinical lore. They are considered to be mechanical prediction rules because statements generated by automated assessment programs are 100% reproducible.

Several strengths of automated assessment programs can be described. First, they are written by clinicians who are generally thought to be experts. Another advantage is that they are mechanical prediction methods, and thus test-retest reliability is perfect (e.g., given a particular MMPI-2 test protocol, the same test report will always be written). Also, the general superiority of mechanical prediction methods was supported by Grove et al. (2000), although results were not analyzed separately for automated assessment programs and statistical prediction rules.

A number of weaknesses can also be described. First, in empirical studies, alleged experts often have been no more accurate than other clinicians (for reviews, see Garb, 1989, 1998; Garb & Schramke, 1996). Second, although test-retest reliability is perfect, interrater reliability is not. Computer-based test reports generated by automated assessment programs are generally used by clinicians along with other information (e.g., history information). One should not assume that psychologists will make similar judgments and decisions when they integrate all of this information. Finally, and perhaps most important, many automated assessment programs for interpreting psychological test results are not validated (Adams & Heaton, 1985; Garb, 1998, 2000b; Garb & Schramke, 1996; Honaker & Fowler, 1990; Lanyon, 1987; Matarazzo, 1986; Snyder, 2000; Snyder, Widiger, & Hoover, 1990; but also see Butcher, Perry, & Atlis, 2000). Thus, automated assessment programs can "lend an unwarranted impression of scientific precision" (Snyder, 2000, p. 52).

Statistical Prediction

One can expect statistical prediction rules to be more accurate than automated assessment programs and clinical judges. After all, statistical prediction rules are usually based on accurate feedback. That is, when deriving statistical prediction rules, accurate criterion scores are usually obtained. Put another way (Garb, 2000a), "In general, statistical prediction rules will do well because they make use of the inductive method. A statistical prediction rule will do well to the extent that one can generalize from a derivation sample to a new sample" (p. 32). In contrast, in the course of clinical practice, it is normally too expensive for clinicians to obtain good criterion scores. For example, clinicians are unable to follow up with patients after a 6 month time period to learn if they have become violent. Similarly, when writing a computer-based test interpretation program, an expert clinician will not normally collect criterion information.

There is another important reason one can expect statistical prediction rules to be more accurate than automated assessment programs and clinical judges. The use of statistical prediction rules can minimize the occurrence of errors and biases, including race bias and gender bias (Garb, 1997). Automated assessment programs may be biased (e.g., descriptions may be more accurate for White clients than Black clients), because criterion scores are not usually obtained to learn whether accuracy varies by client characteristic (e.g., race). Errors and biases that occur when clinicians make judgments will be described in a later section. Suffice it to say that a carefully derived statistical rule will not make predictions that vary as a function of race or gender unless race or gender has been shown to be related to the behavior one is predicting. To make sure that statistical predictions are unbiased, the effects of client characteristics (e.g., race, gender) need to be investigated.

Although there are reasons to believe that statistical prediction rules will transform psychological assessment, it is important to realize that present-day rules are of limited value (Garb, 1994, 1998, 2000a). For tasks involving diagnosis or describing personality traits or psychiatric symptoms, many statistical prediction rules make use of only limited information (e.g., results from only a single psychological test). This might be satisfactory if investigators first determined that the assessment information represents the best information that is available. However, this is not the case. For tasks involving diagnosis and describing personality traits and psychiatric symptoms, investigators rarely collect a large amount of information and identify optimal predictors.

There is a methodological reason why optimal information has rarely been used for the tasks of diagnosis and describing personality traits and psychiatric symptoms. When statistical prediction rules have been derived for these tasks, criterion ratings have usually been made by psychologists who use information that is available in clinical practice (e.g., history and interview information). If information used by criterion judges is also used as input information for statistical prediction rules, criterion contamination can occur. To avoid criterion contamination, information that is given to criterion judges is not used as input information for statistical prediction rules, even though this information may be optimal. Thus, in many studies, statistical predictions are made using results from a psychological test but not results from history and interview information.

To avoid criterion contamination, new methods need to be used to construct and validate statistical rules for the tasks of diagnosis and describing personality traits and psychiatric symptoms (Garb, 1994, 1998, 2000a). For example, by collecting longitudinal information, one can obtain criterion scores that are not based on information that is normally used by mental health professionals. Thus, if a statistical rule makes a diagnosis of major depression, but longitudinal data reveal that the client later developed a manic episode, then we could say that this diagnosis was incorrect.

Criterion contamination is not a problem for behavioral prediction (e.g., predicting suicide), so it is not surprising that statistical prediction rules that have been used to predict behavior have been based on optimal information. For behavioral prediction, outcome scores are obtained after assessment information has been collected and predictions have been made. All of the information that is normally available in clinical practice can be used by a statistical prediction rule without fear of criterion contamination.

Most present-day statistical prediction rules have *not* been shown to be powerful. As already noted, statistical prediction rules for making diagnoses and describing personality traits and psychiatric symptoms have almost always made use of limited information that has not been shown to be optimal (e.g., Carlin & Hewitt, 1990; Danet, 1965; Goldberg, 1965, 1969, 1970; Grebstein, 1963; Hiler & Nesvig, 1965; Janzen & Coe, 1975; Kleinmuntz, 1967; Lindzey, 1965; Meehl, 1959; Oskamp, 1962; Stricker, 1967; Todd, 1954; Vanderploeg, Sison, & Hickling, 1987). Typically, the statistical prediction rules, and the clinicians to which they have been compared, have been given results from only a single test.

An example will be given. In one of the best known studies on clinical versus statistical prediction (Goldberg, 1965), MMPI (Hathaway & McKinley, 1942) results were used to discriminate between neurotic and psychotic clients. Goldberg constructed a formula that involves adding and subtracting MMPI T scores: Lie (L) + Paranoia (Pa) + Schizophrenia (Sc) − Hysteria (Hy) − Psychasthenia (Pt). Using data collected by Meehl (1959), hit rates were 74% for the Goldberg index and only 68% for the average clinician. Clinicians in this study were not given any information other than the MMPI protocols. The study is well known not so much because the statistical rule did better than clinicians, but because a simple linear rule was more accurate than complex statistical rules including regression equations, profile typologies, Bayesian techniques, density estimation procedures, the Perceptron algorithm, and sequential analyses. However, one can question whether the Goldberg index should be used by itself in clinical practice to make differential diagnoses of neurosis versus psychosis. As observed by Graham (2000), "It is important to note that the index is useful only when the clinician is relatively sure that the person being considered is either psychotic or neurotic. When the index is applied to the scores of normal persons or those with personality disorder diagnoses, most of them are considered to be psychotic" (p. 252). Thus, before using the Goldberg index, one needs to rule out diagnoses of normal and of personality disorder, either by relying on clinical judgment or another statistical prediction rule. Of course, the other limitation of the Goldberg index is that it is possible, and perhaps even likely, that clinicians could outperform the index if they were given history and interview information in addition to MMPI results.

In contrast to diagnosis and the description of personality traits and psychiatric symptoms, present-day rules are more promising for the task of prediction. Statistical prediction rules have been developed for predicting violence (e.g., Gardner et al., 1996; Lidz et al., 1993; Monahan et al., 2000), but they are not yet ready for clinical use. In commenting on their prediction rule, Monahan et al. (p. 318) noted that "the extent to which the accuracy of the actuarial tool developed here generalizes to other types of clinical settings (e.g., forensic hospitals) is unknown." One can anticipate (and hope) that actuarial rules for predicting violence will soon be available for widespread use in clinical practice.

Although valuable actuarial rules for predicting violence may soon be available, prospects are less promising for the prediction of suicide. This is such an important task that if a rule could obtain even a low level of accuracy, it might be of use in clinical practice. However, results for actuarial rules have been disappointing. For example, in one study (R. B. Goldstein, Black, Nasrallah, & Winokur, 1991), predictions were made for 1,906 patients who had been followed for several years. Forty-six of the patients committed suicide. Several risk factors for suicide were identified (e.g., history of suicide attempts, suicidal ideation on index admission, and gender). However, these risk factors could not be meaningfully used to make predictions. When the risk factors were incorporated into a statistical rule, five predictions of suicide were made, but only one of them was valid and predictions of no suicide were made for 45 of the 46 patients who did kill themselves. The statistical rule did not do well even though it was derived and validated on the same data set.

Among the most valuable statistical prediction rules currently available are those in the area of behavioral assessment. These rules are helpful for conducting functional analyses. As observed by Schlundt and Bell (1987),

> when clients keep a self-monitoring diary, a large amount of data is often generated. Typically, clinicians review the records and use clinical judgment to identify patterns and draw inferences about functional relationships among antecedents, behaviors, and consequences. Although the clinical review of self-monitoring records provides data that might not be otherwise obtained, clinical judgment is known to be subject to inaccuracies . . . and statistical prediction is typically more accurate and reliable than clinical judgment. (p. 216)

The shortcomings of clinical judgment for functional analyses were illustrated in a study by O'Brien (1995). In this study, the self-monitoring data for a client who complained of headaches were given to eight clinical psychology graduate students. Over a period of 14 days, the client monitored a number of variables including stress level, arguments, hours of sleep, number of headaches, headache severity, duration of headaches, and number of painkillers taken. The task for the graduate students was to estimate "the magnitude of functional relationships that existed between pairs of target behaviors and controlling factors by generating a subjective correlation" (p. 352). Results were both surprising and disappointing: The graduate students identified the controlling variables that were most strongly correlated with each headache symptom only 51% of the time.

Given the shortcomings of clinical judgment for describing functional relationships, it is important to note that sequential and conditional probability analyses have been used to analyze self-monitoring data. These statistical analyses have been used to clarify the functional relationships involved in a variety of problems including smoking addiction, bulimia, hypertension, and obesity (e.g., Schlundt & Bell, 1987; Shiffman, 1993).

In conclusion, there are reasons one can expect statistical prediction rules to be more accurate than automated assessment programs and clinical judges. However, relatively few statistical prediction rules can be recommended for clinical use. Substantial progress has occurred with predicting violence, child abuse and neglect among the offenders and it does seem likely that powerful statistical rules for these tasks will become available for use in clinical practice in the near future (see Wood, Garb, Lilienfeld, & Nezworski, 2002). Also, statistical rules for analyzing functional relationships are impressive. On the other hand, before powerful statistical rules become available for other tasks, such as diagnosis, the description of personality era psychopathology, and planning methodological barriers will have to be overcome.

CRITIQUE OF CLINICAL JUDGMENT

A strength of clinical judgment is that mental health professionals can make use of a wide range of information. Automated assessment programs and present-day statistical prediction rules generally make use of limited information, for example, results from a single psychological test. In contrast, mental health professionals can make judgments after reviewing all of the information that is normally available in clinical practice. As noted earlier, in seven of the eight studies that found clinicians to be substantially more accurate than mechanical prediction rules (Grove et al., 2000), clinicians had more information available than did the mechanical prediction rules.

Mental health professionals can make reliable and valid judgments if they are careful about the information they use, if they avoid making judgments for tasks that are extremely difficult (tasks that are so difficult the clinicians are unable to make reliable and valid judgments), and if they are careful in how they make their judgments (Garb, 1998). For example, they can make reliable and valid diagnoses if they adhere to diagnostic criteria. Similarly, they can make moderately valid predictions of violence.

The focus of this section is on the limitations of clinical judgment. Results from empirical studies reveal that it can be surprisingly difficult for mental health professionals to learn from clinical experience. That is, a large body of research contradicts the popular belief that the more experience clinicians have, the more likely it is that they will be able to make accurate judgments. Numerous studies have demonstrated that when different groups of clinicians are given identical sets of information, experienced clinicians are no more accurate than are less experienced clinicians (Dawes, 1994; Garb, 1989, 1998; Garb & Boyle, in press; Garb & Schramke, 1996; Goldberg, 1968; Wiggins, 1973; also see Meehl, 1997). Remarkably, these results even extend to comparisons of mental health professionals and graduate students in mental health fields. These results, along with results on the value of training, will be described. Afterward, the reasons clinicians have trouble learning from experience will be described.

Experience and Validity

The validity of judgments will be described for presumed expert versus nonexpert clinicians, experienced versus less experienced clinicians, clinicians versus graduate students, and graduate students followed over time. Also described will be research on illusory correlations. Results from all of these studies describe the relations among presumed expertise, experience, and validity.

For the task of interpreting objective and projective personality test results, alleged experts have been no more accurate than other clinicians, and experienced clinicians have been no more accurate than less experienced clinicians (Graham, 1967; Levenberg, 1975; Silverman, 1959; Turner, 1966; Walters, White, & Greene, 1988; Wanderer, 1969; Watson, 1967). In these studies, all of the clinicians were given the assessment information. For example, in one study (Turner), expert judges were "25 Fellows in the Society for Projective Techniques with at least 10 years of clinical experience with the Rorschach" (p. 5). In this study, different groups of judges were to use

Rorschach results to describe the personality functioning of clients. Not only were the presumed expert judges no more accurate than a group of recently graduated psychologists (PhDs) and a group of graduate students in clinical psychology, they were not even more accurate than a group of "25 undergraduate psychology majors who were unfamiliar with the technique" (p. 5). In another study (Graham, 1967), one group of PhD-level psychologists had used the MMPI much more frequently than a less experienced group of psychologists. Also, the experienced group, but not the inexperienced group, demonstrated a broad knowledge of the research literature on the MMPI. In this study, as in the others, judgmental validity was *not* related to experience and presumed expertise.

The relation between experience and validity has also been investigated among psychiatrists. Results indicate that experience is unrelated to the validity of diagnoses and treatment decisions, at least under some circumstances (Hermann, Ettner, Dorwart, Langman-Dorwart, & Kleinman, 1999; Kendell, 1973; Muller & Davids, 1999). For example, in one study (Muller & Davids, 1999), psychiatrists who described themselves as being experienced in the treatment of schizophrenic patients were no more adept than less experienced psychiatrists when the task was to assess positive and negative symptoms of schizophrenia. In another study (Hermann et al., 1999), the number of years of clinical experience was *negatively* related to validity. Hermann et al. found that "psychiatrists trained in earlier eras were more likely to use ECT [electroconvulsive therapy] for diagnoses outside evidence-based indications" (p. 1059). In this study, experienced psychiatrists may have made less valid judgments than younger psychiatrists because education regarding the appropriate use of ECT has improved in recent years. If this is true, then the value of having years of clinical experience did not compensate for not having up-to-date training.

Results have been slightly different in the area of neuropsychology. Neuropsychologists with national reputations did better than PhD psychologists when using the Bender-Gestalt Test to diagnose organic brain damage (Goldberg, 1959) and when using the Halstead-Reitan Neuropsychological Test Battery to describe neurological impairment (Wedding, 1983). Otherwise, results in the area of neuropsychology have been similar to results obtained in the areas of personality assessment and diagnosis. For example, neuropsychologists with the American Board of Professional Psychology (ABPP) diploma have generally been no more accurate than less experienced and presumably less qualified doctoral-level neuropsychologists (Faust et al., 1988; Gaudette, 1992; Heaton, Smith, Lehman, & Vogt, 1978; Wedding, 1983).

One of the neuropsychology studies will be described. In this study (Faust et al., 1988), 155 neuropsychologists evaluated results from several commonly used neuropsychological tools (including the Halstead-Reitan Neuropsychological Test Battery). The judgment task was to detect the presence of neurological impairment and describe the likely location, process, and etiology of any neurologic injury that might exist. Clinicians' levels of training and experience were *not* related to the validity of their judgments. Measures of training included amount of practicum experience in neuropsychology, number of supervised neuropsychology hours, relevant coursework, specialized neuropsychology internship training, and the completion of postdoctoral training in neuropsychology. Measures of experience included years of practice in neuropsychology and number of career hours spent on issues related to neuropsychology. Status in the ABPP was used as a measure of presumed expertise. The results indicated that there is no meaningful relationship between validity, on the one hand, and training, experience, and presumed expertise, on the other.

An assumption that is frequently made without our even being aware that we are making the assumption is that clinical and counseling psychologists are more accurate than psychology graduate students. However, with few exceptions, this assumption has not been supported. In empirical studies, psychologists and other types of mental health professionals have rarely been more accurate than graduate students, regardless of the type of information provided to clinicians. This has been true when judgments have been made on the basis of interviews (Anthony, 1968; Grigg, 1958; Schinka & Sines, 1974), case history information (Oskamp, 1965; Soskin, 1954), behavioral observations (Garner & Smith, 1976; E. Walker & Lewine, 1990), recordings of psychotherapy sessions (Brenner & Howard, 1976), MMPI protocols (Chandler, 1970; Danet, 1965; Goldberg, 1965, 1968; Graham, 1967, 1971; Oskamp, 1962; Walters et al., 1988; Whitehead, 1985), human figure drawing protocols (Levenberg, 1975; Schaeffer, 1964; Stricker, 1967), Rorschach protocols (Gadol, 1969; Turner, 1966; Whitehead, 1985), screening measures for detecting neurological impairment (Goldberg, 1959; Leli & Filskov, 1981, 1984; Robiner, 1978), and all of the information that clinical and counseling psychologists normally have available in clinical practice (Johnston & McNeal, 1967).

Although mental health professionals have rarely been more accurate than graduate students, two exceptions can be described. In both instances, the graduate students were just beginning their training. In the first study (Grebstein, 1963; reanalyzed by Hammond, Hursch, & Todd, 1964), the task was to use Rorschach results to estimate IQ. Clinical psychologists were more accurate than graduate students who had not yet had practicum training, although they were not more accurate than advanced graduate students. In a second

study (Falvey & Hebert, 1992), the task was to write treatment plans after reading case histories. Certified clinical mental health counselors wrote better treatment plans than graduate students in master's degree programs, but half of the graduate students had not yet completed a single class related to diagnosis or treatment planning.

Although mental health professionals were sometimes more accurate than beginning graduate students, this was not always the case. In one study (Whitehead, 1985), psychologists, first-year clinical psychology graduate students, and fully trained clinical psychology graduate students were instructed to make differential diagnoses on the basis of Rorschach or MMPI results. For example, one task they were given was to differentiate patients with schizophrenia from those with bipolar disorder. The first-year graduate students had received training in the use of the MMPI, but they had not yet received training in the use of the Rorschach. For this reason, the only Rorschach data given to beginning graduate students were transcripts of the Rorschach sessions. In contrast, the Rorschach data given to psychologists and fully trained graduate students included transcripts, response location sheets, and Rorschach scores (using the Comprehensive System Structural Summary; Exner, 1974). In general, all three groups of judges were able to make valid judgments (accuracy was better than chance), although they were significantly less accurate when the Rorschach was used as the sole source of data. A repeated measures analysis of variance indicated that accuracy did not vary for the three groups of judges, both for the Rorschach data and the MMPI data.

To learn about the relation between experience and validity, one can conduct a longitudinal study. In one study (Aronson & Akamatsu, 1981), 12 graduate students made judgments using the MMPI before and after they completed a year-long assessment and therapy practicum. All of the students had already completed a course on MMPI interpretation. To determine validity, graduate students' judgments were compared with criterion ratings made on the basis of patient and family interviews. Results revealed that validity increased from .42 to only .44 after graduate students completed their practicum. The practicum experience did not serve to improve accuracy significantly.

Studies on illusory correlations (Chapman & Chapman, 1967, 1969; Dowling & Graham, 1976; Golding & Rorer, 1972; Kurtz & Garfield, 1978; Lueger & Petzel, 1979; Mowrey, Doherty, & Keeley, 1979; Rosen, 1975, 1976; Starr & Katkin, 1969; R. W. Waller & Keeley, 1978) also demonstrate that it can be difficult for clinicians to learn from clinical experience (for a review, see Garb, 1998, pp. 23–25). An *illusory correlation* occurs when a person believes that events are correlated even though they really are not.

In a classic study that established the paradigm for studying illusory correlations, Chapman and Chapman (1967) hoped to learn why psychologists use the sign approach to interpret the draw-a-person test despite research that reflects negatively on its validity (Groth-Marnat & Roberts, 1998; Joiner & Schmidt, 1997; Kahill, 1984; Lilienfeld, Wood, & Garb, 2000, 2001; Motta, Little, & Tobin, 1993; Swensen, 1957; Thomas & Jolley, 1998). The *sign approach* involves interpreting a single feature of a drawing (e.g., size of figure, unusual eyes). It can be contrasted to the *global approach,* in which a number of indicators are summed to yield a total score. The global approach has a stronger psychometric foundation than the sign approach (e.g., Naglieri, McNeish, & Bardos, 1991).

In their study, Chapman and Chapman (1967) instructed psychologists to list features of drawings (signs) that are associated with particular symptoms and traits. They then presented human figure drawings to undergraduates. On the back of each drawing was a statement that described a trait or symptom that was said to be descriptive of the client who had drawn the picture. Undergraduates were to examine each drawing and then read the statement on the back. Afterwards, they were to describe signs that were associated with the traits and symptoms. The undergraduates were unaware that the experimenters had randomly paired the drawings and the statements on the back of the drawings. Remarkably, the undergraduates reported observing the same relations that had been reported by the clinicians.

The results of the Chapman and Chapman (1967) study indicate that clinicians respond to the verbal associations of human figure drawings. For example, both clinicians and undergraduates reported that there is a positive relation between unusually drawn eyes and watchfulness or suspiciousness.

The results from the Chapman and Chapman study help to explain why clinicians continue to interpret specific drawing signs even though the overwhelming majority of human figure drawing signs possess negligible or zero validity. Psychologists believe they have observed these relations in their clinical experience, even when they have not. Along with results from other studies on illusory correlation, the results from the Chapman and Chapman study show that clinicians can have a difficult time learning from experience.

Unanswered questions remain. Do psychologists who interpret projective drawings know the research literature on the validity of specific drawing signs? Would they stop making invalid interpretations if they became aware of negative findings or would they weigh their clinical experiences more heavily than the research findings? Research on experience and validity is important because it helps us understand the problems that can occur when psychologists ignore research findings and are guided only by their clinical experiences.

Training and Validity

Empirical results support the value of training. In some, but not all, studies, clinicians and graduate students were more accurate than lay judges. In other studies, mental health professionals with specialized training were more accurate than health professionals without specialized training.

When the task was to describe psychopathology using interview data, psychologists and graduate students outperformed undergraduate students (Grigg, 1958; Waxer, 1976; also see Brammer, 2002). However, for a similar task, they did not outperform physical scientists (Luft, 1950). Additional research needs to be done to clarify whether psychologists and graduate students did better than undergraduates because of the training they received or because they are more intelligent and mature.

When asked to describe psychopathology on the basis of case history data, clinicians outperformed lay judges when judgments were made for psychiatric patients (Horowitz, 1962; Lambert & Wertheimer, 1988; Stelmachers & McHugh, 1964; also see Holmes & Howard, 1980), but not when judgments were made for normal participants (Griswold & Dana, 1970; Oskamp, 1965; Weiss, 1963). Of course, clinicians rarely make judgments for individuals who are not receiving treatment. As a consequence, clinicians may incorrectly describe normals as having psychopathology because they are not used to working with them.

In other studies, judgments were made on the basis of psychological test results. Psychologists were *not* more accurate than lay judges (e.g., undergraduates) when they were given results from projective techniques, such as Rorschach protocols (Cressen, 1975; Gadol, 1969; Hiler & Nesvig, 1965; Levenberg, 1975; Schaeffer, 1964; Schmidt & McGowan, 1959; Todd, 1954, cited in Hammond, 1955; C. D. Walker & Linden, 1967). Nor were they more accurate than lay judges when the task was to detect brain impairment using screening instruments (Goldberg, 1959; Leli & Filskov, 1981, 1984; Nadler, Fink, Shontz, & Brink, 1959; Robiner, 1978). For example, in a study on the Bender-Gestalt Test (Goldberg, 1959) that was later replicated (Robiner, 1978), clinical psychologists were no more accurate than their own secretaries! Finally, positive results have been obtained for the MMPI. In several studies on the use of the MMPI, psychologists and graduate students were more accurate than lay judges (Aronson & Akamatsu, 1981; Goldberg & Rorer, 1965, and Rorer & Slovic, 1966, described in Goldberg, 1968; Karson & Freud, 1956; Oskamp, 1962). For example, in a study that was cited earlier, Aronson and Akamatsu (1981) compared the ability of graduate and undergraduate students to perform Q-sorts to describe the personality characteristics of psychiatric patients on the basis of MMPI protocols. Graduate students had completed coursework on the MMPI and had some experience interpreting the instrument. Undergraduates had attended two lectures on the MMPI. Validity was determined by using criterion ratings based on family and patient interviews. Validity coefficients were .44 and .24 for graduate and undergraduate students, respectively. Graduate students were significantly more accurate than undergraduates.

The value of specialized training in mental health has also been supported. For example, neuropsychologists are more accurate than clinical psychologists at detecting neurological impairment (e.g., S. G. Goldstein, Deysach, & Kleinknecht, 1973), psychologists with a background in forensic psychology are more accurate than other psychologists when the task is to detect lying (Ekman, O'Sullivan, & Frank, 1999), and psychiatrists make more appropriate decisions than other physicians when prescribing antidepressant medicine (e.g., making sure a patient is on a therapeutic dose; Fairman, Drevets, Kreisman, & Teitelbaum, 1998).

IMPEDIMENTS TO LEARNING FROM EXPERIENCE

It is important to understand why it can be difficult for mental health professionals to learn from experience. Invalid assessment information, fallible cognitive processes, and inadequate feedback are some of the factors that can lead to poor judgments and a failure to learn from experience (Arkes, 1981; Brehmer, 1980; Dawes, 1994; Dawes et al., 1989; Einhorn, 1988; Garb, 1998).

Assessment Information

It will be difficult for clinicians to learn from experience if they are using invalid, or marginally valid, information. This point was made by Trull and Phares (2001):

> The accuracy of predictions is limited by the available measures and methods that are used as aids in the prediction process. If scores from psychological tests, for example, are not strongly correlated with the criterion of interest (that is, highly valid), then it is unlikely one could ever observe an effect for clinical experience. The accuracy of predictions will remain modest at best and will not depend on how "clinically experienced" the clinician is. (p. 277)

Bearing this in mind, one should be aware that some psychological techniques are controversial, at least when they are used for some tasks. For example, there is a controversy surrounding the use of the Rorschach (Lilienfeld et al., 2000, 2001). One problem is that the norms of the Rorschach Comprehensive System (Exner, 1993) may be inaccurate and may tend to make individuals look pathological even when no pathology exists. This issue has been hotly contested (Aronow, 2001; Exner, 2001; Hunsley & Di Giulio, 2001; Meyer, 2001; Widiger, 2001; Wood, Nezworski, Garb, & Lilienfeld, 2001a, 2001b).

Cognitive Processes

Cognitive biases, cognitive heuristics, and memory processes can exert a major negative impact on judgment and decision-making strategies. *Cognitive biases* are preconceptions or beliefs that can negatively influence clinical judgment. *Cognitive heuristics* are simple rules that describe how clinicians, and other people, make judgments and treatment decisions. Reliance on cognitive heuristics can be efficient because they are simple and they allow us to make judgments and decisions quickly and with little effort, but they are fallible and can lead clinicians to fail to learn from their experiences. With regard to memory, it should be obvious that clinicians will not learn from their experiences when their memories of those experiences are incorrect.

Several cognitive biases and heuristics will be described. *Confirmatory bias* occurs when clinicians seek, attend to, and remember information that can support but not counter their hunches or hypotheses. When psychologists ask questions that can confirm but not refute their impressions of a client, they are unlikely to make good judgments and decisions and they are unlikely to learn from their experiences. Similarly, psychologists are unlikely to learn from experience if their memories are distorted to support their preconceptions. Empirical research indicates that confirmatory bias does occur when psychologists work with clients (Haverkamp, 1993; Lee, Barak, Uhlemann, & Patsula, 1995; Murdock, 1988; Strohmer, Shivy, & Chiodo, 1990).

Hindsight bias describes how individuals, including mental health professionals, generate explanations for events that have occurred. Psychologists are generally unaware that knowledge of an outcome influences the perceived likelihood of that outcome (Fischhoff, 1975). In other words, after an event has occurred, people are likely to believe that the event was bound to occur. Results on hindsight bias have been replicated across a range of judgment tasks (Hawkins & Hastie, 1990), including the diagnosis of neurological impairment (Arkes, Faust, Guilmette, & Hart, 1988). Hindsight bias is important for understanding why mental health professionals have difficulty learning from clinical experience because it suggests that they think in deterministic (not probabilistic) terms. As observed by Einhorn (1988):

> The clinical approach to diagnosis and prediction can be characterized by its strong reliance on attempting to explain all the data. Indeed, a significant feature of diagnostic thinking is the remarkable speed and fluency that people have for generating explanations to explain any result. For example, "discussion sections" in journal articles are rarely at a loss to explain why the results did not come out as predicted (cf. Slovic & Fischhoff, 1977); psychotherapists are quick to point out that a patient's suicide should have been anticipated; and commissions, panels, committees, and the like, place blame on administrators for not knowing what is "obvious" in hindsight. As Fischhoff (1975) has pointed out, the past has few surprises but the future has many. (p. 63)

Mental health professionals will have trouble learning from experience if they do not recognize that all assessment information is fallible and that we frequently cannot make predictions with a high degree of certainty. That is, they will believe they have learned many things from a case when they have not. In conclusion, the cognitive processes described by the hindsight bias can lead clinicians to the erroneous belief that a particular combination of symptoms or behaviors is almost invariably associated with a particular outcome.

With regard to cognitive heuristics, the heuristic that is most relevant to understanding why clinicians can have a difficult time learning from experience is the *availability heuristic* (Kahneman, Slovic, & Tversky, 1982). This heuristic describes how selective memory can lead to judgmental error. Mental health professionals typically recall only selected information about a case because it is difficult, or even impossible, to remember all the details about a client. If their memories of a case are inadequate, they will have trouble learning from the case. According to the availability heuristic, the strength of a memory is related to the vividness of information and the strength of verbal associative connections between events. For example, a mental health professional is likely to remember a client who is striking or unusual in some way. Similarly, when trying to remember if a test indicator and a symptom or behavior co-occurred, a mental health professional may be influenced by the verbal associative connections between the test indicator and the symptom or behavior.

Finally, a large body of research on *covariation misestimation* suggests that mental health professionals are more likely to remember instances in which a test indicator and symptom are present than those in which a test indicator is absent and a symptom is either present or absent (Arkes, 1981; Kayne & Alloy, 1988). To learn whether a test indicator can be used to describe a symptom, one has to remember instances when the test indicator is absent as well as instances when it is present. Of course, an illusory correlation is said to be present when clinicians cannot accurately determine how two events covary. Thus, in the Chapman and Chapman (1967) study on illusory correlation, when undergraduates mistakenly remembered that there is a positive relation between unusually drawn eyes and watchfulness or suspiciousness, they may have been remembering cases when clients drew unusual eyes but forgetting cases when this drawing characteristic was not present. To be more specific, if a significant proportion of clients who draw unusual eyes are watchful or suspicious, then clinicians may believe this is a valid indicator. However, if a significant proportion of clients who do not draw unusual eyes are also watchful or suspicious, then it would be inappropriate to conclude that unusual eyes is a valid indicator. Thus, covariation misestimation, in addition to verbal associative connections (as mentioned by Chapman & Chapman), may in part explain the occurrence of illusory correlation phenomena.

One other theory about memory and clinical judgment will be mentioned. The act of making a diagnosis can influence how a mental health professional remembers a client's symptoms (Arkes & Harkness, 1980). According to this theory, a mental health professional may forget that a client has a particular symptom because the symptom is not typical of the symptoms associated with the client's diagnosis. Similarly, a symptom that is typical of the diagnosis may be "recalled," even though the client may not have that symptom. Of course, it is difficult to learn from experience when the details of cases are remembered incorrectly.

Environmental Factors

Mental health professionals learn from experience when they receive unbiased feedback, but the benefits of feedback are likely to be setting specific. In several studies (Goldberg & Rorer, 1965 and Rorer & Slovic, 1966, cited in Goldberg, 1968; Graham, 1971), psychologists made diagnoses using MMPI profiles. They became more accurate when they were told whether their diagnoses were valid or invalid, but only when all of the MMPI protocols came from the same setting.

Unfortunately, mental health professionals typically do not receive accurate feedback on whether their judgments and decisions are valid. For example, after making a diagnosis, no one comes along and tells them whether the diagnosis is correct or incorrect. They sometimes receive helpful feedback from a client, but *client feedback* is subjective and can be misleading. In contrast, when physicians make judgments, they frequently receive accurate feedback from laboratory results, radiology studies, and, in some cases, autopsies. In most cases, for mental health professionals to determine the accuracy of a judgment or decision, longitudinal or outcome data would have to be collected. Longitudinal and outcome data are collected in empirical studies, but most clinicians find this data to be too expensive and time consuming to collect in clinical practice.

Client feedback can be misleading for several reasons. First, clients may be reluctant to dispute their therapists' hypotheses. This can occur if clients are passive, suggestible, fearful of authority, or motivated to be pleasing. Second, clients may be unable to give accurate feedback because they may not be able to describe all of their traits and symptoms accurately. Even their reports of whether they have improved will be subjective and will be influenced by how they feel when they are asked. Finally, mental health professionals may describe clients in general terms. Their descriptions may be true of clients in general and may not describe traits that are specific to a client (e.g., "You have a superb sense of humor" and "You have too strong a need for others to admire you"—from Logue, Sher, & Frensch, 1992, p. 228). This phenomenon has been labeled the *Barnum effect,* after the circus figure P. T. Barnum (Meehl, 1954). Occurrence of the Barnum effect will be misleading to clinicians if they believe their judgments and decisions are valid for a specific client and not for clients in general.

Client feedback will also be misleading if clinicians make incorrect interpretations but convince their clients that they are correct. For example, after being told by their therapists that they were abused, some clients falsely remember having been abused (Loftus, 1993; Ofshe & Watters, 1994). These therapists have used a variety of techniques to help clients believe they remember having been abused, including telling them that they were abused, repeatedly asking them to remember the events, interpreting their dreams, hypnotizing them, and referring them to incest-survivor groups. Of course, clinicians will have a hard time learning from experience if they convince clients to accept incorrect interpretations and judgments.

SUMMARY AND DISCUSSION

It was not possible to cover all areas of research on clinical judgment and mechanical prediction in this chapter. Most notably, little was said about the validity of judgments made by mental health professionals (e.g., the reliability of diagnoses, the validity of descriptions of personality). An entire book on these topics has been written (Garb, 1998). However, conclusions from key areas of research were described. First, many automated assessment programs for interpreting psychological test results are not validated. Second, although there are reasons to believe that statistical prediction rules will transform psychological assessment, present-day rules are of limited value. Finally, the value of training in psychology and other mental health fields is supported, but research illustrates the difficulty of learning from clinical experience. These last results highlight the importance of continuing education, although continuing education may be of limited value unless it capitalizes on the findings of empirical research.

It is likely that clinical experience is valuable under certain circumstances. Experienced mental health professionals may be more adept at structuring judgment tasks (Brammer, 2002). In virtually of the studies that have been done, the tasks were already structured for clinicians: They were told what judgments to make and they were given information. However, in clinical practice, supervision can be helpful because questions are raised about what judgments and decisions need to be made (Do you think she is suicidal? Has the client ever had a manic episode?). Similarly, supervision can be helpful because supervisors provide direction on what information should be collected. Just the same, although experience may be helpful under certain circumstances, it does *not* seem to be useful for helping clinicians evaluate the validity of an assessment instrument. Nor does it seem to help clinicians make more valid judgments than graduate students when those judgments are made for a structured task.

A number of recommendations can be made for improving the way that judgments and decisions are made. The recommendations are made for both practicing clinicians and research investigators. First, mental health professionals should not use automated assessment programs to interpret test results unless they are appropriately validated. Second, as discussed earlier, new methods for building and validating statistical prediction rules need to be utilized. Data need to be collected for judgment tasks that have not yet been studied. Also, new analyses, including neural network models and multivariate taxometric analyses, should be used to build statistical rules (Marshall & English, 2000; Price, Spitznagel, Downey, Meyer, & Risk, 2000; N. G. Waller & Meehl, 1998). Third, mental health professionals need to become familiar with the research literature on clinical judgment. By becoming familiar with the results of studies on the validity of judgments made by mental health professionals, they can avoid making judgments for tasks that are surprisingly difficult and for which they are unlikely to be accurate. Fourth, clinicians should rely more on their notes and less on their memories. Fifth, to decrease confirmatory bias, clinicians should consider alternative hypotheses when making judgments and decisions. Sixth, when deciding whether to use an assessment instrument or treatment method, clinicians should weigh empirical findings more heavily than clinical experiences. That is, they should not use an assessment instrument or treatment method simply because it seems to work. In conclusion, to improve clinical practice dramatically, powerful statistical prediction rules need to be constructed and clinicians need to place less emphasis on their clinical experiences and greater emphasis on scientific findings.

REFERENCES

Adams, K. M., & Heaton, R. K. (1985). Automated interpretation of neuropsychological test data. *Journal of Consulting and Clinical Psychology, 53,* 790–802.

Ambady, N., & Rosenthal, R. (1992). Thin slices of expressive behavior as predictors of interpersonal consequences: A meta-analysis. *Psychological Bulletin, 111,* 256–274.

Anthony, N. (1968). The use of facts and cues in clinical judgments from interviews. *Journal of Clinical Psychology, 24,* 37–39.

Arkes, H. R. (1981). Impediments to accurate clinical judgment and possible ways to minimize their impact. *Journal of Consulting and Clinical Psychology, 49,* 323–330.

Arkes, H. R., Faust, D., Guilmette, T. J., & Hart, K. (1988). Eliminating the hindsight bias. *Journal of Applied Psychology, 73,* 305–307.

Arkes, H. R., & Harkness, A. R. (1980). Effect of making a diagnosis on subsequent recognition of symptoms. *Journal of Experimental Psychology: Human Learning and Memory, 6,* 568–575.

Aronow, E. (2001). CS norms, psychometrics, and possibilities for the Rorschach technique. *Clinical Psychology: Science and Practice, 8,* 383–385.

Aronson, D. E., & Akamatsu, T. J. (1981). Validation of a Q-sort task to assess MMPI skills. *Journal of Clinical Psychology, 37,* 831–836.

Brammer, R. (2002). Effects of experience and training on diagnostic accuracy. *Psychological Assessment, 14,* 110–113.

Brehmer, B. (1980). In one word: Not from experience. *Acta Psychologica, 45,* 223–241.

Brenner, D., & Howard, K. I. (1976). Clinical judgment as a function of experience and information. *Journal of Clinical Psychology, 32,* 721–728.

Butcher, J. N., Dahlstrom, W. G., Graham, J. R., Tellegen, A., & Kaemmer, B. (1989). *Minnesota Multiphasic Personality Inventory-2 (MMPI-2): Manual for administration and scoring.* Minneapolis: University of Minnesota Press.

Butcher, J. N., Perry, J. N., & Atlis, M. M. (2000). Validity and utility of computer-based test interpretation. *Psychological Assessment, 12,* 6–18.

Carlin, A. S., & Hewitt, P. L. (1990). The discrimination of patient generated and randomly generated MMPIs. *Journal of Personality Assessment, 54,* 24–29.

Chandler, M. J. (1970). Self-awareness and its relation to other parameters of the clinical inference process. *Journal of Consulting and Clinical Psychology, 35,* 258–264.

Chapman, L. J., & Chapman, J. P. (1967). Genesis of popular but erroneous psychodiagnostic observations. *Journal of Abnormal Psychology, 72,* 193–204.

Chapman, L. J., & Chapman, J. P. (1969). Illusory correlation as an obstacle to the use of valid psychodiagnostic signs. *Journal of Abnormal Psychology, 74,* 271–280.

Cressen, R. (1975). Artistic quality of drawings and judges' evaluations of the DAP. *Journal of Personality Assessment, 39,* 132–137.

Danet, B. N. (1965). Prediction of mental illness in college students on the basis of "nonpsychiatric" MMPI profiles. *Journal of Consulting Psychology, 29,* 577–580.

Dawes, R. M. (1994). *House of cards: Psychology and psychotherapy built on myth.* New York: Free Press.

Dawes, R. M., Faust, D., & Meehl, P. E. (1989). Clinical versus actuarial judgment. *Science, 243,* 1668–1674.

Dawes, R. M., Faust, D., & Meehl, P. E. (1993). Statistical prediction versus clinical prediction: Improving what works. In G. Keren & C. Lewis (Eds.), *A handbook for data analysis in the behavioral sciences: Methodological issues* (pp. 351–367). Hillsdale, NJ: Erlbaum.

Dowling, J. F., & Graham, J. R. (1976). Illusory correlation and the MMPI. *Journal of Personality Assessment, 40,* 531–538.

Einhorn, H. J. (1988). Diagnosis and causality in clinical and statistical prediction. In D. C. Turk & P. Salovey (Eds.), *Reasoning, inference, and judgment in clinical psychology* (pp. 51–70). New York: Free Press.

Ekman, P., O'Sullivan, M., & Frank, M. G. (1999). A few can catch a liar. *Psychological Science, 10,* 263–266.

Exner, J. E., Jr. (1974). *The Rorschach: A comprehensive system* (Vol. 1). New York: Wiley.

Exner, J. E., Jr. (1993). *The Rorschach: A comprehensive system, Vol. 1: Basic foundations* (3rd ed.). New York: Wiley.

Exner, J. E. (2001). A comment on *The misperception of psychopathology:* Problems with the norms of the Comprehensive System for the Rorschach. *Clinical Psychology: Science and Practice, 8,* 386–388.

Fairman, K. A., Drevets, W. C., Kreisman, J. J., & Teitelbaum, F. (1998). Course of antidepressant treatment, drug type, and prescriber's specialty. *Psychiatric Services, 49,* 1180–1186.

Falvey, J. E., & Hebert, D. J. (1992). Psychometric study of the Clinical Treatment Planning Simulations (CTPS) for assessing clinical judgment. *Journal of Mental Health Counseling, 14,* 490–507.

Faust, D., Guilmette, T. J., Hart, K., Arkes, H. R., Fishburne, F. J., & Davey, L. (1988). Neuropsychologists' training, experience, and judgment accuracy. *Archives of Clinical Neuropsychology, 3,* 145–163.

Fischhoff, B. (1975). Hindsight ≠ foresight: The effect of outcome knowledge on judgment under uncertainty. *Journal of Experimental Psychology: Human Perception and Performance, 1,* 288–299.

Gadol, I. (1969). The incremental and predictive validity of the Rorschach test in personality assessments of normal, neurotic, and psychotic subjects. *Dissertation Abstracts, 29,* 3482-B. (UMI No. 69-4469)

Garb, H. N. (1989). Clinical judgment, clinical training, and professional experience. *Psychological Bulletin, 105,* 387–396.

Garb, H. N. (1994). Toward a second generation of statistical prediction rules in psychodiagnosis and personality assessment. *Computers in Human Behavior, 10,* 377–394.

Garb, H. N. (1997). Race bias, social class bias, and gender bias in clinical judgment. *Clinical Psychology: Science and Practice, 4,* 99–120.

Garb, H. N. (1998). *Studying the clinician: Judgment research and psychological assessment.* Washington, DC: American Psychological Association.

Garb, H. N. (2000a). Computers will become increasingly important for psychological assessment: Not that there's anything wrong with that! *Psychological Assessment, 12,* 31–39.

Garb, H. N. (2000b). Introduction to the Special Section on the use of computers for making judgments and decisions. *Psychological Assessment, 12,* 3–5.

Garb, H. N., & Boyle, P. (in press). Understanding why some clinicians use pseudoscientific methods: Findings from research on clinical judgment. In S. O. Lilienfeld, J. M. Lohr, & S. J. Lynn (Eds.), *Science and pseudoscience in contemporary clinical psychology.* New York: Guilford Press.

Garb, H. N., & Schramke, C. J. (1996). Judgment research and neuropsychological assessment: A narrative review and meta-analyses. *Psychological Bulletin, 120,* 140–153.

Gardner, W., Lidz, C. W., Mulvey, E. P., & Shaw, E. C. (1996). Clinical versus actuarial predictions of violence by patients with mental illnesses. *Journal of Consulting and Clinical Psychology, 64,* 602–609.

Garner, A. M., & Smith, G. M. (1976). An experimental videotape technique for evaluating trainee approaches to clinical judging. *Journal of Consulting and Clinical Psychology, 44,* 945–950.

Gaudette, M. D. (1992). Clinical decision making in neuropsychology: Bootstrapping the neuropsychologist utilizing Brunswik's lens model (Doctoral dissertation, Indiana University of Pennsylvania, 1992). *Dissertation Abstracts International, 53,* 2059B.

Goldberg, L. R. (1959). The effectiveness of clinicians' judgments: The diagnosis of organic brain damage from the Bender-Gestalt test. *Journal of Consulting Psychology, 23,* 25–33.

Goldberg, L. R. (1965). Diagnosticians versus diagnostic signs: The diagnosis of psychosis versus neurosis from the MMPI. *Psychological Monographs, 79*(9, Whole No. 602).

Goldberg, L. R. (1968). Simple models or simple processes? Some research on clinical judgments. *American Psychologist, 23,* 483–496.

Goldberg, L. R. (1969). The search for configural relationships in personality assessment: The diagnosis of psychosis versus neurosis from the MMPI. *Multivariate Behavioral Research, 4,* 523–536.

Goldberg, L. R. (1970). Man versus model of man. *Psychological Bulletin, 73,* 422–432.

Goldberg, L. R. (1991). Human mind versus regression equation: Five contrasts. In W. M. Grove & D. Cicchetti (Eds.), *Thinking clearly about psychology: Vol. 1. Matters of public interest* (pp. 173–184). Minneapolis: University of Minnesota Press.

Golding, S. L., & Rorer, L. G. (1972). Illusory correlation and subjective judgment. *Journal of Abnormal Psychology, 80,* 249–260.

Goldstein, R. B., Black, D. W., Nasrallah, M. A., & Winokur, G. (1991). The prediction of suicide. *Archives of General Psychiatry, 48,* 418–422.

Goldstein, S. G., Deysach, R. E., & Kleinknecht, R. A. (1973). Effect of experience and amount of information on identification of cerebral impairment. *Journal of Consulting and Clinical Psychology, 41,* 30–34.

Graham, J. R. (1967). A Q-sort study of the accuracy of clinical descriptions based on the MMPI. *Journal of Psychiatric Research, 5,* 297–305.

Graham, J. R. (1971). Feedback and accuracy of clinical judgments from the MMPI. *Journal of Consulting and Clinical Psychology, 36,* 286–291.

Graham, J. R. (2000). *MMPI-2: Assessing personality and psychopathology* (3rd ed). New York: Oxford University Press.

Grebstein, L. (1963). Relative accuracy of actuarial prediction, experienced clinicians, and graduate students in a clinical judgment task. *Journal of Consulting Psychology, 37,* 127–132.

Grigg, A. E. (1958). Experience of clinicians, and speech characteristics and statements of clients as variables in clinical judgment. *Journal of Consulting Psychology, 22,* 315–319.

Griswold, P. M., & Dana, R. H. (1970). Feedback and experience effects on psychological reports and predictions of behavior. *Journal of Clinical Psychology, 26,* 439–442.

Groth-Marnat, G., & Roberts, L. (1998). Human Figure Drawings and House Tree Person drawings as indicators of self-esteem: A quantitative approach. *Journal of Clinical Psychology, 54,* 219–222.

Grove, W. M., Zald, D. H., Lebow, B. S., Snitz, B. E., & Nelson, C. (2000). Clinical versus mechanical prediction: A meta-analysis. *Psychological Assessment, 12,* 19–30.

Grove, W. M., & Meehl, P. E. (1996). Comparative efficiency of informal (subjective, impressionistic) and formal (mechanical, algorithmic) prediction procedures: The clinical-statistical controversy. *Psychology, Public Policy, and Law, 2*, 293–323.

Hammond, K. R. (1955). Probabilistic functioning and the clinical method. *Psychological Review, 62*, 255–262.

Hammond, K. R., Hursch, C. J., & Todd, F. J. (1964). Analyzing the components of clinical inference. *Psychological Review, 71*, 438–456.

Hathaway, S. R., & McKinley, J. C. (1942). *The Minnesota Multiphasic Personality Inventory*. Minneapolis: University of Minnesota Press.

Haverkamp, B. E. (1993). Confirmatory bias in hypothesis testing for client-identified and counselor self-generated hypotheses. *Journal of Counseling Psychology, 40*, 303–315.

Hawkins, S. A., & Hastie, R. (1990). Hindsight: Biased judgments of past events after the outcomes are known. *Psychological Bulletin, 107*, 311–327.

Heaton, R. K., Smith, H. H., Jr., Lehman, R. A. W., & Vogt, A. T. (1978). Prospects for faking believable deficits on neuropsychological testing. *Journal of Consulting and Clinical Psychology, 46*, 892–900.

Hermann, R. C., Ettner, S. L., Dorwart, R. A., Langman-Dorwart, N., & Kleinman, S. (1999). Diagnoses of patients treated with ECT: A comparison of evidence-based standards with reported use. *Psychiatric Services, 50*, 1059–1065.

Hiler, E. W., & Nesvig, D. (1965). An evaluation of criteria used by clinicians to infer pathology from figure drawings. *Journal of Consulting Psychology, 29*, 520–529.

Holmes, C. B., & Howard, M. E. (1980). Recognition of suicide lethality factors by physicians, mental health professionals, ministers, and college students. *Journal of Consulting and Clinical Psychology, 48*, 383–387.

Honaker, L. M., & Fowler, R. D. (1990). Computer-assisted psychological assessment. In G. Goldstein & M. Hersen (Eds.), *Handbook of psychological assessment* (2nd ed., pp. 521–546). New York: Pergamon Press.

Horowitz, M. J. (1962). A study of clinicians' judgments from projective test protocols. *Journal of Consulting Psychology, 26*, 251–256.

Hunsley, J., & Di Giulio, G. (2001). Norms, norming, and clinical assessment. *Clinical Psychology: Science and Practice, 8*, 378–382.

Janzen, W. B., & Coe, W. C. (1975). Clinical and sign prediction: The Draw-A-Person and female homosexuality. *Journal of Clinical Psychology, 31*, 757–765.

Johnston, R., & McNeal, B. F. (1967). Statistical versus clinical prediction: Length of neuropsychiatric hospital stay. *Journal of Abnormal Psychology, 72*, 335–340.

Joiner, T. E., & Schmidt, K. L. (1997). Drawing conclusions–or not–from drawings. *Journal of Personality Assessment, 69*, 476–481.

Kahill, S. (1984). Human figure drawing in adults: An update of the empirical evidence, 1967–1982. *Canadian Psychology, 25*, 269–292.

Kahneman, D., Slovic, P., & Tversky, A. (Eds.). (1982). *Judgment under uncertainty: Heuristics and biases*. New York: Cambridge University Press.

Karson, S., & Freud, S. L. (1956). Predicting diagnoses with the MMPI. *Journal of Clinical Psychology, 12*, 376–379.

Kayne, N. T., & Alloy, L. B. (1988). Clinician and patient as aberrant actuaries: Expectation-based distortions in assessment of covariation. In L. Y. Abramson (Ed.), *Social cognition and clinical psychology: A synthesis* (pp. 295–365). New York: Guilford Press.

Kendell, R. E. (1973). Psychiatric diagnoses: A study of how they are made. *British Journal of Psychiatry, 122*, 437–445.

Kleinmuntz, B. (1967). Sign and seer: Another example. *Journal of Abnormal Psychology, 72*, 163–165.

Kleinmuntz, B. (1990). Why we still use our heads instead of formulas: Toward an integrative approach. *Psychological Bulletin, 107*, 296–310.

Kurtz, R. M., & Garfield, S. L. (1978). Illusory correlation: A further exploration of Chapman's paradigm. *Journal of Consulting and Clinical Psychology, 46*, 1009–1015.

Lambert, L. E., & Wertheimer, M. (1988). Is diagnostic ability related to relevant training and experience? *Professional Psychology: Research and Practice, 19*, 50–52.

Lanyon, R. I. (1987). The validity of computer-based personality assessment products: Recommendations for the future. *Computers in Human Behavior, 3*, 225–238.

Lee, D. Y., Barak, A., Uhlemann, M. R., & Patsula, P. (1995). Effects of preinterview suggestion on counselor memory, clinical impression, and confidence in judgments. *Journal of Clinical Psychology, 51*, 666–675.

Leli, D. A., & Filskov, S. B. (1981). Clinical-actuarial detection and description of brain impairment with the W-B Form I. *Journal of Clinical Psychology, 37*, 623–629.

Leli, D. A., & Filskov, S. B. (1984). Clinical detection of intellectual deterioration associated with brain damage. *Journal of Clinical Psychology, 40*, 1435–1441.

Levenberg, S. B. (1975). Professional training, psychodiagnostic skill, and Kinetic Family Drawings. *Journal of Personality Assessment, 39*, 389–393.

Lidz, C. W., Mulvey, E. P., & Gardner, W. (1993). The accuracy of predictions of violence to others. *Journal of the American Medical Association, 269*, 1007–1011.

Lilienfeld, S. O., Wood, J. M., & Garb, H. N. (2000). The scientific status of projective techniques. *Psychological Science in the Public Interest, 1*, 27–66.

Lilienfeld, S. O., Wood, J. M., & Garb, H. N. (2001, May). What's wrong with this picture? *Scientific American*, 80–87.

Lindzey, G. (1965). Seer versus sign. *Journal of Experimental Research in Personality, 1*, 17–26.

Loftus, E. F. (1993). The reality of repressed memories. *American Psychologist, 48,* 518–537.

Logue, M. B., Sher, K. J., & Frensch, P. A. (1992). Purported characteristics of adult children of alcoholics: A possible "Barnum Effect." *Professional Psychology: Research and Practice, 23,* 226–232.

Lueger, R. J., & Petzel, T. P. (1979). Illusory correlation in clinical judgment: Effects of amount of information to be processed. *Journal of Consulting and Clinical Psychology, 47,* 1120–1121.

Luft, J. (1950). Implicit hypotheses and clinical predictions. *Journal of Abnormal and Social Psychology, 45,* 756–760.

Marchese, M. C. (1992). Clinical versus actuarial prediction: A review of the literature. *Perceptual and Motor Skills, 75,* 583–594.

Marshall, D. B., & English, D. J. (2000). Neural network modeling of risk assessment in child protective services. *Psychological Methods, 5,* 102–124.

Matarazzo, J. D. (1986). Computerized clinical psychological test interpretations: Unvalidated plus all mean and no sigma. *American Psychologist, 41,* 14–24.

McFall, R. M., & Treat, T. A. (1999). Quantifying the information value of clinical assessments with signal detection theory. *Annual Review of Psychology, 50,* 215–241.

Meehl, P. E. (1954). *Clinical versus statistical prediction: A theoretical analysis and a review of the evidence.* Minneapolis: University of Minnesota Press.

Meehl, P. E. (1959). A comparison of clinicians with five statistical methods of identifying psychotic MMPI profiles. *Journal of Counseling Psychology, 6,* 102–109.

Meehl, P. E. (1986). Causes and effects of my disturbing little book. *Journal of Personality Assessment, 50,* 370–375.

Meehl, P. E. (1997). Credentialed persons, credentialed knowledge. *Clinical Psychology: Science and Practice, 4,* 91–98.

Meyer, G. J. (2001). Evidence to correct misperceptions about Rorschach norms. *Clinical Psychology: Science and Practice, 8,* 389–396.

Monahan, J., Steadman, H. J., Appelbaum, P. S., Robbins, P. C., Mulvey, E. P., Silver, E., Roth, L. H., & Grisso, T. (2000). Developing a clinically useful actuarial tool for assessing violence risk. *British Journal of Psychiatry, 176,* 312–319.

Mossman, D. (1994). Assessing predictions of violence: Being accurate about accuracy. *Journal of Consulting and Clinical Psychology, 62,* 783–792.

Motta, R. W., Little, S. G., & Tobin, M. I. (1993). The use and abuse of human figure drawings. *School Psychology Quarterly, 8,* 162–169.

Mowrey, J. D., Doherty, M. E., & Keeley, S. M. (1979). The influence of negation and task complexity on illusory correlation. *Journal of Abnormal Psychology, 88,* 334–337.

Muller, M. J., & Davids, E. (1999). Relationship of psychiatric experience and interrater reliability in assessment of negative symptoms. *Journal of Nervous and Mental Diseases, 187,* 316–318.

Murdock, N. L. (1988). Category-based effects in clinical judgment. *Counseling Psychology Quarterly, 1,* 341–355.

Nadler, E. B., Fink, S. L., Shontz, F. C., & Brink, R. W. (1959). Objective scoring vs. clinical evaluation of the Bender-Gestalt. *Journal of Clinical Psychology, 15,* 39–41.

Naglieri, J. A., McNeish, T. J., & Bardos, A. N. (1991). *Draw-A-Person: Screening procedure for emotional disturbance.* Austin, TX: ProEd.

O'Brien, W. H. (1995). Inaccuracies in the estimation of functional relationships using self-monitoring data. *Journal of Behavior Therapy and Experimental Psychiatry, 26,* 351–357.

Ofshe, R., & Watters, E. (1994). *Making monsters: False memories, psychotherapy, and sexual hysteria.* New York: Scribner's.

Oskamp, S. (1962). The relationship of clinical experience and training methods to several criteria of clinical prediction. *Psychological Monographs, 76*(28, Whole No. 547).

Oskamp, S. (1965). Overconfidence in case-study judgments. *Journal of Consulting Psychology, 29,* 261–265.

Price, R. K., Spitznagel, E. L., Downey, T. J., Meyer, D. J., & Risk, N. K. (2000). Applying artificial neural network models to clinical decision making. *Psychological Assessment, 12,* 40–51.

Rice, M. E., & Harris, G. T. (1995). Violent recidivism: Assessing predictive validity. *Journal of Consulting and Clinical Psychology, 63,* 737–748.

Robiner, W. N. (1978). *An analysis of some of the variables influencing clinical use of the Bender-Gestalt.* Unpublished manuscript.

Rosen, G. M. (1975). On the persistence of illusory correlations with the Rorschach. *Journal of Abnormal Psychology, 84,* 571–573.

Rosen, G. M. (1976). "Associative homogeneity" may affect the persistence of illusory correlations but does not account for their occurrence. *Journal of Abnormal Psychology, 85,* 239.

Schaeffer, R. W. (1964). Clinical psychologists' ability to use the Draw-A-Person Test as an indicator of personality adjustment. *Journal of Consulting Psychology, 28,* 383.

Schinka, J. A., & Sines, J. O. (1974). Correlates of accuracy in personality assessment. *Journal of Clinical Psychology, 30,* 374–377.

Schlundt, D. G., & Bell, C. (1987). Behavioral assessment of eating patterns and blood glucose in diabetes using the self-monitoring analysis system. *Behavior Research Methods, Instruments, and Computers, 19,* 215–223.

Schmidt, L. D., & McGowan, J. F. (1959). The differentiation of human figure drawings. *Journal of Consulting Psychology, 23,* 129–133.

Shiffman, S. (1993). Assessing smoking patterns and motives. *Journal of Consulting and Clinical Psychology, 61,* 732–742.

Silverman, L. H. (1959). A Q-sort study of the validity of evaluations made from projective techniques. *Psychological Monographs, 73*(7, Whole No. 477).

Slovic, P., & Fischhoff, B. (1977). On the psychology of experimental surprises. *Journal of Experimental Psychology: Human Perception and Performance, 3,* 544–551.

Snyder, D. K. (2000). Computer-assisted judgment: Defining strengths and liabilities. *Psychological Assessment, 12,* 52–60.

Snyder, D. K., Widiger, T. A., & Hoover, D. W. (1990). Methodological considerations in validating computer-based test interpretations: Controlling for response bias. *Psychological Assessment, 2,* 470–477.

Soskin, W. F. (1954). Bias in postdiction from projective tests. *Journal of Abnormal and Social Psychology, 49,* 69–74.

Starr, B. J., & Katkin, E. S. (1969). The clinician as an aberrant actuary: Illusory correlation and the Incomplete Sentences Blank. *Journal of Abnormal Psychology, 74,* 670–675.

Stelmachers, Z. T., & McHugh, R. B. (1964). Contribution of stereotyped and individualized information to predictive accuracy. *Journal of Consulting Psychology, 28,* 234–242.

Stricker, G. (1967). Actuarial, naive clinical, and sophisticated clinical prediction of pathology from figure drawings. *Journal of Consulting Psychology, 31,* 492–494.

Strohmer, D. C., Shivy, V. A., & Chiodo, A. L. (1990). Information processing strategies in counselor hypothesis testing: The role of selective memory and expectancy. *Journal of Counseling Psychology, 37,* 465–472.

Swensen, C. H. (1957). Empirical evaluations of human figure drawings. *Psychological Bulletin, 54,* 431–466.

Thomas, G. V., & Jolley, R. P. (1998). Drawing conclusions: A re-examination of empirical and conceptual bases for psychological evaluation of children from their drawings. *British Journal of Clinical Psychology, 37,* 127–139.

Trull, T. J., & Phares, E. J. (2001). *Clinical Psychology* (6th ed.). Belmont, CA: Wadsworth.

Turner, D. R. (1966). Predictive efficiency as a function of amount of information and level of professional experience. *Journal of Projective Techniques and Personality Assessment, 30,* 4–11.

Vanderploeg, R. D., Sison, G. F. P., Jr., & Hickling, E. J. (1987). A reevaluation of the use of the MMPI in the assessment of combat-related Posttraumatic Stress Disorder. *Journal of Personality Assessment, 51,* 140–150.

Walker, C. D., & Linden, J. D. (1967). Varying degrees of psychological sophistication in the interpretation of sentence completion data. *Journal of Clinical Psychology, 23,* 229–231.

Walker, E., & Lewine, R. J. (1990). Prediction of adult-onset schizophrenia from childhood home movies of the patients. *American Journal of Psychiatry, 147,* 1052–1056.

Waller, N. G., & Meehl, P. E. (1998). *Multivariate taxometric procedures.* Thousand Oaks, CA: Sage.

Waller, R. W., & Keeley, S. M. (1978). Effects of explanation and information feedback on the illusory correlation phenomenon. *Journal of Consulting and Clinical Psychology, 46,* 342–343.

Walters, G. D., White, T. W., & Greene, R. L. (1988). Use of the MMPI to identify malingering and exaggeration of psychiatric symptomatology in male prison inmates. *Journal of Consulting and Clinical Psychology, 56,* 111–117.

Wanderer, Z. W. (1969). Validity of clinical judgments based on human figure drawings. *Journal of Consulting and Clinical Psychology, 33,* 143–150.

Watson, C. G. (1967). Relationship of distortion to DAP diagnostic accuracy among psychologists at three levels of sophistication. *Journal of Consulting Psychology, 31,* 142–146.

Waxer, P. (1976). Nonverbal cues for depth of depression: Set versus no set. *Journal of Consulting and Clinical Psychology, 44,* 493.

Wedding, D. (1983). Clinical and statistical prediction in neuropsychology. *Clinical Neuropsychology, 5,* 49–55.

Weiss, J. H. (1963). The effect of professional training and amount and accuracy of information on behavioral prediction. *Journal of Consulting Psychology, 27,* 257–262.

Whitehead, W. C. (1985). Clinical decision making on the basis of Rorschach, MMPI, and automated MMPI report data (Doctoral dissertation, University of Texas at Southwestern Medical Center at Dallas, 1985). *Dissertation Abstracts International, 46*(08), 2828B.

Widiger, T. A. (2001). The best and the worst of us? *Clinical Psychology: Science and Practice, 8,* 374–377.

Wiggins, J. S. (1973). *Personality and prediction: Principles of personality assessment.* Reading, MA: Addison-Wesley.

Wiggins, J. S. (1981). Clinical and statistical prediction: Where are we and where do we go from here? *Clinical Psychology Review, 1,* 3–18.

Wood, J. M., Nezworski, M. T., Garb, H. N., & Lilienfeld, S. O. (2001a). Problems with the norms of the Comprehensive System for the Rorschach: Methodological and conceptual considerations. *Clinical Psychology: Science and Practice, 8,* 397–402.

Wood, J. M., Nezworski, M. T., Garb, H. N., & Lilienfeld, S. O. (2001b). The misperception of psychopathology: Problems with the norms of the Comprehensive System for the Rorschach. *Clinical Psychology: Science and Practice, 8,* 350–373.

Wood, J. M. Garb, H. N., Lilienfeld, S. O., & Nezworski, M. T. (2002). Clinical assessment. *Annual Review of Psychology, 53,* 519–543.

CHAPTER 3

Psychometric Characteristics of Assessment Procedures

JOHN D. WASSERMAN AND BRUCE A. BRACKEN

"Whenever you can, count!" advised Sir Francis Galton (as cited in Newman, 1956, p. 1169), the father of contemporary psychometrics. Galton is credited with originating the concepts of regression, the regression line, and regression to the mean, as well as developing the mathematical formula (with Karl Pearson) for the correlation coefficient. He was a pioneer in efforts to measure physical, psychophysical, and mental traits, offering the first opportunity for the public to take tests of various sensory abilities and mental capacities in his London Anthropometric Laboratory. Galton quantified everything from fingerprint characteristics to variations in weather conditions to the number of brush strokes in two portraits for which he sat. At scientific meetings, he was known to count the number of times per minute members of the audience fidgeted, computing an average and deducing that the frequency of fidgeting was inversely associated with level of audience interest in the presentation.

Of course, the challenge in contemporary assessment is to know what to measure, how to measure it, and whether the measurements are meaningful. In a definition that still remains appropriate, Galton defined psychometry as the "art of imposing measurement and number upon operations of the mind" (Galton, 1879, p. 149). Derived from the Greek *psyche*

(ψυχή, meaning *soul*) and *metro* (μετρώ, meaning *measure*), psychometry may best be considered an evolving set of scientific rules for the development and application of psychological tests. Construction of psychological tests is guided by psychometric theories in the midst of a paradigm shift. Classical test theory, epitomized by Gulliksen's (1950) *Theory of Mental Tests,* has dominated psychological test development through the latter two thirds of the twentieth century. Item response theory, beginning with the work of Rasch (1960) and Lord and Novick's (1968) *Statistical Theories of Mental Test Scores,* is growing in influence and use, and it has recently culminated in the "new rules of measurement" (Embretson, 1995).

In this chapter, the most salient psychometric characteristics of psychological tests are described, incorporating elements from both classical test theory and item response theory. Guidelines are provided for the evaluation of test technical adequacy. The guidelines may be applied to a wide array of psychological tests, including those in the domains of academic achievement, adaptive behavior, cognitive-intellectual abilities, neuropsychological functions, personality and psychopathology, and personnel selection. The guidelines are based in part upon conceptual extensions of the *Standards for*

Educational and Psychological Testing (American Educational Research Association, 1999) and recommendations by such authorities as Anastasi and Urbina (1997), Bracken (1987), Cattell (1986), Nunnally and Bernstein (1994), and Salvia and Ysseldyke (2001).

PSYCHOMETRIC THEORIES

The psychometric characteristics of mental tests are generally derived from one or both of the two leading theoretical approaches to test construction: classical test theory and item response theory. Although it is common for scholars to contrast these two approaches (e.g., Embretson & Hershberger, 1999), most contemporary test developers use elements from both approaches in a complementary manner (Nunnally & Bernstein, 1994).

Classical Test Theory

Classical test theory traces its origins to the procedures pioneered by Galton, Pearson, Spearman, and E. L. Thorndike, and it is usually defined by Gulliksen's (1950) classic book. Classical test theory has shaped contemporary investigations of test score reliability, validity, and fairness, as well as the widespread use of statistical techniques such as factor analysis.

At its heart, classical test theory is based upon the assumption that an obtained test score reflects both true score and error score. Test scores may be expressed in the familiar equation

Observed Score = True Score + Error

In this framework, the observed score is the test score that was actually obtained. The true score is the hypothetical amount of the designated trait specific to the examinee, a quantity that would be expected if the entire universe of relevant content were assessed or if the examinee were tested an infinite number of times without any confounding effects of such things as practice or fatigue. Measurement error is defined as the difference between true score and observed score. Error is uncorrelated with the true score and with other variables, and it is distributed normally and uniformly about the true score. Because its influence is random, the average measurement error across many testing occasions is expected to be zero.

Many of the key elements from contemporary psychometrics may be derived from this core assumption. For example, internal consistency reliability is a psychometric function of random measurement error, equal to the ratio of the true score variance to the observed score variance. By comparison, validity depends on the extent of nonrandom measurement error. Systematic sources of measurement error negatively influence validity, because error prevents measures from validly representing what they purport to assess. Issues of test fairness and bias are sometimes considered to constitute a special case of validity in which systematic sources of error across racial and ethnic groups constitute threats to validity generalization. As an extension of classical test theory, generalizability theory (Cronbach, Gleser, Nanda, & Rajaratnam, 1972; Cronbach, Rajaratnam, & Gleser, 1963; Gleser, Cronbach, & Rajaratnam, 1965) includes a family of statistical procedures that permits the estimation and partitioning of multiple sources of error in measurement. Generalizability theory posits that a response score is defined by the specific conditions under which it is produced, such as scorers, methods, settings, and times (Cone, 1978); generalizability coefficients estimate the degree to which response scores can be generalized across different levels of the same condition.

Classical test theory places more emphasis on test score properties than on item parameters. According to Gulliksen (1950), the essential item statistics are the proportion of persons answering each item correctly (item difficulties, or *p* values), the point-biserial correlation between item and total score multiplied by the item standard deviation (reliability index), and the point-biserial correlation between item and criterion score multiplied by the item standard deviation (validity index).

Hambleton, Swaminathan, and Rogers (1991) have identified four chief limitations of classical test theory: (a) It has limited utility for constructing tests for dissimilar examinee populations (sample dependence); (b) it is not amenable for making comparisons of examinee performance on different tests purporting to measure the trait of interest (test dependence); (c) it operates under the assumption that equal measurement error exists for all examinees; and (d) it provides no basis for predicting the likelihood of a given response of an examinee to a given test item, based upon responses to other items. In general, with classical test theory it is difficult to separate examinee characteristics from test characteristics. Item response theory addresses many of these limitations.

Item Response Theory

Item response theory (IRT) may be traced to two separate lines of development. Its origins may be traced to the work of Danish mathematician Georg Rasch (1960), who developed a family of IRT models that separated person and item parameters. Rasch influenced the thinking of leading European and American psychometricians such as Gerhard Fischer and Benjamin Wright. A second line of development stemmed from research at the Educational Testing Service that culminated in Frederick Lord and Melvin Novick's (1968) classic textbook, including four chapters on IRT written by Allan Birnbaum. This book provided a unified statistical treatment of test theory and moved beyond Gulliksen's earlier classical test theory work.

IRT addresses the issue of how individual test items and observations map in a linear manner onto a targeted construct (termed *latent trait,* with the amount of the trait denoted by θ). The frequency distribution of a total score, factor score, or other trait estimates is calculated on a standardized scale with a mean θ of 0 and a standard deviation of 1. An item characteristic curve (ICC) can then be created by plotting the proportion of people who have a score at each level of θ, so that the probability of a person's passing an item depends solely on the ability of that person and the difficulty of the item. This item curve yields several parameters, including item difficulty and item discrimination. Item *difficulty* is the location on the latent trait continuum corresponding to chance responding. Item *discrimination* is the rate or slope at which the probability of success changes with trait level (i.e., the ability of the item to differentiate those with more of the trait from those with less). A third parameter denotes the probability of guessing. IRT based on the one-parameter model (i.e., item difficulty) assumes equal discrimination for all items and negligible probability of guessing and is generally referred to as the Rasch model. Two-parameter models (those that estimate both item difficulty and discrimination) and three-parameter models (those that estimate item difficulty, discrimination, and probability of guessing) may also be used.

IRT posits several assumptions: (a) *unidimensionality and stability* of the latent trait, which is usually estimated from an aggregation of individual item; (b) *local independence* of items, meaning that the only influence on item responses is the latent trait and not the other items; and (c) *item parameter invariance,* which means that item properties are a function of the item itself rather than the sample, test form, or interaction between item and respondent. Knowles and Condon (2000) argue that these assumptions may not always be made safely. Despite this limitation, IRT offers technology that makes test development more efficient than classical test theory.

SAMPLING AND NORMING

Under ideal circumstances, individual test results would be referenced to the performance of the entire collection of individuals (*target population*) for whom the test is intended. However, it is rarely feasible to measure performance of every member in a population. Accordingly, tests are developed through *sampling* procedures, which are designed to estimate the score distribution and characteristics of a target population by measuring test performance within a subset of individuals

selected from that population. Test results may then be interpreted with reference to sample characteristics, which are presumed to accurately estimate population parameters. Most psychological tests are norm referenced or criterion referenced. *Norm-referenced* test scores provide information about an examinee's standing relative to the distribution of test scores found in an appropriate peer comparison group. *Criterion-referenced* tests yield scores that are interpreted relative to predetermined standards of performance, such as proficiency at a specific skill or activity of daily life.

Appropriate Samples for Test Applications

When a test is intended to yield information about examinees' standing relative to their peers, the chief objective of sampling should be to provide a reference group that is representative of the population for whom the test was intended. Sample selection involves specifying appropriate stratification variables for inclusion in the sampling plan. Kalton (1983) notes that two conditions need to be fulfilled for stratification: (a) The population proportions in the strata need to be known, and (b) it has to be possible to draw independent samples from each stratum. Population proportions for nationally normed tests are usually drawn from Census Bureau reports and updates.

The stratification variables need to be those that account for substantial variation in test performance; variables unrelated to the construct being assessed need not be included in the sampling plan. Variables frequently used for sample stratification include the following:

- Sex.
- Race (White, African American, Asian/Pacific Islander, Native American, Other).
- Ethnicity (Hispanic origin, non-Hispanic origin).
- Geographic Region (Midwest, Northeast, South, West).
- Community Setting (Urban/Suburban, Rural).
- Classroom Placement (Full-Time Regular Classroom, Full-Time Self-Contained Classroom, Part-Time Special Education Resource, Other).
- Special Education Services (Learning Disability, Speech and Language Impairments, Serious Emotional Disturbance, Mental Retardation, Giftedness, English as a Second Language, Bilingual Education, and Regular Education).
- Parent Educational Attainment (Less Than High School Degree, High School Graduate or Equivalent, Some College or Technical School, Four or More Years of College).

The most challenging of stratification variables is socioeconomic status (SES), particularly because it tends to be associated with cognitive test performance and it is difficult to operationally define. Parent educational attainment is often used as an estimate of SES because it is readily available and objective, and because parent education correlates moderately with family income. Parent occupation and income are also sometimes combined as estimates of SES, although income information is generally difficult to obtain. Community estimates of SES add an additional level of sampling rigor, because the community in which an individual lives may be a greater factor in the child's everyday life experience than his or her parents' educational attainment. Similarly, the number of people residing in the home and the number of parents (one or two) heading the family are both factors that can influence a family's socioeconomic condition. For example, a family of three that has an annual income of $40,000 may have more economic viability than a family of six that earns the same income. Also, a college-educated single parent may earn less income than two less educated cohabiting parents. The influences of SES on construct development clearly represent an area of further study, requiring more refined definition.

When test users intend to rank individuals relative to the special populations to which they belong, it may also be desirable to ensure that proportionate representation of those special populations are included in the normative sample (e.g., individuals who are mentally retarded, conduct disordered, or learning disabled). Millon, Davis, and Millon (1997) noted that tests normed on special populations may require the use of base rate scores rather than traditional standard scores, because assumptions of a normal distribution of scores often cannot be met within clinical populations.

A classic example of an inappropriate normative reference sample is found with the original Minnesota Multiphasic Personality Inventory (MMPI; Hathaway & McKinley, 1943), which was normed on 724 Minnesota white adults who were, for the most part, relatives or visitors of patients in the University of Minnesota Hospitals. Accordingly, the original MMPI reference group was primarily composed of Minnesota farmers! Fortunately, the MMPI-2 (Butcher, Dahlstrom, Graham, Tellegen, & Kaemmer, 1989) has remediated this normative shortcoming.

Appropriate Sampling Methodology

One of the principal objectives of sampling is to ensure that each individual in the target population has an equal and independent chance of being selected. Sampling methodologies include both probability and nonprobability approaches, which have different strengths and weaknesses in terms of accuracy, cost, and feasibility (Levy & Lemeshow, 1999).

Probability sampling is a random selection approach that permits the use of statistical theory to estimate the properties of sample estimators. Probability sampling is generally too expensive for norming educational and psychological tests, but it offers the advantage of permitting the determination of the degree of sampling error, such as is frequently reported with the results of most public opinion polls. Sampling error may be defined as the difference between a sample statistic and its corresponding population parameter. Sampling error is independent from measurement error and tends to have a systematic effect on test scores, whereas the effects of measurement error by definition is random. When sampling error in psychological test norms is not reported, the estimate of the true score will always be less accurate than when only measurement error is reported.

A probability sampling approach sometimes employed in psychological test norming is known as *multistage stratified random cluster sampling;* this approach uses a multistage sampling strategy in which a large or dispersed population is divided into a large number of groups, with participants in the groups selected via random sampling. In two-stage cluster sampling, each group undergoes a second round of simple random sampling based on the expectation that each cluster closely resembles every other cluster. For example, a set of schools may constitute the first stage of sampling, with students randomly drawn from the schools in the second stage. Cluster sampling is more economical than random sampling, but incremental amounts of error may be introduced at each stage of the sample selection. Moreover, cluster sampling commonly results in high standard errors when cases from a cluster are homogeneous (Levy & Lemeshow, 1999). Sampling error can be estimated with the cluster sampling approach, so long as the selection process at the various stages involves random sampling.

In general, sampling error tends to be largest when nonprobability-sampling approaches, such as convenience sampling or quota sampling, are employed. *Convenience samples* involve the use of a self-selected sample that is easily accessible (e.g., volunteers). *Quota samples* involve the selection by a coordinator of a predetermined number of cases with specific characteristics. The probability of acquiring an unrepresentative sample is high when using nonprobability procedures. The weakness of all nonprobability-sampling methods is that statistical theory cannot be used to estimate sampling precision, and accordingly sampling accuracy can only be subjectively evaluated (e.g., Kalton, 1983).

Adequately Sized Normative Samples

How large should a normative sample be? The number of participants sampled at any given stratification level needs to be sufficiently large to provide acceptable sampling error, stable parameter estimates for the target populations, and sufficient power in statistical analyses. As rules of thumb, group-administered tests generally sample over 10,000 participants per age or grade level, whereas individually administered tests typically sample 100 to 200 participants per level (e.g., Robertson, 1992). In IRT, the minimum sample size is related to the choice of calibration model used. In an integrative review, Suen (1990) recommended that a minimum of 200 participants be examined for the one-parameter Rasch model, that at least 500 examinees be examined for the two-parameter model, and that at least 1,000 examinees be examined for the three-parameter model.

The minimum number of cases to be collected (or clusters to be sampled) also depends in part upon the sampling procedure used, and Levy and Lemeshow (1999) provide formulas for a variety of sampling procedures. Up to a point, the larger the sample, the greater the reliability of sampling accuracy. Cattell (1986) noted that eventually diminishing returns can be expected when sample sizes are increased beyond a reasonable level.

The smallest acceptable number of cases in a sampling plan may also be driven by the statistical analyses to be conducted. For example, Zieky (1993) recommended that a minimum of 500 examinees be distributed across the two groups compared in differential item function studies for group-administered tests. For individually administered tests, these types of analyses require substantial oversampling of minorities. With regard to exploratory factor analyses, Riese, Waller, and Comrey (2000) have reviewed the psychometric literature and concluded that most rules of thumb pertaining to minimum sample size are not useful. They suggest that when communalities are high and factors are well defined, sample sizes of 100 are often adequate, but when communalities are low, the number of factors is large, and the number of indicators per factor is small, even a sample size of 500 may be inadequate. As with statistical analyses in general, minimal acceptable sample sizes should be based on practical considerations, including such considerations as desired alpha level, power, and effect size.

Sampling Precision

As we have discussed, sampling error cannot be formally estimated when probability sampling approaches are not used, and most educational and psychological tests do not employ probability sampling. Given this limitation, there are no objective standards for the sampling precision of test norms. Angoff (1984) recommended as a rule of thumb that the maximum tolerable sampling error should be no more than 14%

of the standard error of measurement. He declined, however, to provide further guidance in this area: "Beyond the general consideration that norms should be as precise as their intended use demands and the cost permits, there is very little else that can be said regarding minimum standards for norms reliability" (p. 79).

In the absence of formal estimates of sampling error, the accuracy of sampling strata may be most easily determined by comparing stratification breakdowns against those available for the target population. The more closely the sample matches population characteristics, the more representative is a test's normative sample. As best practice, we recommend that test developers provide tables showing the composition of the standardization sample within and across all stratification criteria (e.g., *Percentages of the Normative Sample* according to combined variables such as *Age by Race by Parent Education*). This level of stringency and detail ensures that important demographic variables are distributed proportionately across other stratifying variables according to population proportions. The practice of reporting sampling accuracy for single stratification variables "on the margins" (i.e., by one stratification variable at a time) tends to conceal lapses in sampling accuracy. For example, if sample proportions of low socioeconomic status are concentrated in minority groups (instead of being proportionately distributed across majority and minority groups), then the precision of the sample has been compromised through the neglect of minority groups with high socioeconomic status and majority groups with low socioeconomic status. The more the sample deviates from population proportions on multiple stratifications, the greater the effect of sampling error.

Manipulation of the sample composition to generate norms is often accomplished through sample weighting (i.e., application of participant weights to obtain a distribution of scores that is exactly proportioned to the target population representations). Weighting is more frequently used with group-administered educational tests than psychological tests because of the larger size of the normative samples. Educational tests typically involve the collection of thousands of cases, with weighting used to ensure proportionate representation. Weighting is less frequently used with psychological tests, and its use with these smaller samples may significantly affect systematic sampling error because fewer cases are collected and because weighting may thereby differentially affect proportions across different stratification criteria, improving one at the cost of another. Weighting is most likely to contribute to sampling error when a group has been inadequately represented with too few cases collected.

Recency of Sampling

How old can norms be and still remain accurate? Evidence from the last two decades suggests that norms from measures of cognitive ability and behavioral adjustment are susceptible to becoming soft or stale (i.e., test consumers should use older norms with caution). Use of outdated normative samples introduces systematic error into the diagnostic process and may negatively influence decision-making, such as by denying services (e.g., for mentally handicapping conditions) to sizable numbers of children and adolescents who otherwise would have been identified as eligible to receive services. Sample recency is an ethical concern for all psychologists who test or conduct assessments. The American Psychological Association's (1992) *Ethical Principles* direct psychologists to avoid basing decisions or recommendations on results that stem from obsolete or outdated tests.

The problem of normative obsolescence has been most robustly demonstrated with intelligence tests. The *Flynn effect* (Herrnstein & Murray, 1994) describes a consistent pattern of population intelligence test score gains over time and across nations (Flynn, 1984, 1987, 1994, 1999). For intelligence tests, the rate of gain is about one third of an IQ point per year (3 points per decade), which has been a roughly uniform finding over time and for all ages (Flynn, 1999). The Flynn effect appears to occur as early as infancy (Bayley, 1993; S. K. Campbell, Siegel, Parr, & Ramey, 1986) and continues through the full range of adulthood (Tulsky & Ledbetter, 2000). The Flynn effect implies that older test norms may yield inflated scores relative to current normative expectations. For example, the Wechsler Intelligence Scale for Children—Revised (WISC-R; Wechsler, 1974) currently yields higher full scale IQs (FSIQs) than the WISC-III (Wechsler, 1991) by about 7 IQ points.

Systematic generational normative change may also occur in other areas of assessment. For example, parent and teacher reports on the Achenbach system of empirically based behavioral assessments show increased numbers of behavior problems and lower competence scores in the general population of children and adolescents from 1976 to 1989 (Achenbach & Howell, 1993). Just as the Flynn effect suggests a systematic increase in the intelligence of the general population over time, this effect may suggest a corresponding increase in behavioral maladjustment over time.

How often should tests be revised? There is no empirical basis for making a global recommendation, but it seems reasonable to conduct normative updates, restandardizations, or revisions at time intervals corresponding to the time expected to produce one standard error of measurement (SE_M) of change. For example, given the Flynn effect and a WISC-III FSIQ SE_M of 3.20, one could expect about 10 to 11 years should elapse before the test's norms would soften to the magnitude of one SE_M.

CALIBRATION AND DERIVATION OF REFERENCE NORMS

In this section, several psychometric characteristics of test construction are described as they relate to building individual scales and developing appropriate norm-referenced scores. *Calibration* refers to the analysis of properties of gradation in a measure, defined in part by properties of test items. *Norming* is the process of using scores obtained by an appropriate sample to build quantitative references that can be effectively used in the comparison and evaluation of individual performances relative to typical peer expectations.

Calibration

The process of item and scale calibration dates back to the earliest attempts to measure temperature. Early in the seventeenth century, there was no method to quantify heat and cold except through subjective judgment. Galileo and others experimented with devices that expanded air in glass as heat increased; use of liquid in glass to measure temperature was developed in the 1630s. Some two dozen temperature scales were available for use in Europe in the seventeenth century, and each scientist had his own scales with varying gradations and reference points. It was not until the early eighteenth century that more uniform scales were developed by Fahrenheit, Celsius, and de Réaumur.

The process of calibration has similarly evolved in psychological testing. In classical test theory, item difficulty is judged by the p value, or the proportion of people in the sample that passes an item. During ability test development, items are typically ranked by p value or the amount of the trait being measured. The use of regular, incremental increases in item difficulties provides a methodology for building scale gradations. Item difficulty properties in classical test theory are dependent upon the population sampled, so that a sample with higher levels of the latent trait (e.g., older children on a set of vocabulary items) would show different item properties (e.g., higher p values) than a sample with lower levels of the latent trait (e.g., younger children on the same set of vocabulary items).

In contrast, item response theory includes both item properties and levels of the latent trait in analyses, permitting item calibration to be sample-independent. The same item difficulty and discrimination values will be estimated regardless of trait distribution. This process permits item calibration to be "sample-free," according to Wright (1999), so that the scale transcends the group measured. Embretson (1999) has stated one of the new rules of measurement as "Unbiased estimates of item properties may be obtained from unrepresentative samples" (p. 13).

Item response theory permits several item parameters to be estimated in the process of item calibration. Among the indexes calculated in widely used Rasch model computer programs (e.g., Linacre & Wright, 1999) are item fit-to-model expectations, item difficulty calibrations, item-total correlations, and item standard error. The conformity of any item to expectations from the Rasch model may be determined by examining item fit. Items are said to have good fits with typical item characteristic curves when they show expected patterns near to and far from the latent trait level for which they are the best estimates. Measures of item difficulty adjusted for the influence of sample ability are typically expressed in logits, permitting approximation of equal difficulty intervals.

Item and Scale Gradients

The item gradient of a test refers to how steeply or gradually items are arranged by trait level and the resulting gaps that may ensue in standard scores. In order for a test to have adequate sensitivity to differing degrees of ability or any trait being measured, it must have adequate item density across the distribution of the latent trait. The larger the resulting standard score differences in relation to a change in a single raw score point, the less sensitive, discriminating, and effective a test is.

For example, on the Memory subtest of the Battelle Developmental Inventory (Newborg, Stock, Wnek, Guidubaldi, & Svinicki, 1984), a child who is 1 year, 11 months old who earned a raw score of 7 would have performance ranked at the 1st percentile for age, whereas a raw score of 8 leaps to a percentile rank of 74. The steepness of this gradient in the distribution of scores suggests that this subtest is insensitive to even large gradations in ability at this age.

A similar problem is evident on the Motor Quality index of the Bayley Scales of Infant Development–Second Edition Behavior Rating Scale (Bayley, 1993). A 36-month-old child with a raw score rating of 39 obtains a percentile rank of 66. The same child obtaining a raw score of 40 is ranked at the 99th percentile.

As a recommended guideline, tests may be said to have adequate item gradients and item density when there are approximately three items per Rasch logit, or when passage of a single item results in a standard score change of less than one third standard deviation (0.33 SD) (Bracken, 1987;

Bracken & McCallum, 1998). Items that are not evenly distributed in terms of the latent trait may yield steeper change gradients that will decrease the sensitivity of the instrument to finer gradations in ability.

Floor and Ceiling Effects

Do tests have adequate breadth, bottom and top? Many tests yield their most valuable clinical inferences when scores are extreme (i.e., very low or very high). Accordingly, tests used for clinical purposes need sufficient discriminating power in the extreme ends of the distributions.

The floor of a test represents the extent to which an individual can earn appropriately low standard scores. For example, an intelligence test intended for use in the identification of individuals diagnosed with mental retardation must, by definition, extend at least 2 standard deviations below normative expectations (IQ < 70). In order to serve individuals with severe to profound mental retardation, test scores must extend even further to more than 4 standard deviations below the normative mean (IQ < 40). Tests without a sufficiently low floor would not be useful for decision-making for more severe forms of cognitive impairment.

A similar situation arises for test ceiling effects. An intelligence test with a ceiling greater than 2 standard deviations above the mean (IQ > 130) can identify most candidates for intellectually gifted programs. To identify individuals as exceptionally gifted (i.e., IQ > 160), a test ceiling must extend more than 4 standard deviations above normative expectations. There are several unique psychometric challenges to extending norms to these heights, and most extended norms are extrapolations based upon subtest scaling for higher ability samples (i.e., older examinees than those within the specified age band).

As a rule of thumb, tests used for clinical decision-making should have floors and ceilings that differentiate the extreme lowest and highest 2% of the population from the middlemost 96% (Bracken, 1987, 1988; Bracken & McCallum, 1998). Tests with inadequate floors or ceilings are inappropriate for assessing children with known or suspected mental retardation, intellectual giftedness, severe psychopathology, or exceptional social and educational competencies.

Derivation of Norm-Referenced Scores

Item response theory yields several different kinds of interpretable scores (e.g., Woodcock, 1999), only some of which are norm-referenced standard scores. Because most test users are most familiar with the use of standard scores, it is the process of arriving at this type of score that we discuss. Transformation of raw scores to standard scores involves a number of decisions based on psychometric science and more than a little art.

The first decision involves the nature of raw score transformations, based upon theoretical considerations (Is the trait being measured thought to be normally distributed?) and examination of the cumulative frequency distributions of raw scores within age groups and across age groups. The objective of this transformation is to preserve the shape of the raw score frequency distribution, including mean, variance, kurtosis, and skewness. *Linear transformations* of raw scores are based solely on the mean and distribution of raw scores and are commonly used when distributions are not normal; linear transformation assumes that the distances between scale points reflect true differences in the degree of the measured trait present. *Area transformations* of raw score distributions convert the shape of the frequency distribution into a specified type of distribution. When the raw scores are normally distributed, then they may be transformed to fit a normal curve, with corresponding percentile ranks assigned in a way so that the mean corresponds to the 50th percentile, -1 *SD* and $+1$ *SD* correspond to the 16th and 84th percentiles, respectively, and so forth. When the frequency distribution is not normal, it is possible to select from varying types of nonnormal frequency curves (e.g., Johnson, 1949) as a basis for transformation of raw scores, or to use polynomial curve fitting equations.

Following raw score transformations is the process of smoothing the curves. Data smoothing typically occurs within groups and across groups to correct for minor irregularities, presumably those irregularities that result from sampling fluctuations and error. Quality checking also occurs to eliminate vertical reversals (such as those within an age group, from one raw score to the next) and horizonal reversals (such as those within a raw score series, from one age to the next). Smoothing and elimination of reversals serve to ensure that raw score to standard score transformations progress according to growth and maturation expectations for the trait being measured.

TEST SCORE VALIDITY

Validity is about the meaning of test scores (Cronbach & Meehl, 1955). Although a variety of narrower definitions have been proposed, psychometric validity deals with the extent to which test scores exclusively measure their intended psychological construct(s) and guide consequential decision-making. This concept represents something of a metamorphosis in understanding test validation because of its emphasis on the meaning and application of test results (Geisinger, 1992). Validity involves the inferences made from test scores and is not inherent to the test itself (Cronbach, 1971).

Evidence of test score validity may take different forms, many of which are detailed below, but they are all ultimately concerned with construct validity (Guion, 1977; Messick, 1995a, 1995b). *Construct validity* involves appraisal of a body of evidence determining the degree to which test score inferences are accurate, adequate, and appropriate indicators of the examinee's standing on the trait or characteristic measured by the test. Excessive narrowness or broadness in the definition and measurement of the targeted construct can threaten construct validity. The problem of excessive narrowness, or *construct underrepresentation,* refers to the extent to which test scores fail to tap important facets of the construct being measured. The problem of excessive broadness, or *construct irrelevance,* refers to the extent to which test scores are influenced by unintended factors, including irrelevant constructs and test procedural biases.

Construct validity can be supported with two broad classes of evidence: *internal* and *external* validation, which parallel the classes of threats to validity of research designs (D. T. Campbell & Stanley, 1963; Cook & Campbell, 1979). Internal evidence for validity includes information intrinsic to the measure itself, including content, substantive, and structural validation. External evidence for test score validity may be drawn from research involving independent, criterion-related data. External evidence includes convergent, discriminant, criterion-related, and consequential validation. This internal-external dichotomy with its constituent elements represents a distillation of concepts described by Anastasi and Urbina (1997), Jackson (1971), Loevinger (1957), Messick (1995a, 1995b), and Millon et al. (1997), among others.

Internal Evidence of Validity

Internal sources of validity include the intrinsic characteristics of a test, especially its content, assessment methods, structure, and theoretical underpinnings. In this section, several sources of evidence internal to tests are described, including content validity, substantive validity, and structural validity.

Content Validity

Content validity is the degree to which elements of a test, ranging from items to instructions, are relevant to and representative of varying facets of the targeted construct (Haynes, Richard, & Kubany, 1995). Content validity is typically established through the use of expert judges who review test content, but other procedures may also be employed (Haynes et al., 1995). Hopkins and Antes (1978) recommended that tests include a table of content specifications, in which the facets and dimensions of the construct are listed alongside the number and identity of items assessing each facet.

Content differences across tests purporting to measure the same construct can explain why similar tests sometimes yield dissimilar results for the same examinee (Bracken, 1988). For example, the universe of mathematical skills includes varying types of numbers (e.g., whole numbers, decimals, fractions), number concepts (e.g., half, dozen, twice, more than), and basic operations (addition, subtraction, multiplication, division). The extent to which tests differentially sample content can account for differences between tests that purport to measure the same construct.

Tests should ideally include enough diverse content to adequately sample the breadth of construct-relevant domains, but content sampling should not be so diverse that scale coherence and uniformity are lost. Construct underrepresentation, stemming from use of narrow and homogeneous content sampling, tends to yield higher reliabilities than tests with heterogeneous item content, at the potential cost of generalizability and external validity. In contrast, tests with more heterogeneous content may show higher validity with the concomitant cost of scale reliability. Clinical inferences made from tests with excessively narrow breadth of content may be suspect, even when other indexes of validity are satisfactory (Haynes et al., 1995).

Substantive Validity

The formulation of test items and procedures based on and consistent with a theory has been termed *substantive validity* (Loevinger, 1957). The presence of an underlying theory enhances a test's construct validity by providing a scaffolding between content and constructs, which logically explains relations between elements, predicts undetermined parameters, and explains findings that would be anomalous within another theory (e.g., Kuhn, 1970). As Crocker and Algina (1986) suggest, "psychological measurement, even though it is based on observable responses, would have little meaning or usefulness unless it could be interpreted in light of the underlying theoretical construct" (p. 7).

Many major psychological tests remain psychometrically rigorous but impoverished in terms of theoretical underpinnings. For example, there is conspicuously little theory associated with most widely used measures of intelligence (e.g., the Wechsler scales), behavior problems (e.g., the Child Behavior Checklist), neuropsychological functioning (e.g., the Halstead-Reitan Neuropsychology Battery), and personality and psychopathology (the MMPI-2). There may be some post hoc benefits to tests developed without theories; as observed by Nunnally and Bernstein (1994), "Virtually every measure

that became popular led to new unanticipated theories" (p. 107).

Personality assessment has taken a leading role in theory-based test development, while cognitive-intellectual assessment has lagged. Describing best practices for the measurement of personality some three decades ago, Loevinger (1972) commented, "Theory has always been the mark of a mature science. The time is overdue for psychology, in general, and personality measurement, in particular, to come of age" (p. 56). In the same year, Meehl (1972) renounced his former position as a "dustbowl empiricist" in test development:

> I now think that all stages in personality test development, from initial phase of item pool construction to a late-stage optimized clinical interpretive procedure for the fully developed and "validated" instrument, theory—and by this I mean all sorts of theory, including trait theory, developmental theory, learning theory, psychodynamics, and behavior genetics—should play an important role. . . . [P]sychology can no longer afford to adopt psychometric procedures whose methodology proceeds with almost zero reference to what bets it is reasonable to lay upon substantive personological horses. (pp. 149–151)

Leading personality measures with well-articulated theories include the "Big Five" factors of personality and Millon's "three polarity" bioevolutionary theory. Newer intelligence tests based on theory such as the Kaufman Assessment Battery for Children (Kaufman & Kaufman, 1983) and Cognitive Assessment System (Naglieri & Das, 1997) represent evidence of substantive validity in cognitive assessment.

Structural Validity

Structural validity relies mainly on factor analytic techniques to identify a test's underlying dimensions and the variance associated with each dimension. Also called *factorial validity* (Guilford, 1950), this form of validity may utilize other methodologies such as multidimensional scaling to help researchers understand a test's structure. Structural validity evidence is generally internal to the test, based on the analysis of constituent subtests or scoring indexes. Structural validation approaches may also combine two or more instruments in cross-battery factor analyses to explore evidence of convergent validity.

The two leading factor-analytic methodologies used to establish structural validity are exploratory and confirmatory factor analyses. Exploratory factor analyses allow for empirical derivation of the structure of an instrument, often without a priori expectations, and are best interpreted according to the psychological meaningfulness of the dimensions or factors that emerge (e.g., Gorsuch, 1983). Confirmatory factor analyses help researchers evaluate the congruence of the test data with a specified model, as well as measuring the relative fit of competing models. Confirmatory analyses explore the extent to which the proposed factor structure of a test explains its underlying dimensions as compared to alternative theoretical explanations.

As a recommended guideline, the underlying factor structure of a test should be congruent with its composite indexes (e.g., Floyd & Widaman, 1995), and the interpretive structure of a test should be the best fitting model available. For example, several interpretive indexes for the Wechsler Intelligence Scales (i.e., the verbal comprehension, perceptual organization, working memory/freedom from distractibility, and processing speed indexes) match the empirical structure suggested by subtest-level factor analyses; however, the original Verbal–Performance Scale dichotomy has never been supported unequivocally in factor-analytic studies. At the same time, leading instruments such as the MMPI-2 yield clinical symptom-based scales that do not match the structure suggested by item-level factor analyses. Several new instruments with strong theoretical underpinnings have been criticized for mismatch between factor structure and interpretive structure (e.g., Keith & Kranzler, 1999; Stinnett, Coombs, Oehler-Stinnett, Fuqua, & Palmer, 1999) even when there is a theoretical and clinical rationale for scale composition. A reasonable balance should be struck between theoretical underpinnings and empirical validation; that is, if factor analysis does not match a test's underpinnings, is that the fault of the theory, the factor analysis, the nature of the test, or a combination of these factors? Carroll (1983), whose factor-analytic work has been influential in contemporary cognitive assessment, cautioned against overreliance on factor analysis as principal evidence of validity, encouraging use of additional sources of validity evidence that move beyond factor analysis (p. 26). Consideration and credit must be given to both theory and empirical validation results, without one taking precedence over the other.

External Evidence of Validity

Evidence of test score validity also includes the extent to which the test results predict meaningful and generalizable behaviors independent of actual test performance. Test results need to be validated for any intended application or decision-making process in which they play a part. In this section, external classes of evidence for test construct validity are described, including convergent, discriminant, criterion-related, and consequential validity, as well as specialized forms of validity within these categories.

Convergent and Discriminant Validity

In a frequently cited 1959 article, D. T. Campbell and Fiske described a multitrait-multimethod methodology for investigating construct validity. In brief, they suggested that a measure is jointly defined by its methods of gathering data (e.g., self-report or parent-report) and its trait-related content (e.g., anxiety or depression). They noted that test scores should be related to (i.e., strongly correlated with) other measures of the same psychological construct (*convergent* evidence of validity) and comparatively unrelated to (i.e., weakly correlated with) measures of different psychological constructs (*discriminant* evidence of validity). The multitrait-multimethod matrix allows for the comparison of the relative strength of association between two measures of the same trait using different methods (monotrait-heteromethod correlations), two measures with a common method but tapping different traits (heterotrait-monomethod correlations), and two measures tapping different traits using different methods (heterotrait-heteromethod correlations), all of which are expected to yield lower values than internal consistency reliability statistics using the same method to tap the same trait.

The multitrait-multimethod matrix offers several advantages, such as the identification of problematic method variance. Method variance is a measurement artifact that threatens validity by producing spuriously high correlations between similar assessment methods of different traits. For example, high correlations between digit span, letter span, phoneme span, and word span procedures might be interpreted as stemming from the immediate memory span recall method common to all the procedures rather than any specific abilities being assessed. Method effects may be assessed by comparing the correlations of different traits measured with the same method (i.e., monomethod correlations) and the correlations among different traits across methods (i.e., heteromethod correlations). Method variance is said to be present if the heterotrait-monomethod correlations greatly exceed the heterotrait-heteromethod correlations in magnitude, assuming that convergent validity has been demonstrated.

Fiske and Campbell (1992) subsequently recognized shortcomings in their methodology: "We have yet to see a really good matrix: one that is based on fairly similar concepts and plausibly independent methods and shows high convergent and discriminant validation by all standards" (p. 394). At the same time, the methodology has provided a useful framework for establishing evidence of validity.

Criterion-Related Validity

How well do test scores predict performance on independent criterion measures and differentiate criterion groups? The relationship of test scores to relevant external criteria constitutes evidence of *criterion-related validity,* which may take several different forms. Evidence of validity may include criterion scores that are obtained at about the same time (*concurrent* evidence of validity) or criterion scores that are obtained at some future date (*predictive* evidence of validity). External criteria may also include functional, real-life variables (*ecological* validity), diagnostic or placement indexes (*diagnostic* validity), and intervention-related approaches (*treatment* validity).

The emphasis on understanding the functional implications of test findings has been termed *ecological validity* (Neisser, 1978). Banaji and Crowder (1989) suggested, "If research is scientifically sound it is better to use ecologically lifelike rather than contrived methods" (p. 1188). In essence, ecological validation efforts relate test performance to various aspects of person-environment functioning in everyday life, including identification of both competencies and deficits in social and educational adjustment. Test developers should show the ecological relevance of the constructs a test purports to measure, as well as the utility of the test for predicting everyday functional limitations for remediation. In contrast, tests based on laboratory-like procedures with little or no discernible relevance to real life may be said to have little ecological validity.

The capacity of a measure to produce relevant applied group differences has been termed *diagnostic validity* (e.g., Ittenbach, Esters, & Wainer, 1997). When tests are intended for diagnostic or placement decisions, diagnostic validity refers to the utility of the test in differentiating the groups of concern. The process of arriving at diagnostic validity may be informed by decision theory, a process involving calculations of decision-making accuracy in comparison to the base rate occurrence of an event or diagnosis in a given population. Decision theory has been applied to psychological tests (Cronbach & Gleser, 1965) and other high-stakes diagnostic tests (Swets, 1992) and is useful for identifying the extent to which tests improve clinical or educational decision-making.

The method of contrasted groups is a common methodology to demonstrate diagnostic validity. In this methodology, test performance of two samples that are known to be different on the criterion of interest is compared. For example, a test intended to tap behavioral correlates of anxiety should show differences between groups of normal individuals and individuals diagnosed with anxiety disorders. A test intended for differential diagnostic utility should be effective in differentiating individuals with anxiety disorders from diagnoses that appear behaviorally similar. Decision-making classification accuracy may be determined by developing cutoff scores or rules to differentiate the groups, so long as the rules show

adequate sensitivity, specificity, positive predictive power, and negative predictive power. These terms may be defined as follows:

- *Sensitivity:* the proportion of cases in which a clinical condition is detected when it is in fact present (true positive).
- *Specificity:* the proportion of cases for which a diagnosis is rejected, when rejection is in fact warranted (true negative).
- *Positive predictive power:* the probability of having the diagnosis given that the score exceeds the cutoff score.
- *Negative predictive power:* the probability of not having the diagnosis given that the score does not exceed the cutoff score.

All of these indexes of diagnostic accuracy are dependent upon the prevalence of the disorder and the prevalence of the score on either side of the cut point.

Findings pertaining to decision-making should be interpreted conservatively and cross-validated on independent samples because (a) classification decisions should in practice be based upon the results of multiple sources of information rather than test results from a single measure, and (b) the consequences of a classification decision should be considered in evaluating the impact of classification accuracy. A false negative classification, in which a child is incorrectly classified as not needing special education services, could mean the denial of needed services to a student. Alternately, a false positive classification, in which a typical child is recommended for special services, could result in a child's being labeled unfairly.

Treatment validity refers to the value of an assessment in selecting and implementing interventions and treatments that will benefit the examinee. "Assessment data are said to be *treatment valid,*" commented Barrios (1988), "if they expedite the orderly course of treatment or enhance the outcome of treatment" (p. 34). Other terms used to describe treatment validity are *treatment utility* (Hayes, Nelson, & Jarrett, 1987) and *rehabilitation-referenced assessment* (Heinrichs, 1990).

Whether the stated purpose of clinical assessment is description, diagnosis, intervention, prediction, tracking, or simply understanding, its ultimate raison d'être is to select and implement services in the best interests of the examinee, that is, to guide treatment. In 1957, Cronbach described a rationale for linking assessment to treatment: "For any potential problem, there is some best group of treatments to use and best allocation of persons to treatments" (p. 680).

The origins of treatment validity may be traced to the concept of aptitude by treatment interactions (ATI) originally proposed by Cronbach (1957), who initiated decades of research seeking to specify relationships between the traits measured by tests and the intervention methodology used to produce change. In clinical practice, promising efforts to match client characteristics and clinical dimensions to preferred therapist characteristics and treatment approaches have been made (e.g., Beutler & Clarkin, 1990; Beutler & Harwood, 2000; Lazarus, 1973; Maruish, 1999), but progress has been constrained in part by difficulty in arriving at consensus for empirically supported treatments (e.g., Beutler, 1998). In psychoeducational settings, test results have been shown to have limited utility in predicting differential responses to varied forms of instruction (e.g., Reschly, 1997). It is possible that progress in educational domains has been constrained by underestimation of the complexity of treatment validity. For example, many ATI studies utilize overly simple modality-specific dimensions (auditory-visual learning style or verbal-nonverbal preferences) because of their easy appeal. New approaches to demonstrating ATI are described in the chapter on intelligence in this volume by Wasserman.

Consequential Validity

In recent years, there has been an increasing recognition that test usage has both intended and unintended effects on individuals and groups. Messick (1989, 1995b) has argued that test developers must understand the social values intrinsic to the purposes and application of psychological tests, especially those that may act as a trigger for social and educational actions. Linn (1998) has suggested that when governmental bodies establish policies that drive test development and implementation, the responsibility for the consequences of test usage must also be borne by the policymakers. In this context, *consequential validity* refers to the appraisal of value implications and the social impact of score interpretation as a basis for action and labeling, as well as the actual and potential consequences of test use (Messick, 1989; Reckase, 1998).

This new form of validity represents an expansion of traditional conceptualizations of test score validity. Lees-Haley (1996) has urged caution about consequential validity, noting its potential for encouraging the encroachment of politics into science. The *Standards for Educational and Psychological Testing* (1999) recognize but carefully circumscribe consequential validity:

> Evidence about consequences may be directly relevant to validity when it can be traced to a source of invalidity such as construct underrepresentation or construct-irrelevant components. Evidence about consequences that cannot be so traced—that in fact reflects valid differences in performance—is crucial in informing policy decisions but falls outside the technical purview of validity. (p. 16)

Evidence of consequential validity may be collected by test developers during a period starting early in test development and extending through the life of the test (Reckase, 1998). For educational tests, surveys and focus groups have been described as two methodologies to examine consequential aspects of validity (Chudowsky & Behuniak, 1998; Pomplun, 1997). As the social consequences of test use and interpretation are ascertained, the development and determinants of the consequences need to be explored. A measure with unintended negative side effects calls for examination of alternative measures and assessment counterproposals. Consequential validity is especially relevant to issues of bias, fairness, and distributive justice.

Validity Generalization

The accumulation of external evidence of test validity becomes most important when test results are generalized across contexts, situations, and populations, and when the consequences of testing reach beyond the test's original intent. According to Messick (1995b), "The issue of generalizability of score inferences across tasks and contexts goes to the very heart of score meaning. Indeed, setting the boundaries of score meaning is precisely what generalizability evidence is meant to address" (p. 745).

Hunter and Schmidt (1990; Hunter, Schmidt, & Jackson, 1982; Schmidt & Hunter, 1977) developed a methodology of validity generalization, a form of meta-analysis, that analyzes the extent to which variation in test validity across studies is due to sampling error or other sources of error such as imperfect reliability, imperfect construct validity, range restriction, or artificial dichotomization. Once incongruent or conflictual findings across studies can be explained in terms of sources of error, meta-analysis enables theory to be tested, generalized, and quantitatively extended.

TEST SCORE RELIABILITY

If measurement is to be trusted, it must be reliable. It must be consistent, accurate, and uniform across testing occasions, across time, across observers, and across samples. In psychometric terms, reliability refers to the extent to which measurement results are precise and accurate, free from random and unexplained error. Test score reliability sets the upper limit of validity and thereby constrains test validity, so that unreliable test scores cannot be considered valid.

Reliability has been described as "fundamental to all of psychology" (Li, Rosenthal, & Rubin, 1996), and its study dates back nearly a century (Brown, 1910; Spearman, 1910).

Concepts of reliability in test theory have evolved, including emphasis in IRT models on the test information function as an advancement over classical models (e.g., Hambleton et al., 1991) and attempts to provide new unifying and coherent models of reliability (e.g., Li & Wainer, 1997). For example, Embretson (1999) challenged classical test theory tradition by asserting that "Shorter tests can be more reliable than longer tests" (p. 12) and that "standard error of measurement differs between persons with different response patterns but generalizes across populations" (p. 12). In this section, reliability is described according to classical test theory and item response theory. Guidelines are provided for the objective evaluation of reliability.

Internal Consistency

Determination of a test's internal consistency addresses the degree of uniformity and coherence among its constituent parts. Tests that are more uniform tend to be more reliable. As a measure of internal consistency, the reliability coefficient is the square of the correlation between obtained test scores and true scores; it will be high if there is relatively little error but low with a large amount of error. In classical test theory, reliability is based on the assumption that measurement error is distributed normally and equally for all score levels. By contrast, item response theory posits that reliability differs between persons with different response patterns and levels of ability but generalizes across populations (Embretson & Hershberger, 1999).

Several statistics are typically used to calculate internal consistency. The split-half method of estimating reliability effectively splits test items in half (e.g., into odd items and even items) and correlates the score from each half of the test with the score from the other half. This technique reduces the number of items in the test, thereby reducing the magnitude of the reliability. Use of the Spearman-Brown prophecy formula permits extrapolation from the obtained reliability coefficient to original length of the test, typically raising the reliability of the test. Perhaps the most common statistical index of internal consistency is Cronbach's alpha, which provides a lower bound estimate of test score reliability equivalent to the average split-half consistency coefficient for all possible divisions of the test into halves. Note that item response theory implies that under some conditions (e.g., adaptive testing, in which the items closest to an examinee's ability level need be measured) short tests can be more reliable than longer tests (e.g., Embretson, 1999).

In general, minimal levels of acceptable reliability should be determined by the intended application and likely consequences of test scores. Several psychometricians have

TABLE 3.1   Guidelines for Acceptable Internal Consistency Reliability Coefficients

Test Methodology	Purpose of Assessment	Median Reliability Coefficient
Group assessment	Programmatic decision-making	.60 or greater
Individual assessment	Screening	.80 or greater
	Diagnosis, intervention, placement, or selection	.90 or greater

proposed guidelines for the evaluation of test score reliability coefficients (e.g., Bracken, 1987; Cicchetti, 1994; Clark & Watson, 1995; Nunnally & Bernstein, 1994; Salvia & Ysseldyke, 2001), depending upon whether test scores are to be used for high- or low-stakes decision-making. *High-stakes* tests refer to tests that have important and direct consequences such as clinical-diagnostic, placement, promotion, personnel selection, or treatment decisions; by virtue of their gravity, these tests require more rigorous and consistent psychometric standards. *Low-stakes* tests, by contrast, tend to have only minor or indirect consequences for examinees.

After a test meets acceptable guidelines for minimal acceptable reliability, there are limited benefits to further increasing reliability. Clark and Watson (1995) observe that "Maximizing internal consistency almost invariably produces a scale that is quite narrow in content; if the scale is narrower than the target construct, its validity is compromised" (pp. 316–317). Nunnally and Bernstein (1994, p. 265) state more directly: "Never switch to a less valid measure simply because it is more reliable."

Local Reliability and Conditional Standard Error

Internal consistency indexes of reliability provide a single average estimate of measurement precision across the full range of test scores. In contrast, local reliability refers to measurement precision at specified trait levels or ranges of scores. Conditional error refers to the measurement variance at a particular level of the latent trait, and its square root is a conditional standard error. Whereas classical test theory posits that the standard error of measurement is constant and applies to all scores in a particular population, item response theory posits that the standard error of measurement varies according to the test scores obtained by the examinee but generalizes across populations (Embretson & Hershberger, 1999).

As an illustration of the use of classical test theory in the determination of local reliability, the Universal Nonverbal Intelligence Test (UNIT; Bracken & McCallum, 1998) presents local reliabilities from a classical test theory orientation. Based on the rationale that a common cut score for classification of individuals as mentally retarded is an FSIQ equal to 70, the reliability of test scores surrounding that decision point was calculated. Specifically, coefficient *alpha* reliabilities were calculated for FSIQs from -1.33 and -2.66 standard deviations below the normative mean. Reliabilities were corrected for restriction in range, and results showed that composite IQ reliabilities exceeded the .90 suggested criterion. That is, the UNIT is sufficiently precise at this ability range to reliably identify individual performance near to a common cut point for classification as mentally retarded.

Item response theory permits the determination of conditional standard error at every level of performance on a test. Several measures, such as the Differential Ability Scales (Elliott, 1990) and the Scales of Independent Behavior—Revised (SIB-R; Bruininks, Woodcock, Weatherman, & Hill, 1996), report local standard errors or local reliabilities for every test score. This methodology not only determines whether a test is more accurate for some members of a group (e.g., high-functioning individuals) than for others (Daniel, 1999), but also promises that many other indexes derived from reliability indexes (e.g., index discrepancy scores) may eventually become tailored to an examinee's actual performance. Several IRT-based methodologies are available for estimating local scale reliabilities using conditional standard errors of measurement (Andrich, 1988; Daniel, 1999; Kolen, Zeng, & Hanson, 1996; Samejima, 1994), but none has yet become a test industry standard.

Temporal Stability

Are test scores consistent over time? Test scores must be reasonably consistent to have practical utility for making clinical and educational decisions and to be predictive of future performance. The stability coefficient, or test-retest score reliability coefficient, is an index of temporal stability that can be calculated by correlating test performance for a large number of examinees at two points in time. Two weeks is considered a preferred test-retest time interval (Nunnally & Bernstein, 1994; Salvia & Ysseldyke, 2001), because longer intervals increase the amount of error (due to maturation and learning) and tend to lower the estimated reliability.

Bracken (1987; Bracken & McCallum, 1998) recommends that a total test stability coefficient should be greater than or equal to .90 for high-stakes tests over relatively short test-retest intervals, whereas a stability coefficient of .80 is reasonable for low-stakes testing. Stability coefficients may be spuriously high, even with tests with low internal consistency, but tests with low stability coefficients tend to have low internal consistency unless they are tapping highly variable state-based constructs such as state anxiety (Nunnally & Bernstein, 1994). As a general rule of thumb, measures of

internal consistency are preferred to stability coefficients as indexes of reliability.

Interrater Consistency and Consensus

Whenever tests require observers to render judgments, ratings, or scores for a specific behavior or performance, the consistency among observers constitutes an important source of measurement precision. Two separate methodological approaches have been utilized to study consistency and consensus among observers: interrater reliability (using correlational indexes to reference consistency among observers) and interrater agreement (addressing percent agreement among observers; e.g., Tinsley & Weiss, 1975). These distinctive approaches are necessary because it is possible to have high interrater reliability with low manifest agreement among raters if ratings are different but proportional. Similarly, it is possible to have low interrater reliability with high manifest agreement among raters if consistency indexes lack power because of restriction in range.

Interrater reliability refers to the proportional consistency of variance among raters and tends to be correlational. The simplest index involves correlation of total scores generated by separate raters. The intraclass correlation is another index of reliability commonly used to estimate the reliability of ratings. Its value ranges from 0 to 1.00, and it can be used to estimate the expected reliability of either the individual ratings provided by a single rater or the mean rating provided by a group of raters (Shrout & Fleiss, 1979). Another index of reliability, Kendall's coefficient of concordance, establishes how much reliability exists among ranked data. This procedure is appropriate when raters are asked to rank order the persons or behaviors along a specified dimension.

Interrater agreement refers to the interchangeability of judgments among raters, addressing the extent to which raters make the same ratings. Indexes of interrater agreement typically estimate percentage of agreement on categorical and rating decisions among observers, differing in the extent to which they are sensitive to degrees of agreement correct for chance agreement. Cohen's *kappa* is a widely used statistic of interobserver agreement intended for situations in which raters classify the items being rated into discrete, nominal categories. Kappa ranges from -1.00 to $+1.00$; kappa values of .75 or higher are generally taken to indicate excellent agreement beyond chance, values between .60 and .74 are considered good agreement, those between .40 and .59 are considered fair, and those below .40 are considered poor (Fleiss, 1981).

Interrater reliability and agreement may vary logically depending upon the degree of consistency expected from specific sets of raters. For example, it might be anticipated that people who rate a child's behavior in different contexts (e.g., school vs. home) would produce lower correlations than two raters who rate the child within the same context (e.g., two parents within the home or two teachers at school). In a review of 13 preschool social-emotional instruments, the vast majority of reported coefficients of interrater congruence were below .80 (range .12 to .89). Walker and Bracken (1996) investigated the congruence of biological parents who rated their children on four preschool behavior rating scales. Interparent congruence ranged from a low of .03 (Temperament Assessment Battery for Children Ease of Management through Distractibility) to a high of .79 (Temperament Assessment Battery for Children Approach/Withdrawal). In addition to concern about low congruence coefficients, the authors voiced concern that 44% of the parent pairs had a mean discrepancy across scales of 10 to 13 standard score points; differences ranged from 0 to 79 standard score points.

Interrater studies are preferentially conducted under field conditions, to enhance generalizability of testing by clinicians "performing under the time constraints and conditions of their work" (Wood, Nezworski, & Stejskal, 1996, p. 4). Cone (1988) has described interscorer studies as fundamental to measurement, because without scoring consistency and agreement, many other reliability and validity issues cannot be addressed.

Congruence Between Alternative Forms

When two parallel forms of a test are available, then correlating scores on each form provides another way to assess reliability. In classical test theory, strict parallelism between forms requires equality of means, variances, and covariances (Gulliksen, 1950). A hierarchy of methods for pinpointing sources of measurement error with alternative forms has been proposed (Nunnally & Bernstein, 1994; Salvia & Ysseldyke, 2001): (a) assess alternate-form reliability with a two-week interval between forms, (b) administer both forms on the same day, and if necessary (c) arrange for different raters to score the forms administered with a two-week retest interval and on the same day. If the score correlation over the two-week interval between the alternative forms is lower than coefficient *alpha* by .20 or more, then considerable measurement error is present due to internal consistency, scoring subjectivity, or trait instability over time. If the score correlation is substantially higher for forms administered on the same day, then the error may stem from trait variation over time. If the correlations remain low for forms administered on the same day, then the two forms may differ in content with one form being more internally consistent than the other. If trait variation and content differences have been ruled out, then

comparison of subjective ratings from different sources may permit the major source of error to be attributed to the subjectivity of scoring.

In item response theory, test forms may be compared by examining the forms at the item level. Forms with items of comparable item difficulties, response ogives, and standard errors by trait level will tend to have adequate levels of alternate form reliability (e.g., McGrew & Woodcock, 2001). For example, when item difficulties for one form are plotted against those for the second form, a clear linear trend is expected. When raw scores are plotted against trait levels for the two forms on the same graph, the ogive plots should be identical.

At the same time, scores from different tests tapping the same construct need not be parallel if both involve sets of items that are close to the examinee's ability level. As reported by Embretson (1999), "Comparing test scores across multiple forms is optimal when test difficulty levels vary across persons" (p. 12). The capacity of IRT to estimate trait level across differing tests does not require assumptions of parallel forms or test equating.

Reliability Generalization

Reliability generalization is a meta-analytic methodology that investigates the reliability of scores across studies and samples (Vacha-Haase, 1998). An extension of validity generalization (Hunter & Schmidt, 1990; Schmidt & Hunter, 1977), reliability generalization investigates the stability of reliability coefficients across samples and studies. In order to demonstrate measurement precision for the populations for which a test is intended, the test should show comparable levels of reliability across various demographic subsets of the population (e.g., gender, race, ethnic groups), as well as salient clinical and exceptional populations.

TEST SCORE FAIRNESS

From the inception of psychological testing, problems with racial, ethnic, and gender bias have been apparent. As early as 1911, Alfred Binet (Binet & Simon, 1911/1916) was aware that a failure to represent diverse classes of socioeconomic status would affect normative performance on intelligence tests. He deleted classes of items that related more to quality of education than to mental faculties. Early editions of the Stanford-Binet and the Wechsler intelligence scales were standardized on entirely White, native-born samples (Terman, 1916; Terman & Merrill, 1937; Wechsler, 1939, 1946, 1949). In addition to sample limitations, early tests also contained items that reflected positively on whites. Early editions of the Stanford-Binet included an Aesthetic Comparisons item in which examinees were shown a white, well-coiffed blond woman and a disheveled woman with African features; the examinee was asked "Which one is prettier?" The original MMPI (Hathaway & McKinley, 1943) was normed on a convenience sample of white adult Minnesotans and contained true-false, self-report items referring to culture-specific games (drop-the-handkerchief), literature (*Alice in Wonderland*), and religious beliefs (the second coming of Christ). These types of problems, of normative samples without minority representation and racially and ethnically insensitive items, are now routinely avoided by most contemporary test developers.

In spite of these advances, the fairness of educational and psychological tests represents one of the most contentious and psychometrically challenging aspects of test development. Numerous methodologies have been proposed to assess item effectiveness for different groups of test takers, and the definitive text in this area is Jensen's (1980) thoughtful *Bias in Mental Testing*. The chapter by Reynolds and Ramsay in this volume also describes a comprehensive array of approaches to test bias. Most of the controversy regarding test fairness relates to the lay and legal perception that any group difference in test scores constitutes bias, in and of itself. For example, Jencks and Phillips (1998) stress that the test score gap is the single most important obstacle to achieving racial balance and social equity.

In landmark litigation, Judge Robert Peckham in *Larry P. v. Riles* (1972/1974/1979/1984/1986) banned the use of individual IQ tests in placing black children into educable mentally retarded classes in California, concluding that the cultural bias of the IQ test was hardly disputed in this litigation. He asserted, "Defendants do not seem to dispute the evidence amassed by plaintiffs to demonstrate that the IQ tests in fact are culturally biased" (Peckham, 1972, p. 1313) and later concluded, "An unbiased test that measures ability or potential should yield the same pattern of scores when administered to different groups of people" (Peckham, 1979, pp. 954–955).

The belief that any group test score difference constitutes bias has been termed the *egalitarian fallacy* by Jensen (1980, p. 370):

> This concept of test bias is based on the gratuitous assumption that all human populations are essentially identical or equal in whatever trait or ability the test purports to measure. Therefore, any difference between populations in the distribution of test scores (such as a difference in means, or standard deviations, or any other parameters of the distribution) is taken as evidence that the test is biased. The search for a less biased test, then, is guided by the criterion of minimizing or eliminating the statistical differences between groups. The perfectly nonbiased test, according to this definition, would reveal reliable individual differences but not reliable (i.e., statistically significant) group differences. (p. 370)

However this controversy is viewed, the perception of test bias stemming from group mean score differences remains a deeply ingrained belief among many psychologists and educators. McArdle (1998) suggests that large group mean score differences are "a necessary but not sufficient condition for test bias" (p. 158). McAllister (1993) has observed, "In the testing community, differences in correct answer rates, total scores, and so on do not mean bias. In the political realm, the exact opposite perception is found; differences mean bias" (p. 394).

The newest models of test fairness describe a systemic approach utilizing both internal and external sources of evidence of fairness that extend from test conception and design through test score interpretation and application (McArdle, 1998; Camilli & Shepard, 1994; Willingham, 1999). These models are important because they acknowledge the importance of the consequences of test use in a holistic assessment of fairness and a multifaceted methodological approach to accumulate evidence of test fairness. In this section, a systemic model of test fairness adapted from the work of several leading authorities is described.

Terms and Definitions

Three key terms appear in the literature associated with test score fairness: *bias, fairness,* and *equity*. These concepts overlap but are not identical; for example, a test that shows no evidence of test score bias may be used unfairly. To some extent these terms have historically been defined by families of relevant psychometric analyses—for example, bias is usually associated with differential item functioning, and fairness is associated with differential prediction to an external criterion. In this section, the terms are defined at a conceptual level.

Test score bias tends to be defined in a narrow manner, as a special case of test score invalidity. According to the most recent *Standards* (1999), bias in testing refers to "construct under-representation or construct-irrelevant components of test scores that differentially affect the performance of different groups of test takers" (p. 172). This definition implies that bias stems from nonrandom measurement error, provided that the typical magnitude of random error is comparable for all groups of interest. Accordingly, test score bias refers to the systematic and invalid introduction of measurement error for a particular group of interest. The statistical underpinnings of this definition have been underscored by Jensen (1980), who asserted, "The assessment of bias is a purely objective, empirical, statistical and quantitative matter entirely independent of subjective value judgments and ethical issues concerning fairness or unfairness of tests and the uses to which they are put" (p. 375). Some scholars consider the characterization of bias as objective and independent of the value judgments associated with fair use of tests to be fundamentally incorrect (e.g., Willingham, 1999).

Test score *fairness* refers to the ways in which test scores are utilized, most often for various forms of decision-making such as selection. Jensen suggests that test fairness refers "to the ways in which test scores (whether of biased or unbiased tests) are used in any selection situation" (p. 376), arguing that fairness is a subjective policy decision based on philosophic, legal, or practical considerations rather than a statistical decision. Willingham (1999) describes a test fairness manifold that extends throughout the entire process of test development, including the consequences of test usage. Embracing the idea that fairness is akin to demonstrating the generalizability of test validity across population subgroups, he notes that "the manifold of fairness issues is complex because validity is complex" (p. 223). Fairness is a concept that transcends a narrow statistical and psychometric approach.

Finally, *equity* refers to a social value associated with the intended and unintended consequences and impact of test score usage. Because of the importance of equal opportunity, equal protection, and equal treatment in mental health, education, and the workplace, Willingham (1999) recommends that psychometrics actively consider equity issues in test development. As Tiedeman (1978) noted, "Test equity seems to be emerging as a criterion for test use on a par with the concepts of reliability and validity" (p. xxviii).

Internal Evidence of Fairness

The *internal* features of a test related to fairness generally include the test's theoretical underpinnings, item content and format, differential item and test functioning, measurement precision, and factorial structure. The two best-known procedures for evaluating test fairness include expert reviews of content bias and analysis of differential item functioning. These and several additional sources of evidence of test fairness are discussed in this section.

Item Bias and Sensitivity Review

In efforts to enhance fairness, the content and format of psychological and educational tests commonly undergo subjective bias and sensitivity reviews one or more times during test development. In this review, independent representatives from diverse groups closely examine tests, identifying items and procedures that may yield differential responses for one group relative to another. Content may be reviewed for cultural, disability, ethnic, racial, religious, sex, and socioeconomic status bias. For example, a reviewer may be asked a series of questions including, "Does the content, format, or structure of the test item present greater problems for students from some backgrounds than for others?" A comprehensive item bias review is available from Hambleton and Rodgers (1995), and useful guidelines to reduce bias in language are available from the American Psychological Association (1994).

Ideally, there are two objectives in bias and sensitivity reviews: (a) eliminate biased material, and (b) ensure balanced and neutral representation of groups within the test. Among the potentially biased elements of tests that should be avoided are

- material that is controversial, emotionally charged, or inflammatory for any specific group.
- language, artwork, or material that is demeaning or offensive to any specific group.
- content or situations with differential familiarity and relevance for specific groups.
- language and instructions that have different or unfamiliar meanings for specific groups.
- information or skills that may not be expected to be within the educational background of all examinees.
- format or structure of the item that presents differential difficulty for specific groups.

Among the prosocial elements that ideally should be included in tests are

- Presentation of universal experiences in test material.
- Balanced distribution of people from diverse groups.
- Presentation of people in activities that do not reinforce stereotypes.
- Item presentation in a sex-, culture-, age-, and race-neutral manner.
- Inclusion of individuals with disabilities or handicapping conditions.

In general, the content of test materials should be relevant and accessible for the entire population of examinees for whom the test is intended. For example, the experiences of snow and freezing winters are outside the range of knowledge of many Southern students, thereby introducing a geographic regional bias. Use of utensils such as forks may be unfamiliar to Asian immigrants who may instead use chopsticks. Use of coinage from the United States ensures that the test cannot be validly used with examinees from countries with different currency.

Tests should also be free of controversial, emotionally charged, or value-laden content, such as violence or religion. The presence of such material may prove distracting, offensive, or unsettling to examinees from some groups, detracting from test performance.

Stereotyping refers to the portrayal of a group using only a limited number of attributes, characteristics, or roles. As a rule, stereotyping should be avoided in test development. Specific groups should be portrayed accurately and fairly, without reference to stereotypes or traditional roles regarding sex, race, ethnicity, religion, physical ability, or geographic setting. Group members should be portrayed as exhibiting a full range of activities, behaviors, and roles.

Differential Item and Test Functioning

Are item and test statistical properties equivalent for individuals of comparable ability, but from different groups? *Differential test and item functioning* (DTIF, or DTF and DIF) refers to a family of statistical procedures aimed at determining whether examinees of the same ability but from different groups have different probabilities of success on a test or an item. The most widely used of DIF procedures is the Mantel-Haenszel technique (Holland & Thayer, 1988), which assesses similarities in item functioning across various demographic groups of comparable ability. Items showing significant DIF are usually considered for deletion from a test.

DIF has been extended by Shealy and Stout (1993) to a test score–based level of analysis known as differential test functioning, a multidimensional nonparametric IRT index of test bias. Whereas DIF is expressed at the item level, DTF represents a combination of two or more items to produce DTF, with scores on a valid subtest used to match examinees according to ability level. Tests may show evidence of DIF on some items without evidence of DTF, provided item bias statistics are offsetting and eliminate differential bias at the test score level.

Although psychometricians have embraced DIF as a preferred method for detecting potential item bias (McAllister, 1993), this methodology has been subjected to increasing criticism because of its dependence upon internal test properties and its inherent circular reasoning. Hills (1999) notes that two decades of DIF research have failed to demonstrate that removing biased items affects test bias and narrows the gap in group mean scores. Furthermore, DIF rests on several assumptions, including the assumptions that items are unidimensional, that the latent trait is equivalently distributed across groups, that the groups being compared (usually racial, sex, or ethnic groups) are homogeneous, and that the overall test is unbiased. Camilli and Shepard (1994) observe, "By definition, internal DIF methods are incapable of detecting constant bias. Their aim, and capability, is only to detect relative discrepancies" (p. 17).

Additional Internal Indexes of Fairness

The demonstration that a test has *equal internal integrity* across racial and ethnic groups has been described as a way to demonstrate test fairness (e.g., Mercer, 1984). Among the internal psychometric characteristics that may be examined for this type of generalizability are internal consistency, item difficulty calibration, test-retest stability, and factor structure.

With indexes of internal consistency, it is usually sufficient to demonstrate that the test meets the guidelines such as those recommended above for each of the groups of interest, considered independently (Jensen, 1980). Demonstration of adequate measurement precision across groups suggests that a test has adequate accuracy for the populations in which it may be used. Geisinger (1998) noted that "subgroup-specific reliability analysis may be especially appropriate when the reliability of a test has been justified on the basis of internal consistency reliability procedures (e.g., coefficient *alpha*). Such analysis should be repeated in the group of special test takers because the meaning and difficulty of some components of the test may change over groups, especially over some cultural, linguistic, and disability groups" (p. 25). Differences in group reliabilities may be evident, however, when test items are substantially more difficult for one group than another or when ceiling or floor effects are present for only one group.

A Rasch-based methodology to compare relative difficulty of test items involves separate calibration of items of the test for each group of interest (e.g., O'Brien, 1992). The items may then be plotted against an identity line in a bivariate graph and bounded by 95 percent confidence bands. Items falling within the bands are considered to have invariant difficulty, whereas items falling outside the bands have different difficulty and may have different meanings across the two samples.

The temporal stability of test scores should also be compared across groups, using similar test-retest intervals, in order to ensure that test results are equally stable irrespective of race and ethnicity. Jensen (1980) suggests,

> If a test is unbiased, test-retest correlation, of course with the
> same interval between testings for the major and minor groups,

should yield the same correlation for both groups. Significantly different test-retest correlations (taking proper account of possibly unequal variances in the two groups) are indicative of a biased test. Failure to understand instructions, guessing, carelessness, marking answers haphazardly, and the like, all tend to lower the test-retest correlation. If two groups differ in test-retest correlation, it is clear that the test scores are not equally accurate or stable measures of both groups. (p. 430)

As an index of construct validity, the underlying factor structure of psychological tests should be robust across racial and ethnic groups. A difference in the factor structure across groups provides some evidence for bias even though factorial invariance does not necessarily signify fairness (e.g., Meredith, 1993; Nunnally & Bernstein, 1994). Floyd and Widaman (1995) suggested, "Increasing recognition of cultural, developmental, and contextual influences on psychological constructs has raised interest in demonstrating measurement invariance before assuming that measures are equivalent across groups" (p. 296).

External Evidence of Fairness

Beyond the concept of internal integrity, Mercer (1984) recommended that studies of test fairness include evidence of *equal external relevance*. In brief, this determination requires the examination of relations between item or test scores and independent external criteria. External evidence of test score fairness has been accumulated in the study of comparative prediction of future performance (e.g., use of the Scholastic Assessment Test across racial groups to predict a student's ability to do college-level work). Fair prediction and fair selection are two objectives that are particularly important as evidence of test fairness, in part because they figure prominently in legislation and court rulings.

Fair Prediction

Prediction bias can arise when a test differentially predicts future behaviors or performance across groups. Cleary (1968) introduced a methodology that evaluates comparative predictive validity between two or more salient groups. The Cleary rule states that a test may be considered fair if it has the same approximate regression equation, that is, comparable slope and intercept, explaining the relationship between the predictor test and an external criterion measure in the groups undergoing comparison. A slope difference between the two groups conveys differential validity and relates that one group's performance on the external criterion is predicted less well than the other's performance. An intercept difference suggests a difference in the level of estimated performance between the

groups, even if the predictive validity is comparable. It is important to note that this methodology assumes adequate levels of reliability for both the predictor and criterion variables. This procedure has several limitations that have been summarized by Camilli and Shepard (1994). The demonstration of equivalent predictive validity across demographic groups constitutes an important source of fairness that is related to validity generalization.

Fair Selection

The consequences of test score use for selection and decision-making in clinical, educational, and occupational domains constitute a source of potential bias. The issue of fair selection addresses the question of whether the use of test scores for selection decisions unfairly favors one group over another. Specifically, test scores that produce adverse, disparate, or disproportionate impact for various racial or ethnic groups may be said to show evidence of selection bias, even when that impact is construct relevant. Since enactment of the Civil Rights Act of 1964, demonstration of *adverse impact* has been treated in legal settings as prima facie evidence of test bias. Adverse impact occurs when there is a substantially different rate of selection based on test scores and other factors that works to the disadvantage of members of a race, sex, or ethnic group.

Federal mandates and court rulings have frequently indicated that adverse, disparate, or disproportionate impact in selection decisions based upon test scores constitutes evidence of unlawful discrimination, and differential test selection rates among majority and minority groups have been considered a bottom line in federal mandates and court rulings. In its *Uniform Guidelines on Employment Selection Procedures* (1978), the Equal Employment Opportunity Commission (EEOC) operationalized adverse impact according to the four-fifths rule, which states, "A selection rate for any race, sex, or ethnic group which is less than four-fifths (4/5) (or eighty percent) of the rate for the group with the highest rate will generally be regarded by the Federal enforcement agencies as evidence of adverse impact" (p. 126). Adverse impact has been applied to educational tests (e.g., the Texas Assessment of Academic Skills) as well as tests used in personnel selection. The U.S. Supreme Court held in 1988 that differential selection ratios can constitute sufficient evidence of adverse impact. The 1991 Civil Rights Act, Section 9, specifically and explicitly prohibits any discriminatory use of test scores for minority groups.

Since selection decisions involve the use of test cutoff scores, an analysis of costs and benefits according to decision theory provides a methodology for fully understanding the consequences of test score usage. Cutoff scores may be varied to provide optimal fairness across groups, or alternative cutoff scores may be utilized in certain circumstances. McArdle (1998) observes, "As the cutoff scores become increasingly stringent, the number of false negative mistakes (or costs) also increase, but the number of false positive mistakes (also a cost) decrease" (p. 174).

THE LIMITS OF PSYCHOMETRICS

Psychological assessment is ultimately about the examinee. A test is merely a tool with which to understand the examinee, and psychometrics are merely rules with which to build the tools. The tools themselves must be sufficiently sound (i.e., valid and reliable) and fair that they introduce acceptable levels of error into the process of decision-making. Some guidelines have been described above for psychometrics of test construction and application that help us not only to build better tools, but to use these tools as skilled craftspersons.

As an evolving field of study, psychometrics still has some glaring shortcomings. A long-standing limitation of psychometrics is its systematic overreliance on internal sources of evidence for test validity and fairness. In brief, it is more expensive and more difficult to collect external criterion-based information, especially with special populations; it is simpler and easier to base all analyses on the performance of a normative standardization sample. This dependency on internal methods has been recognized and acknowledged by leading psychometricians. In discussing psychometric methods for detecting test bias, for example, Camilli and Shepard cautioned about circular reasoning: "Because DIF indices rely only on internal criteria, they are inherently circular" (p. 17). Similarly, there has been reticence among psychometricians in considering attempts to extend the domain of validity into consequential aspects of test usage (e.g., Lees-Haley, 1996). We have witnessed entire testing approaches based upon internal factor-analytic approaches and evaluation of content validity (e.g., McGrew & Flanagan, 1998), with negligible attention paid to the external validation of the factors against independent criteria. This shortcoming constitutes a serious limitation of psychometrics, which we have attempted to address by encouraging the use of both internal and external sources of psychometric evidence.

Another long-standing limitation is the tendency of test developers to wait until the test is undergoing standardization to establish its validity. A typical sequence of test development involves pilot studies, a content tryout, and finally a national standardization and supplementary studies (e.g.,

Robertson, 1992). Harkening back to the stages described by Loevinger (1957), the external criterion-based validation stage comes last in the process—after the test has effectively been built. It constitutes a limitation in psychometric practice that many tests only validate their effectiveness for a stated purpose at the end of the process, rather than at the beginning, as MMPI developers did over half a century ago by selecting items that discriminated between specific diagnostic groups (Hathaway & McKinley, 1943). The utility of a test for its intended application should be partially validated at the pilot study stage, prior to norming.

Finally, psychometrics has failed to directly address many of the applied questions of practitioners. Tests results often do not readily lend themselves to functional decision-making. For example, psychometricians have been slow to develop consensually accepted ways of measuring growth and maturation, reliable change (as a result of enrichment, intervention, or treatment), and atypical response patterns suggestive of lack of effort or dissimulation. The failure of treatment validity and assessment-treatment linkage undermines the central purpose of testing. Moreover, recent challenges to the practice of test profile analysis (e.g., Glutting, McDermott, & Konold, 1997) suggest a need to systematically measure test profile strengths and weaknesses in a clinically relevant way that permits a match to prototypal expectations for specific clinical disorders. The answers to these challenges lie ahead.

REFERENCES

Achenbach, T. M., & Howell, C. T. (1993). Are American children's problems getting worse? A 13-year comparison. *Journal of the American Academy of Child and Adolescent Psychiatry, 32,* 1145–1154.

American Educational Research Association. (1999). *Standards for educational and psychological testing.* Washington, DC: Author.

American Psychological Association. (1992). Ethical principles of psychologists and code of conduct. *American Psychologist, 47,* 1597–1611.

American Psychological Association. (1994). *Publication manual of the American Psychological Association* (4th ed.). Washington, DC: Author.

Anastasi, A., & Urbina, S. (1997). *Psychological testing* (7th ed.). Upper Saddle River, NJ: Prentice Hall.

Andrich, D. (1988). *Rasch models for measurement.* Thousand Oaks, CA: Sage.

Angoff, W. H. (1984). *Scales, norms, and equivalent scores.* Princeton, NJ: Educational Testing Service.

Banaji, M. R., & Crowder, R. C. (1989). The bankruptcy of everyday memory. *American Psychologist, 44,* 1185–1193.

Barrios, B. A. (1988). On the changing nature of behavioral assessment. In A. S. Bellack & M. Hersen (Eds.), *Behavioral assessment: A practical handbook* (3rd ed., pp. 3–41). New York: Pergamon Press.

Bayley, N. (1993). Bayley Scales of Infant Development second edition manual. San Antonio, TX: The Psychological Corporation.

Beutler, L. E. (1998). Identifying empirically supported treatments: What if we didn't? *Journal of Consulting and Clinical Psychology, 66,* 113–120.

Beutler, L. E., & Clarkin, J. F. (1990). *Systematic treatment selection: Toward targeted therapeutic interventions.* Philadelphia, PA: Brunner/Mazel.

Beutler, L. E., & Harwood, T. M. (2000). *Prescriptive psychotherapy: A practical guide to systematic treatment selection.* New York: Oxford University Press.

Binet, A., & Simon, T. (1916). New investigation upon the measure of the intellectual level among school children. In E. S. Kite (Trans.), *The development of intelligence in children* (pp. 274–329). Baltimore: Williams and Wilkins. (Original work published 1911).

Bracken, B. A. (1987). Limitations of preschool instruments and standards for minimal levels of technical adequacy. *Journal of Psychoeducational Assessment, 4,* 313–326.

Bracken, B. A. (1988). Ten psychometric reasons why similar tests produce dissimilar results. *Journal of School Psychology, 26,* 155–166.

Bracken, B. A., & McCallum, R. S. (1998). *Universal Nonverbal Intelligence Test examiner's manual.* Itasca, IL: Riverside.

Brown, W. (1910). Some experimental results in the correlation of mental abilities. *British Journal of Psychology, 3,* 296–322.

Bruininks, R. H., Woodcock, R. W., Weatherman, R. F., & Hill, B. K. (1996). *Scales of Independent Behavior—Revised comprehensive manual.* Itasca, IL: Riverside.

Butcher, J. N., Dahlstrom, W. G., Graham, J. R., Tellegen, A., & Kaemmer, B. (1989). *Minnesota Multiphasic Personality Inventory-2 (MMPI-2): Manual for administration and scoring.* Minneapolis: University of Minnesota Press.

Camilli, G., & Shepard, L. A. (1994). *Methods for identifying biased test items* (Vol. 4). Thousand Oaks, CA: Sage.

Campbell, D. T., & Fiske, D. W. (1959). Convergent and discriminant validation by the multitrait-multimethod matrix. *Psychological Bulletin, 56,* 81–105.

Campbell, D. T., & Stanley, J. C. (1963). *Experimental and quasi-experimental designs for research.* Chicago: Rand-McNally.

Campbell, S. K., Siegel, E., Parr, C. A., & Ramey, C. T. (1986). Evidence for the need to renorm the Bayley Scales of Infant Development based on the performance of a population-based sample of 12-month-old infants. *Topics in Early Childhood Special Education, 6,* 83–96.

Carroll, J. B. (1983). Studying individual differences in cognitive abilities: Through and beyond factor analysis. In R. F. Dillon & R. R. Schmeck (Eds.), *Individual differences in cognition* (pp. 1–33). New York: Academic Press.

Cattell, R. B. (1986). The psychometric properties of tests: Consistency, validity, and efficiency. In R. B. Cattell & R. C. Johnson (Eds.), *Functional psychological testing: Principles and instruments* (pp. 54–78). New York: Brunner/Mazel.

Chudowsky, N., & Behuniak, P. (1998). Using focus groups to examine the consequential aspect of validity. *Educational Measurement: Issues and Practice, 17,* 28–38.

Cicchetti, D. V. (1994). Guidelines, criteria, and rules of thumb for evaluating normed and standardized assessment instruments in psychology. *Psychological Assessment, 6,* 284–290.

Clark, L. A., & Watson, D. (1995). Constructing validity: Basic issues in objective scale development. *Psychological Assessment, 7,* 309–319.

Cleary, T. A. (1968). Test bias: Prediction of grades for Negro and White students in integrated colleges. *Journal of Educational Measurement, 5,* 115–124.

Cone, J. D. (1978). The behavioral assessment grid (BAG): A conceptual framework and a taxonomy. *Behavior Therapy, 9,* 882–888.

Cone, J. D. (1988). Psychometric considerations and the multiple models of behavioral assessment. In A. S. Bellack & M. Hersen (Eds.), *Behavioral assessment: A practical handbook* (3rd ed., pp. 42–66). New York: Pergamon Press.

Cook, T. D., & Campbell, D. T. (1979). *Quasi-experimentation: Design and analysis issues for field settings.* Chicago: Rand-McNally.

Crocker, L., & Algina, J. (1986). *Introduction to classical and modern test theory.* New York: Holt, Rinehart, and Winston.

Cronbach, L. J. (1957). The two disciplines of scientific psychology. *American Psychologist, 12,* 671–684.

Cronbach, L. J. (1971). Test validation. In R. L. Thorndike (Ed.), *Educational measurement* (2nd ed., pp. 443–507). Washington, DC: American Council on Education.

Cronbach, L. J., & Gleser, G. C. (1965). *Psychological tests and personnel decisions.* Urbana: University of Illinois Press.

Cronbach, L. J., Gleser, G. C., Nanda, H., & Rajaratnam, N. (1972). *The dependability of behavioral measurements: Theory of generalizability scores and profiles.* New York: Wiley.

Cronbach, L. J., & Meehl, P. E. (1955). Construct validity in psychological tests. *Psychological Bulletin, 52,* 281–302.

Cronbach, L. J., Rajaratnam, N., & Gleser, G. C. (1963). Theory of generalizability: A liberalization of reliability theory. *British Journal of Statistical Psychology, 16,* 137–163.

Daniel, M. H. (1999). Behind the scenes: Using new measurement methods on the DAS and KAIT. In S. E. Embretson & S. L. Hershberger (Eds.), *The new rules of measurement: What every psychologist and educator should know* (pp. 37–63). Mahwah, NJ: Erlbaum.

Elliott, C. D. (1990). *Differential Ability Scales: Introductory and technical handbook*. San Antonio, TX: The Psychological Corporation.

Embretson, S. E. (1995). The new rules of measurement. *Psychological Assessment, 8,* 341–349.

Embretson, S. E. (1999). Issues in the measurement of cognitive abilities. In S. E. Embretson & S. L. Hershberger (Eds.), *The new rules of measurement: What every psychologist and educator should know* (pp. 1–15). Mahwah, NJ: Erlbaum.

Embretson, S. E., & Hershberger, S. L. (Eds.). (1999). *The new rules of measurement: What every psychologist and educator should know*. Mahwah, NJ: Erlbaum.

Fiske, D. W., & Campbell, D. T. (1992). Citations do not solve problems. *Psychological Bulletin, 112,* 393–395.

Fleiss, J. L. (1981). Balanced incomplete block designs for interrater reliability studies. *Applied Psychological Measurement, 5,* 105–112.

Floyd, F. J., & Widaman, K. F. (1995). Factor analysis in the development and refinement of clinical assessment instruments. *Psychological Assessment, 7,* 286–299.

Flynn, J. R. (1984). The mean IQ of Americans: Massive gains 1932 to 1978. *Psychological Bulletin, 95,* 29–51.

Flynn, J. R. (1987). Massive IQ gains in 14 nations: What IQ tests really measure. *Psychological Bulletin, 101,* 171–191.

Flynn, J. R. (1994). IQ gains over time. In R. J. Sternberg (Ed.), *The encyclopedia of human intelligence* (pp. 617–623). New York: Macmillan.

Flynn, J. R. (1999). Searching for justice: The discovery of IQ gains over time. *American Psychologist, 54,* 5–20.

Galton, F. (1879). Psychometric experiments. *Brain: A Journal of Neurology, 2,* 149–162.

Geisinger, K. F. (1992). The metamorphosis of test validation. *Educational Psychologist, 27,* 197–222.

Geisinger, K. F. (1998). Psychometric issues in test interpretation. In J. Sandoval, C. L. Frisby, K. F. Geisinger, J. D. Scheuneman, & J. R. Grenier (Eds.), *Test interpretation and diversity: Achieving equity in assessment* (pp. 17–30). Washington, DC: American Psychological Association.

Gleser, G. C., Cronbach, L. J., & Rajaratnam, N. (1965). Generalizability of scores influenced by multiple sources of variance. *Psychometrika, 30,* 395–418.

Glutting, J. J., McDermott, P. A., & Konold, T. R. (1997). Ontology, structure, and diagnostic benefits of a normative subtest taxonomy from the WISC-III standardization sample. In D. P. Flanagan, J. L. Genshaft, & P. L. Harrison (Eds.), *Contemporary intellectual assessment: Theories, tests, and issues* (pp. 349–372). New York: Guilford Press.

Gorsuch, R. L. (1983). *Factor analysis* (2nd ed.). Hillsdale, NJ: Erlbaum.

Guilford, J. P. (1950). *Fundamental statistics in psychology and education* (2nd ed.). New York: McGraw-Hill.

Guion, R. M. (1977). Content validity: The source of my discontent. *Applied Psychological Measurement, 1,* 1–10.

Gulliksen, H. (1950). *Theory of mental tests*. New York: McGraw-Hill.

Hambleton, R. K., & Rodgers, J. H. (1995). *Item bias review*. Washington, DC: The Catholic University of America, Department of Education. (ERIC Clearinghouse on Assessment and Evaluation, No. EDO-TM-95-9)

Hambleton, R. K., Swaminathan, H., & Rogers, H. J. (1991). *Fundamentals of item response theory*. Newbury Park, CA: Sage.

Hathaway, S. R., & McKinley, J. C. (1943). *Manual for the Minnesota Multiphasic Personality Inventory*. New York: The Psychological Corporation.

Hayes, S. C., Nelson, R. O., & Jarrett, R. B. (1987). The treatment utility of assessment: A functional approach to evaluating assessment quality. *American Psychologist, 42,* 963–974.

Haynes, S. N., Richard, D. C. S., & Kubany, E. S. (1995). Content validity in psychological assessment: A functional approach to concepts and methods. *Psychological Assessment, 7,* 238–247.

Heinrichs, R. W. (1990). Current and emergent applications of neuropsychological assessment problems of validity and utility. *Professional Psychology: Research and Practice, 21,* 171–176.

Herrnstein, R. J., & Murray, C. (1994). *The bell curve: Intelligence and class in American life*. New York: Free Press.

Hills, J. (1999, May 14). Re: Construct validity. *Educational Statistics Discussion List (EDSTAT-L)*. (Available from edstat-l @jse.stat.ncsu.edu)

Holland, P. W., & Thayer, D. T. (1988). Differential item functioning and the Mantel-Haenszel procedure. In H. Wainer & H. I. Braun (Eds.), *Test validity* (pp. 129–145). Hillsdale, NJ: Erlbaum.

Hopkins, C. D., & Antes, R. L. (1978). *Classroom measurement and evaluation*. Itasca, IL: F. E. Peacock.

Hunter, J. E., & Schmidt, F. L. (1990). *Methods of meta-analysis: Correcting error and bias in research findings*. Newbury Park, CA: Sage.

Hunter, J. E., Schmidt, F. L., & Jackson, C. B. (1982). *Advanced meta-analysis: Quantitative methods of cumulating research findings across studies*. San Francisco: Sage.

Ittenbach, R. F., Esters, I. G., & Wainer, H. (1997). The history of test development. In D. P. Flanagan, J. L. Genshaft, & P. L. Harrison (Eds.), *Contemporary intellectual assessment: Theories, tests, and issues* (pp. 17–31). New York: Guilford Press.

Jackson, D. N. (1971). A sequential system for personality scale development. In C. D. Spielberger (Ed.), *Current topics in clinical and community psychology* (Vol. 2, pp. 61–92). New York: Academic Press.

Jencks, C., & Phillips, M. (Eds.). (1998). *The Black-White test score gap*. Washington, DC: Brookings Institute.

Jensen, A. R. (1980). *Bias in mental testing*. New York: Free Press.

Johnson, N. L. (1949). Systems of frequency curves generated by methods of translation. *Biometika, 36,* 149–176.

Kalton, G. (1983). Introduction to survey sampling. Beverly Hills, CA: Sage.

Kaufman, A. S., & Kaufman, N. L. (1983). *Kaufman Assessment Battery for Children.* Circle Pines, MN: American Guidance Service.

Keith, T. Z., & Kranzler, J. H. (1999). The absence of structural fidelity precludes construct validity: Rejoinder to Naglieri on what the Cognitive Assessment System does and does not measure. *School Psychology Review, 28,* 303–321.

Knowles, E. S., & Condon, C. A. (2000). Does the rose still smell as sweet? Item variability across test forms and revisions. *Psychological Assessment, 12,* 245–252.

Kolen, M. J., Zeng, L., & Hanson, B. A. (1996). Conditional standard errors of measurement for scale scores using IRT. *Journal of Educational Measurement, 33,* 129–140.

Kuhn, T. (1970). *The structure of scientific revolutions* (2nd ed.). Chicago: University of Chicago Press.

Larry P. v. Riles, 343 F. Supp. 1306 (N.D. Cal. 1972) (order granting injunction), *aff'd* 502 F.2d 963 (9th Cir. 1974); 495 F. Supp. 926 (N.D. Cal. 1979) (decision on merits), *aff'd* (9th Cir. No. 80-427 Jan. 23, 1984). Order modifying judgment, C-71-2270 RFP, September 25, 1986.

Lazarus, A. A. (1973). Multimodal behavior therapy: Treating the BASIC ID. *Journal of Nervous and Mental Disease, 156,* 404–411.

Lees-Haley, P. R. (1996). Alice in validityland, or the dangerous consequences of consequential validity. *American Psychologist, 51,* 981–983.

Levy, P. S., & Lemeshow, S. (1999). *Sampling of populations: Methods and applications.* New York: Wiley.

Li, H., Rosenthal, R., & Rubin, D. B. (1996). Reliability of measurement in psychology: From Spearman-Brown to maximal reliability. *Psychological Methods, 1,* 98–107.

Li, H., & Wainer, H. (1997). Toward a coherent view of reliability in test theory. *Journal of Educational and Behavioral Statistics, 22,* 478–484.

Linacre, J. M., & Wright, B. D. (1999). *A user's guide to Winsteps/ Ministep: Rasch-model computer programs.* Chicago: MESA Press.

Linn, R. L. (1998). Partitioning responsibility for the evaluation of the consequences of assessment programs. *Educational Measurement: Issues and Practice, 17,* 28–30.

Loevinger, J. (1957). Objective tests as instruments of psychological theory [Monograph]. *Psychological Reports, 3,* 635–694.

Loevinger, J. (1972). Some limitations of objective personality tests. In J. N. Butcher (Ed.), *Objective personality assessment* (pp. 45–58). New York: Academic Press.

Lord, F. N., & Novick, M. (1968). *Statistical theories of mental tests.* New York: Addison-Wesley.

Maruish, M. E. (Ed.). (1999). *The use of psychological testing for treatment planning and outcomes assessment.* Mahwah, NJ: Erlbaum.

McAllister, P. H. (1993). Testing, DIF, and public policy. In P. W. Holland & H. Wainer (Eds.), *Differential item functioning* (pp. 389–396). Hillsdale, NJ: Erlbaum.

McArdle, J. J. (1998). Contemporary statistical models for examining test-bias. In J. J. McArdle & R. W. Woodcock (Eds.), *Human cognitive abilities in theory and practice* (pp. 157–195). Mahwah, NJ: Erlbaum.

McGrew, K. S., & Flanagan, D. P. (1998). *The intelligence test desk reference (ITDR): Gf-Gc cross-battery assessment.* Boston: Allyn and Bacon.

McGrew, K. S., & Woodcock, R. W. (2001). *Woodcock-Johnson III technical manual.* Itasca, IL: Riverside.

Meehl, P. E. (1972). Reactions, reflections, projections. In J. N. Butcher (Ed.), *Objective personality assessment: Changing perspectives* (pp. 131–189). New York: Academic Press.

Mercer, J. R. (1984). What is a racially and culturally nondiscriminatory test? A sociological and pluralistic perspective. In C. R. Reynolds & R. T. Brown (Eds.), *Perspectives on bias in mental testing* (pp. 293–356). New York: Plenum Press.

Meredith, W. (1993). Measurement invariance, factor analysis and factorial invariance. *Psychometrika, 58,* 525–543.

Messick, S. (1989). Meaning and values in test validation: The science and ethics of assessment. *Educational Researcher, 18,* 5–11.

Messick, S. (1995a). Standards of validity and the validity of standards in performance assessment. *Educational Measurement: Issues and Practice, 14,* 5–8.

Messick, S. (1995b). Validity of psychological assessment: Validation of inferences from persons' responses and performances as scientific inquiry into score meaning. *American Psychologist, 50,* 741–749.

Millon, T., Davis, R., & Millon, C. (1997). *MCMI-III: Millon Clinical Multiaxial Inventory-III manual* (3rd ed.). Minneapolis, MN: National Computer Systems.

Naglieri, J. A., & Das, J. P. (1997). *Das-Naglieri Cognitive Assessment System interpretive handbook.* Itasca, IL: Riverside.

Neisser, U. (1978). Memory: What are the important questions? In M. M. Gruneberg, P. E. Morris, & R. N. Sykes (Eds.), *Practical aspects of memory* (pp. 3–24). London: Academic Press.

Newborg, J., Stock, J. R., Wnek, L., Guidubaldi, J., & Svinicki, J. (1984). *Battelle Developmental Inventory.* Itasca, IL: Riverside.

Newman, J. R. (1956). *The world of mathematics: A small library of literature of mathematics from A'h-mose the Scribe to Albert Einstein presented with commentaries and notes.* New York: Simon and Schuster.

Nunnally, J. C., & Bernstein, I. H. (1994). *Psychometric theory* (3rd ed.). New York: McGraw-Hill.

O'Brien, M. L. (1992). A Rasch approach to scaling issues in testing Hispanics. In K. F. Geisinger (Ed.), *Psychological testing of Hispanics* (pp. 43–54). Washington, DC: American Psychological Association.

Peckham, R. F. (1972). Opinion, *Larry P. v. Riles. Federal Supplement, 343,* 1306–1315.

Peckham, R. F. (1979). Opinion, *Larry P. v. Riles. Federal Supplement, 495,* 926–992.

Pomplun, M. (1997). State assessment and instructional change: A path model analysis. *Applied Measurement in Education, 10,* 217–234.

Rasch, G. (1960). *Probabilistic models for some intelligence and attainment tests.* Copenhagen: Danish Institute for Educational Research.

Reckase, M. D. (1998). Consequential validity from the test developer's perspective. *Educational Measurement: Issues and Practice, 17,* 13–16.

Reschly, D. J. (1997). Utility of individual ability measures and public policy choices for the 21st century. *School Psychology Review, 26,* 234–241.

Riese, S. P., Waller, N. G., & Comrey, A. L. (2000). Factor analysis and scale revision. *Psychological Assessment, 12,* 287–297.

Robertson, G. J. (1992). Psychological tests: Development, publication, and distribution. In M. Zeidner & R. Most (Eds.), *Psychological testing: An inside view* (pp. 159–214). Palo Alto, CA: Consulting Psychologists Press.

Salvia, J., & Ysseldyke, J. E. (2001). *Assessment* (8th ed.). Boston: Houghton Mifflin.

Samejima, F. (1994). Estimation of reliability coefficients using the test information function and its modifications. *Applied Psychological Measurement, 18,* 229–244.

Schmidt, F. L., & Hunter, J. E. (1977). Development of a general solution to the problem of validity generalization. *Journal of Applied Psychology, 62,* 529–540.

Shealy, R., & Stout, W. F. (1993). A model-based standardization approach that separates true bias/DIF from group differences and detects test bias/DTF as well as item bias/DIF. *Psychometrika, 58,* 159–194.

Shrout, P. E., & Fleiss, J. L. (1979). Intraclass correlations: Uses in assessing rater reliability. *Psychological Bulletin, 86,* 420–428.

Spearman, C. (1910). Correlation calculated from faulty data. *British Journal of Psychology, 3,* 171–195.

Stinnett, T. A., Coombs, W. T., Oehler-Stinnett, J., Fuqua, D. R., & Palmer, L. S. (1999, August). *NEPSY structure: Straw, stick, or brick house?* Paper presented at the Annual Convention of the American Psychological Association, Boston, MA.

Suen, H. K. (1990). *Principles of test theories.* Hillsdale, NJ: Erlbaum.

Swets, J. A. (1992). The science of choosing the right decision threshold in high-stakes diagnostics. *American Psychologist, 47,* 522–532.

Terman, L. M. (1916). *The measurement of intelligence: An explanation of and a complete guide for the use of the Stanford revision and extension of the Binet Simon Intelligence Scale.* Boston: Houghton Mifflin.

Terman, L. M., & Merrill, M. A. (1937). *Directions for administering: Forms L and M, Revision of the Stanford-Binet Tests of Intelligence.* Boston: Houghton Mifflin.

Tiedeman, D. V. (1978). In O. K. Buros (Ed.), *The eight mental measurements yearbook.* Highland Park: NJ: Gryphon Press.

Tinsley, H. E. A., & Weiss, D. J. (1975). Interrater reliability and agreement of subjective judgments. *Journal of Counseling Psychology, 22,* 358–376.

Tulsky, D. S., & Ledbetter, M. F. (2000). Updating to the WAIS-III and WMS-III: Considerations for research and clinical practice. *Psychological Assessment, 12,* 253–262.

Uniform guidelines on employee selection procedures. (1978). *Federal Register, 43,* 38296–38309.

Vacha-Haase, T. (1998). Reliability generalization: Exploring variance in measurement error affecting score reliability across studies. *Educational and Psychological Measurement, 58,* 6–20.

Walker, K. C., & Bracken, B. A. (1996). Inter-parent agreement on four preschool behavior rating scales: Effects of parent and child gender. *Psychology in the Schools, 33,* 273–281.

Wechsler, D. (1939). *The measurement of adult intelligence.* Baltimore: Williams and Wilkins.

Wechsler, D. (1946). *The Wechsler-Bellevue Intelligence Scale: Form II. Manual for administering and scoring the test.* New York: The Psychological Corporation.

Wechsler, D. (1949). *Wechsler Intelligence Scale for Children manual.* New York: The Psychological Corporation.

Wechsler, D. (1974). *Manual for the Wechsler Intelligence Scale for Children–Revised.* New York: The Psychological Corporation.

Wechsler, D. (1991). *Wechsler Intelligence Scale for Children* (3rd ed.). San Antonio, TX: The Psychological Corporation.

Willingham, W. W. (1999). A systematic view of test fairness. In S. J. Messick (Ed.), *Assessment in higher education: Issues of access, quality, student development, and public policy* (pp. 213–242). Mahwah, NJ: Erlbaum.

Wood, J. M., Nezworski, M. T., & Stejskal, W. J. (1996). The comprehensive system for the Rorschach: A critical examination. *Psychological Science, 7,* 3–10.

Woodcock, R. W. (1999). What can Rasch-based scores convey about a person's test performance? In S. E. Embretson & S. L. Hershberger (Eds.), *The new rules of measurement: What every psychologist and educator should know* (pp. 105–127). Mahwah, NJ: Erlbaum.

Wright, B. D. (1999). Fundamental measurement for psychology. In S. E. Embretson & S. L. Hershberger (Eds.), *The new rules of measurement: What every psychologist and educator should know* (pp. 65–104). Mahwah, NJ: Erlbaum.

Zieky, M. (1993). Practical questions in the use of DIF statistics in test development. In P. W. Holland & H. Wainer (Eds.), *Differential item functioning* (pp. 337–347). Hillsdale, NJ: Erlbaum.

CHAPTER 4

Bias in Psychological Assessment: An Empirical Review and Recommendations

CECIL R. REYNOLDS AND MICHAEL C. RAMSAY

Much writing and research on test bias reflects a lack of understanding of important issues surrounding the subject and even inadequate and ill-defined conceptions of test bias itself. This chapter of the *Handbook of Assessment Psychology* provides an understanding of ability test bias, particularly cultural bias, distinguishing it from concepts and issues with which it is often conflated and examining the widespread assumption that a mean difference constitutes bias. The topics addressed include possible origins, sources, and effects of test bias. Following a review of relevant research and its results, the chapter concludes with an examination of issues suggested by the review and with recommendations for researchers and clinicians.

Few issues in psychological assessment today are as polarizing among clinicians and laypeople as the use of standardized tests with minority examinees. For clients, parents, and clinicians, the central issue is one of long-term consequences that may occur when mean test results differ from one ethnic group to another—Blacks, Hispanics, Asian Americans, and

so forth. Important concerns include, among others, that psychiatric clients may be overdiagnosed, students disproportionately placed in special classes, and applicants unfairly denied employment or college admission because of purported bias in standardized tests.

Among researchers, also, polarization is common. Here, too, observed mean score differences among ethnic groups are fueling the controversy, but in a different way. Alternative explanations of these differences seem to give shape to the conflict. Reynolds (2000a, 2000b) divides the most common explanations into four categories: (a) genetic influences; (b) environmental factors involving economic, social, and educational deprivation; (c) an interactive effect of genes and environment; and (d) biased tests that systematically underrepresent minorities' true aptitudes or abilities. The last two of these explanations have drawn the most attention. Williams (1970) and Helms (1992) proposed a fifth interpretation of differences between Black and White examinees: The two groups have qualitatively different cognitive structures, which must be measured using different methods (Reynolds, 2000b).

The problem of cultural bias in mental tests has drawn controversy since the early 1900s, when Binet's first intelligence scale was published and Stern introduced procedures for testing intelligence (Binet & Simon, 1916/1973; Stern, 1914). The conflict is in no way limited to cognitive ability tests, but the so-called IQ controversy has attracted most of the public attention. A number of authors have published works on the subject that quickly became controversial (Gould, 1981; Herrnstein & Murray, 1994; Jensen, 1969). IQ tests have gone to court, provoked legislation, and taken thrashings from the popular media (Reynolds, 2000a; Brown, Reynolds, & Whitaker, 1999). In New York, the conflict has culminated in laws known as truth-in-testing legislation, which some clinicians say interferes with professional practice.

In statistics, *bias* refers to systematic error in the estimation of a value. A biased test is one that systematically overestimates or underestimates the value of the variable it is intended to assess. If this bias occurs as a function of a nominal cultural variable, such as ethnicity or gender, cultural test bias is said to be present. On the Wechsler series of intelligence tests, for example, the difference in mean scores for Black and White Americans hovers around 15 points. If this figure represents a true difference between the two groups, the tests are not biased. If, however, the difference is due to systematic underestimation of the intelligence of Black Americans or overestimation of the intelligence of White Americans, the tests are said to be culturally biased.

Many researchers have investigated possible bias in intelligence tests, with inconsistent results. The question of test bias remained chiefly within the purlieu of scientists until the 1970s. Since then, it has become a major social issue, touching off heated public debate (e.g., Editorial, *Austin-American Statesman*, October 15, 1997; Fine, 1975). Many professionals and professional associations have taken strong stands on the question.

MINORITY OBJECTIONS TO TESTS AND TESTING

Since 1968, the Association of Black Psychologists (ABP) has called for a moratorium on the administration of psychological and educational tests with minority examinees (Samuda, 1975; Williams, Dotson, Dow, & Williams, 1980). The ABP brought this call to other professional associations in psychology and education. The American Psychological Association (APA) responded by requesting that its Board of Scientific Affairs establish a committee to study the use of these tests with disadvantaged students (see the committee's report, Cleary, Humphreys, Kendrick, & Wesman, 1975).

The ABP published the following policy statement in 1969 (Williams et al., 1980):

> The Association of Black Psychologists fully supports those parents who have chosen to defend their rights by refusing to allow their children and themselves to be subjected to achievement, intelligence, aptitude, and performance tests, which have been and are being used to (a) label Black people as uneducable; (b) place Black children in "special" classes and schools; (c) potentiate inferior education; (d) assign Black children to lower educational tracks than whites; (e) deny Black students higher educational opportunities; and (f) destroy positive intellectual growth and development of Black children.

Subsequently, other professional associations issued policy statements on testing. Williams et al. (1980) and Reynolds, Lowe, and Saenz (1999) cited the National Association for the Advancement of Colored People (NAACP), the National Education Association, the National Association of Elementary School Principals, and the American Personnel and Guidance Association, among others, as organizations releasing such statements.

The ABP, perhaps motivated by action and encouragement on the part of the NAACP, adopted a more detailed resolution in 1974. The resolution described, in part, these goals of the ABP: (a) a halt to the standardized testing of Black people until culture-specific tests are made available, (b) a national policy of testing by competent assessors of an examinee's own ethnicity at his or her mandate, (c) removal of standardized test results from the records of Black students and employees, and (d) a return to regular programs of Black students inappropriately diagnosed and placed in special education classes (Williams et al., 1980). This statement presupposes that flaws in standardized tests are responsible for the unequal test results of Black examinees, and, with them, any detrimental consequences of those results.

ORIGINS OF THE TEST BIAS CONTROVERSY

Social Values and Beliefs

The present-day conflict over bias in standardized tests is motivated largely by public concerns. The impetus, it may be argued, lies with beliefs fundamental to democracy in the United States. Most Americans, at least those of majority ethnicity, view the United States as a land of opportunity—increasingly, equal opportunity that is extended to every person. We want to believe that any child can grow up to be president. Concomitantly, we believe that everyone is created equal, that all people harbor the potential for success and achievement. This equality of opportunity seems most reasonable if everyone is equally able to take advantage of it.

Parents and educational professionals have corresponding beliefs: *The children we serve have an immense potential for success and achievement; the great effort we devote to teaching or raising children is effort well spent; my own child is intelligent and capable.* The result is a resistance to labeling and alternative placement, which are thought to discount students' ability and diminish their opportunity. This terrain may be a bit more complex for clinicians, because certain diagnoses have consequences desired by clients. A disability diagnosis, for example, allows people to receive compensation or special services, and insurance companies require certain serious conditions for coverage.

The Character of Tests and Testing

The nature of psychological characteristics and their measurement is partly responsible for long-standing concern over test bias (Reynolds & Brown, 1984a). Psychological characteristics are internal, so scientists cannot observe or measure them directly but must infer them from a person's external behavior. By extension, clinicians must contend with the same limitation.

According to MacCorquodale and Meehl (1948), a psychological process is an *intervening variable* if it is treated only as a component of a system and has no properties beyond the ones that operationally define it. It is a *hypothetical construct* if it is thought to exist and to have properties beyond its defining ones. In biology, a *gene* is an example of a hypothetical construct. The gene has properties beyond its use to describe the transmission of traits from one generation to the next. Both intelligence and personality have the status of hypothetical constructs. The nature of psychological processes and other unseen hypothetical constructs are often subjects of persistent debate (see Ramsay, 1998b, for one approach). Intelligence, a highly complex psychological process, has given rise to disputes that are especially difficult to resolve (Reynolds, Willson, et al., 1999).

Test development procedures (Ramsay & Reynolds, 2000a) are essentially the same for all standardized tests. Initially, the author of a test develops or collects a large pool of items thought to measure the characteristic of interest. Theory and practical usefulness are standards commonly used to select an item pool. The selection process is a rational one.

That is, it depends upon reason and judgment; rigorous means of carrying it out simply do not exist. At this stage, then, test authors have no generally accepted evidence that they have selected appropriate items.

A common second step is to discard items of suspect quality, again on rational grounds, to reduce the pool to a manageable size. Next, the test's author or publisher administers the items to a group of examinees called a *tryout sample.* Statistical procedures then help to identify items that seem to be measuring an unintended characteristic or more than one characteristic. The author or publisher discards or modifies these items.

Finally, examiners administer the remaining items to a large, diverse group of people called a standardization sample or *norming sample.* This sample should reflect every important characteristic of the population who will take the final version of the test. Statisticians compile the scores of the norming sample into an array called a *norming distribution.*

Eventually, clients or other examinees take the test in its final form. The scores they obtain, known as *raw scores,* do not yet have any interpretable meaning. A clinician compares these scores with the norming distribution. The comparison is a mathematical process that results in new, *standard scores* for the examinees. Clinicians can interpret these scores, whereas interpretation of the original, raw scores would be difficult and impractical (Reynolds, Lowe, et al., 1999).

Standard scores are relative. They have no meaning in themselves but derive their meaning from certain properties—typically the mean and standard deviation—of the norming distribution. The norming distributions of many ability tests, for example, have a mean score of 100 and a standard deviation of 15. A client might obtain a standard score of 127. This score would be well above average, because 127 is almost 2 standard deviations of 15 above the mean of 100. Another client might obtain a standard score of 96. This score would be a little below average, because 96 is about one third of a standard deviation below a mean of 100.

Here, the reason why raw scores have no meaning gains a little clarity. A raw score of, say, 34 is high if the mean is 30 but low if the mean is 50. It is very high if the mean is 30 and the standard deviation is 2, but less high if the mean is again 30 and the standard deviation is 15. Thus, a clinician cannot know how high or low a score is without knowing certain properties of the norming distribution. The standard score is the one that has been compared with this distribution, so that it reflects those properties (see Ramsay & Reynolds, 2000a, for a systematic description of test development).

Charges of bias frequently spring from low proportions of minorities in the norming sample of a test and correspondingly small influence on test results. Many norming samples include only a few minority participants, eliciting suspicion that the tests produce inaccurate scores—misleadingly low ones in the case of ability tests—for minority examinees. Whether this is so is an important question that calls for scientific study (Reynolds, Lowe, et al., 1999).

Test development is a complex and elaborate process (Ramsay & Reynolds, 2000a). The public, the media, Congress, and even the intelligentsia find it difficult to understand. Clinicians, and psychologists outside the measurement field, commonly have little knowledge of the issues surrounding this process. Its abstruseness, as much as its relative nature, probably contributes to the amount of conflict over test bias. Physical and biological measurements such as height, weight, and even risk of heart disease elicit little controversy, although they vary from one ethnic group to another. As explained by Reynolds, Lowe, et al. (1999), this is true in part because such measurements are absolute, in part because they can be obtained and verified in direct and relatively simple ways, and in part because they are free from the distinctive social implications and consequences of standardized test scores. Reynolds et al. correctly suggest that test bias is a special case of the uncertainty that accompanies all measurement in science. Ramsay (2000) and Ramsay and Reynolds (2000b) present a brief treatment of this uncertainty incorporating Heisenberg's model.

Divergent Ideas of Bias

Besides the character of psychological processes and their measurement, differing understandings held by various segments of the population also add to the test bias controversy. Researchers and laypeople view bias differently. Clinicians and other professionals bring additional divergent views. Many lawyers see bias as illegal, discriminatory practice on the part of organizations or individuals (Reynolds, 2000a; Reynolds & Brown, 1984a).

To the public at large, bias sometimes conjures up notions of prejudicial attitudes. A person seen as prejudiced may be told, "You're biased against Hispanics." For other laypersons, bias is more generally a characteristic slant in another person's thinking, a lack of objectivity brought about by the person's life circumstances. A sales clerk may say, "I think sales clerks should be better paid." "Yes, but you're biased," a listener may retort. These views differ from statistical and research definitions for bias as for other terms, such as *significant, association,* and *confounded.* The highly specific research definitions of such terms are unfamiliar to almost everyone. As a result, uninitiated readers often misinterpret research reports.

Both in research reports and in public discourse, the scientific and popular meanings of bias are often conflated, as if even the writer or speaker had a tenuous grip on the distinction. Reynolds, Lowe, et al. (1999) suggest that the topic would be less controversial if research reports addressing test bias as a scientific question relied on the scientific meaning alone.

EFFECTS AND IMPLICATIONS OF THE TEST BIAS CONTROVERSY

The dispute over test bias has given impetus to an increasingly sophisticated corpus of research. In most venues, tests of reasonably high statistical quality appear to be largely unbiased. For neuropsychological tests, results are recent and still rare, but so far they appear to indicate little bias. Both sides of the debate have disregarded most of these findings and have emphasized, instead, a mean difference between ethnic groups (Reynolds, 2000b).

In addition, publishers have released new measures such as nonverbal and "culture fair" or "culture-free" tests; practitioners interpret scores so as to minimize the influence of putative bias; and, finally, publishers revise tests directly, to expunge group differences. For minority group members, these revisions may have an undesirable long-range effect: to prevent the study and thereby the remediation of any bias that might otherwise be found.

The implications of these various effects differ depending on whether the bias explanation is correct or incorrect, assuming it is accepted. An incorrect bias explanation, if accepted, would lead to modified tests that would not reflect important, correct information and, moreover, would present the incorrect information that unequally performing groups had performed equally. Researchers, unaware or unmindful of such inequalities, would neglect research into their causes. Economic and social deprivation would come to appear less harmful and therefore more justifiable. Social programs, no longer seen as necessary to improve minority students' scores, might be discontinued, with serious consequences.

A correct bias explanation, if accepted, would leave professionals and minority group members in a relatively better position. We would have copious research correctly indicating that bias was present in standardized test scores. Surprisingly, however, the limitations of having these data might outweigh the benefits. Test bias would be a correct conclusion reached incorrectly.

Findings of bias rely primarily on mean differences between groups. These differences would consist partly of bias and partly of other constituents, which would project them upward or downward, perhaps depending on the particular groups involved. Thus, we would be accurate in concluding that bias was present but inaccurate as to the amount of bias and, possibly, its direction: that is, which of two groups it favored. Any modifications made would do too little, or too much, creating new bias in the opposite direction.

The presence of bias should allow for additional explanations. For example, bias and *Steelean effects* (Steele & Aronson, 1995), in which fear of confirming a stereotype impedes minorities' performance, might both affect test results. Such additional possibilities, which now receive little attention, would receive even less. Economic and social deprivation, serious problems apart from testing issues, would again appear less harmful and therefore more justifiable. Efforts to improve people's scores through social programs would be difficult to defend, because this work presupposes that factors other than test bias are the causes of score differences. Thus, Americans' belief in human potential would be vindicated, but perhaps at considerable cost to minority individuals.

POSSIBLE SOURCES OF BIAS

Minority and other psychologists have expressed numerous concerns over the use of psychological and educational tests with minorities. These concerns are potentially legitimate and substantive but are often asserted as true in the absence of scientific evidence. Reynolds, Lowe, et al. (1999) have divided the most frequent of the problems cited into seven categories, described briefly here. Two categories, inequitable social consequences and qualitatively distinct aptitude and personality, receive more extensive treatments in the "Test Bias and Social Issues" section.

1. *Inappropriate content.* Tests are geared to majority experiences and values or are scored arbitrarily according to majority values. Correct responses or solution methods depend on material that is unfamiliar to minority individuals.
2. *Inappropriate standardization samples.* Minorities' representation in norming samples is proportionate but insufficient to allow them any influence over test development.
3. *Examiners' and language bias.* White examiners who speak standard English intimidate minority examinees and communicate inaccurately with them, spuriously lowering their test scores.
4. *Inequitable social consequences.* Ethnic minority individuals, already disadvantaged because of stereotyping and past discrimination, are denied employment or relegated to dead-end educational tracks. Labeling effects are another example of invalidity of this type.

5. *Measurement of different constructs.* Tests largely based on majority culture are measuring different characteristics altogether for members of minority groups, rendering them invalid for these groups.
6. *Differential predictive validity.* Standardized tests accurately predict many outcomes for majority group members, but they do not predict any relevant behavior for their minority counterparts. In addition, the criteria that tests are designed to predict, such as achievement in White, middle-class schools, may themselves be biased against minority examinees.
7. *Qualitatively distinct aptitude and personality.* This position seems to suggest that minority and majority ethnic groups possess characteristics of different *types,* so that test development must begin with different definitions for majority and minority groups.

Researchers have investigated these concerns, although few results are available for labeling effects or for long-term social consequences of testing. As noted by Reynolds, Lowe, et al. (1999), both of these problems are relevant to testing in general, rather than to ethnic issues alone. In addition, individuals as well as groups can experience labeling and other social consequences of testing. Researchers should investigate these outcomes with diverse samples and numerous statistical techniques. Finally, Reynolds et al. suggest that tracking and special education should be treated as problems with education rather than assessment.

WHAT TEST BIAS IS AND IS NOT

Bias and Unfairness

Scientists and clinicians should distinguish bias from *unfairness* and from *offensiveness*. Thorndike (1971) wrote, "The presence (or absence) of differences in mean score between groups, or of differences in variability, tells us nothing directly about fairness" (p. 64). In fact, the concepts of test bias and unfairness are distinct in themselves. A test may have very little bias, but a clinician could still use it unfairly to minority examinees' disadvantage. Conversely, a test may be biased, but clinicians need not—and must not—use it to unfairly penalize minorities or others whose scores may be affected. Little is gained by anyone when concepts are conflated or when, in any other respect, professionals operate from a base of misinformation.

Jensen (1980) was the author who first argued cogently that fairness and bias are separable concepts. As noted by Brown et al. (1999), fairness is a moral, philosophical, or legal issue on which reasonable people can legitimately disagree. By contrast, bias is an empirical property of a test, as used with two or more specified groups. Thus, bias is a statistically estimated quantity rather than a principle established through debate and opinion.

Bias and Offensiveness

A second distinction is that between test bias and item *offensiveness*. In the development of many tests, a minority review panel examines each item for content that may be offensive to one or more groups. Professionals and laypersons alike often view these examinations as tests of bias. Such *expert reviews* have been part of the development of many prominent ability tests, including the Kaufman Assessment Battery for Children (K-ABC), the Wechsler Preschool and Primary Scale of Intelligence–Revised (WPPSI-R), and the Peabody Picture Vocabulary Test–Revised (PPVT-R). The development of personality and behavior tests also incorporates such reviews (e.g., Reynolds, 2001; Reynolds & Kamphaus, 1992). Prominent authors such as Anastasi (1988), Kaufman (1979), and Sandoval and Mille (1979) support this method as a way to enhance rapport with the public.

In a well-known case titled PASE v. Hannon (Reschly, 2000), a federal judge applied this method rather quaintly, examining items from the Wechsler Intelligence Scales for Children (WISC) and the Binet intelligence scales to personally determine which items were biased (Elliot, 1987). Here, an authority figure showed startling naivete and greatly exceeded his expertise—a telling comment on modern hierarchies of influence. Similarly, a high-ranking representative of the Texas Education Agency argued in a televised interview (October 14, 1997, KEYE 42, Austin, TX) that the Texas Assessment of Academic Skills (TAAS), controversial among researchers, could not be biased against ethnic minorities because minority reviewers inspected the items for biased content.

Several researchers have reported that such expert reviewers perform at or below chance level, indicating that they are unable to identify biased items (Jensen, 1976; Sandoval & Mille, 1979; reviews by Camilli & Shepard, 1994; Reynolds, 1995, 1998a; Reynolds, Lowe, et al., 1999). Since initial research by McGurk (1951), studies have provided little evidence that anyone can estimate, by personal inspection, how differently a test item may function for different groups of people.

Sandoval and Mille (1979) had university students from Spanish, history, and education classes identify items from the WISC-R that would be more difficult for a minority child than for a White child, along with items that would be equally difficult for both groups. Participants included Black, White, and Mexican American students. Each student judged 45 items, of which 15 were most difficult for Blacks, 15 were most difficult for Mexican Americans, and 15 were most nearly equal in difficulty for minority children, in comparison with White children.

The participants read each question and identified it as easier, more difficult, or equally difficult for minority versus White children. Results indicated that the participants could not make these distinctions to a statistically significant degree and that minority and nonminority participants did not differ in their performance or in the types of misidentifications they made. Sandoval and Mille (1979) used only extreme items, so the analysis would have produced statistically significant results for even a relatively small degree of accuracy in judgment.

For researchers, test bias is a deviation from examinees' real level of performance. Bias goes by many names and has many characteristics, but it always involves scores that are too low or too high to accurately represent or predict some examinee's skills, abilities, or traits. To show bias, then—to greatly simplify the issue—requires estimates of scores. Reviewers have no way of producing such an estimate. They can suggest items that may be offensive, but statistical techniques are necessary to determine test bias.

Culture Fairness, Culture Loading, and Culture Bias

A third pair of distinct concepts is cultural *loading* and cultural *bias,* the former often associated with the concept of culture fairness. Cultural loading is the degree to which a test or item is specific to a particular culture. A test with greater cultural loading has greater potential bias when administered to people of diverse cultures. Nevertheless, a test can be culturally loaded without being culturally biased.

An example of a culture-loaded item might be, "Who was Eleanor Roosevelt?" This question may be appropriate for students who have attended U.S. schools since first grade, assuming that research shows this to be true. The cultural specificity of the question would be too great, however, to permit its use with European and certainly Asian elementary school students, except perhaps as a test of knowledge of U.S. history. Nearly all standardized tests have some degree of cultural specificity. Cultural loadings fall on a continuum, with some tests linked to a culture as defined very generally and liberally, and others to a culture as defined very narrowly and distinctively.

Cultural loading, by itself, does not render tests biased or offensive. Rather, it creates a potential for either problem, which must then be assessed through research. Ramsay (2000;

Ramsay & Reynolds, 2000b) suggested that some characteristics might be viewed as desirable or undesirable in themselves but others as desirable or undesirable only to the degree that they influence other characteristics. Test bias against Cuban Americans would itself be an undesirable characteristic. A subtler situation occurs if a test is both culturally loaded and culturally biased. If the test's cultural loading is a cause of its bias, the cultural loading is then *indirectly* undesirable and should be corrected. Alternatively, studies may show that the test is culturally loaded but unbiased. If so, indirect undesirability due to an association with bias can be ruled out.

Some authors (e.g., Cattell, 1979) have attempted to develop culture-fair intelligence tests. These tests, however, are characteristically poor measures from a statistical standpoint (Anastasi, 1988; Ebel, 1979). In one study, Hartlage, Lucas, and Godwin (1976) compared Raven's Progressive Matrices (RPM), thought to be culture fair, with the WISC, thought to be culture loaded. The researchers assessed these tests' predictiveness of reading, spelling, and arithmetic measures with a group of disadvantaged, rural children of low socio-economic status. WISC scores consistently correlated higher than RPM scores with the measures examined.

The problem may be that intelligence is defined as adaptive or beneficial behavior within a particular culture. Therefore, a test free from cultural influence would tend to be free from the influence of intelligence—and to be a poor predictor of intelligence in any culture. As Reynolds, Lowe, et al. (1999) observed, if a test is developed in one culture, its appropriateness to other cultures is a matter for scientific verification. Test scores should not be given the same interpretations for different cultures without evidence that those interpretations would be sound.

Test Bias and Social Issues

Authors have introduced numerous concerns regarding tests administered to ethnic minorities (Brown et al., 1999). Many of these concerns, however legitimate and substantive, have little connection with the scientific estimation of test bias. According to some authors, the unequal results of standardized tests produce inequitable social consequences. Low test scores relegate minority group members, already at an educational and vocational disadvantage because of past discrimination and low expectations of their ability, to educational tracks that lead to mediocrity and low achievement (Chipman, Marshall, & Scott, 1991; Payne & Payne, 1991; see also "Possible Sources of Bias" section).

Other concerns are more general. Proponents of tests, it is argued, fail to offer remedies for racial or ethnic differences (Scarr, 1981), to confront societal concerns over racial discrimination when addressing test bias (Gould, 1995, 1996), to respect research by cultural linguists and anthropologists (Figueroa, 1991; Helms, 1992), to address inadequate special education programs (Reschly, 1997), and to include sufficient numbers of African Americans in norming samples (Dent, 1996). Furthermore, test proponents use massive empirical data to conceal historic prejudice and racism (Richardson, 1995). Some of these practices may be deplorable, but they do not constitute test bias. A removal of group differences from scores cannot combat them effectively and may even remove some evidence of their existence or influence.

Gould (1995, 1996) has acknowledged that tests are not statistically biased and do not show differential predictive validity. He argues, however, that defining cultural bias statistically is confusing: The public is concerned not with statistical bias, but with whether Black-White IQ differences occur because society treats Black people unfairly. That is, the public considers tests biased if they record biases originating elsewhere in society (Gould, 1995). Researchers consider them biased only if they introduce additional error because of flaws in their design or properties. Gould (1995, 1996) argues that society's concern cannot be addressed by demonstrations that tests are statistically unbiased. It can, of course, be addressed empirically.

Another social concern, noted briefly above, is that majority and minority examinees may have qualitatively different aptitudes and personality traits, so that traits and abilities must be conceptualized differently for different groups. If this is not done, a test may produce lower results for one group because it is conceptualized most appropriately for another group. This concern is complex from the standpoint of construct validity and may take various practical forms.

In one possible scenario, two ethnic groups can have different patterns of abilities, but the sums of their abilities can be about equal. Group A may have higher verbal fluency, vocabulary, and usage, but lower syntax, sentence analysis, and flow of logic, than Group B. A verbal ability test measuring only the first three abilities would incorrectly represent Group B as having lower verbal ability. This concern is one of construct validity.

Alternatively, a verbal fluency test may be used to represent the two groups' verbal ability. The test accurately represents Group B as having lower verbal fluency but is used inappropriately to suggest that this group has lower verbal ability per se. Such a characterization is not only incorrect; it is unfair to group members and has detrimental consequences for them that cannot be condoned. Construct invalidity is difficult to argue here, however, because this concern is one of test use.

RELATED QUESTIONS

Test Bias and Etiology

The etiology of a condition is distinct from the question of test bias (review, Reynolds & Kaiser, 1992). In fact, the need to research etiology emerges only after evidence that a score difference is a real one, not an artifact of bias. Authors have sometimes inferred that score differences themselves indicate genetic differences, implying that one or more groups are genetically inferior. This inference is scientifically no more defensible—and ethically much less so—than the notion that score differences demonstrate test bias.

Jensen (1969) has long argued that mental tests measure, to some extent, the intellectual factor g, found in behavioral genetics studies to have a large genetic component. In Jensen's view, group differences in mental test scores may reflect largely genetic differences in g. Nonetheless, Jensen made many qualifications to these arguments and to the differences themselves. He also posited that other factors make considerable, though lesser, contributions to intellectual development (Reynolds, Lowe, et al., 1999). Jensen's theory, if correct, may explain certain intergroup phenomena, such as differential Black and White performance on digit span measures (Ramsay & Reynolds, 1995).

Test Bias Involving Groups and Individuals

Bias may influence the scores of individuals, as well as groups, on personality and ability tests. Therefore, researchers can and should investigate both of these possible sources of bias. An overarching statistical method called the general linear model permits this approach by allowing both *group* and *individual* to be analyzed as independent variables. In addition, item characteristics, motivation, and other nonintellectual variables (Reynolds, Lowe, et al., 1999; Sternberg, 1980; Wechsler, 1975) admit of analysis through recoding, categorization, and similar expedients.

EXPLAINING GROUP DIFFERENCES

Among researchers, the issue of cultural bias stems largely from well-documented findings, now seen in more than 100 years of research, that members of different ethnic groups have different levels and patterns of performance on many prominent cognitive ability tests. Intelligence batteries have generated some of the most influential and provocative of these findings (Elliot, 1987; Gutkin & Reynolds, 1981; Reynolds, Chastain, Kaufman, & McLean, 1987; Spitz, 1986). In many countries worldwide, people of different ethnic and racial groups, genders, socioeconomic levels, and other demographic groups obtain systematically different intellectual test results. Black-White IQ differences in the United States have undergone extensive investigation for more than 50 years. Jensen (1980), Shuey (1966), Tyler (1965), and Willerman (1979) have reviewed the greater part of this research. The findings occasionally differ somewhat from one age group to another, but they have not changed substantially in the past century.

On average, Blacks differ from Whites by about 1.0 standard deviation, with White groups obtaining the higher scores. The differences have been relatively consistent in size for some time and under several methods of investigation. An exception is a reduction of the Black-White IQ difference on the intelligence portion of the K-ABC to about .5 standard deviations, although this result is controversial and poorly understood (see Kamphaus & Reynolds, 1987, for a discussion). In addition, such findings are consistent only for African Americans. Other, highly diverse findings appear for native African and other Black populations (Jensen, 1980).

Researchers have taken into account a number of demographic variables, most notably socioeconomic status (SES). The size of the mean Black-White difference in the United States then diminishes to .5–.7 standard deviations (Jensen, 1980; Kaufman, 1973; Kaufman & Kaufman, 1973; Reynolds & Gutkin, 1981) but is robust in its appearance.

Asian groups, although less thoroughly researched than Black groups, have consistently performed as well as or better than Whites (Pintner, 1931; Tyler, 1965; Willerman, 1979). Asian Americans obtain average mean ability scores (Flynn, 1991; Lynn, 1995; Neisser et al., 1996; Reynolds, Willson, & Ramsay, 1999).

Matching is an important consideration in studies of ethnic differences. Any difference between groups may be due neither to test bias nor to ethnicity but to SES, nutrition, and other variables that may be associated with test performance. Matching on these variables controls for their associations.

A limitation to matching is that it results in regression toward the mean. Black respondents with high self-esteem, for example, may be selected from a population with low self-esteem. When examined later, these respondents will test with lower self-esteem, having regressed to the lower mean of their own population. Their extreme scores—high in this case—were due to chance.

Clinicians and research consumers should also be aware that the similarities between ethnic groups are much greater than the differences. This principle holds for intelligence, personality, and most other characteristics, both psychological and physiological. From another perspective, the variation among members of any one ethnic group greatly exceeds the differences between groups. The large similarities among groups appear repeatedly in statistical analyses as large, statistically significant constants and great overlap between different groups' ranges of scores.

Some authors (e.g., Schoenfeld, 1974) have disputed whether racial differences in intelligence are real or even researchable. Nevertheless, the findings are highly reliable from study to study, even when study participants identify their own race. Thus, the existence of these differences has gained wide acceptance. The differences are real and undoubtedly complex. The tasks remaining are to describe them thoroughly (Reynolds, Lowe, et al., 1999) and, more difficult, to explain them in a causal sense (Ramsay, 1998a, 2000). Both the lower scores of some groups and the higher scores of others must be explained, and not necessarily in the same way.

Over time, exclusively genetic and environmental explanations have lost so much of their credibility that they can hardly be called current. Most researchers who posit that score differences are real now favor an interactionist perspective. This development reflects a similar shift in psychology and social science as a whole. However, this relatively recent consensus masks the subtle persistence of an earlier assumption that test score differences must have either a genetic or an environmental basis. The relative contributions of genes and environment still provoke debate, with some authors seemingly intent on establishing a predominantly genetic or a predominantly environmental basis. The interactionist perspective shifts the focus of debate from *how much* to *how* genetic and environmental factors contribute to a characteristic. In practice, not all scientists have made this shift.

CULTURAL TEST BIAS AS AN EXPLANATION

The bias explanation of score differences has led to the cultural test bias hypothesis (CTBH; Brown et al., 1999; Reynolds, 1982a, 1982b; Reynolds & Brown, 1984b). According to the CTBH, differences in mean performance for members of different ethnic groups do not reflect real differences among groups but are artifacts of tests or of the measurement process. This approach holds that ability tests contain systematic error occurring as a function of group membership or other nominal variables that should be irrelevant. That is, people who should obtain equal scores obtain unequal ones because of their ethnicities, genders, socioeconomic levels, and the like.

For SES, Eells, Davis, Havighurst, Herrick, and Tyler (1951) summarized the logic of the CTBH as follows: If (a) children of different SES levels have experiences of different kinds and with different types of material, and if (b) intelligence tests contain a disproportionate amount of material

drawn from cultural experiences most familiar to high-SES children, then (c) high-SES children should have higher IQ scores than low-SES children. As Eells et al. observed, this argument tends to imply that IQ differences are artifacts that depend on item content and "do not reflect accurately any important underlying ability" (p. 4) in the individual.

Since the 1960s, the CTBH explanation has stimulated numerous studies, which in turn have largely refuted the explanation. Lengthy reviews are now available (e.g., Jensen, 1980; Reynolds, 1995, 1998a; Reynolds & Brown, 1984b). This literature suggests that tests whose development, standardization, and reliability are sound and well documented are not biased against native-born, American racial or ethnic minorities. Studies do occasionally indicate bias, but it is usually small, and it most often favors minorities.

Results cited to support content bias indicate that item biases account for < 1% to about 5% of variation in test scores. In addition, it is usually counterbalanced across groups. That is, when bias against an ethnic group occurs, comparable bias favoring that group occurs also and cancels it out. When apparent bias is counterbalanced, it may be random rather than systematic, and therefore not bias after all. Item or subtest refinements, as well, frequently reduce and counterbalance bias that is present.

No one explanation is likely to account for test score differences in their entirety. A contemporary approach to statistics, in which effects of zero are rare or even nonexistent, suggests that tests, test settings, and nontest factors may all contribute to group differences (see also Bouchard & Segal, 1985; Flynn, 1991; Loehlin, Lindzey, & Spuhler, 1975).

Some authors, most notably Mercer (1979; see also Lonner, 1985; Helms, 1992), have reframed the test bias hypothesis over time. Mercer argued that the lower scores of ethnic minorities on aptitude tests can be traced to the anglocentrism, or adherence to White, middle-class value systems, of these tests. Mercer's assessment system, the System of Multicultural Pluralistic Assessment (SOMPA), effectively equated ethnic minorities' intelligence scores by applying complex demographic corrections. The SOMPA was popular for several years. It is used less commonly today because of its conceptual and statistical limitations (Reynolds, Lowe, et al., 1999). Helms's position receives attention below (Helms and Cultural Equivalence).

HARRINGTON'S CONCLUSIONS

Harrington (1968a, 1968b), unlike such authors as Mercer (1979) and Helms (1992), emphasized the proportionate but small numbers of minority examinees in norming samples.

Their low representation, Harrington argued, made it impossible for minorities to exert any influence on the results of a test. Harrington devised an innovative experimental test of this proposal.

The researcher (Harrington, 1975, 1976) used six genetically distinct strains of rats to represent ethnicities. He then composed six populations, each with different proportions of the six rat strains. Next, Harrington constructed six intelligence tests resembling Hebb-Williams mazes. These mazes, similar to the Mazes subtest of the Wechsler scales, are commonly used as intelligence tests for rats. Harrington reasoned that tests normed on populations dominated by a given rat strain would yield higher mean scores for that strain.

Groups of rats that were most numerous in a test's norming sample obtained the highest average score on that test. Harrington concluded from additional analyses of the data that a test developed and normed on a White majority could not have equivalent predictive validity for Blacks or any other minority group.

Reynolds, Lowe, et al. (1999) have argued that Harrington's generalizations break down in three respects. Harrington (1975, 1976) interpreted his findings in terms of predictive validity. Most studies have indicated that tests of intelligence and other aptitudes have equivalent predictive validity for racial groups under various circumstances and with many criterion measures.

A second problem noted by Reynolds, Lowe, et al. (1999) is that Chinese Americans, Japanese Americans, and Jewish Americans have little representation in the norming samples of most ability tests. According to Harrington's model, they should score low on these tests. However, they score at least as high as Whites on tests of intelligence and of some other aptitudes (Gross, 1967; Marjoribanks, 1972; Tyler, 1965; Willerman, 1979).

Finally, Harrington's (1975, 1976) approach can account for group differences in overall test scores but not for patterns of abilities reflected in varying subtest scores. For example, one ethnic group often scores higher than another on some subtests but lower on others. Harrington's model can explain only inequality that is uniform from subtest to subtest. The arguments of Reynolds, Lowe, et al. (1999) carry considerable weight, because (a) they are grounded directly in empirical results, rather than rational arguments such as those made by Harrington, and (b) those results have been found with humans; results found with nonhumans cannot be generalized to humans without additional evidence.

Harrington's (1975, 1976) conclusions were overgeneralizations. Rats are simply so different from people that rat and human intelligence cannot be assumed to behave the same. Finally, Harrington used genetic populations in his studies.

However, the roles of genetic, environmental, and interactive effects in determining the scores of human ethnic groups are still topics of debate, and an interaction is the preferred explanation. Harrington begged the nature-nurture question, implicitly presupposing heavy genetic effects.

The focus of Harrington's (1975, 1976) work was reduced scores for minority examinees, an important avenue of investigation. Artifactually low scores on an intelligence test could lead to acts of race discrimination, such as misassignment to educational programs or spurious denial of employment. This issue is the one over which most court cases involving test bias have been contested (Reynolds, Lowe, et al., 1999).

MEAN DIFFERENCES AS TEST BIAS

A view widely held by laypeople and researchers (Adebimpe, Gigandet, & Harris, 1979; Alley & Foster, 1978; Hilliard, 1979, 1984; Jackson, 1975; Mercer, 1976; Padilla, 1988; Williams, 1974; Wright & Isenstein, 1977–1978) is that group differences in mean scores on ability tests constitute test bias. As adherents to this view contend, there is no valid, a priori reason to suppose that cognitive ability should differ from one ethnic group to another. However, the same is true of the assumption that cognitive ability should be the same for all ethnic groups and that any differences shown on a test must therefore be effects of bias. As noted by Reynolds, Lowe, et al. (1999), an a priori acceptance of either position is untenable from a scientific standpoint.

Some authors add that the distributions of test scores of each ethnic group, not merely the means, must be identical before one can assume that a test is fair. Identical distributions, like equal means, have limitations involving accuracy. Such alterations correct for any source of score differences, including those for which the test is not responsible. Equal scores attained in this way necessarily depart from reality to some degree.

The Egalitarian Fallacy

Jensen (1980; Brown et al., 1999) contended that three fallacious assumptions were impeding the scientific study of test bias: (a) the *egalitarian fallacy,* that all groups were equal in the characteristics measured by a test, so that any score difference must result from bias; (b) the *culture-bound fallacy,* that reviewers can assess the culture loadings of items through casual inspection or armchair judgment; and (c) the *standardization fallacy,* that a test is necessarily biased when used with any group not included in large numbers in the norming sample. In Jensen's view, the mean-difference-as-bias approach is an example of the egalitarian fallacy.

A prior assumption of equal ability is as unwarranted scientifically as the opposite assumption. Studies have shown group differences for many abilities and even for sensory capacities (Reynolds, Willson, et al., 1999). Both equalities and inequalities must be found *empirically,* that is, through scientific observation. An assumption of equality, if carried out consistently, would have a stultifying effect on research. Torrance (1980) observed that disadvantaged Black children in the United States have sometimes earned higher creativity scores than many White children. This finding may be important, given that Blacks are underrepresented in classes for gifted students. The egalitarian assumption implies that these Black children's high creativity is an artifact of tests, foreclosing on more substantive interpretations—and on possible changes in student placement.

Equal ability on the part of different ethnic groups is not a defensible egalitarian fallacy. A fallacy, as best understood, is an error in judgment or reasoning, but the question of equal ability is an empirical one. By contrast, an *a priori assumption* of either equal or unequal ability can be regarded as fallacious. The assumption of equal ability is most relevant, because it is implicit when any researcher interprets a mean difference as test bias.

The impossibility of proving a null hypothesis is relevant here. Scientists never regard a null hypothesis as proven, because the absence of a counterinstance cannot prove a rule. If 100 studies do not provide a counterinstance, the 101st study may. Likewise, the failure to reject a hypothesis of equality between groups—that is, a null hypothesis—cannot prove that the groups are equal. This hypothesis, then, is not falsifiable and is therefore problematic for researchers.

Limitations of Mean Differences

As noted above, a mean difference by itself does not show bias. One may ask, then, what (if anything) it does show. It indicates simply that two groups differ when means are taken to represent their performance. Thus, its accuracy depends on how well means, as opposed to other measures of the typical score, represent the two groups; on how well *any* measure of the typical score *can* represent the two groups; and on how well *differences* in typical scores, rather than in variation, asymmetry, or other properties, can represent the relationships between the two groups. Ramsay (2000) reanalyzed a study in which mean differences between groups had been found. The reanalysis showed that the two groups differed much more in variation than in typical scores.

Most important, a mean difference provides no information as to *why* two groups differ: because of test bias, genetic influences, environmental factors, a gene-environment

interaction, or perhaps biases in society recorded by tests. Rather than answering this question, mean differences raise it in the first place. Thus, they are a starting point—but are they a good one? Answering this question is a logical next step.

A difference between group means is easy to obtain. In addition, it permits an easy, straightforward interpretation—but a deceptive one. It provides scant information, and none at all regarding variation, kurtosis, or asymmetry. These additional properties are needed to understand any group's scores.

Moreover, a mean difference is often an inaccurate measure of center. If a group's scores are highly asymmetric—that is, if the high scores taper off gradually but the low scores clump together, or vice versa—their mean is always too high or too low, pulled as it is toward the scores that taper gradually. Symmetry should never be assumed, even for standardized test scores. A test with a large, national norming sample can produce symmetric scores with that sample but asymmetric or *skewed* scores for particular schools, communities, or geographic regions. Results for people in these areas, if skewed, can produce an inaccurate mean and therefore an inaccurate mean difference. Even a large norming sample can include very small samples for one or more groups, producing misleading mean differences for the norming sample itself.

Finally, a mean is a point estimate: a single number that summarizes the scores of an entire group of people. A group's scores can have little skew or kurtosis but vary so widely that the mean is not typical of the highest and lowest scores. In addition to being potentially inaccurate, then, a mean can be unrepresentative of the group it purports to summarize.

Thus, means have numerous potential limitations as a way to describe groups and differences between groups. In addition to a mean, measures of shape and spread, sometimes called *distribution* and *variation,* are necessary. Researchers, including clinical researchers, may sometimes need to use different centroids entirely: medians, modes, or modified *M* statistics. Most basically, we always need a thoroughgoing description of each sample. Furthermore, it is both possible and necessary to test the characteristics of each sample to assess their representativeness of the respective population characteristics. This testing can be a simple process, often using group confidence intervals.

Once we know what we have found—which characteristics vary from group to group—we can use this information to start to answer the question *why.* That is, we can begin to investigate causation. Multivariate techniques are often suitable for this work. Bivariate techniques address only two variables, as the name implies. Thus, they are ill suited to pursue possible causal relationships, because they cannot rule out alternative explanations posed by additional variables (Ramsay, 2000).

Alternatively, we can avoid the elusive causal question *why* and instead use measurement techniques developed to assess bias. Reynolds (1982a) provides copious information about these techniques. Such procedures cannot tell us if group differences result from genetic or environmental factors, but they can suggest whether test scores may be biased. Researchers have generated a literature of considerable size and sophistication using measurement techniques for examining test bias. This chapter now addresses the results of such research.

RESULTS OF BIAS RESEARCH

Jensen's Review

Jensen (1980) compiled an extensive early review of test bias studies. One concern addressed in the review was rational judgments that test items were biased based on their content or phrasing. For scientists, *rational* judgments are those based on reason rather than empirical findings. Such judgments may seem sound or even self-evident, but they often conflict with each other and with scientific evidence.

A WISC-R item often challenged on rational grounds is, "What is the thing to do if a boy/girl much smaller than yourself starts to fight with you?" Correct responses include, "Walk away," and, "Don't hit him back." CTBH proponents criticized this item as biased against inner-city Black children, who may be expected to hit back to maintain their status, and who may therefore respond incorrectly for cultural reasons. Jensen (1980) reviewed large-sample research indicating that proportionately more Black children than White children responded correctly to this item. Miele (1979), who also researched this item in a large-*N* study, concluded that the item was easier for Blacks than for Whites. As with this item, empirical results often contradict rational judgments.

Predictive and Construct Validity

Jensen (1980) addressed bias in predictive and construct validity, along with situational bias. Bias in predictive validity, as defined by Jensen, is systematic error in predicting a criterion variable for people of different groups. This bias occurs when one regression equation is incorrectly used for two or more groups. The review included studies involving Blacks and Whites, the two most frequently researched groups. The conclusions reached by Jensen were that (a) a large majority of studies showed that tests were equally valid for these groups and that (b) when differences were found, the tests overpredicted Black examinees when compared with White examinees. CTBH would have predicted the opposite result.

Bias in construct validity occurs when a test measures groups of examinees differently. For example, a test can be more difficult, valid, or reliable for one group than for another. Construct bias involves the test itself, whereas predictive bias involves a test's prediction of a result outside the test.

Jensen (1980) found numerous studies of bias in construct validity. As regards difficulty, when item scores differed for ethnic groups or social classes, the differences were not consistently associated with the culture loadings of the tests. Score differences between Black and White examinees were larger on nonverbal than on verbal tests, contrary to beliefs that nonverbal tests are culture fair or unbiased. The sizes of Black-White differences were positively associated with tests' correlations with *g*, or general ability. In tests with several item types, such as traditional intelligence tests, the rank orders of item difficulties for different ethnic groups were very highly correlated. Items that discriminated most between Black and White examinees also discriminated most between older and younger members of each ethnic group. Finally, Blacks, Whites, and Mexican Americans showed similar correlations between raw test scores and chronological ages.

In addition, Jensen (1980) reviewed results pertaining to validity and reliability. Black, White, and Mexican American examinees produced similar estimates of internal consistency reliability. As regards validity, Black and White samples showed the same factor structures. Jensen wrote that the evidence was generally inconclusive for infrequently researched ethnic groups, such as Asian Americans and Native Americans.

Situational Bias

Jensen's (1980) term *situational bias* refers to "influences in the test situation, but independent of the test itself, that may bias test scores" (p. 377). These influences may include, among others, characteristics of the test setting, the instructions, and the examiners themselves. Examples include anxiety, practice and coaching effects, and examiner dialect and ethnic group (Jensen, 1984). As Jensen (1980) observed, situational influences would not constitute test bias, because they are not attributes of the tests themselves. Nevertheless, they should emerge in studies of construct and predictive bias. Jensen concluded that the situational variables reviewed did not influence group differences in scores.

Soon after Jensen's (1980) review was published, the National Academy of Sciences and the National Research Council commissioned a panel of 19 experts, who conducted a second review of the test bias literature. The panel concluded that well-constructed tests were not biased against African Americans or other English-speaking minority groups (Wigdor

& Garner, 1982). Later, a panel of 52 professionals signed a position paper that concluded, in part, "Intelligence tests are not culturally biased against American blacks or other native-born, English-speaking peoples in the U. S. Rather, IQ scores predict equally accurately for all such Americans, regardless of race and social class" ("Mainstream Science," 1994, p. A18). That same year, a task force of 11 psychologists, established by the American Psychological Association, concluded that no test characteristic reviewed made a substantial contribution to Black-White differences in intelligence scores (Neisser et al., 1996). Thus, several major reviews have failed to support CTBH (see also Reynolds, 1998a, 1999).

Review by Reynolds, Lowe, and Saenz

Content Validity

Reynolds, Lowe, et al. (1999) categorized findings under content, construct, and predictive validity. Content validity is the extent to which the content of a test is a representative sample of the behavior to be measured (Anastasi, 1988). Items with content bias should behave differently from group to group for people of the same standing on the characteristic being measured. Typically, reviewers judge an intelligence item to have content bias because the information or solution method required is unfamiliar to disadvantaged or minority individuals, or because the tests' author has arbitrarily decided on the correct answer, so that minorities are penalized for giving responses that are correct in their own culture but not in the author's culture.

The issue of content validity with achievement tests is complex. Important variables to consider include exposure to instruction, general ability of the group, and accuracy and specificity of the items for the sample (Reynolds, Lowe, et al., 1999; see also Schmidt, 1983). Little research is available for personality tests, but cultural variables that may be found to influence some personality tests include beliefs regarding discipline and aggression, values related to education and employment, and perceptions concerning society's fairness toward one's group.

Camilli and Shepard (1994; Reynolds, 2000a) recommended techniques based on item-response theory (IRT) to detect differential item functioning (DIF). DIF statistics detect items that behave differently from one group to another. A statistically significant DIF statistic, by itself, does not indicate bias but may lead to later findings of bias through additional research, with consideration of the construct meant to be measured. For example, if an item on a composition test were about medieval history, studies might be conducted to determine if the item is measuring composition skill or some

unintended trait, such as historical knowledge. For smaller samples, a contingency table (CT) procedure is often used to estimate DIF. CT approaches are relatively easy to understand and interpret.

Nandakumar, Glutting, and Oakland (1993) used a CT approach to investigate possible racial, ethnic, and gender bias on the Guide to the Assessment of Test Session Behavior (GATSB). Participants were boys and girls aged 6–16 years, of White, Black, or Hispanic ethnicity. Only 10 of 80 items produced statistically significant DIFs, suggesting that the GATSB has little bias for different genders and ethnicities.

In very-large-N studies, Reynolds, Willson, and Chatman (1984) used a partial correlation procedure (Reynolds, 2000a) to estimate DIF in tests of intelligence and related aptitudes. The researchers found no systematic bias against African Americans or women on measures of English vocabulary. Willson, Nolan, Reynolds, and Kamphaus (1989) used the same procedure to estimate DIF on the Mental Processing scales of the K-ABC. The researchers concluded that there was little apparent evidence of race or gender bias.

Jensen (1976) used a chi-square technique (Reynolds, 2000a) to examine the distribution of incorrect responses for two multiple-choice intelligence tests, RPM and the Peabody Picture-Vocabulary Test (PPVT). Participants were Black and White children aged 6–12 years. The errors for many items were distributed systematically over the response options. This pattern, however, was the same for Blacks and Whites. These results indicated bias in a general sense, but not racial bias. On RPM, Black and White children made different types of errors, but for few items. The researcher examined these items with children of different ages. For each of the items, Jensen was able to duplicate Blacks' response patterns using those of Whites approximately two years younger.

Scheuneman (1987) used linear methodology on Graduate Record Examination (GRE) item data to show possible influences on the scores of Black and White test-takers. Vocabulary content, true-false response, and presence or absence of diagrams were among the item characteristics examined. Paired, experimental items were administered in the experimental section of the GRE General Test, given in December 1982. Results indicated that certain characteristics common to a variety of items may have a differential influence on Blacks' and Whites' scores. These items may be measuring, in part, test content rather than verbal, quantitative, or analytical skill.

Jensen (1974, 1976, 1977) evaluated bias on the Wonderlic Personnel Test (WPT), PPVT, and RPM using correlations between P decrements (Reynolds, 2000a) obtained by Black students and those obtained by White students. P is the probability of passing an item, and a P decrement is the size of the

TABLE 4.1 Ethnic Correlations for *P* Decrements and for Rank Orders of Item Difficulties

Scale	Black-White				Mexican American-White			
	Rank Orders		*P* Decrements		Rank Orders		*P* Decrements	
PPVT (Jensen, 1974)	.99[a]	.98[b]	.79[a]	.65[b]	.98[a]	.98[b]	.78[a]	.66[b]
RPM (Jensen, 1974)	.99[a]	.99[b]	.98[a]	.96[b]	.99[a]	.99[b]	.99[a]	.97[b]
SB L-M (Jensen, 1976)	.96[c]							
WISC-R (Jensen, 1976)	.95[c]							
(Sandoval, 1979)	.98[c]		.87[c]		.99[c]		.91[c]	
WISC (Miele, 1979)	.96[a]	.95[b]						
WPT (Jensen, 1977)	.94[c]		.81[c]					

Notes. PPVT = Peabody Picture Vocabulary Test; RPM = Raven's Progressive Matrices; SB L-M = Stanford-Binet, Form LM; WISC-R = Wechsler Intelligence Scale for Children–Revised; WPT = Wonderlic Personnel Test; Sandoval, 1979 = Medians for 10 WISC-R subtests, excluding Coding and Digit Span.
[a]Males. [b]Females. [c]Males and females combined.

difference between *P*s for one item and the next. Jensen also obtained correlations between the rank orders of item difficulties for Black and Whites. Results for rank orders and *P* decrements, it should be noted, differ from those that would be obtained for the scores themselves.

The tests examined were RPM; the PPVT; the WISC-R; the WPT; and the Revised Stanford-Binet Intelligence Scale, Form L-M. Jensen (1974) obtained the same data for Mexican American and White students on the PPVT and RPM. Table 4.1 shows the results, with similar findings obtained by Sandoval (1979) and Miele (1979). The correlations showed little evidence of content bias in the scales examined. Most correlations appeared large. Some individual items were identified as biased, but they accounted for only 2% to 5% of the variation in score differences.

Hammill (1991) used correlations of P decrements to examine the Detroit Tests of Learning Aptitude (DTLA-3). Correlations exceeded .90 for all subtests, and most exceeded .95. Reynolds and Bigler (1994) presented correlations of *P* decrements for the 14 subtests of the Test of Memory and Learning (TOMAL). Correlations again exceeded .90, with most exceeding .95, for males and females and for all ethnicities studied.

Another procedure for detecting item bias relies on the partial correlation between an item score and a nominal variable such as ethnic group. The correlation partialed out is that between total test score and the nominal variable. If the variable and the item score are correlated after the partialed correlation is removed, the item is performing differently from group to group, which suggests bias. Reynolds, Lowe, et al. (1999) describe this technique as "the simplest and perhaps the most powerful" means of detecting item bias. They note, however, that it is a relatively recent application. Thus, it may have limitations not yet known.

Research on item bias in personality measures is sparse but has produced results similar to those with ability tests (Moran,

1990; Reynolds, 1998a, 1998b; Reynolds & Harding, 1983). The few studies of behavior rating scales have produced little evidence of bias for White, Black, and Hispanic and Latin populations in the United States (James, 1995; Mayfield & Reynolds, 1998; Reynolds & Kamphaus, 1992).

Not all studies of content bias have focused on items. Researchers evaluating the WISC-R have defined bias differently. Few results are available for the WISC-III; future research should utilize data from this newer test. A recent book by Prifitera and Saklofske (1998), however, addresses the WISC-III and ethnic bias in the United States. These results are discussed later (see the "Construct Validity" and "Predictive Validity" sections).

Reynolds and Jensen (1983) examined the 12 WISC-R subtests for bias against Black children using a variation of the group by item analysis of variance (ANOVA). The researchers matched Black children to White children from the norming sample on the basis of gender and Full Scale IQ. SES was a third matching variable and was used when a child had more than one match in the other group. Matching controlled for *g*, so a group difference indicated that the subtest in question was more difficult for Blacks or for Whites.

Black children exceeded White children on Digit Span and Coding. Whites exceeded Blacks on Comprehension, Object Assembly, and Mazes. Blacks tended to obtain higher scores on Arithmetic and Whites on Picture Arrangement. The actual differences were very small, and variance due to ethnic group was less than 5% for each subtest. If the WISC-R is viewed as a test measuring only *g*, these results may be interpretable as indicating subtest bias. Alternatively, the results may indicate differences in Level II ability (Reynolds, Willson, et al., 1999) or in specific or intermediate abilities.

Taken together, studies of major ability and personality tests show no consistent evidence for content bias. When bias is found, it is small. Tests with satisfactory reliability, validity, and norming appear also to have little content bias. For numerous standardized tests, however, results are not yet available. Research with these tests should continue, investigating possible content bias with differing ethnic and other groups.

Construct Validity

Anastasi (1988) defines construct validity as the extent to which a test may be said to measure a theoretical construct or trait. Test bias in construct validity, then, may be defined as the extent to which a test measures different constructs for different groups.

Factor analysis is a widely used method for investigating construct bias (Reynolds, 2000a). This set of complex techniques groups together items or subtests that correlate highly among themselves. When a group of items correlates highly together, the researcher interprets them as reflecting a single characteristic. The researcher then examines the pattern of correlations and induces the nature of this characteristic. Table 4.2 shows a simple example.

In the table, the subtests picture identification, matrix comparison, visual search, and diagram drawing have high correlations in the column labeled "Factor 1." Definitions, antonyms, synonyms, and multiple meanings have low correlations in this column but much higher ones in the column labeled "Factor 2." A researcher might interpret these results as indicating that the first four subtests correlate with factor 1 and the second four correlate with factor 2. Examining the table, the researcher might see that the subtests correlating highly with factor 1 require visual activity, and he or she might therefore label this factor Visual Ability. The same researcher might see that the subtests correlating highly with factor 2 involve the meanings of words, and he or she might label this factor Word Meanings. To label factors in this way, researchers must be familiar with the subtests or items, common responses to them, and scoring of these responses (see also Ramsay & Reynolds, 2000a). The results in Table 4.2 are called a *two-factor*

TABLE 4.2   A Sample Factor Structure

Subtest	Factor 1	Factor 2
Picture Identification	.78	.17
Matrix Comparison	.82	.26
Visual Search	.86	.30
Diagram Drawing	.91	.29
Definitions	.23	.87
Antonyms	.07	.92
Synonyms	.21	.88
Multiple Meanings	.36	.94

solution. Actual factor analysis is a set of advanced statistical techniques, and the explanation presented here is necessarily a gross oversimplification.

Very similar factor analytic results for two or more groups, such as genders or ethnicities, are evidence that the test responses being analyzed behave similarly as to the constructs they represent and the extent to which they represent them. As noted by Reynolds, Lowe, et al. (1999), such comparative factor analyses with multiple populations are important for the work of clinicians, who must know that a test functions very similarly from one population to another to interpret scores consistently.

Researchers most often calculate a coefficient of congruence or simply a Pearson correlation to examine factorial similarity, often called *factor congruence* or *factor invariance*. The variables correlated are one group's item or subtest correlations (shown in Table 4.2) with another's. A coefficient of congruence may be preferable, but the commonly used techniques produce very similar results, at least with large samples (Reynolds & Harding, 1983; Reynolds, Lowe, et al., 1999). Researchers frequently interpret a value of .90 or higher as indicating factor congruity. For other applicable techniques, see Reynolds (2000a).

Extensive research regarding racial and ethnic groups is available for the widely used WISC and WISC-R. This work consists largely of factor analyses. Psychometricians are trained in this method, so its usefulness in assessing bias is opportune. Unfortunately, many reports of this research fail to specify whether exploratory or confirmatory factor analysis has been used. In factor analyses of construct and other bias, exploratory techniques are most common. Results with the WISC and WISC-R generally support factor congruity. For preschool-age children also, factor analytic results support congruity for racial and ethnic groups (Reynolds, 1982a).

Reschly (1978) conducted factor analyses comparing WISC-R correlations for Blacks, Whites, Mexican Americans, and Papagos, a Native American group, all in the southwestern United States. Reschly found that the two-factor solutions were congruent for the four ethnicities. The 12 coefficients of congruence ranged from .97 to .99. For the less widely used three-factor solutions, only results for Whites and Mexican Americans were congruent. The one-factor solution showed congruence for all four ethnicities, as Miele (1979) had found with the WISC.

Oakland and Feigenbaum (1979) factor analyzed the 12 WISC-R subtests separately for random samples of normal Black, White, and Mexican American children from an urban school district in the northwestern United States. Samples were stratified by race, age, sex, and SES. The researchers used a Pearson r for each factor to compare it for the three ethnic groups. The one-factor solution produced rs of .95 for Black and White children, .97 for Mexican American and White children, and .96 for Black and Mexican American children. The remaining results were $r = .94 - .99$. Thus, WISC-R scores were congruent for the three ethnic groups.

Gutkin and Reynolds (1981) compared factor analytic results for the Black and White children in the WISC-R norming sample. Samples were stratified by age, sex, race, SES, geographic region, and community size to match 1970 U.S. Census Bureau data. The researchers compared one-, two-, and three-factor solutions using magnitudes of unique variances, proportion of total variance accounted for by common factor variance, patterns of correlations with each factor, and percentage of common factor variance accounted for by each factor. Coefficients of congruence were .99 for comparisons of the unique variances and of the three solutions examined. Thus, the factor correlations were congruent for Black and White children.

Dean (1979) compared three-factor WISC-R solutions for White and Mexican American children referred because of learning difficulties in the regular classroom. Analyzing the 10 main WISC-R subtests, Dean found these coefficients of congruence: .84 for Verbal Comprehension, .89 for Perceptual Organization, and .88 for Freedom from Distractibility.

Gutkin and Reynolds (1980) compared one-, two-, and three-factor principal-factor solutions of the WISC-R for referred White and Mexican American children. The researchers also compared their solutions to those of Reschly (1978) and to those derived from the norming sample. Coefficients of congruence were .99 for Gutkin and Reynolds's one-factor solutions and .98 and .91 for their two-factor solutions. Coefficients of congruence exceeded .90 in all comparisons of Gutkin and Reynolds's solutions to Reschly's solutions for normal Black, White, Mexican American, and Papago children and to solutions derived from the norming sample. Three-factor results were more varied but also indicated substantial congruity for these children.

DeFries et al. (1974) administered 15 ability tests to large samples of American children of Chinese or Japanese ancestry. The researchers examined correlations among the 15 tests for the two ethnic groups and concluded that the cognitive organization of the groups was virtually identical. Willerman (1979) reviewed these results and concluded, in part, that the tests were measuring the same abilities for the two groups of children.

Results with adults are available as well. Kaiser (1986) and Scholwinski (1985) have found the Wechsler Intelligence Scale–Revised (WAIS-R) to be factorially congruent for Black and White adults from the norming sample. Kaiser conducted separate hierarchical analyses for Black and White participants and calculated coefficients of congruence for the General, Verbal, and Performance factors. Coefficients for the

three factors were .99, .98, and .97, respectively. Scholwinski (1985) selected Black and White participants closely matched in age, sex, and Full Scale IQ, from the WAIS-R norming sample. Results again indicated factorial congruence.

Researchers have also assessed construct bias by estimating internal consistency reliabilities for different groups. *Internal consistency reliability* is the extent to which all items of a test are measuring the same construct. A test is unbiased with regard to this characteristic to the extent that its reliabilities are similar from group to group.

Jensen (1977) used Kuder-Richardson formula 21 to estimate internal consistency reliability for Black and White adults on the Wonderlic Personnel Test. Reliability estimates were .86 and .88 for Blacks and Whites, respectively. In addition, Jensen (1974) used Hoyt's formula to obtain internal consistency estimates of .96 on the PPVT for Black, White, and Mexican American children. The researcher then subdivided each group of children by gender and obtained reliabilities of .95–.97. Raven's colored matrices produced internal consistency reliabilities of .86–.91 for the same six race-gender groupings. For these three widely used aptitude tests, Jensen's (1974, 1976) results indicated homogeneity of test content and consistency of measurement by gender and ethnicity.

Sandoval (1979) and Oakland and Feigenbaum (1979) have extensively examined the internal consistency reliability of the WISC-R subtests, excluding Digit Span and Coding, for which internal consistency analysis is inappropriate. Both studies included Black, White, and Mexican American children. Both samples were large, and Sandoval's exceeded 1,000.

Sandoval (1979) estimated reliabilities to be within .04 of each other for all subtests except Object Assembly. This subtest was most reliable for Black children at .95, followed by Whites at .79 and Mexican Americans at .75. Oakland and Feigenbaum (1979) found reliabilities within .06, again excepting Object Assembly. In this study, the subtest was most reliable for Whites at .76, followed by Blacks at .64 and Mexican Americans at .67. Oakland and Feigenbaum also found consistent reliabilities for males and females.

Dean (1979) assessed the internal consistency reliability of the WISC-R for Mexican American children tested by White examiners. Reliabilities were consistent with, although slightly larger than, those reported by Wechsler (1975) for the norming sample.

Results with the WISC-III norming sample (Prifitera, Weiss, & Saklofske, 1998) suggested a substantial association between IQ and SES. WISC-III Full Scale IQ was higher for children whose parents had high education levels, and parental education is considered a good measure of SES. The children's Full Scale IQs were 110.7, 103.0, 97.9, 90.6, and 87.7, respectively, in the direction of highest (college or above) to lowest (< 8th grade) parental education level. Researchers have reported similar results for other IQ tests (Prifitera et al.). Such results should not be taken as showing SES bias because, like ethnic and gender differences, they may reflect real distinctions, perhaps influenced by social and economic factors. Indeed, IQ is thought to be associated with SES. By reflecting this theoretical characteristic of intelligence, SES differences may support the construct validity of the tests examined.

Psychologists view intelligence as a developmental phenomenon (Reynolds, Lowe, et al., 1999). Hence, similar correlations of raw scores with age may be evidence of construct validity for intelligence tests. Jensen (1976) found that these correlations for the PPVT were .73 with Blacks, .79 with Whites, and .67 with Mexican Americans. For Raven's colored matrices, correlations were .66 for Blacks, .72 for Whites, and .70 for Mexican Americans. The K-ABC produced similar results (Kamphaus & Reynolds, 1987).

A review by Moran (1990) and a literature search by Reynolds, Lowe, et al. (1999) indicated that few construct bias studies of personality tests had been published. This limitation is notable, given large mean differences on the Minnesota Multiphasic Personality Inventory (MMPI), and possibly the MMPI-2, for different genders and ethnicities (Reynolds et al.). Initial results for the Revised Children's Manifest Anxiety Scale (RCMAS) suggest consistent results by gender and ethnicity (Moran, 1990; Reynolds & Paget, 1981).

To summarize, studies using different samples, methodologies, and definitions of bias indicate that many prominent standardized tests are consistent from one race, ethnicity, and gender to another (see Reynolds, 1982b, for a review of methodologies). These tests appear to be reasonably unbiased for the groups investigated.

Predictive Validity

As its name implies, predictive validity pertains to *prediction* from test scores, whereas content and construct validity pertain to *measurement*. Anastasi (1988) defines predictive or criterion-related validity as "the effectiveness of a test in predicting an individual's performance in specified activities" (p. 145). Thus, test bias in predictive validity may be defined as systematic error that affects examinees' performance differentially depending on their group membership. Cleary et al. (1975) defined predictive test bias as constant error in an inference or prediction, or error in a prediction that exceeds the smallest feasible random error, as a function of membership in a particular group. Oakland and Matuszek (1977) found that fewer children were wrongly placed using these criteria than using other, varied models of bias. An early court ruling also favored Cleary's definition (*Cortez v. Rosen*, 1975).

Of importance, inaccurate prediction sometimes reflects inconsistent measurement of the characteristic being predicted, rather than bias in the test used to predict it. In addition, numerous investigations of predictive bias have addressed the selection of employment and college applicants of different racial and ethnic groups. Future studies should also address personality tests (Moran, 1990). As the chapter will show, copious results for intelligence tests are available.

Under the definition presented by Cleary et al. (1975), the regression line formed by any predictor and criterion (e.g., total test score and a predicted characteristic) must be the same for each group with whom the test is used. A regression line consists of two parameters: a slope a and an intercept b. Too great a group difference in either of these parameters indicates that a regression equation based on the combined groups would predict inaccurately (Reynolds, Lowe, et al., 1999). A separate equation for each group then becomes necessary with the groups and characteristics for which bias has been found.

Hunter, Schmidt, and Hunter (1979) reviewed 39 studies, yielding 866 comparisons, of Black-White test score validity in personnel selection. The researchers concluded that the results did not support a hypothesis of differential or single-group validity. Several studies of the Scholastic Aptitude Test (SAT) indicated no predictive bias, or small bias against Whites, in predicting grade point average (GPA) and other measures of college performance (Cleary, 1968; Cleary et al., 1975).

Reschly and Sabers (1979) examined the validity of WISC-R IQs in predicting the Reading and Math subtest scores of Blacks, Whites, Mexican Americans, and Papago Native Americans on the Metropolitan Achievement Tests (MAT). The MAT has undergone item analysis procedures to eliminate content bias, making it especially appropriate for this research: Content bias can be largely ruled out as a competing explanation for any invalidity in prediction. WISC-R IQs underpredicted MAT scores for Whites, compared with the remaining groups. Overprediction was greatest for Papagos. The intercept typically showed little bias.

Reynolds and Gutkin (1980) conducted similar analyses for WISC-R Verbal, Performance, and Full Scale IQs as predictors of arithmetic, reading, and spelling. The samples were large groups of White and Mexican American children from the southwestern United States. Only the equation for Performance IQ and arithmetic achievement differed for the two groups. Here, an intercept bias favored Mexican American children.

Likewise, Reynolds and Hartlage (1979) assessed WISC and WISC-R Full Scale IQs as predictors of Blacks' and Whites' arithmetic and reading achievement. The children's teachers had referred them for psychological services in a rural, southern school district. The researchers found no statistically significant differences for these children. Many participants, however, had incomplete data (34% of the total).

Prifitera, Weiss, and Saklofske (1998) noted studies in which the WISC-III predicted achievement equally for Black, White, and Hispanic children. In one study, Weiss and Prifitera (1995) examined WISC-III Full Scale IQ as a predictor of Wechsler Individual Achievement Test (WIAT) scores for Black, White, and Hispanic children aged 6 to 16 years. Results indicated little evidence of slope or intercept bias, a finding consistent with those for the WISC and WISC-R. Weiss, Prifitera, and Roid (1993) reported similar results.

Bossard, Reynolds, and Gutkin (1980) analyzed the 1972 Stanford-Binet Intelligence Scale when used to predict the reading, spelling, and arithmetic attainment of referred Black and White children. No statistically significant bias appeared in comparisons of either correlations or regression analyses.

Reynolds, Willson, and Chatman (1985) evaluated K-ABC scores as predictors of Black and White children's academic attainment. Some of the results indicated bias, usually overprediction of Black children's attainment. Of 56 Potthoff comparisons, however, most indicated no statistically significant bias. Thus, evidence for bias had low method reliability for these children.

In addition, Kamphaus and Reynolds (1987) reviewed seven studies on predictive bias with the K-ABC. Overprediction of Black children's scores was more common than with other tests and was particularly common with the Sequential Processing Scale. The differences were small and were mitigated by using the K-ABC Mental Processing Composite. Some underprediction of Black children's scores also occurred.

A series of very-large-N studies reviewed by Jensen (1980) and Sattler (1974) have compared the predictive validities of group IQ tests for different races. This procedure has an important limitation. If validities differ, regression analyses must also differ. If validities are the same, regression analyses may nonetheless differ, making additional analysis necessary (but see Reynolds, Lowe, et al., 1999). In addition, Jensen and Sattler found few available studies. Lorge-Thorndike Verbal and Nonverbal IQs were the results most often investigated. The reviewers concluded that validities were comparable for Black and White elementary school children. In the future, researchers should broaden the range of group intelligence tests that they examine. Emphasis on a small subset of available measures is a common limitation of test research.

Guterman (1979) reported an extensive analysis of the Ammons and Ammons Quick Test (QT), a verbal IQ measure, with adolescents of different social classes. The variables predicted were (a) social knowledge measures; (b) school grades obtained in Grades 9, 10, and 12; (c) Reading Comprehension Test scores on the Gates Reading Survey; and (d) Vocabulary and Arithmetic subtest scores on the General Aptitude Test Battery (GATB). Guterman found little evidence of slope or intercept bias with these adolescents, except that one social knowledge measure, sexual knowledge, showed intercept bias.

Another extensive analysis merits attention, given its unexpected results. Reynolds (1978) examined seven major preschool tests: the Draw-a-Design and Draw-a-Child subtests of the McCarthy Scales, the Mathematics and Language subtests of the Tests of Basic Experiences, the Preschool Inventory–Revised Edition, and the Lee-Clark Readiness Test. Variables predicted were four MAT subtests: Word Knowledge, Word Discrimination, Reading, and Arithmetic. Besides increased content validity, the MAT had the advantage of being chosen by teachers in the district as the test most nearly measuring what was taught in their classrooms. Reynolds compared correlations and regression analyses for the following race-gender combinations: Black females versus Black males, White females versus White males, Black females versus White females, and Black males versus White males. The result was 112 comparisons each for correlations and regression analyses.

For each criterion, scores fell in the same rank order: White females < White males < Black females < Black males. Mean validities comparing pre- and posttest scores, with 12 months intervening, were .59 for White females, .50 for White males, .43 for Black females, and .30 for Black males. In spite of these overall differences, only three differences between correlations were statistically significant, a chance finding with 112 comparisons. Potthoff comparisons of regression lines, however, indicated 43 statistically significant differences. Most of these results occurred when race rather than gender was compared: 31 of 46 comparisons ($p < .01$). The Preschool Inventory and Lee-Clark Test most frequently showed bias; the MRT never did. The observed bias overpredicted scores of Black and male children.

Researchers should investigate possible reasons for these results, which may have differed for the seven predictors but also by the statistical results compared. Either Potthoff comparisons or comparisons of correlations may be inaccurate or inconsistent as analyses of predictive test bias (see also Reynolds, 1980).

Brief screening measures tend to have low reliability compared with major ability and aptitude tests such as the WISC-III and the K-ABC. Low reliability can lead to bias in prediction (Reynolds, Lowe, et al., 1999). More reliable measures, such as the Metropolitan Readiness Tests (MRT), the

WPPSI, and the McCarthy Scales, have shown little evidence of internal bias. The WPPSI and McCarthy Scales have not been assessed for predictive bias with differing racial or ethnic groups (Reynolds, Lowe, et al., 1999).

Reynolds (1980) examined test and subtest scores for the seven tests noted above when used to predict MAT scores for males and females and for diverse ethnic groups. The researcher examined *residuals,* the differences between predicted scores and actual scores obtained by examinees. Techniques used were multiple regression to obtain residuals and race by gender ANOVA to analyze them.

ANOVA results indicated no statistically significant differences in residuals for ethnicities or genders, and no statistically significant interactions. Reynolds (1980) then examined a subset of the seven-test battery. No evidence of racial bias appeared. The results indicated gender bias in predicting two of the four MAT subtests, Word Discrimination and Word Knowledge. The seven tests consistently underpredicted females' scores. The difference was small, on the order of .13 to .16 standard deviation.

For predictive validity, as for content and construct validity, the results reviewed above suggest little evidence of bias, be it differential or single-group validity. Differences are infrequent. Where they exist, they usually take the form of small overpredictions for lower scoring groups, such as disadvantaged, low-SES, or ethnic minority examinees. These overpredictions are unlikely to account for adverse placement or diagnosis of these groups. On a grander scale, the small differences found may be reflections, but would not be major causes, of sweeping social inequalities affecting ethnic group members. The causes of such problems as employment discrimination and economic deprivation lie primarily outside the testing environment.

Path Modeling and Predictive Bias

Keith and Reynolds (1990; see also Ramsay, 1997) have suggested path analysis as a means of assessing predictive bias. Figure 4.1 shows one of their models. Each arrow represents a path, and each oblong or rectangle represents a variable.

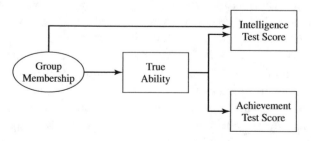

Figure 4.1 A path model showing predictive bias. The arrow from Group Membership to Intelligence Test Score represents bias.

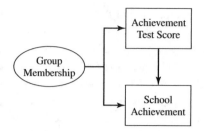

Figure 4.2 A revised path model showing predictive bias. The arrow from Group Membership to Predictor of School Achievement represents bias.

The path from group membership to intelligence test score denotes bias. Its beta value, then, should be small. The absence of this path would represent bias of zero.

A limitation of this approach is that no true ability measures exist. Thus, a path model could not incorporate true ability unless it was measured by three or more existing variables. Figure 4.2 shows a proposed model that disposes of this limitation. Here, true ability drops out, and a path leads from the predictor, *Achievement Test Score,* to the criterion, *School Achievement.* The path from group membership to the predictor denotes bias; as before, its beta value should be small. The absence of this path would, again, reflect zero bias.

THE EXAMINER-EXAMINEE RELATIONSHIP

Contrary findings notwithstanding, many psychological professionals continue to assert that White examiners impede the test performance of minority group members (Sattler, 1988). Sattler and Gwynne (1982) reviewed 27 published studies on the effects of examiners' race on the test scores of children and youth on a wide range of cognitive tests. Participants were students in preschool through Grade 12, most from urban areas throughout the United States. Tests included the Wechsler Scales; the Stanford-Binet, Form L-M; the PPVT; the Draw-a-Man Test; the Iowa Test of Preschool Development; and others. In 23 of these studies, examiner's race (Black or White) and test scores of racial groups (Black or White) had no statistically significant association. Sattler and Gwynne reported that the remaining 4 studies had methodological limitations, including inappropriate statistical tests and designs. Design limitations included lack of a comparison group and of external criteria to evaluate the validity of procedures used.

The question of possible examiner-examinee effects has taken numerous forms. Minority examinees might obtain reduced scores because of their *responses* to examiner-examinee differences. An examiner of a different race, for example, might evoke anxiety or fear in minority children. Research has lent little support to this possibility. Kaufman

(1994), for example, found that Black populations obtained their highest scores on tests most sensitive to anxiety.

White examiners may be less effective than Hispanic American examiners when testing Hispanic American children and adolescents. This proposal, too, has received little support. Gerkin (1978) found that examiner's ethnicity (White or Hispanic American) and examiner's bilingual ability (monolingual or bilingual) had no statistically significant association with the WPPSI IQs or the Leiter International Performance Scale scores of children aged 4, 5, and 6 years. Morales and George (1976) found that Hispanic bilingual children in Grades 1–3 obtained higher WISC-R scores with monolingual non-Hispanic examiners than with bilingual Hispanic examiners, who tested the children in both Spanish and English (Sattler, 1988; Reynolds, Lowe, et al., 1999).

These findings suggest that examiner ethnicity has little adverse effect on minority scores. Examiners need to be well trained and competent, however, in administering standardized tests to diverse minority group members. Rapport may be especially crucial for minority examinees, and approaches that are effective with one ethnic group may be less so with another. As usual, research in this area should continue. Neither researchers nor clinicians can assume that the results reviewed above typify all future results.

HELMS AND CULTURAL EQUIVALENCE

As noted above, Helms (1992) and other authors have reframed the CTBH approach over time. Helms has addressed the implicit biological and environmental philosophical perspectives used to explain racial and ethnic group differences in tested cognitive ability. Helms's position is that these perspectives stem from inadequate notions of culture and that neither perspective provides useful information about the cultural equivalence of tests for diverse ethnic groups. Assessment of cultural equivalence is necessary to account for minority groups' cultural, social, and cognitive differences from the majority.

For Helms (1992), cultural equivalence should take seven forms (Butcher, 1982): (a) functional equivalence, the extent to which test scores have the same meaning for different cultural groups; (b) conceptual equivalence, whether test items have the same meaning and familiarity in different groups; (c) linguistic equivalence, whether tests have the same linguistic meaning to different groups; (d) psychometric equivalence, the extent to which tests measure the same thing for different groups; (e) testing condition equivalence, whether groups are equally familiar with testing procedures and view testing as a means of assessing ability; (f) contextual equivalence, the

extent to which a cognitive ability is assessed similarly in different contexts in which people behave; and (g) sampling equivalence, whether comparable samples of each cultural group are available at the test development, validation, and interpretation stages.

Helms (1992) argues for the diversification of existing tests, the development of new standardized tests, and the formation of explicit principles, hypotheses, assumptions, and theoretical models for investigating cultural differences. In addition, Helms argues that existing frameworks—biological, environmental, and cultural—should be operationally defined.

For future research, Helms (1992) recommends (a) development of measures for determining interracial cultural dependence and levels of acculturation and assimilation in test items, (b) modification of test content to include items that reflect cultural diversity, (c) examination of incorrect responses, (d) incorporation of cognitive psychology into interactive modes of assessment, (e) use of theories to examine environmental content of criteria, and (f) separate racial group norms for existing tests. Researchers should interpret test scores cautiously, Helms suggests, until psychometricians develop more diverse procedures to address cultural concerns.

Helms' (1992) approach, or one like it, is likely to become a future trend. As observed by Reynolds, Lowe, et al. (1999), however, much of the work recommended by Helms has been well under way for several decades (for an extensive treatment, see Cronbach & Drenth, 1972; see also Hambleton, 1994; Van de Vijver & Hambleton, 1996). Reynolds et al. contend that Helms has coined new terms for old constructs and dismissed many studies already addressing the issues she raises. At best, Helms has organized and called attention to long-recognized empirical issues.

TRANSLATION AND CULTURAL TESTING

The findings reviewed above do not apply to translations of tests. Use of a test in a new linguistic culture requires that it be redeveloped from the start. One reason for the early success of the Stanford-Binet Intelligence Scale was that Terman reconceptualized it for the United States, reexamining Binet's theory of intelligence, writing and testing new items, and renorming the scales (Reynolds, Lowe, et al., 1999).

Terman's work was an exception to a rule of simple translation of the Binet Scales. Even today, few researchers are versant in procedures for adapting tests and establishing score equivalence. Nonetheless, the procedures are available, and they increase the validity of the adapted tests (Hambleton & Kanjee, 1995). Adaptation of educational and psychological tests most frequently occurs for one of three reasons: to facilitate comparative ethnic studies, to allow individuals to be tested in their own language, or to reduce the time and cost of developing new tests.

Test adaptation has been common for more than 90 years, but the field of cross-cultural and cross-national comparisons is relatively recent. This field presently focuses on development and use of adaptation guidelines (Hambleton, 1994), ways to interpret and use cross-cultural and cross-national data (Hambleton & Kanjee, 1995; Poortinga & Malpass, 1986), and especially procedures for establishing item equivalence (Ellis, 1991; Hambleton, 1993; Poortinga, 1983; Van de Vijver & Poortinga, 1991). Test items are said to be equivalent when members of each linguistic or cultural group who have the same standing on the construct measured by the tests have the same probability of selecting the correct item response.

The designs used to establish item equivalence fall into two categories, judgmental and statistical. Judgmental designs rely on a person's or group's decision regarding the degree of translation equivalence of an item. Two common designs are forward translation and back translation (Hambleton & Bollwark, 1991). In the first design, translators adapt or translate a test to the target culture or language. Other translators then assess the equivalency of the two versions. If the versions are not equivalent, changes are made. In the second design, translators adapt or translate a test to the target culture or language as before. Other translators readapt the items back to the original culture or language. An assessment of equivalence follows. Judgmental designs are a preliminary approach. Additional checks, such as DIF or other statistical analyses, are also needed (Reynolds, Lowe, et al., 1999).

Three statistical designs are available, depending on the characteristics of the sample. In the bilingual examinees design, participants who take both the original and the target version of the test are bilingual (Hambleton & Bollwark, 1991). In the source and target language monolinguals design, monolinguals in the original language take the original or back-translated version, and monolinguals in the target language take the target version (Ellis, 1991). In the third design, monolinguals in the original language take the original and back-translated versions.

After administration and scoring, statistical procedures are selected and performed to assess DIF. Procedures can include factor analysis, item response theory, logistic regression, and the Mantel-Haenszel technique. If DIF is statistically significant, additional analyses are necessary to investigate possible bias or lack of equivalence for different cultures or languages.

A study by Arnold, Montgomery, Castaneda, and Longoria (1994) illustrates the need to evaluate item equivalence. The researchers found that acculturation affected several subtests of the Halstead-Reitan neuropsychological test when used with unimpaired Hispanics. By contrast, Boivin et al. (1996) conducted a study with Lao children and identified variables such as nutritional development, parental education, and home environment that may influence scores on several tests, including the K-ABC, the Tactual Performance Test (TPT), and the computerized Tests of Variables of Attention (TOVA). These results suggest that tests can potentially be adapted to different cultures, although the challenges of doing so are formidable. Such results also show that psychologists have addressed cultural equivalence issues for some time, contrary to the view of Helms (1992).

NATURE AND NURTURE

Part of the emotion surrounding the test bias controversy stems from its association in the human mind with the troubling notion of innate, genetic inferiority. Given real differences, however, a genetic explanation is by no means inevitable. Absence of bias opens up the possibility of environmental causes, as well, and explanations span the sociopolitical spectrum. Discrimination; economic disadvantage; exclusion from educational opportunity, personal development, social support, practical information, and achievement-oriented values—all become possible causes, if differences are real.

All sides of the nature-nurture debate depend on the existence of real differences. Therefore, the debate must eventually prove irresolvable unless the test bias question is somehow answered. The reverse, however, is not true. Test bias research can continue indefinitely with the nature-nurture question unresolved. Psychometricians are attempting to disentangle the nature-nurture debate from the empirical investigation of test bias, but the separation is unlikely to be a neat one (Reynolds , Lowe, et al., 1999).

CONCLUSIONS AND RECOMMENDATIONS

The conclusion reached in most of the research reviewed above was that test bias did not exist. Today, the same research would lead to different conclusions. Test bias exists but is small, which raises questions about its importance. It most often overestimates or overpredicts minority examinees' performance, so that its social consequences may be very different from those typically ascribed to it, and appropriate responses to it may differ from those typically made. Finally, just as purely genetic and environmental paradigms have given way, the interpretation of zero bias should cede to a better informed understanding that bias cannot be understood in isolation from other possible influences.

We recommend that rigorous examination of possible test bias and inaccuracy should continue, employing the latest and most diverse techniques. Nonetheless, we caution against labeling tests biased in the absence of, or in opposition to, reliable evidence. To do so is of questionable effectiveness in the struggle to identify and combat real discrimination and to ensure that everyone is treated fairly.

Discrimination is a legitimate and compelling concern. We do not argue that it is rare, unimportant, or remotely acceptable. We do, however, suggest from research findings that standardized test bias is not a major source of discrimination. Accordingly, resources meant to identify and alleviate discrimination might better be directed toward real-world causes rather than standardized tests. In addition, we question whether the goal of equal opportunity is served if possible evidence of discrimination, or of inequalities resulting from it, is erased by well-meaning test publishers or other professionals.

The issue of bias in mental testing, too, is an important concern with strong historical precedence in the social sciences and with formidable social consequences. The controversy is liable to persist as long as we entangle it with the nature-nurture question and stress mean differences in standardized test scores. Similarly, the use of aptitude and achievement measures is long-standing and widespread, extending back more than 2000 years in some cultures and across most cultures today. It is unlikely to disappear soon.

The news media may be partly responsible for a popular perception that tests and testing are uniformly biased or unfair. As indicated by the findings reviewed here, the view that tests are substantially biased has little support at present, at least in cultures with a common language and a degree of common experience. In addition, public pressure has pushed the scientific community to refine its definitions of bias, scrutinize the practices used to minimize bias in tests, and develop increasingly sophisticated statistical techniques to detect bias (Reynolds, Lowe, et al., 1999; Samuda, 1975). Finally, the findings reviewed here give indications that fair testing is an attainable goal, albeit a challenging one that demands skill and training.

Reynolds, Lowe, et al. (1999) suggest four guidelines to help ensure equitable assessment: (a) investigate possible referral source bias, because evidence suggests that people are not always referred for services on impartial, objective grounds; (b) inspect test developers' data for evidence that sound statistical analyses for bias have been completed; (c) conduct assessments with the most reliable measure available; and, finally, (d) assess multiple abilities and use multiple methods. In summary, clinicians should use accurately

derived data from multiple sources before making decisions about an individual.

Clinicians should be cognizant of a person's environmental background and circumstances. Information about a client's home, community, and the like must be evaluated in an individualized decision-making process. Likewise, clinicians should not ignore evidence that disadvantaged, ethnic minority clients with unfavorable test results are as likely to encounter difficulties as are middle-class, majority clients with unfavorable test results, given the same environmental circumstances. The purpose of the assessment process is to beat the prediction—to suggest hypotheses for interventions that will prevent a predicted failure or adverse outcome (Reynolds, Lowe, et al., 1999). This perspective, although developed primarily around ability testing, is relevant to personality testing as well.

We urge clinicians to use tests fairly and in the interest of examinees, but we see little benefit in discarding standardized tests entirely. We recommend that test consumers evaluate each measure separately to ensure that results pertaining to bias are available and satisfactory. If results are unsatisfactory, local norming may produce less biased scores. If results are unavailable, additional testing may be possible given samples of sufficient size. In addition, clinical practice and especially research should reflect an understanding of the conceptual distinctions, such as bias versus unfairness, described above.

A philosophical perspective emerging in the bias literature is that, before publication, test developers should not only demonstrate content, construct, and predictive validity but should also conduct content analysis in some form to ensure that offensive material is absent from the test. Expert reviews of test content can have a role, and the synergistic relationship between test use and psychometrics must be accommodated in an orderly manner before tests gain increased acceptance in society.

Nevertheless, informal reviews cannot meet the need to assess for bias. Test authors and publishers must demonstrate factorial congruence with all groups for whom a test is designed, to permit accurate interpretation. Comparisons of predictive validity with ethnic and gender groups are also important. Such research should take place during test development, a window during which measures can be altered using numerous item analysis procedures to minimize gender or ethnic bias. This practice has been uncommon, except with some recent achievement tests.

Scant available findings for personality tests are a major weakness in the bias literature. Only recently have researchers begun to respond appropriately to this problem (e.g., Reynolds & Kamphaus, 1992). Increased research is needed also for neuropsychological tests, for ability and achievement tests not yet investigated, for SES, and for minority examinees tested by majority examiners. Future results, it is expected, will continue to indicate consistency for different genders, races, ethnicities, and similar groups.

Finally, a clear consensus on fairness, and on steps to be taken to attain it, is needed between persons with humanitarian aims and those with scientific interest in test bias. Accommodation toward this end would ensure that everyone concerned with a given test was satisfied that it was unbiased and that the steps taken to achieve fairness could be held up to public scrutiny without reservation (Reynolds, Lowe, et al., 1999). Test bias and fairness is a domain in great need of consensus, and this goal is attainable only with concessions on all sides.

REFERENCES

Adebimpe, V. R., Gigandet, J., & Harris, E. (1979). MMPI diagnosis of black psychiatric patients. *American Journal of Psychiatry, 136,* 85–87.

Alley, G., & Foster, C. (1978). Nondiscriminatory testing of minority and exceptional children. *Focus on Exceptional Children, 9,* 1–14.

Anastasi, A. (1988). *Psychological testing* (6th ed.). New York: MacMillan.

Arnold, B., Montgomery, G., Castaneda, I., & Longoria, R. (1994). Acculturation and performance of Hispanics on selected Halstead-Reitan neuropsychological tests. *Assessment, 1,* 239–248.

Binet, A., & Simon, T. (1973). *The development of intelligence in children.* New York: Arno. (Original work published 1916)

Boivin, M., Chounramany, C., Giordani, B., Xaisida, S., Choulamountry, L., Pholsena, P., et al. (1996). Validating a cognitive ability testing protocol with Lao children for community development applications. *Neuropsychology, 10,* 1–12.

Bossard, M., Reynolds, C. R., & Gutkin, T. B. (1980). A regression analysis of test bias on the Stanford-Binet Intelligence Scale. *Journal of Clinical Child Psychology, 9,* 52–54.

Bouchard, T. J., & Segal, N. L. (1985). *Environment and IQ.* In B. Wolman (Ed.), *Handbook of intelligence* (pp. 391–464). New York: Wiley-Interscience.

Brown, R. T., Reynolds, C. R., & Whitaker, J. S. (1999). Bias in mental testing since "Bias in Mental Testing." *School Psychology Quarterly, 14,* 208–238.

Butcher, J. N. (1982). Cross-cultural research methods in clinical psychology. In P. C. Kendall & J. N. Butcher (Eds.), *Black children: Social educational and parental environments* (pp. 33–51). Beverly Hills, CA: Sage.

Camilli, G., & Shepard, L. A. (1994). *Methods for identifying biased test items.* Thousand Oaks, CA: Sage.

Cattell, R. B. (1979). Are culture fair intelligence tests possible and necessary? *Journal of Research and Development in Education, 12,* 3–13.

Chipman, S., Marshall, S., & Scott, P. (1991). Content effect on word-problem performance: A possible source of test bias? *American Educational Research Journal, 28,* 897–915.

Cleary, T. A. (1968). Test bias: Prediction of grades of negro and white students in integrated universities. *Journal of Educational Measurement, 5,* 118–124.

Cleary, T. A., Humphreys, L. G., Kendrick, S. A., & Wesman, A. (1975). Educational uses of tests with disadvantaged students. *American Psychologist, 30,* 15–41.

Cortez v. Rosen (1975).

Cronbach, L. J., & Drenth, P. J. D. (Eds.). (1972). *Mental tests and cultural adaptation.* The Hague, The Netherlands: Mouton.

Dean, R. S. (1979, September). *WISC-R factor structure for Anglo and Hispanic children.* Paper presented at the annual meeting of the American Psychological Association, New York.

DeFries, J. C., Vandenberg, S. G., McClearn, G. E., Kuse, A. R., Wilson, J. R., Ashton, G. C., et al. (1974). Near identity of cognitive structure in two ethnic groups. *Science, 183,* 338–339.

Dent, H. E. (1996). Non-biased assessment or realistic assessment? In R. L. Jones (Ed.), *Handbook of tests and measurement for Black populations* (Vol. 1, pp. 103–122). Hampton, VA: Cobb & Henry.

Ebel, R. L. (1979). Intelligence: A skeptical view. *Journal of Research and Development in Education, 12,* 14–21.

Eells, K., Davis, A., Havighurst, R. J., Herrick, V. E., & Tyler, R. W. (1951). *Intelligence and cultural differences: A study of cultural learning and problem-solving.* Chicago: University of Chicago Press.

Elliot, R. (1987). *Litigating intelligence.* Dover, MA: Auburn House.

Ellis, B. B. (1991). Item response theory: A tool for assessing the equivalence of translated tests. *Bulletin of the International Test Commission, 18,* 33–51.

Figueroa, R. A. (1991). Bilingualism and psychometrics. *Diagnostique, 17*(1), 70–85.

Fine, B. (1975). *The stranglehold of the IQ.* Garden City, NY: Doubleday.

Flynn, J. R. (1991). *Asian-Americans: Achievement beyond IQ.* Hillsdale, NJ: Erlbaum.

Gerkin, K. C. (1978). Performance of Mexican-American children on intelligence tests. *Exceptional Children, 44,* 438–443.

Gould, S. J. (1981). *The mismeasure of man.* New York: Norton.

Gould, S. J. (1995). Curveball. In S. Fraser (Ed.), *The bell curve wars: Race, intelligence, and the future of America* (pp. 11–22). New York: Basic Books.

Gould, S. J. (1996). *The mismeasure of man* (Rev. ed.). New York: Norton.

Gross, M. (1967). *Learning readiness in two Jewish groups.* New York: Center for Urban Education.

Guterman, S. S. (1979). IQ tests in research on social stratification: The cross-class validity of the tests as measures of scholastic aptitude. *Sociology of Education, 52,* 163–173.

Gutkin, T. B., & Reynolds, C. R. (1980). Factorial similarity of the WISC-R for Anglos and Chicanos referred for psychological services. *Journal of School Psychology, 18,* 34–39.

Gutkin, T. B., & Reynolds, C. R. (1981). Factorial similarity of the WISC-R for white and black children from the standardization sample. *Journal of Educational Psychology, 73,* 227–231.

Hambleton, R. K. (1993). Translating achievement tests for use in cross-national studies. *European Journal of Psychological Assessment, 9,* 54–65.

Hambleton, R. K. (1994). Guidelines for adapting educational and psychological tests: A progress report. *European Journal of Psychological Assessment, 10,* 229–244.

Hambleton, R. K., & Bollwark, J. (1991). Adapting tests for use in different cultures: Technical issues and methods. *Bulletin of the International Test Commission, 18,* 3–32.

Hambleton, R. K., & Kanjee, A. (1995). Increasing the validity of cross-cultural assessments: Use of improved methods for adaptations. *European Journal of Psychological Assessment, 11,* 147–157.

Hammill, D. (1991). *Detroit Tests of Learning Aptitude* (3rd ed.). Austin, TX: Pro-Ed.

Harrington, G. M. (1968a). Genetic-environmental interaction in "intelligence": I. Biometric genetic analysis of maze performance of *Rattus norvegicus. Developmental Psychology, 1,* 211–218.

Harrington, G. M. (1968b). Genetic-environmental interaction in "intelligence": II. Models of behavior, components of variance, and research strategy. *Developmental Psychology, 1,* 245–253.

Harrington, G. M. (1975). Intelligence tests may favor the majority groups in a population. *Nature, 258,* 708–709.

Harrington, G. M. (1976, September). *Minority test bias as a psychometric artifact: The experimental evidence.* Paper presented at the annual meeting of the American Psychological Association, Washington, DC.

Hartlage, L. C., Lucas, T., & Godwin, A. (1976). Culturally biased and culturally fair tests correlated with school performance in culturally disadvantaged children. *Journal of Consulting and Clinical Psychology, 32,* 325–327.

Helms, J. E. (1992). Why is there no study of cultural equivalence in standardized cognitive ability testing? *American Psychologist, 47,* 1083–1101.

Herrnstein, R. J., & Murray, C. (1994). *The bell curve.* New York: Free Press.

Hilliard, A. G. (1979). Standardization and cultural bias as impediments to the scientific study and validation of "intelligence." *Journal of Research and Development in Education, 12,* 47–58.

Hilliard, A. G., III. (1984). IQ testing as the emperor's new clothes: A critique of Jensen's Bias in Mental Testing. In C. R. Reynolds & R. T. Brown (Eds.), *Perspectives on bias in mental testing* (pp. 139–169). New York: Plenum.

Hunter, J. E., Schmidt, F. L., & Hunter, R. (1979). Differential validity of employment tests by race: A comprehensive review and analysis. *Psychological Bulletin, 86,* 721–735.

Jackson, G. D. (1975). Another psychological view from the Association of Black Psychologists. *American Psychologist, 30,* 88–93.

James, B. J. (1995). *A test of Harrington's experimental model of ethnic bias in testing applied to a measure of emotional functioning in adolescents.* Doctoral dissertation, Texas A&M University, College Station.

Jensen, A. R. (1969). How much can we boost IQ and scholastic achievement? *Harvard Educational Review, 39,* 1–123.

Jensen, A. R. (1974). How biased are culture loaded tests? *Genetic Psychology Monographs, 90,* 185–224.

Jensen, A. R. (1976). Test bias and construct validity. *Phi Delta Kappan, 58,* 340–346.

Jensen, A. R. (1977). An examination of culture bias in the Wonderlic Personnel Test. *Intelligence, 1,* 51–64.

Jensen, A. R. (1980). *Bias in mental testing.* New York: Free Press.

Jensen, A. R. (1984). Test Bias: Concepts and criticisms. In C. R. Reynolds & R. T. Brown (Eds.), *Perspectives on bias in mental testing* (pp. 507–586). New York: Plenum.

Kaiser, S. (1986). *Ability patterns of black and white adults on the WAIS-R independent of general intelligence and as a function of socioeconomic status.* Doctoral dissertation, Texas A&M University, College Station.

Kamphaus, R. W., & Reynolds, C. R. (1987). *Clinical and research applications of the K-ABC.* Circle Pines, MN: American Guidance Service.

Kaufman, A. S. (1973). Comparison of the performance of matched groups of black children and white children on the Wechsler Preschool and Primary Scale of Intelligence. *Journal of Consulting and Clinical Psychology, 41,* 186–191.

Kaufman, A. S. (1979). *Intelligent testing with the WISC-R.* New York: Wiley-Interscience.

Kaufman, A. S. (1994). *Intelligent testing with the WISC-III.* New York: Wiley.

Kaufman, A. S., & Kaufman, N. L. (1973). Black-white differences on the McCarthy Scales of Children's Abilities. *Journal of School Psychology, 11,* 196–206.

Keith, T. Z., & Reynolds, C. R. (1990). Measurement and design issues in child assessment research. In C. R. Reynolds & R. W. Kamphaus (Eds.), *Handbook of psychological and educational assessment of children.* New York: Guilford.

Loehlin, J. C., Lindzey, G., & Spuhler, J. N. (1975). *Race differences in intelligence.* San Francisco, CA: Freeman.

Lonner, W. J. (1985). Issues in testing and assessment in cross-cultural counseling. *The Counseling Psychologist, 13,* 599–614.

Lynn, R. (1995). Cross-cultural differences in intelligence and personality. In D. Sakolfske & M. Zeidner (Eds.), *The international handbook of personality and intelligence* (pp. 107–134). New York: Plenum.

MacCorquodale, K., & Meehl, P. E. (1948). On a distinction between hypothetical constructs and intervening variables. *Psychological Review, 55*, 95–107.

Mainstream science on intelligence. (1994, December 13). *Wall Street Journal*, p. A18.

Marjoribanks, K. (1972). Ethnic and environmental influences on mental abilities. *American Journal of Sociology, 78*, 323–337.

Mayfield, J. W., & Reynolds, C. R. (1998). Are ethnic differences in diagnosis of childhood psychopathology an artifact of psychometric methods? An experimental evaluation of Harrington's hypothesis using parent report symptomatology. *Journal of School Psychology, 36*, 313–334.

McGurk, F. V. J. (1951). *Comparison of the performance of Negro and white high school seniors on cultural and noncultural psychological test questions*. Washington, DC: Catholic University of American Press.

Mercer, J. R. (1976, August). *Cultural diversity, mental retardation, and assessment: The case for nonlabeling*. Paper presented to the Fourth International Congress of the International Association for the Scientific Study of Mental Retardation, Washington, DC.

Mercer, J. R. (1979). *System of Multicultural Pluralistic Assessment (SOMPA): Conceptual and technical manual*. San Antonio, TX: Psychological Corporation.

Miele, F. (1979). Cultural bias in the WISC. *Intelligence, 3*, 149–164.

Morales, E. S., & George, C. (1976, September). *Examiner effects in the testing of Mexican-American children*. Paper presented at the annual meeting of the American Psychological Association, Washington, DC.

Moran, M. P. (1990). The problem of cultural bias in personality assessment. In C. R. Reynolds & R. W. Kamphaus (Eds.), *Handbook of psychological and educational assessment of children. Vol. 2: Personality, behavior, and context* (pp. 524–545). New York: Guilford.

Nandakumar, R., Glutting, J. J., & Oakland, T. (1993). Mantel-Haenszel methodology for detecting item bias: An introduction and example using the Guide to the Assessment of Test Session Behavior. *Journal of Psychoeducational Assessment, 11*(2), 108–119.

Neisser, U., Boodoo, G., Bouchard, T. J., Jr., Boykin, A. W., Brody, N., Ceci, S. J., et al. (1996). Intelligence: Knowns and unknowns. *American Psychologist, 51*, 77–101.

Oakland, T., & Feigenbaum, D. (1979). Multiple sources of test bias on the WISC-R and the Bender-Gestalt Test. *Journal of Consulting and Clinical Psychology, 47*, 968–974.

Oakland, T., & Matuszek, P. (1977). Using tests in nondiscriminatory assessment. In T. Oakland (Ed.), *Psychological and educational assessment of minority children*. New York: Brunner/Mazel.

Padilla, A. M. (1988). Early psychological assessment of Mexican-American children. *Journal of the History of the Behavioral Sciences, 24*, 113–115.

Payne, B., & Payne, D. (1991). The ability of teachers to identify academically at-risk elementary students. *Journal of Research in Childhood education, 5*(2), 116–126.

Pintner, R. (1931). *Intelligence testing*. New York: Holt, Rinehart, & Winston.

Poortinga, Y. H. (1983). Psychometric approaches to intergroup comparison: The problem of equivalence. In S. H. Irvine & J. W. Berry (Eds.), *Human assessment and cross-cultural factors* (pp. 237–258). New York: Plenum.

Poortinga, Y. H., & Malpass, R. S. (1986). Making inferences from cross-cultural data. In W. J. Lonner & J. W. Berry (Eds.), *Field methods in cross-cultural psychology* (pp. 17–46). Beverly Hills, CA: Sage.

Prifitera, A., & Saklofske, D. H. (Eds.). (1998). *WISC-III clinical use and interpretation: Scientist-practitioner perspectives*. San Diego, CA: Academic Press.

Prifitera, A., Weiss, L. G., & Saklofske, D. H. (1998). The WISC-III in context. In A. Prifitera & D. H. Saklofske (Eds.), *WISC-III clinical use and interpretation: Scientist-practitioner perspectives* (pp. 1–37). San Diego, CA: Academic Press.

Ramsay, M. C. (1997, November). *Structural equation modeling and test bias*. Paper presented at the annual meeting of the Educational Research Exchange, Texas A&M University, College Station.

Ramsay, M. C. (1998a, February). *Proposed theories of causation drawn from social and physical science epistemology*. Paper presented at the annual meeting of the Education Research Exchange, Texas A&M University, College Station.

Ramsay, M. C. (1998b, February). *The processing system in humans: A theory*. Paper presented at the annual meeting of the Education Research Exchange, Texas A&M University, College Station.

Ramsay, M. C. (2000). *The putative effects of smoking by pregnant women on birthweight, IQ, and developmental disabilities in their infants: A methodological review and multivariate analysis*. Unpublished doctoral dissertation, Texas A&M University, College Station.

Ramsay, M. C., & Reynolds, C. R. (1995). Separate digits tests: A brief history, a literature review, and a reexamination of the factor structure of the Test of Memory and Learning (TOMAL). *Neuropsychology Review, 5*, 151–171.

Ramsay, M. C., & Reynolds, C. R. (2000a). Development of a scientific test: A practical guide. In G. Goldstein & M. Hersen (Eds.), *Handbook of psychological assessment* (3rd ed.). Amsterdam: Pergamon.

Ramsay, M. C., & Reynolds, C. R. (2000b). Does smoking by pregnant women influence birth weight, IQ, and developmental disabilities in their infants? A methodological review and multivariate analysis. *Neuropsychology Review, 10*, 1–49.

Reschly, D. J. (1978). WISC-R factor structures among Anglos, Blacks, Chicanos, and Native American Papagos. *Journal of Consulting and Clinical Psychology, 46,* 417–422.

Reschly, D. J. (1997). Diagnostic and treatment utility of intelligence tests. In D. P. Flanagan, J. L. Genshaft, & P. L. Harrison (Eds.), *Contemporary intellectual assessment: Theories, tests, and Issues* (pp. 437–456). New York: Guilford.

Reschly, D. J. (2000). PASE v. Hannon. In C. R. Reynolds & E. Fletcher-Janzen (Eds.), *Encyclopedia of special education* (2nd ed., pp. 1325–1326). New York: Wiley.

Reschly, D., & Sabers, D. (1979). Analysis of test bias in four groups with the regression definition. *Journal of Educational Measurement, 16,* 1–9.

Reynolds, C. R. (1978). *Differential validity of several preschool assessment instruments for blacks, whites, males, and females.* Unpublished doctoral dissertation, University of Georgia, Athens.

Reynolds, C. R. (1980). Differential construct validity of intelligence as popularly measured: Correlation of age and raw scores on the WISC-R for blacks, whites, males and females. *Intelligence: A Multidisciplinary Journal, 4,* 371–379.

Reynolds, C. R. (1982a). Construct and predictive bias. In R. A. Berk (Ed.), *Handbook of methods for detecting test bias* (pp. 199–227). Baltimore: Johns Hopkins University Press.

Reynolds, C. R. (1982b). The problem of bias in psychological assessment. In C. R. Reynolds & T. B. Gutkin (Eds.), *The handbook of school psychology* (pp. 178–208). New York: Wiley.

Reynolds, C. R. (1995). Test bias in the assessment of intelligence and personality. In D. Saklofsky & M. Zeidner (Eds.), *International handbook of personality and intelligence* (pp. 545–576). New York: Plenum.

Reynolds, C. R. (1998a). Cultural bias in testing of intelligence and personality. In A. Bellack & M. Hersen (Series Eds.) and C. Belar (Vol. Ed.), *Comprehensive clinical psychology: Vol. 10. Cross Cultural Psychology* (pp. 53–92). New York: Elsevier Science.

Reynolds, C. R. (1998b). Need we measure anxiety separately for males and females? *Journal of Personality Assessment, 70,* 212–221.

Reynolds, C. R. (1999). Cultural bias in testing of intelligence and personality. In M. Hersen & A. Bellack (Series Eds.) and C. Belar (Vol. Ed.), *Comprehensive clinical psychology: Vol. 10. Sociocultural and individual differences* (pp. 53–92). Oxford, England: Elsevier Science.

Reynolds, C. R. (2000a). Methods for detecting and evaluating cultural bias in neuropsychological tests. In E. Fletcher-Janzen, T. L. Strickland, & C. R. Reynolds (Eds.), *Handbook of cross-cultural neuropsychology* (pp. 249–285). New York: Kluwer Academic/Plenum.

Reynolds, C. R. (2000b). Why is psychometric research on bias in mental testing so often ignored? *Psychology, Public Policy, and Law, 6,* 144–150.

Reynolds, C. R. (2001). *Professional manual for the Clinical Assessment Scales for the Elderly.* Odessa, FL: Psychological Assessment Resources.

Reynolds, C. R., & Bigler, E. D. (1994). *Test of Memory and Learning (TOMAL).* Austin, TX: Pro-Ed.

Reynolds, C. R., & Brown, R. T. (1984a). Bias in mental testing: An introduction to the issues. In C. R. Reynolds & R. T. Brown (Eds.), *Perspectives on bias in mental testing* (pp. 1–39). New York: Plenum.

Reynolds, C. R., & Brown, R. T. (1984b). *Perspectives on bias in mental testing.* New York: Plenum.

Reynolds, C. R., Chastain, R., Kaufman, A. S., & McLean, J. (1987). Demographic influences on adult intelligence at ages 16 to 74 years. *Journal of School Psychology, 25,* 323–342.

Reynolds, C. R., & Gutkin, T. B. (1980, September). *WISC-R performance of blacks and whites matched on four demographic variables.* Paper presented at the annual meeting of the American Psychological Association, Montreal, Canada.

Reynolds, C. R., & Gutkin, T. B. (1981). A multivariate comparison of the intellectual performance of blacks and whites matched on four demographic variables. *Personality and Individual Differences, 2,* 175–180.

Reynolds, C. R., & Harding, R. E. (1983). Outcome in two large sample studies of factorial similarity under six methods of comparison. *Educational and Psychological Measurement, 43,* 723–728.

Reynolds, C. R., & Hartlage, L. C. (1979). Comparison of WISC and WISC-R regression lines for academic prediction with black and white referred children. *Journal of Consulting and Clinical Psychology, 47,* 589–591.

Reynolds, C. R., & Jensen, A. R. (1983, September). *Patterns of intellectual performance among blacks and whites matched on "g."* Paper presented at the annual meeting of the American Psychological Association, Montreal, Canada.

Reynolds, C. R., & Kaiser, S. (1992). Test bias in psychological assessment. In T. B. Gutkin & C. R. Reynolds (Eds.), *The handbook of school psychology* (2nd ed., pp. 487–525). New York: Wiley.

Reynolds, C. R., & Kamphaus, R. W. (1992). *Behavior Assessment System for Children (BASC): Manual.* Circle Pines, MN: American Guidance Service.

Reynolds, C. R., Lowe, P. A., & Saenz, A. (1999). The problem of bias in psychological assessment. In T. B. Gutkin & C. R. Reynolds (Eds.), *The handbook of school psychology* (3rd ed., 549–595). New York: Wiley.

Reynolds, C. R., & Paget, K. (1981). Factor analysis of the Revised Children's Manifest Anxiety Scale for blacks, whites, males, and females with a national normative sample. *Journal of Consulting and Clinical Psychology, 49,* 349–352.

Reynolds, C. R., Willson, V. L., & Chatman, S. P. (1984). Item bias on the 1981 revisions of the Peabody Picture Vocabulary Test using a new method of detecting bias. *Journal of Psychoeducational Assessment, 2,* 219–221.

Reynolds, C. R., Willson, V. L., & Chatman, S. P. (1985). Regression analyses of bias on the Kaufman Assessment Battery for Children. *Journal of School Psychology, 23,* 195–204.

Reynolds, C. R., Willson, V. L., & Ramsay, M. C. (1999). Intellectual differences among Mexican Americans, Papagos and Whites, independent of *g. Personality and Individual Differences, 27,* 1181–1187.

Richardson, T. Q. (1995). The window dressing behind the Bell Curve. *School Psychology Review, 24,* 42–44.

Samuda, A. J. (1975). *Psychological testing of American minorities: Issues and consequences.* New York: Dodd.

Sandoval, J. (1979). The WISC-R and internal evidence of test bias with minority groups. *Journal of Consulting and Clinical Psychology, 47,* 919–927.

Sandoval, J., & Mille, M. P. W. (1979). *Accuracy judgments of WISC-R item difficulty for minority groups.* Paper presented at the annual meeting of the American Psychological Association.

Sattler, J. M. (1974). *Assessment of children's intelligence.* Philadelphia: Saunders.

Sattler, J. M. (1988). *Assessment of children* (3rd ed.). San Diego, CA: Author.

Sattler, J. M., & Gwynne, J. (1982). White examiners generally do not impede the intelligence test performance of black children: To debunk a myth. *Journal of Consulting and Clinical Psychology, 50,* 196–208.

Scarr, S. (1981). Implicit messages: A review of bias in mental testing. *American Journal of Education, 89*(3), 330–338.

Scheuneman, J. D. (1987). An experimental, exploratory study of the causes of bias in test items. *Journal of Educational Measurement, 29,* 97–118.

Schmidt, W. H. (1983). Content biases in achievement tests. *Journal of Educational Measurement, 20,* 165–178.

Schoenfeld, W. N. (1974). Notes on a bit of psychological nonsense: "Race differences in intelligence." *Psychological Record, 24,* 17–32.

Scholwinski, E. (1985). *Ability patterns of blacks and whites as determined by the subscales on the Wechsler Adult Intelligence Scale–Revised.* Unpublished doctoral dissertation, Texas A&M University, College Station.

Shuey, A. M. (1966). *The testing of Negro intelligence* (2nd ed.). New York: Social Science Press.

Spitz, H. (1986). *The raising of intelligence.* Hillsdale, NJ: Erlbaum.

Steele, C. M., & Aronson, J. (1995). Stereotype threat and the intellectual test performance of African Americans. *Journal of Personality and Social Psychology, 69,* 797–811.

Stern, W. (1914). *The psychological methods of testing intelligence.* Baltimore: Warwick & York.

Sternberg, R. J. (1980). Intelligence and test bias: Art and science. *Behavioral and Brain Sciences, 3,* 353–354.

Thorndike, R. L. (1971). Concepts of culture-fairness. *Journal of Educational Measurement, 8,* 63–70.

Torrance, E. P. (1980). Psychology of gifted children and youth. In W. M. Cruickshank (Ed.), *Psychology of exceptional children and youth.* Englewood Cliffs, NJ: Prentice-Hall.

Tyler, L. E. (1965). *The psychology of human differences.* New York: Appleton-Century-Crofts.

Van de Vijver, F., & Hambleton, R. K. (1996). Translating tests: Some practical guidelines. *European Psychologists, 1,* 89–99.

Van de Vijver, F., & Poortinga, Y. H. (1991). Culture-free measurement in the history of cross-cultural psychology. *Bulletin of the International Test Commission, 18,* 72–87.

Wechsler, D. (1975). Intelligence defined and undefined: A relativistic appraisal. *American Psychologist, 30,* 135–139.

Weiss, L. G., & Prifitera, A. (1995). An evaluation of differential prediction of WIAT achievement scores from WISC-III FSIQ across ethnic and gender groups. *Journal of School Psychology, 33,* 297–304.

Weiss, L. G., Prifitera, A., & Roid, G. H. (1993). The WISC-III and fairness of predicting achievement across ethnic and gender groups. *Journal of Psychoeducational Assessment,* 35–42.

Wigdor, A. K., & Garner, W. R. (Eds.). (1982). *Ability testing: Uses, consequences, and controversies.* Washington, DC: National Academy of Sciences.

Willerman, L. (1979). *The psychology of individual and group differences.* San Francisco, CA: Freeman.

Williams, R. L. (1970). Danger: Testing and dehumanizing Black children. *Clinical Child Psychology Newsletter, 9,* 5–6.

Williams, R. L. (1974). From dehumanization to black intellectual genocide: A rejoinder. In G. J. Williams & S. Gordon (Eds.), *Clinical child psychology: Current practices and future perspectives.* New York: Behavioral Publications.

Williams, R. L., Dotson, W., Dow, P., & Williams, W. S. (1980). The war against testing: A current status report. *Journal of Negro Education, 49,* 263–273.

Willson, V. L., Nolan, R. F., Reynolds, C. R., & Kamphaus, R. W. (1989). Race and gender effects on item functioning on the Kaufman Assessment Battery for Children. *Journal of School Psychology, 27,* 289–296.

Wright, B. J., & Isenstein, V. R. (1977–1978). *Psychological tests and minorities* (DHEW Publication No. ADM 78–482). Rockville, MD: National Institutes of Mental Health.

CHAPTER 5

Testing and Assessment in Cross-Cultural Psychology

KURT F. GEISINGER

Some say that the world is shrinking. We know that worldwide cable news programs and networks, the Internet, and satellites are making communications across cultures and around the world much easier, less expensive, and remarkably faster. *Cross-cultural psychology* studies the psychological differences associated with cultural differences. (In a strictly experimental design sense, in much of cross-cultural research, cultures typically serve as independent variables and behaviors of interest as dependent variables.) At one time, such research implied crossing the borders of countries, and generally, it still may. However, as countries become more multicultural due to immigration (made much easier in Europe with the advent of the European Union, or EU), different cultures may exist within a country as well as in differing countries. Research in psychology, too, has been affected by these worldwide changes.

The world context has also shifted. The cultural makeup of the United States is certainly changing rapidly; recent U.S. Census Bureau analyses indicate the rapid increase in ethnic minorities, especially Hispanic Americans and Asian Americans, to the extent that the historical European American majority in American is likely to become a minority group

within the next decade or so (see Geisinger, 2002, or Sandoval, 1998, for an elaboration of these data). While the United States is experiencing population changes with a considerable increase in groups traditionally identified as ethnic minorities, so have other parts of the world experienced these same population shifts. Many of these changes are occurring as "the direct consequence of cross-immigration and globalization of the economy" (Allen & Walsh, 2000, p. 63). Cultures change due to population changes caused by immigration and emigration, birth and death rates, and other factors, but they also change due to historical influences apart from population shifts. Countries that have suffered famine, aggression on the part of other nations, or other traumatic changes may experience significant cultural transformations as well as population changes. Most psychologists have studied human behavior within a single, broad culture, sometimes called *Euro-American culture* (Moreland, 1996; Padilla & Medina, 1996). In more recent years, psychologists have begun to recognize the importance of culture; in 1995 the American Psychological Association (APA) began publishing the journal *Culture and Psychology*. Such an event may be seen as an indication of the increased recognition of the importance of culture in psychology.

According to Berry (1980), *cross-cultural psychology* seeks to explore the relationships between cultural and behavioral variables. He included ecological and societal factors within the realm of cultural variables. Likewise, he included as part of behavioral variables those that must be inferred from behavior, such as personality, attitudes, interests, and so on. The variables that are studied in cross-cultural psychology, of course, must be measured and they have traditionally been examined using standardized tests, interviews, and a variety of formal and informal assessments. In fact, Triandis, Malpass, and Davidson (1971) describe cross-cultural psychology as follows: "Cross-cultural psychology includes studies of subjects from two or more cultures, using equivalent methods of measurement, to determine the limits within which general psychological theories do hold, and the kinds of modifications of these theories that are needed to make them universal" (p. 1; also cited in Berry, 1980, p. 4). The previous statement emphasizes the need for equivalent methods of measurement. If the findings of cross-cultural psychology are to have validity, then equivalent measurement is required. This point is the general theme of this chapter. It is argued that to note cross-cultural differences or similarities in terms of psychological variables and theories, one must have confidence that the measures used in research are equivalent measures in each culture.

When one is comparing two cultures with respect to a psychological or other variable, there are a number of factors that can invalidate the comparison. For example, if one selects well-educated individuals from one culture and less well-educated persons from the second culture, the comparison is likely to be flawed. (See van de Vijver & Leung, 1997, for a more complete listing and explanation of these confounding factors.) However, one of the primary sources of invalidity, one that is often not understood as easily as the previous sampling example, relates to measurement instruments. When the two cultures to be compared do not employ the same language to communicate and have other cultural differences, the measures that are used in the comparison must of necessity be somewhat different. A number of the possible options are discussed and evaluated in this chapter. Depending upon the use and other factors, cross-cultural psychologists and psychologists dealing with testing issues in applied use are provided with some strategies for solving the dilemmas that they face. Language is generally not the only disparity when making cross-cultural comparisons. Cultural differences in idioms, personal styles, experiences in test taking, and a plethora of other variables must also be considered in making cross-cultural or multicultural assessments. These factors are often more subtle than language differences.

Thus, there are theoretical reasons to examine testing within cross-cultural psychology. There are also applied reasons that testing is important in cross-cultural settings. Obviously, the applied uses of tests and assessment across cultures must rely on the theoretical findings from cross-cultural psychology. Tests and assessment devices have been found to have substantial validity in aiding in various kinds of decision making in some cultures. Thus, other cultures may wish to employ these measures, or adaptations of them, in what appear to be similar applied settings in cultures other than those where they were first developed and used.

Test development, test use, and other psychometric issues have long held an important role in cross-cultural psychology. Berry (1980) differentiated cross-cultural psychology from many other areas of psychology, and aligned it closely to measurement and methodology by reflecting that "most areas of psychological enquiry are defined by their *content;* however, cross-cultural psychology is defined primarily by its *method*" (p. 1; emphasis in the original). The words *testing* and *assessment* are used interchangeably by some psychologists, but differentially by others. When they are distinguished, *testing* involves the administration and scoring of a measurement instrument; *assessment,* on the other hand, is a broader term that includes score and behavioral interpretation in the context of the culture or the individual being evaluated.

Some Basic Distinctions

Before beginning a formal discussion of testing in cross-cultural psychology, a few fundamental features must be differentiated. When one uses measures in two cultures, one engages in *cross-cultural* work. On the other hand, when one studies the various subcultures within a country, such as the United States of America, then one performs *multicultural* analyses. The distinction is somewhat more complex, however, and this demarcation in described in the next section. Next, one of the fundamental distinctions in cross-cultural psychology—the concepts of *etic* and *emic*—are described; these terms in some ways parallel the distinction between cross-cultural and multicultural analyses. In brief, etic studies compare a variable across cultures whereas emic studies are performed within a single culture. Finally, a distinction between the uses of tests in relatively pure research as opposed to the testing of individuals in real-life, often high-stakes decisions is described.

Cross-Cultural and Multicultural Psychology

The differences between *cross-cultural* and *multicultural* are not entirely clear. Allen and Walsh (2000), for example, make the distinction that use of tests across cultural groups ("often internationally") is a cross-cultural application of tests whereas the use of tests with individuals of differing ethnic minority (or perhaps cultural) status within a nation is a multicultural application of tests (p. 64). They note that there is often overlap between culture and minority group status. Clearly, the distinction blurs.

Thus, the techniques used in cross-cultural psychology have great applicability to multicultural, psychological issues. The questions and concerns involved in adapting a test to make a comparison between U.S. and Mexican cultures, for example, are certainly applicable to the testing of Spanish-speaking Chicanos in the United States.

The Concepts of Etic and Emic

Linguists often use two important words in their work: *phonetic* and *phonemic*. According to Domino (2000), "Phonetic refers to the universal rules for all languages, while phonemic refers to the sounds of a particular language. From these terms, the word 'etic' and 'emic' were derived and used in the cross-cultural literature. Etic studies compare the same variable across cultures. . . . Emic studies focus on only one culture and do not attempt to compare cultures" (p. 296). These terms were originally coined by Pike (1967). The words *etic* and *emic* also refer to local and universal qualities, respectively. Thus, the terms have been used to describe both behaviors and investigations.

Emics are behaviors that apply only in a single society or culture and etics are those that are seen as universal, or without the restrictions of culture. A complaint made about traditional psychology is that it has presumed that certain findings in the field are etics, even though they have not been investigated in non-Western arenas (Berry, 1980; Moreland, 1996). Thus, some findings considered etics are only so-called *pseudo etics* (Triandis et al., 1971). The emic-etic distinction is one that has broad applicability to the adaptation of tests developed in America to other cultural spheres.

The emic-etic distinction also applies to the goals of and approaches to cross-cultural research: The first goal is to document valid principles that describe behavior in any one culture by using constructs that the people themselves conceive as meaningful and important; this is an emic analysis. The second goal of cross-cultural research is to make generalizations across cultures that take into account all human behavior. The goal, then is theory building; that would be an etic analysis (Brislin, 1980, p. 391). In searching for emic findings, we are attempting to establish behavioral systems (or rules) that appear to hold across cultures. That is, we are endeavoring to verify that certain behavioral patterns exist

universally. Etic studies look at the importance of a given behavior within a specific culture.

The Use of Tests and Assessments for Research and Applied Use

The goal of most cross-cultural psychologists and other researchers is the development of knowledge and the correlated development, expansion, and evaluation of theories of human behavior. Many applied psychologists, however, are more concerned with the use of tests with specific individuals, whether in clinical practice, school settings, industrial applications, or other environments in which tests are effectively used. The difference in the use of tests in these settings is significant; differences in the type or nature of the tests that they need for their work, however, may well be trivial. If we assume that the psychological variable or construct to be measured is the same, then differences required for such varied uses are likely to be minor. Both uses of tests, whether for research or application, require that the measure be assessed accurately and validly. Part of *validity,* it is argued, is that the measure is free from bias, including those biases that emerge from cultural and language differences. Some writers (e.g., Padilla & Medina, 1996) have accentuated the need for valid and fair assessments when the nature of the assessment is for high-stakes purposes such as admissions in higher education, placement into special education, employment, licensure, or psychodiagnosis.

THE NATURE OF EQUIVALENCE

The very nature of cross-cultural psychology places a heavy emphasis upon assessment. In particular, measures that are used to make comparisons across cultural groups need to measure the characteristic unvaryingly in two or more cultural groups. Of course, in some settings, this procedure may be rather simple; a comparison of British and American participants with regard to a variable such as depression or intelligence may not produce unusual concerns. The language, English, is, of course the same for both groups. Minor adjustments in the spelling of words (e.g., *behavioral* becomes *behavioural*) would first be needed. Some more careful editing of the items composing scales would also be needed, however, to assure that none of the items include content that has differing cultural connotations in the two countries. A question about baseball, for example, could affect resultant comparisons. These examples are provided simply to present the nature of the issue. Cross-cultural psychologists have focused upon the nature of equivalence and, in particular, have established qualitative levels of equivalence.

Many writers have considered the notion of *equivalence* in cross-cultural testing. Lonner (1979) is acknowledged often for systematizing our conception of equivalence in testing in cross-cultural psychology. He described four kinds of equivalence: linguistic equivalence, conceptual equivalence, functional equivalence, and metric equivalence (Nichols, Padilla, & Gomez-Maqueo, 2000). Brislin (1993) provided a similar nomenclature with three levels of equivalence: translation, conceptual, and metric, leaving out functional equivalence, an important kind of equivalence, as noted by Berry (1980), Butcher and Han (1998), and Helms (1992). van de Vijver and Leung (1997) operationalized four hierarchical levels of equivalence as well, encompassing construct inequivalence, construct equivalence, measurement unit equivalence, and scalar or full-score comparability. It should be noted, however, that like the concepts of test reliability and validity, equivalence is not a property resident in a particular test or assessment device (van de Vijver & Leung). Rather, the construct is tied to a particular instrument and the cultures involved. Equivalence is also time dependent, given the changes that may occur in cultures. Lonner's approach, which would appear to be most highly accepted in the literature, is described in the next section, followed by an attempt to integrate some other approaches to equivalence.

Linguistic Equivalence

When a cross-cultural study involves two or more settings in which different languages are employed for communication, the quality and fidelity of the translation of tests, testing materials, questionnaires, interview questions, open-ended responses from test-takers, and the like are critical to the validity of the study. Differences in the wording of questions on a test, for example, can have a significant impact on both the validity of research results and the applicability of a measure in a practice setting. If items include idioms from the home language in the original form, the translation of those idioms is typically unlikely to convey the same meaning in the target language. The translation of tests from host language to target language has been a topic of major concern to cross-cultural psychologists and psychometricians involved in this work. A discussion of issues and approaches to the translation of testing materials appears later in this chapter.

Most of the emphasis on this topic has concerned the translation of tests and testing materials. Moreland (1996) called attention to the translation of test-taker responses and of testing materials. Using objective personality inventories, for example, in a new culture when they were developed in another requires substantial revisions in terms of language and cultural differences. It is relatively easy to use a projective device such as the Rorschach inkblots in a variety of languages. That is

because such measures normally consist of nonverbal stimuli, which upon first glance do not need translating in terms of language. However, pictures and stimuli that are often found in such measures may need to be changed to be consistent with the culture in which they are to be used. (The images of stereotypic people may differ across cultures, as may other aspects of the stimuli that appear in the projective techniques.) Furthermore, it is critical in such a case that the scoring systems, including rubrics when available, be carefully translated as well. The same processes that are used to insure that test items are acceptable in both languages must be followed if the responses are to be evaluated in equivalent manners.

Conceptual Equivalence

The question asked in regard to conceptual equivalence may be seen as whether the test measures the same construct in both (or all) cultures, or whether the construct underlying the measure has the same meaning in all languages (Allen & Walsh, 2000). Conceptual equivalence therefore relates to test validity, especially construct validity.

Cronbach and Meehl (1955) established the conceptual structure for construct validity with the model of a nomological network. The *nomological network* concept is based upon our understanding of psychological constructs (hypothetical psychological variables, characteristics, or traits) through their relationships with other such variables. What psychologists understand about in vivo constructs emerges from how those constructs relate empirically to other constructs. In naturalistic settings, psychologists tend to measure two or more constructs for all participants in the investigation and to correlate scores among variables. Over time and multiple studies, evidence is amassed so that the relationships among variables appear known. From their relationships, the structure of these constructs becomes known and a nomological network can be imagined and charted; variables that tend to be highly related are closely aligned in the nomological network and those that are not related have no connective structure between them. The *construct validity* of a particular test, then, is the extent to which it appears to measure the theoretical construct or trait that it is intended to measure. This construct validity is assessed by determining the extent to which the test correlates with variables in the patterns predicted by the nomological network. When the test correlates with other variables with which it is expected to correlate, evidence of construct validation, called *convergent validation,* is found (Campbell & Fiske, 1959; Geisinger, 1992). Conversely, when a test does not correlate with a measure that the theory of the psychological construct suggests that it should not, positive evidence of construct validation, called *discriminant validation* (Campbell & Fiske, 1959) is also found.

Consider the following simple example. *Intelligence* and *school performance* are both constructs measured by the Wechsler Intelligence Scale for Children–III (WISC-III) and grade point average (GPA)—in this instance, in the fourth grade. Numerous investigations in the United States provide data showing the two constructs to correlate moderately. The WISC-III is translated into French and a similar study is performed with fourth-graders in schools in Quebec, where a GPA measure similar to that in U.S. schools is available. If the correlation is similar between the two variables (intelligence and school performance), then some degree of conceptual equivalence between the English and French versions of the WISC-III is demonstrated. If a comparable result is not found, however, it is unclear whether (a) the WISC-III was not properly translated and adapted to French; (b) the GPA in the Quebec study is different somehow from that in the American studies; (c) one or both of the measured constructs (intelligence and school performance) does not exist in the same fashion in Quebec as they do in the United States; or (d) the constructs simply do not relate to each other the way they do in the United States. Additional research would be needed to establish the truth in this situation. This illustration is also an example of what van de Vijver and Leung (1997) have termed *construct inequivalence,* which occurs when an assessment instrument measures different constructs in different languages. No etic comparisons can be made in such a situation, because the comparison would be a classic apples-and-oranges contrast.

Ultimately and theoretically, conceptual equivalence is achieved when a test that has considerable evidence of construct validity in the original or host language and culture is adapted for use in a second language and culture, and the target-language nomological network is identical to the original one. When such a nomological network has been replicated, it might be said that the construct validity of the test *generalizes* from the original test and culture to the target one. *Factor analysis* has long been used as a technique of choice for this equivalence evaluation (e.g., Ben-Porath, 1990). Techniques such as *structural equation modeling* are even more useful for such analyses (e.g., Byrne, 1989, 1994; Loehlin, 1992), in which the statistical model representing the nomological network in the host culture can be applied and tested in the target culture. Additional information on these approaches is provided later in this chapter. (Note that, throughout this chapter, the terms *conceptual equivalence* and *construct equivalence* are used synonymously.)

Functional Equivalence

Functional equivalence is achieved when the domain of behaviors sampled on a test has the same purpose and meaning in both cultures in question. "For example, in the United States the handshake is functionally equivalent to the head bow with hands held together in India" (Nichols et al., 2000, p. 260). When applied to testing issues, functional equivalence is generally dealt with during the translation phase. The individuals who translate the test must actually perform a more difficult task than a simple translation. They frequently must adapt questions as well. That is, direct, literal translation of questions may not convey meaning because the behaviors mentioned in some or all of the items might not generalize across cultures. Therefore, those involved in adapting the original test to a new language and culture must remove or change those items that deal with behavior that does not generalize equivalently in the target culture. When translators find functionally equivalent behaviors to use to replace those that do not generalize across cultures, they are adapting, rather than translating, the test; for this reason, it is preferable to state that the test is *adapted* rather than translated (Geisinger, 1994; Hambleton, 1994). Some researchers appear to believe that functional equivalence has been subsumed by conceptual equivalence (e.g., Brislin, 1993; Moreland, 1996).

Metric Equivalence

Nichols et al. (2000) have defined *metric equivalence* as "the extent to which the instrument manifests similar psychometric properties (distributions, ranges, etc.) across cultures" (p. 256). According to Moreland (1996), the standards for meeting metric equivalence are higher than reported by Nichols et al. First, metric equivalence presumes conceptual equivalence. The measures must quantify the same variable in the same way across the cultures. Specifically, scores on the scale must convey the same meaning, regardless of which form was administered. There are some confusing elements to this concept. On one hand, such a standard does not require that the arithmetic means of the tests to be the same in both cultures (Clark, 1987), but does require that individual scores be indicative of the same psychological meaning. Thus, it is implied that scores must be criterion referenced. An individual with a given score on a measure of psychopathology would need treatment, regardless of which language version of the form was taken. Similarly, an individual with the same low score on an intelligence measure should require special education, whether that score is at the 5th or 15th percentile of his or her cultural population. Some of the statistical techniques for establishing metric equivalence are described later in this chapter.

Part of metric equivalence is the establishment of comparable reliability and validity across cultures. Sundberg and Gonzales (1981) have reported that the reliability of measures is unlikely to be influenced by translation and adaptation. This writer finds such a generalization difficult to accept as a conclusion. If the range of scores is higher or lower in one culture, for example, that reliability as traditionally defined will also be reduced in that testing. The quality of the test adaptation, too, would have an impact. Moreland (1996) suggests that investigators would be wise to ascertain *test stability* (i.e., test-retest reliability) and internal consistency in any adapted measure, and this writer concurs with this recommendation.

Geisinger (1992) has considered the validation of tests for two populations or in two languages. There are many ways to establish validity evidence: content-related approaches, criterion-related approaches, and construct-related approaches. Construct approaches were already discussed with respect to conceptual equivalence.

In regard to establishing *content validity,* the adequacy of sampling of the domain is critical. To establish comparable content validity in two forms of a measure, each in a different language for a different cultural group, one must gauge first whether the content domain is the same or different in each case. In addition, one must establish that the domain is sampled with equivalent representativeness in all cases. Both of these determinations may be problematic. For example, imagine the translation of a fourth-grade mathematics test that, in its original country, is given to students who attend school 10 months of the year, whereas in the target country, the students attend for only 8 months. In such an instance, the two domains of mathematics taught in the 4th year of schooling are likely to be overlapping, but not identical. Because the students from the original country have already attended three longer school years prior to this year, they are likely to begin at a more advanced level. Furthermore, given that the year is longer, they are likely to cover more material during the academic year. In short, the domains are not likely to be identical. Finally, the representativeness of the domains must be considered.

Other Forms of Equivalence

van de Vijver and Leung (1997) have discussed two additional types of equivalence, both of which can probably be considered as subtypes of metric equivalence: measurement unit equivalence and scalar or full-score equivalence. Both of these concepts are worthy of brief consideration because they are important for both theoretical and applied cross-cultural uses of psychological tests.

Measurement Unit Equivalence

This level of equivalence indicates that a measure that has been adapted for use in a target culture continues to have the same units of measurement in the two culture-specific forms. That is, both forms of the measure must continue to yield assessments that follow an interval scale, and in addition, it must be the same interval scale. If a translated form of a test were studied using a sample in the target culture comparable to the original norm group and the new test form was found to have the same raw-score standard deviation as the original, this finding would be strong evidence of measurement unit equivalence. If the norms for the target population were extremely similar to that in the original population, these data would also be extremely strong substantiation of measurement unit equivalence.

Scalar (full-score) Equivalence

Scalar equivalence assumes measurement unit equivalence and requires one additional finding: Not only must the units be equivalent, the zero-points of the scales must also be identical. Thus, the units must both fall along the same ratio scale. It is unlikely that many psychological variables will achieve this level of equivalence, although some physiological variables, such as birth weight, certainly do.

THE NATURE OF BIAS

There have been many definitions of *test bias* (Flaugher, 1978; and see chapter 4 of this volume). Messick's (1980, 1989, 1995) conceptions of test bias are perhaps the most widely accepted and emerge from the perspective of construct validity. Messick portrayed *bias* as a specific source of test variance other than the valid variance associated with the desired construct. Bias is associated with some irrelevant variable, such as race, gender, or in the case of cross-cultural testing, culture (or perhaps country of origin). van de Vijver and his associates (van de Vijver, 2000; van de Vijver & Leung, 1997; van de Vijver & Poortinga, 1997) have perhaps best characterized bias within the context of cross-cultural assessment. "Test bias exists, from this viewpoint, when an existing test does not measure the equivalent underlying psychological construct in a new group or culture, as was measured within the original group in which it was standardized" (Allen & Walsh, 2000, p. 67). van de Vijver describes bias as "a generic term for all nuisance factors threatening the validity of cross-cultural comparisons. Poor item translations, inappropriate item content, and lack of standardization in administration procedures are just a few examples" (van de Vijver & Leung, p. 10). He also describes bias as "a lack of similarity of psychological meaning of test scores across cultural groups" (van de Vijver, p. 88).

The term *bias,* as can be seen, is very closely related to *conceptual equivalence*. van de Vjver describes the distinction as follows: "The two concepts are strongly related, but have a somewhat different connotation. Bias refers to the presence or absence of validity-threatening factors in such assessment, whereas equivalence involves the consequences of these factors on the comparability of test scores" (van de Vijver, 2000, p. 89). In his various publications, van de Vijver identifies three groupings of bias: construct, method, and item bias. Each is described in the following sections.

Construct Bias

Measures that do not examine the same construct across cultural groups exhibit *construct bias,* which clearly is highly related to the notion of conceptual equivalence previously described. Contstruct bias would be evident in a measure that has been (a) factor analyzed in its original culture with the repeated finding of a four-factor solution, and that is then (b) translated to another language and administered to a sample from the culture in which that language is spoken, with a factor analysis of the test results indicating a two-factor and therefore different solution. When the constructs underlying the measures vary across cultures, with culture-specific components of the construct present in some cultures, such evidence is not only likely to result, it *should* result if both measures are to measure the construct validly in their respective cultures. Construct bias can occur when constructs only partially overlap across cultures, when there is a differential appropriateness of behaviors comprising the construct in different cultures, when there is a poor sampling of relevant behaviors constituting the construct in one or more cultures, or when there is incomplete coverage of all relevant aspects of the construct (van de Vijver, 2000).

An example of construct bias can be seen in the following. In many instances, inventories (such as personality inventories) are largely translated from the original language to a second or target language. If the culture that uses the target language has culture-specific aspects of personality that either do not exist or are not as prevalent as in the original culture, then these aspects will certainly not be translated into the target-language form of the assessment instrument.

The concept of construct bias has implications for both cross-cultural research and cross-cultural psychological practice. Cross-cultural or etic comparisons are unlikely to be very meaningful if the construct means something different in the two or more cultures, or if it is a reasonably valid representation of the construct in one culture but less so in the other. The practice implications in the target language emerge from the fact that the measure may not be valid as a measure of culturally relevant constructs that may be of consequence for diagnosis and treatment.

Method Bias

van de Vijver (2000) has identified a number of types of method bias, including sample, instrument, and administration bias. The different issues composing this type of bias were given the name *method bias* because they relate to the kinds of topics covered in methods sections of journal articles (van de Vijver). Method biases often affect performance on the assessment instrument as a whole (rather than affecting only components of the measure). Some of the types of method bias are described in the following.

Sample Bias

In studies comparing two or more cultures, the samples from each culture may differ on variables related to test-relevant background characteristics. These differences may affect the comparison. Examples of such characteristics would include fluency in the language in which testing occurs, general education levels, and underlying motivational levels (van de Vijver, 2000). Imagine an essay test that is administered in a single language. Two groups are compared: Both have facility with the language, but one has substantially more ability. Regardless of the knowledge involved in the answers, it is likely that the group that is more facile in the language will provide better answers on average because of their ability to employ the language better in answering the question.

Instrument Bias

This type of bias is much like sample bias, but the groups being tested tend to differ in less generic ways that are more specific to the testing method itself, as when a test subject has some familiarity with the general format of the testing or some other form of test sophistication. van de Vijver (2000) states that the most common forms of this bias exist when groups differ by response styles in answering questions, or by their familiarity with the materials on the test. As is described later in this chapter, attempts to develop culture-fair or culture-free intelligence tests (e.g., Bracken, Naglieri, & Baardos, 1999; Cattell, 1940; Cattell & Cattell, 1963) have often used geometric figures rather than language in the effort to avoid dependence upon language. Groups that differ in educational experience or by culture also may have differential exposure to geometric figures. This differential contact with the stimuli composing the test may bias the comparison in a manner that is difficult to disentangle from the construct of intelligence measured by the instrument.

Alternatively, different cultures vary in the tendency of their members to disclose personal issues about themselves.

When two cultures are compared, depending upon who is making the comparison, it is possible that one group could look overly self-revelatory or the other too private.

Imagine the use of a measure such as the Thematic Apperception Test (TAT) in a cross-cultural comparison. Not only do the people pictured on many of the TAT cards not look like persons from some cultures, but the scenes themselves have a decidedly Western orientation. Respondents from some cultures would obviously find such pictures more foreign and strange.

Geisinger (1994) recommended the use of enhanced test-practice exercises to attempt to reduce differences in test-format familiarity. Such exercises could be performed at the testing site or in advance of the testing, depending upon the time needed to gain familiarity.

Administration Bias

The final type of method bias emerges from the interactions between test-taker or respondent and the individual administering the test, whether the test, questionnaire, or interview, is individually administered or is completed in more of a large-group situation. Such biases could come from language problems on the part of an interviewer, who may be conducting the interview in a language in which he or she is less adept than might be ideal (van de Vijver & Leung, 1997). Communications problems may result from other language problems—for example, the common mistakes individuals often make in second languages in regard to the use of the familiar second person.

Another example of administration bias may be seen in the multicultural testing literature in the United States. The theory of *stereotype threat* (Steele, 1997; Steele & Aronson, 1995) suggests that African Americans, when taking an individualized intellectual assessment or other similar measure that is administered by someone whom the African American test-takers believe holds negative stereotypes about them, will perform at the level expected by the test administrator. Steele's theory holds that negative stereotypes can have a powerful influence on the results of important assessments—stereotypes that can influence test-takers' performance and, ultimately, their lives. Of course, in a world where there are many cultural tensions and cultural preconceptions, it is possible that this threat may apply to groups other than Whites and Blacks in the American culture. van de Vijver (2000) concludes his chapter, however, with the statement that with notable exceptions, responses to either interviews or most cognitive tests do not seem to be strongly affected by the cultural, racial, or ethnic status of administrators.

Item Bias

In the late 1970s, those involved in large-scale testing, primarily psychometricians, began studying the possibility that items could be biased—that is, that the format or content of items could influence responses to individual items on tests in unintended ways. Because of the connotations of the term *biased,* the topic has more recently been termed *differential item functioning,* or *dif* (e.g., Holland & Wainer, 1993). van de Vijver and his associates prefer continuing to use the term *item bias,* however, to accentuate the notion that these factors are measurement issues that, if not handled appropriately, may bias the results of measurement. Essentially, on a cognitive test, an item is biased for a particular group if it is more difficult for individuals of a certain level of overall ability than it is for members of the other group who have that same level of overall ability. Items may appear biased in this way because they deal with content that is not uniformly available to members of all cultures involved. They may also be identified as biased because translations have not been adequately performed.

In addition, there may be factors such as words describing concepts that are *differentially more difficult* in one language than the other. A number of studies are beginning to appear in the literature describing the kinds of item problems that lead to differential levels of difficulty (e.g., Allalouf, Hambleton, & Sireci, 1999; Budgell, Raju, & Quartetti, 1995; Hulin, 1987; Tanzer, Gittler, & Sim, 1994). Some of these findings may prove very useful for future test-translation projects, and may even influence the construction of tests that are likely to be translated. For example, in an early study of Hispanics and Anglos taking the Scholastic Aptitude Test, Schmitt (1988) found that verbal items that used roots common to English and Spanish appeared to help Hispanics. Limited evidence suggested that words that differed in cognates (words that appear to have the same roots but have different meanings in both languages) and homographs (words spelled alike in both languages but with different meanings in the two) caused difficulties for Hispanic test-takers. Allalouf et al. found that on a verbal test for college admissions that had been translated from Hebrew to Russian, analogy items presented the most problems. Most of these difficulties (items identified as differentially more difficult) emerged from word difficulty, especially in analogy items. Interestingly, many of the analogies were easier in Russian, the target language. Apparently, the translators chose easier words, thus making items less difficult. Sentence completion items had been difficult to translate because of different sentence structures in the two languages. Reading Comprehension items also lead to some problems, mostly related to the specific content of the reading passages in question. In some cases, the content was seen as culturally specific. Allalouf et al. also concluded that differences in item difficulty can emerge from differences in wording, differences in content, differences in format, or differences in cultural relevance.

If the responses to questions on a test are not objective in format, *differences in scoring rubrics* can also lead to item bias. Budgell et al. (1995) used an expert committee to review the results of statistical analyses that identified items as biased; in many cases, the committee could not provide logic as to why an item translated from English to French was differentially more difficult for one group or the other.

Item bias has been studied primarily in cognitive measures: ability and achievement tests. van de Vijver (2000) correctly notes that measures such as the Rorschach should also be evaluated for item bias. It is possible that members of different cultures could differentially interpret the cards on measures such as the Rorschach or the TAT.

THE TRANSLATION AND ADAPTATION OF TESTS

During the 1990s, considerable attention was provided to the translation and adaptation of tests and assessment devices in the disciplines of testing and psychometrics and in the literature associated with these fields. The International Testing Commission developed guidelines that were shared in various draft stages (e.g., Hambleton, 1994, 1999; van de Vijver & Leung, 1997; the resulting guidelines were a major accomplishment for testing and for cross-cultural psychology, and they are provided as the appendix to this chapter). Seminal papers on test translation (Berry, 1980; Bracken & Barona, 1991; Brislin, 1970, 1980, 1986; Butcher & Pancheri, 1976; Geisinger, 1994; Hambleton, 1994; Lonner, 1979; Werner & Campbell, 1970) appeared and helped individuals faced with the conversion of an instrument from one language and culture to another. The following sections note some of the issues to be faced regarding language and culture, and then provide a brief description of the approaches to test translation.

The Role of Language

One of the primary ways that cultures differ is through language. In fact, in considering the level of acculturation of individuals, their language skills are often given dominant (and sometimes mistaken) importance. Even within countries and regions of the world where ostensibly the same language is spoken, accents can make oral communication difficult. *Language skill* is, ultimately, the ability to communicate. There are different types of language skills. Whereas some language

scholars consider competencies in areas such as grammar, discourse, language strategy, and sociolinguistic facility (see Durán, 1988), the focus of many language scholars has been on more holistic approaches to language. Generally, language skills may be considered along two dimensions, one being the oral and written dimension, and the other being the understanding and expression dimension.

Depending upon the nature of the assessment to be performed, different kinds and qualities of language skills may be needed. Academically oriented, largely written language skills may require 6 to 8 years of instruction and use to develop, whereas the development of the spoken word for everyday situations is much faster. These issues are of critical importance for the assessment of immigrants and their children (Geisinger, 2002; Sandoval, 1998). Some cross-cultural comparisons are made using one language for both groups, even though the language may be the second language for one of the groups. In such cases, language skills may be a confounding variable. In the United States, the issue of language often obscures comparisons of Anglos and Hispanics. Pennock-Roman (1992) demonstrated that English-language tests for admissions to higher education may not be valid for language minorities when their English-language skills are not strong.

Culture and language may be very closely wedded. However, not all individuals who speak the same language come from the same culture or are able to take the same test validly. Also within the United States, the heterogeneous nature of individuals who might be classified as Hispanic Americans is underscored by the need for multiple Spanish-language translations and adaptations of tests (Handel & Ben-Porath, 2000). For example, the same Spanish-language measure may not be appropriate for Mexicans, individuals from the Caribbean, and individuals from the Iberian Peninsula. Individuals from different Latin American countries may also need different instruments.

Measurement of Language Proficiency

Before making many assessments, we need to establish whether the individuals being tested have the requisite levels of language skills that will be used on the examination. We also need to develop better measures of language skills (Durán, 1988). In American schools, English-language skills should be evaluated early in the schooling of a child whose home language is not English to determine whether that child can profit from English-language instruction (Durán). Handel and Ben-Porath (2000) argue that a similar assessment should be made prior to administration of the Minnesota Multiphasic Personality Inventory–2 (MMPI-2) because studies have shown that it does not work as effectively with individuals whose language skills are not robust, and that the validity of at least some of the scales is compromised if the respondent does not have adequate English reading ability. Many school systems and other agencies have developed tests of language skills, sometimes equating tests of English- and Spanish-language skills so that the scores are comparable (e.g., O'Brien, 1992; Yansen & Shulman, 1996).

The Role of Culture

One of the primary and most evident ways that cultures often differ is by spoken and written language. They also differ, of course, in many other ways. Individuals from two different cultures who take part in a cross-cultural investigation are likely to differ according to other variables that can influence testing and the study. Among these are speed of responding, the amount of education that they have received, the nature and content of that schooling, and their levels of motivation. All of these factors may influence the findings of cross-cultural studies.

Culture may be envisioned as an antecedent of behavior. *Culture* is defined as a set of contextual variables that have either a direct or an indirect effect on thought and behavior (Cuéllar, 2000). Culture provides a context for all human behavior, thought, and other mediating variables, and it is so pervasive that it is difficult to imagine human behavior that might occur without reference to culture. As noted at the beginning of this chapter, one of the goals of cross-cultural psychology is to investigate and differentiate those behaviors, behavior patterns, personalities, attitudes, worldviews, and so on that are universal from those that are culture specific (see van de Vijver & Poortinga, 1982). "The current field of cultural psychology represents a recognition of the cultural specificity of all human behavior, whereby basic psychological processes may result in highly diverse performance, attitude, self-concepts, and world views in members of different cultural populations" (Anastasi & Urbina, 1997, p. 341). *Personality* has sometimes been defined as an all-inclusive characteristic describing one's patterns of responding to others and to the world. It is not surprising that so many anthropologists and cross-cultural psychologists have studied the influence of culture and personality—the effects of the pervasive environment on the superordinate organization that mediates behavior and one's interaction with the world.

For much of the history of Western psychology, investigators and theorists believed that many basic psychological processes were universal, that is, that they transcended individual cultures (e.g., Moreland, 1996; Padilla & Medina, 1996). More psychologists now recognize that culture has the omnipresent impact. For example, the APA's current

Diagnostic and Statistical Manual of Mental Disorders (fourth edition, or *DSM-IV*) was improved over its predecessor, *DSM-III-R*, by "including an appendix that gives instructions on how to understand culture and descriptions of culture-bound syndromes" (Keitel, Kopala, & Adamson, 1996, p. 35).

Malgady (1996) has extended this argument. He has stated that we should actually assume cultural nonequivalence rather than cultural equivalence. Of course, much of the work of cross-cultural psychologists and other researchers is determining whether our measures are equivalent and appropriate (not biased). Clearly, if we are unable to make parallel tests that are usable in more than one culture and whose scores are comparable in the varying cultures, then we do not have an ability to compare cultures. Helms (1992), too, has asked this question with a particular reference to intelligence testing, arguing that intelligence tests are oriented to middle-class, White Americans.

What about working with individuals with similar-appearing psychological concerns in different cultures, especially where a useful measure has been identified in one culture? Can we use comparable, but not identical, psychological measures in different cultures? Indeed, we should probably use culture-specific measures, even though these measures cannot be used for cross-cultural comparisons (van de Vijver, 2000). If we use measures that have been translated or adapted from other cultures, we need to revalidate them in the new culture. In some circumstances, we may also need to use assessments of acculturation as well as tests of language proficiency before we use tests with clients requiring assessment. (See Geisinger, 2002, for a description of such an assessment paradigm.)

There are problems inherent in even the best translations of tests. For example, even when professional translators, content or psychological specialists, and test designers are involved, "direct translations of the tests are often not possible as psychological constructs may have relevance in one culture and not in another.... Just because the content of the items is preserved does not automatically insure that the item taps the same ability within the cultural context of the individual being tested" (Suzuki, Vraniak, & Kugler, 1996). This lack of parallelism is, of course, what has already been seen as construct bias and a lack of conceptual equivalence. Brislin (1980) has also referred to this issue as *translatability*. A test is poorly translated when salient characteristics in the construct to be assessed cannot be translated. The translation and adaptation of tests is considered later in this section.

Intelligence tests are among the most commonly administered types of tests. Kamin (1974) demonstrated in dramatic form how tests of intelligence were once used in U.S. governmental decision making concerning the status of immigrants. In general, immigration policies were affected by analyses of the intelligence of immigrants from varying countries and regions of the world. Average IQs were computed from country and region of origin; these data were shared widely and generally were believed to be the results of innate ability, even though one of the strongest findings of the time was that the longer immigrants lived in the United States, the higher their levels of intelligence were (Kamin). The tests used for many of these analyses were the famous Army Alpha and Army Beta, which were early verbal and nonverbal tests of intelligence, respectively. It was obvious even then that language could cause validity problems in the intelligence testing of those whose English was not proficient. Leaders in the intelligence-testing community have also attempted to develop tests that could be used cross-culturally without translation. These measures have often been called *culture-free* or *culture-fair* tests of intelligence.

Culture-Free and Culture-Fair Assessments of Intelligence

Some psychologists initially attempted to develop so-called culture-free measures of intelligence. In the 1940s, for example, Cattell (1940) attempted to use very simple geometric forms that were not reliant upon language to construct what he termed *culture-free* tests. These tests were based on a notion that Cattell (1963) conceptualized and later developed into a theory that intelligence could be decomposed into two types of ability: fluid and crystallized mental abilities. *Fluid abilities* were nonverbal and involved in adaptation and learning capabilities. *Crystallized abilities* were developed as a result of the use of fluid abilities and were based upon cultural assimilation (Sattler, 1992). These tests, then, were intended to measure only fluid abilities and, according to this theory, would hence be culture-free: that is, implicitly conceptually equivalent.

It was soon realized that it was not possible to eliminate the effects of culture from even these geometric-stimulus-based, nonverbal tests. "Even those designated as 'culture-free' do not eliminate the effects of previous cultural experiences, both of impoverishment and enrichment. Language factors greatly affect performance, and some of the tasks used to measure intelligence have little or no relevance for cultures very different from the Anglo-European" (Ritzler, 1996, p. 125). Nonlanguage tests may even be more culturally loaded than language-based tests. Larger group differences with nonverbal tests than with verbal ones have often been found. "Nonverbal, spatial-perceptual tests frequently require relatively abstract thinking processes and analytic cognitive styles characteristic of middle-class Western cultures" (Anastasi & Urbina, 1997, p. 344). In retrospect, "cultural influences will

and should be reflected in test performance. It is therefore futile to try to devise a test that is free from cultural influences" (Anastasi & Urbina, p. 342).

Noting these and other reactions, Cattell (Cattell & Cattell, 1963) tried to balance cultural influences and build what he termed *culture-fair* tests. These tests also tend to use geometric forms of various types. The items frequently are complex patterns, classification tasks, or solving printed mazes; and although the tests can be paper-and-pencil, they can also be based on performance tasks and thus avoid language-based verbal questions. They may involve pictures rather than verbal stimuli. Even such tests were not seen as fully viable:

> It is unlikely, moreover, that any test can be equally "fair" to more than one cultural group, especially if the cultures are quite dissimilar. While reducing cultural differentials in test performance, cross-cultural tests cannot completely eliminate such differentials. Every test tends to favor persons from the culture in which it was developed. (Anastasi & Urbina, 1997, p. 342)

Some cultures place greater or lesser emphases upon abstractions, and some cultures value the understanding of contexts and situations more than Western cultures (Cole & Bruner, 1971).

> On the other hand, there is a substantial literature that suggests culture-fair tests like the Cattell fulfill not only theoretical and social concerns but practical needs as well. . . . Smith, Hays, and Solway (1977) compared the Cattell Culture-Fair Test and the WISC-R in a sample of juvenile delinquents, 53% of whom were black or Mexican-Americans. . . . The authors concluded that the Cattell is a better measure of intelligence for minority groups than the WISC-R, as it lessens the effect of cultural bias and presents a "more accurate" picture of their intellectual capacity. (Domino, 2000, p. 300)

Some of our top test developers continue to develop tests intended to be culture-fair (Bracken et al., 1999). Although such measures may not be so culture-fair that they would permit cross-cultural comparisons that would be free of cultural biases, they nevertheless have been used effectively in a variety of cultures and may be transported from culture to culture without many of the translation issues so incumbent on most tests of ability that are used in more than one culture. Such tests should, however, be evaluated carefully for what some have seen as their middle-class, Anglo-European orientation.

Acculturation

Cuéllar (2000) has described *acculturation* as a moderator variable between personality and behavior, and *culture* as "learned behavior transmitted from one generation to the next" (p. 115). When an individual leaves one culture and joins a second, a transition is generally needed. This transition is, at least in part, acculturation. "Most psychological research defines the construct of acculturation as the product of learning due to contacts between the members of two or more groups" (Marín, 1992, p. 345). Learning the language of the new culture is only one of the more obvious aspects of acculturation. It also involves learning the history and traditions of the new culture, changing personally meaningful behaviors in one's life (including the use of one's language), and changing norms, values, worldview, and interaction patterns (Marín).

In practice settings, when considering the test performance of an individual who is not from the culture in which the assessment instrument was developed, one needs to consider the individual's level of acculturation. Many variables have been shown to be influenced by the level of acculturation in the individual being assessed. Sue, Keefe, Enomoto, Durvasula, and Chao (1996), for example, found that acculturation affected scales on the MMPI-2. It has also been shown that one's level of acculturation affects personality scales to the extent that these differences could lead to different diagnoses and, perhaps, hospitalization decisions (Cuéllar, 2000).

Keitel et al. (1996) have provided guidelines for conducting ethical multicultural assessments. Included among these guidelines are assessing acculturation level, selecting tests appropriate for the culture of the test taker, administering tests in an unbiased fashion, and interpreting results appropriately and in a manner that a client can understand. Dana (1993) and Moreland (1996) concur that acculturation should be assessed as a part of an in-depth evaluation. They suggest, as well, that the psychologist first assess an individual's acculturation and then use instruments appropriate for the individual's dominant culture. Too often, they fear, psychologists use instruments from the dominant culture and with which the psychologist is more likely to be familiar. They also propose that a psychologist dealing with a client who is not fully acculturated should consider test results with respect to the individual's test sophistication, motivation, and other psychological factors that may be influenced by the level of his or her acculturation. Because of the importance of learning to deal with clients who are not from dominant cultures, it has been argued that in training psychologists and other human-service professionals, practicums should provide students with access to clients from different cultures (Geisinger & Carlson, 1998; Keitel et al., 1996).

There are many measures of acculturation. Measurement is complex, in part because it is not a unidimensional characteristic (even though many measures treat it as such). Discussion of this topic is beyond the scope of the present chapter;

however, the interested reader is referred to Cuéllar (2000), Marín (1992), or Olmeda (1979).

Approaches to Test Adaptation and Translation

The translation and adaptation of tests was one of the most discussed testing issues in the 1990s. The decade ended with a major conference held in Washington, DC, in 1999 called the "International Conference on Test Adaptation: Adapting Tests for Use in Multiple Languages and Cultures." The conference brought together many of the leaders in this area of study for an exchange of ideas. In a decade during which many tests had been translated and adapted, and some examples of poor testing practice had been noted, one of the significant developments was the publication of the International Test Commission guidelines on the adapting of tests. These guidelines, which appear as the appendix to this chapter, summarize some of the best thinking on test adaptation. They may also be found in annotated form in Hambleton (1999) and van de Vijver and Leung (1997). The term *test adaptation* also took prominence during the last decade of the twentieth century; previously, the term *test translation* had been dominant. This change was based on the more widespread recognition that changes to tests were needed to reflect both cultural differences and language differences. These issues have probably long been known in the cross-cultural psychology profession, but less so in the field of testing. (For excellent treatments on the translation of research materials, see Brislin, 1980, 1986.)

There are a variety of qualitatively different approaches to test adaptation. Of course, for some cross-cultural testing projects, one might develop a new measure altogether to meet one's needs. Such an approach is not test adaptation per se, but nonetheless would need to follow many of the principles of this process. Before building a test for use in more than one culture, one would need to ask how universal the constructs to be tested are (Anastasi & Urbina, 1997; van de Vijver & Poortinga, 1982). One would also have to decide how to validate the measure in the varying cultures. If one imagines a simple approach to validation (e.g., the criterion-related approach), one would need equivalent criteria in each culture. This requirement is often formidable. A more common model is to take an existing and generally much-used measure from one culture and language to attempt to translate it to a second culture and language.

van de Vijver and Leung (1997) have identified three general approaches to adapting tests: back-translation, decentering, and the committee approach. Each of these is described in turn in the following sections. Prior to the development of any of these general approaches, however, some researchers and test developers simply translated tests from one language to a second. For purposes of this discussion, this unadulterated technique is called *direct translation;* it has sometimes been called *forward translation,* but this writer does not prefer that name because the process is *not* the opposite of the back-translation procedure. The techniques embodied by these three general approaches serve as improvements over the direct translation of tests.

Back-Translation

This technique is sometimes called the *translation/back-translation technique* and was an initial attempt to advance the test adaptation process beyond a direct test translation (Brislin, 1970; Werner & Campbell, 1970). In this approach, an initial translator or team of translators alters the test materials from the original language to the target language. Then a second translator or team, without having seen the original test, begins with the target language translation, and renders this form back to the original language. At this point, the original test developer (or the individuals who plan to use the translated test, or their representatives) compares the original test with the back-translated version, both of which are in the original language. The quality of the translation is evaluated in terms of how accurately the back-translated version agrees with the original test. This technique was widely cited as the procedure of choice (e.g., Butcher & Pancheri, 1976) for several decades and it has been very useful in remedying certain translation problems (van de Vijver & Leung, 1997). It may be especially useful if the test user or developer lacks facility in the target language. It also provides an attempt to evaluate the quality of the translation. However, it also has other disadvantages. The orientation is on a language-only translation; there is no possibility of changes in the test to accommodate cultural differences. Thus, if there are culture-specific aspects of the test, this technique should generally not be used. In fact, this technique can lead to special problems if the translators know that their work will be evaluated through a back-translation procedure. In such an instance, they may use stilted language or wording to insure an accurate back-translation rather than a properly worded translation that would be understood best by test takers in the target language. In short, "a translation-back translation procedure pays more attention to the semantics and less to connotations, naturalness, and comprehensibility" (van de Vijver & Leung, 1997, p. 39).

Decentering

The process of culturally decentering test materials is somewhat more complex than either the direct translation or translation/back-translation processes (Werner & Campbell, 1970). *Cultural decentering* does involve translation of an instrument from an original language to a target language. However, unlike direct translation, the original measure is changed prior to being adapted (or translated) to improve its translatability; those components of the test that are likely to be specific to the original culture are removed or altered. Thus, the cultural biases, both construct and method, are reduced. In addition, the wording of the original measure may be changed in a way that will enhance its translatability. The process is usually performed by a team composed of multilingual, multicultural individuals who have knowledge of the construct to be measured and, perhaps, of the original measure (van de Vijver & Leung, 1997). This team then changes the original measure so that "there will be a smooth, natural-sounding version in the second language" (Brislin, 1980, p. 433). If decentering is successful, the two assessment instruments that result, one in each language, are both generally free of culture-specific language and content. "Tanzer, Gittler, and Ellis (1995) developed a test of spatial ability that was used in Austria and the United States. The instructions and stimuli were simultaneously in German and English" (van de Vijver & Leung, 1997, pp. 39–40).

There are several reasons that cultural decentering is not frequently performed, however. First, of course, is that the process is time consuming and expensive. Second, data collected using the original instrument in the first language cannot be used as part of cross-cultural comparisons; only data from the two decentered methods may be used. This condition means that the rich history of validation and normative data that may be available for the original measure are likely to have little use, and the decentered measure in the original language must be used in regathering such information for comparative purposes. For this reason, this process is most likely to be used in comparative cross-cultural research when there is not plentiful supportive data on the original measure. When the technique is used, it is essentially two test-construction processes.

The Committee Approach

This approach was probably first described by Brislin (1980), has been summarized by van de Vijver and Leung (1997), and is explained in some detail by Geisinger (1994). In this method, a group of bilingual individuals translates the test from the original language to the target language. The members of the committee need to be not only bilingual, but also thoroughly familiar with both cultures, with the construct(s) measured on the test, and with general testing principles. Like most committee processes, this procedure has advantages and disadvantages. A committee will be more expensive than a single translator. A committee may not work well together, or may be dominated by one or more persons. Some members of the committee may not contribute fully or may be reticent to participate for personal reasons. On the other hand, members of the committee are likely to catch mistakes of others on the committee (Brislin, 1980). It is also possible that the committee members can cooperate and help each other, especially if their expertise is complementary (van de Vijver & Leung, 1997). This method, however, like the decentering method, does not include an independent evaluation of its effectiveness. Therefore, it is useful to couple the work of a committee with a back-translation.

Rules for Adapting Test and Assessment Materials

Brislin (1980, p. 432) provided a listing of general rules for developing research documents and instruments that are to be translated. These are rules that generate documents written in English that are likely to be successfully translated or adapted, similar to decentering. Most appear as rules for good writing and effective communication, and they have considerable applicability. These 12 rules have been edited slightly for use here.

1. Use short, simple sentences of fewer than 16 words.
2. Employ active rather than passive words.
3. Repeat nouns instead of using pronouns.
4. Avoid metaphors and colloquialisms. Such phrases are least likely to have equivalents in the target language.
5. Avoid the subjunctive mood (e.g., verb forms with *could* or *would*).
6. Add sentences that provide context for key ideas. Reword key phrases to provide redundancy. This rule suggests that longer items and questions be used only in single-country research.
7. Avoid adverbs and prepositions telling where or when (e.g., *frequently, beyond, around*).
8. Avoid possessive forms where possible.
9. Use specific rather than general terms (e.g., the specific animal name, such as *cows, chickens,* or *pigs,* rather than the general term *livestock*).
10. Avoid words indicating vagueness regarding some event or thing (e.g., *probably, frequently*).
11. Use wording familiar to the translators where possible.
12. Avoid sentences with two different verbs if the verbs suggest two different actions.

Steps in the Translation and Adaptation Process

Geisinger (1994) elaborated 10 steps that should be involved in any test-adaptation process. In general, these steps are an adaptation themselves of any test-development project. Other writers have altered these procedural steps to some extent, but most modifications are quite minor. Each step is listed and annotated briefly below.

1. *Translate and adapt the measure.* "Sometimes an instrument can be translated or adapted on a question-by-question basis. At other times, it must be adapted and translated only in concept" (Geisinger, 1994, p. 306). This decision must be made based on the concept of whether the content and constructs measured by the test are free from construct bias. The selection of translators is a major factor in the success of this stage, and Hambleton (1999) provides good suggestions in this regard. Translators must be knowledgeable about the content covered on the test, completely bilingual, expert about both cultures, and often able to work as part of a team.

2. *Review the translated or adapted version of the instrument.* Once the measure has been adapted, the quality of the new document must be judged. Back-translation can be employed at this stage, but it may be more effective to empanel individual or group reviews of the changed document. Geisinger (1994) suggested that members of the panel review the test individually in writing, share their comments with one another, and then meet to resolve differences of opinion and, perhaps, to rewrite portions of the draft test. The individual participants in this process must meet a number of criteria. They must be fluent in both languages and knowledgeable about both cultures. They must also understand the characteristics measured with the instrument and the likely uses to which the test is to be put. If they do not meet any one of these criteria, their assessment may be flawed.

3. *Adapt the draft instrument on the basis of the comments of the reviewers.* The individuals involved in the translation or adaptation process need to receive the feedback that arose in Step 2 and consider the comments. There may be reasons not to follow some of the suggestions of the review panel (e.g., reasons related to the validity of the instrument), and the original test author, test users, and the translator should consider these comments.

4. *Pilot-test the instrument.* It is frequently useful to have a very small number of individuals who can take the test and share concerns and reactions that they may have. They should be as similar as possible to the eventual test

takers, and they should be interviewed (or should complete a questionnaire) after taking the test. They may be able to identify problems or ambiguities in wording, in the instructions, in timing, and so on. Any changes that are needed after the pilot test should be made, and if these alterations are extensive, the test may need to be pilot-tested once again.

5. *Field-test the instrument.* This step differs from the pilot test in that it involves a large and representative sample. If the population taking the test in the target language is diverse, all elements of that diversity should be represented and perhaps overrepresented. After collection of these data, the reliability of the test should be assessed and item analyses performed. Included in the item analyses should be analyses for item bias (both as compared to the original-language version and, perhaps, across elements of diversity within the target field-testing sample). van de Vijver and Poortinga (1991) describe some of the analyses that should be performed on an item-analysis basis.

6. *Standardize the scores.* If desirable and appropriate, equate them with scores on the original version. If the sample size is large enough, it would be useful (and necessary for tests to be used in practice) to establish norms. If the field-test sample is not large enough, and the test is to be used for more than cross-cultural research in the target language, then collection of norm data is necessary. Scores may be equated back to the score scale of the original instrument, just as may be performed for any new form of a test. These procedures are beyond the scope of the present chapter, but may be found in Angoff (1971), Holland and Rubin (1982), or Kolen and Brennan (1995).

7. *Perform validation research as needed.* The validation research that is needed includes at least research to establish the equivalence to the original measure. However, as noted earlier, the concepts of construct validation represent the ideal to be sought (Embretson, 1983). Some forms of appropriate revalidation are needed before the test can be used with clients in the target language. It is appropriate to perform validation research before the test is used in research projects, as well.

8. *Develop a manual and other documents for users of the assessment device.* Users of this newly adapted instrument are going to need information so that they may employ it effectively. A manual that describes administration, scoring, and interpretation should be provided. To provide information that relates to interpretation, summarization of norms, equating (if any), reliability analyses, validity analyses, and investigations of bias should all be provided. Statements regarding the process of adaptation should be also included.

9. *Train users.* New users of any instrument need instruction so that they may use it effectively. There may be special problems associated with adapted instruments because users may tend to use materials and to employ knowledge that they have of the original measure. Although transfer of training is often positive, if there are differences between the language versions negative consequences may result.

10. *Collect reactions from users.* Whether the instrument is to be used for cross-cultural research or with actual clients, it behooves the test adaptation team to collect the thoughts of users (and perhaps of test takers as well) and to do so on a continuing basis. As more individuals take the test, the different experiential backgrounds present may identify concerns. Such comments may lead to changes in future versions of the target-language form.

METHODS OF EVALUATING TEST EQUIVALENCE

Once a test has been adapted into a target language, it is necessary to establish that the test has the kinds of equivalence that are needed for proper test interpretation and use. Methodologists and psychometricians have worked for several decades on this concern, and a number of research designs and statistical methods are available to help provide data for this analysis, which ultimately informs the test-development team to make a judgment regarding test equivalence. Such research is essential for tests that are to be used with clients in settings that differ from that in which the test was originally developed and validated.

Methods to Establish Equivalence of Scores

Historically, a number of statistical methods have been used to establish the equivalence of scores emerging from a translated test. Four techniques are noted in this section: exploratory factor analysis, structural equation modeling (including confirmatory factor analysis), regression analysis, and item-response theory. Cook, Schmitt, and Brown (1999) provide a far more detailed description of these techniques. Individual items that are translated or adapted from one language to another also should be subjected to item bias (or dif) analyses as well. Holland and Wainer (1993) have provided an excellent resource on dif techniques, and van de Vijver and Leung (1997) devote the better part of an outstanding chapter (pp. 62–88) specifically to the use of item bias techniques. Allalouf et al. (1999) and Budgell et al. (1995) are other fine examples of this methodology in the literature.

Exploratory, Replicatory Factor Analysis

Many psychological tests, especially personality measures, have been subjected to factor analysis, a technique that has often been used in psychology in an exploratory fashion to identify dimensions or consistencies among the items composing a measure (Anastasi & Urbina, 1997). To establish that the internal relationships of items or test components hold across different language versions of a test, a factor analysis of the translated version is performed. A *factor analysis* normally begins with the correlation matrix of all the items composing the measure. The factor analysis looks for patterns of consistency or factors among the items. There are many forms of factor analysis (e.g., Gorsuch, 1983) and techniques differ in many conceptual ways. Among the important decisions made in any factor analysis are determining the number of factors, deciding whether these factors are permitted to be correlated (*oblique*) or forced to be uncorrelated (*orthogonal*), and interpreting the resultant factors. A component of the factor analysis is called *rotation,* whereby the dimensions are changed mathematically to increase interpretability. The exploratory factor analysis that bears upon the construct equivalence of two measures has been called *replicatory factor analysis* (*RFA;* Ben-Porath, 1990) and is a form of cross-validation. In this instance, the number of factors and whether the factors are orthogonal or oblique are constrained to yield the same number of factors as in the original test. In addition, a rotation of the factors is made to attempt to maximally replicate the original solution; this technique is called *target rotation*. Once these procedures have been performed, the analysts can estimate how similar the factors are across solutions. van de Vijver and Leung (1997) provide indices that may be used for this judgment (e.g., the *coefficient of proportionality*). Although RFA has probably been the most used technique for estimating congruence (van de Vijver & Leung), it does suffer from a number of problems. One of these is simply that newer techniques, especially confirmatory factor analysis, can now perform a similar analysis while also testing whether the similarity is statistically significant through hypothesis testing. A second problem is that different researchers have not employed standard procedures and do not always rotate their factors to a target solution (van de Vijver & Leung). Finally, many studies do not compute indices of factor similarity across the two solutions and make this discernment only judgmentally (van de Vijver & Leung). Nevertheless, a number of outstanding researchers (e.g., Ben-Porath, 1990; Butcher, 1996)

have recommended the use of RFA to establish equivalence and this technique has been widely used, especially in validation efforts for various adaptations of the frequently translated MMPI and the Eysenck Personality Questionnaire.

Regression

Regression approaches are generally used to establish the relationships between the newly translated measure and measures with which it has traditionally correlated in the original culture. The new test can be correlated statistically with other measures, and the correlation coefficients that result may be compared statistically with similar correlation coefficients found in the original population. There may be one or more such correlated variables. When there is more than one independent variable, the technique is called *multiple regression*. In this case, the adapted test serves as the dependent variable, and the other measures as the independent variables. When multiple regression is used, the independent variables are used to predict the adapted test scores. Multiple regression weights the independent variables mathematically to optimally predict the dependent variable. The regression equation for the original test in the original culture may be compared with that for the adapted test; where there are differences between the two regression lines, whether in the slope or the intercept, or in some other manner, bias in the testing is often presumed.

If the scoring of the original- and target-language measures is the same, it is also possible to include cultural group membership in a multiple regression equation. Such a nominal variable is added as what has been called *dummy-coded* variable. In such an instance, if the dummy-coded variable is assigned a weighting as part of the multiple regression equation, indicating that it predicts test scores, evidence of cultural differences across either the two measures or the two cultures may be presumed (van de Vijver & Leung, 1997).

Structural Equation Modeling, Including Confirmatory Factor Analysis

Structural equation modeling (*SEM;* Byrne, 1994; Loehlin, 1992) is a more general and statistically sophisticated procedure that encompasses both factor analysis and regression analysis, and does so in a manner that permits elegant hypothesis testing. When SEM is used to perform factor analysis, it is typically called a *confirmatory factor analysis,* which is defined by van de Vijver and Leung (1997) as "an extension of classical exploratory factor analysis. Specific to confirmatory factor analysis is the testing of a priori specified hypotheses about the underlying structure, such as the number of factors, loadings of variables on factors, and factor correlations" (p. 99). Essentially, the results of factor-analytic studies of the measure in the original language are constrained upon the adapted measure, data from the adapted measure analyzed, and a goodness-of-fit statistical test is performed.

Regression approaches to relationships among a number of tests can also be studied with SEM. Elaborate models of relationships among other tests, measuring variables hypothesized and found through previous research to be related to the construct measured by the adapted test, also may be tested using SEM. In such an analysis, it is possible for a researcher to approximate the kind of nomological net conceptualized by Cronbach and Meehl (1955), and test whether the structure holds in the target culture as it does in the original culture. Such a test should be the ideal to be sought in establishing the construct equivalence of tests across languages and cultures.

Item-Response Theory

Item-response theory (IRT) is an alternative to classical psychometric true-score theory as a method for analyzing test data. Allen and Walsh (2000) and van de Vijver and Leung (1997) provide descriptions of the way that IRT may be used to compare items across two forms of a measure that differ by language. Although a detailed description of IRT is beyond the scope of this chapter, the briefest of explanations may provide a conceptual understanding of how the procedure is used, especially for cognitive tests. An *item characteristic curve (ICC)* is computed for each item. This curve has as the *x* axis the overall ability level of test takers, and as the *y* axis, the probability of answering the question correctly. Different IRT models have different numbers of parameters, with one-, two- and three-parameter models most common. These parameters correspond to difficulty, discrimination, and the ability to get the answer correct by chance, respectively. The ICC curves are plotted as normal ogive curves. When a test is adapted, each translated item may be compared across languages graphically by overlaying the two ICCs as well as by comparing the item parameters mathematically. If there are differences, these may be considered conceptually. This method, too, may be considered as one technique for identifying item bias.

Methods to Establish Linkage of Scores

Once the conceptual equivalence of an adapted measure has been met, researchers and test developers often wish to provide measurement-unit and metric equivalence, as well. For most measures, this requirement is met through the process of *test equating*. As noted throughout this chapter, merely translating a test from one language to another, even if cultural biases have been eliminated, does not insure that the two different-language forms of a measure are equivalent. Conceptual or construct equivalence needs to be established first. Once such a step has been taken, then one can consider higher levels of equivalence. The mathematics of equating may be found in a variety of sources (e.g., Holland & Rubin, 1982; Kolen & Brennan, 1995), and Cook et al. (1999) provide an excellent integration of research designs and analysis for test adaptation; research designs for such studies are abstracted in the following paragraphs.

Sireci (1997) clarified three experimental designs that can be used to equate adapted forms to their original-language scoring systems and, perhaps, norms. He refers to them as (a) the separate-monolingual-groups design, (b) the bilingual-group design, and (c) the matched-monolingual-groups design. A brief description of each follows.

Separate-Monolingual-Groups Design

In the separate-monolingual-groups design, two different groups of test takers are involved, one from each language or cultural group. Although some items may simply be assumed to be equivalent across both tests, data can be used to support this assumption. These items serve as what is known in equating as *anchor items*. IRT methods are then generally used to calibrate the two tests to a common scale, most typically the one used by the original-language test (Angoff & Cook, 1988; O'Brien, 1992; Sireci, 1997). Translated items must then be evaluated for invariance across the two different-language test forms; that is, they are assessed to determine whether their difficulty differs across forms. This design does not work effectively if the two groups actually differ, on average, on the characteristic that is assessed (Sireci); in fact, in such a situation, one cannot disentangle differences in the ability measured from differences in the two measures. The method also assumes that the construct measured is based on a single, unidimensional factor. Measures of complex constructs, then, are not good prospects for this method.

Bilingual-Group Design

In the bilingual-group design, a single group of bilingual individuals takes both forms of the test in counterbalanced order. An assumption of this method is that the individuals in the group are all equally bilingual, that is, equally proficient in each language. In Maldonado and Geisinger (in press), all participants first were tested in both Spanish and English competence to gain entry into the study. Even under such restrictive circumstances, however, a ceiling effect made a true assessment of equality impossible. The problem of finding equally bilingual test takers is almost insurmountable. Also, if knowledge of what is on the test in one language affects performance on the other test, it is possible to use two randomly assigned groups of bilingual individuals (where their level of language skill is equated via randomization). In such an instance, it is possible either to give each group one of the tests or to give each group one-half of the items (counterbalanced) from each test in a nonoverlapping manner (Sireci, 1997). Finally, one must question how representative the equally bilingual individuals are of the target population; thus the external validity of the sample may be questioned.

Matched-Monolingual-Groups Design

This design is conceptually similar to the separate-monolingual-groups design, except that in this case the study participants are matched on the basis of some variable expected to correlate highly with the construct measured. By being matched in this way, the two groups are made more equal, which reduces error. "There are not many examples of the matched monolingual group linking design, probably due to the obvious problem of finding relevant and available matching criteria" (Sireci, 1997, p. 17). The design is nevertheless an extremely powerful one.

CONCLUSION

Psychology has been critiqued as having a Euro-American orientation (Moreland, 1996; Padilla & Medina, 1996). Moreland wrote,

> Koch (1981) suggests that American psychologists . . . are trained in scientific attitudes that Kimble (1984) has characterized as emphasizing objectivity, data, elementism, concrete mechanisms, nomothesis, determinism, and scientific values. Dana (1993) holds that multicultural research and practice should emanate from a human science perspective characterized by the opposite of the foregoing terms: intuitive theory, holism, abstract concepts, idiography, indeterminism, and humanistic values. (p. 53)

Moreland believed that this dichotomy was a false one. Nevertheless, he argued that a balance of the two approaches was needed to understand cultural issues more completely. One of the advantages of cross-cultural psychology is that it challenges many of our preconceptions of psychology. It is often said that one learns much about one's own language when learning a foreign tongue. The analogy for psychology is clear.

Assessment in cross-cultural psychology emphasizes an understanding of the context in which assessment occurs. The notion that traditional understandings of testing and assessment have focused solely on the individual can be tested in this discipline. Cross-cultural and multicultural testing help us focus upon the broader systems of which the individual is but a part.

Hambleton (1994) stated,

> The common error is to be rather casual about the test adaptation process, and then interpret the score differences among the samples or populations as if they were real. This mindless disregard of test translation problems and the need to validate instruments in the cultures where they are used has seriously undermined the results from many cross cultural studies. (p. 242)

This chapter has shown that tests that are adapted for use in different languages and cultures need to be studied for equivalence. There are a variety of types of equivalence: linguistic equivalence, functional equivalence, conceptual or construct equivalence, and metric equivalence. Linguistic equivalence requires sophisticated translation techniques and an evaluation of the effectiveness of the translation. Functional equivalence requires that those translating the test be aware of cultural issues in the original test, in the construct, in the target culture, and in the resultant target test. Conceptual equivalence requires a relentless adherence to a construct-validation perspective and the conduct of research using data from both original and target tests. Metric equivalence, too, involves careful analyses of the test data. The requirements of metric equivalence may not be met in many situations regardless of how much we would like to use scoring scales from the original test with the target test.

If equivalence is one side of the coin, then bias is the other. Construct bias, method bias and item bias can all influence the usefulness of a test adaptation in detrimental ways. The need for construct-validation research on adapted measures is reiterated; there is no more critical point in this chapter. In addition, however, it is important to replicate the construct validation that had been found in the original culture with the original test. Factor analysis, multiple regression, and structural equation modeling permit researchers to assess whether conceptual equivalence is achieved.

The future holds much promise for cross-cultural psychology and for testing and assessment within that subdiscipline of psychology. There will be an increase in the use of different forms of tests used in both the research and the practice of psychology. In a shrinking world, it is clearer that many psychological constructs are likely to hold for individuals around the world, or at least throughout much of it. Knowledge of research from foreign settings and in foreign languages is much more accessible than in the recent past. Thus, researchers may take advantage of theoretical understandings, constructs, and their measurement from leaders all over the world. In applied settings, companies such as Microsoft are already fostering a world in which tests (such as for software literacy) are available in dozens of languages. Costs of test development are so high that adaptation and translation of assessment materials can make the cost of professional assessment cost-effective even in developing nations, where the benefits of psychological testing are likely to be highest. Computer translations of language are advancing rapidly. In some future chapter such as this one, the author may direct that the first step is to have a computer perform the first translation of the test materials. As this sentence is being written, we are not yet there; human review for cultural and language appropriateness continues to be needed. Yet in the time it will take for these pages to be printed and read, these words may have already become an anachronism.

The search for psychological universals will continue, as will the search for cultural and language limitations on these characteristics. Psychological constructs, both of major import and of more minor significance, will continue to be found that do not generalize to different cultures. The fact that the world is shrinking because of advances in travel and communications does not mean we should assume it is necessarily becoming more Western—more American. To do so is, at best, pejorative.

These times are exciting, both historically and psychometrically. The costs in time and money to develop new tests in each culture are often prohibitive. Determination of those aspects of a construct that are universal and those that are culturally specific is critical. These are new concepts for many psychologists; we have not defined cultural and racial concepts carefully and effectively and we have not always incorporated these concepts into our theories (Betancourt & López, 1993; Helms, 1992). Good procedures for adapting tests are available and the results of these efforts can be evaluated. Testing can help society and there is no reason for any country to hoard good assessment devices. Through the adaptation procedures discussed in this chapter they can be shared.

APPENDIX

Guidelines of the International Test Commission for Adapting Tests (van de Vijver & Leung, 1997, and Hambleton, 1999)

The initial guidelines relate to the testing context, as follows.

1. Effects of cultural differences that are not relevant or important to the main purposes of the study should be minimized to the extent possible.

2. The amount of overlap in the constructs in the populations of interest should be assessed.

The following guidelines relate to test translation or test adaptation.

3. Instrument developers/publishers should ensure that the translation/adaptation process takes full account of linguistic and cultural differences among the populations for whom the translated/adapted versions of the instrument are intended.

4. Instrument developers/publishers should provide evidence that the language used in the directions, rubrics, and items themselves as well as in the handbook [is] appropriate for all cultural and language populations for whom the instruments is intended.

5. Instrument developers/publishers should provide evidence that the testing techniques, item formats, test conventions, and procedures are familiar to all intended populations.

6. Instrument developers/publishers should provide evidence that item content and stimulus materials are familiar to all intended populations.

7. Instrument developers/publishers should implement systematic judgmental evidence, both linguistic and psychological, to improve the accuracy of the translation/adaptation process and compile evidence on the equivalence of all language versions.

8. Instrument developers/publishers should ensure that the data collection design permits the use of appropriate statistical techniques to establish item equivalence between the different language versions of the instrument.

9. Instrument developers/publishers should apply appropriate statistical techniques to (a) establish the equivalence of the different versions of the instrument and (b) identify problematic components or aspects of the instrument which may be inadequate to one or more of the intended populations.

10. Instrument developers/publishers should provide information on the evaluation of validity in all target populations for whom the translated/adapted versions are intended.

11. Instrument developers/publishers should provide statistical evidence of the equivalence of questions for all intended populations.

12. Nonequivalent questions between versions intended for different populations should *not* be used in preparing a common scale or in comparing these populations.

However, they may be useful in enhancing content validity of scores reported for each population separately. [emphasis in original]

The following guidelines relate to test administration.

13. Instrument developers and administrators should try to anticipate the types of problems that can be expected and take appropriate actions to remedy these problems through the preparation of appropriate materials and instructions.

14. Instrument administrators should be sensitive to a number of factors related to the stimulus materials, administration procedures, and response modes that can moderate the validity of the inferences drawn from the scores.

15. Those aspects of the environment that influence the administration of an instrument should be made as similar as possible across populations for whom the instrument is intended.

16. Instrument administration instructions should be in the source and target languages to minimize the influence of unwanted sources of variation across populations.

17. The instrument manual should specify all aspects of the instrument and its administration that require scrutiny in the application of the instrument in a new cultural context.

18. The administration should be unobtrusive, and the examiner-examinee interaction should be minimized. Explicit rules that are described in the manual for the instrument should be followed.

The final grouping of guidelines relate to documentation that is suggested or required of the test publisher or user.

19. When an instrument is translated/adapted for use in another population, documentation of the changes should be provided, along with evidence of the equivalence.

20. Score differences among samples of populations administered the instrument should *not* be taken at face value. The researcher has the responsibility to substantiate the differences with other empirical evidence. [emphasis in original]

21. Comparisons across populations can only be made at the level of invariance that has been established for the scale on which scores are reported.

22. The instrument developer should provide specific information on the ways in which the sociocultural and ecological contexts of the populations might affect performance on the instrument and should suggest procedures to account for these effects in the interpretation of results.

REFERENCES

Allalouf, A., Hambleton, R. K., & Sireci, S. G. (1999). Identifying the causes of DIF in translated verbal items. *Journal of Educational Measurement, 36,* 185–198.

Allen, J., & Walsh, J. A. (2000). A construct-based approach to equivalence: Methodologies to cross-cultural/multicultural personality assessment research. In R. H. Dana (Ed.), *Handbook of cross-cultural and multicultural personality assessment* (pp. 63–85). Mahwah, NJ: Erlbaum.

Anastasi, A., & Urbina, S. (1997). *Psychological testing* (7th ed.). Upper Saddle River, NJ: Prentice Hall.

Angoff, W. H. (1971). Scales, norms, and equivalent scores. In R. L. Thorndike (Ed.), *Educational measurement* (2nd ed., pp. 508–600). Washington, DC: American Council on Education.

Angoff, W. H., & Cook, L. L. (1988). *Equating the scores of the "Prueba de Aptitud Academica" and the "Scholastic Aptitude Test"* (Report No. 88-2). New York: College Entrance Examination Board.

Ben-Porath, Y. S. (1990). Cross-cultural assessment of personality: The case of replicatory factor analysis. In J. N. Butcher & C. D. Spielberger (Eds.), *Advances in personality assessment* (Vol. 8, pp. 27–48). Hillsdale, NJ: Erlbaum.

Berry, J. W. (1980). Introduction to methodology. In H. C. Triandis & J. W. Berry (Eds.), *Handbook of cross-cultural psychology* (Vol. 2, pp. 1–28). Boston: Allyn and Bacon.

Betancourt, H., & López, S. R. (1993). The study of culture, ethnicity, and race in American psychology. *American Psychologist, 48,* 629–637.

Bracken, B. A., & Barona, A. (1991). State of the art procedures for translating, validating, and using psychoeducational tests in cross-cultural assessment. *School Psychology International, 12,* 119–132.

Bracken, B. A., Naglieri, J., & Bardos, A. (1999, May). *Nonverbal assessment of intelligence: An alternative to test translation and adaptation.* Paper presented at the International Conference on Test Adaptation, Washington, DC.

Brislin, R. W. (1970). Back translation for cross-cultural research. *Journal of Cross-Cultural Psychology, 1,* 185–216.

Brislin, R. W. (1980). Translation and content analysis of oral and written material. In H. C. Triandis & J. W. Berry (Eds.), *Handbook of cross-cultural psychology, Vol. 2: Methodology* (pp. 389–444). Needham Heights, MA: Allyn and Bacon.

Brislin, R. W. (1986). The wording and translation of research instruments. In W. J. Lonner & J. W. Berry (Eds.), *Field methods in cross-cultural research* (pp. 137–164). Newberry Park, CA: Sage.

Brislin, R. W. (1993). *Understanding culture's influence on behavior.* New York: Harcourt Brace.

Budgell, G. R., Raju, N. S., & Quartetti, D. A. (1995). Analysis of differential item functioning in translated assessment instruments. *Applied Psychological Measurement, 19,* 309–321.

Butcher, J. N. (1996). Translation and adaptation of the MMPI-2 for international use. In J. N. Butcher (Ed.), *International adaptations of the MMPI-2* (pp. 393–411). Minneapolis: University of Minnesota Press.

Butcher, J. N., & Han, K. (1998). Methods of establishing cross-cultural equivalence. In J. N. Butcher (Ed.), *International adaptations of the MMPI-2: Research and clinical applications* (pp. 44–63). Minneapolis: University of Minnesota Press.

Butcher, J. N., & Pancheri, P. (1976). *A handbook of cross-cultural MMPI research*. Minneapolis: University of Minnesota Press.

Byrne, B. M. (1989). *A primer of LISREL: Basic applications and programming for confirmatory factor analytic models*. New York: Springer.

Byrne, B. M. (1994). *Structural equation modeling with EQS and EQS/Windows: Basic concepts, applications and programming*. Thousand Oaks, CA: Sage.

Campbell, D. T., & Fiske, D. W. (1959). Convergent and discriminant validity by the multitrait-multimethod matrix. *Psychological Bulletin, 56,* 81–105.

Cattell, R. B. (1940). A culture-free intelligence test. *Journal of Educational Psychology, 31,* 176–199.

Cattell, R. B. (1963). Theory of fluid and crystallized intelligence: A critical experiment. *Journal of Educational Psychology, 54,* 1–22.

Cattell, R. B., & Cattell, A. K. S. (1963). *A culture fair intelligence test*. Champaign, IL: Institute for Personality and Ability Testing.

Clark, L. A. (1987). Mutual relevance of mainstream and cross-cultural psychology. *Journal of Consulting and Clinical Psychology, 55,* 461–470.

Cole, M., & Bruner, J. S. (1971). Cultural differences and inferences about psychological processes. *American Psychologist, 26,* 867–876.

Cook, L., Schmitt, A., & Brown, C. (1999, May). *Adapting achievement and aptitude tests: A review of methodological issues.* Paper presented at the International Conference on Test Adaptation, Washington, DC.

Cronbach, L. J., & Meehl, P. E. (1955). Construct validity in psychological tests. *Psychological Bulletin, 52,* 281–302.

Cuéllar, I. (2000). Acculturation as a moderator of personality and psychological assessment. In R. H. Dana (Ed.), *Handbook of cross-cultural and multicultural personality assessment* (pp. 113–130). Mahwah, NJ: Erlbaum.

Dana, R. H. (1993). *Multicultural assessment perspectives for professional psychology*. Boston: Allyn and Bacon.

Domino, G. (2000). *Psychological testing: An introduction*. Upper Saddle River, NJ: Prentice Hall.

Durán, R. P. (1988). Validity and language skills assessment: Non-English background students. In H. Wainer & H. I. Braun (Eds.), *Test validity* (pp. 105–127). Hillsdale, NJ: Erlbaum.

Embretson, S. E. (1983). Construct validity: Construct representation versus nomothetic span. *Psychological Bulletin, 93,* 179–193.

Flaugher, R. J. (1978). The many definitions of test bias. *American Psychologist, 33,* 671–679.

Geisinger, K. F. (1992). Fairness and selected psychometric issues in the psychological assessment of Hispanics. In K. F. Geisinger (Ed.), *Psychological testing of Hispanics* (pp. 17–42). Washington, DC: American Psychological Association.

Geisinger, K. F. (1994). Cross-cultural normative assessment: Translation and adaptation issues influencing the normative interpretation of assessment instruments. *Psychological Assessment, 6,* 304–312.

Geisinger, K. F. (2002). Testing the members of an increasingly diverse society. In J. F. Carlson & B. B. Waterman (Eds.), *Social and personal assessment of school-aged children: Developing interventions for educational and clinical use* (pp. 349–364). Boston: Allyn and Bacon.

Geisinger, K. F., & Carlson, J. F. (1998). Training psychologists to assess members of a diverse society. In J. Sandoval, C. L. Frisby, K. F. Geisinger, J. D. Schueneman, & J. R. Grenier (Eds.), *Test interpretation and diversity: Achieving equity in assessment* (pp. 375–386). Washington, DC: American Psychological Association.

Gorsuch, R. L. (1983). *Factor analysis* (2nd ed.). Hillsdale, NJ: Erlbaum.

Hambleton, R. K. (1994). Guidelines for adapting educational and psychological tests: A progress report. *European Journal of Psychological Assessment, 10,* 229–244.

Hambleton, R. K. (1999). *Issues, designs, and technical guidelines for adapting tests in multiple languages and cultures* (Laboratory of Psychometric and Evaluative Research Report No. 353). Amherst: University of Massachusetts, School of Education.

Handel, R. W., & Ben-Porath, Y. S. (2000). Multicultural assessment with the MMPI-2: Issues for research and practice. In R. H. Dana (Ed.), *Handbook of cross-cultural and multicultural personality assessment* (pp. 229–245). Mahwah, NJ: Erlbaum.

Helms, J. E. (1992). Why is there no study of cultural equivalence in standardized cognitive ability testing? *American Psychologist, 47,* 1083–1101.

Holland, P. W., & Rubin, D. B. (Eds.). (1982). *Test equating*. New York: Academic Press.

Holland, P. W., & Wainer, H. (Eds.). (1993). *Differential item functioning*. Hillsdale, NJ: Erlbaum.

Hulin, C. L. (1987). A psychometric theory of evaluations of item and scale translations: Fidelity across languages. *Journal of Cross-Cultural Psychology, 18,* 721–735.

Kamin, L. J. (1974). *The science and politics of I.Q.* Potomac, MD: Erlbaum.

Keitel, M. A., Kopala, M., & Adamson, W. S. (1996). Ethical issues in multicultural assessment. In L. A. Suzuki, P. J. Meller, & J. G. Ponterotto (Eds.), *Handbook of multicultural assessment:*

Clinical, psychological and educational applications (pp. 28–48). San Francisco: Jossey-Bass.

Kolen, M. J., & Brennan, D. B. (1995). *Test equating: Methods and practices.* New York: Springer.

Loehlin, J. C. (1992). *Latent variable models: An introduction to factor, path, and structural equations analysis.* Hillsdale, NJ: Erlbaum.

Lonner, W. J. (1979). Issues in cross-cultural psychology. In A. J. Marsella, R. Tharp, & T. Ciborowski (Eds.), *Perspectives on cross-cultural psychology* (pp. 17–45). New York: Academic Press.

Maldonado, C. Y., & Geisinger, K. F. (in press). Conversion of the Wechsler Adult Intelligence Scale into Spanish: An early test adaptation effort of considerable consequence. In R. K. Hambleton, P. F. Merenda, & C. D. Spielberger (Eds.), *Adapting educational and psychological tests for cross-cultural assessment.* Hillsdale, NJ: Erlbaum.

Malgady, R. G. (1996). The question of cultural bias in assessment and diagnosis of ethnic minority clients: Let's reject the null hypothesis. *Professional Psychology: Research and Practice, 27,* 33–73.

Marín, G. (1992). Issues in the measurement of acculturation among Hispanics. In K. F. Geisinger (Ed.), *The psychological testing of Hispanics* (pp. 235–272). Washington, DC: American Psychological Association.

Messick, S. (1980). Test validity and the ethics of assessment. *American Psychologist, 35,* 1012–1027.

Messick, S. (1989) Validity. In R. L. Linn (Ed.), *Educational measurement* (3rd ed., pp. 13–104). New York: American Council on Education/Macmillan.

Messick, S. (1995). Validity of psychological assessment: Validation of inferences from persons' responses and performances as scientific inquiry into score meaning. *American Psychologist, 50,* 741–749.

Moreland, K. L. (1996). Persistent issues in multicultural assessment of social and emotional functioning. In L. A. Suzuki, P. J. Meller, & J. G. Ponterotto (Eds.), *Handbook of multicultural assessment: Clinical, psychological and educational applications* (pp. 51–76). San Francisco: Jossey-Bass.

Nichols, D. S., Padilla, J., & Gomez-Maqueo, E. L. (2000). Issues in the cross-cultural adaptation and use of the MMPI-2. In R. H. Dana (Ed.), *Handbook of cross-cultural and multicultural personality assessment* (pp. 247–266). Mahwah, NJ: Erlbaum.

O'Brien, M. L. (1992). A Rausch approach to scaling issues in testing Hispanics. In K. F. Geisinger (Ed.), *Psychological testing of Hispanics* (pp. 43–54). Washington, DC: American Psychological Association.

Olmeda, E. L. (1979). Acculturation: A psychometric perspective. *American Psychologist, 34,* 1061–1070.

Padilla, A. M. (1992). Reflections on testing: Emerging trends and new possibilities. In K. F. Geisinger (Ed.), *The psychological testing of Hispanics* (pp. 271–284). Washington, DC: American Psychological Association.

Padilla, A. M., & Medina, A. (1996). Cross-cultural sensitivity in assessment: Using tests in culturally appropriate ways. In L. A. Suzuki, P. J. Meller, & J. G. Ponterotto (Eds.), *Handbook of multicultural assessment: Clinical, psychological and educational applications* (pp. 3–28). San Francisco: Jossey-Bass.

Pennock-Roman, M. (1992). Interpreting test performance in selective admissions for Hispanic students. In K. F. Geisinger (Ed.), *The psychological testing of Hispanics* (pp. 99–136). Washington, DC: American Psychological Association.

Pike, K. L. (1967). *Language in relation to a unified theory of the structure of human behavior.* The Hague, The Netherlands: Mouton.

Ritzler, B. A. (1996). Projective techniques for multicultural personality assessment: Rorschach, TEMAS and the Early Memories Procedure. In L. A. Suzuki, P. J. Meller, & J. G. Ponterotto (Eds.), *Handbook of multicultural assessment: Clinical, psychological and educational applications* (pp. 115–136). San Francisco: Jossey-Bass.

Sandoval, J. (1998). Test interpretation in a diverse future. In J. Sandoval, C. L. Frisby, K. F. Geisinger, J. D. Schueneman, & J. R. Grenier (Eds.), *Test interpretation and diversity: Achieving equity in assessment* (pp. 387–402). Washington, DC: American Psychological Association.

Sattler, J. M. (1992). *Assessment of children* (Revised and updated 3rd ed.). San Diego, CA: Author.

Schmitt, A. P. (1988). Language and cultural characteristics that explain differential item functioning for Hispanic examinees on the Scholastic Aptitude Test. *Journal of Educational Measurement, 25,* 1–13.

Sireci, S. G. (1997). Problems and issues in linking assessments across languages. *Educational Measurement: Issues and Practice, 16,* 12–17.

Steele, C. M. (1997). A threat in the air: How stereotypes shape intellectual identity and performance. *American Psychologist, 52,* 613–629.

Steele, C. M., & Aronson, J. (1995). Stereotype threat and the intellectual test performance of African Americans. *Journal of Personality and Social Psychology, 69,* 797–811.

Sue, S., Keefe, K., Enomoto, K., Durvasula, R., & Chao, R. (1996). Asian American and White college students' performance on the MMPI-2. In J. N. Butcher (Ed.), *International adaptations of the MMPI-2: Research and clinical applications* (pp. 206–220). Minneapolis: University of Minnesota Press.

Sundberg, N. D., & Gonzales, L. R. (1981). Cross-cultural and cross-ethnic assessment: Overview and issues. In P. McReynolds (Ed.), *Advances in psychological assessment* (Vol. 5, pp. 460–541). San Francisco: Jossey-Bass.

Suzuki, L. A., Vraniak, D. A., & Kugler, J. F. (1996). Intellectual assessment across cultures. In L. A. Suzuki, P. J. Meller, & J. G. Ponterotto (Eds.), *Handbook of multicultural assessment: Clinical, psychological and educational applications* (pp. 141–178). San Francisco: Jossey-Bass.

Tanzer, N. K., Gittler, G., & Sim, C. Q. E. (1994). Cross-cultural validation of item complexity in an LLTM-calibrated spatial ability test. *European Journal of Psychological Assessment, 11,* 170–183.

Triandis, H. C., Malpass, R. S., & Davidson, A. (1971). Cross-cultural psychology. In B. J. Siegel (Ed.), *Biennial review of anthropology* (pp. 1–84). Palo Alto, CA: Annual Reviews.

van de Vijver, F. (2000). The nature of bias. In R. H. Dana (Ed.), *Handbook of cross-cultural and multicultural personality assessment* (pp. 87–106). Mahwah, NJ: Erlbaum.

van de Vijver, F., & Leung, K. (1997). *Methods and data analysis for cross-cultural research.* Thousand Oaks, CA: Sage.

van de Vijver, F., & Poortinga, Y. H. (1982). Cross-cultural generalization and universality. *Journal of Cross-Cultural Psychology, 13,* 387–408.

van de Vijver, F., & Poortinga, Y. H. (1991). Testing across cultures. In R. K. Hambleton & J. N. Zall (Eds.), *Advances in educational and psychological testing* (pp. 277–308). Boston: Kluwer Academic.

van de Vijver, F. J. R., & Poortinga, Y. H. (1997). Towards an integrated analysis in cross-cultural assessment. *European Journal of Psychological Assessment, 13,* 29–37.

Werner, O., & Campbell, D. T. (1970). Translating, working through interpreters, and the problem of decentering. In R. Narroll & R. Cohen (Eds.), *A handbook of cultural anthropology* (pp. 398–419). New York: American Museum of Natural History.

Yansen, E. A., & Shulman, E. L. (1996). Language testing: Multicultural considerations. In L. A. Suzuki, P. J. Meller, & J. G. Ponterotto (Eds.), *Handbook of multicultural assessment: Clinical, psychological and educational applications* (pp. 353–394). San Francisco: Jossey-Bass.

CHAPTER 6

Psychological Assessment in Treatment

MARK E. MARUISH

Society's need for behavioral health care services provides an opportunity for trained providers of mental health and substance abuse services to become part of the solution to a major health care problem. Each of the behavioral health professions has the potential to make a particular contribution to this solution. Not the least of these contributions are those that can be made by clinical psychologists. The use of psychological tests in the assessment of the human condition is one of the hallmarks of clinical psychology. The training and acquired level of expertise in psychological testing distinguishes the clinical psychologist from other behavioral health care professionals. Indeed, expertise in test-based psychological assessment can be said to be *the* unique contribution that clinical psychologists make to the behavioral health care field.

For decades, clinical psychologists and other behavioral health care providers have come to rely on psychological assessment as a standard tool to be used with other sources of information for diagnostic and treatment planning purposes. However, changes that have taken place during the past several years in the delivery of health care in general, and behavioral health care services in particular, have led to changes in the way in which third-party payers and clinical psychologists themselves think about and use psychological assessment in day-to-day clinical practice. Some question the value of psychological assessment in the current time-limited, capitated service delivery arena, where the focus has changed from clinical priorities to fiscal priorities (Sederer, Dickey, & Hermann, 1996). Others argue that it is in just such an arena that the benefits of psychological assessment can be most fully realized and contribute significantly to the delivery of cost-effective treatment for behavioral health disorders (Maruish, 1999a). Consequently, psychological assessment could assist the health care industry in appropriately controlling or reducing the utilization and cost of health care over the long term.

Portions adapted from M. E. Maruish (1999a) with permission from Erlbaum. Portions adapted from M. E. Maruish (1999b) with permission from Elsevier Science. Portions adapted from M. E. Maruish (2002) with permission from Erlbaum.

In developing this chapter, I intended to provide students and practitioners of clinical psychology with an overview of how psychological assessment can be used in the treatment of behavioral health problems. In doing so, I present a discussion of how psychological assessment in currently being used in the therapeutic environment and the many ways in which it might be used to the ultimate benefit of patients.

As a final introductory note, it is important for the reader to understand that the term *psychological assessment,* as it is used in this chapter, refers to the evaluation of a patient's mental health status using psychological tests or related instrumentation. Implicit here is the use of additional information from patient or collateral interviews, review of medical or other records, or other sources of relevant information about the patient as part of this evaluation.

PSYCHOLOGICAL ASSESSMENT AS A TREATMENT ADJUNCT: AN OVERVIEW

Traditionally, the role of psychological assessment in therapeutic settings has been quite limited. Those who did not receive their clinical training within the past few years were probably taught that the value of psychological assessment is found only at the front end of treatment. That is, they were probably instructed in the power and utility of psychological assessment as a means of assisting in the identification of symptoms and their severity, personality characteristics, and other aspects of the individual (e.g., intelligence, vocational interests) that are important in understanding and describing the patient at a specific point in time. Based on these data and information obtained from patient and collateral interviews, medical records, and the individual's stated goals for treatment, a diagnostic impression was given and a treatment plan was formulated and placed in the patient's chart, to be reviewed, it is hoped, at various points during the course of treatment. In some cases, the patient was assigned to another practitioner within the same organization or referred out, never to be seen or contacted again, much less be reassessed by the one who performed the original assessment.

Fortunately, during the past few years psychological assessment has come to be recognized for more than just its usefulness at the beginning of treatment. Consequently, its utility has been extended beyond being a mere tool for describing an individual's current state, to a means of facilitating the treatment and understanding behavioral health care problems throughout and beyond the episode of care. There are now many commercially available and public domain measures that can be employed as tools to assist in clinical decision-making and outcomes assessment, and, more directly, as a treatment technique in and of itself. Each of these uses contributes value to the therapeutic process.

Psychological Assessment for Clinical Decision-Making

Traditionally, psychological assessment has been used to assist psychologists and other behavioral health care clinicians in making important clinical decisions. The types of decision-making for which it has been used include those related to screening, diagnosis, treatment planning, and monitoring of treatment progress. Generally, screening may be undertaken to assist in either (a) identifying the patient's need for a particular service or (b) determining the likely presence of a particular disorder or other behavioral/emotional problems. More often than not, a positive finding on screening leads to a more extensive evaluation of the patient in order to confirm with greater certainty the existence of the problem or to further delineate the nature of the problem. The value of screening lies in the fact that it permits the clinician to quickly identify, with a fairly high degree of confidence, those who are likely to need care or at least require further evaluation.

Psychological assessment has long been used to obtain information necessary to determine the diagnoses of mental health patients. It may be used routinely for diagnostic purposes or to obtain information that can assist in differentiating one possible diagnosis from another in cases that present particularly complicated pictures. Indeed, even under current restrictions, managed care companies are likely to authorize payment for psychological assessment when a diagnostic question impedes the development of an appropriate treatment plan for one of its so-called covered lives.

In many instances, psychological assessment is performed in order to obtain information that is deemed useful in the development of a patient-specific treatment plan. Typically, this type of information is not easily (if at all) accessible through other means or sources. When combined with other information about the patient, information obtained from a psychological assessment can aid in understanding the patient, identifying the most important problems and issues that need to be addressed, and formulating recommendations about the best means of addressing them.

Another way psychological assessment plays a valuable role in clinical decision-making is through treatment monitoring. Repeated assessment of the patient at regular intervals during the treatment episode can provide the clinician with valuable feedback regarding therapeutic progress. Depending on the findings, the therapist will be encouraged either to continue with the original therapeutic approach or, in the case of no change or exacerbation of the problem, to modify or abandon the approach in favor of an alternate one.

Psychological Assessment for Outcomes Assessment

Currently, one of the most common reasons for conducting psychological assessment in the United States is to assess the outcomes of behavioral health care treatment. The interest in and focus on outcomes assessment can probably be traced to the continuous quality improvement (CQI) movement that was initially implemented in business and industrial settings. The impetus for the movement was a desire to produce quality products in the most efficient manner, resulting in increased revenues and decreased costs.

In health care, outcomes assessment has multiple purposes, not the least of which is as a tool for marketing the organization's services. Those provider organizations vying for lucrative contracts from third-party payers frequently must present outcomes data demonstrating the effectiveness of their services. Equally important are data that demonstrate patient satisfaction with the services they have received. However, perhaps the most important potential use of outcomes data within provider organizations (although it is not always recognized as such) is the knowledge it can yield about what works and what does not. In this regard, outcomes data can serve as a means for ongoing program evaluation. It is the knowledge obtained from outcomes data that, if acted upon, can lead to improvement in the services the organization offers. When used in this manner, outcomes assessment can become an integral component of the organization's CQI initiative.

More importantly, for the individual patient, outcomes assessment provides a means of objectively measuring how much improvement he or she has made from the time of treatment initiation to the time of treatment termination, and in some cases extending to some time after termination. Feedback to this effect may serve to instill in the patient greater self-confidence and self-esteem, or a more realistic view of where he or she is (from a psychological standpoint) at that point in time. It also may serve as an objective indicator to the patient of the need for continued treatment.

Psychological Assessment as a Treatment Technique

The degree to which the patient is involved in the assessment process has changed. One reason for this is the relatively recent revision of the ethical standards of the American Psychological Association (1992). This revision includes a mandate for psychologists to provide feedback to clients whom they assess. According to ethical standard 2.09, "psychologists ensure that an explanation of the results is provided using language that is reasonably understandable to the person assessed or to another legally authorized person on behalf of the client" (p. 8).

Finn and Tonsager (1992) offer other reasons for the recent interest in providing patients with assessment feedback. These include the recognition of patients' right to see their medical and psychiatric health care records, as well as clinically and research-based findings and impressions that suggest that *therapeutic assessment* (described below) facilitates patient care. Finn and Tonsager also refer to Finn and Butcher's (1991) summary of potential benefits that may accrue from providing test results feedback to patients about their results. These include increased feelings of self-esteem and hope, reduced symptomatology and feelings of isolation, increased self-understanding and self-awareness, and increased motivation to seek or be more actively involved in their mental health treatment. In addition, Finn and Martin (1997) note that the therapeutic assessment process provides a model for relationships that can result in increased mutual respect, lead to increased feelings of mastery and control, and decrease feelings of alienation.

Therapeutic use of assessment generally involves a presentation of assessment results (including assessment materials such as test protocols, profile forms, and other assessment summary materials) directly to the patient; an elicitation of the patient's reactions to them; and an in-depth discussion of the meaning of the results in terms of patient-defined assessment goals. In essence, assessment data can serve as a catalyst for the therapeutic encounter via (a) the objective feedback that is provided to the patient, (b) the patient self-assessment that is stimulated, and (c) the opportunity for patient and therapist to arrive at mutually agreed-upon therapeutic goals.

The purpose of the foregoing was to present a broad overview of psychological assessment as a multipurpose behavioral health care tool. Depending on the individual clinician or provider organization, it may be employed for one or more of the purposes just described. The preceding overview should provide a context for better understanding the more in-depth and detailed discussion about each of these applications that follows.

PSYCHOLOGICAL ASSESSMENT AS A TOOL FOR SCREENING AND DIAGNOSIS

One of the most apparent ways in which psychological assessment can contribute to the development of an economical and efficient behavioral health care delivery system is by using it to screen potential patients for need for behavioral health care services and to determine the likelihood that the problem identified is a particular disorder or problem of interest. Probably the most concise, informative treatment of the topic of the use of psychological tests in screening for behavioral health care disorders is provided by Derogatis and Lynn (1999). They clarify the nature and the use of screening procedures, stating that the screening process represents a relatively unrefined sieve that is designed to segregate the cohort under assessment into "positives," who presumably have the condition, and "negatives," who are ostensibly free of the disorder. Screening is not a diagnostic procedure per se. Rather, it represents a preliminary filtering operation that identifies those individuals with the highest probability of having the disorder in question for subsequent specific diagnostic evaluation. Individuals found negative by the screening process are not evaluated further (p. 42).

The most important aspect of any screening procedure is the efficiency with which it can provide information useful to clinical decision-making. In the area of clinical psychology, the most efficient and thoroughly investigated screening procedures involve the use of psychological assessment instruments. As implied by the foregoing, the power or utility of a psychological screener lies in its ability to determine, with a high level of probability, whether the respondent is or is not a member of a group with clearly defined characteristics. In daily clinical practice, the most commonly used screeners are those designed specifically to identify some aspect of psychological functioning or disturbance or provide a broad overview of the respondent's point-in-time mental status. Examples of screeners include the Beck Depression Inventory-II (BDI-II; Beck, Steer, & Brown, 1996) and the Brief Symptom Inventory (BSI; Derogatis, 1992).

The establishment of a system for screening for a particular disorder or condition involves determining what it is one wants to screen in or screen out, at what level of probability one feels comfortable about making that decision, and how many incorrect classifications or what percentage of errors one is willing to tolerate. Once one decides what one wishes to screen for, one must then turn to the instrument's classification efficiency statistics—sensitivity, specificity, positive predictive power (PPP), negative predictive power (NPP), and receiver operating characteristic (ROC) curves—for the information necessary to determine if a given instrument is suitable for the intended purpose(s). These statistics are discussed in detail in the chapter by Wasserman and Bracken in this volume.

A note of caution is warranted when evaluating sensitivity, specificity, and the two predictive powers of a test. First, the cutoff score, index value, or other criterion used for classification can be adjusted to maximize either sensitivity or specificity. However, maximization of one will necessarily result in a decrease in the other, thus increasing the percentage of false positives (with maximized sensitivity) or false negatives (with maximized specificity). Second, unlike sensitivity

and specificity, both PPP and NPP are affected and change according to the prevalence or base rate at which the condition or characteristic of interest (i.e., that which is being screened by the test) occurs within a given setting. As Elwood (1993) reports, the lowering of base rates results in lower PPPs, whereas increasing base rates results in higher PPPs. The opposite trend is true for NPPs. He notes that this is an important consideration because clinical tests are frequently validated using samples in which the prevalence rate is .50, or 50%. Thus, it is not surprising to see a test's PPP drop in real-life applications where the prevalence is lower.

DIAGNOSIS

Key to the development of any effective plan of treatment for mental health and substance abuse patients is the ascertainment of an accurate diagnosis of the problem(s) for which the patient is seeking intervention. As in the past, assisting in the differential diagnosis of psychiatric disorders continues to be one of the major functions of psychological assessment (Meyer et al., 1998). In fact, managed behavioral health care organizations (MBHOs) are more likely to authorize reimbursement of testing for this purpose than for most other reasons (Maruish, 2002). Assessment with well-validated, reliable psychological test instruments can provide information that might otherwise be difficult (if not impossible) to obtain through psychiatric or collateral interviews, medical record reviews, or other clinical means. This is generally made possible through the inclusion of (a) test items representing diagnostic criteria from an accepted diagnostic classification system, such as the fourth edition of the *Diagnostic and Statistical Manual of Mental Disorders* (*DSM-IV;* American Psychiatric Association, 1994) or (b) scales that either alone or in combination with other scales have been empirically tied (directly or indirectly) to specific diagnoses or diagnostic groups.

In most respects, considerations related to the use of psychological testing for diagnostic purposes are the same as those related to their use for screening. In fact, information obtained from screening can be used to help determine the correct diagnosis for a given patient. As well, information from either source should be used only in conjunction with other clinical information to arrive at a diagnosis. The major differentiation between the two functions is that screening generally involves the use of a relatively brief instrument for the identification of patients with a specific diagnosis, a problem that falls within a specific diagnostic grouping (e.g., affective disorders), or a level of impairment that falls within a problematic range. Moreover, it represents the first step in a process designed to separate those who do not exhibit indications of the problem being screened for from those with a higher probability of experiencing the target problem and thus warrant further evaluation for its presence. Diagnostic instruments such as those just mentioned generally tend to be lengthier, differentiate among multiple disorders or broad diagnostic groups (e.g., anxiety disorders vs. affective disorders), or are administered further along in the evaluation process than is the case with screeners. In many cases, these instruments also allow for a formulation of description of personality functioning.

Diagnosis-Specific Instruments

There are many instruments available that have been specifically designed to help identify individuals with disorders that meet a diagnostic classification system's criteria for the disorder(s). In the vast majority of the cases, these types of tests will be designed to detect individuals meeting the diagnostic criteria of *DSM-IV* or the 10th edition of the *International Classification of Diseases* (*ICD-10;* World Health Organization, 1992). Excellent examples of such instruments include the Millon Clinical Multiaxial Inventory-III (MCMI-III; Millon, 1994), the Primary Care Evaluation of Mental Disorders (PRIME-MD; Spitzer et al., 1994), the Patient Health Questionnaire (PHQ, the self-report version of the PRIME-MD; Spitzer, Kroenke, Williams, & Patient Health Questionnaire Primary Care Study Group, 1999); the Mini-International Neuropsychiatric Interview (MINI; Sheehan et al., 1998).

Like many of the instruments developed for screening purposes, most diagnostic instruments are accompanied by research-based diagnostic efficiency statistics—sensitivity, specificity, PPP, NPP, and overall classification rates—that provide the user with estimates of the probability of accurate classification of those having or not having one or more specific disorders. One typically finds classification rates of the various disorders assessed by any of these types of instrument to vary considerably. For example, the PPPs for those disorders assessed by the PRIME-MD (Spitzer et al., 1999) range from 19% for minor depressive disorder to 80% for major depressive disorder. For the self-report version of the MINI (Sheehan et al., 1998), the PPPs ranged from 11% for dysthymia to 75% for major depressive disorder. Generally, NPPs and overall classification rates are found to be relatively high and show a lot less variability across diagnostic groups. For the PRIME-MD, overall accuracy rates ranged from 84% for anxiety not otherwise specified to 96% for panic disorder, whereas MINI NPPs ranged from 81% for major depressive disorder to 99% for anorexia. Thus, it would appear that one can feel more confident in the results from these instruments when they indicate that the patient does *not* have a particular disorder. This, of course, is going to vary from instrument to instrument and disorder to disorder. For diagnostic instruments such as these, it is therefore important for the user to be aware of what the research has demonstrated as far the instrument's classification accuracy for *each individual disorder,* since this may vary within and between measures.

Personality Measures and Symptom Surveys

There are a number of instruments that, although not specifically designed to arrive at a diagnosis, can provide information that is suggestive of a diagnosis or diagnostic group (e.g., affective disorders) or can assist in the differential diagnosis of complicated cases. These include multiscale instruments that list symptoms and other aspects of psychiatric disorders and ask respondents to indicate if or how much they are bothered by each of these, or whether certain statements are true or false as they apply to them. Generally, research on these instruments has found elevated scores on individual scales, or patterns or profiles of multiple elevated scores, to be associated with specific disorders or diagnostic groups. Thus, when present, these score profiles are suggestive of the presence of the associated type of pathology and bear further investigation. This information can be used either as a starting place in the diagnostic process or as additional information to support an already suspected problem.

Probably the best known of this type of instrument is the Minnesota Multiphasic Personality Inventory–2 (MMPI-2; Butcher, Dahlstrom, Graham, Tellegen, & Kaemmer, 1989). It has a substantial body of research indicating that certain elevated scale and subscale profiles or code types are strongly associated with specific diagnoses or groups of diagnoses (see Graham, 2000, and Greene, 2000). For example, an 8-9/9-8 highpoint code type (Sc and Ma scales being the highest among the significantly elevated scales) is associated with schizophrenia, whereas the 4-9/9-4 code type is commonly associated with a diagnosis of antisocial personality disorder. Similarly, research on the Personality Assessment Inventory (PAI; Morey, 1991, 1999) has demonstrated typical patterns of PAI individual and multiple-scale configurations that also are diagnostically related. For one PAI profile cluster—prominent elevations on the DEP and SUI scales with additional elevations on the SCZ, STR, NON, BOR, SOM, ANX, and ARD scales—the most frequently associated diagnoses were major depression (20%), dysthymia (23%), and anxiety disorder (23%). Sixty-two percent of those with a profile cluster consisting of prominent elevations on ALC and SOM with additional elevations on DEP, STR, and ANX were diagnosed with alcohol abuse or dependence.

In addition, there are other well-validated, single- or multi-scale symptom checklists that can also be useful for diagnostic purposes. They provide means of identifying symptom domains (e.g., anxiety, depression, somatization) that are problematic for the patient, thus providing diagnostic clues and guidance for further exploration to the assessing psychologist. The BDI-II and STAI are good examples of well validated, single-scale symptom measures. Multiscale instruments include measures such as the Symptom Checklist-90-Revised (SCL-90-R; Derogatis, 1983) and the Symptom Assessment-45 Questionnaire (SA-45; Strategic Advantage, Inc., 1996).

Regardless of the psychometric property of any given instrument for any disorder or symptom domain evaluated by that instrument, or whether it was developed for diagnostic purposes or not, one should never rely on test findings alone when assigning a diagnosis. As with any other psychological test instruments, diagnosis should be based on findings from the test and from other sources, including findings from other instruments, patient and collateral interviews, reviews of psychiatric and medical records (when available), and other pertinent documents.

PSYCHOLOGICAL ASSESSMENT AS A TOOL FOR TREATMENT PLANNING

Psychological assessment can provide information that can greatly facilitate and enhance the planning of a specific therapeutic intervention for the individual patient. It is through the implementation of a tailored treatment plan that the patient's chances of problem resolution are maximized. The importance of treatment planning has received significant attention during recent years. The reasons for this recognition include

> concerted efforts to make psychotherapy more efficient and cost effective, the growing influence of "third parties" (insurance companies and the federal government) that are called upon to foot the bill for psychological as well as medical treatments, and society's disenchantment with open-ended forms of psychotherapy without clearly defined goals. (Maruish, 1990, p. iii)

The role that psychological assessment can play in planning a course of treatment for behavioral health care problems is significant. Butcher (1990) indicated that information available from instruments such as the MMPI-2 not only can assist in identifying problems and establishing communication with the patient, but can also help ensure that the plan for treatment is consistent with the patient's personality and external resources. In addition, psychological assessment

may reveal potential obstacles to therapy, areas of potential growth, and problems that the patient may not be consciously aware of. Moreover, both Butcher (1990) and Appelbaum (1990) viewed testing as a means of quickly obtaining a second opinion. Other benefits of the results of psychological assessment identified by Appelbaum include assistance in identifying patient strengths and weaknesses, identification of the complexity of the patient's personality, and establishment of a reference point during the therapeutic episode. And as Strupp (cited in Butcher, 1990) has noted, "It will predictably save money and avoid misplaced therapeutic effort; it can also enhance the likelihood of favorable treatment outcomes for suitable patients" (pp. v–vi).

The Benefits of Psychological Assessment for Treatment Planning

As has already been touched upon, there are several ways in which psychological assessment can assist in the planning of treatment for behavioral health care patients. The more common and evident contributions can be organized into four general categories: problem identification, problem clarification, identification of important patient characteristics, and prediction of treatment outcomes.

Problem Identification

Probably the most common use of psychological assessment in the service of treatment planning is for problem identification. Often, the use of psychological testing per se is not needed to identify what problems the patient is experiencing. He or she will either tell the clinician directly without questioning or admit his or her problem(s) while being questioned during a clinical interview. However, this is not always the case.

The value of psychological testing becomes apparent in those cases in which the patient is hesitant or unable to identify the nature of his or her problems. In addition, the nature of some of the more commonly used psychological test instruments allows for the identification of secondary, but significant, problems that might otherwise be overlooked. Note that the type of problem identification described here is different from that conducted during screening (see earlier discussion). Whereas screening is commonly focused on determining the presence or absence of a single problem, problem identification generally takes a broader view and investigates the possibility of the presence of multiple problem areas. At the same time, there also is an attempt to determine problem severity and the extent to which the problem area(s) affect the patient's ability to function.

Problem Clarification

Psychological testing can often assist in the clarification of a known problem. Through tests designed for use with populations presenting problems similar to those of the patient, aspects of identified problems can be elucidated. Information gained from these tests can both improve the patient's and clinician's understanding of the problem and lead to the development of a better treatment plan. The three most important types of information that can be gleaned for this purpose are the severity of the problem, the complexity of the problem, and the degree to which the problem impairs the patient's ability to function in one or more life roles.

Identification of Important Patient Characteristics

The identification and clarification of the patient's problems is of key importance in planning a course of treatment. However, there are numerous other types of patient information not specific to the identified problem that can be useful in planning treatment and that may be easily identified through the use of psychological assessment instruments. The vast majority of treatment plans are developed or modified with consideration to at least some of these nonpathological characteristics. The exceptions are generally found with clinicians or programs that take a one-size-fits-all approach to treatment.

Probably the most useful type of information that is not specific to the identified problem but can be gleaned from psychological assessment is the identification of patient characteristics that can serve as assets or areas of strength for the patient in working to achieve his or her therapeutic goals. For example, Morey and Henry (1994) point to the utility of the PAI's Nonsupport scale in identifying whether the patient perceives an adequate social support network, which is a predictor of positive therapeutic change.

Similarly, knowledge of the patient's weaknesses or deficits may also affect the type of treatment plan that is devised. Greene and Clopton (1999) provided numerous types of deficit-relevant information from the MMPI-2 content scales that have implications for treatment planning. For example, a clinically significant score (T > 64) on the Anger scale should lead one to consider the inclusion of training in assertiveness or anger control techniques as part of the patient's treatment. On the other hand, uneasiness in social situations, as suggested by a significantly elevated score on either the Low Self-Esteem or Social Discomfort scale, suggests that a supportive approach to the intervention would be beneficial, at least initially.

Moreover, use of specially designed scales and procedures can provide information related to the patient's ability to

become engaged in the therapeutic process. For example, the Therapeutic Reactance Scale (Dowd, Milne, & Wise, 1991) and the MMPI-2 Negative Treatment Indicators content scale developed by Butcher and his colleagues (Butcher, Graham, Williams, & Ben-Porath, 1989) may be useful in determining whether the patient is likely to resist therapeutic intervention.

Other types of patient characteristics that can be identified through psychological assessment have implications for selecting the best therapeutic approach for a given patient and thus can contribute significantly to the treatment planning process. Moreland (1996), for example, pointed out how psychological assessment can assist in determining whether the patient deals with problems through internalizing or externalizing behaviors. He noted that, all other things being equal, internalizers would probably profit more from an insight-oriented approach than a behaviorally oriented approach. The reverse would be true for externalizers. Through their work over the years, Beutler and his colleagues (Beutler & Clarkin, 1990; Beutler, Wakefield, & Williams, 1994) have identified several other patient characteristics that are important to matching patients and treatment approaches for maximized therapeutic effectiveness.

Prediction of Treatment Outcomes

An important consideration in the development of a treatment plan has to do with the likely outcome of treatment. In other words, how likely is it that a given patient with a given set of problems or level of dysfunction will benefit from any of the treatment options that are available? In some cases, the question is, what is the probability that the patient will significantly benefit from *any* type of treatment? In many cases, psychological test results can yield empirically based predictions that can assist in answering these questions. In doing so, the most effective treatment can be implemented immediately, saving time, health care benefits, and potential exacerbation of problems that might result from implementation of a less than optimal course of care.

The ability to predict outcomes is going to vary from test to test and even within individual tests, depending on the population being assessed and what one would like to predict. For example, Chambless, Renneberg, Goldstein, and Gracely (1992) were able to detect predictive differences in MCMI-II-identified (Millon, 1987) personality disorder patients seeking treatment for agoraphobia and panic attacks. Patients classified as having an MCMI-II avoidant disorder were more likely to have poorer outcomes on measures of depression, avoidance, and social phobia than those identified as having dependent or histrionic personality disorders. Also, paranoid personality disorder patients were likely to drop out before receiving

10 sessions of treatment. In another study, Chisholm, Crowther, and Ben-Porath (1997) did not find any of the seven MMPI-2 scales they investigated to be particularly good predictors of early termination in a sample of university clinic outpatients. They did find that the Depression (DEP) and Anxiety (ANX) content scales were predictive of other treatment outcomes. Both were shown to be positively associated with therapist-rated improvement in current functioning and global psychopathology, with ANX scores also being related to therapist- rated progress toward therapy goals.

The reader is referred to Meyer et al. (1998) for an excellent overview of the research supporting the use of objective and projective test results for outcomes prediction as well as for other clinical decision-making purposes. Moreover, the use of patient profiling for the prediction of treatment outcome is discussed later in this chapter.

PSYCHOLOGICAL ASSESSMENT AS A TREATMENT INTERVENTION

The use of psychological assessment as an adjunct to or means of therapeutic intervention in and of itself has received more than passing attention during the past several years (e.g., Butcher, 1990; Clair & Prendergast, 1994). Therapeutic assessment with the MMPI-2 has received particular attention primarily through the work of Finn and his associates (Finn, 1996a, 1996b; Finn & Martin, 1997; Finn & Tonsager, 1992). Finn's approach appears to be applicable with instruments or batteries of instruments that provide multidimensional information relevant to the concerns of patients seeking answers to questions related to their mental health status. The approach espoused by Finn will thus be presented here as a model for deriving direct therapeutic benefits from the psychological assessment experience.

What Is Therapeutic Assessment?

In discussing the use of the MMPI-2 as a therapeutic intervention, Finn (1996b) describes an assessment procedure whose goal is to "gather accurate information about clients . . . and then use this information to help clients understand themselves and make positive changes in their lives" (p. 3). Simply stated, therapeutic assessment may be considered an approach to the assessment of mental health patients in which the patient is not only the primary provider of information needed to answer questions but also actively involved in formulating the questions that are to be answered by the assessment. Feedback regarding the results of the assessment is provided to the patient and is considered a primary, if not *the* primary, element of the assessment process. Thus, the patient becomes a partner

in the assessment process; as a result, therapeutic and other benefits accrue.

The Therapeutic Assessment Process

Finn (1996b) has outlined a three-step procedure for therapeutic assessment using the MMPI-2 in those situations in which the patient is seen *only* for assessment. It should work equally well with other multidimensional instruments and with patients the clinician later treats.

Step 1: The Initial Interview

According to Finn (1996b), the initial interview with the patient serves multiple purposes. It provides an opportunity to build rapport, or to increase rapport if a patient-therapist relationship already exists. The assessment task is presented as a collaborative one. The therapist gathers background information, addresses concerns, and gives the patient the opportunity to identify questions that he or she would like answered using the assessment data. Step 1 is completed as the instrumentation and its administration are clearly defined and the particulars (e.g., time of testing) are agreed upon.

Step 2: Preparing for the Feedback Session

Upon the completion of the administration and scoring of the instrumentation used during the assessment, the clinician first outlines all results obtained from the assessment, including those not directly related to the patient's previously stated questions. This is followed by a determination of how to present the results to the patient (Finn, 1996b). The clinician must also determine the best way to present the information to the patient so that he or she can accept and integrate it while maintaining his or her sense of identity and self-esteem.

Step 3: The Feedback Session

As Finn (1996b) states, "The overriding goal of feedback sessions is to have a therapeutic interaction with clients" (p. 44). This begins with the setting of the stage for this type of encounter before the clinician answers the questions posed by the patient during Step 1. Beginning with a positive finding from the assessment, the clinician proceeds first to address those questions whose answers the patient is most likely to accept. He or she then carefully moves to the findings that are more likely to be anxiety-arousing for the patient or challenge his or her self-concept. A key element to this step is to have the patient verify the accuracy of each finding and provide a real-life example of the interpretation that is offered. Alternately, the clinician asks the patient to modify the interpretation to make it more in line with how the patient sees him- or herself and the situation. Throughout the session, the clinician maintains a supportive stance with regard to any affective reactions to the findings.

Additional Steps

Finn and Martin (1997) indicate two additional steps that may be added to the therapeutic assessment process. The purpose of the first additional step, referred to as an *assessment intervention session,* is essentially to clarify initial test findings through the administration of additional instruments. The other additional step discussed by Finn and Martin (1997) is the provision of a written report of the findings to the patient.

Empirical Support for Therapeutic Assessment

Noting the lack of direct empirical support for the therapeutic effects of sharing test results with patients, Finn and Tonsager (1992) investigated the benefits of providing feedback to university counseling center clients regarding their MMPI-2 results. Thirty-two participants underwent therapeutic assessment and feedback procedures similar to those described above while on the counseling center's waiting list. Another 28 participants were recruited from the same waiting list to serve as a control group. Instead of receiving feedback, Finn and Tonsager's (1992) control group received nontherapeutic attention from the examiner. However, they were administered the same dependent measures as the feedback group at the same time that the experimental group received feedback. They were also administered the same dependent measures as the experimental group two weeks later (i.e., two weeks after the experimental group received the feedback) in order to determine if there were differences between the two groups on those dependent measures. These measures included a self-esteem questionnaire, a symptom checklist (the SCL-90-R), a measure of private and public self-consciousness, and a questionnaire assessing the subjects' subjective impressions of the feedback session.

The results of Finn and Tonsager's (1992) study indicated that compared to the control group, the feedback group demonstrated significantly less distress at the two-week postfeedback follow-up and significantly higher levels of self-esteem and hope at both the time of feedback and the two-week postfeedback follow-up. In other findings, feelings about the feedback sessions were positively and significantly correlated with changes in self-esteem from testing to feedback, both from feedback to follow-up and from testing to follow-up among those who were administered the MMPI-2. In addition, change in level of distress from feedback to follow-up correlated significantly with private self-consciousness (i.e., the tendency to

focus on the internal aspects of oneself) but not with public self-consciousness.

M. L. Newman and Greenway (1997) provided support for Finn and Tonsager's findings in their study of 60 Australian college students. Clients given MMPI-2 feedback reported an increase in self-esteem and a decrease in psychological distress that could not be accounted for by their merely completing the MMPI-2. At the same time, changes in self-esteem or symptomatology were not found to be related to either the level or type of symptomatology at the time of the first assessment. Also, the clients' attitudes toward mental health professionals (as measured by the MMPI-2 TRT scale) were not found to be related to level of distress or self-esteem. Their results differed from those of Finn and Tonsager in that general satisfaction scores were not associated with change in self-esteem or change in symptomatology, nor was private self-consciousness found to be related to changes in symptomatology. Recognizing the limitations of their study, Newman and Greenway's recommendations for future research in this area included examination of the components of therapeutic assessment separately and the use of different patient populations and different means of assessing therapeutic change (i.e., use of both patient and therapist/third party report).

Overall, the research on the benefits of therapeutic assessment is limited but promising. The work of Finn and others should be extended to include other patient populations with more severe forms of psychological disturbance and to reassess study participants over longer periods of follow-up. Moreover, the value of the technique when used with instrumentation other than the MMPI-2 warrants investigation.

TREATMENT MONITORING

Monitoring treatment progress with psychological assessment instruments can prove to be quite valuable, especially with patients who are seen over relatively long periods of time. If the treatment is inefficient, inappropriate or otherwise not resulting in the expected effects, changes in the treatment plan can be formulated and deployed. These adjustments may reflect the need for (a) more intensive or aggressive treatment (e.g., increased number of psychotherapeutic sessions each week, addition of a medication adjunct); (b) less intensive treatment (e.g., reduction or discontinuation of medication, transfer from inpatient to outpatient care); or (c) a different therapeutic approach (e.g., a change from humanistic therapy to cognitive-behavioral therapy). Regardless, any modifications require later reassessment of the patient to determine if the treatment revisions have affected patient progress in the expected direction. This process may be repeated any number of times. These in-treatment reassessments also can provide information relevant to the decision of when to terminate treatment.

Monitoring Change

Methods for determining if statistically and clinically significant change has occurred from one point in time to another have been developed and can be used for treatment monitoring. Many of these methods are the same as those that can be used for outcomes assessment and are discussed later in this chapter. In addition, the reader is also referred to an excellent discussion of analyzing individual and group change data in F. L. Newman and Dakof (1999) and F. L. Newman and Tejeda (1999).

Patient profiling is yet another approach to monitoring therapeutic change that can prove to be more valuable than looking at simple changes in test scores from one point in time to another. Patient profiling involves the generation of an expected curve of recovery over the course of psychotherapy based on the observed recovery of similar patients (Howard, Moras, Brill, Martinovich, & Lutz, 1996; Leon, Kopta, Howard, & Lutz, 1999). An individual recovery curve is generated from selected clinical characteristics (e.g., severity and chronicity of the problem, attitudes toward treatment, scores on treatment-relevant measures) present at the time of treatment onset. This curve will enable the clinician to determine if the patient is on the expected track for recovery through the episode of care. Multiple measurements of the clinical characteristics during the course of treatment allow a comparison of the patient's actual score with that which would be expected from similar individuals after the same number of treatment sessions. The therapist thus knows when the treatment is working and when it is not working so that any necessary adjustments in the treatment strategy can be made.

Other Uses for Patient Profiling

Aside from its obvious treatment value, treatment monitoring data can support decisions regarding the need for continued treatment. This holds true whether the data are nothing more than a set of scores from a relevant measure (e.g., a symptom inventory) administered at various points during treatment, or are actual and expected recovery curves obtained by the Howard et al. (1996) patient profiling method. Expected and actual data obtained from patient profiling can easily point to the likelihood that additional sessions are needed or would be significantly beneficial for the patient. Combined with clinician impressions, these data can make a powerful case for the patient's need for additional treatment sessions or, conversely, for treatment termination.

As well as the need for supporting decisions regarding additional treatment sessions for patients already in treatment, there are indications that patient profiling may also be useful in making initial treatment-related decisions. Leon et al. (1999) sought to determine whether patients whose actual response curve matched or exceeded (i.e., performed better than) the expectancy curve could be differentiated from those whose actual curve failed to match their expectancy curve on the basis of pretreatment clinical characteristics. They first generated patient profiles for 821 active outpatients and found a correlation of .57 ($p < .001$) between the actual and expected slopes. They then used half of the original sample to develop a discriminate function that was able to significantly discriminate ($p < .001$) patients whose recovery was predictable (i.e., those with consistent actual and expected curves) from those whose recovery was not predictable (i.e., those with inconsistent curves). The discriminant function was based on 15 pretreatment clinical characteristics (including the subscales and items of the Mental Health Index, or MHI; Howard, Brill, Lueger, O'Mahoney, & Grissom, 1993) and was cross-validated with the other half of the original sample. In both subsamples, lower levels of symptomatology and higher levels of functioning were associated with those in the predictable group of patients.

The implications of these findings are quite powerful. According to Leon et al. (1999),

> The patient profiling-discriminant approach provides promise for moving toward the reliable identification of patients who will respond more rapidly in psychotherapy, who will respond more slowly in psychotherapy, or who will demonstrate a low likelihood of benefiting from this type of treatment.
>
> The implications of these possibilities for managed mental health care are compelling. . . . [A] reliable prediction system—even for a proportion of patients—would improve efficiency, thereby reducing costs in the allocation and use of resources for mental health care. For instance, patients who would be likely to drain individual psychotherapeutic resources while achieving little or no benefit could be identified at intake and moved into more promising therapeutic endeavors (e.g., medication or group psychotherapy). Others, who are expected to succeed but are struggling could have their treatment reviewed and then modified in order to get them back on track. . . . Patients who need longer term treatment could justifiably get it because the need would be validated by a reliable, empirical methodology. (p. 703)

The Effects of Providing Feedback to the Therapist

Intuitively, one would expect that patient profiling information would result in positive outcomes for the patient. Is this really the case, though? Lambert et al. (1999) sought to answer this question by conducting a study to determine if patients whose therapists receive feedback about their progress (experimental group) would have better outcomes and better treatment attendance (an indicator of cost-effective psychotherapy) than those patients whose therapists did not receive this type of feedback (control group). The feedback provided to the experimental group's therapists came in the form of a weekly updated numerical and color-coded report based on the baseline and current total scores of the Outcome Questionnaire (OQ-45; Lambert et al., 1996) and the number of sessions that the patient had completed. The feedback report also contained one of four possible interpretations of the patient's progress (not making expected level of progress, may have negative outcome or drop out of treatment, consider revised or new treatment plan, reassess readiness for change).

The Lambert et al. (1999) findings from this study were mixed and lend only partial support for benefits accruing from the use of assessment-based feedback to therapists. They also suggested that information provided in a feedback report alone is not sufficient to maximize its impact on the quality of care provided to a patient; that is, the information must be put to use. The use of feedback to therapists appears to be beneficial, but further research in this area is called for.

Notwithstanding whether it is used as fodder for generating complex statistical predictions or for simple point-in-time comparisons, psychological test data obtained for treatment monitoring can provide an empirically based means of determining the effectiveness of mental health and substance abuse treatment during an episode of care. Its value lies in its ability to support ongoing treatment decisions that must be made using objective data. Consequently, it allows for improved patient care while supporting efforts to demonstrate accountability to the patient and interested third parties.

OUTCOMES ASSESSMENT

The 1990s witnessed accelerating growth in the level of interest and development of behavioral health care outcomes programs. The interest in and necessity for outcomes measurement and accountability in this era of managed care provide a unique opportunity for psychologists to use their training and skills in assessment (Maruish, 1999a). However, the extent to which psychologists and other trained professionals become a key and successful contributor to an organization's outcomes initiative will depend on their understanding of what outcomes and their measurement and applications are all about.

What Are Outcomes?

Outcomes is a term that refers to the results of the specific treatment that was rendered to a patient or group of patients.

Along with structure and process, outcomes is one component of what Donabedian (1980, 1982, 1985) refers to as "quality of care." The first component is *structure*. This refers to various aspects of the organization providing the care, including how the organization is organized, the physical facilities and equipment, and the number and professional qualifications of its staff. *Process* refers to the specific types of services that are provided to a given patient (or group of patients) during a specific episode of care. These might include various tests and assessments (e.g., psychological tests, lab tests, magnetic resonance imaging), therapeutic interventions (e.g., group psychotherapy, medication), and discharge planning activities. *Outcomes,* on the other hand, refers to the results of the specific treatment that was rendered.

In considering the types of outcomes that might be assessed in behavioral health care settings, a substantial number of clinicians would probably identify symptomatic change in psychological status as being the most important. However, no matter how important change in symptom status may have been in the past, psychologists and other behavioral health care providers have come to realize that change in many other aspects of functioning identified by Stewart and Ware (1992) are equally important indicators of treatment effectiveness. As Sederer et al. (1996) have noted,

> Outcome for patients, families, employers, and payers is not simply confined to symptomatic change. Equally important to those affected by the care rendered is the patient's capacity to function within a family, community, or work environment or to exist independently, without undue burden to the family and social welfare system. Also important is the patient's ability to show improvement in any concurrent medical and psychiatric disorder. . . . Finally, not only do patients seek symptomatic improvement, but they want to experience a subjective sense of health and well being. (p. 2)

The Use of Outcomes Assessment in Treatment

Following are considerations and recommendations for the development and implementation of outcomes assessment by psychologists. Although space limitations do not allow a comprehensive review of all issues and solutions, the information that follows touches upon matters that are most important to psychologists who wish to incorporate outcomes assessment into their standard therapeutic routine.

Measurement Domains

The specific aspects or dimensions of patient functioning that are measured as part of outcomes assessment will depend on the purpose for which the assessment is being conducted. Probably the most frequently measured variable is that of symptomatology or psychological/mental health status. After all, disturbance or disruption in this dimension is probably the most common reason why people seek behavioral health care services in the first place. However, there are other reasons for seeking help. Common examples include difficulties in coping with various types of life transitions (e.g., a new job, a recent marriage or divorce, other changes in the work or home environment), an inability to deal with the behavior of others (e.g., spouse, children), or general dissatisfaction with life. Additional assessment of related variables may therefore be necessary or even take precedence over the assessment of symptoms or other indicators.

For some patients, measures of one or more specific psychological disorders or symptom clusters are at least as important as, if not more important than, overall symptom or mental health status. Here, if interest is in only one disorder or symptom cluster (e.g., depression), one may choose to measure only that particular set of symptoms using an instrument designed specifically for that purpose (e.g., the BDI-II would be used with depressed patients). For those interested in assessing the outcomes of treatment relative to multiple psychological dimensions, the administration of more than one disorder-specific instrument or a single, multiscale instrument that assesses all or most of the dimensions of interest (e.g., BSI) would be required. Again, instruments such as the SA-45 or the BSI can provide a quick, broad assessment of several symptom domains.

It is not always a simple matter to determine exactly what should be measured. However, careful consideration of the following questions should greatly facilitate the decision: Why did the patient seek services? What does the patient hope to gain from treatment? What are the patient's criteria for successful treatment? What are the clinician's criteria for the successful completion of the current therapeutic episode? What, if any, are the outcomes initiatives within the provider organization? Note that the selection of the variables to be assessed may address more than one of the above issues. Ideally, this is what should happen. However, one needs to ensure that the task of gathering outcomes data does not become too burdensome. The key is to identify the point at which the amount of data that can be obtained from a patient or collaterals and the ease at which they can be gathered are optimized.

Measurement Methodology

Once the decision of *what* to measure has been made, one must then decide *how* it should be measured. In many cases, the most important data will be those that are obtained directly from the patient using self-report instruments. Underlying

this assertion is the assumption that valid and reliable instrumentation, appropriate to the needs of the patient, is available to the clinician; the patient can read at the level required by the instruments; and the patient is motivated to respond honestly to the questions asked. Barring one or more of these conditions, other options should be considered.

Other types of data-gathering tools may be substituted for self-report measures. Rating scales completed by the clinician or other members of the treatment staff may provide information that is as useful as that elicited directly from the patient. In those cases in which the patient is severely disturbed, unable to give valid and reliable answers (as in the case of younger children), unable to read, or otherwise an inappropriate candidate for a self-report measure, clinical rating scales, such as the Brief Psychiatric Rating Scale (BPRS; Faustman & Overall, 1999; Overall & Gorham, 1962) and the Child and Adolescent Functional Assessment Scale (CAFAS; Hodges, 1994), can serve as a valuable substitute for gathering information about the patient. Related to these instruments are parent-completed instruments for child and adolescent patients, such as the Child Behavior Checklist (CBCL; Achenbach, 1991) and the Personality Inventory for Children-2 (PIC-2; Lachar & Gruber, 2001). Collateral rating instruments and parent-report instruments can also be used to gather information in addition to that obtained from self-report measures. When used in this manner, these instruments provide a mechanism by which the clinician, other treatment staff, and parents, guardians, or other collaterals can contribute data to the outcomes assessment endeavor.

When to Measure

There are no hard and fast rules or widely accepted conventions related to when outcomes should be assessed. The common practice is to assess the patient at least at treatment initiation and again at termination or discharge. Additional assessment of the patient on the variables of interest can take place at other points as part of postdischarge follow-up.

Many would argue that postdischarge or posttermination follow-up assessment provides the best or most important indication of the outcomes of therapeutic intervention. In general, postdischarge outcomes assessment should probably take place no sooner than 1 month after treatment has ended. When feasible, waiting 3–6 months to assess the variables of interest is preferred. A longer interval between discharge and postdischarge follow-up should provide a more valid indication of the lasting effects of treatment. Comparison of the patient's status on the variables of interest at the time of follow-up with that found at the time of either treatment initiation or termination will provide an indication of the more lasting effects of the intervention. Generally, the variables of interest for this type of comparison include symptom presence and intensity, feeling of well-being, frequency of substance use, and social or role functioning.

Although it provides what is arguably the best and most useful outcomes information, a program of postdischarge follow-up assessment is also the most difficult to successfully implement. There must be a commitment of staff and other resources to track terminated patients; contact them at the appropriate times to schedule a reassessment; and process, analyze, report, and store the follow-up data. The task is made more difficult by frequently noted difficulties in locating terminated patients whose contact information has changed, or convincing those who can be located to complete a task from which they will not directly benefit. However, those organizations and individual clinicians who are able to overcome the barriers will find the fruits of their efforts quite rewarding.

Analysis of Outcomes Data

There are two general approaches to the analysis of treatment outcomes data. The first is by determining whether changes in patient scores on outcomes measures are statistically significant. The other is by establishing whether these changes are clinically significant. Use of standard tests of statistical significance is important in the analysis of group or population change data. Clinical significance is more relevant to change in the individual patient's scores.

The issue of clinical significance has received a great deal of attention in psychotherapy research during the past several years. This is at least partially owing to the work of Jacobson and his colleagues (Jacobson, Follette, & Revenstorf, 1984, 1986; Jacobson & Truax, 1991) and others (e.g., Christensen & Mendoza, 1986; Speer, 1992; Wampold & Jenson, 1986). Their work came at a time when researchers began to recognize that traditional statistical comparisons do not reveal a great deal about the efficacy of therapy. In discussing the topic, Jacobson and Truax broadly define the clinical significance of treatment as "its ability to meet standards of efficacy set by consumers, clinicians, and researchers" (p. 12).

From their perspective, Jacobson and his colleagues (Jacobson et al., 1984; Jacobson & Truax, 1991) felt that clinically significant change could be conceptualized in one of three ways. Thus, for clinically significant change to have occurred, the measured level of functioning following the therapeutic episode would either (a) fall outside the range of the dysfunctional population by at least 2 standard deviations from the mean of that population, in the direction of functionality; (b) fall within 2 standard deviations of the mean for the normal or functional population; or (c) be closer to the mean of the functional population than to that of the dysfunctional population. Jacobson and Truax viewed option (c) as being the least arbitrary, and they provided different recommendations for determining cutoffs for clinically significant change, depending upon the availability of normative data.

At the same time, these investigators noted the importance of considering the change in the measured variables of interest from pre- to posttreatment in addition to the patient's functional status at the end of therapy. To this end, Jacobson et al. (1984) proposed the concomitant use of a reliable change (RC) index to determine whether change is clinically significant. This index, modified on the recommendation of Christensen and Mendoza (1986), is nothing more than the pretest score minus the posttest score divided by the standard error of the difference of the two scores.

The demand to demonstrate the outcomes of treatment is pervasive throughout the health care industry. Regulatory and accreditation bodies are requiring that providers and provider organizations show that their services are having a positive impact on the people they treat. Beyond that, the behavioral health care provider also needs to know whether what he or she does works. Outcomes information derived from psychological assessment of individual patients allows the provider to know the extent to which he or she has helped each patient. At the same time, in aggregate, this information can offer insight about what works best for whom under what circumstances, thus facilitating the treatment of future patients.

PSYCHOLOGICAL ASSESSMENT IN THE ERA OF MANAGED BEHAVIORAL HEALTH CARE

Numerous articles (e.g., Ficken, 1995) have commented on how the advent of managed care has limited the reimbursement for (and therefore the use of) psychological assessment. Certainly, no one would argue with this assertion. In an era of capitated behavioral health care coverage, the amount of money available for behavioral health care treatment is limited. Managed behavioral health care organizations therefore require a demonstration that the amount of money spent for testing will result in a greater amount of treatment cost savings. As of this writing, this author is unaware of any published research that can provide this demonstration. Moreover, Ficken asserts that much of the information obtained from psychological assessment is not relevant to the treatment of patients within a managed care environment. If this indeed is how MBHOs view psychological assessment information, it is not surprising that MBHOs are reluctant to pay for gathering it.

Current Status

Where does psychological assessment currently fit into the daily scope of activities for practicing psychologists in this age of managed care? In a survey conducted in 1995 by the American Psychological Association's Committee for the Advancement of Professional Practice (Phelps, Eisman, & Kohut, 1998), almost 16,000 psychological practitioners responded to questions related to workplace settings, areas of practice concerns, and range of activities. Even though there were not any real surprises, there were several interesting findings. The principal professional activity reported by the respondents was psychotherapy, with 44% of the sample acknowledging involvement in this service. Assessment was the second most prevalent activity, with only 16% reporting this activity. In addition, the results showed that 29% were involved in outcomes assessment.

Taking a closer look at the impact that managed care has had on assessment, Piotrowski, Belter, and Keller (1998) surveyed 500 psychologists randomly selected from that year's *National Register of Health Service Providers in Psychology* in the fall of 1996 to investigate how managed care has affected assessment practices. One hundred thirty-seven usable surveys (32%) were returned. Sixty-one percent of the respondents saw no positive impact of managed care; and, consistent with the CAPP survey findings, 70% saw managed care as negatively affecting clinicians or patients. The testing practices of 72% of the respondents were affected by managed care, as reflected in their performing less testing, using fewer instruments when they did test patients, and having lower reimbursement rates. Overall, they reported less reliance on those tests requiring much clinician time—such as the Weschler scales, Rorschach, and Thematic Apperception Test—along with a move to briefer, problem-focused tests. The results of their study led Piotrowski et al. to describe many possible scenarios for the future of assessment, including providers relying on briefer tests or briefer test batteries, changing the focus of their practice to more lucrative types of assessment activities (e.g., forensic assessment), using computer-based testing, or, in some cases, referring testing out to another psychologist.

In yet another survey, Stout and Cook (1999) contacted 40 managed care companies regarding their viewpoints concerning reimbursement for psychological assessment. The good news is that the majority (70%) of these companies reported that they did reimburse for these services. At the same time, the authors pointed to the possible negative implications for the covered lives of those other 12 or so companies that do not reimburse for psychological assessment. That is, these people may not be receiving the services they need because of missing information that might have been revealed through the assessment.

Piotrowski (1999) summed up the current state of psychological assessment by stating,

> Admittedly, the emphasis on the standard personality battery over the past decade has declined due to the impact of brief therapeutic approaches with a focus on diagnostics, symptomatology, and treatment outcome. That is, the clinical emphasis has been on addressing referral questions and not psychodynamic, defenses, character structure, and object relations. Perhaps the managed care environment has brought this issue to the forefront. Either way, the role of clinical assessment has, for the most part, changed. To the dismay of proponents of clinical methods, the future is likely to focus more on specific domain-based rather than comprehensive assessment. (p. 793)

Opportunities for Psychological Assessment

The foregoing representations of the current state of psychological assessment in behavioral health care delivery could be viewed as an omen of worse things to come. In my opinion, they are not. Rather, the limitations that are being imposed on psychological assessment and the demand for justification of its use in clinical practice represent part of health care customers' dissatisfaction with the way things were done in the past. In general, this author views the tightening of the purse strings as a positive move for both behavioral health care and the profession of psychology. It is a wake-up call to those who have contributed to the health care crisis by uncritically performing costly psychological assessments, being unaccountable to the payers and recipients of those services, and generally not performing assessment services in the most responsible, cost-effective way possible. Psychologists need to evaluate how they have used psychological assessment in the past and then determine the best way to use it in the future.

Consequently, this is an opportunity for psychologists to reestablish the value of the contributions they can make to improve the quality of care delivery through their knowledge and skills in the area of psychological assessment. As has been shown throughout this chapter, there are many ways in which the value of psychological assessment can be demonstrated in traditional mental health settings during this era of managed behavioral health care. However, the health care industry is now beginning to recognize the value of psychological assessment in the more traditional *medical* arenas. This is where potential opportunities are just now beginning to be realized.

Psychological Assessment in Primary Care Settings

The past three decades have witnessed a significant increase in the number of psychologists who work in general health care settings (Groth-Marnat & Edkins, 1996). This can be attributed to several factors, including the realization that psychologists can improve a patient's physical health by helping to reduce overutilization of medical services and prevent stress-related disorders, offering alternatives to traditional medical interventions, and enhancing the outcomes of patient care. The recognition of the financial and patient-care benefits that can accrue from the integration of primary medical care and behavioral health care has resulted in the implementation of various types of integrated behavioral health programs in primary care settings. Regardless of the extent to which these services are merged, these efforts attest to the belief that any steps toward integrating behavioral health care services—including psychological testing and assessment—in primary care settings represents an improvement over the more traditional model of segregated service delivery.

The alliance of primary and behavioral health care providers is not a new phenomenon; it has existed in one form or another for decades. Thus, it is not difficult to demonstrate that clinical psychologists and other trained behavioral health care professionals can uniquely contribute to efforts to fully integrate their services in primary care settings through the establishment and use of psychological assessment services. Information obtained from psychometrically sound self-report tests and other assessment instruments (e.g., clinician rating scales, parent-completed instruments) can assist the primary care provider in several types of clinical decision-making activities, including screening for the presence of mental health or substance abuse problems, planning a course of treatment, and monitoring patient progress. Testing can also be used to assess the outcome of treatment that has been provided to patients with mental health or substance abuse problems, thus assisting in determining what works for whom.

Psychological Assessment in Disease Management Programs

Beyond the primary care setting, the medical populations for which psychological assessment can be useful are quite varied and may even be surprising to some. Todd (1999) observed that "Today, it is difficult to find any organization in the healthcare industry that isn't in some way involved in disease management. . . . This concept has quickly evolved from a marketing strategy of the pharmaceutical industry to an entrenched discipline among many managed care organizations" (p. xi). It is here that opportunities for the application of psychological screening and other assessment activities are just beginning to be realized.

What is *disease management,* or (as some prefer) disease state management? Gurnee and DaSilva (1999, p. 12)

described it as "an integrated system of interventions, measurements, and refinements of health care delivery designed to optimize clinical and economic outcomes within a specific population. . . . [S]uch a program relies on aggressive prevention of complications as well as treatment of chronic conditions." The focus of these programs is on a systems approach that treats the entire disease rather than its individual components, such as is the case in the more traditional practice of medicine. The payoff comes in improvement in the quality of care offered to participants in the program as well as real cost savings.

Where can psychological assessment fit into these programs? In some MBHOs, for example, there is a drive to work closer with health plan customers in their disease management programs for patients facing diabetes, asthma, and recovery from cardiovascular diseases. This has resulted in a recognition on the part of the health plans of the value that MBHOs can bring to their programs, including the expertise in selecting or developing assessment instruments and developing an implementation plan that can help identify and monitor medical patients with comorbid behavioral health problems. These and other medical disorders are frequently accompanied by depression and anxiety that can significantly affect quality of life, morbidity, and, in some cases, mortality. Early identification and treatment of comorbid behavioral health problems in patients with chronic medical diseases can thus dramatically affect the course of the disease and the toll it takes on the patient. In addition, periodic (e.g., annual) monitoring of the patient can be incorporated into the disease management process to help ensure that there has been no recurrence of the problem or development of a different behavioral health problem over time.

A Concluding Note

It is difficult to imagine that any behavioral health care organization—managed or otherwise—would not find value in at least one or two of the previously described applications. The issue becomes whether there are funds for these applications. These might include funds for assessment materials, reimbursing network providers or other third-party contractors (e.g., disease management companies) for their assessment work, an in-house staff position to conduct or oversee the implementation of this work, or any combination of the three. Regardless, it is highly unlikely that any MBHO is going to spend money on any service that is not considered essential for the proper care of patients unless that service can demonstrate value in short-term or long-term money savings or offset costs in other ways. The current restrictions for authorizing assessment are a reflection of this fact. As Dorfman (2000) succinctly put it,

> Until the value of testing can be shown unequivocally, support and reimbursement for evaluation and testing will be uneven with [MBHOs] and frequently based on the psychologist's personal credibility and competence in justifying such expenditures. In the interim, it is incumbent on each psychologist to be aware of the goals and philosophy of the managed care industry, and to understand how the use of evaluation and testing with his or her patients not only is consistent with, but also helps to further, those goals. To the extent that these procedures can be shown to enhance the value of the managed care product by ensuring quality of care and positive treatment outcome, to reduce treatment length without sacrificing that quality, to prevent overutilization of limited resources and services, and to enhance patient satisfaction with care, psychologists can expect to gain greater support for their unique testing skill from the managed care company. (pp. 24–25)

FUTURE DIRECTIONS

The ways in which psychologists and other behavioral health care clinicians conduct the types of psychological assessment described in this chapter have undergone dramatic changes during the 1990s, and they will continue to change in this new millennium. Some of those involved in the delivery of psychological assessment services may wonder (with some fear and trepidation) where the health care revolution is leading the behavioral health care industry and, in particular, how their ability to practice will be affected in the twenty-first century. At the same time, others are eagerly awaiting the inevitable advances in technology and other resources that will come with the passage of time. What ultimately will occur is open to speculation. However, close observation of the practice of psychological assessment and the various industries that support it has led this author to arrive at a few predictions as to where the field of psychological assessment is headed and the implications they have for patients, clinicians, and provider organizations.

What the Field Is Moving Away From

One way of discussing what the field is moving toward is to first talk about what it is moving away from. In the case of psychological assessment, two trends are becoming quite clear. First, as just noted, the use of (and reimbursement for) psychological assessment has gradually been curtailed. In particular, this has been the case with regard to indiscriminate administration of lengthy and expensive psychological test batteries. Payers began to demand evidence that the knowledge gained from

the administration of these instruments in fact contributes to the delivery of cost-effective, efficient care to patients. This author sees no indications that this trend will stop.

Second, as the Piotrowski et al. (1998) findings suggest, the form of assessment commonly used is moving away from lengthy, multidimensional objective instruments (e.g., MMPI) or time-consuming projective techniques (e.g., Rorschach) that previously represented the standard in practice. The type of assessment authorized now usually involves the use of brief, inexpensive, problem-oriented instruments that have demonstrated validity for the purpose for which they will be used. This reflects modern behavioral health care's time-limited, problem-oriented approach to treatment. Today, the clinician can no longer afford to spend a great deal of time in assessment when the patient is only allowed a limited number of payer-authorized sessions. Thus, brief instruments will become more commonly employed for problem identification, progress monitoring, and outcomes assessment in the foreseeable future.

Trends in Instrumentation

In addition to the move toward the use of brief, problem-oriented instruments, another trend in the selection of instrumentation is the increasing use of public domain tests, questionnaires, rating scales, and other measurement tools. In the past, these free-use instruments were not developed with the same rigor that is applied by commercial test publishers in the development of psychometrically sound instruments. Consequently, they commonly lacked the validity and reliability data that are necessary to judge their psychometric integrity.

Recently, however, there has been significant improvement in the quality and documentation of the public domain, free-use, and nominal cost tests that are available. Instruments such as the SF-36 Health Survey (SF-36; Ware, Snow, Kosinski, & Gandek, 1993) and the SF-12 Health Survey (SF-12; Ware, Kosinski, & Keller, 1995) health measures are good examples of such tools. These and instruments such as the Behavior and Symptom Identification Scale (BASIS-32; Eisen, Grob, & Klein, 1986) and the Outcome Questionnaire (OQ-45; Lambert, Lunnen, Umphress, Hansen, & Burlingame, 1994) have undergone psychometric scrutiny and have gained widespread acceptance. Although copyrighted, these instruments may be used for a nominal one-time or annual licensing fee; thus, they generally are treated much like public domain assessment tools. In the future, one can expect that other high quality, useful instruments will be made available for use at little or no cost.

As for the types of instrumentation that will be needed and developed, one can probably expect some changes.

Accompanying the increasing focus on outcomes assessment is a recognition by payers and patients that positive change in several areas of functioning is at least as important as change in level of symptom severity when evaluating treatment effectiveness. For example, employers are interested in the patient's ability to resume the functions of his or her job, whereas family members are probably concerned with the patient's ability to resume his or her role as spouse or parent. Increasingly, measurement of the patient's functioning in areas other than psychological or mental status has come to be included as part of behavioral health care outcomes systems. Probably the most visible indication of this is the incorporation of the SF-36 or SF-12 in various behavioral health care studies. One will likely see other public domain and commercially available, non-symptom-oriented instruments, especially those emphasizing social and occupational role functioning, in increasing numbers over the next several years.

Other types of instrumentation will also become prominent. These may well include measures of variables that support outcomes and other assessment initiatives undertaken by provider organizations. What one organization or provider believes is important, or what payers determine is important for reimbursement or other purposes, will dictate what is measured. Instrumentation may also include measures that will be useful in predicting outcomes for individuals seeking specific psychotherapeutic services from those organizations.

Trends in Technology

Looking back to the mid-1980s and early 1990s, the cutting-edge technology for psychological testing at that time included optical mark reader (OMR) scanning technologies. Also, there were those little black boxes that facilitated the per-use sale and security of test administration, scoring, and interpretations for test publishers while making computer-based testing convenient and available to practitioners. As has always been the case, someone has had the foresight to develop applications of several current technological advances that we use every day to the practice of psychological testing. Just as at one time the personal computer held the power of facilitating the testing and assessment process, the Internet, the fax, and interactive voice response, technologies are being developed to make the assessment process easier, quicker, and more cost effective.

Internet Technology

The Internet has changed the way we do many things, so that the possibility of using it for the administration, scoring, and interpretation of psychological instruments should not be a surprise to anyone. The process here is straightforward. The clinician accesses the Web site on which the desired instrumentation resides. The desired test is selected for administration, and then the patient completes the test online. There may also be an option of having the patient complete a paper-and-pencil version of the instrument and then having administrative staff key the responses into the program. The data are scored and entered into the Web site's database, and a report is generated and transmitted back to the clinician through the Web. Turnaround time on receiving the report will be only a matter of minutes. The archived data can later be used for any of a number of purposes. The most obvious, of course, is to develop scheduled reporting of aggregated data on a regular basis. Data from repeated testing can be used for treatment monitoring and report card generation. These data can also be used for psychometric test development or other statistical purposes.

The advantages of an Internet-based assessment system are rather clear-cut. This system allows for online administration of tests that include branching logic for item selection. Any instruments available through a Web site can be easily updated and made available to users, which is not the case with disk-distributed software, for which updates and fixes are sometimes long in coming. The results of a test administration can be made available almost immediately. In addition, data from multiple sites can be aggregated and used for normative comparisons, test validation and risk adjustment purposes, generation of recovery curves, and any number of other statistically based activities that require large data sets.

There are only a couple of major disadvantages to an Internet-based system. The first and most obvious is the fact that it requires access to the Internet. Not all clinicians have Internet access. The second disadvantage has to do with the general Internet data security issue. With time, the access and security issues will likely become of less concern as the use of the Internet in the workplace becomes more of the standard and advances in Internet security software and procedures continue to take place.

Faxback Technology

The development of facsimile and faxback technology that has taken place over the past decade has opened an important application for psychological testing. It has dealt a huge blow to the optical scanning industry's low-volume customer base while not affecting sales to their high-volume scanning customers.

The process for implementing faxback technology is fairly simple. Paper-and-pencil answer sheets for those tests available through the faxback system are completed by the patient. The answer sheet for a given test contains numbers or other types of code that tell the scoring and reporting software which test is being submitted. When the answer sheet is completed, it is faxed in—usually through a toll-free number that the scoring service has provided—to the central scoring facility, where the data are entered into a database and then scored. A report is generated and faxed back to the clinician within about 5 minutes, depending on the number of phone lines that the vendor has made available and the volume of submissions at that particular time. At the scoring end of the process, the whole system remains paperless. Later, the stored data can be used in the same ways as those gathered by an Internet-based system.

Like Internet-based systems, faxback systems allow for immediate access to software updates and fixes. As is the case with the PC-based testing products that are offered through most test publishers, its paper-and-pencil administration format allows for more flexibility as to where and when a patient can be tested. In addition to the types of security issues that come with Internet-based testing, the biggest disadvantage of or problem with faxback testing centers around the identification and linking data. Separate answer sheets are required for each instrument that can be scored through the faxback system.

Another disadvantage is that of developing the ability to link data from multiple tests or multiple administrations of the same test to a single patient. At first glance, this may not seem to be a very challenging task. However, there are issues related to the sometimes conflicting needs of maintaining confidentiality while at the same time ensuring the accuracy of patient identifiers that link data over an episode or multiple episodes of care. Overcoming this challenge may be the key to the success of any faxback system. If a clinician cannot link data, then the data will be limited in its usefulness.

IVR Technology

One of the more recent applications of new technology to the administration, scoring, and reporting of results of psychological tests can be found in the use of interactive voice response, or IVR, systems. Almost everyone is familiar with the IVR technology. When we place a phone call to order products, address billing problems, or find out what the balance is in our checking accounts, we are often asked to provide information to an automated system in order to facilitate the meeting of our requests. This is IVR, and its applicability to test administration, data processing, and data storage should be obvious. What may not be obvious is how the data can be accessed and used.

Interactive voice response technology is attractive from many standpoints. It requires no extra equipment beyond a touch-tone telephone for administration. It is available for use 24 hours a day, 7 days a week. One does not have to be concerned about the patient's reading ability, although oral comprehension levels need to be taken into account when determining which instruments are appropriate for administration via IVR or any audio administration format. As with fax- and Internet-based assessment, the system is such that branching logic can be used in the administration of the instrument. Updates and fixes are easily implemented systemwide. Also, the ability to store data allows for comparison of results from previous testings, aggregation of data for statistical analyses, and all the other data analytic capabilities available through fax- and Internet-based assessment. As for the down side of IVR assessment, probably the biggest issue is that in many instances the patient must be the one to initiate the testing. Control of the testing is turned over to a party that may or may not be amenable to assessment. With less cooperative patients, this may mean costly follow-up efforts to encourage full participation in the process.

Overall, the developments in instrumentation and technology that have taken place over the past several years suggest two major trends. First, there will always be a need for the commercially published, multidimensional assessment instruments in which most psychologists received training. These instruments can efficiently provide the type of information that is critical in forensic, employment, or other evaluations that generally do not involve ongoing treatment-related decision-making. However, use of these types of instruments will become the exception rather than the rule in day-to-day, in-the-trenches clinical practice. Instead, brief, valid, problem-oriented instruments whose development and availability were made possible by public or other grant money will gain prominence in the psychologist's armamentarium of assessment tools. As for the second trend, it appears that the Internet will eventually become the primary medium for automated test administration, scoring, and reporting. Access to the Internet will soon become universal, expanding the possibilities for in-office and off-site assessment and making test administration simple, convenient, and cost effective for patients and psychologists.

REFERENCES

Achenbach, T. M. (1991). *Manual for the Child Behavior Checklist/4-18 and 1991 Profile.* Burlington: University of Vermont, Department of Psychiatry.

American Psychiatric Association. (1994). *Diagnostic and statistical manual of mental disorders* (4th ed.). Washington, DC: Author.

American Psychological Association. (1992). *Ethical principles.* Washington, DC: Author.

Appelbaum, S. A. (1990). The relationship between assessment and psychotherapy. *Journal of Personality Assessment, 54,* 791–801.

Beck, A. T., Steer, R. A., & Brown, G. K. (1996). *Manual for the Beck Depression Inventory-II.* San Antonio, TX: The Psychological Corporation.

Beutler, L. E., & Clarkin, J. (1990). *Systematic treatment selection: Toward targeted therapeutic interventions.* New York: Brunner/Mazel.

Beutler, L. E., Wakefield, P., & Williams, R. E. (1994). Use of psychological tests/instruments for treatment planning. In M. E. Maruish (Ed.), *The use of psychological testing for treatment planning and outcome assessment* (pp. 55–74). Hillsdale, NJ: Erlbaum.

Butcher, J. N. (1990). *The MMPI-2 in psychological treatment.* New York: Oxford University Press.

Butcher, J. N., Dahlstrom, W. G., Graham, J. R., Tellegen, A. M., & Kaemmer, B. (1989). *MMPI-2: Manual for administration and scoring.* Minneapolis: University of Minnesota Press.

Butcher, J. N., Graham, J. R., Williams, C. L., & Ben-Porath, Y. (1989). *Development and use of the MMPI-2 content scales.* Minneapolis: University of Minnesota Press.

Chambless, D. L., Renneberg, B., Goldstein, A., & Gracely, E. J. (1992). MCMI-diagnosed personality disorders among agoraphobic outpatients: Prevalence and relationship to severity and treatment outcome. *Journal of Anxiety Disorders, 6,* 193–211.

Chisholm, S. M., Crowther, J. H., & Ben-Porath, Y. S. (1997). Selected MMPI-2 scales' ability to predict premature termination and outcome from psychotherapy. *Journal of Personality Assessment, 69,* 127–144.

Christensen, L., & Mendoza, J. L. (1986). A method of assessing change in a single subject: An alteration of the RC index [Letter to the Editor]. *Behavior Therapy, 17,* 305–308.

Clair, D., & Prendergast, D. (1994). Brief psychotherapy and psychological assessments: Entering a relationship, establishing a focus, and providing feedback. *Professional Psychology: Research and Practice, 25,* 46–49.

Derogatis, L. R. (1983). *SCL-90-R: Administration, scoring and procedures manual-II.* Baltimore: Clinical Psychometric Research.

Derogatis, L. R. (1992). *BSI: Administration, scoring and procedures manual-II.* Baltimore: Clinical Psychometric Research.

Derogatis, L. R., & Lynn, L. L. (1999). Psychological tests in screening for psychiatric disorder. In M. E. Maruish (Ed.), *The use of psychological testing for treatment planning and outcomes assessment* (2nd ed., pp. 41–79). Mahwah, NJ: Erlbaum.

Donabedian, A. (1980). *Explorations in quality assessment and monitoring: Vol. 1. The definition of quality and approaches to its assessment.* Ann Arbor, MI: Health Administration Press.

Donabedian, A. (1982). *Explorations in quality assessment and monitoring: Vol. 2. The criteria and standards of quality.* Ann Arbor, MI: Health Administration Press.

Donabedian, A. (1985). *Explorations in quality assessment and monitoring: Vol. 3. The methods and findings in quality assessment: An illustrated analysis.* Ann Arbor, MI: Health Administration Press.

Dorfman, W. I. (2000). Psychological assessment and testing under managed care. In A. J. Kent & M. Hersen (Eds.), *A psychologist's proactive guide to managed mental health care* (pp. 23–39). Mahwah, NJ: Erlbaum.

Dowd, E. T., Milne, C. R., & Wise, S. L. (1991). The therapeutic Reactance Scale: A measure of psychological reactance. *Journal of Counseling and Development, 69,* 541–545.

Eisen, S. V., Grob, M. C., & Klein, A. A. (1986). BASIS: The development of a self-report measure for psychiatric inpatient evaluation. *The Psychiatric Hospital, 17,* 165–171.

Elwood, R. W. (1993). Psychological tests and clinical discrimination: Beginning to address the base rate problem. *Clinical Psychology Review, 13,* 409–419.

Faustman, W. O., & Overall, J. E. (1999). Brief Psychiatric Rating Scale. In M. E. Maruish (Ed.), *The use of psychological testing for treatment planning and outcomes assessment* (2nd ed., pp. 791–830). Mahwah, NJ: Erlbaum.

Ficken, J. (1995). New directions for psychological testing. *Behavioral Health Management, 20,* 12–14.

Finn, S. E. (1996a). Assessment feedback integrating MMPI-2 and Rorschach findings. *Journal of Personality Assessment, 67,* 543–557.

Finn, S. E. (1996b). *Manual for using the MMPI-2 as a therapeutic intervention.* Minneapolis: University of Minnesota Press.

Finn, S. E., & Butcher, J. N. (1991). Clinical objective personality assessment. In M. Hersen, A. E. Kazdin, & A. S. Bellack (Eds.), *The clinical psychology handbook* (2nd ed., pp. 362–373). New York: Pergamon Press.

Finn, S. E., & Martin, H. (1997). Therapeutic assessment with the MMPI-2 in managed health care. In J. N. Butcher (Ed.), *Objective personality assessment in managed health care: A practitioner's guide* (pp. 131–152). Minneapolis: University of Minnesota Press.

Finn, S. E., & Tonsager, M. E. (1992). Therapeutic effects of providing MMPI-2 test feedback to college students awaiting therapy. *Psychological Assessment, 4,* 278–287.

Graham, J. R. (2000). *MMPI-2: Assessing personality and psychopathology* (3rd ed.). New York: Oxford University Press.

Greene, R. L. (2000). *The MMPI-2: An interpretive manual* (2nd ed.). Boston: Allyn and Bacon.

Greene, R. L., & Clopton, J. R. (1999). Minnesota Multiphasic Personality Inventory-2 (MMPI-2). In M. E. Maruish (Ed.), *The use of psychological testing for treatment planning and outcomes assessment* (2nd ed., pp. 1023–1049). Mahwah, NJ: Erlbaum.

Groth-Marnat, G., & Edkins, G. (1996). Professional psychologists in general medical settings: A review of the financial efficacy of direct treatment interventions. *Professional Psychology: Research and Practice, 2,* 161–174.

Gurnee, M. C., & DaSilva, R. V. (1999). Constructing disease management programs. In S. Heffner (Ed.), *Disease management sourcebook 2000: Resources and strategies for program design and implementation* (pp. 12–18). New York: Faulkner and Gray.

Hodges, K. (1994). *Child and Adolescent Functional Assessment Scale.* Ypsilanti: Eastern Michigan University.

Howard, K. I., Brill, P. L., Lueger, R. J., O'Mahoney, M. T., & Grissom, G. R. (1993). *Integra outpatient tracking assessment.* Philadelphia: Compass Information Services.

Howard, K. I., Moras, K., Brill, P. B., Martinovich, Z., & Lutz, W. (1996). Evaluation of psychotherapy: Efficacy, effectiveness, and patient progress. *American Psychologist, 51,* 1059–1064.

Jacobson, N. S., Follette, W. C., & Revenstorf, D. (1984). Psychotherapy outcome research: Methods for reporting variability and evaluating clinical significance. *Behavior Therapy, 15,* 336–352.

Jacobson, N. S., Follette, W. C., & Revenstorf, D. (1986). Toward a standard definition of clinically significant change [Letter to the Editor]. *Behavior Therapy, 17,* 309–311.

Jacobson, N. S., & Truax, P. (1991). Clinical significance: A statistical approach defining meaningful change in psychotherapy research. *Journal of Consulting and Clinical Psychology, 59,* 12–19.

Lachar, D., & Gruber, C. P. (2001). *Personality Inventory for Children-2 (PIC-2) manual.* Los Angeles: Western Psychological Services.

Lambert, M. J., Hansen, N. B., Umphress, V., Lunnen, K., Okiishi, J., Burlingame, G., Huefner, J. C., & Reisinger, C. W. (1996). *Administration and scoring manual for the Outcome Questionnaire (OQ 45.2).* Wilmington, DL: American Professional Credentialing Services.

Lambert, M. J., Lunnen, K., Umphress, V., Hansen, N. B., & Burlingame, G. M. (1994). *Administration and scoring manual for the Outcome Questionnaire (OQ-45.1).* Salt Lake City, UT: IHC Center for Behavioral Healthcare Efficacy.

Lambert, M. J., Whipple, J. L., Smart, D. W., Vermeesch, D. A., Nielsen, S. L., & Hawkins, E. J. (1999). *The effects of providing therapists with feedback on patient progress during psychotherapy: Are outcomes enhanced?* Manuscript submitted for publication.

Leon, S. C., Kopta, S. M., Howard, K. I., & Lutz, W. (1999). Predicting patients' responses to psychotherapy: Are some more predictable than others? *Journal of Consulting and Clinical Psychology, 67,* 698–704.

Maruish, M. E. (1990, Fall). Psychological assessment: What will its role be in the future? *Assessment Applications,* pp. 7–8.

Maruish, M. E. (1999a). Introduction. In M. E. Maruish (Ed.), *The use of psychological testing for treatment planning and outcome assessment* (pp. 1–39). Hillsdale, NJ: Erlbaum.

Maruish, M. E. (1999b). Therapeutic assessment: Linking assessment and treatment. In M. Hersen, A. Bellack (Series Eds.), & C. R. Reynolds (Vol. Ed.), *Comprehensive Clinical Psychology: Volume: 4. Assessment* (pp. 563–600). New York: Elsevier Science.

Maruish, M. E. (2002). *Applications of psychological testing in managed behavioral healthcare systems.* Mahwah, NJ: Erlbaum.

Meyer, G. J., Finn, S. E., Eyde, L. D., Kay, G. G., Kubiszyn, T. W., Moreland, K. L., Eisman, E. J., & Dies, R. R. (1998). *Benefits and costs of psychological assessment in healthcare delivery: Report of the Board of Professional Affairs Psychological Assessment Work Group, Part I.* Washington, DC: American Psychological Association.

Millon, T. (1987). *Manual for the MCMI-II.* Minneapolis, MN: National Computer Systems.

Millon, T. (1994). *MCMI-III manual.* Minneapolis, MN: National Computer Systems.

Moreland, K. L. (1996). How psychological testing can reinstate its value in an era of cost containment. *Behavioral Healthcare Tomorrow, 5,* 59–61.

Morey, L. C. (1991). *The Personality Assessment Inventory professional manual.* Odessa, FL: Psychological Assessment Resources.

Morey, L. C. (1999). Personality Assessment Inventory. In M. E. Maruish (Ed.), *The use of psychological testing for treatment planning and outcomes assessment* (2nd ed., pp. 1083–1121). Mahwah, NJ: Erlbaum.

Morey, L. C., & Henry, W. (1994). Personality Assessment Inventory. In M. E. Maruish (Ed.), *The use of psychological testing for treatment planning and outcome assessment* (pp. 185–216). Hillsdale, NJ: Erlbaum.

Newman, F. L., & Dakof, G. A. (1999). Progress and outcomes assessment of individual patient data: Selecting single-subject design and statistical procedures. In M. E. Maruish (Ed.), *The use of psychological testing for treatment planning and outcomes assessment* (2nd ed., pp. 211–223). Mahwah, NJ: Erlbaum.

Newman, F. L., & Tejeda, M. J. (1999). Selecting statistical procedures for progress and outcome assessment: The analysis of group data. In M. E. Maruish (Ed.), *The use of psychological testing for treatment planning and outcomes assessment* (2nd ed., pp. 225–266). Mahwah, NJ: Erlbaum.

Newman, M. L., & Greenway, P. (1997). Therapeutic effects of providing MMPI-2 test feedback to clients at a university counseling service: A collaborative approach. *Psychological Assessment, 9,* 122–131.

Overall, J. E., & Gorham, D. R. (1962). The Brief Psychiatric Rating Scale. *Psychological Reports, 10,* 799–812.

Phelps, R., Eisman, E. J., & Kohut, J. (1998). Psychological practice and managed care: Results of the CAPP practitioner survey. *Professional Psychology: Research and Practice, 29,* 31–36.

Piotrowski, C. (1999). Assessment practices in the era of managed care: Current status and future directions. *Journal of Clinical Psychology, 55,* 787–796.

Piotrowski, C., Belter, R. W., & Keller, J. W. (1998). The impact of "managed care" on the practice of psychological testing: Preliminary findings. *Journal of Personality Assessment, 70,* 441–447.

Sederer, L. I., Dickey, B., & Hermann, R. C. (1996). The imperative of outcomes assessment in psychiatry. In L. I. Sederer & B. Dickey (Eds.), *Outcomes assessment in clinical practice* (pp. 1–7). Baltimore: Williams and Wilkins.

Sheehan, D. V., Lecrubier, Y., Sheehan, K. H., Amorim, P., Janavs, J., Weiller, E., Thierry, H., Baker, R., & Dunbar, G. C. (1998). The Mini-International Neuropsychiatric Interview (M.I.N.I.): The development and validation of a structured diagnostic interview for DSM-IV and ICD-10. *Journal of Clinical Psychiatry, 59*(Suppl. 20), 22–33.

Speer, D. C. (1992). Clinically significant change: Jacobson and Truax (1991) revisited. *Journal of Consulting and Clinical Psychology, 60,* 402–408.

Spitzer, R. L., Kroenke, K., Williams, J. B., & Patient Health Questionnaire Primary Care Study Group (1999). Validation and utility of a self-report version of PRIME-MD: The PHQ primary care study. *Journal of the American Medical Association, 282,* 1737–1744.

Spitzer, R. L., Williams, J. B., Kroenke, K., Linzer, M., duGruy, F. V., Hahn, S. R., Brody, D., & Johnson, J. G. (1994). Utility of a new procedure for diagnosing mental disorders in primary care: The PRIME–MD 1000 study. *Journal of the American Medical Association, 272,* 1749–1756.

Stewart, A. L., & Ware, J. E., Jr. (1992). *Measuring functioning and well-being.* Durham, NC: Duke University Press.

Stout, C. E., & Cook, L. P. (1999). New areas for psychological assessment in general health care settings: What to do today to prepare for tomorrow. *Journal of Clinical Psychology, 55,* 797–812.

Strategic Advantage, Inc. (1996). *Symptom Assessment-45 Questionnaire manual.* Minneapolis, MN: Author.

Todd, W. E. (1999). Introduction: Fulfilling the promise of disease management: Where are we today? Where are we headed? In S. Heffner (Ed.), *Disease management sourcebook 2000: Resources and strategies for program design and implementation* (pp. xi–xxiii). New York: Faulkner and Gray.

Wampold, B. E., & Jenson, W. R. (1986). Clinical significance revisited [Letter to the Editor]. *Behavior Therapy, 17,* 302–305.

Ware, J. E., Kosinski, M., & Keller, S. D. (1995). *SF-12: How to Score the SF-12 Physical and Mental summary scales* (2nd ed.). Boston: New England Medical Center, The Health Institute.

Ware, J. E., Snow, K. K., Kosinski, M., & Gandek, B. (1993). *SF-36 Health Survey manual and interpretation guide.* Boston: New England Medical Center, The Health Institute.

World Health Organization. (1992). *International classification of diseases, tenth revision.* Geneva, Switzerland: Author.

CHAPTER 7

Computerized Psychological Assessment

JAMES N. BUTCHER

Computers have become an integral part of modern life. No longer are they mysterious, giant electronic machines that are stuck away in some remote site at a university or government facility requiring a bunch of engineers with PhDs to operate. Computers are everywhere—doing tasks that were once considered to be sheer human drudgery (managing vast unthinkable inventories with lightening speed), happily managing chores that no one could accomplish (like monitoring intricate internal engine functions), or depositing a letter to a friend all the way around the world in microseconds, a task that used to take months.

Computers have served in several capacities in the field of psychological assessment since their introduction almost a half

century ago, although initially only in the processing of psychological test information. Over the past several decades, their uses in mental health care settings have broadened, and computers have become important and necessary aids to assessment. The benefits of computers to the field of psychology continue to expand as technology becomes more advanced, allowing for more sophisticated operations, including integrative test interpretation, which once was the sole domain of humans. How can an electronic and nonintuitive gadget perform a complex cognitive process such as psychological test interpretation (which requires extensive knowledge, experience, and a modicum of intuition)?

The theoretical rationale underlying computer-based test interpretation was provided in 1954 when Meehl published a monograph in which he debated the merits of actuarial or statistical (objective) decision-making methods versus more subjective or clinical strategies. Meehl's analysis of the relative

I would like to express my appreciation to Reneau Kennedy for providing case material used in this chapter.

strengths of actuarial prediction over clinical judgment led to the conclusion that decisions based upon objectively applied interpretive rules were ultimately more valid than judgments based on subjective strategies. Subsequently, Dawes, Faust, and Meehl (1989) and Grove and Meehl (1996) have reaffirmed the finding that objective assessment procedures are equal or superior to subjective methods. More recently, in a meta-analysis of 136 studies, Grove, Zald, Lebow, Smith, and Nelson (2000) concluded that the advantage in accuracy for statistical prediction over clinical prediction was approximately 10%.

In spite of the common foundations and comparable rationales that actuarial assessment and computerized assessment share, they are not strictly the same. Computer-based test interpretation (CBTI) can be either clinical or actuarial in foundation. It is an actuarial task only if its interpretive output is determined strictly by statistical rules that have been demonstrated empirically to exist between the input and the output data. A computer-based system for describing or predicting events that are not actuarial in nature might base its interpretations on the work of a clinician (or even an astrologer) who hypothesizes relationships using theory, practical experience, or even lunar phases and astrology charts.

It is important in the field of psychological assessment that the validity of computerized assessment instruments be demonstrated if they are to be relied upon for making crucial dispositions or decisions that can affect people. In 1984 the Committee on Professional Standards of the American Psychological Association (APA) cautioned psychologists who used interpretive reports in business and school settings against using computer-derived narrative test summaries in the absence of adequate data to validate their accuracy.

WAYS COMPUTERS ARE USED IN CLINICAL ASSESSMENT

In the history of psychological assessment, the various computer-based test applications evolved differently. The relatively more routine tasks were initially implemented, and the applications of more complex tasks, such as interpretation, took several decades to become available.

Scoring and Data Analysis

The earliest computer-based applications of psychological tests involved scoring and data processing in research. Almost as soon as large mainframe computers became available for general use in the 1950s, researchers began to use them to process test development information. In the early days, data were input for scoring by key entry, paper tape, or cards. Today optical readers or scanners are used widely but not

exclusively. It is also common to find procedures in which the respondent enters his or her responses directly into the machine using a keyboard. Allard, Butler, Faust, and Shea (1995) found that computer scoring was more reliable than manual scoring of test responses.

Profiling and Charting of Test Results

In the 1950s, some commercial services for scoring psychological tests for both research and clinical purposes emerged. These early services typically provided summary scores for the test protocols, and in some cases, they provided a profile graph with the appropriate levels of the scale elevation designated. The technology of computer graphics of the time did not allow for complex visual displays or graphing a profile by connecting the dots, and the practitioner needed to connect the dots manually to complete the profile.

Listing of Possible Interpretations

As computer use became more widespread, its potential advantage to the process of profiling of scores and assigning meaning to significantly elevated scores came to be recognized. A research group at Mayo Clinic in Rochester, Minnesota developed a computer program that actually provided rudimentary interpretations for the Minnesota Multiphasic Personality Inventory (MMPI) results of patients being seen at the hospital (Rome et al., 1962). The interpretive program was comprised of 110 statements or descriptions that were based on empirical correlates for particular MMPI scale elevations. The program simply listed out the most relevant statements for each client's profile. This system was in use for many years to assess psychopathology of patients undergoing medical examinations at Mayo Clinic.

In 1963 Piotrowski completed a very elaborate computer program for Rorschach interpretation (Exner, 1987). The program was based on his own interpretive logic and included hundreds of parameters and rules. Because the program was too advanced for the computer technology available at that time, Piotrowski's program never became very popular. However, it was a precursor of modern computer programs for calculating scores and indexes and generating interpretations of Rorschach data.

Evolution of More Complex Test Interpretation and Report Generation

It wasn't long until others saw the broader potential in computer-based test interpretation. Fowler (1969) developed a computer program for the drug company, Hoffman-La Roche Laboratories, that not only interpreted the important scales of the MMPI but also combined the interpretive statements into a narrative report. Several other computer-based systems became available in the years that followed—for example, the Caldwell Report (Caldwell, 1996) and the Minnesota Report (Butcher, 1982).

Adapting the Administration of Test Items

Computer administration has been widely used as a means of obtaining response data from clients. This response format has many advantages over traditional manual processing methods—particularly the potential time savings, elimination of the possibility that respondents would make errors while filling out handwritten answer sheets, and elimination of the possibility that clinicians and technicians would make errors while hand-scoring items .

The flexibility of the computer offers the option of adapting the test to suit the needs and preferences of the test taker. The administration of test items in a paper-and-pencil inventory requires that the test taker respond to each and every question regardless of whether it applies. Psychologists have been interested in modifying the administration of test items to fit the respondent—that is, to tailor a test administration to be analogous to an interview. For example, in an interview, if a question such as *Are you married?* is answered *no,* then all subsequent questions take this response into account and are *branched away* from seeking responses to items pertinent to being married. In other words, the items are administered in an adapted or tailored manner for the specific test taker. The comparability and validity of this method (known as computerized adaptive testing) have been explored in several studies (e.g., Butcher, Keller, & Bacon, 1985). Roper, Ben-Porath, and Butcher (1995) examined an adaptive version of the MMPI-2. Five hundred and seventy-one undergraduate psychology students were administered three versions of the MMPI-2: a booklet version, an adaptive computerized version, and a conventional computerized version. Each participant took the same format twice, took the booklet and adaptive computerized versions (in counterbalanced order), or took the conventional and adaptive computerized versions (again, in counterbalanced order). There were few statistically significant differences in the resulting mean scale scores between the booklet and adaptive computerized formats.

Decision Making by Computer

Available computer interpretation systems, even the most sophisticated report-generating programs, are essentially look up, list out programs—that is, they provide canned interpretations that have been stored in the computer to be called up when various test scores and indexes are obtained. The computer does not actually make decisions but simply follows instructions (often very complex and detailed ones) about the statements or paragraphs that are to be printed out. The use of computers to actually make decisions or simulate what the human brain does in making decisions—an activity that has been referred to as *artificial intelligence*—has not been fully accomplished in the assessment field. One program that comes closest to having the computer actually make the decisions is available in the Minnesota Personnel Screening Report (Butcher, 1995). In this system, the computer has been programmed with decision rules defining an array of test scores and decisions (e.g., *manages stress well*). The computer program determines the scores and indexes and then decides which of the summary variables are most appropriate for the range of scores obtained.

Butcher (1988) investigated the usefulness of this computer-based MMPI assessment strategy for screening in personnel settings. A group of 262 airline pilot applicants were evaluated by both expert clinicians and by computer-based decision rules. The overall level of adjustment of each applicant was rated by experts (using only an MMPI profile) on a Likert-type scale with three categories: *adequate, problems possible,* and *problems likely.* The computer-based decision rules were also used to make determinations about the applicants. Here, the categories of *excellent, good, adequate, problems possible,* and *poor* were used to classify the profiles. The results showed high agreement between the computer-based decisions and those made by clinicians in rating overall adjustment. Over 50% of individuals falling into the *adequate* category based on the computer-based rules were given ratings of *adequate* by the clinicians. There was agreement between the computer rules and clinician judgment on the possibility of problems being present in 26.7% of cases. Over 60% of individuals rated as *poor* by the computer rules were given *problems likely* ratings by the clinicians. This study indicated that there can be substantial agreement between clinicians and the computer when an objectively interpreted test is used. The study did not, however, provide information on the external validity of either approach because no criteria were available to allow for an assessment of the relative accuracy of either method.

Internet-Based Test Applications

Computer-based technological developments are advancing more rapidly than is the psychological technology to support psychological test usage on the Internet. The growth of the Internet and broadening commercial uses have increased the potential to administer, score, and interpret psychological tests online. Commercial test publishers have been receiving a great deal of pressure from test users to make more test-based services available on the Internet. The ethics of psychological test usage, standards of care, and the basic psychological test research have not kept up with the growth spurt of the Internet itself. Consequently, there are many unanswered questions as psychologists move into the twenty-first century with the almost limitless potential of test applications facing the field. Later in this chapter, we address a number of these issues.

EQUIVALENCE OF COMPUTER-ADMINISTERED TESTS AND TRADITIONAL METHODS

Several authorities have raised questions about the equivalence of computer-based assessment methods and traditional psychological testing procedures. Hofer and Green (1985), for example, pointed out that there are several conditions related to computerized test administration that could produce noncomparable results. Some people might be uncomfortable with computers and feel awkward dealing with them; this would make the task of taking tests on a computer different from standard testing procedures. Moreover, factors such as the type of equipment used and the nature of the test material (i.e., when item content deals with sensitive and personal information) might make respondents less willing (or more willing) to reveal their true feelings to a computer than to a human being. These situations might lead to atypical results for computerized assessment compared to a traditional format. Another possible disadvantage of computer assessment is that computer-generated interpretations may be excessively general in scope and not specific enough for practical use. Finally, there is a potential for computer-based results to be misused because they might be viewed as more scientific than they actually are, simply because they came out of a computer (Butcher, 1987). It is therefore important that the issues of measurement comparability and, of course, validity of the interpretation be addressed. The next section addresses the comparability of computer-administered tests and paper-and-pencil measures or other traditional methods of data collection.

Comparability of Psychiatric Screening by Computer and Clinical Interview

Several studies have reported on adaptations of psychiatric interviews for computer-based screening, and these adaptations are discussed in the chapter by Craig in this volume. Research has shown that clients in mental health settings report feeling comfortable with providing personal information through computer assessment (e.g., Hile & Adkins, 1997). Moreover, research has shown that computerized assessment programs were generally accurate in being able to diagnose the presence of behavioral problems. Ross, Swinson, Larkin, and Doumani (1994) used the Computerized Diagnostic

Interview Schedule (C-DIS) and a clinician-administered Structural Clinical Interview for the *Diagnostic and Statistical Manual of Mental Disorders–Third Edition–Revised* (*DSM-III-R;* SCID) to evaluate 173 clients. They reported the congruence between the two instruments to be acceptable except for substance abuse disorders and antisocial personality disorder, in which the levels of agreement were poor. The C-DIS was able to rule out the possibility of comorbid disorders in the sample with approximately 90% accuracy.

Farrell, Camplair, and McCullough (1987) evaluated the capability of a computerized interview to identify the presence of target complaints in a clinical sample. Both a face-to-face, unstructured intake interview and the interview component of a computerized mental health information system, the Computerized Assessment System for Psychotherapy Evaluation and Research (CASPER), were administered to 103 adult clients seeking outpatient psychological treatment. Results showed relatively low agreement (mean $r = .33$) between target complaints as reported by clients on the computer and as identified by therapists in interviews. However, 9 of the 15 complaints identified in the computerized interview were found to be significantly associated with other self-report and therapist-generated measures of global functioning.

Comparability of Standard and Computer-Administered Questionnaires

The comparability of computer and standard administrations of questionnaires has been widely researched. Wilson, Genco, and Yager (1985) used a test-attitudes screening instrument as a representative of paper-and-pencil tests that are administered also by computer. Ninety-eight female college freshman were administered the Test Attitude Battery (TAB) in both paper-and-pencil and computer-administered formats (with order of administration counterbalanced). The means and variances were found to be comparable for paper-and-pencil and computerized versions.

Holden and Hickman (1987) investigated computerized and paper-and-pencil versions of the Jenkins Activity Scale, a measure that assesses behaviors related to the Type A personality. Sixty male undergraduate students were assigned to one of the two administration formats. The stability of scale scores was comparable for both formats, as were mean scores, variances, reliabilities, and construct validities. Merten and Ruch (1996) examined the comparability of the German versions of the Eysenck Personality Questionnaire (EPQ-R) and the Carroll Rating Scale for Depression (CRS) by having people complete half of each instrument with a paper-and-pencil administration and the other half with computer administration (with order counterbalanced). They compared the results from the two formats to one another as well as to data from another sample, consisting of individuals who were administered only the paper-and-pencil version of the EPQ-R. As in the initial study, means and standard deviations were comparable across computerized and more traditional formats.

In a somewhat more complex and comprehensive evaluation of computer-based testing, Jemelka, Wiegand, Walker, and Trupin (1992) administered several computer-based measures to 100 incarcerated felons. The measures included brief mental health and personal history interviews, the group form of the MMPI, the Revised Beta IQ Examination, the Suicide Probability Scale, the Buss-Durkee Hostility Inventory, the Monroe Dyscontrol Scale, and the Veteran's Alcohol Screening Test. From this initial sample, they developed algorithms from a CBTI system that were then used to assign to each participant rakings of potential for violence, substance abuse, suicide, and victimization. The algorithms were also used to describe and identify the presence of clinical diagnoses based on the *DSM-III-R*. Clinical interviewers then rated the felons on the same five dimensions. The researchers then tested a new sample of 109 participants with eight sections of the computer-based DIS and found the agreement between the CBTI ratings and the clinician ratings to be fair. In addition, there was also high agreement between CBTI- and clinician-diagnosed *DSM-III-R* disorders, with an overall concordance rate of 82%.

Most of the research concerning the comparability of computer-based and standard personality assessment measures has been with the MMPI or the MMPI-2. Several studies reported possible differences between paper-and-pencil and computerized testing formats (e.g., Lambert, Andrews, Rylee, & Skinner, 1987; Schuldberg, 1988; Watson, Juba, Anderson, & Manifold, 1990). Most of the studies suggest that the differences between administrative formats are few and generally of small magnitude, leading to between-forms correlations of .68–.94 (Watson et al., 1990). Moreover, some researchers have reported very high (Sukigara, 1996) or near-perfect (i.e., 92% to 97%) agreement in scores between computer and booklet administrations (Pinsoneault, 1996). Honaker, Harrell, and Buffaloe (1988) investigated the equivalency of a computer-based MMPI administration with the booklet version among 80 community volunteers. They found no significant differences in means or standard deviations between various computer formats for validity, clinical, and 27 additional scales. However, like a number of studies investigating the equivalency of computer and booklet forms of the MMPI, the power of their statistical analyses did not provide conclusive evidence regarding the equivalency of the paper-and-pencil and computerized administration format (Honaker et al., 1988).

The question of whether computer-administered and paper-and-pencil forms are equivalent was pretty much laid to rest by a comprehensive meta-analysis (Finger & Ones, 1999). Their analysis included 14 studies, all of which included computerized and standard formats of the MMPI or MMPI-2, that had been conducted between 1974 and 1996. They reported that the differences in *T* score means and standard deviations between test formats across the studies were negligible. Correlations between forms were consistently near 1.00. Based on these findings, the authors concluded that computer-administered inventories are comparable to booklet-administered forms.

The equivalence of conventional computerized and computer-adapted test administrations was demonstrated in the study cited earlier by Roper et al. (1995). In this study, comparing conventional computerized to adaptive computerized administrations of the MMPI, there were no significant differences for either men or women. In terms of criterion-related validity, there were no significant differences between formats for the correlations between MMPI scores and criterion measures that included the Beck Depression Inventory, the Trait Anger and Trait Anxiety scales from the State-Trait Personality Inventory, and nine scales from the Symptoms Checklist—Revised.

Equivalence of Standard and Computer-Administered Neuropsychological Tests

Several investigators have studied computer-adapted versions of neuropsychological tests with somewhat mixed findings. Pellegrino, Hunt, Abate, and Farr (1987) compared a battery of 10 computerized tests of spatial abilities with these paper-and-pencil counterparts and found that computer-based measures of static spatial reasoning can supplement currently used paper-and-pencil procedures. Choca and Morris (1992) compared a computerized version of the Halstead Category Test to the standard version with a group of neurologically impaired persons and reported that the computer version was comparable to the original version.

However, some results have been found to be more mixed. French and Beaumont (1990) reported significantly lower scores on the computerized version than on the standard version of the Standard Progressive Matrices Test, indicating that these two measures cannot be used interchangeably. They concluded, however, that the poor resolution of available computer graphics might have accounted for the differences. With the advent of more sophisticated computer graphics, these problems are likely to be reduced in future studies. It should also be noted that more than a decade ago, French and Beaumont (1990) reported that research participants expressed a clear preference for the computer-based response format over the standard administration procedures for cognitive assessment instruments.

Equivalence of Computer-Based and Traditional Personnel Screening Methods

Several studies have evaluated computer assessment methods with traditional approaches in the field of personnel selection. Carretta (1989) examined the usefulness of the computerized Basic Attributes Battery (BAT) for selecting and classifying United States Air Force pilots. A total of 478 Air Force officer candidates completed a paper-and-pencil qualifying test and the BAT, and they were also judged based on undergraduate pilot training performance. The results demonstrated that the computer-based battery of tests was adequately assessing abilities and skills related to flight training performance, although the results obtained were variable.

In summary, research on the equivalence of computerized and standard administration has produced variable results. Standard and computerized versions of paper-and-pencil personality measures appear to be the most equivalent, and those involving more complex stimuli or highly different response or administration formats appear less equivalent. It is important for test users to ensure that a particular computer-based adaptation of a psychological test is equivalent before their results can be considered comparable to those of the original test (Hofer & Green, 1985).

COMPUTER-BASED PERSONALITY NARRATIVES

Computer-based psychological interpretation systems usually provide a comprehensive interpretation of relevant test variables, along with scores, indexes, critical item responses, and so forth. The narrative report for a computer-based psychological test interpretation is often designed to read like a psychological report that has been prepared by a practitioner. However, psychological tests differ with respect to the amount of valid and reliable information available about them and consequently differ in terms of the time required to program the information into an effective interpretive system. Of course, if more research is available about a particular instrument, the more likely it is that the interpretations will be accurate. Instruments that have been widely researched, such as the MMPI and MMPI-2 (which have a research base of more than 10,000 articles) will likely have a more defensible interpretive system than a will test that has little or no research base. Test users need to be aware of the fact that some test interpretation systems that are commercially available are published with minimal established validity research. Simply being available commercially by computer does not assure test validity.

Steps in the Development of a Narrative Report

In developing a computer-based narrative report, the system developer typically follows several steps:

- Develops a systematic strategy for storing and retrieving relevant test information. This initial phase of development sets out the rationale and procedure for incorporating the published research findings into a coherent theme.

- Designs a computer program that scores the relevant scales and indexes and presents the information in a consistent and familiar form. This step may involve development of a program that accurately plots test profiles.

- Writes a dictionary of appropriate and validated test behaviors or correlates that can serve as the narrative data base. The test index definitions stored into memory can vary in complexity, ranging from discrete behaviors (e.g., if Scale 1 receives a T score greater than 70, print the following: *Reports many physical symptoms*) to extensive descriptors (e.g., if Scale 2 receives a T score greater than 65, then print the following: *This client has obtained a significant scale elevation on the depression scale. It is likely that he is reporting extensive mental health symptoms including depression, worry, low self-esteem, low energy, feelings of inadequacy, lacking in self-confidence, social withdrawal, and a range of physical complaints*). The dictionary of stored test information can be quite extensive, particularly if the test on which it is based has a broad research base. For example, a comprehensive MMPI-2 based interpretive system would likely include hundreds of pages of stored behavioral correlates.

- Specifies the interpretive algorithms for combining test indexes and dictionary text. This component of the interpretive system is the engine for combining the test indexes to use in particular reports and locating the appropriate dictionary text relevant for the particular case.

- Organizes the narrative report in a logical and user-friendly format. Determines what information is available in the test being interpreted and organizes the information into a structure that maximizes the computer-generated hypotheses.

- Tests the system extensively before it is offered to the public. This may involve generating sample reports that test the system with a broad range of possible test scores and indexes.

- Eliminates internal contradictions within the system. This phase involves examining a broad range of reports on clients with known characteristics in order to modify the program to prevent contradictory or incorrect statements from appearing in the narrative.

- Revises the system periodically to take into account new research on the test instrument.

Responsibilities of Users of Computer-Based Reports

As Butcher (1987, 1995; Butcher et al., 1985) has discussed, there are definite responsibilities that users of computer-based psychological reports assume, and these responsibilities are especially important when the reports are used in forensic evaluations:

- It is important to ensure that appropriate custody of answer sheets and generated test materials be maintained (i.e., kept in a secure place). Practitioners should see to it that the client's test materials are properly labeled and securely stored so that records can be identified if circumstances call for recovery at a later date—for example, in a court case.
- The practitioner should closely follow computer-based validity interpretations because clients in both clinical and forensic cases may have motivation to distort their answers in order to present a particular pattern in the evaluation.
- It is up to the practitioner to ensure that there is an appropriate match between the prototypal report generated by the computer and background and other test information available about a particular client. Does the narrative report match the test scores generated by the scoring program? Please refer to the note at the end of the sample computerized narrative report presented in the appendix to this chapter. It is customary for reports to contain language that stresses the importance of the practitioner, making sure that the case matches the report.
- The practitioner must integrate congruent information from the client's background and other sources into evaluation based on test results. Computer-based reports are by necessity general personality or clinical descriptions based on prototypes.
- It is the responsibility of the practitioner using computer-based test interpretations to account for any possible discrepancies between the report and other client data.

Illustration of a Computer-Based Narrative Report

Although the output of various interpretive systems can vary from one service to another or from one test to another, the Minnesota Report for the MMPI-2 offers a fairly representative example of what one might expect when using computerized interpretation services. The MMPI-2 responses for the case of Della B. were submitted to National Computer Systems, and the resulting report is presented in the appendix to this chapter.

Della, a 22-year-old woman, was evaluated by a forensic psychologist at the request of her attorney. She and her husband had been charged with the murder of their 16-month-old child. Della, who was 5 months pregnant at the time of the evaluation, had been living with her husband and daughter in a small apartment.

About 2 months before the death of her daughter, the parents were investigated by the county protection agency for possible child abuse or neglect after a neighbor had reported to the authorities that their apartment was a shambles and that the child appeared to be neglected. The neighbors reported that the couple kept the child in a small room in the apartment along with cages for the parents' four rabbits, which were allowed to run free around the room most of the time. The parents also kept two Russian wolfhounds in their living room. The family periodically volunteered to take care of animals for the animal recovery shelter, and on two previous occasions the animals died mysterious deaths while in the family's care. Although the house was found to be in shambles, the child protection worker did not believe that the child was endangered and recommended that the parents retain custody. The family apparently lived a very chaotic life. Della and her husband drank heavily almost every day and argued almost constantly. The day that their daughter died, the couple had been drinking and arguing loudly enough for the neighbors to hear. Della reported her daughter's death through a 911 call indicating that the child had apparently suffocated when she became trapped between her bed and the wall. After a police investigation, however, both parents were charged with homicide because of the extensive bruises on the child's body. During the pretrial investigation (and after Della's second child was born), her husband confessed to killing his daughter to allow his wife to go free. He was sentenced to 18 years in prison. Although there was much evidence to indicate Della's complicity in the killing, she was released from custody after serving a 5-month sentence for conspiracy and rendering false statements.

VALIDITY RESEARCH ON COMPUTERIZED NARRATIVE REPORTS

Interpretive reports generated by computer-based psychological assessment systems need to have demonstrated validity even if the instruments on which the interpretations are based are supported by research literature. Computerized outputs are typically one step removed from the test index-validity data relationships from the original test; therefore, it is important to demonstrate that the inferences included in the computerized report are reliable and valid in the settings where they are used. Some computer interpretation programs now in use also provide comprehensive personality assessment by combining test findings into narrative descriptions and conclusions. Butcher, Perry, and Atlis (2000) recently reviewed the extensive validity research for computer-based interpretation systems. Highlights from their evaluation are summarized in the following sections.

In discussing computer-based assessment, it is useful to subdivide computerized reports into two broad categories: descriptive summaries and consultative reports. Descriptive summaries (e.g., for the 16 Personality Factor Test or 16PF) are usually on a scale-by-scale basis without integration of the results into a narrative. Consultative reports (e.g., those for the MMPI-2 and DTREE, a computer-based *DSM-IV* diagnostic program) provide detailed analysis of the test data and emulate as closely as possible the interpretive strategies of a trained human consultant.

Narrative Reports in Personality Assessment

The validity of computerized reports has been extensively studied in both personality testing and psychiatric screening (computer-based diagnostic interviewing). Research aimed at exploring the accuracy of narrative reports has been conducted for several computerized personality tests, such as the Rorschach Inkblot Test (e.g., Harris, Niedner, Feldman, Fink, & Johnson, 1981; Prince & Guastello, 1990), the 16PF (e.g., Guastello & Rieke, 1990; O'Dell, 1972), the Marital Satisfaction Questionnaire (Hoover & Snyder, 1991) and the Millon Clinical Multiaxial Inventory (MCMI; Moreland & Onstad, 1987; Rogers, Salekin, & Sewell, 1999). Moreland (1987) surveyed results from the most widely studied computer-based personality assessment instrument, the MMPI. Evaluation of diagnostic interview screening by computer (e.g., the DIS) has also been reported (First, 1994).

Moreland (1987) provided an overview of studies that investigated the accuracy of computer-generated MMPI narrative reports. Some studies compared computer-generated narrative interpretations with evaluations provided by human interpreters. One methodological limitation of this type of study is that the clinician's interpretation might not be valid and accurate (Moreland, 1987). For example, Labeck, Johnson, and Harris (1983) asked three clinicians (each with at least 12 years of clinical experience) to rate the quality and the accuracy of code-type interpretations generated by an automated MMPI program (the clinicians did not rate the fit of a narrative to a particular patient, however). Results indicated that the MMPI code-type, diagnostic, and overall profile interpretive statements were consistently rated by the expert judges as strong interpretations. The narratives provided by automated

MMPI programs were judged to be substantially better than average when compared to the blind interpretations of similar profiles that were produced by the expert clinicians. The researchers, however, did not specify how they judged the quality of the blind interpretation and did not investigate the possibility that statements in the blind interpretation could have been so brief and general (especially when compared to a two-page narrative CBTI) that they could have artificially inflated the ratings of the CBTI reports. In spite of these limitations, this research design was considered useful in evaluating the overall congruence of computer-generated decision and interpretation rules.

Shores and Carstairs (1998) evaluated the effectiveness of the Minnesota Report in detecting faking. They found that the computer-based reports detected fake-bad profiles in 100% of the cases and detected fake-good profiles in 94% of the cases.

The primary way researchers have attempted to determine the accuracy of computer-based tests is through the use of raters (usually clinicians) who judge the accuracy of computer interpretations based on their knowledge of the client (Moreland, 1987). For example, a study by Butcher and colleagues (1998) explored the utility of computer-based MMPI-2 reports in Australia, France, Norway, and the United States. In all four countries, clinicians administered the MMPI-2 to their patients being seen for psychological evaluation or therapy; they a booklet format in the language of each country. The tests were scored and interpreted by the Minnesota Report using the American norms for MMPI-2. The practitioner, familiar with the client, rated the information available in each narrative section as *insufficient, some, adequate, more than adequate,* or *extensive.* In each case, the clinicians also indicated the percentage of accurate descriptions of the patient and were asked to respond to open-ended questions regarding ways to improve the report. Relatively few raters found the reports inappropriate or inaccurate. In all four countries, the Validity Considerations, Symptomatic Patterns, and Interpersonal Relations sections of the Minnesota Report were found to be the most useful sections in providing detailed information about the patients, compared with the Diagnostic Considerations section. Over two thirds of the records were considered to be highly accurate, which indicated that clinicians judged 80–100% of the computer-generated narrative statements in them to be appropriate and relevant. Overall, in 87% of the reports, at least 60% of the computer-generated narrative statements were believed to be appropriate and relevant to understanding the client's clinical picture.

Although such field studies are valuable in examining the potential usefulness of computer-based reports for various applications, there are limitations to their generalizability. Moreland concluded that this type of study has limitations, in part because estimates of interrater reliability are usually not practical. Raters usually are not asked to provide descriptions of how their judgments were made, and the appropriateness of their judgments was not verified with information from the patients themselves and from other sources (e.g., physicians or family members). Moreland (1985) suggested that in assessing the validity of computer-generated narrative reports, raters should evaluate individual interpretive statements because global accuracy ratings may limit the usefulness of ratings in developing the CBTI system.

Eyde, Kowal, and Fishburne (1991) followed Moreland's recommendations in a study that investigated the comparative validity of the narrative outputs for several CBTI systems. They used case histories and self-report questionnaires as criteria against which narrative reports obtained from seven MMPI computer interpretation systems could be evaluated. Each of the clinicians rated six protocols. Some of the cases were assigned to all raters; they consisted of an African American patient and a Caucasian patient who were matched for a 7-2 (Psychasthenia-Depression) code-type and an African American soldier and a Caucasian soldier who had all clinical scales in the subclinical range ($T < 70$). The clinicians rated the relevance of *each sentence* presented in the narrative CBTI as well as the global accuracy of each report. Some CBTI systems studied showed a high degree of accuracy (The Minnesota Report was found to be most accurate of the seven). However, the overall results indicated that the validity of the narrative outputs varied, with the highest accuracy ratings being associated with narrative lengths in the short-to-medium range. The longer reports tended to include less accurate statements. For different CBTI systems, results for both sentence-by-sentence and global ratings were consistent, but they differed for the clinical and subclinical normal profiles. The subclinical normal cases had a high percentage ($Mdn = 50\%$) of unratable sentences, and the 7-2 profiles had a low percentage ($Mdn = 14\%$) of sentences that could not be rated. One explanation for such differences may come from the fact that the clinical cases were inpatients for whom more detailed case histories were available. Because the length of time between the preparation of the case histories and the administrations of the MMPI varied from case to case, it was not possible to control for changes that a patient might have experienced over time or as a result of treatment.

One possible limitation of the published accuracy-rating studies is that it is usually not possible to control for a phenomenon referred to as the P. T. Barnum effect (e.g., Meehl, 1956) or Aunt Fanny effect (e.g., Tallent, 1958), which suggests that a narrative report may contain high base-rate descriptions that apply to virtually anybody. One factor to consider is that personality variables, such as extraversion, introversion, and neuroticism (Furnham, 1989), as well as the extent of private self-consciousness (Davies, 1997), also have been found to be connected to individuals' acceptance of Barnum feedback.

Research on the Barnum rating effect has shown that participants can usually detect the nature of the overly general feedback if asked the appropriate questions about it (Furnham & Schofield, 1987; Layne, 1979). However, this criticism might not be appropriate for clinical studies because this research has most often been demonstrated for situations involving acceptance of positive statements in self-ratings in normally functioning individuals. For example, research also has demonstrated that people typically are more accepting of favorable Barnum feedback than they are of unfavorable feedback (Dickson & Kelly, 1985; Furnham & Schofield, 1987; C. R. Snyder & Newburg, 1981), and people have been found to perceive favorable descriptions as more appropriate for themselves than for people in general (Baillargeon & Danis, 1984).

Dickson and Kelly (1985) suggested that test situations, such as the type of assessment instruments used, can be significant in eliciting acceptance of Barnum statements. However, Baillargeon and Danis (1984) found no interaction between the type of assessment device and the favorability of statements. Research has suggested that people are more likely to accept Barnum descriptions that are presented by persons of authority or expertise (Lees-Haley, Williams, & Brown, 1993). However, the relevance of this interpretation to studies of testing results has been debated.

Some researchers have made efforts to control for Barnum-type effects on narrative CBTIs by comparing the accuracy of ratings to a stereotypical client or an average subject and by using multireport-multirating intercorrelation matrices (Moreland, 1987) or by examining differences in perceived accuracy between bogus and real reports (Moreland & Onstad, 1987; O'Dell, 1972). Several studies have compared bogus with genuine reports and found them to be statistically different in judged accuracy. In one study, for example, Guastello, Guastello, and Craft (1989) asked college students to complete the Comprehensive Personality Profile Compatibility Questionnaire (CPPCQ). One group of students rated the real computerized test interpretation of the CPPCQ, and another group rated a bogus report. The difference between the accuracy ratings for the bogus and real profiles (57.9% and 74.5%, respectively) was statistically significant. In another study (Guastello & Rieke, 1990), undergraduate students enrolled in an industrial psychology class evaluated a real computer-generated Human Resources Development Report (HRDR) of the 16PF and a bogus report generated from the average 16PF profile of the entire class. Results indicated no statistically significant difference between the ratings for the real reports and the bogus reports (which had mean accuracy ratings of 71.3% and 71.1%, respectively). However, when the results were analyzed separately, four out of five sections of the real 16PF output had significantly higher accuracy ratings than did the bogus report. Contrary to these findings, Prince and Guastello (1990) found no statistically significant differences between descriptions of a bogus and real CBTI interpretations when they investigated a computerized version of the Exner Rorschach interpretation system.

Moreland and Onstad (1987) asked clinical psychologists to rate genuine MCMI computer-generated reports and randomly generated reports. The judges rated the accuracy of the reports based on their knowledge of the client as a whole as well as the global accuracy of each section of the report. Five out of seven sections of the report exceeded chance accuracy when considered one at a time. Axis I and Axis II sections demonstrated the highest incremental validity. There was no difference in accuracy between the real reports and the randomly selected reports for the Axis IV psychosocial stressors section. The overall pattern of findings indicated that computer reports based on the MCMI can exceed chance accuracy in diagnosing patients (Moreland & Onstad, 1987, 1989).

Overall, research concerning computer-generated narrative reports for personality assessment has typically found that the interpretive statements contained in them are comparable to clinician-generated statements. Research also points to the importance of controlling for the degree of generality of the reports' descriptions in order to reduce the confounding influence of the Barnum effect (Butcher et al., 2000).

Neuropsychological Assessment

Computer-based test batteries have also been used in making assessment decisions for cognitive evaluation and in neuropsychological evaluations. The 1960s marked the beginning of investigations into the applicability of computerized testing to this field (e.g., Knights & Watson, 1968). Because of the inclusion of complex visual stimuli and the requirement that participants perform motor response tasks, the computer development of computerized assessment of cognitive tasks has not proceeded as rapidly as that of paper-and-pencil personality measures. Therefore, neuropsychology computerized test interpretation was slower to develop procedures that are equal in accuracy to those achieved by human clinicians (Adams & Heaton, 1985, p. 790; see also Golden, 1987). Garb and Schramke (1996) reviewed and performed a meta-analysis of studies involving computer analyses for neuropsychological assessment, concluding that they were promising but that they needed improvement. Specifically, they pointed out that programs needed to be created that included such information

as patient history and clinician observation in addition to the psychometric and demographic data that are more typically used in the prediction process for cognitive measures.

Russell (1995) concluded that computerized testing procedures were capable of aiding in the detection and location of brain damage accurately but not as precisely as clinical judgment. For example, the Right Hemisphere Dysfunction Test (RHDT) and Visual Perception Test (VPT) were used in one study (Sips, Catsman-Berrevoets, van Dongen, van der Werff, & Brook, 1994) in which these computerized measures were created for the purpose of assessing right-hemisphere dysfunction in children and were intended to have the same validity as the Line Orientation Test (LOT) and Facial Recognition Test (FRT) had for adults. Fourteen children with acquired cerebral lesions were administered all four tests. Findings indicated that the computerized RHDT and VPT together were sensitive (at a level of 89%) to right-hemisphere lesions, had relatively low specificity (40%), had high predictive value (72%), and accurately located the lesion in 71% of cases. Fray, Robbins, and Sahakian (1996) reviewed findings regarding a computerized assessment program, the Cambridge Neuropsychological Test Automated Batteries (CANTAB). Although specificity and sensitivity were not reported, the reviewers concluded that CANTAB could detect the effects of progressive, neurogenerative disorders sometimes before other signs manifested themselves. They concluded that the CANTAB has been found successful in detecting early signs of Alzheimer's, Parkinson's, and Huntington's diseases.

Evaluation of Computerized Structured Interviews

Research on computer-assisted psychiatric screening has largely involved the development of logic-tree decision models to assist the clinician in arriving at clinical diagnoses (Erdman, Klein, & Greist, 1985; see also the chapter by Craig in this volume). Logic-tree systems are designed to establish the presence of symptoms specified in diagnostic criteria and to arrive at a particular diagnosis (First, 1994). For example, the DTREE is a recent program designed to guide the clinician through the diagnostic process (First, 1994) and provide the clinician with diagnostic consultation both during and after the assessment process. A narrative report is provided that includes likely diagnoses as well as an extensive narrative explaining the reasoning behind diagnostic decisions included. Research on the validity of logic-tree programs typically compares diagnostic decisions made by a computer and diagnostic decisions made by clinicians. In an initial evaluation, First et al. (1993) evaluated the use of DTREE in an inpatient setting by comparing case conclusions by expert clinicians with the results of DTREE output.

Psychiatric inpatients ($N = 20$) were evaluated by a consensus case conference and by their treating psychiatrist (five psychiatrists participated in the rating) who used DTREE software. Although the number of cases within each of the diagnostic categories was small, the results are informative. On the primary diagnosis, perfect agreement was reached between the DTREE and the consensus case conference in 75% of cases ($N = 15$). The agreement was likely to be inflated because some of the treating psychiatrists participated in both the DTREE evaluation and the consensus case conference. This preliminary analysis, however, suggested that DTREE might be useful in education and in evaluation of diagnostically challenging clients (First et al., 1993), although the amount of rigorous research on the system is limited.

A second logic-tree program in use is a computerized version of the World Health Organization (WHO) Composite International Diagnostic Interview (CIDI-Auto). Peters and Andrews (1995) conducted an investigation of the validity of the CIDI-Auto in the *DSM-III-R* diagnoses of anxiety disorders, finding generally variable results ranging from low to high accuracy for the CIDI-auto administered by computer. However, there was only modest overall agreement for the procedure. Ninety-eight patients were interviewed by the first clinician in a brief clinical intake interview prior to entering an anxiety disorders clinic. When the patients returned for a second session, a CIDI-Auto was administered and the client was interviewed by another clinician. The order in which CIDI-Auto was completed varied depending upon the availability of the computer and the second clinician. At the end of treatment, clinicians reached consensus about the diagnosis in each individual case ($\kappa = .93$). When such agreement could not be reached, diagnoses were not recorded as the LEAD standard against which CIDI-Auto results were evaluated. Peters and Andrews (1995) concluded that the overdiagnosis provided by the CIDI might have been caused by clinicians' using stricter diagnostic rules in the application of duration criteria for symptoms.

In another study, 37 psychiatric inpatients completed a structured computerized interview assessing their psychiatric history (Carr, Ghosh, & Ancill, 1983). The computerized interview agreed with the case records and clinician interview on 90% of the information. Most patients (88%) considered computer interview to be no more demanding than a traditional interview, and about one third of them reported that the computer interview was easier. Some patients felt that their responses to the computer were more accurate than those provided to interviewers. The computer program in this study elicited about 9.5% more information than did traditional interviews.

Psychiatric screening research has more frequently involved evaluating computer-administered versions of the DIS (Blouin, Perez, & Blouin, 1988; Erdman et al., 1992; Greist et al., 1987; Mathisen, Evans, & Meyers, 1987; Wyndowe, 1987). Research has shown that in general, patients tend to hold favorable attitudes toward computerized DIS systems, although diagnostic validity and reliability are questioned when such programs are used alone (First, 1994).

PAST LIMITATIONS AND UNFULFILLED DREAMS

So far I have explored the development of computer-based assessment strategies for clinical decision making, described how narrative programs are developed, and examined their equivalence and accuracy or validity. In this section I provide a summary of limitations of computer-based assessment and indicate some directions that further studies will likely or should go.

Computer-based testing services have not maximally incorporated the flexibility and graphic capabilities in presenting test-based stimuli. Psychologists have not used to a great degree the extensive powers of the computer in presenting stimuli to test takers. Much could be learned from the computer game industry about presenting items in an interesting manner. With the power, graphic capability, and flexibility of the computer, it is possible to develop more sophisticated, real-world stimulus environments than are currently available in computer-administered methods. For example, the test taker might be presented with a virtual environment and be asked to respond appropriately to the circumstances presented.

It is likely that assessment will improve in quality and effectiveness as technology—particularly graphic displays and voice-activated systems—improves in quality. At the present time, the technology exists for computer-based assessment of some complex motor activities, but they are extremely expensive to develop and maintain. For example, airlines use complex flight simulators that mimic the flight environment extremely well. Similar procedures could be employed in the assessment of cognitive functioning; however, the psychotechnology is lacking for developing more sophisticated uses. The computer assessment field has not kept up with the electronic technology that allows developing test administration strategies along the lines of the virtual reality environment. A great deal more could be done in this area to provide more realistic and interesting stimulus situations to test takers. At present, stimulus presentation of personality test items simply follows the printed booklet form. A statement is printed on the screen and the client simply presses a *yes* or *no* key. Many response behaviors that are important to test interpretation are not incorporated in computer-based interpretation at present (e.g., stress-oriented speech patterns, facial expressions, or the behavior of the client during testing). Further advancements from the test development side need to come to fruition in order to take full advantage of the present and future computer technology.

Computer-based reports are not stand-alone clinical evaluations. Even after almost 40 years of development, most computer-based interpretive reports are still considered to be broad, generic descriptions rather than integrated, stand-alone psychological reports. Computer-generated reports should be considered as potentially valuable adjuncts to clinical judgment rather than stand-alone assessments that are used in lieu of an evaluation of a skilled clinician (Fowler, 1969). The reports are essentially listings of the most likely test interpretations for a particular set of test scores—an electronic dictionary of interpretive hypotheses that have been stored in the computer to be called out when those variables are obtained for a client.

Many people would not, however, consider this feature to be a limitation of the computer-based system but actually prefer this more limited role as the major goal rather than development of final-product reports for an instrument that emerge from the computer. There has not been a clamoring in the field for computer-based finished-product psychological reports.

Computer-based assessment systems often fail to take into consideration client uniqueness. Matarazzo (1986) criticized computerized test interpretation systems because of their seeming failure to recognize the uniqueness of the test takers—that is, computer-based reports are often amorphous descriptions of clients that do not tap the uniqueness of the individual's personality.

It is true that computer-based reports seem to read a lot alike when one sees a number of them for different patients in a particular setting. This sense of sameness results from two sources. First, computerized reports are the most general summaries for a particular test score pattern and do not contain much in the way of low-frequency and specifically tailored information. Second, it is natural for reports to contain similar language because patients in a particular setting *are* alike when it comes to describing their personality and symptoms. For example, patients in a chronic pain program tend to cluster into four or five MMPI-2 profile types—representing a few scales, Hypochondriasis (Hs), Hysteria (Hy), Depression (D), and Psychasthenia (Pt; Keller & Butcher, 1991). Patients seen in an alcohol treatment setting tend to cluster into about four clusters, usually showing Paranoid (Pd), D, Pt, and Hypomania (Ma). Reports across different settings are more recognizably different. It should be noted that attempting to tailor test results to unique individual characteristics is a complex process and may not always increase their validity

because it is then necessary to include low base rate or rare hypotheses into the statement library.

The use of computer-based reports in clinical practice might dilute responsibility in the psychological assessment. Matarazzo (1986) pointed out that the practice of having unsigned computer-based reports creates a problem—a failure of responsibility for the diagnostic evaluation. According to Matarazzo, no one feels directly accountable for the contents of the reports when they come from a computer. In most situations today, this is not considered a problem because computer-based narrative reports are clearly labeled *professional-to-professional consultations.* The practitioner chooses to (or not to) incorporate the information from the report into his or her own signed evaluation report. Computer-based reports are presented as likely relevant hypotheses and labeled as consultations; they are not sold as stand-alone assessment evaluations. In this way, computerized interpretation systems are analogous to electronic textbooks or reference works: They provide a convenient lookup service. They are not finished products.

Computer-based reporting services do not maximally use the vast powers of the computer in integrating test results from different sources. It is conceptually feasible to developing an integrated diagnostic report—one that incorporates such elements or components as

- Behavioral observations.
- Personal history.
- Personality data from an omnibus personality measure such as the MMPI-2.
- Intellectual-cognitive abilities such as those reported by the Wechsler scales or performance on a neuropsychological battery such as the Reitan Neuropsychological Battery.
- Life events.
- Current stressors.
- Substance use history.

Moreover, it would be possible (and some research supports its utility) to administer this battery adaptively (i.e., tailored to the individual client), reducing the amount of testing time by eliminating redundancy. However, although a fully integrated diagnostic system that incorporates different measures from different domains is conceptually possible, it is not a practical or feasible undertaking for a number of reasons. First, there are issues of copyright with which to contend. Tests are usually owned and controlled by different—often competing—commercial publishers. Obtaining cooperation between such groups to develop an integrated system is unlikely. Second, there is insufficient research information on integrated interpretation with present-day measures to guide their integration into a single report that is internally consistent.

The idea of having the computer substitute for the psychologist's integrative function has not been widely proclaimed as desirable and in fact has been lobbied against. (Matarazzo, 1986), for example, cautioned that computerized testing must be subjected to careful study in order to preserve the integrity of psychological assessment. Even though decision-making and interpretation procedures may be automated with computerized testing, personal factors must still be considered in some way. Research by Styles (1991) investigated the importance of a trained psychologist during computerized testing with children. Her study of Raven's Progressive Matrices demonstrated the need for the psychologist to establish and maintain rapport and interest prior to, during, and after testing. These factors were found to have important effects on the reliability and validity of the test data, insofar as they affected test-taking attitudes, comprehension of test instructions, on-task behavior, and demeanor. Carson (1990) has also argued for the importance of a sound clinicianship, both in the development of psychological test systems and in their use.

Tests should not be used for tasks beyond their capability. If a test has not been developed for or validated in a particular setting, computer-based applications of it in that setting are not warranted. Even though computer-based psychological tests have been validated in some settings, it does not guarantee their validity and appropriateness for all settings. In their discussion of the misuse of psychological tests, Wakefield and Underwager (1993) cautioned against the use of computerized test interpretations of the MCMI and MCMI-II, which were designed for clinical populations, in other settings, such as for forensic evaluations. The danger of misusing data applies to all psychological test formats, but the risk seems particularly high when one considers the convenience of computerized outputs—that is (as noted by Garb, 1998), some of the consumers of computer interpretation services are nonpsychologists who are unlikely to be familiar with the validation research on a particular instrument. It is important for scoring and interpretation services to provide computer-based test results only to qualified users.

Research evaluations of computer-based systems have often been slow to appear for some assessment methods. The problems with computer-based assessment research have been widely discussed (Butcher, 1987; Maddux & Johnson, 1998; Moreland, 1985). Moreland (1985), for example, concluded that the existing research on computer-based interpretation

has been limited because of several methodological problems, including small sample sizes, inadequate external criterion measures to which one can compare the computer-based statements, lack of information regarding the reports' base-rate accuracy, failure to assess the ratings' reliability across time or across raters, failure to investigate the internal consistency of the reports' interpretations, and issues pertaining to the report raters (e.g., lack of familiarity with the interpretive system employed), lack of expertise in the area of interest, and possible bias secondary to the theoretical orientation of the rater. D. K. Snyder, Widiger, and Hoover (1990) expressed concerns over computer-based interpretation systems, concluding that the literature lacks rigorously controlled experimental studies that examine methodological issues. They recommended specifically that future studies include representative samples of both computer-based test consumers and test respondents and use characteristics of each as moderator variables in analyzing reports' generalizability.

In fairness to computer-based assessment, there has been more research into validity and accuracy for this approach than there has been for the validity of interpretation by human interpreters—that is, for clinical interpretation strategies. Extensive research on some computer-assisted assessments has shown that automated procedures can provide valid and accurate descriptions and predictions. Research on the accuracy of some computer-based systems (particularly those based on the MMPI and MMPI-2, which have been subjected to more scrutiny) has shown promising results with respect to accuracy. However, reliability and utility of computer-based interpretations vary as a function of the instruments and the settings included, as illustrated by Eyde et al. (1991) in their extensive study of the accuracy of computer-based reports.

Computer-based applications need to be evaluated carefully. Computer system developers have not always been sensitive to the requirement of validation of procedures. It is important for all computer-based systems to be evaluated to the extent that MMPI-based programs have been subjected to such evaluation (Butcher, 1987; Fowler, 1987; Moreland, 1985).

It should be kept in mind that just because a report comes from a computer, it is not necessarily valid. The caution required in assessing the utility of computer-based applications brings about a distinct need for specialized training in their evaluation. It is also apparent that instruction in the use (and avoidance of misuse) of computer-based systems is essential for all professionals who use them (Hofer & Green, 1985). There is also a need for further research focusing on the accuracy of the information contained in computer-based reports.

OFFERING PSYCHOLOGICAL ASSESSMENT SERVICES VIA THE INTERNET

As noted earlier, the expansion of psychological assessment services through the Internet brings to the field special problems that have not been sufficiently dealt with by psychologists. In this section I address several important issues that need to be taken into consideration before making psychological tests available on the Internet.

Test Security

The question of test security has several facets.

• One must assure that the test items are secure and not made available to the public. Most psychologists are aware that test items are considered protected items and should not be made public to prevent the test from being compromised. Making test items available to the general public would undermine the value of the test for making important decisions. The security of materials placed on the Internet is questionable. There have been numerous situations in which hackers have gotten into highly secure files of banks, the State Department, and so forth. It is important for test security to be assured before items are made available through the Internet.
• Some psychological tests are considered to require higher levels of expertise and training to interpret and are not made available to psychologists without clear qualifications to use them. Many psychological tests—particularly those involved in clinical assessment—require careful evaluation of user qualifications. Wide availability of tests on the Internet could result in access to the test for nonqualified test users.
• Most psychological tests are copyrighted and cannot be copied. Making test items available through the Internet increases the likelihood that copyright infringement will occur.

Of course, there are ways of controlling access to test materials in a manner similar to the way they are controlled in traditional clinical practice—that is, the tests would only be available to practitioners who would administer them in controlled office settings. The item responses could then be sent to the test scoring-interpreting service through the Internet for processing. The results of the testing could then be returned to the practitioner electronically in a coded manner that would not be accessible to nonauthorized persons.

Assurance That the Norms for the Test Are Appropriate for Internet Application

Most psychological tests are normed in a standard manner—that is, by having the normative population taking the test in

a standard, carefully monitored test situation. Relatively few traditional psychological tests are administered through the Internet. (One exception to this was the Dutch-language version of the MMPI-2; see Sloore, Derksen, de Mey, & Hellenbosch, 1996.) Consequently, making tests available to clients through the Internet would represent a test administration environment very different from the one for which the test was developed.

Assurance That the Individual Taking the Test Has the Cooperative Response Set Present in the Normative Sample

Response sets for Internet administration versus standard administration have not been widely studied. It would be important to ensure that Internet administration would not produce results different from those of standard administration. As noted earlier, computer-administered versus booklet-administered tests have been widely studied. However, if Internet administration involves procedures that are different from those of typical computer administration, these conditions should also be evaluated.

The Internet Version of the Test Needs to Have Reliability and Validity Demonstrated

It is important to ensure that the scores for the test being administered through the Internet are equivalent to those on which the test was originally developed and that the correlates for the test scores apply equally well for the procedure when the test administration procedures are altered.

Psychological test distributors need to develop procedures to assure that the problems noted here do not occur. As previously noted, it is possible that although the tests are processed through the Internet, they could still be administered and controlled through individual clinicians—that is, it is possible that the problems described here could be resolved by limiting access to the test in much the same way that credit card numbers are currently protected. Practitioners who wish to process their test results through the Internet could administer the test to the client in their office and then enter the client's responses into the computer from their own facility keyboard or scanner before dialing up the Internet server. In this manner, the clinician (who has been deemed a qualified test user and is eligible to purchase the test) can assume the responsibility for test security as well as determine which psychological tests meet the essential criteria for the test application involved.

THE ACCEPTANCE AND ETHICS OF COMPUTER-BASED PSYCHOLOGICAL ASSESSMENT

Now after almost 40 years, where does computer-based psychological assessment stand in the field of professional psychology in terms of user acceptance? Recent evidence shows that applied psychologists have substantially endorsed computer-based psychological assessment, although as a group, clinicians are seemingly reluctant to endorse or use new technological developments in their practice (McMinn, Buchanan, Ellens, & Ryan, 1999). The actual use of computer-scored test results is unclear. One recent survey of practitioners found that 67.8% of respondents used computer scoring of psychological tests and 43.8% also used computer-derived reports in their practice (Downey, Sinnett, & Seeberger, 1998). However, Camara, Nathan, and Puente (2000) reported that only about 10% of neuropsychologists and clinical psychologists score tests by computer.

When computer-based assessment was in its infancy, there was a concern that ethical problems could result from handing over a professionally sensitive task like personality assessment to computers. Some authorities (e.g., Matarazzo, 1986) expressed concerns that individual clinicians might defer important clinical decisions to computers, thereby ignoring the client in the assessment process. Such reliance upon machines to provide clinical assessments could result in unethical and irresponsible judgments on the part of the practitioner. However, these arguments were answered by Fowler and Butcher (1986), who noted that psychologists use computer-based psychological reports not as a final polished report but as one source of information that is available to the practitioner who is responsible for decisions made about clients. Most authorities in the computer-based area as well as several professional organizations that have provided practical guidelines for computer based assessment, such the *Guidelines for Computer-Based Tests and Interpretations* of the American Psychological Association (1986) and the *Standards for Educational and Psychological Testing* by the American Educational Research Association, American Psychological Association, and National Council on Measurement in Education (1999) have supported the ethical use of computer-based psychological assessment.

How do present-day clinicians feel about the ethics of computerized assessment? The earlier concerns over computer-based test usage seem to have waned considerably with the growing familiarity with computerized assessment. For example, in a recent survey concerning computer-based test use (McMinn et al. 1999), most respondents thought that use of computer-based assessment was an ethical practice.

SUMMARY

Computer-based psychological assessment has come far since it began to evolve over 40 years ago. As a group, assessment practitioners have accepted computerized testing. Many clinicians use some computer scoring, computer-based interpretation, or both. Most practitioners today consider computer-assisted test interpretation to be an ethical professional activity. Computers have been important to the field of applied psychology almost since they were introduced, and the application of computerized methods has expanded over the past several decades. Since that time, the application of computerized methods has broadened both in scope and in depth.

The merger of computer technology and psychological test interpretation has not, however, been a perfect relationship. Past efforts at computerized assessment have not gone far enough in making optimal use of the flexibility and power of computers for making complex decisions. At present, most interpretive systems largely perform a look up, list out function—a broad range of interpretations is stored in the computer for various test scores and indexes, and the computer simply lists out the stored information for appropriate scale score levels. Computers are not involved as much in decision making.

Computerized applications are limited to some extent by the available psychological expertise and psychotechnology. To date, computer-human interactions are confined to written material. Potentially valuable information, such as critical nonverbal cues (e.g., speech patterns, vocal tone, and facial expressions), is presently not incorporated in computer-based assessments. Furthermore, the response choices are usually provided to the test taker in a fixed format (e.g., true-false).

On the positive side, the earlier suggestion made by some researchers that computer-administered and traditional administration approaches were nonequivalent has not been supported by more recent findings. Research has supported the view that computer-administered tests are essentially equivalent to booklet-administered instruments.

In spite of what have been described as limitations and unfulfilled hopes, computer-based psychological assessment is an enormously successful endeavor. Research thus far appears to point to the conclusion that computer-generated reports should be viewed as valuable adjuncts to clinical judgment rather than as substitutes for skilled clinicians. Computer-based assessment has brought accountability and reliability into the assessment field. It is apparent that whatever else computerized assessment has done for the field of psychology, it clearly has focused attention upon objective and accurate assessment in the fields of clinical evaluation and diagnosis.

APPENDIX

MMPI-2™

The Minnesota Report:™

Reports for Forensic Settings

James N. Butcher, PhD

ID Number 1359303

Female

Age 22

Married

12 Years of Education

Pre-trial Criminal Report

9/18/2000

Profile Validity

This is a valid MMPI-2 profile. The client's attitude toward the testing was appropriate. She responded to the items in a frank and open manner, freely admitting to some psychological problems, which are described in the narrative report.

Symptomatic Patterns

The personality and behavioral descriptions for this very well-defined MMPI-2 profile code, which incorporates correlates of *Pd and Pa,* are likely to clearly reflect her current per-

Copyright © 1997 REGENTS OF THE UNIVERSITY OF MINNESOTA. All rights reserved.
Portions reproduced from the MMPI-2 test. Copyright © 1942, 1943, (renewed 1970), 1989 REGENTS OF THE UNIVERSITY OF MINNESOTA. All rights reserved. Distributed exclusively by National Computer Systems, Inc.
"Minnesota Multiphasic Personality Inventory-2," "MMPI-2," and "The Minnesota Report" are trademarks of the University of Minnesota.
[13 / 1.0 / 1.0]

sonality functioning. Her profile is a good match with the empirical literature from which the correlates were derived. Individuals with this MMPI-2 clinical profile tend to have an extreme pattern of chronic psychological maladjustment. The client appears to be very immature and alienated, tending to manipulate others for her own gratification. She also seems quite self-indulgent, hedonistic, and narcissistic, with a grandiose conception of her capabilities. She may be quite aggressive with others. She tends to be very impulsive and acts out her problems. She rationalizes her difficulties and denies responsibility for her actions, preferring instead to blame other people. She tends to be very hostile, resentful, and irritable.

In addition, the following description is suggested by the content of the client's item responses. She endorsed a number of items suggesting that she is experiencing low morale and a depressed mood. She endorsed a number of items reflecting a high degree of anger. She appears to have a high potential for explosive behavior at times. She feels somewhat self-alienated and expresses some personal misgivings or a vague sense of remorse about past acts. She feels that life is unrewarding and dull, and she finds it hard to settle down. She views the world as a threatening place, sees herself as having been unjustly blamed for others' problems, and feels that she is getting a raw deal from life. She endorsed statements that indicate some inability to control her anger. She may physically or verbally attack others when she is angry.

Profile Frequency

Profile interpretation can be greatly facilitated by examining the relative frequency of clinical scale patterns in various settings. The client's high-point clinical scale score (Pd) occurs in 9.5% of the MMPI-2 normative sample of women. However, only 4.7% of the sample have Pd scale peak scores at or above a T score of 65, and only 2.9% have well-defined Pd spikes. Her elevated MMPI-2 two-point profile configuration (4-6/6-4) is very rare in samples of normals, occurring in less than 1% of the MMPI-2 normative sample of women.

The relative frequency of her high-point Pd profile in inpatient settings is useful information for clinical interpretation. In the Graham and Butcher (1988) sample, Pd is the second most frequent peak score, occurring as the high point in 14.5% of the females (13.7% are at or above a T score of 65, and 6.9% are well defined in that range). In the NCS inpatient sample, this high-point clinical scale score (Pd) occurs in 15.7% of the women (the second most frequent peak score). Additionally, 14% of the inpatient women have the Pd spike equal to or greater than a T score

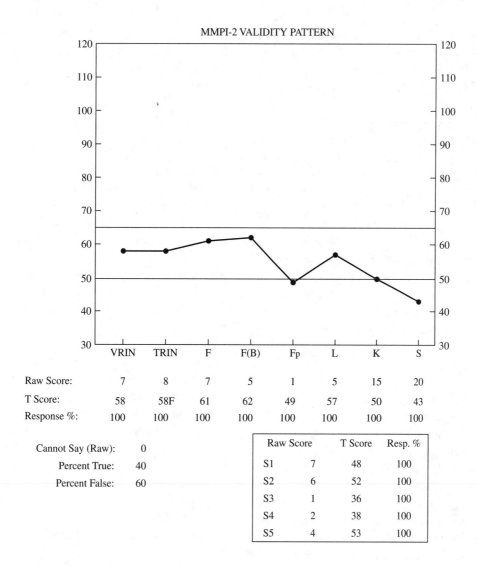

MMPI-2 VALIDITY PATTERN

	VRIN	TRIN	F	F(B)	Fp	L	K	S
Raw Score:	7	8	7	5	1	5	15	20
T Score:	58	58F	61	62	49	57	50	43
Response %:	100	100	100	100	100	100	100	100

Cannot Say (Raw):   0
Percent True: 40
Percent False: 60

	Raw Score	T Score	Resp. %
S1	7	48	100
S2	6	52	100
S3	1	36	100
S4	2	38	100
S5	4	53	100

of 65, and 7.7% produce well-defined Pd peak scores in that range.

As the highest peak score in the profile, this spike on Pd is found in 15.1% of the women in a Veterans Administration inpatient sample (Arbisi & Ben-Porath, 1997). The high-point Pd score was the second highest in frequency among the clinical scale high points. It was found to be well defined and elevated at or above a T of 65 in 11.6% of the cases.

The frequency of Pd spike scores on MMPI-2 was also high for women in the general psychiatric inpatient study conducted by Arbisi, Ben-Porath, Marshall, Boyd, and Strauman (1997). They found that this high-point score occurred in 23.1% of the high-point codes (the second most frequent peak score for women) and that 12.8% of high-point Pd scores were well-defined high-point profiles.

This elevated MMPI-2 two-point profile configuration (4-6/6-4) is found in 6.9% of the females in the Graham and Butcher (1988) sample and in 4.6% of the females in the NCS inpatient sample. A similar frequency (4.7%) was obtained in the sample of female veterans in the VA hospital inpatient sample (Arbisi & Ben-Porath, 1997). Only 1.2% of these profiles were well defined at or above a T score of 65. Interestingly, this code type was found to be one of the most common profile configurations in the sample studied by Arbisi, Ben-Porath, Marshall, Boyd, and Strauman (1997). They reported that this high-point configuration occurred with 11.1% frequency (the second highest code type), with 4.4% having well-defined code types.

Ben-Porath and Stafford (1997) reported high-point and code type frequencies for men and women undergoing competency assessments. The high-point MMPI-2 score on Pd that the client received occurred with very high frequency (25.4%) in that sample. Additionally, this high point occurred with high frequency (14.1%) in terms of well-defined profiles

at or above a T score of 65. The Pd spike was the most frequent clinical scale elevation for women undergoing competency evaluations. This MMPI-2 high-point code (4-6/6-4)
can best be understood in the context of cases reported by
Ben-Porath and Stafford (1997) in their study of individuals
undergoing competency evaluations. This profile configuration (the most frequent two-point code) occurred with high
frequency (12.7%) and with 3.5% frequency as a well-
defined score at or above a T of 65.

Profile Stability

The relative elevation of the highest scales in her clinical profile shows very high profile definition. Her peak scores are
likely to be very prominent in her profile pattern if she
is retested at a later date. Her high-point score on Pd is likely
to remain stable over time. Short-term test-retest studies have
shown a correlation of 0.79 for this high-point score.

Interpersonal Relations

She has a great deal of difficulty in her social relationships.
She feels that others do not understand her and do not give
her enough sympathy. She is somewhat aloof, cold, non-
giving, and uncompromising, attempting to advance herself
at the expense of others. She may have a tendency to be verbally abusive toward her husband when she feels frustrated.

The content of this client's MMPI-2 responses suggests
the following additional information concerning her interpersonal relationships. She feels intensely angry, hostile, and resentful toward others, and she would like to get back at them.
She is competitive and uncooperative and tends to be very
critical of others.

Mental Health Considerations

An individual with this profile is usually viewed as having
a severe personality disorder, such as an antisocial or paranoid
personality. The possibility of a paranoid disorder should also
be considered. Her self-reported tendency toward experiencing depressed mood should be taken into consideration in any
diagnostic formulation.

Individuals with this profile tend not to seek psychological
treatment on their own and are usually not good candidates
for psychotherapy. They resist psychological interpretation,
argue, and tend to rationalize and blame others for their problems. They also tend to leave therapy prematurely and blame
the therapist for their own failings.

If psychological treatment is being considered, it may be
profitable for the therapist to explore the client's treatment

motivation early in therapy. The item content she endorsed
includes some feelings and attitudes that could be unproductive in psychological treatment and in implementing
change.

Pre-Trial Criminal Considerations

Her approach to the test was open and cooperative and should
provide valuable information for the case disposition. She
endorsed some psychological symptoms without a great deal
of exaggeration.

Some distinctive problems are evident in her MMPI-2
profile. She presented some clear personality problems that
are probably relevant to an assessment of her day-to-day
functioning. Her high elevations on the Pd and Pa scales may
reflect a tendency to engage in angry, irresponsible, immature, and possibly antisocial behavior. In pre-trial situations,
individuals with this personality pattern are usually suspicious of others and resentful of demands made on them. They
may make excessive and unrealistic demands on others. They
tend not to accept responsibility for their own behavior and
are unrealistic and grandiose in their self-appraisal.

Individuals with this pattern are usually mistrustful of the
people close to them and tend to have trouble with emotional
involvement. Their irritable, sullen, argumentative, and generally obnoxious behavior can strain relationships. The extent
to which this individual's behavior has caused her current
problem situation should be further evaluated. Her tendency
to resent and disregard authority might make her vulnerable to encountering problems with the law or with supervisors in the work place.

In addition to the problems indicated by the MMPI-2 clinical scales, she endorsed some items on the Content Scales
that could reflect difficulties for her. Her proneness to experience depression might make it difficult for her to think
clearly or function effectively. Her anger-control problems
are likely to interfere with her functioning in relationships.
The sources of her anger problems should be identified, and
effective strategies for helping her gain better control over
her aggressiveness should be implemented.

NOTE: This MMPI-2 interpretation can serve as a useful source of
hypotheses about clients. This report is based on objectively derived
scale indices and scale interpretations that have been developed
with diverse groups of people. The personality descriptions, inferences, and recommendations contained herein should be verified by
other sources of clinical information because individual clients may
not fully match the prototype. The information in this report should
be considered confidential and should be used by a trained, qualified
test interpreter.

MMPI-2 BASIC AND SUPPLEMENTARY SCALES PROFILE

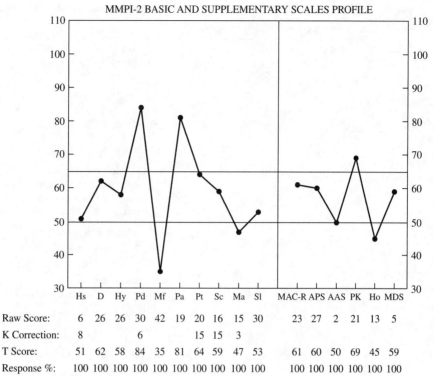

	Hs	D	Hy	Pd	Mf	Pa	Pt	Sc	Ma	Si		MAC-R	APS	AAS	PK	Ho	MDS
Raw Score:	6	26	26	30	42	19	20	16	15	30		23	27	2	21	13	5
K Correction:	8			6			15	15	3								
T Score:	51	62	58	84	35	81	64	59	47	53		61	60	50	69	45	59
Response %:	100	100	100	100	100	100	100	100	100	100		100	100	100	100	100	100
Non-Gendered T Score:	53	64	60	83		81	66	58	46								

Welsh Code: 46ᵐ+72-8301/9:5# F-LK/

Profile Elevation: 63.30

MMPI-2 CONTENT SCALES PROFILE

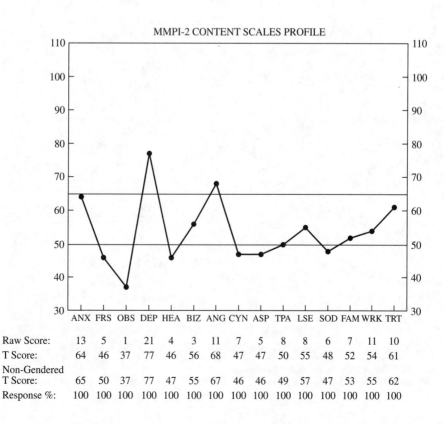

	ANX	FRS	OBS	DEP	HEA	BIZ	ANG	CYN	ASP	TPA	LSE	SOD	FAM	WRK	TRT
Raw Score:	13	5	1	21	4	3	11	7	5	8	8	6	7	11	10
T Score:	64	46	37	77	46	56	68	47	47	50	55	48	52	54	61
Non-Gendered T Score:	65	50	37	77	47	55	67	46	46	49	57	47	53	55	62
Response %:	100	100	100	100	100	100	100	100	100	100	100	100	100	100	100

Supplementary Score Report

	Raw Score	T Score	Resp %
Anxiety (A)	18	58	100
Repression (R)	12	39	100
Ego Strength (Es)	32	45	100
Dominance (Do)	14	42	100
Social Responsibility (Re)	23	56	100
Depression Subscales			
(Harris-Lingoes)			
Subjective Depression (D1)	12	60	100
Psychomotor Retardation (D2)	5	46	100
Physical Malfunctioning (D3)	5	63	100
Mental Dullness (D4)	4	57	100
Brooding (D5)	6	68	100
Hysteria Subscales			
(Harris-Lingoes)			
Denial of Social Anxiety (Hy1)	6	61	100
Need for Affection (Hy2)	8	55	100
Lassitude-Malaise (Hy3)	7	67	100
Somatic Complaints (Hy4)	1	41	100
Inhibition of Aggression (Hy5)	3	46	100
Psychopathic Deviate Subscales			
(Harris-Lingoes)			
Familial Discord (Pd1)	2	50	100
Authority Problems (Pd2)	4	61	100
Social Imperturbability (Pd3)	5	58	100
Social Alienation (Pd4)	8	70	100
Self-Alienation (Pd5)	9	77	100
Paranoia Subscales			
(Harris-Lingoes)			
Persecutory Ideas (Pa1)	6	75	100
Poignancy (Pa2)	4	59	100
Naivete (Pa3)	7	60	100
Schizophrenia Subscales			
(Harris-Lingoes)			
Social Alienation (Sc1)	5	57	100
Emotional Alienation (Sc2)	4	76	100
Lack of Ego Mastery, Cognitive (Sc3)	0	43	100
Lack of Ego Mastery, Cognitive (Sc4)	4	59	100
Lack of Ego Mastery, Defective Inhibition (Sc5)	2	53	100
Bizarre Sensory Experiences (Sc6)	2	50	100
Hypomania Subscales			
(Harris-Lingoes)			
Amorality (Ma1)	3	62	100
Psychomotor Acceleration (Ma2)	3	40	100
Imperturbability (Ma3)	3	50	100
Ego Inflation (Ma4)	1	37	100
Social Introversion Subscales			
(Ben-Porath, Hostetler, Butcher, and Graham)			
Shyness/Self-Consciousness (Si1)	3	44	100
Social Avoidance (Si2)	4	56	100
Alienation–Self and Others (Si3)	5	49	100

Uniform T scores are used for Hs, D, Hy, Pd, Pa, Pt, Sc, Ma, and the Content Scales; all other MMPI-2 scales use linear T scores.

Content Component Scales (Ben-Porath & Sherwood)

	Raw Score	T Score	Resp %
Fears Subscales			
Generalized Fearfulness (FRS1)	1	48	100
Multiple Fears (FRS2)	4	43	100
Depression Subscales			
Lack of Drive (DEP1)	6	70	100
Dysphoria (DEP2)	6	87	100
Self-Depreciation (DEP3)	5	75	100
Suicidal Ideation (DEP4)	3	93	100
Health Concerns Subscales			
Gastrointestinal Symptoms (HEA1)	0	43	100
Neurological Symptoms (HEA2)	2	50	100
General Health Concerns (HEA3)	1	48	100
Bizarre Mentation Subscales			
Psychotic Symptomatology (BIZ1)	1	57	100
Schizotypal Characteristics (BIZ2)	2	54	100
Anger Subscales			
Explosive Behavior (ANG1)	3	61	100
Irritability (ANG2)	7	70	100
Cynicism Subscales			
Misanthropic Beliefs (CYN1)	4	45	100
Interpersonal Suspiciousness (CYN2)	3	49	100
Antisocial Practices Subscales			
Antisocial Attitudes (ASP1)	4	45	100
Antisocial Behavior (ASP2)	1	51	100
Type A Subscales			
Impatience (TPA1)	5	64	100
Competitive Drive (TPA2)	2	41	100
Low Self-Esteem Subscales			
Self-Doubt (LSE1)	6	66	100
Submissiveness (LSE2)	1	45	100
Social Discomfort Subscales			
Introversion (SOD1)	4	49	100
Shyness (SOD2)	1	40	100
Family Problems Subscales			
Family Discord (FAM1)	5	57	100
Familial Alienation (FAM2)	1	50	100
Negative Treatment Indicators Subscales			
Low Motivation (TRT1)	3	56	100
Inability to Disclose (TRT2)	3	60	100

REFERENCES

Adams, K. M., & Heaton, R. K. (1985). Automated interpretation of the neuropsychological test data. *Journal of Consulting and Clinical Psychology, 53,* 790–802.

Allard, G., Butler, J., Faust, D., & Shea, M. T. (1995). Errors in hand scoring objective personality tests: The case of the Personality Diagnostic Questionnaire—Revised (PDQ-R). *Professional Psychology: Research and Practice, 26,* 304–308.

American Educational Research Association, American Psychological Association, & National Council on Measurement in Education. (1999). *Standards for educational and psychological testing.* Washington, DC: American Educational Research Association.

American Psychological Association. (1986). *Guidelines for computer-based tests and interpretations.* Washington, DC: American Psychological Association.

American Psychological Association, Committee on Professional Standards. (1984). Casebook for providers of psychological services. *American Psychologist, 39,* 663–668.

Baillargeon, J., & Danis, C. (1984). Barnum meets the computer: A critical test. *Journal of Personality Assessment, 48,* 415–419.

Blouin, A. G., Perez, E. L., & Blouin, J. H. (1988). Computerized administration of the Diagnostic Interview Schedule. *Psychiatry Research, 23,* 335–344.

Butcher, J. N. (1982). *User's guide for the MMPI-2 Minnesota Report: Adult clinical system.* Minneapolis, MN: National Computer Systems.

Butcher, J. N. (Ed). (1987a). *Computerized psychological assessment.* New York: Basic Books.

Butcher, J. N. (1987b). The use of computers in psychological assessment: An overview of practices and issues. In J. N. Butcher (Ed.), *Computerized psychological assessment: A practitioner's guide* (pp. 3–15). New York: Basic Books.

Butcher, J. N. (1988*). Personality profile of airline pilot applicants.* Unpublished manuscript, University of Minnesota, Department of Psychology, MMPI-2 Workshops.

Butcher, J. N. (1995a). Clinical use of computer-based personality test reports. In J. N. Butcher (Ed.), *Clinical personality assessment: Practical approaches* (pp. 3–9). New York: Oxford University Press.

Butcher, J. N. (1995b). *User's guide for the MMPI-2 Minnesota Report: Personnel system.* Minneapolis, MN: National Computer Systems.

Butcher, J. N. (1997). *User's guide for the MMPI-2 Minnesota Report: Forensic system.* Minneapolis, MN: National Computer Systems.

Butcher, J. N., Berah, E., Ellersten, B., Miach, P., Lim, J., Nezami, E., Pancheri, P., Derksen, J., & Almagor, M. (1998). Objective personality assessment: Computer-based MMPI-2 interpretation in international clinical settings. In C. Belar (Ed.), *Comprehensive clinical psychology: Sociocultural and individual differences* (pp. 277–312). New York: Elsevier.

Butcher, J. N., Keller, L., & Bacon, S. (1985). Current developments and future directions in computerized personality assessment. *Journal of Consulting and Clinical Psychology, 53,* 803–815.

Butcher, J. N., Perry, & Atlis (2000). Validity and utility of computer-based test interpretation. *Psychological Assessment, 12,* 6–18.

Caldwell, A. B. (1996). *Forensic questions and answers on the MMPI/MMPI-2.* Los Angeles, CA: Caldwell Reports.

Camara, W. J., Nathan, J. S., & Puente, A. E. (2000). Psychological test usage: Implications in professional psychology. *Professional Psychology: Research and Practice, 31,* 141–154.

Carr, A. C., Ghosh, A., & Ancill, R. J. (1983). Can a computer take a psychiatric history? *Psychological Medicine, 13,* 151–158.

Carretta, T. R. (1989). USAF pilot selection and classification systems. *Aviation, Space, and Environmental Medicine, 60,* 46–49.

Carson, R. C. (1990). Assessment: What role the assessor? *Journal of Personality, 54,* 435–445.

Choca, J., & Morris, J. (1992). Administering the Category Test by computer: Equivalence of results. *The Clinical Neurologist, 6,* 9–15.

Davies, M. F. (1997). Private self-consciousness and the acceptance of personality feedback: Confirmatory processing in the evaluation of general vs. specific self-information. *Journal of Research in Personality, 31,* 78–92.

Dawes, R. M., Faust, D., & Meehl, P. E. (1989). Clinical versus actuarial judgment. *Science, 24,* 1668–1674.

Dickson, D. H., & Kelly, I. W. (1985). The "Barnum effect" in personality assessment: A review of the literature. *Psychological Reports, 57,* 367–382.

Downey, R. B., Sinnett, E. R., & Seeberger, W. (1998). The changing face of MMPI practice. *Psychological Reports, 83*(3, Pt 2), 1267–1272.

Erdman, H. P., Klein, M. H., & Greist, J. H. (1985). Direct patient computer interviewing. *Journal of Consulting and Clinical Psychology, 53,* 760–773.

Erdman, H. P., Klein, M. H., Greist, J. H., Skare, S. S., Husted, J. J., Robins, L. N., Helzer, J. E., Goldring, E., Hamburger, M., & Miller, J. P. (1992). A comparison of two computer-administered versions of the NMIH Diagnostic Interview schedule. *Journal of Psychiatric Research, 26,* 85–95.

Exner, J. E. (1987). Computer assistance in Rorschach interpretation. In J. N. Butcher (Ed.), *Computerized psychological assessment: A practitioner's guide* (pp. 218–235). New York: Basic Books.

Eyde, L., Kowal, D. M., & Fishburne, F. J. (1991). The validity of computer-based test interpretations of the MMPI. In T. B. Gutkin & S. L. Wise (Eds.), *The computer and the decision-making process* (pp. 75–123). Hillsdale, NJ: Erlbaum.

Farrell, A. D., Camplair, P. S., & McCullough, L. (1987). Identification of target complaints by computer interview: Evaluation of the Computerized Assessment System for Psychotherapy Evaluation and Research. *Journal of Consulting and Clinical Psychology, 55,* 691–700.

Finger, M. S., & Ones, D. S. (1999). Psychometric equivalence of the computer and booklet forms of the MMPI: A meta-analysis. *Psychological Assessment, 11,* 58–66.

First, M. B. (1994). Computer-assisted assessment of DSM-III-R diagnosis. *Psychiatric Annals, 24,* 25–29.

First, M. B., Opler, L. A., Hamilton, R. M., Linder, J., Linfield, L. S., Silver, J. M., Toshav, N. L., Kahn, D., Williams, J. B. W., & Spitzer, R. L. (1993). Evaluation in an inpatient setting of

DTREE, a computer-assisted diagnostic assessment procedure. *Comprehensive Psychiatry, 34,* 171–175.

Fowler, R. D. (1969). Automated interpretation of personality test data. In J. N. Butcher (Ed.), *MMPI: Research developments and clinical applications* (pp. 325–342). New York: McGraw-Hill.

Fowler, R. D. (1987). Developing a computer-based test interpretation system. In J. N. Butcher (Ed.), *Computerized psychological assessment* (pp. 50–63). New York: Basic Books.

Fowler, R. D., & Butcher, J. N. (1986). Critique of Matarazzo's views on computerized testing: All sigma and no meaning. *American Psychologist, 41,* 94–96.

Fray, P. J., Robbins, T. W., & Sahakian, B. J. (1996). Neuropsychological applications of CANTAB. *International Journal of Geriatric Psychiatry, 11,* 329–336.

French, C. C., & Beaumont, J. G. (1990). A clinical study of the automated assessment of intelligence by the Mill Hill Vocabulary Test and the Standard Progressive Matrices Test. *Journal of Clinical Psychology, 46,* 129–140.

Furnham, A. (1989). Personality and the acceptance of diagnostic feedback. *Personality and Individual Differences, 10,* 1121–1133.

Furnham, A., & Schofield, S. (1987). Accepting personality test feedback: A review of the Barnum effect. *Current Psychological Research and Reviews, 6,* 162–178.

Garb, H. N. (1998). *Studying the clinician: Judgment research and psychological assessment.* Washington, DC: American Psychological Association.

Garb, H. N., & Schramke, C. J. (1996). Judgement research and neuropsychological assessment: A narrative review and meta-analyses. *Psychological Bulletin, 120,* 140–153.

Golden, C. J. (1987). Computers in neuropsychology. In J. N. Butcher (Ed.), *Computerized psychological assessment: A practitioner's guide* (pp. 344–355). New York: Basic Books.

Greist, J. H., Klein, M. H., Erdman, H. P., Bires, J. K., Bass, S. M., Machtinger, P. E., & Kresge, D. G. (1987). Comparison of computer- and interviewer-administered versions of the Diagnostic Interview Schedule. *Hospital and Community Psychiatry, 38,* 1304–1310.

Grove, W. M., & Meehl, P. E. (1996). Comparative efficiency of information (subjective, impressionistic) and formal (mechanical, algorithmic) prediction procedures: The clinical-statistical controversy. *Psychology, Public Policy, and Law, 2,* 293–323.

Grove, W. M., Zald, D. H., Lebow, B., Smith, E., & Nelson, C. (2000). Clinical versus mechanical prediction: A meta-analysis. *Psychological Assessment, 12,* 19–30.

Guastello, S. J., Guastello, D., & Craft, L. (1989). Assessment of the Barnum effect in computer-based test interpretations. *The Journal of Psychology, 123,* 477–484.

Guastello, S. J., & Rieke, M. L. (1990). The Barnum effect and validity of computer-based test interpretations: The Human Resource Development Report. *Psychological Assessment, 2,* 186–190.

Harris, W. G., Niedner, D., Feldman, C., Fink, A., & Johnson, J. N. (1981). An on-line interpretive Rorschach approach: Using Exner's comprehensive system. *Behavior Research Methods and Instrumentation, 13,* 588–591.

Hile, M. G., & Adkins, R. E. (1997). Do substance abuse and mental health clients prefer automated assessments? *Behavior Research Methods, Instruments, and Computers, 29,* 146–150.

Hofer, P. J., & Green, B. F. (1985). The challenge of competence and creativity in computerized psychological testing. *Journal of Consulting and Clinical Psychology, 53,* 826–838.

Holden, R. R., & Hickman, D. (1987). Computerized versus standard administration of the Jenkins Activity Survey (Form T). *Journal of Human Stress, 13,* 175–179.

Honaker, L. M., Harrell, T. H., & Buffaloe, J. D. (1988). Equivalency of Microtest computer MMPI administration for standard and special scales. *Computers in Human Behavior, 4,* 323–337.

Hoover, D. W., & Snyder, D. K. (1991). Validity of the computerized interpretive report for the Marital Satisfaction Inventory. *Psychological Assessment: A Journal of Consulting and Clinical Psychology, 3,* 213–217.

Jemelka, R. P., Wiegand, G. A., Walker, E. A., & Trupin, E. W. (1992). Computerized offender assessment: Validation study. *Psychological Assessment, 4,* 138–144.

Keller, L. S., & Butcher, J. N. (1991). *Use of the MMPI-2 with chronic pain patients.* Minneapolis: University of Minnesota Press.

Knights, R. M., & Watson, P. (1968). The use of computerized test profiles in neuropsychological assessment. *Journal of Learning Disabilities, 1,* 6–19.

Labeck, L. J., Johnson, J. H., & Harris, W. G. (1983). Validity of a computerized on-line MMPI interpretive system. *Journal of Clinical Psychology, 39,* 412–416.

Lambert, M. E., Andrews, R. H., Rylee, K., & Skinner, J. (1987). Equivalence of computerized and traditional MMPI administration with substance abusers. *Computers in Human Behavior, 3,* 139–143.

Layne, C. (1979). The Barnum effect: Rationality versus gullibility? *Journal of Consulting and Clinical Psychology, 47,* 219–221.

Lees-Haley, P. R., Williams, C. W., & Brown, R. S. (1993). The Barnum effect and personal injury litigation. *American Journal of Forensic Psychology, 11,* 21–28.

Maddux, C. D., & Johnson, L. (1998). Computer assisted assessment. In H. B. Vance (Ed.), *Psychological assessment in children* (2nd ed., pp. 87–105). New York: Wiley.

Matarazzo, J. D. (1986). Computerized clinical psychological interpretations: Unvalidated plus all mean and no sigma. *American Psychologist, 41,* 14–24.

Mathisen, K. S., Evans, F. J., & Meyers, K. M. (1987). Evaluation of the computerized version of the Diagnostic Interview Schedule. *Hospital and Community Psychiatry, 38,* 1311–1315.

McMinn, M. R., Buchanan, T., Ellens, B. M., & Ryan, M. (1999). Technology, professional practice, and ethics: Survey findings and implications. *Professional Psychology: Research and Practice, 30,* 165–172.

Meehl, P. E. (1954). *Clinical versus statistical prediction: A theoretical analysis and a review of the evidence.* Minneapolis: University of Minnesota Press.

Meehl, P. E. (1956). Wanted—A good cookbook. *American Psychologist, 11,* 263–272.

Merten, T., & Ruch, W. (1996). A comparison of computerized and conventional administration of the German versions of the Eysenck Personality Questionnaire and the Carroll Rating Scale for depression. *Personality and Individual Differences, 20,* 281–291.

Moreland, K. L. (1985). Validation of computer-based interpretations: Problems and prospects. *Journal of Consulting and Clinical Psychology, 53,* 816–825.

Moreland, K. L. (1987). Computerized psychological assessment: What's available. In J. N. Butcher (Ed.), *Computerized psychological assessment: A practitioner's guide* (pp. 64–86). New York: Basic Books.

Moreland, K. L., & Onstad, J. A. (1987). Validity of Millon's computerized interpretation system of the MCMI: A controlled study. *Journal of Consulting and Clinical Psychology, 55,* 113–114.

Moreland, K. L., & Onstad, J. A. (1989). Yes, our study could have been better: Reply to Cash, Mikulka, and Brown. *Journal of Consulting and Clinical Psychology, 57,* 313–314.

O'Dell, J. W. (1972). P. T. Barnum explores the computer. *Journal of Consulting and Clinical Psychology, 38,* 270–273.

Pellegrino, J. W., Hunt, E. B., Abate, R., & Farr, S. (1987). A computer-based test battery for the assessment of static and dynamic spatial reasoning abilities. *Behavior Research Methods, Instruments, and Computers, 19,* 231–236.

Peters, L., & Andrews, G. (1995). Procedural validity of the computerized version of the Composite International Diagnostic Interview (CIDI-Auto) in the anxiety disorders. *Psychological Medicine, 25,* 1269–1280.

Pinsoneault, T. B. (1996). Equivalency of computer-assisted and paper and pencil administered versions of the Minnesota Multiphasic Personality Inventory-2. *Computers in Human Behavior, 12,* 291–300.

Prince, R. J., & Guastello, S. J. (1990). The Barnum effect in a computerized Rorschach interpretation system. *Journal of Psychology, 124,* 217–222.

Rogers, R., Salekin, R. T., & Sewell, K. W. (1999). Validation of the Millon Clinical Multiaxial Inventory for Axis II disorders: Does it meet Daubert standard? *Law and Human Behavior, 23,* 425–443.

Rome, H. P., Swenson, W. M., Mataya, P., McCarthy, C. E., Pearson, J. S., Keating, F. R., & Hathaway, S. R. (1962). Symposium on automation techniques in personality assessment. *Proceedings of the Staff Meetings of the Mayo Clinic, 37,* 61–82.

Roper, B. L., Ben-Porath, Y. S., & Butcher, J. N. (1995). Comparability and validity of computerized adaptive testing with the MMPI-2. *Journal of Personality Assessment, 65,* 358–371.

Ross, H. E., Swinson, R., Larkin, E. J., & Doumani, S. (1994). Diagnosing comorbidity in substance abusers: Computer assessment and clinical validation. *Journal of Nervous and Mental Disease, 182,* 556–563.

Russell, E. W. (1995). The accuracy of automated and clinical detection of brain damage and lateralization in neuropsychology. *Neuropsychology Review, 5,* 1–68.

Schuldberg, D. (1988). The MMPI is less sensitive to the automated testing format than it is to repeated testing: Item and scale effects. *Computers in Human Behaviors, 4,* 285–298.

Shores, A., & Carstairs, J. R. (1998). Accuracy of the Minnesota Report in identifying fake-good and fake-bad response sets. *Clinical Neuropsychologist, 12,* 101–106.

Sips, H. J. W. A., Catsman-Berrevoets, C. E., van Dongen, H. R., van der Werff, P. J. J., & Brook, L. J. (1994). Measuring right-hemisphere dysfunction in children: Validity of two new computerized tests. *Developmental Medicine and Child Neurology, 36,* 57–63.

Sloore, H., Derksen, J., de Mey, H., & Hellenbosch, G. (1996). The Flemish/Dutch version of the MMPI-2: Development and adaptation of the inventory for Belgium and the Netherlands. In J. N. Butcher (Ed.), *International adaptations of the MMPI-2: Research and clinical applications* (pp. 329–349). Minneapolis: University of Minnesota Press.

Snyder, C. R., & Newburg, C. L. (1981). The Barnum effect in a group setting. *Journal of Personality Assessment, 45,* 622–629.

Snyder, D. K., Widiger, T. A., & Hoover, D. W. (1990). Methodological considerations in validating computer-based test interpretations: Controlling for response bias. *Psychological Assessment, 2,* 470–477.

Styles, I. (1991). Clinical assessment and computerized testing. *International Journal of Man-Machine Studies, 35,* 133–150.

Sukigara, M. (1996). Equivalence between computer and booklet administrations of the new Japanese version of the MMPI. *Educational and Psychological Measurement, 56,* 570–584.

Tallent, N. (1958). On individualizing the psychologist's clinical evaluation. *Journal of Clinical Psychology, 14,* 243–245.

Wakefield, H., & Underwager, R. (1993). Misuse of psychological tests in forensic settings: Some horrible examples. *American Journal of Forensic Psychology, 11,* 55–75.

Watson, C. G., Juba, M., Anderson, P. E., & Manifold, V. (1990). What does the Keane et al. PTSD scale for the MMPI measure? *Journal of Clinical Psychology, 46,* 600–606.

Wilson, F. R., Genco, K. T., & Yager, G. G. (1985). Assessing the equivalence of paper-and-pencil vs. computerized tests: Demonstration of a promising methodology. *Computers in Human Behavior, 1,* 265–275.

Wyndowe, J. (1987). The microcomputerized Diagnostic Interview Schedule: Clinical use in an outpatient setting. *Canadian Journal of Psychiatry, 32,* 93–99.

CHAPTER 8

Ethical Issues in Psychological Assessment

GERALD P. KOOCHER AND CELIANE M. REY-CASSERLY

Psychological assessment is unique among the services provided by professional psychologists. Unlike psychotherapy, in which clients may come seeking help for themselves, psychological evaluation services are seldom performed solely at the request of a single individual. In the most common circumstances, people are referred to psychologists for assessment by third parties with questions about school performance, suitability for potential employment, disability status, competence to stand trial, or differential clinical diagnosis. The referring parties are invariably seeking answers to questions with varying degrees of specificity, and these answers may or may not be scientifically addressable via the analysis of psychometric data. In addition, the people being tested may benefit (e.g., obtain remedial help, collect damages, or gain a job offer) or suffer (e.g., lose disability benefits, lose custody of a child, or face imprisonment) as a consequence of the assessment, no matter how competently it is carried out.

Psychological assessment is founded on a scientific base and has the capacity to translate human behavior, characteristics, and abilities into numbers or other forms that lend themselves to description and comparison across individuals and groups of people. Many of the behaviors studied in the course of an evaluation appear to be easily comprehensible to the layperson unfamiliar with test development and psychometrics

(e.g., trace a path through a maze, perform mental arithmetic, repeat digits, or copy geometric shapes)—thereby implying that the observed responses must have some inherent validity for some purpose. Even common psychological assessment tasks that may be novel to most people (e.g., *Put this unusual puzzle together quickly. What does this inkblot look like to you?*) are imbued by the general public with some implied valuable meaning. After all, some authority suggested that the evaluation be done, and the person conducting the evaluation is a licensed expert. Unfortunately, the statistical and scientific underpinnings of the best psychological assessments are far more sophisticated than most laypersons and more than a few psychologists understand them to be. When confronted with an array of numbers or a computer-generated test profile, some people are willing to uncritically accept these data as simple answers to incredibly complex questions. This is the heart of the ethical challenge in psychological assessment: the appropriate use of psychological science to make decisions with full recognition of its limitations and the legal and human rights of the people whose lives are influenced.

In attempting to address the myriad issues that challenge psychologists undertaking to conduct assessments in the most ethically appropriate manner, it is helpful to think in terms of the prepositions *before, during,* and *after.* There are ethical considerations best addressed before the assessment is begun, others come into play as the data are collected and analyzed, and still other ethical issues crop up after the actual assessment is completed. This chapter is organized to explore the ethical problems inherent in psychological assessment using that same sequence.

In the beginning—prior to meeting the client and initiating data collection—it is important to consider several questions. What is being asked for and by whom (i.e., who is the client and what use does that person hope to make of the data)? Is the proposed evaluator qualified to conduct the evaluation and interpret the data obtained? What planning is necessary to assure the adequacy of the assessment? What instruments are available and most appropriate for use in this situation?

As one proceeds to the actual evaluation and prepares to undertake data collection, other ethical issues come to the fore. Has the client (or his or her representative) been given adequate informed consent about both the nature and intended uses of the evaluation? Is it clear who will pay for the evaluation, what is included, and who will have access to the raw data and report? What are the obligations of the psychologist with respect to optimizing the participants' performance and assuring validity and thoroughness in documentation? When the data collection is over, what are the examiner's obligations with respect to scoring, interpreting, reporting, and explaining the data collected?

Finally, after the data are collected and interpreted, what are the ongoing ethical responsibilities of the psychologist with respect to maintenance of records, allowing access to the data, and providing feedback or follow-up services? What is appropriate conduct when one psychologist is asked to review and critique another psychologist's work? How should one respond upon discovery of apparent errors or incompetence of a colleague in the conduct of a now-completed evaluation?

This chapter was completed during a period of flux in the evolution of the American Psychological Association's (APA) *Ethical Standards of Psychologists and Code of Conduct*. The current, in-force version of this document was adopted in 1992 (APA, 1992), but work on a revision is nearing completion (Ethics Code Task Force, 2001); a vote on adoption of the newest revision should take place in 2002. Many of the proposed revisions deal with psychological assessment. The Ethics Code Task Force (ECTF) charged with revising the code set out to avoid fixing that which is not broken—that is, the proposed changes focused on problems raised in a critical incident survey of psychologists, intended to ascertain where clarification and change were needed to improve professional and scientific practices. We have chosen to focus this chapter on key ethical foundations, but we also identify areas of controversy throughout. Whenever possible, we

discuss trends and likely policy decisions based on the work of the ECTF; however, readers are encouraged to visit the APA Web site (http://www.apa.org/ethics) to view the most current version of the code and standards, which will continue to evolve long after this chapter appears in print.

IN THE BEGINNING

Who Is the Client?

The first step in undertaking the evaluator role is often seductively automatic. The simple act of accepting the referral and setting up the appointment may occur almost automatically; not much thought may be devoted to the question of what specific duties or professional obligations are owed to which parties. Is the client simply the person to be evaluated, or are there layers of individuals and institutions to whom the psychologist owes some degree of professional obligation? For example, is the person to be evaluated a legally competent adult? If not—as in the case of children or dependent adults—the party seeking the evaluation may be a parent, guardian, government agency, institution, or other legally responsible authority. The evaluator must pause to consider what rights each layer of authority has in terms of such factors as the ability to compel cooperation of the person to be assessed, the right of access to test data and results, and the right to dictate components of the evaluation or the manner in which it is conducted. Sometimes there is uniform agreement by all parties, and no conflicts of interest take place. In other circumstances, the person being evaluated may have had little choice in the matter or may wish to reserve the right to limit access to results of the evaluation. In still other instances, there may be direct conflicts between what one party is seeking and the objectives of another party with some degree of client status.

Evaluations conducted in the context of the educational system provide a good example of the complex layers of client status that can be involved. Suppose that a schoolchild is failing and an assessment is requested by the child's family for use in preparation of an individualized educational plan (IEP) as specified under state or federal special education laws. If a psychologist employed by the public school system undertakes the task, that evaluator certainly owes a set of professional duties (e.g., competence, fairness, etc.) to the child, to the adults acting on behalf of the child (i.e., parents or guardians), to the employing school system, and—by extension—to the citizens of the community who pay school taxes. In the best of circumstances, there may be no problem—that is to say, the evaluation will identify the child's needs, parents and school will agree, and an appropriate effective remediation or treatment component for the IEP will be put in place.

The greater ethical challenge occurs when parents and school authorities disagree and apply pressure to the evaluator to interpret the data in ways that support their conflicting demands. One set of pressures may apply when the psychologist is employed by the school, and another may apply when the evaluation is funded by the parents or another third party. From an ethical perspective, there should be no difference in the psychologist's behavior. The psychologist should offer the most scientifically and clinically sound recommendations drawn from the best data while relying on competence and personal integrity without undue influence from external forces.

Similar conflicts in competing interests occur frequently within the legal system and the business world—a person may agree to psychological assessment with a set of hopes or goals that may be at variance or in direct conflict with the data or the outcomes desired by another party in the chain of people or institutions to whom the evaluator may owe a professional duty. Consider defendants whose counsel hope that testing will support insanity defenses, plaintiffs who hope that claims for psychological damages or disability will be supported, or job applicants who hope that test scores will prove that they are the best qualified. In all such instances, it is critical that the psychologist conducting the assessment strive for the highest level of personal integrity while clarifying the assessment role and its implications to all parties to whom a professional duty is owed.

Other third parties (e.g., potential employers, the courts, and health insurers) are involved in many psychological assessment contexts. In some cases, when the psychologist is an independent practitioner, the third party's interest is in making use of the assessment in some sort of decision (e.g., hiring or school placement); in other cases, the interest may simply be contract fulfillment (e.g., an insurance company may require that a written report be prepared as a condition of the assessment procedure). In still other situations, the psychologist conducting the evaluation may be a full-time employee of a company or agency with a financial interest in the outcome of the evaluation (e.g., an employer hoping to avoid a disability claim or a school system that wishes to avoid expensive special education placements or services). For all these reasons, it is critical that psychologists clearly conceptualize and accurately represent their obligations to all parties.

Informed Consent

The current revision of the ECTF (2001) has added a proposed standard referring specifically to obtaining informed consent for psychological assessment. The issue of consent is also discussed extensively in the professional literature

in areas of consent to treatment (Grisso & Appelbaum, 1998) and consent for research participation, but references to consent in the area of psychological assessment had been quite limited. Johnson-Greene, Hardy-Morais, Adams, Hardy, and Bergloff (1997) review this issue and propose a set of recommendations for providing informed consent to clients. These authors also propose that written documentation of informed consent be obtained; the APA ethical principles allow but do not require this step. We believe that psychologists would be wise to establish consistent routines and document all discussions with clients related to obtaining consent, explaining procedures, and describing confidentiality and privacy issues. It is particularly wise to obtain written informed consent in situations that may have forensic implications, such as personal injury lawsuits and child custody litigation.

Psychologists are expected to explain the nature of the evaluation, clarify the referral questions, and discuss the goals of the assessment, in language the client can readily understand. It is also important to be aware of the limitations of the assessment procedures and discuss these procedures with the client. To the extent possible, the psychologist also should be mindful of the goals of the client, clarify misunderstandings, and correct unrealistic expectations. For example, parents may seek a psychological evaluation with the expectation that the results will ensure that their child will be eligible for a gifted and talented program, accident victims may anticipate that the evaluation will document their entitlement to damages, and job candidates may hope to become employed or qualify for advancement. These hopes and expectations may come to pass, but one cannot reasonably comment on the outcome before valid data are in hand.

Whether the assessment takes place in a clinical, employment, school, or forensic settings, some universal principles apply. The nature of assessment must be described to all parties involved before the evaluation is performed. This includes explaining the purpose of the evaluation, who will have access to the data or findings, who is responsible for payment, and what any relevant limitations are on the psychologist's duties to the parties. In employment contexts, for example, the psychologist is usually hired by a company and may not be authorized to provide feedback to the employee or candidate being assessed. Similarly, in some forensic contexts, the results of the evaluation may ultimately be open to the court or other litigants over the objections of the person being assessed. In each case, it is the psychologist's responsibility to recognize the various levels of people and organizations to whom a professional duty may be owed and to clarify the relationship with all parties at the outset of the assessment activity.

The key elements of consent are information, understanding, and voluntariness. First, do the people to be evaluated have all the information that might reasonably influence their willingness to participate? Such information includes the purpose of the evaluation, who will have access to the results, and any costs or charges to them. Second, is the information presented in a manner that is comprehensible to the client? This includes use of appropriate language, vocabulary, and explanation of any terms that are confusing to the client. Finally, is the client willing to be evaluated? There are often circumstances in which an element of coercion may be present. For example, the potential employee, admissions candidate, criminal defendant, or person seeking disability insurance coverage might prefer to avoid mandated testing. Such prospective assessment clients might reluctantly agree to testing in such a context because they have no other choice if they wish to be hired, gain admission, be found not criminally responsible, or adjudicated disabled, respectively. Conducting such externally mandated evaluations do not pose ethical problems as long as the nature of the evaluation and obligations of the psychologist are carefully delineated at the outset. It is not necessary that the person being evaluated be happy about the prospect—he or she must simply understand and agree to the assessment and associated risks, much like people referred for a colonoscopy or exploratory surgery.

Additional issues of consent and diminished competence come into play when a psychologist is called upon to evaluate a minor child, an individual with dementia, or other persons with reduced mental capacity as a result of significant physical or mental disorder. When such an evaluation is undertaken primarily for service to the client (e.g., as part of treatment planning), the risks to the client are usually minimal. However, if the data might be used in legal proceedings (e.g., a competency hearing) or in any way that might have significant potentially adverse future consequences that the client is unable to competently evaluate, a surrogate consent process should be used—that is to say, a parent or legal guardian ought to be involved in granting permission for the evaluation. Obtaining such permission helps to address and respect the vulnerabilities and attendant obligations owed to persons with reduced personal decision-making capacities.

Test User Competence

Before agreeing to undertake a particular evaluation, the clinician should be competent to provide the particular service to the client, but evaluating such competence varies with the eye of the beholder. Psychologists are ethically bound not to promote the use of psychological assessment techniques by unqualified persons, except when such use is conducted for training purposes with appropriate supervision. Ascertaining what constitutes competence or qualifications in the area of

psychological assessment has been a difficult endeavor due to the complex nature of assessment, the diverse settings and contexts in which psychological assessments are performed, and the differences in background and training of individuals providing psychological assessment services. Is a doctoral degree in clinical, counseling, or school psychology required? How about testing conducted by licensed counselors or by individuals with master's degrees in psychology? Are some physicians competent to use psychological tests? After all, Hermann Rorschach was a psychiatrist, and so was J. Charnley McKinley, one of the two originators of the Minnesota Multiphasic Personality Inventory (MMPI). Henry Murray, a nonpsychiatric physician, coinvented the thematic apperception test (TAT) with Christiana Morgan, who had no formal training in psychology.

Historically, the APA addressed this issue only in a very general manner in the *Ethical Principles and Code of Conduct for Psychologists*. In earliest versions of the *Ethical Standards of Psychologists* (APA, 1953), the ethical distribution and sale of psychological tests was to be limited to unspecified "qualified persons." A system of categorization of tests and concordant qualifications that entailed three levels of tests and expertise was subsequently developed. Vocational guidance tools, for example, were at the low end in terms of presumed required expertise. At the high end of required competence were tests designed for clinical assessment and diagnoses such as intelligence and personality assessment instruments. The rationale involved in this scheme was based on the need to understand statistics, psychopathology, and psychometrics in order to accurately draw clinical inference or make actuarial predictions based on the test data. Although the three-tier system is no longer discussed in APA ethical standards, it was adopted by many test publishers, and variations continue in use. When attempting to place orders for psychological test materials, would-be purchasers are often asked to list their credentials, cite a professional license number, or give some other indication of presumed competence. Decisions about the actual sale are generally made by the person processing the order—often a clerk who has little understanding of the issues and considerable incentive to help the test publisher make the sale. Weaknesses and inconsistencies in the implementation of these criteria are discussed in a recent Canadian study (Simner, 1994).

Further efforts to delineate qualifications of test users included the lengthy efforts of the Test User Qualifications Working Group (TUQWG) sponsored by an interdisciplinary group, the Joint Committee on Testing Practices, which was convened and funded by the APA. To study competence problems, this group of professionals and academics attempted to quantify and describe factors associated with appropriate test use by using a data-gathering (as opposed to a specification of qualifications) approach (Eyde, Moreland, Robertson, Primoff, & Most, 1988; Eyde et al., 1993; Moreland, Eyde, Robertson, Primoff, & Most, 1995).

International concerns regarding competent test use—perhaps spurred by expansion of the European Economic Community and the globalization of industry—prompted the British Psychological Society (BPS) to establish a certification system that delineates specific competencies for the use of tests (BPS, 1995, 1996) in employment settings. Under this system, the user who demonstrates competence in test use is certified and listed in an official register. Professionals aspiring to provide psychological assessment services must demonstrate competence with specific tests to be listed. The International Test Commission (2000) recently adopted test-use guidelines describing the knowledge, competence, and skills.

Within the United States, identifying test user qualifications and establishing competence in test use have been complicated by political and practical issues, including the potential for nonprofit professional groups to be accused of violating antitrust laws, the complexity of addressing the myriad settings and contexts in which tests are used, and the diversity of experience and training in assessment among the professionals who administer and interpret psychological tests. Further complicating matters is the trend in recent years for many graduate programs in psychology to de-emphasize psychological assessment theory and practice in required course work, producing many licensed doctoral psychologists who are unfamiliar with contemporary measurement theory (Aiken, West, Sechrest, & Reno, 1990).

In October of 1996, the APA formed a task force to develop more specific guidelines in the area of test user qualifications and competence (Task Force on Test User Qualifications). Members of the task force were selected to represent the various settings and areas of expertise in psychological assessment (clinical, industrial/organizational, school, counseling, educational, forensic, and neuropsychological). Instead of focusing on qualifications in terms of professional degrees or licenses, the task force elected to delineate a core set of competencies in psychological assessment and then describe more specifically the knowledge and skills expected of test users in specific contexts. The core competencies included not only knowledge of psychometric and measurement principles and appropriate test administration procedures but also appreciation of the factors affecting tests' selection and interpretation in different contexts and across diverse individuals.

Other essential competencies listed by the task force included familiarity with relevant legal standards and regulations relevant to test use, including civil rights laws, the Americans with Disabilities Act (ADA), and the Individuals with Disabil-

ities Education Act (IDEA). Public commentary in response to the Task Force's preliminary report emphasized the variety of settings and purposes involved and generally argued against a focus on degrees and licenses as providing adequate assurance of competence. The Task Force delineated the purposes for which tests are typically used (e.g., classification, description, prediction, intervention planning, and tracking) and described the competencies and skills required in specific settings (e.g., employment, education, career-vocational counseling, health care, and forensic). The task force's recommendations were drafted as aspirational guidelines describing the range of knowledge and skills for optimal test use in various contexts. The task force report also expressed the hope that the guidelines would serve to bolster the training of future psychologists in the area of assessment. The final report of the task force was approved by the APA Council of Representatives in August 2000.

The chief ethical problems in this area involve matters of how to objectively determine one's own competence and how to deal with the perceived lack of competence in others whose work is encountered in the course of professional practice. The key to the answer lies in peer consultation. Discussion with colleagues, teachers, and clinical supervisors is the best way to assess one's emerging competence in assessment and focus on additional training needs. Following graduation and licensing, continuing professional education and peer consultation are the most effective strategies for assessing and maintaining one's own competence. When in doubt, presenting samples of one's work to a respected senior colleague for review and critique is a useful strategy. If one's competence is ever challenged before a court, ethics committee, or licensing board, the expert testimony of senior colleagues will be used in an effort to prove incompetence or negligence. By consulting with such colleagues regularly, one can be continuously updated on any perceived problems with one's own work and minimize the risk of criticism in this regard.

Dealing with the less-than-adequate work of others poses a different set of ethical concerns. At times psychologists may become aware of inadequate assessment work or misuse of psychological tests by colleagues or individuals from other professions (e.g., physicians or nonpsychologist counselors). Such individuals may be unaware of appropriate testing standards or may claim that they disagree with or are not bound by them. Similarly, some psychologists may attempt to use assessment tools they are not qualified to administer or interpret. The context in which such problems come to light is critical in determining the most appropriate course of action. The ideal circumstance is one in which the presumed malefactor is amenable to correcting the problem as a result of an informal conversation, assuming that you have the consent of the party who has consulted you to initiate such a dialogue. Ideally, a professional who is the recipient of an informal contact expressing concern about matters of assessment or test interpretation will be receptive to and interested in remedying the situation. When this is not the case, the client who has been improperly evaluated should be advised about potential remedies available through legal and regulatory channels.

If one is asked to consult as a potential expert witness in matters involving alleged assessment errors or inadequacies, one has no obligation to attempt informal consultation with the professional who rendered the report in question. In most cases, such contact would be ethically inappropriate because the client of the consulting expert is not the person who conducted the assessment. In such circumstances, the people seeking an expert opinion will most likely be attorneys intent on challenging or discrediting a report deemed adverse to their clients. The especially complex issues raised when there are questions of challenging a clinician's competence in the area of neuropsychological assessment are effectively discussed by Grote, Lewin, Sweet, and van Gorp (2000).

Planning the Evaluation

As an essential part of accepting the referral, the psychologist should clarify the questions to be answered in an interactive process that refines the goals of the evaluation in the context of basic assessment science and the limitations of available techniques; this is especially important when the referral originates with nonpsychologists or others who may be unaware of the limitations of testing or may have unrealistic expectations regarding what they may learn from the test data.

Selection of Instruments

In attempting to clarify the ethical responsibilities of psychologists conducting assessments, the APA's ECTF charged with revision of the code concluded that psychologists should base their assessments, recommendations, reports, opinions, and diagnostic or evaluative statements on information and techniques sufficient to substantiate their findings (ECTF, 2001). The psychologist should have a sound knowledge of the available instruments for assessing the particular construct related to the assessment questions. This knowledge should include an understanding of the psychometric properties of the instruments being employed (e.g., their validity, reliability, and normative base) as well as an appreciation of how the instrument can be applied in different contexts or with different individuals across age levels, cultures, languages, and other variables. It is also important for psychologists to differentiate between the

instrument's strengths and weaknesses such that the most appropriate and valid measure for the intended purpose is selected. For example, so-called floor and ceiling constraints can have special implications for certain age groups. As an illustration, the Stanford-Binet, Fourth Edition, has limited ability to discriminate among children with significant intellectual impairments at the youngest age levels (Flanagan & Alfonso, 1995). In evaluating such children, the use of other instruments with lower floor capabilities would be more appropriate.

Adequacy of Instruments

Consistent with both current and revised draft APA standards (APA, 1992; ECTF, 2001), psychologists are expected to develop, administer, score, interpret, or use assessment techniques, interviews, tests, or instruments only in a manner and for purposes that are appropriate in light of the research on or evidence of the usefulness and proper application of the techniques in question. Psychologists who develop and conduct research with tests and other assessment techniques are expected to use appropriate psychometric procedures and current scientific or professional knowledge in test design, standardization, validation, reduction or elimination of bias, and recommendations for use of the instruments. The ethical responsibility of justifying the appropriateness of the assessment is firmly on the psychologist who uses the particular instrument. Although a test publisher has some related obligations, the APA ethics code can only be enforced against individuals who are APA members, as opposed to corporations. The reputations of test publishers will invariably rise or fall based on the quality of the tools they develop and distribute. When preparing new assessment techniques for publication, the preparation of a test manual that includes the data necessary for psychologists to evaluate the appropriateness of the tool for their work is of critical importance. The psychologist in turn must have the clinical and scientific skill needed to evaluate the data provided by the publisher.

Appropriate Assessment in a Multicultural Society

In countries with a citizenry as diverse as that of the United States, psychologists are invariably confronted with the challenge of people who by reason of race, culture, language, or other factors are not well represented in the normative base of frequently used assessment tools. The Reynolds and Ramsay chapter in this volume considers these issues in detail. Such circumstances demand consideration of a multiplicity of issues. When working with diverse populations, psychologists are expected to use assessment instruments whose validity and reliability have been established for that particular population. When such instruments are not available, the psychologist is expected to take care to interpret test results cautiously and with regard to the potential bias and potential misuses of such results. When appropriate tests for a particular population have not been developed, psychologists who use existing standardized tests may ethically adapt the administration and interpretation procedures only if the adaptations have a sound basis in the scientific and experiential foundation of the discipline. Psychologists have an ethical responsibility to document any such adaptations and clarify their probable impact on the findings. Psychologists are expected to use assessment methods in a manner appropriate to an individual's language preference, competence, and cultural background, unless the use of an alternative language is relevant to the purpose of the assessment.

Getting Around Language Barriers

Some psychologists incorrectly assume that the use of an interpreter will compensate for a lack of fluency in the language of the person being tested. Aside from the obvious nuances involved in vocabulary, the meaning of specific instructions can vary widely. For example, some interpreters may tend to simplify instructions or responses rather than give precise linguistic renditions. At other times, the relative rarity of the language may tempt an examiner to use family or community members when professional interpreters are not readily available. Such individuals may have personal motives that could lead to alterations in the meaning of what was actually said, or their presence may compromise the privacy of the person being assessed. Psychologists using the services of an interpreter must assure themselves of the adequacy of the interpreter's training, obtain the informed consent of the client to use that particular interpreter, and ensure that the interpreter will respect the confidentiality of test results and test security. In addition, any limitations on the data obtained via the use of an interpreter must be discussed in presenting the results of the evaluation.

Some psychologists mistakenly assume that they can compensate for language or educational barriers by using measures that do not require verbal instructions or responses. When assessing individuals of diverse cultural and linguistic backgrounds, it is not sufficient to rely solely on nonverbal procedures and assume that resulting interpretations will be valid. Many human behaviors, ranging from the nature of eye contact; speed, spontaneity, and elaborateness of response; and persistence on challenging tasks may be linked to social or cultural factors independent of language or semantics. It has been demonstrated, for example, that performance on nonverbal tests can be significantly affected both by culture (Ardila & Moreno, 2001) and by educational level (Ostrosky, Ardila, Rosselli, Lopez-Arango, & Uriel-Mendoza, 1998).

What's in a Norm?

Psychologists must have knowledge of the applicability of the instrument's normative basis to the client. Are the norms up-to-date and based on people who are compatible with the client? If the normative data do not apply to the client, the psychologist must be able to discuss the limitations in interpretation. In selecting tests for specific populations, it is important that the scores be corrected not only with respect to age but also with respect to educational level (Heaton, Grant, & Matthews, 1991; Vanderploeg, Axelrod, Sherer, Scott, & Adams, 1997). For example, the assessment of dementia in an individual with an eighth-grade education would demand very different considerations from those needed for a similar assessment in a person who has worked as a college professor.

Psychologists should select and interpret tests with an understanding of how specific tests and the procedures they entail interact with the specific individual undergoing evaluation. Several tests purporting to evaluate the same construct (e.g., general cognitive ability) put variable demands on the client and can place different levels of emphasis on specific abilities. For example, some tests used with young children have different expectations for the amount of language used in the instructions and required of the child in a response. A child with a specific language impairment may demonstrate widely discrepant scores on different tests of intelligence as a function of the language load of the instrument because some tests can place a premium on verbal skills (Kamphaus, Dresden, & Kaufman, 1993).

It is important to remember that psychologists must not base their assessment, intervention decisions, or recommendations on outdated data or test results. Similarly, psychologists do not base such decisions or recommendations on test instruments and measures that are obsolete. Test kits can be expensive, and more than a few psychologists rationalize that there is no need to invest in a newly revised instrument when they already own a perfectly serviceable set of materials of the previous edition. In some instances, a psychologist may reasonably use an older version of a standardized instrument, but he or she must have an appropriate and valid rationale to justify the practice. For example, a psychologist may wish to assess whether there has been deterioration in a client's condition and may elect to use the same measure as used in prior assessments such as the Wechsler Adult Intelligence

Scales–Revised (WAIS-R), even if a newer improved version such as the WAIS-III is now available. The chapter in this volume by Wasserman and Bracken discusses psychometric issues relevant to such comparisons.

Bases for Assessment

The current APA ethics code holds that psychologists typically provide opinions on the psychological characteristics of individuals only after conducting an examination of the individuals that is adequate to support the psychologists' statements or conclusions. This provision is confusing in some contexts. At times such an examination is not practical (e.g., when a psychologist serving as an expert witness is asked to offer hypothetical opinions regarding data sets collected by others). Another example would occur when a psychologist is retained to provide confidential assistance to an attorney. Such help might be sought to explore the accuracy of another's report or to help the attorney frame potential cross-examination questions to ask the other side's expert. In such situations, psychologists document the efforts they made to obtain their own data (if any) and clarify the potential impact of their limited information on the reliability and validity of their opinions.

The key to ethical conduct in such instances is to take great care to appropriately limit the nature and extent of any conclusions or recommendations. Related areas of the current APA code include Standards 2.01 (Boundaries of Competence) and 9.06 (Interpreting Assessment Results). When psychologists conduct record review and an individual examination is not warranted or necessary for their opinions, psychologists explain this situation and the bases upon which they arrived at this opinion in their conclusions and recommendations. This same issue is addressed in the pending revision (ECTF, 2001) as part of a new section—Section 9 (Assessment). Subsection c of 9.01 (Bases for Assessments) indicates that when despite reasonable efforts, examination of an individual is impractical, "psychologists document the efforts they made and the result of those efforts, clarify the probable impact of their limited information on the reliability and validity of their opinions, and appropriately limit the nature and extent of their conclusions or recommendations" (ECTF, 2001, p. 18).

Subsection d addresses the issue of record review. This practice is especially common in the forensic arena; attorneys often want their own expert to examine the complete data set and may not wish to disclose the identity of the expert to the other side. When psychologists conduct record reviews and when "an individual examination is not warranted or necessary for the opinion, psychologists explain this and the bases upon which they arrived at this opinion in their conclusions and recommendations" (ECTF, 2001, p. 18).

This circumstance of being able to ethically offer an opinion with limitations—absent a direct assessment of the client—is also germane with respect to requests for the release of raw test data, as discussed later in this chapter.

CONDUCTING THE EVALUATION

The requirements for and components of informed consent—including contracting details (i.e., who is the client, who is paying for the psychologist's services, and who will have access to the data)—were discussed earlier in this chapter. We proceed with a discussion of the conduct of the evaluation on the assumption that adequate informed consent has been obtained.

Conduct of the Assessment

A conducive climate is critical to collection of valid test data. In conducting their assessments, psychologists strive to create appropriate rapport with clients by helping them to feel physically comfortable and emotionally at ease, as appropriate to the context. The psychologist should be well-prepared and work to create a suitable testing environment. Most psychological tests are developed with the assumption that the test takers' attitudes and motivations are generally positive. For example, attempting to collect test data in a noisy, distracting environment or asking a client to attempt a lengthy test (e.g., an MMPI-2) while the client is seated uncomfortably with a clipboard balanced on one knee and the answer form on another would be inappropriate.

The psychologist should also consider and appreciate the attitudes of the client and address any issues raised in this regard. Some test takers may be depressed or apathetic in a manner that retards their performance, whereas others may engage in dissimulation, hoping to fake bad (i.e., falsely appear to be more pathological) or to fake good (i.e., conceal psychopathology). If there are questions about a test taker's motivation, ability to sustain adequate concentration, or problems with the test-taking environment, the psychologist should attempt to resolve these issues and is expected to discuss how these circumstances ultimately affect test data interpretations in any reports that result from the evaluation. Similarly, in circumstances in which subtle or obvious steps by clients to fake results appear to be underway, it is important for psychologists to note these steps and consider additional instruments or techniques useful in detecting dissimulation.

Another factor that can affect the test-taking environment is the presence of third-party observers during the interview and testing procedures. In forensic evaluations, psychologists are occasionally faced by a demand from attorneys to be present as observers. Having a third-party observer present can compromise the ability of the psychologist to follow standardized procedures and can affect the validity and reliability of the data collection (McCaffrey, Fisher, Gold, & Lynch, 1996; McSweeney et al., 1998). The National Academy of Neuropsychology has taken a position that third-party observers should be excluded from evaluations (NAN, 2000b). A reasonable alternative that has evolved in sexual abuse assessment interviewing, in which overly suggestive interviewing by unskilled clinicians or the police is a well-known problem, can include video recording or remote monitoring of the process when appropriate consent is granted. Such recording can have a mixed effect. It can be very useful in demonstrating that a competent evaluation was conducted, but it can also provide a strong record for discrediting poor-quality work.

Data Collection and Report Preparation

Psychologists are expected to conduct assessments with explicit knowledge of the procedures required and to adhere to the standardized test administration prescribed in the relevant test manuals. In some contexts—particularly in neuropsychological assessment, in which a significant number and wide range of instruments may be used—technicians are sometimes employed to administer and score tests as well as to record behaviors during the assessment. In this situation, it is the neuropsychologist who is responsible for assuring adequacy of the training of the technician, selecting test instruments, and interpreting findings (see National Academy of Neuropsychology [NAN], 2000a). Even in the case of less sophisticated evaluations (e.g., administration of common IQ or achievement testing in public school settings), psychologists charged with signing official reports are responsible for assuring the accuracy and adequacy of data collection, including the training and competence of other personnel engaged in test administration. This responsibility is especially relevant in circumstances in which classroom teachers or other nonpsychologists are used to proctor group-administered tests.

Preparation of a report is a critical part of a psychological assessment, and the job is not complete until the report is finished; this sometimes leads to disputes when payment for assessment is refused or delayed. Although it is not ethically appropriate to withhold a completed report needed for critical decision making in the welfare of a client, psychologists are not ethically required to prepare a report if payment is refused. Many practitioners require advance payment or a retainer as a prerequisite for undertaking a lengthy evaluation. In some instances, practitioners who have received partial payment that covers the time involved in record review and data collection will pause prior to preparing the actual report and await additional payment before writing the report. Such strategies are not unethical per se but should be carefully spelled out and agreed to as part of the consent process before the evaluation is begun. Ideally, such agreements should be made clear in written form to avoid subsequent misunderstandings.

Automated Test Scoring and Interpretation

The psychologist who signs the report is responsible for the contents of the report, including the accuracy of the data scoring and validity of the interpretation. When interpreting assessment results—including automated interpretations—psychologists must take into account the purpose of the assessment, the various test factors, the client's test-taking abilities, and the other characteristics of the person being assessed (e.g., situational, personal, linguistic, and cultural differences) that might affect psychologists' judgments or reduce the accuracy of their interpretations. If specific accommodations for the client (e.g., extra time, use of a reader, or availability of special appliances) are employed in the assessment, these accommodations must be described; automated testing services cannot do this. Although mechanical scoring of objective test data is often more accurate than hand scoring, machines can and do make errors. The psychologist who makes use of an automated scoring system should check the mechanically generated results carefully.

Psychologists are ethically responsible for indicating any significant reservations they have about the accuracy or limitations of their interpretations in the body of their reports, including any limitations on automated interpretative reports that may be a part of the case file. For example, psychologists who obtain computer-generated interpretive reports of MMPI-2 protocols may choose to use some or all of the information so obtained in their personally prepared reports. The individually prepared report of the psychologist should indicate whether a computer-assisted or interpretive report was used and explain any modified interpretations made or confirm the validity of the computerized findings, as appropriate. A summary of criteria helpful in evaluating psychological assessment reports (Koocher, 1998) is presented in Table 8.1.

AFTER THE EVALUATION

Following completion of their evaluations and reports, psychologists often receive requests for additional clarification, feedback, release of data, or other information and materials related to the evaluation. Release of confidential client

TABLE 8.1   Assessing the Quality of a Psychological Testing Report

Item to be Included	Comments in Report Should Address
Referral information	Who referred the person? What questions are to be addressed?
Informed consent	Was the person (or parent or guardian) advised about the nature and purpose of the evaluation, as well as who is to pay, what charges are anticipated, who will have access to the data, and what feedback will be provided?
Contextual issues	What is the relevant psychosocial ecology (e.g., school failure, recent divorce, criminal charges, etc.)?
Third-party involvement	Is a statement about any third party obligations or entitlements (e.g., responsibility for payment or access to findings) noted?
Current status observations	What behaviors were observed during the interview (e.g., mood, rapport, concentration, language barriers, physical handicaps, etc.)?
Deviations from standard practice	Were any deviations from standard practice in test administration needed to accommodate the client?
Listing of instruments used	Is a complete list of the tests administered provided? Does the list specify the full names of the instruments and version or form used? Does the report provide descriptive information or references for any unusual instruments or techniques used? If more than one set of norms exist, are the norms used in evaluating the particular client reported on specified?
Reliability and validity	Are the test results obtained deemed reliable and valid, or should they be considered in light of any mediating factors?
Data presentation	Are scores for each instrument administered presented and explained? Are the meanings of the data discussed in the context of the referral questions? Are homogeneity, variability, or scatter in patterns of scores discussed? Are technical terms and jargon avoided?
Summary	If a summary is provided, does it err by mentioning material not addressed in the body of the report?
Recommendations	If recommendations are made, is it evident how these flow from the data? Do recommendations relate cogently to the referral questions?
Diagnosis	If a diagnosis is requested or if differential diagnosis was a referral question, does the report address this issue?
Authentication	Is the report signed by the person who conducted the evaluation? Are the degree(s) and title of the person signing provided? If the signer is unlicensed or a trainee, has a licensed supervisor countersigned the report?

Source: Koocher (1998).

information is addressed in the ethics code and highly regulated under many state and federal laws, but many other issues arise when psychological testing is involved.

Feedback Requests

Psychologists are expected to provide explanatory feedback to the people they assess unless the nature of the client relationship precludes provision of an explanation of results. Examples of relationships in which feedback might not be owed to the person tested would include some organizational consulting, preemployment or security screening, and some forensic evaluations. In every case the nature of feedback to be provided and any limitations must be clearly explained to the person being assessed in advance of the evaluation. Ideally, any such limitations are provided in both written and oral form at the outset of the professional relationship. In normal circumstances, people who are tested can reasonably expect an interpretation of the test results and answers to questions they may have in a timely manner. Copies of actual test reports may also be provided as permitted under applicable law.

Requests for Modification of Reports

On some occasions, people who have been evaluated or their legal guardians may request modification of a psychologist's assessment report. One valid reason for altering or revising a report would be to allow for the correction of factual errors. Another appropriate reason might involve release of information on a need-to-know basis for the protection of the client. For example, suppose that in the course of conducting a psychological evaluation of a child who has experienced sexual abuse, a significant verbal learning disability is uncovered. This disability is fully described in the psychologist's report. In an effort to secure special education services for the learning problem, the parents of the child ask the psychologist to tailor a report for the school focusing only on matters relevant to the child's educational needs—that is to say, the parents would prefer that information on the child's sexual abuse is not included in the report sent to the school's learning disability assessment team. Such requests to tailor or omit certain information gleaned during an evaluation may be appropriately honored as long as doing so does not tend to mislead or misrepresent the relevant findings.

Psychologists must also be mindful of their professional integrity and obligation to fairly and accurately represent relevant findings. A psychologist may be approached by a case management firm with a request to perform an independent examination and to send a draft of the report so that editorial changes can be made. This request presents serious ethical considerations, particularly in forensic settings. Psychologists are ethically responsible for the content of all reports issued over their signature. One can always listen to requests or suggestions, but professional integrity and oversight of one's work cannot be delegated to another. Reports should not be altered to conceal crucial information, mislead recipients, commit fraud, or otherwise falsely represent findings of a psychological evaluation. The psychologist has no obligation to modify a valid report at the insistence of a client if the ultimate result would misinform the intended recipient.

Release of Data

Who should have access to the data on which psychologists predicate their assessments? This issue comes into focus most dramatically when the conclusions or recommendations resulting from an assessment are challenged. In such disputes, the opposing parties often seek review of the raw data by experts not involved in the original collection and analyses. The purpose of the review might include actual rescoring raw data or reviewing interpretations of scored data. In this context, test data may refer to any test protocols, transcripts of responses, record forms, scores, and notes regarding an individual's responses to test items in any medium (ECTF, 2001). Under long-standing accepted ethical practices, psychologists may release test data to a psychologist or another qualified professional after being authorized by a valid release or court order. Psychologists are exhorted to generally refrain from releasing test data to persons who are not qualified to use such information, except (a) as required by law or court order, (b) to an attorney or court based on a client's valid release, or (c) to the client as appropriate (ECTF, 2001). Psychologists may also refrain from releasing test data to protect a client from harm or to protect test security (ECTF, 2001).

In recent years, psychologists have worried about exactly how far their responsibility goes in upholding such standards. It is one thing to express reservations about a release, but it is quite another matter to contend within the legal system. For example, if a psychologist receives a valid release from the client to provide the data to another professional, is the sending psychologist obligated to determine the specific competence of the intended recipient? Is it reasonable to assume that any other psychologist is qualified to evaluate all psychological test data? If psychologists asked to release data are worried about possible harm or test security, must they retain legal counsel at their own expense to vigorously resist releasing the data?

The intent of the APA ethical standards is to minimize harm and misuse of test data. The standards were never intended to require psychologists to screen the credentials of intended recipients, become litigants, or incur significant legal expenses in defense of the ethics code. In addition, many attorneys do not want the names of their potential experts released to the other side until required to do so under discovery rules. Some attorneys may wish to show test data to a number of potential experts and choose to use only the expert(s) most supportive of their case. In such situations, the attorney seeing the file may prefer not to provide the transmitting psychologist with the name of the intended recipient. Although such strategies are alien to the training of many psychologists trained to think as scientific investigators, they are quite common and ethical in the practice of law. It is ethically sufficient for transmitting psychologists to express their concerns and rely on the assurance of receiving clinicians or attorneys that the recipients are competent to interpret those data. Ethical responsibility in such circumstances shifts to receiving experts insofar as justifying their own competence and the foundation of their own expert opinions is concerned, if a question is subsequently raised in that regard. The bottom line is that although psychologists should seek appropriate confidentiality and competence assurances, they cannot use the ethics code as a shield to bar the release of their complete testing file.

Test Security

The current APA ethics code requires that psychologists make reasonable efforts to maintain the integrity and security of copyright-protected tests and other assessment techniques consistent with law and with their contractual obligations (ECTF, 2001). Most test publishers also elicit such a pledge from those seeking to purchase test materials. Production of well-standardized test instruments represents a significant financial investment to the publisher. Breaches of such security can compromise the publisher's proprietary rights and vitiate the utility of the test to the clinician by enabling coaching or otherwise inappropriate preparation by test takers.

What is a reasonable effort as envisioned by the authors of the ethics code? Close reading of both the current and proposed revision of the code indicate that psychologists may rely on other elements of the code in maintaining test security. In that context, psychologists have no intrinsic professional obligation to contest valid court orders or to resist appropriate requests for disclosure of test materials—that is to say, the psychologist is not obligated to litigate in the support of a test publisher or to protect the security of an instrument at significant personal cost. When in doubt, a psychologist always has the option of contacting the test publisher. If publishers, who sold the tests to the psychologist eliciting a promise that the test materials be treated confidentially, wish to object to requested or court-ordered disclosure, they should be expected to use their own financial and legal resources to defend their own copyright-protected property.

Psychologists must also pay attention to the laws that apply in their own practice jurisdiction(s). For example, Minnesota has a specific statute that prohibits a psychologist from releasing psychological test materials to individuals who are unqualified or if the psychologist has reason to believe that releasing such material would compromise the integrity of the testing process. Such laws can provide additional protective leverage but are rare exceptions.

An editorial in the *American Psychologist* (APA, 1999) discussed test security both in the context of scholarly publishing and litigation, suggesting that potential disclosure must be evaluated in light of both ethical obligations of psychologists and copyright law. The editorial also recognized that the psychometric integrity of psychological tests depends upon the test taker's not having prior access to study or be coached on the test materials. The National Academy of Neuropsychology (NAN) has also published a position paper on test security (NAN, 2000c). There has been significant concern among neuropsychologists about implications for the validity of tests intended to assess malingering if such materials are freely circulated among attorneys and clients. Both the *American Psychologist* editorial and the NAN position paper ignore the implications of this issue with respect to preparation for high-stakes testing and the testing industry, as discussed in detail later in this chapter. Authors who plan to publish information about tests should always seek permission from the copyright holder of the instrument and not presume that the fair use doctrine will protect them from subsequent infringement claims. When sensitive test documents are subpoenaed, psychologists should also ask courts to seal or otherwise protect the information from unreasonable public scrutiny.

SPECIAL ISSUES

In addition to the basic principles described earlier in this chapter (i.e., the preparation, conduct, and follow-up of the actual assessment), some special issues regard psychological testing. These issues include automated or computerized assessment services, high-stakes testing, and teaching of psychological assessment techniques. Many of these topics fall under the general domain of the testing industry.

The Testing Industry

Psychological testing is big business. Test publishers and other companies offering automated scoring systems or national testing programs are significant business enterprises. Although precise data are not easy to come by, Walter Haney and his colleagues (Haney, Madaus, & Lyons, 1993) estimated gross revenues of several major testing companies for 1987–1988 as follows: Educational Testing Service, $226 million; National Computer Systems, $242 million; The Psychological Corporation (then a division of Harcort General), $50–55 million; and the American College Testing Program, $53 million. The Federal Reserve Bank suggests that multiplying the figures by 1.56 will approximate the dollar value in 2001 terms, but the actual revenue involved is probably significantly higher, given the increased numbers of people taking such tests by comparison with 1987–1988.

The spread of consumerism in America has seen increasing criticism of the testing industry (Haney et al., 1993). Most of the ethical criticism leveled at the larger companies fall into the categories of marketing, sales to unauthorized users, and the problem of so-called impersonal services. Publishers claim that they do make good-faith efforts to police sales so that only qualified users obtain tests. They note that they cannot control the behavior of individuals in institutions where tests are sent. Because test publishers must advertise in the media provided by organized psychology (e.g., the *APA Monitor*) to influence their prime market, most major firms are especially responsive to letters of concern from psychologists and committees of APA. At the same time, such companies are quite readily prepared to cry antitrust fouls when professional organizations become too critical of their business practices.

The Center for the Study of Testing, Evaluation, and Educational Policy (CSTEEP), directed by Walt Haney, is an educational research organization located at Boston College in the School of Education (http://wwwcsteep.bc.edu). CSTEEP has been a valuable ally to students who have been subjected to bullying and intimidation by testing behemoths such as Educational Testing Service and the SAT program when the students' test scores improve dramatically. In a number of circumstances, students have had their test results canceled, based on internal statistical formulas that few people other than Haney and his colleagues have ever analyzed. Haney has been a valuable expert in helping such students obtain legal remedies from major testing companies, although the terms of the settlements generally prohibit him from disclosing the details. Although many psychologists are employed by large testing companies, responses to critics have generally been issued by corporate attorneys rather than psychometric experts. It is difficult to assess the degree to which insider psychologists in these big businesses exert any influence to assure ethical integrity and fairness to individual test takers.

Automated Testing Services

Automated testing services and software can be a major boon to psychologists' practices and can significantly enhance the accuracy and sophistication of diagnostic decision making, but there are important caveats to observe. The draft revision of the APA code states that psychologists who offer assessment or scoring services to other professionals should accurately describe the purpose, norms, validity, reliability, and applications of the procedures and any special qualifications applicable to their use (ECTF, 2001). Psychologists who use such scoring and interpretation services (including automated services) are urged to select them based on evidence of the validity of the program and analytic procedures (ECTF, 2001). In every case, ethical psychologists retain responsibility for the appropriate application, interpretation, and use of assessment instruments, whether they score and interpret such tests themselves or use automated or other services (ECTF, 2001).

One key difficulty in the use of automated testing is the aura of validity conveyed by the adjective *computerized* and its synonyms. Aside from the long-standing debate within psychology about the merits of actuarial versus clinical prediction, there is often a kind of magical faith that numbers and graphs generated by a computer program somehow equate with increased validity of some sort. Too often, skilled clinicians do not fully educate themselves about the underpinnings of various analytic models. Even when a clinician is so inclined, the copyright holders of the analytic program are often reluctant to share too much information, lest they compromise their property rights.

In the end, the most reasonable approach is to use automated scoring and interpretive services as only one component of an evaluation and to carefully probe any apparently discrepant findings. This suggestion will not be a surprise to most competent psychologists, but unfortunately they are not the only users of these tools. Many users of such tests are nonpsychologists with little understanding of the interpretive subtleties. Some take the computer-generated reports at face value as valid and fail to consider important factors that make their client unique. A few users are simply looking for a quick and dirty source of data to help them make a decision in the absence of clinical acumen. Other users inflate the actual cost of the tests and scoring services to enhance their own billings. When making use of such tools,

psychologists should have a well-reasoned strategy for incorporating them in the assessment and should interpret them with well-informed caution.

High-Stakes Testing

The term *high-stakes tests* refers to cognitively loaded instruments designed to assess knowledge, skill, and ability with the intent of making employment, academic admission, graduation, or licensing decisions. For a number of public policy and political reasons, these testing programs face considerable scrutiny and criticism (Haney et al., 1993; Sackett, Schmitt, Ellingson, & Kabin, 2001). Such testing includes the SAT, Graduate Record Examination (GRE), state examinations that establish graduation requirements, and professional or job entry examinations. Such tests can provide very useful information but are also subject to misuse and a degree of tyranny in the sense that individuals' rights and welfare are easily lost in the face of corporate advantage and political struggles about accountability in education.

In May, 2001 the APA issued a statement on such testing titled "Appropriate Use of High Stakes Testing in Our Nation's Schools" (APA, 2001). The statement noted that the measurement of learning and achievement are important and that tests—when used properly—are among the most sound and objective ways to measure student performance. However, when tests' results are used inappropriately, they can have highly damaging unintended consequences. High-stakes decisions such as high school graduation or college admissions should not be made on the basis of a single set of test scores that only provide a snapshot of student achievement. Such scores may not accurately reflect a student's progress and achievement, and they do not provide much insight into other critical components of future success, such as motivation and character.

The APA statement recommends that any decision about a student's continued education, retention in grade, tracking, or graduation should not be based on the results of a single test. The APA statement noted that

- When test results substantially contribute to decisions made about student promotion or graduation, there should be evidence that the test addresses only the specific or generalized content and skills that students have had an opportunity to learn.
- When a school district, state, or some other authority mandates a test, the intended use of the test results should be clearly described. It is also the responsibility of those who mandate the test to monitor its impact—particularly on racial- and ethnic-minority students or students of lower

socioeconomic status—and to identify and minimize potential negative consequences of such testing.

- In some cases, special accommodations for students with limited proficiency in English may be necessary to obtain valid test scores. If students with limited English skills are to be tested in English, their test scores should be interpreted in light of their limited English skills. For example, when a student lacks proficiency in the language in which the test is given (students for whom English is a second language, for example), the test could become a measure of their ability to communicate in English rather than a measure of other skills.

- Likewise, special accommodations may be needed to ensure that test scores are valid for students with disabilities. Not enough is currently known about how particular test modifications may affect the test scores of students with disabilities; more research is needed. As a first step, test developers should include students with disabilities in field testing of pilot tests and document the impact of particular modifications (if any) for test users.

- For evaluation purposes, test results should also be reported by sex, race-ethnicity, income level, disability status, and degree of English proficiency.

One adverse consequence of high-stakes testing is that some schools will almost certainly focus primarily on teaching-to-the-test skills acquisition. Students prepared in this way may do well on the test but find it difficult to generalize their learning beyond that context and may find themselves unprepared for critical and analytic thinking in their subsequent learning environments. Some testing companies such as the Educational Testing Service (developers of the SAT) at one time claimed that coaching or teaching to the test would have little meaningful impact and still publicly attempt to minimize the potential effect of coaching or teaching to the test.

The best rebuttal to such assertions is the career of Stanley H. Kaplan. A recent article in *The New Yorker* (Gladwell, 2001) documents not only Kaplan's long career as an entrepreneurial educator but also the fragility of so-called test security and how teaching strategies significantly improves test scores in exactly the way the industry claimed was impossible. When Kaplan began coaching students on the SAT in the 1950s and holding posttest pizza parties to debrief the students and learn about what was being asked, he was considered a kind of subverter of the system. Because the designers of the SAT viewed their work as developing a measure of enduring abilities (such as IQ), they assumed that coaching would do little to alter scores. Apparently little thought was given to the notion that people are affected by what they know and that what they know is affected by what they are

taught (Gladwell, 2001). What students are taught is dictated by parents and teachers, and they responded to the high-stakes test by strongly supporting teaching that would yield better scores.

Teaching Psychological Testing

Psychologists teaching assessment have a unique opportunity to shape their students' professional practice and approach to ethics by modeling how ethical issues are actively integrated into the practice of assessment (Yalof & Brabender, 2001). Ethical standards in the areas of education and training are relevant. "Psychologists who are responsible for education and training programs take reasonable steps to ensure that the programs are designed to provide appropriate knowledge and proper experiences to meet the requirements for licensure, certification and other goals for which claims are made by the program" (ECTF, 2001). A primary responsibility is to ensure competence in assessment practice by providing the requisite education and training.

A recent review of studies evaluating the competence of graduate students and practicing psychologists in administration and scoring of cognitive tests demonstrates that errors occur frequently and at all levels of training (Alfonso & Pratt, 1997). The review also notes that relying only on practice assessments as a teaching methodology does not ensure competent practice. The authors conclude that teaching programs that include behavioral objectives and that focus on evaluating specific competencies are generally more effective. This approach is also more concordant with the APA guidelines for training in professional psychology (APA, 2000).

The use of children and students' classmates as practice subjects in psychological testing courses raises ethical concern (Rupert, Kozlowski, Hoffman, Daniels, & Piette, 1999). In other teaching contexts, the potential for violations of privacy are significant in situations in which graduate students are required to take personality tests for practice. Yalof and Brabender (2001) address ethical dilemmas in personality assessment courses with respect to using the classroom for in vivo training. They argue that the student's introduction to ethical decision making in personality assessment occurs in assessment courses with practice components. In this type of course, students experience firsthand how ethical problems are identified, addressed, and resolved. They note that the instructor's demonstration of how the ethical principles are highlighted and explored can enable students to internalize a model for addressing such dilemmas in the future. Four particular concerns are described: (a) the students' role in procuring personal experience with personality testing, (b) identification of participants with which to practice, (c) the development of informed consent procedures for assessment participants, and (d) classroom presentations. This discussion does not provide universally applicable concrete solutions to ethical problems; however, it offers a consideration of the relevant ethical principles that any adequate solution must incorporate.

RECOMMENDATIONS

In an effort to summarize the essence of good ethical practice in psychological assessment, we offer this set of suggestions:

- Clients to be tested (or their parents or legal guardians) must be given full informed consent about the nature of the evaluation, payment for services, access to results, and other relevant data prior to initiating the evaluation.
- Psychologists should be aware of and adhere to published professional standards and guidelines relevant to the nature of the particular type of assessment they are conducting.
- Different types of technical data on tests exist—including reliability and validity data—and psychologists should be sufficiently familiar with such data for any instrument they use so that they can justify and explain the appropriateness of the selection.
- Those administering psychological tests are responsible for assuring that the tests are administered and scored according to standardized instructions.
- Test users should be aware of potential test bias or client characteristics that might reduce the validity of the instrument for that client and context. When validity is threatened, the psychologists should specifically address the issue in their reports.
- No psychologist is competent to administer and interpret all psychological tests. It is important to be cautiously self-critical and to agree to undertake only those evaluations that fall within one's training and sphere of competence.
- The validity and confidence of test results relies to some degree on test security. Psychologists should use reasonable caution in protecting the security of test items and materials.
- Automated testing services create a hazard to the extent that they may generate data that are inaccurate for certain clients or that are misinterpreted by improperly trained individuals. Psychologists operating or making use of such services should take steps to minimize such risks.
- Clients have a right to feedback and a right to have confidentiality of data protected to the extent agreed upon at the outset of the evaluation or in subsequent authorized releases.

- Test users should be aware of the ethical issues that can develop in specific settings and should consult with other professionals when ethical dilemmas arise.

REFERENCES

Aiken, L. S., West, S. G., Sechrest, L., & Reno, R. R. (1990). Graduate training in statistics, methodology and measurement in psychology: A survey of PhD programs in North America. *American Psychologist, 45,* 721–734.

American Psychological Association (APA). (1953). *Ethical standards of psychologists.* Washington, DC: Author.

American Psychological Association (APA). (1992). *Ethical standards of psychologists and code of conduct.* Washington, DC: Author.

American Psychological Association (APA). (1999). Test security: Protecting the integrity of tests. *American Psychologist, 54,* 1078.

American Psychological Association (APA). (2000). *Guidelines and principles for accreditation of programs in professional Psychology.* Washington, DC: Author.

American Psychological Association (APA). (2001). *Appropriate use of high stakes testing in our nation's schools.* Washington, DC: Author.

Ardila, A., & Moreno, S. (2001). Neuropsychological test performance in Aruaco Indians: An exploratory study. *Neuropsychology, 7,* 510–515.

British Psychological Society (BPS). (1995). *Certificate statement register: Competencies in occupational testing, general information pack (Level A).* (Available from the British Psychological Society, 48 Princess Road East, Leicester, England LEI 7DR)

British Psychological Society (BPS). (1996). *Certificate statement register: Competencies in occupational testing, general information pack (Level B).* (Available from the British Psychological Society, 48 Princess Road East, Leicester, England LEI 7DR)

Ethics Code Task Force (ECTF). (2001). *Working draft ethics code revision, October, 2001.* Retrieved from http://www.apa.org/ethics.

Eyde, L. E., Moreland, K. L., Robertson, G. J., Primoff, E. S., & Most, R. B. (1988). *Test user qualifications: A data-based approach to promoting good test use. Issues in scientific psychology* (Report of the Test User Qualifications Working Group of the Joint Committee on Testing Practices). Washington, DC: American Psychological Association.

Eyde, L. E., Robertson, G. J., Krug, S. E., Moreland, K. L., Robertson, A.G., Shewan, C. M., Harrison, P. L., Porch, B. E., Hammer, A. L., & Primoff, E. S. (1993). *Responsible test use: Case studies for assessing human behavior.* Washington, DC: American Psychological Association.

Flanagan, D. P., & Alfonso, V. C. (1995). A critical review of the technical characteristics of new and recently revised intelligence tests for preschool children. *Journal of Psychoeducational Assessment, 13,* 66–90.

Gladwell, M. (2001, December 17). What Stanley Kaplan taught us about the S.A.T. *The New Yorker.* Retrieved from http://www .newyorker.com/PRINTABLE/?critics/011217crat_atlarge

Grisso, T., & Appelbaum, P. S. (1998). *Assessing competence to consent to treatment: A guide for physicians and other health professionals.* New York: Oxford University Press.

Grote, C. L., Lewin, J. L., Sweet, J. J., & van Gorp, W. G. (2000). Courting the clinician. Responses to perceived unethical practices in clinical neuropsychology: Ethical and legal considerations. *The Clinical Neuropsychologist, 14,* 119–134.

Haney, W. M., Madaus, G. F., & Lyons, R. (1993). *The fractured marketplace for standardized testing.* Norwell, MA: Kluwer.

Heaton, R. K., Grant, I., & Matthews, C. G. (1991). *Comprehensive norms for an Expanded Halstead-Reitan Battery: Demographic corrections, research findings, and clinical applications.* Odessa, FL: Psychological Assessment Resources.

International Test Commission. (2000). *International guidelines for test use: Version 2000.* (Available from Professor Dave Bartram, President, SHL Group plc, International Test Commission, The Pavilion, 1 Atwell Place, Thames Ditton, KT7, Surrey, England)

Johnson-Greene, D., Hardy-Morais, C., Adams, K., Hardy, C., & Bergloff, P. (1997). Informed consent and neuropsychological assessment: Ethical considerations and proposed guidelines. *The Clinical Neuropsychologist, 11,* 454–460.

Kamphaus, R. W., Dresden, J., & Kaufman, A. S. (1993). Clinical and psychometric considerations in the cognitive assessment of preschool children. In J. Culbertson & D. Willis. (Eds.), *Testing young children: A reference guide for developmental, psychoeducational, and psychosocial assessments* (pp. 55–72). Austin, TX: PRO-ED.

Koocher, G. P. (1998). Assessing the quality of a psychological testing report. In G. P. Koocher, J. C. Norcross, & S. S. Hill (Eds.), *PsyDR: Psychologists' desk reference* (pp. 169–171). New York: Oxford University Press.

McCaffrey, R. J., Fisher, J. M., Gold, B. A., & Lynch, J. K. (1996). Presence of third parties during neuropsychological evaluations: Who is evaluating whom? *The Clinical Neuropsychologist, 10,* 435–449.

McSweeney, A. J., Becker, B. C., Naugle, R. I., Snow, W. G., Binder, L. M., & Thompson, L. L. (1998). Ethical issues related to third party observers in clinical neuropsychological evaluations. *The Clinical Neuropsychologist, 12,* 552–559.

Moreland, K. L., Eyde, L. D., Robertson, G. J., Primoff, E. S., & Most, R. B. (1995). Assessment of test user qualifications: a research-based measurement procedure. *American Psychologist, 50,* 14–23.

National Academy of Neuropsychology (NAN). (2000a). The use of neuropsychology test technicians in clinical practice. *Archives of Clinical Neuropsychology, 15,* 381–382.

National Academy of Neuropsychology (NAN). (2000b). Presence of third party observers during neuropsychological testing. *Archives of Clinical Neuropsychology, 15,* 379–380.

National Academy of Neuropsychology (NAN). (2000c). Test security. *Archives of Clinical Neuropsychology, 15,* 381–382.

Ostrosky, F., Ardila, A., Rosselli, M., López-Arango, G., & Uriel-Mendoza, V. (1998). Neuropsychological test performance in illiterates. *Archives of Clinical Neuropsychology, 13,* 645–660.

Rupert, P. A., Kozlowski, N. F., Hoffman, L. A., Daniels, D. D., & Piette, J. M. (1999). Practical and ethical issues in teaching psychological testing. *Professional Psychology: Research and Practice, 30,* 209–214.

Sackett, P. R., Schmitt, N., Ellingson, J. E., & Kabin, M. B. (2001). High-stakes testing in employment, credentialing, and higher education: Prospects in a post-affirmative action world. *American Psychologist, 56,* 302–318.

Simner, M. L. (1994*). Draft of final report of the Professional Affairs Committee Working Group on Test Publishing Industry Safeguards.* Ottawa, ON: Canadian Psychological Association.

Vanderploeg, R. D., Axelrod, B. N., Sherer, M., Scott, J., & Adams, R. (1997). The importance of demographic adjustments on neuropsychological test performance: A response to Reitan and Wolfson (1995). *The Clinical Neuropsychologist, 11,* 210–217.

Yalof, J., & Brabender, V. (2001). Ethical dilemmas in personality assessment courses: Using the classroom for in vivo training. *Journal of Personality Assessment, 77,* 203–213.

CHAPTER 9

Education and Training in Psychological Assessment

LEONARD HANDLER AND AMANDA JILL CLEMENCE

We begin this chapter with a story about an assessment done by one of us (Handler) when he was a trainee at a Veterans Administration hospital outpatient clinic. He was asked by the chief of psychiatry to reassess a patient the psychiatrist had been seeing in classical psychoanalysis, which included heavy emphasis on dream analysis and free association, with little input from the analyst, as was the prevailing approach at the time. The patient was not making progress, despite the regimen of three sessions per week he had followed for over a year.

The patient was cooperative and appropriate in the interview and in his responses to the Wechsler Adult Intelligence Scale (WAIS) items, until the examiner came to one item of the Comprehension subtest, "What does this saying mean: 'Strike while the iron is hot'?" The examiner was quite surprised when the patient, who up to that point had appeared to be relatively sound, answered: "Strike is to hit. Hit my wife. I should say push, and then pull the cord of the iron. Strike in baseball—one strike against you. This means you have to hit and retaliate to make up that strike against you—or if you feel you have a series of problems—if they build up, you will strike." The first author still remembers just beginning to understand what needed to be said to the chief of psychiatry about the type of treatment this patient needed.

As the assessment continued, it became even more evident that the patient's thinking was quite disorganized, especially on less structured tests. The classical analytic approach, without structure, eliciting already disturbed mentation, caused this man to become more thought disordered than he had been before treatment: His WAIS responses before treatment were quite sound, and his projective test responses showed only some significant anxiety and difficulty with impulse control. Although a previous assessor had recommended a more structured, supportive approach to therapy, the patient was unfortunately put in this unstructured approach that probed an unconscious that contained a great deal of turmoil and few adequate defenses.

This assessment was a significant experience in which the assessor learned the central importance of using personality assessment to identify the proper treatment modality for patients and to identify patients' core life issues. Illuminating experiences such as this one have led us to believe that assessment should be a central and vital part of any doctoral curriculum that prepares students to do applied work. We have had many assessment experiences that have reinforced our belief in the importance of learning assessment to facilitate the treatment process and to help guide patients in constructive directions.

The approach to teaching personality assessment described in this chapter emphasizes the importance of viewing assessment as an interactive process—emphasizing the interaction of teacher and student, as well as the interaction of patient and assessor. The process highlights the use of critical thinking and continued questioning of approaches to assessment and to their possible interpretations, and it even extends to the use of such a model in the application of these activities in the assessment process with the patient. Throughout the chapter we have emphasized the integration of research and clinical application.

DIFFERENCES BETWEEN TESTING AND ASSESSMENT

Unfortunately, many people use the terms *testing* and *assessment* synonymously, but actually these terms mean quite different things. *Testing* refers to the process of administering, scoring, and perhaps interpreting individual test scores by applying a descriptive meaning based on normative, nomothetic data. The focus here is on the individual test itself. Assessment,

on the other hand, consists of a *process* in which a number of tests, obtained from the use of multiple methods, are administered and the results of these tests are integrated among themselves, along with data obtained from observations, history, information from other professionals, and information from other sources—friends, relatives, legal sources, and so on. All of these data are integrated to produce, typically, an in-depth understanding of the individual, focused on the reasons the person was referred for assessment. This process is *person* focused or *problem issue* focused (Handler & Meyer, 1998). The issue is not, for example, what the person scored on the Minnesota Multiphasic Personality Inventory-2 (MMPI-2), or what the Rorschach Structural Summary yielded, but, rather, what we can say about the patient's symptomatology, personality structure, and dynamics, and how we can answer the referral questions. Tests are typically employed in the assessment process, but much more information and much more complexity are involved in the assessment process than in the simple act of testing itself.

Many training programs teach testing but describe it as assessment. The product produced with this focus is typically a report that presents data from each test, separately, with little or no integration or interpretation. There are often no valid clear-cut conclusions one can make from interpreting tests individually, because the results of other test and nontest data often modify interpretations or conclusions concerning the meaning of specific test signs or results on individual tests. In fact, the data indicate that a clinician who uses a single method will develop an incomplete or biased understanding of the patient (Meyer et al., 2000).

WHY TEACH AND LEARN PERSONALITY ASSESSMENT?

When one considers the many advantages offered by learning personality assessment, its emphasis in many settings becomes quite obvious. Therefore, we have documented the many reasons personality assessment should be taught in doctoral training programs and highlighted as an important and respected area of study.

Learning Assessment Teaches Critical Thinking and Integrative Skills

The best reason, we believe, to highlight personality assessment courses in the doctoral training curriculum concerns the importance of teaching critical thinking skills through the process of learning to integrate various types of data. Typically, in most training programs until this point, students have amassed a great deal of information from discrete courses by reading, by attending lectures, and from discussion. However, in order to learn to do competent assessment work students must now learn to organize and integrate information from many diverse courses. They are now asked to bring these and other skills to bear in transversing the scientist-practitioner bridge, linking nomothetic and ideographic data. These critical thinking skills, systematically applied to the huge task of data integration, provide students with a template that can be used in other areas of psychological functioning (e.g., psychotherapy, or research application).

Assessment Allows the Illumination of a Person's Experience

Sometimes assessment data allow us to observe a person's experience as he or she is being assessed. This issue is important because it is possible to generalize from these experiences to similar situations in psychotherapy and to the patient's environment. For example, when a 40-year-old man first viewed Card II of the Rorschach, he produced a response that was somewhat dysphoric and poorly defined, suggesting possible problems with emotional control, because Card II is the first card containing color that the patient encounters. He made a sound that indicated his discomfort and said, "A bloody wound." After a minute he said, "A rocket, with red flames, blasting off." This response, in contrast to the first one, was of good form quality. These responses illuminate the man's style of dealing with troubling emotions: He becomes angry and quickly and aggressively leaves the scene with a dramatic show of power and force. Next the patient gave the following response: "Two people, face to face, talking to each other, discussing." One could picture the sequence of intrapsychic and interpersonal events in the series of these responses. First, it is probable that the person's underlying depression is close to the surface and is poorly controlled. With little pressure it breaks through and causes him immediate but transitory disorganization in his thinking and in the ability to manage his emotions. He probably recovers very quickly and is quite capable, after an unfortunate release of anger and removing himself from the situation, of reestablishing an interpersonal connection. Later in therapy this man enacted just such a pattern of action in his work situation and in his relationships with family members and with the therapist, who was able to understand the pattern of behavior and could help the patient understand it.

A skilled assessor can explore and describe with empathic attunement painful conflicts as well as the ebb and flow of dynamic, perhaps conflictual forces being cautiously contained. The good assessor also attends to the facilitating and creative aspects of personality, and the harmonious interplay

of intrapsychic and external forces, as the individual copes with day-to-day life issues (Handler & Meyer, 1998). It is possible to generate examples that provide moving portraits of a person's experience, such as the woman who saw "a tattered, torn butterfly, slowly dying" on Card I of the Rorschach, or a reclusive, schizoid man whom the first author had been seeing for some time, who saw "a mushroom" on the same card. When the therapist asked, "If this mushroom could talk, what would it say?" the patient answered, "Don't step on me. Everyone likes to step on them and break them." This response allowed the therapist to understand this reserved and quiet man's experience of the therapist, who quickly altered his approach and became more supportive and affiliative.

Assessment Can Illuminate Underlying Conditions

Responses to assessment stimuli allow us to look beyond a person's pattern of self-presentation, possibly concealing underlying emotional problems. For example, a 21-year-old male did not demonstrate any overt signs of gross pathology in his initial intake interview. His Rorschach record was also unremarkable for any difficulties, until Card IX, to which he gave the following response: "The skull of a really decayed or decaying body . . . with some noxious fumes or odor coming out of it. It looks like blood and other body fluids are dripping down on the bones of the upper torso and the eyes are glowing, kind of an orange, purplish glow." To Card X he responded, "It looks like someone crying for help, all bruised and scarred, with blood running down their face." The student who was doing the assessment quickly changed her stance with this young man, providing him with rapid access to treatment.

Assessment Facilitates Treatment Planning

Treatment planning can focus and shorten treatment, resulting in benefits to the patient and to third-party payors. Informed treatment planning can also prevent hospitalization, and provide more efficient and effective treatment for the patient. Assessment can enhance the likelihood of a favorable treatment outcome and can serve as a guide during the course of treatment (Applebaum, 1990).

Assessment Facilitates the Therapeutic Process

The establishment of the initial relationship between the patient and the therapist is often fraught with difficulty. It is important to sensitize students to this difficult interaction because many patients drop out of treatment prematurely. Although asking the new patient to participate in an assessment before beginning treatment would seem to result in greater dropout than would a simple intake interview because it may seem to be just another bothersome hurdle the patient must jump over to receive services, recent data indicate that the situation is just the opposite (Ackerman, Hilsenroth, Baity, & Blagys, 2000). Perhaps the assessment procedure allows clients to slide into therapy in a less personal manner, desensitizing them to the stresses of the therapy setting.

An example of an assessment approach that facilitates the initial relationship between patient and therapist is the recent research and clinical application of the Early Memories Procedure. Fowler, Hilsenroth, and Handler (1995, 1996) have provided data that illustrate the power of specific early memories to predict the patient's transference reaction to the therapist.

The Assessment Process Itself Can Be Therapeutic

Several psychologists have recently provided data that demonstrate the therapeutic effects of the assessment process itself, when it is conducted in a facilitative manner. The work of Finn (1996; Finn & Tonsager, 1992) and Fischer (1994) have indicated that assessment, done in a facilitative manner, will typically result in the production of therapeutic results. The first author has developed a therapeutic assessment approach that is ongoing in the treatment process with children and adolescents to determine whether therapeutic assessment changes are long-lasting.

Assessment Provides Professional Identity

There are many mental health specialists who do psychotherapy (e.g., psychologists, psychiatrists, social workers, marriage and family counselors, ministers), but only psychologists are trained to do assessment. Possession of this skill allows us to be called upon by other professionals in the mental health area, as well as by school personnel, physicians, attorneys, the court, government, and even by business and industry, to provide evaluations.

Assessment Reflects Patients' Relationship Problems

More and more attention has been placed on the need for assessment devices to evaluate couples and families. New measures have been developed, and several traditional measures have been used in unique ways, to illuminate relational patterns for therapists and couples. Measures range from pencil-and-paper tests of marital satisfaction to projective measures of relational patterns that include an analysis of a person's interest in, feelings about, and cognitive conceptualizations of

relationships, as well as measures of the quality of relationships established.

The Rorschach and several selected Wechsler verbal subtests have been used in a unique manner to illustrate the pattern and style of the interaction between or among participants. The Rorschach or the WAIS subtests are given to each person separately. The participants are then asked to retake the test together, but this time they are asked to produce an answer (on the WAIS; e.g., Handler & Sheinbein, 1987) or responses on the Rorschach (e.g., Handler, 1997) upon which they both agree. The quality of the interaction and the outcome of the collaboration are evaluated. People taking the test can get a realistic picture of their interaction and its consequences, which they often report are similar to their interactions in everyday relationships.

Personality Assessment Helps Psychologists Arrive at a Diagnosis

Assessment provides information to make a variety of diagnostic statements, including a *Diagnostic and Statistical Manual (DSM)* diagnosis. Whether the diagnosis includes descriptive factors, cognitive and affective factors, interaction patterns, level of ego functions, process aspects, object relations factors, or other dynamic aspects of functioning, it is an informed and comprehensive diagnosis, with or without a diagnostic label.

Assessment Is Used in Work-Related Settings

There is a huge literature on the use of personality assessment in the workplace. Many studies deal with vocational choice or preference, using personality assessment instruments (e.g., Krakowski, 1984; Muhlenkamp & Parsons, 1972; Rezler & Buckley, 1977), and there is a large literature in which personality assessment is used as an integral part of the study of individuals in work-related settings and in the selection and promotion of workers (Barrick & Mount, 1991; Tett, Jackson, & Rothstein, 1991).

Assessment Is Used in Forensic and Medical Settings

Psychologists are frequently asked to evaluate people for a wide variety of domestic, legal, or medical problems. Readers should see the chapters in this volume by Ogloff and Douglas and by Sweet, Tovian, and Suchy, which discuss assessment in forensic and medical settings, respectively.

Assessments are often used in criminal cases to determine the person's ability to understand the charges brought against him or her, or to determine whether the person is competent to stand trial or is malingering to avoid criminal responsibility.

Assessments are also requested by physicians and insurance company representatives to determine the emotional correlates of various physical disease processes or to help differentiate between symptoms caused by medical or by emotional disorders. There is now an emphasis on the *biopsychosocial* approach, in which personality assessment can target emotional factors along with the physical problems that are involved in the person's total functioning. In addition, *psychoneuroimmunology,* a term that focuses on complex mind-body relationships, has spawned new psychological assessment instruments. There has been a significant increase in the psychological aspects of various health-related issues (e.g., smoking cessation, medical compliance, chronic pain, recovery from surgery). Personality assessment has become an integral part of this health psychology movement (Handler & Meyer, 1998).

Assessment Procedures Are Used in Research

Assessment techniques are used to test a variety of theories or hypothesized relationships. Psychologists search among a large array of available tests for assessment tools to quantify the variables of interest to them. There are now at least three excellent journals in the United States as well as some excellent journals published abroad that are devoted to research in assessment.

Assessment Is Used to Evaluate the Effectiveness of Psychotherapy

In the future, assessment procedures will be important to insure continuous improvement of psychotherapy through more adequate treatment planning and outcome assessment. Maruish (1999) discusses the application of test-based assessment in Continuous Quality Improvement, a movement to plan treatment and systematically measure improvement. Psychologists can play a major role in the future delivery of mental health services because their assessment instruments can quickly and economically highlight problems that require attention and can assist in selecting the most cost-effective, appropriate treatment (Maruish, 1990). Such evidence will also be necessary to convince legislators that psychotherapy services are effective. Maruish believes that our psychometrically sound measures, which are sensitive to changes in symptomatology and are administered pre- and posttreatment, can help psychology demonstrate treatment effectiveness. In addition, F. Newman (1991) described a way in which personality assessment data, initially used to determine progress or outcome, "can be related to treatment approach, costs, or reimbursement criteria, and can provide objective support for

decisions regarding continuation of treatment, discharge, or referral to another type of treatment" (Maruish, 1999, p. 15). The chapter by Maruish in this volume discusses the topic of assessment and treatment in more detail.

Assessment Is Important in Risk Management

Assessment can substantially reduce many of the potential legal liabilities involved in the provision of psychological services (Bennet, Bryan, VandenBos, & Greenwood, 1990; Schutz, 1982) in which providers might perform routine baseline assessments of their psychotherapy patients' initial level of distress and of personality functioning (Meyer et al., 2000).

PROBLEMS OF LEARNING PERSONALITY ASSESSMENT: THE STUDENT SPEAKS

The first assessment course typically focuses on teaching students to give a confusing array of tests. Advanced courses are either didactic or are taught by the use of a group process model in which hypothesis generation and data integration are learned. With this model, *depression, anxiety, ambivalence*, and similar words take on new meaning for students when they are faced with the task of integrating personality assessment data. These words not only define symptoms seen in patients, but they also define students' experiences.

Early in their training, students are often amazed at the unique responses given to the most obvious test stimuli. Training in assessment is about experiencing for oneself what it is like to be with patients in a variety of situations, both fascinating and unpleasant, and what it is like to get a glimpse of someone else's inner world. Fowler (1998) describes students' early experience in learning assessment with the metaphor of being in a "psychic nudist colony." With this metaphor he is referring to the realization of the students that much of what they say or do reveals to others and to themselves otherwise private features of their personality. No further description was necessary in order for the second author (Clemence) to realize that she and Fowler shared a common experience during their assessment training. However, despite the feeling that one can no longer insure the privacy of one's inner world, or perhaps because of this, the first few years of training in personality assessment can become an incredibly profound educational experience. If nothing else, students can learn something many of them could perhaps learn nowhere else—what it is like to feel examined and assessed from all angles, often against their will. This approach to learning certainly allows students to become more empathic and sensitive to their patients' insecurities throughout the assessment procedure. Likewise, training in assessment has the potential to greatly enrich one's ability to be with clients during psychotherapy. Trainees learn how to observe subtleties in behavior, how to sit through uncomfortable moments with their patients, and how to endure scrutiny by them as well.

Such learning is enhanced if students learn assessment in a safe environment, such as a group learning class, to be described later in this chapter. However, with the use of this model there is the strange sense that our interpretation of the data may also say something about ourselves and our competence in relation to our peers. Are we revealing part of our inner experience that we would prefer to keep hidden, or at least would like to have some control over revealing?

Although initially one cannot escape scrutiny, eventually there is no need to do so. With proper training, students will develop the ability to separate their personal concerns and feelings from those of their patients, which is an important step in becoming a competent clinician. Much of their ignorance melts away as they develop increased ability to be excited about their work in assessment. This then frees students to wonder about their own contributions to the assessment experience. They wonder what they are projecting onto the data that might not belong there. Fortunately, in the group learning model, students have others to help keep them in check. Hearing different views of the data helps to keep projections at a minimum and helps students recognize the many different levels at which the data can be understood. It is certainly a more enriching experience when students are allowed to learn from different perspectives than it is when one is left on one's own to digest material taught in a lecture.

The didactic approach leaves much room for erroneous interpretation of the material once students are on their own and are trying to make sense of the techniques discussed in class. This style of learning encourages students to be more dependent on the instructor's method of interpretation, whereas group learning fosters the interpretative abilities of individual students by giving each a chance to confirm or to disconfirm the adequacy of his or her own hypothesis building process. This is an important step in the development of students' personal assessment styles, which is missed in the didactic learning model. Furthermore, in the didactic learning model it is more difficult for the instructor to know if the pace of teaching or the material being taught is appropriate for the skill level of the students, whereas the group learning model allows the instructor to set a pace matched to their abilities and expectations for learning.

During my (Clemence) experience in a group learning environment, what became increasingly more important over time was the support we received from learning as a group. Some students seemed to be more comfortable consulting with peers than risking the instructor's criticism upon revealing a lack of understanding. We also had the skills to continue our training when the instructor was not available. Someone from the group was often nearby for consultation and discussion, and this proved quite valuable during times when one of us had doubts about our approach or our responsibilities.

After several classes in personality assessment and after doing six or seven practice assessments, students typically feel they are beginning to acquire the skills necessary to complete an assessment, until their supervisor asks them to schedule a feedback session with the patient. Suddenly, newfound feelings of triumph and mastery turn again into fear and confusion because students find it awkward and discomforting to be put in a position of having to reveal to the patient negative aspects of his or her functioning. How do new students communicate such disturbing and seemingly unsettling information to another person? How can the patient ever understand what it has taken the student 2–3 years to even begin to understand? Students fear that it will surely devastate someone to hear he or she has a thought disorder or inadequate reality testing. However, when the emphasis of assessment (as in a therapeutic assessment approach) is on the facilitation of the client's questions about him- or herself, in addition to the referral question(s), this seemingly hopeless bind becomes much less of a problem. This approach makes the patient an active participant in the feedback process.

PROBLEMS OF TEACHING PERSONALITY ASSESSMENT: THE INSTRUCTOR SPEAKS

The problems encountered in teaching the initial assessment course, in which the emphasis is on learning the administration and scoring of various instruments, are different from those involved in teaching an advanced course, in which assessment of patients is the focus and the primary issue is integration of data. It must be made clear that the eventual goal is to master the integration of diverse data.

The instructor should provide information about many tests, while still giving students enough practice with each instrument. However, there may only be time to demonstrate some tests or have the student read about others. The instructor should introduce each new test by describing its relevance to an assessment battery, discussing what it offers that other tests do not offer. Instructors should resist students' efforts to ask for cookbook interpretations. Students often ask what each variable means. The response to the question of meaning is a point where the instructor can begin shifting from a test-based approach to one in which each variable is seen in context with many others.

Learning to do assessment is inherently more difficult for students than learning to do psychotherapy, because the former activity does not allow for continued evaluation of hypotheses. In contrast, the therapeutic process allows for continued discussion, clarification, and reformulation of hypotheses, over time, with the collaboration of the patient. This problem is frightening to students, because they fear making interpretive errors in this brief contact with the patient. More than anything else they are concerned that their inexperience will cause them to harm the patient. Their task is monumental: They must master test administration while also being empathic to patient needs, and their learning curve must be rapid. At the same time they must also master test interpretation and data integration, report writing, and the feedback process.

Sometimes students feel an allegiance to the patient, and the instructor might be seen as callous because he or she does not feel this personal allegiance or identification. Students' attitudes in this regard must be explored, in a patient, non-confrontational manner. Otherwise, the students might struggle to maintain their allegiance with the patient and might turn against learning assessment.

Not unlike some experienced clinicians who advocate for an actuarial process, many students also resist learning assessment because of the requirement to rely on intuitive processes, albeit those of disciplined intuition, and the fear of expressing their own conflicts in this process, rather than explaining those of the patient. The students' list of newfound responsibilities of evaluating, diagnosing, and committing themselves to paper concerning the patients they see is frightening. As one former student put it, "Self-doubt, anxiety, fear, and misguided optimism are but a few defenses that cropped up during our personality assessment seminar" (Fowler, 1998, p. 34).

Typically, students avoid committing themselves to sharply crafted, specific interpretations, even though they are told by the instructor that these are only hypotheses to try out. Instead, they resort to vague Barnum statements, statements true of most human beings (e.g., "This patient typically becomes anxious when under stress"). Students also often refuse to recognize pathology, even when it is blatantly apparent in the test data, ignoring it or reinterpreting it in a much less serious manner. They feel the instructor is overpathologizing the patient. The instructor should not challenge these defenses directly but instead should explore them in a patient, supportive manner, helping to provide additional clarifying data and

trying to understand the source of the resistance. There is a large body of literature concerning these resistances in learning assessment (e.g., Berg, 1984; Schafer, 1967; Sugarman, 1981, 1991). Time must also be made available outside the classroom for consultation with the instructor, as well as making use of assessment supervisors. Most of all, students who are just learning to integrate test data need a great deal of encouragement and support of their efforts. They also find it helpful when the instructor verbalizes an awareness of the difficulties involved in this type of learning.

LEARNING TO INTERVIEW

All too often the importance of interviewing is ignored in doctoral training programs. Sometimes it is taken for granted that a student will already know how to approach a person who comes for assessment in order to obtain relevant information. In the old days this was the role of the social worker, who then passed the patient on for assessment. We prefer the system in which the person who does the assessment also does the interview before any tests are given, since the interview is part of the assessment. In this way rapport can be built, so that the actual testing session is less stressful. Just as important, however, is that the assessor will have a great deal of information and impressions that can be used as a reference in the interpretation of the other data. Test responses take on additional important meaning when seen in reference to history data.

There are many ways to teach interviewing skills. In the interviewing class taught by the first author (Handler), students first practice using role playing and psychodrama techniques. Then they conduct videotaped interviews with student volunteers, and their interviews are watched and discussed by the class. Students learn to identify latent emotions produced in the interview, to handle their anxiety in productive ways, to manage the interviewee's anxiety, to go beyond mere chitchat with the interviewee, and to facilitate meaningful conversation. Students also learn to examine relevant life issues of the people they interview; to conceptualize these issues and describe them in a report; to ask open-ended questions rather than closed-ended questions, which can be answered with a brief "yes" or "no"; to reflect the person's feelings; and to encourage more open discussion.

There are many types of clinical interviews one might teach, depending upon one's theoretical orientation, but this course should be designed to focus on interviewing aspects that are probably of universal importance. Students should know that in its application the interview can be changed and modified, depending on its purpose and on the theoretical orientation of the interviewer.

THE IMPORTANCE OF RELIABILITY AND VALIDITY

It is essential when teaching students about the use of assessment instruments that one also teaches them the importance of sound psychometric properties for any measure used. By learning what qualities make an instrument useful and meaningful, students can be more discerning when confronted with new instruments or modifications of traditional measures. "In the absence of additional interpretive data, a raw score on any psychological test is meaningless" (Anastasi & Urbina, 1998, p. 67). This statement attests to the true importance of gathering appropriate normative data for all assessment instruments. Without a reference sample with which to compare individual scores, a single raw score tells the examiner little of scientific value. Likewise, information concerning the reliability of a measure is essential in understanding each individual score that is generated. If the measure has been found to be reliable, this then allows the examiner increased accuracy in the interpretation of variations in scores, such that differences between scores are more likely to result from individual differences than from measurement error (Nunnally & Bernstein, 1994). Furthermore, reliability is essential for an instrument to be valid.

The assessment instruments considered most useful are those that accurately measure the constructs they intend to measure, demonstrating both *sensitivity,* the true positive rate of identification of the individual with a particular trait or pattern, and *specificity,* the true negative rate of identification of individuals who do not have the personality trait being studied. In addition, the overall correct classification, the *hit rate,* indicates how accurately test scores classify both individuals who meet the criteria for the specific trait and those who do not. A measure can demonstrate a high degree of sensitivity but low specificity, or an inability to correctly exclude those individuals who do not meet the construct definition. When this occurs, the target variable is consistently correctly classified, but other variables that do not truly fit the construct definition are also included in the categorization of items. As a result, many false positives will be included along with the correctly classified variables, and the precision of the measure suffers. Therefore, it is important to consider both the sensitivity and the specificity of any measure being used. One can then better understand the possible meanings of their findings. For a more detailed discussion of these issues, see the chapter by Wasserman and Bracken in this volume.

TEACHING AN INTRODUCTORY COURSE IN PERSONALITY ASSESSMENT

Given that students have had an adequate course in psychometrics, the next typical step in training is an introductory course in assessment, in which they learn the many details of test administration, scoring, and initial interpretation. Assessment is taught quite differently in doctoral programs throughout the country. As mentioned previously, in some programs testing is actually taught, but the course is labeled *assessment.* In some programs this course is taught entirely as a survey course; students do little or no practice testing, scoring, or interpretation (Childs & Eyde, 2002; Durand, Blanchard, & Mindell, 1988; Hilsenroth & Handler, 1995). We believe this is a grave error, because each assessment course builds on the previous one(s). A great deal can be learned about assessment from reading textbooks and test manuals, but there is no substitute for practical experience.

Some doctoral training programs require only one assessment course in which there is actual practice with various tests. Many other programs have two courses in their curriculum but require only one, whereas other programs require two courses. In some programs only self-report measures are taught, and in others only projective measures are taught. In some programs there are optional courses available, and in others no such opportunities exist. The variability of the required and optional personality assessment courses in training programs is astounding, especially since assessment is a key area of proficiency, required by the American Psychological Association (APA) for program accreditation. In our opinion, students cannot become well grounded in assessment unless they learn interviewing skills and have taken both an introductory course focused on the administration and scoring of individual tests and an advanced course focused on the integration of assessment data and their communication to referral sources and to the person who took the tests.

Many times the required assessment courses are determined by a prevailing theoretical emphasis in the program. In these settings, assessment techniques chosen for study are limited to those instruments that are believed to fit the prevailing point of view. This is unfortunate, because students should be exposed to a wide variety of instruments and approaches to personality assessment, and because no instrument belongs to a particular theoretical approach; each test can be interpreted from a wide variety of theoretical viewpoints.

Some programs do not include the training of students in assessment as one of their missions, despite the APA requirement. Instead, they believe that the responsibility for teaching personality assessment lies with the internship site. Relegating this important area of clinical experience to the internship is a bad idea, because students learn under a great deal of pressure in these settings, pressure far greater than that of graduate school. Learning assessment in this type of pressured environment is truly a trial by fire.

Most students do not know the history of the testing and assessment movement and the relevance of assessment to clinical psychology. We recommend that this information be shared with students, along with the long list of reasons to learn assessment, which was discussed earlier in this chapter, and the reasons some psychologists eschew assessment.

The necessary emphasis on each test as a separate entity in the first course must eventually give way to a more integrated approach. In addition, although it is necessary to teach students to administer tests according to standardized instructions, they must also be introduced to the idea that in some cases it will not be possible or perhaps advisable to follow standardized instructions. They must also be helped to see that test scores derived in a nonstandardized manner are not necessarily invalid. Although they should be urged to follow the standardized procedures whenever possible, modifying instructions can sometimes help students understand the patient better.

We believe that it is important to draw students' attention to the similarities and differences among the tests, emphasizing the details of the stimuli, the ability of different tests to tap similar factors, the style of administration, and so on. Students should be taught the relevance of the variables they are measuring and scoring for each test. Otherwise, their administration is often rote and meaningless. For example, it makes little sense to students to learn to do a Rorschach Inquiry if they are not first acquainted with the relevance of the variables scored. Therefore, conceptualization of the perceptual, communicative, and representational aspects of perceiving the inkblots, and any other stimuli, for that matter, must first be discussed. We recommend beginning with stimuli other than the test stimuli, in order to demonstrate that aspects of the stimuli to which we ask patients to respond are no different from aspects of ordinary, real-life stimuli.

In our opinion, the most important function of this first course is to discuss the reasons each test was chosen to be studied and to help students become proficient in the administration, scoring, and initial interpretation of each test. Once students have mastered test administration, the instructor should begin to emphasize the establishment of rapport with the patient, which involves knowing the directions well enough to focus on the patient rather than on one's manual.

The introductory course usually has an assigned laboratory section, in which students practice with volunteer subjects to improve proficiency. Checkouts with volunteer subjects or with the instructor are routine. Students must be able to administer the tests smoothly and in an error-free manner and then score them properly before moving on to the next course.

In many programs students are required to administer, score, and begin to interpret several of each test they are learning. The number of practice protocols varies considerably, but it is typical to require two or three, depending on each student's level of proficiency. In the classroom there should be discussion of the psychometric properties and the research findings for each test and a discussion of the systematic administration and scoring errors produced by students.

Students should be taught that each type of data collected in an assessment has its strengths and its weaknesses. For example, observational and history data are especially helpful in assessment, but these sources can also be quite misleading. Anyone who has done marital therapy or custody evaluations has experienced a situation in which each spouse's story sounds quite plausible, but the husband and the wife tell opposite stories. Such are the limitations of history and observational data. People typically act differently in different situations, and they interpret their behaviors and intentions, and the behaviors and intentions of others, from their own biased vantage points. It soon becomes obvious that additional methods of understanding people are necessary in order to avoid the types of errors described above. Adding test data to the history and observational data should increase the accuracy of the assessment and can allow access to other key variables involved in knowing another person. However, test-derived data also contain sources of error, and at times they are also distorted by extratest effects or by impression management attempts, but many tests include systematic methods of determining test-taking attitude and the kind and degree of impression management attempted. Students should be taught that because no assessment method is error-free and no test, by itself, is comprehensive, it is important to use a number of assessment methods and a number of different types of tests and to aggregate and integrate them in order to answer referral questions adequately and to obtain a meaningful picture of the person assessed. This orientation leads the students directly to the advanced assessment course.

TEACHING AN ADVANCED COURSE IN PERSONALITY ASSESSMENT

What follows is a description of an advanced course in personality assessment much like the one taught by the first author (Handler). We will present this model to the reader for consideration because it is based on data culled from work on creative reasoning processes and is supported by research. In addition, we have added the use of integration approaches based on the use of metaphor, as well as an approach with which to facilitate empathic attunement with the patient. To this experiential approach we have also added an approach that asks the interpreter to imagine interacting with the person who produced the test results.

A second important reason we have used the following description as a suggested model is that the model can be used with *any* test battery the instructor wishes to teach, because the approach is not test specific. We suggest that the reader attempt to use this model in communicating integrative and contextual approaches to assessment teaching, modifying and tailoring the approach to fit individual needs and style.

Nevertheless, we recognize that this approach will not be suitable in its entirety for some clinicians who teach personality assessment. However, readers should nevertheless feel free to use any part or parts of this model that are consistent with their theoretical point of view and their preferred interpretive style. We believe the approach described here can be of use to those with an emphasis on intuition, as well as to those who prefer a more objective approach, because the heart of the approach to data integration is the use of convergent and divergent reasoning processes. This approach can be applicable to self-report data as well as to projective test data. Indeed, in the class described, the first author models the same approaches to the interpretation of the MMPI-2 and the Personality Assessment Inventory (PAI), for example, that we do to the Rorschach and the Thematic Apperception Test (TAT).

In this second course, students typically begin assessing patients. They must now focus on using their own judgment and intuitive skills to make interpretations and to integrate data. The task now, as we proceed, is the use of higher-level integrative approaches to create an accurate picture of the person they are assessing. The instructor should describe the changed focus and the difficult and complex problem of interpretation, along with the assurance that students will be able to master the process. Nevertheless, students are typically quite anxious, because interpretation places novel demands on them; for the first time they are being placed in a position of authority as experts and are being called upon to use themselves as an assessment tool. They have difficulty in the integration of experiential data and objective data, such as test scores and ratios. The complexity of the data is often overwhelming, and this pressure often leads students to search instead for cookbook answers.

With no attention to the interpretive process, students make low-level interpretations; they stay too close to the data, and therefore little meaningful integration is achieved. Hypotheses generated from this incomplete interpretive process are mere laundry lists of disconnected and often meaningless technical jargon. An approach is needed that systematically focuses on helping students develop meaningful interpretations and on

the integration of these interpretations to produce a meaningful report (Handler, Fowler, & Hilsenroth, 1998).

Emphasis is now placed on the communication of the experiential and cognitive aspects involved in the process of interpretation. Students are told that the interpretive process is systematized at each step of their learning, that each step will be described in detail, and that the focus will be on the development of an experience-near picture of the person assessed. First they observe the instructor making interpretations from assessment data. In the next step the focus is on group interpretation, to be described subsequently. Next, the student does the interpretation and integration with the help of a supervisor and then writes a report free of technical jargon, responding to the referral questions. Reports are returned to the students with detailed comments about integration, style, accuracy, and about how well the referral questions were answered. The students rewrite or correct them and return them to the instructor for review.

The group interpretation focuses on protocols collected by students in their clinical setting. Only the student who did the assessment knows the referral issue, the history, and any other relevant information. The remainder of the class and the instructor are ignorant of all details. Only age and gender are supplied.

Tests typically included in many test batteries include the WAIS-III, the Symptom Checklist-90-Revised (SCL-90-R), the MMPI-2, the PAI, the Bender Gestalt, a sentence completion test, figure drawings, the Rorschach, the TAT, a variety of self-report depression and anxiety measures, and early memories. However, instructors might add or delete tests depending upon their interests and the students' interests. Although this is much more than a full battery, these tests are included to give students wide exposure to many instruments.

The instructor describes various systematic ways in which one can interpret and integrate the data. The first two methods are derived from research in creativity. The first, *divergent thinking,* is derived from measures of creativity that ask a person to come up with as many ways as he or she can in which a specific object, such as a piece of string, or a box can be used. Those who find many novel uses for the object are said to be creative (Torrance, 1966, 1974; Williams, 1980). Handler and Finley (1994) found that people who scored high on tests of divergent thinking were significantly better Draw-a-Person (DAP) interpreters than those who were low on divergent thinking. (Degree of accuracy in the interpretation of the DAP protocols was determined by first generating a list of questions about three drawings, each list generated from an interview with that person's therapist). The participants were asked to look at each drawing and to mark each specific statement as either true or false. This approach asks students to come up with more than one interpretation for each observation or group of observations of the data.

Rather than seeking only one isolated interpretation for a specific test response, students are able to see that several interpretations might fit the data, and that although one of these might be the best choice as a hypothesis, it is also possible that several interpretations can fit the data simultaneously. This approach is especially useful in preventing students from ignoring possible alternatives and in helping them avoid the problem of *confirmatory bias:* ignoring data that do not fit the hypothesis and selecting data that confirm the initial hypothesis. Gradually, the students interpret larger and larger pieces of data by searching for additional possibilities, because they understand that it is premature to focus on certainty.

The second interpretive method based on creativity research is called *convergent thinking*. It asks how different bits of information can be brought together so that they reflect something unique and quite different from any of the pieces but are related to those pieces. Convergent thinking has been measured by the Remote Associates Test (RAT; Mednick & Mednick, 1967), in which the respondent is asked to come up with a word that is related in some way to three other presented stimulus words. For example, for the following three words: "base," round," and "dance," the correct answer is "ball." The interpretive process concerns "seeing relationships among seemingly mutually remote ideas" (Mednick & Mednick, 1967, p. 4). This is essentially the same type of task that is required in effective assessment interpretation, in which diverse pieces of data are fitted together to create an interpretive hypothesis. Burley and Handler (1997) found that the RAT significantly differentiated good and poor DAP interpreters (determined as in the Handler & Finley study cited earlier) in groups of undergraduate students and in a group of graduate students in clinical psychology.

A helpful teaching heuristic in the interpretive process is the use of the metaphor (Hilsenroth, 1998), in which students are taught to offer an interpretive response as though it were an expression of the patient's experience. They are asked to summarize the essential needs, wishes, expectations, major beliefs, and unresolved issues of the patient through the use of a short declarative statement, typically beginning with "I wish," "I feel," "I think," "I want," or "I am." This "metaphor of the self" facilitates interpretation because it allows for a quick and easy way to frame the response to empathize vicariously with the patient. When this approach is combined with the cognitive approaches of divergent and convergent thinking, students generate meaningful hypotheses not only about self-experience, but also about how others might experience the patient in other settings. To facilitate this latter approach, students are asked how they would feel interacting with the patient who gave a certain response if they met the person at a party or in some other interpersonal setting (Potash, 1998).

At first students focus on individual findings, gradually branching out to include patterns of data from a series of responses, and finally integrating these interpretations across various tests. Initial attempts at interpretation are little more than observations, couched as interpretations, such as "This response is an F-"; "She drew her hands behind her back"; "He forgot to say how the person was feeling in this TAT story." The student is surprised when the instructor states that the interpretation was merely an observation. To discourage this descriptive approach the instructor typically asks the student to tell all the things that such an observation could mean, thereby encouraging divergent thinking.

At the next level, students typically begin to shift their interpretations to a somewhat less descriptive approach, but the interpretations are still test based, rather than being psychologically relevant. Examples of this type of interpretation are "She seems to be experiencing anxiety on this card" and "The patient seems to oscillate between being too abstract and too concrete on the WAIS-III." Again, the instructor asks the student to generate a *psychologically relevant* interpretation concerning the meaning of this observation in reference to the person's life issues, or in reference to the data we have already processed.

Efforts are made to sharpen and focus interpretations. Other students are asked to help by attempting to clarify and focus a student's overly general interpretation, and often a discussion ensues among several students to further define the original interpretation. The instructor focuses the questions to facilitate the process. The task here is to model the generation of detailed, specific hypotheses that can be validated once we have completed all the interpretation and integration of the data.

Whenever a segment of the data begins to build a picture of the person tested, students are asked to separately commit themselves to paper in class by writing a paragraph that summarizes and integrates the data available so far. The act of committing their interpretations to paper forces students to focus and to be responsible for what they write. They are impressed with each other's work and typically find that several people have focused on additional interpretations they had not noticed.

Anyone who uses this teaching format will inevitably encounter resistance from students who have been trained to stick closely to empirical findings. Sometimes a student will feel the class is engaging in reckless and irresponsible activities, and/or that they are saying negative and harmful things about people, without evidence. It is necessary to patiently but persistently work through these defensive barriers. It is also sometimes frightening for students to experience blatant pathology so closely that it becomes necessary to back away from interpretation and, perhaps, to condemn the entire process.

The instructor should be extremely supportive and facilitative, offering hints when a student feels stuck and a helpful direction when the student cannot proceed further. The entire class becomes a protective and encouraging environment, offering suggestions, ideas for rephrasing, and a great deal of praise for effort expended and for successful interpretations. It is also important to empower students, reassuring them that they are on the correct path and that even at this early stage they are doing especially creative work. Students are also introduced to relatively new material concerning the problem of test integration. The work of Beutler and Berren (1995), Ganellen (1996), Handler et al. (1998), Meyer (1997), and Weiner (1998) have focused on different aspects of this issue.

Once the entire record is processed and a list of specific hypotheses is recorded, the student who did the assessment tells the class about the patient, including history, presenting problem(s), pattern and style of interaction, and so forth. Each hypothesis generated is classified as "correct," "incorrect," or "cannot say," because of lack of information. Typically, correct responses range from 90 to 95%, with only one or two "incorrect" hypotheses and one or two "cannot say" responses.

In this advanced course students might complete three reports. They should continue to do additional supervised assessments in their program's training clinic and, later, in their clinical placements throughout the remainder of their university training.

IMPROVING ASSESSMENT RESULTS THROUGH MODIFICATION OF ADMINISTRATION PROCEDURES

Students learning assessment are curious about ways to improve the accuracy of their interpretations, but they nevertheless adhere strictly to standardized approaches to administration, even when, in some situations, these approaches result in a distortion of findings. They argue long, hard, and sometimes persuasively that it is wrong to modify standardized procedures, for any reason. However, we believe that at certain times changing standardized instructions will often yield data that are a more accurate measure of the individual than would occur with reliance on standardized instructions. For example, a rather suspicious man was being tested with the WAIS-R. He stated that an orange and a banana were not alike and continued in this fashion for the other pairs of items. The examiner then reassured him that there really was a way in which the pairs of

items were alike and that there was no trick involved. The patient then responded correctly to almost all of the items, earning an excellent score. When we discuss this alteration in the instructions, students express concern about how the examiner would score the subtest results. The response of the instructor is that the students are placing the emphasis in the wrong area: They are more interested in the test and less in the patient. If the standardized score was reported, it would also not give an accurate measure of this patient's intelligence or of his emotional problems. Instead, the change in instructions can be described in the report, along with a statement that says something like, "The patient's level of suspicion interferes with his cognitive effectiveness, but with some support and assurance he can give up this stance and be more effective."

Students are also reluctant to modify standardized instructions by merely adding additional tasks after standardized instructions are followed. For example, the first author typically recommends that students ask patients what they thought of each test they took, how they felt about it, what they liked and disliked about it, and so on. This approach helps in the interpretation of the test results by clarifying the attitude and approach the patient took to the task, which perhaps have affected the results. The first author has designed a systematic Testing of the Limits procedure, based on the method first employed by Bruno Klopfer (Klopfer, Ainsworth, Klopfer, & Holt, 1954). In this method the patient is questioned to amplify the meanings of his or her responses and to gain information about his or her expectations and attitudes about the various tests and subtests. This information helps put the responses and the scores in perspective. For example, when a patient gave the response, "A butterfly coming out of an iceberg" to Card VII of the Rorschach, he was asked, after the test had been completed, "What's that butterfly doing coming out of that iceberg?" The patient responded, "That response sounds kind of crazy; I guess I saw a butterfly and an iceberg. I must have been nervous; they don't actually belong together." This patient recognized the cognitive distortion he apparently experienced and was able to explain the reason for it and correct it. Therefore, this response speaks to a less serious condition, compared with a patient who could not recognize that he or she had produced the cognitive slip. Indeed, later on, the patient could typically recognize when he had made similar cognitive misperceptions, and he was able to correct them, as he had done in the assessment.

Other suggestions include asking patients to comment on their responses or asking them to amplify these responses, such as amplifying various aspects of their figure drawings and Bender Gestalt productions, their Rorschach and TAT response, and the critical items on self-report measures. These amplifications of test responses reduce interpretive errors by providing clarification of responses.

TEACHING STUDENTS HOW TO CONSTRUCT AN ASSESSMENT BATTERY

Important sources of information will of course come from an interview with the patient and possibly with members of his or her family. Important history data and observations from these contacts form a significant core of data, enriched, perhaps, by information derived from other case records and from referral sources. In our clinical setting patients take the SCL-90-R before the intake interview. This self-report instrument allows the interviewer to note those physical and emotional symptoms or problems the patients endorse as particularly difficult problems for them. This information is typically quite useful in structuring at least part of the interview. The construction of a comprehensive assessment battery is typically the next step.

What constitutes a comprehensive assessment battery differs from setting to setting. Certainly, adherents of the five-factor model would constitute an assessment battery differently than someone whose theoretical focus is object relations. However, there are issues involved in assessment approaches that are far more important than one's theoretical orientation. No test is necessarily tied to any one theory. Rather, it is the clinician who interprets the test who may imbue it with a particular theory.

It is difficult to describe a single test battery that would be appropriate for everyone, because referral questions vary, as do assessment settings and their requirements; physical and emotional needs, educational and intellectual levels, and cultural issues might require the use of somewhat different instruments. Nevertheless, there are a number of guiding principles used to help students construct a comprehensive assessment battery, which can and should be varied given the issues described above.

Beutler and Berren (1995) compare test selection and administration in assessment to doing research. They view each test as an "analogue environment" to be presented to the patient. In this process the clinician should ask which types of environments should be selected in each case. The instructions of each test or subtest are the clinician's way of manipulating these analogue environments and presenting them to the patient. Responding to analogue environments is made easier or more difficult as the degree of structure changes from highly structured to ambiguous or vague. Some people do much better in a highly structured environment, and some do worse.

Assessment is typically a stressful experience because the examiner constantly asks the patient to respond in a certain manner or in a certain format, as per the test instructions. When the format is unstructured there is sometimes less stress because the patient has many options in the way in which he or she can respond. However, there are marked differences in the ways that people experience this openness. For some people a vague or open format is gratifying, and for others it is terrifying. For this reason it is helpful to inquire about the patient's experience with each format, to determine its effect.

Beutler and Berren make another important point in reference to test selection: Some tests are measures of enduring internal qualities (*traits*), whereas others tap more transitory aspects of functioning (*states*), which differ for an individual from one situation to another. The clinician's job is to determine which test results are measuring states and which reflect traits. When a specific test in some way resembles some aspects of the patient's actual living environment, we can assume that his or her response will be similar to the person's response in the real-world setting (Beutler & Berren, 1995). The assessor can often observe these responses, which we call *stylistic* aspects of a person's personality.

One question to be answered is whether this approach is typical of the patient's performance in certain settings in the environment, whether it is due to the way in which the person views this particular task (or the entire assessment), or whether it is due to one or more underlying personality problems, elicited by the test situation itself. It is in part for this reason that students are taught to carefully record verbatim exactly what the patient answers, the extratest responses (e.g., side comments, emotional expressions, etc.), and details of how each task was approached.

Important aspects of test choice are the research that supports the instrument, the ease of administration for the patient, and the ability of the test to tap specific aspects of personality functioning that other instruments do not tap. We will discuss choosing a comprehensive assessment battery next.

First, an intellectual measure should be included, even if the person's intelligence level appears obvious, because it allows the assessor to estimate whether there is emotional interference in cognitive functioning. For this we recommend the WAIS-III or the WISC-III, although the use of various short forms is acceptable if time is an important factor. For people with language problems of one type or another, or for people whose learning opportunities have been atypical for any number of reasons (e.g., poverty, dyslexia, etc.), a nonverbal intelligence test might be substituted if an IQ measure is necessary. The Wechsler tests also offer many clues concerning personality functioning, from the pattern of interaction with the examiner, the approach to the test, the patient's attitude while taking it, response content, as well as from the style and approach to the subtest items, and the response to success or failure. If these issues are not relevant for the particular referral questions, the examiner could certainly omit this test completely.

Additionally, one or more self-report inventories should be included, two if time permits. The MMPI-2 is an extremely well-researched instrument that can provide a great deal more information than the patient's self-perception. Students are discouraged from using the descriptive printout and instead are asked to interpret the test using a more labor-intensive approach, examining the scores on the many supplementary scales and integrating them with other MMPI-2 data. The PAI is recommended because it yields estimates of adaptability and emotional health that are not defined merely as the absence of pathology, because it has several scales concerning treatment issues, and because it is psychometrically an extremely well-constructed scale. Other possible inventories include the Millon Clinical Multiaxial Inventory-III (MCMI-III), because it focuses on Axis II disorders, and the SCL-90-R or its abbreviated form, because it yields a comprehensive picture concerning present physical and emotional symptoms the patient endorses. There are a host of other possible self-report measures that can be used, depending on the referral issues (e.g., the Beck Depression Inventory and the Beck Anxiety Inventory).

Several projective tests are suggested, again depending upon the referral questions and the presenting problems. It is helpful to use an array of projective tests that vary on a number of dimensions, to determine whether there are different patterns of functioning with different types of stimuli. We recommend a possible array of stimuli that range from those that are very simple and specific (e.g., the Bender Gestalt Test) to the opposite extreme, the DAP Test, because it is the only test in the battery in which there is no external guiding stimulus. Between these two extremes are the TAT, in which the stimuli are relatively clear-cut, and the Rorschach, in which the stimuli are vague and unstructured.

Although the research concerning the symbolic content in the interpretation of the Bender Gestalt Test (BG) is rather negative, the test nevertheless allows the assessor a view of the person's stylistic approach to the rather simple task of copying the stimuli. The Rorschach is a multifaceted measure that may be used in an atheoretical manner, using the Comprehensive System (Exner, 1993), or it may be used in association with a number of theoretical approaches, including self psychology, object relations, ego psychology, and even Jungian psychology. In addition, many of the variables scored in the Exner system could very well be of interest to psychologists with a cognitive-behavioral approach. The Rorschach is a good choice as a projective instrument because it is multidimensional, tapping many areas of functioning, and because there has been a great deal of recent research that supports its validity (Baity & Hilsenroth, 1999; Ganellen, 1999; Kubeszyn et al., 2000; Meyer, 2000; Meyer, Riethmiller, Brooks, Benoit, & Handler, 2000; Meyer & Archer, 2001; Meyer & Handler, 1997; Viglione, 1999; Viglione & Hilsenroth, 2001; Weiner, 2001). There are also several well-validated Rorschach content scoring systems

that were generated from research and have found application in clinical assessment as well (e.g., the Mutuality of Autonomy Scale, Urist, 1977; the Holt Primary Process Scale, Holt, 1977; the Rorschach Oral Dependency Scale, or ROD, Masling, Rabie, & Blondheim, 1967; and the Lerner Defense Scale, Lerner & Lerner, 1980).

The TAT is another instrument frequently used by psychologists that can be used with a variety of theoretical approaches. The TAT can be interpreted using content, style, and coherence variables. There are several interpretive systems for the TAT, but the systematic work of Cramer (1996) and Westen (1991a, 1991b; Westen, Lohr, Silk, Gold, & Kerber, 1990) seems most promising.

One assessment technique that might be new to some psychologists is the early memories technique, in which the assessor asks the patient for a specific early memory of mother, father, first day of school, eating or being fed, of a transitional object, and of feeling snug and warm (Fowler et al., 1995, 1996). This approach, which can also be used as part of an interview, has demonstrated utility for predicting details of the therapeutic relationship, and it correlates with a variety of other measures of object relations. The approach can be used with a wide variety of theoretical approaches, including various cognitive approaches (Bruhn, 1990, 1992).

Additional possible tests include various drawing tests (e.g., the DAP test and the Kinetic Family Drawing Test, or K-F-D). The research findings for these tests are not consistently supportive (Handler, 1996; Handler & Habenicht, 1994). However, many of the studies are not well conceived or well controlled (Handler & Habenicht, 1994; Riethmiller & Handler, 1997a, 1997b). The DAP and/or the K-F-D are nevertheless recommended for possible use for the following reasons:

1. They are the only tests in which there is no standard stimulus to be placed before the patient. This lack of structure is an asset because it allows the examiner to observe organizing behavior in situations with no real external structure. Therefore, the DAP taps issues concerning the quality of internal structuring. Poor results are often obtained if the person tested has problems with identity or with the ability to organize self-related issues.

2. Drawing tests are helpful if the person being assessed is not very verbal or communicative, because a minimum of talking is required in the administration.

3. Drawing tests are quick and easy to administer.

4. Drawings have been demonstrated to be excellent instruments to reflect changes in psychotherapy (Handler, 1996; Hartman & Fithian, 1972; Lewinsohn, 1965; Maloney & Glasser, 1982; Robins, Blatt, & Ford, 1991; Sarel, Sarel, & Berman, 1981; Yama, 1990).

Much of the research on drawing approaches is poorly conceived, focusing on single variables, taken out of context, and interpreted with a sign approach (Riethmiller & Handler, 1997a, 1997b). There is also confusion between the interpretation of distortions in the drawings that reflect pathology and those that reflect poor artistic ability. There are two ways to deal with these problems. The first is to use a control figure of equal task difficulty to identify problems due primarily to artistic ability. Handler and Reyher (1964, 1966) have developed such a control figure, the drawing of an automobile. In addition, sensitizing students to the distortions produced by people with pathology and comparing these with distortions produced by those with poor artistic ability helps students differentiate between those two situations (Handler & Riethmiller, 1998).

A sentence completion test (there are many different types) is a combination of a self-report measure and a projective test. The recommended version is the Miale-Holsopple Sentence Completion Test (Holsopple & Miale, 1954) because of the type of items employed. Patients are asked to complete a series of sentence stems in any way they wish. Most of the items are indirect, such as "Closer and closer there comes . . . ," "A wild animal . . . ," and "When fire starts . . . ." Sentence completion tests also provide information to be followed up in an interview.

ASSESSMENT AND CULTURAL DIVERSITY

No assessment education is complete without an understanding of the cultural and subcultural influences on assessment data. This is an important issue because often the effects of cultural variables may be misinterpreted as personality abnormality. Therefore, traditional tests might be inappropriate for some people, and for others adjustments in interpretation should be made by reference to cultural or subcultural norms. Students should recognize that it is unethical to use typical normative findings to evaluate members of other cultures unless data are available suggesting cross-cultural equivalence. The reader should refer to the chapter by Geisinger in this volume on testing and assessment in cross-cultural psychology.

In many cases traditional test items are either irrelevant to the patient or have a different meaning from that intended. Often, merely translating a test into the patient's language is not adequate because the test items or even the test format may still be inappropriate. Knowledge of various subgroups obtained from reading, consulting with colleagues, and interacting with members of the culture goes a long way to sensitize a person to the problems encountered in personality assessment with members of that subgroup. It is also important to understand

the significant differences among various ethnic and cultural groups in what is considered normal or typical behavior. Cultural factors play a critical role in the expression of psychopathology; unless this context is understood, it is not possible to make an accurate assessment of the patient. The instructor should introduce examples of variations in test performance from members of different cultural groups. For example, figure drawings obtained from children in different cultures are shown to students (Dennis, 1966). In some groups the drawings look frighteningly like those produced by retarded or by severely emotionally disturbed children.

Another problem concerning culturally competent personality assessment is the importance of determining the degree of acculturation the person being assessed has made to the prevailing mainstream culture. This analysis is necessary to determine what set of norms the assessor might use in the interpretive process. Although it is not possible to include readings about assessment issues for all available subcultures, it is possible to include research on the subgroups the student is likely to encounter in his or her training. There are a number of important resources available to assist students in doing competent multicultural assessments (e.g., Dana, 2000a, 2000b). Allen (1998) reviews personality assessment with American Indians and Alaska Natives; Lindsey (1998) reviews such work with African American clients; Okazaki (1998) reviews assessment with Asian Americans; and Cuéllar (1998) reviews cross-cultural assessment with Hispanic Americans.

TEACHING ETHICAL ISSUES OF ASSESSMENT

As students enter the field and become professional psychologists, they must have a clear understanding of how legal and ethical responsibilities affect their work. However, Plante (1995) found that ethics courses in graduate training programs tend to focus little on practical strategies for adhering to ethical and legal standards once students begin their professional careers.

One way to reduce the risks associated with the practice of assessment is to maintain an adequate level of competency in the services one offers (Plante, 1999). Competency generally refers to the extent to which a psychologist is appropriately trained and has obtained up-to-date knowledge in the areas in which he or she practices. This principle assumes that professional psychologists are aware of the boundaries and limitations of their competence. Determining this is not always easy, because there are no specific guidelines for measuring competence or indicating how often training should be conducted. To reduce the possibility of committing ethical violations, the psychologist should attend continuing education classes and workshops at professional conferences and local psychology organizations.

The APA (1992) publication *Ethical Principles of Psychologists and Code of Conduct* also asserts that psychologists who use assessment instruments must use them appropriately, based on relevant research on the administration, scoring, and interpretation of the instrument. To adhere to this principle, psychologists using assessment instruments must be aware of the data concerning reliability, validity, and standardization of the instruments. Consideration of normative data is essential when interpreting test results. There may be occasions when an instrument has not been tested with a particular group of individuals and, as a result, normative data do not exist for that population. If this is the case, use of the measure with an individual of that population is inappropriate.

Information regarding the psychometric properties of an instrument and its intended use must be provided in the test manual to be in accordance with the ethical standards of publication or distribution of an assessment instrument (Koocher & Keith-Spiegel, 1998). Anyone using the instrument should read the manual thoroughly and understand the measure's limitations before using it. "The responsibility for establishing whether the test measures the construct or reflects the content of interest is the burden of both the developers and the publishers," (Koocher & Keith-Spiegel, 1998, p. 147) but the person administering it is ultimately responsible for knowing this information and using it appropriately. The reader should refer to the chapter by Koocher and Rey-Casserly in this volume, on ethical issues in psychological assessment, for a more detailed discussion of this topic.

ASSESSMENT APPROACHES AND PERSONALITY THEORY

In the past those with behavioral and cognitive approaches typically used self-report measures in their assessments, whereas those with psychodynamic orientations tended to rely on projective tests. Since those old days, during which the two sides crossed swords on a regular basis in the literature and in the halls of academia, we now seem more enlightened. We now tend to use each other's tools, but in a more flexible manner. For example, although psychoanalytically oriented clinicians use the Rorschach, it can also be interpreted from a more cognitive and stylistic approach. In fact, Exner has been criticized by some psychodynamically oriented psychologists for having developed an atheoretical, nomothetic system.

Tests can be interpreted using any theoretical viewpoint. For example, psychodynamically oriented psychologists sometimes interpret the MMPI-2 using a psychodynamic orientation (Trimboli & Kilgore, 1983), and cognitive psychologists

interpret the TAT from a variety of cognitive viewpoints (Ronan, Date, & Weisbrod, 1995; Teglasi, 1993), as well as from a motivational viewpoint (McClelland, 1987). Martin Mayman's approach to the interpretation of the Early Memories Procedure (EMP) is from an object relations perspective, but the EMP is also used by adherents of social learning theory and cognitive psychology (e.g., Bruhn, 1990, 1992).

Many psychologists believe that the use of theory in conducting an assessment is absolutely necessary because it serves as an organizing function, a clarifying function, a predictive function, and an integrative function, helping to organize and make sense of data (Sugarman, 1991). Theory serves to "recast psychological test data as psychological constructs whose relationship is already delineated by the theory in mind" (Sugarman & Kanner, 2000). In this way the interpreter can organize data, much of it seemingly unrelated, into meaningful descriptions of personality functioning, and can make predictions about future functioning. Theory often helps students make sense of inconsistencies in the data.

Students should be helped to understand that although assessment instruments can be derived from either an atheoretical or a theoretical base, the data derived from any assessment instrument can be interpreted using almost any theory, or no theory at all. No test is necessarily wedded to any theory, but theory is often useful in providing the glue, as it were, that allows the interpreter to extend and expand the meaning of the test findings in a wide variety of ways. Students must ask themselves what can be gained by interpreting test data through the lens of theory. Some would say that what is gained is only distortion, so that the results reflect the theory and not the person. Others say it is possible to enrich the interpretations made with the aid of theory and to increase the accuracy and meaningfulness of assessment results, and that a theory-based approach often allows the assessor to make predictions with greater specificity and utility than can be made if one relies only on test signs.

LEARNING THROUGH DOING: PROFICIENCY THROUGH SUPERVISED PRACTICE

Something interesting happens when a student discusses data with his or her supervisor. The supervisee often says and does things that reveal information about the nature and experience of the client being assessed, in metaphors used to describe assessment experiences, slips of the tongue when discussing a client, or an actual recreation of the dynamics present in the relationship between client and assessor in the supervisory relationship. This reenactment has come to be known as *parallel process* (e.g., Deering, 1994; Doehrman, 1976; Whitman & Jacobs, 1998), defined by Deering (1994) as "an unconscious process that takes place when a trainee replicates problems and symptoms of patients during supervision" with the purpose "of causing the supervisor to demonstrate how to handle the situation" (p. 1). If the supervisor and supervisee can become aware of its presence in the supervision, it can be a powerful diagnostic and experiential tool. It is important for the supervisor to note when students act in a way that is uncharacteristic of their usual behavior, often the first clue that parallel process is occurring (Sigman, 1989). Students sometimes take on aspects of their clients' personality, especially when they identify with some facet of a patient's experience or character style.

The supervisor should always strive to model the relationship with the supervisee after that which he or she would want the supervisee to have with the client. With this approach, the supervisor becomes an internalized model or standard for the trainee. Supervisors often serve as the template for how to behave with a client during assessment because many students have no other opportunities to observe seasoned clinicians at their work. It is also important to remember that problems in the supervisor-supervisee relationship can trickle down into the supervisee-client relationship, so issues such as power, control, competition, and inferiority may arise between the supervisee and the client as well if these emotions happen to be present in the supervision relationship. Nevertheless, given the inevitable occurrence of parallel process, going over data with the student is not sufficient supervision or training. The supervisory relationship itself should be used to facilitate growth and development of the student. There must also be a good alliance between the supervisor and the student, and a sense of confidence from both parties involved that each has sound judgement and good intentions toward the assessment process and the client.

It is important for the supervisor to encourage a sense of hopefulness in the student that will translate into hope for the client that this new information will be helpful. Otherwise, it is difficult for students to know or at least to believe that what they are doing is meaningful. When the characteristics of trust, confidence, collaboration, and hopefulness are not present in the supervision relationship, this should be discussed during the supervision hour. It is crucial that the relationship be examined when something impedes the ability to form a strong alliance.

ASSESSMENT TEACHING IN GRADUATE SCHOOL: A REVIEW OF THE SURVEYS

According to the recent survey literature, training in assessment continues to be emphasized in clinical training programs (Belter & Piotrowski, 1999; Piotrowski, 1999;

Piotrowski & Zalewski, 1993; Watkins, 1991), although there is evidence that those in academic positions view assessment as less important than other areas of clinical training (Kinder, 1994; Retzlaff, 1992). Those instruments that have consistently received the most attention during graduate training are MMPI, Rorschach, Wechsler scales, and TAT (Belter & Piotrowski, 1999; Hilsenroth & Handler, 1995; Piotrowski & Zalewski, 1993; Ritzler & Alter, 1986; Watkins, 1991). Some concern, however, has been expressed about the level of training being conducted in the area of projective assessment (Dempster, 1990; Hershey, Kopplin, & Cornell, 1991; Hilsenroth & Handler, 1995; Rossini & Moretti, 1997). Watkins (1991) found that clinical psychologists in academia generally believe that projective techniques are less important assessment approaches now than they have been in the past and that they are not grounded in empirical research (see also Watkins, Campbell, & Manus, 1990).

Academic training often emphasizes objective assessment over projective techniques. Clinical training directors surveyed by Rossini and Moretti (1997) reported that the amount of formal instruction or supervision being conducted in the use of the TAT was little to none, and Hilsenroth and Handler (1995) found that graduate students were often dissatisfied with the quality and degree of training they received in the Rorschach. Piotrowski and Zalewski (1993) surveyed directors of clinical training in APA-approved Psy.D. and Ph.D. programs and found that behavioral testing and objective personality testing were expected to increase in use in academic settings, whereas projective personality assessment was predicted to decrease according to almost one half of those surveyed. In addition, 46% of training directors answered "no" to the question, "Do you feel that the extent of projective test usage in various applied clinical settings is warranted?" (Piotrowski & Zalewski, 1993, p. 399).

It is apparent that although training in assessment remains widely emphasized, this does not mean that students are well prepared, especially in the area of projective assessment. Specific qualities and approaches to training may vary widely from program to program and may not meet the needs of applied settings and internship programs. In fact, Durand et al. (1988) found that 47% of graduate training directors felt that projective assessment was less important than in the past, whereas 65% of internship directors felt projective assessment had remained an important approach for training in assessment. Such disagreement is not rare; much of the literature reflects the discrepancy between graduate training in assessment and internship needs (Brabender, 1992; Durand et al., 1988; Garfield & Kurtz, 1973; Shemberg & Keeley, 1970; Shemberg & Leventhal, 1981; Watkins, 1991). Furthermore, given the report by Camara, Nathan, and Puente (2000), who found that the most frequently used instruments by professional psychologists are the WAIS-R/WISC-R, the MMPI-2, the Rorschach, BG, and the TAT, it is clear that the discrepancy between training and application of assessment goes beyond that of internship needs and includes real-world needs as well.

ASSESSMENT ON INTERNSHIP: REPORT OF A SURVEY

Clemence and Handler (2001) sought to examine the expectations that internship training directors have for students and to ascertain the specific psychological assessment methods most commonly used at internship programs in professional psychology. Questionnaires designed to access this information were mailed to all 563 internships listed in the 1998–1999 Association of Psychology Postdoctoral and Internship Centers Directory. Only two sites indicated that no patients are assessed, and 41% responded that testing instruments are used with the majority of their patients.

Each intern is required to administer an average of 27 full battery or 33 partial battery assessments per year, far exceeding the number of batteries administered by most students during their graduate training. Of those rotations that utilize a standard assessment battery (86%), over 50% include the WISC/WAIS (91%), the MMPI-2/MMPI-A (80%), the Rorschach (72%), or the TAT (56%) in their battery. These results are consistent with previous research investigating the use of assessment on internship (Garfield & Kurtz, 1973; Shemberg & Keeley, 1974). Piotrowski and Belter (1999) also found the four most commonly used assessment instruments at internship facilities to be the MMPI-2/MMPI-A (86%), the WAIS (83%), the Rorschach (80%), and the TAT (76%).

To ensure that students are fully prepared to perform in the area of assessment on their internship, training is frequently offered to bridge the gap that exists between the type and amount of training conducted in most graduate programs and that desired by internship sites. In the Clemence and Handler study, 99% of the internships surveyed reported offering training in assessment, and three approaches to training in personality assessment were most commonly endorsed by training directors: intellectual assessment (79%), interviewing (76%), and psychodynamic personality assessment (64%). These three methods seem to be the predominant training approaches used by the sites included in the survey. This finding suggests that these are important directions for training at the graduate level, as well.

Of the topics being offered in the area of assessment training, report writing is most often taught (92%); 86% of the rotations conduct training in advanced assessment, 84% in providing feedback to clients, 74% in providing feedback to

referral sources, 56% in introductory assessment, and 44% in the study of a specific test. This breakdown may reflect the priorities internship training directors place on areas of assessment, or the areas in which students are less prepared upon leaving graduate school.

Piotrowski and Belter (1999) surveyed 84 APA-approved internship programs and found that 87% of their respondents required interns to participate in assessment seminars. If the demand for training is as critical as these surveys seem to indicate, it is curious that graduating students do not appear to be especially well-prepared in this area, as this and previous studies indicate (Watkins, 1991). Training in basic assessment should be the job of graduate training programs and not internship sites, whose primary function should be in providing supervised practical experience in the field.

From our findings and other surveys (Petzel & Berndt, 1980; Stedman, 1997; Watkins, 1991), it appears that internship training directors prefer students who have been properly trained in a variety of assessment approaches, including self-report, projective, and intelligence testing. Distinct differences were found between the types of assessment techniques utilized across various facilities. The WISC and WAIS were found to be routinely used at each of the various internship facilities; the MMPI-2 and MMPI-A are used regularly at all but the child facilities, where only 36% reported using these instruments routinely. The Rorschach is part of a full battery at the majority of internships surveyed, ranging from 58% for Veterans Administration hospitals to 95% for community mental health centers, and the TAT is used in full batteries primarily at private general hospitals (88%) and community mental health centers (73%).

AMERICAN PSYCHOLOGICAL ASSOCIATION DIVISION 12 GUIDELINES

The discrepancy between the real-world use of assessment and training in graduate schools is troubling and seems to be oddly encouraged by certain groups within the psychological community. For example, Division 12 of the APA (1999) set up a task force ("Assessment for the Twenty-First Century") to examine issues concerning clinical training in psychological assessment. They defined their task as one of creating a curriculum model for graduate programs that would include proper and appropriate assessment topics for the next century.

The task force, made up of psychologists experienced in various areas of assessment, was asked to recommend class topics that should be included in this ideal curriculum. They came up with 105 topics, which they then ranked according to their beliefs about their usefulness. Rankings ranged from "essential" ("no proper clinical training program should be without appropriate coverage of this item") to "less important" ("inessential and would not greatly improve the curriculum"; APA Division 12, 1999, p. 11). What is surprising about the final curriculum rankings, given the previously discussed research in the area of assessment in the real world, was that the curriculum seemed to be heavily weighted toward self-report assessment techniques, with only three class topics in the area of projective assessment: (a) Learning Personality Assessment: Projective—Rorschach (or related methods); (b) Learning Personality Assessment: Projective—Thematic Apperception Test; and (c) Learning Personality Assessment: Projective—Drawing Tests. What is even more striking is that these three classes were ranked extremely low in the model curriculum, with the Rorschach class ranked 95th in importance, the TAT class ranked 99th, and the projective drawings class ranked 102nd out of the possible 105 topics proposed. It is clear that the task force considers these topics as primarily useless and certainly inessential in the training of future psychologists. Furthermore, the low rankings then led to the omission of any training in projective techniques from the final Division 12 model syllabus. The omission of these classes leaves us with a model for training that is quite inconsistent with previously cited research concerning the importance of projective testing in applied settings and seems to ignore the needs of students and internships. This Division 12 task force appears to have missed the mark in its attempt to create a model of training that would prepare students for the future of assessment.

The Division 12 model widens the gap between training and use of assessment in applied settings instead of shrinking it. In fact, the model reinforces the division discussed previously between psychologists in academia and those in the field. A better approach to designing a model curriculum of assessment training for the future would be to combine topics relevant to the application of assessment in the real world with those deemed relevant by academicians. Data from research concerning the use of assessment demonstrate that a multidimensional approach is most valid and most useful in providing worthwhile diagnostic and therapeutic considerations of clinicians. This point must not be ignored due to personal preferences. The Division 12 model of assessment training demonstrates that even as late as 1999, models of training continued to be designed that ignored the importance of teaching students a balance of methods so that they would be able to proceed with multifunctional approaches to assessment.

POSTGRADUATE ASSESSMENT TRAINING

Although assessment practice during internship helps to develop skills, it is important to continue to refine these skills and add to them and to continue reading the current research literature in assessment. There are many opportunities to attend workshops that focus on particular tests or on the development of particular assessment skills. For example, there is a series of workshops available at various annual meetings of professional groups devoted to assessment, taught by assessment experts. This is an excellent way to build skills and to learn about the development of new instruments. Also, workshops, often offered for continuing education credit, are available throughout the year and are listed in the APA *Monitor*.

ASSESSMENT AND MANAGED CARE ISSUES

Restrictions by managed care organizations have affected the amount of assessment clinicians are able to conduct (Piotrowski, 1999). Consistent with this assertion, Piotrowski, Belter, and Keller (1998) found that 72% of psychologists in applied settings are conducting less assessment in general and are using fewer assessment instruments, especially lengthy assessment instruments (e.g., Rorschach, MMPI, TAT, and Wechsler scales), due to restrictions by managed care organizations. Likewise, Phelps, Eisman, and Kohout (1998) found that 79% of licensed psychologists felt that managed care had a negative impact on their work, and Acklin (1996) reported that clinicians are limiting their use of traditional assessment measures and are relying on briefer, problem-focused procedures.

With the growing influence of managed care organizations (MCOs) in mental health settings, it is inevitable that reimbursement practices will eventually affect training in assessment techniques and approaches (Piotrowski, 1999). We hope this will not be the case because of the many important training functions facilitated in assessment training, mentioned earlier in this chapter. Also, since we are training for the future, we must train students for the time when managed care will not dictate assessment practice. If, as we indicated earlier, assessment serves important training functions, it should continue to be enthusiastically taught, especially for the time when managed care will be merely a curiosity in the history of assessment. However, managed care has served us well in some ways, because we have sharpened and streamlined our approach to assessment and our instruments as well. We have focused anew on issues of reliability and validity of our measures, not merely in nomothetic research, but in research that includes reference to a test's positive predictive power, negative predictive power, sensitivity, and specificity to demonstrate the validity of our measures. Psychologists have turned more and more to assessment in other areas, such as therapeutic assessment, disability assessment, assessment in child custody, and other forensic applications. The Society for Personality Assessment has reported an increase in membership and in attendance at their annual meetings. We are optimistic that good evaluations, done in a competent manner and meaningfully communicated to the patient and referral source, will always be in great demand.

Nevertheless, an investigation concerning the impact of managed care on assessment at internship settings found that there has been a decrease in the training emphasis of various assessment techniques; 43% of directors reported that managed care has had an impact on their program's assessment curriculum (Piotrowski & Belter, 1999). Although approximately one third of the training directors surveyed reported a decrease in their use of projectives, the Rorschach and TAT remain 2 of the top 10 assessment instruments considered essential by internship directors of the sites surveyed. These studies indicate that MCOs are making an impact on the way assessment is being taught and conducted in clinical settings. Therefore, it is essential that psychologists educate themselves and their students in the practices of MCOs. Furthermore, psychologists should continue to provide research demonstrating the usefulness of assessment so that MCO descriptions of what is considered appropriate do not limit advancements. Empirical validation can help to guarantee psychologists reasonable options for assessment approaches so that we do not have to rely primarily on the clinical interview as the sole source of assessment and treatment planning information.

It is important to remember that MCOs do not dictate our ethical obligations, but the interests of our clients do. It is the ethical psychologist's responsibility to persistently request compensation for assessment that can best serve the treatment needs of the client. However, even if psychologists are denied reimbursement, it does not mean they should not do assessments when they are indicated. Therefore, options for meeting both financial needs of the clinician and health care needs of the client should be considered. One solution may be the integration of assessment into the therapy process. Techniques such as the Early Memories Procedure, sentence completion tasks, brief questionnaires, and figure drawings may be incorporated into the therapy without requiring a great deal of additional contact or scoring time. Other possibilities include doing the assessment as the clinician sees fit and making financial arrangements with the client or doing a condensed battery. Maruish, in his chapter in this volume, deals in more detail with the issues discussed in this section.

THE POLITICS AND MISUNDERSTANDINGS IN PERSONALITY ASSESSMENT

For many years there has been very active debate, and sometimes even animosity and expressions of derision, between those who preferred a more objective approach to personality

assessment (read self-report and MMPI) and those who preferred a more subjective approach (read projective tests and Rorschach). This schism was fueled by researchers and teachers of assessment. Each group disparaged the other's instruments, viewing them as irrelevant at best and essentially useless, while championing the superiority of its own instruments (e.g., Holt, 1970; Meehl, 1954, 1956).

This debate seems foolish and ill-advised to us, and it should be described in this way to students, in order to bring assessment integration practices to the forefront. These misleading attitudes have unfortunately been transmitted to graduate students by their instructors and supervisors over many years. Gradually, however, the gulf between the two seemingly opposite approaches has narrowed. Clinicians have come to use both types of tests, but there is still a great deal of misperception about each type, which interferes with productive integration of the two types of measures and impairs clinicians' efforts to do assessment rather than testing. Perhaps in the future teachers of personality assessment will make fewer and fewer pejorative remarks about each other's preferred instruments and will concentrate more and more on the focal issue of test integration.

Another issue is the place of assessment in the clinical psychology curriculum. For many years graduate curricula contained many courses in assessment. The number of courses has gradually been reduced, in part because the curricula have become crowded with important courses mandated by the APA, such as professional ethics, biological bases of behavior, cognitive and affective aspects of behavior, social aspects of behavior, history and systems, psychological measurement, research methodology, techniques of data analysis, individual differences, human development, and psychopathology, as well as courses in psychotherapy and in cultural and individual diversity (Committee on Accreditation, Education Directorate, & American Psychological Association, 1996). Courses have also been added because they have become important for clinical training (e.g., child therapy, marital therapy, health psychology, neuropsychology, hypnosis). Therefore, there is sometimes little room for assessment courses. To complicate matters even more, some instructors question the necessity of teaching assessment at all. Despite the published survey data, we know of programs that have no identified courses in assessment, and programs in which only one type of measure (e.g., self-report, interview, or projective measures) is taught. While most programs do have courses in assessment, the content of some courses does not prepare students to do effective assessment. Sometimes the courses offered are merely survey courses, or courses in which the student administers and scores one of each type of test. Unfortunately, with this type of inadequate training students do poor applied work and even poorer research, both of which reflect poorly on the discipline of personality assessment.

With the impact of cognitive therapy there have been radical changes in the ways in which some training programs teach assessment, seemingly without knowledge of the significant improvements in assessment research and practice that have taken place in the last 15 years or so. There seems to be a "Throw the baby out with the bathwater" approach, whereby traditional instruments are derided and replaced primarily with self-report measures. This is an important issue because it has major implications for teaching assessment in graduate school and in internship settings.

For example, Wetzler (1989) describes a hospital-based assessment approach in which a general broadly focused assessment has been replaced with a so-called focal approach, using self-report instruments. These changes, he indicates, have come about because of shorter hospitalization stays, and because what he calls "the standard battery" (Rapaport, Gill, & Schafer, 1968) "is no longer appropriate." He believes the questions that need to be answered in this acute problem setting cannot be adequately addressed using the "traditional" assessment approach: "What was well-suited to the psychiatric community of the 1930s, 1940s, and 1950s is no longer appropriate" (p. 5). "No matter what the referral question, they administer the standard battery," he states (p. 7). He lists a number of reported dissatisfactions with "traditional assessment" procedures, which include the problem that "test findings do not respond to [the] referral questions." His solution is to replace "traditional assessment" with "focal assessment," which includes the use of observer rating scales, self-report inventories, and a number of questionnaires derived from psychological research rather than from clinical observation or theory. He describes focal tests as specialized instruments considering specific areas of psychopathology, which have a much narrower focus and are "more concrete and descriptive, focused on surface symptoms and behavior, with clearly defined criteria for scoring, and with normative data available."

Wetzler concludes that "In light of [its] scientific foundation focal assessment is frequently more valid and therefore more effective than projective testing and/or informal interviewing" and that "focal assessment is more appropriate to the parameters of contemporary treatment than is traditional assessment" (p. 9), especially because in his setting assessment findings and clinical decisions must be made within 72 hours.

We do not agree with Wetzler in a number of his conclusions; we believe the approach he described comes closer to the definition we used earlier of *testing* than it does to *assessment,* since only self-report measures are employed, and test scores are emphasized rather than the development of

integrated findings. The overemphasis on the validity of test scores does not take into account the validity of their use in a particular clinical setting without the concomitant understanding of the patient's feelings and his or her experience of being hospitalized, as well as other important issues that would make these disembodied test scores more meaningful. What is lacking is an understanding of and an appreciation for the patient's contextual world, which we emphasize in our teaching. We have no way of knowing whether the patient responded to these instruments in a meaningful manner. The reduction in personal contact with the patient and its replacement with standardized self-report instruments does not seem to us to be an improvement in the assessment process. Validity of the instrument may be only an illusion in many cases, in which patients take a test with perhaps questionable motivation and a nonfacilitative orientation.

This approach to assessment is a prototype of other similar approaches that are convenience-driven, test-driven, and technician-driven; it is a most dangerous approach, in which the role of the assessor is primarily to choose the right test, and the test scores are said to provide the appropriate answers.

Earlier in this chapter we emphasized that psychologists should be well trained in the area of psychometrics and in the limitations of tests, especially problems of reliability and validity. In testing, one seeks the assistance of confidence limits of the results, but in assessment one determines the validity of the results of the test scores by taking into account a host of variables determined from interview data, from observations of the patient during the assessment, and the similarities and differences among the various assessment findings. In the focused approach it is doubtful whether the proper evaluation of the test scores can be accomplished. More to the point, however, is the criticism that there is actually a rigid adherence to a traditional battery. Our survey of test use in internship settings suggests otherwise; internship directors reported that a wide variety of tests are employed in assessment in their setting. We do not recommend or teach adherence to a traditional test battery, although these assessment devices are among those recommended for use, for reasons discussed in this chapter. We believe innovations in assessment should be employed to improve the validity of the assessment procedure and to improve the delivery of assessment services to those who request them. If the referral questions are not answered in an assessment it is the fault of the assessor, who has not paid attention to the referral issue or who has not sufficiently clarified the referral issue with the person requesting the assessment.

To describe an approach we believe is more typical of assessment rather than testing, also in a hospital setting, we will review the approaches of Blais and Eby (1998), in which psychologists have even more stringent demands on them to provide focal answers, often within a day. Blais and Eby train their internship students to assist the referring physician in clarifying referral questions. After a brief discussion with the nurse in charge of the patient, a review of the patient's chart, or both, the student selects the appropriate tests and procedures to answer the referral questions, taking into account the necessary turnaround time and both the physical and psychological limitations of the patient.

In a training case example in which the turnaround time was less than a day, Blais and Eby describe a battery that included a seven-subtest short form of the WAIS-R, the Rorschach, four TAT cards, and the PAI. The brief WAIS-R took less than 30 minutes to administer. Since the patient was described by the staff as extremely guarded, projective testing was viewed as crucial. The Rorschach and the TAT were chosen, the latter to identify the patient's object relations and core interpersonal themes, and both tests served to determine the degree of suicidal ideation. The PAI was chosen rather than the MMPI-2 because it is significantly shorter and the patient had poor physical stamina, and because it can be scored as a short form, using only 199 of its 344 items. It also contained several treatment planning scales that could possibly provide important information relevant to a referral question about treatment.

Although the battery described for this individual patient did include the traditional tests, batteries designed for other patients might not include any of the traditional tests. In addition, these traditional tests were employed not because they were traditional but, rather, because each offered something that the other measures did not offer. Also, the manner in which they are scored is directly tied to a large body of research, including, in the case of the Rorschach, extensive normative findings and reliability and validity data. The Rorschach was scored using the Comprehensive System (Exner, 1993), which includes a well-validated suicide constellation measure along with a host of other scores of importance to the referral issue, and with the P. Lerner and H. Lerner Defense Scale (1980). The TAT was scored as well, using the Social Cognition and Object Relations Scale (SCORS) system, a research-based interpretive system that measures eight aspects of object relations (Westen, 1991a, 1991b). The data were integrated into a picture of the patient's current psychological functioning and categorized according to thought quality, affect, defenses, and relationship to self and others, all issues directly related to the referral questions. Verbal report was given to the referring psychiatrist by telephone well before rounds the next morning, along with treatment recommendations.

The assessment approach designed by Blais and Eby is an example of a hospital-based assessment that demonstrates

that traditional tests can be employed with quite rapid turnaround time and that a test battery that includes traditional tests need not be rigidly fixed. In Blais and Eby's approach the clinicians responded flexibly and actively in the assessment process, integrating data from several different sources and responding in an efficient and rapid manner to focalized referral issues generated from several sources. In Wetzler's approach, the response was to develop a test-focused approach rather than a person-focused approach. Sharing the information in this section of our chapter with students helps to impress them with the importance of taking a person-focused approach to personality assessment.

PERSONALITY ASSESSMENT IN THE FUTURE

In this section we describe several changes we foresee in personality assessment teaching and practice, as well as changes we would like to see.

The Assessment of Psychological Health and the Rise of Positive Psychology

Psychological assessment has typically been tied to the medical model, in which health is defined as the absence of pathology rather than as an aggregate of positive psychological traits that differentiate the psychologically healthy person from others (e.g., Adler, 1958; Erikson, 1963; Maslow, 1954; May, Angel, & Ellenberger, 1958; Rogers, 1961). Seligman and Csikszentmihalyi (2000) have suggested using the term *positive psychology* instead. Such variables as playfulness, the ability to self-soothe and to be soothed by others, psychological-mindedness, flexibility, and the ability to establish intimacy and to express tenderness in relationships are important variables to consider. Seligman has discussed the concept of optimism, and several of the variables discussed by the Big Five theorists, such as openness to experience (McCrae, 1996), surgency, and agreeableness (Goldberg, 1992) describe positive aspects of personality functioning. The surgency factor includes such concepts as extroversion, energy level, spontaneity, assertiveness, sociability, and adventurousness. The agreeableness factor includes interpersonal warmth, cooperativeness, unselfishness, and generosity. In the future we expect to see a number of scoring systems to measure the variables described above using traditional tests, as well as a number of new tests specially designed to tap positive psychology variables. The *Journal of Personality Assessment* recently published a special series, *The Assessment of Psychological Health* (Handler & Potash, 1999), which included a discussion of four variables that were measured using traditional tests: optimism, creativity, playfulness, and transitional relatedness. Handler and Potash (1999) suggest that in the future students should be taught to routinely measure these variables and discuss them in feedback.

Focused Measures of Important Personality Variables

There has been a major movement toward the use of instruments that focus on more detailed aspects of personality functioning, either by scoring systems devised for traditional measures or the construction of new measures. For example, there are a very large number of MMPI and MMPI-2 scales constructed to predict various types of behaviors or to identify various problems (Graham, 2000). Some of these scales, the Harris-Lingoes and Si subscales, the Content scales, and the Supplementary scales, have now been included in the complex analysis of the MMPI-2, allowing for increased specificity in personality description, dynamics, and so on. These scales provide a way to focus interpretation when they are used in context with other data. There is an increasing press to provide such measures of specificity, supported by adequate research. We expect to see an increase in the construction and use of tests that are focused on the therapy process. For example, Fowler, Hilsenroth, and Handler (1995, 1996) found that early memories responses were related to the pattern of the relationship patients established with their therapists. The Holt Primary Process Scale, the Lerner Defense Scale, and the Mutuality of Autonomy Scale have made the transition from a research setting to clinical application. Another more complex measure, derived from scoring the TAT, is the SCORS, developed by Westen (1991a, 1991b) to measure various aspects of object relations. These scales have excellent validity and excellent clinical utility. They are used as focal estimates of object relations when such issues are a central aspect of the referral issue (e.g., Kelly, 1997). Students should be taught to use these research-based measures to generate more focused interpretations.

Recently there has been a proliferation of self-report measures designed for the evaluation of very specific personality questions. These include rapid screening instruments for the presence of specific personality problems, plus inventories that contain fewer items than the MMPI-2 and will therefore be less time consuming. However, we are concerned that test publishers perhaps promise too much. For example, one reputable publisher, describing a reputable test in its recent catalog, announced, "In a relatively short time you will determine whether your clients have characteristics that will aid or impede their treatment program in as few as 80 items, but not more than 120 items." What concerns us is the proliferation of tests that purport to answer complex personality questions

(e.g., suicidality or adaptation to psychotherapy). It is possible that hurried students, unable to take time for proper assessment, will use these tests with apparent face validity, but without data on clinically important types of validity. Complex personality questions cannot be answered with confidence with the use of a single focal instrument. A number of studies support this contention (see Meyer et al., 2000). In addition, some of these tests are quite easy to fake (e.g., the Battelle Developmental Inventory, Beebe, Finer, & Holmbeck, 1996). However, in class we should teach focal instruments in conjunction with other more complex measures.

Therapeutic Assessment

Many patients feel alienated by the traditional approach to assessment; they are often troubled by the procedures, feeling that the tasks requested of them are foolish, meaningless, and ultimately useless. These attitudes can lead to poor cooperation and uneven results. Students have more difficulty with assessment feedback than with any other aspect of assessment. An antidote for this problem, as well as a means to make assessment more meaningful and therapeutic for the person assessed, is the concept of Therapeutic Assessment (Finn, 1996; Finn & Martin, 1997; Finn & Tonsager, 1992; Fischer, 1994). Assessment questions are formulated collaboratively, with the patient, and the feedback is also done collaboratively. In this procedure a facilitative and constructive atmosphere is necessarily established, and the patient's investment in the assessment procedure is increased. Finn indicates that practically any test or test battery can be used as a vehicle for therapeutic assessment. He has also developed a manual for the use of the MMPI-2 as a therapeutic assessment device (Finn, 1996).

The goal of the assessment in this setting is for the person being assessed to come away with answers to his or her initially posed questions and an awareness of problems that can result in personal growth. The process by which this new awareness occurs is the exploration of the patient's subjective experience in the process that develops between the assessor and the patient. These interactions are accessed through intervention by the assessor from assessment data already collected, or in an intervention using particular assessment stimuli or procedures to tap into the patient's life issues, thereby producing them in the presence of the assessor. The facilitation of the occurrence of the problem issue is explored with the person, drawing connections to outside problems and to referral issues. The assessor then names, clarifies, and amplifies these issues, exploring the factors that are necessary and sufficient to produce the problem behavior—what elicits it, what reinforces it, and what maintains it—and provides the person with a new awareness about his or her problems and perhaps their roots. This process has understandably resulted in very substantial therapeutic gains for patients assessed (e.g., Ackerman et al., 2000; Finn & Martin, 1997; Finn & Tonsager, 1992; Hanson, Claiborn, & Kerr, 1997; M. Newman & Greenway, 1997). Students seem very motivated to use these procedures. They are eager to use a method that brings assessment and psychotherapy together very effectively. Students are also more at ease in providing feedback in this manner. We believe this method should be routinely taught in assessment classes.

Assessment on the Internet

Schlosser (1991) envisioned a future in which computers would present test-takers with stimuli ranging from verbal items to moving projective stimuli, including stimuli with synthesized smells. He conceived of the use of virtual reality techniques, computer-generated simulations in which images, sounds, and tactile sensations would be produced to create a synthetic, three-dimensional representation of reality. Ten years later we find a great deal of testing (not assessment) is being done on the Internet, but we have not yet approached Schlosser's vision. This procedure offers the psychologist a number of fascinating opportunities, but it also presents a number of professional and ethical problems (Barak & English, in press). Much research needs to be done to determine the effects of differences in the interpersonal setting with this more artificial Internet approach for various clinical populations. Just because the interaction simulates the traditional approach does not mean the experience of the assessor and the patient will be similar to that of the traditional approach. More disturbed patients would probably have more difficulty with such distance assessment compared with less impaired patients.

These issues seem modest to some psychologists, who even now offer screening tests for depression, anxiety, sexual disorders, attention-deficit disorder, and various personality disorders. Students should be made aware that such blunt feedback of test results does not meet APA ethics requirements. There is also a long list of other ethical issues in this approach that should be discussed in class, because these problems will face students in the future. Nevertheless, Internet testing promises to be a great help for people who for one reason or another cannot get to a psychologist's office to be tested or for people in rural communities in which there are no such services available.

Research on the Interpretive Process

More research should be done to illuminate the interpretive-integrative process in personality assessment, beyond the variables of convergent and divergent thinking. One method that needs exploration is the analysis of the thinking patterns of those who are adept at synthesizing data. By this we mean the study of people who are talented in the integrative process. Emphasis should be placed on studying these experts and on the analysis of heretofore unverbalized methods these people use to integrate data. In other words, we should attempt to focus on these often hidden processes so that the so-called magic of intuition can be described and taught in the classroom. Such studies would be directly relevant for the teaching process. The description of the teaching process in the section describing the advanced assessment course is an effort in that direction.

Expanded Conception of Intelligence

Wechsler's definition of intelligence—"the aggregate or global capacity to act purposefully, think rationally, and to deal effectively with [the] environment" (Wechsler, 1958, p. 7)—is hardly reflected in his intelligence tests. The definition implies that being interpersonally effective and thinking clearly are important intellectual variables. However, these and other variables suggested by Wechsler's definition are personality variables as well. Thus, it appears that personality variables and so-called intelligence variables overlap to some extent. Indeed, Daniel Goleman, in his book *Emotional Intelligence* (1995), highlights the importance of emotional and social factors as measures of intelligence. He describes an expanded model of what it means to be intelligent, emphasizing such variables as being able to motivate oneself and persist in the face of frustration; the ability to control impulses; the ability to delay gratification; the ability to regulate one's moods and to keep distress from interfering with thought processes; the ability to empathize and to hope. Other researchers in the area of intelligence have discussed similar issues. For example, Gardner (1993), and Salovey (Mayer & Salovey, 1993; Salovey & Mayer, 1989–1990) have discussed the importance of *interpersonal intelligence,* defined as "the ability to understand other people; what motivates them, how they work; how to work cooperatively with them" (Goleman, 1995, p. 39), and *intrapersonal intelligence,* defined as "the capacity to form an accurate, veridical model of oneself and to be able to use that model to operate effectively in life" (Goleman, 1995, p. 43). In a recent chapter, Mayer, Caruso, and Parker (2000) focus on four areas of emotional intelligence: perception, facilitation, understanding, and management of emotions. Bar-On and Parker (2000) have compiled a handbook of emotional intelligence, in which they also include the concepts of alexithymia and what they term *practical intelligence.* Nevertheless, researchers and test constructors seem to focus on a more traditional definition of intelligence variables. Although clinical psychologists take these important variables into account in describing personality functioning, they do not typically construct intelligence tests with these interpersonal and intrapersonal variables in mind. Although there are now measures of emotional intelligence available for adults (e.g., the Bar On Emotional Quotient Inventory; Bar-On, 1997), and for children (e.g., The Emotional Intelligence Scale for Children; Sullivan, 1999), emotional intelligence measures have yet to be integrated as parts of more traditional tests measuring other intelligence factors. However, their future use will undoubtedly go a long way toward a more integrated view of human functioning than exists in the somewhat arbitrary split between the concepts of intelligence and personality.

REFERENCES

Ackerman, S., Hilsenroth, M., Baity, M., & Blagys, M. (2000). Interaction of therapeutic process and alliance during psychological assessment. *Journal of Personality Assessment, 75,* 82–109.

Acklin, M. (1996). Personality assessment and managed care. *Journal of Personality Assessment, 66,* 194–201.

Adler, A. (1958). *What life should mean to you.* New York: Capricorn.

Allen, J. (1998). Personality assessment with American Indians and Alaska Natives: Instrument considerations and service delivery style. *Journal of Personality Assessment, 70,* 17–42.

American Psychological Association (APA). (1992). Ethical principles of psychologists and code of conduct. *American Psychologist, 47,* 1597–1611.

American Psychological Association Division 12 (Clinical) Presidential Task Force. (1999). Assessment for the twenty-first century: A model curriculum. *The Clinical Psychologist, 52,* 10–15.

Anastasi, A., & Urbina, S. (1998). *Psychological testing* (7th ed.). Upper Saddle River, NJ: Prentice Hall.

Applebaum, S. (1990). The relationship between assessment and psychotherapy. *Journal of Personality Assessment, 54,* 79–80.

Baity, M., & Hilsenroth, M. (1999). The Rorschach aggression variables: A study of reliability and validity. *Journal of Personality Assessment, 72*(1), 93–110.

Barak, A., & English, N. (in press). Prospects and limitations of psychological testing on the Internet. *Journal of Technology in Human Services.*

Bar-On, R. (1997). *The Bar On Emotional Quotient Inventory.* North Tonawanda, New York: Multi-Health Systems.

Bar-On, R., & Parker, J. (Eds.). (2000). *The handbook of emotional intelligence.* San Francisco: Jossey-Bass.

Barrick, M., & Mount, M. (1991). The big five personality dimensions and job performance: A meta-analysis. *Personnel Psychology, 44,* 1–26.

Beebe, D., Finer, E., & Holmbeck, G. (1996). Low end specificity of four depression measures: Findings and suggestions for the research use of depression tests. *Journal of Personality Assessment, 67,* 272–284.

Belter, R., & Piotrowski, C. (1999). Current status of Master's-level training in psychological assessment. *Journal of Psychological Practice, 5,* 1–5.

Bennett, B. E., Bryant, B. K., VandenBos, G. R., & Greenwood, A. (1990). *Professional liability and risk management.* Washington, DC: American Psychological Association.

Berg, M. (1984). Expanding the parameters of psychological testing. *Bulletin of the Menninger Clinic, 48,* 10–24.

Beutler, L., & Berren, M. (1995). *Integrative assessment of adult personality.* New York: Guilford Press.

Blais, M., & Eby, M. (1998). Jumping into fire: Internship training in personality assessment. In L. Handler & M. Hilsenroth (Eds.), *Teaching and learning personality assessment* (pp. 485–500). Mahwah, NJ: Erlbaum.

Brabender, V. (1992, March). *Graduate program training models.* Paper presented at the meeting of the Society for Personality Assessment, Washington, DC.

Bruhn, A. (1990). *Earliest childhood memories, Vol. 1: Theory and application to clinical practice.* New York: Praeger.

Bruhn, A. (1992). The early memories procedure: I. A projective test of autobiographical memory. *Journal of Personality Assessment, 58,* 1–25.

Burley, T., & Handler, L. (1997). Personality factors in the accurate interpretation of projective tests: The Draw-A-Person Test. In E. Hammer (Ed.), *Advances in projective test interpretation* (pp. 359–380). Springfield, IL: Charles Thomas.

Camara, W., Nathan, J., & Puente, A. (2000). Psychological test usage: Implications in professional psychology. *Professional Psychology: Research and Practice, 31,* 141–154.

Childs, R., & Eyde, L. (2002). Assessment training in clinical psychology doctoral programs: What should we teach? What do we teach? *Journal of Personality Assessment, 78*(1), 130–144.

Clemence, A., & Handler, L. (2001). Psychological assessment on internship: A survey of training directors and their expectations for students. *Journal of Personality Assessment, 76,* 18–47.

Committee on Accreditation, Education Directorate, & American Psychological Association. (1996). *Guidelines and principles for accreditation of programs in professional psychology, January 1, 1996.* Washington, DC: American Psychological Association.

Cramer, P. (1996). *Storytelling, narrative and the Thematic Apperception Test.* New York: Guilford Press.

Cuéllar, I. (1998). Cross-cultural clinical psychological assessment of Hispanic Americans. *Journal of Personality Assessment, 70,* 71–86.

Dana, R. H. (2000a). Culture and methodology in personality assessment. In I. Cueller & F. A. Paniagua (Eds.), *Handbook of multicultural mental health* (pp. 97–120). San Diego, CA: Academic Press.

Dana, R. H. (Ed.). (2000b). *Handbook of cross-cultural and multicultural personality assessment.* Mahwah, NJ: Erlbaum.

Deering, C. (1994). Parallel process in the supervision of child psychotherapy. *American Journal of Psychotherapy, 48,* 102–108.

Dempster, I. (1990). How mental health professionals view their graduate training. *Journal of Training and Practice in Professional Psychology, 6*(2), 59–66.

Dennis, W. (1966). *Group values through children's drawings.* New York: Wiley.

Doehrman, M. (1976). Parallel process in supervision and psychotherapy. *Bulletin of the Menninger Clinic, 40,* 9–83.

Durand, V., Blanchard, E., & Mindell, J. (1988). Training in projective testing: Survey of clinical training directors and internship directors. *Professional Psychology: Research and Practice, 19,* 236–238.

Erikson, E. (1963). *Childhood and society* (2nd ed.). New York: Wiley.

Exner, J. E., Jr. (1993). *The Rorschach: A comprehensive system* (3rd ed., Vol. 1). New York: Wiley.

Finn, S. (1996). *A manual for using the MMPI-2 as a therapeutic intervention.* Minneapolis, MN: University of Minnesota Press.

Finn, S., & Martin, H. (1997). Therapeutic assessment with the MMPI-2 in managed healthcare. In J. Butcher (Ed.), *Objective psychological assessment in managed healthcare: A practitioner's guide* (pp. 131–152). New York: Oxford University Press.

Finn, S., & Tonsager, M. (1992). The therapeutic effects of providing MMPI-2 test feedback to college students awaiting psychotherapy. *Psychological Assessment, 4,* 278–287.

Fischer, C. (1994). *Individualizing psychological assessment.* Hillsdale, NJ: Erlbaum.

Fowler, J. (1998). The trouble with learning personality assessment. In L. Handler & M. Hilsenroth (Eds.), *Teaching and learning personality assessment* (pp. 31–44). Mahwah, NJ: Erlbaum.

Fowler, J., Hilsenroth, M., & Handler, L. (1995). Early memories: An exploration of theoretically derived queries and their clinical utility. *Bulletin of the Menninger Clinic, 59,* 79–98.

Fowler, J., Hilsenroth, M., & Handler, L. (1996). A mulitmethod approach to assessing dependency: The early memory dependency probe. *Journal of Personality Assessment, 67,* 399–413.

Ganellen, R. (1996). *Integrating the Rorschach and the MMPI-2 in personality assessment.* Mahwah, NJ: Erlbaum.

Ganellen, R. (1999). Weighing the evidence for the Rorschach's validity: A response to Wood et al. *Journal of Personality Assessment, 77,* 1–15.

Gardner, H. (1993). *Multiple intelligences: The theory in practice.* New York: Basic Books.

Garfield, S., & Kurtz, R. (1973). Attitudes toward training in diagnostic testing: A survey of directors of internship training. *Journal of Consulting and Clinical Psychology, 40,* 350–355.

Goldberg, L. (1992). The development of markers for the Big-Five factor structure. *Psychological Assessment, 4,* 26–42.

Goleman, D. (1995). *Emotional intelligence.* New York: Bantam.

Graham, J. (2000). *MMPI-2: Assessing personality and psychopathology.* New York: Oxford University Press.

Handler, L. (1996). The clinical use of the Draw-A-Person Test (DAP), the House-Tree-Person Test and the Kinetic Family Drawing Test. In C. Newmark (Ed.), *Major psychological assessment techniques* (2nd ed., pp. 206–293). Englewood Cliffs, NJ: Allyn and Bacon.

Handler, L. (1997). He says, she says, they say: The Consensus Rorschach in marital therapy. In J. Meloy, C. Peterson, M. Acklin, C. Gacono, & J. Murray (Eds.), *Contemporary Rorschach interpretation* (pp. 499–533). Hillsdale, NJ: Erlbaum.

Handler, L., & Finley, J. (1994). *Convergent and divergent thinking and the interpretation of figure drawings.* Unpublished manuscript.

Handler, L., Fowler, J., & Hilsenroth, M. (1998). Teaching and learning issues in an advanced course in personality assessment. In L. Handler & M. Hilsenroth (Eds.), *Teaching and learning personality assessment* (pp. 431–452). Mahwah, NJ: Erlbaum.

Handler, L., & Habenicht, D. (1994). The Kinetic Family Drawing Technique: A review of the literature. *Journal of Personality Assessment, 62,* 440–464.

Handler, L., & Meyer, G. (1998). The importance of teaching and learning personality assessment. In L. Handler & M. Hilsenroth (Eds.), *Teaching and learning personality assessment* (pp. 3–30). Mahwah, NJ: Erlbaum.

Handler, L., & Potash, H. (1999). The assessment of psychological health [Introduction, Special series]. *Journal of Personality Assessment, 72,* 181–184.

Handler, L., & Reyher, J. (1964). The effects of stress in the Draw-A-Person test. *Journal of Consulting and Clinical Psychology, 28,* 259–264.

Handler, L., & Reyher, J. (1966). Relationship between GSR and anxiety indexes on projective drawings. *Journal of Consulting and Clinical Psychology, 30,* 605–607.

Handler, L, & Riethmiller, R. (1998). Teaching and learning the interpretation of figure drawings. In L. Handler & M. Hilsenroth (Eds.), *Teaching and learning personality assessment* (pp. 267–294). Mahwah, NJ: Erlbaum.

Handler, L., & Sheinbein, M. (1987, March). *Decision-making patterns in couples satisfied with their marriage and couples dissatisfied with their marriage.* Paper presented at the Midwinter Meeting of the Society of Personality Assessment, San Francisco.

Hanson, W., Claiborn, C., & Kerr, B. (1997). Differential effects of two test interpretation styles in counseling: A field study. *Journal of Counseling Psychology, 44,* 400–405.

Hartman, W., & Fithian, M. (1972). *Treatment of sexual dysfunction.* Long Beach, CA: Center for Marital and Sexual Studies.

Hershey, J., Kopplin, D., & Cornell, J. (1991). Doctors of Psychology: Their career experiences and attitudes toward degree and training. *Professional Psychology: Research and Practice, 22,* 351–356.

Hilsenroth, M. (1998). Using metaphor to understand projective test data: A training heuristic. In L. Handler & M. Hilsenroth (Eds.), *Teaching and learning personality assessment* (pp. 391–412). Mahwah, NJ: Erlbaum.

Hilsenroth, M., & Handler, L. (1995). A survey of graduate students' experiences, interests, and attitudes about learning the Rorschach. *Journal of Personality Assessment, 64,* 243–257.

Holsopple, J., & Miale, F. (1954). *Sentence completion: A projective method for the study of personality.* Springfield, IL: Charles Thomas.

Holt, R. (1970). Yet another look at clinical and statistical prediction: Or, is clinical psychology worthwhile? *American Psychologist, 25,* 337–349.

Holt, R. (1977). A method for assessing primary process manifestations and their control in Rorschach responses. In M. Rickers-Ovsiankina (Ed.), *Rorschach psychology* (pp. 375–420). Huntington, NY: Kreiger.

Kelly, F. (1997). *The assessment of object relations phenomena in adolescents: TAT and Rorschach measures.* Mahwah, NJ: Erlbaum.

Kinder, B. (1994). Where the action is in personality assessment. *Journal of Personality Assessment, 62,* 585–588.

Klopfer, B., Ainsworth, M., Klopfer, W., & Holt, R. (1954). *Development in the Rorschach technique* (Vol. 1). New York: World Book.

Koocher, G., & Keith-Spiegel, P. (1998). *Ethics in psychology: Professional standards and cases* (2nd ed.). New York: Oxford University Press.

Krakowski, A. (1984). Stress and the practice of medicine: III. Physicians compared with lawyers. *Psychotherapy and Psychosomatics, 42,* 143–151.

Kubeszyn, T., Meyer, G., Finn, S., Eyde, L., Kay, G., Moreland, K., Dies, R., & Eisman, E. (2000). Empirical support for psychological assessment in health care settings. *Professional Psychology: Research and Practice, 31*(2), 119–130.

Lerner, P., & Lerner, H. (1980). Rorschach assessment of primitive defenses in borderline personality structure. In J. Kwarer, H. Lerner, P. Lerner, & A. Sugarman (Eds.), *Borderline phenomena and the Rorschach test* (pp. 257–274). New York: International Universities Press.

Lewinsohn, P. (1965). Psychological correlates of overall quality of figure drawings. *Journal of Consulting Psychology, 29,* 504–512.

Lindsey, M. (1998). Culturally competent assessment of African American clients. *Journal of Personality Assessment, 70,* 43–53.

Maloney, M., & Glasser, A. (1982). An evaluation of the clinical utility of the Draw-A-Person Test. *Journal of Clinical Psychology, 38,* 183–190.

Maruish, M. (1990, Fall). Psychological assessment: What will its role be in the future? *Assessment Applications,* p. 5.

Maruish, M. (1999). The use of psychological testing for treatment planning and outcome assessment (2nd ed.). Hillsdale, NJ: Erlbaum.

Masling, J., Rabie, L., & Blondheim, S. (1967). Relationships of oral imagery to yielding behavior and birth order. *Journal of Consulting Psychology, 32,* 89–91.

Maslow, A. (1954). *Motivation and personality.* New York: Harper and Row.

May, R., Angel, M., & Ellenberger, H. (Eds.). (1958). *Existence: A new dimension in psychiatry and psychology.* New York: Basic Books.

Mayer, J., & Salovey, P. (1993). The intelligence of emotional intelligence. *Intelligence, 7,* 433–442.

Mayer, J., Caruso, D., & Salovey, P. (2000). Selecting a measure of emotional intelligence: The case for ability scales. In R. Bar-On & J. Parker (Eds.), *The handbook of emotional intelligence* (pp. 320–342). San Francisco: Jossey-Bass.

McClelland, D. (1987). *Human motivation.* New York: Cambridge University Press.

McCrae, R. (1996). Social consequences of experiential openness. *Psychological Bulletin, 120,* 323–337.

Mednick, S., & Mednick, M. (1967). *Examiner's manual: Remote Associates Test.* Boston: Houghton Mifflin.

Meehl, P. (1954). *Clinical versus statistical prediction.* Minneapolis: University of Minnesota Press.

Meehl, P. (1956). Wanted: A good cookbook. *American Psychologist, 11,* 263–272.

Meyer, G. (1997). On the integration of personality assessment methods: The Rorschach and the MMPI-2. *Journal of Personality Assessment, 68,* 297–330.

Meyer, G. (2000). Incremental validity of the Rorschach Prognostic Rating Scale over the MMPI Ego Strength Scale and IQ. *Journal of Personality Assessment, 74*(3), 356–370.

Meyer, G., & Archer, R. (2001). The hard science of Rorschach research: What do we know and where do we go? *Psychological Assessment, 13*(4), 486–502.

Meyer, G., Finn, S., Eyde, L., Kay, G., Moreland, K., Dies, R., Eisman, E., Kubiszyn, T., & Reed, J. (2000). Psychological testing and psychological assessment: A review of evidence and issues. *American Psychologist, 56,* 128–165.

Meyer, G., & Handler, L. (1997). The ability of the Rorschach to predict subsequent outcome: A meta-analytic analysis of the Rorschach Prognostic Rating Scale. *Journal of Personality Assessment, 69*(1), 1–38.

Meyer, G., Riethmiller, R., Brooks, R., Benoit, W., & Handler, L. (2000). A replication of Rorschach and MMPI-2 convergent validity. *Journal of Personality Assessment, 74*(2), 175–215.

Muhlenkamp, A., & Parsons, J. (1972). An overview of recent research publications in a nursing research periodical. *Journal of Vocational Behavior, 2,* 261–273.

Newman, F. (1991, Summer). Using assessment data to relate patient progress to reimbursement criteria. *Assessment Applications,* pp. 4–5.

Newman, M., & Greenway, P. (1997). Therapeutic effects of providing MMPI-2 test feedback to clients at a university counseling service: A collaborative approach. *Psychological Assessment, 9,* 122–131.

Nunnally, J., & Bernstein, I. (1994). *Psychometric theory* (3rd ed.). New York: McGraw-Hill.

Okazaki, S. (1998). Psychological assessment of Asian-Americans: Research agenda for cultural competency. *Journal of Personality Assessment, 70,* 54–70.

Petzel, T., & Berndt, D. (1980). APA internship selection criteria: Relative importance of academic and clinical preparation. *Professional Psychology, 11,* 792–796.

Phelps, R., Eisman, E., & Kohout, J. (1998). Psychological practice and managed care: Results of the CAPP practitioner study. *Professional Psychology: Research and Practice, 29,* 31–36.

Piotrowski, C. (1999). Assessment practices in the era of managed care: Current status and future directions. *Journal of Clinical Psychology, 55,* 787–796.

Piotrowski, C., & Belter, R. W. (1999). Internship training in psychological assessment: Has managed care had an impact? *Assessment, 6,* 381–389.

Piotrowski, C., Belter, R., & Keller, J. (1998). The impact of managed care on the practice of psychological testing: Preliminary findings. *Journal of Personality Assessment, 70,* 441–447.

Piotrowski, C., & Zalewski, C. (1993). Training in psychodiagnostic testing in APA-approved PsyD and PhD clinical psychology programs. *Journal of Personality Assessment, 61,* 394–405.

Plante, T. (1995). Training child clinical predoctoral interns and postdoctoral fellows in ethics and professional issues: An experiential model. *Professional Psychology: Research and Practice, 26,* 616–619.

Plante, T. (1999). Ten strategies for psychology trainees and practicing psychologists interested in avoiding ethical and legal perils. *Psychotherapy, 36,* 398–403.

Potash, H. (1998). Assessing the social subject. In L. Handler & M. Hilsenroth (Eds.), *Teaching and learning personality assessment* (pp. 137–148). Mahwah, NJ: Erlbaum.

Rapaport, D., Gill, M., & Schafer, R. (1968). In R. Holt (Ed.), *Diagnostic psychological testing* (2nd ed.). New York: International Universities Press.

Retzlaff, P. (1992). Professional training in psychological testing: New teachers and new tests. *Journal of Training and Practice in Professional Psychology, 6,* 45–50.

Rezler, A., & Buckley, J. (1977). A comparison of personality types among female student health professionals. *Journal of Medical Education, 52,* 475–477.

Riethmiller, R., & Handler, L. (1997a). Problematic methods and unwarranted conclusions in DAP research: Suggestions for improved procedures [Special series]. *Journal of Personality Assessment, 69,* 459–475.

Riethmiller, R., & Handler, L. (1997b). The great figure drawing controversy: The integration of research and practice [Special series]. *Journal of Personality Assessment, 69,* 488–496.

Ritzler, B., & Alter, B. (1986). Rorschach teaching in APA-approved clinical graduate programs: Ten years later. *Journal of Personality Assessment, 50,* 44–49.

Robins, C., Blatt, S., & Ford, R. (1991). Changes on human figure drawings during intensive treatment. *Journal of Personality Assessment, 57,* 477–497.

Rogers, C. (1961). *On becoming a person: A therapist's view of psychotherapy.* Boston: Houghton Mifflin.

Ronan, G., Date, A., & Weisbrod, M. (1995). Personal problem-solving scoring of the TAT: Sensitivity to training. *Journal of Personality Assessment, 64,* 119–131.

Rossini, E., & Moretti, R. (1997). Thematic Apperception Test (TAT) interpretation: Practice recommendations from a survey of clinical psychology doctoral programs accredited by the American Psychological Association. *Professional Psychology: Research and Practice, 28,* 393–398.

Salovey, P., & Mayer, J. (1989–1990). Emotional intelligence. *Imagination, Cognition, and Personality, 9,* 185–211.

Sarrel, P., Sarrel, L., & Berman, S. (1981). Using the Draw-A-Person (DAP) Test in sex therapy. *Journal of Sex and Martial Therapy, 7,* 163–183.

Schafer, R. (1967). *Projective testing and psychoanalysis.* New York: International Universities Press.

Schlosser, B. (1991). The future of psychology and technology in assessment. *Social Science Computer Review, 9,* 575–592.

Schutz, B. (1982). *Legal liability in psychotherapy: A practitioner's guide to risk management.* San Fransisco: Jossey-Bass.

Seligman, M., & Csikszentmihalyi, M. (2000). Positive psychology: An introduction. *American Psychologist, 55,* 5–14.

Shemberg, K., & Keeley, S. (1970). Psychodiagnostic training in the academic setting: Past and present. *Journal of Consulting and Clinical Psychology, 34,* 205–211.

Shemberg, K., & Keeley, S. (1974). Training practices and satisfaction with preinternship preparation. *Professional Psychology, 5,* 98–105.

Shemberg, K., & Leventhal, D. B. (1981). Attitudes of internship directors towards preinternship training and clinical models. *Professional Psychology, 12,* 639–646.

Sigman, S. (1989). Parallel process at case conferences. *Bulletin of the Menninger Clinic, 53,* 340–349.

Stedman, J. (1997). What we know about predoctoral internship training: A review. *Professional Psychology: Research and Practice, 28,* 475–485.

Sugarman, A. (1981). The diagnostic use of countertransference reactions in psychological testing. *Bulletin of the Menninger Clinic, 45,* 475–490.

Sugarman, A. (1991). Where's the beef? Putting personality back into personality assessment. *Journal of Personality Assessment, 56,* 130–144.

Sugarman, A., & Kanner, K. (2000). The contribution of psychoanalytic theory to psychological testing. *Psychoanalytic Psychology, 17,* 1–21.

Sullivan, A. (1999, July). The Emotional Intelligence Scale for Children. *Dissertation Abstracts International, 60*(01), 0068A.

Teglasi, H. (1993). *Clinical use of story telling.* Needham Heights, NJ: Allyn and Bacon.

Tett, R., Jackson, D., & Rothstein, M. (1991). Personality measures as predictors of job performance: A meta-analytic review. *Personnel Psychology, 44,* 703–742.

Torrance, E. (1966). *Torrance tests of creative thinking: Directions, manual and scoring guide (Verbal test booklet A).* Princeton, NJ: Scholastic Testing Service.

Torrance, E. (1974). *Torrance tests of creative thinking: Norms— technical manual.* Princeton, NJ: Scholastic Testing Service.

Trimboli, F., & Kilgore, R. (1983). A psychodynamic approach to MMPI interpretation. *Journal of Personality Assessment, 47,* 614–625.

Urist, J. (1977). The Rorschach test and the assessment of object relations. *Journal of Personality Assessment, 41,* 3–9.

Viglione, D. (1999). A review of the recent research addressing the utility of the Rorschach. *Psychological Assessment, 11*(3), 251–265.

Viglione, D., & Hilsenroth, M. (2001). The Rorschach: Facts, fictions, and the future. *Psychological Assessment, 13,* 452–471.

Watkins, C. E., Jr. (1991). What have surveys taught us about the teaching and practice of psychological assessment? *Journal of Personality Assessment, 56,* 426–437.

Watkins, C. E., Jr., Campbell, V., & Manus, M. (1990). Personality assessment training in counseling psychology programs. *Journal of Personality Assessment, 55,* 380–383.

Wechsler, D. (1958). *The measurement and approval of adult intelligence* (4th ed.). Baltimore: Williams & Wilkins.

Weiner, I. (1998). *Principles of Rorschach interpretation.* Mahwah, NJ: Erlbaum.

Weiner, I. (2001). Advancing the science of psychological assessment: The Rorschach Inkblot Method. *Psychological Assessment, 13*(4), 423–432.

Westen, D. (1991a). Clinical assessment of object relations using the Thematic Apperception Test. *Journal of Personality Assessment, 56,* 56–74.

Westen, D. (1991b). Social cognition and object relations. *Psychological Bulletin, 109,* 429–455.

Westen, D., Lohr, N., Silk, K., Gold, L., & Kerber, K. (1990). Object relations and social cognition in borderlines, major depressives, and normals: A Thematic Apperception Test analysis. *Psychological Assessment, 2,* 355–364.

Wetzler, S. (1989). Parameters of psychological assessment. In S. Wetzler & M. Katz (Eds.), *Contemporary approaches to psychological assessment* (pp. 3–15). New York: Brunner/Mazel.

Whitman, S., & Jacobs, E. (1998). Responsibilities of the psychotherapy supervisor. *American Journal of Psychotherapy, 52,* 166–175.

Williams, F. (1980). *Creativity assessment packet (CAP).* Buffalo, NY: DOK Publishers.

Yama, M. (1990). The usefulness of human figure drawings as an index of overall adjustment inferred from human figure drawings. *Journal of Personality Assessment, 54,* 78–86.

PART TWO

ASSESSMENT SETTINGS

CHAPTER 10

Psychological Assessment in Adult Mental Health Settings

R. MICHAEL BAGBY, NICOLE WILD, AND ANDREA TURNER

Several chapters in this volume address issues related to psychological assessment in adult mental health settings, such as the merits and usage of projective and objective tests, neuropsychological and intelligence testing, and cultural influences on the assessment procedure. This chapter serves to provide systematic guidelines for assessing adult inpatients and outpatients. The chapter is organized into several sections. First, we examine the rationale for conducting psychological assessment in adult mental health settings. Second, we discuss the foundations and goals of a general approach to psychological assessment in adult mental health settings. Third, we consider various psychological assessment tools. Fourth, we examine the general approach to assessment as well as our recommended approach to psychological assessment in adult mental health settings. Finally, we explore issues relevant to psychological assessment and, in particular, those relevant to assessing inpatients.

WHY CONDUCT
PSYCHOLOGICAL ASSESSMENTS?

We conceptualize psychological assessment as a problem-solving process in which psychological tests, interviews, and other sources of data function as tools used to answer questions

(e.g., to address a referral request) and resolve perplexities (e.g., to assist in differential diagnosis; Maloney & Ward, 1976; see also chapter by Weiner in this volume). The primary purpose of psychological assessments in adult inpatient and outpatient mental health settings is to evaluate patients' cognitions, affect, behaviors, personality traits, strengths, and weaknesses in order to make judgments, diagnoses, predictions, and treatment recommendations concerning the clients (Maruish, 1994). The functional utility of psychological assessments, we believe, lies in the ability to provide information about clients' symptoms, but also their stable personality characteristics, defensive patterns, identifications, interpersonal styles, self-concepts, and beliefs (Smith, 1998). Furthermore, comprehensive assessments address the factors that led to the problems and difficulties that presumably led to the referral (Wakefield, 1998). Thus, the general goals of psychological assessment include providing an accurate description of the client's problems, determining what interpersonal and environmental factors precipitated and are sustaining the problems, and making predictions concerning outcome with or without intervention (Aiken, 2000; Lilienfeld, Wood, & Garb, 2001). In addition, assessments can support or challenge clinical impressions and previous working diagnoses, as well as identifying obstacles to therapy (Appelbaum, 1990; Butcher, 1990; Clarkin & Mattis,

1991; Hurt, Reznikoff, & Clarkin, 1991; Maruish, 1994, 1999).

Finally, assessments can also provide assistance in developing and evaluating the effectiveness of a treatment plan consistent with the client's personality and external resources, as well as allowing the client to find out more about himself or herself (Butcher, 1990). As clients continue to adapt and deal with their symptoms after their discharge, assessments can guide discharge planning and subsequent treatment of the individual.

GENERAL APPROACH TO PSYCHOLOGICAL ASSESSMENT IN AN ADULT MENTAL HEALTH SETTING

Foundations of the General Approach to Psychological Assessment

Psychological assessments must be founded upon specific theoretical premises that guide the assessment process. The history of psychological assessment is quite extensive, resulting in many theoretical stances upon which assessments are based. It is our belief, however, that psychological assessment of adults in mental health settings is based on two founding premises: assessments must be evidence-based and multimodal.

Evidence-Based Assessment

Psychological assessment in mental health settings must be evidence-based. That is, a client's psychiatric symptoms must be systematically assessed in relation to the *Diagnostic and Statistical Manual of Mental Disorders* (*DSM-IV;* American Psychiatric Association, 1994) criteria for particular disorders. This criteria analysis is then supplemented with results from empirically validated psychological tests and structured interviews. The client's responses on these measures are used to indicate likely diagnoses and appropriate treatment implications based on empirical research. Consequently, an evidence-based approach to psychological assessment requires empirical support for any conclusions or recommendations, as opposed to relying solely on clinical impression and judgment.

The evidence-based approach was initially practiced in general medicine and recently has been incorporated in psychology. Evidence-based medicine (EBM) integrates clinical expertise with external evidence based on systematic research, while considering the values and expectations of patients or clients (Gambrill, 1999). Within the medical community, EBM is defined as a set of strategies designed to ensure that the clinicians form opinions and base subsequent decisions on the best available external evidence (Geddes, 1997). Thus, decisions pertaining to the client are made in light of the most up-to-date information available. The steps involved in EBM include a precise definition of the clinical problem, an efficient search for the best available evidence, critical appraisal of the evidence, and integration of the research findings with clinical expertise (Geddes, 1997; Olson, 1996). At each stage of EBM, recent developments in clinical findings and information technology are harnessed and utilized (Geddes, 1997). As physicians have acknowledged that no single authority has comprehensive scientific knowledge, the EBM approach is viewed as an improvement over the authoritative knowledge approach to practicing medicine (Kennell, 1999).

Within the domain of psychological assessment, an evidence-based approach emphasizes the importance of systematic observation and the use of rules of evidence in hypothesis testing. Thus, psychologists base their assessments and diagnoses on the best available evidence (Bensing, 2000). This approach to psychological assessment affords the opportunity to integrate real clinical problems with critical evaluation of the psychiatric research literature (Gilbody, 1996). In essence, an evidence-based approach to psychological assessment is premised on obtaining actuarial evidence from both structured interviews and objective measures that have been empirically supported. Empirical and clinical literature suggests patterns of symptoms that are associated with specific diagnoses and provide treatment implications, thereby enhancing the likelihood of making an accurate diagnosis.

The evidence-based approach is distinct from the more established and popular approach based on clinical judgment. Evidence-based actuarial assessments proceed in accordance with a prespecified routine and are based on empirically derived relations between data and the trait or event of interest (Dawes, Faust, & Meehl, 1989; Wiens, 1991). In contrast, clinical judgment consists of decisions made in the clinician's mind. In its most polar form, this distinction is analogous to a dimension with objectivity (evidence-based) on one end and subjectivity (clinical impression) at the other end.

The clinicians who base their assessments on clinical judgment highlight the advantages of their technique. First, certain assessment tools, such as unstructured interviews and behavioral observations, cannot be empirically evaluated or subjected to statistical analyses required by the evidence-based model. In fact, clinical judgment is required to evaluate the results of such tools. The results provide clinicians with a plethora of information, including clinical impressions as to the nature of clients' difficulties and distresses. Second, clinicians' impressions and judgments structure the rest of the assessment and provide a framework around which the client's symptoms and difficulties are conceptualized and understood. Third, many clinicians contend that their clinical impressions and judgments are rarely disputed by empirical test results. Thus, in the interest of conducting an efficient assessment, they rely solely on their judgment gleaned from information obtained from unstructured interviews. Fourth, some clinicians fear that by basing a diagnosis on empirical findings, they will be treating the client nonoptimally through reliance on actual experience (Meehl, 1973). Furthermore, many clinicians often shun actuarial-based data for fear that the data themselves will involve significant error, thereby leading to misdiagnosis of a client. Consequently, reliance on one's own experience and judgment rather than actuarial-based data when making diagnoses and treatment recommendations remains a popular method by which clinicians conduct psychological assessments.

Despite the historical popularity of basing assessments on clinical judgments, the validity of such judgments is often low, thereby placing the client at potential risk for underdiagnosis, overdiagnosis, or misdiagnosis (Faust & Ziskin, 1988; see also chapter by Garb in this volume). Clinical inference and judgment involve probabilistic transitions from clients' observable or reported episodes to their dispositions. Ideally, such inferences should be based upon an extensive actuarial experience providing objective probability statements (Meehl, 1973). However, in reality, this ideal is rarely achieved, because often the conditional probabilities are judged based solely on a clinician's experience, rather than on empirical findings. Consequently, permitting a weak or moderately strong clinical inference to countervail a well-supported set of actuarial data on patients similar to one's client will lead to an increase in erroneous clinical decisions (Meehl, 1973).

Faust and Ziskin (1988) also highlighted some of the disadvantages of clinical judgment. For example, they noted that clinicians often overvalue supportive evidence and undervalue evidence contrary to their hypotheses. They stated that clinicians tend to find evidence of abnormality in those they assess, regardless of whether they have any psychopathology. In addition, they argued that clinicians tend not to receive any outcome information about their clients; therefore, they are unable to learn whether their predictions were accurate and their suggestions were helpful. In summary, although the clinical impression approach has some merits, the validity and utility of the evidence-based approach is making this new format the standard for psychological assessment. Indeed, Hersen, Kazdin, and Bellack (1991) suggested that as the extent of the relevant research increases, the use of actuarial procedures will also increase.

Finally, contrary to popular opinion, clinical judgments and evidence-based models do not generate the same conclusions. Meehl (1973) contends that human judgment and statistical predictions concerning diagnosis, prognosis, and decisions based on the same set of information have a less than perfect correlation. Dawes et al. (1989) reviewed research comparing clinical judgment to actuarial judgment. They pointed out that with the same set of data, different actuarial procedures lead to the same conclusion, whereas different human judgments may result in several different conclusions. Moreover, Dawes et al. stated that clinicians' diagnoses can fall prey to self-fulfilling prophecy in that their predictions of diagnoses can influence their decisions about symptom prevalence and, later, diagnosis. Moreover, they noted that the mathematical nature of actuarial procedures ensures that each variable has predictive power and is related to the criterion in question (valid vs. invalid association with the criteria). In contrast, clinicians may deal with a limited and unrepresentative sample of individuals; therefore, they may not be able to determine accurate relations between variables. Furthermore, clinical judgment is prone to human error. Neither procedure, however, is infallible. Therefore, the actuarial procedures should be reassessed periodically.

Multimodal Assessment

The approach to psychological assessment in mental health settings should also be multimodal. One assessment tool is not sufficient to tap into complex human processes. Moreover, given that empirical support is critical to the validity of a psychological assessment, it is just as essential that there is concordance among the results from the client's history, structured interview, self-report, objective tests, and clinical impression. Because the results and interpretations are obtained from several sources, the multimodal approach increases reliability of the information gathered and helps corroborate hypotheses (Hertzman, 1984). Moreover, this approach draws on the strengths of each test and reduces the limitations associated with each test. A multimodal approach has the benefit of relying on shared methods and thus minimizing any potential biases associated with specific assessment methods or particular instruments. Finn and Butcher (1991) note that objective tests are imperfect and the results should not be seen as definitive conclusions but, rather, as hypotheses that should be compared with information from other sources. A diagnosis can be made with more confidence when several independent sources of information converge than when inferences are based on a single source. Moreover, the multimodal approach prevents the influence of a single perspective from biasing the results (Beutler, Wakefield, & Williams, 1994).

Goals of Psychological Assessment

An evidence-based and multimodal approach to psychological assessment enables the clinician to attain the main goals of assessment, namely clarifying diagnosis and providing treatment recommendations. Whereas other authors have emphasized additional assessment goals such as insight into a client's personality, interpersonal style, and underlying drives, we think that the goals of clarifying diagnosis and guiding treatment are the mainstays of psychological assessment and, in fact, incorporate many of the other goals.

Diagnostic Clarification

A primary reason for conducting psychological assessments of adults in a mental health setting is to make or clarify a diagnosis based on the client's presenting symptomatology. This is a common issue when the client presents with symptoms that are common to several diagnoses or when there is a concern that the symptoms of one disorder may be masking the symptoms of another disorder (Olin & Keatinge, 1998). Adhering to an evidence-based multimodal approach ensures that cross-validated actuarial evidence is obtained, thereby enhancing the validity of the diagnosis and increasing the clinician's confidence in the diagnosis.

Clinicians are often asked to make a differential diagnosis. However, the either-or implication of differential diagnosis is problematic. Often, clients manifest criteria of several disorders simultaneously, or they may manifest symptoms that do not meet criteria for a specific disorder despite the fact that their behaviors and cognitions are maladaptive (Maloney & Ward, 1976; Westen & Arkowitz-Westen, 1998). Thus, clinicians may find it beneficial to use multiple diagnostic impressions and, if possible, determine which disorder is generating the most distress and requires immediate attention.

Making or clarifying one or more diagnoses can benefit the clinician in many ways. These benefits include the following: enhancing communication between clinicians about clients who share certain features; enhancing communication between a clinician and the client through feedback; helping put the client's symptoms into a manageable and coherent form for the client; giving the client some understanding of his or her distress; guiding treatment; and enhancing research that, in turn, should feed back into clinical knowledge (Westen, 1998). Nonetheless, difficulties of psychological diagnosis should also be mentioned. Gunderson, Autry, Mosher, and Buchsbaum (1974) summarized the controversy associated with making a diagnosis:

> Diagnosis, to be meaningful, must serve a function. Too often its function becomes subservient to the process of choosing a label.

Thus, although the intent of diagnosis may be the communication of information in summary form, it may actually convey misinformation if insufficient attention is paid to the complexities and variability of human behavior during the diagnostic process. (p. 22)

According to Kellerman and Burry (1981), diagnosis involves several interconnected features that must be taken into account. These include the potential for shift within any diagnostic formulation, the relationship between the presenting problem and the client's personality, acute versus chronic dimension of the pathology, the presence of various levels and types of pathology and their interconnections, and the impact of diagnostic features on the development of intervention strategies and prognostic formulations. In essence, the diagnosis of the problem is not a discrete final step but, rather, a process that begins with the referral question and continues through the collecting of data from interviews and test results (Maloney & Ward, 1976). Diagnosis is thus a complex process that incorporates a myriad of potential questions and data.

Diagnoses are dependent on meeting *DSM-IV* criteria for Axis I and Axis II disorders, because the *DSM-IV* is currently the gold standard by which to diagnose psychopathology and personality disorders. It is an operational system in which each diagnosis must be met by a necessary and sufficient number of criteria that must occur on multiple dimensions (Hertzman, 1984).

Unfortunately, there are problems inherent in making a diagnosis based on the *DSM-IV*, because the *DSM-IV* itself has certain limitations. First, it is based on a medical model and does not consider underlying processes (i.e., it is concerned only with the signs and associations of the disorder) and overall manifestations of disorders. Second, it does not address etiological contributions to disorders and how they affect the manifestation and outcome of disorders. Third, the Axis I and Axis II disorder criteria represent a consensual opinion of a committee of experts that labeled a particular pattern of symptoms a disorder. Traditionally, the committee's decision to assign a certain cluster of symptoms to a diagnosable condition has been based on the presence and frequency of symptoms, an empirical analysis of the symptoms' social significance, and the specificity of the symptomatic response to various classes of drugs (Beutler et al., 1994). Thus, the process of developing *DSM-IV* diagnoses lacked the very characteristic valued in the assessment process: relying on empirical evidence and ensuring the collection of data from a variety of sources. Fourth, the *DSM-IV* is categorical in nature, requiring a specified number of criteria to meet a diagnosis, even though human nature, mental illness, and mental health are distributed dimensionally.

There are numerous limitations to such a categorical approach in which mental disorders are divided into types based on criteria sets with defining features. It becomes restricted in its clinical utility when diagnostic classes are heterogeneous, when there are unclear boundaries between classes, and when the different classes are not mutually exclusive (*DSM-IV-TR;* American Psychiatric Association, 2000). In addition, the *DSM-IV* categories have overlapping boundaries, resulting in multiple diagnoses and the problem of comorbidity (Barron, 1998). Moreover, a categorical approach does not provide as powerful predictions about etiology, pathology, prognosis, and treatment as a dimensional approach (Gunderson, Links, & Reich, 1991). Fifth, the *DSM-IV* is skewed toward the nomothetic end of the spectrum, resulting in static diagnoses whose operational definitions may be inaccurate, unsupported by research findings, and camouflaging questionable construct validity (Barron, 1998). Other criticisms of the *DSM-IV* include excessive focus on reliability at the expense of validity, arbitrary cutoff points, proliferation of personality disorders, and questionable validity of the personality disorder clusters (Blatt & Levy, 1998).

The American Psychiatric Association has attempted to make the *DSM-IV* more empirical, accessible, reliable, and useful (Nathan, 1998), as well as to create an optimal balance between a respect for historical tradition, compatibility with the *International Statistical Classification of Diseases and Related Health Problems,* 10th edition (*ICD-10;* World Health Organization, 1992), evidence from reviews of the literature, analysis of data sets, results of field trials, and consensus of the field (*DSM-IV-TR;* American Psychiatric Association, 2000). Furthermore, many diagnostic categories are supported by empirical literature (i.e., data from *DSM* field trials). In summary, the *DSM-IV* is a descriptive classificatory system, ostensibly unbound to a specific theory of development, personality organization, etiology, or theoretical approach (Barron, 1998). Moreover, it is an official nomenclature that is applicable in a wide number of contexts, can be used by clinicians and researchers from various theoretical orientations, and has been used across psychological settings. The *DSM-IV* also attempts to address the heterogeneity of clinical presentation of symptoms by adopting a polythetic approach. That is, clients must present with a subset of items from a list of criteria in order to meet a diagnosis. In addition, the *DSM-IV* includes several axes to take social, medical, and economic factors into account. These merits of the *DSM-IV,* particularly in the absence of another comprehensive diagnostic system, suggest that assessment of psychological disorders should adhere to this multiaxial system.

The potential problem with the *DSM* is that it undergoes periodic revision; thus, the clinician relying on this diagnostic system would seem to be continually chasing a moving target or construct. However, except for the changes made from *DSM-II* to *DSM-III,* this system does not undergo substantial structural changes with each new version. Moreover, most tests, for example, the MMPI-2, cover most symptoms associated with a variety of syndromes. The changes in *DSM* from version to version usually involved carving sets of symptoms into different syndromes. Thus, the omnibus inventories designed to assess a variety of psychiatric symptoms are not necessarily affected by these changes, because the fundamental symptoms of most disorders remain captured.

Guide for Treatment

A second and equally important goal of psychological assessments of adults in a mental health setting is to offer a guide for treatment by developing an individualized treatment plan for the client (and family). A psychological assessment offers the opportunity to link symptomatology, personality attributes, and other information with certain treatment modalities or therapeutic targets. Therefore, giving treatment recommendations allows psychologists to proceed past the level of diagnosis and provide suggestions about how to deal with the diagnosed disorder. In fact, diagnosis has most utility when it can be related to treatment. Ideally, an outline of treatment recommendations should include plans to immediately deal with the client's acute symptoms, as well as long-term treatment plans that address the client's chronic symptoms, personality features, coping mechanisms, and interpersonal problems, and stressors within the client's environment (Hertzman, 1984). Moreover, treatment recommendations must provide suggested changes as well as methods for implementing these changes (Maloney & Ward, 1976). In short, treatment recommendations should include short-term and long-term goals, procedures to reach the goals, possible obstacles to treatment, and prognosis of the client.

The process of diagnostic clarification, often the first and primary goal of psychological assessment, often serves as a guide to treatment. Certain treatment protocols are suggested by way of the diagnosis, whereas other treatments may be excluded by virtue of failing to meet criteria for a certain disorder (Hertzman, 1984). However, treatment planning is complicated, because the relationship between diagnosis and treatment is not always simple. Due to the nature of psychiatric difficulties, a client's symptomatology may result from multiple causal pathways, thereby contributing to imprecise treatment (Clarkin & Mattis, 1991). Nonetheless, diagnosis can provide important useful information.

Although diagnosis is often a first step in the treatment planning process, the ability to offer treatment recommendations must go beyond diagnosis and assess a variety of qualities and variables that best describe the client (Halleck, 1991). Treatment planning should take into account information about symptom severity, stage of problem resolution, general personality attributes, interpersonal style, coping mechanisms, and patient resistance. Further sources of information include the client's psychiatric and medical history, psychological mindedness, current levels of stress, motivation levels, and history of prior treatments, as well as physical condition, age, sex, intelligence, education, occupational status, and family situation (Halleck, 1991). This information is relevant to treatment planning in two ways. First, demographic variables and a history of prior treatments can dictate or modify current treatment modalities. Second, other variables might help formulate certain etiological models that can in turn guide treatment (Halleck, 1991). Thus, information from various sources obtained in a psychological assessment can be integrated to provide treatment recommendations as well as to predict the prognosis of the client and expected effects of treatment.

In addition, Clarkin and Hurt (1988) listed several areas of patient functioning that must be evaluated to adequately inform treatment planning. These include patient symptoms, personality traits (strengths and weaknesses) and disorders, cognitive abilities and functioning, patient psychodynamics, patient variables that enable the patient to engage in various kinds of treatments, environmental demands, and general therapeutic enabling factors (Clarkin & Hurt, 1988). In particular, *patient enabling factors* refer to patient dimensions that are important for treatment planning and engaging in particular forms of psychological intervention (Clarkin & Mattis, 1991). For example, the patient's defensive structure, coping style, interpersonal sensitivity, and basic tendencies and characteristics adaptations may dictate the most appropriate psychological intervention (Beutler & Clarkin, 1990; Harkness & Lilienfeld, 1997).

Psychological tests have been widely used to guide treatment. Unfortunately, the information they provide is not necessarily useful in guiding the choice of specific therapeutic modality. However, test scores can guide treatment recommendations. For example, symptom severity, stage of client resolution, recurrent interpersonal themes, level of resistance to treatment, and coping styles can be obtained from various psychological tests, and all serve as indicators for the focus and prognosis of psychotherapeutic procedures (Beutler et al., 1994). In particular, clients' scores on the MMPI-2 (Butcher, Dahlstrom, Graham, Tellegen, & Kaemmer, 1989) validity scales offer predictions about treatment based on factors such as compliance, level of insight, current psychological status, risk of premature termination of therapy, and level of motivation. Both individual scores and profiles of scores

on the content and clinical scales, as well as endorsement of critical items, can also be used for treatment planning, including determining needs to be met, issues with which to deal, and structure and style of therapy (Greene & Clopton, 1994). Similarly, the Personality Assessment Inventory (PAI; Morey, 1991) can also guide treatment recommendations by providing information about a client's level of functional impairment, potential for self-harm, risk of danger to others, chemical dependency, traumatic stress reaction, and likelihood of need for medication (Morey & Henry, 1994). Furthermore, the PAI contains a number of scales that serve as either positive or negative indicators of potential for psychotherapy. Positive indicators include level of perceived distress, positive attitude toward treatment, capacity to utilize psychotherapy, availability of social supports, and ability to form a therapeutic alliance. These suitability indicators should then be weighed against negative indicators, including having disorganized thought processes, being nonpsychologically minded, and being characterologically unsuited for therapy (Morey & Henry, 1984).

PSYCHOLOGICAL ASSESSMENT TOOLS

Types of Psychological Assessment Tools

Clinicians should generally not rely on only one data source, scale, or set of test results to infer the nature of a client's psychological status. Any diagnosis or treatment recommendation should be based on a configuration of impressions from client history, other clinical data, and the results of several tests. Following is a list of various types of assessment tools that can guide the psychological assessment when used in collaboration with other sources of data.

Interviews

Clinical interviews provide comprehensive and detailed analysis of clients' past and current psychological symptomatology. Furthermore, they offer insight into clients' personality features, coping styles, interpersonal styles, and behaviors. Interviews help the clinician generate and evaluate hypotheses and then select appropriate psychological tests to clarify diagnostic impressions. Consequently, clinical interviews play a central role in the assessment process (see also chapter by Craig in this volume). Interviews can be unstructured, semistructured, or structured. Unstructured interviews are often conducted to obtain a clinical impression (person-centered) view of the client, build rapport, clarify symptomatology, and test for discrepancies between self- and other reports. They allow for greater depth and insight into the nature of the client's problems, behaviors, and other modes of functioning. Interpretation of the client's responses relies primarily on the expertise of the clinician. In contrast, semistructured and structured interviews are often scored and interpreted against normative (variable-focused) data. Thus, they provide the potential for greater objectivity and less bias in interpretation. Examples of semistructured and structured interviews include the Structured Clinical Interview for *DSM-IV* Axis I (SCID-I/P; First, Spitzer, Gibbon, & Williams, 1995) and Axis II disorders (SCID-II; First, Gibbon, Spitzer, Williams, & Benjamin, 1997), and the Diagnostic Interview for Personality Disorders (DIPD; Zanarini, Frankenburg, Chauncey, & Gunderson, 1987). A primary advantage of such diagnostic interviews is that the questions ensure that certain criteria are directly questioned, such as whether a syndrome has persisted for a minimum period of time (*DSM-IV-TR;* American Psychiatric Association, 2000). Thus, diagnosis follows directly from the results.

Whereas interviews often provide a plethora of information and help with both diagnostic clarification and treatment recommendation, their clinical utility is reduced by limitations typically associated with such techniques. For example, results of interviews are solely based on the client's self-report and are, therefore, subject to client overreporting, underreporting, or memory distortions. Moreover, the dynamics of directly interviewing clients engender potential biases in clients' responses, as a result of their need to present themselves favorably to the clinician or as a plea for help. Thus, interviews should be supplemented with objective tests in order to assess client reporting style and confirm diagnosis.

Objective Tests

We advocate the use of objective tests primarily in three ways: (a) to assess the frequency and intensity of psychiatric symptoms; (b) to determine a clinical diagnosis; and (c) to assess enduring traits that predict future behaviors, symptoms, or treatment implications. Objective tests vary in the degree of expertise required to accurately evaluate and interpret the results. These tests may have fixed, precise scoring standards and may be scored manually or by computer, or require interpretation by the clinician (Aiken, 2000). Many of these tests are often based on certain criterion groups of people with known symptoms or characteristics, so that the selection of the test items suggests these symptoms.

The self-report modality of this form of assessment has several advantages; namely, empirical validity, brevity, low cost, and generalized utility among various settings. As well, many of the objective tests are empirically based and have

been extensively researched, providing a sound basis on which to evaluate their reliability and validity along with other psychometric criteria (see also the chapter by Ben-Porath in this volume). Moreover, the respondent completing these tests is the person who is actually experiencing the psychological symptoms. Thus, the client is directly expressing his or her actual experience and state of distress. However, disadvantages of this modality also include client bias, conscious or unconscious distortion of responses (although most objective tests have scales designed to assess such response distortion), and the inflexibility of the tests to alter the types of questions depending on the client's responses. Consequently, objective tests should be used to supplement, not supplant, interview and behavioral observation data.

Projective Tests

Projective tests, in general, are unstructured, disguised, and global. Although certain administration and scoring systems allow for the quantification of response scoring, extensive training is required. Furthermore, psychologists often disagree about the interpretations of clients' responses. Unfortunately, most projective tests fail to meet conventional standards of reliability and validity (Aiken, 2000; Lilienfeld et al., 2001). Possible obstacles to the clinical utility of these tests include low validity coefficients of the instruments, the influence of situational factors on client's responses, and clinician subjectivity in scoring and interpreting responses. Thus, the lack of objectivity in scoring and the paucity of representative normative data on projective tests, in our opinion, limit their use with an adult clinical population. Their use is also limited because projective tests may require more time to administer, score, and interpret than many objective psychological tests, and the assessment procedure is usually under strict time constraints.

It is important to note that both objective and projective tests, by themselves, are typically insufficient in answering referral questions, making differential diagnoses, or deciding upon treatment recommendations. These three tasks can only be effectively performed if the clinician develops a conceptual model of the client based on a hypothetical deductive reasoning approach (Maloney & Ward, 1976) and if the clinician utilizes multiple assessment tools, including tests, interviews, and other sources of data. Clinicians seem to be polarized as to whether they should use projective tests or rely solely on objective measures. It is our opinion that within the EBM, projective tests are not appropriate.

Clinical Judgment

The use of unstructured interviews (and even structured interviews) introduces clinical judgment into the assessment process, thereby allowing for both expertise and greater flexibility in clarifying and delving into areas that can provide relevant information in the assessment. However, clinician bias can never be eliminated, and clinician skills may affect interpretation. Thus, to adhere to the evidence-based muiltimodal approach to assessment, clinicians should use other assessment tools to evaluate and confirm their clinical judgments.

Choosing the Tests to Use

In order to choose which tests to use, clinicians must be familiar with the effectiveness and efficiency of the tests that could help answer the referral question (Olin & Keatinge, 1998). Furthermore, clinicians should select tests that, together, measure a variety of dimensions and are of importance for making treatment recommendations (Beutler et al., 1994).

Four major considerations important in selecting which tests to administer are the test's psychometric properties, clinical utility, client factors, and clinician variables (Olin & Keatinge, 1998). The first two speak to the ability of the psychological tests to answer the referral question based on an evidenced-based approach, whereas the latter two consider factors such as client ethnicity, age, level of education, functional capacity, motivation, and clinician experience, all of which may confound test results or interpretation. One must also take into account the client's ability to speak the language in which the tests are written. For example, if the client speaks Italian and is being assessed in an English-speaking setting, the clinician can utilize versions of some self-report questionnaires that have been translated into Italian and later validated. It may also be necessary to use a translator and modified versions of interviews and other self-report questionnaires. Furthermore, the client's ability to remain focused for extended periods of time must be taken into account. In addition, the length of time required to complete the test must be considered. The utility of the results must be weighed against the time to administer the test and to score and interpret the results.

During the assessment, the clinician may decide to add, eliminate, or modify some tests if the client appears to have a limited attention span or cognitive ability or to be functionally illiterate. In addition, the emphasis of the assessment may change depending on the symptoms the client describes and the clinician's impression. The assessment tools might change accordingly. Finally, a number of tests contain validity scales that measure inconsistent responding, response biases, exaggeration of psychopathology, and feigning of memory or of cognitive deficits. Consequently, the clinician should pay careful attention to the validity scales included in tests such as the MMPI-2 and the PAI. These tests allow the clinician to determine whether the client is presenting an accurate picture of his or her symptoms. If the results of the validity scales indicate that the clinician should be concerned about the validity of the results, the clinician can follow up with specific measures to test for the exaggeration of psychological symptoms and cognitive deficits. For example, if malingering is suspected, tests specifically designed to assess symptom overreporting, such as the Structured Interview of Reported Symptoms (Rogers, Bagby, & Dickens, 1992) can assess the extent to which the client is intentionally overreporting symptoms to attain secondary gains from the diagnosis.

Choosing the Number of Tests

Although the multimodal approach to assessment encourages the use of more than one test, it does not specify the exact number of tests clinicians should use. The clinician must prevent the assessment from becoming too cumbersome yet still obtain enough information to provide an empirically supported diagnosis. Those tests selected should assess for the presence of the primary disorder or problem as well as other disorders that either share similar essential features or typically co-occur (Olin & Keatinge, 1998). Although it is less time-consuming and costly to use fewer tests, taking a multimodal approach and using several objective tests allows for cross-validation, assessment of a client's responses to different situations, identification of previously unrecognized problems, and provision of a more comprehensive evaluation (Olin & Keatinge). There may be instances in which a focal assessment is more appropriate than a comprehensive one. However, given fewer time and financial restraints, a comprehensive assessment is usually considered better practice. On a note of caution, clinicians can give too many tests, which can result in interpreting chance effects as real (O'Neill, 1993).

In summary, employing a variety of assessment tests in a systematic sample of situations, while being aware of the possibility of bias in test selection and interpretation, as well as knowing the degree of generalizability of test findings, will help reduce misinterpretations and overgeneralizations and provide a more comprehensive analysis of the client's functioning, thereby enhancing the clinical utility of psychological assessment (Aiken, 2000).

Integration and Interpretation of Tests

After each of the test results has been discerned, it is important to interpret and integrate the results. Although each test presents a discrete analysis of the client's psychological functioning, the results must be logically and coherently related to other test results and to the individual as a whole. The results of any test should be cross-referenced with other test results, interview findings, current behaviors, and client history to search for convergence of symptoms, personality traits, coping and interpersonal styles, environmental situations, and any other pertinent information that will guide diagnosis and treatment recommendations. Discrepancies between results can also provide valuable information.

Test interpretation involves integrating all the information from the various test results into a cohesive and plausible account. Proficient integration of the tests should explain the presenting problem, answer the referral question, and offer additional information to clarify diagnoses and guide treatment. Integrating psychological assessment results should also provide empirical support for the clinician's hypothetico-deductive reasoning skills, since integration of the tests strengthens some hypotheses and invalidates others. Essentially, analysis of test results and integration and interpretation of the tests enable the clinician to make inferences and, ultimately, decisions concerning the most appropriate care for the client.

O'Neill (1993) described three levels of test interpretation that can help the clinician gain insight into the nature of the client's psychological status. First, the concrete level involves interpretation that is limited to the subtest and subscale scores and does not draw conclusions beyond the scores. Level two, the mechanical level, is concerned with the pattern of subscales and subtests, particularly significant differences between scores. Level three, the individualized level, involves interpreting the test results in the context of a larger picture, incorporating specific details that are particularly characteristic of the client. This last level offers the best clinical interpretation of the client and helps guide treatment goals.

In general, the primary goal of test integration is to discover what O'Neill terms the "internal connection" (1993), that is, to use the test results in conjunction with the client's behavior and history to arrive at an understanding of the client's current state of psychological functioning. Furthermore, integrating the test results helps the clinician make objective observations, infer internal psychological states, make generalized descriptions about the client's behavior and functioning, and give probable explanations for the client's psychological difficulties.

ASSESSMENT PROCEDURE IN ADULT MENTAL HEALTH SETTINGS: THE GENERAL APPROACH

A psychological assessment within an adult inpatient setting can be of intermediate or extensive depth. The range of information required, the sampling of a number of areas of a

client's life, series of psychological tests, and multiple sources of information, all systematically collected and interpreted, testify to the breadth and complexity of psychological assessment in such a setting. This, in turn, generates a plethora of information and recommendations. Olin and Keatinge (1998) have proposed an 11-step model for the assessment procedure: (a) determine the information needed to answer the referral question(s), (b) identify who is to be involved, (c) obtain informed consent and releases, (d) collect and examine medical records, (e) identify what is to be measured, (f) identify and select appropriate measures, (g) administer assessment and modify as needed, (h) score measures and analyze and interpret results, (i) seek consultation if necessary, (j) write the report, and (k) provide feedback to appropriate parties.

The Referral Question

Referral questions are the foundation of any psychological assessment. They provide the rationale for conducting an assessment and dictate the types of questions to ask and the selection of psychological tests to be employed. The referral question acts as a base around which all other information revolves, and it guides the entire assessment process, from the choice of tests and test interpretation to diagnosis and treatment recommendations. Typically, as the examiner starts to clarify the referral question, the process of collecting and interpreting data and formulating hypotheses has already begun (Maloney & Ward, 1976). In essence, the referral question sets the focus of the assessment, which in turn shapes the information gathered. The assessment process thus involves linking the information with the problem (referral question) by a configural web of explanations (O'Neill, 1993).

The nature of the referral question is dependent on the severity and complexity of the client's psychological symptoms and personality, as well as the goals and theoretical orientation of the referring physician or other mental health professional. The clinician must take into account who made the referral and tailor the report to that person's discipline and level of expertise. Moreover, the potential use of the test results (e.g., disability insurance, workplace competency) must be clarified and given careful consideration. Too often, the referral question is relatively brief and vague, and it may necessitate contacting the immediate referral source to determine its nature. It is recommended that the referral form for psychological evaluation include explicit questions about the reasons, purpose, and potential uses of the test and whether or not the patient consented to testing for such purposes.

Although psychological assessment can address a variety of referral questions, there are several questions that psychologists commonly encounter in assessing mental health inpatients. The following are examples of typical referral questions: Clarify a previous working diagnosis or the referring physician's impression of the client; differentiate the client's symptom presentation; identify the cause of the client's symptoms; and determine what characterological features may be interfering with the client's ability to engage in treatment.

Unfortunately, psychologists may receive inappropriate referral questions to which the assessment is unable to provide clear answers. In these situations the clinician must be aware of the limitations of psychological tests and clearly communicate these limitations to the referral source. Regardless of the nature and specificity of the referral question, an effective psychological assessment should take a generic approach to any question and comprehensibly perform four generalfunctions: diagnostic clarification of Axis I; diagnostic clarification of Axis II, description of personality dimensions, or both; description of the client's coping mechanisms and interpersonal styles; and treatment recommendations.

Preliminary Information

Sources of Information

Like any detective work, a psychological assessment involves amassing preliminary information that will further guide the nature of the assessment. Preliminary information about the client's history and current psychological state can be obtained from many sources. Often, the clients themselves are asked to provide this information, because it is helpful to understand their impressions of their history and current problems. This general information is typically gained using an unstructured interview format. However, clients may have memory distortions or biases and may wish to portray themselves in an overly positive or negative manner. Medical records should also be examined, because they contain pertinent information regarding clients' psychiatric histories, medications, previous treatments, and working diagnoses. Furthermore, discussions with the clients' past and current mental health professionals may provide additional insight. Sometimes it is advisable to obtain information from family members or close friends of the clients. This is particularly useful if the clinician suspects that the clients are not portraying themselves in an accurate manner and if the clinician desires insight into the clients' interactions in other environments. However, individuals close to the client may also have their own biases and motives that must be considered.

In general, it is advisable that the psychologist obtain preliminary information from both the client and the medical and general (mental and physical) health care community (usually through a review of the medical records) in order to

increase the reliability of the client's symptom presentation, obtain a more comprehensive picture of the client, and determine whether there are any discrepancies that should be addressed during the assessment.

Chronology of Psychological Symptoms

First and foremost, the psychologist should record the client's chief complaint, including current signs and symptoms of presentation. Equally important is recording symptom chronology, which includes symptom onset and progress, as well as changes in behavior, emotional state, mentation, and personality from the time the client was last considered well until the current assessment (Halleck, 1991; Hertzman, 1984). This should be followed by noting the relevant preceding events, the length and severity of the problem, precipitants and effects, patterns of recurrence, and past psychological treatments (Halleck, 1991; Hertzman, 1984). In addition, a history of the client's previous hospitalizations and medications should be obtained. Moreover, assessing the client's current life situation, including family, living and working environment, and stressors, and how these aspects contribute to the client's symptomatology, will help clarify the manner in which the client's symptoms developed and are being maintained.

Overall Client History

Obtaining information pertaining to the client's developmental, family, emotional, academic, vocational, social, economic, legal, cultural, and medical history is also an essential feature of psychological assessment. Such information provides an understanding of the subtleties of the client's problems and the context in which they exist. Furthermore, this information can help inform diagnosis, identify and clarify stressors, and guide treatment.

Developmental and family history should include attainment of developmental milestones, relationships among family members, history of childhood abuse, and a family history of mental illness. Social history should contain information about past and current friendships, intimate relationships, sexual history, religious participation, social support, and hobbies and activities. A basic appraisal of the client's academic and vocational history should include details about the client's problematic academic areas, special education, grades (including courses failed or skipped), best and worst subjects, highest level of education completed, school behavior, extracurricular activities, attendance, occupational history, current occupational status, and relationships with coworkers and employers. A legal history pertains to any difficulties the client has had with the law, and an economic history relates to the client's financial status and stability. With respect to cultural history, information should be obtained about the client's feelings of closeness, distance, or alienation from his or her cultural group and about the beliefs and meanings associated with the culture. Finally, a medical history should cover previous head injuries, serious accidents or illnesses, surgeries, past and current medical problems, and medications (Halleck, 1991; Hertzman, 1984; Olin & Keatinge, 1998). This list is by no means extensive but, rather, provides a guideline for discovering information that may be pertinent to the client's current psychological state.

Mental Status Examination

Additional preliminary information should be obtained by conducting a Mental Status Exam (MSE). The MSE originated from medical interviews and is now commonly part of psychological assessments. It is a summary of the client's current emotional and cognitive states and provides information about the client's current level of functioning and severity of impairment. Information obtained from the MSE is vital in that it describes the client's level of functioning at the time of testing. Key sections in the MSE include the following: appearance, mood, affect, behavior and activity, intellectual functioning, language, orientation, memory, attention, thought processes (form and content), perception, dangerousness (including suicidal and homicidal ideation), degree of impulse control, insight, judgment, and emotional state (Aiken, 2000; Halleck, 1991; Hertzman, 1984; Olin & Keatinge, 1998). The presence of normal and the absence of abnormal processes should be noted, as well as any observations of unusual, strange, or significant thoughts, emotions, or behaviors.

Clarification of Axis I Diagnoses

Diagnostic clarification of an Axis I condition organizes the presenting symptomatology into a framework in which the nature, severity, and extent of the client's problems can be understood and addressed. Many clinicians depend on the medical chart and clinical interview to make Axis I diagnoses. However, the ideal practice is to use a multimodal approach and rely on several sources of information, including the medical chart, unstructured interview, structured clinical interviews, and psychological tests. Reliable diagnosis must always rest on clear operational or behavioral criteria that can be assessed by the clinician.

Interviews Used to Clarify Axis I Diagnoses

(For a more detailed discussion of clinical interviewing see the chapter by Craig in this volume.) It is useful to begin an assessment with an unstructured interview as a means of surveying the client's past experiences and chief complaints. The art of an unstructured psychological interview is being able to extract relevant information without interrupting the client's flow of thoughts (Hertzman, 1984). This should be followed by semistructured or structured interviews that systematically assess whether the client's symptoms meet the criteria for any Axis I disorders. One widely used interview is the SCID-I/P. The SCID-I/P assesses the presence and lifetime occurrence of current disorders, as well as severity and chronology of symptoms. An important point to note is that the SCID-I/P requires the use of some clinical judgment, because conflicting sources of information and open-ended responses must be evaluated, extrapolated, and coded based on the client's responses (Rubinson & Asnis, 1989).

Psychological Tests Used to Clarify Axis I Diagnoses

The information gathered from the interviews should be supplemented by the results of both omnibus and specific psychological tests. Examples of omnibus tests of general symptom impairment include such inventories as the MMPI-2 and the PAI. In particular, the MMPI-2 and PAI provide actuarial-based clinical hypotheses for Axis I disorders. Although there are a variety of other tests used to examine the presence of Axis I disorders, we will focus on the MMPI-2 because it is the instrument that is most widely used. As indicated earlier, we believe that projective tests are not appropriate for an evidenced-based approach for psychological evaluation, particularly in psychiatric diagnosis, and we do not recommend their use. Consequently, we do not review their use in this section. We realize, however, that many clinicians do use them and have confidence in their validity and reliability.

The MMPI-2 is often used to clarify coexisting diagnoses, validate the clinical impression of a client from the structured interviews, assess emotional functioning, and obtain information about the client's level of psychopathology. The MMPI-2 demonstrates good reliability and validity and provides rapid diagnostic information as well as information about the client's emotional and personality functioning (Olin & Keatinge, 1998). In particular, the 10 clinical scales are actuarially based, because they were developed to identify patients with specific psychiatric disorders. In addition, a client's profile pattern provides information about the individual's overall psychological structure. For example, configural interpretation of clients' code types can inform a clinician about clients' moods, cognitions, interpersonal relations, and other problem areas, as well as their symptoms and personality characteristics (Greene, 2000). Similar information can be obtained from the content scales and the recently developed Psychopathology Five personality scales (PSY-5; Harkness, McNulty, & Ben-Porath, 1995). All of this information is then used to formulate a diagnostic impression. Furthermore, the MMPI-2 profiles and specific scales provide recommendations for treatment. As well, the MMPI-2 contains various critical items that provide insight into the nature and intensity of clients' symptoms. In particular, items dealing with suicidal ideation and psychotic features highlight issues that must be further considered and evaluated. Garb (1984) and Finn and Butcher (1991) reviewed assessment literature and concluded that the MMPI-2 has incremental validity when added to an interview.

Clinicians should make themselves aware of measures that assess specific symptoms. In fact, there is practically a test designed for every disorder or psychological difficulty. These tests may provide incremental validity or consensual validity to omnibus tests. Examples of such specific tests are the State-Trait Anxiety Inventory (Spielberger, 1983), the Beck Anxiety Inventory (BAI; Beck, Epstein, Brown, & Steer, 1988), the Hamilton Anxiety Rating Scale (Hamilton, 1959), the Posttraumatic Stress Disorder Symptom Scale (Foa, Riggs, Dancu, & Rothbaum, 1993), the Trauma Symptom Inventory (TSI; Briere, 1995), the Maudsley Obsessional-Compulsive Inventory (Hodgson & Rachman, 1977), the Beck Depression Inventory (BDI; Beck, Ward, Mendelson, Mock, & Erbaugh, 1961), the Hamilton Rating Scale for Depression (Hamilton, 1960), the Suicide Risk Assessment Scale (Motto, 1985), and the Alcohol Use Inventory (Wanberg, Horn, & Foster, 1977). However, the clinician must consider the efficiency of using specific measures given that many omnibus tests are able to assess a variety of specific disorders and psychological difficulties.

Clarification of Axis II Diagnoses

Clients in an adult mental health setting may present with characterological features that are contributing to, and possibly even magnifying, the current state of psychological distress. If these features are severe and are interfering in a client's daily life, they constitute a personality disorder. A comorbid Axis II disorder also becomes a focus of intervention or a moderating variable in the treatment of an Axis I disorder.

It is important to note that current research suggests that Axis II diagnoses are not usually helpful in explaining presenting symptomatology or in providing mental health care professionals with information that will help guide the treatment of the client. Furthermore, comorbidity of personality disorders is a frequent occurrence and thus both an empirical and clinical dilemma. Nonetheless, knowing about the presence of an Axis II disorder may, in some cases, be useful.

Personality psychopathology is typically clarified in the adult clinical setting by identifying Axis II disorders. Certain so-called normal personality traits that should also be assessed include the client's degree of likability, dependency, passivity, aggressiveness, attention-seeking, controllingness, and exploitativeness, as well as personal values and thoughts about himself or herself and others (Halleck, 1991). Extreme dimensions of these traits tend to be maladaptive and often constitute criteria for personality disorders that can be assessed using psychological tests for personality psychopathology. As is the case with Axis I disorders, medical charts, unstructured and structured clinical interviews, and psychological tests should be used to determine the presence of a personality disorder.

Interviews Used to Clarify Axis II Diagnoses

There are several structured and semistructured interviews that assess personality disorders, personality pathology, or both, according to the *DSM-IV* criteria (see the chapter by Craig in this volume). These include such instruments as the SCID-II (First et al., 1997), DIPD (Zanarini et al., 1987), the Structured Interview for DSM-IV Personality (SIDP-IV; Pfohl, Blum, & Zimmerman, 1995), and the Personality Disorder Interview-IV (PDI-IV; Widiger, Mangine, Corbitt, Ellis, & Thomas, 1995). Interviews are particularly useful to clarify personality disorder diagnoses, because this format allows clinicians to discern the chronology of clients' symptoms and the effect these symptoms have made on their interpersonal relationships and their daily functioning and to determine how clients' characterological patterns are currently affecting their psychological functioning.

Psychological Tests Used to Clarify Axis II Diagnoses

Similar to Axis I diagnoses, various self-report measures designed to assess Axis II disorders exist, including the Personality Diagnostic Questionnaire-4+ (PDQ-4+; Hyler, 1994), the SCID-II Personality Questionnaire (SCID-II-PQ; First et al., 1997), and the Wisconsin Personality Disorders Inventory (Klein et al., 1993). In addition, omnibus tests, such as the MMPI-2 and PAI, contain sets of scales that directly assess the Axis II disorders (Somwaru & Ben-Porath, 1994) or provide actuarial-based diagnostic suggestions for Axis II disorder psychopathology, for example, the MMPI-2 and the PAI. The Millon Clinical Multiaxial Inventory (MCMI-III; Millon, 1993) also has scales specifically designed to assess *DSM-IV* Axis II disorders, although Millon's conceptualization of these disorders differs slightly from *DSM-IV* (Millon, 1981).

Other self-report measures exist that measure personality psychopathology traits other than those in *DSM-IV*. Many of these measures are the direct outcome of different dimensional models of personality psychopathology, developed to address the well-known limitations of the *DSM*, Axis II categorical system. These include the Dimensional Assessment of Personality Psychopathology (DAPP; Livesley, 1998); the Schedule for Non-Adaptive and Adaptive Personality (SNAP; Clark, 1993); the Personality Psychopathology Five (PSY-5; Harkness et al., 1995), which are measured with a set of MMPI-2 scales (Harkness et al., 1995); and the Temperament and Character Inventory (TCI; Cloninger, Przybeck, Svrakic, & Wetzel, 1994). Another alternative to the Axis II system has been to apply existing measures of so-called normal dimensions of personality to personality pathology, with extreme scores representing clinically significant personality pathology when accompanied by psychological distress. Most prominent, in this regard, is the Five-Factor Model of Personality (FFM; Costa & McCrae, 1992), which has garnered considerable empirical support and is thought by many researchers to be the best alternative to the Axis II system (Widiger, 1998). The revised NEO Personality Inventory (NEO PI-R; Costa & McCrae, 1992) measures the domains and facets of this model.

ASSESSMENT PROCEDURE IN ADULT MENTAL HEALTH SETTINGS: THE RECOMMENDED APPROACH

Our recommended approach to psychological assessment in adult mental health settings is not intended to be the sole method of assessment. Rather, it is presented as a model that adheres to the foundations and goals of psychological assessment. It is an approach that is both evidence-based and multimodal, thereby allowing for accurate and valid diagnostic clarification and treatment recommendations. It is also important to note that our assessment approach adheres to a multidimensional approach. Whenever possible, we incorporate clients' biological, developmental, adaptational, and ecological histories in our case conceptualizations.

In addition, it is important to note that with the increasing cost of health care and the trend toward shorter hospital stays, the psychological assessment procedure must be efficient. We strive to contact the client or caregiver and begin testing within two days of receiving the referral. Furthermore, the report is usually written and presented to the referring physician within two to four working days following testing (this is especially the case for inpatient assessment, where longer hospitalizations are costly). Nonetheless, we recognize the importance of ensuring that the assessment process is thorough.

Review of Referral and Preliminary Information

Upon receiving a referral, we review it and proceed with attaining extensive preliminary information. This process includes contacting the referral source (typically a psychiatrist) to gather information and clarify the referral question, if necessary. Next, we review the client's medical record so as to have clearer insight into the nature of the client's problems and to guide the assessment process by determining the assessment tools that are necessary and sufficient to answer the referral question.

Assessment Procedure

Before beginning any psychological assessment, we first explain the process to the client, including who requested the assessment, what is expected of the client, and what the client can hope to gain by participating. We also insure that the patient clearly understands the reason for the referral, often paraphrasing the referral question posed by the referral source and obtain verbal informed consent to use the results from the assessment to address the specific reasons for the referral. Patients are then given the opportunity to pose any of their questions. We then follow with an unstructured clinical interview. Often these two steps allow us to build rapport with the client, ease their anxieties, and motivate them to be open, honest, and forthcoming with information. Moreover, beginning with a general open-ended interview and then progressing to more specific questions in a structured or semistructured format gives the client the opportunity to expand and focus on whatever he or she is most concerned about at the moment. We use the information attained from the unstructured interview to determine which psychological symptoms require further inquiry and to test for discrepancies between the client's self-report and other information sources. In essence, the unstructured clinical interview assists us in generating and testing (i.e., confirming, invalidating, or moderating) hypotheses about the client. In addition, the clinical interview enables us to conduct firsthand observations and evaluations of the client's coping and interpersonal styles. These psychological features provide essential data that are used to assess the client's overall functioning.

Additionally, a specific component of this process involves noting the client's behaviors. Often, the assessment situation represents a microcosm of the client's behavioral and psychological functioning. Thus, observation of the client is an essential source of information, since it represents a sample of the patient's pattern of functioning and can reveal some of the problems that brought the client to the assessment in the first place (Kellerman & Burry, 1981).

The second phase of psychological assessment involves the use of structured interviews and objective self-report measures to clarify Axis I and Axis II diagnoses. These types of assessment tools are used to assure that the assessment process adheres to an evidence-based model that is grounded in empirical data. As noted previously, such a process ensures that the assessment outcome is valid and clinically useful, thereby enhancing the likelihood that clients' symptoms, problems, and distresses are correctly interpreted, that they are given accurate diagnoses, and that they are provided with treatment recommendations that are most likely to help them.

Axis I Diagnostic Clarification

Clients are often referred for psychological assessments because they are presenting with acute symptoms that are causing distress or are impeding their functioning to an extent that warrants being admitted to a mental health setting as an inpatient. Whereas some clients present with symptoms that are stereotypical of a specific disorder, often they present with symptoms that appear to overlap across multiple disorders. The goal of the assessment is thus to make a differential diagnosis that captures and explains the nature of the client's symptoms so that the proper treatment can be established. Other clients have been involved with the mental health care system for many years but have never received a formal assessment or diagnosis. In this case, our goal is to clarify the nature of the client's symptoms, again to be used as a guide for treatment.

Consistent with our objectives, our assessments aimed at clarifying Axis I disorders are grounded on evidence-based principles. All assessment tools we use have been subjected to extensive empirical testing, meet acceptable standards for reliability and validity, and provide actuarial-based data. Currently, the *DSM-IV* manual is the basis upon which diagnoses are met, and clients must meet a certain number of criteria of specific severity and duration in order to receive a diagnosis. Consequently, we use the SCID-I/P (Patient Version 2.0; First et al., 1995) to guide our diagnoses because it is derived directly from the *DSM-IV*. This interview systematically and comprehensively assesses for the symptoms and syndromes of major mental illnesses, the results of which afford clinical diagnoses based on objective and evidence-based information. In particular, the SCID-I/P allows us to make differential diagnoses among overlapping and conflicting symptoms and to examine whether a client's presenting symptomatology is better accounted for by another disorder or a medical condition. For example, symptoms typically associated with panic disorder with agoraphobia may be better explained as the sequelae of posttraumatic stress disorder (PTSD; e.g., hyperarousal and avoidance) if the other diagnostic criteria

for PTSD are met. However, we are aware of the time constraints placed on the assessment process. Thus, we first use the SCID-I/P screener to screen briefly for the presence or absence of anxiety, substance abuse, and eating disorders. We find this screener to be a valuable and time-efficient test, because it determines which disorders should be further questioned and which warrant no further investigation.

Establishing a chronology of symptoms is essential for disentangling and clarifying diagnoses. As much as possible, we obtain dates of symptom onset and get a clinical picture of the course of client symptoms, including periods of remission, maintenance, and intensification. This information is helpful in differentiating between similar disorders.

Although the SCID-I/P enables us to assess directly *DSM-IV* diagnostic criteria, we supplement our assessment with various objective tests so that our clinical judgments are evidence-based. In so doing, we believe that we enhance the validity of our diagnostic impressions. Given that the clinical picture of the client is often quite complex, we seek validation of our clinical impressions from empirically supported test results. Moreover, as we realize the potential impact of diagnosing any client with a disorder, we recognize the importance of providing accurate and valid diagnoses. With regard to the assessment tools themselves, we use both general and specialized measures, all of which have been empirically validated for diagnostic use in a clinical population.

The one global test that we administer to almost all clients is the MMPI-2, because it offers evidence-based interpretive value to client's symptoms. As discussed previously, the MMPI-2 is an excellent example of a carefully developed psychological test with attention to details of reliability, validity, and normative information. Moreover, it provides a great deal of information in a variety of areas of client functioning. However, if the MMPI-2 is deemed invalid, the client is often asked to complete an alternative inventory such as the PAI. The PAI also has validity scales, can provide information about both psychopathology and personality, and offers actuarial-based information about clients' symptoms. Other self-report measures we use include the BDI and the BAI, since both provide indexes of the nature and intensity of clients' current depressive and anxiety symptoms, respectively.

These general measures supplement the SCID-I/P, add evidence-based information to the client's clinical picture, provide empirical support for a diagnosis, offer insight into the client's coping styles, and provide treatment recommendations based on the client's profile. However, the client may present with specific problems that should be further investigated by more specialized measures. For example, we often encounter clients that meet diagnostic criteria for acute or chronic PTSD. In such cases we typically administer the TSI to these clients in order to gain greater insight into the nature and severity of their posttraumatic symptomatology. The TSI also divides clients' symptoms into factors that, in turn, help clarify diagnosis and determine which types of symptoms result in the most distress.

Axis II Diagnostic Clarification

Diagnostic clarification of Axis II disorders adheres to the same rationale as that used to clarify Axis I disorders. That is, we use an evidence-based multimodal approach when selecting tests and interpreting the results. Consequently, we base our diagnoses directly on *DSM-IV* criteria and on empirically validated and actuarial-based assessment tests. To ensure an efficient testing process, we screen for Axis II disorders by first administering the SCID-II Personality Questionnaire. If clients meet the minimum required number of criteria for a particular personality disorder, we follow up with either the SCID-II interview or the DIPD. Assessing personality disorders using an interview format is particularly advantageous because it allows us to clarify whether the presenting symptomatology has been present throughout a client's life or whether it is a recent manifestation reflecting the client's current psychological state or recent events.

As with the Axis I testing procedure, we supplement our Axis II diagnoses with general objective tests. Although various personality inventories are available, we rely on the NEO PI-R (Costa & McCrae, 1992). The NEO PI-R is advantageous because there are both self-report (first person: Form S), other report (third person: Form R), and structured interview formats available (Structured Interview for the Five-Factor Model, SIFFM; Trull & Widiger, 1997). These empirically based tests assess clients' characterological psychopathology and provide directions for treatment.

Personality Profile, Coping, Self-Concept, and Interpersonal Styles

Clients' personality profiles, coping styles, self-concept, and interpersonal patterns provide insightful and extended information that is directly pertinent to diagnosis and treatment recommendations. Information gleaned from these areas of a client's psychological functioning serves several roles. First, it clarifies diagnosis. Examination of actuarial-based interpersonal and coping patterns associated with particular disorders can often assist with differential diagnosis. Second, the information, especially that which relates to a client's personality style, offers added insight and clarification of Axis II personality disorders, including clarification of symptom criteria, intensity and duration of symptoms, and the pervasiveness of

clients' symptoms in their everyday functioning. Third, this information can provide insight into the extent of a client's distress, the manner in which a client attempts to handle and adjust to difficulties, the effect that the symptoms have on significant people in the client's life, and the degree to which the symptoms are affecting the client's life. Fourth, integration of the information helps summarize the client's functioning, problems, and strengths; clarifies the nature of the problem; and encapsulates the client's functioning as well as the role that the client's symptoms play in his or her daily functioning. This insight, in turn, is a powerful tool in guiding treatment recommendations.

The tests we use to assess clients' personality profiles, coping styles, self-concept, and interpersonal patterns include the NEO PI-R, MMPI-2, PAI, and SIFFM. These tests are actuarial-based measures of clients' enduring attributes, stylistic characteristics, and general personality structure. Of course, one critical issue is whether the client has the capacity to read at an appropriate grade level for these self-report inventories. Typically, we do not assess formally for reading level but do have the patient read out loud three to five questions from each of the tests. If we determine sufficient capacity, we proceed. If the reading level is not adequate, we administer the tape recorded versions of the MMPI-2 and PAI and administer only the SIFFM to assess personality.

Treatment Implications and Recommendations

Finally, the information we obtain from clinical structured and unstructured interviews, objective test results, behavioral observations, and additional information from client chart reviews is integrated and interpreted. In effect, the initial problems of the client "have been given a context that serves as a . . . map in which the relevant details of the problem can be made visible and related to each other" (Kellerman & Burry, 1981, p. 4). In addition, the relations among the client's responses, the client's meanings, and the situational context are all assessed and integrated. This integration provides the most valid indicator of whether the client is suffering from a disorder and, if so, the type of disorder (Wakefield, 1998). Each detail of the client's symptoms, behaviors, and history is encapsulated into larger concepts that are then organized in relation to one another. Thus, the presenting problem is demonstrated to be part of a larger system that includes the client's history, personality, coping style, and interpersonal pattern of relating to others. This integration reveals the meaning of the presenting symptoms and provides both information and guidelines in the treatment of the initial problem. Again, we stress that the integration and interpretation of a client's psychological status must be validated by empirical data.

As previously stated, the conceptualization of each client, including his or her diagnoses, symptoms, behaviors, and characterological patterns, is used to provide treatment recommendations. The nature of the recommendations depends on the client and on the referral question. Based on our experience, treatment recommendations tend to focus on several areas, including recommending a medication review, commencing a certain therapeutic intervention or changing current treatment, or discussing suitability for therapy. Additional information tends to pertain to the client's prognosis and preexisting factors, as well as precautions and restrictions.

SKILL SETS AND OTHER ISSUES TO CONSIDER IN PSYCHOLOGICAL ASSESSMENT

Clinicians must be familiar with the following set of issues so as to provide the most effective psychological assessments. It is important to note that clinicians must have numerous skills in order to be proficient in psychological assessment. The following section, although not inclusive, highlights several of these skills that we feel are critical for accurate, insightful, and beneficial assessment of adult patients in a psychiatric setting. Clinicians must first be able to define and clarify the referral question. Clinicians also must possess psychological knowledge about a variety of psychopathology and personality content areas so they can be attentive to important and relevant areas of client functioning, know the relevant data to collect and the methods to obtain this data, and recognize the meaning of test results. With specific reference to the client, clinicians must possess the ability to obtain accurate descriptions of abnormal behavior from the patient or other sources, have an extensive and comprehensive understanding of the patient's history, and determine when patients are presenting insufficient or inaccurate information. Clinicians must additionally possess proficient interpersonal skills, such as establishing a professional relationship and trust with the patient, acting as a participant observer, knowing how to ask questions about inner experiences that the patient will be able to understand and answer, being aware of the patient's interaction with self and others, and engaging in skillful interviewing. Another area of expertise involves the ability to effectively interpret interviews, behavioral observations, and test results; draw valid inferences; determine how behavioral and experiential difficulties may be related; and, finally, consider, evaluate, check, and integrate the data from the various sources in developing the results, diagnosis, and treatment recommendations (Halleck, 1991; Maloney & Ward, 1976).

Second, an integrated approach to psychological assessment must involve specifying the effects of situational variables on clients' symptomatology and behavioral patterns. Clinicians must examine and evaluate potential situational elements and how they interact with the client's cognitive, emotional, and behavioral functioning. Thus a psychological assessment should include the nature, intensity, and duration of the demands placed on the client (Maloney & Ward, 1976).

Mental disorders are often influenced by a client's physical, social, and interpersonal environment. Consequently, the nature of a client's environment, particularly psychological stressors, is an important source of information to obtain in a psychological assessment. Common environmental stressors include marital, familial, financial, occupational, legal, and physical difficulties. Other stressors to examine include specific events, such as a natural disaster or a life cycle transition. The Axis-IV of *DSM-IV* addresses such environmental factors. Unfortunately, despite their importance and contribution to the onset, maintenance, and exacerbation of a client's current psychological symptoms, these factors are often not considered in the assessment process.

The interaction between an individual and his or her environment as it relates to mental illness is complex in nature. When individuals behave in a certain way, they have an impact on their surrounding environment. Unfortunately, responses to an individual with a mental disorder often create new stresses for that individual, thereby perpetuating a cycle of increasing stress. Conversely, some symptoms can elicit reinforcing responses from the surrounding environment, thus making the symptoms difficult to treat (Halleck, 1991). Assessing a client's environment, and obtaining knowledge of the relationship between the individual and his or her environment can help explain the nature of the client's symptoms and even guide therapeutic interventions. Halleck (1991) suggests obtaining this information through three general types of inquiries, namely how characteristics of the client's environment adversely influenced the client, how characteristics of the client interfered with his or her capacity to meet environmental expectations, and how the environment responded to the client's deficiencies. In addition, clinicians must attempt to distinguish between paranoia and appropriate and justified reactions to situations that may have occurred (although the client may be unable to corroborate these situations) and to distinguish between deleterious personality styles and appropriate reactions to difficult situations.

Third, one common goal of adult assessment is to make differential diagnoses and attribute a client's symptoms to specific disorders. It is important to be familiar with the key diagnostic signs that differentiate disorders that have similar criteria (Olin & Keatinge, 1998).

Fourth, a related challenge in adult assessment is the issue of multiple diagnoses. Often, both inpatients and outpatients meet diagnostic criteria for more than one diagnosis, particularly Axis II disorders (Barron, 1998). This raises several important questions. First, what is the clinical utility in making multiple diagnoses? Second, what are the treatment implications? If the client presents with comorbid disorders, how are they treated?

Fifth, another issue in psychological assessment is that a comprehensive intake must include ascertaining information about the clients' past and present medications, as well as determining possible misuse (under- or overmedicating). Clients' reactions to, and the side effects of, their medications can easily influence their presenting symptomatology. Thus, clients' medication may confound diagnostic impressions.

Sixth, another important issue is that of discrepancies. Test scores can sometimes lead to conclusions opposite to those obtained from test behavior, background information, and previous tests (O'Neill, 1993). Moreover, actuarial and clinical judgments may conflict, as can patient self-report and either test results or clinical impression. This is particularly problematic if the discrepant information influences the conclusions drawn. Clinicians must examine the validity of the test results and other potential reasons (e.g., test behavior) for the inconsistencies before documenting them in the report.

Thus, the accuracy of client reports (self-reports or interviews) must also be considered. Even when clients are skillfully interviewed, their reports may be insufficient, inaccurate, or distorted (Halleck, 1991). They may bias or present misleading information, either unknowingly or purposefully, or may be experiencing problems with their memory either independent of, or associated with, their presenting symptomatology. Moreover, clients' motivations for reporting their symptoms often influence the accuracy of their communications.

Regarding underreporting or withholding information, unintentional factors include poor cognitive or expressive capacities to communicate essential information and high levels of anxiety during the assessment that diminishes a client's capacity to think and communicate clearly (Halleck, 1991). In contrast, some clients intentionally choose to withhold information to avoid humiliation, the discovery of previously hidden shortcomings, and the revelation of personal inadequacies in order to prevent the often accompanying feelings of shame and fear (Halleck, 1991). Furthermore, clients may withhold information if they are skeptical or distrustful of the psychologist (which may relate to paranoia) or feel that they will be blamed for willfully creating their symptoms.

A more common occurrence is the tendency for clients to overreport their symptoms and exaggerate their level of dysfunction. Again, the motivation for symptom exaggeration can be either unintentional or intentional. Unintentional overreporting is often attributed to distorted memories. Furthermore, people who are seriously depressed or diagnosed with personality disorders or somatoform disorders may unconsciously exaggerate their symptoms (Halleck, 1991). In contrast, potential gains for intentionally exaggerating one's symptoms include the attention and nurturance of loved ones or medical personnel, a social or interpersonal advantage, power over their physicians, forensic reasons, and receiving disability compensation. Furthermore, individuals who experience memory loss or a factitious disorder may confabulate (Halleck, 1991).

During psychological assessments, certain cues can help alert the psychologist as to whether clients' reports may be inaccurate. Such cues include brief answers to questions even when clients are encouraged to expand their answers; inability or unwillingness to provide details of symptomatology history; presentation of contradictory information; attempts to take control of the interview; descriptions of symptomatology that are unusual in terms of severity, type, or frequency; denial of universal experiences such as sometimes feeling angry or sad; and presentation of an excessively idyllic or abysmal situation (Halleck, 1991). Furthermore, clinicians can review validity scales on psychological tests to help determine whether clients are reporting accurately.

A specific form of symptom overreporting is malingering. *DSM-IV* defines malingering as the voluntary presentation of false, or grossly exaggerated, physical or psychological symptoms. Psychologists should be alerted to the possibility of malingering if any of the following are present: a medical or legal context to the referral, discrepancy between objective findings and reported symptoms, compliance problems, a high number of obvious and improbable symptoms, symptoms that have an unlikely course and severity, sudden onset with vague and inconsistent symptoms, inconsistent test results, an inexplicable decrease from premorbid functioning, and significant gains associated with being impaired (Olin & Keatinge, 1998).

Clinicians should be particularly attentive to signs of malingering when conducting assessments requested from domains such as insurance companies, because these patients may receive secondary gains from presenting with severe symptomatology. When considering malingering, one must distinguish between symptom exaggeration and symptom fabrication, as well as between conscious and unconscious distortion of symptoms. In addition, when assessing whether a client may be overreporting, either generally or in reference to symptoms associated with a specific disorder, the clinician should be cognizant that according to analogue research, it is easier to detect global fakers than specific fakers (Berry, Baer, & Harris, 1991; Berry, Wetter, & Baer, 1995). Malingering may also be more difficult to detect if clients are coached by other individuals (Rogers, Bagby, & Chakraborty, 1993; Storm & Graham, 2000) and as they gain more knowledge of mental disorders and the validity scales embedded within many questionnaires. A final issue in the assessment of malingering relates to the significant and serious consequences of such a diagnosis. Thus, the clinician must recognize the damage of a false positive error and consequently ensure that there is considerable evidence to support a malingering diagnosis. However, one must also consider that the failure to diagnose malingering results in the expenditure of a great deal of money—money that is therefore not available to those who are in genuine serious distress.

Seventh, another aspect of assessment that can be challenging is distinguishing between chronic personality traits and current symptomatology. Clients are often unable to distinguish between the two, especially if they are in an acute state of distress. In addition, they may be unable to recall much of their childhood, or they may be experiencing overall difficulties with memory. It is important to clarify with clients when you are questioning them about lifelong symptoms and when you are inquiring about current problems. We strongly advise clinicians to obtain several examples from their clients that can be dated in order to formulate more accurate client conceptualizations and chronology of symptoms.

Eighth, sometimes psychological testing of Axis I and Axis II disorders requires additional screening for neuropsychological disorders that might be mediating or moderating a client's psychological profile and pattern of functioning. For example, early stages of dementia are often marked by the presence of depressive and anxiety symptoms. Whenever a clinician suspects the presence of a neuropsychological disorder, clients should receive a full neuropsychological battery. The results of neuropsychological assessments can guide diagnoses and affect treatment recommendations.

Conversely, neuropsychological assessments should assess clients' current mood, because the presence of psychological symptomatology, particularly depressive symptoms, can influence test results and interpretations. Thus, clients should receive a comprehensive clinical interview assessing for the presence of psychological symptoms, and they should be screened for Axis I disorders. The results of such a psychological assessment should then guide interpretation of neurological findings.

Ninth, clinicians must also keep in mind the limitations of diagnosis. Psychological diagnoses cannot always provide specific guidelines for treatment, because most mental disorders are classified descriptively on the basis of behavior and experience, rather than etiologically, as has been the practice of medicine. Because mental disorders often have multiple etiological pathways, including both genetics and the environment, the best we can do is classify them on the basis of their clinical features that over time, and with substantial empirical research, have been associated with particular outcomes (Halleck, 1991). Consequently, there is no linear path between diagnosis and treatment.

Regardless of such limitations, clinicians often confer diagnoses or are even legally obligated to diagnose. Moreover, they may provide an overall description of the client, including their clinical impressions. When writing their reports, clinicians must take into account the fact that the client may have access to the report. That is, the clinician must recognize the consequences of using labels (including diagnoses) and negative statements to describe the client.

Tenth, another issue pertaining to psychological assessment is the multiple roles of the psychologist. Within an inpatient setting, the psychologist conducting an assessment has numerous roles and relationships that can affect the assessment process and outcome. First and foremost, the clinician has a unique relationship with the client. Second, the clinician is involved in a teaching relationship with the referring psychiatrists or other mental health professional. The clinician is responsible for communicating the results and recommendations in as succinct but comprehensive a form as possible. However, even in this role, the clinician is advocating for the client, by ensuring that the client's difficulties and needs are clearly articulated and will be subsequently addressed by the treating mental health professional(s).

Finally, psychologists must note that they can only provide recommendations for possible treatment. Although the end result of a psychological assessment can provide extensive and invaluable information about the client's psychological profile, style of functioning, strengths, and weaknesses, as well as guiding treatment recommendations and predicting outcomes, the utility of the assessment depends on the referring physician's judgment. Unfortunately, we can only provide diagnoses and recommend possible treatments. The outcome of the assessment and the potential benefit to the client are ultimately in the hands of the referring psychiatrists.

ISSUES SPECIFIC TO THE PSYCHOLOGICAL ASSESSMENT OF INPATIENTS IN THE MENTAL HEALTH SETTING

There are also some issues regarding psychological assessment that are particularly relevant to assessing inpatients in adult mental health settings. First, unfortunately, time constraints may dictate the depth and breadth of psychological assessments. Clinicians find themselves having to triage because of the cost of keeping inpatients at the facility and the fact that clients often stay at the facility for short periods of time. Consequently, a comprehensive, in-depth assessment that measures all aspects of a client's psychological functioning, including current symptomatology, history, chronic difficulties, coping patterns, interaction styles, personality, and environmental factors, is rarely done. However, we feel that despite the time constraints, a psychological assessment should be as inclusive and comprehensive as possible, in order to best answer the referral question, make a diagnosis, and provide accurate treatment recommendations. To demand any less than this can cause great risk, detriment, and harm to the client.

Second, it is important to note that the severity of clients' psychopathology may affect their self-reports, both within the interview and on psychological tests. Many clients who are in an acute state of distress tend to generalize and over-pathologize their symptoms, to the extent that results from various instruments, such as the MMPI-2 and the PAI, become invalid. It is important for the clinician to tease apart the most salient problems from the client's tendency to use the psychological assessment as a cry for help.

Third, comorbidity of psychological disorders is high within the adult clinical population. Another problem is determining which disorder should be addressed first in treatment, particularly since the symptomatology, etiology, and environmental factors influencing one disorder may also present in another disorder. Of particular concern to the adult inpatient population is the high prevalence of substance abuse or dependence disorders in conjunction with another Axis I or Axis II disorder. Clinicians assessing inpatients should always test for possible substance abuse, because this affects the treatment plan and likely outcome for the client.

Fourth, another critical area to assess is the client's risk of harm to self and others, particularly with respect to suicidal ideology. This matter should not be taken lightly. Any suicidal ideation, plan, or intent should be documented and the appropriate measures taken to decrease the risk of harm. Furthermore, it is important that the clinician examine specific stressors, events, or other variables that are likely to increase a patient's risk of suicide.

Fifth, in psychiatry, an analysis of the influence of the environment on a patient's symptomatology is indispensable. Research suggests that the environment (both positive and negative) exerts an impact on symptom occurrence, development, and maintenance (Clarkin & Mattis, 1991; Halleck, 1991). The environment also exerts a long-term influence on the patient's experiences and behaviors that in turn can contribute to the patient's current psychological state or can develop into certain personality dimensions that complicate symptomatology (Halleck, 1991). The relationship between environment and symptoms is acknowledged in the *DSM-IV* Axis IV. Even more important, understanding a patient's social, developmental, and familial history can guide therapeutic interventions.

It is our opinion that adult inpatients are experiencing a greater number of, and often more intense, Axis IV problems, particularly in the areas of interpersonal difficulty, financial constraints, and employment difficulties. This observation highlights the multidimensional nature of psychopathology, specifically that people's surrounding environmental situations and constraints often influence the onset, severity, maintenance, and outcome of their psychological symptoms. As previously mentioned, Axis IV difficulties must be given strong consideration and value in a psychological assessment.

CONCLUSION

Formulation has been defined as the process by which we systematically, comprehensibly, and objectively assemble and integrate available information to arrive at an understanding of what is happening with the patient (Hertzman, 1984). It is essentially a working hypothesis upon which we base our diagnoses and treatment recommendations. Hertzman recommends integrating the patient's symptoms, functions with which the symptoms interfere, history, premorbid personality structure, external stressors, and defenses and coping styles into a working formulation, which in turn guides diagnostic impression and treatment suggestions.

An effective psychological assessment should have high clinical utility. All of the information obtained about a client's symptomatology, personality, and coping and interpersonal styles within a psychological assessment should be used to guide treatment recommendations.

REFERENCES

American Psychiatric Association. (1994). *Diagnostic and statistical manual of mental disorders* (4th ed.). Washington, DC: Author.

American Psychiatric Association. (2000). *Diagnostic and statistical manual of mental disorders* (4th ed., Text Revision). Washington, DC: Author.

Aiken, L. R. (2000). *Psychological testing and assessment: Tenth edition.* Needham Heights, MA: Allyn and Bacon.

Appelbaum, S. A. (1990). The relationship between assessment and psychotherapy. *Journal of Personality Assessment, 54,* 791–801.

Barron, J. (1998). *Making diagnosis meaningful: Enhancing evaluation and treatment of psychological disorders.* Washington, DC: American Psychological Association.

Beck, A. T., Epstein, N., Brown, G., & Steer, R. A. (1988). An inventory for measuring clinical anxiety: Psychometric properties. *Journal of Consulting and Clinical Psychology, 56,* 893–897.

Beck, A. T., Ward, C. H., Mendelson, M., Mock, J., & Erbaugh, J. (1961). An inventory for measuring depression. *Archives of General Psychiatry, 4,* 561–571.

Bensing, J. (2000). Bridging the gap: The separate worlds of evidence-based medicine and patient-centered medicine. *Patient Education and Counseling, 39,* 17–25.

Berry, D. T., Baer, R., & Harris, M. (1991). Detection of Malingering on the MMPI: A meta-analysis. *Clinical Psychology Review, 11,* 585–598.

Berry, D. T., Wetter, M. W., & Baer, R. A. (1995). Assessment of malingering. In J. N. Butcher (Ed.), *Clinical personality assessment: Practical approaches* (pp. 236–250). New York: Oxford University Press.

Beutler, L. E., & Clarkin, J. F. (1990). *Systematic treatment selection.* New York: Brunner/Mazel.

Beutler, L. E., Wakefield, P., & Williams, R. E. (1994). Use of psychological tests/instruments for treatment planning. In M. E. Maruish (Ed.), *The use of psychological testing for treatment planning and outcome assessment* (pp. 55–74). Hillsdale, NJ: Erlbaum.

Blatt, S. J., & Levy, K. N. (1998). *A psychodynamic approach to the diagnosis of psychopathology.* Washington, DC: American Psychological Association.

Briere, J. (1995). *Trauma Symptom Inventory Professional manual.* Odessa, FL: Psychological Assessment Resources.

Butcher, J. N. (1990). *The MMPI-2 in psychological treatment.* New York: Oxford University Press.

Butcher, J. N., Dahlstrom, W. G., Graham, J. R., Tellegen, A., & Kaemmer, B. (1989). *Manual for the administration and scoring of the MMPI-2.* Minneapolis: University of Minnesota Press.

Clark, L. A. (1993). *The Schedule for Nonadaptive and Adaptive Personality: Manual for administration and scoring.* Minneapolis: University of Minnesota Press.

Clarkin, J. F., & Hurt, S. W. (1988). Psychological assessment: Tests and rating scales. In J. Talbott, R. J. Hales, & S. Yudofsky (Eds.), *Textbook of psychiatry* (pp. 225–246). Washington, DC: American Psychiatric Press.

Clarkin, J. F., & Mattis, S. (1991). Psychological assessment. In L. I. Sederer (Ed.), *Inpatient psychiatry: Diagnosis and treatment* (3rd ed., pp. 360–378). Baltimore: Williams and Wilkens.

Cloninger, C. R., Przybeck, T. R., Svrakic, D. R., & Wetzel, R. D. (1994). *The Temperament and Character Inventory (TCI): A guide to its development and use.* St. Louis, Missouri: Center for Psychobiology of Personality.

Costa, P. T., Jr., & McCrae, R. R. (1992). *Revised NEO Personality Inventory: Professional manual.* Odessa, FL: Psychological Assessment Resources.

Dawes, R. M., Faust, D., & Meehl, P. E. (1989). Clinical versus actuarial judgment. *Science, 243,* 1668–1674.

Faust, D., & Ziskin, J. (1988). The expert witness in psychology and psychiatry. *Science, 241,* 31–35.

Finn, S. E., & Butcher, J. N. (1991). Clinical objective personality assessment. In M. Hersen, A. E. Kazdin, & A. S. Bellack (Eds.), *The clinical psychology handbook* (2nd ed., pp. 362–373). New York: Pergamon Press.

First, M. B., Gibbon, M., Spitzer, M. D., Williams, J. B. W., & Benjamin, L. (1997). *Users guide for the Structured Clinical Interview for DSM-IV Axis II Personality Disorders (SCID-II).* Washington, DC: American Psychiatric Press.

First, M. B., Spitzer, R. L., Gibbon, M., & Williams, J. B. W. (1995). *Structured Clinical Interview for DSM-IV Axis I Disorders— Patient Edition (SCID-I/P, Version 2.0).* New York: New York State Psychiatric Institute.

Foa, E. B., Riggs, D. S., Dancu, C. V., & Rothbaum, B. O. (1993). Reliability and validity of a brief instrument for assessing post-traumatic stress disorder. *Journal of Traumatic Stress, 6,* 459–473.

Gambrill, E. (1999). Evidence-based clinical behavior analysis, evidence-based medicine and the Cochrane collaboration. *Journal of Behavior Therapy and Experimental Psychiatry, 30,* 1–14.

Garb, H. N. (1984). The incremental validity of information used in personality assessment. *Clinical Psychology Review, 4,* 641–655.

Geddes, J. (1997). Using evidence about clinical effectiveness in everyday psychiatric practice. *Psychiatric Bulletin, 21,* 390–393.

Gilbody, S. (1996). Evidence-based medicine: An improved format for journal clubs. *Psychiatric Bulletin, 20,* 673–675.

Greene, R. L. (2000). *The MMPI-2: An interpretive manual* (2nd ed.). Boston: Allyn and Bacon.

Greene, R. L., & Clopton, J. R. (1994). Minnesota Multiphasic Personality Inventory–2. In M. E. Maruish (Ed.), *The use of psychological testing for treatment planning and outcome assessment* (pp. 137–159). Hillsdale, NJ: Erlbaum.

Gunderson, J. G., Autry, J. H., Mosher, L. R., & Buchsbaum, S. (1974). Special report: Schizophrenia. *Schizophrenia Bulletin, 9,* 15–54.

Gunderson, J. G., Links, P. S., & Reich, J. H. (1991). Competing models of personality disorders. *Journal of Personality Disorders, 5,* 60–68.

Halleck, S. L. (1991). *Evaluation of the psychiatric patient: A primer.* New York: Plenum.

Hamilton, M. (1959). The assessment of anxiety states by rating. *British Journal of Medical Psychology, 32,* 50–55.

Hamilton, M. (1960). A rating scale for depression. *Journal of Neurology, Neurosurgery and Psychiatry, 23,* 56–62.

Harkness, A. R., & Lilienfeld, S. O. (1997). Individual differences science for treatment planning: Personality traits. *Psychological Assessment, 9,* 349–360.

Harkness, A. R., McNulty, J. L., & Ben-Porath, Y. S. (1995). The Personality Psychopathology Five (PSY-5): Constructs and MMPI-2 scales. *Psychological Assessment, 7,* 104–114.

Hersen, M., Kazdin, A. E., & Bellack, A. S. (Eds.). (1991). *The clinical psychology handbook* (2nd ed.). Elmsford, NY: Pergamon Press.

Hertzman, M. (1984). *Inpatient psychiatry: Toward rapid restoration of function.* New York: Human Sciences Press.

Hodgson, R. J., & Rachman, S. (1977). Obsessional compulsive complaints. *Behavior Therapy, 15,* 389–395.

Hurt, S. W., Reznikoff, M., & Clarkin, J. F. (1991). *Psychological assessment, psychiatric diagnosis, and treatment planning.* Philadelphia: Brunner/Mazel.

Hyler, S. E. (1994). *PDQ-4+ Personality Questionnaire.* New York: Author.

Kellerman, H., & Burry, A. (1981). *Handbook of psychodiagnostic testing: Personality analysis and report writing.* New York: Grune and Stratton.

Kennell, J. H. (1999). Authoritative knowledge, evidence-based medicine, and behavioral pediatrics. *Journal of Developmental and Behavioral Pediatrics, 20,* 439–445.

Klein, M. H., Benjamin, L. S., Rosenfeld, R., Treece, L., Husted, J., & Greist, J. H. (1993). The Wisconsin Personality Disorders Inventory: I. Development, reliability and validity. *Journal of Personality Disorders, 7,* 285–303.

Lerner, P. (1991). *Psychoanalytic theory and the Rorschach.* Hillsdale, NJ: Analytic Press.

Lilienfeld, S. O., Wood, J. M., & Garb, H. N. (2001). What's wrong with this picture? *Scientific American, 284,* 80–87.

Livesley, W. J. (1998). Suggestions for a framework for an empirically based classification of personality disorder. *Canadian Journal of Psychiatry, 43,* 137–147.

Maloney, M. P., & Ward, M. P. (1976). *Psychological assessment: A conceptual approach.* New York: Oxford University Press.

Maruish, M. E. (1994). Introduction. In M. E. Maruish (Ed.), *The use of psychological testing for treatment planning and outcome assessment* (pp. 3–21). Hillsdale, NJ: Erlbaum.

Maruish, M. E. (1999). *The use of psychological testing for treatment planning and outcome assessment* (2nd ed.). Mahwah, NJ: Erlbaum.

Meehl, P. E. (1973). *Psychodiagnosis: Selected papers.* Minneapolis: University of Minnesota Press.

Millon, T. (1981). *Disorders of Personality: DSM III, Axis II.* New York: Wiley.

Millon, T. (1993). *Millon Clinical Multiaxial Inventory Inventory manual.* Minneapolis, MN: National Computer Systems.

Morey, L. C. (1991). *The Personality Assessment Inventory professional manual.* Odessa, FL: Psychological Assessment Resources.

Morey, L. C., & Henry, W. (1994). Personality Assessment Inventory. In M. E. Maruish (Ed.), *The use of psychological testing for treatment planning and outcome assessment* (pp. 185–216). Hillsdale, NJ: Erlbaum.

Motto, J. A. (1985). Preliminary field testing of a risk estimator for suicide, suicide and life threatening behavior. *American Journal of Psychiatry, 15*(3), 139–150.

Nathan, E. P. (1998). The *DSM-IV* and its antecedents: Enhancing syndromal diagnosis. In J. W. Barron (Ed.), *Making diagnosis meaningful: Enhancing evaluation and treatment of psychological disorders* (pp. 3–27). Washington, DC: American Psychological Association.

O'Neill, A. M. (1993). *Clinical inference: How to draw meaningful conclusions from tests.* Brandon, Vermont: Clinical Psychology Publishing.

Olin, J. T., & Keatinge, C. (1998). *Rapid psychological assessment.* New York: Wiley.

Olson, E. A. (1996). Evidence-based practice: A new approach to teaching the integration of research and practice in gerontology. *Educational Gerontology, 22,* 523–537.

Pfohl, B., Blum, N., & Zimmerman, M. (1995). *Structured Interview for DSM-IV Personality (SIDP-IV).* Iowa City: University of Iowa, Department of Psychiatry.

Robins, L. N., Helzer, J. E., Croughan, J. L., & Ratcliff, K. S. (1981). National Institute of Mental Health Diagnostic Interview Schedule. *Archives of General Psychiatry, 38,* 381–389.

Rogers, R., Bagby, R. M., & Chakraborty, D. (1993). Feigning schizophrenic disorders on the MMPI-2: Detection of coached simulators. *Journal of Personality Assessment, 60,* 215–226.

Rogers, R., Bagby, R. M., & Dickens, S. E. (1992). *Structured Interview of Reported Symptoms: Professional manual.* Odessa, FL: Psychological Assessment Resources.

Rubinson, E. P., & Asnis, G. M. (1989). Use of structured interviews for diagnosis. In S. Wetzler (Ed.), *Measuring mental illness: Psychometric assessment for clinicians* (pp. 43–68). Washington, DC: American Psychiatric Press.

Smith, B. L. (1998). Psychological testing, psychodiagnosis, and psychotherapy. In J. W. Barron (Ed.), *Making diagnosis meaningful: Enhancing evaluation and treatment of psychological disorders* (pp. 227–245). Washington, DC: American Psychological Association.

Somwaru, D. P., & Ben-Porath, Y. S. (1994). *MMPI-2 personality disorders scales.* Unpublished manuscript, Kent State University, Kent, OH.

Spielberger, C. D. (1983). *Manual for the State-Trait Anxiety Inventory.* Palo Alto, CA: Consulting Psychological Press.

Storm, J., & Graham, J. R. (2000). Detection of cached general malingering on the MMPI-2. *Psychological Assessment, 12,* 158–165.

Trull, T. J., & Widiger, T. A. (1997). *Structured Interview for the Five-Factor Model of Personality (SIFFM): Professional manual.* Odessa, FL: Psychological Assessment Resources.

Wakefield, J. C. (1998). Meaning and melancholia: Why the *DSM-IV* cannot (entirely) ignore the patient's intentional system.

In J. W. Barron (Ed.), *Making diagnosis meaningful: Enhancing evaluation and treatment of psychological disorders* (pp. 29–72). Washington, DC: American Psychological Association.

Wanberg, K. W., Horn, J. L., & Foster, F. M. (1977). A differential assessment model for alcoholism: The scales of the Alcohol Use Inventory. *Journal of Studies on Alcohol, 38,* 512–543.

Westen, D. (1998). Case formulation and personality diagnosis: Two processes or one? In J. W. Barron (Ed.), *Making diagnosis meaningful: Enhancing evaluation and treatment of psychological disorders* (pp. 111–137). Washington, DC: American Psychological Association.

Westen, D., & Arkowitz-Westen, L. (1998). Limitations of Axis II in diagnosing personality pathology in clinical practice. *American Journal of Psychiatry, 155,* 1767–1771.

Widiger, T. A. (1998). Four out of five ain't bad. *Archives of General Psychiatry, 55,* 865–866.

Widiger, T. A., Mangine, S., Corbitt, E. M., Ellis, C. G., & Thomas, G. V. (1995). *Personality Disorder Interview-IV: A semistructured interview for the assessment of personality disorders.* Odessa, FL: Psychological Assessment Resources.

Wiens, A. N. (1991). Diagnostic interviewing. In M. Hersen, A. E. Kazdin, & A. S. Bellack (Eds.), *The clinical psychology handbook* (2nd ed., pp. 345–361). New York: Pergamon Press.

World Health Organization. (1992). *ICD: International Statistical Classification of Diseases and Related Health Problems* (Vol. 10). Geneva, Switzerland: Author.

Zanarini, M., Frankenburg, F. R., Chauncey, D. L., & Gunderson, J. G. (1987). The Diagnostic Interview for Personality Disorders: Interrater and test-retest reliability. *Comprehensive Psychiatry, 28,* 467–480.

CHAPTER 11

Psychological Assessment in Child Mental Health Settings

DAVID LACHAR

Although most children receive mental health services because some concern has been raised regarding their emotional and behavioral adjustment, these mental health services are provided in a variety of settings by a variety of professionals. Core evaluation and treatment services may be provided by educational or health care organizations through outpatient clinics, inpatient facilities, or residential care agencies. Such services may be supported by an annual institutional budget from which resources are allocated on some rational basis, or each service may be available only to the extent to which associated expenses can be reimbursed. The latter consideration is always of central importance in private practice settings that provide the majority of fee-based or insurance-reimbursed mental health care. Psychological assessment services may be routinely integrated into intake evaluation, treatment planning, and subsequent outcome review, or may be obtained on a referral basis.

Routine psychological assessment in child mental health settings focuses on the identification and quantification of symptom dimensions and problem behaviors and the collection of information relevant to the development of treatment strategies. In contrast, psychological assessment provided in response to referral may incorporate any of the varied testing

methodologies appropriate for the understanding of youth. Of necessity, routine assessment is designed to be cost and time efficient, requiring relatively narrowly defined skills that are easily acquired. The information provided in such routine assessments must be easily understood and applied by the variety of mental health professionals who evaluate and treat children, adolescents, and their families. This chapter provides a detailed discussion of the forms of psychological assessment that can be either applied routinely or integrated into assessments designed to answer specific diagnostic inquiries.

Psychological assessment services requested by referral are usually provided by, or under the supervision of, doctoral-level psychologists with specialized training who are certified or licensed to provide mental health services independently. For example, the training necessary to provide assessment with projective techniques or neuropsychological assessment requires specific graduate or postgraduate coursework and considerable supervised clinical experience delivered within structured practica, internships, and postdoctoral fellowships. Referral for psychological assessment is often requested to achieve an effective differential diagnosis. Such referrals are made following the collection of a complicated and contradictory history obtained from parent and child interview or subsequent to completion of an ineffective course of treatment.

Surveys of senior doctoral psychologists who maintain specific professional memberships often associated with the use of psychological testing or who conduct research using psychological tests provide some insight regarding valued tests and test-related procedures. Two of these surveys, conducted in 1990 and 1998, have focused on the provision of assessment services to adolescents (Archer, Maruish, Imhof, & Piotrowski, 1991; Archer & Newsom, 2000). The first of these surveys noted the prominence of the Wechsler intelligence scales, Rorschach Inkblot Method, Bender-Gestalt Test, Thematic Apperception Test, Sentence Completion Test, and Minnesota Multiphasic Personality Inventory, often (84%) also administered in a standard battery. The most recent of these surveys suggests the continuing prominence of all but the Bender-Gestalt, the growing use of parent and teacher rating scales, and the influence of managed care in discouraging the use of the most labor-intensive procedures in psychological testing. Unfortunately, such surveys identify neither the degree to which youth receiving mental health services are evaluated using psychological tests, nor the context of such applications (e.g., differential diagnosis, treatment planning, outcome assessment).

MENTAL HEALTH EVALUATION OF YOUTH

This chapter focuses on the ways in which the evaluation of the adjustment of children and adolescents benefits from the use of objective rating scales and questionnaires. The routine use of such procedures within mental health settings supports the primary mission of evaluation and treatment, although other assessment techniques make a positive contribution in this regard. The evaluation of child and adolescent adjustment may benefit from the additional application of projective techniques (cf. Exner & Weiner, 1982; McArthur & Roberts, 1982), the evaluation of cognitive and academic dysfunction, and the assessment of family status. Such efforts are applied to gain a fuller understanding of a child's adjustment, to arrive at an accurate differential diagnosis, to support treatment planning, and to monitor ongoing efforts. The case examples in Lachar and Gruber (2001) demonstrate the considerable contribution that projective techniques, psychoeducational evaluation, and neuropsychological assessment may make to the understanding of child adjustment, although any examination of the issues involved in such applications would merit a separate chapter. The overall goal of this chapter is to examine the routine application of objective

methods in youth evaluation and treatment, and to discuss in some depth the issues related to such application.

Characteristics of Children and Adolescents

The evaluation of youth is substantially different from the comparable evaluation of adults by mental health professionals. Children function in uniform social contexts and consistently perform in standard contexts. That is, they are routinely observed by parents and other guardians, and once they reach the age of 5 years, spend a substantial amount of their lives in the classroom and pursuing school-related activities. Many behavioral expectations are related to a child's specific age, and childhood is characterized by the attainment of a succession of developmental, academic, and social goals. Children and adolescents typically are not self-referred for mental health services, but are referred by parents and teachers. Problems in child adjustment are usually defined and identified by adults, not by the child. These adults are routinely involved in assessment and treatment, because treatment efforts routinely incorporate modification of the home and classroom environments (cf. LaGreca, Kuttler, & Stone, 2001).

Developmental and Motivational Issues

The Dimensions and Content of Adjustment Problems

The same or quite similar core presenting symptoms and problems may be associated with different diagnoses. Presenting problems such as inattention may suggest the presence of attention-deficit/hyperactivity disorder (ADHD), depression, anxiety, defective reality testing, a learning disability, or an acquired cognitive deficit. The same core disability may be demonstrated by quite different symptoms and behaviors at different ages, problem behaviors may change substantially with maturation, and problems may appear as a consequence of a prior untreated condition.

Psychosocial Development

Young children are routinely characterized as unable to contribute meaningfully to the assessment process through the completion of self-report questionnaires (Ammerman & Hersen, 1993). Children under the age of 10 have not been reliable reporters of their own behaviors (Edelbrock, Costello, Dulcan, Kalas, & Conover, 1985). Relevant challenges to test construction and test application most certainly include normative limitations of a child's age-appropriate language comprehension and reading skills. The task of self-evaluation and self-description may also be compromised by a fundamental developmental immaturity in the understanding of the principles of psychosocial adjustment. Hence, developmental immaturity represents a challenge to test validity because of the presence of inadequately developed introspective skills, such as a lack of appreciation for the relation between thoughts and feelings (cf. Flavell, Flavell, & Green, 2001).

Intrinsic Motivation

In contrast to adults who request services from mental health professionals, children and adolescents seldom request such assistance. Children are unlikely to find the completion of a self-description of adjustment consistent with their expectations and are unlikely to experience completion of such a questionnaire as positive. It is quite reasonable to anticipate that most youth will not be motivated to contribute information that is useful in the diagnostic process. In the mental health setting, youth contribution to a formal test-based assessment process may be even more problematic. Youth are frequently referred to mental health professionals because they have been unwilling or unable to comply with the requests of adults. Such youth frequently also present with cognitive or academic disabilities that represent additional obstacles to the use of formal assessment techniques.

UNIQUE CHALLENGES OF THE MENTAL HEALTH SETTING

Assessment of Comorbid Conditions

Comorbidity, the simultaneous occurrence of two or more unrelated conditions, is very commonly observed in youth evaluated in mental health settings. This expectation of comorbid conditions should be seriously considered in the conduct of initial evaluations. Comprehensive multidimensional evaluations of adjustment, and therefore the use of tests that simultaneously assess multiple dimensions of problematic adjustment (or multiple unidimensional tests that provide comparable information) are employed by mental health professionals because of the nature of the problems of the youth they evaluate. Children and adolescents troubled by multiple disorders are most likely to be assessed by a mental health professional because the probability of referral of such a child is determined by the combined likelihood of the referral for each separate disorder (Caron & Rutter, 1991). This *referral bias* has been demonstrated by clinical interviews and in the separate application of standardized questionnaires completed by parents, teachers, and students (McConaughy &

Achenbach, 1994). It is therefore always reasonable to assume that conditions other than the one presented as the primary problem are contributing to the referral process and influencing current adjustment; this possibility must be considered in the selection of assessment procedures. In addition, it is important to consider the developmental implications of current conditions, in that the presence of specific unresolved problems may increase the subsequent likelihood of other specific conditions.

It is important to be alert to the possible presence of the various conditions that are frequently comorbid in youth seen by mental health professionals. Considerable effort has been applied in identifying frequent patterns of comorbidity. For example, as many as two thirds of elementary school children with ADHD referred for clinical evaluation have been found to have at least one other diagnosable psychiatric disorder. Measurement and treatment of these other disorders are often of comparable importance to the assessment and treatment of ADHD itself (Cantwell, 1996). Such comorbid conditions may delineate meaningful subgroups of children with ADHD (Biederman, Newcorn, & Sprich, 1991). Even studies of non-referred samples demonstrate that the majority of children with ADHD also qualify for an additional *disruptive behavior disorder* (e.g., oppositional defiant disorder [ODD], conduct disorder [CD]). These patterns of comorbidity are more common in boys than girls, are associated with increased severity and persistence of symptoms, and have negative implications for future family and societal adjustment (Jensen, Martin, & Cantwell, 1997). *Internalizing disorders* (anxiety, depression) are frequently diagnosed in children with ADHD; this pattern of problems appears to have important implications for treatment effectiveness. The presence of comorbid internalizing symptoms decreases the likelihood of positive response to stimulant medications (cf. Voelker, Lachar, & Gdowski, 1983) and suggests the need to consider alternative treatment with antidepressants. Jensen et al. (1997) noted that underachievement, Tourette's syndrome, bipolar disorder, and a variety of medical conditions should also be considered as possibly comorbid when ADHD has been established as a current diagnosis (see also Pliszka, 1998).

Conduct disorder and ODD demonstrate substantial comorbidity in epidemiological studies and obtain rates of comorbidity in excess of 90% in referred samples. Some authors have even considered these two diagnostic categories not to be independent phenomenon, but points on a continuum, perhaps representing variation in developmental stage and symptom severity (cf. Loeber, Lahey, & Thomas, 1991; Nottelmann & Jensen, 1995). The majority of referred children with CD or ODD also meet the diagnostic criterion for ADHD. Comorbid internalizing conditions are less frequent, although gender may play a role. Girls are more likely than boys to have a comorbid internalizing condition at any age. The co-occurrence of depression is more likely in preadolescence for boys, and such comorbidity in girls increases significantly with age. Indeed, the majority of referred youth (except for adolescent boys) with CD have one or more additional diagnoses (Offord, Boyle, & Racine, 1991). Comorbid anxiety may be associated with fewer CD symptoms of aggression, whereas comorbid depression is associated with increased risk for suicidal behavior (Loeber & Keenan, 1994). Conduct disorder is also often associated with substantial academic underachievement (Hinshaw, Lahey, & Hart, 1993). The conjoint presence of CD and depression may represent an even greater risk for a variety of problems than is represented by each condition alone. These problems may include substance dependence, academic problems, problematic social competence and peer relationships, a predisposition not to experience positive emotions, treatment seeking, treatment resistance, and increased long-term negative implications (Marmorstein & Iacono, 2001).

The comorbidity of depression and anxiety is substantial in clinically referred youth (Brady & Kendall, 1992). Indeed, substantial evidence exists that anxiety and depression are part of a broader construct of emotional distress in children and adolescents (Finch, Lipovsky, & Casat, 1989; King, Ollendick, & Gullone, 1991). Anxiety may more frequently appear before depression, and their joint occurrence suggests a higher degree of disability. Many of these youth have a comorbid externalizing disorder. ADHD occurs with anxiety or depression 25 to 33% of the time, whereas CD or ODD is present at least 50% of the time (Nottelmann & Jensen, 1995).

Multidimensional inventories may be especially valuable in the assessment of children with a known disability. For example, comorbid conditions in youth classified as mentally retarded are typically underdiagnosed (Nanson & Gordon, 1999). This phenomenon is so prevalent that unique descriptive labels have been proposed. *Diagnostic overshadowing* is the tendency for clinicians to overlook additional psychiatric diagnoses once the presence of mental retardation has been established (Spengler, Strohmer, & Prout, 1990); *masking* is the process by which the clinical characteristics of a mental disorder are assumed instead to be features of developmental delay (cf. Pearson et al., 2000). Studies suggest comorbidity for various behavioral or psychiatric disorders of 30 to 60% for children with mental retardation (McLaren & Bryson, 1987).

Problem Intensity and Chronicity

Referral to a mental health professional, whether for hospitalization or residential care or for outpatient evaluation at a clinic or other tertiary referral center, assures the presence a high proportion of difficult and complicated cases that will include high levels of comorbidity (Caron & Rutter, 1991). Such referrals often represent a pattern of maladjustment that does not remit over time and that is also resistant to primary corrective efforts in the home or the school, or through consultation with a pediatrician or family physician. An extended symptomatic course suggests the presence of conditions that are secondary to primary chronic problems (e.g., primary disruptive behavior contributes to peer rejection that results in social isolation that leads to dysphoria). Chronicity and intensity of current adjustment problems represent an assessment challenge to establish the historical sequence of problem emergence and the consequences of previous intervention efforts. Such a history may seduce a clinician into making significant diagnostic leaps of inference that may not be warranted. Such errors may be avoided through systematic use of a multidimensional instrument during the intake process. When current problems have a significant history, the significant adults who will participate in the assessment process (parents, teachers) are likely to bring with them a high degree of emotional commitment to problem resolution. Such informant intensity may decrease the clarity of their contribution as a questionnaire informant to the assessment.

The Referral Process

Youth generally come to mental health settings only because they are referred for specific services, although other evaluations may be conducted at school or in the physician's office secondary to some routine, setting-specific observation or other data-gathering process. Some consideration of the referral process provides insight into the challenges inherent in assessments conducted by mental health professionals. Requests for mental health evaluation often originate with a request by a professional or from a setting that is distant from the mental health professional, allowing less than complete communication. The mental health professional or mental health service delivery agency cannot assume that the detail that accompanies the request for service is either sufficient or accurate. Rather, at least one adult has been motivated to initiate this referral and at least one or more focused concerns may be communicated to some degree.

In other instances the referral for an evaluation may come from a behavioral health managed care company and may represent only the information provided by a parent who has called the number on the back of an insurance card. In such instances the referral assures the clinician of some financial reimbursement for services rendered, but provides no independent meaningful clinical information. That is, the clinician must first document problem presence, then type, pattern, and severity. In such cases, the clinician must be especially vigilant regarding potential errors in focus—that is, assuming that specific behaviors represent one problem, while they actually represent another (i.e., similar behaviors reflect dissimilar problems).

The Challenges of Managed Care

Maruish (2002), although focusing on mental health services for adults, provides a balanced discussion of the changes in psychometric practice that have accompanied behavioral health benefits management. Requests for psychological testing must be preauthorized if these services will be reimbursed. Approval of such requests will be most successful when psychological testing is proposed to support the development of a differential diagnosis and a plan of treatment. Collection of this information is consistent with an emphasis on the application of treatments with proven effectiveness (Roberts & Hurley, 1997). Psychological testing routinely applied without focus, or supporting such goals as the development of an understanding of "the underlying personality structure," as well as administration of collections of tests that incorporate duplicative or overlapping procedures, are inconsistent with the goals and philosophy of managed care. This review process may reduce the use of psychological testing and limit more time-consuming procedures, while supporting the use of brief, easily scored measures and checklists (Piotrowski, Belter, & Keller, 1998).

In contrast, the objectives and general philosophy of managed care are consistent with the application of objective multidimensional measures in the evaluation and treatment of children and adolescents. These goals include the efficient and rapid definition of current problems, the development of an effective treatment program, the monitoring of such intervention, and the evaluation of treatment effectiveness. Of greatest efficiency will be the application of procedures that generate information that supports all of these goals. The information generated by objective ratings and questionnaires are time and cost effective, and provide information that can be easily assimilated by the significant adults in a child's life, therapists with various training backgrounds, and the organizations that ultimately monitor and control mental health resources.

It is useful to contrast contemporary descriptions of effective diagnostic and psychological assessment procedures to the expectation of managed mental health care that the information necessary for accurate diagnosis and treatment planning can be obtained in a 1-hr clinical interview. Cantwell (1996) outlined the necessary diagnostic components in the evaluation

of ADHD. These components are as follows: (a) a comprehensive interview with all parenting figures to review current symptoms and developmental, medical, school, family social, medical, and mental health history; (b) a developmentally appropriate interview with the child that incorporates screening for comorbid disorders; (c) a medical evaluation; (d) assessment of cognitive ability and academic achievement; (e) application of both broad-spectrum and more narrowly focused parent and teacher rating scales; and (f) other adjunct assessments such as speech and language assessment. Cordell (1998) described the range of psychological assessment services often requested by a child psychiatry service. She provided outlines of assessment protocols for preschoolers, preteens, and adolescents. Each of these protocols requires three to five sessions for a total of up to 6 hrs of patient contact.

The assessment methods that are the focus of this chapter may be applied to meet the goals of managed care. In routine (not crisis) evaluation, parents may be mailed a teacher rating form to be completed and returned before the intake interview. Parents may be asked to complete a questionnaire in a similar fashion. Completion of such rating forms not only provides valuable independent assessment of the child, but also represents a sample of positive parent behavior. This compliant behavior may predict an increased likelihood of parent attendance at the first scheduled appointment. This is an important consideration, because an acutely distressed parent may make an appointment for mental health services, yet not appear if the specific conditions that generated the distress resolve before the scheduled appointment.

When a parent completes a questionnaire to describe the child before the intake interview, this additional information can add an efficient focus to the topics subsequently discussed. Because of the central role of family and school in child treatment, the feedback to parents and teachers from these measures is usually accepted with little if any resistance. When these profiles are inconsistent with the global opinions that have motivated the mental health consultation, the presentation and discussion of such results may facilitate realignment of parent or teacher opinion and the development of an alliance with the therapist.

THE CONDUCT OF ASSESSMENT BY QUESTIONNAIRE AND RATING SCALE

Contemporary models of the assessment of psychiatric disorders in youth are, in contrast to the models proposed by managed care, likely to be comprehensive. For example, although early approaches to the behavioral assessment of CD focused on identifying the parenting skills deficits conceptualized as causative and therefore in need of primary remediation, the increased understanding of the developmental aspects of this disorder has substantially influenced assessment. McMahon (1987) noted:

> As our knowledge of the multiple factors influencing the development, manifestation, and maintenance of conduct disorders has grown, it has become apparent that a proper assessment of the conduct disordered child must make use of the multiple methods (e.g., behavioral rating scales, direct observation, interviews) completed by multiple informants (parents, teachers, the children themselves) concerning the child's behavior in multiple settings (e.g., home, school). Furthermore, it is essential that the familial and extra-familial contexts in which the conduct disordered child functions be assessed as well. (p. 246)

This assessment process is often described as *sequential* (Mash & Lee, 1993). The presence of specific problems is first established. Multidimensional inventories can make an efficient and effective contribution to this process. Each problem must be placed in its developmental and historical context, and assessed in relation to recent experiences. Such information is most efficiently gathered by a focused and tailored interview. Once a treatment plan is developed, its effectiveness should be monitored through additional assessment. Repetition of baseline assessment procedures or the use of more focused or narrowly defined questionnaires during and at the completion of treatment can be applied in the support of this process. Such efforts can support modification of ongoing treatment, quantify change at termination, and estimate stability of such improvement by follow-up survey.

Introducing a Family of Multidimensional, Multisource Measures

Personality Inventory for Children, Second Edition

First published in 1977, this questionnaire completed by parent or other guardian was completely revised in 2001. The Personality Inventory for Children has been described as "one of the earliest and remains among the most well known of parent rating scales. . . . the grandparent of many modern rating scales" (Kamphaus & Frick, 1996). The Personality Inventory for Children, Second Edition (PIC-2) is provided in two formats. The first format consists of a reusable 275-statement administration booklet and a separate answer sheet for the recording of parent responses to booklet statements. Various answer sheets can be scored by hand with templates, or the recorded responses (True-False) can be entered for processing into a personal computer; answer sheets may also be mailed or faxed to the test publisher for processing. A multiscale profile (the PIC-2 Behavioral Summary) interpreted using guidelines presented in the test manual (Lachar & Gruber, 2001) is

obtained by completion of the first 96 items, which takes about 15 min. A second, similarly interpreted comprehensive profile (the Standard Format) and responses to a critical item list may be obtained by completing the entire administration booklet, which takes about 40 min or less. The second published format provides the 96 statements of the PIC-2 Behavioral Summary and a simple efficient method to generate and profile its 12 scores. The PIC-2 gender-specific T-score values are derived from a contemporary national sample of parent descriptions of youth 5 to 18 years of age. (A preschool version of the PIC for children 3 to 5 years of age is currently being developed.)

Table 11.1 lists the components of these two profiles and some of their associated psychometric characteristics. PIC-2 statements are written at a low- to mid-fourth-grade reading level and represent current and previous behaviors, feelings, accomplishments, and interactions, both common to and relatively infrequent among youth evaluated by mental health professionals. These statements reflect both variations in problem frequency and severity. PIC-2 adjustment scales were constructed using an iterative procedure. Potential scale items were first assigned to initial dimensions on the basis of previous scale structure or manifest statement content, whereas final item-scale assignment reflected a demonstrated strong and primary correlation with the dimension on which it was finally assigned. The nine scales of the standard profile were then further refined with the assistance of factor analysis to construct 21 subscales of greater content homogeneity applied to facilitate scale interpretation. The PIC-2 Behavioral Summary profile presents eight core scales and four composites or combinations of these values designed to measure change in symptomatic status. Each of these core scales consists of 12 statements selected from the full-length standard form to support treatment planning and to measure behavioral change. Each short scale correlates .92 to .96 with its full-length equivalent.

A significant element of the PIC-2 Standard Format profile is the provision of three response validity scales. The first of these scales (Inconsistency) consists of 35 pairs of statements. Because each pair of statements is highly correlated, two of the four possible pairs of responses (True-True and False-False, or True-False and False-True) are classified as inconsistent and their presence adds a unit weight to the Inconsistency scale raw score that can range from 0 to 35. Review of several examples of inconsistent response pairs clarifies this concept; for example, "My child has many friends. (True)/My child has very few friends. (True)"; "My child often disobeys me. (True)/My child often breaks the rules. (False)." An elevated T score on this scale ($T > 69$) suggests that the parent who completed the PIC-2 failed to attend sufficiently to, or to achieve adequate comprehension of, PIC-2 statement content.

TABLE 11.1 PIC-2 Adjustment Scales and Subscales and Selected Psychometric Performance

SCALE or Subscale (abbreviation)	Items	α	r_{tt}	Subscale Representative Item
	STANDARD FORMAT PROFILE			
COGNITIVE IMPAIRMENT (COG)	39	.87	.94	
Inadequate Abilities (COG1)	13	.77	.95	My child seems to understand everything that is said.
Poor Achievement (COG2)	13	.77	.91	Reading has been a problem for my child.
Developmental Delay (COG3)	13	.79	.82	My child could ride a tricycle by age five years.
IMPULSIVITY AND DISTRACTIBILITY (ADH)	27	.92	.88	
Disruptive Behavior (ADH1)	21	.91	.87	My child cannot keep attention on anything.
Fearlessness (ADH2)	6	.69	.86	My child will do anything on a dare.
DELINQUENCY (DLQ)	47	.95	.90	
Antisocial Behavior (DLQ1)	13	.88	.83	My child has run away from home.
Dyscontrol (DLQ2)	17	.91	.91	When my child gets mad, watch out!
Noncompliance (DLQ3)	17	.92	.87	My child often breaks the rules.
FAMILY DYSFUNCTION (FAM)	25	.87	.90	
Conflict Among Members (FAM1)	15	.83	.90	There is a lot of tension in our home.
Parent Maladjustment (FAM2)	10	.77	.91	One of the child's parents drinks too much alcohol.
REALITY DISTORTION (RLT)	29	.89	.92	
Developmental Deviation (RLT1)	14	.84	.87	My child needs protection from everyday dangers.
Hallucinations and Delusions (RLT2)	15	.81	.79	My child thinks others are plotting against him/her.
SOMATIC CONCERN (SOM)	28	.84	.91	
Psychosomatic Preoccupation (SOM1)	17	.80	.90	My child is worried about disease.
Muscular Tension and Anxiety (SOM2)	11	.68	.88	My child often has back pains.
PSYCHOLOGICAL DISCOMFORT (DIS)	39	.90	.90	
Fear and Worry (DIS1)	13	.72	.76	My child will worry a lot before starting something new.
Depression (DIS2)	18	.87	.91	My child hardly ever smiles.
Sleep Disturbance/Preoccupation with Death (DIS3)	8	.76	.86	My child thinks about ways to kill himself/herself.
SOCIAL WITHDRAWAL (WDL)	19	.81	.89	
Social Introversion (WDL1)	11	.78	.90	Shyness is my child's biggest problem.
Isolation (WDL2)	8	.68	.88	My child often stays in his/her room for hours.
SOCIAL SKILL DEFICITS (SSK)	28	.91	.92	
Limited Peer Status (SSK1)	13	.84	.92	My child is very popular with other children.
Conflict with Peers (SSK2)	15	.88	.87	Other children make fun of my child's ideas.
	BEHAVIORAL SUMMARY PROFILE			
SHORT ADJUSTMENT SCALES				
Impulsivity and Distractibility-Short (ADH-S)	12	.88	.87	
Delinquency-Short (DLQ-S)	12	.89	.85	
Family Dysfunction-Short (FAM-S)	12	.82	.86	
Reality Distortion-Short (RLT-S)	12	.82	.87	
Somatic Concern-Short (SOM-S)	12	.73	.85	
Psychological Discomfort-Short (DIS-S)	12	.81	.87	
Social Withdrawal-Short (WDL-S)	12	.76	.88	
Social Skill Deficits-Short (SSK-S)	12	.82	.89	
COMPOSITE SCALES				
Externalizing (EXT-C)	24	.94	.89	
Internalizing (INT-C)	36	.89	.89	
Social Adjustment (SOC-C)	24	.86	.89	
Total Score (TOT-C)	96	.95	.89	

Note: Scale and subscale alpha (α) values based on a referred sample $n = 1,551$. One-week clinical retest correlation (r_{tt}) sample $n = 38$.
Selected material from the PIC-2 copyright © 2001 by Western Psychological Services. Reprinted by permission of the publisher, Western Psychological Services, 12031 Wilshire Boulevard, Los Angeles, California, 90025, U.S.A., www.wpspublish.com. Not to be reprinted in whole or in part for any additional purpose without the expressed, written permission of the publisher. All rights reserved.

The second validity scale, Dissimulation, evaluates the likelihood that the responses to PIC-2 statements represent an exaggeration of current problems in adjustment, or the description of nonexistent problems and symptoms. These scale items were identified through an analytic process in which three samples were compared: a normative sample, a referred sample, and a sample in which parents were asked to describe their asymptomatic children as if they were in need of mental health services (i.e., a malingering sample). The average endorsement rate for these 35 items was 6.3% in normative, 15.3% in referred, and 54.5% in directed malingered protocols. Elevation of Dissimulation may reflect the presence of informant distress that may distort youth description.

The third validity scale, Defensiveness, includes 12 descriptions of infrequent or highly improbable positive attributes ("My child always does his/her homework on time. [True]") and 12 statements that represent the denial of common child behaviors and problems ("My child has some bad habits. [False]"). Scale values above 59T suggest that significant problems may be minimized or denied on the PIC-2 profile. The PIC-2 manual provides interpretive guidelines for seven patterns of these three scales that classified virtually all cases (99.8%) in a study of 6,370 protocols.

Personality Inventory for Youth

The Personality Inventory for Youth (PIY) and the PIC-2 are closely related in that the majority of PIY items were derived from rewriting content-appropriate PIC items into a first-person format. As demonstrated in Table 11.2, the PIY profile is very similar to the PIC-2 Standard Format profile. PIY scales were derived in an iterative fashion with 270 statements assigned to one of nine clinical scales and to three validity response scales (Inconsistency, Dissimulation, Defensiveness). As in the PIC-2, each scale is further divided into two or three more homogenous subscales to facilitate interpretation. PIY materials include a reusable administration booklet and a separate answer sheet that can be scored by hand with templates, processed by personal computer, or mailed to the test publisher to obtain a narrative interpretive report, profile, and responses to a critical item list. PIY items were intentionally written at a low readability level, and a low- to mid-fourth-grade reading comprehension level is adequate for understanding and responding to the PIY statements. When students have at least an age-9 working vocabulary, but do not have a

TABLE 11.2   PIY Clinical Scales and Subscales and Selected Psychometric Performance

SCALE or Subscale (abbreviation)	Items	α	r_{tt}	Subscale Representative Item
COGNITIVE IMPAIRMENT (COG)	20	.74	.80	
Poor Achievement and Memory (COG1)	8	.65	.70	School has been easy for me.
Inadequate Abilities (COG2)	8	.67	.67	I think I am stupid or dumb.
Learning Problems (COG3)	4	.44	.76	I have been held back a year in school.
IMPULSIVITY AND DISTRACTIBILITY (ADH)	17	.77	.84	
Brashness (ADH1)	4	.54	.70	I often nag and bother other people.
Distractibility and Overactivity (ADH2)	8	.61	.71	I cannot wait for things like other kids can.
Impulsivity (ADH3)	5	.54	.58	I often act without thinking.
DELINQUENCY (DLQ)	42	.92	.91	
Antisocial Behavior (DLQ1)	15	.83	.88	I sometimes skip school.
Dyscontrol (DLQ2)	16	.84	.88	I lose friends because of my temper.
Noncompliance (DLQ3)	11	.83	.80	Punishment does not change how I act.
FAMILY DYSFUNCTION (FAM)	29	.87	.83	
Parent-Child Conflict (FAM1)	9	.82	.73	My parent(s) are too strict with me.
Parent Maladjustment (FAM2)	13	.74	.76	My parents often argue.
Marital Discord (FAM3)	7	.70	.73	My parents' marriage has been solid and happy.
REALITY DISTORTION (RLT)	22	.83	.84	
Feelings of Alienation (RLT1)	11	.77	.74	I do strange or unusual things.
Hallucinations and Delusions (RLT2)	11	.71	.78	People secretly control my thoughts.
SOMATIC CONCERN (SOM)	27	.85	.76	
Psychosomatic Syndrome (SOM1)	9	.73	.63	I often get very tired.
Muscular Tension and Anxiety (SOM2)	10	.74	.72	At times I have trouble breathing.
Preoccupation with Disease (SOM3)	8	.60	.59	I often talk about sickness.
PSYCHOLOGICAL DISCOMFORT (DIS)	32	.86	.77	
Fear and Worry (DIS1)	15	.78	.75	Small problems do not bother me.
Depression (DIS2)	11	.73	.69	I am often in a good mood.
Sleep Disturbance (DIS3)	6	.70	.71	I often think about death.
SOCIAL WITHDRAWAL (WDL)	18	.80	.82	
Social Introversion (WDL1)	10	.78	.77	Talking to others makes me nervous.
Isolation (WDL2)	8	.59	.77	I almost always play alone.
SOCIAL SKILL DEFICITS (SSK)	24	.86	.79	
Limited Peer Status (SSK1)	13	.79	.76	Other kids look up to me as a leader.
SSK2: Conflict with Peers (SSK2)	11	.80	.72	I wish that I were more able to make and keep friends.

Note: Scale and subscale alpha (α) values based on a clinical sample $n = 1,178$. One-week clinical retest correlation (r_{tt}) sample $n = 86$.

Selected material from the PIY copyright © 1995 by Western Psychological Services. Reprinted by permission of the publisher, Western Psychological Services, 12031 Wilshire Boulevard, Los Angeles, California, 90025, U.S.A., www.wpspublish.com. Not to be reprinted in whole or in part for any additional purpose without the expressed, written permission of the publisher. All rights reserved.

comparable level of reading ability, or when younger students have limited ability to attend and concentrate, an audiotape recording of the PIY items is available and can be completed in less than 1 hr. Scale raw scores are converted to *T* scores using contemporary gender-specific norms from students in Grades 4 through 12, representing ages 9 through 19 (Lachar & Gruber, 1995).

Student Behavior Survey

This teacher rating form was developed through reviewing established teacher rating scales and by writing new statements that focused on content appropriate to teacher observation (Lachar, Wingenfeld, Kline, & Gruber, 2000). Unlike ratings that can be scored on parent or teacher norms (Naglieri, LeBuffe, & Pfeiffer, 1994), the Student Behavior Survey (SBS) items demonstrate a specific school focus. Fifty-eight of its 102 items specifically refer to in-class or in-school behaviors and judgments that can be rated only by school staff (Wingenfeld, Lachar, Gruber, & Kline, 1998). SBS items provide a profile of 14 scales that assess student academic status and work habits, social skills, parental participation in the educational process, and problems such as aggressive or atypical behavior and emotional stress (see Table 11.3). Norms that generate linear *T* scores are gender specific and derived from two age groups: 5 to 11 and 12 to 18 years.

SBS items are presented on one two-sided form. The rating process takes 15 min or less. Scoring of scales and completion of a profile are straightforward clerical processes that

take only a couple of minutes. The SBS consists of two major sections. The first section, Academic Resources, includes four scales that address positive aspects of school adjustment, whereas the second section, Adjustment Problems, generates seven scales that measure various dimensions of problematic adjustment. Unlike the PIC-2 and PIY statements, which are completed with a True or False response, SBS items are mainly rated on a 4-point frequency scale. Three additional disruptive behavior scales each consist of 16 items nominated as representing phenomena consistent with the characteristics associated with one of three major *Diagnostic and Statistical Manual, Fourth Edition (DSM-IV)* disruptive disorder diagnoses: ADHD, combined type; ODD; and CD (Pisecco et al., 1999).

Multidimensional Assessment

This author continues to champion the application of objective multidimensional questionnaires (Lachar, 1993, 1998) because there is no reasonable alternative to their use for baseline evaluation of children seen in mental health settings. Such questionnaires employ consistent stimulus and response demands, measure a variety of useful dimensions, and generate a profile of scores standardized using the same normative reference. The clinician may therefore reasonably assume that differences obtained among dimensions reflect variation in content rather than some difference in technical or stylistic characteristic between independently constructed unidimensional measures (e.g., true-false vs. multiple-choice format, application of regional vs. national norms, or statement sets

TABLE 11.3   SBS Scales, Their Psychometric Characteristics, and Sample Items

Scale Name (abbreviation)	Items	α	r_{tt}	$r_{1,2}$	Example of Scale Item
Academic Performance (AP)	8	.89	.78	.84	Reading Comprehension
Academic Habits (AH)	13	.93	.87	.76	Completes class assignments
Social Skills (SS)	8	.89	.88	.73	Participates in class activities
Parent Participation (PP)	6	.88	.83	.68	Parent(s) encourage achievement
Health Concerns (HC)	6	.85	.79	.58	Complains of headaches
Emotional Distress (ED)	15	.91	.90	.73	Worries about little things
Unusual Behavior (UB)	7	.88	.76	.62	Says strange or bizarre things
Social Problems (SP)	12	.87	.90	.72	Teased by other students
Verbal Aggression (VA)	7	.92	.88	.79	Argues and wants the last word
Physical Aggression (PA)	5	.90	.86	.63	Destroys property when angry
Behavior Problems (BP)	15	.93	.92	.82	Disobeys class or school rules
Attention-Deficit/Hyperactivity (ADH)	16	.94	.91	.83	Waits for his/her turn
Oppositional Defiant (OPD)	16	.95	.94	.86	Mood changes without reason
Conduct Problems (CNP)	16	.94	.90	.69	Steals from others

Note: Scale alpha (α) values based on a referred sample *n* = 1,315. Retest correlation (r_{tt}) 5- to 11-year-old student sample (*n* = 52) with average rating interval of 1.7 weeks. Interrater agreement ($r_{1,2}$), sample *n* = 60 fourth- and fifth-grade, team-taught or special-education students.

Selected material from the SBS copyright © 2000 by Western Psychological Services. Reprinted by permission of the publisher, Western Psychological Services, 12031 Wilshire Boulevard, Los Angeles, California, 90025, U.S.A., www.wpspublish.com. Not to be reprinted in whole or in part for any additional purpose without the expressed, written permission of the publisher. All rights reserved.

that require different minimum reading requirements). In addition, it is more likely that interpretive materials will be provided in an integrated fashion and the clinician need not select or accumulate information from a variety of sources for each profile dimension.

Selection of a multidimensional instrument that documents problem presence *and* absence demonstrates that the clinician is sensitive to the challenges inherent in the referral process and the likelihood of comorbid conditions, as previously discussed. This action also demonstrates that the clinician understands that the accurate assessment of a variety of child and family characteristics that are independent of diagnosis may yet be relevant to treatment design and implementation. For example, the PIY *FAM1* subscale (Parent-Child Conflict) may be applied to determine whether a child's parents should be considered a treatment resource or a source of current conflict. Similarly, the PIC-2 and PIY *WDL1* subscale (Social Introversion) may be applied to predict whether an adolescent will easily develop rapport with his or her therapist, or whether this process will be the first therapeutic objective.

Multisource Assessment

The collection of standardized observations from different informants is quite natural in the evaluation of children and adolescents. Application of such an approach has inherent strengths, yet presents the clinician with several challenges. Considering parents or other guardians, teachers or school counselors, and the students themselves as three distinct classes of informant, each brings unique strengths to the assessment process. Significant adults in a child's life are in a unique position to report on behaviors that they—not the child—find problematic. On the other hand, youth are in a unique position to report on their thoughts and feelings. Adult ratings on these dimensions must of necessity reflect, or be inferred from, child language and behavior. Parents are in a unique position to describe a child's development and history as well as observations that are unique to the home. Teachers observe students in an environment that allows for direct comparisons with same-age classmates as well as a focus on cognitive and behavioral characteristics prerequisite for success in the classroom and the acquisition of knowledge. Collection of independent parent and teacher ratings also contributes to comprehensive assessment by determining classes of behaviors that are unique to a given setting or that generalize across settings (Mash & Terdal, 1997).

Studies suggest that parents and teachers may be the most attuned to a child's behaviors that they find to be disruptive (cf. Loeber & Schmaling, 1985), but may underreport the presence

of internalizing disorders (Cantwell, 1996). Symptoms and behaviors that reflect the presence of depression may be more frequently endorsed in questionnaire responses and in standardized interviews by children than by their mothers (cf. Barrett et al., 1991; Moretti, Fine, Haley, & Marriage, 1985). In normative studies, mothers endorse more problems than their spouses or the child's teacher (cf. Abidin, 1995; Duhig, Renk, Epstein, & Phares, 2000; Goyette, Conners, & Ulrich, 1978). Perhaps measured parent agreement reflects the amount of time that a father spends with his child (Fitzgerald, Zucker, Maguin, & Reider, 1994). Teacher ratings have (Burns, Walsh, Owen, & Snell, 1997), and have not, separated ADHD subgroups (Crystal, Ostrander, Chen, & August, 2001). Perhaps this inconsistency demonstrates the complexity of drawing generalizations from one or even a series of studies. The ultimate evaluation of this diagnostic process must consider the dimension assessed, the observer or informant, the specific measure applied, the patient studied, and the setting of the evaluation.

An influential meta-analysis by Achenbach, McConaughy, and Howell (1987) demonstrated that poor agreement has been historically obtained on questionnaires or rating scales among parents, teachers, and students, although relatively greater agreement among sources was obtained for descriptions of externalizing behaviors. One source of informant disagreement between comparably labeled questionnaire dimensions may be revealed by the direct comparison of scale content. Scales similarly named may not incorporate the same content, whereas scales with different titles may correlate because of parallel content. The application of standardized interviews often resolves this issue when the questions asked and the criteria for evaluating responses obtained are consistent across informants. When standardized interviews are independently conducted with parents and with children, more agreement is obtained for visible behaviors and when the interviewed children are older (Lachar & Gruber, 1993).

Informant agreement and the investigation of comparative utility of classes of informants continue to be a focus of considerable effort (cf. Youngstrom, Loeber, & Stouthamer-Loeber, 2000). The opinions of mental health professionals and parents as to the relative merits of these sources of information have been surveyed (Loeber, Green, & Lahey, 1990; Phares, 1997). Indeed, even parents and their adolescent children have been asked to suggest the reasons for their disagreements. One identified causative factor was the deliberate concealment of specific behaviors by youth from their parents (Bidaut-Russell et al., 1995). Considering that youth seldom refer themselves for mental health services, routine assessment of their motivation to provide full disclosure would seem prudent.

The parent-completed Child Behavior Checklist (CBCL; Achenbach, 1991a) and student-completed Youth Self-Report (YSR; Achenbach, 1991b), as symptom checklists with parallel content and derived dimensions, have facilitated the direct comparison of these two sources of diagnostic information. The study by Handwerk, Larzelere, Soper, and Friman (1999) is at least the twenty-first such published comparison, joining 10 other studies of samples of children referred for evaluation or treatment. These studies of referred youth have consistently demonstrated that the CBCL provides more evidence of student maladjustment than does the YSR. In contrast, 9 of the 10 comparable studies of nonreferred children (classroom-based or epidemiological surveys) demonstrated the opposite relationship: The YSR documented more problems in adjustment than did the CBCL. One possible explanation for these findings is that children referred for evaluation often demonstrate a defensive response set, whereas nonreferred children do not (Lachar, 1998).

Because the YSR does not incorporate response validity scales, a recent study of the effect of defensiveness on YSR profiles of inpatients applied the PIY Defensiveness scale to assign YSR profiles to defensive and nondefensive groups (see Wrobel et al., 1999, for studies of this scale). The substantial influence of measured defensiveness was demonstrated for five of eight narrow-band and all three summary measures of the YSR. For example, only 10% of defensive YSR protocols obtained an elevated ($> 63T$) Total Problems score, whereas 45% of nondefensive YSR protocols obtained a similarly elevated Total Problems score (Lachar, Morgan, Espadas, & Schomer, 2000). The magnitude of this difference was comparable to the YSR versus CBCL discrepancy obtained by Handwerk et al. (1999; i.e., 28% of YSR vs. 74% of CBCL Total Problems scores were comparably elevated). On the other hand, youth may reveal specific problems on a questionnaire that they denied during a clinical or structured interview.

Clinical Issues in Application

Priority of Informant Selection

When different informants are available, who should participate in the assessment process, and what priority should be assigned to each potential informant? It makes a great deal of sense first to call upon the person who expresses initial or primary concern regarding child adjustment, whether this be a guardian, a teacher, or the student. This person will be the most eager to participate in the systematic quantification of problem behaviors and other symptoms of poor adjustment. The nature of the problems and the unique dimensions assessed by certain informant-specific scales may also influence

the selection process. If the teacher has not referred the child, report of classroom adjustment should also be obtained when the presence of disruptive behavior is of concern, or when academic achievement is one focus of assessment. In these cases, such information may document the degree to which problematic behavior is situation specific and the degree to which academic problems either accompany other problems or may result from inadequate motivation. When an intervention is to be planned, all proposed participants should be involved in the assessment process.

Disagreements Among Informants

Even estimates of considerable informant agreement derived from study samples are not easily applied as the clinician processes the results of one evaluation at a time. Although the clinician may be reassured when all sources of information converge and are consistent in the conclusions drawn, resolving inconsistencies among informants often provides information that is important to the diagnostic process or to treatment planning. Certain behaviors may be situation specific or certain informants may provide inaccurate descriptions that have been compromised by denial, exaggeration, or some other inadequate response. Disagreements among family members can be especially important in the planning and conduct of treatment. Parents may not agree about the presence or the nature of the problems that affect their child, and a youth may be unaware of the effect that his or her behavior has on others or may be unwilling to admit to having problems. In such cases, early therapeutic efforts must focus on such discrepancies in order to facilitate progress.

Multidimensional Versus Focused Assessment

Adjustment questionnaires vary in format from those that focus on the elements of one symptom dimension or diagnosis (i.e. depression, ADHD) to more comprehensive questionnaires. The most articulated of these instruments rate current and past phenomena to measure a broad variety of symptoms and behaviors, such as externalizing symptoms or disruptive behaviors, internalizing symptoms of depression and anxiety, and dimensions of social and peer adjustment. These questionnaires may also provide estimates of cognitive, academic, and adaptive adjustment as well as dimensions of family function that may be associated with problems in child adjustment and treatment efficacy. Considering the unique challenges characteristic of evaluation in mental health settings discussed earlier, it is thoroughly justified that every intake or baseline assessment should employ a multidimensional instrument.

Questionnaires selected to support the planning and monitoring of interventions and to assess treatment effectiveness must take into account a different set of considerations. Response to scale content must be able to represent behavioral change, and scale format should facilitate application to the individual and summary to groups of comparable children similarly treated. Completion of such a scale should represent an effort that allows repeated administration, and the scale selected must measure the specific behaviors and symptoms that are the focus of treatment. Treatment of a child with a single focal problem may require the assessment of only this one dimension. In such cases, a brief depression or articulated ADHD questionnaire may be appropriate. If applied within a specialty clinic, similar cases can be accumulated and summarized with the same measure. Application of such scales to the typical child treated by mental health professionals is unlikely to capture all dimensions relevant to treatment.

SELECTION OF PSYCHOLOGICAL TESTS

Evaluating Scale Performance

Consult Published Resources

Although clearly articulated guidelines have been offered (cf. Newman, Ciarlo, & Carpenter, 1999), selection of optimal objective measures for either a specific or a routine assessment application may not be an easy process. An expanded variety of choices has become available in recent years and the demonstration of their value is an ongoing effort. Manuals for published tests vary in the amount of detail that they provide. The reader cannot assume that test manuals provide comprehensive reviews of test performance, or even offer adequate guidelines for application. Because of the growing use of such questionnaires, guidance may be gained from graduate-level textbooks (cf. Kamphaus & Frick, 2002; Merrell, 1994) and from monographs designed to review a variety of specific measures (cf. Maruish, 1999). An introduction to more established measures, such as the Minnesota Multiphasic Personality Inventory (MMPI) adapted for adolescents (MMPI-A; Butcher et al., 1992), can be obtained by reference to chapters and books (e.g., Archer, 1992, 1999; Graham, 2000).

Estimate of Technical Performance: Reliability

Test performance is judged by the adequacy of demonstrated reliability and validity. It should be emphasized from the onset that reliability and validity are not characteristics that reside in a test, but describe a specific test application

(i.e., assessment of depression in hospitalized adolescents). A number of statistical techniques are applied in the evaluation of scales of adjustment that were first developed in the study of cognitive ability and academic achievement. The generalizability of these technical characteristics may be less than ideal in the evaluation of psychopathology because the underlying assumptions made may not be achieved.

The core of the concept of *reliability* is performance consistency; the classical model estimates the degree to which an obtained scale score represents the true phenomenon, rather than some source of error (Gliner, Morgan, & Harmon, 2001). At the item level, reliability measures internal consistency of a scale—that is, the degree to which scale item responses agree. Because the calculation of internal consistency requires only one set of responses from any sample, this estimate is easily obtained. Unlike an achievement subscale in which all items correlate with each other because they are supposed to represent a homogenous dimension, the internal consistency of adjustment measures will vary by the method used to assign items to scales. Scales developed by the identification of items that meet a nontest standard (*external* approach) will demonstrate less internal consistency than will scales developed in a manner that takes the content or the relation between items into account (*inductive* or *deductive* approach; Burisch, 1984). An example is provided by comparison of the two major sets of scales for the MMPI-A (Butcher et al., 1992). Of the 10 profile scales constructed by empirical keying, 6 obtained estimates of internal consistency below 0.70 in a sample of referred adolescent boys. In a second set of 15 scales constructed with primary concern for manifest content, only one scale obtained an estimate below 0.70 using the same sample. Internal consistency may also vary with the homogeneity of the adjustment dimension being measured, the items assigned to the dimension, and the scale length or range of scores studied, including the influence of multiple scoring formats.

Scale reliability is usually estimated by comparison of repeated administrations. It is important to demonstrate stability of scales if they will be applied in the study of an intervention. Most investigators use a brief interval (e.g., 7–14 days) between measure administrations. The assumption is made that no change will occur in such time. It has been our experience, however, with both the PIY and PIC-2 that small reductions are obtained on several scales at the retest, whereas the Defensiveness scale *T* score increases by a comparable degree on retest. In some clinical settings, such as an acute inpatient unit, it would be impossible to calculate test-retest reliability estimates in which an underlying change would not be expected. In such situations, *interrater comparisons,* when feasible, may be more appropriate. In this design it is assumed that each rater has had comparable experience with the youth to be rated and that any differences obtained would therefore represent a source of error across raters. Two clinicians could easily participate in the conduct of the same interview and then independently complete a symptom rating (cf. Lachar et al., 2001). However, interrater comparisons of mothers to fathers, or of pairs of teachers, assume that each rater has had comparable experience with the youth—such an assumption is seldom met.

Estimate of Technical Performance: Validity

Of major importance is the demonstration of scale *validity* for a specific purpose. A valid scale measures what it was intended to measure (Morgan, Gliner, & Harmon, 2001). Validity may be demonstrated when a scale's performance is consistent with expectations (*construct* validity) or predicts external ratings or scores (*criterion* validity). The foundation for any scale is *content* validity, that is, the extent to which the scale represents the relevant content universe for each dimension. Test manuals should demonstrate that items belong on the scales on which they have been placed and that scales correlate with each other in an expected fashion. In addition, substantial correlations should be obtained between the scales on a given questionnaire and similar measures of demonstrated validity completed by the same and different raters. Valid scales of adjustment should separate meaningful groups (*discriminant* validity) and demonstrate an ability to assign cases into meaningful categories.

Examples of such demonstrations of scale validity are provided in the SBS, PIY, and PIC-2 manuals. When normative and clinically and educationally referred samples were compared on the 14 SBS scales, 10 obtained a difference that represented a large effect, whereas 3 obtained a medium effect. When the SBS items were correlated with the 11 primary academic resources and adjustment problems scales in a sample of 1,315 referred students, 99 of 102 items obtained a substantial and primary correlation with the scale on which it was placed. These 11 nonoverlapping scales formed three clearly interpretable factors that represented 71% of the common variance: externalization, internalization, and academic performance. The SBS scales were correlated with six clinical rating dimensions (n = 129), with the scales and subscales of the PIC-2 in referred (n = 521) and normative (n = 1,199) samples, and with the scales and subscales of the PIY in a referred (n = 182) sample. The SBS scales were also correlated with the four scales of the Conners' Teacher Ratings Scale, Short Form, in 226 learning disabled students and in 66 students nominated by their elementary school teachers as having most challenged their teaching skills over the previous school year. SBS scale

discriminant validity was also demonstrated by comparison of samples defined by the Conners' Hyperactivity Index. Similar comparisons were also conducted across student samples that had been classified as intellectually impaired (n = 69), emotionally impaired (n = 170), or learning disabled (n = 281; Lachar, Wingenfeld, et al., 2000).

Estimates of PIY validity were obtained through the correlations of PIY scales and subscales with MMPI clinical and content scales (n = 152). The scales of 79 PIY protocols completed during clinical evaluation were correlated with several other self-report scales and questionnaires: Social Support, Adolescent Hassles, State-Trait Anxiety, Reynolds Adolescent Depression, Sensation-Seeking scales, State-Trait Anger scales, and the scales of the Personal Experience Inventory. PIY scores were also correlated with adjective checklist items in 71 college freshmen and chart-derived symptom dimensions in 86 adolescents hospitalized for psychiatric evaluation and treatment (Lachar & Gruber, 1995).

When 2,306 normative and 1,551 referred PIC-2 protocols were compared, the differences on the nine adjustment scales represented a large effect for six scales and a moderate effect for the remaining scales. For the PIC-2 subscales, these differences represented at least a moderate effect for 19 of these 21 subscales. Comparable analysis for the PIC-2 Behavioral Summary demonstrated that these differences were similarly robust for all of its 12 dimensions. Factor analysis of the PIC-2 subscales resulted in five dimensions that accounted for 71% of the common variance: Externalizing Symptoms, Internalizing Symptoms, Cognitive Status, Social Adjustment, and Family Dysfunction. Comparable analysis of the eight narrow-band scales of the PIC-2 Behavioral Summary extracted two dimensions in both referred and standardization protocols: Externalizing and Internalizing. Criterion validity was demonstrated by correlations between PIC-2 values and six clinician rating dimensions (n = 888), the 14 scales of the teacher-rated SBS (n = 520), and the 24 subscales of the self-report PIY (n = 588). In addition, the PIC-2 manual provides evidence of discriminant validity by comparing PIC-2 values across 11 *DSM-IV* diagnosis-based groups (n = 754; Lachar & Gruber, 2001).

Interpretive Guidelines: The Actuarial Process

The effective application of a profile of standardized adjustment scale scores can be a daunting challenge for a clinician. The standardization of a measure of general cognitive ability or academic achievement provides the foundation for score interpretation. In such cases, a score's comparison to its standardization sample generates the IQ for the test of general cognitive ability and the grade equivalent for the test of

TABLE 11.4   Examples of PIC-2 Subscale External Correlates and Their Performance

Subscale	External Correlate (source)	r	Rule	Performance
COG1	Specific intellectual deficits (clinician)	.30	>69T	18%/47%
COG2	Poor mathematics (teacher)	.51	>59T	18%/56%
COG3	Vineland Communication (psychometric)	.60	>59T	32%/69%
ADH1	Teachers complain that I can't sit still (self)	.34	>59T	23%/47%
ADH2	Irresponsible behavior (clinician)	.44	>59T	26%/66%
DLQ1	Expelled/suspended from school (clinician)	.52	>59T	6%/48%
DLQ2	Poorly modulated anger (clinician)	.58	>59T	23%/80%
DLQ3	Disobeys class or school rules (teacher)	.49	>59T	27%/70%
FAM1	Conflict between parents/guardians (clinician)	.34	>59T	14%/43%
FAM2	Parent divorce/separation (clinician)	.52	>59T	24%/76%
RLT1	WRAT Arithmetic (psychometric)	.44	>59T	14%/61%
RLT2	Auditory hallucinations (clinician)	.31	>79T	4%/27%
SOM1	I often have stomachaches (self)	.24	>69T	26%/52%
SOM2	I have dizzy spells (self)	.27	>59T	24%/44%
DIS1	I am often afraid of little things (self)	.26	>69T	19%/39%
DIS2	Becomes upset for little or no reason (teacher)	.33	>59T	25%/56%
DIS3	Suicidal threats (clinician)	.39	>69T	8%/34%
WDL1	Shyness is my biggest problem (self)	.28	>69T	12%/60%
WDL2	Except for going to school, I often stay in the house for days at a time (self)	.31	>69T	21%/48%
SSK1	Avoids social interaction in class (teacher)	.31	>59T	19%/42%
SSK2	I am often rejected by other kids (self)	.36	>69T	17%/46%

Note: r = point biserial correlation between external dichotomous rating and PIC-2 T score; Rule = incorporate correlate content above this point; Performance = frequency of external correlate below and above rule; Dichotomy established as follows: Self-report (True-False), Clinician (Present-Absent), Teacher (average, superior/below average, deficient; never, seldom/sometimes, usually), Psychometric (standard score > 84/standard score < 85). Selected material from the PIC-2 copyright © 2001 by Western Psychological Services. Reprinted by permission of the publisher, Western Psychological Services, 12031 Wilshire Boulevard, Los Angeles, California, 90025, U.S.A., www.wpspublish.com. Not to be reprinted in whole or in part for any additional purpose without the expressed, written permission of the publisher. All rights reserved.

academic achievement. In contrast, the same standardization process that provides *T*-score values for the raw scores of scales of depression, withdrawal, or noncompliance does not similarly provide interpretive guidelines. Although this standardization process facilitates direct comparison of scores from scales that vary in length and rate of item endorsement, there is not an underlying theoretical distribution of, for example, depression to guide scale interpretation in the way that the normal distribution supports the interpretation of an IQ estimate. Standard scores for adjustment scales represent the likelihood of a raw score within a specific standardization sample. A depression scale *T* score of 70 can be interpreted with certainty as an infrequent event in the standardization sample. Although a specific score is infrequent, the prediction of significant clinical information, such as likely symptoms and behaviors, degree of associated disability, seriousness of distress, and the selection of a promising intervention cannot be derived from the standardization process that generates a standard score of 70*T*.

Comprehensive data that demonstrate criterion validity can also be analyzed to develop actuarial, or empirically based, scale interpretations. Such analyses first identify the fine detail of the correlations between a specific scale and

nonscale clinical information, and then determine the range of scale standard scores for which this detail is most descriptive. The content so identified can be integrated directly into narrative text or provide support for associated text (cf. Lachar & Gdowski, 1979). Table 11.4 provides an example of this analytic process for each of the 21 PIC-2 subscales. The PIC-2, PIY, and SBS manuals present actuarially based narrative interpretations for these inventory scales and the rules for their application.

Review for Clinical Utility

A clinician's careful consideration of the content of an assessment measure is an important exercise. As this author has previously discussed (Lachar, 1993), item content, statement and response format, and scale length facilitate or limit scale application. *Content validity* as a concept reflects the adequacy of the match between questionnaire elements and the phenomena to be assessed. It is quite reasonable for the potential user of a measure to first gain an appreciation of the specific manifestations of a designated delinquency or psychological discomfort dimension. Test manuals should facilitate this process by listing scale content and relevant item endorsement rates. Questionnaire content should be representative and include frequent and infrequent manifestations that reflect mild, moderate, and severe levels of maladjustment. A careful review of scales constructed solely by factor analysis will identify manifest item content that is inconsistent with expectation; review across scales may identify unexpected scale overlap when items are assigned to more than one dimension. Important dimensions of instrument utility associated with content are instrument readability and the ease of scale administration, completion, scoring, and interpretation.

It is useful to identify the typical raw scores for normative and clinical evaluations and to explore the amount and variety of content represented by scores that are indicative of significant problems. It will then be useful to determine the shift in content when such raw scores representing significant maladjustment are reduced to the equivalents of standard scores within the normal range. Questionnaire application can be problematic when its scales are especially brief, are composed of statements that are rarely endorsed in clinical populations, or apply response formats that distort the true raw-score distribution. Many of these issues can be examined by looking at a typical profile form. For example, CBCL standard scores of $50T$ often represent raw scores of only 0 or 1. When clinically elevated baseline CBCL scale values are reduced to values within normal limits upon retest, treatment effectiveness and the absence of problems would appear to have been demonstrated. Actually, the shift from baseline to posttreatment assessment may represent the process in which as few as three items that were first rated as a 2 (*very true* or *often true*) at baseline remain endorsed, but are rated as a 1 (*somewhat* or *sometimes true*) on retest (cf. Lachar, 1993).

SELECTED ADJUSTMENT MEASURES FOR YOUTH ASSESSMENT

An ever-increasing number of assessment instruments may be applied in the assessment of youth adjustment. This chapter concludes by providing a survey of some of these instruments. Because of the importance of considering different informants, all four families of parent-, teacher-, and self-report measures are described in some detail. In addition, several multidimensional, single-informant measures, both the well established and the recently published, are described. Each entry has been included to demonstrate the variety of measures that are available. Although each of these objective questionnaires is available from a commercial test publisher, no other specific inclusion or exclusion criteria have been applied. This section concludes with an even more selective description of a few of the many published measures that

restrict their assessment of adjustment or may be specifically useful to supplement an otherwise broadly based evaluation of the child. Such measures may contribute to the assessment of youth seen in a specialty clinic, or support treatment planning or outcome assessment. Again, the selection of these measures did not systematically apply inclusion or exclusion criteria.

Other Families of Multidimensional, Multisource Measures

Considering their potential contribution to the assessment process, a clinician would benefit from gaining sufficient familiarity with at least one parent-report questionnaire, one teacher rating form, and one self-report inventory. Four integrated families of these measures have been developed over the past decade. Some efficiency is gained from becoming familiar with one of these sets of measures rather than selecting three independent measures. Manuals describe the relations between measures and provide case studies that apply two or all three measures. Competence in each class of measures is also useful because it provides an additional degree of flexibility for the clinician. The conduct of a complete multi-informant assessment may not be feasible at times (e.g., teachers may not be available during summer vacation), or may prove difficult for a particular mental health service (e.g., the youth may be under the custody of an agency, or a hospital may distance the clinician from parent informants). In addition, the use of self-report measures may be systematically restricted by child age or some specific cognitive or motivational characteristics that could compromise the collection of competent questionnaire responses. Because of such difficulties, it is also useful to consider the relationship between the individual components of these questionnaire families. Some measures are complementary and focus on informant-specific content, whereas others make a specific effort to apply duplicate content and therefore represent parallel forms. One of these measure families, consisting of the PIC-2, the PIY, and the SBS, has already been described in some detail. The PIC-2, PIY, and SBS are independent comprehensive measures that both emphasize informant-appropriate and informant-specific observations and provide the opportunity to compare similar dimensions across informants.

Behavior Assessment System for Children

The Behavior Assessment System for Children (BASC) family of multidimensional scales includes the Parent Ratings Scales (PRS), Teacher Rating Scales (TRS), and Self-Report of Personality (SRP), which are conveniently described in one integrated manual (Reynolds & Kamphaus, 1992). BASC ratings are marked directly on self-scoring pamphlets or on one-page forms that allow the recording of responses for subsequent computer entry. Each of these forms is relatively brief (126–186 items) and can be completed in 10 to 30 min. The PRS and TRS items in the form of mainly short, descriptive phrases are rated on a 4-point frequency scale (*never, sometimes, often,* and *almost always*), while SRP items in the form of short, declarative statements are rated as either True or False. Final BASC items were assigned through multistage iterative item analyses to only one narrow-band scale measuring clinical dimensions or adaptive behaviors; these scales are combined to form composites. The PRS and TRS forms cover ages 6 to 18 years and emphasize across-informant similarities; the SRP is provided for ages 8 to 18 years and has been designed to complement parent and teacher reports as a measure focused on mild to moderate emotional problems and clinically relevant self-perceptions, rather than overt behaviors and externalizing problems.

The PRS composites and component scales are Internalizing Problems (Anxiety, Depression, Somatization), Externalizing Problems (Hyperactivity, Aggression, and Conduct Problems), and Adaptive Skills (Adaptability, Social Skills, Leadership). Additional profile scales include Atypicality, Withdrawal, and Attention Problems. The TRS Internalizing and Externalizing Problems composites and their component scales parallel the PRS structure. The TRS presents 22 items that are unique to the classroom by including a Study Skills scale in the Adaptive Skills composite and a Learning Problems scale in the School Problems composite. The BASC manual suggests that clinical scale elevations are potentially significant over 59*T* and that adaptive scores gain importance under 40*T*. The SRP does not incorporate externalization dimensions and therefore cannot be considered a fully independent measure. The SRP composites and their component scales are School Maladjustment (Attitude to School, Attitude to Teachers, Sensation Seeking), Clinical Maladjustment (Atypicality, Locus of Control, Social Stress, Anxiety, Somatization), and Personal Adjustment (Relations with Parents, Interpersonal Relations, Self-Esteem, Self-Reliance). Two additional scales, Depression and Sense of Inadequacy, are not incorporated into a composite. The SRP includes three validity response scales, although their psychometric characteristics are not presented in the manual.

Conners' Rating Scales–Revised

The Conners' parent and teacher scales were first used in the 1960s in the study of pharmacological treatment of disruptive behaviors. The current published Conners' Rating

Scales-Revised (CRS-R; Conners, 1997) require selection of one of four response alternatives to brief phrases (parent, teacher) or short sentences (adolescent): 0 = *Not True at All* (*Never, Seldom*), 1 = *Just a Little True* (*Occasionally*), 2 = *Pretty Much True* (*Often, Quite a Bit*), and 3 = *Very Much True* (*Very Often, Very Frequent*). These revised scales continue their original focus on disruptive behaviors (especially ADHD) and strengthen their assessment of related or comorbid disorders. The Conners' Parent Rating Scale–Revised (CPRS-R) derives from 80 items seven factor-derived nonoverlapping scales apparently generated from the ratings of the regular-education students (i.e., the normative sample): Oppositional, Cognitive Problems, Hyperactivity, Anxious-Shy, Perfectionism, Social Problems, and Psychosomatic. A review of the considerable literature generated using the original CPRS did not demonstrate its ability to discriminate among psychiatric populations, although it was able to separate psychiatric patients from normal youth. Gianarris, Golden, and Greene (2001) concluded that the literature had identified three primary uses for the CPRS: as a general screen for psychopathology, as an ancillary diagnostic aid, and as a general treatment outcome measure. Perhaps future reviews of the CPRS-R will demonstrate additional discriminant validity.

The Conners' Teacher Rating Scale–Revised (CTRS-R) consists of only 59 items and generates shorter versions of all CPRS-R scales (Psychosomatic is excluded). Because Conners emphasizes teacher observation in assessment, the lack of equivalence in scale length and (in some instances) item content for the CPRS-R and CTRS-R make the interpretation of parent-teacher inconsistencies difficult. For parent and teacher ratings the normative sample ranges from 3 to 17 years, whereas the self-report scale is normed for ages 12 to 17. The CRS-R provides standard linear *T* scores for raw scores that are derived from contiguous 3-year segments of the normative sample. This particular norm conversion format contributes unnecessary complexity to the interpretation of repeated scales because several of these scales demonstrate a large age effect. For example, a 14-year-old boy who obtains a raw score of 6 on CPRS-R Social Problems obtains a standard score of 68*T*—if this lad turns 15 the following week the same raw score now represents 74*T*, an increase of more than half of a standard deviation. Conners (1999) also describes a serious administration artifact, in that the parent and teacher scores typically drop on their second administration. Pretreatment baseline therefore should always consist of a second administration to avoid this artifact. *T* values of at least 60 are suggestive, and values of at least 65*T* are indicative of a clinically significant problem. General guidance provided as to scale application is quite limited: "Each factor can be interpreted according to the predominant conceptual unity implied by the item content" (Connors, 1999, p. 475).

The Conners-Wells' Adolescent Self-Report Scale consists of 87 items, written at a sixth-grade reading level, that generate six nonoverlapping factor-derived scales, each consisting of 8 or 12 items (Anger Control Problems, Hyperactivity, Family Problems, Emotional Problems, Conduct Problems, Cognitive Problems). Shorter versions and several indices have been derived from these three questionnaires. These additional forms contribute to the focused evaluation of ADHD treatment and would merit separate listing under the later section "Selected Focused (Narrow) or Ancillary Objective Measures." Although Conners (1999) discussed in some detail the influence that response sets and other inadequate responses may have on these scales, no guidance or psychometric measures are provided to support this effort.

Child Behavior Checklist; Teacher's Report Form; Youth Self-Report

The popularity of the CBCL and related instruments in research application since the CBCL's initial publication in 1983 has influenced thousands of research projects; the magnitude of this research application has had a significant influence on the study of child and adolescent psychopathology. The 1991 revision, documented in five monographs totaling more than 1,000 pages, emphasizes consistencies in scale dimensions and scale content across child age (4–18 years for the CBCL/4–18), gender, and respondent or setting (Achenbach, 1991a, 1991b, 1991c, 1991d, 1993). A series of within-instrument item analyses was conducted using substantial samples of protocols for each form obtained from clinical and special-education settings. The major component of parent, teacher, and self-report forms is a common set of 89 behavior problems described in one to eight words ("Overtired," "Argues a lot," "Feels others are out to get him/her"). Items are rated as 0 = Not True, 1 = Somewhat or Sometimes True, or 2 = Very True or Often True, although several items require individual elaboration when these items are positively endorsed. These 89 items generate eight narrow-band and three composite scale scores similarly labeled for each informant, although some item content varies. Composite Internalizing Problems consists of Withdrawn, Somatic Complaints, and Anxious/Depressed and composite Externalizing Problems consists of Delinquent Behavior and Aggressive Behavior; Social Problems, Thought Problems, and Attention Problems contribute to a summary Total scale along with the other five narrow-band scales.

The 1991 forms provide standard scores based on national samples. Although the CBCL and the Youth Self-Report (YSR) are routinely self-administered in clinical application, the CBCL normative data and some undefined proportion of the YSR norms were obtained through interview of the informants. This process may have inhibited affirmative response to checklist items. For example, six of eight parent informant scales obtained average normative raw scores of less than 2, with restricted scale score variance. It is important to note that increased problem behavior scale elevation reflects increased problems, although these scales do not consistently extend below 50T. Because of the idiosyncratic manner in which T scores are assigned to scale raw scores, it is difficult to determine the interpretive meaning of checklist T scores, the derivation of which has been of concern (Kamphaus & Frick, 1996; Lachar, 1993, 1998). The gender-specific CBCL norms are provided for two age ranges (4–11 and 12–18). The Teacher's Report Form (TRF) norms are also gender-specific and provided for two age ranges (5–11 and 12–18). The YSR norms are gender-specific and incorporate the entire age range of 11 to 18 years, and require a fifth-grade reading ability. Narrow-band scores 67 to 70T are designated as borderline; values above 70T represent the clinical range. Composite scores of 60 to 63T are designated as borderline, whereas values above 63T represent the clinical range.

The other main component of these forms measures adaptive competence using a less structured approach. The CBCL competence items are organized by manifest content into three narrow scales (Activities, Social, and School), which are then summed into a total score. Parents are asked to list and then rate (frequency, performance level) child participation in sports, hobbies, organizations, and chores. Parents also describe the child's friendships, social interactions, performance in academic subjects, need for special assistance in school, and history of retention in grade. As standard scores for these scales increase with demonstrated ability, a borderline range is suggested at 30 to 33T and the clinical range is designated as less than 30T. Youth ethnicity and social and economic opportunities may effect CBCL competence scale values (Drotar, Stein, & Perrin, 1995). Some evidence for validity, however, has been provided in their comparison to the PIC in ability to predict adaptive level as defined by the Vineland Adaptive Behavior Scales (Pearson & Lachar, 1994).

In comparison to the CBCL, the TRF measures of competence are derived from very limited data: an average rating of academic performance based on as many as six academic subjects identified by the teacher, individual 7-point ratings on four topics (how hard working, behaving appropriately, amount learning, and how happy), and a summary score derived from these four items. The TRF designates a borderline interpretive range for the mean academic performance and the summary score of 37 to 40*T*, with the clinical range less than 37*T*. The TRF avoids the measurement of a range of meaningful classroom observations to maintain structural equivalence with the CBCL. The YSR provides seven adaptive competency items scored for Activities, Social, and a Total Competence scale. Reference to the YSR manual is necessary to score these multipart items, which tap competence and levels of involvement in sports, activities, organizations, jobs, and chores. Items also provide self-report of academic achievement, interpersonal adjustment, and level of socialization. Scales Activities and Social are classified as borderline at 30 to 33*T* with the clinical range less than 30*T*. The YSR Total Competence scale is classified as borderline at 37 to 40*T* with the clinical range at less than 37*T*. The strengths and weaknesses of these forms have been presented in some detail elsewhere (Lachar, 1998). The CBCL, TRF, and YSR provide quickly administered and easily scored parallel problem-behavior measures that facilitate direct comparison. The forms do not provide validity scales and the test manuals provide neither evidence of scale validity nor interpretive guidelines.

Selected Single-Source Multidimensional Measures

Minnesota Multiphasic Personality Inventory–Adolescent

The Minnesota Multiphasic Personality Inventory (MMPI) has been found to be useful in the evaluation of adolescents for more than 50 years (cf. Hathaway & Monachesi, 1953), although many questions have been raised as to the adequacy of this inventory's content, scales, and the application of adult norms (cf. Lachar, Klinge, & Grisell, 1976). In 1992 a fully revised version of the MMPI custom designed for adolescents, the MMPI-A, was published (Butcher et al., 1992). Although the traditional empirically constructed validity and profile scales have been retained, scale item content has been somewhat modified to reflect contemporary and developmentally appropriate content (for example, the *F* scale was modified to meet statistical inclusion criteria for adolescents). In addition, a series of 15 content scales have been constructed that take advantage of new items that reflect peer interaction, school adjustment, and common adolescent concerns: Anxiety, Obsessiveness, Depression, Health Concerns, Alienation, Bizarre Mentation, Anger, Cynicism, Conduct Problems, Low Self-Esteem, Low Aspirations, Social Discomfort, Family Problems, School Problems, and Negative Treatment Indicators (Williams, Butcher, Ben-Porath, & Graham, 1992).

The MMPI-A normative sample for this 478-statement true-false questionnaire consists of 14 to 18-year-old students collected in eight U.S. states. Inventory items and directions are written at the sixth-grade level. The MMPI-A has also incorporated a variety of test improvements associated with the revision of the MMPI for adults: the development of uniform *T* scores and validity measures of response inconsistency that are independent of specific dimensions of psychopathology. Substantive scales are interpreted as clinically significant at values above 65*T*, while scores of 60 to 65*T* may be suggestive of clinical concerns. Archer (1999) concluded that the MMPI-A continues to represent a challenge for many of the adolescents who are requested to complete it and requires extensive training and expertise to ensure accurate application. These opinions are voiced in a recent survey (Archer & Newsom, 2000).

Adolescent Psychopathology Scale

This 346-item inventory was designed to be a comprehensive assessment of the presence and severity of psychopathology in adolescents aged 12 to 19. The Adolescent Psychopathology Scale (APS; Reynolds, 1998) incorporates 25 scales modeled after Axis I and Axis II *DSM-IV* criteria. The APS is unique in the use of different response formats depending on the nature of the symptom or problem evaluated (e.g., True-False; *Never or almost never, Sometimes, Nearly all the time*) and across different time periods depending on the dimension assessed (e.g., past 2 weeks, past month, past 3 months, in general). One computer-generated profile presents 20 Clinical Disorder scales (such as Conduct Disorder, Major Depression), whereas a second profile presents 5 Personality Disorder scales (such as Borderline Personality Disorder), 11 Psychosocial Problem Content scales (such as Interpersonal Problem, Suicide), and four Response Style Indicators.

Linear *T* scores are derived from a mixed-gender representative standardization sample of seventh- to twelfth-grade students ($n = 1,827$), although gender-specific and age-specific score conversions can be selected. The 12-page administration booklet requires a third-grade reading level and is completed in 1 hr or less. APS scales obtained substantial estimates of internal consistency and test-retest reliability (median values in the .80s); mean scale score differences between APS administrations separated by a 14-day interval were small (median = 1.8*T*). The detailed organized manuals provide a sensible discussion of scale interpretation and preliminary evidence of scale validity. Additional study will be necessary to determine the relationship between scale *T*-score elevation and diagnosis and clinical description for this innovative measure. Reynolds (2000) also developed a 20-min, 115-item APS short form that generates 12 clinical scales and 2 validity scales. These shortened and combined versions of full-length scales were selected because they were judged to be the most useful in practice.

Beck Youth Inventories of Emotional and Social Impairment

Recently published and characterized by the ultimate of simplicity, the Beck Youth Inventories of Emotional and Social Impairment (BYI; Beck, Beck, & Jolly, 2001) consist of five separately printed 20-item scales that can be completed individually or in any combination. The child selects one of four frequency responses to statements written at the second-grade level: *Never, Sometimes, Often, Always*. Raw scores are converted to gender-specific linear *T*-scores for ages 7 to 10 and 11 to 14. The manual notes that 7-year-olds and students in second grade may need to have the scale items read to them. For scales Depression (BDI: "I feel sorry for myself"), Anxiety (BAI: "I worry about the future"), Anger (BANI: "People make me mad"), Disruptive Behavior (BDBI: "I break the rules"), and Self-Concept (BSCI: "I feel proud of the things I do"), the manual provides estimates of internal consistency (α = .86–.92, median = .895) and 1-week temporal stability (r_{tt} = .63–.89, median = .80). Three studies of scale validity are also described: Substantial correlations were obtained between each BYI scale and a parallel established scale (BDI and Children's Depression Inventory, r = .72; BAI and Revised Children's Manifest Anxiety Scale, r = .70; BSCI and Piers-Harris Children's Self-Concept Scale, r = .61; BDBI and Conners-Wells' Self-Report Conduct Problems, r = .69; BANI and Conners-Wells' Self-Report AD/HD Index, r = .73). Each BYI scale significantly separated matched samples of special-education and normative children, with the special-education sample obtaining higher ratings on Depression, Anxiety, Anger, and Disruptive Behavior and lower ratings on Self-Concept. In a comparable analysis with an outpatient sample, four of five scales obtained a significant difference from matched controls. A secondary analysis demonstrated that outpatients who obtained a diagnosis of a mood disorder rated themselves substantially lower on Self-Concept and substantially higher on Depression in comparison to other outpatients. Additional study will be necessary to establish BYI diagnostic utility and sensitivity to symptomatic change.

Comprehensive Behavior Rating Scale for Children

The Comprehensive Behavior Rating Scale for Children (CBRSC; Neeper, Lahey, & Frick, 1990) is a 70-item teacher rating scale that may be scored for nine scales that focus on learning problems and cognitive processing (Reading Problems, Cognitive Deficits, Sluggish Tempo), attention and hyperactivity (Inattention-Disorganization, Motor Hyperactivity, Daydreaming), conduct problems (Oppositional-Conduct Disorders), anxiety (Anxiety), and peer relations (Social Competence). Teachers select one of five frequency descriptors for each item in 10 to 15 min. Scales are profiled as linear *T* values based on a mixed-gender national sample of students between the ages of 6 and 14, although the manual provides age- and gender-specific conversions. Scale values above 65*T* are designated clinically significant.

Millon Adolescent Clinical Inventory

The Millon Adolescent Clinical Inventory (MACI; Millon, 1993), a 160-item true-false questionnaire, may be scored for 12 Personality Patterns, 8 Expressed Concerns, and 7 Clinical Syndromes dimensions, as well as three validity measures (modifying indices). Gender-specific raw score conversions, or Base Rate scores, are provided for age ranges 13 to 15 and 16 to 19 years. Scales were developed in multiple stages, with item composition reflecting theory, *DSM-IV* structure, and item-to-scale performance. The 27 substantive scales require 888 scored items and therefore demonstrate considerable item overlap, even within scale categories. For example, the most frequently placed item among the Personality Patterns scales is "I've never done anything for which I could have been arrested"—an awkward double-negative as a scored statement. The structures of these scales and the effect of this characteristic are basically unknown because scales, or classes of scales, were not submitted to factor analysis. Additional complexity is contributed by the weighting of items (3, 2, or 1) to reflect assigned theoretical or demonstrated empirical importance.

Given the additional complexity of validity adjustment processes, it is accurate to state that it is possible to hand-score the MACI, although any reasonable application requires computer processing. Base rate scores range from 1 to 115, with specific importance given to values 75 to 84 and above 84. These values are tied to "target prevalence rates" derived from clinical consensus and anchor points that are discussed in this manual without the use of clarifying examples. These scores are supposed to relate in some fashion to performance in clinical samples; no representative standardization sample of nonreferred youth was collected for analysis. Base rate scores are designed to identify the pattern of problems, not to demonstrate the presence of adjustment problems. Clearly the MACI should not be used for screening or in settings in which some referred youth may not subsequently demonstrate significant problems.

MACI scores demonstrate adequate internal consistency and temporal stability. Except for some minimal correlational evidence purported to support validity, no evidence of scale performance is provided, although dimensions of psychopathology and scale intent are discussed in detail. Manual readers reasonably expect test authors to demonstrate the wisdom of their psychometric decisions. No evidence is provided to establish the value of item weighting, the utility of correction procedures, or the unique contribution of scale dimensions. For example, a cursory review of the composition of the 12 Personality Patterns scales revealed that the majority of the 22 Forceful items also are also placed on the dimension labeled Unruly. These dimensions correlate .75 and may not represent unique dimensions. Analyses should demonstrate whether a 13-year-old's self-description is best represented by 27 independent (vs. nested) dimensions. A manual should facilitate the review of scale content by assigned value and demonstrate the prevalence of specific scale elevations and their interpretive meaning.

Selected Focused (Narrow) or Ancillary Objective Measures

Attention Deficit Hyperactivity

BASC Monitor for ADHD (Kamphaus & Reynolds, 1998). Parent (46-item) and teacher (47-item) forms were designed to evaluate the effectiveness of treatments used with ADHD. Both forms provide standard scores (ages 4–18) for Attention Problems, Hyperactivity, Internalizing Problems, and Adaptive Skills, and a listing of *DSM-IV* items.

Brown Attention-Deficit Disorder Scales for Children and Adolescents (BADDS; Brown, 2001). This series of brief parent-, teacher-, and self-report questionnaires evaluates dimensions of ADHD that reflect cognitive impairments and symptoms beyond current *DSM-IV* criteria. As many as six subscales may be calculated from each form: Activation ("Seems to have exceptional difficulty getting started on tasks or routines [e.g., getting dressed, picking up toys]"); Focus/Attention ("Is easily sidetracked; starts one task and then switches to a less important task"); Effort ("Do your parents or teachers tell you that you could do better by trying harder?"); Emotion/Affect ("Seems easily irritated or impatient in response to apparently minor frustrations"); Memory ("Learns something one day, but doesn't remember it the next day"); and Action ("When you're supposed to sit still and be quiet, is it really hard for you to do that?"). Three item formats and varying gender-specific age-normative references are provided: 44-item parent and teacher forms normed by gender for ages 3 to 5 and 6 to 7; 50-item parent, teacher, and

self-report forms normed by gender for ages 8 to 9 and 10 to 12; and a 40-item self-report form (also used to collect collateral responses) for ages 12 to 18. All forms generate an ADD Inattention Total score and the multiinformant questionnaires also provide an ADD Combined Total score.

The BADDS manual provides an informative discussion of ADHD and a variety of psychometric studies. Subscales and composites obtained from adult informants demonstrated excellent internal consistency and temporal stability, although estimates derived from self-report data were less robust. Children with ADHD obtained substantially higher scores when compared to controls. Robust correlations were obtained for BADDS dimensions both across informants (parent-teacher, parent-child, teacher-child) and between BADDS dimensions and other same-informant measures of ADHD (CBCL, TRF, BASC Parent and Teacher Monitors, CPRS-R Short Form, CTRS-R Short Form). This manual does not provide evidence that BADDS dimensions can separate different clinical groups and quantify treatment effects.

Internalizing Symptoms

Children's Depression Inventory (CDI; Kovacs, 1992). This focused self-report measure may be used in the early identification of symptoms and the monitoring of treatment effectiveness, as well as contributing to the diagnostic process. The CDI represents a unique format because children are required to select one statement from each of 27 statement triads to describe their past 2 weeks. The first option is scored a 0 (symptom absence), the second a 1 (mild symptom), and the third a 2 (definite symptom). It may therefore be more accurate to characterize the CDI as a task requiring the child to read 81 short statements presented at a third-grade reading level and make a selection from statement triplets. The Total score is the summary of five factor-derived subscales: Negative Mood, Interpersonal Problems, Ineffectiveness, Anhedonia, and Negative Self-esteem. An Inconsistency Index is provided to exclude protocols that may reflect inadequate attention to CDI statements or comprehension of the required task response. Also available is a 10-item short form that correlates .89 to the Total score. Regional norms generate a profile of gender- and age-specific (7–12/13–17 years) *T* scores, in which values in the 60s (especially those above 65*T*) in children referred for evaluation are clinically significant (Sitarenios & Kovacs, 1999). Although considerable emphasis has been placed on the accurate description of the CDI as a good indicator of self-reported distress and not a diagnostic instrument, the manual and considerable literature focus on classification based on a Total raw score cutoff (Fristad, Emery, & Beck, 1997).

Revised Children's Manifest Anxiety Scale (RCMAS; Reynolds & Richmond, 1985).   Response of *Yes-No* to 37 statements generate a focused Total Anxiety score that incorporates three subscales (Physiological Anxiety, Worry/Oversensitivity, Social Concerns/ Concentration); the other nine items provide a validity scale (Lie). Standard scores derived from a normative sample of approximately 5,000 protocols are gender and age specific (6–17+ years). Independent response to scale statements requires a third-grade reading level; each anxiety item obtained an endorsement rate between .30 and .70 and correlated at least .40 with the total score. Anxiety as a disorder is suggested with a total score that exceeds 69*T*; symptoms of anxiety are suggested by subscale elevations when Total Anxiety remains below 70*T* (Gerard & Reynolds, 1999).

Family Adjustment

Marital Satisfaction Inventory–Revised (MSI-R; Snyder, 1997).   When the marital relationship becomes a potential focus of treatment, it often becomes useful to define areas of conflict and the differences manifest by comparison of parent descriptions. The MSI-R includes 150 true-false items comprising two validity scales (Inconsistency, Conventionalization), one global scale (Global Distress), and 10 scales that assess specific areas of relationship stress (Affective Communication, Problem-Solving Communication, Aggression, Time Together, Disagreement About Finances, Sexual Dissatisfaction, Role Orientation, Family History of Distress, Dissatisfaction With Children, Conflict Over Child Rearing). Items are presented on a self-scoring form or by personal computer, and one profile facilitates direct comparison of paired sets of gender-specific normalized *T* scores that are subsequently applied in evaluation, treatment planning, and outcome assessment. Empirically established *T*-score ranges suggesting adjustment problems are designated on the profile (usually scores above 59*T*). The geographically diverse, representative standardization sample included more than 2,000 married adults. Because of substantial scale internal consistency (median $\alpha = .82$) and temporal stability (median 6-week $r_{tt} = .79$), a difference between spouse profiles or a shift on retest of as little as 6 *T*-points represents a meaningful and stable phenomenon. Evidence of scale discriminant and actuarial validity has been summarized in detail (Snyder & Aikman, 1999).

Parenting Stress Index (PSI), Third Edition (Abidin, 1995).   This unique 120-item questionnaire measures excessive stressors and stress within families of children aged 1 to 12 years. Description is obtained by parent selection from five

response options to statements often presented in the form of *strongly agree, agree, not sure, disagree, strongly agree*. A profile of percentiles from maternal response to the total mixed-gender normative sample includes a Child Domain score (subscales Distractibility/Hyperactivity, Adaptability, Reinforces Parent, Demandingness, Mood, Adaptability) and a Parent Domain score (subscales Competence, Isolation, Attachment, Health, Role Restriction, Depression, Spouse), which are combined into a Total Stress composite. Additional measures include a Life Stress scale of 19 *Yes-No* items and a Defensive Responding scale. Interpretive guidelines are provided for substantive dimensions at 1 standard deviation above and for Defensiveness values at 1 standard deviation below the mean. A 36-item short form provides three subscales: Parental Distress, Parent-Child Dysfunctional Interaction, and Difficult Child. These subscales are summed into a Total Stress score; a Defensiveness Responding scale is also scored.

CURRENT STATUS AND FUTURE DIRECTIONS

Multidimensional, multiinformant objective assessment makes a unique contribution to the assessment of youth adjustment. This chapter presents the argument that this form of assessment is especially responsive to the evaluation of the evolving child and compatible with the current way in which mental health services are provided to youth. The growing popularity of these instruments in clinical practice (cf. Archer & Newsom, 2000), however, has not stimulated comparable efforts in research that focuses on instrument application. Objective measures of youth adjustment would benefit from the development of a research culture that promotes the study and demonstration of measure validity. Current child clinical literature predominantly applies objective measures in the study of psychopathology and does not focus on the study of test performance as an important endeavor. The journals that routinely publish studies on test validity (e.g., *Psychological Assessment, Journal of Personality Assessment, Assessment*) seldom present articles that focus on instruments that measure child or adolescent adjustment. An exception to this observation is the MMPI-A, for which research efforts have been influenced by the substantial research culture of the MMPI and MMPI-2 (cf. Archer, 1997).

Considerable effort will be required to establish the construct and actuarial validity of popular child and adolescent adjustment measures. It is not sufficient to demonstrate that a distribution of scale scores separates regular-education students from those referred for mental health services to establish scale validity. Indeed, the absence of such evidence may not exclude a scale from consideration, because it is possible that the measurement of some normally distributed personality characteristic, such as social introversion, may contribute to the development of a more effective treatment plan. Once a child is referred for mental health services, application of a screening measure is seldom of value. The actuarial interpretive guidelines of the PIC-2, PIY, and SBS have established one standard of the significant scale score by identifying the minimum T-score elevation from which useful clinical information may be reliably predicted. Although other paradigms might establish such a minimum scale score standard as it predicts the likelihood of significant disability or caseness scale validity will be truly demonstrated only when a measure contributes to the accuracy of routine decision making that occurs in clinical practice. Such decisions include the successful solution of a representative differential diagnosis (cf. Forbes, 1985), or the selection of an optimal plan of treatment (cf. Voelker et al., 1983).

Similarly, traditional evidence of scale reliability is an inadequate standard of scale performance as applied to clinical situations in which a scale is sequentially administered over time. To be applied in the evaluation of treatment effectiveness, degree of scale score change must be found to accurately track some independent estimate of treatment effectiveness (cf. Sheldrick, Kendall, & Heimberg, 2001). Of relevance here will be the consideration of scale score range and the degree to which a ceiling or floor effect restricts scale performance.

Considering that questionnaire-derived information may be obtained from parents, teachers, and the child, it is not unusual that the study of agreement among informants continues to be of interest. In this regard, it will be more useful to determine the clinical implications of the results obtained from each informant rather than the magnitude of correlations that are so easily derived from samples of convenience (cf. Hulbert, Gdowski, & Lachar, 1986). Rather than attributing obtained differences solely to situation specificity, other explanations should be explored. For example, evidence suggests that considerable differences between informants may be attributed to the effects of response sets, such as respondent defensiveness. Perhaps the study of informant agreement has little value in increasing the contribution of objective assessment to clinical application. Rather, it may be more useful for research to apply paradigms that focus on the *incremental validity* of applications of objective assessment. Beginning with the information obtained from an intake interview, a parent-derived profile could be collected and its additional clinical value determined. In a similar fashion, one could evaluate the relative individual and combined contribution of parent and teacher description in making a meaningful

differential diagnosis, say, between ADHD and ODD. The feasibility of such psychometric research should increase as routine use of objective assessment facilitates the development of clinical databases at clinics and inpatient units.

REFERENCES

Abidin, R. R. (1995). *Parenting Stress Index, third edition, professional manual*. Odessa, FL: Psychological Assessment Resources.

Achenbach, T. M. (1991a). *Integrative guide for the 1991 CBCL/4-18, YSR, and TRF profiles*. Burlington: University of Vermont, Department of Psychiatry.

Achenbach, T. M. (1991b). *Manual for the Child Behavior Checklist/4-18 and 1991 Profile*. Burlington: University of Vermont, Department of Psychiatry.

Achenbach, T. M. (1991c). *Manual for the Teacher's Report Form and 1991 Profile*. Burlington: University of Vermont, Department of Psychiatry.

Achenbach, T. M. (1991d). *Manual for the Youth Self-Report and 1991 Profile*. Burlington: University of Vermont, Department of Psychiatry.

Achenbach, T. M. (1993) *Empirically based taxonomy: How to use syndromes and profile types derived from the CBCL/4-18, TRF, and YSR*. Burlington: University of Vermont, Department of Psychiatry.

Achenbach, T. M., McConaughy, S. H., & Howell, C. T. (1987). Child/adolescent behavioral and emotional problems: Implications of cross-informant correlations for situational specificity. *Psychological Bulletin, 101*, 213–232.

Ammerman, R. T., & Hersen, M. (1993). Developmental and longitudinal perspectives on behavior therapy. In R.T. Ammerman & M. Hersen (Eds.), *Handbook of behavior therapy with children and adults* (pp. 3–9). Boston: Allyn and Bacon.

Archer, R. P. (1992). *MMPI-A: Assessing adolescent psychopathology*. Hillsdale, NJ: Erlbaum.

Archer, R. P. (1997). Future directions for the MMPI-A: Research and clinical issues. *Journal of Personality Assessment, 68*, 95–109.

Archer, R. P. (1999). Overview of the Minnesota Multiphasic Personality Inventory–Adolescent (MMPI-A). In M. E. Maruish (Ed.), *The use of psychological testing for treatment planning and outcomes assessment* (2nd ed., pp. 341–380). Mahwah, NJ: Erlbaum.

Archer, R. P., Maruish, M., Imhof, E. A., & Piotrowski, C. (1991). Psychological test usage with adolescent clients: 1990 survey findings. *Professional Psychology: Research and Practice, 22*, 247–252.

Archer, R. P., & Newsom, C. R. (2000). Psychological test usage with adolescent clients: Survey update. *Assessment, 7*, 227–235.

Barrett, M. L., Berney, T. P., Bhate, S., Famuyiwa, O. O., Fundudis, T., Kolvin, I., & Tyrer, S. (1991). Diagnosing childhood depression. Who should be interviewed—parent or child? The Newcastle child depression project. *British Journal of Psychiatry, 159* (Suppl. 11)*, 22–27.*

Beck, J. S., Beck, A. T., & Jolly, J. B. (2001). *Beck Youth Inventories of Emotional and Social Impairment manual.* San Antonio, TX: The Psychological Corporation.

Bidaut-Russell, M., Reich, W., Cottler, L. B., Robins, L. N., Compton, W. M., & Mattison, R. E. (1995). The Diagnostic Interview Schedule for Children (PC-DISC v.3.0): Parents and adolescents suggest reasons for expecting discrepant answers. *Journal of Abnormal Child Psychology, 23,* 641–659.

Biederman, J., Newcorn, J., & Sprich, S. (1991). Comorbidity of attention deficit hyperactivity disorder with conduct, depressive, anxiety, and other disorders. *American Journal of Psychiatry, 148,* 564–577.

Brady, E. U., & Kendall, P. C. (1992). Comorbidity of anxiety and depression in children in children and adolescents. *Psychological Bulletin, 111,* 244–255.

Brown, T. E. (2001). *Brown Attention-Deficit Disorder Scales for Children and Adolescents manual.* San Antonio, TX: The Psychological Corporation.

Burisch, M. (1984). Approaches to personality inventory construction. *American Psychologist, 39,* 214–227.

Burns, G. L., Walsh, J. A., Owen, S. M., & Snell, J. (1997). Internal validity of attention deficit hyperactivity disorder, oppositional defiant disorder, and overt conduct disorder symptoms in young children: Implications from teacher ratings for a dimensional approach to symptom validity. *Journal of Clinical Child Psychology, 26,* 266–275.

Butcher, J. N., Williams, C. L., Graham, J. R., Archer, R. P., Tellegen, A., Ben-Porath, Y. S., & Kaemmer, B. (1992). *Minnesota Multiphasic Personality Inventory–Adolescent: Manual for administration, scoring, and interpretation.* Minneapolis: University of Minnesota Press.

Cantwell, D. P. (1996). Attention deficit disorder: A review of the past 10 years. *Journal of the American Academy of Child and Adolescent Psychiatry, 35,* 978–987.

Caron, C., & Rutter, M. (1991). Comorbidity in child psychopathology: Concepts, issues, and research strategies. *Journal of Child Psychology and Psychiatry, 32,* 1063–1080.

Conners, C. K. (1997). *Conners' Rating Scales–Revised technical manual.* North Tonawanda, NY: Multi-Health Systems.

Conners, C. K. (1999). Conners' Rating Scales–Revised. In M. E. Maruish (Ed.), *The use of psychological testing for treatment planning and outcome assessment* (2nd ed., pp. 467–495). Mahwah, NJ: Erlbaum.

Cordell, A. (1998). Psychological assessment of children. In W. M. Klykylo, J. Kay, & D. Rube (Eds.), *Clinical child psychiatry* (pp. 12–41). Philadelphia: W. B. Saunders.

Crystal, D. S., Ostrander, R., Chen, R. S., & August, G. J. (2001). Multimethod assessment of psychopathology among DSM-IV subtypes of children with attention-deficit/hyperactivity disorder: Self-, parent, and teacher reports. *Journal of Abnormal Child Psychology, 29,* 189–205.

Drotar, D., Stein, R. E., & Perrin, E. C. (1995). Methodological issues in using the Child Behavior Checklist and its related instruments in clinical child psychology research. *Journal of Clinical Child Psychology, 24,* 184–192.

Duhig, A. M., Renk, K., Epstein, M. K., & Phares, V. (2000). Interparental agreement on internalizing, externalizing, and total behavior problems: A meta-analysis. *Clinical Psychology: Science and Practice, 7,* 435–453.

Edelbrock, C., Costello, A. J., Dulcan, M. K., Kalas, D., & Conover, N. (1985). Age differences in the reliability of the psychiatric interview of the child. *Child Development, 56,* 265–275.

Exner, J. E., Jr., & Weiner, I. B. (1982). *The Rorschach: A comprehensive system: Vol. 3. Assessment of children and adolescents.* New York: Wiley.

Finch, A. J., Lipovsky, J. A., & Casat, C. D. (1989). Anxiety and depression in children and adolescents: Negative affectivity or separate constructs. In P. C. Kendall & D. Watson (Eds.), *Anxiety and depression: Distinctive and overlapping features* (pp. 171–202). New York: Academic Press.

Fitzgerald, H. E., Zucker, R. A., Maguin, E. T., & Reider, E. E. (1994). Time spent with child and parental agreement about preschool children's behavior. *Perceptual and Motor Skills, 79,* 336–338.

Flavell, J. H., Flavell, E. R., & Green, F. L. (2001). Development of children's understanding of connections between thinking and feeling. *Psychological Science, 12,* 430–432.

Forbes, G. B. (1985). The Personality Inventory for Children (PIC) and hyperactivity: Clinical utility and problems of generalizability. *Journal of Pediatric Psychology, 10,* 141–149.

Fristad, M. A., Emery, B. L., & Beck, S. J. (1997). Use and abuse of the Children's Depression Inventory. *Journal of Consulting and Clinical Psychology, 65,* 699–702.

Gerard, A. B., & Reynolds, C. R. (1999). Characteristics and applications of the Revisd Children's Manifest Anxiety Scale (RCMAS). In M. E. Maruish (Ed.), *The use of psychological testing for treatment planning and outcomes assessment* (2nd ed., pp. 323–340). Mahwah, NJ: Erlbaum.

Gianarris, W. J., Golden, C. J., & Greene, L. (2001). The Conners' Parent Rating Scales: A critical review of the literature. *Clinical Psychology Review, 21,* 1061–1093.

Gliner, J. A., Morgan, G. A., & Harmon, R. J. (2001). Measurement reliability. *Journal of the American Academy of Child and Adolescent Psychiatry, 40,* 486–488.

Goyette, C. H., Conners, C. K., & Ulrich, R. F. (1978). Normative data on Revised Conners' Parent and Teacher Rating Scales. *Journal of Abnormal Child Psychology, 6,* 221–236.

Graham, J. R. (2000). *MMPI-2: Assessing personality and psychopathology*. New York: Oxford University Press.

Handwerk, M. L., Larzelere, R. E., Soper, S. H., & Friman, P. C. (1999). Parent and child discrepancies in reporting severity of problem behaviors in three out-of-home settings. *Psychological Assessment, 11,* 14–23.

Hathaway, S. R., & Monachesi, E. D. (1953). *Analyzing and predicting juvenile delinquency with the MMPI*. Minneapolis: University of Minnesota Press.

Hinshaw, S. P., Lahey, B. B., & Hart, E. L. (1993). Issues of taxonomy and comorbidity in the development of conduct disorder. *Development and Psychopathology, 5,* 31–49.

Hulbert, T. A., Gdowski, C. L., & Lachar, D. (1986). Interparent agreement on the Personality Inventory for Children: Are substantial correlations sufficient? *Journal of Abnormal Child Psychology, 14,* 115–122.

Jensen, P. S., Martin, D., & Cantwell, D. P. (1997). Comorbidity in ADHD: Implications for research, practice, and *DSM-IV*. *Journal of the American Academy of Child and Adolescent Psychiatry, 36,* 1065–1079.

Kamphaus, R. W., & Frick, P. J. (1996). *Clinical assessment of child and adolescent personality and behavior*. Boston: Allyn and Bacon.

Kamphaus, R. W., & Frick, P. J. (2002). *Clinical assessment of child and adolescent personality and behavior* (2nd ed.). Boston: Allyn and Bacon.

Kamphaus, R. W., & Reynolds, C. R. (1998). *BASC Monitor for ADHD manual*. Circle Pines, MN: American Guidance Service.

King, N. J., Ollendick, T. H., & Gullone, E. (1991). Negative affectivity in children and adolescents: Relations between anxiety and depression. *Clinical Psychology Review, 11,* 441–459.

Kovacs, M. (1992). *Children's Depression Inventory (CDI) manual*. North Tonawanda, NY: Multi-Health Systems.

Lachar, D. (1993). Symptom checklists and personality inventories. In T. R. Kratochwill & R. J. Morris (Eds.), *Handbook of psychotherapy for children and adolescents* (pp. 38–57). New York: Allyn and Bacon.

Lachar, D. (1998). Observations of parents, teachers, and children: Contributions to the objective multidimensional assessment of youth. In A. S. Bellack, M. Hersen (Series Eds.), & C. R. Reynolds (Vol. Ed.), *Comprehensive clinical psychology: Vol. 4. Assessment* (pp. 371–401). New York: Pergamon Press.

Lachar, D., & Gdowski, C. L. (1979). *Actuarial assessment of child and adolescent personality: An interpretive guide for the Personality Inventory for Children profile*. Los Angeles: Western Psychological Services.

Lachar, D., & Gruber, C. P. (1993). Development of the Personality Inventory for Youth: A self-report companion to the Personality Inventory for Children. *Journal of Personality Assessment, 61,* 81–98.

Lachar, D., & Gruber, C. P. (1995). *Personality Inventory for Youth (PIY) manual: Administration and interpretation guide. Technical guide*. Los Angeles: Western Psychological Services.

Lachar, D., & Gruber, C. P. (2001). *Personality Inventory for Children, Second Edition (PIC-2). Standard Form and Behavioral Summary manual*. Los Angeles: Western Psychological Services.

Lachar, D., Klinge, V., & Grisell, J. L. (1976). Relative accuracy of automated MMPI narratives generated from adult-norm and adolescent-norm profiles. *Journal of Consulting and Clinical Psychology, 46,* 1403–1408.

Lachar, D., Morgan, S. T., Espadas, A., & Schomer, O. (2000, August). *Effect of defensiveness on two self-report child adjustment inventories*. Paper presented at the 108th annual meeting of the American Psychological Association, Washington DC.

Lachar, D., Randle, S. L., Harper, R. A., Scott-Gurnell, K. C., Lewis, K. R., Santos, C. W., Saunders, A. E., Pearson, D. A., Loveland, K. A., & Morgan, S. T. (2001). The Brief Psychiatric Rating Scale for Children (BPRS-C): Validity and reliability of an anchored version. *Journal of the American Academy of Child and Adolescent Psychiatry, 40,* 333–340.

Lachar, D., Wingenfeld, S. A., Kline, R. B., & Gruber, C. P. (2000). *Student Behavior Survey manual*. Los Angeles: Western Psychological Services.

LaGreca, A. M., Kuttler, A. F., & Stone, W. L. (2001). Assessing children through interviews and behavioral observations. In C. E. Walker & M. C. Roberts (Eds.), *Handbook of clinical child psychology* (3rd ed., pp. 90–110). New York: Wiley.

Loeber, R., Green, S. M., & Lahey, B. B. (1990). Mental health professionals' perception of the utility of children, mothers, and teachers as informants on childhood psychopathology. *Journal of Clinical Child Psychology, 19,* 136–143.

Loeber, R., & Keenan, K. (1994). Interaction between conduct disorder and its comorbid conditions: Effects of age and gender. *Clinical Psychology Review, 14,* 497–523.

Loeber, R., Lahey, B. B., & Thomas, C. (1991). Diagnostic conundrum of oppositional defiant disorder and conduct disorder. *Journal of Abnormal Psychology, 100,* 379–390.

Loeber, R., & Schmaling, K. B. (1985). The utility of differentiating between mixed and pure forms of antisocial child behavior. *Journal of Abnormal Child Psychology, 13,* 315–336.

Marmorstein, N. R., & Iacono, W. G. (2001). An investigation of female adolescent twins with both major depression and conduct disorder. *Journal of the American Academy of Child and Adolescent Psychiatry, 40,* 299–306.

Maruish, M. E. (1999). *The use of psychological testing for treatment planning and outcomes assessment* (2nd ed.) Mahwah, NJ: Erlbaum.

Maruish, M. E. (2002). *Psychological testing in the age of managed behavioral health care*. Mahwah, NJ: Erlbaum.

Mash, E. J., & Lee, C. M. (1993). Behavioral assessment with children. In R. T. Ammerman & M. Hersen (Eds.), *Handbook of behavior therapy with children and adults* (pp. 13–31). Boston: Allyn and Bacon.

Mash, E. J., & Terdal, L. G. (1997). Assessment of child and family disturbance: A behavioral-systems approach. In E. J. Mash & L. G. Terdal (Eds.), *Assessment of childhood disorders* (3rd ed., pp. 3–69). New York: Guilford Press.

McArthur, D. S., & Roberts, G. E. (1982). *Roberts Apperception Test for Children manual.* Los Angeles: Western Psychological Services.

McConaughy, S. H., & Achenbach, T. M. (1994). Comorbidity of empirically based syndromes in matched general population and clinical samples. *Journal of Child Psychology and Psychiatry, 35,* 1141–1157.

McLaren, J., & Bryson, S. E. (1987). Review of recent epidemiological studies of mental retardation: Prevalence, associated disorders, and etiology. *American Journal of Mental Retardation, 92,* 243–254.

McMahon, R. J. (1987). Some current issues in the behavioral assessment of conduct disordered children and their families. *Behavioral Assessment, 9,* 235–252.

Merrell, K. W. (1994). *Assessment of behavioral, social, and emotional problems. Direct and objective methods for use with children and adolescents.* New York: Longman.

Millon, T. (1993). *Millon Adolescent Clinical Inventory (MACI) manual.* Minneapolis: National Computer Systems.

Moretti, M. M., Fine, S., Haley, G., & Marriage, K. (1985). Childhood and adolescent depression: Child-report versus parent-report information. *Journal of the American Academy of Child Psychiatry, 24,* 298–302.

Morgan, G. A., Gliner, J. A., & Harmon, R. J. (2001). Measurement validity. *Journal of the American Academy of Child and Adolescent Psychiatry, 40,* 729–731.

Naglieri, J. A., LeBuffe, P. A., & Pfeiffer, S. I. (1994). *Devereux Scales of Mental Disorders manual.* San Antonio, TX: The Psychological Corporation.

Nanson, J. L., & Gordon, B. (1999). Psychosocial correlates of mental retardation. In V. L. Schwean & D. H. Saklofske (Eds.), *Handbook of psychosocial characteristic of exceptional children* (pp. 377–400). New York: Kluwer Academic/Plenum Publishers.

Neeper, R., Lahey, B. B., & Frick, P. J. (1990). *Comprehensive behavior rating scale for children.* San Antonio, TX: The Psychological Corporation.

Newman, F. L., Ciarlo, J. A., & Carpenter, D. (1999). Guidelines for selecting psychological instruments for treatment planning and outcome assessment. In M. E. Maruish (Ed.), *The use of psychological testing for treatment planning and outcomes assessment* (2nd ed., pp. 153–170). Mahwah, NJ: Erlbaum.

Nottelmann, E. D., & Jensen, P. S. (1995). Comorbidity of disorders in children and adolescents: Developmental perspectives. In

T. H. Ollendick & R. J. Prinz (Eds.), *Advances in clinical child psychology* (Vol. 17, pp. 109–155). New York: Plenum Press.

Offord, D. R., Boyle, M. H., & Racine, Y. A. (1991). The epidemiology of antisocial behavior in childhood and adolescence. In D. J. Pepler & K. H. Rubin (Eds.), *The development and treatment of childhood aggression* (pp. 31–54). Hillsdale, NJ: Erlbaum.

Pearson, D. A., & Lachar, D. (1994). Using behavioral questionnaires to identify adaptive deficits in elementary school children. *Journal of School Psychology, 32,* 33–52.

Pearson, D. A., Lachar, D., Loveland, K. A., Santos, C. W., Faria, L. P., Azzam, P. N., Hentges, B. A., & Cleveland, L. A. (2000). Patterns of behavioral adjustment and maladjustment in mental retardation: Comparison of children with and without ADHD. *American Journal on Mental Retardation, 105,* 236–251.

Phares, V. (1997). Accuracy of informants: Do parents think that mother knows best? *Journal of Abnormal Child Psychology, 25,* 165–171.

Piotrowski, C., Belter, R. W., & Keller, J. W. (1998). The impact of "managed care" on the practice of psychological testing: Preliminary findings. *Journal of Personality Assessment, 70,* 441–447.

Pisecco, S., Lachar, D., Gruber, C. P., Gallen, R. T., Kline, R. B., & Huzinec, C. (1999). Development and validation of disruptive behavior DSM-IV scales for the Student Behavior Survey (SBS). *Journal of Psychoeducational Assessment, 17,* 314–331.

Pliszka, S. R. (1998). Comorbidity of attention-deficit/hyperactivity disorder with psychiatric disorder: An overview. *Journal of Clinical Psychiatry, 59*(Suppl. 7), 50–58.

Reynolds, C. R., & Kamphaus, R. W. (1992). *Behavior Assessment System for Children manual.* Circle Pines, MN: American Guidance Service.

Reynolds, C. R., & Richmond, B. O. (1985). *Revised Children's Manifest Anxiety Scale manual.* Los Angeles: Western Psychological Services.

Reynolds, W. M. (1998). *Adolescent Psychopathology Scale (APS): Administration and interpretation manual. Psychometric and technical manual.* Odessa, FL: Psychological Assessment Resources.

Reynolds, W. M. (2000). *Adolescent Psychopathology Scale–Short Form (APS-SF) professional manual.* Odessa, FL: Psychological Assessment Resources.

Roberts, M. C., & Hurley, L. (1997). *Managing managed care.* New York: Plenum Press.

Sheldrick, R. C., Kendall, P. C., & Heimberg, R. G. (2001). The clinical significance of treatments: A comparison of three treatments for conduct disordered children. *Clinical Psychology: Science and Practice, 8,* 418–430.

Sitarenios, G., & Kovacs, M. (1999). Use of the Children's Depression Inventory. In M. E. Maruish (Ed.), *The use of psychological testing for treatment planning and outcomes assessment* (2nd ed., pp. 267–298). Mahwah, NJ: Erlbaum.

Snyder, D. K. (1997). *Manual for the Marital Satisfaction Inventory–Revised.* Los Angeles: Western Psychological Services.

Snyder, D. K., & Aikman, G. G. (1999). Marital Satisfaction Inventory–Revised. In M. E. Maruish (Ed.), *The use of psychological testing for treatment planning and outcomes assessment* (2nd ed., pp. 1173–1210). Mahwah, NJ: Erlbaum.

Spengler, P. M., Strohmer, D. C., & Prout, H. T. (1990). Testing the robustness of the diagnostic overshadowing bias. *American Journal on Mental Retardation, 95,* 204–214.

Voelker, S., Lachar, D., & Gdowski, C. L. (1983). The Personality Inventory for Children and response to methylphenidate: Preliminary evidence for predictive utility. *Journal of Pediatric Psychology, 8,* 161–169.

Williams, C. L., Butcher, J. N., Ben-Porath, Y. S., & Graham, J. R. (1992). *MMPI-A content scales. Assessing psychopathology in adolescents.* Minneapolis: University of Minnesota Press.

Wingenfeld, S. A., Lachar, D., Gruber, C. P., & Kline, R. B. (1998). Development of the teacher-informant Student Behavior Survey. *Journal of Psychoeducational Assessment, 16,* 226–249.

Wrobel, T. A., Lachar, D., Wrobel, N. H., Morgan, S. T., Gruber, C. P., & Neher, J. A. (1999). Performance of the Personality Inventory for Youth validity scales. *Assessment, 6,* 367–376.

Youngstrom, E., Loeber, R., & Stouthamer-Loeber, M. (2000). Patterns and correlates of agreement between parent, teacher, and male adolescent ratings of externalizing and internalizing problems. *Journal of Consulting and Clinical Psychology, 68,* 1038–1050.

CHAPTER 12

Psychological Assessment in School Settings

JEFFERY P. BRADEN

PSYCHOLOGICAL ASSESSMENT IN SCHOOL SETTINGS

Psychological assessment in school settings is in many ways similar to psychological assessment in other settings. This may be the case in part because the practice of modern psychological assessment began with an application to schools (Fagan, 1996). However, the practice of psychological assessment in school settings may be discriminated from practices in other settings by three characteristics: populations, problems, and procedures (American Psychological Association, 1998).

Psychological assessment in school settings primarily targets children, and secondarily serves the parents, families, and educators of those children. In the United States, schools offer

This work was supported in part by a grant from the U.S. Department of Education, Office of Special Education and Rehabilitative Services, Office of Special Education Programs (#H158J970001) and by the Wisconsin Center for Education Research, School of Education, University of Wisconsin—Madison. Any opinions, findings, or conclusions are those of the author and do not necessarily reflect the views of the supporting agencies.

services to preschool children with disabilities as young as 3 years of age and are obligated to provide services to individuals up to 21 years of age. Furthermore, schools are obligated to educate all children, regardless of their physical, behavioral, or cognitive disabilities or gifts. Because public schools are free and attendance is compulsory for children, schools are more likely than private or fee-for-service settings to serve individuals who are poor or members of a minority group or have language and cultural differences. Consequently, psychological assessment must respond to the diverse developmental, cultural, linguistic, ability, and individual differences reflected in school populations.

Psychological assessment in school settings primarily targets problems of learning and school adjustment. Although psychologists must also assess and respond to other developmental, social, emotional, and behavioral issues, the primary focus behind most psychological assessment in schools is understanding and ameliorating learning problems. Children and families presenting psychological problems unrelated to learning are generally referred to services in nonschool settings. Also, school-based psychological assessment addresses problem prevention, such as reducing academic or social failure. Whereas psychological assessment in other settings is frequently not invoked until a problem is presented, psychological assessment in schools may be used to prevent problems from occurring.

Psychological assessment in school settings draws on procedures relevant to the populations and problems served in schools. Therefore, school-based psychologists emphasize assessment of academic achievement and student learning, use interventions that emphasize educational or learning approaches, and use consultation to implement interventions. Because children experience problems in classrooms, playgrounds, homes, and other settings that support education, interventions to address problems are generally implemented in the setting where the problem occurs. School-based psychologists generally do not provide direct services (e.g., play therapy) outside of educational settings. Consequently, psychologists in school settings consult with teachers, parents, and other educators to implement interventions. Psychological assessment procedures that address student learning, psychoeducational interventions, and intervention implementation mediated via consultation are emphasized to a greater degree in schools than in other settings.

The remainder of this chapter will address aspects of psychological assessment that distinguish practices in school-based settings from practices in other settings. The chapter is organized into four major sections: the purposes, current practices, assessment of achievement and future trends of psychological assessment in schools.

PURPOSES OF PSYCHOLOGICAL ASSESSMENT IN SCHOOLS

There are generally six distinct, but related, purposes that drive psychological assessment. These are screening, diagnosis, intervention, evaluation, selection, and certification. Psychological assessment practitioners may address all of these purposes in their school-based work.

Screening

Psychological assessment may be useful for detecting psychological or educational problems in school-aged populations. Typically, psychologists employ screening instruments to detect students at risk for various psychological disorders, including depression, suicidal tendencies, academic failure, social skills deficits, poor academic competence, and other forms of maladaptive behaviors. Thus, screening is most often associated with selected or targeted prevention programs (see Coie et al., 1993, and Reiss & Price, 1996, for a discussion of contemporary prevention paradigms and taxonomies).

The justification for screening programs relies on three premises: (a) individuals at significantly higher than average risk for a problem can be identified prior to onset of the problem; (b) interventions can eliminate later problem onset or reduce the severity, frequency, and duration of later problems; and (c) the costs of the screening and intervention programs are justified by reduced fiscal or human costs. In some cases, psychologists justify screening by maintaining that interventions are more effective if initiated prior to or shortly after problem onset than if they are delivered later.

Three lines of research validate the assumptions supporting screening programs in schools. First, school-aged children who exhibit later problems may often be identified with reasonable accuracy via screening programs, although the value of screening varies across problem types (Durlak, 1997). Second, there is a substantial literature base to support the efficacy of prevention programs for children (Durlak, 1997; Weissberg & Greenberg, 1998). Third, prevention programs are consistently cost effective and usually pay dividends of greater than 3:1 in cost-benefit analyses (Durlak, 1997).

Although support for screening and prevention programs is compelling, there are also concerns about the value of screening using psychological assessment techniques. For example, the consequences of screening mistakes (i.e., false positives and false negatives) are not always well understood. Furthermore, assessment instruments typically identify children as being at risk, rather than identifying the social, educational, and other environmental conditions that put them at risk. The focus on the child as the problem (i.e., the so-called "disease model") may undermine necessary social and educational reforms (see Albee, 1998). Screening may also be more appropriate for some conditions (e.g., suicidal tendencies, depression, social skills deficits) than for others (e.g., smoking), in part because students may not be motivated to change (Norman, Velicer, Fava, & Prochaska, 2000). Placement in special programs or remedial tracks may reduce, rather than increase, students' opportunity to learn and develop. Therefore, the use of psychological assessment in screening and prevention programs should consider carefully the consequential validity of the assessment process and should ensure that inclusion in or exclusion from a prevention program is based on more than a single screening test score (see standard 13.7, American Educational Research Association, American Psychological Association, & National Council on Measurement in Education, 1999, pp. 146–147).

Diagnosis

Psychological assessment procedures play a major, and often decisive, role in diagnosing psychoeducational problems. Generally, diagnosis serves two purposes: establishing eligibility for services and selecting interventions. The use of assessment to select interventions will be discussed in the next section. Eligibility for special educational services in the United States is contingent upon receiving a diagnosis of a psychological or psychoeducational disability. Students may qualify for special programs (e.g., special education) or privileges (e.g., testing accommodations) under two different types of legislation. The first type is statutory (e.g., the Americans with Disabilities Act), which requires schools to provide a student diagnosed with a disability with accommodations to the general education program (e.g., extra time, testing accommodations), but not educational programs. The second type of legislation is entitlement (e.g., Individuals with Disabilities Education Act), in which schools must provide special services to students with disabilities when needed. These special services may include accommodations to the general education program and special education services (e.g., transportation, speech therapy, tutoring, placement in a special education classroom). In either case, diagnosis of a disability or disorder is necessary to qualify for accommodations or services.

Statutory legislation and educational entitlement legislation are similar, but not identical, in the types of diagnoses recognized for eligibility purposes. In general, statutory legislation is silent on how professionals should define a disability. Therefore, most diagnoses to qualify children under statutory legislation invoke medical (e.g., American Psychiatric Association, 2000) nosologies. Psychological assessment leading to a recognized medical or psychiatric diagnosis is a necessary, and in some cases sufficient, condition for establishing a student's eligibility for services. In contrast, entitlement legislation is specific in defining who is (and is not) eligible for services. Whereas statutory and entitlement legislation share many diagnostic categories (e.g., learning disability, mental retardation), they differ with regard to specificity and recognition of other diagnoses. For example, entitlement legislation identifies "severely emotionally disturbed" as a single category consisting of a few broad diagnostic indicators, whereas most medical nosologies differentiate more types and varieties of emotional disorders. An example in which diagnostic systems differ is attention deficit disorder (ADD): The disorder is recognized in popular psychological and psychiatric nosologies (e.g., American Psychiatric Association, 2000), but not in entitlement legislation.

Differences in diagnostic and eligibility systems may lead to somewhat different psychological assessment methods and procedures, depending on the purpose of the diagnosis. School-based psychologists tend to use diagnostic categories defined by entitlement legislation to guide their assessments, whereas psychologists based in clinics and other nonschool settings tend to use medical nosologies to guide psychological assessment. These differences are generally compatible, but they occasionally lead to different decisions about who is, and is not, eligible for accommodations or special education services. Also, psychologists should recognize that eligibility for a particular program or accommodation is not necessarily linked to treatment or intervention for a condition. That is, two students who share the same diagnosis may have vastly different special programs or accommodations, based in part on differences in student needs, educational settings, and availability of resources.

Intervention

Assessment is often invoked to help professionals select an intervention from among an array of potential interventions (i.e., treatment matching). The fundamental assumption is that the knowledge produced by a psychological assessment improves treatment or intervention selection. Although most psychologists would accept the value for treatment matching at a general level of assessment, the notion that psychological assessment results can guide treatment selection is more controversial with respect to narrower levels of assessment. For example, determining whether a student's difficulty with written English is caused by severe mental retardation, deafness, lack of exposure to English, inconsistent prior instruction, or a language processing problem would help educators select interventions ranging from operant conditioning approaches to placement in a program using American Sign Language, English as a Second Language (ESL) programs, general writing instruction with some support, or speech therapy.

However, the utility of assessment to guide intervention is less clear at narrower levels of assessment. For example, knowing that a student has a reliable difference between one or more cognitive subtest or composite scores, or fits a particular personality category or learning style profile, may have little value in guiding intervention selection. In fact, some critics (e.g., Gresham & Witt, 1997) have argued that there is no incremental utility for assessing cognitive or personality characteristics beyond recognizing extreme abnormalities (and such recognition generally does not require the use of psychological tests). Indeed, some critics argue that data-gathering techniques such as observation, interviews, records reviews, and curriculum-based assessment of academic deficiencies (coupled with common sense) are sufficient to guide treatment matching (Gresham & Witt, 1997; Reschly & Grimes, 1995). Others argue that knowledge of cognitive processes, and in particular neuropsychological processes, is useful for treatment matching (e.g., Das, Naglieri, & Kirby, 1994; Naglieri, 1999; Naglieri & Das, 1997). This issue will be discussed later in the chapter.

Evaluation

Psychologists may use assessment to evaluate the outcome of interventions, programs, or other educational and psychological processes. Evaluation implies an expectation for a certain outcome, and the outcome is usually a change or improvement (e.g., improved reading achievement, increased social skills). Increasingly, the public and others concerned with psychological services and education expect students to show improvement as a result of attending school or participating in a program. Psychological assessment, and in particular, assessment of student learning, helps educators decide whether and how much students improve as a function of a curriculum, intervention, or program. Furthermore, this information is increasingly of interest to public and lay audiences concerned with accountability (see Elmore & Rothman; 1999; McDonnell, McLaughlin, & Morrison, 1997).

Evaluation comprises two related purposes: formative evaluation (e.g., ongoing progress monitoring to make instructional decisions, providing feedback to students), and summative evaluation (e.g., assigning final grades, making pass/fail decisions, awarding credits). Psychological assessment is helpful for both purposes. Formative evaluation may focus on students (e.g., curriculum-based measurement of academic progress; changes in frequency, duration, or intensity of social behaviors over time or settings), but it may also focus on the adults involved in an intervention. Psychological assessment can be helpful for assessing treatment acceptability (i.e., the degree to which those executing an intervention find the procedure acceptable and are motivated to comply with it; Fairbanks & Stinnett, 1997), treatment integrity (i.e., adherence to a specific intervention or treatment protocol; Wickstrom, Jones, LaFleur, & Witt, 1998), and goal attainment (the degree to which the goals of the intervention are met; MacKay, Somerville, & Lundie, 1996). Because psychologists in educational settings frequently depend on others to conduct interventions, they must evaluate the degree to which interventions are acceptable and determine whether interventions were executed with integrity before drawing conclusions about intervention effectiveness. Likewise, psychologists should use assessment to obtain judgments of treatment success from adults in addition to obtaining direct measures of student change to make formative and summative decisions about student progress or outcomes.

Selection

Psychological assessment for selection is an historic practice that has become controversial. Students of intellectual assessment may remember that Binet and Simon developed the first practical test of intelligence to help Parisian educators select students for academic or vocational programs. The use of psychological assessment to select—or assign—students to educational programs or tracks was a major function of U.S. school-based psychologists in the early to mid-1900s (Fagan, 2000). However, the general practice of assigning students to different academic tracks (called *tracking*) fell out of favor with educators, due in part to the perceived injustice of limiting students' opportunity to learn. Furthermore, the use of intellectual ability tests to assign students to tracks was deemed illegal by U.S. federal district court, although later judicial decisions have upheld the assignment of students to different academic tracks if those assignments are based on direct measures of student performance (Reschly, Kicklighter, & McKee, 1988). Therefore, the use of psychological assessment to select or assign students to defferent educational tracks is allowed if the assessment is nonbiased and is directly tied to the educational process. However, many educators view tracking as ineffective and immoral (Oakes, 1992), although recent research suggests tracking may have beneficial effects for all students, including those in the lowest academic tracks (Figlio & Page, 2000). The selection activities likely to be supported by psychological assessment in schools include determining eligibility for special education (discussed previously in the section titled "Diagnosis"), programs for gifted children, and academic honors and awards (e.g., National Merit Scholarships).

Certification

Psychological assessment rarely addresses certification, because psychologists are rarely charged with certification decisions. An exception to this rule is certification of student learning, or achievement testing. Schools must certify student learning for graduation purposes, and incresingly for other purposes, such as promotion to higher grades or retention for an additional year in the same grade.

Historically, teachers make certification decisions with little use of psychological assessment. Teachers generally certify student learning based on their assessment of student progress in the course via grades. However, grading practices vary substantially among teachers and are often unreliable within teachers, because teachers struggle to reconcile judgments of student performance with motivation and perceived ability when assigning grades (McMillan & Workman, 1999). Also, critics of public education have expressed grave concerns regarding teachers' expectations and their ability and willingness to hold students to high expectations (Ravitch, 1999).

In response to critics' concerns and U.S. legislation (e.g., Title I of the Elementary and Secondary Education Act), schools have dramatically increased the use and importance of standardized achievement tests to certify student knowledge. Because states often attach significant student consequences to their standardized assessments of student learning, these tests are called *high-stakes tests* (see Heubert & Hauser, 1999). About half of the states in the United States currently use tests in whole or in part for making promotion and graduation decisions (National Governors Association, 1998); consequently, psychologists should help schools design and use effective assessment programs. Because these high-stakes tests are rarely given by psychologists, and because they do not assess more psychological attributes such as intelligence or emotion, one could exclude a discussion of high-stakes achievement tests from this chapter. However, I include them here and in the section on achievement testing, because these assessments are playing an increasingly prominent role in schools and in the lives of students, teachers, and parents. I also differentiate high-stakes achievement tests from diagnostic assessment. Although diagnosis typically includes assessment of academic achievement and also has profound effects on students' lives (i.e., it carries high stakes), two features distinguish high-stakes achievement tests from other forms of assessment: (a) all students in a given grade must take high-stakes achievement tests, whereas only students who are referred (and whose parents consent) undergo diagnostic assessment; and (b) high-stakes tests are used to make general educational decisions (e.g., promotion, retention, graduation), whereas diagnostic assessment is used to determine eligibility for special education.

CURRENT STATUS AND PRACTICES OF PSYCHOLOGICAL ASSESSMENT IN SCHOOLS

The primary use of psychological assessment in U.S. schools is for the diagnosis and classification of educational disabilities. Surveys of school psychologists (e.g., Wilson & Reschly, 1996) show that most school psychologists are trained in assessment of intelligence, achievement, and social-emotional disorders, and their use of these assessments comprises the largest single activity they perform. Consequently, most school-based psychological assessment is initiated at the request of an adult, usually a teacher, for the purpose of deciding whether the student is eligible for special services.

However, psychological assessment practices range widely according to the competencies and purposes of the psychologist. Most of the assessment technologies that school psychologists use fall within the following categories:

1. Interviews and records reviews.
2. Observational systems.
3. Checklists and self-report techniques.
4. Projective techniques.
5. Standardized tests.
6. Response-to-intervention approaches.

Methods to measure academic achievement are addressed in a separate section of this chapter.

Interviews and Records Reviews

Most assessments begin with interviews and records reviews. Assessors use interviews to define the problem or concerns of primary interest and to learn about their history (when the problems first surfaced, when and under what conditions problems are likely to occur); whether there is agreement across individuals, settings, and time with respect to problem occurrence; and what individuals have done in response to the problem. Interviews serve two purposes: they are useful for generating hypotheses and for testing hypotheses. Unstructured or semistructured procedures are most useful for hypothesis generation and problem identification, whereas structured protocols are most useful for refining and testing hypotheses. Garb's chapter on interviewing in this volume examines these various approaches to interviewing in greater detail.

Unstructured and semistructured interview procedures typically follow a sequence in which the interviewer invites the interviewee to identify his or her concerns, such as the nature of the problem, when the person first noticed it, its frequency, duration, and severity, and what the interviewee has done in response to the problem. Most often, interviews begin with open-ended questions (e.g., "Tell me about the problem") and proceed to more specific questions (e.g., "Do you see the problem in other situations?"). Such questions are helpful in establishing the nature of the problem and in evaluating the degree to which the problem is stable across individuals, settings, and time. This information will help the assessor evaluate who has the problem (e.g., "Do others share the same perception of the problem?") and to begin formulating what might influence the problem (e.g., problems may surface in unstructured situations but not in structured ones). Also, evidence of appropriate or nonproblem behavior in one setting or at one time suggests the problem may be best addressed via motivational approaches (i.e., supporting the student's performance of the appropriate behavior). In contrast, the failure to find any prior examples of appropriate behavior suggests the student has not adequately learned the appropriate behavior and thus needs instructional support to learn the appropriate behavior.

Structured interview protocols used in school settings are usually driven by instructional theory or by behavioral theory. For example, interview protocols for problems in reading or mathematics elicit information about the instructional practices the teacher uses in the classroom (see Shapiro, 1989). This information can be useful in identifying more and less effective practices and to develop hypotheses that the assessor can evaluate through further assessment.

Behavioral theories also guide structured interviews. The practice of functional assessment of behavior (see Gresham, Watson, & Skinner, 2001) first identifies one or more target behaviors. These target behaviors are typically defined in specific, objective terms and are defined by the frequency, duration, and intensity of the behavior. The interview protocol then elicits information about environmental factors that occur before, during, and after the target behavior. This approach is known as the ABCs of behavior assessment, in that assessors seek to define the antecedents (A), consequences (C), and concurrent factors (B) that control the frequency, duration, or intensity of the target behavior. Assessors then use their knowledge of the environment-behavior links to develop interventions to reduce problem behaviors and increase appropriate behaviors. Examples of functional assessment procedures include systems developed by Dagget, Edwards, Moore, Tingstrom, and Wilczynski (2001), Stoiber and Kratochwill (2002), and Munk and Karsh (1999). However, functional assessment of behavior is different from functional analysis of behavior. Whereas a functional assessment generally relies on interview and observational data to identify links between the environment and the behavior, a functional analysis requires that the assessor actually manipulate suspected links (e.g., antecedents or consequences) to test the environment-behavior link. Functional analysis procedures are described in greater detail in the section on response-to-intervention assessment approaches.

Assessors also review permanent products in a student's record to understand the medical, educational, and social history of the student. Among the information most often sought in a review of records is the student's school attendance history, prior academic achievement, the perspectives of previous teachers, and whether and how problems were defined in the past. Although most records reviews are informal, formal procedures exist for reviewing educational records (e.g., Walker, Block-Pedego, Todis, & Severson, 1991). Some of the key questions addressed in a records review include whether the student has had adequate opportunity to learn (e.g., are current academic problems due to lack of or poor instruction?) and whether problems are unique to the current setting or year. Also, salient social (e.g., custody problems, foster care) and medical conditions (e.g., otitis media, attention deficit disorder) may be identified in student records. However, assessors should avoid focusing on less salient aspects of records (e.g., birth weight, developmental milestones) when defining problems, because such a focus may undermine effective problem

solving in the school context (Gresham, Mink, Ward, MacMillan, & Swanson, 1994). Analysis of students' permanent products (rather than records about the student generated by others) is discussed in the section on curriculum-based assessment methodologies.

Together, interviews and records reviews help define the problem and provide an historical context for the problem. Assessors use interviews and records reviews early in the assessment process, because these procedures focus and inform the assessment process. However, assessors may return to interview and records reviews throughout the assessment process to refine and test their definition and hypotheses about the student's problem. Also, psychologists may meld assessment and intervention activities into interviews, such as in behavioral consultation procedures (Bergan & Kratochwill, 1990), in which consultants use interviews to define problems, analyze problem causes, select interventions, and evaluate intervention outcomes.

Observational Systems

Most assessors will use one or more observational approaches as the next step in a psychological assessment. Although assessors may use observations for purposes other than individual assessment (e.g., classroom behavioral screening, evaluating a teacher's adherence to an intervention protocol), the most common use of an observation is as part of a diagnostic assessment (see Shapiro & Kratochwill, 2000). Assessors use observations to refine their definition of the problem, generate and test hypotheses about why the problem exists, develop interventions within the classroom, and evaluate the effects of an intervention.

Observation is recommended early in any diagnostic assessment process, and many states in the United States require classroom observation as part of a diagnostic assessment. Most assessors conduct informal observations early in a diagnostic assessment because they want to evaluate the student's behavior in the context in which the behavior occurs. This allows the assessor to corroborate different views of the problem, compare the student's behavior to that of his or her peers (i.e., determine what is typical for that classroom), and detect features of the environment that might contribute to the referral problem.

Observation systems can be informal or formal. The informal approaches are, by definition, idiosyncratic and vary among assessors. Most informal approaches rely on narrative recording, in which the assessor records the flow of events and then uses the recording to help refine the problem definition and develop hypotheses about why the problem occurs. These narrative qualitative records provide rich data for understanding a problem, but they are rarely sufficient for problem definition, analysis, and solution.

As is true for interview procedures, formal observation systems are typically driven by behavioral or instructional theories. Behavioral observation systems use applied behavioral analysis techniques for recording target behaviors. These techniques include sampling by events or intervals and attempt to capture the frequency, duration, and intensity of the target behaviors. One system that incorporates multiple observation strategies is the Ecological Behavioral Assessment System for Schools (Greenwood, Carta, & Dawson, 2000); another is !Observe (Martin, 1999). Both use laptop or handheld computer technologies to record, summarize, and report observations and allow observers to record multiple facets of multiple behaviors simultaneously.

Instructional observation systems draw on theories of instruction to target teacher and student behaviors exhibited in the classroom. The Instructional Environment Scale-II (TIES-II; Ysseldyke & Christenson, 1993) includes interviews, direct observations, and analysis of permanent products to identify ways in which current instruction meets and does not meet student needs. Assessors use TIES-II to evaluate 17 areas of instruction organized into four major domains. The Instructional Environment Scale-II helps assessors identify aspects of instruction that are strong (i.e., matched to student needs) and aspects of instruction that could be changed to enhance student learning. The ecological framework presumes that optimizing the instructional match will enhance learning and reduce problem behaviors in classrooms. This assumption is shared by curriculum-based assessment approaches described later in the chapter. Although TIES-II has a solid foundation in instructional theory, there is no direct evidence of its treatment utility reported in the manual, and one investigation of the use of TIES-II for instructional matching (with the companion *Strategies and Tactics for Educational Interventions,* Algozzine & Ysseldyke, 1992) showed no clear benefit (Wollack, 2000).

The Behavioral Observation of Student in School (BOSS; Shapiro, 1989) is a hybrid of behavioral and instructional observation systems. Assessors use interval sampling procedures to identify the proportion of time a target student is on or off task. These categories are further subdivided into active or passive categories (e.g., actively on task, passively off task) to describe broad categories of behavior relevant to instruction. The BOSS also captures the proportion of intervals teachers actively teach academic content in an effort to link teacher and student behaviors.

Formal observational systems help assessors by virtue of their precision, the ability to monitor change over time and circumstances, and their structured focus on factors relevant to the problem at hand. Formal observation systems often report fair to good interrater reliability, but they often fail to report stability over time. Stability is an important issue in classroom observations, because observer ratings are gener-

ally unstable if based on three or fewer observations (see Plewis, 1988). This suggests that teacher behaviors are not consistent. Behavioral observation systems overcome this limitation via frequent use (e.g., observations are conducted over multiple sessions); observations based on a single session (e.g., TIES-II) are susceptible to instability but attempt to overcome this limitation via interviews of the teacher and student. Together, informal and formal observation systems are complementary processes in identifying problems, developing hypotheses, suggesting interventions, and monitoring student responses to classroom changes.

Checklists and Self-Report Techniques

School-based psychological assessment also solicits information directly from informants in the assessment process. In addition to interviews, assessors use checklists to solicit teacher and parent perspectives on student problems. Assessors may also solicit self-reports of behavior from students to help identify, understand, and monitor the problem.

Schools use many of the checklists popular in other settings with children and young adults. Checklists to measure a broad range of psychological problems include the Child Behavior Checklist (CBCL; Achenbach, 1991a, 1991b), Devereux Rating Scales (Naglieri, LeBuffe, & Pfeiffer, 1993a, 1993b), and the Behavior Assessment System for Children (BASC; C. R. Reynolds & Kamphaus, 1992). However, school-based assessments also use checklists oriented more specifically to schools, such as the Connors Rating Scale (for hyperactivity; Connors, 1997), the Teacher-Child Rating Scale (T-CRS; Hightower et al., 1987), and the Social Skills Rating System (SSRS; Gresham & Elliott, 1990). Lachar's chapter in this volume examines the use of these kinds of measures in mental health settings.

The majority of checklists focus on quantifying the degree to which the child's behavior is typical or atypical with respect to age or grade level peers. These judgments can be particularly useful for diagnostic purposes, in which the assessor seeks to establish clinically unusual behaviors. In addition to identifying atypical social-emotional behaviors such as internalizing or externalizing problems, assessors use checklists such as the Scales of Independent Behavior (Bruininks, Woodcock, Weatherman, & Hill, 1996) to rate adaptive and maladaptive behavior. Also, some instruments (e.g., the Vineland Adaptive Behavior Scales; Sparrow, Balla, & Cicchetti, 1984) combine semistructured parent or caregiver interviews with teacher checklists to rate adaptive behavior. Checklists are most useful for quantifying the degree to which a student's behavior is atypical, which in turn is useful for differential diagnosis of handicapping conditions. For example, diagnosis of severe emotional disturbance implies elevated maladaptive or clinically atypical behavior levels, whereas diagnosis of mental retardation requires depressed adaptive behavior scores.

The Academic Competence Evaluation Scale (ACES; DiPerna & Elliott, 2000) is an exception to the rule that checklists quantify abnormality. Teachers use the ACES to rate students' academic competence, which is more directly relevant to academic achievement and classroom performance than measures of social-emotional or clinically unusual behaviors. The ACES includes a self-report form to corroborate teacher and student ratings of academic competencies. Assessors can use the results of the teacher and student forms of the ACES with the Academic Intervention Monitoring System (AIMS; S. N. Elliott, DiPerna, & Shapiro, 2001) to develop interventions to improve students' academic competence. Most other clinically oriented checklists lend themselves to diagnosis but not to intervention.

Self-report techniques invite students to provide open- or closed-ended response to items or probes. Many checklists (e.g., the CBCL, BASC, ACES, T-CRS, SSRS) include a self-report form that invites students to evaluate the frequency or intensity of their own behaviors. These self-report forms can be useful for corroborating the reports of adults and for assessing the degree to which students share perceptions of teachers and parents regarding their own behaviors. Triangulating perceptions across raters and settings is important because the same behaviors are not rated identically across raters and settings. In fact, the agreement among raters, and across settings, can vary substantially (Achenbach, McConaughy, & Howell, 1987). That is, most checklist judgments within a rater for a specific setting are quite consistent, suggesting high reliability. However, agreement between raters within the same setting, or agreement within the same rater across setting, is much lower, suggesting that many behaviors are situation specific, and there are strong rater effects for scaling (i.e., some raters are more likely to view behaviors as atypical than other raters).

Other self-report forms exist as independent instruments to help assessors identify clinically unusual feelings or behaviors. Self-report instruments that seek to measure a broad range of psychological issues include the Feelings, Attitudes, and Behaviors Scale for Children (Beitchman, 1996), the Adolescent Psychopathology Scale (W. M. Reynolds, 1988), and the Adolescent Behavior Checklist (Adams, Kelley, & McCarthy, 1997). Most personality inventories address adolescent populations, because younger children may not be able to accurately or consistently complete personality inventories due to linguistic or developmental demands. Other checklists solicit information about more specific problems, such as social support (Malecki & Elliott, 1999), anxiety (March, 1997), depression (Reynolds, 1987), and internalizing disorders (Merrell & Walters, 1998).

One attribute frequently associated with schooling is self-esteem. The characteristic of self-esteem is valued in schools, because it is related to the ability to persist, attempt difficult or challenging work, and successfully adjust to the social and academic demands of schooling. Among the most popular instruments to measure self-esteem are the Piers-Harris Children's Self-Concept Scale (Piers, 1984), the Self-Esteem Inventory (Coopersmith, 1981), the Self-Perception Profile for Children (Harter, 1985), and the Multi-Dimensional Self-Concept Scale (Bracken, 1992).

One form of a checklist or rating system that is unique to schools is the peer nomination instrument. Peer nomination methods invite students to respond to items such as "Who in your classroom is most likely to fight with others?" or "Who would you most like to work with?" to identify maladaptive and prosocial behaviors. Peer nomination instruments (e.g., the Oregon Youth Study Peer Nomination Questionnaire, Capaldi & Patterson, 1989) are generally reliable and stable over time (Coie, Dodge, & Coppotelli, 1982). Peer nomination instruments allow school-based psychological assessment to capitalize on the availability of peers as indicators of adjustment, rather than relying exclusively on adult judgement or self-report ratings.

The use of self-report and checklist instruments in schools is generally similar to their use in nonschool settings. That is, psychologists use self-report and checklist instruments to quantify and corroborate clinical abnormality. However, some instruments lend themselves to large-scale screening programs for prevention and early intervention purposes (e.g., the Reynolds Adolescent Depression Scale) and thus allow psychologists in school settings the opportunity to intervene prior to onset of serious symptoms. Unfortunately, this is a capability that is not often realized in practice.

Projective Techniques

Psychologists in schools use instruments that elicit latent emotional attributes in response to unstructured stimuli or commands to evaluate social-emotional adjustment and abnormality. The use of projective instruments is most relevant for diagnosis of emotional disturbance, in which the psychologist seeks to evaluate whether the student's atypical behavior extends to atypical thoughts or emotional responses.

Most school-based assessors favor projective techniques requiring lower levels of inference. For example, the Rorschach tests are used less often than drawing tests. Draw-a-person tests or human figure drawings are especially popular in schools because they solicit responses that are common (children are often asked to draw), require little language mediation or other culturally specific knowledge, and can be group administered for screening purposes, and the same drawing can be used to estimate mental abilities and emotional adjustment. Although human figure drawings have been popular for many years, their utility is questionable, due in part to questionable psychometric characteristics (Motta, Little, & Tobin, 1993). However, more recent scoring system have reasonable reliability and demonstrated validity for evaluating mental abilities (e.g., Naglieri, 1988) and emotional disturbance (Naglieri, McNeish, & Bardos, 1991). The use of projective drawing tests is controversial, with some arguing that psychologists are prone to unwarranted interpretations (Smith & Dumont, 1995) and others arguing that the instruments inherently lack sufficient reliability and validity for clinical use (Motta et al., 1993). However, others offer data supporting the validity of drawings when scored with structured rating systems (e.g., Naglieri & Pfeiffer, 1992), suggesting the problem may lie more in unstructured or unsound interpretation practices than in drawing tests per se.

Another drawing test used in school settings is the Kinetic Family Drawing (Burns & Kaufman, 1972), in which children are invited to draw their family "doing something." Assessors then draw inferences about family relationships based on the position and activities of the family members in the drawing. Other projective assessments used in schools include the Rotter Incomplete Sentences Test (Rotter, Lah, & Rafferty, 1992), which induces a projective assessment of emotion via incomplete sentences (e.g., "I am most afraid of _____"). General projective tests, such as the Thematic Apperception Test (TAT; Murray & Bellak, 1973), can be scored for attributes such as achievement motivation (e.g., Novi & Meinster, 2000). There are also apperception tests that use educational settings (e.g., the Education Apperception Test; Thompson & Sones, 1973) or were specifically developed for children (e.g., the Children's Apperception Test; Bellak & Bellak, 1992). Despite these modifications, apperception tests are not widely used in school settings. Furthermore, psychological assessment in schools has tended to reduce projective techniques, favoring instead more objective approaches to measuring behavior, emotion, and psychopathology.

Standardized Tests

Psychologists use standardized tests primarily to assess cognitive abilities and academic achievement. Academic achievement will be considered in its own section later in this chapter. Also, standardized assessments of personality and psychopathology using self-report and observational ratings are described in a previous section. Consequently, this section will describe standardized tests of cognitive ability.

Standardized tests of cognitive ability may be administered to groups of students or to individual students by an examiner. Group-administered tests of cognitive abilities were popular for much of the previous century as a means for matching students to academic curricula. As previously mentioned, Binet and Simon (1914) developed the first practical test of intelligence to help Parisian schools match students to academic or vocational programs, or *tracks*. However, the practice of assigning students to academic programs or tracks based on intelligence tests is no longer legally defensible (Reschly et al., 1988). Consequently, the use of group-administered intelligence tests has declined in schools. However, some schools continue the practice to help screen for giftedness and cognitive delays that might affect schooling. Instruments that are useful in group-administered contexts include the Otis-Lennon School Ability Test (Otis & Lennon, 1996), the Naglieri Nonverbal Ability Test (Naglieri, 1993), the Raven's Matrices Tests (Raven, 1992a, 1992b), and the Draw-A-Person (Naglieri, 1988). Note that, with the exception of the Otis-Lennon School Ability Test, most of these screening tests use culture-reduced items. The reduced emphasis on culturally specific items makes them more appropriate for younger and ethnically and linguistically diverse students. Although culture-reduced, group-administered intelligence tests have been criticized for their inability to predict school performance, there are studies that demonstrate strong relationships between these tests and academic performance (e.g., Naglieri & Ronning, 2000).

The vast majority of cognitive ability assessments in schools use individually administered intelligence test batteries. The most popular batteries include the Weschler Intelligence Scale for Children—Third Edition (WISC-III; Wechsler, 1991), the Stanford Binet Intelligence Test—Fourth Edition (SBIV; Thorndike, Hagen, & Sattler, 1986), the Woodcock-Johnson Cognitive Battery—Third Edition (WJ-III COG; Woodcock, McGrew, & Mather, 2000b), and the Cognitive Assessment System (CAS; Naglieri & Das, 1997). Psychologists may also use Wechsler Scales for preschool (Wechsler, 1989) and adolescent (Wechsler, 1997) assessments and may use other, less popular, assessment batteries such as the Differential Ability Scales (DAS; C. D. Elliott, 1990) or the Kaufman Assessment Battery for Children (KABC; Kaufman & Kaufman, 1983) on occasion.

Two approaches to assessing cognitive abilities other than broad intellectual assessment batteries are popular in schools: nonverbal tests and computer-administered tests. Nonverbal tests of intelligence seek to reduce prior learning and, in particular, linguistic and cultural differences by using language- and culture-reduced test items (see Braden, 2000). Many nonverbal tests of intelligence also allow for nonverbal responses and may

TABLE 12.1   Intelligence Test Battery Scores, Subtests, and Availability of Conormed Achievement Tests

Instrument	General Ability	Cognitive Factors	Tests or Subtests	Co-Normed Achievement Tests
CAS	1 (Full scale score)	4 cognitive	12	Yes (22 tests on the Woodcock-Johnson-Revised Achievement Battery)
DAS	1 (General conceptual ability)	4 cognitive, 5 diagnostic	17	Yes (3 test on the Basic Academic Skills Inventory Screener)
KABC	1 (Mental processing composite)	2 cognitive	10	Yes (6 achievement tests in the KABC battery)
SBIV	1 (Composite score)	4 cognitive	15	No
WISC-III	1 (Full scale IQ)	2 IQs, 4 factor scores	13	Yes (9 tests on the Wechsler Individual Achievement Test)
WJ-III COG	3 (Brief, standard, & extended general intellectual ability)	7 cognitive, 5 clinical	20	Yes (22 tests on the Achievement Battery)

be administered via gestures or other nonverbal or language-reduced means. Nonverbal tests include the Universal Nonverbal Intelligence Test (UNIT; Bracken & McCallum, 1998), the Comprehensive Test of Nonverbal Intelligence (CTONI; Hammill, Pearson, & Wiederholt, 1997), and the Leiter International Performance Scale—Revised (LIPS-R; Roid & Miller, 1997). The technical properties of these tests is usually good to excellent, although they typically provide less data to support their validity and interpretation than do more comprehensive intelligence test batteries (Athanasiou, 2000).

Computer-administered tests promise a cost- and time-efficient alternative to individually administered tests. Three examples are the General Ability Measure for Adults (Naglieri & Bardos, 1997), the Multidimensional Aptitude Battery (Jackson, 1984), and the Computer Optimized Multimedia Intelligence Test (TechMicro, 2000). In addition to reducing examiner time, computer-administered testing can improve assessment accuracy by using adaptive testing algorithms that adjust the items administered to most efficiently target the examinee's ability level. However, computer-administered tests are typically normed only on young adult and adult populations, and many examiners are not yet comfortable with computer technologies for deriving clinical information. Therefore, these tests are not yet widely used in school settings, but they are likely to become more popular in the future.

Intelligence test batteries use a variety of item types, organized into tests or subtests, to estimate general intellectual ability. Batteries produce a single composite based on a large number of tests to estimate general intellectual ability and typically combine individual subtest scores to produce composite or factor scores to estimate more specific intellectual

abilities. Most batteries recommend a successive approach to interpreting the myriad of scores the battery produces (see Sattler, 2001). The successive approach reports the broadest estimate of general intellectual ability first and then proceeds to report narrower estimates (e.g., factor or composite scores based on groups of subtests), followed by even narrower estimates (e.g., individual subtest scores). Assessors often interpret narrower scores as indicators of specific, rather than general, mental abilities. For each of the intellectual assessment batteries listed, Table 12.1 describes the estimates of general intellectual ability, the number of more specific score composites, the number of individual subtests, and whether the battery has a conormed achievement test.

The practice of drawing inferences about a student's cognitive abilities from constellations of test scores is usually known as *profile analysis* (Sattler, 2001), although it is more precisely termed *ipsative analysis* (see Kamphaus, Petoskey, & Morgan, 1997). The basic premise of profile analysis is that individual subtest scores vary, and the patterns of variation suggest relative strengths and weaknesses within the student's overall level of general cognitive ability. Test batteries support ipsative analysis of test scores by providing tables that allow examiners to determine whether differences among scores are reliable (i.e., unlikely given that the scores are actually equal in value) or unusual (i.e., rarely occurring in the normative sample). Many examiners infer unusual deficits or strengths in a student's cognitive abilities based on reliable or unusual differences among cognitive test scores, despite evidence that this practice is not well supported by statistical or logical analyses (Glutting, McDermott, Watkins, Kush, & Konold, 1997; but see Naglieri, 2000).

Examiners use intelligence test scores primarily for diagnosing disabilities in students. Examiners use scores for diagnosis in two ways: to find evidence that corroborates the presence of a particular disability (confirmation), or to find evidence to disprove the presence of a particular disability (disconfirmation). This process is termed *differential diagnosis,* in that different disability conditions are discriminated from each other on the basis of available evidence (including test scores). Furthermore, test scores are primary in defining cognitive disabilities, whereas test scores may play a secondary role in discriminating other, noncognitive disabilities from cognitive disabilities.

Three examples illustrate the process. First, mental retardation is a cognitive disability that is defined in part by intellectual ability scores falling about two standard deviations below the mean. An examiner who obtains a general intellectual ability score that falls more than two standard deviations below the mean is likely to consider a diagnosis of mental retardation in a student (given other corroborating data), whereas a score above the level would typically disconfirm a diagnosis of mental retardation. Second, learning disabilities are cognitive disabilities defined in part by an unusually low achievement score relative to the achievement level that is predicted or expected given the student's intellectual ability. An examiner who finds an unusual difference between a student's actual achievement score and the achievement score predicted on the basis of the student's intellectual ability score would be likely to consider a diagnosis of a learning disability, whereas the absence of such a discrepancy would typically disconfirm the diagnosis. Finally, an examiner who is assessing a student with severe maladaptive behaviors might use a general intellectual ability score to evaluate whether the student's behaviors might be due to or influenced by limited cognitive abilities; a relatively low score might suggest a concurrent intellectual disability, whereas a score in the low average range would rule out intellectual ability as a concurrent problem.

The process and logic of differential diagnosis is central to most individual psychological assessment in schools, because most schools require that a student meet the criteria for one or more recognized diagnostic categories to qualify for special education services. Intelligence test batteries are central to differential diagnosis in schools (Flanagan, Andrews, & Genshaft, 1997) and are often used even in situations in which the diagnosis rests entirely on noncognitive criteria (e.g., examiners assess the intellectual abilities of students with severe hearing impairments to rule out concomitant mental retardation). It is particularly relevant to the practice of identifying learning disabilities, because intellectual assessment batteries may yield two forms of evidence critical to confirming a learning disability: establishing a discrepancy between expected

and obtained achievement, and identifying a deficit in one or more basic psychological processes. Assessors generally establish aptitude-achievement discrepancies by comparing general intellectual ability scores to achievement scores, whereas they establish a deficit in one or more basic psychological processes via ipsative comparisons of subtest or specific ability composite scores.

However, ipsative analyses may not provide a particularly valid approach to differential diagnosis of learning disabilities (Ward, Ward, Hatt, Young, & Mollner, 1995), nor is it clear that psychoeducational assessment practices and technologies are accurate for making differential diagnoses (MacMillan, Gresham, Bocian, & Siperstein, 1997). Decision-making teams reach decisions about special education eligibility that are only loosely related to differential diagnostic taxonomies (Gresham, MacMillan, & Bocian, 1998), particularly for diagnosis mental retardation, behavior disorders, and learning disabilities (Bocian, Beebe, MacMillan, & Gresham, 1999; Gresham, MacMillan, & Bocian, 1996; MacMillan, Gresham, & Bocian, 1998). Although many critics of traditional psychoeducational assessment believe intellectual assessment batteries cannot differentially diagnose learning disabilities primarily because defining learning disabilities in terms of score discrepancies is an inherently flawed practice, others argue that better intellectual ability batteries are more effective in differential diagnosis of learning disabilities (Naglieri, 2000, 2001).

Differential diagnosis of noncognitive disabilities, such as emotional disturbance, behavior disorders, and ADD, is also problematic (Kershaw & Sonuga-Barke, 1998). That is, diagnostic conditions may not be as distinct as educational and clinical classification systems imply. Also, intellectual ability scores may not be useful for distinguishing among some diagnoses. Therefore, the practice of differential diagnosis, particularly with respect to the use of intellectual ability batteries for differential diagnosis of learning disabilities, is a controversial—yet ubiquitous—practice.

Response-to-Intervention Approaches

An alternative to differential diagnosis in schools emphasizes students' responses to interventions as a means of diagnosing educational disabilities (see Gresham, 2001). The logic of the approach is based on the assumption that the best way to differentiate students with disabilities from students who have not yet learned or mastered academic skills is to intervene with the students and evaluate their response to the intervention. Students without disabilities are likely to respond well to the intervention (i.e., show rapid progress), whereas students without disabilities are unlikely to respond well (i.e., show slower or no progress). Studies of students with diagnosed disabilities suggest that they indeed differ from nondisabled peers in their initial levels of achievement (low) and their rate of response (slow; Speece & Case, 2001).

The primary benefit of a response-to-intervention approach is shifting the assessment focus from diagnosing and determining eligibility for special services to a focus on improving the student's academic skills (Berninger, 1997). This benefit is articulated within the problem-solving approach to psychological assessment and intervention in schools (Batsche & Knoff, 1995). In the problem-solving approach, a problem is the gap between current levels of performance and desired levels of performance (Shinn, 1995). The definitions of current and desired performance emphasize precise, dynamic measures of student performance such as rates of behavior. The assessment is aligned with efforts to intervene and evaluates the student's response to those efforts. Additionally, a response-to-intervention approach can identify ways in which the general education setting can be modified to accommodate the needs of a student, as it focuses efforts on closing the gap between current and desired behavior using pragmatic, available means.

The problems with the response-to-intervention are logical and practical. Logically, it is not possible to diagnose based on response to a treatment unless it can be shown that only people with a particular diagnosis fail to respond. In fact, individuals with and without disabilities respond to many educational interventions (Swanson & Hoskyn, 1998), and so the premise that only students with disabilities will fail to respond is unsound. Practically, response-to-intervention judgments require accurate and continuous measures of student performance, the ability to select and implement sound interventions, and the ability to ensure that interventions are implemented with reasonable fidelity or integrity. Of these requirements, the assessor controls only the accurate and continuous assessment of performance. Selection and implementation of interventions is often beyond the assessor's control, as nearly all educational interventions are mediated and delivered by the student's teacher. Protocols for assessing treatment integrity exist (Gresham, 1989), although treatment integrity protocols are rarely implemented when educational interventions are evaluated (Gresham, MacMillan, Beebe, & Bocian, 2000).

Because so many aspects of the response-to-treatment approach lie beyond the control of the assessor, it has yet to garner a substantial evidential base and practical adherents. However, a legislative shift in emphasis from a diagnosis/ eligibility model of special education services to a response-to-intervention model would encourage the development and practice of response-to-intervention assessment approaches (see Office of Special Education Programs, 2001).

Summary

The current practices in psychological assessment are, in many cases, similar to practices used in nonschool settings. Assessors use instruments for measuring intelligence, psychopathology, and personality that are shared by colleagues in other settings and do so for similar purposes. Much of contemporary assessment is driven by the need to differentially diagnose disabilities so that students can qualify for special education. However, psychological assessment in schools is more likely to use screening instruments, observations, peer-nomination methodologies, and response-to-intervention approaches than psychological assessment in other settings. If the mechanisms that allocate special services shift from differential diagnosis to intervention-based decisions, it is likely that psychological assessment in schools would shift away from traditional clinical approaches toward ecological, intervention-based models for assessment (Prasse & Schrag, 1998).

ASSESSMENT OF ACADEMIC ACHIEVEMENT

Until recently, the assessment of academic achievement would not merit a separate section in a chapter on psychological assessment in schools. In the past, teachers and educational administrators were primarily responsible for assessing student learning, except for differentially diagnosing a disability. However, recent changes in methods for assessing achievement, and changes in the decisions made from achievement measures, have pushed assessment of academic achievement to center stage in many schools. This section will describe the traditional methods for assessing achievement (i.e., individually administered tests used primarily for diagnosis) and then describe new methods for assessing achievement. The section concludes with a review of the standards and testing movement that has increased the importance of academic achievement assessment in schools. Specifically, the topics in this section include the following:

1. Individually administered achievement tests.
2. Curriculum-based assessment and measurement.
3. Performance assessment and portfolios.
4. Large-scale tests and standards-based educational reform.

Individually Administered Tests

Much like individually administered intellectual assessment batteries, individually administered achievement batteries provide a collection of tests to broadly sample various academic achievement domains. Among the most popular achievement batteries are the Woodcock-Johnson Achievement Battery—Third Edition (WJ-III ACH; Woodcock, McGrew, & Mather, 2000a) the Wechsler Individual Achievement Test—Second Edition (WIAT-II; The Psychological Corporation, 2001), the Peabody Individual Achievement Test—Revised (PIAT-R; Markwardt, 1989), and the Kaufman Test of Educational Achievement (KTEA; Kaufman & Kaufman, 1985).

The primary purpose of individually administered academic achievement batteries is to quantify student achievement in ways that support diagnosis of educational disabilities. Therefore, these batteries produce standard scores (and other norm-reference scores, such as percentiles and stanines) that allow examiners to describe how well the student scores relative to a norm group. Often, examiners use scores from achievement batteries to verify that the student is experiencing academic delays or to compare achievement scores to intellectual ability scores for the purpose of diagnosing learning disabilities. Because U.S. federal law identifies seven areas in which students may experience academic difficulties due to a learning disability, most achievement test batteries include tests to assess those seven areas. Table 12.2 lists the tests within each academic achievement battery that assess the seven academic areas identified for learning disability diagnosis.

Interpretation of scores from achievement batteries is less hierarchical or successive than for intellectual assessment batteries. That is, individual test scores are often used to represent an achievement domain. Some achievement test batteries combine two or more test scores to produce a composite. For example, the WJ-III ACH combines scores from the Passage Comprehension and Reading Vocabulary tests to produce a

Reading Comprehension cluster score. However, most achievement batteries use a single test to assess a given academic domain, and scores are not typically combined across academic domains to produce more general estimates of achievement.

Occasionally, examiners will use specific instruments to assess academic domains in greater detail. Examples of more specialized instruments include the Woodcock Reading Mastery Test—Revised (Woodcock, 1987), the Key Math Diagnostic Inventory—Revised (Connolly, 1988), and the Oral and Written Language Scales (Carrow-Woolfolk, 1995). Examiners are likely to use these tests to supplement an achievement test battery (e.g., neither the KTEA nor PIAT-R includes tests of oral language) or to get additional information that could be useful in refining an understanding of the problem or developing an academic intervention. Specialized tests can help examiners go beyond a general statement (e.g., math skills are low) to more precise problem statements (e.g., the student has not yet mastered regrouping procedures for multidigit arithmetic problems). Some achievement test batteries (e.g., the WIAT-II) also supply error analysis protocols to help examiners isolate and evaluate particular skills within a domain.

One domain not listed among the seven academic areas in federal law that is of increasing interest to educators and assessors is the domain of phonemic awareness. Phonemic awareness comprises the areas of grapheme-phoneme relationships (e.g., letter-sound links), phoneme manipulation, and other skills needed to analyze and synthesize print to language. Reading research increasingly identifies low phonemic awareness as a major factor in reading failure and recommends early assessment and intervention to enhance phonemic awareness

TABLE 12.2   Alignment of Achievement Test Batteries to the Seven Areas of Academic Deficit Identified in Federal Legislation

Academic Area	KTEA	PIAT-R	WIAT-II	WJ-III ACH
Listening comprehension	[none]	[none]	Listening comprehension	Understanding directions, oral comprehension
Oral expression	[none]	[none]	Oral expression	Story recall, picture vocabulary
Reading skills	Reading decoding	Reading recognition	Word reading, pseudoword decoding	Letter-word identification, word attack, reading fluency
Reading comprehension	Reading comprehension	Reading comprehension	Reading comprehension	Passage comprehension, reading vocabulary
Math skills	Mathematics computation	Mathematics*	Numerical operations	Calculation, math fluency
Math applications	Mathematics applications		Math reasoning	Applied problems, quantitative concepts
Written expression	Spelling*	Written expression, spelling*	Written expression, spelling*	Writing samples

* A related but indirect measure of the academic area.

skills (National Reading Panel, 2000). Consequently, assessors serving younger elementary students may seek and use instruments to assess phonemic awareness. Although some standardized test batteries (e.g., WIAT-II, WJ-III ACH) provide formal measures of phonemic awareness, most measures of phonemic awareness are not standardized and are experimental in nature (Yopp, 1988). Some standardized measures of phonemic awareness not contained in achievement test batteries include the Comprehensive Test of Phonological Processing (Wagner, Torgesen, & Rashotte, 1999) and The Phonological Awareness Test (Robertson & Salter, 1997).

Curriculum-Based Assessment and Measurement

Although standardized achievement tests are useful for quantifying the degree to which a student deviates from normative achievement expectations, such tests have been criticized. Among the most persistent criticisms are these:

1. The tests are not aligned with important learning outcomes.
2. The tests are unable to provide formative evaluation.
3. The tests describe student performance in ways that are not understandable or linked to instructional practices.
4. The tests are inflexible with respect to the varying instructional models that teachers use.
5. The tests cannot be administered, scored, and interpreted in classrooms.
6. The tests fail to communicate to teachers and students what is important to learn (Fuchs, 1994).

Curriculum-based assessment (CBA; see Idol, Nevin, & Paolucci-Whitcomb, 1996) and measurement (CBM; see Shinn, 1989, 1995) approaches seek to respond to these criticisms. Most CBA and CBM approaches use materials selected from the student's classroom to measure student achievement, and they therefore overcome issues of alignment (i.e., unlike standardized batteries, the content of CBA or CBM is directly drawn from the specific curricula used in the school), links to instructional practice, and sensitivity and flexibility to reflect what teachers are doing. Also, most CBM approaches recommend brief (1–3 minute) assessments 2 or more times per week in the student's classroom, a recommendation that allows CBM to overcome issues of contextual value (i.e., measures are taken and used in the classroom setting) and allows for formative evaluation (i.e., decisions about what is and is not working). Therefore, CBA and CBM approaches to assessment provide technologies that are embedded in the learning context by using classroom materials and observing behavior in classrooms.

The primary distinction between CBA and CBM is the intent of the assessment. Generally, CBA intends to provide information for instructional planning (e.g., deciding what curricular level best meets a student's needs). In contrast, CBM intends to monitor the student's progress in response to instruction. Progress monitoring is used to gauge the outcome of instructional interventions (i.e., deciding whether the student's academic skills are improving). Thus, CBA methods provide teaching or planning information, whereas CBM methods provide testing or outcome information. The metrics and procedures for CBA and CBM are similar, but they differ as a function of the intent of the assessment.

The primary goal of most CBA is to identify what a student has and has not mastered and to match instruction to the student's current level of skills. The first goal is accomplished by having a repertoire of curriculum-based probes that broadly reflect the various skills students should master. The second goal (instructional matching) varies the difficulty of the probes, so that the assessor can identify the ideal balance between instruction that is too difficult and instruction that is too easy for the student. Curriculum-based assessment identifies three levels of instructional match:

1. *Frustration level.* Task demands are too difficult; the student will not sustain task engagement and will generally not learn because there is insufficient understanding to acquire and retain skills.
2. *Instructional level.* Task demands balance task difficulty, so that new information and skills are presented and required, with familiar content or mastered skills, so that students sustain engagement in the task. Instructional level provides the best trade-off between new learning and familiar material.
3. *Independent/Mastery level.* Task demands are sufficiently easy or familiar to allow the student to complete the tasks with no significant difficulty. Although mastery level materials support student engagement, they do not provide many new or unfamiliar task demands and therefore result in little learning.

Instructional match varies as a function of the difficulty of the task and the support given to the student. That is, students can tolerate more difficult tasks when they have direct support from a teacher or other instructor, but students require lower levels of task difficulty in the absence of direct instructional support.

Curriculum-based assessment uses direct assessment using behavioral principles to identify when instructional demands are at frustration, instruction, or mastery levels. The behavioral principles that guide CBA and CBM include defining behaviors in their smallest meaningful unit of behavior (e.g., a word read aloud in context); objectivity and precision of assessment (e.g., counting the frequency of a specific behavior); and repeated measurement over time. Therefore, CBA and CBM approaches tend to value metrics that are discrete, that can be counted and measured as rates of behavior, and that are drawn from students' responses in their classroom context using classroom materials. For example, reading skills might be counted as the proportion of words the student can identify in a given passage or the number of words the student reads aloud in 1 minute. Mathematics skills could be measured as the proportion of problems solved correctly in a set, or the number or correct digits produced per minute in a 2-minute timed test.

Curriculum-based assessment protocols define instructional match between the student and the material in terms of these objective measures of performance. For example, a passage in which a student recognizes less than 93% of the words is deemed to be at frustration level. Likewise, a third-grade student reading aloud at a rate of 82 words/min with 3 errors/min is deemed to be reading a passage that is at instructional level; a passage that the student could read aloud at a rate of more than 100 words/min. with 5 errors would be deemed to be at the student's mastery level. Table 12.3 provides examples of how assessors can use CBA and CBM metrics to determine the instructional match for task demands in reading and mathematics.

Whereas assessors vary the type and difficulty of task demands in a CBA approach to identify how best to match instruction to a student, CBM approaches require assessors to hold task type and difficulty constant and interpret changes in the metrics as evidence of improving student skill. Thus, assessors might develop a set of 20 reading passages, or 20 probes of mixed mathematics problem types of similar difficulty levels, and then randomly and repeatedly administer these probes to a student over time to evaluate the student's academic progress. In most instances, the assessor would chart the results of these 1-min or 2-min samples of behavior to create a time series. Increasing rates of desired behavior (e.g., words read aloud per minute) and stable or decreasing rates of errors (e.g., incorrect words per minute) indicate an increase in a student's skills.

Figures 12.1 and 12.2 present oral reading fluency rates for a student. Figure 12.1 plots the results of eight 1-min reading probes, indicating the number of words the student read correctly, and the number read incorrectly, in one minute. The assessor calculated the median words/min correct for the eight data points and placed an X in the middle of the collected (baseline) data series. The assessor then identified an instructional goal—that is, that the student would read 100 words/min correctly within 30 days. The line connecting the student's current median performance and the assessor's goal is an aim line, or the rate of improvement needed to ensure that the student meets the goal. Figure 12.2 shows the intervention selected to achieve the goal (choral reading) and the chart reflecting the student's progress toward the goal. Given the tendency of the student's progress to fall below the aim line, the assessor concluded that this instructional intervention was not sufficient to meet the performance goal. Assuming that the assessor determined that the choral reading approach was conducted appropriately, these results would lead the assessor to select a more modest goal or a different intervention.

Curriculum-based assessment and CBM approaches promise accurate instructional matching and continuous monitoring of progress to enhance instructional decision-making. Also, school districts can develop CBM norms to provide scores similar to standardized tests (see Shinn, 1989)

TABLE 12.3   Sample Values of Curriculum-Based Metrics for Instructional Matching in Reading and Mathematics

Academic Skill	Support Level	Frustration	Instruction	Mastery
Proportion of unique known words in a passage	Independent Supported	0–92% 0–69%	93–96% 70–85%	97–100% 86–100%
Oral reading rate grades 1–2	Independent	0–39 words/min or more than 4 errors/min	40–60 words/min and 4 or fewer errors/min	More than 60 words/min and 4 or fewer errors/min
Oral reading rate grades 3–6	Independent	0–69 words/min or more than 6 errors/min	70–100 words/min and 6 or fewer errors/min	More than 100 words/min and 6 or fewer errors/min
Proportion of mathematics problems correct	Supported	0–74%	75–90%	91–100%
Correct digits/min grades 1–3	Independent	0–9	10–19	20 or more
Correct digits/min grades 4 and up	Independent	0–19	20–39	40 or more

Source: Data in this table based on Fuchs and Fuchs (1982), Shapiro (1988), and Braden, Kovaleski, and Prasse (1996).

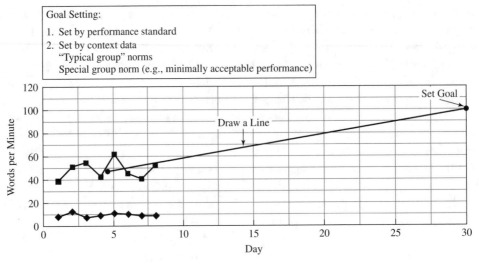

Figure 12.1   Using CBM to set current and desired performance for oral reading fluency.

for screening and diagnostic purposes (although it is expensive to do so). Generally, research supports the value of these approaches. They are reliable and consistent (Hintze, Owen, Shapiro, & Daly, 2000), although there is some evidence of slight ethnic and gender bias (Kranzler, Miller, & Jordan, 1999). The validity of CBA and CBM measures is supported by correspondence to standardized achievement measures and other measures of student learning (e.g., Hintze, Shapiro, Conte, & Basile, 1997; Kranzler, Brownell, & Miller, 1998) and evidence that teachers value CBA methods more than standardized achievement tests (Eckert & Shapiro, 1999). Most important, CBA matching and CBM monitoring of mathematics performance yields more rapid increases in aca-

demic achievement among mildly disabled students than among peers who were not provided with CBM monitoring (Allinder, Bolling, Oats, & Gagnon, 2000; Stecker & Fuchs, 2000).

However, CBA and CBM have some limitations. One such limitation is the limited evidence supporting the positive effects of CBA and CBM for reading achievement (Nolet & McLaughlin, 1997; Peverly & Kitzen, 1998). Others criticize CBA and CBM for failing to reflect constructivist, cognitively complex, and meaning-based learning outcomes and for having some of the same shortcomings as standardized tests (Mehrens & Clarizio, 1993). Still, CBA and CBM promise to align assessment with learning and intervention

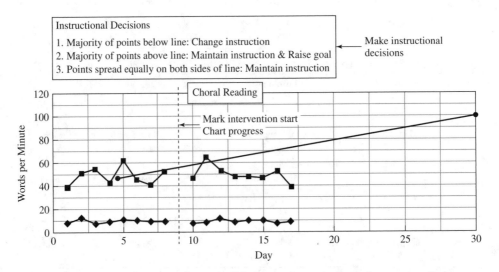

Figure 12.2   Using CBM to make instructional decisions using an aim line and progress monitoring.

more directly than standardized tests of achievement and to lend themselves to continuous progress monitoring in ways that traditional tests cannot match.

Performance Assessment and Portfolios

Performance assessment was inspired in part by the perception that reductionist (e.g., CBM) and standardized testing approaches to assessment failed to capture constructivist, higher order thinking elements of student performance. Performance assessment developed in large part because of the premise that that which is tested is taught. Therefore, performance assessment advocates argued that educators needed tests worth teaching to (Wiggins, 1989). Performance assessment of complex, higher order academic achievement developed to assess complex, challenging academic skills, which in turn support school reforms (Glatthorn, Bragaw, Dawkins, & Parker, 1998) and teachers' professional development (Stiggins & Bridgeford, 1984).

Performance assessment is characterized by complex tasks that require students to understand problems in context, accurately integrate and apply academic knowledge and skills to solve the problems, and communicate their problem-solving process and solutions via written, graphic, oral, and demonstrative exhibits (Braden, 1999). Performance assessments are characterized by tasks embedded in a problem-solving context that require students to construct responses, usually over an extended time frame, and that may require collaboration among group members. Scores produced by performance assessments are criterion referenced to levels of proficiency. An example of a mathematics performance assessment appears in Figure 12.3.

Scoring of performance assessments is a critical issue. Because responses are constructed rather than selected, it is not possible to anticipate all possible answers. Therefore, assessors use scoring guides called rubrics to judge responses against a criterion. Scores are generally rank ordered to reflect increasing levels of proficiency and typically contain four or five categories (e.g., Novice, Basic, Proficient, Advanced). Rubrics may be holistic (i.e., providing a single score for the response) or analytic (i.e., providing multiple scores reflecting various aspects of performance). An example of the rubric used to score the example mathematics performance assessment appears in Figure 12.4. Note that the rubric is analytic (i.e., it provides scores in more than one dimension) and can be used across a variety of grade levels and problems to judge the quality of student work. As is true of most rubrics, the sample rubric emphasizes conceptual aspects of mathematics, rather than simple computation or other low-level aspects of performance.

Portfolios complement performance assessment by providing a means for collecting student work over time. Essentially, a portfolio is a collection of student work that demonstrates the student's proficiency in one or more academic areas. Although portfolios could include results from standardized tests or CBA and CBM results, portfolios generally emphasize complex works that integrate multiple dimensions of proficiency, such as performance assessments, essays, recordings of student performances, and the like (see Barton & Collins, 1997).

Two features generally define a portfolio: rules for including or excluding student work, and rules regarding how work will be judged. Rules for including student work may emphasize work in progress (i.e., a working portfolio) or completed work; also, rules may call for representative works (random work sampling) or best works (optimal work sampling). Most portfolio systems share negotiation of these issues among teachers, students, and occasionally parents, so that rules about including and judging work take on a collaborative quality. Finally, most portfolio systems invoke a summative evaluation process, so that students are required to present their work (a portfolio exhibition) to the teacher or a panel of judges that may include parent and community representatives. These judgments occur even if the individual parts of a portfolio are already scored, so that exhibitions create the opportunity for reflection and longitudinal evaluation of student performance. Portfolio exhibitions may be used to make educational decisions, such as promotion to the next grade or high school graduation, or they may have no specific consequences beyond inviting reflection, engagement, and progress monitoring.

Although performance assessment and portfolios are argued to have strong educational benefits, there are also challenges to performance assessment and portfolio approaches. One significant problem is the reliability of judgments of student work. Performance assessment and portfolio judgments often show unacceptably poor interrater agreement, and portfolio contents may present skewed perceptions of student work (Shapley & Bush, 1999). However, interrater reliability can be increased to acceptable levels with rubric use and adequate rater training, which are resource-intensive activities (Ediger, 2000). Even when interrater agreement is good, performance assessments have limited agreement across tasks purporting to measure the same domain (Shavelson, Ruiz-Primo, & Wiley, 1999), which creates a significant assessment dilemma: to achieve good generalization of results, one must use many performance assessment tasks, yet performance assessment tasks are complex, long, and expensive. Performance assessments and portfolios may not reduce gaps between ethnic groups relative to standardized tests (Braden, 1999), and they may increase gender gaps for early elementary

Illinois Standards Achievement Test Third Grade

Anna and her little brother, Mark, are going to the ice cream store to buy ice cream treats. They have $4.00 to spend on two different ice cream treats. Each must have ice cream and at least one topping. Use price lists to choose a treat for Anna and a treat for Mark.

- List what is on Anna's treat and Mark's treat.
- Give the total cost for both treats.
- Tell how much money is left over after buying the two treats.

Show all your work. **Explain in words** *how* you got your answer and *why* you did the steps you did to solve the problem.

Ice Cream	Cost
Small scoop of ice cream	$0.75
Large scoop of ice cream	$1.25

Toppings	Cost
Chocolate sauce	$0.50
Hot fudge sauce	$0.50
Butterscotch sauce	$0.25
Strawberries	$1.00
Crushed peanuts	$0.20
Whipped cream	$0.15
Banana slices	$0.65
Cherry	$0.05

Anna's Treat

Mark's Treat

For this response, make sure you

- Show all your work in solving the problem.
- Clearly label your answer.
- Tell in words *how* you solved the problem.
- Tell in words *why* you did the steps you did to solve the problem.
- Write as clearly as you can.

Anna's Treat

Mark's Treat

Figure 12.3   Sample performance assessment in mathematics for third grade.   *Source:* Illinois State Board of Education (2001), p. 69.

MATHEMATICS SCORING RUBRIC: A GUIDE TO SCORING EXTENDED-RESPONSE ITEMS			
Score Level	**Mathematical Knowledge** Knowledge of mathematical principles and concepts that result in a correct solution to a problem	**Strategic Knowledge** Identification of important elements of the problem and the use of models, diagrams, symbols, and/or algorithms to systematically represent and integrate concepts	**Explanation** Written explanation and rationales that translate into words the steps of the solution process and provide justification for each step (although important, the length of response, grammar, and syntax are not the critical elements of this dimension)
4	• Shows complete understanding of the problem's mathematical concepts and principles • Uses appropriate mathematical terminology & notations including labeling the answer if appropriate; that is, whether or not the unit is called for in the stem of the item • Executes algorithms completely and correctly	• Identifies all the important elements of the problem and shows complete understanding of the relationships among elements • Reflects an appropriate and systematic strategy for solving the problem • Gives clear evidence of a complete and systematic solution process	• Gives a complete written explanation of the solution process employed; explanation addresses both *what* was done and *why* it was done • May include a diagram with a complete explanation of all its elements
3	• Shows nearly complete understanding of the problem's mathematical concepts and principles • Uses nearly correct mathematical terminology and notations • Executes algorithms completely; computations are generally correct but may contain minor errors	• Identifies most of the important elements of the problem and shows general understanding of the relationships among them • Reflects an appropriate strategy for solving the problem • Solution process is nearly complete	• Gives a nearly complete written explanation of the solution process employed; clearly explains *what* was done and begins to address *why* it was done • May include a diagram with most of the elements explained
2	• Shows some understanding of the problem's mathematical concepts and principles • May contain major computational errors	• Identifies some important elements of the problem but shows only limited understanding of the relationships among them • Appears to reflect an appropriate strategy but the application of strategy is unclear, or a related strategy is applied logically and consistently • Gives some evidence of a solution process	• Gives some written explanation of the solution process employed, either explains *what* was done or addresses *why* it was done; explanation is vague or difficult to interpret • May include a diagram with some of the elements explained
1	• Shows limited to no understanding of the problem's mathematical concepts and principles • May misuse or fail to use mathematical terms • May contain major computational errors	• Fails to identify important elements or places too much emphasis on unimportant elements • May reflect an inappropriate or inconsistent strategy for solving the problem • Gives minimal evidence of a solution process; process may be difficult to identify • May attempt to use irrelevant outside information	• Gives minimal written explanation of the solution process; may fail to explain *what* was done and *why* it was done • Explanation does not match the presented solution process • May include minimal discussion of the elements in a diagram; explanation of significant elements is unclear
0	No answer attempted	No apparent strategy	No written explanation of the solution process is provided

Figure 12.4 Scoring rubric for mathematics performance assessment.

students (Supovitz & Brennan, 1997). Performance assessments and portfolios require substantial resources, such as task and rubric development and teacher training (Ediger, 2000), which may lead schools to avoid portfolio assessments (Underwood, 1998). An advantage to performance and portfolio assessment is the ability to include group work, yet doing so raises the question of whose work is actually rated in the assessment (Gearhart & Herman, 1998).

These problems have not prevented the large-scale adoption of performance assessment and portfolios. For example, Kentucky, Maryland, and Vermont require on-demand portfolio assessments or portfolios as part of their annual assessment programs (Education Week, 2001). Performance assessments and portfolios are likely to remain popular with educators as mechanisms to inspire constructivist, higher order learning and teaching. These methods can also attain reasonable technical adequacy for reliability and validity, but they are likely to do so only if schools invest substantial resources for developing tasks and rubrics and train raters in their use.

Large-Scale Tests and Standards-Based Educational Reform

Educators have used large-scale assessments or group tests to measure academic achievement for decades. Historically, a school district would give a test at one or more elementary and middle school grades, report the scores to its school board and community, and use the results for self-evaluations (e.g., adequacy of curriculum). However, beginning in the late 1980s, the local, informal use of large-scale achievement tests gave way to standards-based education reform.

The logic of standards-based education reform is straightforward: Establish standards for what students should know and do, select assessments to evaluate the degree to which students meet these standards, and report results back to educational stakeholders (e.g., students, teachers, parents, administrators) with the expectation that educators would use assessment results to guide educational reforms (see Ravitch, 1999; Thomas B. Fordham Foundation, 1998). Standards-based reforms at the state and federal levels introduced two key changes from previous educational practices: first, that standards would be high, and second, that test results have formal consequences for schools, states, and possibly individual students and teachers.

The impetus for these changes was reflected in federal funding of public education. Title I of the Elementary and Secondary Education Act (ESEA) requires states to adopt "challenging educational standards" and to institute assessment procedures to judge whether schools are demonstrating continuous progress in preparing elementary, junior high, and high school students to meet these standards. Because every

state accepts Title I ESEA funding, all states have large-scale assessment programs in three or more grades (Education Week, 2001). The ESEA reauthorization will expand the testing requirement to include annual testing in reading and mathematics in grades 3–8 and increase accountability requirements for states (Bush, 2001).

Most states meet the federal requirement to annually assess student achievement by purchasing one of the so-called Big Three group achievement tests: the Iowa Tests of Basic Skills (ITBS; Hoover, Hieronymus, Frisbie, & Dunbar, 1993), the Stanford Achievement Tests—9th Edition (SAT-9; The Psychological Corporation, 1996), or the TerraNova (CTB/McGraw-Hill, 1998). These achievement test batteries appear in 10 or more forms for kindergarten through high school grade levels and usually provide tests of reading, language arts, mathematics, social studies, and science. Some batteries include tests for more specific areas, such as spelling or reading vocabulary. Although large-scale tests are often criticized for their limited ability to assess complex student achievement, most batteries have adapted formats to mimic more authentic forms of assessment. For example, most batteries now include longer (1–2 page) reading passages and extended response writing prompts and may provide performance assessments to supplement the traditional selected-response formats. Therefore, some of the criticisms leveled at group tests of achievement may be aimed at superficial aspects of the assessment (e.g., selected response formats) and consequently overlook the depth of assessment these batteries may provide (Cizek, 1998; S. N. Elliott, Braden, & White, 2001).

States may purchase the test as is from the test publisher or (more commonly) contract with the publisher to provide a test version customized to the state's educational standards. For example, California, Arizona, and Florida use a customized version of the SAT-9 for their annual testing programs. A few states (e.g., Vermont) contract with a test development company to build test specifically tailored to the state's educational standards. All but a few states use group achievement tests composed primarily of selected response (i.e., multiple-choice) items as their primary accountability mechanism, although most states include at least a constructed response essay in their assessments. A few states (e.g., Kentucky, Vermont) rely primarily or exclusively on performance assessments or portfolios, and a few states (e.g., Maryland) mix performance and selected response assessments (Education Week, 2001).

In addition to increasing their use of large-scale achievement tests, states are also increasing the consequences associated with test results. Consequences have moved from low-stakes uses, such as simply reporting results to the public, to high-stakes uses, such as tracking, retention, promotion, and graduation (see Heubert & Hauser, 1999). The increased importance of test scores for students has inspired professional psychology and education organizations to produce policies to guide the appropriate and effective uses of large-scale tests for high-stakes decisions (e.g., American Educational Research Association, 2000; American Educational Research Association, American Psychological Association, National Council on Measurement in Education, 1999; American Psychological Association, 2001). These policies encourage the use of multiple data sources (rather than a single test score), improving students' opportunities to learn, and adopting effective alternatives to grade retention for students not meeting standards.

The increased use of large-scale achievement tests to stimulate standards-based reforms and educational accountability is not without critics. Although there have been episodes of parent-supported boycotts of testing (Schrag, 2000), surveys of parents show overwhelming support for tests as a tool for systemic accountability and even for making high-stakes decisions (Driesler, 2001). Within the educational community, critics (e.g., Labaree, 2000; Nave, Miech, & Moesteller, 2000) have argued against state standards, although most critics focus their criticisms on large-scale achievement tests as a tool for educational reform (e.g., Kohn, 2000; Wiggins, 1989). Others argue that standards are antithetical to profound individual differences among students (Coffman, 1993), whereas still others counter that individual differences can be reconciled with high achievement standards (Tomlinson, 2000). Although not unanimous, support for standards and educational accountability is widespread, even among teacher unions (e.g., Feldman, 2000). The specific value of standardized achievement tests as a tool for instructional reform remains more controversial, even among proponents of standards (e.g., Kinder, 2000).

Summary

Assessment of academic achievement is often informal and conducted primarily by teachers in classrooms with little or no input from psychologists. However, individually administered academic achievement test batteries have a strong diagnostic focus and are typically used only by assessment specialists. Curriculum-based assessment and measurement technologies are increasingly popular with professionals concerned with intervening in classroom settings to improve student performance. Performance assessment and portfolios are embraced by many in the educational enterprise as tools to enhance student learning and instructional reforms. Finally, the use of large-scale assessment techniques, particularly group achievement test batteries, is increasing among states as they seek to comply with federal legislation and spur

standards-based educational reforms. Except for individually administered achievement test batteries, psychological assessors have traditionally delegated assessment of student achievement to nonspecialists. This may change, as educational systems will increasingly require knowledge of assessment principles, procedures, and products to make appropriate high-stakes decisions. Experts in psychological assessments within schools may help systems acquire the capacity for understanding and using assessment procedures wisely.

THE FUTURE OF PSYCHOLOGICAL ASSESSMENT IN SCHOOLS

In addition to describing the current practice of psychological assessment in schools, I will prognosticate about the future of assessment. The future is a child of the present, and consequently predictions will reflect trends already evident in contemporary practice. The trends I will discuss with respect to their impact on the future are aligning assessment to scientific advances, aligning assessment to educational standards, accommodating diverse learners in assessment, and treatment utility.

Aligning Assessment to Scientific Advances

The trend to align assessment with scientific advances means developing and using assessment instruments and procedures that reflect the field's knowledge of psychology. This trend is already evident in the assessment of intelligence. For example, newer intelligence test batteries (e.g., CAS, WJ-III) draw on contemporary theories of cognitive processing and are more explicit about the links between the tests and the theories than traditional intelligence test batteries (e.g., WISC-III). The last revision of the Stanford-Binet intelligence battery (i.e., the SBIV) was substantially more aligned with hierarchical intelligence theories than its predecessors; likewise, even the venerable Wechsler batteries are likely to morph into new forms that better reflect contemporary thinking about cognitive abilities.

The shape of these new intelligence test batteries is as yet unclear. The major influence on recent revisions in intelligence tests is a hierarchical taxonomy of mental abilities, in which general intellectual ability is a superordinate construct, and under which various mental abilities are organized into increasingly narrow cognitive processes (e.g., Carroll, 1993; Jensen, 1998). This model is increasingly promoted as a unifying framework for cognitive assessment (e.g., Flanagan, 2000; McGrew, Keith, Flanagan, & Vanderwood, 1997). However, at least one alternative model, based on Luria's neuropsychological framework, has emerged (i.e., the CAS). It is not yet clear whether Luria's framework is viable for assessing individual differences in cognitive abilities and, if so, whether the CAS successfully represents the framework with practical assessment technologies (Keith, Kranzler, & Flanagan, 2001; cf. Naglieri, 1999).

Aligning assessment to scientific advances in the affective domain will most likely mean pushing instruments and classification systems toward an empirical approach to defining psychopathology (e.g., Achenbach & McConaughy, 1996). That is, assessment instruments and procedures are likely to focus on broad dimensions of externalizing versus internalizing disorders and will be less likely to adopt diagnostic categories developed for adults and extended into childhood (e.g., American Psychiatric Association, 2000). Additionally, the trend away from projective measures in favor of observational and checklist approaches, which is already evident in school-based practices, is likely to continue, so that projective measures will be increasingly marginalized in school-based assessment practice.

A way in which scientific advances will affect assessment comes from outside psychology: the domain of technology. Clearly, computer-assisted assessment is already making inroads into school-based assessment practices. This trend will continue, not only for supporting the scoring and interpretation of traditional assessment tools (e.g., the WJ-III can be scored only with the assistance of a computer), but also in the administration of assessment instruments. To date, computer-based assessment of students has been slow to develop because of technological limitations and the relative inability of younger students to use computers. Those barriers will fall as computers become more available and easier to use. Three aspects of computer-administered assessments are likely to develop: (a) computer-assisted technologies for selecting a set of items customized to the student's ability level (increasing assessment efficiency), (b) repeated assessments of student performance to provide progress monitoring and support instructional decision-making (e.g., using the computer to administer and score oral reading rate from student speech), and (c) increased use of computers to assess domains that cannot be assessed with assessor-driven technologies (e.g., correct decision speed, Nettelbeck, 1998, or physiological indicators of autonomic arousal).

Aligning Assessment to Educational Standards

The standards-based education movement will demand two changes in standardized tests of academic achievement: a shift in how results are described and a change in the content assessed. Currently, standardized achievement tests report results primarily as norm-referenced scores, which accurately define where a student's score places relative to others of the same age or grade. However, the standards-based education reform movement emphasizes student proficiency with respect to objectively defined criterion measures, not relative student standing. Most states use bookmarking procedures to define proficiency levels that are not dependent on norm-referenced descriptions via the use of item response theory scores such as scale scores (see Braden, 2002; Elliott, Braden, et al., 2001, Chap. 3). In a bookmarking procedure, educators use item books, in which there is one item per page, and the items are ordered so that the first page presents the easiest item and the last page presents the hardest item. They then insert bookmarks to reflect their judgment of the item difficulties that divide proficiency categories (e.g., basic, proficient, advanced) for a given grade. This process is typically followed by discussion and consensus-building activities until standards for proficiency (e.g., a proficient student in the fourth grade should pass all items below the bookmark separating the proficient from lower categories).

However, individually administered achievement test batteries provide norm-referenced standard scores. These tests should begin to report a student's score relative to the criterion-referenced proficiency levels used in the state or at least by major test publishers to make individually administered batteries relevant to the standards-based educational environment.

The second change in achievement tests will likely be a shift in item content so that tests are aligned with educational standards. Fortunately, most states have adopted standards that resemble (in some cases, verbatim) the standards passed by professional organizations. For example, the National Council of Teachers of Mathematics (2000) has developed standards describing what students should know and do at various grade levels in mathematics; similar standards are available for reading, language arts, science, and social studies. As test publishers begin to align test content to these standards, the subject matter assessed by the tests will change (e.g., probability problems will be included even for young children, as directed by standards), and the nature of the items will also change (e.g., publishers will begin to include more extended response and performance assessment items). It is also likely that publishers will begin to capitalize on computer technology to administer, score, and report assessments, so that student progress toward mastering standards may be frequently monitored. Finally, it is also likely that computer-based systems will allow for multiple forms of measurement, rather than focusing on a single instrument, which would allow more accurate decisions regarding high-stakes consequences using multiple sources of information (e.g., teacher judgments, portfolio scores, test scores).

Accommodating Diverse Learners in Assessment

At the present time, procedures for accommodating diverse learners in assessments are largely a subjective process driven by examiner judgments. As scientific advances and educational standards will more clearly define the constructs to be assessed, assessment instruments and processes will need to be more rigorous in adequately assessing constructs without capturing construct-irrelevant influences on test scores introduced by student diversity. Historically, test authors and publishers have directly addressed issues of ethnic and gender diversity but have generally avoided or only indirectly addressed issues of linguistic differences and disabilities in their assessment procedures. This will begin to change, in part because the proportion of students speaking languages other than English is rapidly increasing, and in part because of pressures to include all students (including those with language differences or disabilities) in educational accountability programs.

Research on these topics is still fairly limited, although the available results are intriguing. For example, research suggests that some accommodations either fail to help or even hinder the performance of students who are English language learners (Abedi, 2001; Abedi, Lord, Hofstetter, & Baker, 2000) or who have disabilities (Elliott, Kratochwill, & McKevitt, 2001). Therefore, test publishers will need to consider ways in which tests can be constructed (e.g., with multiple language forms) or adapted (e.g., with accommodations) to help assessors accurately assess the constructs targeted in the assessment. Consequently, it is likely that test publishers are likely to offer increasingly diverse arrays of assessment forms (e.g., formal language translations) as they publish tests, and the directions accompanying tests are likely to be more explicit regarding ways in which assessors can (and cannot) accommodate diverse student needs without compromising the validity of the assessment. One example of this trend is the publication of an American Sign Language (ASL) translation of the WAIS-III (Kostrubala & Braden, 1998), which provides a language translation from English to ASL and explicit directions for accommodating individuals who are deaf and hard of hearing in the assessment.

Treatment Utility

The final issue that is likely to influence psychological assessment in schools is the increasing expectation that assessment have utility for treatment. Treatment utility of assessment refers to "the degree to which assessment is shown to contribute to beneficial treatment outcome" (Hayes, Nelson, & Jarrett, 1987, p. 963). This benefit may be realized in many ways, including selecting, implementing, or monitoring a treatment or intervention. In school contexts, treatment utility may also be understood to include instructional utility—that is, the value of assessment for selecting, implementing, or monitoring instruction.

Contemporary methods of assessment using individually administered tests of intelligence and emotion contribute to diagnosis but may not contribute to intervention or treatment. Although interpretive protocols promise utility for selecting interventions or treatments (e.g., Sattler, 2001), there is no evidence that these tests have treatment utility (Gresham & Witt, 1997). The use of assessment for treatment selection is warranted only when the cost (human and financial) of assessment is less than the treatment, and there are substantially different treatment responses among individuals with similar problems (Braden & Kratochwill, 1997). It is not clear that these conditions are met for most academic and social problems experienced in school settings (e.g., the same instructional intervention tends to work regardless of diagnostic category; Kavale, 1990; Reschly & Grimes, 1995). However, some newer approaches to assessment may provide better value for treatment matching (e.g., Naglieri & Gottling, 1997; Naglieri & Johnson, 2000). Although it may be debated whether tests of latent psychological traits, such as cognitive abilities or emotional status, will ever contribute to treatment selection (Gresham & Witt, 1997), the notion that assessment should contribute to treatment utility is becoming a shared expectation that will challenge those who develop assessment techniques (e.g., Naglieri & Das, 1997) and procedures to show how the procedures contribute to treatment utility.

The other two aspects of treatment utility (i.e., implementing and monitoring interventions) will also receive greater attention in the future. Currently, methods for evaluating the degree to which teachers or others adhere to an intervention protocol (i.e., treatment integrity) are limited to global, indirect, qualitative approaches (Sterling-Turner, Watson, Wildman, Watkins, & Little, 2001). It is likely that protocols for evaluating treatment integrity will increase in sophistication and will be aligned with the movement to ensure that interventions have demonstrated effectiveness for helping students. All treatments are not equal in quality or outcome; likewise, psychologists will be under increasing pressure from internal and external sources to ensure that they select and implement evidence-based interventions for the students they serve (see Stoiber & Kratochwill, 2001). Assessment procedures and techniques must provide more compelling evidence to show that they respond to these pressures than do most current approaches, particularly diagnostic assessment instruments. Some early examples of assessment-to-intervention protocols include the ACES and AIMS (DiPerna & Elliott, 2000; S. N. Elliott, DiPerna, et al., 2001) and the Process

Assessment of the Learner (PAL; Berninger, 2001). Future developments will expand these efforts, most likely by including treatment integrity protocols. However, the available technology for evaluating treatment integrity is not well developed and is resource intensive (Sterling-Turner et al., 2001); furthermore, it is not clear that educators will necessarily welcome the scrutiny inherent in evaluations of their adherence to intervention protocols.

The final way in which assessment may have treatment utility is via progress monitoring. The tools for progress monitoring appear to be present or nearly so in the form of observational systems, ratings of nonacademic behaviors and skills, and CBM metrics. The largest changes in progress monitoring will come from two influences already discussed in this section: technology and alignment to educational standards. Technology will most likely improve observational and rating recording systems, allow for more natural administration and scoring of progress monitoring (e.g., it will allow students to write or say their responses), and incorporate academic content aligned to educational standards.

Treatment utility will also be enhanced by the alignment and integration of assessment techniques and processes. Current assessment procedures lack alignment and integration. For example, diagnostic instruments are qualitatively different from the assessment approaches used for assessing treatment integrity, and these in turn are different from progress-monitoring techniques. An exception to this general conclusion is the alignment and integration of techniques and processes that use CBA for instructional matching (treatment selection), followed by CBM for progress monitoring. Future methods of assessment in schools will align assessment, so that procedures used early in the problem identification process contribute meaningfully and directly to intervention selection, monitoring treatment integrity, and evaluating treatment outcomes. Also, these processes will be integrated into unified systems of assessment. It is likely that this integration will proceed by adding modules to existing instruments, so that assessors can add functions as they see the need. For example, modules that add treatment integrity and progress monitoring to ACES/AIMS or PAL approaches are likely targets for integrating and aligning assessment across problem identification, intervention, and evaluation stages. Once again, in school contexts, interventions could include treatments (special procedures to solve atypical problems), interventions (changes in the environment to accommodate individual differences among students), or instruction (methods of teaching to enhance learning).

Summary

The near future of psychological assessment in schools is likely to respond to pressures already in existence. These pressures will come from within the field of psychology (e.g., aligning procedures to scientific advances and evidence-based evaluations of interventions) and from without (e.g., technology, standards-based education reform, student diversity). In most cases, I have identified trends that have already elicited new instruments, approaches, or changes in assessments. However, the degree to which things actually change will depend in large part on the degree to which pressures maintaining current practices and procedures change. If the current pressures for differential diagnosis in education change, it is likely that assessment procedures will more rapidly adapt to achieve treatment utility (see Office of Special Education Programs, 2001; Reschly & Ysseldyke, 1995). However, if these pressures remain stable, psychological assessment will continue to emphasize diagnosis and thus will struggle to meet competing—and perhaps irreconcilable—needs for intervention and progress monitoring.

REFERENCES

Abedi, J. (2001). *Assessment and accommodations for English language learners: Issues and recommendations* (Policy Brief No. 4). Los Angeles, CA: National Center for Research on Education, Standards, and Student Testing. Retrieved September 22, 2001, from http://www.cse.ucla.edu/CRESST/Newsletters/polbrf4web.pdf

Abedi, J., Lord, C., Hofstetter, C., & Baker, E. (2000). Impact of accommodation strategies on English language learners' test performance. *Educational Measurement: Issues and Practice, 19,* 16–26.

Achenbach, T. M. (1991a). *Child Behavior Checklist & Profile for Ages 4–18.* Burlington, VT: Child Behavior Checklist.

Achenbach, T. M. (1991b). *Youth Self-Report Form & Profile for Ages 11–18.* Burlington, VT: Child Behavior Checklist.

Achenbach, T. M., & McConaughy, S. H. (1996). Relations between DSM-IV and empirically based assessment. *School Psychology Review, 25,* 329–341.

Achenbach, T. M., McConaughy, S. H., & Howell, C. T. (1987). Child/adolescent behavioral and emotional problems: Implications of cross-informant correlations for situational specificity. *Psychological Bulletin, 101,* 213–232.

Adams, C. D., Kelley, M. L., & McCarthy, M. (1997). The Adolescent Behavior Checklist: Development and initial psychometric properties of a self-report measure for adolescents with ADHD. *Journal of Clinical Child Psychology, 25,* 77–86.

Albee, G. (1998). The politics of primary prevention. *Journal of Primary Prevention, 19,* 117–127.

Algozzine, B., & Ysseldyke, J. E. (1992). *Strategies and tactics for effective instruction.* Longmont, CO: Sopris West.

Allinder, R. M., Bolling, R. M., Oats, R. G., & Gagnon, W. A. (2000). Effects of teacher self-monitoring on implementation of curriculum-based measurement and mathematics computation achievement of students with disabilities. *Remedial and Special Education, 21*(4), 219–226.

American Education Research Association. (2000). *AERA position statement concerning high-stakes testing preK-12 education.* Washington, DC: Author. Retrieved November 11, 2001, from http://www.aera.net/ about/policy/stakes.htm

American Educational Research Association, American Psychological Association, & National Council on Measurement in Education. (1999). *Standards for educational and psychological testing* (3rd ed.). Washington, DC: Author.

American Psychiatric Association. (2000). *Diagnostic and statistical manual of mental disorders: DSM-IV-TR* (4th ed., text rev.). Washington, DC: Author.

American Psychological Association. (1998). *Archival description of school psychology.* Washington, DC: Author. Retrieved April 10, 2000, from http://www.apa.org/crsppp/schpsych.html

American Psychological Association. (2001). *Appropriate use of high-stakes testing in our nations schools.* Washington, DC: Author. Retrieved from http://www.apa.org/pubinfo/testing.html

Athanasiou, M. S. (2000). Current nonverbal assessment instruments: A comparison of psychometric integrity and test fairness. *Journal of Psychoeducational Assessment, 18,* 211–229.

Barton, J., & Collins, A. (Eds.). (1997). *Portfolio assessment: A handbook for educators.* Menlo Park, CA: Innovative Learning Publications.

Batsche, G. M., & Knoff, H. M. (1995). Best practices in linking assessment to intervention. In A. Thomas & J. P. Grimes (Eds.), *Best practices in school psychology* (4th ed., pp. 569–586). Bethesda, MD: National Association of School Psychologists.

Beitchman, J. H. (1996). *Feelings, Attitudes and Behaviors Scale for Children.* North Tonawanda, NY: Multi-Health Systems.

Bellak, L., & Bellak, S. S. (1992). *Children's Apperception Test.* Larchmont, NY: C.P.S.

Bergan, J. R., & Kratochwill, T. R. (1990). *Behavioral consultation and therapy.* New York: Plenum Press.

Berninger, V. W. (1997). Introduction to interventions for students with learning and behavior problems: Myths and realities. *School Psychology Review, 26,* 326–332.

Berninger, V. W. (2001). *Process assessment of the learner.* San Antonio, TX: The Psychological Corporation.

Binet, A., & Simon, T. (1914). *Mentally defective children.* London: E. Arnold.

Bocian, K. M., Beebe, M. E., MacMillan, D. L., & Gresham, F. M. (1999). Competing paradigms in learning disabilities classification by schools and the variations in the meaning of discrepant achievement. *Learning Disabilities Research and Practice, 14,* 1–14.

Bracken, B. A. (1992). *Multi-Dimensional Self-Concept Scale.* Austin, TX: PRO-ED.

Bracken, B. A., & McCallum, R. S. (1998). *Universal Nonverbal Intelligence Test.* Itasca, IL: Riverside.

Braden, J. P. (1999). Performance assessment and diversity. *School Psychology Quarterly, 14,* 304–326.

Braden, J. P. (2000). Editor's introduction: Perspectives on the non-verbal assessment of intelligence. *Journal of Psychoeducational Assessment, 18,* 204–210.

Braden, J. P. (2002). Best practices in educational accountability, high stakes testing, and educational reform. In A. Thomas & J. P. Grimes (Eds.), *Best practices in school psychology* (4th ed.). Bethesda, MD: National Association of School Psychologists.

Braden, J. P., Kovaleski, J. F., & Prasse, D. P. (1996). *Facilitator's training manual* (301–319). Chicago, IL: Chicago Public Schools.

Braden, J. P., & Kratochwill, T. R. (1997). Treatment utility of assessment: Myths and realities. *School Psychology Review, 26,* 475–485.

Bruininks, R. H., Woodcock, R. W., Weatherman, R. F., & Hill, B. K. (1996). *Scales of Independent Behavior—Revised.* Chicago: Riverside.

Burns, R., & Kaufman, S. H. (1972). *Actions, styles, and symbols in kinetic family drawings: An interpretive manual.* New York: Brunner/Mazel.

Bush, G. W. (2001). *No child left behind.* Washington, DC: Office of the President of the United States. Retrieved from http://www.whitehouse.gov/news/reports/no-child-left-behind.html

Capaldi, D. M., & Pattersen, G. R. (1989). *Psychometric properties of fourteen latent constructs from the Oregon Youth Study.* New York: Springer-Verlag.

Carroll, J. B. (1993). *Human cognitive abilities: A survey of factor-analytic studies.* New York: Cambridge University Press.

Carrow-Woolfolk, E. (1995). *Oral and Written Language Scales—Listening Comprehension and Oral Expression.* Circle Pines, MN: American Guidance Service.

Cizek, G. J. (1998). Filling in the blanks: Putting standardized tests to the test. *Fordham Report, 2.* Retrieved May 5, 2001, from http://www.edexcellence.net/library/cizek.pdf

Coffman, W. E. (1993). A king over Egypt, which knew not Joseph. *Educational Measurement: Issues and Practice, 12,* 5–8.

Coie, J. D., Dodge, K. A., & Coppotelli, H. (1982). Dimensions and type of status: A cross age perspective. *Developmental Psychology, 18,* 557–570.

Coie, J. D., Norman, F. W., West, S. G., Hawkins, J. D., Asarnow, J. R., Markman, H. J., Ramey, S. L., Shure, M. B., & Long, B. (1993). The science of prevention: A conceptual framework and some directions for a national research program. *American Psychologist, 48,* 1013–1022.

Conners, C. K. (1997). *Manual for the Conners' Rating Scales–Revised.* North Tonawanda, NY: Multi-Health Systems.

Connolly, A. J. (1988). *Key Math Forms A and B—Revised: A diagnostic inventory of essential mathematics.* Circle Pines, MN: American Guidance Service.

Coopersmith, S. (1981). *Self-Esteem Inventory.* Palo Alto, CA: Consulting Psychologists Press.

CTB/McGraw-Hill. (1998). *TerraNova.* Monterey, CA: Author.

Das, J. P., Naglieri, J. A., & Kirby, J. R. (1994). *Assessment of cognitive processes: The PASS theory of intelligence.* Boston: Allyn and Bacon.

DiPerna, J. C., & Elliott, S. N. (2000). *Academic Competence Evaluation Scales.* San Antonio, TX: The Psychological Corporation.

Doggett, R. A., Edwards, R. P., Moore, J. W., Tingstrom, D. H., & Wilczynski, S. M. (2001). An approach to functional assessment in general education classroom settings. *School Psychology Review, 30,* 313–328.

Driesler, S. D. (2001). Whiplash from backlash? The truth about public support for testing. *National Council on Measurement in Education Newsletter, 9*(3), 3–5.

Durlak, J. A. (1997). *Successful prevention programs for children and adolescents.* New York: Plenum Press.

Eckert, T. L., & Shapiro, E. S. (1999). Methodological issues in analog acceptability research: Are teachers' acceptability ratings of assessment methods influenced by experimental design? *School Psychology Review, 28,* 5–16.

Education Week. (2001). *Quality counts 2001: A better balance. Standards, tests, and the tools to succeed.* Bethesda, MD: Author. Retrieved January 31, 2001, from http://www.edweek.org/sreports/qc01/

Ediger, M. (2000). *Assessment with portfolio and rubric use.* (ERIC Document Reproduction Service No. ED440127) Retrieved from http://orders.edrs.com/members/sp.cfm?AN=ED440127

Elliott, C. D. (1990). *Differential Ability Scales.* San Antonio, TX: The Psychological Corporation.

Elliott, S. N., Braden, J. P., & White, J. L. (2001). *Assessing one and all: Educational accountability for students with disabilities.* Reston, VA: Council for Exceptional Children.

Elliott, S. N., DiPerna, J. C., & Shapiro, E. S. (2001). *Academic Intervention Monitoring System.* San Antonio, TX: The Psychological Corporation.

Elliott, S. N., Kratochwill, T. R., & McKevitt, B. C. (2001). Experimental analysis of the effects of testing accommodations on the scores of students with and without disabilities. *Journal of School Psychology, 39,* 3–24.

Elmore, R. F., & Rothman, R. (Eds.). (1999). *Testing, teaching, and learning: A guide for states and school districts* (Committee on Title I Testing and Assessment, National Research Council). Washington, DC: National Academy Press. Retrieved July 12, 2001, from http://www.nap.edu/catalog/9609.html

Fagan, T. K. (1996). Witmer's contribution to school psychological services. *American Psychologist, 51,* 241–243.

Fagan, T. K. (2000). Practicing school psychology: A turn-of-the-century perspective. *American Psychologist, 55,* 754–757.

Fairbanks, L. D., & Stinnett, T. A. (1997). Effects of professional group membership, intervention type, and diagnostic label on treatment acceptability. *Psychology in the Schools, 34,* 329–335.

Feldman, S. (2000). Standards are working, but states and districts need to make some mid-course corrections. *American Educator, 24,* 5–7.

Figlio, D. N., & Page, M. E. (2000). *School choice and the distributional effects of ability tracking: Does separation increase equality?* (Working Paper No. W8055). Cambridge, MA: National Bureau of Economic Research. Retrieved June 5, 2001, from http://papers.nber.org/papers/W8055

Flanagan, D. P. (2000). Wechsler based CHC cross-battery assessment and reading achievement: Strengthening the validity of interpretations drawn from Wechsler test scores. *School Psychology Quarterly, 15,* 295–329.

Flanagan, D. P., Andrews, T. J., & Genshaft, J. L. (1997). The functional utility of intelligence tests with special education populations. In D. P. Flanagan, J. L. Genshaft, & P. A. Harrison (Eds.), *Contemporary intellectual assessment: Theories, tests, and issues* (pp. 457–483). New York: Guilford Press.

Fuchs, L. S. (1994). *Connecting performance assessment to instruction.* Reston, VA: Council for Exceptional Children.

Fuchs, L. S., Fuchs, O., & Deno, S. L. (1982). Reliability and validity of curriculum-based informal reading inventories. *Reading Research Quartely, 18*(1), 6–26.

Gearhart, M., & Herman, J. L. (1998). Portfolio assessment: Whose work is it? Issues in the use of classroom assignments for accountability. *Educational Assessment, 5,* 41–55.

Glatthorn, A. A., Bragaw, D., Dawkins, K., & Parker, J. (1998). *Performance assessment and standards-based curricula: The achievement cycle.* Larchmont, NY: Eye On Education.

Glutting, J. J., McDermott, P. A., Watkins, M. M., Kush, J. C., & Konold, T. R. (1997). The base rate problem and its consequences for interpreting children's ability profiles. *School Psychology Review, 26,* 176–188.

Greenwood, C. R., Carta, J. J., & Dawson, H. (2000). Ecobehavioral Assessment Systems Software (EBASS): A system for observation in education settings. In T. Thompson & D. Felce (Eds.), *Behavioral observation: Technology and applications in developmental disabilities* (pp. 229–251). Baltimore, MD: Paul H. Brookes.

Gresham, F. M.(1989). Assessment of treatment integrity in school consultation and prereferral intervention. *School Psychology Review, 18,* 37–50.

Gresham, F. M., Mink, J., Ward, C., MacMillan, D. L., & Swanson, H. L. (1994). *Behavioral profiles of students considered at-risk using school records.* Riverside, CA: Research Programs for Students At-Risk, University of California. (ERIC Document Reproduction Service No. ED393024)

Gresham, F. M. (2001, August). *Responsiveness to intervention: An alternative approach to the identification of learning disabilities.* Presented at the Learning Disabilities Summit: Building a Foundation for the Future, Office of Special Education Programs, Washington, DC. Retrieved September 12, 2001, from http://www.air.org/ldsummit/ paper.htm

Gresham, F. M., & Elliott, S. N. (1990). *Social Skills Rating System.* Circle Pines, MN: American Guidance Service.

Gresham, F. M., MacMillan, D. L., Beebe, F. M. E., & Bocian, K. M. (2000). Treatment integrity in learning disabilities intervention research: Do we really know how treatments are implemented? *Learning Disabilities—Research and Practice, 15,* 198–205.

Gresham, F. M., MacMillan, D. L., & Bocian, K. M. (1996). Learning disabilities, low achievement, and mild mental retardation: More alike than different? *Journal of Learning Disabilities, 29,* 570–581.

Gresham, F. M., MacMillan, D. L., & Bocian, K. M. (1998). Agreement between school study team decisions and authoritative definitions in classification of students at-risk for mild disabilities. *School Psychology Quarterly, 13,* 181–191.

Gresham, F., Watson, T. S., & Skinner, C. H. (2001). Functional behavioral assessment: Principles, procedures, and future directions. *School Psychology Review, 30*(2), 156–172.

Gresham, F. M., & Witt, J. C. (1997). Utility of intelligence tests for treatment planning, classification, and placement decisions: Recent empirical findings and future directions. *School Psychology Quarterly, 12,* 249–267.

Hammill, D. D., Pearson, N. A., & Wiederholt, J. L. (1997). *Comprehensive Test of Nonverbal Intelligence.* Austin, TX: PRO-ED.

Harter, S. (1985). *Manual for the Self-Perception Profile for Children.* Denver, CO: University of Denver.

Hayes, S. C., Nelson, R. O., & Jarrett, R. B. (1987). The treatment utility of assessment: A functional approach to evaluating assessment quality. *American Psychologist, 42,* 963–974.

Heubert, J. P., & Hauser, R. M. (Eds.). (1999). *High stakes: Testing for tracking, promotion, and graduation* (Committee on Appropriate Test Use, National Research Council). Washington, DC: National Academy Press. Retrieved from http://books.nap.edu/catalog/6336.html

Hightower, A. D., Work, W. C., Cowen, E. L., Ltyscewski, B. X., Spinell, A. P., Guare, J. C., & Rorhbeck, C. A. (1987). The Child Rating Scale: The development of a socioemotional self-rating scale for elementary school children. *School Psychology Review, 16,* 239–255.

Hintze, J. M., Owen, S. V., Shapiro, E. S., & Daly, E. J. (2000). Generalizability of oral reading fluency measures: Application of G theory to curriculum-based measurement. *School Psychology Quarterly, 15,* 52–68.

Hintze, J. M., Shapiro, E. S., Conte, K. L., & Basile, I. M. (1997). Oral reading fluency and authentic reading material: Criterion validity of the technical features of CBM survey-level assessment. *School Psychology Review, 26,* 535–553.

Hoover, H. D., Hieronymus, A. N., Frisbie, D. A., & Dunbar, S. B. (1993). *Iowa Tests of Basic Skills.* Chicago: Riverside.

Idol, L., Nevin, A., & Paolucci-Whitcomb, P. (1996). *Models of curriculum-based assessment: A blueprint for learning* (2nd ed.). Austin, TX: PRO-ED.

Illinois State Board of Education. (2001). *Illinois Standards Achievement Test sample mathematics materials 2002.* Springfield, IL: Author. Retrieved July 13, 2001, from http://www.isbe.state.il.us/assessment/PDF/2002%20Math%20Sample%20Book.pdf

Jackson, D. N. (1984). *Multidimensional Aptitude Battery.* Port Huron, MI: Sigma Assessment Systems.

Jensen, A. R. (1998). *The g factor: The science of mental ability.* Westport, CN: Praeger.

Kamphaus, R. W., Petoskey, M. D., & Morgan, A. W. (1997). A history of intelligence test interpretation. In D. P. Flanagan, J. L. Genshaft, & P. A. Harrison (Eds.), *Contemporary intellectual assessment: Theories, tests, and issues* (pp. 32–47). New York: Guilford Press.

Kaufman, A. S., & Kaufman, N. L. (1983). *Kaufman Assessment Battery for Children.* Circle Pines, MN: American Guidance Service.

Kaufman, A. S., & Kaufman, N. L. (1985). *Kaufman Test of Educational Achievement.* Circle Pines, MN: American Guidance Service.

Kavale, K. (1990). The effectiveness of special education. In T. B. Gutkin & C. R. Reynolds (Eds.), *The handbook of school psychology* (2nd ed., pp. 868–898). New York: Wiley.

Keith, T. Z., Kranzler, J. H., & Flanagan, D. P. (2001). What does the Cognitive Assessment System (CAS) measure? Joint confirmatory factor analysis of the CAS and the Woodcock-Johnson Tests of Cognitive Ability (3rd ed.). *School Psychology Review, 30,* 89–119.

Kershaw, P., & Sonuga-Barke, E. (1998). Emotional and behavioural difficulties: Is this a useful category? The implications of clustering and co-morbidity: The relevance of a taxonomic approach. *Educational and Child Psychology, 15,* 45–55.

Kinder, A. (2000). Setting standards for excellence. *NCREL's Learning Point, 2*(3), 4–7.

Kohn, A. (2000). Burnt at the high stakes. *Journal of Teacher Education, 51,* 315–327.

Kostrubala, C. E., & Braden, J. P. (1998). *Administration of the WAIS-III in American Sign Language* [videotape]. San Antonio, TX: The Psychological Corporation.

Kranzler, J. H., Brownell, M. T., & Miller, M. D. (1998). The construct validity of curriculum-based measurement of reading: An empirical test of a plausible rival hypothesis. *Journal of School Psychology, 36,* 399–415.

Kranzler, J. H., Miller, M. D., & Jordan, L. (1999). An examination of racial/ethnic and gender bias on curriculum-based measurement of reading. *School Psychology Quarterly, 14,* 327–342.

Labaree, D. F. (2000). Resisting educational standards. *Phi Delta Kappan, 82,* 28–33.

MacKay, G., Somerville, W., & Lundie, J. (1996). Reflections on goal attainment scaling (GAS): Cautionary notes and proposals for development. *Educational Research, 38,* 161–172.

MacMillan, D. L., Gresham, F. M., & Bocian, K. M. (1998). Discrepancy between definitions of learning disabilities and school practices: An empirical investigation. *Journal of Learning Disabilities, 31*(4), 314–326.

MacMillan, D. L., Gresham, F. M., Bocian, K. M., & Siperstein, G. N. (1997). The role of assessment in qualifying students as eligible for special education: What is and what's supposed to be. *Focus on Exceptional Children, 30,* 1–18.

Malecki, C. K., & Elliott, S. N. (1999). Adolescents' ratings of perceived social support and its importance: Validation of the Student Social Support Scale. *Psychology in the Schools, 36,* 473–483.

March, J. S. (1997). *Multidimensional Anxiety Scale for Children (MASC).* North Tonawanda, NY: Multi-Health Systems.

Markwardt, F. C. (1989). *Peabody Individual Achievement Test—Revised.* Circle Pines, MN: American Guidance Service.

Martin, S. (1999). !Observe: *A behavior recording and reporting software program.* Longmont, CO: Sopris West.

McDonnell, L. M., McLaughlin, M. J., & Morrison, P. (Eds.). (1997). *Educating one and all: Students with disabilities and standards-based reform* (Committee on Goals 2000 and the Inclusion of Students with Disabilities, National Research Council). Washington, DC: National Academy Press. Retrieved from http://www.nap.edu/catalog/5788.html

McGrew, K. S., Keith, T. Z., Flanagan, D. P., & Vanderwood, M. (1997). Beyond "g": The impact of "Gf-Gc" specific cognitive abilities research on the future use and interpretation of intelligence test batteries in the schools. *School Psychology Review, 26,* 189–210.

McMillan, J. H., & Workman, D. (1999). *Teachers' classroom assessment and grading practices: Phase I and II.* Richmond, VA: Metropolitan Educational Research Consortium. (ERIC Document Reproduction Service No. 442840) Retrieved August 3, 2001, from http://orders.edrs.com/members/sp.cfm?AN=ED 442840

Mehrens, W. A., & Clarizio, H. F. (1993). Curriculum-based measurement: Conceptual and psychometric considerations. *Psychology in the Schools, 30,* 241–254.

Merrell, K. W., & Walters, A. S. (1998). *Internalizing Symptoms Scale for Children.* Austin, TX: PRO-ED.

Motta, R. W., Little, S. G., & Tobin, M. I. (1993). The use and abuse of human figure drawings. *School Psychology Quarterly, 8,* 162–169.

Munk, D. D., & Karsh, K. G. (1999). Antecedent curriculum and instructional variables as classwide interventions for preventing or reducing problem behaviors. In A. C. Repp & R. H. Horner (Eds.), *Functional analysis of problem behavior: From effective assessment to effective support* (pp. 259–276). Belmont, CA: Wadsworth.

Murray, H. A., & Bellak, L. (1973). *Thematic Apperception Test.* San Antonio, TX: The Psychological Corporation.

Naglieri, J. A. (1985). *Matrix Analogies Test—Short Form.* San Antonio, TX: The Psychological Corporation.

Naglieri, J. A. (1988). *Draw A Person—A quantitative scoring system.* San Antonio, TX: The Psychological Corporation.

Naglieri, J. A. (1993). *Naglieri Nonverbal Abilities Test.* San Antonio, TX: The Psychological Corporation.

Naglieri, J. A. (1999). How valid is the PASS theory and CAS? *School Psychology Review, 28,* 145–162.

Naglieri, J. A. (2000). Can profile analysis of ability test scores work? An illustration using the PASS theory and CAS with an unselected cohort. *School Psychology Quarterly, 15,* 419–433.

Naglieri, J. A. (2001). Using the Cognitive Assessment System (CAS) with learning-disabled children. In A. S. Kaufman & N. L. Kaufman (Eds.), *Specific learning disabilities and difficulties in children and adolescents: Psychological assessment and evaluation. Cambridge child and adolescent psychiatry* (pp. 141–177). New York: Cambridge University Press.

Naglieri, J. A., & Bardos, A. N. (1997). *General Ability Measure for Adults.* Minnetonka, MN: NCS Assessments.

Naglieri, J. A., & Das, J. P. (1997). *Das-Naglieri Cognitive Assessment System.* Itasca, IL: Riverside.

Naglieri, J. A., & Gottling, S. H. (1997). Mathematics instruction and PASS cognitive processes: An intervention study. *Journal of Learning Disabilities, 30,* 513–520.

Naglieri, J. A., & Johnson, D. (2000). Effectiveness of a cognitive strategy intervention in improving arithmetic computation based on the PASS theory. *Journal of Learning Disabilities, 33,* 591–597.

Naglieri, J. A., LeBuffe, P. A., & Pfeiffer, S. I. (1993a). *Devereux Behavior Rating Scale—School Form—Adolescents.* San Antonio, TX: The Psychological Corporation.

Naglieri, J. A., LeBuffe, P. A., & Pfeiffer, S. I. (1993b). *Devereux Behavior Rating Scale—School Form—Children.* San Antonio, TX: The Psychological Corporation.

Naglieri, J. A., McNeish, T. J., & Bardos, A. N. (1991). *Draw a Person: Screening procedure for emotional disturbance.* Austin, TX: PRO-ED.

Naglieri, J. A., & Pfeiffer, S. I. (1992). Validity of the Draw A Person: Screening procedure for emotional disturbance with a socially-emotionally disturbed sample. *Journal of Consulting and Clinical Psychology: Psychological Assessment, 4,* 156–159.

Naglieri, J. A., & Ronning, M. E. (2000). The relationship between general ability using the Naglieri Nonverbal Ability Test (NNAT) and Stanford Achievement Test (SAT) reading achievement. *Journal of Psychoeducational Assessment, 18,* 230–239.

National Council of Teachers of Mathematics. (2000). *Principles and standards for school mathematics.* Reston, VA: Author. Retrieved October 17, 2000, from http://standards.nctm.org/document/index.htm

National Governors Association. (1998). *High school exit exams: Setting high expectations.* Washington, DC: Author. Retrieved October 17, 2000, from http://www.nga.org/center/divisions/1,1188, C_ISSUE_BRIEF^D_1478,00.html

National Reading Panel. (2000). *Teaching children to read: An evidence-based assessment of the scientific research literature on reading and its implications for reading instruction* (National Institute of Child Health and Human Development NIH Pub. No. 00-4769). Bethesda, MD: U.S. Department of Health and Human Services. Retrieved October 17, 2000, from http://www.nichd.nih.gov/publications/nrp/smallbook.htm

Nave, B., Miech, E., & Mosteller, F. (2000). A lapse in standards: Linking standards-based reform with student achievement. *Phi Delta Kappan, 82,* 128–132.

Nettelbeck, T. (1998). Jensen's chronometric research: Neither simple nor sufficient but a good place to start. *Intelligence, 26,* 233–241.

Nolet, V., & McLaughlin, M. (1997). Using CBM to explore a consequential basis for the validity of a state-wide performance assessment. *Diagnostique, 22,* 146–163.

Norman, G. J., Velicer, W. F., Fava, J. L., & Prochaska, J. O. (2000). Cluster subtypes within stage of change in a representative sample of smokers. *Addictive Behaviors, 25,* 183–204.

Novi, M. J., & Meinster, M. O. (2000). Achievement in a relational context: Preferences and influences in female adolescents. *Career Development Quarterly, 49,* 73–84.

Oakes, J. (1992). Can tracking research inform practice? Technical, normative, and political considerations. *Educational Researcher, 21,* 12–21.

Office of Special Education Programs. (2001). *Learning disabilities summit: Building a foundation for the future.* Washington, DC: Author. Retrieved October 15, 2000, from http://www.air.org/ldsummit/letter.htm

Otis, A. S., & Lennon, R. T. (1996). *Otis-Lennon School Ability Test—Seventh Edition.* San Antonio, TX: The Psychological Corporation.

Peverly, S. T., & Kitzen, K. R. (1998). Curriculum-based assessment of reading skills: Considerations and caveats for school psychologists. *Psychology in the Schools, 35,* 29–47.

Piers, E. V. (1984). *Piers-Harris Children's Self Concept Scale.* Los Angeles, CA: Western Psychological Services.

Plewis, I. (1988). Estimating generalizability in systematic observation studies. *British Journal of Mathematical and Statistical Psychology, 41,* 53–62.

Prasse, D. P., & Schrag, J. A. (1998). Providing noncategorical, functional, classroom-based supports for students with disabilities: Legal parameters. In D. J. Reschly, W. D. Tilly, & J. P. Grimes (Eds.), *Functional and noncategorical identification and intervention in special education* (pp. 259–283). Des Moines, IA: Iowa State Department of Education.

The Psychological Corporation. (1996). *Stanford Achievement Test—Ninth Edition—Test Batteries.* San Antonio, TX: Author.

The Psychological Corporation. (2001). *Wechsler Individual Achievement Test—Second Edition.* San Antonio, TX: Author.

Raven, J. C. (1992a). *Raven's Coloured Progressive Matrices.* San Antonio, TX: The Psychological Corporation.

Raven, J. C. (1992b). *Raven's Progressive Matrices.* San Antonio, TX: The Psychological Corporation.

Ravitch, D. (1999). Student performance: The national agenda in education. In M. Kanstoroom & C. E. Finn (Eds.), *New directions: Federal education policy in the twenty-first century.* Washington, DC: Thomas B. Fordham Foundation and The Manhattan Policy

Institute. Retrieved January 14, 2001, from http://www.edexcellence.net/library/ newdrct.htm

Reiss, D., & Price, R. H. (1996). National research agenda for prevention research: The National Institute of Mental Health report. *American Psychologist, 51,* 1109–1115.

Reschly, D. J., & Grimes, J. P. (1995). Best practices in intellectual assessment. In A. Thomas & J. Grimes (Eds.), *Best practices in school psychology* (3rd ed.). Bethesda, MD: National Association of School Psychologists.

Reschly, D. J., Kicklighter, R. H., & McKee, P. (1988). Recent placement litigation. Pt. III: Analysis of differences in Larry P. Marshall and S-1, and implications for future practices. *School Psychology Review, 17,* 37–48.

Reschly, D. J., & Ysseldyke, J. E. (1995). School psychology paradigm shift. In A. Thomas & J. Grimes (Eds.), *Best practices in school psychology* (3rd ed., pp. 17–32). Washington, DC: National Association of School Psychologists.

Reynolds, C. R., & Kamphaus, R. W. (1992). *Behavior Assessment System for Children.* Circle Pines, MN: American Guidance Service.

Reynolds, W. M. (1987). *Reynolds Adolescent Depression Scale.* Odessa, FL: Psychological Assessment Resources.

Reynolds, W. M. (1988). *Adolescent Psychopathology Scale.* Odessa, FL: Psychological Assessment Resources.

Robertson, C., & Salter, W. (1997). *The Phonological Awareness Test.* East Moline, IL: Linguisystems.

Roid, G. H., & Miller, L. J. (1997). *Leiter International Performance Scale—Revised.* Wood Dale, IL: Stoeling.

Rotter, J. B., Lah, M. I., & Rafferty, J. E. (1992). *Rotter Incomplete Sentences Blank—Second Edition.* San Antonio, TX: The Psychological Corporation.

Sattler, J. M. (2001). *Assessment of children: Cognitive applications* (4th ed.). La Mesa, CA: Author.

Schrag, P. (2000). High stakes are for tomatoes. *Atlantic Monthly, 286.* Retrieved September 10, 2001, from http://www.theatlantic.com/issues/2000/08/ schrag.htm

Shapiro, E. S. (1988). Preventing academic failure. *School Psychology Review, 17*(4), 601–613.

Shapiro, E. S. (1989). *Academic skills problems: Direct assessment and intervention.* New York: Guilford Press.

Shapiro, E. S., & Kratochwill, T. K. (Eds.). (2000). *Conducting school-based assessments of child and adolescent behavior.* New York: Guilford Press.

Shapley, K. S., & Bush, M. J. (1999). Developing a valid and reliable portfolio assessment in the primary grades: Building on practical experience. *Applied Measurement in Education, 12,* 11–32.

Shavelson, R. J., Ruiz-Primo, M. A., & Wiley, E. W. (1999). Note on sources of sampling variability in science performance assessments. *Journal of Educational Measurement, 36,* 61–71.

Shinn, M. R. (Ed.). (1989). *Curriculum-based measurement: Assessing special children.* New York: Guilford Press.

Shinn, M. R. (1995). Best practices in curriculum-based measurement and its use in a problem-solving model. In A. Thomas & J. Grimes (Eds.), *Best practices in school psychology* (3rd ed., pp. 547–568). Washington, DC: National Association of School Psychologists.

Smith, D., & Dumont, F. (1995). A cautionary study: Unwarranted interpretations of the Draw-A-Person Test. *Professional Psychology: Research and Practice, 26,* 298–303.

Sparrow, S., Balla, D., & Cicchetti, P. (1984). *Vineland Adaptive Behavior Scales.* Circle Pines, MN: American Guidance Service.

Speece, D. L. , & Case, L. P. (2001). Classification in context: An alternative approach to identifying early reading disability. *Journal of Educational Psychology, 93*(4), 735–749.

Stecker, P. M., & Fuchs, L. S. (2000). Effecting superior achievement using curriculum-based measurement: The importance of individual progress monitoring. Learning Disabilities: *Research and Practice, 15,* 128–134.

Sterling-Turner, H. E., Watson, T. S., Wildman, M., Watkins, C., & Little, E. (2001). Investigating the relationship between training type and treatment integrity. *School Psychology Quarterly, 16,* 56–67.

Stiggins, R. J., & Bridgeford, N. J. (1984). *Performance assessment for teacher development.* Portland, OR: Center for Performance Assessment, Northwest Regional Educational Laboratory.

Stoiber, K. C., & Kratochwill, T. R. (2001). Evidence-based intervention programs: Rethinking, refining, and renaming the new standing section of *School Psychology Quarterly. School Psychology Quarterly, 16,* 1–8.

Stoiber, K. C., & Kratochwill, T. R. (2002). *Functional assessment and intervention system.* San Antonio, TX: The Psychological Corporation.

Supovitz, J. A., & Brennan, R. T. (1997). Mirror, mirror on the wall, which is the fairest test of all? An examination of the equitability of portfolio assessment relative to standardized tests. *Harvard Educational Review, 67,* 472–506.

Swanson, H. L., & Hoskyn, M. (1998). Experimental intervention research on students with learning disabilities: A meta-analysis of treatment outcomes. *Review of Educational Research, 68,* 277–321.

TechMicro. (2000). *Computer Optimized Multimedia Intelligence Test.* New York: Author.

Thomas B. Fordham Foundation. (1998). *A nation still at risk: An educational manifesto.* Washington, DC: Author. (ERIC Document Reproduction Service ED429988) Retrieved January 14, 2000, from http://orders.edrs.com/DocLibrary/0999/ED429988 .PDF

Thompson, J. M., & Sones, R. A. (1973). *Education Apperception Test.* Los Angeles: Western Psychological Services.

Thorndike, R. L., Hagen, E. P., & Sattler, J. M. (1986). *The Stanford-Binet Intelligence Scale.* Chicago: Riverside.

Tomlinson, C. A. (2000). Reconcilable differences: Standards-based teaching and differentiation. *Educational Leadership, 58,* 6–11.

Underwood, T. (1998). The consequences of portfolio assessment: A case study. *Educational Assessment, 5,* 147–194.

Wagner, R. K., Torgesen, J. K., & Rashotte, C. A. (1999). *Comprehensive Test of Phonological Processing.* Austin, TX: PRO-ED.

Walker, H. M., Block-Pedego, A., Todis, B., & Severson, H. H. (1991). *School Archival Records Search.* Longmont, CO: Sopris West.

Ward, S. B., Ward, T. J., Hatt, C. V., Young, D. L., & Mollner, N. R. (1995). The incidence and utility of the ACID, ACIDS, and SCAD profiles in a referred population. *Psychology in the Schools, 32,* 267–276.

Wechsler, D. (1989). *Wechsler Preschool and Primary Scale of Intelligence—Revised.* San Antonio, TX: The Psychological Corporation.

Wechsler, D. (1991). *Wechsler Intelligence Scale for Children— Third Edition.* San Antonio, TX: The Psychological Corporation.

Wechsler, D. (1997). *Wechsler Adult Intelligence Scale—Third Edition.* San Antonio, TX: The Psychological Corporation.

Weissberg, R. P., & Greenberg, M. T. (1998). School and community competence-enhancement and prevention programs. In W. Damon (Ed.), *Handbook of child psychology: Vol. 4. Child psychology in practice* (pp. 877–954). New York: Wiley.

Wickstrom, K. F., Jones, K. M., LaFleur, L. H., & Witt, J. C. (1998). An analysis of treatment integrity in school-based behavioral consultation. *School Psychology Quarterly, 13,* 41–54.

Wiggins, G. (1989). A true test: Toward more authentic and equitable assessment. *Phi Delta Kappan, 70,* 703–713.

Wilson, M. S., & Reschly, D. J. (1996). Assessment in school psychology training and practice. *School Psychology Review, 25,* 9–23.

Woodcock, R. W. (1987). *Woodcock Reading Mastery Test— Revised.* Circle Pines, MN: American Guidance Service.

Woodcock, R. W., McGrew, K. S., & Mather, N. (2000a). *Woodcock-Johnson Tests of Achievement.* Itasca, IL: Riverside.

Woodcock, R. W., McGrew, K. S., & Mather, N. (2000b). *Woodcock-Johnson Tests of Cognitive Ability.* Itasca, IL: Riverside.

Wollack, J. E. (2000). *A treatment utility study of The Instructional Environment System-II and Strategies and Tactics for Effective Instruction* (Doctoral dissertation, University of Wisconsin— Madison, 2000). *Dissertations Abstracts International, 61*(08), 3059A. Retrieved October 16, 2001, from http://wwwlib.umi.com/ dissertations/dlnow/9983802

Yopp, H. (1988). The validity and reliability of phonemic awareness tests. *Reading Research Quarterly, 23,* 159–177.

Ysseldyke, J. E., & Christenson, S. L. (1993). *The Instructional Environment System-II.* Longmont, CO: Sopris West.

CHAPTER 13

Psychological Assessment in Medical Settings

JERRY J. SWEET, STEVEN M. TOVIAN, AND YANA SUCHY

Historically, medical settings have provided a fertile environment for formal psychological assessment. In fact, primarily as a consequence of the large number of training opportunities provided by Veteran's Administration hospitals, a majority of clinical psychologists have had internship and other levels of training within medical settings. Moreover, the specialties of clinical health psychology and clinical neuropsychology had their genesis and seminal growth within medical settings. Within a wide range of medical settings, formal assessment activities by psychologists have become so commonplace as to now be taken for granted by physician colleagues who have trained recently in major urban American medical schools. That is, recently trained physicians now expect to have psychological assessment resources available within the hospital systems in which they practice because these resources were present within the institutions in which they were trained.

In this chapter, we discuss and delineate general and specific issues that currently are important to psychological assessment activities in medical settings. Included in the topics we discuss are unique aspects of the environment and unique assessment issues, assessment with specific medical populations, and opportunities for psychologists practicing assessment in medical settings. Unless otherwise specified, our use of the terms *psychological assessment* encompass all traditional (e.g., personality, intellectual, academic) *and* specialized (e.g., health-illness coping styles, specific neuropsychological) testing. We endeavor to be explicit when issues pertain only to a subset of formal psychological assessment procedures.

UNIQUE GENERAL ASPECTS OF THE MEDICAL ENVIRONMENT THAT AFFECT PSYCHOLOGICAL PRACTICE

In general, there are a number of characteristics of medical settings that influence—and in some instances even guide—practice activities of psychologists. These characteristics include the organizational structure of some medical settings (e.g., hospitals), the ubiquitous nature of the medical model of conceptualizing and delivering services, the predominant power and authority conferred to the medical degree (MD), the increased pressure for accountability associated with physical health care, opportunities for clinical collaboration with physicians, opportunities for professional learning and growth, possible involvement in medical education, possible involvement in medical research, and multidisciplinary aspects of health care in some medical settings. We consider each of these factors individually.

Organizational Structure

The decision-making power and authority of hospitals and other medical service delivery institutions is structured—like most large businesses—in a hierarchical administrative tree. Although in the past many of the top leadership positions in hospitals were occupied by physicians, the vast majority are filled currently by individuals who have earned a master's of business administration (MBA) degree, specializing in hospital administration or health services administration. The chief administrators (e.g., chairman of the board, chief executive officer, chief financial officer, president, vice president) make business decisions, such as those related to marketing, limiting expenses and developing revenues from day-to-day operations, and planning for future growth. As the administrative structure reaches downward to clinical departments and then to clinical programs, the leadership is much more likely to have had training in a health care delivery field (e.g., nursing or medicine) and to be licensed clinicians as well as administrators. The important decisions regarding targeting of health care problems and effective delivery and quality control of relevant services occur at this level. Although a sharing of financial responsibility occurs throughout the administrative structure of hospitals, it is a relatively recent event at most health care institutions that individual health care providers, who occupy the lowest level of the administrative tree and therefore have the least amount of power and authority, are held accountable for a personal budget of expenses and revenue. This latter event has caused a paradigm shift with regard to the clinical expectations and daily activities of practitioners, including psychologists, within large organized medical settings, such as hospitals. Essentially, there is now a clear burden for a practitioner to earn the equivalent of salary and benefits, *plus* a substantial amount that is typically defined by top administrators, through collection of real dollars in order to justify the practitioner's clinical position. The influence of this environment extends to psychologists practicing assessment in medical settings.

Power and Authority Conferred to Holders of MD

Although their amount of unquestioned power is decreasing with the passage of time, individuals who have earned an MD continue to be at the top of that part of the administrative tree that governs clinicians providing services within medical settings. For example, in a multidisciplinary rehabilitation program, the top leadership position is almost always an MD. This physician is referred to as a medical director and is conferred a position of decision-making power over other individuals—even fellow physicians and others licensed as independent practitioners who do not require medical supervision. Although some notable exceptions can be identified (i.e., psychologists sometimes serve as clinical directors with a purview over physicians), most psychologists working in medical settings work in some sense under a medical director, who may or may not appreciate the unique aspects of psychological service provision. Moreover, awareness and knowledge of specialty assessment services delivered by psychologists may be limited.

Pressure for Accountability Associated With Physical Health Care

American society has come to believe that when it comes to medical care, a negative outcome—regardless of whether it is associated with quality care—potentially may raise the issue of accountability. With impressive developments in science and technology that have fostered true medical advances has come unyielding optimism that nearly all illnesses can and should be controlled or ameliorated with early diagnosis followed by appropriate, good care. This perspective is an understandable outgrowth of rapid progress in recent decades and represents a human attribute that drives us incessantly toward higher accomplishments. The other side of the coin consists of perfectionistic expectations that errors can be reduced to zero and that effectiveness can be maximized at all times. As health care practitioners who work closely with physicians, psychologists are placed under the same expectations of accountability. One has only to explore litigation against psychologists to understand that although the damages may or may not be as visible as those resulting from use of a scalpel, accountability for psychological diagnostic and treatment activities is just as real as for more seemingly tangible medical fields, such as dermatology. Within medical settings, accountability for accuracy of providers individually and clinical procedures in general often is readily apparent among health care workers operating in close proximity. This close accountability for efficacious outcomes is applied in the same manner for psychological assessment outcomes of an individual provider and—for better or worse—will be readily apparent to the nonpsychologists working alongside psychologists within a medical setting.

Opportunities for Clinical Collaboration With Physicians

Within medical settings, psychologists can encounter numerous unique opportunities for collaboration with physician colleagues. Physicians are more than just a referral source for patients; psychologists working in medical settings with physicians can encounter opportunities to work more closely together for the purpose of providing a wider range of services or perhaps reaching a more diverse medical population than would otherwise be seen for psychological services. For example, the close monitoring of mental status changes in patients with acute medical conditions—such as those found in patients hospitalized with onset of central nervous system infections or cerebrovascular stroke—makes for a close clinical collaboration that is not present in outpatient private practice settings. These sorts of close clinical relationships have at times led to improved clinical service delivery that would not have occurred otherwise. For example, monitoring via repeat neuropsychological screenings of patients suffering from brain involvement of AIDS during intense inpatient medical treatment often provides earlier indication of treatment effectiveness than would be possible using only traditional medical markers of brain function. Similarly, psychological screening of candidates for surgical procedures ranging from high-risk, resource-draining procedures (e.g., organ transplantation) to common surgeries, the outcomes of which are known to be affected by psychosocial variables, has increased the frequency of positive outcomes. Finally, from a very different perspective, when one considers the medical cost offset literature (cf. Sobel, 2000), which has demonstrated that appropriate psychological assessment and intervention can produce savings on what would have been unnecessary medical assessment and treatment, it is apparent that utilization of psychological assessment services has a meaningful impact in reducing health care costs. Although it is often overlooked, this latter point is perhaps the most unique contribution of psychological services to overall improved health care, an effect produced as a direct by-product of close collaboration between physicians and psychologists.

Multidisciplinary Aspects of Current Health Care in Medical Settings

Perhaps nowhere has there been more opportunity for psychologists than in multidisciplinary clinical programs, which are almost invariably housed within medical settings and staffed partly by physicians. These programs have grown from the recognition that in order to provide the best care for some medical conditions, the special skills of more than one field are needed. For example, a psychologist working within a hospital may have the opportunity to become part of a multidisciplinary inpatient oncology program, thereby assessing and treating patients who are more acutely ill or who have progressed to the point in their illness that outpatient care is no longer feasible. This multidisciplinary type of endeavor may

involve physicians from multiple specialties and specialists from other disciplines, such as physical therapy, speech therapy, and nursing. Similar examples of common real-life collaborations between psychologists in medical settings and various health care professionals can be seen with multidisciplinary rehabilitation, cardiac disorders, epilepsy, neurodegenerative disorders (e.g., Parkinson's disease, Alzheimer's disease), stroke, traumatic brain injury, chronic pain treatment, dental problems, and organ transplant programs. Within these programs, psychologists often play a key role—in a well-integrated fashion with other specialists—in evaluating and treating psychosocial, cognitive, and family problems associated with the respective medical disorder.

Unique Opportunities for Professional Learning and Growth

Accompanying opportunities for meaningful and close collaborative involvement with physicians are opportunities for professional learning and growth in what would be considered nontraditional areas for psychologists. For example, neuropsychologists may be able to participate in invasive diagnostic procedures, such as the Wada procedure (i.e., assessment of cognitive and motor function during intracarotid sodium amytal injection to each hemisphere of the brain) that take place in surgical rooms. Such multidisciplinary assessment procedures are administered to patients who are under consideration for surgical intervention in areas of the brain where loss of language may occur. These types of sophisticated, highly specialized assessment opportunities only take place in medical settings.

Possible Involvement in Medical Education

Some medical settings—particularly hospitals and medical centers associated with university medical schools—provide psychologists practicing assessment with opportunities to become involved in the educational process of physicians in training. In fact, psychologists have been well represented in physician training programs for many years. More than two decades ago a survey revealed that 98% of all medical schools in the United States employed psychologists, at a ratio of 1 psychologist for every 24 medical students (Gentry & Matarazzo, 1981). The professional identity of psychologists in medical schools crystallized with the formation of the Association of Medical School Professors of Psychology, an organization that subsequently evolved into the Association of Medical School Psychologists. This organization has recently adopted the *Journal of Clinical Psychology in Medical Settings* as its official publication and achieved the status of an official section within Division 12 (Clinical Psychology) of the American Psychological Association.

In a different vein, involvement in assessment activities within academic medical settings is likely to bring clinical involvement with medical students and residents who are struggling academically. Such involvement may be in the form of assessment of apparent psychological difficulties, possible substance abuse, or possible learning disability.

Possible Involvement in Medical Research

Following from the latter three points elaborated previously, some medical settings and some collaborations between psychologists and physicians offer unique medical research opportunities. For example, a neuropsychologist may contribute to medical research by assessing patients' psychological and cognitive functioning before and after the implementation of pharmacological or surgical intervention. Specifically, a neuropsychologist may conduct pre- and postoperative evaluations of patients suspected of normal-pressure hydrocephalus. There may also be an opportunity to work with patients to evaluate their neuropsychological status immediately before and after surgical intervention for an intractable movement disorder. In this manner, the assessment instruments of a neuropsychologist may provide the most salient outcome measure for groups of patients assigned to different types of surgical interventions in an attempt to determine the most effective treatment of a medical disorder. In addition, quality-of-life measures from health psychology have also been utilized in medical treatment outcome studies of cancer patients (and other medical patients) in an attempt to objectify the possible psychosocial benefits of medical interventions to prolong life.

UNIQUE PSYCHOLOGICAL ASSESSMENT ISSUES WITHIN MEDICAL SETTINGS

Here, we individually consider the following factors that can affect the assessment practices of psychologists in medical settings: reimbursement, ethical-legal, logistics, and special instrumentation. The reader should note that in some instances, these factors create a favorable effect, whereas in other instances they create an untoward effect for clinicians as compared to those not practicing in medical settings.

Reimbursement

Although obtaining reimbursement for services legitimately rendered has become more difficult for all health care providers in recent years, there have been particular issues and emphases for those practicing within medical settings. These factors fundamentally all relate to characteristics and expectations of payer sources.

Managed Care

Piotrowski (1999) presented evidence that ". . . managed care policies are having an onerous influence on the majority of practicing clinicians, particularly in the area of assessment" (p. 792). For psychologists practicing assessment in medical settings, managed care has presented a mixed picture of challenges and—in some instances—some advantages. Beginning with the latter, among the advantages of practicing within medical settings may be easier access to managed care panels that are intent on offering a continuum of care that includes outpatient and inpatient services from the entire range of health care disciplines, including psychology. The restriction of access to patients by exclusion of some psychologists from managed care panels has been significant enough to cause the American Psychological Association (APA) to engage in lawsuits against some managed care companies (see Nessman & Herndon, 2000). When psychologists providing clinical services are fully integrated into larger medical practice groups, inclusion in managed care panels may be facilitated. Individual clinicians not associated with large groups of providers of medical care (e.g., hospitals, independent physician associations) within a given economic geography may not appear as attractive to managed care organizations, who may prefer to sign up the entire continuum of care in one major agreement with a well-established medical institution. This appears to have been particularly true in well-populated, urban areas, within which large medical delivery systems already had earned a positive reputation that made for very favorable marketing once signed up by a particular managed care organization.

Moreover, after they are accepted by the managed care company for inclusion on provider panels and therefore accessible to their subscribers, psychologists in large, well-organized medical settings also benefit from the available infrastructure of their employer's organization. Pandemic to at least the current iteration of managed care have been a number of burdensome tasks for clinicians. For psychologists practicing in large medical settings, such as hospitals, there is more likely to be a better support system for the incredibly time consuming tasks of (a) completing unrelenting paper work associated with initial applications and maintenance of panel memberships, (b) accurate completion of extensive and obfuscated precertification procedures, and (c) effective submission and resubmission of proper service delivery and billing documentation. Although subsequent collection procedures are by no means more likely to be effective in large medical institutions, and in many may even be far less effective, the employment relationships of many psychologists to their institutions may be less concerned with actual collections than are those in the private sector.

On the negative side of the ledger, psychologists practicing within the organized multidisciplinary practice group of a medical setting may have to accept panel inclusion for managed care plans that provide relatively better medical coverage than do carved-out (i.e., separately administered and often separately owned) behavioral health plans. Providing services to patients with carved out insurance can be problematic, inasmuch as psychologists are more frequently being reimbursed from the behavioral health portion, rather than the medical portion, of health insurance benefits. In fact, particularly discouraging is the fact that carved-out behavioral health plans proactively may discourage thorough and formal psychological assessments, preferring a less expensive, routine diagnostic interview; a few have a blanket prohibition against neuropsychological evaluations, and some do not ever cover testing for learning disabilities.

Within our own large medical group practice, psychologists have at times been forced to provide services to the patients of our own physician practice group, even though doing so under the *capitated* insurance benefit (i.e., when clinicians assume risk of inadequate monies to cover necessary care for their patients) meant operating at a loss for that subset of patients. Similarly, when the patient's primary care services have been paid from a different portion of the patient's health insurance coverage, there have been instances of no reimbursement's being available for some psychological and neuropsychological assessment services—a situation that can prove very awkward in maintaining a good working relationship with a referral source.

Medicare

Within each region of the United States, Medicare establishes what it considers to be acceptable (i.e., reimbursable) clinical care and the billing procedures required in order to obtain partial reimbursement of standard charges for clinical services. Although the specifics are well known to vary from region to region (e.g., the maximum number of hours for neuropsychological assessment per patient that can be considered without special documentation), there are some general overarching issues in all Medicare regions. For example, the most important consideration in providing psychological assessments to Medicare patients is the documentation of *medical necessity.* In most instances, the documentation of medical necessity is provided by the fact that a physician generated the referral. When bills are submitted, the referring physician's unique physician identifier number (UPIN) is submitted along with patient and provider identification and billing charges.

However, Medicare can deem certain clinical procedures, identified by current procedural terminology (CPT) codes—often linked to certain diagnoses, identified by International

Classification of Diseases (ICD) codes—as not medically necessary, even with physician referral. For example, in the Illinois and Wisconsin Medicare region, evaluation with neuropsychological instruments when the diagnosis involves adjustment disorder is considered *not* medically necessary and therefore not permissible to submit for billing. Despite the fact that the diagnosis cannot be known in advance, providers must take responsibility for understanding the Medicare rules and policies concerning psychological and neuropsychological assessments within their region. Also, such procedures as the Minnesota Multiphasic Personality Inventory–2 (MMPI-2) must be billed using a psychological test procedure code, even if contained within a neuropsychological testing battery, and a Mini Mental Status Examination (MMSE) is considered part of a diagnostic interview and should not be billed with a neuropsychological assessment code. Those who fail to follow such rules run the risk of rejected bills at the minimum and audits and possible legal and financial penalties at the maximum. A second major issue pertaining to Medicare and especially relevant to psychological assessment in medical settings is the *incident to* provision. Basically, with regard to clinical psychology, this provision requires that when providing psychological assessment or treatment to hospitalized patients, the licensed psychologist whose name appears on the bill must provide all services submitted to Medicare for partial reimbursement. That is, the time and associated charges for assistants who are in the employ of the psychologist and who provide part of the services to a Medicare inpatient will not be reimbursed. This problem can be substantial for busy hospital-based consultation programs. In fact, survey data indicate that in 1999, 69% of board-certified neuropsychologists in Division 40 (the Division of Clinical Neuropsychology within the American Psychological Association) used assistants in carrying out formal evaluations (Sweet, Moberg, & Suchy, 2000). From a broader and larger sample of the memberships of Division 40 and the National Academy of Neuropsychology (NAN) in 2000, Sweet, Peck, Abramowitz, and Etzweiler (in press) found that 54% of clinical neuropsychologists were using assistants.

The relatively recent education of professionals and aggressive enforcement by Medicare related to *incident to* services has curtailed and changed some inpatient assessment activities, either through use of different personnel, reducing services, or billing fewer hours. Specifically, the survey data from Division 40 and NAN members found that 85% of inpatient Medicare providers reported administering fewer tests than normal, and of these 45% reported that quality of care with these patients suffered as a result. Moreover, 12% reported that they have stopped seeing Medicare patients as a result of restrictive practices. Medicare's *incident to* billing restriction is apparently related to 24% of neuropsychologists reporting that because of the restriction assistants are not used and to another 45% of neuropsychologists not billing for assistant time. This factor as well as the additional limitation of a maximum allowable billing time have likely been causative factors leading 69% of clinicians to report writing off without billing some portion of the actual hours spent providing services to Medicare inpatients.

Payor Mix

As noted previously, psychologists working in medical settings such as hospitals and other types of formal health care organizations may be part of large health care provider groups. As such, individual members may be forced to take referrals from a variety of payer sources, including those for whom there is very poor reimbursement for psychological and neuropsychological assessment services as defined by managed care contracts for those for whom there is no reimbursement possible at all. Unlike clinicians in private practice, providers working in institutions are likely to not have the choice of so-called cherry picking (i.e., accepting referrals with ability to pay most or all of billing charges while declining to see patients with little or no insurance coverage). Similarly, a recent national survey of clinical neuropsychologists (e.g., Sweet et al., in press) showed a lower proportion of forensic cases, which are known to pay full fee, and self-pay cases among those providing assessment services in medical institutions compared to private practice. As was discussed previously in the section regarding managed care, loss of freedom to decline patients can be a negative incentive for psychologists who practice as employees or affiliates to provider groups in some medical settings.

Reimbursement Obstacles to Timeliness and Length of Testing

Clinical psychologists engaged in formal testing, especially neuropsychologists, have for some time been struggling with the ability to self-determine when assessments can be delivered and the length of time spent in a single neuropsychological evaluation. In fact, with regard to the latter issue of length of testing, Piotrowski (1999) has opined that what traditionally was considered a "comprehensive test battery" by clinical psychologists will be a "moribund clinical activity, at least where third-party reimbursement and managed care constraints are an issue" (p. 792). The forces against which psychologists have struggled to provide timely assessments that are clinically appropriate in length of spent time with the patient are managed care and Medicare. Both the managed care industry and Medicare have attempted to contain costs

of psychological assessment services by limiting the number of hours of testing per evaluation that will be reimbursed. For example, it has become common for a managed care company to approve only a diagnostic interview, which is then followed by a negotiation between the clinician and a managed care representative with regard to which procedures will be reimbursable and how many hours of testing will be reimbursed. This circumstance is common both within and outside of medical settings. What is particularly difficult for those practicing within medical settings is that the immediate management of the very ill medical inpatient (e.g., new stroke patient) or acutely disordered but less ill medical setting outpatient (e.g., Parkinson's disease or epileptic patient under deteriorating medication control) may or may not allow for the slow and efficient authorization process. Even more problematic in some instances is the real possibility that the managed care company may authorize substantially fewer hours or not authorize *any* hours of formal testing. Frequently, psychologists feel obligated to provide services that may then be either underreimbursed or not reimbursed at all.

In contrast to managed care, Medicare insurance coverage does not normally delay delivery of services; however, Medicare coverage is limited to a set number of reimbursable hours of testing annually. When more than the allowed number of hours are delivered, reimbursement requires special written documentation of greater-than-normal medical necessity. Because the special authorization must take place at the time of billing (i.e., after the delivery of services), denial of the request results in nonreimbursement, which is essentially an unexpected contribution to free care.

Consultation-Liaison and Emergency Referrals

Some of the formal assessment services provided within medical settings are associated with a degree of timeliness that requires special consideration not normally seen outside of medical settings. Psychologists providing assessment services within medical settings may be asked to interrupt their daily activities to provide very rapid response to an inpatient. For example, a brief baseline neuropsychological screening of a patient scheduled for imminent surgery may be requested, or the abrupt change of mental status in a hospitalized cardiac patient with heretofore normal neurological status may bring in requests for rapid consultations from neurology, psychiatry, and neuropsychology. Such requests are unique to medical settings in their requirements of extremely rapid assessment and feedback to the referral source. There is no time for insurance carriers to authorize services in advance of this type of clinical psychological assessment.

Financial Efficacy of Assessment

As the expenditure of health care monies has come under closer scrutiny, questions regarding containing costs of insurance coverage for psychological assessment have grown to include demonstration of financial efficacy. Responding to this exigent situation, made more so by the fact that little research has gathered data relevant to this issue (Ambrose, 1997), Groth-Marnat (1999) proposed seven rational strategies that can be used to enhance financial efficacy of clinical assessment. Given the increased pressure for rapid services, efficiency of service delivery (often related to needing to see more patients within the same amount of time), and cost containment within institutional medical settings, Groth-Marnat's recommendations seem particularly well suited to psychological assessment within medical settings. These recommendations were as follows:

- Focus on domains most relevant for treatment planning and outcomes.
- Use formal assessment for risk management.
- Target conditions most likely to result in financial efficacy.
- Use computer-assisted assessment.
- Use time-efficient instruments.
- More closely link assessment, feedback, and intervention.
- Integrate treatment planning, monitoring progress, and evaluating outcome.

With these considerations in mind, Groth-Marnat suggested that research pertaining to financial efficacy of formal psychological assessment include specific impacts on cost benefit (financial gain resulting from an expenditure), cost effectiveness (gains in such areas as quality of life and wellness that cannot easily be expressed in monetary units), cost offset (expenses reduced by utilizing a less expensive procedure in place of one that is more expensive), and cost containment (general efforts to reduce costs through limiting procedures covered or frequency of service utilization). To be clear, the question being addressed to the clinical psychologist practicing in medical settings is not whether there is empirical support for psychological assessment activities in health care settings (see reviews of empirical support by Kubiszyn et al., 2000; Meyer et al., 2001); it is whether these activities can be justified on an economic basis. It is not difficult to imagine that although relevant financial efficacy research data will be very helpful in answering this question at the national level, which can affect managed care policy positively, the most salient information may be that which is gathered at the local level and targeted to specific service delivery systems. In this latter regard, the prominence of the scientist-practitioner approach, a mainstay

of individual and programmatic service delivery of clinical psychologists in medical settings (Rozensky, Sweet, & Tovian, 1997; Sweet, Rozensky, & Tovian, 1991), seems ideally suited to the task.

Ethical and Legal Issues

Ability to Give Informed Consent for Assessment

Concerns regarding the need for documenting informed consent for assessment—as has been more common with treatment—have been well articulated and appear cogent (see Johnson-Greene, Hardy-Morais, Adams, Hardy, & Bergloff, 1997, for a discussion pertaining to neuropsychological assessment). Yet, there are unique aspects of medical settings that increase the likelihood that ethical guidelines may conflict with patient-related situations that may be uncommon—or even nonexistent—in other practice settings. First, within medical settings there are more likely to be seriously ill patients whose conditions may impair or at least bring into question their ability to give consent for diagnostic testing and treatment. As the APA has moved toward more explicit guidelines and expectations regarding the need for informed written consent for treatment *and* assessment, the ethical dilemma for practitioners engaged in assessments with seriously ill patients has increased meaningfully. For example, when a medical inpatient becomes a management problem and also refuses treatment, it is appropriate for physicians to call upon colleagues such as clinical psychologists and neuropsychologists to better determine the problem and related solutions. A medical inpatient who is not able to understand the dire consequences of refusing treatment that would correct the underlying medical situation and also return the patient to competent cognitive status may not have the legal right to refuse the treatment agreed upon by physicians and responsible family members. However, what if the assessment that objectively would document the cognitive incapacity and the need for others to judge the medical necessity of treatment is not possible because the patient also will not cooperate in providing written informed consent? Is a psychologist vulnerable to legal or ethics action if the assessment is carried out without informed consent?

At present, there is no completely satisfying answer for this difficult situation. When informed consent cannot be obtained because the patient is either uncooperative due to delirium or not competent to be truly informed due to dementia, many practitioners rely on the direction and approval of close family members before proceeding. The notion of considering and including family members in a process of medical decision making rests on a philosophical position that views informed consent as a collaborative decision making *process* in which values and thinking related to informed consent "are not the hidden and privileged property of the individual" (Kuczewski, 1996, p. 35). The direction of decisions derived in such a process is best documented in writing, with an endorsing signature of a family member, if possible. However, it is also noteworthy that inpatient services will at times be requested when it appears that no patient family member is available to sign consent for the evaluation or for the release of information. Under such circumstances, the psychologist may have no choice but to document in writing that consent could not be obtained, before proceeding. This topic brings us to the next section, which is related.

Competency Issues in Medical Settings

Inpatient medical settings are more likely than any other type of outpatient clinical setting to involve questions pertaining to competency. Competency is a legal concept, not a medical concept, which—in order to be established as present or absent by legal standards—relies upon observations, opinions, and data from health care providers. Melton, Petrila, Poythress, and Slobogin (1997) note multiple delineations of competency pertaining to criminal matters, including competency to consent to search or seizure, competency to confess, competency to plead guilty, competency to waive the right to counsel, competency to refuse an insanity defense, competency to testify, and competency to be sentenced and executed. These authors also note numerous civil competencies, which have more bearing in psychological assessment with medical inpatients. These are competency to make treatment decisions, competency to consent to research, and testamentary competency. Although the latter two types have relevance, competency to make treatment decisions is perhaps the most salient within medical settings (e.g., Feenan, 1996; Pollack & Billick, 1999), and in particular for psychologists performing inpatient psychological assessments. Setting aside the legal discussion of relevant constructs, the sum of which surpasses the space limitations of this chapter, competence to accept or refuse treatment fundamentally requires the following, subsequent to appropriated disclosure regarding treatment:

> At a minimum the clinician will want to learn the patient's understanding of the nature and purpose of the treatment; its risks and benefits; and the nature, risks, and benefits of alternative treatments. Under the "appreciation" and "reasonable process" test of competency, it will also be important to determine the patient's reasons for consenting or refusing consent. (Melton et al., 1997, p. 355)

The notion of whether a patient is capable of understanding relevant facts and circumstances is part of virtually all types of competency and is the fundamental reason that psychologists are often called upon to provide quantitative evidence of cognitive capacities when issues regarding competency arise. To serve this purpose, psychological test data pertaining to verbal reasoning, learning and memory, and other cognitive domains can be used—in conjunction with information and observations of physicians and others—to assist a judge in establishing the legal presence of competence or incompetence (e.g., Marson, Chatterjee, Ingram, & Harrell, 1996; Marson & Harrell, 1999; Marson, Hawkins, McInturff, & Harrell, 1997). A variety of specific quantified cognitive measures have been constructed for the purpose of addressing issues of competency in medical settings (e.g., Billick, Bella, & Burgert, 1997; Etchells et al., 1999; Glass, 1997; Grisso, Appelbaum, & Hill-Fotouhi, 1997; Holzer, Gansler, Moczynski, & Folstein, 1997; Marson, McInturff, Hawkins, Bartolucci, & Harrell, 1997).

Whereas it has been advocated that children and adolescents—within the limits of cognitive and social development—be involved in medical decision making (McCabe, 1996), minors may not have an absolute right to consent to or refuse medical treatment (cf. Williams, Harris, Thompson, & Brayshaw, 1997). That is, although it may be best from a psychological standpoint to involve children and adolescents in decision making regarding their own medical care, legal standards ultimately bestow final authority to parents or legal guardians.

From both legal and medical perspectives, lack of competence to undergo informed consent and make decisions with regard to treatment has implications for helping patients make decisions regarding advanced directives, such as health care power of attorney and a living will (Ahmed, 1998; Chen & Grossberg, 1997). These decisions require adequate cognitive capacity. For that reason, patients with medical conditions in which illness progression is likely to lead to cognitive incapacity should be educated early regarding the importance of completing advance directives and taking care of personal financial matters (including a legal will that requires that legal standards of testamentary competence be met) while it is still possible to do so.

Unique Quality-of-Life Versus Death Issues

With the advent of sophisticated medical technology that can prolong life, occasionally at the cost of *quality of life,* some seriously ill patients within medical settings may confront physicians, psychologists, and other health care professionals with very complex decisions. With examples such as choosing to forego kidney disease for renal disease (Tobe & Senn, 1996) and determining a consensual threshold beyond which slowing the progression of Alzheimer's disease may not serve the patient (Post, 1997) and hastened death requests associated with terminal illness (Farberman, 1997; Hendin, 1999), it seems the choice to discontinue life-prolonging treatment becomes an issue worthy of consideration. Psychologists working in certain specialty programs, especially as technology to keep very ill patients alive continues to improve, can expect to be involved with other health care professionals in attempting to establish the presence or absence of certain factors (e.g., treatable depression, serious cognitive compromise) in an individual case. In part, the contribution of the psychologist in assisting with this differential diagnosis may come from formal psychological assessment. For example, Smithline, Mader, and Crenshaw (1999) demonstrated that on the basis of formal intellectual testing, as many as 20–32% patients with acute myocardial infarction probably had insufficient capacity to give informed consent to participate in emergency medicine research. Without formal psychological testing, only 8% of these patients were suspected of having insufficient capacity for informed consent.

Limits of Confidentiality

Medical settings may present rather unique concerns regarding confidentiality. Whether inpatient or outpatient, numerous medical settings involve multiple clinicians and sometimes multiple disciplines. Patients and other health care professionals outside of psychology may or may not understand the realities of confidentiality with regard to such settings. For example, multidisciplinary outpatient clinics and inpatient medical settings often maintain, at the specific direction of the Joint Commission on Accreditation of Healthcare Organizations (JCAHO), a single centralized chart, wherein all medical, nursing, and mental health records are stored. For psychologists providing formal assessment services within such settings, there may be a pressure to store psychological test results in this single patient chart, even though state law and professional guidelines and ethics standards may require storage in a separate chart. In order to maintain adequate test security of the test forms, questions, and answers, as well as to protect unnecessary disclosure by another party (e.g., medical records department staff) of detailed personal and psychological information, a separate psychological testing record should be maintained. In order to accomplish this task, clinic, hospital, and office support staffs need to be educated about the special circumstances pertaining to storage and maintenance of psychological test records. When applicable (e.g., when a formal psychological test report is to be placed in a common inpatient hospital

chart), patients should be informed of the degree to which psychological test information may be accessed by others. Alternatively, policies can be adopted proactively by the psychologist to safeguard against unimpeded access; for example, psychological test reports can be provided only to the referral source rather than placed in a common file.

Some unique ethical and legal issues associated with medical settings relate to the dying patient. In the course of an assessment of an inpatient whose terminal condition has just been discovered, a psychologist might be asked by the patient for information that has not yet been shared with the patient by the rest of the health care team. Or the dying patient may divulge important and previously unknown psychological information that would be destructive to the rest of the family if that information were shared and divulged by the health care team, who in turn may not understand the patient's reactions without being informed of the provocative information. Alternatively, what should a psychologist do if while evaluating a dying patient, the patient confesses to serious illegal activities that, *if* he or she survived, would almost certainly be prosecuted?

Limits of Recommendations for Medical Patients

Medical patients have a variety of assessment and treatment needs, some of which are addressed by psychologists and others of which are either (a) outside the scope of psychological practice or (b) not part of the services requested by the physician referral source. The first category may appear at first glance to be clear-cut in that psychologists do not practice outside the scope of their training and the limits of licensure. However, there can be a conflict stimulated by referral questions raised by the referral source that may, for an individual psychologist, not be within his or her expertise (e.g., frequent questions from physicians regarding the psychologist's suggested choice of particular medication after an assessment-based recommendation for an antidepressant medication evaluation has been made). Whether the psychologist has considerable relevant expertise pertaining to such a scenario determines the limits of responses that can be made, all of which must be within current licensing limits.

Response to the second category can be even thornier. For example, if an assessment pertaining only to impaired memory uncovers suicidal ideation and a suicidal plan, presumably no one would suggest that the psychologist should not recommend appropriate treatment, regardless of the specialty or original referral interests of the referring physician. However, in less emergent circumstances, when asked to assess a particular facet of an individual (e.g., psychological readiness for surgery intended to relieve chronic back pain), if there are additional unrelated needs that are identified (e.g., a long-standing learning disability that obstructs a lifelong dream of obtaining a college degree), should treatment recommendations related to the latter issue be included, even if they are not relevant to the reason for the consultation and not within the purview of the referral source? To elaborate further, psychological assessment services are often delivered within medical settings when the psychologist is in the role of a consultant to another health care professional, most often a physician. In such a situation, the purview and associated latitude of recommendations appear more limited than they would be if the psychologist were being consulted directly by a patient who held the expectation that the psychologist would be in the role of primary responsibility for the broad range of caring for the patient's psychological needs.

Logistics

Medical settings, especially hospitals, have some unique characteristics that affect the provision of care, including psychological and neuropsychological assessments. First and perhaps foremost is that the provision of care within hospitals and some other medical settings requires credentialing and privileging of the provider—that is, each provider must have his or her professional *credentials* (e.g., degree programs, formal nondegree coursework, certifications of training or competence, etc.) placed under peer review that allows a determination of which *privileges* (e.g., professional procedures associated with the individual's field of study and practice, such as personality testing or neuropsychological testing) the person will be allowed to perform while working within a given facility. In other words, a psychologist may not simply enter and provide services in a medical facility merely because someone has referred a patient. In most instances, credentialing and privileging at a medical facility implies that the provider will provide services intermittently or with some regularity. However, when a one-time evaluation is requested, temporary privileges can usually be granted expeditiously. These requirements are an expectation of agencies such as the JCAHO. Therefore, it is important to note that merely being hired as an employee of a medical facility is not enough to begin practicing within the facility; credentialing and privileging must still take place, even for a full-time employee of the institution. The facility must still document that an adequate review of credentials and an appropriate granting of privileges for the practice of psychology have taken place. As more psychologists have been hired within medical facilities, more sophisticated and specific credentialing and privileging procedures have been created and entrusted to psychologists rather than medical staff. Thus,

currently this intended *peer* review process is more likely to be a review by one's true peers (other practicing psychologists) than it has been in the past.

Second, the amount of time within which a psychologist provides assessment services to patients is quite different on an inpatient unit than it is in outpatient practice. In fact, there are three separate time intervals that are considered critical to the provision of responsive inpatient services: (a) starting with the referral being received, time to begin the evaluation; (b) time to complete the evaluation; and (c) time to provide feedback (usually in the form of a written report) regarding the evaluation findings. Currently, as a result of shortened hospital stays, the total time available for all three phases of completing a psychological or neuropsychological evaluation of an inpatient is frequently less than 3 days. Barring difficulties that cannot be controlled, such as patient unavailability and patient lack of cooperation, it is not uncommon in our own hospital system to complete all three phases within 2 days.

A very different and unique logistical problem associated with assessment of inpatients is what Medicare terms *incident to* restrictions. Essentially, as discussed previously, psychologists must personally provide all the services for Medicare inpatients that are billed. The time spent by paid testing technicians and other assistants in providing psychological or neuropsychological assessment services is deemed not reimbursable by Medicare. Thus, psychologists and neuropsychologists who are hospital-based—and therefore likely to receive numerous inpatient referrals and to use testing assistants—must either organize their practice time differently to provide all services themselves or must write off time spent delivering inpatient assessment services by paid assistants. Although applicable to all psychologists and neuropsychologists—whether in private practice or working within organized medical systems—this policy is particularly difficult for those whose practices are located within hospitals.

Special Instruments and Issues

Assessments in some medical settings require particular attention to the possibilities that (a) the patient may have limited ability to respond, (b) the patient may be seriously ill and possibly infectious, and (c) the nature of the case may require unusual or special testing procedures, equipment, or both. These types of issues are usually not found outside of medical settings. The presence of such issues requires that the psychologist performing assessments (a) maintain a wide array of testing options in order to be able to assess even the most frail medically ill patients at bedside in their hospital rooms; (b) be aware of universal precautions (generally accepted practices for preventing the spread of infection within hospitals) and the possible need to disinfect or dispose of test materials if they become contaminated; and (c) be able to foresee and employ assessment techniques for patients who may be recently or chronically physically, sensorily, or cognitively handicapped. Given the greater acuity of illness currently required to satisfy admission requirements to inpatient hospital programs and the shorter length of hospital stays, decreasing numbers of these patients are suitable for traditional standardized testing instruments.

ASSESSMENT WITHIN A BIOPSYCHOSOCIAL MODEL

In medicine, the goals of clinical diagnosis are to identify the ongoing disease process and to formulate a plan to deal with the disease. When psychosocial factors are added to the medical symptomatology, the patient cannot be seen as a single entity that carries a group of predictable or constant symptoms requiring evaluation. Rather, psychosocial factors interact with the patient's premorbid personality to create a changing pattern. Under these circumstances, clinical analysis must not only systematically evaluate these varied elements, but also clarify their interrelationships and changes over time. Current behaviors and attitudes are assessed in conjunction with the physical basis of the presenting problem. Premorbid background is delineated in an effort to clarify the person's baseline and the historical context for the medical condition. Moreover, using the biopsychosocial model (Belar & Deardorff, 1995; Engel, 1977; Nicassio & Smith, 1995) clinical health psychology has been able to move from an ineffectual model supporting mind-body duality to a model that considers influences of culture, environment, behavior, and beliefs on physiology and symptomatology. This model is not an endpoint in understanding medical patients, but it can serve as an organizing schema for identifying diagnostic questions. Within this approach an attempt is made to assess the interaction of the *type* of data collected (affective, behavioral, cognitive, or physiological information) with the *source* from which the data can be collected (the patient, his or her environment, or both).

The goal of a psychologist performing assessments in medical settings is to contribute to a broader understanding of the patient. This information can include an understanding of the patient within his or her physical and social environment; the patient's relative psychological assets and weaknesses; evidence of psychopathology contributing to, in reaction to, or separate from the physical disease process; the patient's response or predicted response to both illness and the medical or surgical treatment regimen; and identification of the coping skills being used by the patient and family (Belar & Deardorff, 1995). In addition, the psychologist can be especially helpful to the health care team, the patient, and the patient's family in assessing the complicated questions surrounding issues of malingering, factious disorders, the interaction of psychological disorders and medical disorders, or the problems of the "worried well" seen in the medical setting (Rozensky et al., 1997).

General Issues

Modalities

Assessment information comes from a variety of sources. These sources include interviews, questionnaires and inventories (self-reporting), self-monitoring, direct observation of behavior, and psychophysiological measurement. Each measurement modality must be evaluated uniquely to determine which is the most effective method to use in achieving a valid assessment.

The interview provides the foundation of the assessment process. Interviewing the medical patient requires the basic skills needed in evaluating patients in any setting. Basic to all effective interviewing, the clinician must be able to empathize and develop rapport, gather relevant information to the referral question, make adjustments as a function of process issues and patient characteristics, understand the importance of timing in the disease process and medical treatment intervention, and utilize a theoretical framework to guide the assessment process. More information on the interview process and other modalities in assessment with medical patients can be found in Pinkerton, Hughes, and Wenrich (1982); Hersen and Turner (1994); and Van Egren and Striepe (1998).

Self-report measures are advantageous when external observers cannot achieve sufficient access to that which is being measured (e.g., affect or attitude), cost is crucial, staff time is at a premium, or trained clinicians are not available. Clinical observer rating scales and interviews are usually preferred in situations in which clinical judgment is essential (e.g., diagnosis), the disease process or disability has robbed the patient of the ability to report accurately (e.g., delirium or dementia), or sophisticated clinical decisions are required (e.g., neuropsychological testing). Clinical experience has demonstrated that certain constructs (e.g., quality of life) are best measured via self-report; other measurement tasks have been determined to often require judgment from clinical observers (e.g., diagnostic assessment from the *Diagnostic and Statistical Manual of Mental Disorders–Fourth Edition;* American Psychiatric Association, 1994). Other aspects of psychological assessment (e.g., psychological distress) may be approached through either modality (Derogatis, Fleming, Sudler, & DellaPietra, 1995).

Timing

Another important general issue involves the specific point in time that an assessment occurs. The natural history of many medical conditions may include specific events that place stress on patients' coping abilities. Medical interventions also have noxious side effects that cause psychological effects. Baseline assessment prior to the introduction of any significant treatment intervention would be useful. In addition, it would be ideal if psychological assessments could coincide with major medical diagnostic evaluations and interventions so that information on a patient's psychological state could be integrated with the overall clinical picture and treatment plan. Finally, with many chronic illnesses, perhaps a comprehensive yearly psychological assessment focussing on quality of life, coping efficacy, and possible psychological distress completed during scheduled medical visits could yield crucial information as the illness, the treatments, or both change over time.

Normative Standards

Crucial to effective psychological assessment of medically ill patients is the selection of the most appropriate normative standards or *norms* to use as referents (e.g., general population norms or illness-specific population norms) when using self-report inventories. The identification of appropriate norms is based upon the nature of the comparison that the psychologist wishes to make and the specific question that is addressed. If the basic question is whether the patient's psychological distress has reached clinical proportions, then the general population norm may be used because it is much more likely to have well-established so-called caseness criteria associated with it. Comparison with a general norm addresses the question *Does this patient have a psychological problem of sufficient clinical magnitude to require a therapeutic intervention?* Alternatively, if the referral question concerns the quality of a patient's adjustment to the illness at a particular stage in comparison with the typical patient, then an illness-specific norm is indicated (Derogatis et al., 1995). Therefore, referral questions involving psychological distress and psychiatric disorder are often sufficiently salient to generalize across groups of patients. Adjustment to a particular illness is a construct that is much more illness-specific and may require the psychologist to interpret adjustment profiles in terms of specific illness stages.

Some variables, such as quality of life, are best assessed in a manner that combines normative data from both general and illness-specific populations. Quality-of-life measures often generate a very broad-spectrum continuum—from a status reflecting optimum health, social functioning, and so forth, to one of indicating serious deterioration of well-being at the other end. In addition, specific medical disorders often involve specific symptoms, problems, and disabilities that require detailed assessment. Investigators assessing quality of life (Derogatis et al., 1995; Mayou, 1990) often use a modular strategy combining both norms. In this paradigm, the illness-specific module may be treated as an additional domain of the general inventory instrument or as a distinct, individual measure.

Assessment Measures

In their review of psychological assessment, Derogatis et al. (1995) identified five constructs or attributes to measure in patients with medical disease: (a) well-being or affect balance, (b) psychological distress, (c) cognitive functioning, (d) psychosocial adjustment to illness, and (e) personality or health-related constructs. To this end, the authors recommend several screening instruments to delineate whether the patient has a psychological disorder requiring treatment or influencing medical treatment. Screening instruments are not diagnostic tests per se; rather, they represent an attempt to describe whether the patient has a high probability of having a certain condition in question (positive) or a low probability of the condition (negative). Those with positive screening can be further evaluated. The screening instrument should both be reliable (i.e., consistent in its performance from one administration to the next—sensitivity) and have predictive validity (i.e., capable of identifying those with the disorder and eliminating those who do not).

Several examples of psychological and cognitive screening measures and a neuropsychological battery are presented in Tables 13.1, 13.2, and 13.3. The examples presented are not intended to be exhaustive. Instead, they represent some of the most popular and frequently cited in literature reviews on assessment in medical settings (Demakis, Mercury, & Sweet, 2000; Keefe & Blumenthal, 1982; Rozensky et al., 1997; Sweet et al., 1991). For more information on most of these measures, the reader is advised to consult Maruish (2000) and Derogatis et al. (1995). With regard to Table 13.2, Sweet et al. (1997) recommended that neuropsychological screening batteries be used with cases involving differential psychiatric versus neurological diagnosis, including patients with subtle to mild dementia, who require more extensive diagnostic information and more complex case management. These authors recommend that more comprehensive neuropsychological

TABLE 13.1   Examples of Affect, Personality, Psychopathology, Interview, and Adjustment Measures Used Within Medical Settings

Affect measures
- Beck Depression Inventory–II (BDI-II)
- Beck Anxiety Inventory (BAI)
- State-Trait Anxiety Inventory (STAI)
- State-Trait Anger Expression Inventory–2 (STAXI-2)
- Center for Epidemiological Studies Depression Scale (CES-D)

Personality measures
- Minnesota Multiphasic Personality Inventory–2 (MMPI-2)
- Personality Assessment Inventory (PAI)
- Millon Clinical Multiaxial Inventory–III (MCMI-III)
- Rorschach inkblots
- Thematic apperception test

Brief measures of psychopathology symptoms
- Symptom Checklist–90–Revised (SCL-90-R)
- Brief Symptom Inventory (BSI)
- Illness Behavior Questionnaire (IBQ)
- Symptom Assessment–45 (SA-45)

Structured clinical interviews
- Structured Clinical Interview for *DSM III-R* (SCID)
- Schedule for Affective Disorders and Schizophrenia (SADS)

Psychological adjustment to illness
- Multidimensional Health Locus of Control (MHLC)
- Ways of Coping Inventory (WOC)
- Sickness Illness Profile (SIP)
- Psychological Adjustment to Illness–Self-Report (PAIS-SR)
- Millon Behavioral Medicine Diagnostic (MBMD)
- SF-36 Health Survey

Note: Adapted from Sweet, Rozensky, & Tovian (1997).

TABLE 13.2   Examples of Measures Used for Neuropsychological Referrals Within Medical and Psychiatric Settings

Dementia and delirium rating scales
- Mattis Dementia Rating Scale–2 (DRS-2)
- Mini-Mental State Exam (MMSE)
- Blessed Dementia Rating Scale (BDRS)
- Delirium Rating Scale (DelRS)

Screening batteries
- Finger Tapping
- Trail Making
- Stroop Color-Word Test
- WAIS-III Digit Symbol
- Luria-Nebraska Pathognomonic Scale
- California Verbal Learning Test–II
- Warrington Recognition Memory Test
- Wechsler Memory Test–Third Edition (WMS-III), select subtests
- Multilingual Aphasia Examination
- Shipley Institute of Living Scale
- Ruff Figural Fluency

Comprehensive batteries
- Halstead-Reitan Battery (selected tests: Sensory-Perceptual Exam, Aphasia Screening Examination, Tactual Performance Test, Category Test, Finger Tapping, Trail Making)
- Wechsler Adult Intelligence Scale–Third Edition (WAIS-III)
- Wechsler Memory Scale–Third Edition (WMS-III)
- California Verbal Learning Test–II
- Warrington Recognition Memory Test
- Grooved Pegboard
- Stroop Color-Word Test
- Shipley Institute of Living Scale
- Ruff Figural Fluency Test
- Multilingual Aphasia Examination (Visual Naming, COWA)
- Gordon Diagnostic System (Vigilance, Distractibility)
- Reading Comprehension (from the Peabody Individual Achievement Test–Third Edition)
- Wide Range Achievement Test–Third Edition (WRAT-III)
- Paced Auditory Serial Addition Test
- Beck Depression Inventory–II (BDI-II)
- Beck Hopelessness Scale
- Minnesota Multiphasic Personality Inventory–2 (MMPI-2)

Note. Adapted from Sweet, Rozensky, & Tovian (1997).

batteries be used with (a) rehabilitation cases, such as stroke and head injury; (b) neurological cases that may involve progression of a brain disorder across time, such as early cases of multiple sclerosis, systemic lupus erythematosus, or acquired immune deficiency syndrome, and those that require baseline and interval testing in which a relatively diverse and unpredictable set of deficits is possible, as in cerebrovascular disease; and (c) presurgical multidisciplinary evaluation of epilepsy cases. Forensic neuropsychological cases also require a comprehensive battery (cf. Sweet, 1999).

Types of Referrals

The nature of a referral question depends upon the psychologist's role in the specific medical program or setting (e.g., consultant or full service) and the referral source. Belar and Geisser (1995) outlined three broad areas of assessment: differential diagnosis, provision of treatment, and treatment planning. Differential diagnosis involves assessment of significant psychological contributions to illness. Assessment of the need for treatment can include assessment of patient readiness to undergo a procedure, need for treatment for a particular problem, reevaluation for readiness for the procedure after treatment is completed, and need for concurrent treatment to

facilitate a favorable outcome. An example of such a referral would involve whether a patient is a good candidate for cardiac transplant despite being a smoker. In this instance, evaluation, recommendation of smoking cessation intervention, and reevaluation after a period of smoking abstinence may be appropriate.

A final referral area involves assessment that provides an understanding of the commitments of a chronic disease, the sequelae of a particular event, or reaction to illness, so as to facilitate either medical or psychological treatment planning. Examples include identifying problems of adherence to diabetic regimens, assessing individual and family coping strategies in a depressed cancer patient, and delineating cognitive deficits in a brain tumor patient to help in planning for appropriate support services.

TABLE 13.3   Examples of Measures Used Within Psychiatric Settings

Objective personality measures
   Minnesota Multiphasic Personality Inventory–2 (MMPI-2)
   Personality Assessment Inventory (PAI)
   Millon Clinical Multiaxial Inventory–III (MCMI-III)
   Neuroticism, Extraversion, Openness Personality Inventory–Revised
      (NEO-PI-R)
   Narcissistic Personality Inventory

Posttraumatic stress disorder
   Clinician Administered Posttraumatic Stress Disorder Scale–Forms
      1 & 2 (CAPS-1 & 2)
   University of Pennsylvania Posttraumatic Stress Disorder Inventory
   Impact of Event Scale–Revised

Additional self-report measures
   Dissociative Experiences Scale (DES)
   Yale-Brown Obsessive Compulsive Scale (Y-BOCS)
   Eating Disorders Inventory–2 (EDI-2)
   State-Trait Anger Expression Inventory–2 (STAXI-2)
   State-Trait Anxiety Inventory (STAI)
   Beck Depression Inventory–II (BDI-II)
   Beck Anxiety Inventory (BAI)
   Beck Hopelessness Scale (BHS)
   Beck Suicide Scale

Projective personality measures
   Rorschach inkblots (Exner Comprehensive System)
   Thematic apperception test

Structured clinical interviews
   Structured Clinical Interview for *DSM-IV* (SCID)
   Schedule for Affective Disorders and Schizophrenia (SADS)

Note: Adapted from Sweet, Rozensky, & Tovian (1997).

Wellisch and Cohen (1985) outline guidelines to be used with medical staff for making assessment referrals. Referral sources are encouraged to refer when emotional or behavioral responses (a) interfere with the ability to seek appropriate treatment or to cooperate with necessary medical procedures, (b) cause greater distress than does the disease itself or increase disease-related impairment, (c) interfere with activities of daily living, (d) result in curtailing of usual sources of gratification or result in disorganization so severe and inappropriate that it results in misinterpretation and distortion of events. Referrals of medical patients are also encouraged when psychological dysfunction is significant from the patient history (e.g., history of suicide attempt, substance abuse).

Surgical Interventions

Positive psychological outcome of surgery is directly correlated with patients' ability to understand the proposed procedure, recognize its necessity, and tolerate the stress and discomfort associated with the procedure. Several problems, however, can require psychological evaluation and can serve as reasons for referral: a dysfunctional relationship with the surgeon or staff secondary to personality disorder, inability to understand and give consent, severe panic and refusal of surgery, and exacerbation of a preexisting psychiatric problem (e.g., depression, suicide risk).

There are two primary groups of determinants in the psychological adaptation of a patient to surgery. The first group consists of such variables as the patient's specific combination of salient medical variables (i.e., surgery site, reason for surgery), functional deficits resulting from surgery, rehabilitation potential, and the surgeon's psychological management of the patient. The second group consists of patient-related variables, such as the meaning that the patient attaches to the need for surgery and the site of the surgery, perception of the surgical consequences, psychological ability of the patient to tolerate a stressful event, and the relationship between patient and surgeon (Jacobsen & Holland, 1989).

Some degree of presurgery apprehension is normal. Patients with traumatic pasts (e.g., sexual or physical abuse) or premorbid psychiatric disorders can be among the most vulnerable to an abnormal level of fear. In addition to fear, patients can feel hopeless, angry, helpless, and depressed. In assessing the presurgery patient, the psychologist needs to consider salient factors associated with a particular site (e.g., mastectomy, which often involves cancer, altered body image, fear of loss of sexual attractiveness; cardiac surgery, with possible altered lifestyle postsurgery and the fact that the heart is viewed as synonymous with life).

Salient interview issues for the presurgery patient involve identifying the exact nature of the symptoms experienced (e.g., cognitive, affective, and somatic components). Interview questions should differentiate several possible characteristics: avoidance often seen in phobias; flashbacks of previous medical, physical, or sexual trauma, all characteristic of a posttraumatic stress disorder (PTSD); nervousness and anxiety for 6 months or more, often seen in generalized anxiety disorders; attacks of panic, fear, and dread for no apparent reason, characteristic of panic disorders; and a maladaptive response to a severe stressor, often seen in adjustment disorders. The interview can also highlight past compliance (or lack thereof) with medical personnel and medical regimen, the patient's perception of situational demands from surgery and sense of personal control, meanings attributed to the procedure and organ site, knowledge of pre- and postoperative procedures, and desire to obtain information about the procedure.

In addition to measures used to assess brief cognitive functioning, psychopathology, and affect, it may be useful to consider questionnaires pertaining to coping (e.g., Ways of Coping; Folkman & Lazarus, 1980) and locus of control (e.g., Multidimensional Health Locus of Control; Wallston, Wallston, & DeVellis, 1978) in presurgery assessment.

A spectrum of postoperative central nervous system dysfunctions, both acute and persistent, has been documented after cardiac surgical procedures, including stroke, subtle neurological signs, and overt neuropsychological impairment (Newman et al., 2001). In fact, Murkin, Newman, Stump, and Blumenthal (1995) summarized a group consensus statement from experts, highlighting the need for a standardized core battery of neuropsychological tests to be employed with cardiac surgery patients. The group consensus also indicated that mood state assessment should be evaluated concurrently because neuropsychological performance can be influenced by mood state. Although it is arguable whether the panel in its specific test recommendations achieved its stated purposes (i.e., identifying specific tests relevant to the postsurgical phenomenon documented in the literature that would minimize practice effects due to necessary repeat testings), the goals were sound. Although supplementary tests could be added as deemed appropriate, it was envisioned that a core battery could provide a basis for rational comparison across clinical outcome studies and eventually allow combination of study results by meta-analysis. The need for a core battery can also be relevant to other chronic illnesses such as diabetes, in which cognitive and affect changes occur over time (Strachan, Frier, & Deary, 1997).

Organ Transplant Surgery

It is beyond the scope of this chapter to present a detailed discussion of the medical and psychological conditions of potential transplant patients. It is important to note, however, that consideration of organ transplantation is often precipitated by a major medical crisis with a chronic medical condition, and the possibility of death during and shortly after transplantation remains salient. Recent advances in bone marrow, renal, hepatic (liver), and cardiac transplantation have made organ transplantation a viable medical practice.

Organ transplantation remains extremely stressful for patients and their families and involves the allocation of scarce resources (Zipel et al., 1998). Noncompliant patient behavior following transplant surgery can endanger a graft and result in death. Serious psychopathology, including schizophrenia, major affective disorders, and certain personality disorders may interfere with optimal self-care. Toward this end, psychological assessment goals with transplant patients may include (a) determining contraindications to transplant, (b) establishing baselines of affect and cognitive and coping skills for future reference or comparison, (c) identifying psychosocial problems and beginning preoperative intervention, and (d) establishing patient ability to understand the realities of program involvement and postsurgical rehabilitation (Olbrisch, Levenson, & Hamer, 1989).

Rozensky et al. (1997) have outlined a protocol for the assessment of transplant patients as well as psychological contraindications for transplantations. The interview can focus on issues involving knowledge of the transplantation experience and procedures, desire for and reservations about transplantation, adherence and compliance with medical regimen, premorbid health habits (e.g., weight control, exercise, substance abuse), and family reactions. In addition, the Psychological Adjustment to Illness Scale–Self-Report (PAIS-SR), with scoring norms using coronary-heart disease patients and dialysis patients, can be helpful in assessing current adjustment to illness and predicting posttransplant patient compliance.

Several authors have assessed psychopathology in both pre- and postcardiac transplantation using diagnostic interviews with *DSM-III* formats (Kay & Bienenfeld, 1991; Kuhn et al., 1990; Olbrisch & Levenson, 1991). From these data it appears that approximately 75% of candidates are accepted for cardiac transplant with no significant psychosocial contraindications, approximately 20% of candidates are accepted with preconditions (i.e., specific criteria to be met prior to acceptance, such as completion of weight loss or smoking cessation programs), and 5% are refused on psychosocial grounds. Olbrisch et al. (1989) summarize the ethical problems in the application of psychosocial criteria to transplant assessment—namely, allocating scarce organs and expensive care and technology to those patients likely to derive maximum benefit and longevity. The authors note ethical problems can involve confusing psychosocial factors predictive of survival with judgments of an individual's social worth (not regarded by most as acceptable grounds for choosing candidates), unjust decisions resulting from inconsistencies in the application of psychosocial criteria across transplantation centers, and use of criteria that are of questionable reliability and validity.

Olbrisch et al. (1989) have developed the Psychosocial Assessment of Candidates for Transplantation (PACT) rating scale to objectify and allow scientific study of clinical decision-making criteria in psychosocial assessment of transplantation candidates. Normed on 47 cardiac and liver transplant patients, the PACT was shown to have high interrater reliability, with 96% overall agreement between raters on whether to perform a transplant on a given patient. Less than 5% of all pairs of ratings disagreed by more than one category. The scale shows promise for studying the pretransplant psychosocial evaluation in process and can aid in learning how different programs weight various factors in selecting patients and how these decisions predict clinical outcome. Sears, Rodrigue, Sirois, Urizar, and Perri (1999) have attempted to extend psychometric norms for precardiac transplant evaluations using several cognitive measures, affective functioning and adjustment measures, coping strategies, and quality-of-life measures.

Recent studies evaluated the quality of life in heart and lung transplant recipients before and after surgery (Cohen, Littlefied, Kelly, Maurer, & Abbey, 1998; Deshields, Mannen, Tait, & Bajaj, 1997). The authors in both studies found correlations between extreme pretransplant anxiety levels and poorer posttransplant quality of life. Stilley, Miller, Gayowski, and Marino (1999) found in a study of 73 candidates for liver transplant that past history of substance abuse correlated with more distress and less adaptable coping styles after transplantation.

Psychiatric Conditions

Patients with psychiatric conditions will be seen by psychologists in medical settings when they develop medical symptoms or because psychiatric treatment facilities exist within or adjacent to medical treatment facilities. In 1991, prevalence rates in the general population for any psychiatric disorder, any substance abuse-dependence disorder, and both mental health and substance abuse disorder were estimated to be 22.9%, 11.3%, and 4.7%, respectively. Prevalence rates for any anxiety disorder and any affective disorder for the same year were estimated to be 17% and 11%, respectively. Lifetime prevalence rates for these conditions were estimated to be 25% and 19%, respectively (Maruish, 2000). As summarized by Maruish, there are significant comorbidity rates of depression with cancer (18–39%), myocardial infarction (15–19%), rheumatoid arthritis (13%), Parkinson's disease (10–37%), stroke (22–50%), and diabetes (5–11%). The author also summarizes studies that indicate between 50 and 70% of visits to primary care physicians have a psychosocial basis. These figures highlight the need for psychological assessment and screening of psychiatric disorders in medical settings.

Toward this end, the most frequently used instruments for screening and treatment planning, monitoring, and outcome assessment are measures of psychopathological symptomatology. These instruments were developed to assess behavioral health problems that typically prompt people to seek treatment. Frequently used psychopathology instruments are summarized in Table 13.1 and are reviewed in more detail by Rozensky et al. (1997); Sweet and Westergaard (1997); and Maruish (2000).

There are several types of these measures of psychological-psychiatric symptoms. The first category is comprised of comprehensive multidimensional measures. These instruments are typically lengthy, multiscale, standardized instruments that measure and provide a graphic profile of the patient on several psychopathological symptom domains (e.g., anxiety, depression) or disorders (schizophrenia, antisocial personality

disorder). Summary indexes provide a global picture of the individual with regard to his or her psychological status or level of distress. Probably the most widely used and recognized example of these multidimensional measures is the restandardized version of the MMPI-2 (Butcher, Dahlstrom, Graham, Tellegen, & Kaemmer, 1989).

Multidimensional instruments can serve a variety of purposes that facilitate therapeutic interventions in medical and behavioral health care settings. They may be used on initial patient contact to screen for the need for service and simultaneously offer information that is useful for treatment planning. These instruments might also be useful in identifying specific problems that may be unrelated to the patient's chief complaints (e.g., poor interpersonal relations). In addition, they generally can be administered numerous times during the course of treatment to monitor the patient's progress toward achieving established goals and to assist in determining what adjustments (if any) are needed to the intervention. In addition, pre- and posttreatment use of such instruments can provide individual treatment outcome data.

In a second category, abbreviated multidimensional measures are similar to the MMPI-2 and other comprehensive multidimensional measures in many respects. First, they contain multiple scales for measuring a variety of symptoms and disorders. They may also allow for the derivation of an index that can indicate the patient's general level of psychopathology or distress. In addition, they may be used for screening, treatment planning and monitoring, and outcome assessment, just like the more comprehensive instruments. These instruments, however, differ by their shorter length and ease by which they are administered and scored. Their brevity does not allow for an in-depth assessment, but this is not the purpose for which they were designed. Probably the most widely used of these brief instruments are Derogatis's family of symptom checklists. These include the Symptom Checklist-90-Revised (SCL-90-R) and the Brief Screening Inventory (BSI; Derogatis et al., 1995; Derogatis & Spencer, 1982).

The major advantage of the abbreviated multiscale instruments is the ability to survey—quickly and broadly—psychological symptom domains and disorders. Their value is evident in settings in which time and costs available for assessment are limited. These instruments provide a lot of information quickly and are much more likely to be completed by patients than are their lengthier counterparts; this is important if one is monitoring treatment or assessing outcomes, which requires at least two or more assessments to obtain the necessary information. Ironically, disadvantages of these instruments also relate primarily to decreased items: potential absence of or reduced effectiveness of validity scale items, decreased reliability, and (as noted earlier) restricted range of clinical content.

A third category consists of disorder-specific measures, which are designed to measure one specific disorder or family of disorders (e.g., anxiety, depression, suicidality, substance abuse). These instruments are usually brief, requiring 5–10 minutes to complete. They have been thoroughly reviewed by Maruish (2000) in chapters 12 through 17.

Neuropsychological Dysfunction

Neuropsychological tests are designed to provide information related to the presence and degree of cognitive impairment resulting from brain disease, disorder, or trauma; in some instances, they also can provide information pertaining to diagnosis and etiology. The results of these tests also are used, for example, to draw inferences about the extent to which an impairment interferes with the patient's daily functioning, ability to return to work, and competency to consent to treatment. There are numerous psychometrically sound neuropsychological measures. Some instruments assess only specific areas of functioning (e.g., immediate visual memory). Others assess broader areas of functioning (e.g., a battery of memory measures that assesses immediate, intermediate, and long-term verbal and nonverbal memory). Still others are part of a battery of measures that aim to provide a more comprehensive assessment of neuropsychological functioning (e.g., a battery that include tests of memory, language, academic skills, abstract thinking, nonverbal auditory perception, sensorimotor skills, etc.). Examples of neuropsychological screening measures as well as examples of comprehensive batteries can be found in Table 13.2.

The top two referral sources for neuropsychologists are psychiatrists and neurologists (Sweet et al., 2000). The typical referral question stemming from a psychiatric setting concerns discriminating between an emotionally based (or psychological) and a brain-based (or neurological) disorder. It is important to avoid the inaccurate and out-of-date conceptualization of functional versus organic as well as either-or dichotomous questions—that is, neurologically disordered individuals can also be psychologically disordered (e.g., depressed), and individuals with significant psychiatric disorders can develop neurological disorders.

Neurology patients are referred for assessment for a variety of reasons, including to (a) establish functioning before and after surgery or other medical intervention, (b) track recovery or deterioration of a known neurological disorder, (c) assist in differentiating psychiatric and neurological disorder, (d) assist in assigning relative contributions of multiple

known disorders to clinical presentation, and (e) assist in identifying difficult diagnostic conditions for which there is little or no abnormality on neurological examination or medical diagnostic procedures. Patients with a wide range of neurological disorders are referred for neuropsychological evaluation, including traumatic brain injury, cortical degenerative diseases (e.g., Alzheimer's disease), subcortical degenerative diseases (e.g., Parkinson's disease), demyelinating disease (e.g., multiple sclerosis), cerebrovascular disease (hemorrhagic and thromboembolic stroke), primary and secondary brain tumors, seizure disorders, and brain infections (e.g., herpes simplex encephalitis).

Neuropsychological assessment referrals of patients in outpatient or inpatient rehabilitation typically are motivated by the need of the multidisciplinary rehabilitation team to understand each patient's emotional status and capacity. The two most common acute neurological conditions that lead to subsequent rehabilitation during which they may be referred for neuropsychological evaluation are cerebrovascular stroke and traumatic brain injury. Further discussion of the nature of referral questions from psychiatry, neurology, and rehabilitating medicine with neuropsychological assessment may be found in Rozensky et al. (1997). Demakis et al. (2000) review neuropsychological screening measures and referral issues in general medicine and primary care.

Psychosomatic Disorders

When patients are referred because one or more careful medical workups identify no clear physical findings, their physicians may proceed by diagnosis by exclusion. Because no somatic cause is found, it is hoped that psychological assessment will identify psychosocial or psychological factors that could be causing or maintaining the somatic symptoms. There is a tendency for somatic patients to be referred for psychological evaluation as a last resort. Rozensky et al. (1997) outline approaches to inform referral sources in making a referral for psychological evaluation as well as introducing the assessment to the somatoform patient to avoid increased resistance. The authors also support a comprehensive evaluation utilizing specific interview questions, self-monitoring by the patient, and several questionnaires found in Table 13.1.

Swartz, Hughes, and George (1986) provide a brief screening index to identify patients with probable somatoform disorders. The index can be used in an interview format or by review of patient records. The patient's physical complaints are categorized according to 11 symptoms: abdominal pain, abdominal gas, diarrhea, nausea, vomiting, dizziness, fainting, weakness, feeling sickly, pain in extremities, and chest pain. To confirm a probable somatoform diagnosis, the patient must have at least 5 of the 11 symptoms *without* demonstrable medical findings.

Katon et al. (1990), focusing on the prognostic value of somatic symptoms, used the SCL-90-R to provide an operational definition of *high distressed—high utilizers*. The investigators observed linear increases in SCL-90-R dimension scores of Somatization, Depression, and Anxiety as they moved progressively through the somatic symptom groups from low to high.

Kellner, Hernandez, and Pathak (1992) related distinct dimensions of the SCL-90-R to different aspects of hypochondriasis. The authors observed high levels of the SCL-90-R Somatization and Anxiety scores to be predictive of hypochondriacal fears and beliefs, whereas elevations on Depression were not. Fear of disease correlated most highly with the SCL-90-R Anxiety score, but the false conviction of having a disease was more highly correlated with somatization.

Difficult Patients

The Difficult Doctor-Patient Relationship Questionnaire (DDPRQ; Hahn, Thompson, Stern, Budner, & Wills, 1994) is a relatively new instrument that can reliably identify a group of patients whose care is experienced as often difficult by physicians. The construct validity of the instrument has been established by demonstrating strong associations between characteristics that have been associated with physician-experienced difficulty. The instrument classified 11–20% of primary care patients as difficult, using a cutoff point that has been shown to distinguish between patients with difficult characteristics and those without. The DDPRQ score can also be used as a continuous measure. The instrument is available in two formats: the DDPRQ-30, a 30-item version that requires 3–5 minutes to complete, and a 10-item version, the DDPRQ-10, requiring less than 1 minute. The DDPRQ is completed by the physician after meeting with the patient.

Prior to the DDPRQ, the study of the difficult patient was limited to anecdote, clinical description, or the evaluation of idiosyncratic characteristics. Patients experienced as difficult are an important group to study because they are more likely to have psychopathology, to use the health care system disproportionately, and to be less satisfied than are patients perceived to be nondifficult when receiving care. Physician-experienced difficulty also takes its toll on physician and health care professionals' morale and job satisfaction (Hahn, 2000). The DDPRQ has been used in a number of studies and has proven to be an effective and reliable assessment tool.

Alcohol and Substance Abuse

It is well documented that alcohol abuse and substance abuse are often comorbid with anxiety and depressive disorders. Johnson, Brems, and Fisher (1996) compared psychopathology levels of substance abusers not receiving substance abuse treatment with those in treatment. They found SCL-90-R scores to be significantly higher for the majority of subscales for the treatment versus the nontreatment group. Drug abusers in treatment were found to have more psychological symptoms than were those not in treatment, except on the Hostility and Paranoid Ideation Scales, on which the nontreatment group had higher levels. The authors suggested that the presence of a comorbid condition is associated with a greater likelihood that drug abusers will seek treatment.

Derogatis and Savitz (2000), in their thorough analysis of the SCL-90-R, reviewed numerous studies in general medical populations in which the SCL-90-R—within the context of interview and historical data—identified alcohol and substance abusers. The authors also found that the SCL-90-R was able to identify comorbid psychopathology among substance abusers.

Shedler (2000) reviewed the Quick Psychodiagnostics Panel (QPD), which includes a 14-item alcohol and substance abuse scale. All patients answer five of the questions; the remaining questions are presented only when previous responses suggest substance abuse (i.e., logic branching). The scale is fully automated or portable and can be administered on hand-held computer tablets, representing an innovation in computerized assessment. Initial diagnostic results were promising among patients enrolled in an HMO plan.

The Self-Administered Alcoholism Screening Test (SAAST) is a 37-item questionnaire that has been shown to have good reliability and validity when administered to a variety of patient samples. Patient acceptance has also been good when the use of alcohol is viewed as a health care issue. Patient endorsement of test items on the SAAST has been an excellent starting point or screening prior to a clinical interview (Davis, 2000).

Trauma and Sexual Abuse

Sexual abuse and physical abuse are factors associated with medical problems that are often overlooked. Individuals who experience such abuse also experience significant emotional distress and personal devaluation, which can lead to a chronic vulnerability and can compromise the effective treatment of their medical conditions. Many individuals who have been sexually abused exhibit clinical manifestations of anxiety or depressive disorders, without a clear understanding of the contribution made by their victim experiences (Derogatis & Savitz, 2000).

Some investigators have established the utility of the BSI in work with patients who have been sexually abused. Frazier and Schauben (1994) investigated the stressors experienced by college-age females in adjusting to the transition of college life. Significant correlations were found between the magnitude of stress and levels of psychological symptoms on the BSI. Survivors of sexual abuse had significantly higher total scores on the BSI. Coffey, Leitenberg, Henning, Turner, and Bennett (1996) also investigated the consequences of sexual abuse in 192 women with a history of childhood sexual abuse. Women who had been sexually abused revealed a higher total distress score on the BSI than did women in a nonabused control group, and a greater proportion of their BSI subscale scores fell in clinical ranges.

Toomey, Seville, Mann, Abashian, and Grant (1995) assessed a heterogeneous group of chronic pain patients and observed that those patients with a history of sexual abuse scored higher on the SCL-90-R than did nonabused patients. Similar findings were reported by Walker et al. (1995), who found that female patients with chronic pelvic pain had significantly higher symptomatic distress levels than did a patient group (tubal ligation) without pain. The mean score for chronic pelvic pain sufferers fell in the 60th percentile of psychiatric outpatient norms on the SCL-90-R. The pain group also revealed a significantly greater incidence of somaticization disorders, phobias, sexual dysfunction, and sexual abuse as compared to the no-pain group. These studies suggest chronic pain may be another condition that is associated with sexual abuse.

Quality of Life and Outcomes Research

Andrews, Peters, and Tesson (1994) indicated that most of the definitions of quality of life (QOL) describe a multidimensional construct encompassing physical affective, cognitive, social, and economic domains. QOL scales are designed to evaluate—from the patient's point of view—the extent to which the patient feels satisfied with his or her level of functioning in the aforementioned life domains. Objective measures of QOL focus on the environmental resources required to meet one's need and can be completed by someone other than the patient. Subjective measures of QOL assess the patient's satisfaction with the various aspects of his or her life and thus must be completed by the patient. Andrews et al. (1994) indicated distinctions between QOL and health-related quality of life (HRQL) and between generic and condition-specific measures of QOL. QOL measures differ from HRQL measures in that the former assess the whole aspect of one's life, whereas the latter assesses quality of life as it is affected by a disease or

disorder or by its treatment. Generic measures are designed to assess aspects of life that are generally relevant to most people; condition-specific measures are focused on aspects of the lives of particular disease-disorder populations. QOL scales also provide a means to gauge treatment success. One of the more widely used QOL measures is the Medical Outcomes Study Short Form Health Status (SF-36; Ware, 1993). The scale consists of 36 items, yielding scores on eight subscales: physical functioning, social functioning, body pain, general mental health, role limitations due to emotional problems, role limitations due to physical functioning, vitality, and general health perception. New scoring algorithms yielded two new summary scales: one for physical functioning and one for mental functioning (Wetzler, Lum, & Bush, 2000).

Wallander, Schmitt, and Koot (2001) provide a thorough review of QOL issues, instruments, and applications with children and adolescents. Much of what they propose is clearly applicable to QOL measurement in adult patients. The authors conclude that QOL is an area that has growing importance but has suffered from methodological problems and has relied on untested instruments and on functional measurement to the neglect of the subjective experience. They offer a set of coherent guidelines about QOL research in the future and support the development of broadly constructed, universal QOL measures, constructed using people with and without identified diseases, rather than disease-specific QOL measures.

Given the expanding interest in assessing QOL and treatment outcomes for the patient, it is not surprising to see an accompanying interest in assessing the patient's (and in some cases, the patient's family's) satisfaction with services received. Satisfaction should be considered a measure of the overall treatment process, encompassing the patient's (and at times, others') view of how the service was delivered, the capabilities and the attentiveness of the service provider, the perceived benefits of the service, and various other aspects of the service the patient received. Whereas QOL may measure the result of the treatment rendered, program evaluation may measure how the patient felt about the treatment he or she received (Maruish, 2000).

TYPES OF MEDICAL SETTINGS

During the past decade, there has been an increasing interest in the assessment of health status in medical and behavioral health care delivery systems. Initially, this interest was shown primarily within those settings that focused on the treatment of physical diseases and disorders. In recent years, psychologists have recognized the value of assessing the general level of health as well.

Measures of health status and physical functioning can be classified into one of two groups: generic and condition-specific (Maruish, 2000). An example of a generic measure assessing psychological adjustment to illness would be the PAIS (Derogatis et al., 1995). Several of these measures are listed in Table 13.1 and are reviewed by Derogatis et al. (1995) and Rozensky et al. (1997). Condition-specific measures have been available for a number of years and are used with specific medical disorders, diseases, or conditions. Some of these measures are discussed within this section and listed in Table 13.4.

General Medical Settings and Primary Care

As the primary care physician becomes the gatekeeper in many managed care and capitated health care organizations and systems, several instruments have been developed to meet the screening and assessment needs of the primary care physician. The Primary Care Evaluation of Mental Disorders (PRIME-MD; Hahn, Kroenke, Williams, & Spitzer, 2000) is a diagnostic instrument designed specifically for use in primary care by internists and other practitioners. The PRIME-MD contains separate modules addressing the five most common categories of psychopathology seen in general medicine: mood disorders, anxiety disorders, alcohol abuse and dependence, eating disorders, and somatoform disorders. The PRIME-MD has been shown to be valid and reliable, is acceptable to patients, and is often selected as a research tool by investigators (Hahn et al., 2000). The central function of the PRIME-MD is detection of psychopathology and treatment planning.

Table 13.4   Examples of Illness- or Condition-Specific Measures Used Within Medical Settings

Disorder	Measure
Cancer	Cancer Inventory of Problem Situations (CCIPS)
	Profile of Mood States for Cancer (PMS-C)
	Mental Adjustment to Cancer Scale
	Cancer Behavior Inventory (CBI)
Rheumatoid arthritis	Arthritis Impact Measurement Scales
Diabetes mellitus	Diabetic Adjustment Scale (DAS)
	Problem Areas in Diabetes (PAID)
Spinal cord injury	Psychosocial Questionnaire for Spinal Cord Injured Persons
Traumatic brain injury	Glasgow Coma Scale
	Portland Adaptability Inventory
	Rancho Los Amigos Scale
Dentistry	Dental Anxiety Scale
Pain	McGill Pain Questionnaire (MPQ)
	West Haven-Yale Multidimensional Pain Inventory (WHYMPI)
	Measure of Overt Pain Behavior
	Pain Patient Profile (P-3)

However, it can also be used in episodic care, in subspecialty consultations, and in consultation-liaison psychiatry and health psychology assessments.

The COMPASS for Primary Care (COMPASS-PC; Grissom & Howard, 2000) is also a valid and reliable instrument designed for internists and primary care physicians. Within the instrument's 68 items are three major scales—Current Well-Being (CWB), Current Symptoms (CS), and Current Life Functioning (CLF). The four-item CWB scale includes items on distress, energy and health, emotional and psychological adjustment, and current life satisfaction. The 40-item CS scale contains at least three symptoms from each of seven diagnoses—depression, anxiety, obsessive-compulsive disorder, adjustment disorder, bipolar disorder, phobia, and substance abuse disorders. The 24-item CLF represents six areas of life functioning—self-management, work-school-homemaker, social and leisure, intimacy, family, and health (Grissom & Howard, 2000). Like the PRIME-MD, the COMPASS-PC can be easily administered over various intervals of treatment.

Some of the brief instruments discussed earlier are also appropriate for general medical settings. These include the QPD, SCL-90-R, and the SF-36.

Specialty Areas

In their review of adaptation to chronic illness and disability, Livneh and Antonak (1997) discuss frequently used general measures of adaptation to illness such as the PAIS (Derogatis et al., 1995). The authors also discuss several unidimensional, general measures of adaptation to disability as well. Numerous condition-specific measures have been developed in various medical specialty areas. For example, several measures of adaptation to specific conditions have been developed in oncology (Shapiro et al., 2001), in cardiology (Derogatis & Savitz, 2000), in rehabilitation medicine (Cushman & Scherer, 1995), for AIDS-HIV patients (Derogatis & Savitz, 2000), for sleep disorders (Rozensky et al., 1997), for diabetes (Rubin & Peyrot, 2001), for pain treatment (Cushman & Scherer, 1995), for geriatric patients (Scogin, Rohen, & Bailey, 2000), in emergency medicine (Rozensky et al., 1997), in neurology (Livneh & Antonak, 1997), and in renal dialysis (Derogatis & Savitz, 2000). Examples of these measures are listed in Table 13.4.

When considering general measures of adaptation or condition-specific measures, the determination of which to use can be based upon the specific referral question posed to the psychologist. If the referral question involves whether the patient's psychological distress is significant enough to warrant clinical intervention, then a general measure of adaptation will be clinically useful and sufficient. However, if the referral question concerns the quality of a patient's adjustment to a specific illness at a particular stage of that illness compared with the typical patient with that illness, then a condition-specific measure—if available—may be more meaningful. Quality of life constructs combine normative data from both general and illness-specific populations. Researchers such as Derogatis et al. (1995) support the use of a modular strategy, combining general instruments with modules developed from illness-specific samples. In this way, an illness-specific measure can be used as an additional domain of the general instrument or as a distinct, stand-alone measure.

SUMMARY

As can be seen from the broad range of topics covered within this chapter, psychological assessment in medical settings is diverse and can in some instances be highly specialized. The individuals practicing in these settings may prefer the professional identity of clinical psychologist, clinical health psychologist, or clinical neuropsychologist. All three of these specialists have a place in performing formal assessments within medical settings, with the latter two being more specialized with regard to particular medical populations and specific medical disorders. With regard to training and employment, medical settings have played an important historical role in the development of psychological assessment and will likely continue to do so in the future.

FUTURE DIRECTIONS

Future developments in the area of psychological assessment in medical settings will center around such concepts as specificity, brevity, and normative standards for particular medical populations. Assessments will be targeted to address specific outcome and quality-of-life questions rather than general psychological status and will be utilized across large health care systems as well as with specific disease entities. This goal will require more precise development of specific normative standards for specific, well-defined patient groups and subgroups. Because of economic pressures, including the need to see patients for less time and to see a greater number of patients, there will continue to be a pressure on test authors and publishers to create short forms and shorter instruments. As the former trend continues to take place, we must bear in mind the psychometric costs associated with accompanying threats to validity (Smith, McCarthy, & Anderson, 2000). Psychological assessment will become incorporated in cost-utility analysis, as outcomes involving patient adjustment,

well-being, and quality of life become more central and quantifiable as part of the economic dimensions of treatment (Kopta, Howard, Lowry, & Beutler, 1994). Brevity, cost-efficiency, minimal intrusiveness, and broader applicability will be salient concepts in the design of future assessment systems (Derogatis et al., 1995).

Although it has been recommended for many years that clinician-based judgments yield to actuarial or mechanical judgments (cf. Grove, Zald, Lebow, Snitz, & Nelson, 2000), and without question there has been a useful trend in this direction of at least partial reliance on empirically derived decision aids, we do not foresee a time in the near future when clinicians will abrogate their assessment roles completely to actuarial or mechanical methods. This position is *not* based on philosophical or scientific disagreement with the relevant decision-making literature; rather, it is based on the belief that a sufficient number of appropriate mechanical algorithms will continue to be lacking for years to come (cf. Kleinmuntz, 1990).

Computer-administered assessment, as well as planning for treatment and prevention, will likely be an important component of the future in psychological assessment in medical settings, as has been suggested regarding psychological assessment in general (see the chapter by Butcher in this volume; Butcher, Perry, & Atlis, 2000; Garb, 2000; Snyder, 2000). Maruish (2000) sampled several computerized treatment and prevention programs involving depression, obsessive-compulsive disorders, smoking cessation, and alcohol abuse. Symptom rating scales, screening measures, diagnostic interviews, and QOL and patient satisfaction scales already have been or can easily be computerized, making administration of these measures efficient and cost-effective. As computer technology advances with interactive voice response (IVR), new opportunities for even more thorough evaluation exist. However, as computer usage and technology develop, so do concerns about patient confidentiality, restricting access to databases, and the integration of assessment findings into effective treatment interventions. Similarly, Rozensky et al. (1997) predicted that there will be less emphasis placed on the diagnosis of psychopathology and more focus on those computerized assessment procedures that directly enhance planning and evaluating treatment strategies. Moreover, as telemedicine or telehealth develops, psychological assessment will need to be an integral part of patient and program evaluation as distance medicine technologies improve continuity of care.

Assessment in medical settings will likely continue to become even more specialized in the future. With this trend, more attention will be paid—both within the discipline and by test publishers—to test user qualifications and credentials (cf. Moreland, Eyde, Robertson, Primoff, & Most, 1995). In this same vein, more specific guidelines will be developed to aid in dealing with difficult ethical and legal dilemmas associated with assessment practices with medical patients, as is already evident within clinical neuropsychology (e.g., Johnson-Greene et al., 1997; Sweet, Grote, & Van Gorp, 2002).

Illness and disability necessitate change, resulting in continuous modification in coping and adjustment by the patient, his or her family, and medical personnel (Derogatis et al., 1995). Psychology's ability to document accurately the patient's response to disease and treatment-induced change is crucial to achieving an optimal treatment plan. Psychological assessment can be an integral part of the patient's care system and will continue to contribute crucial information to the patient's treatment regimen. Carefully planned, programmatic, integrated assessments of the patient's psychological coping and adjustment will always serve to identify problematic patients as well as those well-adjusted patients who are entering problematic phases of illness and treatment. Assessments that identify taxed or faltering coping responses can signal the need for interventions designed to avert serious adjustment problems, minimize deterioration of well-being, and restore patient QOL. Cost-effectiveness of medical interventions will continue to be enhanced by appropriate use of psychological assessment in medical settings.

REFERENCES

Ahmed, M. (1998). Psychological and legal aspects of mental incompetence. *Texas Medicine, 94,* 64–67.

Ambrose, P., Jr. (1997). Challenges for mental health service providers: The perspective of managed care organizations. In J. Butcher (Ed.), *Personality assessment in managed health care* (pp. 61–72). New York: Oxford University Press.

American Psychiatric Association. (1994). *Diagnostic and statistical manual of mental disorders* (4th ed.). Washington, DC: Author.

Andrews, G., Peters, L., & Tesson, M. (1994). *The measurement of consumer outcomes in mental health.* Canberra, Australia: Australian Government Publishing Service.

Belar, C., & Deardorff, W. (1995). *Clinical health psychology in medical settings: A practitioner's guidebook.* Washington, DC: American Psychological Association.

Belar, C., & Geisser, M. (1995). Roles of the clinical health psychologist in the management of chronic illness. In P. Nicassio & T. Smith (Eds.), *Managing chronic illness: A biopsychosocial perspective* (pp. 33–58). Washington, DC: American Psychological Association.

Billick, S., Bella, P., & Burgert, W. (1997). Competency to consent to hospitalization in the medical patient. *Journal of the American Academy of Psychiatry and Law, 25,* 191–196.

Butcher, J. N., Dahlstrom, W. G., Graham, J. R., Tellegen, A. M., & Kaemmer, B. (1989). *MMPI-2: Manual for administration and scoring.* Minneapolis: University of Minnesota Press.

Butcher, J. N., Perry, J., & Atlis, M. (2000). Validity and utility of computer-based test interpretation. *Psychological Assessment, 12,* 6–18.

Chen, F., & Grossberg, G. (1997). Issues involved in assessing competency. *New Directions for Mental Health Services, 76,* 71–83.

Coffey, P., Leitenberg, H., Henning, K., Turner, T., & Bennett, R. T. (1996). The relation between methods of coping during adulthood with a history of childhood sexual abuse and current psychological adjustment. *Journal of Consulting and Clinical Psychology, 64,* 1090–1093.

Cohen, L., Littlefied, C., Kelly, P., Maurer, J., & Abbey, S. (1998). Predictors of quality of life and adjustment after lung transplantation. *Chest, 113,* 633–644.

Cushman, L. A., & Scherer, M. J. (Eds.). (1995). *Psychological assessment in medical rehabilitation.* Washington, DC: American Psychological Association.

Davis, L. (2000). Self-administered alcohol screening test (SAAST). In M. Maruish (Ed.), *Handbook of psychological assessment in primary care settings* (pp. 537–554). Mahwah, NJ: Erlbaum.

Demakis, G. J., Mercury, M. G., & Sweet, J. J. (2000). Screening for cognitive impairments in primary care settings. In M. E. Maruish (Ed.), *Handbook of psychological assessment in primary care settings* (pp. 555–582). Mahwah, NJ: Erlbaum.

Derogatis, L. R., Fleming, M. P., Sudler, N. C., & DellaPietra, L. (1995). Psychological assessment. In P. M. Nicassio & T. W. Smith (Eds.), *Managing Chronic illness: A biopsychosocial perspective* (pp. 59–116). Washington, DC: American Psychological Association.

Derogatis, L. R., & Savitz, K. L. (2000). The SCL-90-R and Brief Symptoms Inventory (BSI) in primary care. In M. E. Maruish (Ed.), *Handbook of psychological assessment in primary care settings* (pp. 297–334). Mahwah, NJ: Erlbaum.

Derogatis, L. R., & Spencer, P. M. (1982). *BSI administration and procedures manual.* Baltimore: Clinical Psychometric Research.

Deshields, T. L., Mannen, K., Tait, R. C., & Bajaj, V. (1997). Quality of life in heart transplant candidates. *Journal of Clinical Psychology in Medical Settings, 4,* 327–341.

Engel, G. L. (1977). The need for a new medical model: A challenge for biomedicine. *Science, 196,* 129–136.

Etchells, E., Darzins, P., Silberfeld, M., Singer, P., McKenny, J., Naglie, G., Katz, M., Guyatt, G., Molloy, D. W., & Strang, D. (1999). Assessment of patient capacity to consent to treatment. *Journal of General Internal Medicine, 14,* 27–34.

Farberman, R. (1997). Terminal illness and hastened death requests: The important role of the mental health professional. *Professional Psychology: Research and Practice, 28,* 544–547.

Feenan, D. (1996). Capacity to decide about medical treatment. *British Journal of Hospital Medicine, 56,* 295–297.

Folkman, S., & Lazarus, R. (1980). An analysis of coping in a middle-aged community sample. *Journal of Health and Social Behavior, 21,* 219–239.

Frazier, P. A., & Schauben, L. J. (1994). Stressful life events and psychological adjustment among female college students. *Measurement and Evaluation in Counseling and Development, 27,* 280–292.

Garb, H. (2000). Computers will become increasingly important for psychological assessment: Not that there's anything wrong with that! *Psychological Assessment, 12,* 31–39.

Gentry, W., & Matarazzo, J. (1981). Medical psychology: Three decades of growth and development. In C. Prokop & L. Bradley (Eds.), *Medical psychology: Contributions to behavioral medicine* (pp. 6–19). New York: Academic Press.

Glass, K. (1997). Refining definitions and devising instruments: Two decades of assessing mental competence. *International Journal of Law and Psychiatry, 20,* 5–33.

Grisso, T., Appelbaum, P., & Hill-Fotouhi, C. (1997). The MacCAT-T: A clinical tool to assess patients' capacities to make treatment decisions. *Psychiatric Services, 48,* 1415–1419.

Grissom, G. R., & Howard, K. I. (2000). Directions and COMPASS-PC. In M. E. Maruish (Ed.), *Handbook of psychological assessment in primary care settings* (pp. 255–276). Mahwah, NJ: Erlbaum.

Groth-Marnat, G. (1999). Financial efficacy of clinical assessment: Rational guidelines and issues for future research. *Journal of Clinical Psychology, 55,* 813–824.

Grove, W., Zald, D., Lebow, B., Snitz, B., & Nelson, C. (2000). Clinical versus mechanical prediction: A meta-analysis. *Psychological Assessment, 12,* 19–30.

Hahn, S. R. (2000). The Difficult Doctor-Patient Relationship Questionnaire. In M. E. Maruish (Ed.), *Handbook of psychological assessment in primary care settings* (pp. 653–684). London: Erlbaum.

Hahn, S. R., Kroenke, K., Williams, J. B. W., & Spitzer, R. L. (2000). Evaluation of mental disorders with the PRIME-MD. In M. E. Maruish (Ed.), *Handbook of psychological assessment in primary care settings* (pp. 191–254). Mahwah, NJ: Erlbaum.

Hahn, S. R., Thompson, K. S., Stern, V., Budner, N. S., & Wills, T. A. (1994). The difficult doctor-patient relationship: Somaticization, personality and psychopathology. *Journal of Clinical Epidemiology, 47,* 647–658.

Hendin, H. (1999). Suicide, assisted suicide, and medical illness. *Journal of Clinical Psychiatry, 60*(Suppl. 2), 46–52.

Hersen, M., & Turner, S. (1994). *Diagnostic interviewing* (2nd ed.). New York: Plenum Press.

Holzer, J., Gansler, D., Moczynski, N., & Folstein, M. (1997). Cognitive functions in the informed consent evaluation process: A pilot study. *Journal of the American Academy of Psychiatry and Law, 25,* 531–540.

Jacobsen, P., & Holland, J. (1989). Psychological reactions to cancer surgery. In J. Holland & J. Rowland (Eds.), *Handbook of psychosocial oncology: Psychological care of the patient with cancer* (pp. 117–133). New York: Oxford University Press.

Johnson, M. E., Brems, C., & Fisher, D. G. (1996). Self-reported levels of psychopathology and drug abusers not currently in treatment. *Journal of Psychopathology and Behavioral Assessment, 18,* 21–34.

Johnson-Greene, D., Hardy-Morais, C., Adams, K., Hardy, C., & Bergloff, P. (1997). Informed consent and neuropsychological assessment: Ethical considerations and proposed guidelines. *The Clinical Neuropsychologist, 11,* 454–460.

Katon, W., Von Korff, M., Lin, E., Lipscomb, P., Russo, J., Wagner, E., & Polk, E. (1990). Distressed high users of medical care: DSM-III-R diagnosis and treatment needs. *General Hospital Psychiatry, 12,* 355–362.

Kay, J., & Bienenfeld, D. (1991). The clinical assessment of the cardiac transplant candidate. *Psychosomatics, 32,* 78–87.

Keefe, F. J., & Blumenthal, J. A. (Eds.). (1982). *Assessment strategies in behavioral medicine.* New York: Grune and Stratton.

Kellner, R., Hernandez, J., & Pathak, D. (1992). Hypochondriacal fears and their relationship to anxiety and somaticization. *British Journal of Psychiatry, 160,* 525–532.

Kleinmuntz, B. (1990). Why we still use our heads instead of formulas: Toward an integrative approach. *Psychological Bulletin, 107,* 296–310.

Kopta, S. M., Howard, L. I., Lowry, J. L., & Beutler, L. E. (1994). Patterns of symptomatic recovery in psychotherapy. *Journal of Consulting and Clinical Psychology, 62,* 1009–1016.

Kubiszyn, T., Meyer, G., Finn, S., Eyde, L., Kay, G., Moreland, K., Dies, R., & Eisman, E. (2000). Empirical support for the psychological assessment in clinical health care settings. *Professional Psychology: Research and Practice, 31,* 119–130.

Kuczewski, M. (1996). Reconceiving the family: The process of consent in medical decision making. *Hastings Center Report, 26,* 30–37.

Kuhn, W., Brennan, A., Lacefield, P., Brohm, J., Skelton, V., & Gray, L. (1990). Psychiatric distress during stages of the heart transplantation protocol. *Journal of Heart Transplant, 9,* 25–29.

Livneh, H., & Antonak, R. F. (1997). *Psychosocial adaptation to chronic illness and disability.* Gaitherburg, MD: Aspen Publishers.

Marson, D., Chatterjee, A., Ingram, K., & Harrell, L. (1996). Toward a neurologic model of competency: Cognitive predictors of capacity to consent in Alzheimer's disease using three different legal standards. *Neurology, 46,* 666–672.

Marson, D., & Harrell, L. (1999). Executive dysfunction and loss of capacity to consent to medical treatment in patients with Alzheimer's disease. *Seminars in Clinical Neuropsychiatry, 4,* 41–49.

Marson, D., Hawkins, L., McInturff, B., & Harrell, L. (1997). Cognitive models that predict physician judgments of capacity to consent in mild Alzheimer's disease. *Journal of the American Geriatric Society, 45,* 458–464.

Marson, D., McInturff, B., Hawkins, L., Bartolucci, A., & Harrell, L. (1997). Consistency of physician judgments of capacity to consent in mild Alzheimer's disease. *Journal of the American Geriatric Society, 45,* 453–457.

Maruish, M. E. (Ed.). (2000). Handbook of psychological assessment in primary care settings. Mahwah, NJ: Erlbaum.

Mayou, R. (1990). Quality of life in cardiovascular disease. *Psychotherapy and Psychosomatics, 54,* 99–109.

McCabe, M. (1996). Involving children and adolescents in medical decision making: Developmental and clinical considerations. *Journal of Pediatric Psychology, 21,* 505–516.

Melton, G., Petrila, J., Poythress, N., & Slobogin, C. (Eds.). (1997). *Psychological evaluations for the courts: A handbook for mental health professionals and lawyers* (2nd ed.). New York: Guilford Press.

Meyer, G., Finn, S., Eyde, L., Kay, G., Moreland, K., Dies, R., Eisman, E., Kubiszyn, T., & Reed, G. (2001). Psychological testing and psychological assessment: A review of evidence and issues. *American Psychologist, 56,* 128–165.

Moreland, K., Eyde, L., Robertson, G., Primoff, E., & Most, R. (1995). Assessment of test user qualifications: A research-based measurement procedure. *American Psychologist, 50,* 14–23.

Murkin, J. M., Newman, S. P., Stump, D. A., & Blumenthal, J. A. (1995). Statement of consensus on assessment of neurobehavioral outcomes after cardiac surgery. *Annals of Thoracic Surgery, 59,* 1289–1295.

Nessman, A., & Herndon, P. (2000, December). New Jersey settlement offers strong protection for psychologists. *Monitor on Psychology, 31*(11), 20–21.

Newman, M., Kirchner, J., Phillips-Bute, B., Gaver, V., Grocott, H., Jones, R., Mark, D., Reves, J., & Blumenthal, J. (2001). Longitudinal assessment of neurocognitive function after coronary-artery bypass surgery. *New England Journal of Medicine, 344,* 395–402.

Nicassio, P. M., & Smith, T. W. (1995). *Managing chronic illness: A biopsychosocial perspective.* Washington, DC: American Psychological Association.

Olbrisch, M. E., & Levenson, J. (1991). Psychosocial evaluation of heart transplant candidates: An international survey of process, criteria, and outcome. *Journal of Heart and Lung Transplantation, 10,* 948–955.

Olbrisch, M. E., Levenson, J., & Hamer, R. (1989). The PACT: A rating scale for the study of clinical decision-making in psychosocial screening of organ transplant candidates. *Clinical Transplantation, 3,* 1–6.

Pinkerton, S. S., Hughes, H., & Wenrich, W. W. (1982). *Behavioral medicine: Clinical applications.* New York: Wiley.

Piotrowski, C. (1999). Assessment practices in the era of managed care: Current status and future directions. *Journal of Clinical Psychology, 55,* 787–796.

Pollack, M., & Billick, S. (1999). Competency to consent to treatment. *Psychiatric Quarterly, 70,* 303–311.

Post, S. (1997). Slowing the progression of Alzheimer Disease: Ethical issues. *Alzheimer Disease and Associated Disorders, 11*(Suppl. 5), S34–S36.

Rozensky, R., Sweet, J., & Tovian, S. (1997). *Psychological assessment in medical settings.* New York: Plenum Press.

Rubin, R. R., & Peyrot, M. (2001). Psychological issues and treatments for people with diabetes. *Journal of Clinical Psychology, 57,* 457–478.

Scogin, F., Rohen, N., & Bailey, E. (2000). Geriatric Depression Scale. In M. E. Maruish (Ed.), *Handbook of psychological assessment in primary care settings* (pp. 491–508). Mahwah, NJ: Erlbaum.

Sears, S. F., Rodrigue, J. R., Siros, B. C., Urizar, G. C., & Perri, M. G. (1999). Extending psychometric norms for pre-cardiac transplantation evaluations: The Florida cohort, 1990–1996. *Journal of Clinical Psychology in Medical Settings, 6,* 303–316.

Shapiro, S. L., Lopez, A. M., Schwartz, G. E., Bootzin, R., Figueredo, A. J., Braden, C. J., & Kurker, S. F. (2001). Quality of life and breast cancer: Relationship to psychosocial variables. *Journal of Clinical Psychology, 57,* 501–520.

Shedler, J. (2000). The Shedler QPD Panel (Quick PsychoDiagnostics Panel): A psychiatric "lab test" for primary care. In M. E. Maruish (Ed.), *Handbook of psychological assessment in primary care settings* (pp. 277–296). Mahwah, NJ: Erlbaum.

Smith, G., McCarthy, D., & Anderson, K. (2000). On the sins of short-form development. *Psychological Assessment, 12,* 102–111.

Smithline, H., Mader, T., & Crenshaw, B. (1999). Do patients with acute medical conditions have the capacity to give informed consent for emergency medicine research? *Academic Emergency Medicine, 6,* 776–780.

Snyder, D. (2000). Computer-assisted judgment: Defining strengths and liabilities. *Psychological Assessment, 12,* 52–60.

Sobel, D. (2000). Mind matters, money matters: The cost-effectiveness of mind/body medicine [Editorial]. *Journal of the American Medical Association, 284,* 1705.

Stilley, C. S., Miller, D. J., Gayowski, T., & Marino, I. R. (1999). Psychological characteristics of candidates for liver transplantation: Differences according to history of substance abuse and UNOS listing. *Journal of Clinical Psychology, 55,* 1287–1297.

Strachan, M. W., Frier, B. M., & Deary, I. J. (1997). Cognitive assessment in diabetes: The need for consensus. *Diabetic Medicine, 14,* 421–422.

Swartz, M., Hughes, D., & George, L. (1986). Developing a screening index for community studies of somaticization disorder. *Journal of Psychiatric Research, 20,* 335–343.

Sweet, J. (Ed.). (1999). *Forensic neuropsychology: Fundamentals and practice.* Lisse, The Netherlands: Swets and Zeitlinger.

Sweet, J., Grote, C., & Van Gorp, W. (2002). Ethical issues in forensic neuropsychology. In S. Bush & M. Drexler (Eds.), *Ethical issues in clinical neuropsychology.* Lisse, The Netherlands: Swets and Zeitlinger.

Sweet, J., Moberg, P., & Suchy, Y. (2000). Ten-year follow-up survey of clinical neuropsychologists: Part I. Practices and beliefs. *The Clinical Neuropsychologist, 14,* 18–37.

Sweet, J., Peck, E., Abramowitz, C., & Etzweiler, S. (in press). *National Academy of Neuropsychology/Division 40 (American Psychological Association) Practice Survey of Clinical Neuropsychology in the United States, Part I: Practitioner and Practice Characteristics, Professional Activities, and Time Requirements. The Clinical Neuropsychologist.*

Sweet, J., Rozensky, R., & Tovian, S. (Eds.). (1991). *Handbook of clinical psychology in medical settings.* New York: Plenum Press.

Sweet, J., & Westergaard, C. (1997). Evaluation of psychopathology in neuropsychological assessment. In G. Goldstein & T. Incagnoli (Eds.), *Contemporary approaches in neuropsychological assessment* (pp. 325–358). New York: Plenum Press.

Tobe, S., & Senn, J. (1996). Foregoing renal dialysis: A case study and review of ethical issues. *American Journal of Kidney Diseases, 28,* 147–153.

Toomey, T. C., Seville, J. L., Mann, J. D., Abashian, S. W., & Grant, J. R. (1995). Relationship of sexual and physical abuse to pain description, psychological distress, and health care utilization in a chronic pain sample. *Clinical Journal of Pain, 11,* 307–315.

Van Egren, L., & Striepe, M. I. (1998). Assessment approaches in health psychology: Issues and practical considerations. In P. M. Camic & S. J. Knight (Eds.), *Clinical handbook of health psychology: A practical guide to effective interventions* (pp. 17–52). Seattle, WA: Hogrefe and Huber.

Walker, E. A., Katon, W. J., Hansom, J., Haerrop-Griffiths, J., Holm, L., Jones, M. L., Hickok, L. R., & Russo, J. (1995). Psychiatric diagnoses and sexual victimization in women with chronic pelvic pain. *Psychosomatics, 36,* 531–540.

Wallander, J. L., Schmitt, M., & Koot, H. M. (2001). Quality of life measurement in children and adolescents: Issues, instruments and applications. *Journal of Clinical Psychology, 57,* 571–586.

Wallston, K., Wallston, B., & DeVellis, R. (1978). Development of the Multidimensional Health Locus of Control (MHLC) scale. *Health Education Monographs, 6,* 160–170.

Ware, J. E. (1993). *SF-36 Health Survey: Manual and interpretation guide.* Boston: New England Medical Center, The Health Institute.

Wellisch, D., & Cohen, R. (1985). Psychosocial aspects of cancer. In C. Haskell (Ed.), *Cancer treatment* (pp. 863–882). Philadelphia: Saunders.

Wetzler, H. P., Lum, D. L., & Bush, D. M. (2000). Using the SF-36 Health Survey in primary care. In M. E. Maruish (Ed.), *Handbook of psychological assessment in primary care settings* (pp. 583–622). Mahwah, NJ: Erlbaum.

Williams, L., Harris, A., Thompson, M., & Brayshaw, A. (1997). Consent to treatment by minors attending accident and emergency departments: Guidelines. *Journal of Accident and Emergency Medicine, 14,* 286–289.

Zipel, S., Lowe, B., Paschke, T., Immel, B., Lange, R., Zimmerman, R., Herzog, W., & Bergman, G. (1998). Psychological distress in patients awaiting heart transplantation. *Journal of Psychosomatic Research, 45,* 465–470.

CHAPTER 14

Psychological Assessment in Industrial/ Organizational Settings

RICHARD J. KLIMOSKI AND LORI B. ZUKIN

CONTEXT OF PSYCHOLOGICAL ASSESSMENTS IN INDUSTRIAL/ORGANIZATIONAL SETTINGS

Psychologists have been active in the assessment of individuals in work settings for almost a century. In light of the apparent success of the applications of psychology to advertising and marketing (Baritz, 1960), it is not surprising that corporate managers were looking for ways that the field could contribute to the solution of other business problems, especially enhancing worker performance and reducing accidents. For example, Terman (1917) was asked to evaluate candidates for municipal positions in California. He used a shortened form of the Stanford-Binet and several other tests and looked for patterns against past salary and occupational level (Austin, Scherbaum, & Mahlman, 2000). Other academic psychologists, notably Walter Dill Scott and Hugo Munsterberg, were also happy to oblige.

In this regard, the approaches used and the tools and techniques developed clearly reflected prevailing thinking among researchers of the time. Psychological measurement approaches in industry evolved from procedures used by Fechner and Galton to assess individual differences (Austin et al., 2000). Spearman's views on generalized intelligence and measurement error had an influence on techniques that

ultimately became the basis of the standardized instruments popular in work applications. Similarly, if instincts were an important theoretical construct (e.g., McDougal, 1908), these became the cornerstone for advertising interventions. When the laboratory experimental method was found valuable for theory testing, it was not long before it was adapted to the assessment of job applicants for the position of street railway operators (Munsterberg, 1913). Vocational interest blanks designed for guiding students into careers were adapted to the needs of industry to select people who would fit in.

Centers of excellence involving academic faculty consulting with organizations were often encouraged as part of the academic enterprise, most notably one established by Walter Bingham at Carnegie Institute in Pittsburgh (now Carnegie Mellon University). It makes sense, then, that programs such those at as Carnegie, Purdue, and Michigan State University were located in the proximity of large-scale manufacturing enterprises. As will become clear through a reading of this chapter, the legacy of these origins can still be seen in the models and tools of contemporary practitioners (e.g., the heavy emphasis on the assessment for the selection of hourly workers for manufacturing firms).

The practice of assessment in work organizations was also profoundly affected by activities and developments during the great wars fought by the United States. Many of the personnel and performance needs of the military during both the first and second World Wars were met by contributions of psychologists recruited from the academy. The work of Otis on the (then) new idea of the multiple-choice test was found extremely valuable in solving the problem of assessing millions of men called to duty for their suitability and, once enlisted, for their assignments to specific work roles. The Army's Alpha test, based on the work of Otis and others, was itself administered to 1,700,000 individuals. Tools and techniques for the assessment of job performance were refined or developed to meet the needs of the military relative to evaluating the impact of training and determining the readiness of officers for promotion. After the war, these innovations were diffused into the private sector, often by officers turned businessmen or by the psychologists no longer employed by the government. Indeed, the creation of the *Journal of Applied Psychology* (1917) and the demand for practicing psychologists in industry are seen as outgrowths of the success of assessment operations in the military (Schmitt & Klimoski, 1991).

In a similar manner, conceptual and psychometric advances occurred as a result of psychology's involvement in government or military activities involved in winning the second World War. Over 1,700 psychologists were to be involved in the research, development, or implementation of assessment procedures in an effort to deal with such things as absenteeism, personnel selection, training (especially leader training), and soldier morale. Moreover, given advances in warfare technology, new problems had to be addressed in such areas as equipment design (especially the user interface), overcoming the limitations of the human body (as in high-altitude flying), and managing work teams. Technical advances in survey methods (e.g., the Likert scale) found immediate applications in the form of soldier morale surveys or studies of farmers and their intentions to plant and harvest foodstuffs critical to the war effort.

A development of particular relevance to this chapter was the creation of assessment procedures for screening candidates for unusual or dangerous assignments, including submarine warfare and espionage. The multimethod, multisource philosophy of this approach eventually became the basis for the assessment center method used widely in industry for selection and development purposes (Howard & Bray, 1988). Finally, when it came to the defining of performance itself, Flanagan's (1954) work on the critical incident method was found invaluable. Eventually, extensions of the approach could be found in applied work on the assessment of training needs and even the measurement of service quality.

Over the years, the needs of the military and of government bureaus and agencies have continued to capture the attention of academics and practitioners, resulting in innovations of potential use to industry. This interplay has also encouraged the development of a large and varied array of measurement tools or assessment platforms. The Army General Classification test has its analogue in any number of multi-aptitude test batteries. Techniques for measuring the requirements of jobs, like Functional Job Analysis or the Position Analysis Questionnaire, became the basis for assessment platforms like the General Aptitude Test Battery (GATB) or, more recently, the Occupational Information Network (O*Net; Peterson, Mumford, Borman, Jeanneret, & Fleishman, 1999). Scales to measure job attitudes (Smith, Kendall, & Hulin, 1969), organizational commitment (Mowday, Steers, & Porter, 1979), or work adjustment (Dawis, 1991) found wide application, once developed. Moreover, there is no shortage of standard measures for cognitive and noncognitive individual attributes (Impara & Plake, 1998).

A final illustration of the importance of cultural context on developments in industry can be found in the implementation of civil rights legislation in America in the 1960s and 1970s (and, a little later, the Americans with Disabilities Act). This provided new impetus to changes in theory, research designs, and assessment practices in work organizations. The litigation of claims under these laws has also had a profound effect on the kinds of measures found to be acceptable for use as well.

THE NATURE OF ASSESSMENT IN INDUSTRIAL AND ORGANIZATIONAL SETTINGS

This chapter is built on a broad view of assessment relative to its use in work organizations. The thrust of the chapter, much like the majority of the actual practice of assessment in organizations, will be to focus on constructs that imply or allow for the inference of job-related individual differences. Moreover, although we will emphasize the activities of psychologists in industry whenever appropriate, it should be clear at the outset that the bulk of individual assessments in work settings are being conducted by others—managers, supervisors, trainers, human resource professionals—albeit often under the guidance of practicing psychologists or at least using assessment platforms that the latter designed and have implemented on behalf of the company.

Most individuals are aware of at least some of the approaches used for individual assessment by psychologists generally. For example, it is quite common to see mention in the popular press of psychologists' use of interviews and questionnaires. Individual assessment in work organizations involves many of these same approaches, but there are some characteristic features worth stressing at the outset. Specifically, with regard to assessments in work settings, we would highlight their multiple (and at times conflicting) purposes, the types of factors measured, the approach used, and the role that assessment must play to insure business success.

Purposes

Business Necessity

For the most part, assessments in work organizations are conducted for business-related reasons. Thus, they might be performed in order to design, develop, implement, or evaluate the impact of a business policy or practice. In this regard, the firm uses assessment information (broadly defined) to index such things as the level of skill or competency (or its obverse, their deficiencies) of its employees or their level of satisfaction (because this might presage quitting). As such, the information so gathered ends up serving an operational feedback function for the firm. It can also serve to address the issue of how well the firm is conforming to its own business plans (Katz & Kahn, 1978).

Work organizations also find it important to assess individuals as part of their risk management obligation. Most conspicuous is the use of assessments for selecting new employees (trying to identify who will work hard, perform well, and not steal) or in the context of conducting performance appraisals. The latter, in turn, serve as the basis for compensation or promotion decisions (Murphy & Cleveland, 1995; Saks, Shmitt, & Klimoski, 2000). Assessments of an individual's level of work performance can become the (only) basis for the termination of employment as well. Clearly, the firm has a business need to make valid assessments as the basis for appropriate and defensible personnel judgments.

In light of the numerous laws governing employment practices in most countries (and because the United States, at least, seems to be a litigious society), assessments of the perceptions, beliefs, and opinions of the workforce with regard to such things as the prevalence of sexual harassment (Fitzgerald, Drasgow, Hulin, Gelfand, & Magley, 1997; Glomb, Munson, Hulin, Bergman, & Drasgow, 1999) or of unlawful discrimination are often carried out as part of management's "due diligence" obligation. Thus, assessed attitudes can be used to complement demographic data supplied by these individuals relative to their race, age, gender, or disability and used in monitoring personnel practice and to insure nondiscriminatory treatment of the workforce (e.g., Klimoski & Donahue, 1997).

Individual Necessity

Individual assessments in industry can also be performed with the goal of meeting the needs of the individual worker as well. The assessment of *individual training needs,* once

made, can become the basis for a specific worker's training and development experiences. Such information would guide the worker to just what programs or assignments would best remedy a particular deficiency. Such data, if gathered regularly over time, can also inform the worker of his or her progress in skill acquisition. In a related manner, assessments may be gathered to guide the worker relative to a *work career*. Whether done in the context of an organizationally managed career-path planning program or done by the worker on his or her initiative, such competency assessments relative to potential future jobs or different careers are ultimately in the service of the worker.

Progressive firms and many others whose workers are covered by collective bargaining agreements might use individual assessment data to help workers find suitable employment elsewhere, a need precipitated by such things as a corporate restructuring effort or downsizing or as an outcome of an acquisition or a merger. Job preferences and skills are typically evaluated as part of an *outplacement* program. Often, however, one is also assessed (and, if found wanting, trained) in such things as the capacity to look for different work or to do well in a job interview that might lead to new work.

Individual assessments are at the core of *counseling and coaching* in the workplace. These activities can be part of a larger corporate program for enhancing the capabilities of the workforce. However, usually an assessment is done because the individual worker is in difficulty. This may be manifested in a career plateau, poor job performance, excessive absenteeism, interpersonal conflict on the job, symptoms of depression, or evidence of substance abuse. In the latter cases such assessments may be part of an *employee assistance program,* specifically set up to help workers deal with personal issues or problems.

Research Necessity

Many work organizations and consultants to industry take an empirical approach to the design, development, and evaluation of personnel practices. In this regard, assessment data, usually with regard to an individual's job performance, work-related attitudes, or job-relevant behavior, are obtained in order to serve as research criterion measures. Thus, in evaluating the potential validity of a selection test, data regarding the performance of individuals on the test and their later performance on the job are statistically compared. Similarly, the impact of a new recruitment program may be evaluated by assessing such things as the on-the-job performance and work attitudes of those brought into the organization under the new system and comparing these to data similarly obtained from individuals who are still being brought in under the old one. Finally, as another example, a proposed new course for training employees may need to be evaluated. Here, evidence of learning or of skill acquisition obtained from a representative sample of workers, both before and again after the program, might be contrasted with scores obtained from a group of employees serving as a comparison group who do not go through the training.

Assessments as Criterion Measures

In the course of almost one hundred years of practice, specialists conducting personnel research have concluded that good criterion measures are hard to develop. This may be due in part to the technical requirements for such measures, as outlined in the next section. However, it also may be simply a reflection that the human attributes and the performances of interest are, by their very nature, quite complex. When it comes to criterion measures, this is most clearly noted in the fact that these almost always must be treated as multidimensional.

The notion of dimensionality itself is seen most clearly in measures of job performance. In this regard, Ghiselli (1956) distinguished three types of criterion dimensionality. He uses the term *static dimensionality* to convey the idea that at any point in time, we can imagine that there are multiple facets to performance. Most of us can easily argue that both quality and quantity are usually part of the construct. In order to define the effective performance of a manager, studies have revealed that it usually requires five or more dimensions to cover this complex role (Campbell, McCloy, Oppler, & Sager, 1993).

Dynamic dimensionality is the term used to capture the notion that the essence of effective performance can change over time, even for the same individual. Thus, we can imagine that the performance of a new worker might be anchored in such things a willingness to learn, tolerance of ambiguity, and persistence. Later, after the worker has been on the job for a while, he or she would be held accountable for such things as high levels of output, occasional innovation, and even the mentoring of other, newer, employees.

Finally, Ghiselli identifies the concept of *individual dimensionality*. In the context of performance measures, this is used to refer to the fact that two employees can be considered equally good (or bad), but for different reasons. One worker may be good at keeping a work team focused on its task, whereas another may be quite effective because he seems to be able to manage interpersonal conflict and tension in the team so that it does not escalate to have a negative effect on team output. Similarly, two artists can be equally well regarded but for manifesting very different artistic styles.

An additional perspectives on the multidimensionality of performance is offered by Borman and Motowidlo (1993). In their model, task performance is defined as "activities that contribute to the organization's technological core either directly by implementing a part of its technological process, or indirectly by providing it with needed materials or services" (p. 72). Task performance, then, involves those activities that are formally recognized as part of a job. However, there are many other activities that are important for organizational effectiveness that do not fall within the task performance category. These include activities such as volunteering, persisting, helping, cooperating, following rules, staying with the organization, and supporting its objectives (Borman & Motowidlo, 1993). Whereas task performance affects organizational effectiveness through the technical core, contextual performance does so through organizational, social, and psychological means. Like Ghisellis's (1956) perspective, the task and contextual performance distinction (Borman & Motowidlo, 1993; Motowidlo, Borman, & Schmit, 1997; Motowidlo & Van Scotter, 1994) shows that the constructs we are assessing will vary depending on the performance dimension of interest. The multidimensionality of many of the constructs of interest to those doing individual assessments in industry places a major burden on those seeking to do high-quality applied research. However, as will be pointed out below, it also has a profound on the nature of the tools and of the specific measures to be used for operational purposes as well.

Thus, assessments for purposes of applied research may not differ much in terms of the specific features of the tools themselves. For example, something as common as a work sample test may be the tool of choice to gather data for validation or for making selection decisions. However, when one is adopted as the source of criterion scores, it implies a requirement for special diligence from the organization in terms of assessment conditions, additional time or resources, and certainly high levels of skill on the part of the practitioner (Campbell, 1990).

Attributes Measured

As implied by the brief historical orientation to this chapter, the traditional focus on what to measure has been on those individual difference factors that are thought to account for worker success. These *person* factors are frequently thought of as inputs to the design and management of work organizations. Most often, the attributes to be assessed derive from an analysis of the worker's job duties and include specific forms of knowledge, skills, abilities, or other attributes (KSAOs) implying work-related interests and motivation. More recently, the focus has been on competencies, the demonstrated capacity to perform job-relevant activities (Schippmann et al.,

2000). Key competencies are ascertained from a careful consideration not of the job but of the role or functions expected to be performed by an employee if he or she is to contribute to business success. Thus, attributes such as speed of learning or teamwork skills might be the focus of assessments. As will be detailed later, these attributes might be the core of any personnel selection program.

Assessments of individuals in work settings may also focus on the *process* used by the employee to get the job done. Operationally, these are the kinds of behaviors that are necessary and must be carried out well in the work place if the worker is to be considered successful. These, too, derive from an analysis of the job and of the behaviors that distinguish effective employees from less effective ones. Process assessments are particularly common in organizational training and worker performance review programs.

For the most part, employees in work organizations are held accountable for generating *products:* outcomes or results. Thus, it is common for assessments to be focused on such things as the quality and quantity of performance, the frequency of accidents, and the number of product innovations proposed. The basis for such assessments might be a matter of record. Often, however, human judgment and skill are required in locating and categorizing work outcomes relative to some standard. Outcome assessments are often used as the basis for compensation and retention decisions. In the course of the year, most individuals in work organizations might be assessed against all three types of assessments.

Approaches Used for Assessment in Industry

Three features of the approach favored by many of those doing assessment work in industry are worth highlighting. The first has been noted already in that many assessment platforms are built on careful development and backed up by empirical evidence. Although it is possible that an assessment technique would be adopted or a particular practitioner hired without evidence of appropriateness for that particular organization, it is not recommended. As stressed throughout this chapter, to do so would place the firm at risk.

A second feature that is somewhat distinctive is that most assessments of individuals in work contexts are not done by psychologists. Instead, managers, supervisors, trainers, and even peers are typically involved in evaluating individuals on the factors of interest. This said, for larger firms, practicing psychologists may have had a hand in the design of assessment tools and programs (e.g., a structured interview protocol for assessing job applicants), or they may have actually trained company personnel on how to use them. However, the assessments themselves are to be done by the latter without

much supervision by program designers. For smaller firms, this would be less likely, because a practicing psychologist might be retained or used on an as-needed basis (e.g., to assist in the selection of a managing partner in a law firm). Under these circumstances, it would be assumed that the psychologist would be using assessment tools that he or she has found valid in other applications.

A final distinction between assessment in industry and other psychological assessments is that quite often assessments are being done on a large number of individuals at the same time or over a short period of time. For example, when the fire and safety service of Nassau County, New York sought to recruit and select about 1,000 new police officers, it had to arrange for 25,000 applicants to sit for the qualifying exam at one time (Schmitt, 1997). This not only has implications for the kinds of assessment tools that can be used but affects such mundane matters as choice of venue (in this case, a sports arena was needed to accommodate all applicants) and how to manage test security (Halbfinger, 1999).

The large-scale nature of assessments in industry implies the common use of aggregate data. Although the individual case will be the focus of the assessment effort, as noted earlier, very often the firm is interested in averages, trends, or establishing the existence of reliable and meaningful differences on some metric between subgroups. For example, individual assessments of skill might be made but then aggregated across cases to reveal, for example, that the average skill of new people hired has gone up as a result of the implementation of a new selection program. Similarly, the performance of individuals might be assessed to show that the mean performance level of employees under one manager is or is not better than the mean for those working under another. Thus, in contrast to other venues, individual assessments conducted in work settings are often used as a means to assess still other individuals, in this case, organizational programs or managers.

Marketplace and the Business Case

Most models of organizational effectiveness make it clear that the capacity to acquire, retain, and efficiently use key resources is essential. In this regard, employees as human resources are no different. At the time that this chapter is being prepared, unemployment levels are at historical lows in the United States. Moreover, given the strength of the so-called new economy, the demand for skilled workers is intense. Added to the convergence of these two marketplace realities is the arrival of new and powerful Internet-based services that give more information than ever to current and prospective employees regarding the human resource needs and practices of various organizations. It is important to note that similar services now provide individuals with a more accurate sense of their own market value than ever. Clearly there are intense competitive pressures to recruit, select, and retain good employees. Those responsible for the design and management of platforms for individual assessment must contribute to meeting such pressures or they will not be retained.

Another marketplace demand is for efficiency. The availability of resources notwithstanding, few organizations can escape investor scrutiny with regard to their effective use of resources. When it comes to assessment programs, this implies that new approaches will be of interest and ultimately found acceptable if it can be demonstrated that (a) they address a business problem, (b) they add value over current approaches, and (c) they have utility, in the sense that the time and costs associated with assessment are substantially less than the gains realized in terms of worker behavior (e.g., quitting) or performance. In fact, the need to make a business case is a hallmark of the practice of individual assessments in work organizations. It is also at the heart of the notion of utility as described in the next section.

A third imperative facing contemporary practitioners is embedded in the notion *speed to market*. All other things considered, new and useful assessment tools or programs need to be brought on line quickly to solve a business problem (e.g., meeting the human resource needs for a planned expansion or reducing high levels of turnover). Similarly, the information on those individuals assessed must be made available quickly so that decisions can be made in a timely manner. These factors may cause an organization to choose to make heavy use of external consultants for assessment work in the context of managing their human resource needs and their bottom line.

In summary, individual assessment in work settings is indeed both similar to and different from many other contexts in which such assessments take place. Although the skills and techniques involved would be familiar to most psychologists, the application of the former must be sensitive and appropriate to particular contextual realities.

PROFESSIONAL AND TECHNICAL CONSIDERATIONS

As described in the overview section, professionals who conduct assessments in industrial settings do so based on the work context. A job analysis provides information on the tasks, duties, and responsibilities carried out by the job incumbents as well as the KSAOs needed to perform the job well (Saks et al., 2000). Job analysis information helps us conduct selection and promotion assessments by determining if there is a fit between

the skills needed for the job and those held by the individual and if the individual has the potential to perform well on the important KSAOs. We can also use job analysis information for career management by providing the individual and the career counselor or coach with information about potential jobs or careers. The individual can then be assessed using various skill and interest inventories to determine fit. Job analysis information can also be used for classification and placement to determine which position within an organization best matches the skills of the individual. We will discuss the purpose, application, and tools for assessments in the next section. In this section, we will focus on how organizations use job analysis tools to develop assessment tools to make organizational decisions.

The Role of Assessment Data for Inferences in Organizational Decisions

Guion (1998) points out that one major purpose of research on assessments in industrial/organizational settings is to evaluate how well these assessments help us in making personnel decisions. The process he describes is prescriptive and plays out especially well for selection purposes. The reader should be aware that descriptively there are several constraints, such as a small number of cases, the rapid pace at which jobs change, and the time it takes to carry out the process, that make this approach difficult. Guion therefore suggests that assessment practices should be guided by theory, but so too should practice inform theory. With that said, his approach for evaluating assessments is described below:

1. Conduct a job and organizational analysis to identify what criterion we are interested in predicting and to provide a rational basis for specifying which applicant characteristics (predictors) are likely to predict that criterion.

2. Choose the specific criterion or criteria that we are trying to predict. Usually, the criteria are some measure of performance (e.g., production quality or earnings) or some valued behavior associated with the job (e.g., adaptability to change).

3. Develop the predictive hypothesis based on strong rationale and prior research.

4. Select the methods of measurement that effectively assess the construct of interest. Guion suggests that we should not limit our assessments to any particular method but that we should look at other methods. The tendency here is to assess candidates on traits for which tests are developed rather than to assess them on characteristics not easily assessed with current testing procedures (Lawshe, 1959).

5. Design the research to assure that findings from research samples can generalize to the population of interest, job applicants.

6. Collect data using standardized procedures and the appropriate treatment of those being assessed.

7. Evaluate the results to see if the predictor correlates with the criterion of interest. This evaluation procedure is often called validation.

8. Justify the selection procedure through the assessment of both incremental validity and utility. The former refers to the degree to which the proposed selection procedure significantly predicts the criterion over and above a procedure already in place. The latter refers to the economic value of utilizing the new procedure.

Technical Parameters

Reliability

Most readers are aware of the various forms of reliability and how they contribute to inferences in assessments. These are discussed in detail in the chapter by Wasserman and Bracken in this volume. This section will note the forms of reliability used in industrial settings.

For the most part, organizations look at internal consistency reliability more than test-retest or parallel forms. In many industrial settings, with the exception of large organizations that conduct testing with many individuals on a regular basis, it is often asserted that time constraints limit the evaluation of the latter forms of reliability.

The kind of reliability sought should be appropriate to the application of the assessment. Of particular importance to industrial settings are retest reliability and interrater reliability. For example, in the context of structured interviews or assessment centers, if raters (or judges) do not agree on an individual's score, this should serve as a warning that the assessment platform should be reviewed. Moreover, political issues may come into play if one of the raters has a significant position of power in the organization. This rater may want the person to be selected even if other raters disagree.

Validity

All test validation involves inferences about psychological constructs (Schmitt & Landy, 1993). It is not some attribute of the tests or test items themselves (e.g., Guion, 1980).

We are not simply interested in whether an assessment predicts performance, but whether the inferences we make with regard to these relationships are correct. Binning and Barrett (1989) lay out an approach for assessing the validity

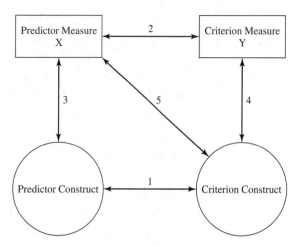

Figure 14.1 Relationships among predictor constructs, predictor measures, criterion constructs, and criterion measures.

(job-relatedness of a predictor) of personnel decisions based on the many inferences we make in validation.

Guion's (1998) simplification of Binning and Barrett's presentation is described in Figure 14.1 to illustrate the relationships among predictor constructs, predictor measures, criterion constructs, and criterion measures.

Line 1 shows that the relationship between the predictor construct (e.g., conscientiousness) is related to the criterion construct (some form of job behavior such as productivity) or a result of the behavior. Relationship 2 is the only inference that is empirically testable. It is the statistical relationship between the predictor measure, a test of conscientiousness such as the Hogan Personality Inventory (HPI; R. T. Hogan & Hogan, 1995), and the criterion measure (some measured criteria of job performance such as scores on a multisource feedback assessment). Tests of inferences 3 and 4 are used in construct validation. Relationship 3 shows whether the predictor measure (HPI) is a valid measure of the predictor construct (conscientiousness). Relationship 4 assesses whether the criterion measure (multisource feedback scores) is effectively measuring the performance of interest (e.g., effective customer service). Finally, relationship 5 is the assessment of whether the predictor measure (conscientiousness) is related to the criterion construct of interest (customer service) in a manner consistent with its presumed relationship to the criterion measure. Relationship 5 is dependent on the inferences we make about our job analysis data and those that we make about our predictor and construct relationships. Although the importance of establishing construct validity is now well established in psychology, achieving the goal of known construct validity in the assessments used in work contexts continues to be elusive.

Political considerations come into play in establishing validity in industrial settings. Austin, Klimoski, and Hunt

(1996) point out that "validity is necessary but not sufficient for effective long-term selection systems." They suggest that in addition to the technical considerations discussed above, procedural justice or fairness and feasibility-utility also be considered. For example, in union environments optimizing all three standards may be a better strategy than maximizing one set.

Fairness

Industrial/organizational psychologists view fairness as a technical issue (Cascio, 1993), a social justice issue (Austin et al., 1996), and a public policy issue (American Educational Research Association, American Psychological Association, & National Council on Measurement in Education, 1999). In industrial/organizational settings, the technical issues of differential validity and differential prediction are assessed for fairness. Differential validity exists when there are differences in subgroup validity coefficients. If a measure that is valid only for one subgroup is used for all individuals regardless of group membership, then the measure may discriminate unfairly against the subgroup for whom it is invalid. Job performance and test performance must be considered because unfair discrimination cannot be said to exist if unfair test performance is associated with inferior job performance by the same group. Differential prediction exists when there are slope and intercept differences between minority and nonminority groups. For example, Cascio (1993) points out that a common differential prediction exists when the prediction system for the nonminority group slightly overpredicts minority group performance. In this case, minorities would tend not to do as well on the job as their test scores would indicate.

As Austin et al. (1996) point out, fairness is also related to the social justice of how the assessment is administered. For example, they point out that that perceptions of neutrality of decision makers, respect given to test takers, and trust in the system are important for the long-term success of assessments. In fact, Gilliland (1993) argues that procedural justice can be decomposed into three components: formal characteristics of procedures, the nature of explanations offered to stakeholders, and the quality of interpersonal treatment as information comes out. These issues must be considered for there to be acceptability of the process.

Additionally, it cannot be stressed enough that there is no consensus on what is fair. Fairness is defined in a variety of ways and is subject to a several interpretations (American Educational Research Association et al., 1999). Cascio (1993) points out that personnel practices, such as testing, must be considered in the total system of personnel decisions and that

each generation should consider the policy implications of testing. The critical consideration is not whether to use tests but, rather, how to use tests (Cronbach, 1984).

Feasibility/Utility

This term has special meaning in the assessment of individuals in industry. It involves the analysis of the interplay among the predictive power of assessment tools and the selection ratio. In general, even a modest correlation coefficient can have utility if there is a favorable selection ratio. Assessments in this context must be evaluated against the cost and potential payoff to the organization. Utility theory does just that. It provides decision makers with information on the costs, benefits, and consequences of all assessment options. For example, through utility analysis, an organization can decide whether a structured interview or a cognitive ability test is more cost effective. This decision would also be concerned with the psychometric properties of the assessment. Cascio (1993) points out the importance of providing the utility unit (criteria) in terms that the user can understand, be it dollars, number of products developed, or reduction in the number of workers needed. Because assessment in industry must concern itself with the bottom line, costs and outcomes are a critical component in evaluating assessment tools.

Robustness

In selecting an assessment, it is also important to assess whether its validity is predictive across many situations. In other words, is the relationship robust? The theory of situation specificity is based on the findings of researchers that validities for similar jobs in different work environments varied significantly. With the increased emphasis on meta-analysis and validity generalization (Schmidt & Hunter, 1977; Schmidt et al., 1993), many researchers believe that these differences were due to statistical and measurement artifacts and were not real differences between jobs.

Legal Considerations

Employment laws exist to prohibit unfair discrimination in employment and provide equal employment opportunity for all. Unfair discrimination occurs when employment decisions are based on race, sex, religion, ethnicity, age, or disability rather than on job-relevant knowledge, skills, abilities, and other characteristics (U.S. Department of Labor, 1999). Employment practices that unfairly discriminate against people are called unlawful or discriminatory employment practices.

Those endeavoring to conduct individual assessments in industry must consider the laws that apply in their jurisdiction. With the increasingly global society of practitioners, they must also consider laws in other countries. In the United States, case law and professional standards and acts must be followed. The following are some standards and acts that must be considered:

- *Title VII of the Civil Rights Act of 1964* (as amended in 1972), which prohibits unfair discrimination in all terms and conditions of employment based on race, color, religion, sex, and national origin.

- *Age Discrimination in Employment Act of 1967 (ADEA)*, which prohibits discrimination against employees or applicants age 40 or older in all aspects of the employment process.

- *Equal Employment Opportunity Commission (EEOC) of 1972*, which is responsible for enforcing federal laws prohibiting employment discrimination.

- *Uniform Guidelines on Employee Selection Procedures of 1978* (Equal Employment Opportunity Commission, Civil Service Commission, U.S. Department of Labor, & U.S. Department of Justice, 1978), which incorporate a set of principles governing the use of employee selection procedures according to applicable laws and provide a framework for employers to determine the proper use of tests and other selection procedures. A basic principle of the guidelines is that it is unlawful to use a test or selection procedure that creates adverse impact, unless justified. When there is no charge of adverse impact, the guidelines do not require that one show the job-relatedness of assessment procedures; however, they strongly encourage one to use only job-related assessment tools. Demonstrating the job-relatedness of a test is the same as establishing that the test may be validly used as desired. Demonstrating the business necessity of an assessment involves showing that its use is essential to the safe and efficient operation of the business and that there are no alternative procedures available that are substantially equally valid to achieve business results with lesser adverse impact.

- *Title I of the Civil Rights Act of 1991*, which specifically requires demonstration of both job-relatedness and business necessity (as described in the previous section). The business necessity requirement is harder to satisfy than the "business purpose test" suggested earlier by the Supreme Court. The act also prohibits score adjustments, the use of different cutoff scores for different groups of test takers, or the alteration of employment-related tests based on the demographics of test takers.

- *Americans with Disabilities Act of 1990 (ADA)*, which requires that qualified individuals with disabilities be given equal opportunity in all aspects of employment. Employers must provide reasonable accommodation to persons with disabilities when doing so would not pose undue hardship.

- *Standards for Educational and Psychological Testing* (American Educational Research Association et al., 1999) and principles for validation and use of *Personnel Selection Procedures (1987)*, which are useful guidelines for individuals developing, evaluating, and using assessments in employment, counseling, and clinical settings. Even though they are guidelines, they are consistent with applicable regulations.

PURPOSE, FOCUS, AND TOOLS FOR ASSESSMENT IN INDUSTRIAL/ORGANIZATIONAL SETTINGS

This section will describe how assessments in industrial/organizational settings are used, the focus of those assessments and the major tools used to conduct these assessments. The reader may notice that the focus of the assessment may be similar for different assessment purposes.

For example, cognitive ability may be the focus of both a selection test and a career planning assessment. Table 14.1 provides the linkage of these components and can serve as a preview of the material to follow.

Purpose of Assessment in Industry

Selection

Selection is relevant to organizations when there are more qualified applicants than positions to be filled. The organization must decide who among those applicants can perform best on the job and should therefore be hired. That decision is based upon the prediction that the person hired will be more satisfactory than the person rejected (Cascio, 1993). The goal of selection is thus to capitalize on individual differences in order to select those persons who possess the greatest amount of particular characteristics judged important for job success. A particular assessment is chosen because it looks as though it may be a valid measure of the attributes that are important for a particular job (Landy, 1989; Saks et al., 2000). One or more predictors are selected that presumably relate to the criteria (performance on the job). These predictor constructs become the basis for an assessment test. For example, if we identified that cognitive ability is an important predictor for performance in the job of customer service representative,

TABLE 14.1   Illustrations of the Interface Between the Purpose and Focus of Assessments

	Selection	Promotion	Career Planning	Classification	Employee Assistance Programs	Compensation
Cognitive ability	X			X		
Personality (e.g., conscientiousness)	X			X		
Teamwork skills (e.g., teamwork KSA test)	X	X	X	X		X
Physical abilities (e.g., strength)	X	X	X	X		
Job-specific knowledge and skills (e.g., competencies)	X	X		X		X
Honesty and integrity	X					
Interpersonal skills	X	X	X	X		X
Learning	X	X	X	X		
Training and experience	X	X	X	X		
Job performance					X	X

then we would develop a test that measures the construct of cognitive ability.

The use of assessment tools for selection varies depending on the job performance domain and the level of individual we are selecting. For example, because routine work (e.g., assembly line) is more structured than novel work (e.g., consulting) and because teamwork requires more interpersonal skills than does individually based work, selection assessments vary greatly for different jobs. Additionally, the level of the position dictates the type of assessment we would use. Selection for a chief executive officer would probably involve several interviews, whereas selection for a secretary might involve a typing test, an interpersonal skills test, and an interview.

Thus, selection in industrial settings varies depending on the context in which it is used. Regardless of this difference, the Uniform Guidelines and Standards for Educational and Psychological Assessment should always be applied.

Promotion

When we are conducting an assessment of performance, we are generally determining an individual's *achievement* at the time of the assessment. However, when we are considering an individual for a promotion, performance can be the basis for inferring his or her *potential* to perform a new job. However, we often try to directly assess traits or qualities thought to be relevant to the new job in practice.

In the context of school, an achievement test would be a final examination. At work, it might be a work sample or job knowledge test (more on these types of tests follows) or multisource feedback on the individual's performance over the past year on the job. In the context of school, an assessment of potential might be the Standardized Aptitude Test, which determines the person's potential to perform well in college (Anastasi &

Urbina, 1996). At work, an assessment might focus on managerial potential and on sales potential (e.g., J. Hogan & Hogan, 1986). These scales have been shown to predict performance of managers and sales representatives, respectively. Additionally, assessment centers and multisource assessment platforms are methods for assessing an individual's potential for promotion.

One challenge faced by psychologists in developing promotion instruments is that we are often promoting individuals based on past performance; however, often a new job requires additional KSAOs. This occurs when an individual is moving from a position in the union to one in management, from being a project member to being a project manager, or into any position requiring new skills. In this situation, the assessment should focus on future potential rather than simply past performance.

Another challenge in the promotion arena is that organizations often intend to use yearly performance appraisals to determine if a candidate should be promoted. However, there is often little variance between candidates on these appraisals. Many raters provide high ratings, often to insure workplace harmony, therefore showing little difference between candidates. Other tools, which involve the use of multiple, trained raters used in conjunction with the performance appraisal, might be used to remedy this problem.

Career Planning

Career planning is the process of helping individuals clarify a purpose and a vocation, develop career plans, set goals, and outline steps for reaching those goals. A typical career plan includes identification of a career path and the skills and abilities needed to progress in that path (Brunkan, 1991). It involves assessment, planning, goal setting, and strategizing to gain the skills and abilities required to implement the plan. It can be supported by coaching and counseling from a psychologist or from managers and human resources (HR) specialists within a company. Assessments for the purpose of career planning would be conducted so that individuals can have a realistic assessment of their own potential (Cascio, 1991) as well as their values, interests, and lifestyles (Brunkan, 1991). Assessments for this purpose include the Strong Occupational Interest Blank (Hansen, 1986) and Holland's Vocational Preferences Inventory (Holland, Fritsche, & Powell, 1994). Additionally, the results of participation in an assessment center (described later) or a multisource feedback instrument might be shared with an employee to identify those areas on which he or she could develop further.

Career management in organizations can take place from the perspective of the individual or the firm. If it is the former, the organization is concerned with ensuring that the individual develops skills that are relevant to succeeding in the firm and adding value as he or she progresses. If it is the latter, the individual seeks to develop skills to be applied either inside or outside of the organization. Additionally, the size of the firm and its stability will dictate the degree to which assessments for the purpose of career management can occur. We would be more likely to see large government organizations focusing on career development than small start-up firms.

Training is often a large part of career planning because it facilitates the transfer of skills that are necessary as the individual takes on new tasks. Assessments in this context are used to see if people are ready for training. A representative part of the training is presented to the applicant (Saks et al., 2000) to see if the applicant is ready for and likely to benefit from the training. Additionally, Noe and Schmitt (1986) have found that trainee attitudes and involvement in careers affected the satisfaction and the benefit from training. They show that understanding of trainee attitudes might benefit the organization so that it can develop interventions (e.g., pretraining workshops devoted to increasing involvement and job commitment of trainees) to enhance the effectiveness of the training program.

Classification

Assessments can also be used to determine how to best use staff. The results of an assessment might provide management with knowledge of the KSAOs of an individual and information on his or her interests. Classification decisions are based upon the need to make the most effective matching of people and positions. The decision maker has a specified number of available positions on one hand and a specific number of people on the other.

Depending on the context, the firm might take the perspective that the firm's needs should be fulfilled first or, if the individual is critical to the firm, that his or her needs should dictate where he or she is placed. In the former case, the organization would place an individual in an open slot rather than in a position where he or she may perform better or wish to work. The individual is placed there simply because there is an immediate business need. The organization knows that this individual can perform well, but he or she may not be satisfied here. On the other hand, organizations may have the flexibility to put the individual in a position he or she wants so that job satisfaction can be increased. Some organizations provide so-called stretch assignments, which allow individuals to learn new skills. Although the organization is taking a risk with these assignments, the hope is that the new skills will increase job satisfaction and also add value to the firm in the future.

Employee Assistance Programs

Many organizations use assessments as part of employee assistance programs (EAPs). Often these programs are viewed as an employee benefit to provide employees with outlets for problems that may affect their work. Assessments are used to diagnose stress- or drug-related problems. The individual might be treated through the firm's EAP or referred to a specialist.

Compensation

Organizations also assess individuals to determine their appropriate compensation. A traditional method is to measure the employee's job performance (job-based compensation). More recently, some organizations are using skill-based pay systems, according to which individuals are compensated on explicitly defined skills deemed important for their organization. Murray and Gerhart (1998) have found that skill-based systems can show greater productivity.

Focus of Assessments in Industry

The focus of assessments in industrial settings involves a number of possible constructs. In this section, we highlight those constructs that are robust and are referenced consistently in the literature.

Cognitive Ability Tests

The literature has established that cognitive ability, and specifically general mental ability, is a suitable predictor of many types of performance in the work setting. The construct of cognitive ability is generally defined as the "hypothetical attributes of individuals that are manifest when those individuals are performing tasks that involve the active manipulation of information" (Murphy, 1996, p. 13). Many agree with the comment of Ree and Earles (1992) that "If an employer were to use only intelligence tests and select the highest scoring applicant for the job, training results would be predicted well regardless of the job, and overall performance from the employees selected would be maximized" (p. 88). The meta-analysis conducted by Schmidt and Hunter (1998) showed that scores on cognitive ability measures predict task performance for all types of jobs and that general mental ability and a work sample test had the highest multivariate validity and utility for job performance.

Additionally, the work conducted for the Army Project A has shown that general mental ability consistently provides the best prediction of task proficiency (e.g., McHenry, Hough, Toquam, Hanson, & Ashworth, 1990). The evidence for this relationship is strong. For example, the meta-analysis of Hunter and Hunter (1984) showed that validity for general mental ability is .58 for professional-managerial jobs, .56 for high-level complex technical jobs, .51 for medium-complexity jobs, .40 for semiskilled jobs, and .23 for unskilled jobs. Despite these strong correlations, there is also evidence that it is more predictive of task performance (formally recognized as part of the job) than of contextual performance (activities such as volunteering, persisting, cooperating).

Personality

As we expand the criterion domain (Borman & Motowidlo, 1993) to include contextual performance, we see the importance of personality constructs. Although there is controversy over just how to define personality operationally (Klimoski, 1993), it is often conceptualized as a dynamic psychological structure determining adjustment to the environment but manifest in the regularities and consistencies in the behavior of an individual over time (Snyder & Ickes, 1985).

Mount and Barrick (1995) suggest that the emergence of the five-factor structure of personality led to empirical research that found "meaningful and consistent" relationships between personality and job performance. Over the past 15 years, researchers have found a great deal of evidence to support the notion that different components of the five-factor model (FFM; also known as the "Big Five") predict various dimensions of performance. Although the FFM is prevalent at this time, it is only one of many personality schema. Others include the 16 Personality Factor Questionnaire (16PF; Cattell, Cattell, & Cattell, 1993) and a nine-factor model (Hough, 1992).

The components of the FFM are agreeableness, extroversion, emotional stability, conscientiousness, and openness to experience. Research has shown that these factors predict various dimensions of job performance and therefore are useful constructs to assess in selection. McHenry et al. (1990) found that scores from ability tests provided the best prediction for job-specific and general task proficiency (i.e., task performance), whereas temperament or personality predictors showed the highest correlations with such criteria as giving extra support, supporting peers, and exhibiting personal discipline (i.e., contextual performance).

The factor of personality that has received the most attention is conscientiousness. For example, Mount and Barrick (1995) conducted a meta-analysis that explored the relationship between conscientiousness and the following performance measures: overall job performance, training proficiency, technical proficiency, employee reliability, effort, quality, administration, and interpersonal orientation. They found that although conscientiousness predicted overall performance (both task and contextual), its relationships with the specific criterion determined by motivational effort (employee reliability and effort) were stronger. Organ and Ryan (1995) conducted a meta-analysis on the predictors of organizational citizenship behaviors (OCBs). They found significant relationships between conscientiousness and the altruism component of OCBs (altruism represents the extent to which an individual gives aid to another, such as a coworker). Schmidt and Hunter's (1998) recent meta-analysis showed a .31 correlation between conscientiousness and overall job performance. They concluded that, in addition to general mental ability and job experience, conscientiousness is the "central determining variable of job performance" (p. 272).

The FFM of personality has also been shown to be predictive of an individual's performance in the context of working in a team (we will discuss this issue in the next section). For example, a meta-analysis conducted by Mount, Barrick, and Stewart (1998) found that conscientiousness, agreeableness, and emotional stability were positively related to overall performance in jobs involving interpersonal interactions. Emotional stability and agreeableness were strongly related to performance in jobs that involve teamwork.

Teamwork Skills

Individuals working in organizations today are increasingly finding themselves working in teams with other people who have different sets of functional expertise (Hollenbeck, LePine, & Ilgen, 1996). This change from a clearly defined set of individual roles and responsibilities to an arrangement in which the individual is required to exhibit both technical expertise and an ability to assimilate quickly into a team is due to the speed and amount of information entering and exiting an organization. No individual has the ability to effectively integrate all of this information. Thus, teams have been introduced as a solution (Amason, Thompson, Hochwarter, & Harrison, 1995).

Although an organization is interested in overall team performance, it is important to focus on the individuals' performance within the team (individual-in-team performance) so that we know how to select and appraise them. Hollenbeck et al. (1996) point out that certain types of individuals will assimilate into teams more easily than others. It is these individuals that we would want to select for a team. In the case of individual-in-team performance, we would suggest that both a contextual and a teamwork analysis be conducted. The contextual analysis provides the framework for team staffing by looking at, first, the reason for selection, be it to fill a vacancy, staff a team, or to transform an organization from individual to team-based work, and, second, the team's functions (as described by Katz & Kahn, 1978), be they productive/technical, related to boundary management, adaptive, maintenance-oriented, or managerial/executive. Additionally, the team analysis focuses on the team's role, the team's division of labor, and the function of the position. The results have implications for the KSAOs needed for the job (Klimoski & Zukin, 1998).

Physical Abilities

Physical abilities are important for jobs in which strength, endurance, and balance are important (Guion, 1998), such as mail carrier, power line repairer, and police officer. Fleishman and Reilly (1992) have developed a taxonomy of these abilities. Measures developed to assess these abilities have predicted work sample criteria effectively (R. T. Hogan, 1991). However, they must be used with caution because they can cause discrimination. The key here is that the level of that ability must be job relevant. Physical ability tests can only be used when they are genuine prerequisites for the job.

Job-Specific Knowledge and Skill

The O*NET system of occupational information (Peterson, Mumford, Borman, Jeanneret, & Fleishman, 1995) suggests that skills can be categorized as basic, cross-functional, and occupational specific. Basic skills are developed over a long period of time and provide the foundation for future learning. Cross-functional skills are useful for a variety of occupations and might include such skills as problem solving and resource management. Occupational (or job-specific) skills focus on those tasks required for a specific occupation. It is

not surprising that research has shown that job knowledge has a direct effect on one's ability to do one's job. In fact, Schmidt, Hunter, and Outerbridge's (1986) path analysis found a direct relationship between job knowledge and performance. Cognitive ability had an indirect effect on performance through job knowledge. Findings like this suggest that under certain circumstances job knowledge may be a more direct predictor of performance than cognitive ability.

Honesty and Integrity

The purpose of honesty/integrity assessments is to avoid hiring people prone to counterproductive behaviors. Sackett, Burris, and Callahan (1989) classify the measurement of these constructs into two types of tests. The first type is overt tests, which directly assess attitudes toward theft and dishonesty. They typically have two sections. One deals with *attitudes* toward theft and other forms of dishonesty (beliefs about the frequency and extent of employee theft, perceived ease of theft, and punitiveness toward theft). The other deals with *admissions* of theft. The second type consists of personality-based tests, which are designed to predict a broad range of counterproductive behaviors such as substance abuse (Ones & Viswesvaran, 1998b; Camera & Schneider, 1994).

Interpersonal Skills

Skills related to social perceptiveness include the work by Goleman (1995) on emotional intelligence and works on social intelligence (e.g., M. E. Ford & Tisak, 1982; Zaccaro, Gilbert, Thor, & Mumford, 1991). Goleman argues that empathy and communication skills, as well as social and leadership skills, are important for success at work (and at home). Organizations are assessing individuals on emotional intelligence for both selection and developmental purposes. Another interpersonal skill that is used in industrial settings is social intelligence, which is defined as "acting wisely in human relations" (Thorndike, 1920) and one's ability to "accomplish relevant objectives in specific social settings" (M. E. Ford & Tisak, 1983, p. 197). In fact, Zaccaro et al. (1991) found that social intelligence is related to sensitivity to social cues and situationally appropriate responses. Socially intelligent individuals can better manage interpersonal interactions.

Interests

Psychologists in industrial settings use interests inventories to help individuals with career development. Large organizations going through major restructuring may have new positions in their organization. Interests inventories can help individuals determine what new positions might be a fit for them (although they may still have to develop new skills to succeed in the new positions). Organizations going through downsizing might use these inventories as part of their outplacement services.

Learning

Psychologists in industry also assess one's ability to learn or the information that one has learned. The former might be assessed for the purpose of determining potential success in a training effort or on the job (and therefore for selection). As mentioned earlier in this chapter, the latter might be assessed to determine whether individuals learned from attending a training course. This information helps the organization to determine whether a proposed new course should be used for a broader audience. Tools used to assess learning can range from knowledge tests to cognitive structures or to behavioral demonstration of competencies under standardized circumstances (J. K. Ford, 1997).

Training and Experience

Organizations often use training and experience information to determine if the individual, based on his or her past, has the KSAOs necessary to perform in the job of interest. This information is mostly used for selection. An applicant might describe his or her training and experience through an application form, a questionnaire, a resume, or some combination of these.

Job Performance

Job performance information is frequently used for compensation or promotion decisions, as well as to refer an individual to an EAP (if job performance warrants the need for counseling). In these situations, job performance is measured to make personnel decisions for the individual. In typical validation studies, job performance is the criterion, and measures discussed above (e.g., training and experience, personality, cognitive ability) are used as predictors.

Tools

Cognitive Ability Tests

Schmidt and Hunter (1998) conducted a meta-analysis of measures used for hiring decisions. They have found that cognitive ability tests (e.g., Wonderlic Personnel Test, 1992) are robust predictors of performance and job-related learning.

TABLE 14.2   Example Tools Associated With the Focus of the Assessment

Focus	Example Tools
Cognitive ability	• Wonderlic Personnel Test (1992). • WAIS-III.
Personality	• Big five factor markers (Goldberg, 1992). • Mini-markers (Saucier, 1994). • Hogan Personality Inventory (R. T. Hogan & Hogan, 1995). • 16PF (Cattell et al., 1993).
Teamwork skills	• Teamwork KSA test (Stevens & Campion, 1994).
Physical abilities	• Handbook of Human Abilities (Fleishman & Reilly, 1992).
Job-specific knowledge and skills (tacit knowledge)	• Work sample tests such as those developed for specific trades (welder, carpenter). • Job knowledge tests.
Honesty and integrity	• Reliability scale of Hogan Personnel Selection Series (J. Hogan & Hogan, 1989).
Interpersonal skills	• Goldberg's measure of interpersonal characteristics. • Structured interviews.[1] • Assessment centers.[2]
Interests	• Vocational Preference Inventory (Holland, Fritsche, & Powell, 1994). • Self-directed search (Holland, 1985). • Strong Vocational Interest Blank (Strong, Hansen, & Campbell, 1985).
Learning	• Job knowledge tests.
Training and experience	• Owens Biographical Questionnaire (Owens & Schoenfeldt, 1979).
Job performance	• Supervisor assessments. • Multi-source feedback.

[1]In addition to assessing interpersonal skills, structured interviews assess a variety of competencies (e.g., leadership skills, technical skills, teamwork skills).
[2]In addition to assessing interpersonal skills, structured interviews assess a variety of competencies (e.g., leadership skills, teamwork skills).

They argue that because cognitive ability is so robust, it should be referred to as a primary measure for hiring decisions and that other measures should be referred to as supplementary measures. Where the information is available, this section will summarize these measures and some of their findings on the incremental validity of these measures in predicting performance. Additionally, the reader we suggest that the reader refer to Table 14.2 for examples of tools linked to each type of assessment.

Personality Assessments

Several tools are available to measure personality. Some focus on the FFM of personality (e.g., Big Five Factor Markers, Goldberg, 1992; Mini-markers, Saucier, 1994; Hogan Personality Inventory; R. T. Hogan & Hogan, 1995), whereas others focus on a broader set of personality characteristics (e.g., 16PF; Cattell et al., 1993).

Teamwork Skills Assessments

Several industrial/organizational psychologists have investigated those knowledges, skills, and abilities (KSAs) and personality dimensions that are important for teamwork. For example, Stevens and Campion (1994) studied several teams and argued that two major categories of KSAs are important for teamwork: interpersonal KSAs and self-management KSAs. Research by Stevens and Campion has shown that that teamwork KSAs (to include interpersonal KSAs and self-management KSAs) predict on-the-job teamwork performance of teams in a southeastern pulp processing mill and a cardboard processing plant. Steve and Campion's teamwork KSAs are conflict resolution, collaborative problem solving, communication, goal setting and performance management, planning, and task coordination.

Physical Abilities Tests

In jobs such as those of police officer, fire fighter, and mail carrier, physical strength (e.g., endurance or speed) is critical to job performance. Therefore, tools have been developed to assess the various types of physical abilities. Fleishman and Reilly's (1992) work in this area identifies nine major physical ability dimensions along with scales for the analysis of job requirements for each of these dimensions that are anchored with specific examples.

Tools to Measure Job-Specific Knowledge and Skill

Work sample tests are used to measure job-specific knowledge and skill. Work sample tests are hands-on job simulations that must be performed by applicants. These tests assess one's procedural knowledge base. For example, as part of a work sample test, an applicant might be required to repair a series of defective electric motors. Often used to hire skilled workers such as welders and carpenters (Schmidt & Hunter, 1998), these assessments must be used with applicants who already know the job. Schmidt and Hunter found that work sample tests show a 24% increase in validity over that of cognitive ability tests. Job knowledge tests are also used to assess job-specific knowledge and skills. Like work sample tests, these assessments cannot be used to hire or evaluate inexperienced employees. They are often constructed by the hiring organization on the basis of a job analysis. Although they can be developed internally, this is often costly and time-consuming. Those purchased off the shelf are less expensive and have

only slightly lower validity than those developed by the organization. Job knowledge tests increase the validity over cognitive ability measures by 14%.

Honesty and Integrity Tests

Schmidt and Hunter (1998) found that these types of assessments show greater validity and utility than do work samples. The reliability scale of the Hogan Personnel Selection Series (J. Hogan & Hogan, 1989) is designed to measure "organizational delinquency" and includes items dealing with hostility toward authority, thrill seeking, conscientiousness, and social insensitivity. Ones, Viswesvaran, and Schmidt (1993) found that integrity tests possess impressive criterion-related validity. Both overt and personality-based integrity tests correlated with measures of broad counterproductive behaviors such as violence on the job, tardiness, and absenteeism. Reviews of validity of these instruments show no evidence of adverse impact against women or racial minorities (Sackett et al., 1989; Sackett & Harris, 1984).

Assessments of Interpersonal Skills

Interpersonal skills are often found in the results of job analyses or competency studies. Therefore, an organization might assess interpersonal skills in an interview by asking the candidate to respond to questions on how they handled past experiences dealing with difficult interpersonal interactions. They might also be assessed through assessment centers by being placed in situations like the leaderless group discussion, in which their ability to interact with others is assessed by trained raters. Structured interviews and assessment centers are discussed in more detail later.

Employment Interviews

Employment interviews can be unstructured or structured (Huffcutt, Roth, & McDaniel, 1996). Schmidt and Hunter (1998) point out that the unstructured interviews have no fixed format or set of questions to be answered. There is no format for scoring responses. Structured interviews includes questions that are determined by a careful job analysis, and they have set questions and a set approach to scoring. Structured interviews have greater validity and show a 24% increase over cognitive ability alone in validity. Although there is no one universally accepted structured interview tool, depending on how structured the interview is, it might be based on detailed protocols so that candidates are asked the same questions and assessed against the same criteria. Interviewers are trained to ensure consistency between candidates (Judge, Higgins, & Cable, 2000).

As has been implied, the structured interview is a platform for assessment and can be designed to be used for developmental applicants. One if its functions can be to get at applicant or candidate interpersonal skills. For example, Landy (1976) found that interviews of prospective police officers were able to assess communication skills and personal stability. Arvey and Campion (1982) summarized evidence that the interview was suitable for determining sociability.

Assessment Centers

In assessment centers, the participant is observed participating in various exercises such as leaderless group discussions, supervisor/subordinate simulations, and business games. The average assessment center includes seven exercises and lasts two days (Gaugler, Rosenthal, Thornton, & Bentson, 1987). They have substantial validity but only moderate incremental validity over cognitive ability because they correlate highly with cognitive ability. Despite the lack of incremental validity, organizations use them because they provide a wealth of information useful for the individual's development.

Interest Inventories

Such tools as Holland's Vocational Preference Inventory (Holland et al., 1994) and Self-Directed Search (Holland, 1985), as well as the Strong Interest Inventory (Harmon, Hansen, Borgen, & Hammer, 1994) are used to help individuals going through a career change. Interest inventories are validated often against their ability to predict occupational membership criteria and satisfaction with a job (R. T. Hogan & Blake, 1996). There is evidence that interest inventories do predict occupational membership criteria (e.g., Cairo, 1982; Hansen, 1986). However, results are mixed with regard to whether there is a significant relationship between interests and job satisfaction (e.g., Cairo, 1982; Worthington & Dolliver, 1977). These results may exist because job satisfaction is affected by many factors, such as pay, security, and supervision. Additionally, there are individual differences in the expression of interests with a job. Regardless of their ability to predict these criteria, interest inventories have been useful to help individuals determine next steps in their career development.

Training and Experience Inventories

Schneider and Schneider (1994) point out that there are two assumptions of experience and training rating techniques. First, they are based on the notion that a person's past behaviors are a valid predictor of what the person is likely to do in

the future. Second, as individuals gain more experience in an occupation, they are more committed to it and will be more likely to perform well in it. There are various approaches to conducting these ratings. As an example, one approach is the point method, in which the raters provide points to candidates based on the type and length of a particular experience. Various kinds of experience and training would be differentially rated depending on the results of the job analysis. The literature on empirical validation of point method approaches suggests that they have sufficient validity. For example, McDaniel, Schmidt, and Hunter's (1988) meta-analysis found a corrected validity coefficient of .15 for point method–based experience and training ratings. Questionnaires on biographical data contain questions about life experiences such as involvement in student organizations, offices held, and the like. This practice is based on the behavioral consistency theory, which suggests that past performance is the best predictor of future performance. Items are chosen because they have been shown to predict some criteria of job performance. Historical data, such as attendance and accomplishments, are included in these inventories. Research indicates that biodata measures correlate substantially with cognitive ability and that they have little or no incremental validity over it. Some psychologists even suggest that perhaps they are indirect measures of cognitive ability. These tools are often developed in-house based on the constructs deemed important for the job. Although there are some biodata inventories that are available for general use, most organizations develop tools suitable to their specific needs. For those interested, an example tool discussed as a predictor of occupational attainment (Snell, Stokes, Sands, & McBride, 1994) is the Owens Biographical Questionnaire (Owens & Schoenfeldt, 1979).

Measures of Job Performance

Measures of job performance are often in the form of supervisory ratings or multisource assessment platforms and can be used for promotions, salary increases, reductions in force, development, and for research purposes. *Supervisory assessments,* in the form of ratings, are the most prevalent assessments of job performance in industrial settings. The content is frequently standardized within an organization with regard to the job category and level. There may also be industry standards (e.g., for police officers or insurance auditors); however, specific ratings suitable for the context are also frequently used. Supervisors generally rate individuals on their *personal* traits and attributes related to the job, the *processes* by which they get the job done, and the *products* that result from their work. *Multisource assessment platforms* are based on evaluations gathered about a target participant from two or more rating sources, including self, supervisors, peers, direct reports, internal customers, external customers, and vendors or suppliers. The ratings are based on KSAOs related to the job. Results of multisource assessments can be either provided purely for development (as with Personnel Decision International Corporation's *Profiler,* 1991) or shared with the supervisor as input to a personnel decision (Dalessio, 1998). The problem with the latter is that often the quality of ratings is poorer when the raters know that their evaluations will be used for personnel decisions (e.g., Murphy & Cleveland, 1995).

MAJOR ISSUES

By virtue of our treatment of the material covered so far in this chapter, it should be clear that the scope of individual assessment activities in work contexts is quite great. Similarly, the number of individuals and the range of professions involved in this activity are diverse. It follows, then, that what constitutes an important issue or a problem is likely to be tied to stakeholder needs and perspective. In deference to this, we will briefly examine in this section issues that can be clustered around major stakeholder concerns related to business necessity, social policy, or technical or professional matters.

It should also be noted that it is not uncommon for psychologists to serve as the assessment tool if they are hired by an organization to advise on a personnel action for an individual. Ryan and Sackett (1987) point out that the input for such a psychologist's decision could come from several sources (like those discussed above), but that the final evaluation is made by this psychologist. In this regard, the consulting psychologist often develops a proprietary assessment battery, which, when used over time, provides a model on which to base his or her recommendations and diagnoses. Client firms often do not see the data on candidates but trust the consultant to administer, score, and integrate the raw material.

The Business Case

Business Strategy

As noted, to be successful, organizations need to manage human resources effectively, but the magnitude of this requirement and the options open will be strongly affected by business strategy. At the most fundamental level, the nature and quality of employees required will depend on the product or service identified by senior management to be sold and the nature of technology available. Thus, for educational institutions and consulting firms, labor costs will be a major part of the cost structure of the firm. For heavy industry (e.g., steel making), these costs will be much less.

At a more operational level, the need for and the nature of the kind of assessment work called for will depend on HR strategy. For example, by virtue of the marketing claims of the firm for its products or services, it may need to perform more complete or complex assessments of prospective personnel. Similarly, exacting performance standards or the need for innovation may lead to more diligent assessment of people for positions of responsibility and leadership.

The supply of labor and availability of the critical skills will also affect the role of assessment in HR strategy. Under current economic conditions, with unemployment in the United States around 4%, most firms are having a difficult time staffing existing positions, much less trying to open new offices. Human resource strategy may have to shift in favor of augmenting the pool (Rynes & Barber, 1990), revising standards, spending a great deal more on assessment, or finding more efficient ways to assess more people.

Finally, the nature and extent of company assessment practices have systemic implications. On the one hand, what a firm does or does not do by way of assessment of individuals conveys an image to the public. It is often taken as a manifestation of company culture, communicating a value orientation toward the managing of employees. Depending on the industry and on the activities of competing firms, this may benefit or disadvantage a company. In the Washington, D.C. metropolitan area, the shortage of information technology professionals is so acute that many firms are all but eliminating the use of assessments for selection and adopting them for classification purposes. That is, given an available candidate, the question shifts from "should we hire him or her?" to "where can we place this person?"

Speed-to-Market

Organizational success is often related to the speed with which a product gets introduced, the speed of service, or the speed of response to a new business opportunity. In order for an organization to be competitive in its speed, the HR management systems must be up to the task. This readiness means, among other things, being able to obtain and use high-quality assessment information in a timely manner.

Often this is difficult because obtaining high-quality data is too time-consuming. In this regard, there is tension relative to what historically been called band width and fidelity features of a measurement protocol. Although quick and course measures may give us some insight about someone, it is often only a high-level cut. Making really good diagnoses or predictions may require more deliberate and diligent assessment.

As a case in point, few firms are willing to spend the time (or expense) required for a five-day assessment center. Instead, practitioners are expected to take no more than one day of staff or candidate time on which to base important personnel decisions.

In addition to the issue of how to assess, the issue of who should provide the information becomes salient. In particular, just what aspects of individual achievement, potential, or weakness can be supplied efficiently by such agents as the worker himself, a manager, a human resource specialist, or a psychologist? Importantly, if it comes to using an assessment professional, the issue then becomes just who is in the best position to provide the service quickly. In this regard, it may actually be that an external consulting firm on retainer is indeed better positioned to provide high-quality assessment information faster than the company's own HR department.

The Dynamics of Change

Related to the points made above is the reality that contemporary work organizations are being exposed to forces that induce constant change. The rate of new business start-ups has never been higher in the United States. All types of new businesses (but especially e-commerce firms) are coming into being. Although many are small, all require attention to the assessment of current or prospective employees. The scale and scope of business are dynamic, with acquisitions, mergers, or consolidations occurring almost daily. As many people know, the number of airlines, auto manufacturers, and book publishers is down. This, too, implies the need for assessment for purposes of selective retention or for outplacement of personnel. As a last example, the life cycle of products, especially in the consumer electronics industry, has never been shorter. Although the skills needed to design and produce products may not change dramatically, to be able to quickly reallocate talent across business units as market demand for products is falling calls for valid assessments of past performance, interests, and potential to contribute to the production and sales of new product lines.

The dynamics of change are no less real for public-sector organizations, albeit for somewhat different reasons. Most notably, an examination of the current demographic makeup of the work force in the United States reveals that many current employees will be eligible for retirement in the next five years (Crenshaw, 1999). More specifically, 35% of the U.S. federal workforce in 1998 will be eligible to retire in 2006 (Walsh, 2001). Additionally, 45% of the U.S. government's most senior executives (the senior executive service) are expected to retire in 2005 (Walsh, 2001). A similar reality is facing most school districts relative to their teaching staff. Even

the U.S. military must confront new challenges to effectively recruit and retain key personnel (Suro, 2000). In all these instances, we maintain that programs for the valid and timely assessment of individuals have an important role to play.

Build It or Buy It

At one point in time in the United States, many large corporations had their own HR research units. They would be located in the HR function, staffed by psychologists, and given the responsibility to design, develop, and implement assessment programs. Today, most firms have elected to purchase such services. In this regard, these firms have shed some fixed expenses arguably well for profitability. By using an outside firm, the company is presumably getting state-of-the-art methods and models for assessment. Moreover, the outside firm usually has greater insight regarding normative practices in the industry (and even competitive assessment data). On the other hand, in going outside, the company may have increased its agency costs.

The challenges facing a company that wishes to buy assessment services are numerous. For instance, it is often difficult to ascertain the professional qualifications of the numerous firms offering services. This is especially true when the consulting firm has a strong internal champion for the services of the outsider. The temptation to latch on to the latest tool or technique may also be irresistible. There is ample evidence that many management practices, including assessment programs, have a fad like quality: they are adopted for their popularity at the moment (Abrahamson, 1996), regardless of their suitability. Finally, there is the very real possibility that the outside firm would not take a steward role and gather appropriate statistical evidence that the assessment program meets technical and legal requirements. Even should a consultant recommend local validation or adverse impact analysis, the extra costs, time, and effort may cause the firm to opt out of this activity.

Proper Training

As noted, most assessments in industry are carried out by individuals who are neither psychologists nor measurement specialists (e.g., psychometricians). Although it is also true that many kinds of assessments may not require a PhD, it still is imperative that the firm insure that, whatever the assessment practice used, those responsible for gathering and interpreting data are qualified to do so.

This aspect of due diligence is increasingly difficult as a result of the increased public access to tests, either because of their frequent use or because of the reluctance of test publishers (due to financial pressures) to insure test user qualifications. It is also exacerbated by the increased use of computer-based test systems, which make it logistically easy for even a novice to offer services.

Privacy

Assessment data or results are often paid for by the firm, even when they are nominally in the service of meeting worker counseling or career needs. More to the point, they are often archived in a worker's personnel file. Thus, there is frequently a great deal of tension regarding just how long information should be retained and, importantly, who should have access.

Increasingly, such records are available electronically as companies go to web-based HR systems. Access to such systems, although protected, can rarely be guaranteed. Moreover, there are an increasing number of instances in which third parties can demand to see such data if they are seen as material to litigation. This also implies that disgruntled employees as well may be expected to seek access to individual assessment data (e.g., performance reviews or assessment of career potential) on other employees.

Finally, certain kinds of assessment methods are viewed as more problematic from a privacy perspective. At this point in time, most applicants will accept and tolerate being assessed on ability and performance tests. They will usually see a job interview as a reasonable intrusion into their affairs. However, such approaches as drug testing, honesty testing, and polygraph testing usually create concerns on the part of applicants and employees alike. Assessments with regard to physical or mental disability, even when they are not prohibited by the ADA, are also likely to lead to perceptions of abuse of power and invasion of privacy (Linowes & Spencer, 1996).

Compensation

There are a variety of factors on which to base an individual's compensation: job duties, title, tenure, seniority, market considerations, and performance. All of these imply careful protocols. However, given that the organization wishes to link compensation to performance, additional considerations are involved (Heneman, 1992; Lawler, 1990). Among these, it is most critical for the organizational managers in charge to have an appropriate assessment platform.

Assessments for purposes of compensation should be based on those work behaviors and outcomes that are of strategic value to the organization (Lawler, 1990). Moreover, from the worker's point of view, variance on the measures used

must reflect individual effectiveness in order to be perceived as fair. All other things being equal, such measures should have relatively small standard errors as well. Finally, because this context represents a case of high-stakes measurement, assessment devices and tools need to be robust and resistant to abuse or unwarranted influence intended to wrongfully benefit certain employees over others. Clearly, the successful use of individual assessments as the basis for compensation presents a challenge to system designers and managers.

When it comes to linking pay to assessments, two special cases are worth pointing out. The first involves recent initiatives aimed at increasing the capacity of organizations to be flexible and adaptable by insuring that they have a well-trained and multiskilled work force. Several organizations have attempted to accomplish this by paying individuals (at least in part) in relationship to the number and nature of the skills that they possess. In skill-based pay systems, individuals qualify for wage premiums by being assessed and performing well on measures specifically set up for this purpose. Depending on the organization, this might be in one or several skill or competency areas felt to be important if the worker is to be able to contribute to the future growth of the firm. Passing performance itself may be set at one of several levels of mastery (Ledford, Lawler, & Mohrman, 1995).

Thus, under this arrangement, the number and nature of the assessment domains to be covered, the tools (e.g., tests, work sample, portfolio), the rules and procedures for allowing workers to be assessed (e.g., they must be performing at certain levels on their current job), the cut or passing scores adopted, and the salary or wage differential associated with a particular skill or score must be worked out. Moreover, if the skills of interest are of the type that can atrophy if not used, it may also be necessary for regular and repeated assessments to be performed over time. One would need not only to qualify but to remain qualified to receive the extra pay.

A second area where there are special challenges for assessment relates to the increased use of work teams by contemporary organizations (Sundstrom, 1998). In general, the assessment of individuals as members of work teams requires new models and techniques. Depending on the purpose of the assessment (e.g., retention or developmental feedback), but especially as the basis for individual compensation, as noted in an earlier section, the protocols to be followed in a team environment would be very different. However, aside from the technical complexities, the choice of just who is to provide the assessment data on individuals in a work team is problematic (Jones & Moffett, 1998). In particular, having team members assessing one another, especially when the information is to be used for compensation decisions, requires careful measurement development work, user training, the regular monitoring of practices, and clear accountabilities in order to insure quality.

In each of the areas examined, the assessment professional, in collaboration with the organization's owner or agent, needs not only to bring to bear the best technical knowledge and practices, but also to insure that the business case can be made or justified in the design or choice of assessment platform.

Technical Issues

In spite of over 100 years of technical developments associated with individual assessment theory and practice, there are a number of issues that remain to be resolved when it comes to applications to work settings.

The Criterion Domain

Just what to measure continues to be an important issue facing practitioners. As noted throughout this chapter, there is certainly no shortage of options. Recent developments, however, have forced attention to just how broad or narrow the focus should be when it comes to assessing individual effectiveness.

Traditionally, individuals in work settings have been assessed relative to job performance. Here, the choices have typically included measuring both the quality and quantity of performance. However, systematic investigations into the nature of individual effectiveness (Campbell, 1990) have made a strong case for a more elaborate conceptualization of the performance domain. In particular, these studies have pointed out the need for and appropriateness of assessing what has become termed contextual performance (Borman & Motowidlo, 1993).

As discussed in the section on selection, contextual performance by workers is reflected in extrajob behaviors and accomplishments, including such things as cooperation, teamwork, loyalty, and self-development. As extrajob behaviors, their role or function relative to the workers' formal job duties is often indirect. However, there is evidence that their manifestation does make for a better workplace and for unit effectiveness.

Competencies

As previously noted, there is reason to believe that there is merit to the concept of competencies when it comes to assessing individuals in the workplace. Here too, however, there is no consensus on just how to incorporate this concept (Schippmann et al., 2000). For example, some might include assessing elements of a worker's value system and needs as part of the process (e.g., Spencer & Spencer, 1993). Others would not try to get at the building blocks underlying or producing the performance, but would focus instead directly on the demonstrated (and observed) capacity to perform job-relevant activities.

A second issue relates to the nature and number of competencies that exist. In particular, it is unclear that their definition should emphasize their links to specific jobs, roles, or firms (e.g., those needed to be effective as a call service representative for an insurance company) or whether they should be thought of as more generic in nature and cross-situational in relevance (e.g., "Telephone service rendering").

Noncognitive Measures

There has been a major shift in thinking about the appropriateness of noncognitive measures, because these can contribute to effective HR management programs in work organizations. This is been especially true regarding their application to personnel selection and screening.

Early reviews of the usefulness of interest and personality inventories had been quite critical (Guion & Gottier, 1965), and with good reason. Many of the inventories used had been designed for the assessment of psychopathology (e.g., the Minnesota Multiphasic Personality Inventory). Moreover, the application of a particular scale was often made without regard to a careful analysis of the requirements of the job (Day & Silverman, 1989). Finally, it was not easy to find studies that were carefully designed relative to the validity data needed to make a business case.

In contrast, greater attention to these technical issues in recent years has resulted in great advances and the increased use of personality and interest measures in personnel work. The empirical record is now convincing enough to most critics (e.g., Schmidt & Hunter, 1998) that they truly can add value over cognitive measures when it comes to predicting or selecting individuals for success on the job.

Much more research is needed, however. For instance, just where to use personality assessments is not yet well understood. Modern, work-relevant personality inventories are found to have acceptable validities, but they do not always have value over cognitive measures (Schmidt & Hunter, 1998). Moreover, the nature of the criterion domain appears to be key. Do we want to assess for success in training, early task performance, contextual performance, career success, or commitment or tenure? The value of noncognitive measures should certainly be linked to the criterion of interest. However, we do not yet have parametric research here to tell us when and where this is the case.

The conceptualization of such measures is problematic. As noted in an earlier section, it is now quite common to make use of inventories that are based on meta-analytic research (e.g., Digman, 1990; Goldberg, 1990; Saucier, 1994) that gives support to the existence of and importance for five key constructs. However, these so-called big five dimensions—conscientiousness, extraversion, openness to experience, agreeableness, and emotional stability are only one approach to conceptualizing and measuring the personality domain. Additional work needs to be done to ascertain just when this set of robust factors is indeed a better way to conceptualize and measure the noncognitive assessment needs than scales that might be more focused on the personnel problem at hand (e.g., individual assessment for placement in work teams).

There is also the issue of just when it may be appropriate to use more clinically oriented noncognitive measures. As noted in an earlier section, these are often found in applications such as individual coaching or in the diagnosis of behavior or performance problems in the workplace. However, their validity and relative utility are not well understood.

The use of noncognitive measures in high-stakes settings, such as screening for employment, has also revealed a key weakness. This is their susceptibility to being faked (Ones, Viswesvaran, & Reiss, 1996; McFarland & Ryan, 2000). Applicants or candidates for promotion who are being assessed on personality measures are likely to try to look good. Very often the measures themselves are transparent to the applicant in the sense that he or she can imagine the right answers to questions, those that would give them an advantage in the scoring.

To be sure, the issue of faking on measures (or intentional distortion) has been investigated for over many years (Ones et al., 1996). However, the emphasis in the past has been on response formats that were felt to make it difficult for someone to deliberately mislead the administrator. Formats like the forced-choice tetrad or the weighted checklists were invented for this purpose (Saks et al., 2000). Although there is evidence that these can help to mitigate the problem, this approach has not been a major breakthrough.

Instead, research is currently under way to try to provide an understanding of faking as a phenomenon in and of itself. Thus, the newer focus includes examining such things as the level of awareness that the test taker may have about his or her behavior as investigators try to distinguish between distortion that is motivated or that which is based on lack of self-insight. Similarly, the role of contextual forces is being examined to understand those situations that may promote honesty. Paradoxically, there also a question of the implications of faking for estimating the future job behavior or performance of one who does so. In this regard, some might argue that faking in a high-stakes situation is more of a manifestation of adaptability than dishonesty and thus might actually imply more, than less, likelihood for being a successful worker. Finally, there is uncertainty regarding the implications of applicant faking for personnel decisions based on data from those measures (e.g., personality) more susceptible to faking. Such things as the prevalence and nonrandom distribution of faking behavior in the applicant pool should make a difference here, but the evidence is not conclusive (Ones & Viswesvaran, 1998b). Clearly there is much research that remains to be done.

Technology-Mediated Testing

The previous sections of this chapter have highlighted the variety of ways that individual assessments in work organizations can be carried out. However, traditionally, the individual of interest is usually assessed when in physical proximity to the assessor. Thus, the latter is usually face to face with the candidate or at least in the same room. In contrast, current practice is moving toward technology-mediated interaction.

The technology involved can vary, depending on the application. In the past, assessment processes have been mediated by such mundane technologies as the telephone and FAX machine. In the case of the former, the person to be tested might be asked to dial in to a number to be talked through a series of questions. The person could respond by using the dial matrix as a key pad, following instructions that translated the standard dial to a scoring matrix. Despite such primitive arrangements, many organizations were able to achieve a cost savings and improve the speed of decisions, while still maintaining test security and standardized administration. By and large, however, the computer is currently the technology of choice.

Burke (1993) identifies and contrasts computer-based testing (CBT) and computer-adaptive testing (CAT) as two major advances in computerized psychological testing. The former builds on optical scanning technology and the capacity for computers not only to summarize responses but, using carefully developed algorithms, to provide interpretations.

As the movement toward the on-line administration of tests converges with developments in the areas of Item Response Theory (IRT) and CAT, new technical issues arise and must be resolved (Green, Bock, Humphreys, Linn, & Reckase, 1994; Kingsbury, 1990). Burke highlights such issues as resolving the best way to develop work attribute-job performance matrices on which to base computer algorithms, establishing the construct equivalence of tests across CAT versions and in relationship to conventional forms, and determining criterion-related validity. Finally, although there is some support for the belief that CAT might represent an improvement in test security (Bunderson, Inouye, & Olsen, 1989), it is possible that a test taker motivated to do so would have an easier time recalling specific test items and communicating them to future test takers.

Validity

The earliest practitioners tended to focus on the relevance of the test to the job (Landy, 1991), thus stressing what we would now call content validity. If one wanted to assess someone for suitability for a manufacturing position, one looked for evidence of the knowledge, skills, or ability to perform. This evidence was usually based on criterion-related validity data. However, as the field matured, and for both theoretical and practical reasons (e.g., the need to identify a worker who does not yet have the skill but has the potential to be an effective worker), most thoughtful practitioners have sought to insure that assessments allow for the valid inference of the individual's status relative to a job-related construct (Schmitt & Landy, 1993).

As described above, the process of establishing construct validity is one of building a case that the measure is appropriate based on a variety of types of evidence, obtained from multiple cases and over numerous settings. Analytic tools and approaches such as factor analysis, scaling, rational methods, multimethod, multitrait analysis, validity generalization, path analysis, and even the experimental method can be used (Schmitt & Landy, 1993). Although data from one study or analyzed by one technique may be less than conclusive, there is reassurance in replication and in finding expected or predicted patterns. Thus, the conceptual models and techniques needed to infer that an assessment tool does indeed measure what it is intended to do so are readily available.

Nevertheless, the problem of construct validity persists. For example, biodata or life history information has been found useful for predicting job outcomes, but the construct nature of such measures is often obscure or overlooked (Mael & Hirsch, 1993; Mumford, Costanza, Connelly, & Johnson, 1996). Similarly, the assessment center method has been adopted by many firms as a way to estimate the developmental needs of workers (usually couched in terms of trait-like constructs). However, the evidence for the construct validity of such applications is weak (Klimoski, 1993; Klimoski & Brickner, 1987).

The problem is likely to become worse, given many of the competitive pressures on companies and practitioners noted above. For example, there is a great emphasis on satisfying the client. Often this means providing custom work within a short time frame, leaving few options for careful development

work. Even if there is some scale or test development, given the proprietary nature of such work products, traditional ways of ascertaining the quality of a test (e.g., requesting and reviewing a technical report) are often thwarted. Similarly, many managerial decisions about who to hire for professional assessment work or just what assessment approach to use are unduly influenced by popular culture and testimonials, and rarely based on rigorous evidence of validity or utility (Abrahamson, 1996).

On a different tack, a more diverse workforce, with English as a second language and the tendency for firms to become multinational, also presents challenges. The successful cross-translation of material is difficult at best. When this must be done for assessment tools, the challenges to construct validity are quite great. Similarly, as practitioners attempt to be responsive to applicants covered under the ADA, variation in testing conditions or test format would seem to have a major, but frequently underexamined, impact on construct validity (Klimoski & Palmer, 1994).

Social Policy Issues

Fairness of Assessment Practices

Regardless of the approach used or the purpose, it would seem that issue of the fairness of assessments in the context of work could be considered the major social policy issue facing practitioners. Indeed, much of the work on noncognitive predictors has been stimulated with the goal of finding valid measures that do not have an adverse impact on subgroups in society (Ryan, Ployhart, & Friedel, 1998).

One approach to this problem has been to investigate the bases for inferior performance of subgroups, often using the tools of cognitive psychology (Sternberg & Wagner, 1993; DeShon, Smith, Chan, & Schmitt, 1998). Here, the goal is to ascertain the state of mind or the test-taking strategy used by individuals, with the goal of assisting them in changing their approach if it is dysfunctional. In a related manner, the use of exposure to and training on problematic assessment tools has also been tried, but with limited success (Ryan et al., 1998).

Still a third approach has been to examine the perceived fairness of assessment devices. Here, the goal is to understand how fair the test is in the eyes of the test taker, because this affects his or her motivation to do well and to challenge the outcome of the assessment (Chan, Schmitt, Sacco, & DeSchon, 1998; Gilliland, 1994).

Finally, it has already been noted that the ADA also presents fairness challenges. Applicants or workers covered under the ADA have the right to request an accommodation to allow them to perform to their potential in an assessment event. However, what is reasonable from the firm's point of view may be viewed as unfair by the test taker. Ironically, even when the company and the worker can agree on disability-mitigating adjustments to the assessment platform, other workers and even supervisors may see this as an injustice, because they had to meet the standard, and frequently more strenuous, testing conditions (Klimoski & Donahue, 1997).

Poor Language Skills

At the time of this writing, unemployment is very low in the United States. On the other hand, immigration is very high. Add to this the observation that American schools are producing graduates who perform poorly on many carefully developed achievement-related assessment programs. All this implies that the current and near-future members of the workforce are poorly prepared to perform well on many of the traditional assessment tools used in the work context. Language and reading skills are not at appropriate levels. In extreme cases, recent immigrants may be illiterate in their own national language. As noted above, these tendencies create problems of both valid inference and perceived social injustice. All this implies that, at a minimum, conventional tools need to be recalibrated in light of such a diverse pool of talent. However, it may also call for entirely new approaches to individual assessment as well.

Open Testing

Given the importance of doing well on assessments as a way to obtain desirable work outcomes, its not surprising that there are tremendous pressures to make the nature of tests, test content, and assessment protocols more public. Of course, over the years, there have always been arrangements for informing both the representative of the firm and prospective test taker about what the measure is all about. More recently, however, there are increasing demands for public disclosure of such things as the exact items or exercises used, response options, and even item operating characteristics. This trend has been accelerated by the availability of social dialogue and ease of information search on the Internet. Now details on items can be made known to millions of people in a matter of seconds and at little cost. Needless to say, full disclosure would quickly compromise the test and dramatically affect its validity and utility.

Thus the challenge here is to find ways of meeting the legitimate needs of stakeholders and to insure the accountability of firms to professional practice and yet to be able to maintain the integrity of the assessment program.

Although these issues are not exhaustive, they highlight the fact that the field continuous to overcome new challenges. As a field of practice that is driven not only by developments in theory but also by trends in the business community, it must continuously respond to and affect major societal changes in the economy, immigration, public policy, culture, and business practices.

REFERENCES

Abrahamson, E. (1996). Management fashion. *Academy of Management Review, 21,* 254–285.

Amason, A. C., Thompson, K. R., Hochwarter, W. A., & Harrison, A. W. (1995). Conflict: An important dimension in successful management teams. *Organizational Dynamics, 23,* 20–35.

American Educational Research Association, American Psychological Association, & National Council on Measurement in Education. (1999). *Standards for educational and psychological testing.* Washington, DC: American Educational Research Association.

Anastasi, A., & Urbina, S. (1996). *Psychological testing* (7th ed.). New York: Macmillan.

Arvey, R. D., & Campion, J. E. (1982). Biographical trait and behavioral sampling predictors of performance in a stressful life situation. *Personnel Psychology, 35,* 281–321.

Austin, J. T., Klimoski, R. J., & Hunt, S. T. (1996). Dilemmatics in public sector assessment: A framework for developing and evaluating selection systems. *Human Performance, 3,* 177–198.

Austin, J. T., Scherbaum, C. A., & Mahlman, R. A. (2000). History of research methods in industrial and organizational psychology: Measurement, design analysis. In S. Rogelberg (Ed.), *Handbook of research methods in industrial and organizational psychology.* Malden, MA: Basil Blackwell.

Baritz, L. (1960). *The servants of power.* Middleton, CT: Wesleyan University Press.

Binning, J. F., & Barrett, G. V. (1989). Validity of personnel decisions: A conceptual analysis of the inferential and evidential bases. *Journal of Applied Psychology, 74,* 478–494.

Borman, W. C., & Motowidlo, S. J. (1993). Expanding the criterion domain to include elements of contextual performance. In N. Schmitt & W. C. Borman (Eds.), *Personnel selection in organizations* (pp. 71–98). San Francisco: Jossey-Bass.

Brunkan, R. J. (1991). Psychological assessment in career development. In C. P. Hansen & K. A. Conrad (Eds.), *A handbook of psychological assessment in business.* New York: Quorum.

Bunderson, C. V., Inouye, D. K., & Olsen, J. B. (1989). The four generations of computerized educational measurement. In R. L. Linn (Ed.), *Educational measurement* (3rd ed.). New York: American Council on Education and Macmillan.

Burke, M. J. (1993). Computerized psychological testing: Impacts on measuring predictor constructs and future job behavior.

In N. Schmitt & W. C. Borman (Eds.), *Personnel selection in organizations* (pp. 203–239). San Francisco: Jossey-Bass.

Cairo, P. C. (1982). Measured interests versus expressed interests as predictors of long-term occupational membership. *Journal of Vocational Behavior, 20,* 343–353.

Camera, W., & Schneider, D. L. (1994). Integrity tests: Facts and unresolved issues. *American Psychologist, 49,* 112–119.

Campbell, J. P. (1990). An overview of the army selection and classification project (Project A). *Personnel Psychology, 43,* 231–240.

Campbell, J. P., McCloy, R. A., Oppler, S. H., & Sager, C. E. (1993). A theory of performance. In N. Schmitt & W. C. Borman (Eds.), *Personnel selection in organizations* (pp. 35–70). San Francisco: Jossey-Bass.

Cascio, W. F. (1991). *Applied psychology in personnel management* (4th ed.). Englewood Cliffs, NJ: Prentice Hall.

Cascio, W. F. (1993). Assessing the utility of selection decisions: Theoretical and practical considerations. In N. Schmitt & W. C. Borman (Eds.), *Personnel selection in organizations* (pp. 71–98). San Francisco: Jossey-Bass.

Cattell, R. B., Cattell, A. K., & Cattell, H. F. (1993). *Sixteen Personality Factors Practical Questionnaire* (5th ed.). Champaign, IL: Institute for Personality and Abilities Testing.

Crenshaw, A. B. (1999, September 22). The rise of phased retirement. *Washington Post,* p. 2.

Cronbach, L. J. (1984). *Essentials of psychological testing* (4th ed.). New York: Harper and Row.

Dalessio, A. T. (1998). Using multisource feedback for employee development and personnel decisions. In J. W. Smither (Ed.), *Performance appraisal: State of the art in practice* (pp. 278–330). San Francisco: Jossey-Bass.

Dawis, R. (1991). Vocational interests, values and preferences. In M. Dunnette & L. Hough (Eds.), *Handbook of industrial and organizational psychology* (2nd ed., pp. 833–872). Palo Alto, CA: Consulting Psychologists Press.

Day, D. V., & Silverman, S. B. (1989). Personality and job performance: Evidence of incremental validity. *Personnel Psychology, 42,* 25–36.

DeShon, R. P., Smith, M. R., Chan, D., & Schmitt, N. (1998). Can racial differences in cognitive test performance be reduced by presenting problems in a social context? *Journal of Applied Psychology, 83,* 438–451.

Digman, J. M. (1990). Personality structure: Emergence of the Five-Factor Model. *Annual Review of Psychology, 41,* 417–440.

Equal Employment Opportunity Commission, Civil Service Commission, U.S. Department of Labor, & U.S. Department of Justice. (1978). *Uniform guidelines on employee selection procedures. Federal Register, 43,* 38290–38315.

Fitzgerald, L. F., Drasgow, F., Hulin, C. L., Gelfand, M. J., & Magley, V. J. (1997). The antecedents and consequences of sexual harassment in organizations: A test of an integrated model. *Journal of Applied Psychology, 82,* 578–589.

Flanagan, J. C. (1954). The Critical Incident Technique. *Psychological Bulletin, 51,* 327–358.

Fleishman, E. A., & Reilly, M. E. (1992). *Handbook of human abilities: Definitions, measurements and job task requirements.* Palo Alto, CA: Consulting Psychologists Press.

Ford, J. K. (1997). *Improving training effectiveness in work organizations.* Mahwah, NJ: Erlbaum.

Ford, M. E., & Tisak, M. S. (1983). A further search for social intelligence. *Journal of Educational Psychology, 75,* 196–206.

Gaugler, B. B., Rosenthal, D. B., Thornton, G. C., & Bentson, C. (1987). Meta-analysis of assessment center validity. *Journal of Applied Psychology, 72,* 493–511.

Ghiselli, E. E. (1956). Dimensional problems of criteria. *Journal of Applied Psychology, 40,* 1–4.

Gilliland, S. W. (1993). The perceived fairness of selection systems: An organizational justice perspective. *Academy of Management Review, 18,* 694–734.

Gilliland, S. W. (1994). Effects of procedural and distributive justice on reactions to selection systems. *Journal of Applied Psychology, 79,* 791–804.

Glomb, T. M., Munson, L. J., Hulin, C. L., Bergman, M. E., & Drasgow, F. (1999). Structural equation models of sexual harassment: Longitudinal explorations and cross-sectional generalizations. *Journal of Applied Psychology, 84,* 14–28.

Goldberg, L. R. (1990). An alternative "description of personality": The Big Five factor structures. *Journal of Personality and Social Psychology, 59,* 1216–1229.

Goldberg, L. R. (1992). The development of markers for the Big-Five structure. *Psychological Assessment, 4,* 26–42.

Goleman, D. (1995). *Emotional intelligence.* New York: Bantam Books.

Green, B. F., Bock, R. D., Humphreys, L. G., Linn, R. L., & Reckase, M. D. (1994). Technical guidelines for assessing computer adaptive tests. *Journal of Educational Measurement, 21,* 347–360.

Guion, R. M. (1980). On trinitarian doctrines of validity. *Professional Psychology, 11,* 385–398.

Guion, R. M. (1998). *Assessment, measurement, and prediction for personnel decisions.* Mahwah, NJ: Erlbaum.

Guion, R. M., & Gottier, R. F. (1965). Validity of personality measures in personnel selection. *Personnel Psychology, 18,* 135–164.

Halbfinger, D. M. (1999, March 21). Police and applicants have big stake in test. *New York Times,* p. I40.

Hansen, J. C. (1986). Strong Vocational Interest Blank/Strong-Campbell Interest Inventory. In W. B. Walsh & S. H. Osipow (Eds.), *Advances in vocational psychology, Vol. 1: The assessment of interests* (pp. 1–29). Hillsdale, NJ: Erlbaum.

Harmon, L. W., Hansen, J. C., Borgen, F. H., & Hammer, A. L. (1994). *Strong Interest Inventory: Applications and technical guide.* Palo Alto, CA: Consulting Psychologists Press.

Heneman, R. L. (1992). *Merit pay*. Reading, MA: Addison-Wesley.

Hogan, J., & Hogan, R. T. (1986). *Hogan Personnel Selection Series manual*. Minneapolis, MN: National Computer Systems.

Hogan, J., & Hogan, R. T. (1989). How to measure employee reliability. *Journal of Applied Psychology, 74*, 273–279.

Hogan, R. T. (1991). Personality and personality management. In M. D. Dunnette & L. M. Hough (Eds.), *Handbook of industrial and organizational psychology* (Vol. 2). Palo Alto, CA: Consulting Psychologists Press.

Hogan, R. T., & Blake, R. J. (1996). Vocational interests: Matching self concept with work environment. In K. R. Murphy (Ed.), *Individual difference and behavior in organizations* (pp. 89–144). San Francisco: Jossey-Bass.

Hogan, R. T., & Hogan, J. (1995). *Hogan Personality Inventory manual*. Tulsa, OK: Hogan Selection Systems.

Holland, J. L. (1985). *Professional manual Self-Directed Search*. Odessa, FL: Psychological Assessment Resources.

Holland, J. L., Fritsche, B. A., & Powell, A. B. (1994). *The Self-Directed Search (SDS): Technical manual*. Odessa, FL: Psychological Assessment Resources.

Hollenbeck, J. R., LePine, J. A., & Ilgen, D. R. (1996). Adapting to roles in decision-making teams. In K. R. Murphy (Ed.), *Individual differences and behavior in organizations* (pp. 300–333). San Francisco: Jossey-Bass.

Hough, L. M. (1992). The "Big Five" personality variables—construct confusion: Description versus prediction. *Human Performance, 5*(1&2), 139–155.

Howard, A., & Bray, D. W. (1988). *Managerial lives in transition: Advancing age and changing times*. New York: Guilford Press.

Huffcutt, A. I., Roth, P. L., & McDaniel, M. A. (1996). A meta-analytic investigation of cognitive ability in employment interview evaluations: Moderating characteristics and implications for incremental validity. *Journal of Applied Psychology, 81*, 459–473.

Hunter, J. E., & Hunter, R. F. (1984). Validity and utility of alternative predictors of job performance. *Psychological Bulletin, 96*, 72–98.

Impara, J. C., & Plake, B. S. (1998). *13th annual mental measurement Yearbook*. Lincoln, NE: Buros Institute for Mental Measurement.

Jones, S., & Moffett, R. G. (1998). Measurement and feedback systems for teams. In E. Sundstrom (Ed.), *Supporting work team effectiveness: Best management practices for fostering high performance* (pp. 157–187). San Francisco: Jossey-Bass.

Judge, T. A., Higgins, C. A., & Cable, D. M. (2000). The employment interview: A review of recent research and recommendations for future research. *Human Resources Management Review, 10*, 383–406.

Katz, D., & Kahn, R. L. (1978). *The social psychology of organizations*. New York: Wiley.

Kingsbury, G. G. (1990). Adapting adaptive testing with the MicroCAT testing system. *Educational Measurement, 9*, 3–6, 29.

Klimoski, R. J. (1993). Predictor constructs and their measurement. In N. Schmitt & W. C. Borman (Eds.), *Personnel selection in organizations* (pp. 71–98). San Francisco: Jossey-Bass.

Klimoski, R. J., & Brickner, M. (1987). Why do assessment centers work? Puzzle of assessment center validity. *Personnel Psychology, 40*, 243–260.

Klimoski, R. J., & Donahue, L. M. (1997). HR Strategies for integrating individuals with disabilities into the workplace. *Human Resources Management Review, 7*(1), 109–138.

Klimoski, R. J., & Palmer, S. N. (1994). Psychometric testing and reasonable accommodation for persons with disabilities. In S. M. Bruyere & J. O'Keeffe (Eds.), *Implications of the Americans with Disabilities Act for psychology* (pp. 37–83). Washington, DC: American Psychological Association.

Klimoski, R. J., & Zukin, L. B. (1998). Selection and staffing for team effectiveness. In E. Sundstrom (Ed.), *Supporting work team effectiveness* (pp. 63–94). San Francisco: Jossey-Bass.

Landy, F. J. (1976). The validity of the interview in police officer selection. *Journal of Applied Psychology, 61*, 193–198.

Landy, F. J. (1989). *The psychology of work behavior* (4th ed.). Pacific Grove, CA: Brooks/Cole.

Landy, F. J. (1991, August). *Hugo Musterberg: Victim, visionary or voyeur*. Paper presented at the Society for Industrial Organizational Psychology, St. Louis, MO.

Lawler, E. E. (1990). *Strategic pay*. San Francisco: Jossey-Bass.

Lawshe, C. H. (1959). Of management and measurement. *American Psychologist, 14*, 290–294.

Ledford, G. E., Lawler, E. E., & Mohrman, S. A. (1995). Reward innovations in fortune 1000 companies. *Compensation and Benefits Review, 27*, 76–80.

Linowes, D. F., & Spencer, R. C. (1996). Privacy I the workplace in perspective. *Human Resources Management Review, 613*, 165–181.

Mael, F., & Hirsch, A. (1993). Rainforest empiricism and quasi-rationality: Two approaches to objective biodata. *Personnel Psychology, 46*, 719–738.

McDaniel, M. A., Schmidt, F. L., & Hunter, J. E. (1988). A meta-analysis of the validity of methods for rating training and experience in personnel selection. *Personnel Psychology, 41*, 283–314.

McDougal, W. (1908). *An introduction to social psychology*. London: Methaen.

McFarland, L. A., & Ryan, A. M. (2000). Variance in faking across noncognitive measures. *Journal of Applied Psychology, 85*, 812–821.

McHenry, J. J., Hough, L. M., Toquam, J. L., Hanson, M. A., & Ashworth, S. (1990). Project A validity results: The relationship between predictors and criterion domains. *Personnel Psychology, 43*, 335–354.

Motowidlo, S. J., Borman, W. C., & Schmit, M. J. (1997). A theory of individual differences in task and contextual performance. *Human Performance, 10*, 71–83.

Motowidlo, S. J., & Van Scotter, J. R. (1994). Evidence that task performance should be distinguished from contextual performance. *Journal of Applied Psychology, 79,* 475–480.

Mount, M. K., & Barrick, M. R. (1995). The Big Five personality dimensions: Implications for research and practice in human resources management. *Research in Personnel and Human Resources Management, 13,* 153–200.

Mount, M. K., Barrick, M. R., & Stewart, G. L. (1998). Five-factor model of personality and performance in jobs involving interpersonal interactions. *Human Performance, 11,* 145–165.

Mowday, R. T., Steers, R. M., & Porter, L. W. (1979). The measurement of organizational commitment. *Journal of Vocational Behavior, 14,* 224–247.

Mumford, M. D., Costanza, D. P., Connelly, M. S., & Johnson, J. F. (1996). Item generation procedures and background data scales: Implications for construct and criterion-related validity. *Personnel Psychology, 49,* 361–398.

Murphy, K. R. (1996). Individual differences and behavior in organizations: Much more than g. In K. R. Murphy (Ed.), *Individual differences in behavior in organizations* (pp. 3–30). San Francisco: Jossey-Bass.

Murphy, K. R., & Cleveland, J. N. (1995). *Understanding performance appraisal: Social, organizational, and goal-based perspectives.* Thousand Oaks, CA: Sage.

Murray, B., & Gerhart, B. (1998). An empirical analysis of a skill-based pay program and plant performance outcomes. *Academy of Management Journal, 41,* 68–78.

Munsterberg, H. L. (1913). *Psychology and industrial efficiency.* Boston: Houghton-Mifflln.

Noe, R. A., & Schmitt, N. (1986). The influence of trainee attitudes on training effectiveness: Test of a model. *Personnel Psychology, 39,* 497–523.

Ones, D. S., & Viswesvaran, C. (1998a). Gender, age and race differences in overt integrity tests: Results across four large-scale job applicant data sets. *Journal of Applied Psychology, 83,* 35–42.

Ones, D. S., & Viswesvaran, C. (1998b). The effects of social desirability and faking on personality and integrity assessment for personnel selection. *Human Performance, 11,* 245–269.

Ones, D. S., Viswesvaran, C., & Reiss, A. D. (1996). Role of social desirability in personality testing for personnel selection: The red herring. *Journal of Applied Psychology, 81,* 660–679.

Ones, D. S., Viswesvaran, C., & Schmidt, F. L. (1993). Comprehensive meta-analysis of integrity test validities: Findings and implications for personnel selection and theories of job performance. *Journal of Applied Psychology, 78,* 679–703.

Organ, D., & Ryan, K. (1995). A meta-analytic review of the attitudinal and dispositional predictors of organizational citizenship behavior. *Personnel Psychology, 48,* 775–802.

Owens, W. A., & Schoenfeldt, L. F. (1979). Toward a classification of persons. *Journal of Applied Psychology, 65,* 569–607.

Personnel Decisions International Corporation. (1991). *The profiler.* Minneapolis, MN: Author.

Peterson, N. G., Mumford, M. D., Borman, W. C., Jeanneret, P. R., & Fleishman, E. A. (1995). *Development of Prototype Occupational Information Network (O*NET).* (Vols. 1–2). Salt Lake City: Utah Department of Employment Security.

Peterson, N. G., Mumford, M. D., Borman, W. C., Jeanneret, P. R., & Fleishman, E. A. (1999). *An occupational information system for the 21st century: The development of the O*Net.* Washington, DC: American Psychological Association.

Ree, M. J., & Earles, J. A. (1992). Intelligence is the best predictor of job performance. *Current Directions in Psychological Science, 1,* 86–89.

Ryan, A. M., Ployhart, R. E., & Friedel, L. A. (1998). Using personality testing to reduce adverse impact: A cautionary note. *Journal of Applied Psychology, 83,* 298–307.

Ryan, A. M., & Sackett, P. R. (1987). A survey of individual assessment practices by I/O psychologists. *Personnel Psychology, 40,* 455–488.

Rynes, S. L., & Barber, A. E. (1990). Applicant attraction strategies: An organizational perspective. *Academy of Management Review, 15,* 286–310.

Sackett, P. R., Burris, L. R., & Callahan, C. (1989). Integrity testing for personnel selection. *Personnel Psychology, 42,* 491–529.

Sackett, P. R., & Harris, M. M. (1984). Honesty testing for personnel selection: A review and critique. *Personnel Psychology, 37,* 221–245.

Saks, A. M., Schmitt, N. W., & Klimoski, R. J. (2000). *Research, measurement and evaluation of human resources.* Scarborough, Ontario: Thompson Learning.

Saucier, G. (1994). Mini-markers: A brief version of Goldberg's unipolar Big-five markers. *Journal of Personality Assessment, 63,* 506–516.

Schippmann, J. S., Asch, R. A., Battista, M., Carr, L., Eyde, L., Hesketh, B., Kehoe, J., Pearlman, K., Prien, E. P., & Sanchez, J. I. (2000). The practice of competency modeling. *Personnel Psychology, 53,* 703–740.

Schmidt, F. L., & Hunter, J. E. (1977). Development of a general solution to the problem of validity generalization. *Journal of Applied Psychology, 62,* 529–540.

Schmidt, F. L., & Hunter, J. E. (1998). The validity and utility of selection methods in personnel psychology: Practical and theoretical implications of 85 years of research findings. *Psychological Bulletin, 2,* 262–274.

Schmidt, F. L., Hunter, J. E., & Outerbridge, A. N. (1986). The impact of job experience and ability on job knowledge, work sample performance, and supervisory ratings of job performance. *Journal of Applied Psychology, 71,* 432–439.

Schmidt, F. L., Law, K., Hunter, J. E., Rothstein, H. R., Pearliman, K., & McDaniel, M. (1993). Refinements in validity generalization methods: Implications for the situational specificity hypothesis. *Journal of Applied Psychology, 78,* 3–13.

Schmitt, N. (1997, April). *Panel discussion: Police selection in Nassau County.* Presentation at the annual conference of the

Society for Industrial and Organizational Psychology, St. Louis, MI.

Schmitt, N., & Klimoski, R. J. (1991). *Research methods for human resources management*. Cincinnati, OH: South Western Publishers.

Schmitt, N., & Landy, F. J. (1993). The concept of validity. In N. Schmitt & W. C. Borman (Eds.), *Personnel selection in organizations* (pp. 275–309). San Francisco: Jossey-Bass.

Schneider, B., & Schneider, J. L. (1994). Biodata: An organizational focus. In G. S. Stokes & M. D. Mumford (Eds.), *Biodata handbook: Theory, research, and use of biographical information in selection and performance prediction* (pp. 423–450). Palo Alto, CA: CPP Books.

Smith, P. C., Kendall, L. M., & Hulin, C. L. (1969). *The measurement of satisfaction in work and retirement: A strategy for the study of attitudes*. Chicago: Rand-McNally.

Snell, A. F., Stokes, G. S., Sands, M. M., & McBride, J. R. (1994). Adolescent life experiences as predictors of occupational attainment. *Journal of Applied Psychology, 79,* 131–141.

Snyder, M., & Ickes, W. (1985). Personality and social behavior. In G. Lindzey & E. Aronson (Eds.), *Handbook of social psychology* (3rd ed., pp. 883–948). New York: Random House.

Spencer, L. M., & Spencer, S. M. (1993). *Competence at work: Models for superior performance*. New York: Wiley.

Sternberg, R. J., & Wagner, R. K. (1993). The g-ocentric view of intelligence and performance is wrong. *Current Directions in Psychological Science, 2,* 1–5.

Stevens, M. J., & Campion, M. A. (1994). The knowledge, skill, and ability requirements for teamwork: Implications for human resource management. *Journal of Management, 20,* 503–530.

Sundstrom, E. D. (1998). *Supporting work team effectiveness: Best management practices for fostering high performance.* San Francisco: Jossey-Bass.

Suro, R. (2000, October 16). Captains' Exodus has army fearing for future. *Washington Post,* p. A2.

Terman, L. M. (1917). A trial of mental and pedagogical tests in a civil service examination for policemen and firemen. *Journal of Applied Psychology, 1,* 17–29.

Thorndike, E. L. (1920). Equality in difficulty of alternative intelligence examinations. *Journal of Applied Psychology, 4,* 283–288.

United States Department of Labor. (1999). *Testing and assessment: An employers guide to good practices.*

Walsh, E. (2001, January 18). GAO says lax management hurts federal work force. *Washington Post,* p. A19.

Wonderlic Personnel Test. (1992). *Wonderlic Personnel Test user's manual.* Libertyville, IL: Author.

Worthington, E. L., & Dolliver, R. H. (1977). Validity studies of the Strong vocational interest inventories. *Journal of Counseling Psychology, 24,* 208–216.

Zaccaro, S. J., Gilbert, J. A., Thor, K. K., & Mumford, M. D. (1991). Leadership and social intelligence: Linking social perceptiveness and behavioral flexibility to leader effectiveness. *Leadership Quarterly, 2,* 317–342.

CHAPTER 15

Psychological Assessment in Forensic Settings

JAMES R. P. OGLOFF AND KEVIN S. DOUGLAS

On the cusp of the new millennium, the American Academy of Forensic Psychology and the American Psychology Law Society/Division 41 of the American Psychological Association (APA) prepared a petition to have forensic psychology recognized as a specialty area (Heilbrun, Bank, Follingstad, & Frederick, 2000). At the meeting of the APA Council of Representatives in August, 2001, the council voted to recognize Forensic Psychology as a specialty area of psychology. Although this recognition is timely, psychology's first entrance to the courts occurred in the early 1900s (Ogloff, 2000). At that time, expert witnesses in psychology appeared in court in their capacity as experimental rather than clinical psychologists (Ogloff, Tomkins, & Bersoff, 1996). This is because clinical psychology as a discipline did not exist at that time. In the 1940s, following the end of World War II, there was an enormous growth in clinical psychology (Ogloff et al., 1996). It was then that clinical psychologists began to make their way into the courts.

Although clinical psychologists gave evidence sporadically in cases in the United States as early as the 1940s (e.g., *People v. Hawthorne,* 1940), it was in 1962 that the U.S. Court of Appeals for the District of Columbia clearly recognized clinical psychologists as experts in courts. In *Jenkins v. U.S.,* the trial court judge instructed the jury to disregard a psychologist's testimony, holding that psychologists were not qualified to diagnose mental illness. The U.S. Court of Appeals, sitting en banc, held that a psychologist's lack of medical training could not, in and of itself, be used to justify an automatic disqualification of psychological testimony. Instead, it asserted that consideration of whether a psychologist could testify required the court to look at the knowledge and experience of a particular witness and the probative value of his or her opinion.

Following *Jenkins,* courts around the United States began to recognize clinical psychologists as expert witnesses in a variety of cases (Ogloff et at., 1996; Melton, Petrila, Poythress, & Slobogin, 1997). Although the road to recognition was long and often bumpy, psychologists are now generally seen by the courts and others in the legal system as competent, independent mental health professionals (Melton et al., 1997).

As psychologists were recognized as experts by the courts, the field of forensic psychology emerged. The development of forensic psychology included the emergence of doctoral training programs in forensic psychology, as well as numerous journals and professional associations (Grisso, 1987, 1991; Ogloff, 1990, 2000; Ogloff et al., 1996; Otto & Heilbrun, 2002; Otto, Heilbrun, & Grisso, 1990). By 1987, Melton (1987) wrote that law and psychology—and forensic psychology—was "psychology's growth industry" (p. 681). Although it was written some 15 years ago, Melton's prognostication has been realized.

Driven largely by the inherent challenge in the work, and partly out of economic necessity due to factors like managed health care, increasingly more psychologists find themselves conducting forensic assessments (see Otto & Heilbrun, 2002, for a review of many important developments that have occurred in forensic psychology since the 1980s).

The term *forensic* in forensic psychology and, in particular, forensic psychological assessments implies that these tools will be employed in the legal system. Given its very serious nature, many unique issues arise in clinical forensic work (Ogloff, 1999a). A review of the field of forensic psychology, or the many issues that arise in forensic assessments, is beyond the scope of this chapter. Many of the issues that we discuss in this chapter are covered in a more general context in volume 11 of this series, a volume dedicated entirely to forensic psychology. However, due to the growth of forensic psychology, and because of the large number of mainstream clinical psychologists who are conducting forensic assessment, we shall provide some foundational information about forensic psychology and highlight some of the contemporary issues that exist in this field. Finally, we shall also look to the future to identify possible issues that will arise.

By way of background, we shall define forensic psychology and discuss where forensic psychology fits within clinical psychology. We shall also note the interface between forensic psychology and law and outline criminal and civil topics addressed by forensic psychologists. Because forensic assessments are grounded in law, it is important to review the legal contours of forensic assessments as well as the legal admissibility of forensic assessments into evidence.

Among the contemporary issues in forensic psychological assessments that will be reviewed in this chapter are clinical versus actuarial prediction models in assessments of risk for violence, the legally informed practitioner model, the roles and limits of general psychological testing in forensic contexts, legal specificity, and training and credentialing in forensic psychology.

DEFINING CLINICAL FORENSIC PSYCHOLOGY

Historically, forensic psychology has evolved as a broad field that includes any application of psychology to the legal field (Brigham, 1999; Ogloff, 2000). This broad construal of the field includes everything from psychological research into legal matters such as eyewitness memory or jury decision-making to applied clinical areas including psychological assessment of defendants for court. For the purposes of this chapter, we shall rely on a narrower definition: "Forensic psychology will be defined as the professional practice by psychologists within the areas of clinical psychology, counseling psychology, neuropsychology, and school psychology, when they are engaged regularly as experts and represent themselves as such, in an activity primarily intended to provide professional psychological expertise to the legal system" (Heilbrun et al., 2000). Although it is still broad, this working definition focuses on the applied clinical aspects of forensic psychology. Therefore, the definition does not include the work done by experimental psychologists who work in the field of psychology and law. Because we are discussing forensic assessment, the definition focuses on assessments conducted by professional psychologists for the courts, or for the legal system more broadly construed. This definition does not encompass the practice of those neuropsychologists or clinical, counseling, or school psychologists whose work only occasionally makes its way into the legal system.

Where Forensic Psychology Fits Within Clinical Psychology

Generally speaking, forensic assessments can be construed as specialized clinical psychological assessments (Melton et al., 1997; Otto & Heilbrun, 2002). As such, forensic assessments build upon the foundational training, knowledge, and experience of clinical psychology. Given the range and depth of specialized knowledge in forensic psychology, however, we must emphasize that a significant degree of expertise is required to competently conduct forensic assessments (Ogloff, 1999a). Others have noted, correctly, that forensic evaluations that were conducted by psychologists in the past did not differ from general clinical assessments (Grisso, 1987; Heilbrun, Rogers, & Otto, 2002). As the field of forensic psychology has evolved over the past 20 years, though, the methods, instruments, and general skills of forensic psychologists have emerged as differing significantly from those employed in general clinical assessments (Heilbrun et al., 2002).

The development of forensic psychology as an area of specialization within psychology has been evidenced, for example, by the development of Specialty Guidelines for Forensic Psychologists (Committee on Ethical Guidelines for Forensic Psychologists, 1991), which were promulgated by the American Psychology-Law Society and the American Academy of Forensic Psychology. In addition, with the 1992 version of the Ethical Principles of Psychologists and Code of Conduct, the APA (1992) recognized the need for specific provisions in the code for forensic psychology (see Ethical Standards 7.01–7.06; see Ogloff, 1999a, for a review of the ethical issues in forensic psychology). Moreover, as noted at the outset, the APA Council has recently recognized forensic psychology as a new specialty area within psychology.

Psychological assessments make their way into the courts or the legal system in one of two general ways. First, psychological assessments may be drawn into a legal context unexpectedly. For example, a clinical psychologist may have conducted an assessment on an individual for employment-related purposes. At some point in the future, the assessment could be subpoenaed or otherwise compelled by the court after the individual is in an automobile accident and the assessment is relevant as evidence of premorbid cognitive functioning. Such assessments cannot properly be referred to as forensic assessments because they are completed for some purpose outside the forensic context. Therefore, the psychologist conducting the assessments would not be held to the standards of the Specialty Guidelines for Forensic Psychologists. The APA has promulgated two sets of aspirational practice guidelines of particular relevance to forensic psychology. In 1994, the APA adopted the Guidelines for Child Custody Evaluations in Divorce Proceedings (American Psychological Association, 1994). Then, in 1998, the APA adopted the "Guidelines for Psychological Evaluations in Child Protection Matters" (American Psychological Association Committee on Professional Practice and Standards, 1998). Although such guidelines are described as being merely aspirational, courts can look to them to help provide an indication of the standard of practice within the field.

Second, psychological assessments can be ordered by courts or otherwise requested specifically for legal purposes. These assessments—in which the psychologist specifically sets out in an assessment to address some legal question—can be properly referred to as forensic assessments. The psychologist conducting them would be required to adhere to the requirements of the APA Ethical Principles of Psychologists (American Psychological Association, 1992), including those that pertain to forensic psychology. In addition, to the extent that the Specialty Guidelines for Forensic Psychologists (Committee on Ethical Guidelines for Forensic Psychologists, 1991) are seen as establishing a standard of care in forensic psychology, those doing forensic assessments are advised to follow them (Ogloff, 1999a).

The Need for Professional Competence in Forensic Psychology

Regardless of their role, forensic psychologists are still obligated to comply with general ethical guidelines, principles, and standards. For example, the Ethical Principles of Psychologists and Code of Conduct (American Psychological Association, 1992) provide that "psychologists who perform forensic functions, such as assessments, interviews, consultations, reports, or expert testimony, must comply with all other provisions of this Ethics Code to the extent that they apply to such

activities" (APA Standard 7.01). In addition, though, the ethics code further requires that "psychologists base their forensic work on appropriate knowledge of and competence in the areas underlying such work, including specialized knowledge concerning special populations" (APA Standard 7.01).

The Specialty Guidelines "provide an aspirational model of desirable professional practice by psychologists, within any subdiscipline of psychology (e.g., clinical, developmental, social, experimental), when they are engaged regularly as experts and represent themselves as such, in an activity primarily intended to provide professional psychological expertise to the judicial system" (p. 656). Thus, psychologists are obligated to adhere to the standards provided in the Ethical Principles of Psychologists and Code of Conduct (American Psychological Association, 1992), whereas the Specialty Guidelines are aspirational in nature and "do not represent an official statement of the American Psychological Association" (p. 656). Nonetheless, the Specialty Guidelines can be seen as contributing to the establishment of a standard of care in forensic psychology. Canadian readers are referred to the revised Canadian Code of Ethics for Psychologists (Canadian Psychological Association, 2000). Psychologists from other countries or jurisdictions must consult the codes that are relevant in their areas.

Although a review of the ethical principles that govern forensic psychology is not necessary here, it is important to emphasize that those psychologists who conduct forensic assessments are obligated to ensure that they are competent in their work (Ogloff, 1999a). Although this might appear obvious, in our experience it is surprising how many clinical psychologists begin doing forensic assessments without proper training or experience, only to find themselves experiencing difficulties either by virtue of their lack of appropriate experience or by becoming the subject of an ethics complaint. Of course, psychologists are ethically obligated to be professionally competent in any realm in which they work. For example, the APA Ethics Code requires that "psychologists provide services, teach, and conduct research only within the boundaries of their competence, based on their training, supervised experience, or appropriate professional experience" (APA Standard 1.04; see also APA Standard 7.01). Therefore, psychologists who work in the legal arena must have professional competence in forensic psychology generally. Furthermore, if the psychologist engages in psychological services that require more specialized training, the psychologist must also demonstrate professional competence in that area of subspecialty (e.g., assessment and treatment of sexual offenders, forensic neuropsychological assessment).

As noted in the ethics code of the APA (Standard 1.04; see also Specialty Guideline III), generally speaking, professional competence in an area of specialization may be obtained and demonstrated by a combination of education and training, supervised experience by a registered psychologist with expertise in the area of specialization, and reading and research in the area of specialization. There is no clear rule about what constitutes professional competence in any given area; however, if challenged, the psychologist bears the burden of demonstrating his or her competence.

In addition to matters concerning the boundaries of their professional competence, forensic psychologists are obligated to have a fundamental understanding of the legal and professional standards in their area (Specialty Guideline III[C]), and they must understand the legal rights of the parties with whom they come into contact to ensure that they do not unwittingly abrogate those rights (Specialty Guideline III[D]). Although it is certainly not necessary for a forensic psychologist to have a law degree, forensic psychologists are ethically obligated to ensure that they become thoroughly familiar with the law that is relevant to their areas of practice.

The Scope of Forensic Psychological Assessments

Given that every law, no matter how simple or complex, has but one purpose—to control human behavior—it should come as no surprise that the range of topics in which forensic assessments can be requested is broad (Ogloff, 2001). We shall present the major divisions of law here and briefly discuss the topics in which forensic psychologists might be retained to conduct assessments. Most readers will have some familiarity with the general areas of law; therefore, this review will focus on the areas most relevant to forensic psychology. Law is generally divided into several areas defined by the nature of issues that emerge (see Rose, 2001, for a discussion of the divisions of law relevant to forensic psychology; see Melton et al., 1997, for a comprehensive review of these areas that are relevant to forensic psychology). The most common division in law is between criminal law and civil law. Criminal law is an area of law that is considered to be public law because crimes are considered to be acts against the public good. In the United States, for example, when one is charged with committing a crime, the case is referred to as "the people," "the state," or "the commonwealth" against the defendant. In countries within the Commonwealth of Nations, such as Britain, Canada, or Australia, cases are referred to as "the Queen" or "Regina" against the defendant because Queen Elizabeth II is the head of state of nations in the Commonwealth.

Within criminal law, there are many matters regarding which a forensic psychologist could be requested to conduct an assessment. The types of assessment that might be requested include presentence court assessments, pretrial assessments—such as evaluations of competence or fitness to stand trial

and mental state at the time of the offense—sentencing evaluations, and other court-ordered or quasi-legal assessments. In criminal matters, psychologists can be retained by the prosecution, the defense, or, in some cases, the court itself. Criminal matters can involve either adult or juvenile defendants, although the specific legal issues that arise and the relevant legal standards will probably differ between these populations.

Beyond criminal law, there is a large area of law known as civil law. Unlike criminal law, civil law is an area of private law because it has developed to resolve conflicts between private parties or companies. Civil law includes the enforcement of contracts and the resolution of private wrongs between individuals or companies. Such wrongs can include matters such as trespass, personal injury, libel or slander, false imprisonment, conversion, and so on. In such matters, the legal dispute is between two or more people or companies who have turned to the courts to resolve the dispute in a fair and impartial manner. Unlike criminal law, then, civil lawsuits name the two or more parties or companies that are in dispute (e.g., *Jones v. Gonzales*). Forensic assessments can be required in these areas for establishing the extent of personal injury (e.g., cognitive impairment or emotional harm), worker's compensation, capacity to make a will, and other matters.

The final major area of law in which forensic psychologists are routinely called upon to conduct assessments is family law. Family law concerns marriage and divorce, custody of children, division of assets, and financial maintenance for the support of family members (or former family members). Psychologists are retained most commonly to conduct assessments to assist courts in deciding matters like the custody of and access to children or matters related to the apprehension of children from their parents by child protective service agencies. Less frequently, psychologists may be asked to conduct assessments of parties in family disputes for matters such as capacity to marry.

LEGAL PARAMETERS OF FORENSIC ASSESSMENTS

The Legal Contours of Forensic Assessments

The primary purpose of most forensic assessments is to assist legal decision-makers to come to a legal decision. Of course, as reviewed above, there are myriad legal decisions to which forensic psychological assessments may contribute relevant information. The common thread that runs throughout these diverse areas of law and, subsequently, forensic assessment, is that legal decisions must be made. The legal decision-maker may be judicial (e.g., a judge or jury) or quasi-judicial (administrative tribunal) in nature, and the source of authority may arise from statute, quasi-statute (regulations, bylaws), or common law.

Regardless of the nature and source of the legal decision that must be made, there are specific legal criteria that will be the basis for the decision. In a very real sense, the legal criteria may be considered the referral questions that underlie the request for forensic assessment. For example, a statute may require that in order to be found incompetent to stand trial, defendants, due to mental impairment or mental disorder, must be unable to understand the nature of the charges against them, to understand the outcome and implications of the case, or to communicate with and instruct their lawyers. In this case, the psychologist conducting an assessment of competence to stand trial must address each of the legal criteria to provide the court with the information necessary to decide whether the defendant is competent to stand trial. As this example shows, the forensic assessment must be linked to the elements of the law that requires the assessment to be completed.

Like any referral question, then, it is ultimately the legal criteria that the forensic psychological assessment must inform. Given this reality, forensic assessments may be considered inherently legal in nature. In many situations, such assessments are mandated by the same legal source (i.e., statute or regulation) that gives the legal decision-maker jurisdiction to decide the issue. In others, the authority is permissive: For example, litigants may choose to offer expert evidence to the court, although such evidence is not required by statute.

As discussed earlier in this chapter, the legal context of forensic psychological assessment is largely what sets it apart from other types of psychological assessments. The practical implication of this situation is that the law dictates, to a lesser or greater degree depending upon the issue, the areas that must be addressed in a forensic psychological assessment. This places some constraints on the freedom that clinicians have in determining what their assessments should cover. Moreover, assessments that either do not address the legal criteria or stray too far beyond the legal questions being asked are not helpful to the courts. The goal for any forensic assessment is to provide an optimal fit between the legal requirements and the corresponding psychological assessment, such that the findings of the assessment optimally map onto the legal criteria that will guide the decision-maker's conclusions.

For forensic clinicians and researchers to provide legally informed assessments and clinical research, it is necessary for them to be knowledgeable about the law that is relevant to their assessments. As discussed earlier, ethical guidelines from both the APA (1992) and the Canadian Psychological Association (2000) require that psychologists have knowledge of the context in which they practice. For forensic psychologists, this context is the law.

Psycholegal Content Analysis: A Method and an Example

Forensic assessment is advanced through a procedure that may be called *psycholegal content analysis* (Douglas, 2000; Ogloff, Roberts, & Roesch, 1993). Assessment questions are derived from legal standards and requirements, and, to the extent that these legal standards vary, so too may the assessment questions. Further, to the extent that these legal-assessment questions vary, so too *ought* the research corpus vary in order to be responsive to the legal-assessment task. This is especially important according to a scientist-practitioner approach, as will be described below.

A psycholegal content analysis requires the following steps. First, the source of the legal authority governing the forensic assessment question—typically a statute—is identified. Statutory principles or requirements provided by that authority that are relevant for the assessment should then be distilled. If there are other legal mechanisms that expand upon the original legal authority—typically legal cases that interpret the statute—these are analyzed for, again, principles that are relevant to the assessment task. Once these assessment-relevant legal principles are distilled and organized, the psychological knowledge or strategies that map onto these legal principles can be discerned. Concerning assessment-related research, study questions can be devised that inform the assessment questions, which themselves have been informed by assessment-related legal principles. In essence, this method combines traditional legal research with psychological traditions of clinical assessment and empirical study. Here, the clinical assessment procedures and research study questions are informed, shaped, or determined by the legal parameters or principles.

Melton et al. (1997) provide numerous illustrations of how clinical-forensic assessments ought to be informed by prevailing relevant legal standards. They have provided both legal and psychological analysis throughout their comprehensive analysis of psychology's application to law. Their book, *Psychological Evaluations for the Courts* (second edition), discusses the legal context, as well as psychological tasks, for numerous applications of psychology and psychiatry to law (e.g., competence, family law, criminal responsibility, civil commitment, violence prediction). In general, they reasoned that it is essential for forensic tests and assessment measures to inform the specific legal judgment that is called for; tests that were not developed or validated within legal contexts and according to legal principles, they argued, should be used with great caution in forensic assessment arenas. As well, in places they highlight the difficulties for clinical practice posed by varying legal definitions and standards across jurisdictions and settings.

The area of violence risk assessment is illustrative of the parameters set by law on forensic assessment. Melton et al. (1997) point out that "dangerousness," legally, can been satisfied in various settings and jurisdictions by extremely diverse outcome criteria. For instance, harm to property or emotional harm may satisfy criteria in some settings and in some jurisdictions (e.g., involuntary civil commitment), whereas in other settings (e.g., death penalty cases or dangerous offender cases; Heilbrun, Ogloff, & Picarello, 1999) the outcome criterion is serious physical violence. These differing legal criteria have implications for the forensic assessment that is carried out and the research that can be used to support the assessment procedures.

Heilbrun (1997) discussed in some depth how different legal contexts have different implications for the most appropriate clinical and scientific approaches to violence risk assessment. For instance, in some settings, such as involuntary civil commitment, the immediate goal may be to maximize the accuracy of the prediction, whereas in others, such as graduated release of those found not guilty by reason of insanity, the goal may be ongoing management. Clearly, the legal questions that arise under these two legal contexts call for different assessment strategies and, correspondingly, different research strategies to inform the clinical endeavors.

As Heilbrun (1997) explains, clinicians faced with management-related legal questions (e.g., can this person's risk reasonably be managed in the community, and under what circumstances?) may be faced with a somewhat different task if the legal question is more heavily weighted toward pure prediction. Similarly, researchers interested in evaluating risk assessment strategies that pertain to one or the other legal context will probably chose different approaches (e.g., the use of survival analysis with time-dependent covariates in the former case and receiver operating characteristic analysis in the latter).

As previously noted, Heilbrun's (1997) analysis used two legal contexts to illustrate his points (civil commitment and release of insanity acquittees). There are literally dozens of others from which he could have chosen (see, for example, Lyon, Hart, & Webster, 2001; Shah, 1978). An additional level of complexity is introduced when one makes cross-jurisdictional comparisons of legal context on top of such legally substantive comparisons. For instance, does the legal setting for civil commitment in, say, California, mirror that in Florida? How similar is either of these to the regimes in the Canadian provinces of Ontario or British Columbia? Douglas and Koch (2001) have described how the statutory criteria for involuntary civil

commitment vary tremendously across Canadian jurisdictions alone in terms of risk-relevant requirements. In turn, this means that the nature of forensic assessment of violence risk across these jurisdictions will also vary. In the United States, there are 50 states across which statutory and case law requirements for civil commitment may vary.

The main points to be taken from this discussion are that (a) the law either shapes or sets the parameters of forensic assessment, and (b) both clinical-forensic assessment and assessment-related research need to be informed by the differing legal requirements that bear upon an assessment question (e.g., violence risk assessment), with respect to both different legal areas (e.g., civil commitment versus release of insanity acquittees) and different legal jurisdictions.

The Admissibility of Forensic Assessments Into Evidence

Although a comprehensive review of the admissibility of psychological evidence is beyond the scope of this chapter, it is important to highlight the relevant legal criteria that courts consider when deciding whether the evidence of a psychologist will be admissible as expert opinion evidence. The specific rules of evidence vary across states and in federal court. Although the Federal Rules of Evidence (FRE) is federal law, many states have incorporated at least some portion of the FRE into their evidence legislation. As with any law that relates to their work, readers should determine the specific local laws that are relevant to the admissibility of expert testimony. In interpreting the FRE, we will take note of *Daubert v. Merrell Dow Pharmaceuticals, Inc.* (1993) and *Kuhmo Tire Co. v. Carmichael* (1999), two of the United States Supreme Court decisions that have considered the standard of acceptance for the admission of scientific evidence.

To be admissible, the psychological evidence must first be found by the court to be relevant. That means that the information provided by the psychological assessment must be related to some matter at issue in the case. Second, the court must be assured that the probative value of the psychologist's evidence is not outweighed by its prejudicial value. This means that the value of the expert's testimony will not be unduly outweighed by the expert's influence on the jury.

After the court has determined whether the expert testimony is relevant and that its probative weight outweighs its prejudicial value, the court can turn to a direct review of the expert testimony itself. The relevant provisions of the FRE governing expert testimony include FRE 702 (testimony by experts), FRE 703 (basis of opinion testimony by experts), FRE 704 (opinion on ultimate issue), and FRE 705 (disclosure of facts or data underlying expert opinion).

For expert testimony to be admissible under FRE 702, three requirements must be satisfied: (a) the judge or jury must require the assistance of the expert's testimony; (b) the expert must be qualified to offer an opinion; and (c) if the expert relies on scientific facts or data, the facts or data must be "reasonably relied upon by experts in [the] particular field." In addition, FRE 702 specifies that the expert's testimony may be in the form of an opinion. Unlike all other witnesses who give evidence in trials, only experts are permitted to state their opinions about matters at issue in the case. Other witnesses must only report fact-based information—that is, information about which they have first-hand knowledge (i.e., what they have seen or heard). Due to their expertise and the fact that their evidence is required to assist the judge or jury, experts are permitted to provide both fact-based information and opinion evidence.

Considerable controversy has surrounded the question of how a court determines whether the information presented by experts was "reasonably relied upon by experts in [the] particular field." Prior to the adoption of the FRE, and in some states even following their adoption, courts relied on the *Frye* Test (*Frye v. U.S.,* 1923) to determine whether the scientific evidence on which expert testimony is based should be admitted into evidence at trial. To satisfy the *Frye* Test, an expert witness who offered opinion evidence had to demonstrate not only that the methods relied upon are generally accepted, but that they are used in the relevant areas of the expert's area of expertise and that the techniques he or she employed comported with the state of the art in the field.

The *Frye* Test enjoyed widespread use and endorsement by federal and state courts until Congress adopted the FRE in 1976. From that time, considerable controversy arose regarding the extent to which the test for the admissibility of novel scientific evidence in *Frye* remained applicable, with different courts arriving at different conclusions. In 1993, the U.S. Supreme Court resolved the controversy by holding in *Daubert v. Merrell Dow Pharmaceuticals* (1993) that the *Frye* Test's general acceptance requirement "is not a necessary precondition to the admissibility of scientific evidence under the Federal Rules of Evidence" (p. 597). In *Daubert* (1993), two infants and their parents brought a lawsuit against a pharmaceutical company, arguing that the mothers' prenatal ingestion of the drug Bendectin caused serious birth defects in the infants. During the trial, the testimony of an expert concluded that the corpus of scientific test results on the drug did not show that it was a significant risk factor for birth defects. As a result, the trial court decided in favor of the drug company. On appeal, the U.S. Court of Appeal for the Ninth Circuit relied on the *Frye* Test and affirmed the lower court's decision. In overruling the decision, the U.S. Supreme Court held that nothing in the FRE incorporated *Frye*'s general acceptance rule and that "a rigid 'general acceptance' requirement would be at odds with the 'liberal thrust' of the Federal Rules and their

'general approach of relaxing the traditional barriers to 'opinion' testimony" (p. 588).

Some states still employ the *Frye* Test to ensure that the expert testimony is based on principles that are generally accepted by the field in which it is offered. Other jurisdictions have adopted the approach set out in *Daubert.* As with other points of law, psychologists should acquaint themselves with the standard of the admissibility of expert evidence that is in force in their jurisdiction.

In footnote 11 of their decision, the Supreme Court in *Daubert* provided further guidance that an assessment of scientific knowledge, as is mentioned in FRE 702, "entails a preliminary assessment of whether the reasoning or methodology underlying the testimony is scientifically valid" (p. 592). In addition, the court noted that scientific validity asks the question "does the principle support what it purports to show?" (p. 590). Finally, in 1999, the United States Supreme Court explicitly expanded its ruling in *Daubert* to federal judges' consideration of all expert evidence (*Kuhmo Tire Co. v. Carmichael,* 1999).

Once the court has ensured that the techniques on which the proposed expert testimony is based are valid, the court must decide whether the proposed witness is qualified as an expert in the area in question (FRE 702). A witness may qualify as an expert based on his or her training or education, knowledge, skill, or experience. Typically, it is not difficult for psychologists to qualify as experts, providing that they demonstrate sufficient training and knowledge about techniques that are employed in a particular area.

The final FRE specifically governing the admissibility of expert testimony involves the expert's opinion on the ultimate issue (FRE 704). Ultimate-issue opinions directly address the legal question being asked (e.g., whether the deceased was competent to make a will, or whether the deceased died as the result of an accident or committed suicide). Authorities from the legal and mental health disciplines have debated whether experts should offer opinions that are similar, or parallel, to the ultimate legal issue (Melton et al., 1997). Regardless of this debate, FRE 704 provides that "testimony in the form of an opinion or inference otherwise admissible is not objectionable because it embraces an ultimate issue to be decided by the trier of fact." There is one major exception to allowing expert testimony on ultimate-issue testimony. In 1984, Congress amended FRE 704(b) in response to the verdict in the case *United States v. Hinckley* (1981) in which the would-be assassin of President Reagan was found not guilty by reason of insanity. The amendment precludes experts in a criminal case from testifying whether they believe the defendant had the mental state or condition required to satisfy an element of the crime or a defense to the crime. This section remains in force despite the U.S. Supreme Court's decisions in *Daubert v. Merrell Dow Pharmaceuticals* (1993) and *Kuhmo Tire Co. v. Carmichael* (1999).

In summary, to be admissible, expert psychological testimony must be relevant to the issues in the case, and its probative value must outweigh its prejudicial impact. If these two general requirements are met, expert psychological testimony will be admissible if it can be demonstrated that (a) an issue at question is beyond the understanding of the judge or jury and the decision reached by the judge or jury would benefit as the result of special expertise, (b) the technique or methods employed in the assessment are accepted by the field, and (c) the proffered witness has expertise with respect to the question at issue. Additionally, the FRE allow experts to base their testimony on their observations (in and out of court) or information introduced outside of court. Experts need only reveal the underlying sources for their opinion if requested to do so upon cross-examination. Finally, the psychologist must be aware of the standard for the admissibility of expert opinion evidence that is employed in the jurisdiction in which he or she practices psychology.

CONTEMPORARY ISSUES IN FORENSIC ASSESSMENT

Clinical Versus Actuarial Predictions Revisited

The clinical-actuarial prediction debate has a long and heated history in the fields of clinical, counseling, educational, industrial/organizational, military, and other branches of psychology. Although it is addressed in Garb's chapter in this volume, we will discuss its manifestation within forensic assessment, in part because it has some unique aspects in this field and in part because it remains the topic of lively debate in some areas of forensic assessment. We will use the area of violence risk assessment to illustrate our points.

There is little doubt that actuarial prediction tends to outperform unstructured clinical prediction in terms of validity indices. Of course, the early work of Meehl (1954) and his more recent work with colleagues (Grove & Meehl, 1996; Grove, Zald, Lebow, Snitz, & Nelson, 2000) has supported this position consistently. In the field of violence risk assessment, the debate continues with respect to *violence risk assessment instruments*. Some instruments adopt pure actuarial decision-making procedures, citing Meehl's and colleagues' work in their support (e.g., see Quinsey, Harris, Rice, & Cormier, 1998). Other instruments are developed that require *structured clinical decision-making* (see, e.g., Webster, Douglas, Eaves, & Hart, 1997). More recently, Douglas and Ogloff (2001) have proposed the structured professional judgment approach to

clinical decision-making in violence risk assessment (see also Douglas & Webster, 1999).

In the latter case, there is warranted concession that unstructured clinical opinion that "relies on an informal, 'in the head,' impressionistic, subjective conclusion, reached (somehow) by a human clinical judge" (Grove & Meehl, 1996, p. 294) has little evidence, empirical or conceptual, to support its use. However, some commentators have argued that a *structured* approach to risk assessment can perhaps overcome some of the weaknesses (i.e., low interrater reliability and validity) inherent in the impressionistic nature of global clinical opinion (Douglas, Cox, & Webster, 1999; Hart, 1998). Further, as Hart (1998) describes, particularly in the field of risk assessment, the clinical task is much broader than prediction, including issues related to prevention and management of violence risk. For this reason, the clinical task has come to be called, in recent times, violence risk assessment, rather than violence prediction per se.

The argument is that structured clinical assessment can achieve a more individualized and comprehensive assessment than can actuarial prediction, while still achieving a respectable level of interrater reliability and validity. Furthermore, instruments that adopt structured professional judgment procedures tend to have been developed rationally or analytically, rather than empirically. In theory, this method of developing the instruments should enhance their generalizability to the numerous contexts in which risk assessment is required and minimize the problems of validity shrinkage inherent in the application of empirically derived actuarial instruments to novel settings or purposes.

Research on three such violence risk assessment measures has supported the predictive validity of the clinical opinions that they call for. In a recent study, Douglas and Ogloff (2001) tested the interrater reliability and predictive validity of violence risk judgments made with the HCR-20 violence risk assessment scheme (Webster et al., 1997). Like all structured professional judgment risk measures, the HCR-20 is an analytically or logically developed guide intended to structure professional decisions about violence risk through encouraging the consideration of 20 key violence risk factors dispersed across three scales: historical (H), clinical (C), and risk management (R). The risk factors identified by the HCR-20 have been found in the literature to relate to an individual's likelihood to engage in violent criminal behavior. The H scale focuses on past, mainly static risk factors, the C on current aspects of mental status and attitudes, and the R on future situational features. Using a sample of 100 forensic psychiatric patients, Douglas and Ogloff (2001) found that the interrater reliability of structured professional judgments regarding the patients' risk for violence risk was good or substantial.

Violence risk judgments were also found to be significantly predictive of postrelease community violence. A direct comparison of the structured professional judgment approach and an actuarial approach, both using the HCR-20, showed that the structured professional violence judgments added incremental validity to the HCR-20 scored actuarially. These results showed that clinical judgment, if made within a structured context, can contribute in meaningful ways to the clinical practice of violence risk assessment.

Similar results have been found for two additional violence risk instruments. Investigating the predictive validity of the SVR-20 (Boer, Hart, Kropp, & Webster, 1997), Dempster (1998) completed the SVR-20 on a sample of 95 sentenced sexual offenders. The SVR-20, modeled on the HCR-20, provides a list of the factors that have been found to predict risk for sexual offending and sexual violence. Dempster (1998) compared the summed total of items (i.e., actuarial prediction) and the ratings of high, medium, and low risk (i.e., structured professional judgment). She found that the structured professional judgment approach provided incremental validity over the scored items on the scales of sexual violence risk. Finally, Kropp and Hart (2000) evaluated the structured clinical judgments produced by the Spousal Assault Risk Assessment guide (SARA; Kropp, Hart, Webster, & Eaves, 1999), a further example of the structured professional judgment model of risk assessment. Kropp and Hart (2000) used a sample of 102 male probationers who had been convicted of offenses involving spousal assault and referred by the courts to attend domestic violence treatment. Kropp and Hart (2000) found that structured professional judgments based on the SARA summary risk ratings of low, moderate, and high risk outperformed the summation of SARA items (actuarial prediction) in terms of their respective relationships to spousal assault recidivism. Kropp and Hart also reported good interrater reliability indexes for the final risk judgments.

Taken together, research investigating the structured professional judgment based on the HCR-20, the SVR-20, and the SARA supports both the interrater reliability and predictive validity of the instruments. There is some emerging support, therefore, for the supposition that a structured professional judgment approach to violence risk assessment, if carried out in a structured, operationalized, and measurable manner, can be reliable and valid, as well as potentially more comprehensive and responsive to idiographic concerns than is actuarial prediction.

Legally Informed Practitioner Model

As is well known, clinical psychology adopted the scientist-practitioner "Boulder" model of training and practice over a half-century ago. This model of practice does have its critics, and it is a persisting source of professional disagreement and argument to this day (Beutler, Williams, Wakefield, & Entwistle, 1995; Fensterheim & Raw, 1996; Goldfried & Wolfe, 1996; Hayes, 1996; Kanfer, 1990; Nezu, 1996; Singer, 1990; Sobell, 1996; Stricker, 1992; Stricker & Trierweiler, 1995; Webster & Cox, 1997). The details of this debate cannot be addressed adequately in this chapter, but it is an operating assumption of this chapter that the scientist-practitioner model remains the theoretical cornerstone of doctoral training in clinical psychology. Consequently, clinical-forensic psychology, as a subfield of clinical psychology more broadly, subscribes to its tenets. Therefore, forensic assessment, as a particular activity within clinical-forensic psychology, also rests upon the scientist-practitioner model. Although we favor the scientist-practitioner model as the choice for those who conduct forensic assessments, we should note that we recognize at the outset that those trained in the scholar-practitioner tradition can become competent forensic psychologists.

Both scientist-practitioner and scholar-practitioner doctoral training programs require students to obtain systematic training and supervised experience in psychological assessment and psychological intervention. Training programs subscribing to the scientist-practitioner model, typically leading to the PhD degree, require students to complete a doctoral thesis or dissertation consisting of an empirical research project. By contrast, training programs based on the scholar-practitioner model that lead to the PsyD degree do not require students to complete empirical research. Instead, these programs require that students obtain expertise in reading, interpreting, and critically analyzing empirical research. Our emphasis here is that, particularly due to the inherently technical nature of forensic assessments, a strong background in experimental methods is an asset to those who conduct forensic assessments. Therefore, rather than focusing on the particular doctoral degree a psychologist has, consideration of a psychologist's suitability for practicing forensic psychology should be based on the individual's ability to understand the empirical research and to incorporate it into his or her work.

There are some modifications to and limitations of the scientist-practitioner and scholar-practitioner models in forensic assessment. First, the models must be conceptualized to be situated within a legal context. In essence, this makes the optimal model of training and practice in forensic psychology a legally informed scientist or scholar-practitioner model. This reality has implications for the meaning of the science employed in clinical-forensic psychology. Some of these implications are similar to the issues discussed with respect to the psycholegal content analysis presented earlier. That is, we discussed how practice must be conducted to inform legal criteria.

Similarly, if science is to inform clinical decision-making, it too must find some inspiration within the law. In other fields of psychology, a scientist's questions may be limited only by his or her imagination. In forensic psychology, there is an overriding limiting factor: the law and the legal standards that can be derived from the particular legal question being asked in an assessment. This is not to say that all forensic psychological science must always line up exactly with legal issues. We would not advocate constraining scientific inquiry in such a manner. In fact, there is abundant nonforensic, primary research that is very applicable and of great benefit to the forensic field. For instance, research on the effects of trauma, on violence, and on major mental disorders is of import to forensic psychological science and practice. However, it is imperative that, in addition to maximizing the utility of this research as it pertains to forensic assessment, researchers *also* design studies that map as closely as possible onto quite strict legal criteria or standards. This necessity explains the existence, for example, of research on the psychometric properties of competence measures whose items are defined largely by the legal definition of incompetence in the particular setting (e.g., incompetence to stand trial, incompetence to manage one's estate or affairs) and jurisdiction.

In some ways, this type of research has an additional evaluative component as part of the validation procedure. Content and construct-related validities must take into account legal definitions and outcome criteria that are meant to be represented in the measure. If a measure of competence, for instance, does not tap a major facet of the legal construct (e.g., ability to instruct counsel), then its validity is questionable in this regard, despite the possible existence of otherwise excellent psychometric properties.

In addition to the regular components of the scientist-practitioner model, then, there is an additional, and sometimes superordinate, layer. Consequently, not only must research be carried out that is clinically meaningful and informative, and not only must clinical practice reciprocate by relying upon this research as much as is reasonable, but both science *and* practice must also follow the lead of the law. It is likely that clinical practice has less flexibility than does science to stray from legal standards. All forensic practice, and much forensic research, however, must be mindful of the law.

Several further aspects of the legally informed practitioner model need explanation. First, the addition of the law to the models of clinical training imposes an inherent limitation on their theoretical utility and, perhaps, on the accumulation of clinical-scientific knowledge that gathers under it. Tomorrow, a high-level court could decide that, for example, all pieces of civil commitment legislation of a certain ilk are unconstitutional and in need of drastic revision. What happens to the established base of science and practice that developed to assist decision-makers in this context? Research and practice must

evolve alongside evolutions in the law. Research can become dated and clinical practice antiquated not only through the passage of time, but through the passage of law.

A further limitation of the legally informed practitioner model within the forensic context involves the limitations placed on research methodology. Certain important issues can never be studied in an ideal methodological manner because of the pragmatic constraints of the law. For instance, nearly all research on violence risk assessment, the prediction of violence, and correlates of violence has been carried out on truncated research samples. That is, certain persons will never be included in research samples simply because they will never or only rarely be released from prisons or other institutions. Risk assessment studies that attempt to study postrelease community violence are forced to use only persons who have been actually released. However, when the clinical task of risk assessment is undertaken, this research is applied to all persons appearing for release.

Another example of a methodological shortcoming is the absence of gold standards for validation. For instance, research on criminal competencies is undertaken to maximize the utility of clinical determinations of competence. There is no inherent gold standard of comparison to validate the decisions that competence instruments yield. If an instrument yields a decision of competence, but a judge declares the petitioner incompetent, this does not mean that the instrument was wrong. Rather, the judge may not have understood the psychological and clinical aspects that were entered into evidence in support of the petitioner's motion for a finding of incompetence. Although these instruments do use judicial decisions as part of the formal validation procedure, they must also rely heavily on content validity and inference. That is, the measures must dissect the legal requirements for competence, construct items that tap these legal requirements, and provide thresholds at which inferences are drawn about whether persons understand what they need to about the legal and court process in order to be found competent.

To summarize, then, three main points can be made about the legally informed practitioner model as it manifests in forensic assessment: (a) Practice and scientific freedom must be constrained, in part, by the legal questions that are being posed; (b) the field must at times readjust itself and its scientific and clinical approaches in response to changes in the law; and (c) legal practicalities sometimes preclude optimal methodological approaches to a topic of inquiry.

The Roles and Limits of General Psychological Testing in Forensic Contexts

In much of this chapter, we have discussed the importance of aligning clinical assessment and research with legal requirements. This logic applies as well to psychological testing that is carried out in forensic contexts. In this section, we will discuss specifically the use of psychological assessment instruments and tests as applied to forensic contexts. Following the theme of the legal specificity and parameters of forensic assessment, we will discuss issues surrounding the use of regular psychological tests in forensic assessment, as well as the development and use of tests that are intended to be forensic in nature.

By way of background, Heilbrun et al. (2002) have proposed a simple yet effective typology of psychological measures relevant to forensic assessment. These include *forensic assessment instruments, forensically relevant instruments,* and *clinical instruments.* Although measures from each category can be useful for assisting with a forensic assessment, the specific nature and utility of each category of psychological measure varies. Similarly, the way in which the measures should be used in assessments vary.

A *forensic assessment instrument* is one that "is directly relevant to a specific legal standard and its included capacities that are needed for the individual being evaluated to meet that legal standard" (p. 10 of in press manuscript). Examples of specific legal standards are criminal competence to stand trial, criminal responsibility (versus insanity), and competence to manage one's estate. An example of a forensic assessment instrument is the MacArthur Competence Assessment Tool—Criminal Adjudication (MacCAT-CA; Poythress, Monahan, Bonnie, & Hoge, 1999; Poythress, Nicholson, et al., 1999). The MacCAT-CA was developed to guide mental health professionals who are assessing a defendant's competence to stand trial. The instrument is specifically designed to assess the legal standards for competence to stand trial as set out by the U.S. Supreme Court (*Dusky v. United States,* 1960). As Heilbrun et al. (2002) point out, there has been a proliferation in the past decade or so of instruments intended to be used in forensic settings. The development of forensic assessment instruments and forensically relevant instruments can be seen as an important development, in that it should, in principle, compensate for some of the pitfalls of using clinical measures for forensic assessments.

Forensically relevant instruments are those that do not address specific legal standards but "clinical constructs that are sometimes pertinent to legal standards" (p. 12 of in press manuscript). Examples may include measures of psychopathy (via the Hare Revised Psychopathy Checklist, or PCL-R; Hare, 1991) or measures of violence risk (such as the HCR-20; Webster et al., 1997). Concerning risk assessment measures, some argument may be made that many uses of these instruments actually should place them in the forensic assessment instrument category, since often they are applied to specific legal standards pertaining to risk for future violence.

Heilbrun et al. (1999) called the third type of instrument, comprised of traditional psychological instruments, *clinical measures.* The implications of using these types of instruments in forensic assessment will be discussed later.

Assessment questions in clinical psychology are usually informed through the use of psychological instruments. Such instruments typically were developed to inform decisions about common or traditional psychological constructs, such as intelligence, memory, depression, or anxiety. A problem emerges when these instruments (e.g., the Wechsler Adult Intelligence Scale—Third Edition, or WAIS-III; Wechsler, 1997, or the Minnesota Multiphasic Personality Inventory-2, or MMPI-2; Butcher, Dahlstrom, Graham, Tellegen, & Kaemmer, 2001) are applied to forensic assessments. The basis of the problem is that forensic constructs and questions rarely map directly onto traditional psychological constructs (Heilbrun et al., 2002; Otto & Heilbrun, 2002). As such, there is a schism between general psychological instruments, on the one hand, and forensic psychological assessment questions, on the other. Traditional psychological instruments were not designed for the purpose of answering questions pertaining to legal constructs such as insanity, competence, or risk for certain types of violence. Although they may perform well, and as they were designed to, with respect to general psychological assessment questions among forensic samples (e.g., determining the intelligence of a particular forensic patient), their ability to inform specific forensic questions is tenuous (how does an IQ score inform a decision about competence?).

Research has supported the problems inherent in using traditional psychological instruments to answer forensic or legal questions. First, there is simply not much research that addresses the validity of traditional psychological instruments as applied to forensic questions (Heilbrun et al., 2002). Second, the research that does exist does not provide strong support for their use in forensic assessments to answer specifically forensic questions. For instance, as reviewed by Heilbrun et al. (2002) and Rogers and Shuman (2000), the MMPI/MMPI-2 is commonly used in insanity evaluations, despite relatively few studies on its application to this task (see Ogloff, 1995, for a review of the legal applications of the MMPI/MMPI-2). Studies that do exist tend not to provide stable estimates of profiles indicative of legal insanity. Although the MMPI-2, or some other measure such as the Personality Assessment Inventory (PAI; Morey, 1991), may have adequate research support with respect to its ability to detect *clinical* insanity or psychopathology (i.e., the presence of delusions or hallucinations), there is far from a one-to-one correspondence between clinical and legal insanity. To the extent that the constructs tapped by the MMPI-2 , the PAI, or comprehensive structured assessments fail to align with the legal construct of insanity, the application of such measures for legal or forensic purposes is questionable.

This state of affairs is neither terribly surprising nor detrimental to the general validity of such measures as the MMPI-2 or WAIS-III. Neither was designed with legal constructs in mind. Hence, in psychometric terms, they were not built to include construct coverage of legal questions such as insanity or violence risk. They do not include items that were meant to tap legal constructs. This situation is akin to a depression measure's failing to include items designed to tap the physical signs and symptoms of depression. Such an instrument would have inadequate construct coverage, and its psychometric properties, particularly its validity indexes, would suffer accordingly. Similarly, the validity indexes of traditional psychological measures tend to suffer when these measures are applied to specific forensic or legal constructs or criteria.

In response to the difficulties associated with the use of traditional psychological measures in forensic assessments, commentators have provided some guidance for the use of tests in forensic psychological assessment. Earlier we discussed the importance of legal context to forensic assessment generally. Similarly, there has been discourse pertaining to the link between legal context and psychological instrumentation. Heilbrun et al. (2002) referred to the importance of correspondence between a (forensic) assessment measure and the legal construct to which it purportedly applies. This correspondence is an important part of the development and validation of forensic instruments. They discussed legal status as a "population-specific influence" on the development and validation of forensic instruments. In essence, they pointed out, forensic instruments (and, consequently, assessments) should only be used within legal settings for which they have been developed and validated. Similarly, writing about the importance of legal context for the practice of forensic assessment generally, Heilbrun (1992) has argued that psychological tests used in such assessments must be germane to the legal issue at hand. Thus, as Heilbrun et al. (2002) point out, the law is an important source of authority for the development of forensic instruments.

Grisso (1987), in discussing the "necessary research" (p. 834) to establish forensic psychological assessment as a credible and legally informative vehicle, discussed several law-related research avenues that could forward such a goal. These included pure legal analyses of specific questions (e.g., criminal responsibility), application of basic psychological principles to legal questions, and research on the applicability of traditional psychological measures (e.g., MMPI-2) to legal issues, as well as the development of "specialized assessment instruments" (p. 835) that link directly to legal questions. These ideas overlap with the notion of psycholegal content analysis presented earlier.

In terms of providing a methodology for constructing forensic instruments, Grisso (1986) provided an example based on the assessment of criminal competence. He noted that the first stage of devising and validating a method for assessing criminal competence is to translate legal standards into functional abilities. Then, psychological test construction and validation procedures can be applied to these functional abilities. For example, if the legal standard for competence to stand trial requires, among other things, that the defendant is able to communicate with his or her lawyer, the first task of a psychologist assessing the defendant's competence is to determine what functional abilities the defendant must have to communicate with his or her lawyer. These functional abilities could include, for example, such things as being able to speak or otherwise communicate and being able to assist the lawyer by discussing the evidence and the weaknesses of the testimony to be given by prospective witnesses.

Legal Specificity

In all areas of psychological assessment, it is beneficial to have referral questions that are as specific as possible. This helps to guide the nature and course of the assessment and prevent unnecessary fishing expeditions. This admonition is particularly apt in forensic assessment. The law, and particularly courts, is loath to address more than is required to answer the legal question at stake. The reason for this is sensible. The adversarial legal system in which we live allows opposing parties to litigate their legal questions in front of judges and juries, in effect educating the court about the particular legal issue(s) in question. For a legal decision-maker to address more than what was argued is undesirable because the parties did not have a chance to address or argue the peripheral matters, and hence the decision-maker was not presented with evidence pertaining to these peripheral matters.

Following the logic presented, it is undesirable for a forensic assessment, which often will be used to educate a legal decision-maker, either to address unduly broad referral questions or to stray beyond the referral questions that were asked. Unduly broad referral questions are those that do not provide the forensic evaluator with sufficient information to proceed with an assessment. For example, without knowing exactly at what stage the defendant is in the legal process and the exact legal matters that are at issue and require a forensic assessment the forensic clinician can do little more than provide something akin to a traditional psychological assessment. Straying beyond the referral question results in the clinician's raising issues or addressing matters that extend beyond the particular legal matter being considered. The following is an actual excerpt from a report prepared by a forensic practitioner who was asked to conduct an assessment to determine whether the defendant's mental state at the time of the offense might be grounds for raising the insanity defense:

> It does not appear that Mr. S. was suffering from any psychosis at the time of the assault. He may have been under the influence of various drugs and alcoholic beverages, which he reported consuming at that time. There is no clinical basis for an insanity defence here. Mr. S. is one of the most dangerous persons I have ever examined; the only appropriate disposition would be a lengthy prison sentence. (Melton et al., 1997, p. 548)

In this case, information that is off the legal point will be introduced into the legal arena without due cause and without a priori notice that such information would be justiciable (i.e., at issue in the trial). This introduces an element of uncertainty into the legal forum, one that could unfairly affect the process or the result of the legal endeavor. Apart from the rather picayune legal point presented, psychologists should refrain from going beyond the legal referral question when preparing reports of forensic assessments because the reports that are prepared in legal cases, more so than those of virtually any other area of clinical practice, have a long shelf life. Thus, extraneous information that appears in a report prepared for a particular purpose can be used, sometimes years later, in a manner that can be harmful to the person who was assessed.

Although it is important that forensic assessments address the legal questions for which they were requested, psychologists are generally advised to use extreme caution if asked to answer the ultimate legal question that is asked. In law, this is referred to as answering the ultimate issue (Melton et al., 1997). The ultimate issue in a case is the question the judge or jury is asked to decide. For example, in a case involving a custody dispute, the ultimate issue is generally what living arrangements would be in the child's best interests. Therefore, a psychologist who offered an opinion about which living arrangement would be in the child's best interests would be answering the ultimate issue. As was discussed in the context of the guidelines for expert testimony, the FRE 704 does allow experts to give an opinion concerning the ultimate issue. Recall that, as discussed with reference to the admissibility of expert evidence earlier in this chapter, FRE 704(b) prohibits experts in a criminal case from testifying whether they believe the defendant had the mental state or condition required to satisfy an element of the crime or a defense to the crime. However, forensic mental health professionals should nonetheless be cautious when deciding to answer the ultimate issue. If the expert is allowed to answer the ultimate question, he or she is basically telling the jury or judge how to decide the case. Formerly, ultimate issue testimony was actually barred in courts (Melton et al., 1997). Although the

current rules of evidence are not as strict, psychologists generally should refrain from answering the ultimate issue, both because doing so can usurp the power of the court or jury and because, most often, the ultimate legal issue does not correspond directly to the relevant psychological construct. For example, there is no construct in psychiatry or psychology that corresponds directly to competence to stand trial.

Despite the convincing arguments against providing an ultimate opinion, forensic psychologists are regularly asked by attorneys and judges to state whether they think, for example, that a defendant is competent to stand trial. Any reluctance to answer the question as asked—that is, to state the ultimate opinion—may be met with suspicion or criticism by the attorneys or the judge for not doing their job as an expert witness. We recommend that, rather than simply providing the answer to the ultimate issue, psychologists take care to ensure that they discuss the psychological information that is relevant to the underlying legal principles that pertain to the construct being addressed. Taking the case of competence to stand trial as an example, we would not recommend that psychologists simply express an opinion that a defendant is, or is not, competent to stand trial. Rather, we would suggest that psychologists provide the court with relevant psychological information that relates to the legal criteria for competence to stand trial. For example, the psychologist could discuss the relevant psychological information that relates to how the defendant's mental state will affect his or her ability to communicate with counsel or to understand the nature of the legal proceedings (see Roesch, Ogloff, & Golding, 1993).

Another important issue concerns the absolute necessity of avoiding the role of advocate in forensic assessment practice. Terms such as *hired gun* or *whore of the court* are well-known monikers used to describe the forensic evaluator who will find certain results, given the right price. Of course, such practice is unethical and will undermine not only the credibility of the individual assessor in a given case, but the profession of psychology as well. Despite the pressure that psychologists might experience, either explicitly or implicitly, from the parties that hire them, it is critical that they do not adopt the position of advocate. Rather, the psychologist should most properly take on the role of an impartial educator. That is, even when he or she is hired by one side or another, the proper role of the forensic evaluator is to impartially arrive at a conclusion based on assessment findings and to deliver this conclusion, along with any uncertainties.

Training in Forensic Assessment

As noted in the introduction to this chapter, along with the emergence of forensic psychology has come the development of graduate training programs in the area (see, e.g., Freeman & Roesch, 1992; Grisso, Sales, & Bayless, 1982; Hafemeister, Ogloff, & Small, 1990; Ogloff, 1990; Ogloff & Schuller, 2001; Ogloff et al., 1996; Roesch, Grisso, & Poythress, 1986; Tomkins & Ogloff, 1990). As with other aspects of the developing field, little attention has been given to the training needs and opportunities in the field. Part of the concern for the lack of attention directed to training in legal psychology has been rectified with the National Invitational Conference on Education and Training in Law and Psychology, which that took place at Villanova Law School in 1995. The Villanova Conference, as it has come to be known, was attended by approximately 60 invited people from across the field of legal psychology. The overarching purpose of the conference was to develop an agenda for legal psychology training into the twenty-first century. A description of the conference can be found in an article written by Bersoff et al. (1997).

People have debated whether psychologists who work in the law and psychology field need to be trained formally in law (see Grisso et al., 1982; Hafemeister et al., 1990; Ogloff et al., 1996; Tomkins & Ogloff, 1990). This debate has culminated in consideration of the joint degree programs in which students can obtain both a law degree and a PhD. Arguments against dual degree training have emphasized the costs of such training and the fact that most people who work in legal psychology as clinicians or researchers focus on one or two specific areas of the law. Those who support dual degree programs, by contrast, argue that although all legal psychologists do not require formal training in law there are considerable advantages to pursuing formal training in law and psychology (Hafemeister et al., 1990). Foremost among these advantages is the ability of psychologists with law degrees to have a sophisticated understanding of the law. Indeed, many psychologists with little appreciation of law have jumped into the field only to produce work that is of questionable validity (see Hafemeister et al., 1990). We want to emphasize here that although it would not be necessary, or even a good idea, for all forensic psychologists to obtain a law degree, it is nevertheless critical that forensic psychologists obtain a clear understanding of, if not true expertise in, the law that relates to their work.

Most forensic psychologists working today obtained their forensic training and experience largely on their own. With the growth in the field, the recent recognition of forensic psychology as a specialty area, and the development of knowledge and sophisticated assessment techniques in the field, there will be continued growth in formal training programs in the field. There are several models and methods by which forensic psychologists are now being trained to work in the area (Ogloff & Schuller, 2001). Information about various training programs and internship opportunities in forensic psychology may be found on the Web site of the American Psychology Law Society (http://www.unl.edu/ap-ls). First is the mentor model. In this model, graduate students learn their skills by working and conducting research with individual faculty members who practice or do research in the field of law and psychology. Although this model affords students with individualized training, the students typically receive little formal training in the broad area of the field, and they are unlikely to have a critical mass of colleagues with whom they can converse and collaborate.

Ogloff and Schuller (2001) refer to the second model as the "limited focus training model." In this model, students study and train in a department in which there is more than one person working in the field of law and psychology. Alternatively, they may study in a department with one person in the field, but have access to psychologists in institutions (e.g., jails or prisons, forensic hospitals) who help enrich their training experiences. Programs of this ilk provide students with a wider range of training experiences than is available to students trained by way of the mentor model. Again, though, it is generally difficult for prospective students to identify psychology departments that do offer some informal training by relying on one or two people in the field.

Another model includes actual programs in law and psychology or forensic psychology. There are several of these programs available, and that number is gradually growing. Although the programs vary considerably in their detail and focus, they provide students with an overview of the field of law and psychology as well as advanced courses, research experiences, and practical or applied training in some area of the field. Some of the courses allow graduate students in psychology to take one or more courses in law schools. At least one program, at the University of Nebraska-Lincoln, allows students the option of completing a nonprofessional degree in law, called the Master of Legal Studies. This degree requires students to complete approximately one third of the course that a law student usually takes. The clear advantage of the programs in law and psychology beyond the opportunity to complete a range of relevant courses in the field is that students have the benefit of being part of a critical mass of students and faculty with common interests. Often the learning and training experiences are enriched by the expanded opportunities a program can afford.

A final training model, which has been adopted in a few universities in North America, is a joint or dual degree program in law and psychology or forensic psychology (Ogloff, 1999b). In these programs, students have the opportunity of simultaneously pursuing a law degree (a Juris Doctor or JD in the United States and a Bachelor of Laws degree or LLB in Canada) and a PhD or PsyD in psychology. Although these programs are very demanding, because they require students to complete all of the requirements for both the law degree and PhD, the programs do allow students to become experts in the law.

Beyond developing training programs, considerable discussion is occurring in the field about whether forensic psychology programs should be accredited. In addition, commentators have noted that there still are few well-established training programs in forensic psychology (Otto & Heilbrun, 2002). Moreover, Otto and Heilbrun (2002) note that there are few accredited internships with specialized training in forensic psychology and even fewer postdoctoral fellowships available. It is our view that with the rapid growth and development in the field, there can be little doubt that forensic programs will continue to emerge and that at some point some form of accreditation might be developed.

FUTURE CONCERNS

Throughout this chapter we have defined the newly recognized area of specialty practice forensic psychology. We noted the growth of forensic psychology, and we reviewed some of the contemporary issues in the field. In the remainder of this chapter, we would like to highlight some of the concerns regarding forensic assessments that will need to be addressed in the future. This list will by no means be exhaustive, but in our view the matters identified here are among the most pressing ones. The matters we shall highlight can be broken into two general topics: the need for quality control in forensic assessment and areas requiring future development (e.g., civil forensic assessment and forensic assessments with youth, women, and visible minorities).

Quality Control in Forensic Assessment

In the good old days, most psychologists viewed forensic psychology as an unattractive and unappealing field. Our comment about the good old days is written somewhat facetiously; however, along with the recent attraction of the field of forensic psychology has come a plethora of related problems. Chief among the problems that we see in the field is the fact that many of the psychologists who are making their way into the forensic field, frankly, are poorly trained and inexperienced and do not do a good job overall. Although this statement may seem too extreme, it points to a very serious problem. Given the force of the law in the lives of the people with whom forensic psychologists work, extreme care must be taken to ensure that our work is competent. As Otto and Heilbrun (2002) note,

> That some psychologists are motivated to enter the forensic arena because of economic concerns is not, in itself, problematic. Those

psychologists who actively seek to increase their forensic knowledge, skills, and abilities through continuing education, supervision, and other methods are to be commended and supported. It becomes problematic, however, when some psychologists, in response to financial concerns, enter and practice in the forensic arena unprepared. Psychological expertise, forensic or otherwise, is not developed overnight. By its very nature forensic work is likely to be subjected to a greater degree of scrutiny than other kinds of psychological services, and there is some support for the claim that this is occurring over time. (p. 1)

Although we are sympathetic to the economic pressures that psychologists feel, particularly in light of the impact of managed care on the delivery of health care services, psychologists must ensure that they are competent before entering forensic practice. Unfortunately, across North America, licensing bodies report that complaints arising from assessments and practice in the forensic arena are among the most frequent they see (Ogloff, 1999a). Although forensic psychologists can expect a greater risk of being the focus of an ethics complaint simply because of the adversarial nature of the law, the fact is that there is substance to a large proportion of the complaints that are lodged. To the extent that psychologists are not policing themselves appropriately, then, the question arises whether we should not move toward a model of credentialing and certification in forensic psychology.

Otto and Heilbrun (2002) discuss the advances in credentialing and certification that have emerged in forensic psychology. In particular, they note that as many as nine states have some program of credentialing psychologists who conduct criminal forensic assessments. In addition, increasing numbers of forensic psychologists are seeking board certification. Preeminent among these credentialing boards is the American Board of Forensic Psychology, which employs a stringent process of reviewing an individual's training, experience, and knowledge prior to granting the individual diplomate status. Sadly, a number of newer boards are emerging that grant diplomate or fellow status without careful scrutiny. Such boards are referred to unkindly as vanity boards, and, generally speaking, psychologists gain little from gaining recognition from such a board (Hanson, 2000; Otto & Heilbrun, 2002).

We are reluctant to advocate that all forensic psychologists ought to be board certified or otherwise specially credentialed. Indeed, little if any evidence exists to show that forensic psychologists who are board certified or otherwise recognized as specialists are more competent than other forensic psychologists or whether credentialed forensic psychologists are more ethical. Nonetheless, board certification, through a rigorous process, can at least provide some assurance that the forensic psychologist meets some accepted threshold of training, experience, and knowledge in the field. As discussed earlier in this chapter, the onus falls on the individual psychologist who enters the forensic area to ensure that he or she is competent in every sense of the word. As with developments in training programs, we can expect that more forensic psychologists will seek board certification or equivalent recognition.

Areas Requiring Future Development

Given that forensic psychology can be seen as being in the developmental stage of adolescence (Grisso, 1991), it is not particularly surprising that many areas of forensic assessment require further development or refinement. Here, we shall focus on two topics that are in great need of more attention at this time. The first is the entire area of civil forensic assessments and the second is the need to focus more attention on forensic assessments conducted with youth, women, and visible minorities.

Civil Forensic Assessments

Traditionally, forensic psychologists have worked primarily in the criminal field. Indeed, most often when people think of forensic psychologists, they think of psychologists who work with criminals. Today, although more forensic psychologists do work in noncriminal areas of law, the focus of the research and development of instruments and techniques in practice is still on topics within criminal law. Without a doubt, though, many more people are affected by civil law than are ever affected by criminal law (Melton et al., 1997; Ogloff, 2001). As a result, forensic psychologists would do well to learn about civil law topics for which psychology has some relevance. More importantly, of course, psychologists need to develop more instruments that are relevant to civil law topics and to develop assessment techniques to address these matters. As discussed previously in this chapter, there are several topics in civil law that require further development.

Forensic Assessments With Youth, Women, and Visible Minorities

Perhaps because of our historical focus on criminal behavior, much of the research and practice in forensic psychology has focused on males, and adult males at that. Moreover, despite the overrepresentation of some visible minorities in the criminal justice system, relatively little attention has been paid in forensic assessments to questions about the validity of forensic assessments for populations other than White adult males (Ogloff, 2001).

Although there has been a dramatic increase in forensic assessment instruments that have been developed over the past 15 years (Otto & Heilbrun, 2002; Heilbrun et al., 2002), surprisingly little attention has been paid to the validation of such tests for the diverse populations with which the instruments are sometimes used. To simply employ an instrument across populations, regardless of age, race, or gender of the person being assessed, is inappropriate. At the very least, then, forensic psychologists need to be assured that the tests they are employing are valid and that there are normative data available for the population from which the person being assessed is drawn. In the extreme, using instruments that have not been normed on the population from which the person being assessed comes is evidence of incompetence, and the results of the assessments will have questionable validity.

As the refinement of legal standards for the admissibility of expert psychological testimony has developed following the decision in *Daubert v. Merrell Dow Pharmaceuticals* (1993), the focus of inquiry by courts has moved from the general acceptance of a measure within the field to an examination of the scientific foundation of the instruments. This, again, increases the need for forensic psychologists to ensure that the psychometric instruments and clinical techniques they employ in their assessments are empirically validated.

CONCLUSION

This is an exciting time for the field of forensic psychology. Now that forensic psychology has been formally recognized as a specialty area of practice within psychology, the need is greater than ever before to ensure that forensic psychology meets the highest standards of the discipline. Unlike most other areas of psychology, forensic psychology is reliant upon the law, which places unique demands on the field. In particular, the legal standards that govern the assessments that forensic psychologists perform establish the parameters of the assessments. Thus, forensic psychologists must be thoroughly knowledgeable about the areas of law in which they work.

As the field of forensic psychology has developed, several contemporary issues have received some attention. In particular, forensic psychologists must not rely solely upon clinical experience when conducting assessments, nor should they limit their assessments to purely actuarial measures. Rather, we advocate the use of structured clinical decision-making. This technique involves some reliance upon actuarial instruments and, more importantly, empirically supported evidence in developing clinical decisions. Given its reliance upon empirically validated instruments and techniques, we support the scientist-practitioner model in forensic psychology.

In addition, we recognize the need for forensic psychologists to be knowledgeable about the law in the areas in which they work. Although general psychological testing has some utility for forensic assessments, gone are the days when standard psychological assessments could satisfy the demands of the legal system for our work. As we noted, it is critical to use the legal criteria that underlie a forensic assessment referral as guidelines for the assessment. At the same time, though, we caution against having forensic psychologists offer their opinions about the ultimate legal issue being addressed by the court or other legal decision-makers. In addition, it is critical that forensic psychologists do not fall into the trap of becoming advocates or hired guns for the party that employed them. Finally, the emergence of forensic psychology has seen some development of forensic training programs. At the present time, there are not enough comprehensive programs to meet the needs of the field. Over time, too, it will become necessary to explore the possibility of accrediting specialized forensic clinical training programs.

Moving beyond the issues that have emerged in the field, we highlighted two major areas that present future concerns. First, with the explosion of the field of forensic psychology, it has become increasingly important to ensure that some quality control mechanism is developed. Although we do not advocate a strict model of board certification, we do recognize the value of such a credentialing mechanism. Moreover, we caution readers to avoid becoming recognized by the increasingly notorious vanity boards.

Of considerable importance in forensic assessment is the need to move beyond the criminal law field and to develop specialized forensic assessment techniques and instruments that will be valid for use in the expansive areas of civil law. Finally, surprisingly little attention has been paid to validating assessment instruments and methods for use with diverse populations, including youth, women, and visible minorities.

On the whole, we in the field of forensic psychology have accomplished a great deal in a relatively short time in forensic psychology. Interested readers need only review the premier books that were in print in the mid-1980s (e.g., Melton, Petrila, Poythress, & Slobogin, 1987; Grisso, 1986) and compare the information in them with the more recent volumes (e.g., Melton et al., 1997) that are available to see how far we have come in so little time. Along with the growth in the field have come several contemporary issues and future concerns that must be addressed. From our perspective, the field of forensic clinical assessment is particularly challenging and rewarding, and we look eagerly toward the future developments that we shall experience in the field.

REFERENCES

American Psychological Association. (1992). Ethical principles of psychologists and code of conduct. *American Psychologist, 47,* 1597–1611.

American Psychological Association. (1994). *Guidelines for child custody evaluations in divorce proceedings.* Washington, DC: Author.

American Psychological Association. (1998). *Guidelines for psychological evaluations in child protection matters.* Washington, DC: Author.

Bersoff, N., Goodman-Delahunty, J., Grisso, T., Hans, V., Poythress, N., & Roesch, R. (1997). Training in law and psychology: Models from the Villanova Conference. *American Psychologist, 52,* 1301–1310.

Beutler, L. R., Williams, R. E., Wakefield, P. J., & Entwistle, S. R. (1995). Bridging scientist and practitioner perspectives in clinical psychology. *American Psychologist, 50,* 984–994.

Boer, D. P., Hart, S. D., Kropp, P. R., & Webster, C. D. (1997). *Manual for the Sexual Violence Risk—20: Professional guidelines for assessing risk of sexual violence.* Vancouver: British Columbia Institute Against Family Violence.

Brigham, J. (1999). What is forensic psychology anyway? *Law and Human Behavior, 23,* 273–298.

Butcher, J. N., Dahlstrom, N. G., Graham, J. R., Tellegen, A., & Kaemmer, B. (2001). *MMPI-2: Manual for administration and scoring* (2nd ed.). Minneapolis: University of Minnesota Press.

Canadian Psychological Association. (2000). *Canadian code of ethics for psychologists.* Ottawa, ON, Canada: Author.

Committee on Ethical Guidelines for Forensic Psychologists. (1991). Specialty guidelines for forensic psychologists. *Law and Human Behavior, 15,* 655–665.

Daubert v. Merrell Dow Pharmaceuticals, Inc., 727 F. Supp. 570 (S.D. Cal. 1989), *aff'd,* 951 F.2d 1128 (9th Cir. 1990), *vacated,* 509 U.S. 579 (1993).

Dempster, R. J. (1998). *Prediction of sexually violent recidivism: A comparison of risk assessment instruments.* Unpublished master's thesis, Simon Fraser University, Burnaby, BC, Canada.

Douglas, K. S. (2000, March). *A psycholegal analysis of violence risk assessment: Bringing law, science, and practice closer together.* Paper presented at the 2000 Biennial Meeting of the American Psychology-Law Society (APA Div. 41), New Orleans, LA.

Douglas, K. S., Cox, D. N., & Webster, C. D. (1999). Violence risk assessment: Science and practice. *Legal and Criminological Psychology, 4,* 149–184.

Douglas, K. S., & Koch, W. J. (2001). Civil commitment and civil competencies: Psychological issues. In R. Schuller & J. R. P. Ogloff (Eds.), *Introduction to psychology and law: Canadian perspectives* (pp. 353–374). Toronto, ON, Canada: University of Toronto Press.

Douglas, K. S., & Ogloff, J. R. P. (2001). *A structured professional judgment approach to violence risk assessment: The reliability and validity of the HCR-20.* Unpublished manuscript.

Douglas, K. S., & Webster, C. D. (1999). Predicting violence in mentally and personality disordered individuals. In R. Roesch, S. D. Hart, & J. R. P. Ogloff (Eds.), *Psychology and law: The state of the discipline* (pp. 175–239). New York: Plenum.

Dusky v. United States, 362 U.S. 402 (1960).

Federal Rules of Evidence, 28 U.S.C. (1976).

Fensterheim, H., & Raw, S. D. (1996). Psychotherapy research is not psychotherapy practice. *Clinical Psychology: Science and Practice, 3,* 168–171.

Freeman, R. J., & Roesch, R. (1992). Psycholegal education: Training for forum and function. In D. K. Kagehiro & W. S. Laufer (Eds.), *Handbook of psychology and law* (pp. 567–576). New York: Springer-Verlag.

Frye v. United States, 293 F. 1013 (D.C. Cir. 1923).

Goldfried, M. R., & Wolfe, B. E. (1996). Psychotherapy practice and research. *American Psychologist, 51,* 1007–1016.

Grisso, T. (1986). *Evaluating competencies: Forensic assessments and instruments.* New York: Plenum.

Grisso, T. (1987). The economic and scientific future of forensic psychological assessment. *American Psychologist, 42,* 831–839.

Grisso, T. (1991). A developmental history of the American Psychology-Law Society. *Law and Human Behavior, 15,* 213–230.

Grisso, T., Sales, B. D., & Bayless, S. (1982). Law-related courses and programs in graduate psychology departments. *American Psychologist, 37,* 267–278.

Grove, W. M., & Meehl, P. E. (1996). Comparative efficiency of informal (subjective, impressionistic) and formal (mechanical, algorithmic) prediction procedures: The clinical-statistical controversy. *Psychology, Public Policy, and Law, 2,* 293–323.

Grove, W. M., Zald, D. H., Lebow, B. S., Snitz, B. E., & Nelson, C. (2000). Clinical versus mechanical prediction: A meta-analysis. *Psychological Assessment, 12,* 19–30.

Hafemeister, T., Ogloff, J. R. P., & Small, M. A. (1990). Training and careers in law and psychology: The perspectives of students and graduates of dual degree programs. *Behavioral Sciences and the Law, 8,* 263–283.

Hanson, M. (2000, February). Expertise to go. *American Bar Association Journal, 108,* 44–52.

Hare, R. D. (1991). *Manual for the Hare Psychopathy Checklist–Revised.* Toronto: Multi-Health Systems.

Hart, S. D. (1998). The role of psychopathy in assessing risk for violence: Conceptual and methodological issues. *Legal and Criminological Psychology, 3,* 121–137.

Hayes, S. C. (1996). Creating the empirical clinician. *Clinical Psychology: Science and Practice, 3,* 179–181.

Heilbrun, K. (1992). The role of psychological testing in forensic assessment. *Law and Human Behavior, 16,* 257–272.

Heilbrun, K. (1997). Prediction versus management models relevant to risk assessment: The importance of legal decision-making context. *Law and Human Behavior, 21,* 347–359.

Heilbrun, K., Bank, S., Follingstad, D., & Frederick, R. (2000, September). *Petition for forensic psychology as an APA specialization.* Presented to the Committee for the Recognition of Specialties and Proficiencies in Professional Psychology. American Psychological Association, Washington, DC.

Heilbrun, K., Ogloff, J. R. P., & Picarello, K. (1999). Dangerous offender statutes: Implications for risk assessment. *International Journal of Psychiatry and Law, 22,* 393–415.

Heilbrun, K., Rogers, R., & Otto, R. K. (2002). Forensic assessment: Current status and future directions. In J. R. P. Ogloff (Ed.), *Psychology and law: Reviewing the discipline* (pp. 119–146). New York: Kluwer Academic/Plenum Press.

Jenkins v. United States, 307 F.2d 637 (D.C. Cir. 1962), *en banc.*

Kanfer, F. H. (1990). The scientist-practitioner connection: A bridge in need of constant attention. *Professional Psychology: Research and Practice, 21,* 264–270.

Kropp, P. R., & Hart, S. D. (2000). The Spousal Assault Risk Assessment (SARA) Guide: Reliability and validity in adult male offenders. *Law and Human Behavior, 24,* 101–118.

Kropp, P. R., Hart, S. D., Webster, C. D., & Eaves, D. (1999). *Manual for the Spousal Assault Risk Assessment Guide* (3rd ed.). Toronto, ON, Canada: Multi-Health Systems.

Kuhmo Tire Co. v. Carmichael, 67 U.S.L.W. 4179, 119 S.Ct. 1167 (1999).

Lyon, D. R., Hart, S. D., & Webster, C. D. (2001). Violence risk assessment. In R. Schuller & J. R. P. Ogloff (Eds.), *Law and psychology: Canadian perspectives* (pp. 271–316). Toronto, ON, Canada: University of Toronto Press.

Meehl, P. E. (1954). *Clinical versus statistical prediction.* Minneapolis: University of Minnesota Press.

Melton, G. B. (1987). Training in psychology and law. In I. B. Weiner & A. K. Hess (Eds.), *Handbook of forensic psychology* (pp. 681–697). New York: Wiley.

Melton, G. B., Petrila, J., Poythress, N., & Slobogin, C. (1987). *Psychological evaluations for the courts: A handbook for attorneys and mental health professionals.* New York: Guilford.

Melton, G. B., Petrila, J., Poythress, N., & Slobogin, C. (1997). *Psychological evaluations for the courts: A handbook for attorneys and mental health professionals* (2nd ed.). New York: Guilford.

Morey, L. C. (1991). *Personality Assessment Inventory: Professional manual.* Tampa, FL: Psychological Assessment Resources.

Nezu, A. M. (1996). What are we doing to our patients and should we care if anyone else knows? *Clinical Psychology: Science and Practice, 3,* 160–163.

Ogloff, J. R. P. (1990). Law and psychology in Canada: The need for training and research. *Canadian Psychology, 31,* 61–73.

Ogloff, J. R. P. (1995). The legal basis of forensic applications of the MMPI-2. In Y. S. Ben-Porath, J. R. Graham, G. Hall, R. D.

Hirschman, & M. Zaragoza (Eds.), *Forensic applications of the MMPI-2* (pp. 18–47). Thousand Oaks, CA: Sage.

Ogloff, J. R. P. (1999a). Ethical and legal contours of forensic psychology. In R. Roesch, S. D. Hart, & J. R. P. Ogloff (Eds.), *Psychology and law: The state of the discipline* (pp. 405–422). New York: Kluwer Academic/Plenum.

Ogloff, J. R. P. (1999b). Graduate training in law and psychology at Simon Fraser University. *Professional Psychology: Research and Practice, 30,* 99–103.

Ogloff, J. R. P. (2000). Two steps forward and one-step backward: The law and psychology movement(s) in the 20th century. *Law and Human Behavior, 24,* 457–483.

Ogloff, J. R. P. (2001). Jingoism, dogmatism and other evils in legal psychology: Lessons learned in the 20th century. In R. Roesch, R. Corrado, & R. Dempster (Eds.), *Psychology in the courts: International advances in knowledge.* Amsterdam: Harwood Academic.

Ogloff, J. R. P., Roberts, C. F., & Roesch, R. (1993). The insanity defense: Legal standards and clinical assessment. *Applied and Preventive Psychology, 2,* 163–178.

Ogloff, J. R. P., & Schuller, R. (2001). Law and psychology: Looking towards the future. In R. Schuller & J. R. P. Ogloff (Eds.), *An introduction to law and psychology: Canadian perspectives* (pp. 356–373). Toronto, ON, Canada: University of Toronto Press.

Ogloff, J. R. P., Tomkins, A. J., & Bersoff, D. N. (1996). Education and training in law/criminal justice: Historical foundations, present structures, and future developments. *Criminal Justice and Behavior, 23,* 200–235.

Otto, R. K., & Heilbrun, K. (2002). The practice of forensic psychology: A look towards the future in light of the past. *American Psychologist, 57,* 5–18.

Otto, R. K., Heilbrun, K., & Grisso, T. (1990). Training and credentialing in forensic psychology. *Behavioral Sciences and the Law, 8,* 217–232.

People v. Hawthorne (1940), 291 N.W. 205.

Poythress, N., Monahan, J., Bonnie, R., & Hoge, S. K. (1999). *MacArthur Competence Assessment Tool–Criminal Adjudication.* Odessa, FL: Psychological Assessment Resources.

Poythress, N. G., Nicholson, R., Otto, R. K., Edens, J. F., Bonnie, R. J., Monahan, J., et al. (1999). *Professional manual for the MacArthur Competence Assessment Tool–Criminal Adjudication.* Odessa, FL: Psychological Assessment Resources.

Quinsey, V. L., Harris, G. T., Rice, G. T., & Cormier, C. A. (1998). *Violent offenders: Appraising and managing risk.* Washington, DC: American Psychological Association.

Roesch, R., Grisso, T., & Poythress, N. G. (1986). Training programs, courses, and workshops in psychology and law. In M. F. Kaplan (Ed.), *The impact of social psychology on procedural justice* (pp. 83–108). Springfield, IL: C. C. Thomas.

Roesch, R., Ogloff, J. R. P., & Golding, S. L. (1993). Competency to stand trial: Legal and clinical issues. *Applied and Preventive Psychology, 2,* 43–51.

Rogers, R., & Shuman, D. W. (2000). *Conducting insanity evaluations.* New York: Guilford.

Rose, V. G. (2001). An introduction to law and the Canadian legal system. In R. Schuller & J. R. P. Ogloff (Eds.), *An introduction to law and psychology: Canadian perspectives* (pp. 26–41). Toronto, ON, Canada: University of Toronto Press.

Shah, S. A. (1978). Dangerousness and mental illness: Some conceptual, prediction and policy dilemmas. In C. Frederick (Ed.), *Dangerous behavior: A problem in law and mental health* (pp. 153–191). Washington, DC: U.S. Government Printing Office.

Singer, J. L. (1990). The scientific basis of psychotherapy practice: A question of values and ethics. *Psychotherapy: Theory, Research, and Practice, 17,* 372–383.

Sobell, L. C. (1996). Bridging the gap between scientists and practitioners: The challenge before us. *Behavior Therapy, 27,* 297–320.

Stricker, G. (1992). The relationship of research to clinical practice. *American Psychologist, 47,* 543–549.

Stricker, G., & Trierweiler, S. J. (1995). The local clinical scientist: A bridge between science and practice. *American Psychologist, 50,* 995–1002.

Tomkins, A. J., & Ogloff, J. R. P. (1990). Training and career options in psychology and law. *Behavioral Sciences and the Law, 8,* 205–216.

United States v. Hinckley, 525 F. Supp. 1342 (D.C. 1981).

Webster, C. D., & Cox, D. N. (1997). Integration of nomothetic and ideographic positions in risk assessment: Implications for practice and the education of psychologists and other mental health professionals. *American Psychologist, 52,* 1245–1246.

Webster, C. D., Douglas, K. S., Eaves, D., & Hart, S. D. (1997b). *HCR-20: Assessing the risk for violence* (Version 2). Vancouver, BC, Canada: Mental Health, Law, and Policy Institute, Simon Fraser University.

Wechsler, D. (1997). *Wechsler Adult Intelligence Scale* (3rd ed.). San Antonio, TX: Psychological Corporation.

CHAPTER 16

Psychological Assessment in Correctional Settings

EDWIN I. MEGARGEE

At the beginning of every episode, viewers of the long-running television series *Law and Order* were informed that the criminal justice system is composed of two parts, the police who investigate crime and the district attorneys who prosecute the offenders. Not so! There is a third, equally important, component: the correctional system. Once a defendant has been convicted, the work of the police and the prosecutors is finished. For the men and women who work in corrections, the job has just begun. For months or years to come, it is they who must deal with the offenders. Correctional psychologists are an integral part of a modern correctional system, and assessment is their most important function.

Today, the correctional system and the psychologists who work within it are facing unprecedented challenges. In the United States alone, more than 5.7 million men and women, 2.8% of the adult population of the United States, are under some form of correctional supervision on any given day. Approximately 3,300,000 are on probation, 560,000 in local jails, 1,200,000 in state or federal prisons, and 690,000 on post-release supervision or parole (A. J. Beck et al., 2000). The number of incarcerated adults alone increased 667% from 1970 to 2000 (American Correctional Association, 2000), and in any given year there are approximately 10 million new admissions to jails across the country (Bureau of Justice Statistics, 1995).

At every stage of the criminal justice system, crucial decisions must be made regarding each offender (Megargee &

Carbonell, 1995). After people are arrested, it must be decided whether they should be released or detained, diverted or prosecuted. For those who are convicted of criminal offenses, judges must decide whether they should be admonished, fined, placed on probation, enrolled in appropriate rehabilitation programs, or sentenced to terms of confinement. Each new admission to a jail or prison must be screened for psychological disorders and developmental disabilities to identify those who (a) are dangerous to themselves or others, (b) are at risk of victimization, or (c) require mental health interventions. In addition, correctional authorities must establish their most appropriate supervision and custody levels and then determine the programs and change agents best suited to their particular needs. Eventually, many prisoners must be screened to determine who can be released on parole, or, in certain cases, who should be confined beyond the ends of their sentences in order to protect the community. Psychological assessment plays a crucial role in many of these decisions.

This chapter describes and discusses psychological assessment in adult correctional settings, emphasizing the initial assessments and evaluations mandated by professional organizations and credentialing bodies. It examines external and internal classification, risk assessment, mental health and psychological screening, and needs assessment for management and treatment programming in jails and correctional institutions as well as probation and parole settings. The emphasis will be on policies and research in countries whose legal systems are rooted in English common law, specifically, Canada, the United Kingdom, and the United States. It will not encompass the evaluation of forensic questions such as legal competency and criminal responsibility, which are dealt with elsewhere in this volume.

Space does not permit descriptions of all the many assessment tools and techniques used to address these questions in correctional settings. Instead, the broader issues of correctional classification will be discussed and a few of the instruments that are most used or most useful will be described.

ASSESSMENT AT VARIOUS STAGES OF THE CORRECTIONAL SYSTEM

Although the correctional system deals almost exclusively with people accused or convicted of committing crimes, it comprises a number of separate and distinct segments. Each has its own tasks and issues, and each is subject to different legal constraints. These segments include jails, probation services, correctional institutions of various types, and aftercare services such as parole. In this section, assessment issues in each of these settings will be discussed.

Standards for Health Care in Corrections

Prisoners are, literally, a captive population. Unlike free-world clients, inmates cannot shop around for mental health services. Nevertheless, mental health assessments can have a major impact on offenders' lives, influencing whether they are set free, imprisoned, or even, in certain jurisdictions, sentenced to death (Cunningham & Reidy, 1999).

Because prisoners are totally dependent on correctional staff for their health care needs, a number of professional health care organizations have formulated standards and guidelines regarding the nature and the extent of the psychological and other services that should be afforded offenders in various settings. They include the American Association for Correctional Psychology (AACP; 1980, 2000), the American Correctional Association (ACA; 1981), the American Psychiatric Association (1989), the American Psychological Association (1991), the American Public Health Association (1976), and the National Commission on Correctional Health Care (NCCHC; 1996, 1997). This chapter will focus on the AACP (2000) standards and, to a lesser extent, those of the NCCHC, since they most directly concern the delivery of mental health services and encompass the full range of correctional settings.

General Provisions

The AACP (2000) standards contain certain general provisions that apply to assessment in all correctional settings. They specify that each setting should employ one or more doctoral-level licensed psychologists experienced in the delivery of psychological services in correctional settings. With millions of people being processed by correctional facilities each year, it is obviously impossible for such highly qualified practitioners to carry out all the assessment procedures that are needed. Instead, they must (a) formulate and implement protocols for psychological screening; (b) supervise assessments conducted by master's-level psychologists, psychology interns, and paraprofessional mental health staff members; and (c) train other correctional staff members to recognize the signs and symptoms of mental disorders (Anno, 1991).

The AACP (2000) standards stipulate that psychological assessments should comply with the ethical standards of the American Psychological Association (1992) as well as with any laws applying in that locality. Specifically, correctional psychologists should, "limit their functioning to their demonstrated areas of professional competence" (p. 452). With regard to assessment, this implies that correctional psychologists should not administer or supervise the administration of unfamiliar assessment techniques. Moreover, they should understand any problems associated with the administration and interpretation of familiar techniques in correctional settings, such as how the test scores might be influenced by deception or malingering, and the norms, base rates, and cutting scores found among criminal offenders in their correctional setting.

Furthermore, assessments should be performed only by qualified personnel. As noted earlier, if fully qualified correctional psychologists do not administer psychological assessments personally, they are responsible for supervising the evaluations carried out by others. Under no circumstances should inmates or offenders be used to administer, score, process, or file other offenders' tests or mental health information.

A primary ethical question in correctional psychology is, "Who is the client?" (Monahan, 1980). Although correctional psychologists work *with* offenders, they work *for* the correctional system. Psychologists must make sure that offenders understand that they have obligations to the system as well as to the offenders. For example, correctional psychologists may have a legal or ethical duty to disclose information bearing on the security of the institution or the safety of the staff or inmates, and to warn potential victims who may be at risk (VandeCreek & Knapp, 1989).

Prior to any assessment, offenders should be informed about all limits on confidentiality, how information they provide may be used, and who may have access to those data. Prior to any formal assessments being carried out, offenders should be provided with full disclosure in writing and asked to sign a form acknowledging receipt of this information.

There should be written documentation of all mental health information and the results of all tests and evaluations. These data and reports should be placed in secure, confidential files that are maintained by the mental health service and kept separate from other agency records. Information in the file should be provided to other correctional staff only on a need-to-know basis and under the supervision of a mental health staff member.

Within these general parameters, there are specific problems, issues, and guidelines for assessments conducted in different settings.

Jails

Jails are local facilities that are typically under the jurisdiction of the county sheriff. They range in size and resources from small rural lockups to huge metropolitan facilities with thousands of inmates. The Cook Country (Chicago) jail, for example, admits more than 100,000 people annually (ACA, 2000). When someone is arrested, the local jail is typically that person's first point of contact with the correctional system.

Few, if any, clinical populations are as heterogeneous as that of the accused and convicted offenders encountered in a county jail. They come from all walks of life, ranging from society's affluent to its effluent. All conceivable ethnicities and nationalities are represented, and, although they speak a variety of languages, English is not always one of them. Testing is further complicated by the fact that their academic and reading skills may be minimal or nonexistent.

The offenders encountered in jails approach assessment with different motivations and perspectives. Some may be malingering, hoping to be declared incompetent or legally insane. Others may try to impress the examiner with their exemplary mental health, hoping it will help them to be released to the community.

Deinstitutionalization of the mentally ill has shifted much of the burden for coping with psychiatric patients from state and local psychiatric hospitals to jails (Torrey et al., 1992). As Kennedy (1993, p. 309) noted, "many ex-patients become prisoners for relatively petty yet socially troublesome behavior related to their psychiatric condition." Teplin (1990, 1996) reported that 6.1% of the men and 15.0% of the women detained in the Cook County jail had symptoms of serious

mental disorders. Suicide is another concern. The rate of suicide among people in custody is 2 to 9 times higher than that in the community, and, of all those in custody, the highest rates are found among defendants awaiting trial (Rowan, 1998).

Functions

A jail is expected to serve three basic functions. First, it serves as a clearinghouse and referral source for arrested individuals. After an arrest, decisions must be made as to who can be released and who should be detained pending arraignment. Those individuals with urgent physical or mental problems must be identified and referred or treated (Anno, 1991). These decisions require assessment.

After arraignment, the second function of the jail is to provide for the secure detention of accused offenders who may flee to avoid prosecution or who may commit further crimes while awaiting trial. Such defendants can remain in the jail awaiting trial for weeks or months, so additional assessment and screening are necessary to decide where and with whom they should be placed, and to determine what services and programs they should be afforded. This last task is complicated by the fact that the correctional system is not supposed to attempt to rehabilitate unconvicted individuals who, at this point in the proceedings, are not considered guilty of any crime (National Advisory Commission on Criminal Justice Standards and Goals, 1973).

The third and final function of the jail is to serve as a correctional facility for those convicted of misdemeanors and sentenced to periods of confinement of less than a year. This requires further screening to identify those offenders with special needs for physical or mental health care or interventions (Anno, 1991). Additional assessment is needed to help formulate a management and treatment plan for each offender to guide his or her placement within the facility and to determine the type of programming that is most appropriate.

Mental Health Staffing

Given the round-the-clock need for both mental and physical screening of new arrivals, it is more difficult to provide adequate psychological services in jails than in any other component of the criminal justice system. Smaller facilities often cannot afford the services of a full-time licensed psychologist. Even if a jail has adequate financial resources, those in rural or isolated areas may not be able to find well-qualified practitioners, especially ones having correctional experience.

The AACP (2000) standards adjust expected staffing levels to the size of the jail. Jails with an average daily population (ADP) of 10 or fewer should have a psychologist on call. Those with an ADP of 11 to 75 inmates are expected to have a contract psychologist in the facility at least 8 hr a week; those with an ADP of 76 to 125 should have one on site at least 16 hr a week; and those with an ADP greater than 125 should have a full-time psychologist on staff. Larger facilities should have one full-time mental health staff person for every 150 to 160 inmates. Furthermore, the standards suggest that the composition of the staff should reflect the ethnic, racial, gender, and linguistic makeup of the inmate population.

It is unlikely that many facilities meet all these ideals. Jails are probably the most underfunded of all the elements in the criminal justice system; sheriffs typically focus more on law enforcement than on corrections, and jails are often hard put to meet the basic physical and security needs of their inmates. Except in the case of the most flagrantly and acutely disturbed inmates, mental health services may regarded as a luxury. Even in those jails that do meet the recommended staffing guidelines, the inmate-to-psychologist ratio is often so high that the best use of the psychologists' time is assessing offenders and training paraprofessionals to recognize the signs and symptoms of mental disorders so they can refer disturbed inmates for further evaluation.

Assessment

People arrive at the jail directly from the street at all hours of the day and night. Often they are in acute need of physical or mental health care. Acute mental health problems can include psychosis, agitation, anger, depression, intoxication, and drug withdrawal. The first requirement in jails is screening new admissions for physical and mental conditions that require immediate intervention, and identifying those who pose a threat to others or to themselves. Reception screening should take place before the inmate is placed in a double cell or into the general population of the jail (AACP, 2000).

The AACP standards state the following:

The reception screening process should include (a) a review of papers or records accompanying the inmate, (b) completion of the reception screening form with the help of the inmate (i.e. a review of the inmate's mental health history concerning suicidal behavior, sexual deviancy, alcohol and other substance abuse, hospitalizations, seizures, and patterns of violence and aggression), and (c) visual observations of the inmate's behavior (i.e. observing for signs of delusions, hallucinations, communication difficulties, peculiar speech and/or posturing, impaired level of consciousness, disorganization, memory deficits, depression, and evidence of self-mutilation). (2000, p. 465)

Intake and reception personnel who have been appropriately trained to recognize the signs of acute mental and physical disorders can screen newly arrived inmates and make appropriate referrals to medical and psychological consultants or agencies. Rowan (1998) noted that the officer who transported the inmate to the jail is another useful source of information.

Inmates referred for additional psychological assessment should be evaluated by qualified mental health personnel within two weeks of referral. This should include reviewing intake records and referral information, contacting the individual's prior therapists or personal physician for information regarding his or her mental health history, conducting an extensive diagnostic interview, and writing and filing a brief report. (Although not specifically called for by the AACP standards, psychological testing is also appropriate if qualified personnel are available to administer and interpret the tests.) If signs of mental disturbance or disorder are found, the inmate should be placed in a separate area where closer supervision is possible. The psychologist should formulate a treatment plan that can be carried out in the jail by staff members or, if release is imminent, by referral to an appropriate mental health resource in the community (AACP, 2000, p. 466).

Probation

Despite the fact that probation is the most common form of correctional supervision in the United States, there has been less written about probation in the psychological literature than there is about any other component of corrections.

Functions

When a juvenile or adult defendant pleads guilty or is convicted of committing a crime, the court often considers probation as an option, especially for younger offenders with relatively benign criminal histories who have been charged with relatively minor, nonviolent offenses. The probationer is expected to report to his or her supervising probation officer at regular intervals and to abide by other conditions of probation, which may include attending school, maintaining gainful employment, participating in various forms of treatment (e.g., anger management or DUI [driving under the influence] school), and, obviously, refraining from further criminal activity. Successful completion of probation may get the original offense expunged from the probationer's record, but failure to comply with the terms of probation may mean that the offender is remanded into custody and sentenced on the original charges.

The clients encountered in a probation service differ from those found in a jail. The most disturbed and acutely ill individuals should have been referred to the mental health system. The adult clients have all been convicted and their attorneys have advised them it is in their best interest to make a favorable impression on the psychologist. Most are quite cooperative. Malingering is rare, but psychologists must be prepared for positive dissimulation.

Mental Health Staffing

Neither the AACP or the NCCHC standards specify mental health staffing levels in outpatient settings such as probation or parole. Some probation departments employ their own staff psychologists. Many employ private practitioners on a contract or consulting basis. Others refer clients to the county's community mental health center for assessment and treatment.

Assessment

Individual assessment is often a primary function of correctional psychologists in probation services. When a juvenile is accused or an adult is convicted of a criminal offense, the court may order a probation report. The investigating probation officer (PO) compiles a detailed case history on the basis of interviews with the defendant and with other relevant sources such as family members, teachers, and employers. As part of this investigation, the PO may request a psychological evaluation. This may focus on *diagnosis* (What is wrong with this person? Why is she running away from home, doing drugs, not attending school? Why is he stealing cars, getting into fights?) or *prognosis* (If we place this person on probation will he or she make us look bad? Will she pass more bad checks? Will he keep hitting his wife?).

After a defendant has been placed on probation, a supervising PO may request an evaluation to assist in management or treatment. (Should I set strict limits or be supportive? Will this probationer benefit from group therapy?)

The first step is to meet with the PO and clarify the reason for the referral. Often the psychologist can answer the referral question using information the PO has already collected. This not only takes care of the referral but helps train the PO.

Often, however, an individual appraisal is indicated. If so, it helps to have as much case-history information as possible, including not only the prosecution's description of the current offense (colloquially referred to as "the D.A.'s short story"), the prior criminal history, and whatever information the PO has been able to glean from the defendant's family, teachers, or employers. If time permits, and the defendant signs a release, reports from other mental health personnel who may have conducted evaluations can also be helpful. The choice of assessment techniques should be geared to the issues raised by the referral question; in addition to a clinical interview, individual intelligence, achievement, and personality tests are often indicated.

Prisons and Correctional Institutions

Most empirical research on correctional assessment has taken place in prisons and correctional institutions. As noted earlier, prisoners are a captive population. The one thing they have in abundance is time, which makes them an excellent source of research participants.

Functions

The basic function of prisons is to confine convicted felons in a secure setting for the period of time specified by the sentencing judge. While they are incarcerated, the courts have held that prisoners (as well as pretrial detainees) have a constitutional right to adequate and sufficient medical care under the Eighth Amendment's prohibition against "cruel and unusual punishments" (Estelle v. Gamble, 429 U.S. 97, [1976], cited by Kay, 1991, p. 3). The courts have further held that this includes mental as well as physical health care, because "there is no underlying distinction between the right to medical care for physical ills and its psychological or psychiatric counterpart" (Bowring v. Godwin, 551 F. 2d 44, 47 [4th Cir. 1977], quoted by Kay, p. 15).

Prisons are expected to do more than confine inmates and preserve their health. Various segments of society also expect prisons to incapacitate, punish, rehabilitate, or reform inmates, while deterring criminal behavior in other potential offenders—a mélange of demands that are often mutually exclusive.

To accomplish these goals, further assessment is required. To protect society and incapacitate offenders, correctional institutions must place them in settings that are sufficiently secure that the prisoners cannot or will not abscond or escape. However, the courts have also held that prisoners are entitled to the "least restrictive custody level that is commensurate with their own safety and the safety of other inmates, staff, and the community" (Solomon & Camp, 1993, p. 9). This means assessing the security and supervision levels required by each inmate (Levinson, 1988). Further evaluations are needed to formulate management and treatment plans designed to rehabilitate or reform offenders. Moreover, overcrowding may require establishing priorities for inmates' access to treatment programs.

Mental Health Staffing

The AACP (2000) standards stipulate that there should be at least one licensed, doctoral-level, full-time psychologist with correctional experience who is responsible for the delivery of psychological services on staff at each correctional facility and at the headquarters of a multisite system. In ordinary correctional institutions, the expected ratio is 1 full-time psychologist for every 150 to 160 inmates; in specialized treatment units, such as those for drug-dependent or mentally ill inmates, the ratio should be 1 for every 50 to 75 adult offenders. As with jails, it is expected that the qualified mental health professionals will train line staff to recognize the signs of mental illness, potential suicide, or mental retardation and refer such inmates for more extensive mental health evaluations.

Assessment

After sentencing, offenders are typically held in the local jail until they can be transferred, along with copies of their legal, medical, and psychological records, to the state correctional system, often to a facility that is set aside for admission and classification. At the classification center, newly admitted inmates should immediately be screened for signs of mental illness, developmental disabilities, and potential suicide by qualified health care professionals.

Within the first week (AACP, 2000) or 14 days (NCCHC, 1997) after admission, a mental health assessment should be conducted. The AACP standards (2000, p. 465) state, "Such routine evaluations should be brief and include (but not be limited to) behavioral observations, record review, group testing to screen for emotional and intellectual abnormalities, and a written report of initial findings." The NCCHC's (1997) prison standards also stipulate that group or brief individual intelligence tests should be administered as part of the initial mental health assessment.

Classification

Classification is the next major assessment task. In 1973, the National Advisory Commission on Criminal Justice Standards and Goals called for the immediate implementation of comprehensive classification systems at all levels of the criminal justice system, arguing that

> classification can make handling large numbers of offenders more efficient through a grouping process based on needs and problems. From an administrative standpoint, classification systems can provide for more orderly processing and handling of individuals. From a financial standpoint, classification schemes can enable administrators to make more efficient use of limited resources and to avoid providing resources for offenders who do not require them. (1973, p. 201)

The courts agreed. In Palmigiano v. Garrahy (443 F. Supp. 956, D.R.I. 1977, cited by Solomon & Camp, 1993, p. 5), the court held, "Classification is essential to the operation of an orderly and safe prison system. It enables the institution to gauge the proper custody level of an inmate, to identify the inmate's educational, vocational and psychological needs, and to separate non-violent inmates from the more predatory."

Parole

The role of the psychologist in parole services is similar to that in probation. In both instances, community placement of convicted offenders is being considered; the difference is that paroled offenders have served part of their sentence and are being released to supervised placement in the community subject to certain specified conditions. If they do not abide by these conditions or if they commit additional crimes, their parole can be revoked and they are returned to serve the balance of their sentence.

Psychological assessments may be requested to help determine whether prison inmates are ready for parole and, if so, what conditions should be imposed. As with initial classification, a number of objective devices have been created to predict both general and violent recidivism, as well as sexual predation. Some of these instruments will be described and discussed in the next section.

Once an offender has been paroled, the supervising parole officer may request a psychological assessment to assist in management or treatment. In these cases, the task is similar to that of psychologists in probation settings.

RISK ASSESSMENT AND EXTERNAL CLASSIFICATION

Risk assessment used to be referred to as *predicting dangerousness* (Heilbrun & Heilbrun, 1995). Today it is recognized that the threat an offender poses to others depends in part on the setting and circumstances.

External classification focuses on assigning prison inmates to the most appropriate facilities in a multisite system. Robert Levinson, an architect of the Federal Bureau of Prisons' (BOP's) classification system, wrote, "The goal of this first stage of the classification process is to designate new arrivals to the least restrictive correctional institution that appropriately matches the offenders' needs for security and control" (1988, p. 25). The latter elements are operationally defined by architectural features such as the presence or absence of walls, fences, gun towers, sally ports, and corridor grills, and by the amount of supervision afforded each offender. In all but the smallest states, security levels for male

prisoners typically range from maximum security penitentiaries, through medium security correctional institutions,
down to minimum security open camps. Women, who comprise only 5% of the incarcerated population, have fewer options available; 19 states have only one correctional facility
for all their female prisoners (ACA, 2000).

Risk assessment is also central to whether offenders can
be placed in the community on probation or parole. Much of
the initial research on risk assessment involved attempts to
predict parole success (Glaser, 1987). More recently, a number of states have passed laws permitting the continued confinement and treatment of mentally disordered sex offenders
(MDSOs) whose prison sentences may have expired, if they
pose a threat to the community. Psychologists are often involved in these determinations.

Approaches to Risk Prediction

A number of approaches to risk prediction have been
adopted. *Clinical judgment* relies on the expertise and experience of correctional professionals, such as caseworkers and
correctional psychologists. *Objective methods* utilize standard instruments such as checklists, scorecards, decision
trees, and regression equations to calculate each offender's
risk for various types of undesirable behavior. In some settings, assessment personnel can override the instrument; in
others, they cannot.

Objective methods can be derived *rationally* or *empirically.* Rationally constructed instruments try to capture the
judgments of classification experts and apply them in a standard fashion. Empirically derived tools typically compare
groups of offenders who differ with regard to the behavior in
question, such as adjustment to prison, and combine the factors that significantly differentiate groups into an objective
instrument. In addition to clinical judgment and specially constructed objective risk assessment devices, certain *psychological scales and tests* have also been applied to risk assessment
in correctional settings. In this section we will describe and
discuss each of these approaches to risk assessment.

Subjective Judgment

The earliest and probably most ubiquitous approach to risk
assessment was the clinical judgment of experienced caseworkers and correctional psychologists. Parole board members in both the United Kingdom and the United States often
base their decisions on their individual evaluations of each
offender (Glaser, 1987; Tidmarsh, 1997). For example, the
British Prison Service's Wakefield model uses expert clinical
judgment to weigh factors and arrive at judgments about the
amount of time (*tariff*) that each convicted lifer should serve
(Clark, 1994).

Clinical risk assessment has been criticized as being
overly subjective and potentially influenced by illusory correlation and hindsight bias (Towl & Crighton, 1995). This
was illustrated by Cooper and Werner's (1990) investigation
of the abilities of 10 psychologists and 11 caseworkers to predict institutional violence, based on 17 variables in a sample
of 33 male federal correctional institution inmates, 8 of
whom (24%) were violent and 25 of whom (76%) were not.
They found that interjudge reliabilities were quite low, aver-
aging only .23 between pairs of judges. Pooled judgments
were substantially more reliable than individual assessments.
Accuracy was appalling; the psychologists' predictive accuracy averaged only −.08 (range = −.25 to +.22), while the
caseworkers' mean accuracy was +.08 (range = −.14 to
+.34). The main reason for the inaccuracy appeared to be
illusory correlation, with judges often using cues that proved
to be unrelated to the criterion.

According to James Austin, the executive vice president
of the National Council on Crime and Delinquency,

> Prior to the development of objective prison classification
> systems in the late 1970s and through the 1980s, classification
> decisions were largely based on the subjective judgment of cor-
> rections professionals who relied on experience and intuition.
> Although agencies sometimes specified criteria to be considered
> by classification staff, the relative importance of each factor was
> left to the subjective judgment of each staff person or the un-
> charted consensus of a classification committee. Such informal
> criteria may have had little or no relationship to actual prison
> behavior and, generally, served to perpetuate myths regarding
> offender conduct. (Austin, 1993, pp. 108–109)

Subjective classification procedures were impossible to
document, which resulted in a lack of oversight and accountability. One result was chronic *overclassification,* with
offenders being assigned to more restrictive conditions of confinement than were necessary. In a series of cases, the courts
held that subjective classifications were too often arbitrary,
capricious, inconsistent, and invalid (Austin, 1993; Solomon
& Camp, 1993). In Laaman v. Helgemoe (437 F. Supp. 318,
D.N.H. 1977, quoted by Solomon & Camp, p. 9), the court
stated that classification systems "cannot be arbitrary, irrational, or discriminatory," and in Alabama the court took over
the entire correctional system and ordered every inmate
reclassified (Fowler, 1976).

Objective Risk Assessment

Objective or standard risk-assessment instruments were created to minimize the subjectivity and unreliability associated
with clinical decision making. Objective tools evaluate each
offender on the same set of criteria. The results are then

tabulated in some fashion, and predetermined, uniform decision functions, such as cutting scores or decision trees, decide the outcome. As long as classification personnel do not override the decision, as they may in some settings, each offender is reliably evaluated according to the same criteria. Whether these criteria and the resulting decisions are valid, is, of course, an empirical question.

A number of objective tools have been devised to aid in risk assessment. One of the earliest applications of objective predictive devices was the construction of a *salient factor score,* which was used in conjunction with the length of the original sentence to assist in parole decision-making by the U.S. Board of Parole (Gottfredson, Wilkins, & Hoffman, 1978). The variables in the Parole Board's salient factor score were prior conviction, prior incarcerations, age at first arrest, type of offense, history of parole revocations, drug use, education, employment history, and release plan. More recently, the Federal BOP and a number of state departments of corrections have devised external classification instruments to indicate appropriate custody and supervision levels in correctional institutions (Austin, 1993; Brennan, 1987, 1993; Glaser, 1987). In Canada, the Level of Supervision Inventory (Bonta & Motiuk, 1985) is used to guide probation and halfway-house placement.

A number of instruments to predict violence have been devised in correctional mental health facilities. In Canada, Webster and his associates contributed both the Dangerous Behaviour Rating Scale (DBRS), based on Megargee's (1982, 1993) "algebra of aggression model" (Webster & Menzies, 1993); and the Violence Risk Assessment Guide (Harris, Rice, & Quinsey, 1993), a record-based assessment tool that, when combined with a 10-item clinical scale (ASSESS-LIST; Webster & Polvi, 1995), comprises (a) the Violence Prediction Scheme (VPS; Webster, Harris, Rice, Cormier, & Quinsey, 1994), (b) the Spousal Assault Risk Assessment Guide (SARA; Kropp, Hart, Webster, & Eeaves, 1994), and, most recently, (c) the HCR-20: Assessing Risk for Violence (Webster, Douglas, Eaves, & Hart, 1997). In the United States, risk assessment tools have been devised by Klassen and O'Connor (1988) and by the MacArthur Risk Assessment Study (Steadman et al., 1994). For more detailed reviews of these schemes see Austin (1993), Brennan (1987, 1993), Glaser (1987), Heilbrun and Heilbrun (1995), Monahan (1996), and Otto (2000).

With the passage of legislation allowing for the continued postsentence detention and treatment of sex offenders deemed likely to reoffend, several tools aimed specifically at predicting sexual recidivism have been constructed. They include the Minnesota Sex Offender Screening Tool (MnSOST; Epperson, Kaul, & Huot, 1995); the Rapid Risk Assessment

for Sexual Offender Recidivism (RRASOR; Hanson, 1997); the Sex Offender Risk Appraisal Guide (SORAG; Quinsey, Harris, Rice, & Cormier, 1998); and the Sexual Violence Risk–20 (SVR-20; Boer, Hart, Kropp, & Webster, 1997).

Rationally Derived Instruments. Some objective risk-assessment schemes are based on clinical intuition and correctional experience; they combine factors that their creators believe are associated with misconduct, violence, or recidivism. The BOP's rationally derived model, which has been adopted or adapted by a number of state correctional systems, bases security-level classification on the expected length of incarceration, offense severity, type of prior commitment, history of violence or escape attempts, and types of detainers (Kane, 1993). Proctor (1994), evaluating Nebraska's adaptation of the BOP model, noted that it accounted for only 3% of the variance in institutional adjustment and concluded, "The results regarding the predictive validity of the Nebraska model suggest that the classification model was not a valid instrument for predicting institutional adjustment" (p. 267).

Empirically Derived Instruments. As one might expect, empirically devised schemes have fared better. Several studies showed that actuarial or statistical predictions of prison misconduct and parole success were superior to experts' subjective judgments (Gendreau, Goggin, & Law, 1997; Glaser, 1955, 1962; Gottfredson & Beverly, 1962), a point made in other contexts by Meehl (1954) approximately half a century ago.

These tools have typically been devised by retrospective comparisons of two criterion groups such as violent versus nonviolent prisoners, or recidivists versus nonrecidivists. Investigators then examine the information available in the case records to determine empirically which social, demographic, criminal-history, or other variables significantly differentiate the criterion groups. These schemes seem to work best in correctional mental health facilities (which typically have more data available, including psychological evaluations, than ordinary correctional institutions).

These risk factors are then combined into a predictive scheme. Some investigators use multiple regression equations or weighted discriminant functions, some use simple additive models in which points are assigned for each risk factor, and some use decision trees. In general, the simpler the model, the more readily it is adopted. As Brennan (1993, p. 65) noted, "Advanced statistical and quantitative procedures have had minimal use in applied corrections. Any method that requires line officers to do much more than simple arithmetic is perceived as being too mathematically cumbersome, too inefficient, or too advanced for successful introduction into applied corrections." However, Gardner, Lidz, Mulvey, and Shaw's (1996) comparison of different actuarial models for identifying mental patients prone to repetitive violence indicated that simpler decision trees and two-stage screening procedures were as accurate as the more complex regression methods.

Many of the same variables turn up in the different schemes. They include such demographic variables as age, race, education, socioeconomic status, marital status, and job stability, as well as criminal history variables (e.g., age at first arrest; the nature of the present offense; the length of the present sentence or the time remaining to be served; and the number of previous arrests, convictions, violent offenses, incarcerations, and escapes). Some of these variables are, of course, highly intercorrelated. Including several highly correlated variables has the effect of weighting whatever factor they represent more heavily. Obviously, instruments based only on past history cannot factor in the success or failure of treatment interventions. Moreover, independent cross-validations frequently show that many are not strongly related to the criterion measures (Brennan, 1987; Hanson & Bussiere, 1998; Towl & Crighton, 1995). The use of race and variables highly correlated with race in some of these predictive schemes is controversial. Inclusion of these variables may promote racial discrimination in classification and parole decisions, but exclusion decreases their predictive accuracy (Petersilia & Turner, 1987).

Instruments used to predict sexual reoffending are apt to add the nature of the sex offense, the gender and age of the victims, and whether the client successfully completed his treatment program. Indices derived in correctional mental health facilities may include such variables as psychiatric diagnosis, psychopathy as measured by Hare's Psychopathy Checklist–Revised (PCL-R; Hare, 1991), and response to or compliance with treatment. Rogers (2000) has criticized these schemes because they typically fail to include protective factors that might diminish risk. Techniques focusing on the prediction of violent recidivism or sexual reoffending should be applied only to offenders who already have a history of violence or sexual predation (Otto, 2000).

Actuarially derived prediction tools have improved the accuracy of correctional classification, but they are far from infallible. Hanson and Bussiere (1998) conducted a meta-analysis of 61 studies of variables associated with recidivism on the part of sex offenders and discovered that many of the commonly used risk factors were not significantly associated with reoffending. They also noted that different variables were associated with general recidivism and sexual reoffending. Brennan (1993) reported that actuarial prediction tables account for about 20% of the variance in the different

outcome measures. Otto (2000) estimated that their application in forensic mental health units had increased the accuracy of predictions of future violence among previously violent psychiatric patients from about 33% to about 50%.

Personality Assessment Instruments

Psychological tests developed in other contexts and for other purposes have also been used in risk assessment. For example, certain scales of the Minnesota Multiphasic Personality Inventory–2 (MMPI-2; Butcher, Dahlstrom, Graham, Tellegen, & Kaemmer, 1989) have been correlated with measures of institutional adjustment and violence (Megargee & Carbonell, 1995). The correlations, although significant, have generally been too low to be of much value in risk assessment, and multiple regression equations were not much better. All in all, the MMPI-2 is better at assessing offenders' mental health, adjustment, and need for treatment or other professional interventions (or *needs assessment*) than it is at estimating how dangerous they are.

Psychopathy Checklist–Revised (PCL-R; Hare, 1991). The psychological assessment device that has the best track record with regard to risk assessment is Hare's (1991) PCL-R. Devised to assess the construct of psychopathy as originally delineated by Cleckley (1941/1976), the PCL-R is a psychometric device that is often used in risk assessment among criminal offenders. Meloy and Gacono (1995) reported that criminal offenders classified as psychopaths on the basis of their PCL-R scores commit a greater number and variety of criminal offenses, including more predatory violent offenses, and have longer criminal careers than nonpsychopathic offenders. Although violent behavior is not a defining characteristic of psychopathy, psychopathic offenders' impulsivity, poor behavioral control, and lack of empathy for others make psychopaths prone to violence (Hart, 1996).

PCL-R assessments require a thorough review of the clinical and legal records. This is followed by a clinical interview in which a complete chronological case history is obtained. Although some researchers compute PCL-R scores based only on file data (e.g., Harris et al., 1993), this is not recommended (Meloy & Gacono, 1995).

The PCL-R consists of 20 symptoms of psychopathy, each of which is scored on a 3-point scale from 0 (*absent*) to 2 (*clearly present*). Interrater reliabilities average .86, and users are advised to base assessments on the average of two or more independent ratings whenever possible (Hare, Harpur, Hakstian, Forth, Hart, & Newman, 1990). Although Hare et al. regard the PCL-R as a homogenous, unidimensional scale based on its average alpha coefficient of .88, there are two well-defined factors. The first reflects an egocentric, self-ish interpersonal style with its principle loadings from such items as glibness/superficial charm (.86), grandiose sense of self-worth (.76), pathological lying (.62), conning/manipulative (.59), shallow affect (.57), lack of remorse or guilt (.53), and callous/lack of empathy (.53). The items loading on the second factor suggest the chronic antisocial behavior associated with psychopathy: impulsivity (.66), juvenile delinquency (.59), and need for stimulation, parasitic life style, early behavior problems, and lack of realistic goals (all loading .56; Hare et al.).

Some use the PCL-R to identify psychopaths; although the conventional cutting score is 30, Meloy and Gacono (1995) recommend a cutting score of 33 for clinical purposes. Others treat the PCL-R as a scale and enter PCL-R scores into predictive equations. These differing practices reflect a fundamental disagreement about the nature of psychopathy; that is, is psychopathy a dimension of deviance, or are psychopaths qualitatively different from other offenders?

A number of studies have shown that PCL-R scores correlate with recidivism in general and violent recidivism in particular. In their follow-up of 618 men discharged from a maximum security psychiatric institution, Harris et al. (1993) reported that, of all the variables they studied, the PCL-R had the highest correlation (+.35) with violent recidivism, and they included psychopathy, as defined by PCL-R scores greater than 25, as a predictor in their VRAG. Rice and Harris (1997) reported the PCL-R was also associated with sexual reoffending by child molesters and rapists. Reviewing a number of empirical investigations, both retrospective and prospective, Hart (1996) reported that psychopaths as diagnosed by the PCL-R had higher rates of violence in the community and in institutions than nonpsychopaths, and that psychopathy, as measured by the PCL-R, was predictive of violence after admission to a hospital ward and also after conditional release from a hospital or correctional institution. He estimated that the average correlation of psychopathy with violence in these studies was about .35. In their meta-analysis of 18 studies relating the original and revised PCLs to violent and nonviolent recidivism, Salekin, Rogers, and Sewell (1996) found 29 reports of effect sizes ranging from 0.42 to 1.92, with a mean of 0.79. They reported, "We found that the PCL and PCL-R had moderate to strong effect sizes and appear to be good predictors of violence and general recidivism" (p. 203). Hart summarized it best when he concluded, "predictions of violence using the PCL-R are considerably better than chance, albeit far from perfect" (1996, p. 64).

As is the case with many risk assessment instruments, PCL-R scores in the clinical range are meaningful but those below the cutoff have no clear relation to behavior. Specifically, low PCL-R scores do not guarantee that an offender will never recidivate or be violent.

Although the PCL-R has been used most often for risk assessment, it also has implications for treatment planning. Suedfeld and Landon (1978, p. 369) summarized the results of attempting to treat psychopaths as "not much to show for the amount of time, effort, and money spent." In correctional facilities where treatment resources are scarce and access must be limited to those most likely to profit from interventions, such findings suggest that psychopaths should have lower priority than other offenders.

The PCL-R has shown rather good generalizability, being associated with recidivism and violence among male offenders in the United States and Sweden (Grann, Längström, Tengström, & Kellgren, 1999), as well as those in Canada. There is some question, however, about its applicability to minorities. Black American men score higher than their White American counterparts, and there is insufficient research on the PCL-R with large samples of Asians, Hispanics, or Native Americans or with women (Meloy & Gacono, 1995).

To obtain reliable and valid PCL-R ratings, it is important to have good case histories and interviewer-raters who are trained in Hare's technique. Such records and personnel are more likely to be found in correctional mental health facilities and neuropsychiatric hospitals than in prisons, and it is not surprising that the PCL-R has been used most successfully in those settings. In ordinary correctional institutions and jails, it would probably not be practical to use the PCL-R for mass screening, although it may be feasible to administer it to select groups, such as previously violent offenders being considered for parole.

Evaluating Risk Assessment Instruments

It is impossible to evaluate the predictive validity of risk assessment instruments accurately. Consider a parole prediction instrument. To evaluate it properly, one must first predict which prisoners eligible for parole are most likely to succeed or fail according to whatever criteria one selected. Then they must all be paroled, regardless of the predicted risk. After a year or so, a follow-up should be conducted that will enable the researcher to calculate whether those predicted to fail actually were more violent, committed more new crimes, or violated the conditions of parole more than those predicted to succeed. If not all applicants were released, it is impossible to determine how many of those who were predicted to fail and denied parole actually would have succeeded had they been released (i.e., the false-positive rate; Megargee, 1976). Unfortunately for researchers, parole boards are understandably reluctant to release all eligible applicants in order to test their predictive devices.

Similar considerations apply to security- and custody-level assignments. To properly assess their accuracy, it would be necessary to assign offenders randomly to different facilities without regard for their estimated risk levels. Otherwise, we cannot know whether a high-risk offender who failed to act out was a classification error or was simply deterred from misconduct by being assigned to a maximum security setting with stringent external controls.

Base rates are another vital concern. The closer the incidence of the behavior in question is to 50%, the greater the potential contribution that a predictive tool can make. The more infrequent the behavior, the greater the number of false positives that can be expected (Brennan, 1993; Finn & Kamphuis, 1995; Meehl & Rosen, 1955; Megargee, 1976, 1981). Since violence is still a rare event, even in prisons, the number of false positives is likely to be high.

For this reason it is important to consider the consequences of incorrect classifications (Megargee, 1976). If the risk assessment merely influences the dormitory to which offenders are assigned and has no impact on their programming or other conditions of confinement, the results of being misclassified are relatively benign. On the other hand, if the outcome is involuntary commitment or preventive detention, the consequences for false positives are quite serious. Campbell (2000) recently argued that the schemes suggested for assessing the likelihood that sexual predators will reoffend are, at best, experimental. Likening them to phrenology, he maintained that, at this stage of their development, using them to decide whether a sex offender should be kept in custody beyond the expiration of his prison term is contrary to the American Psychological Association's (1992) ethical standards governing the use of psychological tests.

The generality of predictive instruments is another concern. In order to economize, predictive devices derived in one setting have frequently been applied in other jurisdictions. For example, the National Institute of Corrections (1981) encouraged other states to adopt the Wisconsin method of risk assessment for probation and parole decisions rather than going to the time and expense of developing their own instruments. However, when Wright, Clear, and Dickson (1984) tested the Wisconsin system in New York, they discovered that "a number of variables in the Wisconsin model were found to be unrelated to outcome" in their sample (p. 117). They advised practitioners to test the generality of prediction models in their settings before using them in actual decision making.

Although the emphasis in risk assessment is on diagnosing the most dangerous offenders, the greatest contribution of these classification tools has been to identify low-risk prisoners who could safely be assigned to less secure correctional programs or placed in the community (Austin, 1993; Glaser, 1987; Solomon & Camp, 1993). When making subjective predictions of violence, classifications personnel are often overly conservative, placing many offenders in higher-than-necessary risk categories (Heilbrun & Heilbrun, 1995; Monahan, 1981, 1996; Proctor, 1994; Solomon & Camp). This is not surprising. The public is rarely incensed if low-risk offenders are retained in more restrictive settings than necessary, but clinicians can expect to be castigated if someone they approved for minimum security or early release goes out to rape, pillage, and plunder the community.

Reducing the extent of overclassification has three important benefits. First, it is the correct thing to do; as noted previously, the courts have consistently ruled that offenders have the right to be maintained in the least restrictive settings consistent with maintaining safety, order, and discipline. Second, less restrictive settings are more economical; confining an offender in a maximum security institution costs $3,000 a year more than a minimum security facility and $7,000 more than a community setting. Third, the residents benefit because more programming is possible in less restrictive settings, and the deleterious effects of crowding are diminished (Proctor, 1994).

Internal Classification

After external classification and risk assessment have determined offenders' custody and security levels and assigned offenders to the most appropriate correctional facilities, *internal classification* is used to further subdivide the institutional population into homogenous subgroups for housing and management. According to Levinson,

> Internal classification is the final stage in the classification process. It is a systematic method that identifies homogeneous prisoner subgroups within a single institution's population. Although the degree of variation among one facility's inhabitants is smaller than that found in the total prison system, every institution has a range of inmates—from the predators at one extreme to their prey at the other end of the continuum. Various labels are used to define these individuals: thugs, toughs, wolves, agitators, con-artists, in contrast to weak sisters, sheep, dependents, victims, and other expressions less acceptable in polite society. (1988, p. 27)

The goal of internal classification is to separate these groups in order to reduce the incidence of problematic and disruptive behavior within the institution.

Other factors that influence management and housing decisions are the amount of supervision each offender is likely to need, his or her sense of responsibility and response to supervision, the approach correctional officers should take in working with him or her, and whether he or she will respond better to strict discipline or a more casual correctional atmosphere (Wright, 1986, 1988). In many BOP facilities, Quay's (1984) Adult Internal Management System (AIMS) is used for internal classification.

The Adult Internal Management System

Based on extensive factor analytic research with juvenile (Jenkins, 1943; Jenkins & Glickman, 1947; Hewitt & Jenkins, 1946; Quay, 1965) and adult offenders, Quay (1973, 1974, 1984) defined five adult-offender types:

- *Type I* (aggressive-psychopathic) offenders are the most antisocial and have the most trouble with authorities. Easily bored, and having little concern for others, they are the ones who are most apt to exploit others and cause difficulties and disturbances in an institution.

- *Type II* (manipulative) offenders are less aggressive and confrontational but no less untrustworthy, unreliable, and hostile to authority. They may organize inmate gangs and manipulate others for their own ends.

- *Type III* (moderate) inmates are neither very aggressive nor very weak. Often situational offenders, they have less extensive criminal histories than the first two types and are more responsible and trustworthy.

- *Type IV* (inadequate-dependent) offenders are weak, immature, and indecisive. Rarely involved in disciplinary infractions, they are seen by staff as emotionally dependent and clinging.

- *Type V* (neurotic-anxious) offenders are anxious, worried, and easily upset. They are apt to be exploited or victimized by other offenders.

The primary goal of the AIMS system is to separate the heavy (Types I and II) from the light (Types IV and V) offenders by assigning them to separate living units and arranging their programs so they have minimal contact with one another (Levinson, 1988). However, Quay (1984) also provides differential programming guidelines for the heavy, moderate, and light offenders with regard to educational programming, work assignments, counseling, and staff approach. For example, correctional staff are advised to adopt a no-nonsense, by-the-book approach for the heavies, to supervise moderates only as needed, and to be highly verbal and supportive with the lights.

Categorization into the Quay types is based on two rating forms, the Correctional Adjustment Checklist (CACL) and the Checklist for the Analysis of Life History Records of Adult Offenders (CALH). The CACL is filled out by trained correctional officers on the basis of their observations of the inmates' behavior during the first 2 to 4 weeks after admission (Quay, 1984). Each of the 41 items, such as "Easily upset" or "Has a quick temper," is scored as 0 (*not observed*) or 1 (*observed*). Each item is indicative of a different Quay type, and the number of items checked determines the raw score on each of the five scales.

The 27-item CALH is filled out by a trained caseworker on the basis of the information contained in the presentence investigation report. It contains such behavioral items as "Has few, if any, friends" or "Thrill-seeking," and, as with the CACL, each is scored as present or absent. Offenders are classified into the category on which they receive the highest score. Quay (1984) did not provide interrater reliability data.

In addition to the factor analytic research that guided the development of the AIMS system, Quay (1984) cites five sources of evidence for the validity and utility of the AIMS system: (a) significant reductions in the number of assaults at penitentiaries where it was adopted, (b) significant reductions in misconduct where it was adopted, (c) testimonials from wardens and administrators, (d) convergence between AIMS classifications and parole board Salient Factor Scores, and (e) convergence between AIMS classifications and BOP custody- and security-level ratings.

One drawback to the AIMS system is the time required to obtain valid CACL ratings. Staff should have 2 to 2 weeks to observe behavior before completing the CACL, and some correctional facilities demand quicker results. Quay (1984) himself acknowledges that AIMS has limited utility in jails that have rapid turnover and sparse case history records.

Another concern is the availability of adequate life history information. Attempting to implement the AIMS system in Scotland's largest prison, Cooke, Walker, and Gardiner (1990) found it was difficult to obtain the biographical information needed to complete the CALH. In some settings, staff members resist spending the time and effort required to observe inmates, review case files, and fill out the rating forms. In Van Voorhis's (1994) comparison of five psychological classification systems for adult male offenders, she reported that the AIMS was the most difficult to complete because of the lack of staff cooperation. Some staff sabotaged the administration by checking every item for every inmate. She eventually had to hire additional personnel in order to get the CACL and CALH forms completed properly. However, she reported, "Despite these difficulties, we observe numerous significant relationships between this typology and important institutional behaviors" (1994, p. 126). Correctional psychologists using the AIMS system should be prepared to devote the time and effort required to working with and motivating the staff members who are responsible for making the assessments on which the system depends.

Needs Assessment

Sooner or later, almost all of the nearly 2 million incarcerated adult offenders will be released to return to their communities and to the approximately 2.6 million children they left behind. The goal of treatment is to maximize the chances that former offenders will become productive citizens and responsible parents instead of continuing to prey on society until they are once more arrested and returned to prison. If the correctional system is to reform or rehabilitate inmates, each offender's educational, vocational, emotional, and mental health needs must be appraised and individual management and treatment programs formulated. Treatment planning requires both of the following:

1. *Psychological assessments in order to identify offenders in need of mental health interventions.* These individuals include those who are depressed, psychotic, emotionally disturbed, and prone to self-injurious behavior, as well as those with problems centering around alcohol and substance abuse. In addition to assessing offenders' needs for treatment, program planning involves estimating each inmate's likely response to and ability to benefit from various types of intervention. In systems with limited mental health resources, each inmate's priority for treatment, based on diagnosis and prognosis, needs to be determined. (Priority for various programs is also likely to be influenced by other factors such as the offender's security level and behavior in the institution. In the 1970s, the Bureau of Prisons used a formula based on the offender's age, prior sentences, and the length of the present sentence, as well as the caseworker's rating, to determine priorities. Caseworker ratings being equal, younger offenders with few priors and short sentences were given priority for programming over older offenders with long records and considerable time left to serve.)

2. *Cognitive appraisals to evaluate each offender's need for and ability to profit from educational programming.* These decisions can be based in part on the educational history; there is no need to place college graduates in a general equivalency diploma (GED) program. However, given the extent of social promotion, a high school diploma does not necessarily guarantee literacy, so intelligence and achievement tests are often needed. As with mental health treatment, when educational resources are limited, it may be necessary to determine offenders' priorities for education based on their ability and motivation.

Intake Screening

Inmates who have just arrived at a jail or prison must be screened for serious mental illness, suicide potential, and retardation before they are placed in a double cell or mingled with the general population (Anno, 1991). In jails, the burden of this screening typically falls on the correctional staff who receive new arrivals. In prisons, the receiving evaluation should include a screening for mental illness and suicide potential by a qualified health care professional who may or may not be part of the mental health staff.

The NCCHC provides intake and mental health evaluation forms that appropriately trained reception personnel can use to screen new admissions to jails (NCCHC, 1996) and prisons (NCCHC, 1997), while the ACA has developed a self-instructional course designed to train correctional officers to recognize the signs of suicide and intervene appropriately (Rowan, 1998). This author has been unable to locate any published reports evaluating the reliability or validity of these screening instruments.

Mental Health Assessment

Many prisoners require mental health treatment and care. Reviewing a number of studies, Anno (1991) estimated that 5% to 7% of the adult prison population suffers from serious mental disorders, not including personality disorders or substance abuse problems, and an additional 10% may be considered mentally retarded.

During the course of confinement, emotional problems will naturally arise. Anno (1991) estimated that, in addition to those suffering from serious psychiatric disorders, another 15% to 20% of a prison's inmates require mental health services or interventions at some time during their incarceration.

As noted earlier, all new inmates should receive a mental health assessment within the first week (AACP, 2000) or two (NCCHC, 1997) after admission. This should include an interview and screening with group tests of intellectual and personality functioning, followed by more extensive evaluations of those who appear to show signs of mental illness or retardation or who appear at risk for self injury or suicide (AACP; NCCHC).

Intake Interview

The NCCHC's prison standards (1997, p. 47) stipulate that the mental health assessment should include a structured interview by a member of the mental health staff who inquires into the offender's (a) current psychotropic medications, (b) suicidal ideation and history, and (c) emotional response to incarceration, as well as his or her history of (d) psychiatric hospitalizations and treatments, (e) drug and alcohol use, (f) sex offenses, (g) expressive (angry) aggression or violence, (h) victimization, (i) special education placement, and (j) cerebral trauma or seizures. In addition to the interview, a group personality test and a brief group or individual test of intelligence should be administered (AACP, 2000; NCCHC). If the initial screening or the subsequent mental health assessment indicates mental illness or retardation or suggests the possibility of suicidal or self-injurious behavior, the inmate should be referred for further evaluation by a qualified mental health professional. (The NCCHC's (1997) prison standards state, "The *mental health staff* includes those qualified health professionals who may not have had formal training in working with the mentally ill or retarded, but who have received instruction in identifying and interacting with individuals in need of mental health services. *Qualified mental health professionals* include psychiatrists, psychologists, psychiatric social workers, psychiatric nurses, and others who by virtue of their education, credentials, and experience are permitted by law to evaluate and care for the mental health needs of patients" (p. 47, italics in the original).)

Minnesota Multiphasic Personality Inventory–2

The MMPI-2 is the most widely used and thoroughly researched personality assessment device in the world (Butcher, 1999). The MMPI-2 and the original MMPI have been used in corrections for almost 60 years. There are well-established correctional norms and cutting scores available (Megargee, Mercer, & Carbonell, 1999) and the correlates of the scales among criminal offenders have been thoroughly studied over the years (Megargee, 2000).

Megargee (2000) has provided detailed instructions for administration in correctional settings. Although MMPI-2 administration is not difficult, it must be done properly to achieve optimal results. A sixth-grade reading level is needed to complete MMPI-2, so it is best to administer it after reading ability has been assessed. Audiotaped forms are available for poor readers. For inmates who are not proficient in English, the MMPI-2 is available in a number of other languages.

There are three levels of analysis available for correctional psychologists using the MMPI-2. The first is to interpret the scores on the various MMPI-2 scales and indices using correctional norms and cutting scores (Megargee, 2000; Megargee et al., 1999). The second is to use Megargee's MMPI-2-based offender classification system (Megargee,

Carbonell, Bohn, & Sliger, 2001). The third is to consult the interpretative scales and possible problem areas identified by Megargee's (2000) recently developed interpretive scheme. Each will be discussed in turn.

The MMPI-2 has four types of scales: validity, basic, supplementary, and content. The eight validity scales enable the user to identify offenders who are (a) answering nonresponsively, (b) malingering (faking bad), or (c) dissembling (faking good). In assessing MMPI-2 validity in correctional settings, it is important to consult appropriate offender norms (Megargee, 2000; Megargee et al., 1999). For example, criminal offenders answering honestly may get elevations on the Infrequency (*F*) scale that would be regarded as invalid in free-world settings.

The basic, supplementary, and content scales assess a broad array of traits and behaviors, many of which are relevant to mental health assessment and treatment planning in correctional settings. For example, elevations on MMPI-2 Scales 1 (*Hs*, Hypochondriasis), 3 (*Hy*, Hysteria), and *HEA* (Health Concerns) identify offenders who are likely to use sick-call frequently. Scales 2 (*D*, Depression) and *DEP* (Depression) identify those who are depressed, and Scales 7 (*Pt*, Psychasthenia) and *ANX* (Anxiety) are associated with anxiety. Scales 4 (*Pd*, Psychopathic Deviate), 9 (*Ma*, Hypomania), and *ASP* (Antisocial Practices) reflect authority problems, antisocial behavior, and acting-out. Scale *ANG* (Anger) indicates problems with anger control, and Scales 4, *MDS* (Marital Distress), and *FAM* (Family Problems) identify offenders who may be alienated or estranged from their families. The *MAC-R* (MacAndrew Alcoholism Scale–Revised) and *AAS* (Addiction Admission Scale) suggest alcohol or substance abuse. Scales 6 (*Pa*, Paranoia), 8 (*Sc*, Schizophrenia) and *BIZ* (Bizarre Mentation) identify those who might have mental disorders that require further assessment. Scales 5 (*Mf*, Masculinity-Femininity), 0 (*Si*; Social Introversion), and *SOD* (Social Discomfort) are associated with passivity, introversion, and awkward interpersonal relations that may lead to exploitation by more predatory inmates in prison settings (Butcher & Williams, 1992; Graham, 2000; Megargee, 2000).

Whereas most measures used in correctional settings assess only negative characteristics, the MMPI-2 can also indicate positive attributes. Offenders with moderate elevations on Scale 0 are unlikely to be defiant or cause problems for those in authority, those high on Scale *Re* (Responsibility) should be more mature and cooperative than most, and those with elevations on Scale *Do* (Dominance) should be leaders.

The second level of analysis is to classify MMPI-2 profiles according to Megargee's empirically derived offender classifications system (Megargee & Bohn with Meyer & Sink, 1979; Megargee et al., 2001). Derived from cluster analyses of criminal offenders' original MMPIs, the system is composed of 10 types labeled with neutral, alphabetic names. Independent studies applying similar clustering procedures to the MMPIs of male and female offenders in various settings have demonstrated the reliability of the typology, consistently replicating most of the 10 groups (Goeke, Tosi, & Eshbaugh, 1993; Mrad, Kabacoff, & Duckro, 1983; Nichols, 1979/1980; Shaffer, Pettigrew, Blouin, & Edwards, 1983).

Independent investigators have reported the successful application of the MMPI-based system among male and female offenders in probation, parole, and correctional settings. Within correctional institutions, it has been utilized in federal, state, military, and local facilities with security levels ranging from minimum to maximum. It has also been applied in halfway houses, community restitution centers, forensic mental health units, and local jails. The specialized populations to which the system has been applied include death row inmates, presidential threateners, and mentally disordered sex offenders (MDSOs; Megargee, 1994; Sliger, 1992; Zager, 1988). Gearing (1981, pp. 106–107) wrote that "this new MMPI system unquestionably defines the present state of the art in correctional classification."

A unique aspect of the MMPI-2-based system is the fact that the characteristics of the 10 types were determined entirely through empirical research in offender populations. The original MMPI research delineating the attributes of male offenders has recently been replicated with the MMPI-2 (Megargee, 1994; Megargee et al., 2001) and a number of new studies have extended the system to female offenders (Megargee, 1997; Megargee et al.; Sliger, 1997). In addition, almost 100 independent investigations have further explored the attributes and behaviors of the 10 types in various criminal justice settings (Megargee et al.).

Based on the patterns of empirically observed differences, individual descriptions of each of the 10 MMPI-2-based types were written that discussed their modal family backgrounds; social and demographic characteristics; patterns of childhood and adult adjustment; and educational, vocational, and criminal histories. In addition, a number of studies have examined how the types differ in their adjustment to prison—which ones are most likely to be disruptive or cause trouble, which are most likely to do well or poorly in educational or vocational programming, and which are most likely to succeed or fail on parole. Strategies for management and treatment have been formulated that address the optimal setting, change agent, and treatment program for each type (Megargee & Bohn, 1977; Megargee, Bohn, et al., 1979; Megargee et al., 2001). Although the system is designed primarily for needs assessment, Bohn (1979) obtained a 46% reduction in serious assaults over a 2-year period when he

used it for internal classification to separate the more predatory inmates from those most likely to be victimized.

One of the advantages of an MMPI-2-based system is that it can reflect changes in offenders over time in a way that systems based on the criminal history or current offense systems cannot. Studies have shown that many offenders' classifications do change over the course of their sentences. Doren and Megargee's (1980) research indicated that these differences reflect changes in the client rather than unreliability in the system. If a year or more has passed since an offender's last MMPI-2, it is advisable to readminister the MMPI-2 and reclassify him or her if important programming or treatment decisions are to be made.

A third level of analysis for evaluating MMPI-2's in correctional settings involves consulting a series of interpretive statements recently devised by Megargee (2000). Unlike risk assessment instruments, these ratings include positive as well as negative aspects of offender behavior. Using algorithms based on the Megargee system of classification and cutting scores on selected MMPI-2 scales, offenders are evaluated as being *high, medium,* or *low,* relative to other criminal offenders on nine behavioral dimensions that are especially relevant to corrections: (a) apparent need for mental health assessment or programming; (b) indications of socially deviant behavior or attitudes; (c) extraversion and need for social participation; (d) leadership ability or dominance; (e) likelihood of hostile or antagonistic peer relations; (f) indications of conflicts with or resentment of authorities; (g) likelihood of mature, responsible behavior and positive response to supervision; (h) likelihood of positive or favorable response to academic programming; and (i) likelihood of positive or favorable response to vocational programming.

In addition to these nine bipolar scales, Megargee (2000) has also developed a list of nine *red flags,* or warnings of possible problem areas, including the possibility of (a) difficulties with alcohol or substance abuse, (b) thought disorder, (c) depressive affect or mood disorder, (d) extensive use of sick call, (e) overcontrolled hostility, (f) manipulation or exploitation others, (g) problems with anger control, (h) awkward or difficult interpersonal relationships, passivity, and submissiveness, and (i) family conflict or alienation from family. The purpose of these warning statements is to raise hypotheses for clinicians to evaluate using case history data, interviews, staff observations, and other psychological tests. These interpretive scales and statements are contained in Megargee's (2000) computerized MMPI-2 *Criminal Justice and Corrections Report,* which also provides MMPI-2 profiles, scores, and indices on all the validity, basic, and content scales as well as selected supplementary scales and the offender's Megargee system classification.

Although Megargee's (2000) interpretive scales and warnings of problem areas are based on well-established correlates of the MMPI-2 scales and offender types, the interpretations themselves have not yet been empirically validated, and as yet they apply only to male offenders. As with any computerized assessments, they should be used only by qualified correctional psychologists in conjunction with other sources of information.

Intelligence Screening

As noted earlier, the NCCHC's (1997) *Prison Standards* stipulate that a brief intellectual assessment should be part of the postadmission mental health evaluation. The primary purpose of this assessment is to identify developmentally disabled inmates who may be victimized or exploited by predatory inmates. However, a more thorough intellectual evaluation should also be conducted as part of offenders' needs assessment, to determine their need for educational programming and their ability to profit from instruction. Two brief screening instruments often used in corrections, one verbal and the other nonverbal, will be described.

Shipley Institute of Living Scale

The Shipley Institute of Living Scale (SILS; Shipley, 1940; Zachary, 1994) is a brief, self-administered verbal test of intellectual functioning in adults aged 16 to 64 that is designed for group or computer-based administration. It has two, timed 10-min subtests. The Vocabulary subtest contains 40 multiple-choice items of increasing difficulty on which the respondent selects which of four terms best conveys the meaning of the stimulus word. It thus involves reading and recognition of vocabulary words.

The Abstraction subtest consists of 44 increasingly difficult sequences of letters, words, and numbers. The respondent's task is to deduce the logical principle governing each sequence and to use it to produce the next symbols in the sequence. It thus involves reading, abstract reasoning, and production (as opposed to recognition) of the correct answer. Age-specific T scores can be computed on each of the subtests and on the total of both subtests (Zachary, 1994).

Shipley (1940) originally designed the SILS as a test of intellectual deterioration or impairment based on the now-discredited notion that deterioration is evidenced by the discrepancy between scores on *hold* tests, such as Vocabulary, and *don't-hold* tests, such as Abstraction. Today the SILS is used as a brief screening instrument for intellectual appraisals.

The SILS manual (Zachary, 1994) reports split-half internal consistency coefficients, corrected by the Spearman-Brown formula, of .87 for Vocabulary, .89 for Abstraction, and .92 for the Total score. Test-retest stability coefficients over the course of 8 to 16 weeks ranged from .62 to .82 with a median of .79. Correlations between the SILS Total score and Wechsler Adult Intelligence Scale (WAIS) Full Scale IQs in 11 samples of psychiatric patients ranged from .74 to .90 with a median of .78; correlations with Wechsler Adult Intelligence Scale–Revised (WAIS-R) Full Scale IQs in two samples of psychiatric patients were .74 and .85 (Zachary). The manual (Zachary) provides a procedure for estimating WAIS-R IQs from SILS Total scores; the estimated IQs correlated .85 with actual WAIS-R Full Scale IQs.

Although the SILS manual has been revised and the norms updated, the SILS items have not been changed since 1940. Perhaps because Shipley (1940) derived the test using high school and college students, the SILS works best in young adults; until age-specific T-score tables became available, it tended to underestimate the IQs of older respondents.

Wood, Conn, and Harrison (1977) administered the SILS and the WAIS to prisoners at a county penal farm and reported that the SILS was an adequate predictor of WAIS scores, but cautioned that the estimates were better for White than for Black offenders. Bowers and Pantle (1998) administered the SILS and the Kaufman Brief Intelligence Test (KBIT; Kaufman & Kaufman, 1990) to 52 female inmates. They reported that the SILS correlated .83 with the KBIT IQ and that there were no significant mean differences between the offenders' mean scores on the two measures.

The SILS manual (Zachary, 1994, p. 2) warns that, "Because the scale is self-administered, it is not recommended for individuals who are either unable or unwilling to cooperate," and notes (p. 3), "While the Shipley may be used to obtain a quick estimate of intellectual functioning, it is not a substitute for more detailed assessment procedures."

In corrections, the SILS is best used as a brief screening device for estimating verbal intelligence. If offenders obtain scores in the average range of intellectual functioning or higher, it can be presumed that their intellectual ability is adequate for the educational programming afforded at most correctional institutions. Those obtaining below average scores should receive a more comprehensive individual intellectual assessment with an instrument such as the Wechsler Adult Intelligence Scale–Third Edition (WAIS-III; Wechsler, 1997), especially if their scores suggest possible retardation.

General Ability Measure for Adults

The General Ability Measure for Adults (GAMA; Naglieri & Bardos, 1997) provides a brief nonverbal measure of general intellectual ability for adults aged 18 and older. The GAMA has 66 items consisting of attractive blue and yellow diagrams, each of which has six possible multiple-choice responses. There are four scales:

1. The *Matching* scale items present the respondent with a stimulus diagram. From an array of six similar diagrams, he or she must select the one that matches the stimulus item in color, shape, and configuration.
2. The *Analogies* subtest presents respondents with logic problems of the nature "A is to B as C is to (?)," but diagrams are used instead of letters. Respondents must choose the correct answer from six possible diagrams.
3. *Sequences* presents test takers with an interrupted sequence of five diagrams showing a figure that is being rotated or otherwise moved through space. In each sequence the middle (third) diagram is missing and test takers must select from an array of six possibilities the one design that correctly completes the sequence.
4. *Construction* presents respondents with fragments of shapes; from an array of six completed figures, they must choose the one diagram that could be built with the fragments.

The GAMA can be scored by hand or by computer, and tables are available for converting raw scores to scaled scores for each of 11 age levels ranging from 18 to 19 years at the lower end to 80 or older at the upper. Although the tasks are nonverbal, a third-grade reading level is needed to follow the directions. (A Spanish version is available for those who should be tested in that language.) Respondents have 25 min to complete the 66 GAMA items.

The authors took great pains in selecting the 2,360 participants in the national normative group. Each of the 11 age groups was stratified on the basis of the 1990 U.S. Census into the two usual genders, five racial or ethnic groups (African American, American Indian, Asian–Pacific Islander, Hispanic, or White), five education levels (grade school, attended high school, graduated high school or GED, attended college, or completed bachelor's degree or more), and four geographic regions of the United States. Detailed tables in the GAMA manual (Naglieri & Bardos, 1997) provide complete comparisons with the 1990 Census data.

Split-half internal consistency coefficients, averaged over the 11 age groups and corrected by the Spearman Brown formula, were .66 for the Matching subtest, .81 for Analogies, .79 for Sequences, .65 for Construction, and .90 for the overall IQ. Test-retest coefficients over the course of 2 to 6 weeks were .55 for the Matching subtest, .65 for Analogies, .74 for Sequences, .38 for Construction, and .67 for the overall IQ. Practice effects were evident on all of the retest means except Matching. The magnitudes of these reliability coefficients

suggest that psychologists should discuss the confidence limits when reporting GAMA scores.

Naglieri and Bardos (1997) reported that GAMA IQs correlated .65 with WAIS-R Verbal IQs, .74 with Performance, and .75 with Full Scale IQs. They also obtained correlations of .72 with the SILS and .70 with the KBIT.

Given the multiplicity of ethnicities and the low reading levels typically encountered among criminal offenders, the GAMA appears to have considerable potential as a brief, nonverbal intellectual screening device for correctional settings, and it is currently being marketed for that purpose. Additional data on the GAMA's use in corrections are needed. As with the SILS, its best use appears to be as an indicator of possible intellectual deficiency, with low-scoring offenders being referred for a more complete individual examination with WAIS-III.

Wechsler Adult Intelligence Scale–Third Edition

Offenders who are suspected of being developmentally disabled or for whom a more definitive appraisal of intelligence is needed should be tested with WAIS-III (Wechsler, 1997) by a qualified administrator (NCCHC, 1997). The gold standard (so to speak) for the appraisal of adult intelligence, the WAIS-III has been updated and undergone several modifications that make it more appropriate for correctional use than its predecessor, the WAIS-R. In addition to updating the 11 familiar WAIS subtests, three new supplementary scales have been added. On the new Verbal scale, Letter-Number Sequencing, the examiner reads a series of randomly ordered letters and numbers that the respondent must recall, reorder, and recite back in ascending order, numbers first. One of the new Performance scales, Symbol Search, is a true-false test on which the respondent indicates whether either of two target stimuli, such as stars or crosses, appears in an array of seven similar stimuli. The other Performance scale, Matrix Reasoning, consists of a series of pictures, each of which shows five geometric shapes that the respondent must identify. The new Performance scales should improve the assessment of intelligence among linguistically challenged inmates and reduce the importance of perceptual speed in assessing Performance IQs (Cohen & Swerdlik, 1999).

Correctional assessment will also be improved by the downward extension of the floor for most subtests, making them more suitable for testing intellectually challenged clients. Despite this, the overall administration time is less for the WAIS-III than it was for the WAIS-R (Aiken, 2000).

Several modifications make the WAIS-III more suitable for older respondents than its predecessors were. They include making some of the stimuli larger so they can be seen better by older clients, and extending the norms to adults aged

74 to 89. Unlike with the WAIS-R, scaled scores are computed based on age-specific norms (Cohen & Swerdlik, 1999).

The WAIS-III was standardized on a national sample of 2,450 adults. Within each of 13 age bands, ranging from 16 to 17 at the lower end and from 85 to 89 at the upper, the sample was stratified according to race or ethnicity (White, Black, Hispanic, other), gender, educational level, and geographic region. In addition to the familiar Verbal, Performance, and Full Scale IQs and the scaled scores on the various subtests, the WAIS-III also provides four new factor scores, Verbal Comprehension, Working Memory, Perceptual Organization, and Processing Speed.

Educational Screening

Although most correctional psychologists are trained in clinical psychology, in correctional settings they may also have to undertake some assessments that would fall to counseling or school psychologists in the free world. One such task is assessing offenders' needs for educational programming.

Intelligence tests, especially nonverbal and performance measures, are supposed to reflect intellectual ability rather than achievement. On an individual test such as the WAIS-III, it is possible to obtain an above average IQ without being able to read. In assessing offenders' needs for educational programming, it is essential to evaluate their present educational level and skills.

Obviously, the best way to determine how many years of formal education an offender has completed is to check the presentence investigation report. Unfortunately, the number of grades attended may not reflect adults' actual skills in reading, mathematics, or language. Aiken (2000, p. 118) recently reported that "at least one out of every four employees is functionally illiterate and must 'bluff it out' in performing a job requiring reading skills." Undoubtedly, the illiteracy rate is higher behind bars than in the free world. Therefore offenders' educational skills should be independently assessed.

Test of Adult Basic Education

The Test of Adult Basic Education (TABE; CTB/McGraw Hill, 1987) is a flexible test of basic adult educational skills that is used in a number of correctional settings. It comes in two forms, 5/6 and 7/8, and five levels: L (Literacy; grades 0.0–1.9), E (Easy; grades 1.6–3.9), M (Medium; 3.6–6.9), D (Difficult; (6.6–8.9), and A (Advanced; 8.6–12.9). Relatively brief Locator tests are used to diagnose what level is appropriate for an offender in each content areas. Form 5/6 covers seven content areas (Reading Vocabulary, Reading Comprehension, Mathematics Computation, Mathematics Concepts and Applications,

Language Expression, Language Mechanics, and Spelling). Form 7/8 covers Reading, Mathematics Computation, Applied Mathematics, Language, and Spelling. Any subtest can be administered independently. For basic screening, Form 7/8's Reading and Mathematics subtests can be administered in less than an hour. The full TABE battery takes about 3 hr; a condensed TABE Survey requires 90 min, and the Locator takes about 35 min (CTB/McGraw-Hill). The choice of instrument depends on how detailed an educational evaluation is needed.

The test materials were prepared by teachers and drawn from adult basic education texts from around the country. The TABE is often administered to minorities, so great pains were taken to eliminate ethnic biases (Rogers, 1998). The basic evidence of validity is how the test was constructed and its manifest content; correlations with external criteria such as grades or GED scores are not provided (M. D. Beck, 1998; Rogers).

Although more technical data are needed, the TABE provides correctional users with a broad array of testing options. In concept and design, it reflects current educational practices (Lissitz, 1992). An especially attractive feature of Form 7/8 for corrections use is that norms are provided based on 1,500 adult and juvenile offenders (M. D. Beck, 1998).

Malingering on Intellectual and Achievement Measures

The basic assumption in most ability and achievement testing is that those being evaluated are motivated to perform at their best. Unfortunately, this is not always the case in assessing criminal offenders, so correctional psychologists must be alert to possible malingering.

Unlike personality assessment devices, intelligence and achievement tests do not have validity scales that reflect fake-bad tendencies, so appraisal of malingering must be based on other criteria. Correctional psychologists should keep the purpose of any assessment in mind, and ask themselves whether poorly performing offenders might think it is advisable to appear intellectually challenged. Although forensic assessment is beyond the scope of this chapter, correctional psychologists might find themselves evaluating offenders who are trying to establish a basis for a challenge to their criminal responsibility or legal competency. To take an extreme example, a death row inmate has an obvious incentive for being evaluated as not competent for execution (Small & Otto, 1991). A marked discrepancy between the intellectual level indicated by the case history and the results of intelligence testing is another red flag.

Although there has been relatively little research on criminal offenders' malingering on intelligence and achievement tests, researchers in other settings have examined the factors associated with deliberately poor performance on these measures. Some of the earliest studies were designed to detect draftees trying to evade induction into the armed services by feigning mental illness. More recent research has focused on patients feigning neurological disorders and memory deficits in conjunction with damage suits.

Individual Intelligence Tests

Schretelen (1988) reviewed 11 studies, many of which used individual intelligence tests such as the WAIS. He reported that the most reliable signs of malingering were absurd or grossly illogical answers, approximations, and inconsistent performance across tests or subtests. He concluded that, "At this point, examination of response 'scatter' appears to be the most powerful and well validated detection strategy. It is based on the finding that fakers tend to fail items genuine patients pass, and pass items genuine patients fail" (p. 458). However, he noted that this guideline is difficult to apply on brief scales and those on which the items are arranged hierarchically in order of difficulty.

Schretelen (1988) also noted that it was easier to detect malingering from a battery of tests than it was from any single measure. If, for example, an intelligence test is administered in conjunction with MMPI-2, and the MMPI-2's validity scales suggest malingering, it would be prudent to question the intelligence test results as well.

Symptom Validity Testing

Originally developed to assist in the diagnosis of conversion reactions (Pankratz, 1979) and later applied to those feigning neurological and memory impairment (Rees, Tombaugh, Gansler, & Moczynski, 1998; Tombaugh, 1997), symptom validity testing (SVT) has recently been applied to correctional assessment by Hiscock and her associates (Hiscock, Laymen, & Hiscock, 1994; Hiscock, Rustemier, & Hiscock, 1993). In SVT, suspected malingerers are administered a forced-choice, two-alternative test that may appear challenging but that is actually very easy. Hiscock employed two very easy 72-item tests, one of General Knowledge and the other of Moral Reasoning. A typical item on the General Knowledge test was, "Salt water is found in: (a) lakes or (b) oceans."

On two-choice tests, a person answering randomly should get half the items correct merely on the basis of chance. On SVT instruments, malingering is indicated by a score that is significantly lower than chance performance.

Hiscock et al. (1994) found that when male prisoners were instructed to take her tests as if they were poorly educated and could not tell the difference between right and wrong, 71% scored below chance on the General Knowledge test and

60% were below chance on the Moral Reasoning measure, whereas none of a control sample of offenders who took the tests under standard instructions scored this low. Coaching inmates on how to fake successfully reduced the hit rates to 60% on General Knowledge and 43% on Moral Reasoning, showing that the SVT technique works best on unsophisticated offenders.

CONCLUDING COMMENTS

Corrections is a growth industry. Scholars at Brown University have projected that, if current trends continue, by 2053 the United States will have more people in prison than out (Alter, 2001; given current ratios, everyone else will probably be on probation or parole). As the correctional population grows, so does the need for reliable, valid, cost-effective assessments. The standards issued by professional organizations concerned with correctional health care are an important first step in encouraging correctional agencies to provide offenders with access to mental health care, including objective, reliable, and valid psychological assessment.

Few psychologists are trained to deliver psychological services, including assessment, in correctional settings, and few psychological tests and instruments have been developed in correctional settings to address correctional issues. Instead, correctional assessment has had to rely on personnel and methods from other settings. Psychologists entering the correctional field should be aware that assessment is different in correctional settings. The clients differ, the issues differ, and the situational factors differ. Therefore, they should seek out instruments developed in or empirically adapted for use in correctional settings, and be prepared to determine the norms, patterns, and cutting scores appropriate in their particular settings.

Those instruments that have been developed or adapted for use in corrections need to be continually reassessed. Risk-assessment devices need to be cross-validated before they are applied in new settings or to new problems. Studies reviewed in the present chapter showed that models developed in one state did not always work in another, and factors related to one criterion, such as general recidivism, did not necessarily apply to another, such as sexual reoffending. Predictors may also change over time; not long ago, having a tattoo was an item on Walters, White, and Denney's (1991) Lifetime Criminality Screening Form. It is questionable whether that item would be valid today.

Despite the difficulties in validating risk-assessment devices, they at least have the advantage of having correctionally relevant criterion measures against which they can be validated. This is not true with needs-assessment instruments. For example, intelligence and achievement tests used in correctional settings have been correlated with other, presumably better, intelligence and achievement tests, but few have been correlated with offenders' performance in educational or vocational programming, nor has their interaction with other possible predictors been explored. Steuber (1975), for example, found that the best predictor of educational achievement in a federal correctional institution was an equation combining the Revised Beta Examination with certain MMPI scales, but such studies are rare.

A neglected topic in correctional assessment is the influence of situational variables. As correctional psychologists, we are prone to make the fundamental attribution error in which we ascribe most of our clients' behavior to their personality characteristics and underestimate situational influences. Further research is needed on how being embroiled in the criminal justice system influences clients' interview and test performances. Virtually the only area in which the influence of the correctional or legal setting is presently being studied is in the investigation of deception and malingering using rather crude designs in which criminal offenders are encouraged or paid to fake on tests. These studies have yielded validity indicators that can be used to identify distorted protocols, but more extensive and sophisticated studies of how the context influences assessments are needed.

Research is also needed on the interaction between situational and personality factors with regard to both external and internal classification. Wright (1986, 1988) assessed correctional institutions along several dimensions such as privacy, structure, strictness, and social support, and classified prisoners into Megargee's MMPI-2 types (Megargee et al., 2001). He obtained significant interactions showing that some MMPI-2 types did better in some settings whereas others did better in other settings. Van Voorhis (1994) found similar differences when she contrasted the adjustment of different types of prisoners in penitentiary and open-camp settings. More research on the interactions of personality with situational factors is needed.

In the last two decades, research on assessment in correctional settings has improved in rigor and sophistication. More complex questions are being posed and advanced research methods are being used to address them. For example, it is now routine for risk-assessment studies to report the specificity and sensitivity of their measures. There is more programmatic research, and meta-analyses are increasingly being used to integrate the findings of the many isolated, one-shot investigations that have plagued the field. As correctional assessment inevitably grows to meet the demands of an expanding correctional system, we can hope that both the quality and the quantity of research on assessment in correctional settings will also increase.

REFERENCES

Aiken, L. R. (2000). *Psychological testing and assessment* (10th ed.) Boston: Allyn and Bacon.

Alter, J. (2001, February 12). The war on addiction. *Newsweek*, pp. 36–39.

American Association for Correctional Psychology, Standards Committee. (1980). Standards for psychological services in jails and prisons. *Criminal Justice and Behavior, 8*, 81–127.

American Association for Correctional Psychology, Standards Committee. (2000). Standards for psychological services in jails, prisons, correctional facilities, and agencies: Second edition. *Criminal Justice and Behavior, 27*, 433–494.

American Correctional Association. (1981). *Standards for adult correctional institutions* (2nd ed.). College Park, MD: Author.

American Correctional Association. (2000). *2000 directory: Juvenile and adult correctional departments, institutions, agencies, and paroling authorities.* Lanham, MD: Author.

American Psychiatric Association. (1989). *Psychiatric services in jails and prisons* (APA WM A 512, No. 29). Washington, DC: Office of Psychiatric Services.

American Psychological Association, Committee on Ethical Guidelines for Forensic Psychologists. (1991). *Specialty guidelines for forensic psychologists.* Washington, DC: Author.

American Psychological Association. (1992). Ethical principles of psychologists and code of conduct. *American Psychologist, 47*, 1597–1611.

American Public Health Association. (1976). *Standards for health services in correctional institutions.* Washington, DC: Author.

Anno, B. J. (1991). *Prison health care: Guidelines for the management of an adequate delivery system.* Chicago: National Commission on Correctional Health Care.

Austin, J. (1993). Objective prison classification systems: A review. In American Correctional Association (Ed.), *Classification: A tool for managing today's offenders* (pp. 108–123). Laurel, MD: Author.

Beck, A. J., Bonczar, T. P., Ditton, P. M., Glaze, L. E., Harlow, C. W., Mumoloa, C. J., et al. (2000). *Correctional populations in the United States, 1997.* Washington, DC: Bureau of Justice Statistics.

Beck, M. D. (1998). Review of Tests of Adult Basic Education, Forms 7, & 8. In J. C. Impara & B. S. Plake (Eds.), *The thirteenth mental measurements yearbook* (pp. 1080–1083). Lincoln: Buros Institute of Mental Measurements of the University of Nebraska, Lincoln.

Boer, D. P., Hart, S. D., Kropp, P. R., & Webster, C. D. (1997). *Manual for the Sexual Violence Risk-20.* Odessa, FL: Psychological Assessment Resources.

Bohn, M. J., Jr. (1979). Inmate classification and the reduction of violence. In *Proceedings of the 109th annual congress of correction* (pp. 63–69). College Park, MD: American Correctional Association.

Bonta, J., & Motiuk, L. L. (1985). Utilization of an interview-based classification instrument: A study of correctional halfway houses. *Criminal Justice and Behavior, 12,* 333–352.

Bowers, T. L., & Pantle, M. L. (1998). Shipley Institute for Living Scale and the Kaufman Brief Intelligence Test as screening instruments for intelligence. *Assessment, 5,* 187–195.

Brennan, T. (1987). Classification: An overview of selected methodological issues. In D. M. Gottfredson & M. Tonry (Eds.), *Prediction and classification in criminal justice decision making* (pp. 201–248). Chicago: University of Chicago Press.

Brennan, T. (1993). Risk assessment: An evaluation of statistical classification methods. In American Correctional Association (Ed.), *Classification: A tool for managing today's offenders* (pp. 46–70). Laurel, MD: American Correctional Association.

Bureau of Justice Statistics. (1995). *Jails and jail inmates, 1993–1994.* Washington, DC: U.S. Department of Justice.

Butcher, J. N. (1999). *A beginner's guide to MMPI-2.* Washington, DC: American Psychological Association.

Butcher, J. N., Dahlstrom, W. G., Graham, J. R., Tellegen, A. M., & Kaemmer, B. (1989). *Minnesota Multiphasic Personality Inventory–2 (MMPI-2): Manual for administration and scoring.* Minneapolis: University of Minnesota Press.

Butcher, J. N., & Williams, C. L. (1992). *Essentials of MMPI-2 and MMPI-A interpretation.* Minneapolis: University of Minnesota Press.

Campbell, T. W. (2000). Sexual predator evaluations and phrenology: Considering issues of evidentiary reliability. *Behavioral Sciences and the Law, 18,* 111–130.

Clark, D. A. (1994). Behavioural risk assessment: A methodology in practice. In N. K. Clark & G. M. Stephenson (Eds.), *Rights and risks: The application of forensic psychology. Issues in criminological and legal psychology, No. 21.* Leicester, UK: British Psychological Society.

Cleckley, H. (1976). *The mask of sanity.* St. Louis, MO: C. V. Mosby. (Original work published 1941)

Cohen, R. J., & Swerdlik, M. E. (1999). *Psychological testing and assessment* (4th ed.). Mountain View, CA: Mayfield.

Cooke, D. J., Walker, A., & Gardiner, W. (1990). Behavioral disturbance in Barlinnie Prison. *Prison Service Journal, 80,* 2–8.

Cooper, R. P., & Werner, P. D. (1990). Predicting violence in newly admitted inmates. A lens model of staff decision making. *Criminal Justice and Behavior, 17,* 431–447.

CTB/McGraw-Hill. (1987). *Tests of Adult Basic Education (TABE).* Monterey, CA: Author.

Cunningham, M. D., & Reidy, T. J. (1999). Don't confuse me with the facts: Common errors in risk assessment at capital sentencing. *Criminal Justice and Behavior, 26,* 20–43.

Doren, D. M., & Megargee, E. I. (1980). The nature and prediction of typological changes when employing the MMPI criminal classification system. *The differential view: A publication of the International Differential Treatment Association. 10*(February), 28–41.

Epperson, D. L., Kaul, J. D., & Huot, S. J. (1995). *Predicting risk for recidivism for incarcerated sex offenders: Updated development of the Sex Offender Screening Test (SOST).* Poster session presented at the annual meeting of the Association for the Treatment of Sexual Abusers, New Orleans, LA.

Finn, S. E., & Kamphuis, J. H. (1995). What a clinician needs to know about base rates. In J. N. Butcher (Ed.), *Clinical personality assessment: Practical approaches* (pp. 224–235) New York: Oxford University Press.

Fowler, R. (1976). Sweeping reforms ordered in Alabama prisons. *APA Monitor, 7*(4), 1, 15.

Gardner, W., Lidz, C. W., Mulvey, E. P., & Shaw, E. C. (1996). A comparison of actuarial methods for identifying repetitively violent patients with mental illness. *Law and Human Behavior, 20,* 35–48.

Gearing, M. I., 2nd. (1981). The new MMPI typology for prisoners: The beginning of a new era in correctional research and (hopefully) practice. [Review of the book *Classifying criminal offenders: A new system based on the MMPI.*] *Journal of Personality Assessment, 45,* 102–107.

Gendreau, P., Goggin, C. E., & Law, M. A. (1997). Predicting prison misconducts. *Criminal Justice and Behavior, 24,* 414–431.

Glaser, D. (1955). The efficacy of alternative approaches to parole prediction. *American Sociological Review, 20,* 283–287.

Glaser, D. (1962). Prediction tables as accounting devices for judges and parole boards. *Crime and Delinquency, 8,* 239–258.

Glaser, D. (1987). Classification for risk. In D. M. Gottfredson & M. Tonry (Eds.), *Prediction and classification in criminal justice decision making* (pp. 249–291). Chicago: University of Chicago Press.

Goeke, R. K., Tosi, D. J., & Eshbaugh, D. M. (1993). Personality patterns of male felons in a correctional halfway house setting: An MMPI typological analysis. *Journal of Clinical Psychology, 49,* 413–422.

Gottfredson, D. M., & Beverly, R. F. (1962). Development and operational use of prediction methods in correctional work. In *Proceedings of the social science section.* Washington, DC: American Statistical Society.

Gottfredson, D. M., Wilkins, L. T., & Hoffman, P. B. (1978). *Guidelines for parole and sentencing.* Lexington, MA: Lexington Books.

Graham, J. R. (2000). *MMPI-2: Assessing personality and psychopathology* (3rd ed.) New York: Oxford University Press.

Grann, M., Längström, N., Tengström, A., & Kellgren, G. (1999). Psychopathy (PCL-R) predicts violent recidivism among criminal offenders with personality disorders in Sweden. *Law and Human Behavior, 23,* 205–217.

Hanson, R. K. (1997). *Development of a brief scale for sexual offender recidivism.* Ottawa, ONT: Public Works and Government Services of Canada.

Hanson, R. K., & Bussiere, M. T. (1998). Predicting relapse: A meta-analysis of sexual offender recidivism studies. *Journal of Consulting and Clinical Psychology, 66,* 348–362.

Hare, R. D. (1991). *The Hare Psychopathy Checklist–Revised manual.* Toronto: Multi-Health Systems.

Hare, R. D., Harpur, T. J., Hakstian, A. R., Forth, A. E., Hart, S. D., & Newman, J. P. (1990). The Revised Psychopathy Checklist: Reliability and factor structure. *Psychological Assessment: A Journal of Consulting and Clinical Psychology, 2,* 338–341.

Harris, G. T., Rice, M. E., & Quinsey, V. L. (1993). Violent recidivism of mentally disordered offenders: The development of a statistical prediction instrument. *Criminal Justice and Behavior, 20,* 315–335.

Hart, S. D. (1996). Psychopathy and risk assessment. In D. J. Cooke, A. E. Forth, J. Newman, & R. D. Hare (Eds.), *International perspectives in psychopathy* (pp. 63–67). *Issues in criminological and legal psychology, No. 24.* Leicester, UK: British Psychological Society, Division of Criminological and Legal Psychology.

Heilbrun, K., & Heilbrun, A. (1995). Risk assessment with MMPI-2 in forensic evaluations. In Y. S. Ben-Porath, J. R. Graham, G. C. N. Hall, R. D. Hirschman, & M. S. Zaragoza (Eds.), *Forensic applications of MMPI-2* (pp. 160–178). Thousand Oaks, CA: Sage.

Hewitt, L. E., & Jenkins, R. L. (1946). *Fundamental patterns of maladjustment: The dynamics of their origin.* Springfield: State of Illinois.

Hiscock, C. K., Layman, L. B., & Hiscock, M. (1994). Cross-validation of two measures for assessing feigned mental incompetence. *Criminal Justice and Behavior, 21,* 443–453.

Hiscock, C. K., Rustemier, P., & Hiscock, M. (1993). Determination of criminal responsibility: Application of the two-alternative forced-choice strategem. *Criminal Justice and Behavior, 20,* 391–405.

Jenkins, R. L. (1943). Child relationships and delinquency and crime. In W. C. Reckless (Ed.), *The etiology of delinquent and criminal behavior.* Social Science Research Council Bulletin No. 50.

Jenkins, R. L., & Glickman, S. (1947). Patterns of personality organization among delinquents. *Neurotic Child, 6,* 329–339.

Kane, P. R. (1993). Classification: Its central role in managing the Federal Bureau of Prisons. In American Correctional Association (Ed.), *Classification: A tool for managing today's offenders* (pp. 124–134). Laurel, MD: Author.

Kaufman, A. S., & Kaufman, N. L. (1990). *Kaufman Brief Intelligence Test (K-BIT) manual.* Circle Pines, MN: American Guidance Service.

Kay, S. I. (1991). *The constitutional dimensions of an inmate's right to health care.* Chicago: National Commission on Correctional Health Care.

Kennedy, D. B. (1993). [Review of the book *Suicide behind bars*]. *Criminal Justice and Behavior, 20,* 306–309.

Klassen, D., & O'Connor, W. A. (1988). A prospective study of predictors of violence in adult male mental patients. *Law and Human Behavior, 12,* 143–158.

Kropp, P. R., Hart, S. D., Webster, C. D., & Eaves, D. (1994). *Manual for the Spousal Assault Risk Assessment guide.* Vancouver, BC: British Columbia Institute on Family Violence.

Levinson, R. (1988). Developments in the classification process: Quay's AIMS approach. *Criminal Justice and Behavior, 15,* 24–38.

Lissitz, R. W. (1992). Review of Tests of Adult Basic Education, Forms 5 & 6 and Survey Form. In J. J. Kramer & J. C. Conley (Eds.), *The eleventh mental measurements yearbook* (pp. 984–985). Lincoln: Buros Institute of Mental Measurements of the University of Nebraska, Lincoln.

Meehl, P. (1954). *Clinical versus statistical prediction.* Minneapolis: University of Minnesota Press.

Meehl, P. E., & Rosen, A. (1955). Antecedent probability and the efficiency of certain psychometric signs, patterns, and cutting scores. *Psychological Bulletin, 52,* 194–216.

Megargee, E. I. (1976). The prediction of dangerous behavior. *Criminal Justice and Behavior, 3,* 3–21.

Megargee, E. I. (1981). Methodological problems in the prediction of violence. In J. R. Hays, T. K. Roberts, & K. S. Solway (Eds.), *Violence and the violent individual* (pp. 179–191). New York: S. P. Scientific and Medical Books.

Megargee, E. I. (1982). Psychological correlates and determinants of criminal violence. In M. Wolfgang & N. Wiener (Eds.), *Criminal violence* (pp. 81–170). Beverly Hills, CA: Sage.

Megargee, E. I. (1993). Aggression and violence. In H. Adams & P. Sutker (Eds.), *Comprehensive handbook of psychopathology* (2nd. ed., pp. 617–644). New York: Plenum Press.

Megargee, E. I. (1994). Using the Megargee MMPI-based classification system with the MMPI-2s of male prison inmates. *Psychological Assessment, 6,* 337–344.

Megargee, E. I. (1997). Using the Megargee MMPI-based classification system with MMPI-2s of female prison inmates. *Psychological Assessment, 9,* 75–82.

Megargee, E. I. (2000). *User's guide for the MMPI-2 Criminal Justice and Correctional Report for Men.* Minneapolis: University of Minnesota Press.

Megargee, E. I., & Bohn, M. J. (1977). A new classification system for criminal offenders, IV: Empirically determined characteristics of the ten types. *Criminal Justice and Behavior, 4,* 149–210.

Megargee, E. I., & Bohn, M. J., Jr., with Meyer, J., Jr., & Sink, F. (1979). *Classifying criminal offenders: A new system based on the MMPI.* Beverly Hills, CA: Sage.

Megargee, E. I., & Carbonell, J. L. (1995). Use of the MMPI-2 in correctional settings. In Y. S. Ben-Porath, J. R. Graham, G. C. N.

Hall, R. D. Hirschman, & M. S. Zaragoza (Eds.), *Forensic applications of MMPI-2* (pp. 127–159). Thousand Oaks, CA: Sage.

Megargee, E. I., Carbonell, J. L., Bohn, M. J., Jr., & Sliger, G. L. (2001). *Classifying criminal offenders with MMPI-2: The Megargee system.* Minneapolis: University of Minnesota Press.

Megargee, E. I., Mercer, S. J., & Carbonell, J. L. (1999). MMPI-2 with male and female state and federal prison inmates. *Psychological Assessment, 11,* 177–185.

Meloy, J. R., & Gacono, C. (1995). Assessing the psychopathic personality. In J. N. Butcher (Ed.), *Clinical personality assessment: Practical approaches* (pp. 410–422). New York: Oxford University Press.

Monahan, J. (1980). *Who is the client? The ethics of psychological intervention in the criminal justice system.* Washington, DC: American Psychological Association.

Monahan, J. (1981). *Predicting violent behavior: An assessment of clinical techniques.* Beverly Hills, CA: Sage.

Monahan, J. (1996). Violence prediction: The past twenty years. *Criminal Justice and Behavior, 23,* 107–120.

Mrad, D. F., Kabacoff, R. A., & Duckro, P. (1983). Validation of the Megargee typology in a halfway house setting. *Criminal Justice and Behavior, 10,* 252–262.

Naglieri, J. A., & Bardos, A. (1997). *GAMA (General Ability Measure for Adults) manual.* Minneapolis, MN: National Computer Systems.

National Advisory Commission on Criminal Justice Standards and Goals. (1973). *Report on corrections.* Washington, DC: U.S. Department of Justice, Law Enforcement Assistance Administration.

National Commission on Correctional Health Care. (1996). *Standards for health services in jails.* Chicago: Author.

National Commission on Correctional Health Care. (1997). *Standards for health services in prisons.* Chicago: Author.

National Institute of Corrections. (1981). *A model classification system for probation and parole.* Washington, DC: Author.

Nichols, W. (1980). The classification of law offenders with the MMPI: A methodological study. (Doctoral dissertation, University of Alabama, 1979). *Dissertation Abstracts International, 41*(01), 333B.

Otto, R. (2000). Assessing and managing violence risk in outpatient settings. *Journal of Clinical Psychology, 56,* 1239–1262.

Pankratz, L. (1979). Symptom validity testing and symptom retraining: Procedures for assessment and treatment of sensory deficits. *Journal of Consulting and Clinical Psychology, 47,* 409–410.

Petersilia, J., & Turner, S. (1987). Guideline-based justice: Prediction and racial minorities. In D. M. Gottfredson & M. Tonry (Eds.), *Prediction and classification in criminal justice decision making* (pp. 151–182). Chicago: University of Chicago Press.

Proctor, J. L. (1994). Evaluating a modified version of the federal prison system's inmate classification model: An assessment of objectivity and predictive validity. *Criminal Justice and Behavior, 21,* 256–272.

Quay, H. C. (1965). Personality and delinquency. In H. C. Quay (Ed.), *Juvenile delinquency.* New York: Litton.

Quay, H. C. (1973, November). *An empirical approach to the differential behavioral assessment of the adult offender.* Paper presented at the meeting of the American Society of Criminology, New York City.

Quay, H. C. (1974). *The differential behavioral classification of the adult male offender: Interim results and procedures.* Technical report prepared for the Bureau of Prisons, U.S. Department of Justice (Contract J-IC-22,253). Philadelphia: Psychology Department, Temple University.

Quay, H. C. (1984). *Managing adult inmates: Classification for housing and program assignments.* College Park, MD: American Correctional Association.

Quinsey, V. L., Harris, G. T., Rice, M. E., & Cormier, C. A., (1998). *Violent offenders: Appraisals and managing risks.* Washington, DC: American Psychological Association.

Rees, L. M., Tombaugh, T. N., Gansler, D. A., & Moczynski, N. P. (1998). Five validation experiments of the Test of Memory Malingering. *Psychological Assessment, 10,* 10–20.

Rice, M. E., & Harris, G. T. (1997). Cross-validation and extension of the Violence Risk Appraisal Guide for child molesters and rapists. *Law and Human Behavior, 21,* 231–241.

Rogers, B. G. (1998). Review of Tests of Adult Basic Education, Forms 7, & 8. In J. C. Impara & B. S. Plake (Eds.), *The thirteenth mental measurements yearbook* (pp. 1083–1085). Lincoln: Buros Institute of Mental Measurements of the University of Nebraska, Lincoln.

Rogers, R. (2000). The uncritical acceptance of risk assessment in forensic practice. *Law and Human Behavior, 24,* 595–605.

Rowan, J. (1998). *Suicide prevention in custody.* Lanham, MD: American Correctional Association.

Salekin, R. T., Rogers, R., & Sewell, K. W. (1996). A review and meta-analysis of the Psychopathy Checklist and the Psychopathy Checklist–Revised: Predictive validity of dangerousness. *Clinical Psychology: Science and Practice, 3,* 203–215.

Schretelen, D. (1988). The use of psychological tests to identify malingered symptoms of mental disorder. *Clinical Psychology Review, 8,* 451–476.

Shaffer, C. E., Pettigrew, C. G., Blouin, D., & Edwards, D. W. (1983). Multivariate classification of female offender MMPI profiles. *Journal of Crime and Justice, 6,* 57–66.

Shipley, W. C. (1940). A self-administering scale for measuring intellectual impairment and deterioration. *The Journal of Psychology, 9,* 371–377.

Sliger, G. L. (1992). *The MMPI-based classification system for adult criminal offenders: A critical review.* Unpublished manuscript, Florida State University, Department of Psychology, Tallahassee, FL.

Sliger, G. L. (1997). *The applicability of the Megargee MMPI-based offender classification system to the MMPI-2s of women inmates.* Unpublished doctoral dissertation, Florida State University, Tallahassee.

Small, M. A., & Otto, R. K. (1991). Evaluations of competency for execution: Legal contours and implications for assessment. *Criminal Justice and Behavior, 18,* 146–158.

Solomon, L., & Camp, A. T. (1993). The revolution in correctional classification. In American Correctional Association (Ed.), *Classification: A tool for managing today's offenders* (pp. 1–16). Laurel, MD: ACA.

Steadman, H., Monahan, J., Appelbaum, P., Grisso, T., Mulvey, E., Roth, L., et al. (1994). Designing a new generation of risk assessment research. In J. Monahan & H. Steadman (Eds.), *Violence and mental disorder: Developments in risk assessment* (pp. 297–318). Chicago: University of Chicago Press.

Steuber, H. (1975). Prediction of academic achievement with the Minnesota Multiphasic Personality Inventory (MMPI) and California Psychological Inventory (CPI) in a correctional institution. *FCI Research Reports, 5*(4), 1–32.

Suedfeld, P., & Landon, P. B. (1978). Approaches to treatment. In R. D. Hare & D. Schalling (Eds.), *Psychopathic behaviour: Approaches to treatment.* New York: Wiley.

Teplin, L. (1990). The prevalence of severe mental disorder among urban jail detainees: Comparison with the Epidemiological Catchment Area program. *American Journal of Public Health, 80,* 663–669.

Teplin, L. (1996). Prevalence of psychiatric disorders among incarcerated women. *Archives of General Psychiatry, 53,* 505–512.

Tidmarsh, D. (1997). Risk assessment among prisoners: A view from a parole board member. *International Review of Psychiatry, 9,* 273–281.

Tombaugh, T. N. (1997). The Test of Memory Malingering (TOMM): Normative data from cognitively intact and cognitively impaired individuals. *Psychological Assessment, 9,* 260–268.

Torrey, E., Stieber, J., Ezekial, J., Wolfe, S. M., Sharfstein, J., Noble, J. H., et al. (1992). *Criminalizing the mentally ill: The abuse of jails as hospitals.* Washington, DC: Public Citizen's Health Research Group and the National Alliance for the Mentally Ill.

Towl, G., & Crighton, D. (1995). Risk assessment in prison: A psychological critique. *Forensic Update, 40,* 6–14.

VandeCreek, L. & Knapp, S. (1989). *Tarasoff and beyond: Legal and clinical considerations in the treatment of life-endangering patients.* Sarasota, FL: Practitioner's Resource Series.

Van Voorhis, P. (1994). *Psychological classification of the adult male prison inmate.* Albany: State University of New York Press.

Walters, G. D., White, T. W., & Denney, D. (1991). The Lifestyle Criminality Screening Form. *Criminal Justice and Behavior, 18,* 406–418.

Webster, C. D., Douglas, K. S., Eaves, D., & Hart, S. D. (1997). *HCR-20: Assessing risk for violence* (Version 2). Burnaby, BC: Mental Health, Law, and Policy Institute, Simon Frazier University.

Webster, C. D., Harris, G. T., Rice, M. E., Cormier, C., & Quinsey, V. L. (1994). *The Violence Prediction Scheme: Assessing dangerousness in high risk men.* Toronto, ONT: University of Toronto.

Webster, C. D., & Menzies, R. J. (1993). Supervision in the deinstitutionalized community. In S. Hodgins (Ed.), *Mental disorder and crime* (pp. 22–38). Newbury Park, CA: Sage.

Webster, C. D., & Polvi, N. H. (1995). Challenging assessments of dangerousness and risk. In J. Ziskind (Ed.), *Coping with psychiatric and psychological testimony* (pp. 221–240). Marina del Rey, CA: Law and Psychology Press.

Wechsler, D. (1997). *Wechsler Adult Intelligence Scale–Third edition.* San Antonio, TX: Psychological Corporation.

Wood, R. W., Conn, D. C., & Harrison, H. D. (1977). The efficacy of using Shipley-Hartford scores to predict WAIS IQ scores. *Quarterly Journal of Corrections, 1,* 39–41.

Wright, K. N. (1986). An exploratory study of transactional classification. *Journal of Research in Crime and Delinquency, 23,* 595–618.

Wright, K. N. (1988). The relationship of risk, needs, and personality classification systems and prison adjustment. *Criminal Justice and Behavior, 15,* 454–471.

Wright, K. N., Clear, T. R., & Dickson, P. (1984). Universal applicability of probation risk-assessment instruments. *Criminology, 22,* 113–134.

Zachary, R. A. (1994). *Shipley Institute of Living Scale–Revised manual.* Los Angeles: Western Psychological Services.

Zager, L. D. (1988). The MMPI-based criminal classification system: A review, current status, and future directions. *Criminal Justice and Behavior, 15,* 39–57.

CHAPTER 17

Psychological Assessment in Geriatric Settings

BARRY A. EDELSTEIN, RONALD R. MARTIN, AND LESLEY P. KOVEN

In 1998 there were 34.4 million adults who were 65 years of age and older in the United States, representing 12.7% of the population (Administration on Aging, 1999). This percentage is expected to increase dramatically as baby boomers reach the age of 65. In addition, the older adult population is getting older. In 1998 there were 12 million adults aged 75 to 84 and 4 million who were 85 years of age and older. When compared to the census figures for 1900, the 75- to 84-year-old group is now 16 times larger, and the 85+ group is 33 times larger (Administration on Aging, 1999).

Although most adults age successfully (cf. Rowe & Kahn, 1998), aging is not without its detractors. Most older adults have at least one chronic health problem, and many have several. In 1996 over 33% of older adults reported that they were limited by a chronic health problem. More than half of older adults have reported having at least one disability, and one third have reported at least one severe disability (Administration on Aging, 1999). The mental health problems of older adults also invite attention, with estimates of approximately

25% of older adults meeting criteria for a diagnosis (Gatz, Kasl-Godley, & Karel, 1996). In addition, comorbid health and mental health problems are common among older adults—particularly among those seen in medical clinics (Lichtenberg, 2000) and long-term care settings. These collections of health and mental health problems are often accompanied by the administration of medications.

The combination of health problems, mental health problems, and medication effects and side effects offers a unique array of challenges for the clinician—particularly the clinician who is unaccustomed to the provision of services to older adults. Although these challenges are sufficiently daunting in and of themselves, the clinician must consider the foregoing factors in the context of age-related changes in biological, psychological, and adaptive functioning.

The principal goal of this chapter is to acquaint the reader with assessment issues that are relatively unique to older adults, with particular attention to factors that could influence the process or outcome of clinical assessment. We begin with the discussions of two intra- and interpersonal variables—bias in the form of ageism and cultural competence. Ignorance of the importance and influence of these variables can lead to the corruption, contamination, and invalidation of the entire assessment enterprise. We then consider biological and medical issues that are more common among older adults that can play a significant role in the interplay between biological and environmental factors. Next, we shift to two conceptual issues, beginning with the assessment paradigms within which the clinician performs the assessment. We then address diagnostic issues and question the prudence of utilizing traditional diagnostic taxonomies with older adults. The complexities of carrying out clinical assessments are then addressed through discussions of multiple-method and multidimensional assessment. We follow this with a discussion of psychometric considerations for developing or selecting assessment instruments suitable for older adults. The chapter is closed with a brief discussion of future directions in the assessment of older adults.

INTRA- AND INTERPERSONAL ISSUES

Ageism

Ageism refers to stereotyping, prejudice, and discrimination based on age (Butler, 1969). Although ageism can apply to any age group, it is especially prevalent with older adults and can have a considerable impact on the assessment process. Butler (1980) describes three components of ageism related to older adults: (a) prejudicial attitudes toward older adults, old age, and the aging process; (b) discriminatory practices against older adults; and (c) institutional practices and policies that limit opportunities and deny older adults respect and freedom.

Negative Myths of Aging

The assessment process is not immune to the effects of ageism. Stereotypes and misconceptions about older adults abound. Mental health professionals must therefore be acutely aware of their perceptions and attitudes towards older adults so that they may be challenged and prevented from influencing the assessment process and outcome. The most common misconception about older adults is that they are sick or disabled (Palmore, 1999). Although older adults have higher rates of chronic illness than do younger adults, they experience lower rates of acute illness, injury, and accidents (Palmore, 1999). Disease is the main barrier to health and longevity, not age.

Another common myth is the belief that mental abilities begin to decline from middle age onward (Rowe & Kahn, 1998). However, most adults retain the majority of their usual mental abilities, including the ability to learn and remember, until their mid-70s (Schaie, 1996). Kaufman (1990) concluded that although mean Verbal, Performance, and Full Scale IQ scores on the Wechsler scales show declines between young adulthood and old age, it is the Performance IQ that suffers significantly. Similarly, fluid abilities tend to decline in early adulthood, whereas crystallized abilities are more likely to be sustained into older adulthood. Of equal importance is Poon's (1995) conclusion that chronological age does not appear to play a large role in learning ability (Poon, 1995).

A similar stereotype to that previously mentioned is that most older adults are senile and that mental illness is a normal part of aging (Palmore, 1999). Whereas 16% of the U.S. population has a major illness or substance abuse problem (National Institute of Mental Health, 2001), less than 10% of community-living older adults have significant or severe mental illness, and another 10–32% have only mild or moderate mental illness (Gurland, 1995). Because of the widespread belief that the typical older adult is disabled by physical or mental illness, many people conclude that older individuals are unable to remain in the workforce and that those who do work are unproductive (Palmore, 1999). Mandatory retirement policies and discrimination in hiring, retraining, and promotion are founded in this myth. However, studies of employed older workers show that they perform as well as or better than younger workers on most measures of job performance (Rix, 1995). Furthermore, upon retirement, many older adults maintain active lifestyles and make significant contributions to their communities. Belief in the aforementioned myths tends to perpetuate the attitude that the typical older adult is also miserable and depressed. A common myth is that major depression is more prevalent among the elderly than among younger persons. However, major depression is less prevalent among older adults than among younger adults, and most older adults report that they are relatively happy most of the time (Palmore, 1999).

Effects of Myths on Assessment

Belief in any of these myths and stereotypes can affect assessment. For example, a common myth that older adults are set in their ways and unable to learn new skills or coping mechanisms may lead to a belief that therapy will not help them (Thompson, Gallagher, & Breckenridge, 1987). Health professionals may therefore be less likely to refer older adults for therapy. However, therapy has been found to be equally as effective with older adults as it is with other age groups (e.g., Knight, 1996; Thompson et al., 1987). In assessing older adults, there is a tendency for medical and psychological problems to be attributed to age (Rodin & Langer, 1980). Although some problems may be a consequence of aging, the misattribution of problems to aging may be dangerous. For example, a belief that depression and sadness are normal parts of aging may preclude a diagnosis of major depression in an older adult who could benefit from treatment. When diagnoses are made, older adults are more likely to receive an organically based diagnosis such as dementia and to receive medications as treatment for depression than are younger adults (Gatz & Pearson, 1988; Rodin & Langer, 1980). This finding likely contributes to the overmedication of many older adults and increases the risk of adverse drug interactions. Because physicians commonly prescribe drugs to treat older adults' mental disorders, referrals to mental health professionals are less frequent for older adults than for younger adults (Gatz & Pearson, 1988).

Positive Ageism

Much less attention has been paid to positive ageism, or positive stereotypes about older adults, than to negative ageism. Positive ageism is less common than negative ageism and is not thought to harm older individuals. There are many positive stereotypes about older adults, and there are many people who have positive attitudes towards older adults. For example, Palmore (1999) maintains that many people believe that older adults hold great wisdom due to their greater years of experience. Others believe that because older adults are often retired, they are free to do anything they want at any time they want and in any way they want. These positive stereotypes in combination with an antidiscrimination response on the part of professionals, whereby they exaggerate the competencies and excuse the failings of the aged, may also lead to maltreatment of older adults (Gatz & Pearson, 1988). By making an effort not to denigrate older adults, therapists may fail to recognize genuine psychological problems with the potential for treatment.

To avoid the effects of ageism, professionals should learn about the aging process, gain more exposure to older adults, and examine their personal feelings about aging and how these feelings may affect their professional performance (Dupree & Patterson, 1985). It is particularly important to appreciate that ageism can affect older adults' behavior as they adopt these attitudes themselves.

CULTURAL AND ETHNIC ISSUES

The role of culture and ethnicity in the assessment process cannot be overemphasized, particularly with older adults who are more likely than their younger counterparts are to have strong cultural identities. The clinician and the client bring unique cultural and ethnic histories and knowledge bases to the assessment process. Indeed, there are suggestions that the biochemical and biophysical architecture of one's brain can be influenced by one's culture and experiences (e.g., Baltes & Singer, 2000). It is not surprising, then, that psychiatric disorders may present and be experienced differently among different cultural groups. For example, the presentation of depression in some cultures varies markedly. The Hopi of Arizona have a disorder that is similar to major depression but does not include the dysphoria component (Mouton & Esparza, 2000). Similarly, the expression of depression among the Flathead people of Montana takes the form of loneliness (O'Nell, 1996).

The unique characteristics of culturally diverse older adults can be quite profound and call for specialized knowledge and skills. In 1998, approximately 15.7% of the older adult (65+) population were minority group members (8.0% African American, 2.1% Asian or Pacific Islander, 5.1% Hispanic, and less than 1% American Indian or Native Alaskan; Administration on Aging, 1999). Older adults are becoming even more racially and ethnically diverse. In 1994, 10% of the older adults were non-White. In 2050 this proportion is expected to be 20%. Hispanic older adults are expected to represent 16% of the older adults (U.S. Bureau of Census, 1995). Such figures reinforce supplications for cultural competence (Dana, 2000) and intercultural approaches to clinical assessment (cf. Jones & Thorne, 1987).

Cultural competence might include knowledge of the prevalence, incidence, and risk factors for mental disorders among older adult ethnic groups, skills for gaining culturally relevant information regarding psychopathology, assessment (including culturally-ethnically unique psychometrics of assessment instruments), and treatment, and knowledge of the unique responses to various psychosocial interventions. At the individual level, such competence might include knowledge of the individual's cultural identity, his or her cultural explanations of the suspected mental disorder, culturally relevant aspects of the client's social environment, and culturally relevant factors in the client's relationship with the clinician (Rubio-Stipec, Hicks, & Tsuang, 2000).

A thorough discussion of culturally relevant information regarding older adult assessment is beyond the scope of this chapter. Moreover, such information varies both within and between cultures. Thus, we only very briefly discuss some of the more general considerations. The interested reader is referred to Dana (2000); Mouton and Esparaza (2000); and Rubio-Stipec, Hicks, and Tsuang (2000) for more complete discussions of the assessment of culturally diverse young and older adults.

The kinship systems of older adult ethnic groups are often an important element of their culture. Such systems are collections of social relationship that often define group life (Morales, 1999). The system governs the individual's relationships and status within the culture. Older adults tend to rely more on members of their kinship systems and their cultural traditions than younger adults. They may also be more devoted to folk beliefs, religious affiliations, and cultural traditions than are their younger counterparts. In general, culturally-ethnically diverse older adults tend to be more devoted to their unique cultures and family ties than are younger ethnic minority adults (Morales, 1999). When these individuals encounter problems, the older adults are more likely than younger minority adults to seek assistance from family or community members and less likely to seek help outside the minority community; this is particularly true with psychological problems (Morales, 1999).

Unfortunately, much of the available information about factors to consider when working with ethnically diverse populations is based on younger individuals. Moreover, few clinical assessment instruments have sound psychometric support for use with older adults. This paucity of relevant instruments is even more apparent when one is seeking culture-free or culturally relevant assessment instruments for older adults. Test items with idioms and colloquialisms unique to a particular culture can yield very different meanings when read by members of other cultures, raising the additional question of whether the same constructs are being measured. The norms and language of the Caucasian majority dominate the assessment literature, notwithstanding the sometimes unique presentation and experience of mental disorders among ethnically diverse populations (Edelstein, Kalish, Drozdick, & McKee, 1999; Futterman, Thompson, Gallagher-Thompson, & Ferris, 1995).

BIOLOGICAL AND MEDICAL FACTORS

Sensory Changes Associated With Aging

Although it is true that as individuals age, they are at greater risk of developing chronic health problems, such conditions are not a normal part of the aging process (Whitbourne, 1996). Recognition of this distinction between disease and the normal physiological changes associated with aging is essential to facilitate accurate assessments and diagnoses. Knowledge of the physiological changes that often occur with aging and how these changes may contribute to clients' presenting problems and affect the veracity of assessments is crucial. Due to space limitations, we address age-related changes in only visual and auditory systems.

Vision

Whereas the majority of older adults have fair to adequate vision (Pfeifer, 1980), some of the most severe age-associated decrements occur in the visual system. Many older adults experience decreasing visual acuity, diminished light sensitivity and visual processing speed, and problems with near vision, visual search, and tracking moving objects (Kosnik, Winslow, Kline, Rasinski, & Sekuler, 1988). Cataracts, another common problem, can cause visual difficulties resulting from a dulling of colors and glare in brightly lit areas. When presenting visual stimuli to older adults, one must be careful to minimize glare. Materials printed on glossy surfaces are particularly vulnerable to glare (Storandt, 1994). During assessment, clinicians should try to balance the older adult's susceptibility to increased glare with the need for sufficient illumination.

With increased age, the lens becomes thicker and less elastic, and it is unable to change shape to focus on close objects (Winograd, 1984). Older adults may have to wear trifocals to achieve good focus of near, far, and middle-distance objects. Older adults may need to shift between these three components of their eyeglasses to achieve good focus on test materials at different distances, which may slow performance (Storandt, 1994). Older adults' trouble with near vision, or presbyopia, often leads to an increasing difficulty reading small print (Kosnik et al., 1988). Whenever possible, stimuli should be made larger for older adults. One should consider having written or self-report instruments produced in larger print for use with older clients. Specifically, a 14-point font for written text has been found to maximize visual clarity for older adults with presbyopia (Vanderplas & Vanderplas, 1981).

The aforementioned visual deficits could result in a number of outcomes, including diminished test performance on tests requiring adequate vision, changes in social behavior resulting from a failure to recognize friends and acquaintances, reluctance to participate in activities requiring visual acuity, falls resulting from difficulties with dark adaptation and depth perception, and automobile accidents resulting from glare and rapid changes in light intensity (Edelstein, Drozdick, & Kogan, 1998).

Other research indicates that visual deficits are also related to intelligence. Specifically, visual acuity accounts for 41.3%

of the variance in older adults' intellectual functioning (Lindenberger & Baltes, 1994). Visual impairment is also related to functional status decline (Stuck et al., 1999; Werner-Wahl, Schilling, Oswald, & Heyl, 1999), anxiety (DeBeurs, Beekman, Deeg, Dyck, & Tillburg, 2000), emotional well-being (Penninx et al., 1998; Werner-Wahl et al., 1999), and everyday activity levels (Marsiske, Klumb, & Baltes, 1997). One should therefore take into account older adults' level of visual deficits when conceptualizing impairment in these areas.

Hearing

Hearing loss is a common problem among older adults; approximately 50% of Americans over the age of 65 experience some form of hearing impairment (Vernon, 1989). Clinicians should be aware of clues that may signal hearing impairment, such as a history of ear infections, loud speech, requests for the interviewer to repeat statements, inability to distinguish the sound of one individual in a group of speakers, and the tendency to keenly watch the speaker's mouth (Vernon, 1989).

Older adults commonly experience a phenomenon known as *masking,* which involves particular difficulties hearing normal speech when there is substantial background noise (Storandt, 1994). Therefore, efforts should be made to interview and assess older adults in a quiet setting. For most older adults, the ability to hear high-frequency tones is impaired earlier and more severely than is the ability to hear low-frequency tones (Whitbourne, 1996). Female speakers with high-pitched voices should be sensitive to the fact that difficulty hearing high frequencies may impair communication with older adults, and attempts may be made to lower the pitch of their voices (Storandt, 1994). Additionally, one should attempt to speak more slowly without overarticulating, which can distort speech and facial gestures (Edelstein, Staats, Kalish, & Northrop, 1996).

Hearing deficits may be due to presbycusis (loss of auditory acuity associated with aging), drugs and allergies, circulatory disorders, central organic impairments, and occupational and recreational noise (Storandt, 1994). Other age-associated changes in the ear may also contribute to hearing loss. The wall of the outer cartilaginous portion of the auditory canal collapses inward with advancing age, narrowing the passage and making the canal less effective at receiving and channeling sound waves to the middle ear (Ferrini & Ferrini, 1993). Additionally, earwax tends to thicken with age. Accumulated earwax may block the auditory canal and may contribute to hearing impairments (Whitbourne, 1996).

Communication problems may be exacerbated as individuals with hearing loss pretend to understand what is being said during the interview. More critically, reduced hearing acuity commonly has psychological effects. Decreased hearing sensitivity may limit one's enjoyment of social activities and the stimulation that other people and television provide. Paranoid ideas and behavior (Zimbardo, Andersen, & Kabat, 1981), withdrawal from other people (Vernon, 1989), depression (Vernon, 1989), denial (Vernon, Grifffen, & Yoken, 1981), anxiety (DeBeurs et al., 2000) decreasing functional status (L. M. Stein & Bienenfeld, 1992), decreased intelligence (Marsiske et al., 1997), and rapid deterioration of cognitive functioning in older adults with dementia of the Alzheimer's type (Uhlmann, Larson, & Koepsell, 1986) may also occur in those with gradual hearing loss. Family members and friends may also withdraw from the hearing-impaired person because they are frustrated by efforts to communicate. Furthermore, older adults with hearing impairments may be misdiagnosed because they appear inattentive or withdrawn (Ferrini & Ferrini, 1993).

Biological Rhythms and Assessment

There is mounting chronobiological and psychological evidence that clinicians should no longer ignore the time of day during which adults are assessed. The human biological clock or circadian system controls a wide range of biological and psychological processes (e.g., body temperature regulation, hormone secretion, sleep-wake cycles) through circadian rhythms. Each of these processes shows peaks and troughs throughout the 24-hour cycle. Recent evidence suggests that various cognitive processes follow similar rhythms, with peak performance associated with peak periods of physiological arousal (e.g., Bodenhausen, 1990). For example, May, Hasher, and Stoltzfus (1993) found memory for prose to be most accurate when participants were tested during their period of peak circadian arousal, typically during the early morning or late afternoon. It is interesting to note that researchers have found that such peak performance periods vary by age (e.g., May et al., 1993). These age-related differences in performance also correspond to subjective ratings of peak and off-peak times of the day (e.g., Horne & Osterberg, 1976). For example, approximately 40% of college students (aged 18–25) tend to experience peak performance in the evening, whereas most (approximately 70%) older adults (aged 60–75) tend to peak in the morning (Yoon, May, & Hasher, 1997). Yoon et al. (1997), as cited in Ishihara, Miyake, Miyasita, and Miyata (1991), note that the shift toward peak morning performance appears to begin around the age of 50.

For purposes of the present chapter, the work of Hasher, May, and their colleagues appears to have the most relevance.

Hasher, Zacks, and May (1999) argue for major roles of excitatory and inhibitory processes to explain the variations in older adult performance across the day. It is these processes that are ostensibly influenced by circadian arousal patterns. The authors attribute a major role to inhibition, which serves three functions related to working memory: (a) deletion, (b) access, and (c) restraint. Inhibitory processes prevent irrelevant information from entering working memory. Inhibitory processes also delete or suppress the activation of irrelevant information. Overall, the inhibitory processes reduce the amount of distracting information.

There is considerable evidence of age-related declines in the inhibition of task-irrelevant information (e.g., Alain & Woods, 1999). Hasher and colleagues suggest that older adults whose inhibitory processes are impaired are more likely to experience impairment in working memory due to the presence of distracting, irrelevant information generated by the individual (e.g., related cognitions) or by the external environment (e.g., noise). Hasher and colleagues (e.g., Hasher & Zacks, 1988; Li, Hasher, Jonas, Rahhal, & May, 1998; May, 1999) have compiled an impressive amount of data suggesting that the changes in cognitive functioning that occur at off-peak times are due to circadian-rhythm-related deficits in inhibition. They have also found that the excitatory processes do not seem to vary across time. Thus, well-learned information (e.g., vocabulary) appears to be unaffected.

The research addressing the performance effects of off-peak assessment has very important implications for the assessment of older adult cognitive functioning. Neuropsychological assessment should probably be conducted during an individual's peak time period if one is seeking optimal performance. More specifically, cognitive assessment of older adults should ideally take into consideration the individual's peak and off-peak performance periods. Finally, the assessment of other domains that involve cognitive performance (e.g., decision-making capacity) is also potentially susceptible to these circadian rhythms. At the very least, clinicians should record the time of day during which each element of the assessment process occurs.

The aforementioned physiological changes can significantly alter the behavior of the client and unintentionally contribute to erroneous conclusions if one is ignorant of these changes and their potential consequences. Clinicians must be vigilant about assessing for the presence and degree of physiological and sensory changes associated with aging and should consider these changes when formulating a conceptualization of the client's presenting problems. Similarly, erroneous assumptions made by clinicians with regard to the characteristics of older adults can lead to faulty conclusions. Clinicians must be careful to not misattribute symptoms of disease to normal aging processes or assume that impairments in sensory symptoms are not amenable to intervention.

Psychological Presentations of Physical Disease

Many of the most common medical conditions experienced by older adults have numerous psychological symptoms. However, medical practitioners are often insufficiently prepared to assess the psychological concomitants of medical illness. Similarly, many physical disorders—when they are undetected—can appear as psychological symptoms, and mental health practitioners are often unaware of the possible underlying medical conditions. We now discuss various physical disorders that can lead to biologically based psychological symptoms as well as those that—when undetected—can present as psychological symptoms.

Parkinson's Disease

Parkinson's disease is manifested by stiff and slow motor movements. Patients may have hand tremors and may be unsteady when standing or walking. Initiating motor activity, such as walking, may be particularly difficult. The course is chronic and progressive. Depression is the primary psychological symptom associated with Parkinson's disease (Frazer, Leicht, & Baker, 1996). Starkstein, Preziosi, Bolduc, and Robinson (1990) reported a 41% rate of depression among outpatients with Parkinson's disease. Half of the depressed patients met criteria for major depression and half for minor depression (dysthymia). Starkstein et al. (1990) suggested that changes in the basal ganglia associated with Parkinson's disease may be an etiological factor in depression. Parkinson's disease can often also initially present as depression. Starkstein et al. (1990) reported that in patients with major depression and Parkinson's disease, 29% suffered a history of depression prior to the appearance of any motor symptoms. Todes and Lee (1985) also found high rates of premorbid depression in patients with Parkinson's disease. In addition to depression, dementia (Cummings, 1988) and anxiety (Schiffer, Kurlan, Rubin, & Boer, 1988; M. B. Stein, Heuser, Juncos, & Uhde, 1990) are also frequently associated with Parkinson's disease.

Cancer

Whereas depression appears to be a common concomitant to cancer, the diagnosis of cancer-related depression is complicated by the somatic features of the disease and the side effects of its treatment (Frazer et al., 1996). Rates of major depression in cancer patients vary from 6% to 42%, with one study reporting a drop from 42% to 24% when somatic criteria were eliminated (Rodin, Craven, & Littlefield, 1993). Clinical knowledge about the specific type of tumor, its course, and its treatment is essential to diagnose depression in individuals with cancer (Greenberg, 1989). Greenberg suggests that symptoms of depression, such as anorexia, fatigue, and insomnia may be caused by radiation, chemotherapy, or intractable pain. However, if the fatigue is worse in the morning, depression may be the causal factor, and if insomnia is not accompanied by pain, depression should also be considered. Greenberg argues that anhedonia is not common in cancer patients without depression. Extensive research indicates that pancreatic cancer can first appear as depression (Gillam, 1990; Holland et al., 1986), and there is some evidence of depression as an early symptom in lung cancer (Hughes, 1985) and in head and neck cancer (Davies, Davies, & Delpo, 1986).

Chronic Obstructive Pulmonary Disease

Chronic obstructive pulmonary disease (COPD) consists of a group of degenerative diseases of the respiratory system. Chronic bronchitis and emphysema are the most common forms of COPD. Dyspnea (inability to obtain enough air), chronic cough, and increased sputum production are the prominent symptoms. Depression is the most common psychological feature associated with COPD; approximately one quarter to one half of individuals with COPD experience some form of depressive symptomology (Murrell, Himmelfarb, & Wright, 1983). Anxiety also appears to be a common feature of COPD, related to the hypoxia and dyspnea associated with the diseases (Frazer et al., 1996). The anxiety that an individual experiences when he or she cannot breathe adequately places further demands on the respiratory system, causing a feedback loop that can exacerbate both respiratory and psychological symptomology (Frazer et al., 1996).

Cardiovascular Disease

Cardiovascular diseases, including hypertension, coronary artery disease, valvular heart disease, arrhythmias and conduction disorders, heart failure, and peripheral vascular diseases, all involve difficulty sustaining a regular, sufficient blood supply throughout the body (Frazer et al., 1996). Patients with chronic heart disease experience depressive symptomatology at a rate between 10% and 20% (Cohen-Cole, 1989). Cohen-Cole also argues that anxiety may be a prominent feature in heart disease because of its unpredictable and life-threatening nature. Anxiety-like symptoms, such as dread, bewilderment, respiratory distress, and sweating may also be a signal of myocardial infarction due to rising levels of catecholamines (G. Cohen, 1991). The relationship between depression and cardiovascular disease is exemplified in coronary artery disease (CAD). Friedman and Booth-Kewley (1987) found depression to be as major a risk factor for CAD as cigarette smoking. In older adults, a sudden change in mental status has been found to be a predictor of myocardial infarction (Frazer et al., 1996).

Cerebrovascular Disease

Cerebrovascular conditions are closely related to cardiovascular conditions. Whenever heart disease or atherosclerosis leads to interruption in blood flow to the brain, the patient experiences cognitive effects from the resulting anoxia. The most common cerebrovascular condition in older adults is stroke. Extensive research has examined the relationship between stroke and depression. Lipsey and Parikh (1989) found clinical depression to be a common psychological consequence of stroke, occurring in 47% of patients immediately following stroke and increasing to 60% of the patients at a 6-month follow-up. Starkstein and Robinson (1993) reported that poststroke major depression tends to resolve after approximately 1 year, whereas poststroke minor depression tends to last for over 2 years. Furthermore, lesion location has been found to be related to poststroke duration, with middle cerebral artery areas associated with longer duration and subcortical lesions associated with briefer durations of depression (Starkstein & Robinson, 1993).

Diabetes Mellitus

Diabetes mellitus involves hyperglycemia (high blood sugar) due to absent or reduced insulin secretion or ineffective insulin action. Diabetes is divided into Type 1 (insulin-dependent diabetes mellitus or IDDM) and Type 2 (non-insulin-dependent diabetes mellitus or NIDDM). NIDDM is the most prevalent form of the disease in older adults. Depression is a common psychological manifestation of diabetes. Lustman, Griffith, Clouse, and Cryer (1986) estimated a lifetime prevalence of major depression among IDDM and NIDDM patients as 32.5%, and point prevalence rates at 14%. Lustman et al. (1986) speculate that depression can either cause or be caused by poor glucose control and that psychiatric illness is associated with poor long-term glucose control. However, depression may also be a reaction to diagnosis, lifestyle changes, control issues, and physical complications such as impotence and blindness (Frazer et al., 1996).

Clinicians must be knowledgeable of the frequent comorbidity of medical and mental disorders, especially when the psychological symptoms are the initial presentation of the disease. To the extent that both medical and mental health practitioners are aware of the complex interactions, assessments can be more thorough and interventions can be more specifically and appropriately focused.

Medication Use

Approximately 80% of older adults suffer from at least one chronic health problem (Knight, Santos, Teri, & Lawton, 1995). Because they have a high prevalence of chronic illnesses, older adults consume more medications than do members of any other age group (Ferrini & Ferrini, 1993). However, older adults are at higher risk of adverse drug reactions than are any other age groups because of age-related changes in physiology and increased use of multiple medications, both prescribed and over-the-counter. Older adults in the United States use a disproportionate amount of both prescription and nonprescription medications. They comprise over 12% of the total population but account for 30% of the total drug expenditures (Ferrini & Ferrini, 1993).

Pharmacokinetics refers to various aspects of drug metabolism, such as absorption, distribution, metabolism, and excretion (Schneider, 1996). Whereas there is little evidence that age-related changes in gastrointestinal function affect drug absorption (Norman, 1993), the age-related changes in total body water and total body fat lead to changes in drug distribution in older adults (Schneider, 1996). Furthermore, decline in liver function due to age-associated changes may cause medications to remain in the body longer, and decreases in kidney blood flow and filtration ability associated with age allow drugs to circulate longer in the body, thus increasing their effect (Ferrini & Ferrini, 1993).

Polypharmacy is the practice of using medications excessively and unnecessarily. Polypharmacy is common in older adults who are taking a number of medications to treat multiple illnesses. Drug interactions are frequent in older adults because of their high consumption of prescription drugs. Those who use drugs to reduce the adverse effects of other drugs (rather than adjust the dosage or change the original drug) are at greater risk for adverse reactions, more health problems, and increased expense of drugs and physician visits (Ferrini & Ferrini, 1993).

Psychological symptoms in older adults may be the result of medications. For example, hallucinations, illusions, insomnia, and psychotic symptoms are possible side effects of various antiparkinsonian agents (Salzman, 1992). Side effects of many cardiovascular drugs include depression, confusion, delusions, paranoia, disorientation, agitation, and fatigue (Salzman, 1992). Finally, delusions, forgetfulness, illogical thoughts, paranoid delusions, and sleep disturbances may be associated with antidepressant use (Salzman, 1992). In light of these potential side effects, clinicians should thoroughly assess their clients' medication use to rule out drug side effects when conceptualizing psychological symptoms.

METHODOLOGICAL AND PROCEDURAL ISSUES

Assessment Paradigms

A variety of assessment paradigms guide our approaches to assessment. A brief discussion of the two dominant paradigms is important before proceeding with our discussion of older adult assessment methods and instruments. An assessment paradigm is "a set of principles, beliefs, values, hypotheses, and methods advocated in an assessment discipline or by it adherents" (Haynes & O'Brien, 2000, p. 10). Consequently, the paradigm determines the nature of the questions addressed, settings in which information is obtained, nature of assessment instruments, the manner in which data obtained from assessment instruments are used, inferences that may be drawn from assessment data, how the clinician proceeds from assessment to intervention when change is desirable, and so on. In summary, a clinician's assessment paradigm determines how he or she approaches the systematic examination of behavior, which is essentially the task of psychological assessment.

The two principal assessment paradigms are traditional and behavioral. It would be simplistic to attempt a clear distinction between these two paradigms because they share some elements. Moreover, neither is monolithic; each has subparadigms (cf. Haynes & O'Brien, 2000). For example, within the traditional paradigm, one might find trait-oriented psychodynamic personality, intellectual, neuropsychological, diagnostic, and family systems subparadigms. Within the behavioral paradigm, one might find behavior—analytic, social learning and cognitive-behavioral subparadigms (see Kazdin & Wilson, 1978).

Behavioral and traditional paradigms can be distinguished in a variety of ways (see Barrios & Hartmann, 1986; Cone, 1986; Haynes & O'Brien, 2000; Nelson & Hayes, 1986). For the purposes of this chapter, two distinctions are useful. First, one can distinguish between behavioral and traditional paradigms in terms of their philosophical assumptions regarding descriptions and causes of behavior. Traditional approaches tend to emphasize descriptions of an individual's dispositional characteristics (e.g., personality traits) or what he or she *has* (cf. Mischel, 1968), which is often inferred from observed behavior and from self-reports of feelings, attitudes, and behavior. The behavior of the individual tends to be explained by these personal characteristics. In contrast, behavioral approaches focus on the identification of environmental conditions that reliably produce the behaviors of interest. The behavior of the individual is explained by describing the conditions under which the behavior of interest occurs; this might include a description, for example, of the environmental conditions and schedule of reinforcement that are maintaining the screaming behavior of an individual with dementia or the low level of social engagement of a depressed individual. A lower level of inference is required in behavioral assessment because the phenomenon of interest is usually behavior (including thoughts or cognitions) rather than inferences drawn from the behavior.

Another way of characterizing the differences between traditional and behavioral paradigms is to distinguish between idiographic and nomothetic approaches to assessment. The idiographic-nomothetic distinction was popularized by Allport (1937) in his discussions of personality assessment. In general, the nomothetic approach is used to examine commonalities among individuals, whereas the idiographic approach is used to ascertain the uniqueness of an individual. Nomothetic assessment typically involves the use of assessment instruments that have been standardized with a large number of individuals. The same instrument is used to assess multiple individuals. The results of the assessment are compared against the results obtained with a standardization population (normative sample). For example, a person might complete a self-report measure of depression. The obtained total score would then be compared against population norms derived from a large, representative group of individuals with presumably similar demographic characteristics.

Idiographic assessment is an individualized approach to assessment that involves methods and measures that are tailored to the individual client. For example, a socially anxious individual might be assessed via a role play with several strangers, a direct observation instrument that targets relevant overt behaviors under a wide range of conditions, and a set of self-report questions that are specifically tailored for the particular client and that focus on cognitions (e.g., self-statements regarding fear of negative evaluation), experiences of anxiety (e.g., increased heart rate, tightening chest, sweaty palms), and knowledge of effective conversational skills. There is typically no attempt to compare the assessment results with those obtained with other individuals. The criteria or standards used by the clinician are individually determined. Mischel (1968) noted that "behavioral assessment involves an exploration of the unique or idiosyncratic aspects of the single case, perhaps to a greater extent than any other approach" (p. 190).

Although the traditional and behavioral paradigms are quite different in many respects, their characteristic assessment methods and instruments can be combined (cf. Nelson-Gray, 1996). For example, a clinician might use a standardized depression assessment instrument to obtain information for use in a behavioral analysis. In addition to comparing a total depression score with population norms (traditional nomothetic approach), the individual depression inventory items could be used to characterize the individual (idiographic). Thus, one might determine that an individual is probably clinically depressed using a total score and then examine individual test items to gain an understanding of how the individual is experiencing and expressing depression.

As one moves from cognitively intact to cognitively impaired individuals, one must necessarily shift from more traditional to more behavioral, idiographic assessment approaches. Moderate to severe cognitive impairment typically precludes accurate and reliable self-report. Thus, assessment questions are less likely to focus on the person's personality, cognitions, and self-reported behavior, and they are more likely to focus on the person's observed behavior and the environmental conditions that are maintaining it. The question *Why is this person behaving this way?* becomes *Under what conditions is this person exhibiting this behavior?* Questions asked might include *What time of day, in whose presence, and how often does the behavior occur?* Similarly one typically asks *What happens after the behavior occurs?* Of equal importance is the question of the conditions under which the behavior does *not* occur. The assessment methods become more circumscribed and direct, relying principally upon report by others and direct observation. In general, the goals of assessment become the increase, decrease, or maintenance of specific target behaviors.

Diagnostic Issues

Differential Diagnosis

The presenting signs and symptoms of older adults may fall within more than one diagnostic category. When this occurs, clinicians are faced with the task of differential diagnosis. This entails determining which disorder or disorders best account for the symptoms that are present. Consider the example of an older adult who presents with the following symptoms: memory difficulties, sleep disturbance, a change in psychomotor activity, and poor concentration. Without any additional information, one might speculate that the older adult is experiencing some form of anxiety or mood disorder, a dementing illness, the sequelae of a medical condition, or the side effects of a medication or other ingested substance. What is needed at this point are data that may be used to differentiate between the possible diagnoses. These data may be acquired from numerous sources, including direct observation, informal and standardized clinical interviews, functional evaluations, self-report questionnaires, standardized psychological tests, physiological data, information gathered from significant others, neuropsychological evaluations, medical examinations and tests, and lists of medications and substances that are being used, along with the individual and compounded side effects that are possible.

Epidemiological Issues

According to Gatz, Kasl-Godley, and Karel (1996), approximately 25% of older adults meet criteria for a diagnosable mental disorder, including cognitive impairment and emotional dysfunction. Knowledge regarding the prevalence of various psychological disorders among older adults in community and inpatient settings may be useful in dispelling some of the myths about mental health and aging (e.g., the myth that depression is quite common among community-dwelling older adults) and providing mental health practitioners with a basic appreciation of the pervasiveness or rarity of various disorders.

The results from epidemiological studies indicate that approximately 2.5% of community-dwelling older adults meet diagnostic criteria for a depressive disorder (Reiger et al., 1988). Specifically, the 1-month prevalence rates for major depressive disorder among older men and women are 0.4% and 0.9%, respectively. The 1-month prevalence rates for dysthymic disorder among older men and women are 1.0% and 2.3%, respectively (Reiger et al., 1988). Higher prevalence rates may be observed among nursing home residents, with approximately 15–25% of residents experiencing depressive disorders (Salzman, 1997). In contrast, depressive symptoms are much more common and have been reported to occur in approximately 15–27% of community-dwelling older adults (Blazer, Hughes, & George, 1987; Koenig & Blazer, 1992; Salzman, 1997).

Results of the Epidemiological Catchment Area survey (ECA) revealed a 1-month prevalence rate of 5.5% for anxiety disorders among older adults (Reiger et al., 1988; Reiger, Narrow, & Rae, 1990). Data from the ECA survey further indicated that anxiety disorders occurred more than twice as often as affective disorders among older adults, which signals the need for further study of anxiety disorders among older adults (Stanley & Beck, 1998). Prevalence rates for schizophrenia have been reported to be less than 1% among adults of all ages (Kessler et al., 1994). Among community-dwelling older adults, the prevalence rate is approximately 0.1% (Zarit & Zarit, 1998). The prevalence among nursing home residents has been estimated to be 12% (Gurland & Cross, 1982). Estimating the prevalence of dementia is difficult

because there are no definitive markers for the disease. However, studies suggest that the prevalence of dementia among older adults in their 60s is approximately 1%. The prevalence rate increases to approximately 7% among older adults in their mid-70s and then rises dramatically in the 80s to between 20% and 30%. Overall, the prevalence of dementia has been reported to double approximately every 5 years after the age of 65 (Jorm, Korten, & Henderson, 1987). It has been suggested that some personality disorders may become less prominent among older adults (e.g., antisocial, borderline, and narcissistic), whereas other disorders may become more prominent (e.g., compulsive, schizotypal, paranoid) in later life (Rosowsky & Gurian, 1991; Sadavoy & Fogel, 1992; Zarit & Zarit, 1998). A meta-analysis conducted by Abrams and Horowitz (1999) examined the prevalence of several personality disorders among adults aged 50 years and over using criteria from present and past editions of the *Diagnostic and Statistical Manual of Mental Disorders–Fourth Edition* (*DSM-IV;* American Psychiatric Association, 1994). The results revealed that the most prevalent personality disorders were paranoid (19.8%), self-defeating (12.3%), and schizoid (10.8%), and the least prevalent were mixed (2.0%), antisocial (2.6%), and narcissistic (4.6%).

Unique Presentations of Disorders Among Older Adults

Age-Related Changes and Differences in Axis I Disorders

The presentation of Axis I disorders may vary greatly between younger and older adults. This finding is not surprising because cross-sectional and longitudinal studies have documented age-related changes and differences across many dimensions of life (e.g., cognitive, biological, and social). In fact, given our knowledge of these changes and differences, one might logically expect that older adults would have unique presentations of disorders. For example, in contrast to younger adults, the clinical presentation of depression among older adults is more likely to include changes in appetite and sleep patterns, loss of interest, lack of energy, increased dependency, social withdrawal, anxiety, psychomotor agitation, delusions, hypochondriacal syndromes, chronic pain, and increased irritability (Gottfries, 1997; Müller-Spahn & Hock, 1994; Salzman, 1997; Yesavage, 1992). The type of symptoms reported by older adults may also differ from types reported by other age groups. Using the example of depression, older adults may be more likely than younger adults to present with masked depression, which involves differential reports of physical rather than psychological symptoms (Yesavage, 1992). In such cases, older adults may be more likely to describe gastrointestinal disorders, poor health, musculoskeletal problems, or cardiovascular problems rather than depressed mood. This difference may be due in part to a hesitancy among older adults to accept a psychiatric explanation for their symptoms because of stereotypes regarding psychiatric disorders (Casey, 1994).

Age-Related Changes and Differences in Axis II Disorders

Personality disorders are defined within the *DSM-IV* (American Psychiatric Association, 1994) as rigid and inflexible personality traits that lead to functional problems and intrapsychic conflict. These disorders are manifested usually during adolescence or early adulthood. Therefore, older adults with personality disorders have most likely had a long history of related symptoms. Information regarding the changes in personality disorders with advancing age is very limited because there is a marked paucity of longitudinal data. Therefore, not much is known about how the symptoms of personality disorders change across adulthood or about the pattern of improvement or deterioration across adulthood (Zarit & Zarit, 1998). However, some evidence suggests that the emotional and dramatic symptoms that are found among antisocial, histrionic, and borderline diagnoses may become less pronounced with age. This change may be due to age-related decreases in impulsivity and activity levels. Other evidence suggests that somatic and depressive features may become more central in personality disorders as adults age (Segal, Coolidge, & Rosowksy, 2000).

Age-Related DSM-IV Criteria

As mentioned previously, age-related changes have been documented to occur across many dimensions (i.e., cognitive, biological, social) of life. In many instances, normative, age-related changes in these dimensions coincide with the diagnostic criteria set forth by the *DSM-IV* (American Psychiatric Association, 1994). For example, consider the following age-related changes: The sleep-wake cycle changes (e.g., total sleep time is reduced and getting to sleep may become more difficult; Ancoli-Israel, Pat-Horencyzk, & Martin, 1998); it becomes more difficult to filter out distractions when working on cognitive tasks (Smith, 1996); and social networks are reduced and made more efficient (i.e., older adults conserve their time and energy by associating with fewer individuals; Carstensen, 1995). All of these changes that are normative in later adulthood may be interpreted as part of the diagnostic criteria for a major depressive episode (i.e., sleep disturbance, poor concentration, and declines in social functioning). This example illustrates how the present diagnostic system may not be especially suited to older populations.

Syndromal Classification and Alternative Approaches

Syndromal Classification

Currently, syndromal classification is the dominant approach used by the majority of clinicians because it underlies the organization and content of the widely used *DSM-IV* (American Psychiatric Association, 1994). This approach involves the identification and classification of syndromes. Syndromes are collections of signs (i.e., what is observed) and symptoms (i.e., the client's complaints) that often lead to the diagnosis of various disorders.

The strategy of using syndromal classification has been criticized on several grounds. Hayes, Wilson, Gifford, Follette, and Strosahl (1996) argued that diagnostic criteria may be continually changed and refined, thus leading to an ever-increasing number of diagnostic categories found within the *DSM* system. Follette and Houts (1996) also noted that the use of syndromal classification steers the clinicians' efforts toward classification—at the expense of investigating factors that may predict or etiologically explain various diseases. Criticisms such as these have led others (e.g., Follette & Houts, 1996; McFall & Townsend, 1998) to reexamine the foundations of psychological assessment and call for viable alternatives to the dominant strategy of syndromal classification. Alternative approaches to syndromal classification may be especially desirable for clinicians who work with older clients because the signs and symptoms of a given disorder may differ between younger and older clients.

Functional Classification

Using this alternative to syndromal classification, Hayes et al. (1996) argued that problematic behaviors may be organized by the functional processes that are hypothesized to have produced and maintained them. Proponents of functional classification may use a functional analysis (for a description of functional analysis, see Hayes & Follette, 1992; G. Martin & Pear, 1996). This type of analysis involves the observation of clients' problematic behaviors in their natural environments to arrive at hypotheses about how the problem behaviors are controlled and maintained by their antecedents and consequences. For example, a functional analysis may be utilized with an older client exhibiting constant yelling or occasional aggressive behavior. The initial occurrence or maintenance of these behaviors may be understood from a functional perspective (e.g., these behaviors may produce attention from others). The use of functional analyses as a means of functional classification has been criticized on several grounds. For example, Hayes et al. (1996) have reported that functional analyses may be vague, hard to replicate and test empirically, and strongly idiographic (i.e., not very generalizable).

Symptom Severity

Other approaches to classification have been described that may benefit older adults. For example, Nease, Volk, and Cass (1999) have suggested that symptom severity should be incorporated into classification strategies. These authors investigated a severity-based classification of mood and anxiety symptoms. In their research, the authors were able to identify valid clusters of symptom severity (e.g., low severity, high severity) and define relations between these clusters and other outcomes (e.g., health-related quality of life and frequency of *DSM* disorders). Severity-based classification strategies may be especially beneficial in the assessment of older clients because they often may exhibit subclinical symptoms of certain disorders (i.e., they may fail to meet all of the diagnostic criteria for a given disorder that are sufficient to warrant clinical attention and intervention). For example, minor depression, a subtype of depression found among older adults, involves a smaller number of the same symptoms identified in major depressive disorder (Fiske, Kasl-Godley, & Gatz, 1998). Although the prevalence of major depressive disorder among older adults is low, the prevalence of depressive symptoms may be substantially higher. Because subclinical symptoms of depression may be somewhat common among older adults, an assessment strategy that focuses on the severity of these symptoms may be more suited for older populations.

MULTIMETHOD ASSESSMENT

Clinicians have long been encouraged to employ multiple methods in the measurement of clinical phenomena (e.g., Campbell & Fiske, 1959). Each method (e.g., interview, direct observation, self-report, report by others, psychophysiological recording) has strengths and weaknesses. Moreover, each method can portray a different picture of the phenomenon of interest, which is often characterized as method variance (cf. Campbell & Fisk, 1959). The relative strengths and weaknesses of each method can be minimized by using multiple assessment methods. For example, one might measure depression of a nursing home resident by using a self-report instrument, a rating scale completed by a staff member, direct observation of relevant behavior, and a brief structured interview completed by a mental health professional. The use of such methods can offer both unique and corroborative information. The strengths and

weaknesses of some of these methods are discussed in the following sections.

Self-Report

The self-report method is arguably the most frequently used assessment method. The reliability and validity of assessment information obtained via self-report with older adults are vulnerable for a variety of reasons, some of which are more likely than others to be age-related. For example, the specific wording of questions, question format, and question context can influence the results one obtains from the self-report method with older adults (Schwarz, 1999). Self-reporting can be particularly problematic with older adults who are experiencing communication-related cognitive deficits. Overall, the evidence supporting the accuracy, reliability, and validity of older adult self-reports is mixed. For example, older adult estimates of their functional ability have been questioned; some overestimate their functional abilities (e.g., Rubenstein, Schairer, Weiland, & Kane, 1984), and others both under- and overestimate their abilities (e.g., Sager et al., 1992). Similarly, self-reports of memory impairment among older adults may be inaccurate (e.g., Perlmutter, 1978; A. Sunderland, Watts, Baddeley, & Harris, 1986; Zelinski, Gilewski, & Thompson, 1980).

A variety of factors can contribute to the inaccuracies of self reported information among older adults. These factors might include, for example, physical and mental health status, affective responses to acute illness, changes from previous levels of physical functioning occurring during hospitalization, and the presence of acute or chronic cognitive impairment (Sager et al., 1992). Cognitively impaired older adults pose a formidable assessment challenge because few instruments are valid for use with such individuals, and they may be unable to comprehend questions or the nature of information requested. Numerous studies have questioned the accuracy of self-reports by cognitively impaired older adults. For example, Feher, Larrabee, and Crook (1992) found that older adults with dementia who denied memory loss also tended to deny the presence of other symptoms . Kiyak, Teri, and Borsom (1994) found that self-reports of functional health of demented individuals were consistently rated as poorer than reports by family members. Similarly, Kelly-Hayes, Jette, Wolf, D'Adostino, and Odell (1992) found low rates of agreement between self-reports of cognitively impaired individuals and performance-based measures. In contrast to the aforementioned findings, Feher et al. (1992) argue that self-report instruments designed to measure mood may be utilized with older adults experiencing mild to moderate dementia, noting that accurate self-report of recent mood requires only minimal memory ability.

Evidence regarding the accuracy of unimpaired older adults is more encouraging. For example, self-reported activities of daily living (ADLs) correlate highly with performance measures in outpatient settings (Sager et al., 1992). Older adults are also as accurate as younger adults when replying to survey questions (Rodgers & Herzog, 1987). Similarly, older adult self-reports of insomnia are accurate when compared against polysomnography (e.g., Reite, Buysse, Reynolds, & Mendelson, 1995), the gold standard for sleep disorder assessment.

The Interview

The interview is the most commonly used clinical assessment instrument (Haynes & Jensen, 1979) and arguably the most important means of gathering assessment data. Interviews afford one the opportunity to observe directly behavioral indicators of psychopathology in addition to obtaining information through strategic queries. Although the principles of young adult interviewing apply to older adults, the interviewing of older adults requires knowledge of possible age-related psychological and physiological changes. For example, when contrasted with younger adults, older adults have been found to refuse to participate in surveys at a higher rate (e.g., DeMaio, 1980; Herzog & Rodgers, 1988), refuse to answer certain types of questions (e.g., Gergen & Back, 1966), and to respond *don't know* (Colsher & Wallace, 1989) more often. Older adults also tend to be more cautious when responding (Okun, 1976) and give more acquiescent responses (N. Kogan, 1961). The older adult's physical stamina, cognitive skills, and sensory deficits can all play a role in determining the accuracy, reliability, and validity of information obtained.

Interviews vary in structure, ranging from structured and semistructured diagnostic interviews (e.g., Comprehensive Assessment and Referral Evaluation, Gurland et al., 1977; Geriatric Mental State Schedule, Copeland et al., 1976) to unstructured, free-flowing, nonstandardized clinical interviews. Although highly structured interviews offer diagnostic precision, they lack the flexibility and forgiving nature of unstructured interviews. The unstructured interview permits rephrasing of questions that appear unclear to the interviewee and the exploration of topic areas that may be tangential but relevant to the presenting problems (Edelstein et al., 1996). Moreover, the unstructured interview permits one to prompt and encourage responses and maintain the attention of interviewees who experience difficulty concentrating.

Self-Report Inventories

Self-report inventories can be very useful in the assessment of older adults, particularly because they permit the older

adult to respond to questions at his or her own pace. Sadly, few existing instruments have psychometric support for use with older adults. However, self-report instruments are gradually being developed specifically for use with older adults (e.g., Northrop & Edelstein, 1998; Wisocki, Handen, & Morse, 1986; also see Bialk & Vosburg, 1996, for list of instruments and descriptions). The physical and cognitive demands of self-report inventories must be considered in the selection of instruments because most require good vision, adequate reading comprehension, and at least modest perceptual-motor skills. Problems in any of these domains can influence the reliability and validity of information obtained via questionnaires and inventories.

Self-report measures continue to be the mainstay of clinicians and are an important source of information. Their uses will undoubtedly grow as more current self-report instruments are revised for use with older adults and as more instruments are developed specifically for use with the older adults. Self-reported information should, however, be considered in combination with information obtained through other assessment methods.

Report by Others

The report-by-other (e.g., spouse, caregiver, adult child) assessment method can be a rich source of unique and verifying data—particularly regarding contextual factors relating to the problem(s) in question (Edelstein, Martin, & McKee, 2000). Reports by others can be particularly valuable with older adults who are incapable of conveying accurate information (e.g., when demented). Even when the ability to self-report is unimpaired, reports by others can offer an additional method for gathering convergent information. As with any source of information, reports by others are subject to the same potential problems of unreliability, invalidity, and inaccuracy as other assessment methods. For example, accuracy of caregiver reports of patient ADLs among individuals with mild dementia can be influenced by the caregiver's depressive symptoms and burden (e.g., Zanetti, Geroldi, Frisoni, Bianchetti, & Trabucchi, 1999). Moreover, the accuracy of the caregiver varies across activities (e.g., walking, telephone use, money use, shopping; Zanetti et al., 1999).

Direct Observation

Direct observation of behavior can be one of the richest and most accurate assessment methods because overt behavior is often the ultimate focus of assessment. This method can be incorporated into many of the other methods discussed. For example, one can begin one's observation with an ambulatory patient as he or she walks down the hall of a clinical facility to one's office, and the observation can continue during an interview and formal testing. Unreported symptoms can also be noted during the assessment process.

There are several advantages of using direct observation. Direct observation can be useful when assessing older adults who are uncooperative, unavailable for self-report, or severely cognitively or physically impaired (Goga & Hambacher, 1977). In addition, simple observational procedures can be taught easily to individuals with little or no previous experience (Edelstein et al., 2000). Direct observation data are of particular value in institutional settings, where the often profound effects of environmental factors can be observed and addressed through institution-wide systems. Moreover, multiple staff can monitor behavior changes over time, thereby offering convergent evidence for sometimes idiosyncratic variations in behavior as a function of environmental stimuli.

The potential disadvantages of direct observation methodology are both financial and practical. Reliable direct observation can be quite time consuming, depending upon the nature and frequency of the behaviors in question. Such observations can become quite complicated when complex behavior coding systems are employed. One must balance the richness of data provided by complex coding systems with the demands of other staff responsibilities.

Psychophysiological Assessment

Psychophysiological assessment is typically performed in the clinical context as an index of autonomic nervous system arousal. For the most part, such assessment is limited to the assessment of anxiety-related responses. Psychophysiological methods have enabled researchers to understand better the basic processes related to the etiology and maintenance of anxiety disorders, clarify the boundaries and relations between subtypes of anxiety disorders, and assess anxiety states and treatment progress (Turpin, 1991). Unfortunately, there are no published studies of the psychophysiological assessment of anxiety in older adults (J. Kogan, Edelstein, & McKee, 2000; Lau, Edelstein, & Larkin, 2001). There are, however, conclusions one can draw from research that has examined psychophysiological arousal in different age groups. In general, autonomic arousal appears to diminish with age (Appenzeller, 1994). Resting heart rate tends to decrease with age. Similarly, skin conductance levels in response to behavioral and sensory stressors diminish with age (Anderson & McNeilly, 1991; Appenzeller, 1994; Juniper & Dykman, 1967). In contrast, older adults exhibit a greater stress-induced blood pressure reactivity than do younger adults when exposed to pharmacological, behavioral, and cognitive challenges (McNeilly & Anderson, 1997).

These changes in autonomic arousal are believed to result from multiple age-related physiological and neurochemical changes (J. Kogan et al., 2000). In light of these apparent changes in responses to stressful stimuli, one might expect similar patterns of responding when older adults face anxiety-arousing stimuli. If this is the case, then one must be cautious in interpreting arousal patterns using normative data based on younger adults.

MULTIDIMENSIONAL ASSESSMENT

"Health-care and social-service providers and organizations tend to specialize, but human beings are general entities with multidimensional functions, needs, and problems" (Janik & Wells, 1982, p. 45). The nature, complexity, and interaction of mental and physical problems among older adults often require the skills and knowledge of multiple disciplines (cf. Zeiss & Steffen, 1996). Such multidisciplinary collaboration in assessment is often termed *comprehensive geriatric assessment* (Rubenstein, 1995). Each of these disciplines focuses on the discipline related functions, needs, and problems. For example, the health status and medical regimen of an individual would be addressed by members of the health care discipline (e.g., nursing and medicine), and economic issues would be addressed by social service professionals (e.g., social work).

Multidimensional assessment can improve outcome in a variety of domains—improved diagnostic accuracy, more appropriate placement, decreased dependency, improved functional status (i.e. ADLs), more appropriate use of prescriptions and other medications, improved coordination of services, improved emotional status and sense of well-being, and greater client satisfaction with services (e.g., Haug, Belgrave, & Gratton, 1984; Marcus-Bernstein, 1986; D. C. Martin, Morycz, McDowell, Snustad, & Karpf, 1985; Moore, 1985; Rubenstein, 1983; Williams, Hill, Fairbank, & Knox, 1973).

The targets of a multidimensional assessment can vary but might include, for example, health status, medication regimen, mental status and cognitive functioning, social functioning, adaptive functioning (e.g., bathing, dressing, eating), psychological functioning, quality of life, and economic and environmental resources (cf. Fry, 1986; D. C. Martin et al., 1985). The assessment is usually sufficiently detailed to permit care planning and the monitoring of progress. A complete discussion of all elements of a multidimensional assessment is beyond the scope of this chapter. We limit our discussion to the following assessment domains: physical health, cognitive functioning, psychological functioning, adaptive functioning, and social functioning.

Assessment of Physical Health

As previously noted, the majority of older adults experience at least one chronic illness. The physical health assessment of older adults is complicated by the interplay of illnesses and the multiple medications prescribed to address these illnesses. Additional problems and assessment complications arise from drug interactions and side effects, which are prevalent among older adults (Appelgate, 1996). Physical illnesses also can mask psychological problems, and psychological problems can mask physical illness (Morrison, 1997). For example, depression and hypothyroidism can share overlapping symptoms. Such complications can be particularly troublesome with older adults experiencing major depression because they are less likely than are younger adults to report depressed mood and more likely to report somatic complaints (Blazer, Bacher, & Hughes, 1987).

The assessment of physical functioning typically includes both a physical examination and laboratory tests (e.g., thyroid, blood sugar, vitamin B12, folic acid levels, medications, lipids). Examinations address both age-related changes (e.g., change in muscle strength, sensory changes) and those changes due to other factors (e.g., diseases, medications). Subsequent assessment depends upon the findings of these preliminary examinations and tests and may involve elaborate and extensive testing and evaluation. For example, one may initially find a single clue upon initial examination (e.g., confusion or diminished mental status), and subsequently learn this symptom was due to pneumonia, appendicitis, or congestive heart failure (Gallo, Fulmer, Paveza, & Reichel, 2000).

Assessment of Cognitive Functioning

Age-related changes in cognitive functioning are not uncommon among older adults. However, these changes are typically observed only within certain domains (e.g., working memory), whereas other domains may evidence stability or even improvement (e.g., semantic memory; Babcock & Salthouse, 1990; Light, 1992). Diminished cognitive functioning may result from a variety of factors beyond aging (e.g., drug side effects, cardiovascular disease, schizophrenia, dementia). The identification of potential sources of cognitive deficits is one of the more complex tasks in multidimensional assessment. Normal age-related cognitive impairment must be distinguished from impairment due to a plethora of possible etiologies.

The starting point for cognitive assessment is typically the administration of a cognitive screening instrument. Such instruments are used to quickly identify individuals who are at risk for cognitive impairment and who might warrant more extensive neuropsychological assessment (Alexopoulos & Mattis, 1991). A variety of such screening instruments exist—for example, the Mini Mental Status Examination (Folstein, Folstein, & McHugh, 1975), Mental Status Questionnaire (Kahn, Goldfarb, Pollack, & Peck, 1960), Dementia Rating Scale (Mattis, 1988), and the Short Portable Mental Status Questionnaire (Pfeiffer, 1975). These instruments vary in content, validity, and utility. The interested reader is referred to Macneil and Lichtenberg (1999) and Albert (1994) for thorough descriptions and evaluations of these and other screening instruments.

More extensive evaluation is often warranted when the screening reveals possible cognitive impairment; such evaluation might include neuroimaging, neuropsychological assessment, or both. A wide range of neuropsychological assessment batteries have been used to further investigate cognitive functioning, ranging from relatively small batteries focusing on dementia (e.g., Consortium to Establish a Registry for Alzheimer's Disease Neuropsycholgical Battery, Morris et al., 1989; Washington University Battery, Storandt, Botwinick, Danziger, Berg, & Hughers, 1984), to very comprehensive neuropsychological batteries (e.g., Reitan & Wolfson, 1985).

Assessment of Psychological Functioning

As noted earlier, older adults experience lower rates of some psychological disorders (e.g., depression and anxiety) than do younger adults (Blazer, 1994; Wolfe, Morrow, & Fredrickson, 1996). For example, the 1-month prevalence rate for anxiety among older adults (65+ years) is 5.5%, in contrast to 7.3% for younger adults (Reiger et al., 1990).

Psychological assessment of older adults often begins with an unstructured interview and a broad, sensitive screening for a wide range of psychopathology, followed by more focused assessment that addresses identified problem areas. A broad variety of standardized assessment instruments have been used to assess psychopathology in older adults, but few have adequate psychometric support for use with this population. On a more positive note, there is growing evidence to support a few of these instruments originally developed for use with younger adults—for example, the Beck Depression Inventory (Stukenberg, Dura, & Kiecolt-Glaser, 1990), the Center for Epidemiologic Studies Depression Scale (Lewinsohn, Seely, Allen, & Roberts, 1997), and the extracted version of the Hamilton Depression Rating Scale (Rapp, Smith, & Britt, 1990). With each of these instruments, older adult norms and evidence of reliability and validity with older adults have been established. Although very few psychopathology assessment instruments have been developed specifically for use with older adults, this trend is changing. For example, the Geriatric Depression Scale (GDS; Yesavage et al., 1983) and the Dementia Mood Assessment Scale (DMAS; T. Sunderland et al., 1988) were both designed for older adults. Evidence for the reliability and validity of the GDS has been established for older, medically ill outpatients (Norris, Gallagher, Wilson, & Winograd, 1987), nursing home residents who are not cognitively impaired (Lesher, 1986), and hospitalized older adults (Rapp, Parisi, Walsh, & Wallace, 1988). In contrast, T. Sunderland et al. (1988) found only weak evidence for the concurrent validity of the DMAS and moderate interrater reliability estimates ($r = .74$ for core raters and $r = .69$ for other raters).

Assessment instruments for older adults also have been designed to assess specific problem or symptom areas. For example, there is a version of the Cohen-Mansfield Agitation Inventory (Cohen-Mansfield, Marx, & Rosenthal, 1989) designed specifically for use in nursing homes with older adults. Similarly, Northrop and Edelstein (1998) developed a measure of assertive behavior specifically for older adults that includes situations encountered by older adults that require assertive behavior.

Assessment of Adaptive Functioning

Adaptive functioning is usually defined in terms of an individual's ability to perform ADLs (e.g., eating, dressing, bathing) and instrumental activities of daily living (IADLs; e.g., meal preparation, money management). Such abilities can be substantially impaired by a variety of problems ranging from acute and chronic diseases (e.g., viral infections, atherosclerosis, chronic obstructive pulmonary disease, diabetes) to various forms of psychopathology, such as depression, dementia, substance abuse, and psychoses (LaRue, 1992). Normal age-related changes also can diminish one's level of adaptive functioning. For example, age-related loss of bone density and muscle strength can limit a wide range of activities of daily living (e.g., mowing, walking, housecleaning, weeding).

ADLs and IADLs can be assessed through self-report, direct observation, or report by others using standardized assessment instruments (e.g., the Katz Activities of Daily Living Scale, Katz, Downs, Cash, & Gratz, 1970; Direct Assessment of Functional Status Scale, Lowenstein et al., 1989). Most of these more popular measures of adaptive functioning have considerable psychometric support. For example, the Katz Activities of Daily Living Scale has shown high rates of interrater reliability (Kane & Kane, 1981), and scores on measures of ADL are related to scores on other

measures of functional and cognitive abilities (Prineas et al., 1995).

Although all of these instruments measure aspects of everyday activities and skills, they range from measures of independence in ADLs of chronically ill and older adults (e.g., Katz Activities of Daily Living Scale) to more comprehensive indexes of perceived mental health, perceived physical health, ADLs, and IADLs (e.g., Multidimensional Assessment Questionnaire; Duke University Center for the Study of Aging and Human Development, 1978).

Assessment of Social Functioning

The assessment of social functioning can be extremely important in the consideration of the mental and physical health of older adults (cf., Burman & Margolin, 1992; Thomas, Goodwin, & Goodwin, 1985). As with younger adults, positive social interactions can enhance physical and emotional functioning (Oxman & Berkman, 1990), and negative interactions can lead to diminished physical and emotional functioning (Rook, 1990). Indeed, Rook (1998) suggests that the negative aspects of relationships can cancel or even outweigh the benefits of the positive aspects.

Relationship patterns change with age, and shifts occur in the motivations for social interactions. Carstensen (1995) suggests that the motivation for social interactions is a function of information seeking, self-concept, and emotional regulation, and each of these factors is differentially influential at different ages. Carstensen (1995) asserts that older adults are more likely to seek emotional regulation by careful selection of those with whom they interact. Thus, the reduced size of an older adult's social network may very well contribute positively to well-being through a concentration of rewarding friendships.

Numerous instruments that have been used to assess social relationships and support among older adults' instruments can be helpful in examining facets of both negative and positive social interactions. These instruments include, for example, the Arizona Social Support Interview Schedule (Barrera, Sandler, & Ramsey, 1981) and the Frequency of Interactions Inventory (Stephens, Kinney, Norris, & Ritchie, 1987). Each of the available instruments measures somewhat different aspects of social support, some require considerable subjective judgment, and most are extremely time consuming for both the interviewer and the participant (Kalish, 1997). Psychometric support for available social support inventories varies considerably. Both of the instruments mentioned previously have moderate psychometric support. For example, the Frequency of Interactions Inventory has moderate 1-week test-retest reliability ($r = .77$) and internal consistency ($\alpha = .67$).

Convergent evidence of construct validity is good, with expected correlations with measures of morale and psychiatric symptoms.

PSYCHOMETRIC CONSIDERATIONS

Although a wide variety of assessment instruments have been used to assess psychopathology in older adults, few have supporting psychometric support for use with this population. Therefore it is beneficial to become familiar with the psychometric properties of the instruments that are used in the assessment of older adults. Pertinent information concerns how the test scores of older adults are interpreted as well as the reliability and validity of the assessment instruments that are used.

Interpretation of Test Scores

Ideally, normative data should be reviewed to ensure that the comparison samples match the older client to a sufficient degree on relevant variables (e.g., age, gender, educational level). After an assessment instrument has been administered to an older client, the clinician is faced with the task of interpreting the results. Barrios and Hartmann (1986) specified two methods of test construction that allow the clinician to derive meaning from test scores. One method involves the traditional, norm-referenced approach, in which the individual's test score is expressed (i.e., given meaning) in relation to the test scores of other individuals on the same instrument. If normative data are available from older populations, the interpretations that are made by clinicians about their older clients are likely to be more accurate. However, clinicians are commonly faced with normative samples that are primarily comprised of younger age groups. The use of instruments that feature younger normative samples would affect the conclusions drawn regarding the performance of an older adult. In some cases, there may be a bias against older adults. For example, clinicians may conclude that an older adult is experiencing cognitive deficits in carrying out tasks that access fluid abilities (e.g., matrix reasoning), given that these abilities typically decline with advancing age. Conversely, clinicians may conclude that an older adult possesses strengths on tasks that tap crystallized intelligence (e.g., vocabulary), as these abilities typically show maintenance or improvement with advancing age.

An alternative method of interpreting the results of test scores involves criterion-referenced testing, which is more characteristic of a behavioral approach to assessment. When criterion-referenced testing is used, the older adult's test scores are interpreted in reference to some criterion. For example, if the aggressive behaviors of an older adult are being assessed, the rate of physical or verbal assaults may be measured at various points in time (e.g., during baseline and intervention phases). The criterion that is selected (i.e., the rate of physical or verbal assaults) is flexible and contextually determined. In this manner, the rate of aggressive behaviors of an older adult is interpreted in relation to the individually determined criterion. Hartmann, Roper, and Bradford (1979) indicated that in contrast to norm-referenced approaches, criterion-referenced testing yields interpretations that are "direct, rather than comparative, emphasizes intra-individual change, rather than inter-individual differences, and gages the level of attainment of relatively narrow, rather than broad, performance objectives" (p. 9). Criterion-referenced testing may be utilized by clinicians when the assessment is focused on a narrowly defined, idiosyncratic aspect of the older adult's behavior. In these cases, commonly used assessment instruments either may be too broad or may fail to measure the unique behavior of interest. This type of testing also may be preferred when no assessment instruments are available that include normative data on older adults. Overall, the selection of criterion-referenced testing or norm-referenced approaches will depend on the clinician's theoretical orientation and the nature of the assessment question.

Reliability

Internal consistency describes estimates of reliability based on the average correlation among test items (Nunnally & Bernstein, 1994). Different measures of internal consistency may be reported, including coefficient α (J. Cohen, 1960), KR-20 for dichotomous items (Kuder & Richardson, 1937), split-half, and alternate forms. If internal consistency is very low, it indicates that either the test is too short or the items have little in common. One way that researchers may address low reliability estimates is to increase the number of test items. There may be limits to this strategy, however, given that chronic health problems (e.g., arthritis) or fatigue may interfere with the completion of longer assessments. Reliability estimates also may be low if different age groups interpret the meaning of test items differently. This possibility is conceivable, given that the life experiences of various age groups may differ substantially.

Content Validity

Content validity involves the extent to which an instrument samples the domain of interest (Cronbach, 1971). In order to establish content validity, it is necessary first to define the relevant domain and then to ensure a representative sampling from this domain when selecting items for inclusion in an assessment instrument. In reference to older populations, it is important for clinicians to confirm that the items on an assessment instrument pertain to the construct of interest as it applies to older adults. This practice is crucial because psychological symptoms among older adults often differ substantially from those of other age groups (Himmelfarb & Murrell, 1983). For example, some evidence suggests that younger and older adults experience different fears (J. N. Kogan & Edelstein, 1997).

The content of assessment instruments also should be examined to ensure that item bias does not exist. For example, Grayson, MacKinnon, Jorm, Creasey, and Broe (2000) reported that scores on the Center for Epidemiologic Studies Depression Scale (CES-D; Radloff, 1977) may be affected by items that are influenced by health conditions. The authors noted that conditions such as mobility disability, chronic lung disease, bone and joint disease, stroke, visual impairments, peripheral vascular disease, gait instability, and cognitive impairment may all have effects on CES-D items, independent of depressive symptoms.

Construct Validity

Constructs (e.g., anxiety, depression) are defined generally as abstract or latent summaries of behavior. For example, the construct of depression is represented by a variety of behaviors (e.g., loss of interest or pleasure, depressed mood) that are believed to correlate with one another. Construct validity is defined as the degree to which scores from an instrument accurately measure the psychological construct of interest (Cronbach & Meehl, 1955). It is important to be aware, however, that constructs may evidence age-related differences. For example, Strauss, Spreen, and Hunter (2000) reported that the construct of intelligence changes across the life span (i.e., different life stages require different elements of what is included in the domain of intelligence). Such changes may be signaled, for example, by the results of factor analyses that indicate different factor structures between age groups. This has been demonstrated by Tulsky, Zhu, and Ledbetter (1997), who reported that the factor loadings on the perceptual organization and processing speed factors differed among age groups on the Wechsler Adult Intelligence Scale–Third Edition (WAIS-III; Wechsler, 1997). Age-related changes in constructs have prompted researchers (e.g., Kaszniak, 1990) to assert that construct validity must be established with different age groups. Ideally, clinicians who work with older clients should check the psychometric data of the assessment instruments that are used for the presence of age-specific validity estimates.

FUTURE DIRECTIONS

Projected demographic changes signal an increase in the proportion of older adults in our society. Currently, individuals over the age of 65 are one of the fastest-growing segments of the population. An estimated one quarter of these individuals demonstrate symptoms that meet *DSM-IV* diagnostic criteria. As this segment of the population continues to grow, the likelihood that clinicians will encounter older adult clients in their practices does as well.

The future assessment of older adults is likely to be affected by advances in technology. Computerized assessments will likely become more commonplace. This possibility raises concerns regarding the interaction between older clients and the computerized assessment format. Although older adults currently have generally positive attitudes toward the use of computers (Morgan, 1994), they report higher levels of anxiety regarding the use of computers than do younger adults (Laguna & Babcock, 1997). It is likely that successive cohorts of older adults may be more at ease with the use of computers, as training programs and computer interfaces are redesigned to accommodate the needs of older users. There are certain advantages to the use of computerized assessments with older populations. For example, ageism or stereotypes that may be harbored by clinicians would be negated by the greater standardization of testing conditions. In addition, it is feasible that assessment software packages could be designed to take into account an older adult's cognitive, sensory, or motor deficits. For example, electronic assessment instruments could be developed to accommodate the cognitive and sensory deficits of the individual being assessed. Individuals with limited motor skills could interact verbally with an assessment device that also takes into consideration the individual's unique hearing deficits by amplifying selected sound frequencies. Partially sighted individuals also could interact with such a device. Fatigue could be minimized through branching programs that permitted the skipping of various contents areas when warranted. The words, sentence structures, and information complexity and quantity used in the assessment process could be tailored to the individual's probable cognitive deficits as determined by a screening instrument. Information also could be conveyed via digital video systems that would permit rapid replays and enhance information recall through the use of multisensory (e.g., olfactory, auditory, visual) contextual cues. With the aid of telemetry devices and satellite technology, patterns of behavior could also be monitored from great distances. For example, rural older persons could have their sleep patterns, motor activity, and psychophysiological responses continuously monitored through the attachment of miniaturized electrodes and telemetry systems. Even stuffed animals, dolls, or other items frequently held by older adults with dementia could contain sensing and recording devices that would be connected to remote monitoring systems. As has been the case in some rural medicine clinics, older adults in rural areas could be assessed by clinicians via live video systems.

While the format of the assessment process may change over time (i.e., toward the greater use of electronics), the underlying goals of the assessment process may also change in the future. As mentioned earlier in the chapter, a departure from the traditional approach of syndromal classification may occur, with a move toward the use of functional classifications or severity-based classification systems. Such changes may result in more age-sensitive assessment instruments and a broader range of age-appropriate strategies for assessing older adults.

The future assessment of older adults also may be affected at a societal level by changes in the nature of health care delivery systems. Managed care has had a major impact on the manner in which health services are rendered in the United States. Managed care organizations already place restrictions on the content and length of psychological services, leaving clinicians with less room to tailor their services to suit the needs of individual clients. If they are not modified for older adults, these restrictions may have a negative impact on the assessment of older clients. For example, older adults may require more time to complete assessment instruments, given age-related declines in various cognitive resources (e.g., processing speed, working memory) and the existence of chronic health conditions (e.g., arthritis, COPD) that may interfere with the assessment process.

In general, the future of older adult assessment will hold benefits from greater attention to the nature of psychological problems as they are experienced and exhibited by older adults, and it will also benefit from the development of new and the refinement of current assessment instruments to meet the specific needs of older adults.

REFERENCES

Abrams, R. C., & Horowitz, S. V. (1999). Personality disorders after age 50: A meta-analytic review of the literature. In E. Rosowsky, R. C. Abrams, & R. A. Zweig (Eds.), *Personality disorders in older adults: Emerging issues in diagnosis and treatment* (pp. 55–68). Mahwah, NJ: Erlbaum.

Administration on Aging. (1999). *Profile of older Americans.* Washington, DC: Author.

Alain, C., & Woods, D. L. (1999). Age-related changes in processing auditory stimuli during visual attention: Evidence for deficits in inhibitory control and sensory memory. *Psychology and Aging, 14,* 507–519.

Albert, M. (1994). Brief assessments of cognitive function in the elderly. In M. P. Lawton & J. A. Teresi (Eds.), *Annual review of gerontology and geriatrics: Focus on assessment techniques* (pp. 93–106). New York: Springer.

Alexopoulos, G. S., & Mattis, S. (1991). Diagnosing cognitive dysfunction in the elderly: Primary screening tests. *Geriatrics, 46,* 33–44.

Allport, G. W. (1937). *Personality: A psychological interpretation.* New York: Holt.

American Psychiatric Association. (1994). *Diagnostic and statistical manual of mental disorders* (4th ed.). Washington, DC: Author.

Ancoli-Israel, S., Pat-Horencyzk, R., & Martin, J. (1998). Sleep disorders. In A. S. Bellack & M. Hersen (Eds.), *Comprehensive clinical psychology* (Vol. 7, pp. 307–326). New York: Elsevier.

Anderson, N. B., & McNeilly, M. (1991). Age, gender, and ethnicity as variables in psychophysiological assessment: Sociodemographics in context. *Psychological Assessment, 3,* 376–384.

Appelgate, W. B. (1996). The medical evaluation. In L. Z. Rubenstein, D. Wieland, & R. Bernabei (Eds.), *Geriatric assessment technology: The state of the art* (pp. 41–50). Milan, Italy: Kurtis.

Appenzeller, O. (1994). Aging, stress, and autonomic control. In M. L. Albert & J. E. Knoefel (Eds.), *Clinical neurology of aging* (pp. 651–673). NewYork: Oxford University Press.

Babcock, R. L., & Salthouse, T. A. (1990). Effects of increased processing demands on age differences in working memory. *Psychology and Aging, 5,* 421–428.

Baltes, P. B., & Singer, T. (2000, July). *Plasticity and the aging mind: An exemplar of the biocultural and biopsychological perspectives.* Paper presented at the meeting of the World Congress on Medicine and Health, EXPO2000, Hannover, Germany.

Barrera, M., Jr., Sandler, I. N., & Ramsey, T. B. (1981). Preliminary development of a scale of social support: Studies on college students. *American Journal of Community Psychology, 9,* 435–447.

Barrios, B., & Hartmann, D. P. (1986). The contributions of traditional assessment: Concepts, issues, and methodologies. In R. O. Nelson & S. C. Hayes (Eds.), *Conceptual foundations of behavioral assessment* (pp. 81–110). New York: Guilford.

Bialk, B. S., & Vosburg, F. (Eds.). (1996). *Geropsychology assessment resource guide.* Milwaukee, WI: National Center for Cost Containment.

Blazer, D. G. (1994). Epidemiology of late life depression. In L. S. Schneider, C. F. Reynolds, B. D. Lebowitz, & A. J. Friedhoff (Eds.), *Diagnosis and treatment of depression in late life* (pp. 9–19). Washington, DC: American Psychiatric Association.

Blazer, D. G., Bacher, J., & Hughes, D. C. (1987). Major depression with melancholia: A comparison of middle-aged and elderly adults. *Journal of the American Geriatrics Society, 34,* 519–525.

Blazer, D., Hughes, D. S., & George, L. K. (1987). The epidemiology of depression in an elderly community population. *Gerontologist, 27,* 281–287.

Bodenhausen, G. V. (1990). Stereotypes and judgmental heuristics: Evidence of circadian variations in discrimination. *Psychological Science, 1,* 319–322.

Burman, B., & Margolin, G. (1992). Analysis of the association between marital relationships and health problems: An interactional perspective. *Psychological Bulletin, 112,* 39–63.

Butler, R. (1969). Ageism: Another form of bigotry. *The Gerontologist, 9,* 243.

Butler, R. (1980). Ageism: A foreword. *Journal of Social Issues, 36,* 8–11.

Campbell, D. T., & Fiske, D. W. (1959). Convergent and discriminant validation by the multitrait-multidimensional maxtrix. *Psychological Bulletin, 56,* 81–105.

Carstensen, L. L. (1995). Evidence for a life-span theory of socioemotional selectivity. *Current Directions in Psychological Science, 4,* 151–156.

Casey, D. A. (1994). Depression in the elderly. *Southern Medical Journal, 87*(5), 561–563.

Cohen, G. (1991). Anxiety and general medical disorders. In C. S. Alzman & B. D. Lebowitz (Eds.), *Anxiety in the elderly* (pp. 47–58). New York: Springer.

Cohen, J. (1960). A coefficient of agreement for nominal scales. *Educational and Psychological Measurement, 20,* 37–46.

Cohen-Cole, S. A. (1989). Depression in heart disease. In R. G. Robinson & P. V. Rabins (Eds.), *Depression in coexisting disease* (pp. 27–39). New York: Igaku-Shoin.

Cohen-Mansfield, J., Marx, M. S., & Rosenthal, A. S. (1989). A description of agitation in a nursing home. *Journals of Gerontology, 44,* M77–M84.

Colsher, P., & Wallace, R. B. (1989). Data quality and age: Health and psychobehavioral correlates of item nonresponse and inconsistent responses. *Journal of Gerontology: Psychological Sciences, 44,* P45–P52.

Cone, J. D. (1986). Idiographic, nomothetic, and related perspectives in behavioral assessment. In R. O. Nelson & S. C. Hayes (Eds.), *Conceptual foundations of behavioral assessment* (pp. 111–128). New York: Guilford.

Copeland, J. R. M., Kelleher, M. J., Kellett, J. M., Gourlay, A. J., Gurland, B. J., Fleiss, J. L., et al. (1976). A semi-structured clinical interview for the assessment of diagnostic and mental state in the elderly—the Geriatric and Mental State Schedule: I. Development and reliability. *Psychological Medicine, 6,* 439–449.

Cronbach, L. J. (1971). Test validation. In R. L. Thorndike (Ed.), *Educational measurement* (2nd ed., pp. 443–507). Washington, DC: American Council on Education.

Cronbach, L. J., & Meehl, P. E. (1955). Construct validity in psychological tests. *Psychological Bulletin, 52,* 281–302.

Cummings, J. L. (1988). Intellectual impairment in Parkinson's disease: Clinical, pathologic, and biochemical correlates. *Journal of Geriatric Psychiatry and Neurology, 1,* 24–36.

Dana, R. H. (Ed.). (2000). *Handbook of cross-cultural and multicultural personality assessment.* Mahwah, NJ: Erlbaum.

Davies, A. D. M., Davies, C., & Delpo, M. C. (1986). Depression and anxiety in patients undergoing diagnostic investigations for head and neck cancers. *British Journal of Psychiatry, 149,* 491–493.

DeBeurs, E., Beekman, A. T. F., Deeg, D. J. H., Dyck, R. V., & Tillburg, W. V. (2000). Predictors of change in anxiety symptoms of older persons: Results form the longitudinal aging study Amsterdam. *Psychological Medicine, 30,* 515–527.

DeMaio, T. (1980). Refusals: Who, where and why. *Public Opinion Quarterly, 44,* 223–233.

Duke University Center for the Study of Aging and Human Development. (1978). *Multidimensional functional assessment: The OARS methodology* (2nd ed.). Durham, NC: Author.

Dupree, L. W., & Patterson, R. L. (1985). Assessing deficits and supports in the elderly. In M. Hersen & S. M. Turner (Eds.), *Diagnostic interviewing* (pp. 337–359). New York: Plenum.

Edelstein, B. A., Drozdick, L. W., & Kogan, J. N. (1998). Assessment of older adults. In A. S. Bellack & M. Hersen (Eds.), *Behavioral assessment: A practical handbook* (4th ed., pp.179–209). Needham Heights, MA: Allyn & Bacon.

Edelstein, B., Kalish, K., Drozdick, L., & McKee, D. (1999). Assessment of depression and bereavement in older adults. In P. Lichtenberg (Ed.), *Handbook of assessment in clinical gerontology* (pp. 11–58). New York: Wiley.

Edelstein, B., Martin, R. R., & McKee, D. R. (2000). Assessment of older adult psychopathology. In S. K. Whitbourne (Ed.), *Psychopathology in later adulthood* (pp. 61–88). New York: Wiley.

Edelstein, B., Staats, N., Kalish, K., & Northrop, L. (1996). Assessment of older adults. In M. Hersen & V. Van Hasselt (Eds.) *Psychological treatment of older adults: An introductory textbook.* New York: Plenum.

Feher, E. P., Larrabee, G. J., & Crook, T. J. (1992). Factors attenuating the validity of the geriatric depression scale in a dementia population. *Journal of the American Geriatrics Society, 40,* 906–909.

Ferrini, A. F., & Ferrini, R. L. (1993). *Health in the later years* (2nd ed.). Dubuque, IA: William C. Brown Communications.

Fiske, A., Kasl-Godley, J. E., & Gatz, M. (1998). Mood disorders in late life. In A. S. Bellack & M. Hersen (Eds.), *Comprehensive clinical psychology* (Vol. 7, pp. 193–229). New York: Elsevier.

Follette, W. C., & Houts, A. C. (1996). Models of scientific progress and the role of theory in taxonomy development: A case study of the *DSM. Journal of Consulting and Clinical Psychology, 64,* 1120–1132.

Folstein, M. F., Folstein, S. E., & McHugh, P. R. (1975). "Mini-Mental State:" A practical method for grading the cognitive state of patients for the clinician. *Journal of Psychiatric Research, 12,* 189–198.

Frazer, D. W., Leicht, M. L., & Baker, M. D. (1996). Psychological manifestations of physical disease in the elderly. In L. L. Carstensen, B. A. Edelstein, & L. Dornbrand (Eds.), *The practical handbook of clinical gerontology* (pp. 217–235). Thousand Oaks, CA: Sage.

Friedman, H. S., & Booth-Kewley, S. (1987). The disease-prone personality: A meta-analytic view of the construct. *American Psychologist, 42,* 539–555.

Fry, P. S. (1986). *Depression, stress, and adaptations in the elderly: Psychological assessment and intervention.* Rockville, MD: Aspen.

Futterman, A., Thompson, L., Gallagher-Thompson, D., & Ferris, R. (1995). Depression in later life: Epidemiology, assessment, and treatment. In E. E. Beckham & W. R. Leber (Eds.), *Handbook of depression* (2nd ed., pp. 494–525). New York: Guilford.

Gallo, J. J., Fulmer, T., Paveza, G. J., & Reichel, W. (2000). Physical assessment. In J. J. Gallo, T. Fulmer, G. J. Paveza, & W. Reichel (Eds.), *Handbook of geriatric assessment* (pp. 213–250). Gaithersburg, MD: Aspen.

Gatz, M., Kasl-Godley, J. E., & Karel, M. J. (1996). Aging and mental disorders. In J. Birren & K. W. Schaie (Eds.), *Handbook of the psychology of aging* (4th ed., pp. 365–382). New York: Academic Press.

Gatz, M., & Pearson, C. G. (1988). Ageism revised and the provision of psychological services. *American Psychologist, 43,* 184–188.

Gergen, K. J., & Back, K. W. (1966). Communication in the interview and the disengaged respondent. *Public Opinion Quarterly, 30,* 385–398.

Gillam, J. H., III. (1990). Pancreatic disorders. In W. R. Hazzard, R. Andres, E. L. Bierman, & J. P. Blass (Eds.), *Principles of geriatric medicine and gerontology* (2nd ed., pp. 640–644). New York: McGraw-Hill.

Goga, J. A., & Hambacher, W. O. (1977). Psychologic and behavioral assessment of geriatric patients: A review. *Journal of the American Geriatrics Society, 25,* 232–237.

Gottfries, C. G. (1997). Recognition and management of depression in the elderly. *International Clinical Psychopharmacology, 12*(Suppl. 7), 31–36.

Grayson, D. A., MacKinnon, A., Jorm, A. F., Creasey, H., & Broe, G. A. (2000). Item bias in the Center for Epidemiologic Studies Depression Scale: Effects of physical disorders and disability in an elderly community sample. *Journal of Gerontology: Psychological Sciences, 55,* P273–P282.

Greenberg, D. B. (1989). Depression and cancer. In R. G. Robinson & P. V. Rabins (Eds.), *Depression and coexisting disease* (pp. 103–115). New York: Igaku-Shoin.

Gurland, B. (1997). Psychopathology. In G. Maddox (Ed.), *The encyclopedia of aging* (pp. 549–550). New York: Springer.

Gurland, B. J., & Cross, P. S. (1982). Epidemiology of psychopathology in old age. *Psychiatric Clinics of North America, 5,* 11–26.

Gurland, B. J., Kuriansky, J. B., Sharpe, L., Simon, R., Stiller, P., & Birkett, P. (1977). The Comprehensive Assessment and Referral and Evaluation (CARE): Rationale, development, and reliability. *International Journal of Aging and Human Development, 8,* 9–42.

Hartmann, D. P., Roper, B. L., & Bradford, D. C. (1979). Some relationships between behavioral and traditional assessment. *Journal of Behavioral Assessment, 1,* 3–21.

Hasher, L., & Zacks, R. T. (1988). Working memory, comprehension, and aging: A review and a new view. In G. H. Bower (Ed.), *The psychology of learning and motivation* (Vol. 22, pp. 193–225). New York: Academic Press.

Hasher, L., Zacks, R. T., & May, C. P. (1999). Inhibitory control, circadian arousal, and age. In D. Gopher & A. Koriat (Eds.), *Attention and performance XVII. Cognitive regulation of performance: Interaction of theory and application* (pp. 653–676). Cambridge, MA: MIT Press.

Haug, M., Belgrave, L. L., & Gratton, B. (1984). Mental health and the elderly: Factors in stability and change over time. *Journal of Health and Social Behavior, 25,* 100–115.

Hayes, S. C., & Follette, W. C. (1992). Can functional analysis provide a substitute for syndromal classification? *Behavioral Assessment, 14,* 345–365.

Hayes, S. C., Wilson, K. G., Gifford, E. V., Follette, V. M., & Strosahl, K. (1996). Experiential avoidance and behavioral disorders: A functional dimensional approach to diagnosis and treatment. *Journal of Consulting and Clinical Psychology, 6,* 1152–1168.

Haynes, S. N., & O'Brien, W. H. (2000). *Principles and practice of behavioral assessment.* New York: Kluwer.

Haynes, S., & Jensen, B. (1979). The interview as a behavioral assessment instrument. *Behavioral Assessment, 1,* 97–106.

Herzog, A. R., & Rodgers, W. L. (1988). Age and response rates to interview sample surveys. *Journals of Gerontology, 43,* S200–S205.

Himmelfarb, S., & Murrell, S. A. (1983). Reliability and validity of five mental health scales in older persons. *Journal of Gerontology, 38,* 333–339.

Holland, J. C., Korzun, A. H., Tross, S., Silberfarb, P., Perry, M., Comis, R., et al. (1986). Comparative psychological disturbance in patients with pancreatic and gastric cancer. *American Journal of Psychiatry, 143,* 982–986.

Horne, J., & Osterberg, O. (1976). A self-assessment questionnaire to determine morningness-eveningness in human circadian rhythms. *International Journal of Chronobiology, 4,* 97–110.

Hughes, J. E. (1985). Depressive illness and lung cancer. *European Journal of Surgical Oncology, 11,* 15–20.

Ishihara, K., Miyake, S., Miyasita, A., & Miyata, Y. (1991). Morningness-eveningness preference and sleep habits in Japanese office workers of different ages. *Chronobiologia, 18,* 9–16.

Janik, S. W., & Wells, K. S. (1982). Multidimensional assessment of the elderly client: A training program for the development of a new specialist. *Journal of Applied Gerontology, 1,* 45–52.

Jones, E. E., & Thorne, A. (1987). Rediscovery of the subject: Intercultural approaches to clinical assessment. *Journal of Consulting and Clinical Psychology, 55,* 488–495.

Jorm, A. F., Korten, A. E., & Henderson, A. S. (1987). The prevalence of dementia: A quantitative integration of the literature. *Acta Psychiatrica Scandinavica, 76,* 465–479.

Juniper, K., & Dykman, R. A. (1967). Skin resistance, sweat gland counts, salivary flow, and gastric secretion: Age, race, and sex differences and intercorrelations. *Psychophysiology, 4,* 216–222.

Kahn, R. L., Goldfarb, A. I., Pollack, M., & Peck, A. (1960). Brief objective measures for the determination of mental status in the aged. *American Journal of Psychiatry, 117,* 326–328.

Kalish, K. (1997). *The relation between negative social interactions and health in older adults: A critical review of selected literature.* Unpublished manuscript, West Virginia University at Morgantown.

Kane, R. A., & Kane, R. L. (1981). *Assessing the elderly.* Lexington, MA: Lexington Books.

Kaszniak, A. W. (1990). Psychological assessment of the aging individual. In J. E. Birren & K. W. Schaie (Eds.), *Handbook of the psychology of aging* (3rd ed., pp. 427–445). New York: Academic Press.

Katz, S., Downs, T. D., Cash, H. R., & Gratz, R. C. (1970). Progress in development of the index of ADL. *The Gerontologist, 10,* 20–30.

Kaufman, A. S. (1990). *Assessing adolescent and adult intelligence.* New York: Allyn & Bacon.

Kazdin, A., & Wilson, G. T. (1978). *Evaluation of behavior therapy: Issues, evidence, and research.* Cambridge, MA: Ballinger.

Kelly-Hayes, M., Jette, A. M., Wolf, P. A, D'Adostino, R. B., & Odell, P. M. (1992). Functional limitations and disability among elders in the Framingham study. *American Journal of Public Health, 82,* 841–845.

Kessler, R. C., McGonagle, K. A., Zhao, S., Nelson, C. B., Hughes, M., Eshleman, S., et al. (1994). Lifetime and 12-month prevalence of *DSM-III-R* psychiatric disorders in the United States: Results from the National Comorbidity Survey. *Archives of General Psychiatry, 51,* 8–19.

Kiyak, H. A., Teri, L., & Borsom, S. (1994). Physical and functional health assessment in normal aging and Alzheimer's disease: Self-reports vs. family reports. *Gerontologist, 34,* 324–330.

Knight, B. G. (1996). *Psychotherapy with older adults* (2nd ed.). Thousand Oaks, CA: Sage.

Knight, B. G., Santos, J., Teri, L., & Lawton, M. P. (1995). The development of training in clinical geropsychology. In B. G. Knight, L. Teri, P. Wholford, & J. Santos (Eds.), *Mental health services for older adults: Implications for training and practice in geropsychology* (pp. 1–8). Washington, DC: American Psychological Association.

Koenig, H. G., & Blazer, D. G. (1992). Mood disorders and suicide. In J. E. Birren, R. B. Sloane, & G. D. Cohen (Eds.), *Handbook of mental health and aging* (2nd ed., pp. 379–407). San Diego, CA: Academic Press.

Kogan, J. N., & Edelstein, B. (1997, November). *Fears in middle-aged and older adults: Relations to daily functioning and life satisfaction.* Paper presented at meeting of the Association for Advancement of Behavior Therapy, Miami, FL.

Kogan, J., Edelstein, B., & McKee, D. (2000). Assessment of anxiety in older adults: Current status. *Journal of Anxiety Disorders, 14,* 109–132.

Kogan, N. (1961). Attitudes towards old people in an older sample. *Journal of Abnormal and Social Psychology, 62,* 616–622.

Kosnik, W., Winslow, L., Kline, D., Rasinski, K., & Sekuler, R. (1988). Visual changes in daily life throughout adulthood. *Journal of Gerontology: Psychologcial Sciences, 43,* P63–P70.

Kuder, G. F., & Richardson, M. W. (1937). The theory of the estimation of reliability. *Psychometrika, 2,* 151–160.

Laguna, K., & Babcock, R. L. (1997). Computer anxiety in young and older adults: Implications for human-computer interactions in older populations. *Computers in Human Behavior, 13,* 317–326.

LaRue, A. (1992). *Aging and neuropsychological assessment.* New York: Plenum.

Lau, A., Edelstein, B., & Larkin, K. (2001). Psychophysiological responses of older adults: A critical review with implications for assessment of anxiety disorders. *Clinical Psychology Review, 21,* 609–630.

Lesher, E. L. (1986). Validation of the Geriatric Depression Scale among nursing home residents. *Clinical Gerontologist, 4,* 21–28.

Lesher, E. L., & Berryhill, J. S. (1994). Validation of the Geriatric Depression Scale–Short Form among inpatients. *Journal of Clinical Psychology, 50,* 256–260.

Lewinsohn, P. M., Seeley, J. R., Allen, N. B., & Roberts, R. E. (1997). Center for Epidemiologic Studies Depression Scale (CESD-D) as a screening instrument for depression among community-residing older adults. *Psychology and Aging, 12,* 277–287.

Li, K., Hasher, L., Jonas, D., Rahhal, T., & May, C. P. (1998). Distractibility, aging, and circadian arousal: A boundary condition. *Psychology & Aging, 13,* 574–583.

Lichtenberg, P. A. (2000). Asssessment of older adults in medical settings. *Clinical Geropsychology News, 7,* 5.

Light, L. L. (1992). The organization of memory in old age. In F. I. M. Craik & T. A. Salthouse (Eds.), *Emergent theories of aging* (pp. 111–165). New York: Springer.

Lindenberger, U., & Baltes, P. B. (1994). Sensory functioning and intelligence in old age: A strong connection. *Psychology and Aging, 9,* 339–355.

Lipsey, J. R., & Parikh, R. M. (1989). In R. G. Robinson & P. V. Rabins (Eds.), *Depression and coexisting disease* (pp. 186–201). New York: Igaku-Shoin.

Lowenstein, D. A., Amigo, E., Duara, R., Guterman, A., Hurwitz, D., Berkowitz, N., Wilkie, F., Weinberg, G., Black, B., Gittelman, B., & Eisdorfer, C. (1989). A new scale for the assessment of functional status in Alzheimer's disease and related disorders. *Journal of Gerontology, 4,* 114–121.

Lustman, P. J., Griffith, L. S., Clouse, R. E., & Cryer, P. E. (1986). Psychiatric illness in diabetes mellitus: Relationship to symptoms and glucose control. *Journal of Nervous and Mental Disease, 174,* 736–742.

Macneil, S., & Lichtenberg, P. (1999). Screening instruments and brief batteries for assessment of dementia. In P. Lichtenberg (Ed.), *Handbook of assessment in clinical gerontology* (pp. 417–441). New York: Wiley.

Marcus-Bernstein, C. (1986). Audiologic and nonaudiologic correlates of hearing handicap in black elderly. *Journal of Speech and Hearing Research, 29,* 301–312.

Marsiske, M., Klumb, P., & Baltes, M. M. (1997). Everyday activity patterns and sensory functioning in old age. *Psychology and Aging, 12,* 444–457.

Martin, D. C., Morycz, R. K., McDowell, J., Snustad, D., & Karpf, M. (1985). Community-based geriatric assessment. *Journal of the American Geriatric Society, 33*(9), 602–606.

Martin, G., & Pear, J. (1996). *Behavior modification: What it is and how to do it* (5th ed.). Upper Saddle River, NJ: Prentice Hall.

Mattis, S. (1988). *The Dementia Rating Scale: Professional manual.* Odessa, FL: Psychological Assessment Resources.

May, C. P. (1999). Synchrony effects in cognition: The costs and benefits. *Psychonomic Bulletin & Review, 6,* 142–147.

May, C. P., Hasher, L., & Stoltzfus, E. R. (1993). Optimal time of day and the magnitude of age differences in memory. *Psychological Science, 4,* 326–330.

McFall, R. M., & Townsend, J. T. (1998). Foundations of psychological assessment: Implications for cognitive assessment in clinical science. *Psychological Assessment, 10,* 316–330.

McNeilly, M., & Anderson, N. B. (1997). Age differences in physiological responses to stress. In P. E. Ruskin & J. A. Talbott (Eds.), *Aging and posttraumatic stress disorder* (pp. 163–201). Washington, DC: American Psychiatric Press.

Mischel, W. (1968). *Personality and assessment.* New York: Wiley.

Moore, J. T. (1985). Dysthymia in the elderly. *Journal of Affective Disorders, 5*(Suppl. 1), S15–S21.

Morales, P. (1999). The impact of cultural differences in psychotherapy with older clients: Sensitive issues and strategies. In M. Duffy (Ed.), *Handbook of counseling and psychotherapy with older adults* (pp. 132–153). New York: Wiley.

Morgan, M. J. (1994). Computer training needs of older adults. *Educational Gerontology, 20,* 541–555.

Morris, J. C., Heyman, A., Mohs, R. C., Hughes, J. P., Van Bell, G., Fillenbaum, G., et al. (1989). The Consortium to Establish a Registry for Alzheimer's Disease (CERAD). *Neurology, 39,* 1159–1165.

Morrison, J. (1997). *When psychological problems mask medical disorders: A guide for psychotherapists.* New York: Guilford.

Mouton, C. P., & Esparza, Y. B. (2000). Ethnicity and geriatric assessment. In J. J. Gallo, T. Fulmer, G. J. Paveza, & W. Reichel (Eds.), *Handbook of geriatric assessment* (pp. 13–28). Gaithersburg, MD: Aspen.

Müller-Spahn, F., & Hock, C. (1994). Clinical presentation of depression in the elderly. *Gerontology, 40*(Suppl. 1), 10–14.

Murrell, S. A., Himmelfarb, S., & Wright, K. (1983). Prevalence of depression and its correlates in older adults. *American Journal of Epidemiology, 117,* 173–185.

National Institute of Mental Health. (2001). *Mental health information and statistics.* Retrieved July 8, 2001, from http://www.mhsource.com/resource/mh.html

Nease, D. E., Jr., Volk, R. J., & Cass, A. R. (1999). Investigation of a severity-based classification of mood and anxiety symptoms in primary care patients. *Journal of the American Board of Family Practice, 12,* 21–31.

Nelson, R. O., & Hayes, S. C. (1986). The nature of behavioral assessment. In R. O. Nelson & S. C. Hayes (Eds.), *Conceptual foundations of behavioral assessment* (pp. 3–41). New York: Guilford.

Nelson-Gray, R. (1996). Treatment outcome measures: Nomothetic or idiographic? *Clinical Psychology: Science and Practice, 3,* 164–167.

Norman, T. R. (1993). Pharmacokinetic aspects of antidepressant treatment in the elderly. *Progress in Neuro-Psychopharmacology and Biological Psychiatry, 17,* 329–344.

Norris, J. T., Gallagher, D., Wilson, A., & Winograd, C. H. (1987). Assessment of depression in geriatric medical outpatients: The validity of two screening measures. *Journal of the American Geriatrics Society, 35,* 989–995.

Northrop, L., & Edelstein, B. (1998). An assertive behavior competence inventory for older adults. *Journal of Clinical Geropsychology, 4,* 315–332.

Nunnally, J. C., & Bernstein, I. H. (1994). *Psychometric theory* (3rd ed.). New York: McGraw-Hill.

Okun, M. (1976). Adult age and cautiousness in decision: A review of the literature. *Human Development, 19,* 220–233.

O'Nell, T. D. (1996). *Disciplined hearts: History, identity, and depression in an American Indian community.* Los Angeles: University of California Press.

Oxman, T. E., & Berkman, L. F. (1990). Assessments of social relationships in the elderly. *International Journal of Psychiatry in Medicine, 21,* 65–84.

Palmore, E. B. (1999). *Ageism: Negative and positive* (2nd ed.). New York: Springer.

Penninx, B. W. J. H., Guralnik, J., Simonsick, E., Kasper, J. D., Ferrucci, L., & Fried, L. P. (1998). Emotional vitality among disabled older women: The women's health and aging study. *Journal of the American Geriatrics Society, 46,* 807–815.

Perlmutter, M. (1978). What is memory aging the aging of? *Developmental Psychology, 14,* 330–345.

Pfeiffer, E. (1975). A short portable mental status questionnaire for the assessment of organic brain deficit in elderly patients. *Journal of the American Geriatrics Society, 23,* 433–441.

Pfeifer, E. (1980). The psychosocial evaluation of the elderly interviewee. In E. W. Busse & D. G. Glazer (Eds.), *Handbook of geriatric psychiatry* (pp. 275–284). New York: Van Nostrand.

Poon, L. (1995). Learning. In G. Maddox (Ed.), *The encyclopedia of aging* (pp. 380–381). New York: Springer.

Prineas, R. J., Demirovic, J., Bean, J. A., Duara, R., Gomez Marin, O., Loewenstein, D., et al. (1995). South Florida program on aging and health: Assessing the prevalence of Alzheimer's disease in three ethnic groups. *Journal of the Florida Medical Association, 82,* 805–810.

Radloff, L. S. (1977). The CES-D scale: A self report depression scale for research in the general population. *Applied Psychological Measurement, 1,* 385–401.

Rapp, S. R., Parisi, S. A., Walsh, D. A., & Wallace, C. E. (1988). Detecting depression in elderly medical inpatients. *Journal of Consulting and Clinical Psychology, 56,* 509–513.

Rapp, S. R., Smith, S. S., & Britt, M. (1990). Identifying comorbid depession in elderly medical patients: Use of the Extracted Hamilton Depression Raging Scale. *Psychological Assessment: A Journal of Consulting and Clinical Psychology, 2,* 243–247.

Reiger, D. A., Boyd, J. H., Burke, J. D., Rae, D. S., Myers, J. K., Kramer, M., et al. (1988). One-month prevalence of mental disorders in the United States. *Archives of General Psychiatry, 45,* 977–986.

Reiger, D. A., Narrow, W. E., & Rae, D. S. (1990). The epidemiology of anxiety disorders: The Epidemiologic Catchment Area (ECA) experience. *Journal of Psychiatric Research, 24,* 3–14.

Reitan, R. M., & Wolfson, D. (1985). *The Halstead-Reitan Neuropsychological Battery: Theory and clinical interpretation.* Tucson, AZ: Neuropsychology Press.

Reite, M., Buysse, D., Reynolds, C., & Mendelson, W. (1995). The use of polysomnography in the evaluation of insomnia. *Sleep, 18,* 58–70.

Rix, S. (1995). Employment. In G. Maddox (Ed.), *The encyclopedia of aging* (pp. 327–328). New York: Springer.

Rodgers, W. L., & Herzog, A. R. (1987). Interviewing older adults: The accuracy of factual information. *Journal of Gerontology, 42*(4), 387–394.

Rodin, G., Craven, J., & Littlefield, C. (1993). *Depression in the medically ill.* New York: Brunner/Mazel.

Rodin, J., & Langer, E. J. (1980). Aging labels: The decline of control and the fall of self-esteem. *Journal of Social Issues, 36,* 12–29.

Rook, K. S. (1990). Stressful aspects of older adults' social relationships. In M. A. P. Stephens, J. H. Crowther, S. E. Hobfoll, & D. L. Tennenbaum (Eds.), *Stress and coping in later-life families* (pp. 173–192). New York: Hemisphere.

Rook, K. S. (1998). Investigating the positive and negative sides of personal relationships: Through a lens darkly? In B. H. Spitzberg & W. R. Cupach (Eds.), *The dark side of close relationships* (pp. 369–393). Mahwah, NJ: Erlbaum.

Rosowsky, E., & Gurian, B. (1991). Borderline personality disorder in late life. *International Psychogeriatrics, 3,* 39–52.

Rowe, J. W., & Kahn, R. L. (1998). *Successful aging.* New York: Pantheon Books.

Rubenstein, L. (1983). The clinical effectiveness of multidimensional geriatric assessment. *Journal of the American Geriatric Society, 31*(12), 758–762.

Rubenstein, L. Z. (1995). An overview of comprehensive geriatric assessment: Rationale, history, program models, basic components. In L. Z. Rubenstein, D. Wieland, & R. Bernabei (Eds.), *Geriatric assessment technology: The state of the art* (pp. 11–26). Milan, Italy: Kurtis.

Rubenstein, L. Z., Schairer, C., Weiland, G. D., & Kane, R. (1984). Systematic biases in functional status assessment of elderly adults: Effects of different data sources. *Journal of Gerontology, 39*(6), 686–691.

Rubio-Stipec, M., Hicks, M., & Tsuang, M. T. (2000). Cultural factors influencing the selection, use, and interpretation of psychiatric measures. In M. B. First (Ed.). *Handbook of psychiatric measures* (pp. 33–41). Washington, DC: American Psychiatric Association.

Sadavoy, J., & Fogel, F. (1992). Personality disorders in old age. In J. E. Birren, R. B. Sloane, & G. D. Cohen (Eds.), *Handbook of mental health and aging* (2nd ed., pp. 433–462). San Diego, CA: Academic Press.

Sager, M. A., Dunham, N. C., Schwantes, A., Mecum, L., Haverson, K., & Harlowe, D. (1992). Measurement of activities of daily living in hospitalized elderly: A comparison of self-report and performance-based methods. *Journal of the American Geriatrics Society, 40,* 457–462.

Salzman, C. (1992). *Clinical geriatric psychopharmacology* (2nd ed.). Baltimore: Williams & Wilkins.

Salzman, C. (1997). Depressive disorders and other emotional issues in the elderly: Current issues. *International Clinical Psychopharmacology, 12*(Suppl. 7), 37–42.

Schaie, K. W. (1996). Intellectual development in adulthood. In J. E. Birren & K. W. Schaie (Eds.), *Handbook of psychology and aging* (4th ed., pp. 266–286). New York: Academic Press.

Schiffer, R. B., Kurlan, R., Rubin, A., & Boer, S. (1988). Evidence for atypical depression in Parkinson's disease. *American Journal of Psychiatry, 145,* 1020–1022.

Schneider, J. (1996). Geriatric psychopharmacology. In L. L. Carstensen, B. A. Edelstein, & L. Dornbrand (Eds.), *The practical handbook of clinical gerontology.* Thousand Oaks, CA: Sage.

Schwarz, N. (1999). Self-reports of behavioral and opinions: Cognitive and communicative processes. In N. Schwarz, D. C. Park, B. Knauper, & S. Sudman (Eds.), *Cognition, aging, and self-reports* (pp. 17–44). Philadelphia: Psychology Press.

Segal, D. L., Coolidge, F. L., & Rosowsky, E. (2000). Personality disorders. In S. K. Whitbourne (Ed.), *Psychopathology in later adulthood* (pp. 89–116). New York: Wiley.

Smith, A. D. (1996). Memory. In J. E. Birren & K. W. Schaie (Eds.), *Handbook of the psychology of aging* (4th ed., pp. 236–250). San Diego, CA: Academic Press.

Stanley, M. A., & Beck, J. G. (1998). Anxiety disorders. In A. S. Bellack & M. Hersen (Eds.), *Comprehensive clinical psychology* (Vol. 7, pp. 171–191). New York: Elsevier.

Starkstein, S. E., Preziosi, T. J., Bolduc, P. L., & Robinson, R. G. (1990). Depression in Parkinson's disease. *Journal of Nervous and Mental Disorders, 178,* 27–31.

Starkstein, S. E., & Robinson, R. G. (1993). Depression in cerebrovascular disease. In S. E. Starkstein & R. G. Robinson (Eds.), *Depression in neurologic disease* (pp. 28–49). Baltimore: Johns Hopkins.

Stein, L. M., & Bienenfeld, D. (1992). Hearing impairment and its impact on elderly patients with cognitive, behavioral, or psychiatric disorders: A literature review. *Journal of Geriatric Psychiatry, 25,* 145–156.

Stein, M. B., Heuser, J. L., Juncos, J. L., & Uhde, T. W. (1990). Anxiety disorders in patients with Parkinson's disease. *American Journal of Psychiatry, 147,* 217–220.

Stephens, M. A. P., Kinney, J. M., Norris, V. K., & Ritchie, S. W. (1987). Social networks as assets and liabilities in recovery from stroke by geriatric patients. *Psychology and Aging, 2,* 125–129.

Storandt, M. (1994). General principles of assessment of older adults. In M. Storandt & G. R. VandenBos (Eds.), *Neuropsychological assessment of dementia and depression in older adults: A clinician's guide* (pp. 7–31). Washington, DC: American Psychological Association.

Storandt, M., Botwinick, J., Danziger, W. L., Berg, L., & Hughers, C. (1984). Psychometric differentiation of mild senile dementia of the Alzheimer type. *Archives of Neurology, 41,* 497–499.

Strauss, E., Spreen, O., & Hunter, M. (2000). Implications of test revisions for research. *Psychological Assessment, 12,* 237–244.

Stuck, A. E., Walthert, J. M., Nikolaus, T., Bula, C. J., Hohmann, C., & Beck, J. C. (1999). Risk factors for functional status decline in community-living elderly people: A systematic literature review. *Social Science & Medicine, 48,* 445–469.

Stukenberg, K. W., Dura, J. R., & Kiecolt-Glaser, J. K. (1990). Depression screening scale validation in an elderly community-dwelling population. *Psychological Assessment: A Journal of Consulting and Clinical Psychology, 2,* 134–138.

Sunderland, A., Watts, K., Baddeley, A. D., & Harris, J. E. (1986). Subjective memory assessment and test performance in elderly adults. *Journal of Gerontology, 41*(3), 376–384.

Sunderland, T., Alterman, I. S., Yount, D., Hill, J. L., Tariot, P. N., Newhouse, P. A., et al. (1988). A new scale for the assessment of depressed mood in demented patients. *American Journal of Psychiatry, 145,* 955–959.

Thomas, P. D., Goodwin, J. M., & Goodwin, J. S. (1985). Effect of social support on stress-related changes in cholesterol level, uric acid, and immune function in an elderly sample. *American Journal of Psychiatry, 121,* 735–737.

Thompson, L. W., Gallagher, D., & Breckenridge, J. S. (1987). Comparative effectiveness of psychotherapies for depressed elders. *Journal of Consulting and Clinical Psychology, 55,* 385–390.

Todes, C. J., & Lee, A. J. (1985). The pre-morbid personality of patients with Parkinson's disease. *Journal of Neurological and Neurosurgical Psychiatry, 48,* 97–100.

Tulsky, D., Zhu, J., & Ledbetter, M. F. (1997). *WAIS-III/WMS-III technical manual.* San Antonio, TX: The Psychological Corporation.

Turpin, G. (1991). The psychophysiological assessment of anxiety disorders: Three-systems measurement and beyond. *Psychological Assessment, 3,* 366–375.

Uhlmann, R. F., Larson, E. B., & Koepsell, T. D. (1986). Hearing impairment and cognitive decline in senile dementia of the Alzheimer's type. *Journal of the American Geriatrics Society, 34,* 207–210.

U.S. Bureau of Census. (1995). *Statistical Brief.* Washington, DC: U.S. Department of Commerce.

Vanderplas, J. H., & Vanderplas, J. M. (1981). Effects of legibility on verbal test performance of older adults. *Perceptual and Motor Skills, 53,* 183–186.

Vernon, M. (1989). Assessment of persons with hearing disabilities. In T. Hunt & C. J. Lindley (Eds.), *Testing older adults: A reference guide for geropsychological assessments* (pp. 150–162). Austin, TX: PRO-ED.

Vernon, M., Griffen, D. H., & Yoken, C. (1981). Hearing loss. *Journal of Family Practice, 12,* 1053–1058.

Wechsler, D. (1997). *Wechsler Memory Scale–Third Edition.* San Antonio, TX: The Psychological Corporation.

Werner Wahl, H., Schilling, O., Oswald, F., & Heyl, V. (1999). Psychosocial consequences of age-related visual impairment: Comparison with mobility-impaired older adults and long-term outcome. *Journal of Gerontology: Psychological Sciences, 54B,* P304–P316.

Whitbourne, S. K. (1996). *The aging individual: Physical and psychological perspectives.* New York: Springer.

Williams, T. F., Hill, J. G., Fairbank, M. E., & Knox, K. G. (1973). Appropriate placement of the chronically ill and aged: A successful approach by evaluation. *Journal of the American Medical Society, 226*(11), 1332–1335.

Winograd, I. R. (1984). Sensory changes with age: Impact on psychological well-being. *Psychiatric Medicine, 2*(1), 1–24.

Wisocki, P. A., Handen, B., & Morse, C. K. (1986). The worry scale as a measure of anxiety among homebound and community active elderly. *The Behavior Therapist, 5,* 369–379.

Wolfe, R., Morrow, J., & Fredrickson, B. L. (1996). Mood disorders in older adults. In L. L. Carstensen, B. A. Edelstein, & L. Dornbrand (Eds.), *The practical handbook of clinical gerontology* (pp. 274–303). Thousand Oaks, CA: Sage.

Yesavage, J. A. (1992). Depression in the elderly: How to recognize masked symptoms and choose appropriate therapy. *Postgraduate Medicine, 91*(1), 255–261.

Yesavage, J. A., Brink, T. L., Rose, T. L., Lum, O., Huang, V., Adey, M., et al. (1983). Development and validation of a geriatric depression screening scale: A preliminary report. *Journal of Psychiatric Research, 17,* 37–49.

Yoon, C., May, C. P., & Hasher, L. (1997). Age differences in consumers' processing strategies: An investigation of moderating influences. *Journal of Consumer Research, 24,* 329–342.

Zanetti, O., Geroldi, C., Frisoni, G. B., Bianchetti, A., & Trabucchi, M. (1999). Contrasting results between caregiver's report and direct assessment of activities of daily living in patients affected by mild and very mild dementia: The contribution of the caregiver's personal characteristics. *Journal of the American Geriatrics Society, 47,* 196–202.

Zarit, S. H., & Zarit, J. M. (1998). *Mental disorders in older adults: Fundamentals of assessment and treatment.* New York: Guilford.

Zeiss, A., & Steffan, A. (1996). Interdisciplinary health care teams: The basic unit of geriatric care. In L. Carstensen, B. Edelstein, & L. Dornbrand (Eds.), *The practical handbook of clinical gerontology* (pp. 423–450). Thousand Oaks, CA: Sage.

Zelinski, E. M., Gilewski, M. J., & Thompson, L. W. (1980). Do laboratory tests relate to self-assessment of memory ability in the young and old? In L. W. Poon, J. L. Fozard, L. S. Cermak, D. Arenberg, & L. W. Thompson (Eds.), *New directions in memory and aging: Proceedings of the George A. Talland memorial conference.* Hillsdale, NJ: Erlbaum.

Zimbardo, P. G., Andersen, S. M., & Kabat, L. G. (1981). Induced hearing deficit generates experimental paranoia. *Science, 212,* 1529–1531.

PART THREE

ASSESSMENT METHODS

CHAPTER 18

Assessment of Intellectual Functioning

JOHN D. WASSERMAN

Life is not so much a conflict of intelligences as a combat of characters.

ALFRED BINET & THÉODORE SIMON (1908/1916, p. 256)

The study of intelligence and cognitive abilities dates back more than a century and is characterized by the best and the worst of science—scholarly debates and bitter rivalries, research breakthroughs and academic fraud, major assessment paradigm shifts, and the birth of a commercial industry that generates hundreds of millions of dollars in annual revenue. Still struggling with unresolved matters dating from its birth, the study of intelligence has seen as many fallow periods in its growth as it has seen steps forward. In this chapter, the history and evolution of intelligence theory and applied intelligence testing are described, along with a vision of intelligence as a field of study grounded in theory and psychological science— aimed at facilitating clinical and educational decision making related to classification and intervention. The essential requirements of a mature clinical science, according to Millon (1999; Millon & Davis, 1996), are (a) a coherent foundational *theory,* from which testable principles and propositions may be derived; (b) a variety of *assessment instruments,* operationalizing the theory and serving the needs of special populations; (c) an applied *diagnostic taxonomy,* derived from and consistent with the theory and its measures; and (d) a compendium of change-oriented *intervention techniques,* aimed at modifying specific behaviors in a manner consistent with the theory. The study of intelligence has yet to claim status as a mature clinical science, but some signs of progress are evident.

The story behind the first intelligence tests is familiar to many psychologists (Wolf, 1973). In the fall of 1904, the French Minister of Public Instruction appointed a commission to study problems with the education of mentally retarded children in Paris, in response to the failures of the children to benefit from universal education laws. Alfred Binet, as an educational activist and leader of the *La Société Libre pour l'Étude Psychologique de l'Enfant* (Free Society for the Psychological Study of the Child) was named to the commission. *La Société* had originally been founded to give teachers and school administrators an opportunity to discuss problems of education and to collaborate in research. Binet's appointment to the commission was hardly an accident because members of *La Société* had already served as principal advocates with the ministry on behalf of schoolchildren. The commission's recommendations included what they called a medico-pedagogical examination for children who do not benefit from education, teaching, or discipline, before such children were removed from primary schools and—if educable—placed in special classes. The commission did not offer any substance for the examination, but having thought about intelligence for over a decade, Binet decided to take advantage of the commission mandate and undertake the task of developing a reliable diagnostic system with his colleague Théodore Simon. The first Binet-Simon Scale was completed in 1905, revised in 1908, and revised again in 1911. By the completion of the 1911 edition, Binet and Simon's scale was extended through adulthood and balanced with five items at each age level.

417

Although many scholars in the United States were introduced to the new intelligence test through Binet's journal *L'Année Psychologique,* it became widely known after Henry H. Goddard, Director of Research at the Training School for the Retarded at Vineland, New Jersey, arranged for his assistant Elizabeth Kite to translate the 1908 scale. Impressed by its effectiveness in yielding scores in accord with the judgments of senior clinicians, Goddard became a vocal advocate of the test, distributing 22,000 copies and 88,000 response sheets by 1915. Within a few years, the test had changed the landscape for mental testing in the United States, spawning an entire testing industry and laying the groundwork for the proliferation in intelligence and achievement tests after World War I. The most successful adaptation of the Binet-Simon Scale was the Stanford-Binet Intelligence Scale, which dominated intelligence testing in the United States until the 1960s, when it was overtaken in popularity by the Wechsler intelligence scales (Lubin, Wallis, & Paine, 1971). The Wechsler scales have remained firmly entrenched as the most widely used intelligence tests in every subsequent psychological test usage survey.

DESCRIPTIONS OF THE MAJOR INTELLIGENCE TESTS

In this section, six of the leading individually administered intelligence tests are described, along with the most common ways to interpret them. The descriptions are limited to intelligence tests that purport to be reasonably comprehensive and multidimensional, covering a variety of content areas; more specialized tests (such as nonverbal cognitive batteries) and group-administered tests (usually administered in large-scale educational testing programs) have been excluded. Students of intellectual assessment will notice considerable overlap and redundancy between many of these instruments—in large part because they tend to measure similar psychological constructs with similar procedures, and in many cases, they have similar origins. With a few exceptions, most intelligence testing procedures can be traced to tasks developed from the 1880s through the 1920s.

The tests are presented in alphabetical order. For each test, its history is briefly recounted followed by a description of its theoretical underpinnings. Basic psychometric features including characteristics of standardization, reliability, and validity are presented. Test administration is described but not detailed because administration can only be learned through a careful reading of the test manuals, and every test seems to offer its own set of unique instructions. Core interpretive indexes are also described in a way that is generally commensurate with descriptions provided in the test manuals,

albeit with some modifications made for the purposes of clarity and precision. Emphasis is placed on the interpretive indexes that are central to the test but not on the plethora of indexes that are available for some tests.

Cognitive Assessment System

The Das-Naglieri Cognitive Assessment System (CAS; Naglieri & Das, 1997a) is a cognitive processing battery intended for use with children and adolescents 5 through 17 years of age. The origins of the CAS may be traced to the work of A. R. Luria, the preeminent Russian neuropsychologist whose work has been highly influential in American psychology (Solso & Hoffman, 1991). Beginning in 1972, Canadian scholar J. P. Das initiated a program of research based upon the simultaneous and successive modes of information processing suggested by Luria. Ashman and Das (1980) first reported the addition of planning measures to the simultaneous-successive experimental tasks, and separate attention and planning tasks were developed by the end of the decade (Naglieri & Das, 1987, 1988). The work of Luria and Das influenced Alan and Nadeen Kaufman, who published the Kaufman Assessment Battery for Children (K-ABC; based on the sequential-simultaneous dichotomy discussed later in this chapter) in 1983. Jack A. Naglieri, a former student of Kaufman's who had assisted with the K-ABC development, met J. P. Das in 1984 and began a collaboration to assess Luria's three functional systems. Thirteen years and more than 100 studies later, the CAS was published. It is available in two batteries: an 8-subtest basic battery and a 12-subtest standard battery.

Theoretical Underpinnings

The CAS has its theoretical underpinnings in the work of Luria's (1973, 1980) three functional units in the brain: (a) The first unit regulates cortical tone and focus of *attention;* (b) the second unit receives, processes, and retains information in two basic modes (*simultaneous* and *successive*); and (c) the third unit involves the formation, execution, and monitoring of behavioral *planning.* These processes are articulated and described in PASS theory, using the acronym for *planning, attention, simultaneous,* and *successive* processing (Das, Naglieri, & Kirby, 1994).

Of the theories and models associated with the major intelligence instruments, PASS theory and Kaufman's sequential-simultaneous theory alone offer an approach with articulated neurobiological underpinnings (although *g* theory has numerous neurophysiological correlates). Moreover, Luria's approaches to restoration of function after brain injury

(Luria, 1963; Luria & Tsvetkova, 1990) has provided a basis for use of his theory to understand and implement treatment and intervention. Accordingly, PASS theory and sequential-simultaneous theory have emphasized intervention more than do other intelligence tests.

Standardization Features and Psychometric Adequacy

The CAS was standardized from 1993 through 1996 on 2,200 children and adolescents from 5 through 17 years of age, stratified on 1990 census figures. Sample stratification variables included race, ethnicity, geographic region, community setting, parent educational attainment, classroom placement, and educational classification. The standardization sample was evenly divided between males and females, with $n = 300$ for the earliest school-age levels and $n = 200$ for levels with older children and adolescents. Demographic characteristics of the standardization sample are reported in detail across stratification variables in the CAS interpretive handbook and closely match the targeted census figures (Naglieri & Das, 1997b).

The reliability of the CAS is fully adequate. Internal consistency is computed through the split-half method with Spearman-Brown correction, and average reliabilities for the PASS and full-scale composite scores range from .84 (Attention, Basic Battery) to .96 (full-scale, Standard Battery). Average subtest reliability coefficients range from .75 to .89, with a median reliability of .82. Score stability coefficients were measured with a test-retest interval from 9 to 73 days, with a median of 21 days. Corrected for variability of scores from the first testing, the stability coefficients have median values of .73 for the CAS subtests and .82 for the Basic and Standard Battery PASS scales.

CAS floors and ceilings tend to be good. Test score floors extend two or more standard deviations below the normative mean, beginning with 6-year-old children; thus, discrimination at the lowest processing levels is somewhat limited with 5-year-olds. Test score ceilings extend more than two standard deviations above the mean at all age levels.

CAS full-scale standard scores correlate strongly with the Wechsler Intelligence Scales for Children–Third Edition Full Scale IQ (WISC-III FSIQ; $r = .69$), Woodcock-Johnson III Tests of Cognitive Abilities Brief Intellectual Ability (WJ III Cog; $r = .70$; from McGrew & Woodcock, 2001) and somewhat more moderately with the Wechsler Preschool and Primary Scale of Intelligence Full Scale IQ (WPPSI FSIQ; $r = .60$). Based upon a large sample ($n = 1,600$) used as a basis for generating ability-achievement comparisons, the CAS full-scale standard scores yield high correlations with broad reading and broad mathematics achievement ($r = .70–.72$).

Exploratory and confirmatory factor analyses of the CAS provide support for either a three- or four-factor solution (Naglieri & Das, 1997b). The four-factor solution is based upon the four PASS dimensions, whereas the three-factor solution combines Planning and Attention to form a single dimension. The decision to use the four-factor solution was based upon the test's underlying theory, meaningful discrepancies between planning and attention performance in criterion populations (e.g., individuals with ADHD, traumatic brain injury), and differential response to treatments in intervention studies (e.g., planning-based intervention). On a data set based on the tryout version of the CAS, Carroll (1995) argued that the planning scale, which is timed, may best be conceptualized as a measure of perceptual speed. Keith, Kranzler, and Flanagan have challenged the CAS factor structure based upon reanalyses of the standardization sample and analysis with a new sample of $n = 155$ (Keith & Kranzler, 1999; Keith, Kranzler, & Flanagan, 2001; Kranzler & Keith, 1999; Kranzler, Keith, & Flanagan, 2000). These investigations have variously reported that the PASS model provides a better fit (but a less-than-optimal fit) to the standardization data—but not the newer sample—than do several competing nonhierarchical models and that planning and attention factors demonstrate inadequate specificity for separate interpretation.

The CAS has also been studied with several special populations, including children and adolescents with ADHD, reading disabilities, mental retardation, traumatic brain injury, serious emotional disturbance, and intellectual giftedness. CAS is unique among tests of cognitive abilities and processes insofar as it has been studied with several research-based programs of intervention, one of which is described at the end of this chapter.

Interpretive Indexes and Applications

The CAS yields four standard scores corresponding to the PASS processes, as well as a full-scale standard score. Although the subtests account for high levels of specific variance, the focus of CAS interpretation is at the PASS scale level—not at the subtest level or full-scale composite level. PASS theory guides the examination of absolute and relative cognitive strengths and weaknesses. Table 18.1 contains interpretations for each of the PASS scales.

In general, children with diverse exceptionalities tend to show characteristic impairment on selected processes or combinations of processes. Children with a reading disability tend as a group to obtain their lowest scores on measures of successive processing (Naglieri & Das, 1997b), presumably due to the slowed phonological temporal processing thresholds

TABLE 18.1   Interpretive Indexes From the Das-Naglieri Cognitive Assessment System (CAS; Naglieri & Das, 1997)

Composite Indexes	Description
Full Scale	Complex mental activity involving the interaction of diverse cognitive processes.
Planning	The process by which an individual determines, selects, applies, and evaluates solutions to problems; involves generation of strategies, execution of plans, self-control, and self-monitoring.
Attention	The process of selectively focusing on particular stimuli while inhibiting response to competing stimuli; involves directed concentration and sustained focus on important information.
Simultaneous Processing	The process of integrating separate stimuli into a single perceptual or conceptual whole; applies to comprehension of verbal relationships and concepts, understanding of inflection, and working with spatial information.
Successive Processing	The process of integrating stimuli into a specific, temporal order that forms a chainlike progression; involves sequential perception and organization of visual and auditory events and execution of motor behaviors in order.

that have been identified as a processing deficit associating with delayed reading acquisition (e.g., Anderson, Brown, & Tallal, 1993). Children diagnosed with the hyperactive-impulsive subtype of ADHD tend to characteristically have weaknesses in planning and attention scales (Paolitto, 1999), consistent with the newest theories reconceptualizing ADHD as a disorder of executive functions (Barkley, 1997). Characteristic weaknesses in planning and attention have also been reported in samples of children with traumatic brain injury (Gutentag, Naglieri, & Yeates, 1998), consistent with the frontal-temporal cortical impairment usually associated with closed head injury.

Like most of the other intelligence tests for children and adolescents, CAS is also empirically linked to an achievement test (Woodcock-Johnson–Revised and the Woodcock-Johnson III Tests of Achievement). Through the use of simple and predicted differences between ability and achievement, children who qualify for special education services under various state guidelines for specific learning disabilities may be identified. Moreover, CAS permits the identification of impaired cognitive processes that may contribute to the learning problems. In contrast, CAS has very low acquired knowledge requirements.

CAS also provides normative reference for the use of metacognitive problem-solving strategies that may be observed by the examiner or reported by the examinee on planning subtests. The inclusion of age-referenced norms for strategy usage provides an independent source of information about the efficiency, implementation, and maturity with which an individual approaches and performs complex tasks. Children with ADHD, for example, tend to utilize developmentally younger strategies during task performance (Wasserman, Paolitto, & Becker, 1999).

Through an emphasis on cognitive processes rather than culture-anchored forms of acquired knowledge, CAS also offers an intellectual assessment approach that may reduce the disproportionately high number of minority children placed in special education settings. Wasserman and Becker (2000) reported a mean 3.5 full-scale standard score difference between demographically matched African Americans and Whites in the CAS standardization sample, compared to an 11.0 difference previously reported using similar matching strategies with the WISC-III FSIQ (Prifitera, Weiss, & Saklofske, 1998). The reduced race-based group mean score differences for CAS relative to WISC-III have been found to ameliorate the problem of disproportionate classification of African American minorities in special education programs for children with mental retardation (Naglieri & Rojahn, 2001). Accordingly, CAS offers promise in improving the equity of intellectual assessments.

By virtue of its theoretical underpinnings and linkages to diagnosis and treatment (discussed later in this chapter), the CAS builds upon the earlier advances offered by the K-ABC (Kaufman & Kaufman, 1983a, 1983b). In a recent review, Meikamp (1999) observed, "The CAS is an innovative instrument and its development meets high standards of technical adequacy. Despite interpretation cautions with exceptional populations, this instrument creatively bridges the gap between theory and applied psychology" (p. 77).

Differential Ability Scales

The Differential Ability Scales (DAS; C. D. Elliott, 1990a, 1990b) offer ability profiling in 17 subtests divided into two overlapping age levels and standardized for ages 2.5 through 17 years. It also includes several tests of school achievement that are beyond the scope of this chapter. The DAS is a U.S. adaptation, revision, and extension of the British Ability Scales (BAS; C. D. Elliott, 1983). Development of the BAS originally began in 1965, with a grant from the British Department of Education and Science to the British Psychological Society to prepare an intelligence scale. Under the direction of F. W. Warburton, more than 1,000 children were tested with a series of tasks developed to measure Thurstone's (1938) seven primary mental abilities and key dimensions from Piagetian theory. Following Warburton's death, the government grant was extended, and in 1973 Colin Elliott became the director of the project. The decision was made to de-emphasize IQ estimation and to provide a profile of meaningful and distinct subtest scores, resulting in the name *British Ability Scales.* New subtests were created, and the use of item response theory was introduced in psychometric analyses. Following a standardization of 3,435 children, the first edition of the BAS was published in 1979, and an amended revised edition was published in 1982. The development of the DAS began in 1984, in an effort to address the strengths and weaknesses of the BAS and apply the test for use in the United States. To enhance clarity and diagnostic utility, six BAS subtests were deleted and four new subtests were added to create the DAS, which was published 25 years after the work on the BAS began. The DAS Cognitive Battery includes a preschool level beginning at age 2.5 and a school-age level beginning at age 6 years.

Theoretical Underpinnings

The DAS was developed to accommodate diverse theoretical perspectives and to permit interpretation at multiple levels of performance. It fits most closely with the work of the hierarchical multifactor theorists through its emphasis on a higher order general intellectual factor (conventionally termed *g*) and lower order broad cognitive factors. The DAS avoids use of the terms *intelligence* and *IQ* to avoid traditional misconceptions, focusing instead on cognitive abilities and processes that are either strongly related to the general factor or thought to have value for diagnostic purposes. The DAS is also characterized by an exceptionally high attention to technical qualities, and C. D. Elliott (1990b) was careful to ensure that all interpretive indexes—from the cluster scores down to the diagnostic subtests—have adequate reliable specificity to support individual interpretation.

The General Conceptual Ability (GCA) score captures test performance on subtests that have high *g* loadings, in contrast to tests such as the Wechsler scales in which all subtests (high and low *g* loading) contribute to the overall index of composite intelligence. At the hierarchical level below a superordinate general factor are cluster scores that have sufficient specific variance for interpretation. For children from ages 2.5 years through 3.5 years, only a single general factor may be derived from the DAS. For older preschool children, the clusters are verbal ability and nonverbal ability, roughly paralleling the verbal-performance dichotomy featured in the Wechsler intelligence scales. For school-age children, the clusters are verbal ability, nonverbal reasoning ability, and spatial ability. The increased cognitive differentiation from one general factor to two preschool clusters to three school-age clusters is consistent

with the developmental tenet that cognitive abilities tend to become differentiated with maturation (Werner, 1948).

At the diagnostic level are four preschool subtests and three school-age subtests, included on the basis of cognitive and neuropsychological bodies of research. The preschool procedures include measures of short-term memory in separate auditory, visual, and crossed modalities, as well as measures tapping visual-spatial abilities. The school-age procedures include measures of short-term auditory memory, short-term cross-modality memory, and processing speed. Each of the subtests has adequate specific variance to be interpreted as an isolated strength or weakness.

Standardization Features and Psychometric Adequacy

The DAS was standardized from 1986 to 1989 on 3,475 children and adolescents, with 175–200 examinees per age level. The sample was balanced by age and sex, representative of 1988 U.S. census proportions, and stratified on race-ethnicity, parent educational level, geographic region, and educational preschool and special education enrollment. The sample excluded children with severe handicaps or limited English proficiency. The sample was largest for the preschool periods ($n = 175$ per 6-month interval), when cognitive development is most rapid. The composition of the normative sample is detailed across stratification variables in the *DAS Introductory and Technical Handbook* (C. D. Elliott, 1990b) and appears to closely match its target figures.

The reliability of the DAS subtests and composites were computed through innovative methodologies utilizing item response theory (IRT). Specifically, DAS subtests are administered in predetermined item sets rather than with formal basal and discontinue rules; this means that starting points and stopping decision points (as well as alternative stopping points) are designated on the record form according to the child's age. If the child does not pass at least three items in the item set, the examiner administers an easier set of items. Accordingly, children receive a form of tailored, adaptive testing, in which they are given items closest to their actual ability levels. Because IRT permits measurement precision to be computed at each level of ability (see the chapter by Wasserman & Bracken in this volume), it was possible for C. D. Elliott (1990b) to provide reliability estimates that are similar to conventional indexes of internal consistency. IRT-based mean subtest reliabilities ranged from .71 to .88 for the preschool battery and from .70 to .92 for the school-age battery. Cluster and GCA reliabilities ranged from .81 to .94 for the preschool battery and .88 to .95 for the school-age battery. These score reliabilities tend to be fully adequate. The inclusion of psychometric statistics on out-of-level subtests (i.e., items that are not normally administered to persons of a given age but that may be appropriate for individuals functioning at an ability level much lower than that typically expected for their age) provides examiners with additional flexibility, especially for older children with significant delay or impairment. Stability coefficients were computed for examinees in three age groups undergoing test and retest intervals of 2–7 weeks, with correction for restriction of range on the initial score. Across these groups, subtest test-retest reliabilities ranged from .38 to .89, whereas cluster and GCA reliabilities ranged from .79 to .94. These results indicate that composite scores tend to be adequately stable, but subtests at specific ages may not be particularly stable. Four subtests with open-ended scorable responses all have interrater reliabilities greater than or equal to .90, which falls within an acceptable range.

DAS floors are sufficiently low so that it can be used with 3-year-old children with developmental delays. Use of IRT scaling extrapolation also permits GCA norms to be extended downward to a standard score of 25, enhancing the discriminability of the DAS with individuals with moderate to severe mental retardation. Test items are also considered by reviewers to be appealing, engaging, and conducive to maintaining high interest in younger children (e.g., Aylward, 1992). Initial investigations with the DAS also suggest that it has promise in accurate identification and discrimination of at-risk preschoolers (McIntosh, 1999), sometimes a challenging group to assess because of test floor limitations.

The DAS tends to show strong convergence with other intelligence tests. According to analyses from C. D. Elliott (1990b), the DAS GCA correlates highly with composite indexes from the WPPSI-R ($r = .89$ for the preschool battery), WISC-III ($r = .92$ for the school-age battery; from Wechsler, 1991), Stanford-Binet (.77 preschool; .88 school-age), and K-ABC (.68 preschool; .75 school-age).

Exploratory and confirmatory factor analyses of the DAS provide general support for the structure of the test (C. D. Elliott, 1990b). In separate confirmatory reanalyses, Keith (1990) reported a structure that is generally consistent with the structure reported in the DAS handbook. He found support for a hierarchical structure with superordinate g and several second-order factors (including the diagnostic subtests) that generally correspond to the test's structure. The nonverbal reasoning ability cluster had the strongest relationship to g for school-age children, whereas the early number concepts subtest had the strongest relationship to g for preschool children. These analyses may be interpreted as consistent with other bodies of research (e.g., Carroll, 1993; Gustafsson, 1984, 1988; Undheim, 1981) suggesting that reasoning ability is largely synonymous with g. In additional investigations,

the DAS has also been found to be factorially stable across racial and ethnic groups (Keith, Quirk, Schartzer, & Elliott, 1999).

Interpretive Indexes and Applications

The DAS involves some score transformation based upon item response theory. Raw scores are converted first to latent trait ability scores, which are in turn translated into T scores and percentiles. T scores may be summed to produce the GCA and cluster scores ($M = 100$, $SD = 15$). The GCA is a composite score derived only from subtests with high g loadings, and cluster scores consist of subtests that tend to factor together. The diagnostic subtests measure relatively independent abilities. The clusters and diagnostic subtests have adequate specific variance to support their interpretation independent from g. Table 18.2 contains the basic composite indexes, with subtests excluded.

TABLE 18.2   Differential Ability Scales Cognitive Battery Composite Indexes (S. N. Elliott, 1990)

Composite Indexes	Description
General Conceptual Ability (GCA)	Ability to perform complex mental processing that involves conceptualization and transformation of information.
Ages 3 years, 6 months through 5 years	
Verbal Ability	Acquired verbal concepts and knowledge.
Nonverbal Ability	Complex nonverbal mental processing, including spatial perception, nonverbal reasoning ability, perceptual-motor skills, and the understanding of simple verbal instructions and visual cues.
Ages 6 years through 17 years	
Verbal Ability	Complex verbal mental processing, including acquired verbal concepts, verbal knowledge, and reasoning; involves knowledge of words, verbal concepts, and general information; also involves expressive language ability and long-term semantic memory.
Nonverbal Reasoning Ability	Nonverbal inductive reasoning and complex mental processing; inductive reasoning, including an ability to identify the rules that govern features or variables in abstract visual problems and an ability to formulate and test hypotheses; understanding of simple verbal instructions and visual cues; and use of verbal mediation strategies.
Spatial Ability	Complex visual-spatial processing; ability in spatial imagery and visualization, perception of spatial orientation (the preservation of relative position, size, and angles in different aspects of the design), analytic thinking (the separation of the whole into its component parts), and attention to visual detail.

Note. Interpretive indexes are adapted from Sattler (1988).

Test reviews in the *Mental Measurements Yearbook* have lauded the technical psychometric quality of the DAS as well as its utility with preschool children; they are critical, however, of selected aspects of administration and scoring. Aylward (1992) noted its utility with delayed or impaired young children: "The combination of developmental and educational perspectives makes the DAS unique and particularly useful in the evaluation of young (3.5–6 years) children suspected of having developmental delays, children with hearing or language difficulties, or school-age students with LDs [learning disabilities] or mild mental retardation" (p. 282). At the same time, Reinehr (1992) expressed concern about its administration and scoring complexity. For example, the Recall of Digits subtest involves presentation of digits at a rate different from the conventional rate in psychological testing, and raw scores must be transformed from raw scores to IRT-based ability scores before undergoing transformation to norm-referenced standard scores. Practice administration and newly available computer-scoring software may help to address some of these concerns.

Kaufman Assessment Battery for Children

Alan S. Kaufman and Nadeen L. Kaufman are married coauthors of the Kaufman Assessment Battery for Children (K-ABC; Kaufman & Kaufman, 1983a, 1983b) and Kaufman Adolescent and Adult Intelligence Test (KAIT; Kaufman & Kaufman, 1993). They have a unique training and academic lineage and have in turn exerted strong influences on several leading test developers. Their history here is summarized from the Kaufmans' own telling, as provided to Cohen and Swerdlik (1999). Alan Kaufman completed his doctorate from Columbia University under Robert L. Thorndike, who would head the restandardization of the Stanford-Binet L-M (Terman & Merrill, 1973) and serve as senior author of the Stanford-Binet Fourth Edition (R. L. Thorndike, Hagen, & Sattler, 1986). Kaufman was employed at the Psychological Corporation from 1968 to 1974, where he worked closely with David Wechsler on the WISC-R. Nadeen Kaufman completed her doctorate in special education with an emphasis in neurosciences from Columbia University, where she acquired a humanistic, intra-individual developmental approach to psychological assessment and learning disabilities that would blend uniquely with her husband's approach. Following his departure from the Psychological Corporation, Alan Kaufman joined the Educational and School Psychology Department at the University of Georgia. According to the Kaufmans, the K-ABC was conceptualized and a blueprint developed on a 2-hour car trip with their children in March of 1978. In a remarkable coincidence, they were contacted the next day by the director of test development at American Guidance Service (AGS), who asked if they were interested in developing an intelligence test to challenge the Wechsler scales. At the University of Georgia, Alan and Nadeen worked with a gifted group of graduate students on the K-ABC. Among their students were Bruce Bracken, Jack Cummings, Patti Harrison, Randy Kamphaus, Jack Naglieri, and Cecil Reynolds, all influential school psychologists and test authors.

Theoretical Underpinnings

The K-ABC was developed to assess Luria's (1980) neuropsychological model of sequential and simultaneous cognitive processing. As conceptualized by the Kaufmans, sequential operations emphasize the processing of stimuli events in sequential or serial order, based upon their temporal relationship to preceding and successive stimuli. Language, for instance, is inherently sequential because one word is presented after another in everyday communications. Simultaneous operations refer to the processing, integration, and interrelationship of multiple stimuli events at the same time. Spatial perception lends itself to simultaneous processing, for example, because it requires that various figural elements be organized into a single perceptual whole. The sequential-simultaneous dichotomy represents two distinctive forms of novel information processing. Factual knowledge and acquired skills are measured separately, in an Achievement scale that is separate from the two mental processing scales.

In what the Kaufmans have described as a theoretical rerouting, the KAIT was based primarily on the Cattell and Horn distinction between fluid and crystallized intelligence and was developed to serve the ages 11–85+ years. The K-ABC and KAIT models may be reconciled if mental processing is considered roughly equivalent to fluid intelligence (reasoning) and achievement is treated as analogous to crystallized intelligence (knowledge; Cohen & Swerdlik, 1999). *Fluid intelligence* refers to forms of analysis that only minimally rely upon recall of knowledge and well-learned skills to draw conclusions, reach solutions, and solve problems. Reasoning is considered to be *fluid* when it takes different forms or utilizes different cognitive skills according to the demands of the situation. Cattell and Horn (1976) describe *crystallized intelligence* as representing a coalescence or organization of prior knowledge and educational experience into functional cognitive systems to aid further learning in future educational situations. *Crystallized intelligence* is dependent upon previously learned knowledge and skills, as well as on forms of knowledge that are culturally and linguistically based. The Stanford-Binet and Woodcock-Johnson III tests of cognitive abilities represent the most frequently used measures based upon a fluid and crystallized model of intelligence. As the most well researched and popular of the Kaufman cognitive-intellectual measures, the K-ABC is now described.

Standardization Features and Psychometric Adequacy

The K-ABC underwent national standardization in 1981, and norms are based on a sample of 2,000 children between the ages of 2.5–12.5 years. The sample was collected to be representative according to 1980 U.S. census figures, based upon the stratification variables of sex, race-ethnicity, geographic region, community size, parental education, and educational placement. Ages were sampled at $n = 200$ per 12-month interval. Exceptional children were included in the K-ABC sample. The sample tends to be fairly representative of census expectations at the time of standardization, although African American and Hispanic minorities tended to have higher parent education levels than expected according to census figures (Bracken, 1985). The use of minorities of high socioeconomic status (SES) may explain the small African American-White and Hispanic-White group mean score differences reported for the K-ABC (Kaufman & Kaufman, 1983b).

The reliabilities of the K-ABC were computed with a Rasch adaptation of the split-half method. Person-ability estimates were computed from each of the odd and even item sets and correlated, with correction for length by the Spearman-Brown formula. For preschool children, the mean subtest reliability coefficients range from .72 to .89 (Mdn = .78); for school-age children, they range from .71 to .85 (Mdn = .81). These score reliabilities approach the lower bounds of acceptability. The K-ABC mean composite scale reliabilities range from .86 to .94, with a mean Mental Processing Composite coefficient of .91 for preschool children and .94 for school-age children. Test-retest stability over an interval of 2–4 weeks (M = 18 days) yielded a median Mental Processing Composite reliability of .88, median processing scale reliabilities of .85, and median subtest reliabilities of .76. Stability coefficients tend to be smaller for preschool than for school-aged children.

The K-ABC offers several unique developmental features, coupled with floor and ceiling limitations. The test consists of developmentally appropriate subtests at specific ages, and several subtests are introduced at age 5. By contrast, the Wechsler scales and the WJ III have similar subtest procedures across the entire life span. The K-ABC also permits out-of-level testing, so that tests intended for 4-year-olds may be given to older children with mental retardation or developmental delays, whereas tests intended for older children may be given to 4-year-olds who are thought to be gifted of

developmentally advanced. At the same time, the K-ABC has some problems with floors because subtests do not consistently extend 2 SDs below the normative mean until age 6. Subtest ceilings do not consistently extend 2 SDs above the normative mean above age 10.

Interpretive Indexes and Applications

The K-ABC consists of 10 processing subtests, each with a normative mean of 10 and standard deviation of 3, intended for specific age ranges between 2.5 and 12.5 years. Six additional subtests are included to test academic achievement. The K-ABC yields four global processing scales: Mental Processing Composite, Sequential Processing, Simultaneous Processing, and Nonverbal, all with a mean of 100 and standard deviation of 15. Table 18.3 includes core interpretations for the K-ABC global processing scales. Kaufman and Kaufman (1983b) recommend a step-by-step approach to interpretation and hypothesis generation, beginning with interpretation of mental processing and achievement composites and proceeding through individual subtest strengths and weaknesses. An emphasis is based upon subtest profile analysis, in which subtest performance is compared with an examinee's own subtest mean in order to identify relative strengths and weaknesses. A number of profile patterns are described to explain achievement performance based upon the Lurian model.

At the time of its publication, the K-ABC was perceived as innovative and progressive, holding considerable promise for changing fundamental aspects of intellectual assessment. To a limited extent, this promise has been realized because many K-ABC features (e.g., easel-based test administration) have become standard for intelligence testing. In a thoughtful review of the impact of the K-ABC, Kline, Snyder, and

TABLE 18.3   Kaufman Assessment Battery for Children

Composite Indexes	Description
Mental Processing Composite (MPC)	An aggregate index of information-processing proficiency; intended to emphasize problem-solving rather than acquired knowledge and skills.
Sequential Processing	An index of proficiency at processing stimuli in sequential or serial order, where each stimulus is linearly or temporally related to the previous one.
Simultaneous Processing	An index of proficiency at processing stimuli all at once, in an integrated manner interrelating each element into a perceptual whole.
Nonverbal	A broad index of cognitive processing based upon K-ABC subtests that are appropriate for use with children who are deaf, have communication disorders, or have limited English proficiency.

Castellanos (1996) noted its laudable intentions to formulate a test based upon a coherent theory, using novel measurement paradigms to assess cognitive skills that are considered directly relevant to school achievement. The main problems with the K-ABC, according to Kline and colleagues (1996), include the degree to which its subtests may be interpreted as tapping constructs other than those intended (e.g., sequential processing subtests may be seen as measures of short-term memory, and simultaneous processing subtests as measures of spatial cognition) and its failure to adequately support its remedial model. It is noted, however, that the K-ABC and CAS are the only major intelligence tests to even make a formal attempt to link cognitive assessment to remediation.

Stanford-Binet Intelligence Scale

The oldest line of intelligence tests is the Stanford-Binet Intelligence Scale, now in its fourth edition (SB4; R. L. Thorndike et al., 1986), with a redesigned fifth edition undergoing standardization at the time of this writing. The Stanford-Binet has a distinguished lineage, having been the only one of several adaptations of Binet's 1911 scales to survive to the present time. According to Théodore Simon (cited in Wolf, 1973, p. 35), Binet gave Lewis M. Terman at Stanford University the rights to publish an American revision of the Binet-Simon scale "for a token of one dollar." Terman (1877–1956) may arguably be considered the person most responsible for spawning the large-scale testing industry that develops educational tests for many states. He was a leading author and advocate for Riverside Press and the World Book Company, as well as a founding vice president at the Psychological Corporation (Sokal, 1981). Terman's (1916) adaptation of the Binet-Simon Scales was followed by his collaboration with Maud A. Merrill beginning in 1926 to produce two parallel forms (Forms L for *Lewis* and M for *Maud*) published in 1937. The 1937 edition of the Stanford-Binet had remarkable breadth, developmentally appropriate procedures, and a highly varied administration pace so that examinees performed many different kinds of activities. It may have constituted an early high point for intelligence testing. McNemar's (1942) analyses of the standardization data included the creation of nonverbal scales and memory scales, none of which were implemented in the 1960 edition. Terman and Merrill merged the best items of each form into Form L-M in 1960. A normative update and restandardization of Form L-M, with only minor content changes, was conducted from 1971 to 1972 under the direction of Robert L. Thorndike. Thorndike's norming approach was unusual because he sampled from the 20,000 student participants (and their siblings) who had participated in the norming of his

group-administered Cognitive Abilities Test (CogAT); specifically, he sought to stratify the Stanford-Binet sample to proportionately represent all ability levels based upon performance on the Verbal CogAT Battery. No effort was made to stratify the sample on demographic variables such as race, ethnicity, or SES, although the sample ultimately was more inclusive and diverse than that used with any previous Stanford-Binet edition.

The Stanford-Binet–Fourth Edition (SB4) was published in 1986, authored by Robert L. Thorndike, Elizabeth P. Hagen, and Jerome M. Sattler. The SB4 covers the age range of 2 through 23 years and offers several significant departures from its predecessors, most notably offering a point-scale format instead of Form L-M's age-scale format and offering factor-based composite scores, whereas Form L-M only yielded a composite intelligence score. The SB4 was the first major intelligence test to include use of IRT in building scales and differential item functioning to minimize item bias. Attempts were made to preserve many of the classic procedures (e.g., picture absurdities) that were prominent in prior editions. In spite of these efforts, the SB4 was poorly executed, receiving considerable criticism for problems with the makeup of its standardization sample, delays in producing test norms and a technical manual, and dissent among the authors that led to the development of several different factor-scoring procedures.

Theoretical Underpinnings

Binet's tests are best remembered for innovative diversity and their emphasis upon a common factor of *judgment,* which may be considered similar to Spearman's g factor. In understanding intelligence, Terman placed an emphasis upon abstract and conceptual thinking over other types of mental processes. In the famous 1921 symposium on intelligence, he asserted that the important intellectual differences among people are "in the capacity to form concepts to relate in diverse ways, and to grasp their significance. *An individual is intelligent in proportion as he is able to carry on abstract thinking.* . . . Many criticisms of the current methods of testing intelligence rest plainly on a psychology which fails to distinguish the levels of intellectual functioning or to assign to conceptual thinking the place that belongs to it in the hierarchy of intelligences" (pp. 128–129). Terman further asserted that measures of abstract thinking using language or other symbols are most strongly associated with educational success, arguing that the Stanford-Binet contained as many of these types of tasks as was practical.

The SB4 sought to recast many of the Stanford-Binet's classical tests in terms of Cattell and Horn's fluid-crystallized model of cognitive abilities, thereby "to wed theory with measurement practice" (R. M. Thorndike & Lohman, 1990, p. 125). The SB4 was conceptualized to measure a hierarchically organized model of intelligence. General ability or *g* is at the apex of this model, and is interpreted "as consisting of the cognitive assembly and control processes that an individual uses to organize adaptive strategies for solving novel problems" (R. L. Thorndike et al., 1986, p. 3). Three broad group factors—crystallized abilities, fluid-analytic abilities, and short-term memory—constitute the second level. First-order factors in the four broad areas of cognitive ability tapped by the SB4 are represented at the base of the model with crystallized abilities represented by both verbal and quantitative reasoning tasks. Accordingly, the SB4 may be considered the first contemporary test to operationalize the fluid and crystallized model of intelligence.

Standardization Features and Psychometric Adequacy

The Stanford-Binet was standardized in 1985 on 5,013 children, adolescents, and adults in 17 age groups. Age groups were generally represented by 200 to 300 participants, although the numbers dip below 200 for older adolescents. The sample was selected to be representative of 1980 U.S. census figures. Stratification variables included sex, ethnicity, geographic region, and community size, with parent educational and occupational levels serving as proxies for SES. The final sample was weighted to adjust for inadequate representation of children from low-SES backgrounds, thereby introducing potential sampling error into the standardization sample. Stratification accuracy is reported in the Stanford-Binet on the margins, so that for example, the percent of the sample classified in varied racial-ethnic groups is reported in isolation without concurrent information about socioeconomic composition. The unpredictable consequences of sample weighting on proportionate representation in specific sampling cells cannot be formally assessed when stratification by several variables is not fully reported. Accordingly, it is difficult to evaluate the representativeness of the Stanford-Binet sample.

The reliabilities of the Stanford-Binet scores are fully adequate. Computed with the Kuder-Richardson Formula 20, the composite standard age score internal consistency reliability ranges from .95 to .99 across age groups. Lower bound reliability estimates for the area scores (based on the two-subtest versions of these composites) are at or above .90 for the verbal reasoning area, the abstract-visual reasoning area, and the quantitative area, but they are at .89 for the short-term memory area. Median subtest reliabilities range from .73 to .94. Test-retest reliability over an interval ranging from 2–8 months (*M* = 16 weeks) appears to be generally adequate; the composite standard age score (SAS) is at .90, the area scores have

a median stability coefficient of .81 (quantitative reasoning has markedly lower stability than do the other area scores), and the subtests have a median stability coefficient of .70. Given the longer-than-typical test-retest interval, these retests tend to be adequate with the possible exception of the quantitative reasoning subtests.

Stanford-Binet floors and ceilings also tend to be adequate. Test score floors extend two or more standard deviations below the normative mean beginning with age 4, indicating that younger children with cognitive delays may show floor effects. Subtest ceilings consistently extend two or more standard deviations above the normative mean up through age 10, so older children who are intellectually gifted may show ceiling effects. The overall composite SAS ranges from −4 *SD* to +4 *SD* across ages.

The factor structure of the Stanford-Binet has yielded several separate solutions (all of which are scored in the test software), marked by Sattler's dissension from his coauthors and publication of new factor analyses and score computations (Sattler, 1988). Robert M. Thorndike, son of the senior author, sought to resolve the divergent solutions in a 1990 study. In brief, he concluded that from ages 2 through 6, a two-factor solution representing primarily verbal ability (defined by vocabulary, comprehension, absurdities, and memory for sentences) and nonverbal ability (defined by pattern analysis, copying, quantitative, and bead memory) was most defensible. From ages 7 through 11, a three-factor solution including verbal ability (defined by vocabulary, comprehension, and memory for sentences), abstract-visual ability (defined by pattern analysis, copying, matrices, bead memory, and absurdities), and memory (defined primarily by memory for digits and memory for objects, although memory for sentences has a secondary load here) was supported. From ages 12 through 23 years, three factors were also supported: verbal ability (vocabulary, comprehension, memory for sentences), abstract-visual ability (pattern analysis, matrices, paper folding and cutting, number series, equation building, and to a lesser extent bead memory), and memory (memory for digits, memory for sentences, and memory for objects). Thorndike was unable to extract a quantitative factor. These results are generally consistent with those offered by Sattler (1988) and suggest that the Stanford-Binet quantitative reasoning standard age scores should be interpreted with caution. The Stanford-Binet permits substantial flexibility in choosing the number and identity of subtests contributing to a composite, but the degree to which subtests are interchangeable (i.e., appropriately substituted for one another) is questionable and should be based upon the factor analytic findings described previously. In a comprehensive review of the factor analytic studies of the Stanford-Binet, Laurent, Swerdlik, and Ryburn

(1992) concluded that the analyses by Sattler and R. M. Thorndike were essentially correct.

The Stanford-Binet composite SAS generally correlates highly with the Wechsler scales ($r = .80–.91$ across the WPPSI, WISC, and WAIS) and $r = .74–.89$ with the K-ABC, according to a review from Kamphaus, 1993). The Stanford-Binet, however, is the only one of the major intelligence tests not systematically linked to an achievement test for identification of ability-achievement discrepancies. According to the SB4 technical manual, the correlation between the composite SAS and the K-ABC Achievement Scale was .74.

Interpretive Indexes and Applications

The Stanford-Binet consists of 15 point-scale tests, in contrast with the developmental age scale utilized for Form L-M. The vocabulary test is used with chronological age to locate the starting point for each test. Each of the tests has a normative $T = 50$ and SD of 8. Four broad areas of cognitive abilities are assessed—Verbal Reasoning, Abstract-Visual Reasoning, Quantitative Reasoning, and Short-Term Memory. SAS composites are all set at a mean of 100 and SD of 16. As discussed previously, the factor studies reported by Sattler (1988) and R. M. Thorndike (1990) provide more support for the interpretation of the factor scores than for the four broad area scores, so the use of the factors is recommended for interpretive purposes: verbal comprehension ability, nonverbal reasoning-visualization ability, and memory ability. The first two factors should be interpreted for children aged 2–6, but all three factors should be interpreted for ages 7–23. Fundamental interpretation of these composite and factor scores appears in Table 18.4. The overall IQ score is termed the Composite Standard Age Score in an attempt to avoid some of the connotations of the term *IQ*. All of the Stanford-Binet subtests are either good or fair measures of *g* (Sattler, 1988).

Although the SB4 does not appear to have the proficiency of its predecessors in identifying intellectually gifted children, it has been shown to have utility in facilitating the identification of mentally retarded and neurologically impaired children (Laurent et al., 1992). The *Examiner's Handbook* and *Inferred Abilities and Influences Chart* (Delaney & Hopkins, 1987) provide additional guidelines for administration and interpretive depth; they also describe appropriate combinations of tests to use with special populations.

The SB4 blended "old tasks and new theory" (R. M. Thorndike & Lohman, 1990, p. 126) to create a much-needed revision to the older L-M edition. It offered factor scores, an easy easel-based administration format, a flexible and versatile administration format, and better psychometric properties than the L-M's. It included numerous technical innovations

TABLE 18.4   Stanford-Binet Intelligence Scale–Fourth Edition (R. L. Thorndike, Hagen, & Sattler, 1986)

Composite/Factor Indexes	Description
Composite Standard Age Score	A global estimate of cognitive ability.
Ages 2 years through 6 years	
Verbal Comprehension Ability	Depth and breadth of accumulated experience and repertoire of verbal knowledge.
Nonverbal Reasoning and Visualization Ability	Nonverbal, fluid problem-solving abilities, particularly when stimuli are presented visually and involve motor, pointing, or verbal responses.
Ages 7 years through 23 years	
Verbal Comprehension Ability	Complex verbal mental processing, including acquired verbal concepts, verbal knowledge, and reasoning; involves knowledge of words, verbal concepts, and general information; also involves expressive language ability and long-term semantic memory.
Nonverbal Reasoning and Visualization Ability	Nonverbal, fluid problem-solving abilities, particularly when stimuli are presented visually and involve motor, pointing, or verbal responses.
Memory Ability	Short-term memory abilities; involves the abilities to attend, encode, use rehearsal strategies, shift mental operations rapidly, and self-monitor.

(e.g., use of IRT and differential item function studies). The major weaknesses of the SB4 involved the boldness of its break with its own tradition and its poor technical execution—particularly in the representativeness of its normative sample and the problems with its disputed factor structure. Cronbach (1989) questioned the factor structure and asked, "How useful is the profile?" (p. 774). Anastasi (1989) noted that the Stanford-Binet's "principal limitation centers on communications with test users, especially in clinical settings" (p. 772).

Wechsler Intelligence Scales

No brand name in psychology is better known than *Wechsler,* now applied to a series of four intelligence scales spanning the ages 3 through 89, an adult memory scale covering ages 16 through 89, and an achievement test covering ages 4 through adult. The remarkable success of the Wechsler measures is attributable to David Wechsler (1896–1981), a gifted clinician and psychometrician with a well-developed sense of what was practical and clinically relevant. Decades after Wechsler's death, his tests continue to dominate intellectual assessment among psychologists (Camera, Nathan, & Puente, 2000). Indeed, even the achievement test bearing his name (but that he did not develop) has become a market leader.

Wechsler's role in the history of intelligence assessment has yet to be formally assessed by historians, but the origins of his tests and interpretive approaches can easily be traced to his early educational and professional experiences. Wechsler was introduced to most of the procedures that would eventually find a home in his intelligence and memory scales as a graduate student at Columbia University (with faculty including J. McKeen Cattell, Edward L. Thorndike, and Robert S. Woodworth), as an assistant for a brief time to Arthur Otis at the World Book Company in the development in the first group intelligence test, and as an army psychological examiner in World War I. As part of a student detachment from the military, Wechsler attended the University of London in 1919, where he spent some 3 months working with Charles E. Spearman. From 1925 to 1927, he would work for the Psychological Corporation in New York, conducting research and developing tests such as his first entitled Tests for Taxicab Drivers. Finally, Wechsler sought clinical training from several of the leading clinicians of his day, including Augusta F. Bronner and William Healy at the Judge Baker Foundation in Boston and Anna Freud at the Vienna Psychoanalytic Institute (for 3 months in 1932). By virtue of his education and training, Wechsler should properly be remembered as one of the first scientist-clinicians in psychology.

Wechsler originally introduced the Bellevue Intelligence Tests in 1939 (Wechsler, 1939), followed by the Wechsler Intelligence Scale for Children (WISC; Wechsler, 1949), the Wechsler Adult Intelligence Scale (WAIS; Wechsler, 1955), and the Wechsler Preschool and Primary Scale of Intelligence (WPPSI; Wechsler, 1967). With some variation, these tests all use the same core set of subtests and interpretive scores. The most recent editions of Wechsler's tests are the WISC-III (Third Edition; Wechsler, 1991), the WAIS-III (Wechsler, 1997), and a short form named the Wechsler Abbreviated Scale of Intelligence (WASI; Wechsler, 1999). The WASI uses the Wechsler Vocabulary, Similarities, Block Design, and Matrix Reasoning subtests.

Theoretical Underpinnings

The Wechsler intelligence scales are decidedly atheoretical (beyond their emphasis on g), and in recent years they have exemplified a test in search of a theory. As originally conceptualized by David Wechsler (1939), they were clearly intended to tap Spearman's general intelligence factor, g: "The only thing we can ask of an intelligence scale is that it measures sufficient portions of intelligence to enable us to use it as a fairly reliable index of the individual's global capacity" (p. 11). Wechsler purposefully included a diverse range of tasks to avoid placing disproportionate emphasis on any one

ability: "My definition of intelligence is that it's not equivalent to any single ability, it's a global capacity. . . . The tests themselves are only modes of communication" (Wechsler, 1976, p. 55). Although he was at Columbia University when the Spearman-Thorndike-Thomson debates on g were occurring in the professional journals, he was sufficiently taken with Spearman's work to later (unsuccessfully) attempt the identification of a parallel general emotional factor (Wechsler, 1925). Wechsler's friendship with and loyalty to Spearman never permitted him to break with g theory, and in 1939 he wrote that Spearman's theory and its proofs constitute "one of the great discoveries of psychology" (p. 6).

Wechsler did not believe that division of his intelligence scales into verbal and performance subtests tapped separate dimensions of intelligence; rather, he felt that this dichotomy was diagnostically useful (e.g., Wechsler, 1967). In essence, the verbal and performance scales constituted different ways to assess g. Late in his life, Wechsler described the verbal and performance tests merely as ways to converse with a person—that is, "to appraise a person in as many different modalities as possible" (Wechsler, 1976, p. 55). Wechsler's scales sought to capitalize on preferences of practitioners to administer both verbal and performance scales by packaging both in a single conformed test battery (a combination previously attempted by Rudolf Pintner, who was responsible, with Donald G. Paterson, for the one of the most popular early performance scales). Wechsler found belatedly that after they were published, his tests were valued more for their verbal-performance dichotomy than for their diverse measures of g:

> It was not until the publication of the Bellevue Scales that any consistent attempt was made to integrate performance and verbal tests into a single measure of intelligence test. The Bellevue tests have had increasingly wider use, but I regret that their popularity seems to derive, not from the fact that they make possible a single global rating, but because they enable the examiner to obtain separate verbal and performance I.Q.'s with one test. (Wechsler, 1950/1974, p. 42)

Wechsler was clearly aware of multifactor theories of human ability. He placed relatively little emphasis upon multifactor ability models in his tests, however, because after the contribution of the general factor of intelligence was removed, the group factors (e.g., verbal, spatial, memory) accounted for little variance in performance (e.g., Wechsler, 1961). Wechsler also rejected the separation of abilities because he saw intelligence as resulting from the collective integration and connectivity of separate neural functions. He believed that intelligence would never be localized in the brain and observed, "While intellectual abilities can be shown to contain several independent factors, intelligence cannot be so broken up" (Wechsler, 1958, p. 23).

Following Wechsler's death in 1981, the test publisher has slowly but inexorably gravitated toward a multifactor interpretive model—expanding coverage to four factors in the 1991 WISC-III (verbal-comprehension, perceptual-organization, freedom from distractibility, and processing speed) and four factors in the 1997 WAIS-III (verbal-comprehension, perceptual-organization, working memory, and processing speed). The WISC-III featured a new subtest called Symbol Search to tap processing speed, and the WAIS-III added Matrix Reasoning to enhance the measurement of fluid reasoning and added Letter-Number Sequencing as a measure of working memory (The Psychological Corporation, 1997). There is a piecemeal quality to these changes in the Wechsler scales, guided less by a coherent approach than by a post hoc effort to impose theory upon existing Wechsler subtests. The theoretical directions to be charted for the Wechsler scales remain to be clearly articulated, but the words of Cronbach (1949) in describing the Wechsler scales remain salient: "One can point to numerous shortcomings. Most of these arise from Wechsler's emphasis on clinical utility rather than upon any theory of mental measurement" (p. 158).

Standardization Features and Psychometric Adequacy

The Wechsler scales are renowned for their rigorous standardizations, and their revisions with normative updates are now occurring about every 15 years, apparently in response to the Flynn effect (see the chapter by Wasserman & Bracken in this volume). The Wechsler scales tend to utilize a demographically stratified (and quasi-random) sampling approach, collecting a sample at most age levels of about $n = 200$ divided equally by sex. Larger sample sizes are most important during ages undergoing changes such as the rapid cognitive development in young school-aged children and the deterioration in older individuals. Unfortunately, the WAIS-III sample reduces its sample size requirements (to $n = 150$ and $n = 100$) at the two age levels between 80 and 90, although these individuals by virtue of their deterioration actually merit an *increased* sample size. Stratification targets are based on the most contemporary census figures for race-ethnicity, educational level (or parent educational level for children), and geographic region. The manuals for the Wechsler scales typically report demographic characteristics of the standardization sample across stratification variables, so it is possible to ascertain that characteristics were accurately and proportionally distributed across groups rather than concentrated in a single group. Individuals with sensory deficits or known or suspected neurological or psychiatric disorders were excluded

from the WAIS-III sample in an effort to enhance the clinical sensitivity of the measure.

Internal consistency tends to be adequate for the Wechsler scales, although there are some isolated subtests with problems. Composite scores (FSIQ; Verbal IQ, VIQ; Performance IQ, PIQ; Verbal Comprehension Index, VCI; Perceptual Organization Index, POI; and Freedom From Distractibility Index and Working Memory Index, FDI-WMI) tend to yield average $rs > .90$ for the WISC-III and WAIS-III, although the FDI tends to be slightly lower. Test-retest stability coefficients are reported instead of internal consistency for the PSI. At the WISC-III subtest level, Arithmetic, Comprehension, and all performance subtests (with the exception of Block Design) have average reliabilities below .80. At the WAIS-III subtest level, only Picture Arrangement, Symbol Search, and Object Assembly have average reliability coefficients below .80, and Object Assembly in particular appears to decline in measurement precision after about age 70. Accordingly, the Wechsler scales show measurement precision slightly less than considered optimal for their intended decision-making applications.

Test-retest reliability tends to be adequate for WISC-III and the WAIS-III composite indexes and verbal scale subtests, although some performance subtests have less-than-optimal stability. For six age groups undergoing serial testing with test-retest intervals ranging from 12 to 63 days (*Mdn* = 23 days), the WISC-III yielded a mean corrected stability coefficient of .94 for FSIQ and in the .80s and .90s for composite scores, with the exception of a low FDI corrected stability coefficient of .74 for 6- to 7-year-old children. Corrected reliability coefficients for individual subtests ranged from a low of .54–.62 for Mazes to a high of .82–.93 for Vocabulary. Four subtests (Vocabulary, Information, Similarities, and Picture Completion) have an average corrected stability coefficient above .80 (Wechsler, 1991). Over an interval ranging from 2 to 12 weeks (*M* = 34.6 days) across four age groups, the WAIS-III FSIQ has a mean stability coefficient of .96 corrected for the variability of scores in the standardization sample. Mean corrected stability coefficients for the WAIS-III subtests range from the .90s for Vocabulary and Information to the .60s and .70s for Picture Arrangement and Picture Completion. Composite indexes all have corrected stability coefficients in the .80s and .90s (The Psychological Corporation, 1997).

The four-factor structure of the WISC-III and the WAIS-III, corresponding to the four interpretive indexes, have been found to be largely resilient across a variety of samples. The WISC-III has been reported to be factorially invariant across age (Keith & Witta, 1997), racial groups (Kush et al., 2001), deaf and hearing samples (Maller & Ferron, 1997), and Canadian and British samples (Cooper, 1995; Roid & Worrall,

1997). Among clinical and exceptional groups, the factor structure is consistent across samples of children in special education (Grice, Krohn, & Logerquist, 1999; Konold, Kush, & Canivez, 1997), children with psychiatric diagnoses (Tupa, Wright, & Fristad, 1997), and children with traumatic brain injury (Donders & Warschausky, 1997). The WAIS-III has been found to be factorially stable across the United States and Canada (Saklofske, Hildebrand, & Gorsuch, 2000) and across mixed psychiatric and neurologically impaired samples (Ryan & Paolo, 2001).

WISC-III and WAIS-III subtest floors and ceilings tend to be good, spanning at least ±2 SDs at every age and usually larger. The lowest possible FSIQ yielded by the WISC-III is 40, and the highest possible FSIQ is 160. The WAIS-III has slightly less range, with FSIQs from 45 to 155. Ceilings on several of the performance subtests are obtained through the use of bonus points for speed. Perhaps one of the central weaknesses of the Wechsler scales is that most performance tests are timed. Although measuring speed of performance on subtests such as Block Design, Picture Arrangement, and Object Assembly allows for heightened ceilings and increased reliabilities, it may detract from the construct validity of the tests. The Wechsler scales now include a processing speed index, so the inclusion of speed dependency in other subtests is unnecessary and redundant.

Interpretive Indexes and Applications

Wechsler is reported to have administered and interpreted his own tests in a way that would be considered unacceptable today. For example, in practice he was known to administer the Vocabulary subtest alone to estimate intelligence and personality (Adam F. Wechsler, personal communication, December 3, 1993). Weider (1995) reports, "He never gave the Wechsler the same way twice" and considered the standardization of his tests to be imposed upon him by the test publisher. Kaufman (1994) has described Wechsler's clinical approach to interpreting the scales, along with his interest in qualitative aspects of examinee responses to emotionally loaded verbal and pictorial stimuli. One need only read Wechsler's (1939) *The Measurement of Adult Intelligence* to see that he interpreted every test behavior, every item response, every response error, and every problem-solving strategy.

Interpretations are derived from a decidedly formulaic and psychometric approach, based upon global composites, verbal and performance standard scores, factor indexes, and subtest scaled scores. Contemporary interpretation of the Wechsler intelligence scales typically involves a hierarchical approach involving (a) interpretation of the FSIQ if there is relatively little scatter in the verbal and performance scales or index composites, (b) interpreting the verbal and performance

standard scores (and meaningful discrepancies) if there is relatively little scatter in the factor-based index scores, (c) interpreting the four factor-based index scores (and meaningful discrepancies) when there is relatively little scatter in each one's constituent subtests, (d) interpreting scores at the subtest level if there is sufficient evidence to support the interpretation of unique and specific variance, and (e) interpreting responses, errors, and strategies on individual items that are clinically relevant and normatively unusual. The composite and factor-based indexes for the WISC-III and WAIS-III appear in Table 18.5, with our own descriptions appended.

After interpretation of the FSIQ, the most common score interpreted on the Wechsler scales is the discrepancy between the verbal and performance IQs. Leading interpretations of the discrepancies are presented in Alan Kaufman's books on the Wechsler scales (Kaufman, 1994; Kaufman & Lichtenberger, 1999, 2000). Logical comparisons between clusters of subtests that may guide interpretation also appear in Kaufman's body of work.

The Wechsler scales are the most widely used intelligence tests for identification of intellectually gifted and learning disabled students, individuals with mental retardation, and older adults with dementias and disabilities. In spite of its deep entrenchment among practitioners and thousands of research publications, its principal value is still based upon its measurement of the general factor *g* and its practical verbal-nonverbal split—both very old concepts.

Woodcock-Johnson Tests of Cognitive Abilities

The Woodcock-Johnson III Tests of Cognitive Abilities (WJ III Cog; Woodcock, McGrew, & Mather, 2001a) represent the most recent revision of an assessment battery with prior editions from 1977 and 1989. Normed for use from ages 2 through 90+ years, the WJ III Cog is conormed with a leading achievement test. The battery's origins may be traced to Richard W. Woodcock's employment in a sawmill and a butcher shop, where he earned about $1.00 per hour, after completion of military duty in the navy during World War II. Upon reading Wechsler's (1939) *Measurement of Adult Intelligence,* Woodcock was inspired to study psychology, quit his previous job, and joined the Veteran's Testing Bureau for a wage of $0.55 per hour! Woodcock began active development of the WJ Cog in 1963 in a series of controlled learning experiments and furthered its development during a 1974–1975 fellowship in neuropsychology at Tufts University, where he adapted the Category Test. The first edition of the WJ Cog was published in 1977. Unlike prior editions, the WJ III Cog yields an intelligence composite score and explicitly presents itself as a multifactor intelligence test.

TABLE 18.5   Wechsler Intelligence Scales (WISC-III and WAIS-III)

Composite Indexes	Description
Full Scale IQ (FSIQ)	Average level of cognitive functioning, sampling performance across a wide variety of complex verbal and performance tasks.
General Ability Index (GAI)	Overall level of cognitive functioning, based on subtests strongly associated with general intelligence or *g*; available for the WISC-III only; see Prifitera, Weiss, and Saklofske (1998).
Verbal IQ (VIQ)	Average cognitive ability on verbal-language-based tasks requiring declarative knowledge and problem solving, varying in the complexity of problem-solving operations, the degree of abstract reasoning required, and the extent of the required verbal response.
Performance IQ (PIQ)	Average cognitive ability on performance tasks with reduced language emphasis; dependent on spatial cognition, fine motor coordination, and ideational and psychomotor speed.
Verbal Comprehension Index (VCI)	Responses to language-based tasks requiring crystallized-declarative knowledge and limited problem solving, varying in the degree of abstract reasoning required and expressive language requirements (based on Information, Similarities, Vocabulary, and Comprehension subtests).
Perceptual Organization Index (POI)	Performance on tasks making high demands on spatial cognition, motor coordination, and ideational speed (based on Picture Completion, Picture Arrangement, Block Design, and Object Assembly subtests).
Freedom From Distractibility Index (FDI) and Working Memory Index (WMI)	Auditory immediate-working memory capacity, dependent on capacity and complexity of mental operations as well as facility with number processing (based on Digit Span and Arithmetic subtests in WISC-III; Arithmetic, Digit Span, and Letter-Number Sequencing in WAIS-III).
Processing Speed Index (PSI)	Efficiency of performance on psychomotor tasks with low to moderate cognitive processing demands; nonspecifically sensitive to nature and severity of disruptions in cognitive processing from a variety of disorders (based on Coding–Digit Symbol and Symbol Search subtests).

Originally finding its primary audience with special educators and best known for its companion Tests of Achievement, the WJ Cog is increasingly being utilized by psychologists in educational settings because of the ease with which it can provide ability-achievement comparisons through its conorming with the WJ III Tests of Achievement. The WJ III Cog consists of two batteries: a 10-test standard battery and a 20-test extended battery. All items are administered from an easel or audiotape. The WJ III Cog requires computer scoring and cannot be scored by hand. The WJ III Cog is distinguished from other intelligence tests by the elegance of its factorial structure, but its strength as a factor-driven instrument is offset by the absence of demonstrated clinical relevance for its factors.

Theoretical Underpinnings

The WJ III Tests of Cognitive Abilities is based upon what has been called the Cattell-Horn-Carroll (CHC) theory of cognitive abilities, but it has also been referred to in the literature as Horn-Cattell theory, fluid and crystallized intelligence theory, and extended Gf-Gc theory. The theory has been described as a hierarchical, multiple-stratum model with *g* or general intelligence at the apex (or highest stratum), 7–10 broad factors of intelligence at the second stratum, and at least 69 narrow factors at the first stratum. The model has recently been termed an integrated or synthesized CHC framework (McGrew, 1997; McGrew & Flanagan, 1998), and it forms the basis for the cross-battery approach to cognitive assessment. With the WJ III Cog as the anchor for (and only relatively complete representation of) this model, it attempts to resolve incongruities between the work of Horn, Carroll, and others. Our focus here is primarily upon the seven broad cognitive abilities tapped by the WJ III Cog (Gc, Glr, Gv, Ga, Gf, Gs, and Gsm; abbreviations are explained in the following discussion) and their contribution to the General Intellectual Ability score, which is a differentially weighted estimate of *g*. The WJ III technical manual (McGrew & Woodcock, 2001) reports the smoothed *g* weights; in descending order, the most weighted tests are Gc, Gf, Glr, Gsm, Ga, Gs, and Gv. This weighting scheme represents a major point of departure from prior investigations (e.g., Carroll, 1993; Gustafsson, 1984, 1988; Undheim, 1981) establishing Gf as the most substantial contributor to *g*. In practical terms, it expresses the idea that learned information contributes more to one's intelligence than does one's ability to reason.

Standardization Features and Psychometric Adequacy

The WJ III Cog was standardized from 1996 through 1999 on 8,818 children, adolescents, and adults from ages 2 through 90+. The school-age sample consisted of 4,783 participants. Stratification targets were based on census projections for the year 2000. Sample stratification variables included sex, race, ethnicity, type of school, geographic region, community size, adult education, and adult occupation. The sample consisted of over 200 participants at each age year, although sample sizes drop below 200 in the decades after age 60. The sample was statistically weighted to correct for proportional under-representation of selected groups, including Hispanics and parents with education levels below high school completion. It is not possible to assess the degree to which the sample is representative of the general population because accuracy is only reported on the margins without detailed reporting across stratification variables. Accordingly, it is possible that minorities in the sample are not representative of the general population in terms of age, sex, or parent education level. Sample weighting under these circumstances may magnify errors associated with inaccuracy in specific sampling cells. Some irregularities appear in the samples reported in the test technical manual (McGrew & Woodcock, 2001)—for example, of the 2,241 children from ages 9 to 13 reported in the norming sample (p. 18), only 1,875 completed the verbal comprehension test, only 1,454 took the planning test, and only 561 obtained scores on the pair cancellation test (p. 161). The pair cancellation sample suggests that as many as 75% of the sample may have not completed some tests for some age groups in the WJ III Cog.

Test internal consistency was calculated with the split-half procedure with Spearman-Brown correction and with Rasch procedures for eight tests that were either speeded or contained multiple point scoring. Test score reliability appears to be fully adequate, with median values across age falling below $r = .80$ for picture recognition and planning only. The clusters also tend to be highly reliable, with all but three having median values above .90 (the exceptions are long-term retrieval at .88, visual-spatial thinking at .81, and short-term memory at .88). The overall composite General Intellectual Ability (GIA) has a median reliability of .97 for the standard battery and .98 for the extended battery. Test-retest score reliabilities are reported in Rasch ability units for selected tests at varying test-retest intervals, with no apparent correction for variability at the time of first testing, thereby probably yielding artificially inflated values because of the large standard deviations. Accordingly, these findings are reported with caution. The five speeded WJ III Cog tests have a median 1-day stability coefficient of .81 (range from .78 to .87) for ages 7–11, .78 (range from .73 to .85) for ages 14–17, and .73 (range from .69 to .86) for ages 26–79. Test-retest reliabilities for selected tests administered over multiyear intervals—apparently collected as part of an unspecified longitudinal study using prior editions of the WJ (tests that no longer appear in the battery are included)—yield a range of stability coefficients from .60 to .86, suggesting that some of the tests have high degrees of stability over extended periods of time.

WJ III Cog floors and ceilings cannot be formally evaluated because the test may only be computer-scored, and no printed norms are available. The examiner's manual reports

that test standard scores extend from 0 to over 200 (p. 72; Mather & Woodcock, 2001), but this range seems inflated, given that adequate test floors tend to be difficult to achieve with certain age groups such as preschool children.

The WJ III GIA score tends to be highly correlated with composites from other intelligence tests, although correlations are not corrected for restricted or expanded ranges. According to the WJ III technical manual, the GIA standard scale correlates .76 with the DAS General Conceptual Ability, .75 with the KAIT Composite Intelligence Scale, .76 with the Stanford-Binet Composite SAS, .76 with the WISC-III FSIQ, and .67 with the WAIS-III FSIQ.

Factor analytic studies of the WJ III constitute an area of concern for a test battery that has historically based its foundation on the work of Cattell, Horn, and Carroll. Exploratory factor analyses are not reported in the technical manual, although the addition of eight new subtests to the WJ III Cog certainly justifies these analyses. The new WJ III Cog subtests purport to measure working memory, planning, naming speed, and attention. Moreover, hierarchical exploratory factor analyses conducted by John B. Carroll (using the same approach described in his 1993 book) have been previously reported for the WJ-R (see McGrew, Werder, & Woodcock, 1991, p. 172); these analyses yield findings of first-order and second-order factors that are not entirely congruent with the structure of the WJ Cog. As a basis for comparison, other tests in their third editions (e.g., WISC-III, WAIS-III) continue to report exploratory factor analyses, and tests that reported only confirmatory analyses (e.g., Stanford-Binet) have proven to have factor structures that have been effectively challenged (e.g., Sattler, 1988; R. M. Thorndike, 1990). With the exception of the Stanford-Binet and the WJ III, every test discussed in this chapter reports the results of exploratory factor analyses.

The confirmatory factor analyses (CFAs) reported in the WJ III technical manual appear to provide marginal support for a seven-factor structure relative to two alternative models, but the root mean squared errors of approximation (RMSEA, which should ideally be less than .05 with good model fit) do not support good model fit at any age level. The CFAs involve a contrast between the seven-factor CHC structure, a WAIS-based model, and a Stanford-Binet-based model, the latter two with model specifications that Wechsler or Stanford-Binet devotees would likely argue are misrepresentations. None of the models are hierarchical, none include a superordinate g, and none include the higher order dimensions suggested by Woodcock in his cognitive performance model. Moreover, only three goodness-of-fit indexes are included, whereas best practice with CFAs suggests that fit statistics should ideally include indexes sensitive to model fit, model comparison, *and* model parsimony. On a model built on multifactor foundations, it may be argued that a more rigorous CFA test of alternative models is appropriate.

Interpretive Indexes and Applications

The WJ III Cog consists of 20 tests purporting to measure seven broad cognitive factors. The tests are organized into a standard battery (Tests 1 through 7, with three supplemental tests) and an extended battery (Tests 1 through 7 and Tests 11 through 17, with six supplemental tests). The WJ III Cog is normed for ages 2 years through 90+ years and is conormed with 22 tests in an achievement battery—WJ III Tests of Achievement (Woodcock, McGrew, & Mather, 2001b).

In spite of the factor analytic findings reported in the preceding section, the WJ III Cog model is an elegant exemplar of the multifactor approach to cognitive abilities. Its factor analytic lineage may be most clearly traced from the pioneering efforts in factor analysis of ability tests by Thurstone (1938) to the encyclopedic tome by Carroll (1993), along with seminal contributions by Cattell and Horn. It is this association to a large body of factor analytic research that constitutes the WJ III Cog's main strength.

Unfortunately, a systematic overreliance on this same body of factor analytic research as evidence of test validity constitutes the most substantial weakness of the WJ III Cog. The WJ III Cog structure is a structural model missing the

integrative, explanatory, and predictive glue that constitutes a scientific theory. To their credit, advocates for the WJ Cog have acknowledged this shortcoming: "Gf-Gc provides little information on how the Gf-Gc abilities develop or how the cognitive processes work together. The theory is largely product oriented and provides little guidance on the dynamic interplay of variables (i.e., the processes) that occur in human cognitive processing" (Flanagan, McGrew, & Ortiz, 2000, p. 61).

The WJ III Cog also has little demonstrated diagnostic value. The technical manual includes no investigations of samples of mentally retarded or intellectually gifted individuals—the only intelligence test in this chapter failing to report findings with these important criterion groups. Three studies with other special populations—two with ADHD and one with a college learning disabled sample—fail to include a normative comparison group or report any indexes of effect size or statistical significance testing. In general, these few studies are consistent with Woodcock's (1998) report of results with 21 diagnostic groups in suggesting that the WJ Cog has limited value in identifying or differentiating clinical and exceptional samples.

Finally, the WJ III Cog offers little in the way of empirically based assessment intervention linkages. Although logical interventions and recommendations have been offered in Mather and Jaffe (1992), there is a conspicuous absence of empirical verification for these assessment-intervention linkages. In spite of its apparent assets, the WJ III Cog is absent a coherent theoretical framework, established clinical correlates, and empirically demonstrated treatment utility—an unsatisfying state of affairs for a factorial model of nearly 70 years' duration and a cognitive battery available for 25 years and now in its third edition. Kaufman (2000), in referring to the Carroll, Horn, and Cattell models, suggested that "there is no empirical evidence that these approaches yield profiles for exceptional children, are directly relevant to diagnosis, or have relevance to eligibility decisions, intervention or instructional planning—all of which are pertinent for school psychologists" (p. 27). Accordingly, the WJ III Cog provides clear evidence that claims of test structural validity are unrelated to its applied utility for clinical and educational decision making.

INTELLECTUAL ASSESSMENT AND DIAGNOSTIC CLASSIFICATION

In this section, general approaches to diagnostic utility of intelligence tests are described, specifically listing several diagnostic categories that are operationally defined through the use of cognitive or intelligence tests. As suggested at the beginning of this chapter, one characteristic of a mature

TABLE 18.6   Woodcock-Johnson III Tests of Cognitive Abilities (Woodcock, McGrew, & Mather, 2001a)

Composite Indexes	Description
General Intellectual Ability (GIA)	A weighted estimate of general cognitive ability.
Comprehension-Knowledge (GC)	The breadth and depth of prior learning about both verbal facts and information.
Long-Term Retrieval (Glr)	The ability to efficiently acquire and store information, measured by long-term and remote retrieval processes.
Visual Processing (Gv)	Analysis and synthesis of spatial-visual stimuli and the ability to hold and manipulate mental images.
Auditory Processing (Ga)	The ability to discriminate, analyze, and synthesize auditory stimuli; also related to phonological awareness.
Fluid Reasoning (Gf)	The ability to solve novel, abstract, visual, and nonverbal problems.
Short-Term Memory (Gsm)	The ability to hold, transform, and act upon auditory information in immediate awareness; the capacity of the auditory loop in mental operating space.
Processing Speed (Gs)	Speed and efficiency in performing simple cognitive tasks.

clinical science is the generation of a coherent *diagnostic taxonomy,* derived from and consistent with theory. A theory of intelligence (and tests developed according to the theory) should have value in generating a classification system by which clusters of individuals sharing common clinical characteristics may be systematically and meaningfully grouped. A classificatory taxonomy based on intelligence test results started at the beginning of the century by assigning individuals who were at the extreme ends of the distribution of general intelligence to diagnostic groups now known as *mental retardation* and *intellectual giftedness.*

The *Diagnostic and Statistical Manual of Mental Disorders–Fourth Edition–Text Revision* (*DSM-IV-TR;* American Psychiatric Association, 2000)—the most recent edition—contains several diagnostic classes based upon criteria related to cognitive or intelligence test results, including mental retardation, learning disorders, dementia, and a proposed new category, mild neurocognitive disorder. Amnestic disorders are defined by a disturbance in memory functioning that may be specifically quantified with neuropsychological testing, although several intelligence tests include measures of long-term memory ability that may be useful in arriving at a diagnosis of amnesia.

Individuals With Mental Retardation

There are several diagnostic approaches to identifying individuals with mental retardation, some of which rely on intellectual disability and impairment in areas of adaptive behavior. The *DSM-IV-TR* requires significantly subaverage general intellectual functioning, accompanied by significant limitations in adaptive functioning in at least two of the following skill areas: communication, self-care, home living, social-interpersonal skills, use of community resources, self-direction, functional academic skills, work, leisure, health, and safety. Table 18.7 contains a summary of these criteria (American Psychological Association Division 33 Editorial Board, 1996). Onset must occur during the developmental period, and deficits are expected to adversely affect a individual's educational performance.

TABLE 18.7   Levels of Mental Retardation

Level	IQ Range	IQ Deviation Cutting Point	Extent of Concurrent Adaptive Limitations
Mild	50–55 to 70–75	−2 SD	Two or more domains.
Moderate	35–40 to 50–55	−3 SD	Two or more domains.
Severe	20–25 to 35–40	−4 SD	All domains.
Profound	below 20 or 25	−5 SD	All domains.

Note. IQ range scores are for a test with a standard score mean of 100 and *SD* of 15. Adapted from American Psychological Association Division 33 Editorial Board (1996).

The 1992 definition from the American Association on Mental Retardation (AAMR; Luckasson et al., 1992) shifts the emphasis from subtyping on the basis of IQ ranges alone toward an assessment of the degrees of support required to function well intellectually, adaptively, psychologically, emotionally, and physically. The AAMR definition involves a three-step procedure for diagnosing, classifying, and determining the needed supports of individuals with mental retardation: (a) an IQ of 70–75 or below, with significant disabilities in two or more adaptive skill areas and age of onset below 18; (b) identification of strengths and weaknesses and the need for support across four dimensions (intellectual functioning and adaptive skills, psychological-emotional considerations, physical-health-etiological considerations, and environmental considerations); and (c) identification of the kinds and intensities of supports needed for each of the four dimensions. The four classification levels for mental retardation are *intermittent* (need for support during stressful or transition periods but not constantly), *limited* (less intense, consistent supports needed but time limited for changing situations), *extensive* (long-term consistent support at work, at home, or both), and *pervasive* (very intense, long-term, constant support needed across most or all situations). Intelligence tests continue to play a role in the diagnosis of mental retardation, although their role has been slightly de-emphasized in the AAMR definition.

Individuals Who Are Intellectually Gifted

Giftedness has traditionally been defined in terms of elevated general intelligence (Hollingworth, 1942; Terman, 1925). In 1972 the U.S. federal government adopted its first definition of gifted and talented students; this definition was based on a report to Congress from former U.S. Commissioner of Education Sidney P. Marland:

> Gifted and talented children are those, identified by professionally qualified persons, who by virtue of outstanding abilities are capable of high performance. These children who require differentiated programs and/or services beyond those normally provided by the regular school program in order to realize their contribution to self and society. Children capable of high performance include those with demonstrated high achievement and/or potential ability in any of the following areas, singly or in combination; general intellectual ability, specific academic aptitude, creative or productive thinking, leadership ability, visual and performing arts, and/or psychomotor ability. (p. 2)

This definition and subsequent public law does not, however, mandate that gifted and talented students are served in special education, and states and individual school districts vary as to how they define giftedness and whom they serve. High level of intelligence remains the most common single criterion of

TABLE 18.8   Levels of Intellectual Giftedness

Level	IQ Range	IQ Deviation Cutting Point
Profoundly gifted	above 175–180	+5 SD
Exceptionally gifted	160–174	+4 SD
Highly gifted	145–159	+3 SD
Gifted	130–144	+2 SD

Note. IQ range scores are for a test with a standard score mean of 100 and SD of 15.

giftedness (Callahan, 1996), although the use of multiple measures and approaches transcending intelligence tests alone is considered to constitute best assessment practice (Gallagher, 1994).

Levels of intellectual giftedness appear in Table 18.8 and have appeared in various forms in the literature (Gross, 1993; Hollingworth, 1942; Terman, 1925). Few intelligence tests have sufficient ceiling to serve the upper levels; as a result, comparatively little research on exceptionally and profoundly gifted children has been conducted.

Individuals With Specific Learning Disabilities

The current reauthorization of Individuals with Disabilities Education Act (IDEA; PL 105-17) defines specific learning disability as "a disorder in one or more of the basic psychological processes" involved in language comprehension, language expression, reading, writing, spelling, or mathematics. Specific learning disabilities are operationally assessed in different ways; the most common ones are (a) significant discrepancies between measured intelligence and academic achievement skills, and (b) isolated relative weaknesses in core cognitive processes such as phonological awareness that are thought to contribute to the development of reading decoding skills and subsequent success in reading. In both of these approaches, the role of cognitive-intellectual assessment is central.

Both assessment approaches have their limitations. The intelligence-achievement discrepancy model as a basis for identifying reading disability has been criticized for its implicit assumption that intelligence predicts reading potential (e.g., Stanovich, 1991a, 1991b). The cognitive processing approach requires that the specific processes contributing to performance in reading, for example, be included as part of an assessment intended to detect reading disability. Most intelligence tests do not include tests of these specialized abilities and processes as part of their battery.

Individuals With Dementias

Dementia refers to a generalized deterioration in cognitive functioning relative to a previously higher level of functioning.

Alzheimer's disease is the most common dementia. Diagnostic criteria for dementia appearing in the *International Classification of Diseases–Tenth Edition* (*ICD-10;* World Health Organization, 1992) include a decline in memory; a decline in other cognitive abilities, characterized by deterioration in judgment and thinking such as planning, organizing, and general processing of information; and preserved awareness of the environment. Other criteria include a decline in emotional control and a minimal duration of 6 months. The use of mental status examination results are sometimes sufficient to arrive at a diagnosis of dementia, but formal cognitive and neuropsychological assessment is often necessary to fully document the nature and extent of any suspected deterioration. Identification of dementias constitute the raison d'être to administer intelligence tests to older adults.

INTELLECTUAL ASSESSMENT AND INTERVENTION

Perhaps the most telling indicator of the existing intervention utility of intelligence tests may be found in Maruish (1999), a 1,500-page tome on the use of psychological testing for treatment planning with *no* mention of intelligence or IQ. After nearly a century and in what must be considered one of applied psychology's greatest failures, intellectual assessment has not been systematically linked to effective interventions. Several high-profile failures to link cognitive profiles to treatment (e.g., Kaufman & Kaufman, 1983b; Kirk, McCarthy, & Kirk, 1968) have deservedly led practitioners toward skepticism about the promise of including research-based recommendations in their psychological reports. There is, however, reason for guarded optimism regarding the future of assessment—intervention linkages based upon new remediation programs that utilize principles from cognitive instruction and neuronal plasticity. In this section, a few of these interventions are examined as well as some historical perspectives in intelligence-related intervention research.

Studies linking intelligence assessment to intervention date to the origins of intelligence testing. Binet (1909/1975) was unequivocal about his belief in the effectiveness of cognitive intervention, arguing that education tailored to a child's aptitudes could increase intelligence: "Twenty-five years of experimentation in schools have led me to believe that the most important task of teaching and education is the identification of children's aptitudes. The child's aptitudes must dictate the kind of education he will receive and the profession toward which he will be oriented" (Binet, 1909/1975, p. 23). He described programs that were antecedents to special education that partitioned mentally retarded students according to their intellectual abilities. Moreover, he described a series of exercises called mental orthopedics that were intended to enhance the efficiency of the cognitive faculties, especially in mentally handicapped children.

Contemporary investigations into intervention utility may be traced to the introduction, by Lee J. Cronbach (1957), of the concept of aptitude by treatment interactions (ATI). In formulating assessment recommendations, Cronbach recommended that applied psychologists consider individual differences and treatments simultaneously in order to select the best group of interventions to use and the optimal allocation of individuals to interventions. Of ATI, he predicted that "ultimately we should design treatments, not to fit the average person, but to fit groups of students with particular aptitude patterns. Conversely, we should seek out the aptitudes which correspond to (interact with) modifiable aspects of the treatment" (Cronbach, 1957, pp. 680–681).

In collaboration with Cronbach, Richard E. Snow developed a sampling-assembly-affordance model of ATI with the objective of elucidating person-treatment matching approaches in learning and instruction. Snow emphasized that ATI involved the complex interaction between persons and situations, with aptitude defined as "relatively stable psychological characteristics of individuals that predispose and thus predict differences in later learning under specified instructional conditions" (Snow, 1998, p. 93). The true focus of study, he argued, should be neither the main effects of the treatment nor the characteristics of the learner, but rather the interface between the two. Moreover, Snow (1998) recommended that ATI serve as additional criteria for construct validation beyond traditional validation approaches, insofar as ATI requires determination of the situational boundaries within which an ability can predict learning and ATI requires experimental manipulation of abilities within circumscribed situations.

The success of cognitive and intelligence tests as tools in establishing ATI has been modest at best. Traditional intelligence tests such as the Wechsler scales have never been empirically linked to intervention, leading authorities to decry the "virtual absence of empirical evidence supporting the existence of aptitude x treatment interactions" with intelligence tests (Gresham & Witt, 1997, p. 249). Witt and Gresham (1985) specifically commented the following on the Wechsler scales: "In short, the WISC-R lacks treatment validity in that its use does not enhance remediation interventions for children who show specific academic skills deficiencies. . . . For a test to have treatment validity, it must lead to better treatments (i.e., better educational programs, teaching strategies, etc.)" (p. 1717). Tests with theory-driven remedial approaches such as the Illinois Test of Psycholinguistic Ability (ITPA; Kirk et al., 1968) and the K-ABC (Kaufman &

Kaufman, 1983b) that sought to match instruction to learning styles have generally tended to yield disappointing findings. Only two major tests, the CAS and the K-ABC, even address treatment and intervention in their manuals.

Assessment-intervention linkages in intelligence and ATI are being explored in both old and new areas: cognitive instruction and computerized instruction. In the following sections, illustrative examples are provided of new types of interventions for individuals with deficits identified through cognitive and intelligence testing. These interventions represent beginnings for a larger body of work likely to evolve in the near future.

Cognitive Instruction

The study of *cognitive instruction* is concerned with the interface between psychology and education—particularly the cognitive processes involved in learning (e.g., Mayer, 1992). In this section, a representative series of studies is described linking cognitive assessment to a program of educational instruction, based upon PASS theory as measured in the CAS (Naglieri & Das, 1997a). Compendiums of other cognitive instructional methods of demonstrated efficacy are available from Ashman and Conway (1993) and Pressley and Woloshyn (1995).

The *planning facilitation* method described by Naglieri (1999) is an intervention that may be applied to individual or groups of children in as few as three 10-min sessions per week. It involves a nondirective emphasis on self-reflection, planning, and use of efficient problem-solving strategies and is taught through classroom group discussions led by teachers. It is intended to stimulate children's use of planning, based on the assumption that planning processes should be facilitated rather than directly instructed so that children discover the value of strategy use without specific instruction.

The planning facilitation method may be administered following a classroom assignment, such as completion of an arithmetic worksheet. After students have worked on the problems, the teacher facilitates a discussion intended to encourage students to consider various ways to be more successful in completion of the assignment. The teacher typically offers probes or nondirective questions such as *How did you do the math?*, *What could you do to get more correct?*, or *What will you do next time?* Student responses become a beginning point for discussions and further development of ideas. Teachers are instructed to make no direct statements like *That is correct* or *Remember to use that same strategy,* nor do they provide feedback on the accuracy on worksheets. Moreover, they do not give mathematics instruction. The sole role of the teacher is to facilitate self-reflection, thereby encouraging the students to plan so that they can more effectively complete their worksheet assignment. In response to the planning facilitation method, students arrive at their own problem-solving approaches, selectively incorporating any ideas from the class discussion that are perceived to be useful.

The initial investigations of planning facilitation were conducted based on PASS theory by Cormier, Carlson, and Das (1990) and Kar, Dash, Das, and Carlson (1992). Both investigations demonstrated that students differentially benefited from a verbalization technique intended to facilitate planning. Participants who initially performed poorly on measures of planning earned significantly higher scores than did those with good scores in planning. The verbalization method encouraged a carefully planned and organized examination of the demands of the task, differentially benefiting the children with low planning scores.

These investigations were the basis for three experiments by Naglieri and Gottling (1995, 1997) and Naglieri and Johnson (2000). The three studies focused on improving math calculation performance through teacher delivery of planning facilitation about two to three times per week. Teachers also consulted with school psychologists on a weekly basis to assist in the application of the intervention, monitor the progress of the students, and consider ways of facilitating classroom discussions. Students completed mathematics worksheets in a sequence of about 7 baseline and 21 intervention sessions over about a 2-month period. In the intervention phase, the students were given a 10-min period for completing a mathematics worksheet, a 10-min period was used for facilitating planning, and a second 10-min period was allocated for another mathematics worksheet. All students were given intervention sessions involving the three 10-min segments of mathematics-discussion-mathematics in 30-min instructional periods.

The first two research studies by Naglieri and Gottling (1995, 1997) demonstrated that planning facilitation led to improved performance on multiplication problems for those with low scores in planning, but minimal improvement was found for those with high planning scores. Thus, students benefited differentially from instruction based on their cognitive processing patterns. Using the planning facilitation method with a larger sample of children with learning problems, Naglieri and Johnson (2000) sought to determine whether children with specific PASS profiles would show different rates of improvement on mathematics performance. Children with cognitive weaknesses (i.e., an individual PASS standard score below 85 and significantly lower than the child's own mean) in either the Planning, Attention, Simultaneous, or Successive scales were selected to form contrast groups. The contrasting groups of children responded very differently to the intervention. Children with a cognitive

TABLE 18.9 Summary of Planning Facilitation Research Investigations: Percentage of Change From Baseline to Intervention for Children With High or Low Planning Scores

Study	High Planning	Low Planning	Difference
Cormier, Carlson, & Das (1990)	5%	29%	24%
Kar, Dash, Das, & Carlson (1992)	15%	84%	69%
Naglieri & Gottling (1995)	26%	178%	152%
Naglieri & Gottling (1997)	42%	80%	38%
Naglieri & Johnson (2000)	11%	143%	132%
Median values across all studies	*15%*	*84%*	*69%*

weakness in Planning improved considerably over baseline rates, whereas those with no cognitive weakness improved only marginally. Children with cognitive weaknesses in the Simultaneous, Successive, and Attention scales also showed substantially lower rates of improvement. These three studies, summarized with the two previous investigations in Table 18.9, illustrate that PASS cognitive processes are relevant to effective educational intervention in children with and without learning disabilities.

Computerized Instruction

The prospects that highly individualized and tailored programs of instruction and remediation may be delivered by computer represents a new trend needing validation and independent verification. Based upon findings that phonemic discrimination deficits contribute to reading problems, decoding impairments, and various language problems (e.g., Anderson et al., 1993), one promising technology-based program of instruction uses acoustically modified sounds and cross-training methods to directly train phoneme discrimination. Known as Fast ForWord (Tallal, 2000), the training program resembles a computer game and features adaptive instruction (centered slightly above the examinee's level of mastery), highly intensive and frequent training (for 100 min per day, 5 days per week, over 4–8 weeks), and high levels of reinforcement (through the use of computer-delivered reinforcement). The Fast ForWord training program reportedly yields statistically significant improvement in temporal processing thresholds, speech discrimination, and listening comprehension, and it results in a significant shift along the normal distribution of language comprehension scores for academically at-risk children (Tallal, 2000). Moreover, the training program purports to exploit the dynamic plasticity of the brain by remapping neural circuitry associated with phonemic discrimination (Tallal, 2000). Independent verification of treatment effectiveness has yet to be reported for this program, but more such programs can be expected to be developed as technological interventions continue to affect educational practices. These new generation interventions may provide opportunities to link cognitive assessment to focused interventions.

TOWARD A MATURE CLINICAL SCIENCE

Whither goeth intellectual assessment? Most of the subtest procedures currently in use were created before 1930, and the leading interpretive models of intelligence date back nearly as far. As Oscar K. Buros commented in 1977, ". . . except for the tremendous advances in electronic scoring, analysis, and reporting of test results, we don't have a great deal to show for fifty years of work" (p. 10).

If the past provides the best prediction of the future, then by around the year 2050 we may expect seventh-edition revisions of the Stanford-Binet, the WISC, and the WAIS. As computer usage and online test scoring applications continue to grow among practitioners, these tests may be expected to feature more sophisticated technology, including online administration, scoring, and interpretation. Computer administration also permits more accurate adaptive testing, so the duration of assessment batteries should grow progressively shorter and focused around an examinee's ability level. Psychometric techniques such as Rasch scaling have had little discernible impact on the material substance of intellectual tests thus far, but as psychometric techniques evolve, the process of test development should become more efficient and streamlined, reducing test development time and costs and offering practitioners more choices in intelligence assessment.

Neurophysiological assessment has been described as one methodology that may eventually supercede psychometric assessment. For example, Matarazzo (1992) speculated that the future of intelligence testing is to "record individual differences in brain functions at the neuromolecular, neurophysiologic, and neurochemical levels" (p. 1007). Among the current neurophysiological techniques that show promise include evoked potentials and nerve conduction velocity, quantitative electroencephalography, and measures of cerebral glucose metabolism.

More important than changes in technology, however, will be changes in fundamental assessment paradigms. Science does not advance slowly and gradually, but rather in brief periods of intense change, reappraisal, and upheaval (e.g., Kuhn, 1970). Challenges to conventional thinking in intelligence assessment have laid the groundwork for a paradigm shift, and that new tests delivering additional applied value to the practitioner have the greatest likelihood of success in the future. It is possible to envision a time when the psychological assessment results for a child referred for learning problems in

school, for example, will (a) yield results commensurate with the ways in which we know learning to occur, (b) describe the impaired cognitive abilities-processes that specifically contribute to the learning problems, (c) assess the degree to which the child's ability-process profile resembles that obtained by other children in diagnostic groups with similar patterns of learning problems, and (d) prescribe a series of interventions that have been demonstrated to be effective in addressing the special needs of children with similar test score profiles. The combination of a well-developed theory, valid and reliable tests, a cognitive diagnostic nomenclature related to abilities and processes, and effective interventions linked to assessment may one day enable the field of intelligence assessment to become a mature applied clinical science.

REFERENCES

American Association on Mental Retardation (AAMR). (1992). *Mental retardation: Definition, classification, and systems of supports* (9th ed.). Washington, DC: Author.

American Psychiatric Association. (2000). *Diagnostic and statistical manual of mental disorders* (4th ed., Text Revision). Washington, DC: Author.

American Psychological Association, Division 33 Editorial Board. (1996). Definition of mental retardation. In J. W. Jacobson & J. A. Mulick (Eds.), *Manual of diagnosis and professional practice in mental retardation* (pp. 13–53). Washington, DC: American Psychological Association.

Anastasi, A. (1989). Review of the Stanford-Binet Intelligence Scale, Fourth Edition. In J. C. Conoley & J. J. Kramer (Eds.), *The tenth mental measurements yearbook* (pp. 771–773). Lincoln, NE: Buros Institute of Mental Measurements.

Anderson, K., Brown, C., & Tallal, P. (1993). Developmental language disorders: Evidence for a basic processing deficit. *Current Opinion in Neurology and Neurosurgery, 6,* 98–106.

Ashman, A. F., & Conway, R. N. F. (1993). *Using cognitive methods in the classroom.* New York: Routledge.

Ashman, A. F., & Das, J. P. (1980). Relation between planning and simultaneous-successive processing. *Perceptual and Motor Skills, 51,* 371–382.

Aylward, G. P. (1992). Differential Abilities Scales. In J. J. Kramer & J. C. Conoley (Eds.), *The eleventh mental measurements yearbook* (pp. 281–282). Lincoln, NE: Buros Institute of Mental Measurements.

Barkley, R. A. (1997). *ADHD and the nature of self-control.* New York: Guilford Press.

Binet, A. (1975). *Modern ideas about children* (S. Heisler, Trans.). Menlo Park, CA: Suzanne Heisler. (Original work published 1909)

Binet, A., & Simon, T. (1916). The development of intelligence in the child. In E. S. Kite (Trans.), *The development of intelligence in children: The Binet-Simon Scale* (pp. 182–273). Baltimore: Williams and Wilkins. (Original work published 1908)

Bracken, B. A. (1985). A critical review of the Kaufman Assessment Battery for Children (K-ABC). *School Psychology Review, 14,* 21–36.

Buros, O. K. (1977). Fifty years in testing: Some reminiscences, criticisms, and suggestions. *Educational Researcher, 6,* 9–15.

Callahan, C. M. (1996). A critical self-study of gifted education: Healthy practice, necessary evil, or sedition? *Journal for the Education of the Gifted, 19,* 148–163.

Camara, W. J., Nathan, J. S., & Puente, A. E. (2000). Psychological test usage: Implications in professional psychology. *Professional Psychology: Research and Practice, 31,* 141–154.

Carroll, J. B. (1993). *Human cognitive abilities: A survey of factor-analytic studies.* New York: Cambridge University Press.

Carroll, J. B. (1995). Review of the book *Assessment of cognitive processing:* The PASS theory of intelligence. *Journal of Psychoeducational Assessment, 13,* 397–409.

Cohen, R. J., & Swerdlik, M. E. (1999). *Psychological testing and assessment: An introduction to tests and measurement* (4th ed.). Mountain View, CA: Mayfield.

Cooper, C. (1995). Inside the WISC-III-UK. *Association of Educational Psychologists Journal, 10,* 215–219.

Cormier, P., Carlson, J. S., & Das, J. P. (1990). Planning ability and cognitive performance: The compensatory effects of a dynamic assessment approach. *Learning and Individual Differences, 2,* 437–449.

Cronbach, L. J. (1949). *Essentials of psychological testing.* New York: Harper.

Cronbach, L. J. (1957). The two disciplines of scientific psychology. *American Psychologist, 12,* 671–684.

Cronbach, L. J. (1989). Review of the Stanford-Binet Intelligence Scale, Fourth Edition. In J. C. Conoley & J. J. Kramer (Eds.), *The tenth mental measurements yearbook* (pp. 773–775). Lincoln, NE: Buros Institute of Mental Measurements.

Das, J. P., Naglieri, J. A., & Kirby, J. R. (1994). *Assessment of cognitive processes: The PASS theory of intelligence.* Needham Heights, MA: Allyn and Bacon.

Delaney, E. A., & Hopkins, T. F. (1987). *The Stanford-Binet Intelligence Scale: Fourth Edition examiner's handbook.* Itasca, IL: Riverside.

Donders, J., & Warschausky, S. (1997). WISC-III factor index score pattern after traumatic head injury in children. *Child Neuropsychology, 3,* 71–78.

Elliott, C. D. (1983). *The British Ability Scales, Manual 1: Introductory handbook.* Windsor, England: NFER-Nelson.

Elliott, C. D. (1990a). *Differential Ability Scales.* San Antonio, TX: The Psychological Corporation.

Elliott, C. D. (1990b). *Differential Ability Scales: Introductory and technical handbook.* San Antonio, TX: The Psychological Corporation.

Elliott, S. N. (1990). The nature and structure of the DAS: Questioning the test's organizing model and use. *Journal of Psychoeducational Assessment, 8,* 406–411.

Flanagan, D. P., McGrew, K. S., & Ortiz, S. O. (2000). *The Wechsler intelligence scales and Gf-Gc theory: A contemporary approach to interpretation.* Needham Heights, MA: Allyn and Bacon.

Gallagher, J. J. (1994). Current and historical thinking on education for gifted and talented students. In P. Ross (Ed.), *National excellence: An anthology of readings* (pp. 83–107). Washington, DC: U.S. Department of Education.

Gresham, F. M., & Witt, J. C. (1997). Utility of intelligence tests for treatment planning, classification, and placement decisions: Recent empirical findings and future directions. *School Psychology Quarterly, 12,* 249–267.

Grice, J. W., Krohn, E. J., & Logerquist, S. (1999). Cross-validation of the WISC-III factor structure in two samples of children with learning disabilities. *Journal of Psychoeducational Assessment, 17,* 236–248.

Gross, M. U. M. (1993). *Exceptionally gifted children.* London: Routledge.

Gustafsson, J.-E. (1984). A unifying model of the structure of intellectual abilities. *Intelligence, 8,* 179–203.

Gustafsson, J.-E. (1988). Hierarchical models for individual differences in cognitive abilities. In R. J. Sternberg (Ed.), *Advances in the psychology of human intelligence* (Vol. 4, pp. 35–71). Hillsdale, NJ: Erlbaum.

Gutentag, S. S., Naglieri, J. A., & Yeates, K. O. (1998). Performance of children with traumatic brain injury on the cognitive assessment system. *Assessment, 5,* 263–272.

Hollingworth, L. S. (1942). *Children above 180 IQ Stanford-Binet: Origin and development.* Yonkers, NY: World Book.

Kar, B. C., Dash, U. N., Das, J. P., & Carlson, J. S. (1992). Two experiments on the dynamic assessment of planning. *Learning and Individual Differences, 5,* 13–29.

Kaufman, A. S. (1994). *Intelligent testing with the WISC-III.* New York: Wiley.

Kaufman, A. S. (2000). Intelligence tests and school psychology: Predicting the future by studying the past. *Psychology in the Schools, 37,* 7–16.

Kaufman, A. S., & Kaufman, N. L. (1983a). *Kaufman Assessment Battery for Children administration and scoring manual.* Circle Pines, MN: American Guidance.

Kaufman, A. S., & Kaufman, N. L. (1983b). *Kaufman Assessment Battery for Children interpretive manual.* Circle Pines, MN: American Guidance.

Kaufman, A. S., & Kaufman, N. L. (1993). *Kaufman Adolescent and Adult Intelligence Test.* Circle Pines, MN: American Guidance.

Kaufman, A. S., & Lichtenberger, E. O. (1999). *Essentials of WAIS-III assessment.* New York: Wiley.

Kaufman, A. S., & Lichtenberger, E. O. (2000). *Essentials of WISC-III and WPPSI-R assessment.* New York: Wiley.

Keith, T. Z. (1990). Confirmatory and hierarchical confirmatory analysis of the Differential Ability Scales. *Journal of Psychoeducational Assessment, 8,* 391–405.

Keith, T. Z., & Kranzler, J. H. (1999). The absence of structural fidelity precludes construct validity: Rejoinder to Naglieri on what the Cognitive Assessment System does and does not measure. *School Psychology Review, 28,* 303–321.

Keith, T. Z., Kranzler, J. H., & Flanagan, D. P. (2001). What does the Cognitive Assessment System (CAS) measure? Joint confirmatory factor analysis of the CAS and the Woodcock-Johnson Tests of Cognitive Ability—3rd Edition. *School Psychology Review, 30,* 89–119.

Keith, T. Z., Quirk, K. J., Schartzer, C., & Elliott, C. D. (1999). Construct bias in the Differential Ability Scales? Confirmatory and hierarchical factor structure across three ethnic groups. *Journal of Psychoeducational Assessment, 17,* 249–268.

Keith, T. Z., & Witta, E. L. (1997). Hierarchical and cross-age confirmatory factor analysis of the WISC-III: What does it measure? *School Psychology Quarterly, 12,* 89–107.

Kirby, J. R., & Das, J. P. (1978). Information processing and human abilities. *Journal of Experimental Psychology, 70,* 58–66.

Kirk, S. A., McCarthy, J. J., & Kirk, W. D. (1968). *Illinois Test of Psycholinguistic Abilities.* Urbana: University of Illinois Press.

Kline, R. B., Snyder, J., & Castellanos, M. (1996). Lessons from the Kaufman Assessment Battery for Children (K-ABC): Toward a new cognitive assessment model. *Psychological Assessment, 8,* 7–17.

Konold, T. R., Kush, J. C., & Canivez, G. L. (1997). Factor replication of the WISC-III in three independent samples of children receiving special education. *Journal of Psychoeducational Assessment, 15,* 123–137.

Kranzler, J. H., & Keith, T. Z. (1999). Independent confirmatory factor analysis of the Cognitive Assessment System (CAS): What does the CAS measure? *School Psychology Review, 28,* 117–144.

Kranzler, J. H., Keith, T. Z., & Flanagan, D. P. (2000). Independent examination of the factor structure of the Cognitive Assessment System (CAS): Further evidence challenging the construct validity of the CAS. *Journal of Psychoeducational Assessment, 18,* 143–159.

Kuhn, T. (1970). *The structure of scientific revolutions* (2nd ed.). Chicago: University of Chicago Press.

Kush, J. C., Watkins, M. W., Ward, T. J., Ward, S. B., Canivez, G. L., & Worrell, F. C. (2001). Construct validity of the WISC-III for White and Black students from the WISC-III standardization sample and for Black students referred for psychological evaluation. *School Psychology Review, 30,* 70–88.

Laurent, J., Swerdlik, M., & Ryburn, M. (1992). Review of validity research on the Stanford-Binet Intelligence Scale: Fourth Edition. *Psychological Assessment, 4,* 102–112.

Lubin, B., Wallis, R. R., & Paine, C. (1971). Patterns of psychological test usage in the United States: 1935–1969. *Professional Psychology, 2,* 70–74.

Luckasson, R., Counter, D. L., Polloway, E. A., Reiss, S., Schalock, R. L., Snell, M. E., et al. (1992). *Mental retardation: Definition, classifications and systems of support* (9th ed.). Washington, DC: American Association on Mental Retardation.

Luria, A. R. (1963). *Restoration of function after brain injury* (B. Haigh, Trans.). New York: Macmillan.

Luria, A. R. (1973). *The working brain: An introduction to neuropsychology.* New York: Basic Books.

Luria, A. R. (1980). *Higher cortical functions in man.* New York: Basic Books.

Luria, A. R., & Tsvetkova, L. S. (1990). *The neuropsychological analysis of problem solving* (A. Mikheyev & S. Mikheyev, Trans.). Orlando, FL: Paul M. Deutsch Press.

Maller, S. J., & Ferron, J. (1997). WISC-III factor invariance across deaf and standardization samples. *Educational and Psychological Measurement, 57,* 987–994.

Marland, S. P. (1972). *Education of the gifted and talented: Vol. 1. Report to the Congress of the United States by the U.S. Commissioner of Education.* Washington, DC: Government Printing Office.

Maruish, M. E. (Ed.). (1999). *The use of psychological testing for treatment planning and outcomes assessment* (2nd ed.). Mahwah, NJ: Erlbaum.

Matarazzo, J. D. (1992). Psychological testing and assessment in the 21st century. *American Psychologist, 47,* 1007–1018.

Mather, N., & Jaffe, L. E. (1992). *Woodcock-Johnson Psychoeducational Battery—Revised: Recommendations and reports.* Brandon, VT: Clinical Psychology Publishing.

Mather, N., & Woodcock, R. W. (2001). *Woodcock-Johnson III Tests of Cognitive Abilities examiner's manual: Standard and extended batteries.* Itasca, IL: Riverside.

Mayer, R. E. (1992). Cognition and instruction: Their historic meeting within educational psychology. *Journal of Educational Psychology, 84,* 405–412.

McGrew, K. S. (1997). Analysis of the major intelligence batteries according to a proposed comprehensive Gf-Gc framework. In D. P. Flanagan, J. L. Genshaft, & P. L. Harrison (Eds.), *Contemporary intellectual assessment: Theories, tests, and issues* (pp. 151–180). New York: Guilford Press.

McGrew, K. S., & Flanagan, D. P. (1998). *The intelligence test desk reference (ITDR): Gf-Gc cross-battery assessment.* Needham Heights, MA: Allyn and Bacon.

McGrew, K. S., Werder, J. K., & Woodcock, R. W. (1991). *WJ-R technical manual.* Itasca, IL: Riverside.

McGrew, K. S., & Woodcock, R. W. (2001). *Technical manual: Woodcock-Johnson III.* Itasca, IL: Riverside.

McIntosh, D. E. (1999). Identifying at-risk preschoolers: The discriminant validity of the Differential Ability Scales. *Psychology in the Schools, 36,* 1–10.

McNemar, Q. (1942). *The revision of the Stanford-Binet scale: An analysis of the standardization data.* Boston: Houghton Mifflin.

Meikamp, J. (1999). Review of the Das-Naglieri Cognitive Assessment System. In B. S. Plake & J. C. Impara (Eds.), *The supplement to the thirteenth mental measurements yearbook* (pp. 75–77). Lincoln, NE: Buros Institute of Mental Measurements.

Millon, T. (1999). Reflections on psychosynergy: A model for integrating science, theory, classification, assessment, and therapy. *Journal of Personality Assessment, 72,* 437–456.

Millon, T., & Davis, R. D. (1996). *Disorders of personality: DSM-IV and beyond* (2nd ed.). New York: Wiley.

Naglieri, J. A. (1999). *Essentials of CAS assessment.* New York: Wiley.

Naglieri, J. A., & Das, J. P. (1987). Construct and criterion related validity of planning, simultaneous, and successive cognitive processing tasks. *Journal of Psychoeducational Assessment, 5,* 353–363.

Naglieri, J. A., & Das, J. P. (1988). Planning-Arousal-Simultaneous-Successive (PASS): A model for assessment. *Journal of School Psychology, 26,* 35–48.

Naglieri, J. A., & Das, J. P. (1997a). *Cognitive Assessment System.* Itasca, IL: Riverside.

Naglieri, J. A., & Das, J. P. (1997b). *Cognitive Assessment System interpretive handbook.* Itasca, IL: Riverside.

Naglieri, J. A., & Gottling, S. H. (1995). A cognitive education approach to math instruction for the learning disabled: An individual study. *Psychological Reports, 76,* 1343–1354.

Naglieri, J. A., & Gottling, S. H. (1997). Mathematics instruction and PASS cognitive processes: An intervention study. *Journal of Learning Disabilities, 30,* 513–520.

Naglieri, J. A., & Johnson, D. (2000). Effectiveness of a cognitive strategy intervention in improving arithmetic computation based on the PASS theory. *Journal of Learning Disabilities, 33,* 591–597.

Naglieri, J. A., & Rojahn, J. (2001). Intellectual classification of Black and White children in special education programs using the WISC-III and the Cognitive Assessment System. *American Journal on Mental Retardation, 106,* 359–367.

Paolitto, A. W. (1999). Clinical validation of the Cognitive Assessment System with children with ADHD. *ADHD Report, 7,* 1–5.

Pressley, M. P., & Woloshyn, V. (1995). *Cognitive strategy instruction that really improves children's academic performance* (2nd ed.). Cambridge, MA: Brookline Books.

Prifitera, A., Weiss, L. G., & Saklofske, D. H. (1998). The WISC-III in context. In A. Prifitera & D. Saklofske (Eds.), *WISC-III clinical use and interpretation: Scientist-practitioner perspectives* (pp. 1–38). San Diego, CA: Academic Press.

The Psychological Corporation. (1997). *WAIS-III–WMS-III technical manual.* San Antonio, TX: Author.

Reinehr, R. C. (1992). Review of the Differential Abilities Scales. In J. J. Kramer & J. C. Conoley (Eds.), *The eleventh mental measurements yearbook* (pp. 282–283). Lincoln, NE: Buros Institute of Mental Measurements.

Roid, G. H., & Worrall, W. (1997). Replication of the Wechsler Intelligence Scale for Children—Third edition four-factor model in the Canadian normative sample. *Psychological Assessment, 9,* 512–515.

Ryan, J. J., & Paolo, A. M. (2001). Exploratory factor analysis of the WAIS-III in a mixed patient sample. *Archives of Clinical Neuropsychology, 16,* 151–156.

Saklofske, D. H., Hildebrand, D. K., & Gorsuch, R. L. (2000). Replication of the factor structure of the Wechsler Adult Intelligence Scale—Third Edition with a Canadian sample. *Psychological Assessment, 12,* 436–439.

Sattler, J. M. (1988). *Assessment of children* (3rd ed.). San Diego, CA: Author.

Snow, R. E. (1998). Abilities at aptitudes and achievements in learning situations. In J. J. McArdle & R. W. Woodcock (Eds.), *Human cognitive abilities in theory and practice* (pp. 93–112). Mahwah, NJ: Erlbaum.

Sokal, M. M. (1981). The origins of the Psychological Corporation. *Journal of the History of the Behavioral Sciences, 17,* 54–67.

Solso, R. L., & Hoffman, C. A. (1991). Influence of Soviet scholars. *American Psychologist, 46,* 251–253.

Stanovich, K. E. (1991a). Conceptual and empirical problems with discrepancy definitions of reading disability. *Learning Disability Quarterly, 14,* 269–280.

Stanovich, K. E. (1991b). Discrepancy definitions of reading disability: Has intelligence led us astray? *Reading Research Quarterly, 26,* 7–29.

Tallal, P. (2000, March 14). The science of literacy: From the laboratory to the classroom. *Proceedings of the National Academy of Sciences of the United States of America, 97,* 2402–2404.

Terman, L. M. (1916). *The measurement of intelligence.* Boston: Houghton Mifflin.

Terman, L. M. (1925). *Genetic studies of genius: Vol. 1. Mental and physical traits of a thousand gifted children.* Stanford, CA: Stanford University Press.

Terman, L. M., & Merrill, M. A. (1937). *Measuring intelligence: A guide to the administration of the new revised Stanford-Binet tests of intelligence.* Boston: Houghton Mifflin.

Terman, L. M., & Merrill, M. A. (1960). *Stanford-Binet Intelligence Scale: Manual for the third revision. Form L-M.* Boston: Houghton Mifflin.

Terman, L. M., & Merrill, M. A. (1973). *Stanford-Binet Intelligence Scale: 1973 norms edition.* Boston: Houghton Mifflin.

Thorndike, R. L., Hagen, E. P., & Sattler, J. M. (1986). *The Stanford-Binet intelligence scale: Fourth edition.* Itasca, IL: Riverside.

Thorndike, R. M. (1990). Would the real factors of the Stanford-Binet Fourth Edition please come forward? *Journal of Psychoeducational Assessment, 8,* 412–435.

Thorndike, R. M., & Lohman, D. F. (1990). *A century of ability testing.* Itasca, IL: Riverside.

Thurstone, L. L. (1938). *Primary mental abilities.* Chicago: University of Chicago Press.

Tupa, D. J., Wright, M. O., & Fristad, M. A. (1997). Confirmatory factor analysis of the WISC-III with child psychiatric inpatients. *Psychological Assessment, 9,* 302–306.

Undheim, J. O. (1981). On intelligence: II. A neo-Spearman model to replace Cattell's theory of fluid and crystallized intelligence. *Scandinavian Journal of Psychology, 22,* 181–187.

Wasserman, J. D., & Becker, K. A. (2000, August). Racial and ethnic group mean score differences on intelligence tests. In J. A. Naglieri (Chair), *Making assessment more fair—taking verbal and achievement out of ability tests.* Symposium conducted at the annual meeting of the American Psychological Association, Washington, DC.

Wasserman, J. D., Paolitto, A. M., & Becker, K. A. (1999, November). *Clinical application of the Das-Naglieri Cognitive Assessment System (CAS) with children diagnosed with Attention-Deficit/ Hyperactivity Disorders.* Paper presented at the annual meeting of the National Academy of Neuropsychology, San Antonio, TX.

Wechsler, D. (1925). On the specificity of emotional reactions. *Journal of Psychology, 36,* 424–426.

Wechsler, D. (1939). *The measurement of adult intelligence.* Baltimore: Williams and Wilkins.

Wechsler, D. (1949). *Wechsler Intelligence Scale for Children manual.* New York: The Psychological Corporation.

Wechsler, D. (1955). *Wechsler Adult Intelligence Scale manual.* New York: The Psychological Corporation.

Wechsler, D. (1958). Intelligence et fonction cérébrale. *Revue de Psychologie Appliquee, 8,* 143–147.

Wechsler, D. (1961). Intelligence, memory, and the aging process. In P. Hoch & J. Zubin (Eds.), *Psychopathology of aging* (pp. 152–159). New York: Grune and Stratton.

Wechsler, D. (1967). *Wechsler Preschool and Primary Scale of Intelligence.* New York: The Psychological Corporation.

Wechsler, D. (1974). Cognitive, conative, and non-intellective intelligence. In D. Wechsler (Ed.), *Selected papers of David Wechsler* (pp. 39–48). New York: Academic Press. (Original work published 1950)

Wechsler, D. (Speaker). (1976, January). *Unpublished interview with David Wechsler* [Transcript]. San Antonio, TX: The Psychological Corporation.

Wechsler, D. (1991). *Wechsler Intelligence Scale for Children— Third Edition manual.* San Antonio, TX: The Psychological Corporation.

Wechsler, D. (1997). *Wechsler Adult Intelligence Scale—Third Edition: Administration and scoring manual.* San Antonio, TX: The Psychological Corporation.

Wechsler, D. (1999). *Wechsler Abbreviated Scale of Intelligence.* San Antonio, TX: The Psychological Corporation.

Weider, A. (Speaker). (1995, August). *An interview with Arthur Weider.* Unpublished manuscript. (Available from John D. Wasserman, George Mason University, 4400 University Drive, MSN 2C6, Fairfax, Virginia 22030-4444)

Werner, H. (1948). *Comparative psychology of mental development.* New York: International Universities Press.

Witt, J. C., & Gresham, F. M. (1985). Review of the Wechsler Intelligence Scale for Children—Revised. In J. V. Mitchell (Ed.), *Ninth mental measurements yearbook* (pp. 1716–1719). Lincoln: University of Nebraska Press.

Wolf, T. H. (1973). *Alfred Binet.* Chicago: University of Chicago Press.

Woodcock, R. W. (1998). *The WJ-R and Batería-R in neuropsychological assessment* (Research Rep. No. 1). Itasca, IL: Riverside.

Woodcock, R. W., McGrew, K. S., & Mather, N. (2001a). *Woodcock-Johnson III Tests of Cognitive Abilities.* Itasca, IL: Riverside.

Woodcock, R. W., McGrew, K. S., & Mather, N. (2001b). *Woodcock-Johnson III Tests of Achievement.* Itasca, IL: Riverside.

World Health Organization. (1992). *The ICD-10 classification of mental and behavioral disorders: Clinical descriptions and diagnostic guidelines.* Geneva, Switzerland: Author.

CHAPTER 19

Assessment of Neuropsychological Functioning

KENNETH PODELL, PHILIP A. DeFINA, PAUL BARRETT, ANNEMARIE McCULLEN, AND ELKHONON GOLDBERG

In scientific fields, both external and internal forces create, change, and shape that field. Neuropsychology is no different; in fact, this field is in the midst of some of the largest growth, advancements, and changes it has ever undergone. Although it is a relatively young science, neuropsychology has been influenced by many factors that have helped to develop and shape the field, both experimentally and clinically. For example, there was a large amount of clinical information obtained from studying World War II survivors who had penetrating missile injuries to the head. Not only did the presence (although not a pleasant event) of war help contribute to our knowledge base, but the use of penicillin in the battlefield also allowed these individuals to survive in the first place in order to be available for study later.

Presently, various internal and external forces have shaped researchers and clinicians in the field of neuropsychology. Internal forces include cutting-edge neuroimaging technology, such as functional magnetic resonance imaging (fMRI) and magnetoencephalography (MEG), the development and application of more sophisticated statistical techniques, and the expansion into new clinical areas (such as sports-related concussion). Similarly, one of the strongest external forces influencing and molding the future of neuropsychology (for the better and the worse) is economics. The current situation in health care has had a particular impact on the development of neuropsychology—especially as a clinical discipline. Some

of the changes have been good and others have been not so good. As for the latter, the rather dismal prospect of finding an adequate, well-paying job as a neuropsychologist is influencing the career choices of many bright and talented individuals and causing them to seriously consider—and probably choose—other professions. Similarly, numerous graduate and postgraduate training sites have closed due to lack of funding or budget cuts. Paradoxically, there has been a slight increase in the number of students entering graduate psychology programs in general. This situation has led to a glut of (quality) students who cannot find adequate training; moreover, even if they do find such training, many cannot find an acceptable position. However, the shrinking health care dollar is causing neuropsychologists to rethink how they administer neuropsychological services (a much-needed self-check) and is also causing neuropsychologists to be creative and develop or enter new venues for generating revenue.

Probably the best example of new revenue opportunities is the explosion of forensic neuropsychology. More and more neuropsychologists have recognized the lucrative area of forensic practice. Although some truly see forensic neuropsychology as a science, others see it as a way of increasing revenue. This situation has caused exponential growth in clinical activity, which has in turn stimulated the critical research required to support this area of neuropsychological practice from a scientific perspective. This research in turn improves its clinical application and the reputations of neuropsychologists (and probably psychology as a whole) in the forensic arena.

The changing face of health care and recent advancements in technology have stimulated the growth of neuropsychology into a more scientific and clinically diverse subspecialty of psychology. However, the field still faces several challenges in the areas of training for and delivery of health care. This chapter focuses on some of these innovative issues in neuropsychology. Our attempt is to introduce these advances and explain some the basic components of each. We focus on how these new developments and progress in neuropsychology advance experimental and clinical neuropsychology, how they contribute to our knowledge of brain-behavior relationships and treatment of patients, and how they are shaping the field of neuropsychology as a whole. Before we discuss the current new developments in neuropsychology, we provide a brief review of the history of neuropsychology as a backdrop and perhaps—at least heuristically—as a context for understanding some of the more recent advancements.

BRIEF HISTORY OF NEUROPSYCHOLOGY

Neuropsychology is a relatively new field that traces its roots back to at least the late 1800s. It is a hybrid discipline representing the confluence of several fields of study: neurology and psychology, neuroanatomy and neurophysiology, and neurochemistry and neuropharmacology (Benton, 1988). Its early status was dependent upon the status of its contributory disciplines. Modern clinical neuropsychology grew out of— or was at least strongly influenced by—clinical neurology (Bradshaw & Mattingley, 1995).

Neuropsychology, although it is closely related to behavioral neurology, distinguishes itself from both neuropsychiatry and behavioral neurology by its ultimate focus on clarifying the mechanisms underlying both abnormal *and* normal behavior. Neuropsychiatry and behavioral neurology focus on the diagnosis and treatment of abnormal behavior only (Bradshaw & Mattingley, 1995). Modern neuropsychology is based upon data from both brain-injured and healthy individuals. In addition to its clinical neurology parentage, neuropsychology makes use of more than 100 years of research in experimental psychology to help explain the patterns of disordered perceptual, cognitive, and motor processes seen in patients with neurological damage (Bradshaw & Mattingley, 1995).

The term *neuropsychology* first began to be used in the 1930s and 1940s (Benton, 1987). According to Bruce (1985, cited in Benton, 1988), the term began gaining currency in the 1950s when it displaced older terms, such as *psychoneurology* and *brain pathology*. The discipline of human neuropsychology was established over a course of about 15 years, roughly between 1950 and 1965 (Benton, 1987). Prior to that time, experimental neuropsychology was largely involved in animal model research. In fact, there was a period, mostly from the 1950s through the early 1970s, during which there was prolific research and understanding in the basic aspects of brain-behavior relationship, mostly through animal model research.

Neuropsychology's status as a discipline was first signaled by the appearance of two international neuropsychological journals between 1963 and 1964—*Neuropsychologia* founded by Henry Hecaen and *Cortex* founded by Ennio De Renzi. The first association specifically oriented toward neuropsychology was the International Neuropsychological Society, which was founded in the late 1960s by a group organized by Louis Costa. In the late 1970s, Louis Costa is credited as the individual who gave birth to clinical neuropsychology as a distinct professional specialty and gave it legitimacy as a subspecialty in psychology (at least in North America). Professor Costa did this by founding (with Byron Rourke) the *Journal of Clinical Neuropsychology* and by developing Division 40 of the APA, the Division of Clinical Neuropsychology.

Modern neuropsychology began by studying the localization of brain function and cognitive and behavioral changes following large lesions to the brain. These advances are perhaps best illustrated by the work of Broca and Wernicke in establishing the major speech areas in the left hemisphere. Some of the seminal researchers of the late 1800s up through the mid-1960s include Broca, Wernicke, Kliest, Goldstein, Henry Hecaen, Denny-Brown, Karl Pribram, Mortimer Mishkin, Hans Lukas-Teuber, Norman Geschwind, Ward Halstead, Ralph Reitan, A. L. Benton, and many others. One individual who requires special attention is A. R. Luria, a Russian psychologist whose contribution to neuropsychology was actual only part of his total contribution to psychology as a whole. Luria, a neurologist trained in psychoanalysis, did extensive research in understanding the cognitive and behavioral alterations following lesions to the brain. *Higher Cortical Functions in Man* (1966/1980), one of several books written by Luria, is considered one of the seminal textbooks on localization neuropsychology. In fact, Luria's name is virtually synonymous with executive control (i.e., prefrontal functions). Luria was perhaps one of the first to describe in detail the qualitative features of the behavioral and cognitive deficits associated with various lesions of the brain.

To give an overview of how neuropsychological research and techniques progressed and evolved over time, one needs to understand the contribution of three general components or phases. The first phase started with efforts to understand brain-behavior relationships by studying the cognitive and behavioral deficits found following focal lesions. Deficits found in these individuals were used to infer normal functions. For example, a large left inferior frontal lesion (Broca's area) caused a deficit in speech output. Thus, the area was inferred to be important in generating speech output. One of the first and most famous cases used in this manner was Phineas Gage (Damasio, Grabowski, Frank, Galaburda, & Damasio, 1994; Harlow, 1868). Gage sustained a large lesion in his prefrontal cortex (primarily orbito-frontal) when a tamping rod accidentally misfired and entered into his head from below his chin and exited through the top of his skull. Gage went on to develop what is now referred to as an orbito-frontal or *pseudo-psychopathic* syndrome.

Studying focal, localized lesions in humans has been going on for over 150 years and has become particularly refined over the past 30–40 years. Although this line of study has been extensively used in humans, there is a long and storied history of animal research that has contributed immensely to the understanding of neuropsychology. In fact, animal neuropsychology was a major force in the contribution to understanding brain-behavior relationships from the 1940s through the 1970s.

The second general phase to contribute to neuropsychology was the study of cytoarchitechtonics and the attempt to better understand brain-behavior relationships as they related to microscopic neuroanatomy (see Barbas & Pandya, 1989). The third and current phase entails in vivo neuroimaging of healthy volunteers. Techniques such as functional magnetic resonance imaging (fMRI), positron emission tomography (PET), regional cerebral blood flow (rCBF), single photon emitting computerized tomography (SPECT), evoked potentials (EP), and MEG have taken neuropsychology to a new level of understanding brain-behavior relationships by allowing us to study, in vivo, behavior in healthy individuals rather than inferring it from the deficits demonstrated by brain-injured individuals (see Goldberg, 2001, for a more detailed description of this method). So far, the evidence coming from fMRI research is generally confirming our findings from studies of lesions, but it is also revealing new and exciting (and sometimes counterintuitive) findings.

The following sections of this chapter discuss various developments and advances in neuropsychology, both clinical and experimental. We attempt to address some of the more current issues and advances—as well as problems—facing neuropsychology today.

DEVELOPMENTS IN CLINICAL APPLICATION

Clinical neuropsychology is in the midst of rapid and (in our opinion) historical change. Most of the change is positive, but some may not be so positive. In part, some of these changes are reactions to the shrinking health care dollar and its effect on psychology in general. Neuropsychologists have adapted and developed unique and novel responses to the lack of funding for neuropsychology and the reduction—and even elimination—of health care insurance for traditional mental health services. The two major clinical services to arise from this challenge are the neuropsychologist's involvement in the new and increasingly popular sports-related concussion assessment and return-to-play decision making and the phenomenal expansion of forensic neuropsychology.

Sports-Related Concussion Assessment

Although their involvement was virtually nonexistent 10 years ago, neuropsychologists are becoming ever more important in helping sport teams assess and manage sports-related concussions. One of the most exciting aspects is that this development is taking place at every level of competition: international, profession, collegiate, and high school. Neuropsychologists are becoming integral participants in the care of athletes who sustain concussions. The neuropsychologist's primary role is to diagnose the presence of concussion effect (e.g., cognitive deficits and symptomatology) and to use this information to help the team trainer and physicians determine when an athlete has recovered fully from the concussion and is able to return to play. One reason that this role has become so important is the amount of potential money involved. With the advent of multimillion dollar contracts, it becomes critical that players are cared for properly. See Echemendia and Julian (2001) for an extensive overview of the entire topic.

Sports-related concussions are no longer considered trivial injuries. Large epidemiological studies by Powell and others (Barth et al., 1989; Guskiewicz, Weaver, Padua, & Garrett, 2000; Powell, 1999; Powell & Barber-Foss, 1999) have shown that 5–10% of football players are concussed each year and approximately 5% from various others sports (e.g., soccer and field hockey). In American high school football alone, that would indicate approximately 25,500 concussions per season (a base rate of 2,460 concussions per 100,000 high school football players). Maroon et al. (2000) have shown that the rate of concussion in college athletes has decreased from about 10% per season (Barth et al., 1989) to about 4%, probably due to rule changes and new and improved equipment (Powell, 1999). Given these base rates, it is clear that there is a need for better diagnosis, management, and treatment. This area is exactly where clinical neuropsychology has played an integral part and is rapidly developing as the standard for measuring the effects of sports-related concussions and return-to-play issues (Aubry et al., 2002).

Besides opening a new area of clinical services and clientele, neuropsychology's role in sports-related concussion assessment and management has done a tremendous job of exposing various areas of clinical care and professional services (e.g., athletic trainers, physicians, and parents) to the expertise of clinical neuropsychology. For example, because of neuropsychology's role in sports-related concussion assessment, neuropsychologists are now presenting to and working with the sports-medicine community, athletic trainers, and other physicians who would not normally have been aware of or utilized this service. Neuropsychologists are publishing in journals that are not typical for them (e.g., *Journal of The American Medical Association, Journal of Sports Medicine, Physician and Sports Medicine*), broadening and increasing neuropsychology's exposure and prominence to an even greater degree.

One neuropsychologist who has led both clinical and experimental neuropsychologists into the area of sports-related concussion is Mark R. Lovell. Through his involvement with concussion committees for both the National Football League (NFL) and National Hockey League (NHL), neuropsychological testing is mandatory in the NHL, and approximately 80% of the NFL teams use neuropsychological testing. Additionally, colleges, high schools, and amateur and professional sports teams worldwide have concussion safety programs in which players undergo baseline testing during the preseason. If concussed during the season, a player is retested, and his or her results are compared to their baseline. This comparison allows for direct intra-individual changes, and the neuropsychologist can use the differences (or lack of differences) in scores to help the team with return-to-play decision making.

Lovell and Collins (1998) have demonstrated little change (outside of practice effect) in preseason versus postseason testing in varsity college football players. However, Collins et al. (1999) demonstrated that sports-related concussion in college football players caused significant decrement in memory and attention-concentration (consistent with the initial seminal studies of Barth (see Barth et al., 1989). In addition, Collins et al. (1999) found that after a concussion, those with a prior history of concussion performed more poorly than did those without a prior history of concussion. Moreover, they found that a history of learning disability was a risk factor for greater cognitive impairment following a concussion.

The standard protocol for performing neuropsychological evaluations in sports-related concussions is to use a serial assessment approach starting with a baseline (e.g., preseason or prior to any concussions) neuropsychological evaluation. Typically, these computerized neuropsychological batteries are relatively short (approximately 20–25 minutes, focusing on working memory, complex attention-concentration, reaction time, and anterograde memory). Although there are variations across institutions, typically a follow-up neuropsychological evaluation is performed within 24 hours of the concussion and is followed by additional postconcussion evaluations at Day 3, Day 5, and Day 7. After this point, if the athlete is still concussed, additional testing can be done weekly or even every other week. Various programs differ from this pattern, but the general idea is to perform a baseline evaluation, an initial postconcussion assessment, and additional follow-up assessments to document recovery of function and help with return-to-play decision making.

The role of neuropsychologists in sports-related concussions has expanded the understanding of concussions and their effects on and recovery of cognition and symptomatology. It has also increased concussion awareness in the general public—particularly parents—and has demystified some of the misconceptions about concussion and placed it alongside other common injuries (e.g., sprains) in sports. Neuropsychology has also improved how athletes' concussions are diagnosed, managed, and treated (see Collins & Hawn, 2002; Grindel, Lovell, & Collins, 2001). Today, concussions are no longer ignored; rather, they are diagnosed and treated as the injury they are. Because of this enlightened attitude and improved awareness and diagnostic accuracy, athletes—especially younger ones—are more accurately (and frequently) diagnosed and treated. This practice allows for appropriate treatment and decreased risk of greater injury by sustaining a second concussion while still concussed from the first one; this may help to reduce greater long-term brain injury and reduce the chance of second-impact syndrome—a rare but often fatal event (Cantu, 1998). Clearly, neuropsychologists' leadership role in this area has had and will continue to have a beneficial effect on these athletes.

Forensic Neuropsychology

Probably the single area within clinical neuropsychology that has seen the greatest growth explosion is forensic neuropsychology; this is due partly to the greater demand by the legal system for expert testimony that can identify neuropsychological deficits (Nies & Sweet, 1994) and also to the potentially lucrative income associated with forensic-related activity. The research related to this area has been explosive in the terms of the quality and wealth of information obtained so far. In just a few short years, the clinical techniques studied and developed have greatly enhanced neuropsychologists' ability to practice in this area.

The one area within forensic neuropsychology that has seen the greatest growth clinically is civil litigation—usually traumatic brain injuries suffered in motor vehicle accidents (Ruff & Richardson, 1999). In fact, motor vehicle accidents account for roughly half of the estimated 2 million traumatic brain injuries yearly (Krauss & McArthur, 1996). The following is a brief introduction into the area of clinical forensic neuropsychological assessment; we use mild traumatic brain injury (MTBI) as a model.

The crux of neuropsychology's involvement in forensic activity is to find evidence for or refute (through test performance) the presence of central nervous system (CNS) dysfunction. Often, standard neurological testing (such as CT or MRI of the brain and EEG) is insensitive to the subtle deficits of MTBI while neuropsychological deficits are present (Bigler & Snyder, 1995; Gronwall, 1991). Typically, considerable monetary compensation is sought in these cases, which augments the importance of the neuropsychological evaluation. Well over half of TBI cases are mild in nature (Ruff & Richardson, 1999). Although most people with MTBI fully recover, a minority of individuals (ranging from estimates of 7–8% to 10–20%) experience more long-term effects (Alexander, 1995; L. M. Binder, 1997). The constellation of subjective complaints often reported by individuals with MTBI has been termed the postconcussion syndrome (PCS). The most commonly reported symptoms include irritability, fatigue, difficulty concentrating, memory deficits, headache, dizziness, blurred vision, photophobia, ringing of the ears, and disinhibition and loss of temper (Lees-Haley & Brown, 1993). There has been a great deal of debate concerning persistent PCS; many suggest that it is psychologically rather than neurologically based or that patients are exaggerating or malingering symptoms in order to receive compensation (Mittenberg & Strauman, 2000; Youngjohn, Burrows, & Erdal, 1995). Because there is no litmus test to determine the presence of residual MTBI, it can become very difficult to differentiate those who truly have residual deficits from those without deficits who are exploiting their past (recovered) injury for monetary compensation solely based upon self-reported symptomatology. In fact, the base rates of self-reported symptomatology cannot distinguish between groups with verified MTBI from healthy controls or from those seeking compensation for non-TBI-related injuries (Lees-Haley & Brown 1993; Lees-Haley, Fox, & Courtney, 2001). Therefore, when this difficulty is combined with the lack of any neuroimaging evidence, the neuropsychologist becomes the key to determining and proving the presence of residual MTBI.

From a forensic perspective, the critical question is *Can a neuropsychologist, who applies various neuropsychological and psychological tests, differentiate between those who truly have residual cognitive or emotional deficits from those who are malingering, exaggerating, or even presenting with a somatoform or factitious disorder?* The task of detecting suboptimal performance carries a great responsibility because

the decision can determine whether services will be provided for a patient or whether the patient will receive large monetary compensation (Davies et al., 1997; Nies & Sweet, 1994). Although the rate of malingering is unknown, estimates range from 7.5–15% (Trueblood & Schmidt, 1993) to 18–33% (L. M. Binder, 1993). However, it is generally believed that the incidence of exaggeration of symptoms is higher than that of actual malingering (Resnick, 1988).

There are several ways in which neuropsychological testing can determine whether the test score actually represents a true cognitive deficit—or alternatively, whether it might indicate symptom exaggeration or even malingering. Some of the procedures or tests are more sophisticated and sensitive than others. First, and foremost, the deficits (one of the most common complaints is anterograde memory impairment) must be consistent with the nature of the injury. For example, one cannot have a dense amnesia if the traumatic brain injury was only mild. Similarly, the deficit patterns must make neuropsychological sense and conform to known brain-behavior relationships. For example, an individual complaining of worsening memory over time after a MTBI is not consistent with what is known about TBIs (that they are static events from which one can only recover—not worsen over time). Another method that neuropsychologists use to detect true versus malingered or exaggerated deficits is through the use of tests specifically designed to test for suboptimal performance.

Test development in the area of the assessment of malingering has flourished over the past several years, and significant strides have been made (see Iverson & Binder, 2000; Sweet, 1999, for comprehensive reviews). The sophistication of the tests developed and refined has improved greatly over the past few years; this is important because lawyers and the clients are becoming more sophisticated and aware of these tests. In fact, plaintiff attorneys have been known to coach their clients about these tests and prepare them for any independent neuropsychological evaluation they may undergo for the defense. Such practices have led some researchers to not publish some of their normative data in journal articles in order to protect the integrity and use of the tests (see Millis, Putnam, Adams, & Ricker, 1995; Sweet et al., 2000).

Forced-Choice Recognition Tests

There are a number of strategies typically employed to identify malingered performance. The first involves the use of a two-alternative forced-choice (e.g., five-digit numbers) method (Hiscock & Hiscock, 1989). When these tests were first designed and employed in clinical assessments, simple binomial distribution theory was applied to interpret performance. In two-choice recognition tests, the probability of responding correctly on all items by chance alone (i.e., guessing) is 50%. Scores significantly below that predicted by chance are unlikely by chance alone; therefore, such performance is assumed to be the result of deliberate selection of incorrect answers, which is suggestive of exaggeration or malingering of deficits. Without any knowledge of the stimulus (as would occur in the case of amnesia) the patient should answer approximately 50% of the items correctly; a score significantly below 50% suggests that the patient knew the correct answer but deliberately chose the incorrect response.

More recently, research has shown that patients with more severe head injury and genuine memory loss typically perform well above the chance level on two-alternative forced-choice tests (L. M. Binder & Pankrantz, 1987; L. M. Binder & Willis, 1991; Guilmette, Hart & Giuliano, 1993; Prigatano & Amin 1993). Prigatano and Amin (1993) demonstrated that the performance of postconcussive patients and those with unequivocal history of cerebral dysfunction averaged over 99% correct compared to a group of suspected malingerers who averaged only 73.8% correct. Guilmette et al. (1993) demonstrated that a group of brain-injured and psychiatric patients obtained almost perfect scores, whereas simulators obtained scores that were significantly lower. However, only 34% of the simulators obtained scores below chance level. These findings suggest that the development of cutoff scores is necessary in order to improve the sensitivity of this method. A 90% cutoff score has typically been established based on the large body of evidence, which suggests that those with genuine brain injury typically perform above this level on digit recognition procedures. A number of forced-choice tests have been developed and are briefly reviewed here; they include the Portland Digit Recognition Test (PDRT; L. M. Binder, 1993), the Victoria Symptom Validity Test (VSVT; Slick, Hopp, & Strauss, 1998), the Recognition Memory Test (RMT; Warrington, 1984), the Validity Indicator Profile (VIP; Frederick, 1997), the Computerized Assessment of Response Bias (CARB; Allen, Conder, Green, & Cox, 1998), and the Test of Memory Malingering (TOMM; Tombaugh, 1996).

Hiscock and Hiscock (1989) developed a test requiring individuals to choose which of two 5-digit numbers was the same as a number seen prior to a brief delay. The five-digit number is presented on a card for 5 s followed by a delay period, after which another card is presented with the correct choice and a foil. The foil items differed from the target item by two or more digits, including either the first or last digit. A total of 72 items are administered. These 72 items are divided into three blocks with either a 5-s, 10-s, or 15-s delay. The examiner tells the patient that the test is difficult for those with memory deficits and after the first and second blocks, that

the test will be more difficult because of the increasing delay period.

In an attempt to improve the test's sensitivity in detecting suboptimal performance, L. M. Binder (1993) refined the Hiscock and Hiscock procedure by developing the PDRT. It is a digit recognition task with three blocks of items differentiated by the length of delay between target presentation and response. Binder's version differed from that of Hiscock and Hiscock in a number of ways such as auditory presentation of the target item followed by visual presentation of the target and distractor item and increased delay periods between presentation and response (5 s, 15 s, and 30 s). Research suggests that difficult items (30-s delay) are more sensitive to malingered performance than are easy items (Hiscock & Hiscock, 1989). In addition, it has an intervening activity, which requires that the patient count backwards during the delay period. This activity makes the task appear even more difficult to the patient.

L. M. Binder (1992) found that non-compensation-seeking (NCS) patients with well-documented brain injury performed better than did both mild head trauma and compensation-seeking (CS) patients with well-documented brain injury on the PDRT, but that the CS brain-injured group's performance was superior to that of the mild head injury group on other tests. Binder (1993) administered the PDRT and the Rey Auditory Verbal Learning Test (RAVLT) to two groups of CS patients, including a mild head injury and well documented brain injury group and a group of NCS brain dysfunction patients. His results showed that patients with financial incentives were significantly more impaired on the PDRT but performed as well as the NCS groups did on the RAVLT. Binder and Willis (1991) demonstrated that those with affective disorders performed at a level similar to that of a group of NCS brain dysfunction patients, which suggests that the performance of the CS groups in this study was not the result of depression. Binder concluded that poor PDRT performance significant enough to raise concern about malingering is probably not caused by either verbal memory deficits or affective disorders, and the PDRT is therefore a useful tool for the detection of exaggerated memory deficits.

Vickery, Berry, Hanlon-Inman, Harris, and Orey (2001) performed a meta-analysis of a number of malingering procedures. The PDRT had high specificity rates at the level of individual classification (97.3%) but only moderate sensitivity (43.3%) because of a high number of performances that were poor but above chance level (Rose, Hall, & Szalda-Petree, 1995). One suggestion to improve the PDRT has been to measure the response latency (Brandt, 1988). It is expected that to purposely respond incorrectly to the test items require increased information processing time. Brandt used a computerized version of the test and found that when response latency and total number correct were used in combination, 32% fewer classification errors were made and overall hit rate increased from 72% to 81%. It was also demonstrated that coaching affected the total number correct in that all subjects scored above the cutoff; however, there was no difference in response latency.

Slick (Slick et al., 1998) also modified the Hiscock and Hiscock procedure. First, administration time was decreased by decreasing the number of items from 72 to 48, which are presented in three blocks of 16 items each. The delay period is increased in each block from 5 to 10 to 15 s. Item difficulty was manipulated by making items appear more difficult (i.e., similarity between the correct item and foils). Strauss et al. (1999) administered the VSVT to simulators and controls three times over a 3-week period. Simulators performed less consistently over the three administrations. Results demonstrated that on the hard items, a deviation of 3 points differentiated the control and malingering groups with 95% probability. A deviation of 1 point differentiated the groups with 95% probability on the easy items. Eighty-eight percent of the control group and 89% of the malingering group were correctly classified.

On the VSVT, both response latency and number correct are recorded. Slick, Hopp, Strauss, Hunter, and Pinch (1994) found that those who produced invalid profiles had significantly longer response latencies, again suggesting the usefulness of this measure. In addition, a new third category of classification is added. Performance below chance is still labeled invalid and performance significantly above chance is still labeled valid. The third category, *questionable,* consists of scores that fall within the remaining 90% confidence interval of chance performance. The three-category classification system has shown high specificity and good sensitivity (Slick et al., 1994).

The VIP (Frederick, 1997) is a computerized, two-alternative forced-choice procedure that incorporates a fourfold classification system based on two test-taking characteristics: motivation (to excel or fail) and effort (high or low). The combination of the concepts of motivation and effort generate four classification schemes; compliant (high effort and motivation), careless (high motivation to perform well but low effort to correctly respond), irrelevant (low effort when motivated to perform poorly), and malingering (high effort and motivation to perform poorly). Only the compliant profile is considered valid. The test contains both verbal (20 min) and nonverbal (30 min) subtests. The nonverbal subtest is a 100-item progressive matrix test modified from the Test of Nonverbal Intelligence (TONI; Brown, Sherbenou, & Johnson, 1982). The verbal subtest contains 78 two-alternative

word knowledge items. The VIP uses a performance curve analysis. The performance curve shows the average performance of the test taker across an increasingly difficult range of test items. Compliant responding results in a curve that starts at about 100% and remains at that level until the test taker reaches his or her ceiling of ability (as items increase in difficulty), at which time the curve goes through a period of transition until it results in about 50% correct performance (or random responding). As a result, performance curves for compliant test takers should be similar in shape regardless of ability levels.

Standard Clinical Tests

Although there have been several tests developed specifically to assess for malingering, several researchers have taken standard clinical tests and studied their ability to distinguish motivated from possibly malingering-exaggerating (or those acting as malingerers) and TBI patients. Some of the more commonly used tests today include the Wechsler Memory Scale–III (Scott Killgore & DellaPietra, 2000) the California Verbal Learning Test (Baker, Donders, & Thompson, 2000; Millis et al., 1995; Sweet et al., 2000), and Wisconsin Card Sorting Test (Suhr & Boyer 1999). Cutoff scores or patterns of performance have been developed that can be used to evaluate those with documented mild TBI.

The development of tests used to assess for suboptimal effort has greatly enhanced the neuropsychologist's ability to accurately detect malingering and thus sincere performance as well. The sophistication of these tests has undergone tremendous and rapid expansion over the past few years. However, a few interesting points should be made regarding the development of normative data for these tests as well as the appropriate application of these tests. First, it is almost impossible to *truly* find a known malingering group. By definition, these individuals are trying to fake brain impairment and thus do not admit to malingering. Therefore, the research used in developing these tasks and their normative data has primarily used groups trained to fake brain impairment or has compared groups of TBI patients matched for severity of injury but differing in CS status (e.g., CS vs. NCS). Although these substitutes are adequate and quite frankly the best that can be achieved, it does not allow for the assessment of a group of clearly defined true malingerers.

All of the aforementioned tests used to help determine level of motivation depend upon a conscious response by the subject. It is this response that is under the individual's control. It is up to the neuropsychologist to determine whether the response actually represents the true ability of the individual or whether it was suboptimal (i.e., possibly malingered or exaggerated). It would be helpful if a test that was able to determine malingering that was not under the conscious control of the client—something akin to a blood test—could be developed. In fact, cognitive evoked response potentials (ERPs) may be the closet thing we have to a cognitive blood test, so to speak (see Rosenfeld & Ellwanger, 1999, for a review). It has been proposed that cognitive ERP (P300) may be the involuntary psychophysiological test that cannot be faked by the individual and thus give one a window into true cognitive deficit or the lack thereof (Ellwanger, Rosenfeld, Sweet, & Bhatt, 1996; Rosenfeld, Ellwanger, & Sweet, 1995). Others have shown (see Ellwanger, Tenhulla, Rosenfeld, & Sweet, 1999) that the P300 amplitude is decreased in traumatic brain injury even if recognition memory is intact (Ellwanger, Rosenfeld, & Sweet, 1997). Since P300 is not under the conscious control of the client, then appropriate changes in P300 would indicate intact electrophysiological functioning, regardless of the client's response. Overall, the evidence suggests that P300 during recognition memory test or during an oddball auditory paradigm was able to accurately detect groups of simulated feigners of memory deficits—especially when it was used in conjunction with other neuropsychological tests of motivation-malingering (Ellwanger et al., 1999; Rosenfeld & Ellwanger, 1999; Tardif, Barry, Fox, & Johnstone, 2000).

One of the major shortfalls in the assessment of malingering is that almost all of these tests are designed for assessment of MTBI, and using them for other populations (e.g., malingering, depression, somatoform or conversion disorders) is difficult. Even if a patient scores in the impaired range on these tests, it is not a guarantee of a diagnosis of malingering; this is why many authors like to think of these tests as measuring suboptimal performance and not malingering, per se. For example, if an individual with MTBI seeking compensation performs near the chance level on a forced-choice recognition test, one can say that the test indicated suboptimal performance. However, one cannot conclude that the patient is malingering because issues of depression, anxiety, and even somatoform and conversion disorders could cause poor performance on these tests. Thus, the use of these tests is highly specific and can only be used with the populations for which they were intended, developed, and normed until experimental evidence is produced that supports their use and interpretation within other clinical populations.

Finally, the ability to detect malingering does not end with cognitive deficits. It typically extends into the assessment of affect and personality. Ample research has been performed with self-report personality questionnaires in determining malingering and distortion. The most commonly used self-report questionnaire, the Minnesota Multiphasic Personality

Inventory–2 (MMPI-2), has been researched extensively in terms of methodology and patterns in detecting malingering or distortion (see Ben-Porath, Graham, Hall, Hirschman, & Zaragoza, 1995). For example, the Fake Bad scale (Lees-Haley, English, & Glen, 1991) was designed to detect the endorsement of items rarely identified in known psychopathology. Also, a neurocorrection factor for use in traumatic brain injury patients (Gass, 1991) was developed to try to tease out items that are common in neurological samples (such as MTBI) but otherwise would inflate psychopathology level on the MMPI-2 scales.

The Personality Assessment Inventory (PAI; Morey, 1991) is becoming a widely used self-report personality questionnaire. Although the PAI is not as popular as the MMPI-2, it is an alternative the MMPI-2 and does have some differences that may serve as unique advantages. It is shorter (344 vs. 567 items). The PAI requires a fourth-grade reading level (the MMPI requires a sixth-grade reading level), uses a 4-point rating scale rather than in the true-false format of the MMPI-2, and its clinical scales are nonoverlapping. Most important, however, is that it has appropriate application in the forensic setting. Various authors have developed malingering scales that are very useful in detecting malingering, exaggeration, or minimalization of psychopathology (see Morey, 1996).

Neuropsychological assessments have other forensic applications in addition to civil litigation. For example, neuropsychologists are often asked to perform assessments to help determine issues of guardianship and conservatorship. From a legal perspective, individuals can be assessed to determine their ability to make independent decisions in medical treatment, finances, and caring for themselves. Daniel Marson has applied the legal standards (that vary by state) to these issues and developed a battery of cognitive-based tasks capable of answering these questions (Dymek, Atchison, Harrell, & Marson, 2001; Earnst, Marson, & Harrell, 2000; Marson 2001; Marson, Annis, McInturff, Bartolucci, & Harrell, 1999; Marson, Chatterjee, Ingram, & Harrell, 1996; Marson, Cody, Ingram, & Harrell, 1995). This area is important for future research in neuropsychological assessment.

ISSUES IN NEUROPSYCHOLOGICAL ASSESSMENT

Within general neuropsychological assessment, there are new developments worth mentioning. In general, test development has become more rigorous over the years, and many of the standard tests have been redesigned and renormed. Moreover, some specific developments—particularly in the areas of computerized assessment and the development of novel assessment techniques—have made some rather significant impacts on the advancement of clinical neuropsychology.

Assessment in clinical neuropsychology historically can trace its roots back to two lines of development that (roughly speaking) can be separated into a North American camp and a European-Russian camp. The European and Russian group based their assessments mainly on qualitative features that were developed over time studying brain injured patients. This approach is very much in the Lurian tradition of neuropsychological assessment. The North American approach is quantitative in nature and has it foundations in more experimentally and empirically based test design. The Halstead-Reitan Neuropsychological Test Battery (Reitan & Wolfson, 1993) is the quintessential example of a strictly formal psychometric approach in neuropsychological assessment. In this approach, all types of patients receive the same tests administered in the exact same way every time. Their data are based almost exclusively on the numerical tests scores. Interpretation is based upon actuarial predictions for diagnosis (see Lezak, 1995, pp. 146–151).

Although there has been much debate over which assessment technique is better—qualitative or quantitative (see Lezak, 1995, pp. 146–151)—there clearly has been a merging of these two camps over time. Edith Kaplan and Muriel Lezak have probably been the most influential in merging both qualitative and quantitative aspects into current-day clinical neuropsychological assessments. Therefore, some of the developments in clinical neuropsychological testing have to do with combining both qualitative and quantitative features.

In addition to merging qualitative and quantitative aspects of testing, other neuropsychological tests have emerged that represent a blending of various specialties within psychology (e.g., educational psychology), as well as combining complex theoretical models of cognition. For example, the Cognitive Assessment System (Naglieri & Das, 1997) is designed to measure basic cognitive processes, including attention-concentration and executive control. It integrates the assessment of cognitive processes from a Lurian perspective with the advantages of a psychometric tradition using a well-developed theory (PASS; planning, attention, simultaneous, and successive processes) and applies the results, often—but not exclusively—in an educational setting (see Naglieri, 1999).

Computerized Assessment

Neuropsychological testing, like most assessments in psychology, has traditionally been conducted with paper-and-pencil tests; however, more and more neuropsychological testing is becoming computerized. Although computerization has made scoring much simpler and more accurate, it has also allowed for more complicated computations and thus more sophisticated and powerful clinical applications. However, the actual computerization of test administration has had the greatest impact. There are some clear and basic advantages to computerized assessment. First, it allows for more efficient and standardized testing. For example, it allows for more accurate reaction time measurement, which is important when testing higher order attention and concentration; also, it can allow for better randomization of stimuli. Computerized test administration can be very economical because it decreases costs and allows for group administration at times (i.e., less need for a technician-based administration). However, as usual, there are some disadvantages as well. It can be rather inflexible, which can lead to problems testing brain-injured individuals or individuals who do not understand test instructions (especially in a group administration setting). Computerized testing can also reduce the ability to pick up qualitative features of test performance, which are more easily detected with paper-and-pencil testing. What will most likely evolve (and is actually being done in most clinical settings at present) is a combination of both paper-and-pencil and computerized testing.

Although it is beyond the scope of this paper to review the full array of computerized neuropsychological assessment, it is worth mentioning its use in one particular area. Neuropsychologists working within sports-related concussion have developed basic assessment techniques to assess and measure the extent of concussion (as defined as decrements in cognitive abilities). Initially, paper-and-pencil tests were used (see Lovell & Collins, 1998), but because of practice effects, accuracy measuring reaction time, and high costs, computerized assessment has become the new standard. Using generic computerized testing techniques (Automated Neuropsychological Assessment Metrics, or ANAM; Reeves, Kane, & Winter, 1996), Joseph Bleiberg and others have demonstrated the cognitive deficits following a concussion and mild traumatic brain injury (Bleiberg, Halpern, Reeves, & Daniel, 1998; Bleiberg, Kane, Reeves, Garmoe, & Halpern, 2000; Warden et al., 2001).

Others have developed specific computerized test batteries specifically designed for use in sports-related concussion work. For example, the Immediate Post-Concussion Assessment and Cognitive Testing (ImPACT; see Maroon et al., 2000) consists of seven modules assessing working memory, anterograde memory, simple and complex reaction time, and impulsivity. It also assesses concussion symptomatology. It was designed to be very easy to administer (so it can be given by athletic trainers), it requires minimal English skills (for athletes for whom English is second language), and it is very sensitive to the effects of concussion. It can be group administered and uses computer-randomized stimuli to create up to five equivalent versions to minimize practice effects with repeat administration. ImPACT uses self-report symptomatology along with scores from memory, reaction time, and impulsivity indexes derived from the individual modules.

Paper-and-Pencil Testing

Although computerized assessment is a new and viable approach, the crux of neuropsychological assessment still depends upon the use of paper-and-pencil testing. Some of the more popular tests continually undergo refinement, redevelopment, and renorming (e.g., the Wechsler Memory Scale and Wechsler Adult Intelligence Scale; Psychological Corporation, 1997). In fact, test developers are being sensitive to the need for shorter, yet still reliable tests (in response to managed care) and are trying to develop such instruments. A few examples would be the Wechsler Abbreviated Scale of Intelligence (WASI; Psychological Corporation, 1999), Kaufman Brief Intelligence Test (K-BIT; Kaufman & Kaufman, 1990), and the General Ability Measure for Adults (GAMA; Naglieri & Bardos, 1997).

Another area in which paper-and-pencil test development has seen some advancement is in the quantification of qualitative aspects of impaired neuropsychological performance. Several prominent neuropsychologists (for example, A. R. Luria and Edith Kaplan) had for decades expressed the importance of understanding *how* the patient responded and not just with *what* the patient responded. In the past, one had to have years of experience in order to develop the skills to perform qualitative analysis. Even then, these skills often differed from practitioner to practitioner. However, some tests have been developed in order to quantify these qualitative features that are often so important in neuropsychological assessments. Edith Kaplan, for example, authored the Wechsler Adult Intelligence Scale—Revised Neuropsychological Investigation. Other tests such as the Boston Qualitative Scoring System for the Rey Complex Figure Test (R. A. Stern et al., 1999) also is an attempt at quantifying various qualitative features found in the responses of brain injured patients. The Executive Control Battery (ECB; Goldberg, Podell, Bilder, & Jaeger, 2000) was developed in order to quantify various features of executive control deficits often not assessed in other, more frequently used, measures of executive control skills (e.g., Wisconsin Card Sorting Test).

Clearly, the development of tests assessing qualitative features has improved neuropsychological testing. However, neuropsychological tests in general are limited in measuring ability only. To take the assessment of qualitative features one

step further, it would be important to understand not only *ability* (i.e., whether the subject could get the correct answer) but perhaps the subject's *preference* in choosing. At times—particularly in brain-injured patients—it is as important to understand an individual's preference when given a choice in problem solving as it is to understand the ability level per se. For example, we know that patients with prefrontal lobe damage have extreme difficulty functioning in everyday life and sometimes cannot complete basic daily skills, but they still maintain intact cognitive abilities (see Goldberg, 2001, for an eloquent description of these types of deficits). Thus, it may not be the individual's ability per se that interferes with daily functioning, but rather their preference, or in the case of brain injured person, the inability to make the appropriate choice.

Goldberg and colleagues (Goldberg & Podell, 1999; Goldberg, Podell, Harner, Lovell, & Riggio, 1994), studied the effects of lateralized prefrontal lesions and developed a task specifically designed to assess a person's response preference rather than ability. The Cognitive Bias Task (Goldberg & Podell, 2001) entails a simple, forced-choice perceptual discrimination task with rather ambiguous instructions. After seeing a target card, participants are presented with two stimulus cards and must choose the one they like the best. Of the two stimulus choice cards, one is perceptually more similar to and one is perceptually more different from the target card. The task is set up so that the individual must decide which way he or she is going to respond—more similar to or more different from the target card. There is no feedback after a response. The ambiguity of the instructions is central to making the task a test of preference rather than ability. In fact, it is this ambiguity that allowed Goldberg and colleagues to demonstrate some of the essential cognitive differences between right and left prefrontal functioning as well as a significant gender difference. When the instructions are disambiguated (e.g., choose the more similar or more different stimulus card), all of the subjects—even patients with prefrontal cortical lesions—performed the tasks well. Thus, it was not an issue of ability (e.g., intact performance with disambiguated instructions), but rather preference (e.g., difference with ambiguous instructions).

RECENT ADVANCEMENTS IN PSYCHOMETRIC APPLICATIONS

Neuropsychologists are typically asked to look at changes in cognitive abilities over time as they relate to a disease process (e.g., dementia), recovery of function (e.g., TBI), or following surgical intervention (e.g., temporal lobectomy for intractable seizure disorder). However, many clinical neuropsychologists (as well as psychologists in general) do not apply well-established, empirically based statistical procedures for determining whether the differences in tests actually represent a *true* (i.e., statistically reliable) change or rather one that can be explained simply by test-retest variance. We believe that this issue is central and pertinent to the practice of clinical neuropsychology and thus worthy of some detailed discussion. Another important development in this area for neuropsychology is the use of receiver operant curves (ROC) in determining the sensitivity of a test. Historically, research using neuropsychological tests has relied on strictly using weaker, discriminant analyses and not relying upon more sophisticated methods such as ROC. As is discussed in the following sections, one can see that the use of more sophisticated statistical methods such as ROC is starting to come of age in neuropsychological research.

Reliability of Change Indexes

Repeated administrations of neuropsychological tests frequently yield varying results, even in people who have not experienced any true change in cognitive functioning (Temkin, Heaton, Grant, & Dikmen, 1999). There are a number of reasons for this variance, including less than perfect reliability of test instruments, less than optimally standardized test administration, fluctuations in a patient's performance related to motivational issues, mood, health status, and so on. The relative contribution of these factors is almost always different for different tests. Many clinical neuropsychologists use a seat-of-the-pants approach to determine whether changes are to be considered significant; they simply examine the change in scores and decide whether the difference is significant based on clinical experience and a basic knowledge of statistics. Others use various rules of thumb, such as the change in test scores must be greater than one half standard deviation of a test's normative sample to be considered significant. Obviously, these methods are highly susceptible to error and seem to occur most often in the direction of concluding that a change is significant when it is in fact not statistically significant.

Any change from one testing occasion to another is considered to be significant if the magnitude of the change is sufficiently large relative to the associated error variance of the test. Determination of the error variance is based on test-retest reliability and variation about the mean of the test (Jacobson & Truax, 1991). Statistical approaches to determining the significance of a change in test scores are based on predicting the likely range of scores that would be obtained if there were no real change in cognitive functioning. Statistical approaches to predicting scores on retest with concomitant prediction or confidence intervals are much more likely to be accurate and

unbiased than is the seat-of-the-pants approach or rules of thumb. Even so, it is not entirely clear what statistical approach is best suited for predicting subsequent scores on a given measure. There is not even a clear consensus about the factors that should be considered in a prediction model beyond the baseline test score and test-retest reliability. Test factors beyond test-retest reliability may be important, such as internal consistency, susceptibility to practice effects, and test floors and ceilings. Potentially important participant variables include age, education, overall level of neuropsychological test performance at baseline, health status, mood, test-taking attitude, medication and other drug use, and various cognitive risk factors.

The prediction interval is the range of scores around the predicted score that is considered to include scores that would likely be obtained if there is no true change in the characteristic being tested. The prediction interval is sometimes known as the confidence interval. For purposes of determining whether there has been change in functioning over time, the size of the interval is based partly on the standard error of difference (S_{diff}) between the two test scores. This in turn is typically based on the standard deviation of scores in the control group and the test's stability coefficient (test-retest reliability). The size of the prediction interval is also based on the clinician or researcher's judgment as to the level of certainty desired. Intervals typically contain 90% of the differences between actual and predicted test scores in a cognitively intact or stable sample (Temkin et al., 1999). The intervals are usually defined so that in a stable sample, 5% of the individuals will be considered to show significant deterioration and 5% will show significant improvement. Intervals of other sizes and the use of one-tailed tests of significance may be more appropriate depending upon the goals of the researcher or clinician (Hinton-Bayre, Geffin, Geffen, McFarland, & Friss, 1999; Jacobson & Truax, 1991).

Various models for determining the significance of changes in test scores have been presented in the research literature. The models have become more sophisticated and the number of potentially important variables considered has increased as this research area has evolved. Early models consisted of simply dividing the change in test scores by the standard error of difference between the two test scores (Christensen & Mendoza, 1986). This value is considered to represent significant change if it exceeds the RC *z* score cut point corresponding to the desired level of certainty. The next step in the evolution of determining the significance of changes involved taking practice effects into account (Chelune, Naugle, Luders, Sedlak, & Awad, 1993). Performance on many neuropsychological measures is expected to improve with subsequent testing simply because of increased familiarity with the material and because strategies to improve performance are often learned.

Another method of determining the significance of changes in test scores is linear regression, which can correct for regression to the mean as well as practice effects (McSweeny, Naugle, Chelune, & Luders, 1993, cited in Temkin et al., 1999). As Atkinson (1991) noted, the obtained score is not the best estimate of an individual's true score because of the tendency for a person with a score that deviates from the mean to obtain a score closer to the mean on a randomly parallel form to the test. The discrepancy between obtained and predicted true scores will be greater when the obtained score is more extreme, and the discrepancy will be less with tests that are more reliable. Another reason for using predicted true scores is that the original or classic RC index makes the statistical assumption that the error components are normally distributed with a mean of zero and that standard errors of measurement of the difference score are equal for all participants (Maassen, 2000). Temkin et al. (1999) presented a model that uses stepwise linear regression to predict retest scores using additional factors that might be important. These factors included the test-retest interval; various demographic variables including age, education, sex, and race; and a measure of overall neuropsychological competence at baseline. They also explored the possibility of a nonlinear relationship between test and retest scores by including the square and the cube of the initial score in the variable selection as well as the square and the cube of the test-retest interval.

Temkin et al. (1999) compared the exemplars of the various models for assessing the significance of change on several neuropsychological tests using multiple measures of prediction accuracy. They also examined the distribution of the residuals and presented distribution-free intervals for those that had particularly nonnormal distributions, and they explored whether prediction accuracy was constant across different levels of predictor variables. They found that initial test performance is the most powerful predictor of follow-up test performance. For example, they found that for the representative measures from the Halstead-Reitan Neuropsychological Test Battery that they analyzed, initial scores alone accounted for 67% to 88% of the variance in follow-up test scores. The addition of other predictors in the multiple regression model increased explained follow-up test scores between 0.8% and 8.5%. In general, demographic variables tended to exert additional influences on follow-up scores in the same direction as they did on initial test scores. For example, older and less well-educated participants tended to perform worse on follow-up than did younger and better educated participants with the same initial test scores. Perhaps surprising to many

clinicians is the finding that practice effects do not decrease very much over the 2- to 16-month time frame considered in these studies (Temkin et al., 1999).

Temkin et al. (1999) noted that of the four models they compared, the original RC index performed least well. They considered this model inadequate because of its wide prediction intervals and its poor prediction accuracy. The RC model with correction for practice effects had much better prediction accuracy, but of course the size of the prediction interval is not affected. In fact, the overall prediction accuracy of the RC model with correction for practice effects was similar to that of the multiple regression model, although there were large differences in predicted retest scores at the extremes of initial test performance and extremes of general neuropsychological competence at baseline. For practical purposes, the differences in the size of the prediction intervals are not always clinically significant. For example, the prediction interval size for WAIS Verbal IQ using the regression model with all predictors was only 0.2 IQ points smaller in each direction (improved and deteriorated) than was the RC index. A larger difference was noted between the two methods for the Halstead Category Test, with a difference of 3.6 errors in each direction. The difference was yet more pronounced when distribution-free intervals were computed for tests with scores that are not normally distributed, such as Trails B and the Tactual Performance Test.

Various authors have reached different conclusions about the most appropriate methods for determining the reliability of change scores. For example, Temkin et al. (1999) concluded from their study that simple models perform less well than do more complex models with patients that are relatively more impaired and those whose demographic characteristics are associated with lower absolute levels of performance. They suggest that because the patients seen in clinical settings are more likely than healthy individuals to obtain relatively extreme test scores, the complex prediction models are likely to be even more advantageous than demonstrated in their study.

Maassen (2000) reached a different conclusion based on theoretical and conceptual considerations. He compared null hypothesis methods, of which the original RC index (originally developed by Jacobson, Follette, & Revenstorf, 1984 and refined by Christensen & Mendoza, 1986) is derived to estimation interval methods, which include the regressed score approach. Although he acknowledges that both general methods probably lead to the same interpretation of observed change, he noted that the probability that observed changes will be erroneously deemed reliable with the null hypothesis method is limited by a low level of significance. This method rules out with high probability that measurement error is a possible explanation for observed change. In contrast, there is no uniform upper limit for the probability of an incorrect conclusion with the estimation interval methods. Trivial effects could potentially lead to an observed change, or even lack of change, being deemed reliable. In fact, an observed change in one direction could be interpreted as reliable change in the other direction.

There are other considerations for the practicing clinical neuropsychologist. For example, the average clinician is highly unlikely to have the data and the necessary time and skills to develop regression models for the other tests that he or she uses in clinical practice. In contrast, the manuals for most standardized tests contain the stability coefficients required for determination of RC indexes with or without practice effects. These approaches are very likely to be much more reliable than a seat-of-the-pants approach or a rule of thumb. Chelune et al. (1993) pointed out another important consideration for the clinician. The formulas that have been developed to date are only concerned with the reliability of change in single test scores. Clinicians very rarely base conclusions about changes in cognitive or other functioning based on a single change score. Rather, they look at patterns of change across a number of tests in a battery. The co-occurrence of two or more changes in the same direction is more reliable and robust than are changes on a single measure (Chelune, Prititera, & Cheek, 1992, cited in Chelune et al., 1993). Two or more change scores that are each not statistically significant in themselves may represent reliable change when considered together. It is of course important to consider the statistical independence of the scores. The fact that two or more related scores from the same test have changed in the same direction inspires much less confidence than do consistent changes across different tests.

Receiver Operating Curves

Most assessment in clinical neuropsychology is geared toward description of a client's overall level of functioning and the pattern of his or her cognitive strengths and weaknesses across multiple cognitive domains (and tests). However, there are times when a particular test is administered to address dichotomous questions, such as whether a particular condition is present or absent. Within clinical neuropsychology, this goal is most often realized with screening tests. In this case, a certain level of performance is taken to suggest the presence of a condition such as dementia or depression. It is also utilized for the assessment of response bias or malingering.

Receiver operating characteristic (ROC) curves describe the accuracy of a test as it relates to the sensitivity and specificity of different scores. ROC curves help the user decide what constitutes normal and abnormal or pathological performance. Virtually no test can discriminate between normal and pathological with 100% accuracy because the distributions of normal and pathological performances overlap. A score in the overlap area might belong to either the normal or the pathological distribution. Consequently, test users choose a cutoff score. Scores on one side of the cutoff are presumed to be normal and the scores on the other side are presumed to be pathological. The position of the cutoff determines the number of true positives, true negatives, false positives, and false negatives. The exact cutoff chosen is based on the particular use of a test and the user's assessment of the relative costs of different types of erroneous decisions.

The sensitivity of a cutoff score refers to the proportion of results considered positive relative to the proportion of the sample that is actually part of the positive distribution. In other words, increasing sensitivity results in an increasing number of true positives, but it does so at the expense of also increasing the number of false positives. Conversely, the specificity of a cutoff score refers to the proportion of results considered negative relative to the proportion of the sample that is actually part of the negative distribution. In other words, increasing specificity reduces the number of false positives at the expense of also increasing the number of false negatives. There is always a trade-off between sensitivity and specificity. Increasing sensitivity will always result in reduced specificity and increasing specificity will always result in reduced sensitivity.

ROC curves are plots of a test's sensitivity or true positive rate along the y axis against (1 – specificity) or false positive rate along the x axis (Tape, 2001). ROC curves graphically demonstrate the trade-off between sensitivity and specificity. The area under the curve is a measure of test accuracy or the potential discriminability of a test. Tests that are more accurate are characterized by ROC curves that closely follow the left-hand border and then the top border of the ROC space. Less accurate tests are characterized by ROC curves that more closely follow a 45° diagonal from the bottom left to the upper right of the ROC space. An area of 1.0 represents a perfect test, whereas an area of 0.5 represents a worthless test (see Figure 19.1).

ROC curve analysis is primarily used in research to compare tests or test indexes. For example, Nicholson et al. (1997) used ROC analysis to evaluate and compare MMPI-2 indicators of response distortion. Storey, Rowland, Basic, and Conforti (2001) compared different clock drawing scoring methods with ROC curve analysis, and Barr and McCrea (2001) used it to determine a test's sensitivity for detecting

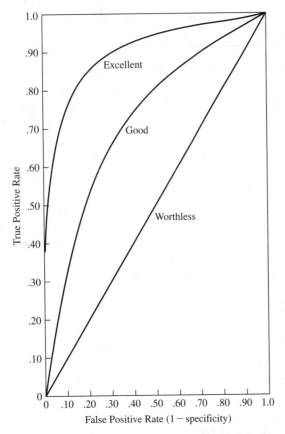

Figure 19.1   Example of a receiver operating characteristic curve.

concussion. The major use of ROC curves for practicing clinical neuropsychologists is in test selection. An ROC curve provides valuable information about the ability of a test to discriminate between normal and pathological or between sufficient and insufficient effort. An ROC curve also provides information about the trade-off between sensitivity and specificity, and it is helpful in guiding decisions about the most appropriate cutoff score to use in a particular situation (e.g., Barr & McCrea, 2001).

Positive and Negative Predictive Power

One final statistical area in which neuropsychology is beginning to show improved sophistication is in the application of positive and negative predictive power in looking at clinical assessment tests' sensitivity and specificity. Historically, neuropsychological research depended upon discriminant analyses when looking at tests' sensitivity and specificity. However, to accurately determine sensitivity and specificity, one must take into account base rates for the clinical population or trait being used or measure; because discriminant

analysis alone does not do this, then a test's true sensitivity and specificity are not truly being measured.

Meehl and Rosen (1955) showed that the probability of valid classifications depends on the base rate or prevalence of the disorder in the clinical sample and that the base rate represents the proportion of valid test positives due to chance alone. They showed that under certain conditions, even tests with very good sensitivity and specificity can result in more classification errors than does chance alone. The sensitivity of a test is most misleading for the clinician when the base rate of a disorder is very low, and the specificity is most misleading when the base rate is very high. Rather than using inflexible cutoffs, Meehl and Rosen argued that cutoffs should be adjusted to local base rates to maximize the probability of valid test discriminations.

Two statistics that are related to sensitivity and specificity but better address the clinician's needs are positive predictive power (PPP) and negative predictive power (NPP). These statistics take the base rates of a disorder into account. PPP is defined as the number of true positives divided by the total number of true and false positives. Similarly, NPP is defined as the number of true negatives divided by the total number of true and false negatives. PPP and NPP are reciprocally influenced by prevalence. A lower prevalence rate results in a loss of PPP and a gain in NPP (Elwood, 1993). Although sensitivity and specificity are independent of prevalence, they are still related to PPP and NPP. A loss of specificity (i.e., an increase in false positives) results in reduced PPP, whereas a loss of sensitivity (i.e., an increase in false negatives) results in reduced NPP.

NEUROIMAGING

With the advent and refinement of various neuroimaging techniques and technology, a new opportunity has opened up for neuropsychology. Initially, neuroimaging was very static and limited to dry (structural) anatomy. Although these earlier methodologies—head X rays, pneumoencephalography, CT scanning and static MRI—were progressive and very useful clinically, they were only capable of eliciting correlative data regarding brain structure and brain functioning.

Modern, state-of-the-art neuroimaging techniques such as SPECT, PET, fMRI, magnetic resonance spectroscopy (MRS), and magnetoencephalography (MEG) have drastically advanced our level of understanding of brain-behavior relationships. In essence, we went from a static, correlative model of matching neuropsychological findings to lesions on CT-MRI or EEG to a more dynamic-causative model through understanding cause and effect in healthy subjects. These technological breakthroughs have expanded our understanding of brain-behavior relationships not only from a scientific-research perspective, but also in terms of clinical applications.

What is unique about functional neuroimaging and neuropsychology is the interdependence they have upon each other. Functional neuroimaging has evolved beyond simple motor-sensory paradigms, and in order to use its full potential, it must rely upon sophisticated neuropsychology paradigms to elicit brain activation in heteromodal cortices and limbic regions (required for complex cognition, memory, and behavior). In the past, although static neuroimaging and neuropsychology were helpful to each other, they were not functionally dependent upon each other and often functioned in separate vacuums. Because we already knew the correlative findings between brain lesion location and deficit, static neuroimaging was all that was needed to infer deficit. However, functional neuroimaging changed all of this. Scientists can now directly test hypotheses of brain-behavior relationships (both experimentally and clinically) and use fundamental experimental psychology principles of manipulating an IV (neuropsychological paradigms) and assess change in the DV (brain activation) rather than correlating changes in test scores with lesion location (as has been the tradition with static neuroimaging). Thus, in order to use functional neuroimaging, especially fMRI, one needs the appropriate cognitive paradigms (unique to the knowledge base of neuropsychologists) in order to elicit brain activation.

Functional neuroimaging has already added an incredible amount of scientific information about brain-behavior relationships and has the potential for adding much more. However, there is also significant clinical application for functional neuroimaging. Probably the best example of this application would be the use of fMRI as a replacement technique for the intracarotid amobarbital procedure (IAP; also referred to as the Wada procedure). The IAP technique is an assessment technique used in the presurgical evaluation for intractable epilepsy (i.e., anterior temporal lobe resections for an intractable seizure disorder). During the IAP, sodium amobarbitol is injected into the carotid arteries in order to anaesthetize each cerebral hemisphere separately to assess for language laterality and memory abilities. Although the Wada is well tested and considered the standard of care in presurgical workups, it is a somewhat invasive procedure that has some risks and limitations. The use of fMRI has been explored and is starting to be used experimentally to determine its efficacy in the evaluation of language laterality (J. R. Binder et al., 1996; Brockway, 2000; Hirsch et al., 2000;

Lehericy et al., 2000) and activation of modality-specific memory systems (Detre et al., 1998; W. D. Killgore et al., 1999). Tantamount to the method's success is the development of the appropriate cognitive assessment paradigms developed by neuropsychologists.

Perhaps one of the most influential findings to come from functional neuroimaging is proof of the concept that complex (and even not-so-complex) behaviors and cognition require the integration of many different brain regions configured into rather large and complex neural systems or networks. This finding clearly dispels the notion of neuropsychological isomorphism between behavior and neuroanatomy (i.e., that discrete areas of the brain were responsible for one and only one function) and the concept of modularity of brain organization. Also, functional neuroimaging—particularly fMRI—is starting to address such issues as cognitive efficiency and how it relates to brain activation (such that more efficient processing requires less activation). Prior to this technological development, such topics were left up to theoretical discussion only.

The following sections are very brief overviews of particular clinical areas or cognitive processes currently being studied using functional neuroimaging.

Language

Functional neuroimaging in normal populations has gone beyond the early focus on primary motor and sensory areas and is now exploring more complex, integrative regions of the brain (secondary unimodal zones and heteromodal or tertiary zones). The studies most related to neuropsychological issues are language, memory, and executive functions. These functional activation studies are aimed at elucidating specificity of functions in underlying neural networks. Beyond the classical language areas of Broca's and Wernicke's new areas continue to be identified. Regions contiguous to these known areas of expressive and receptive speech also play important roles in language. New areas identified as playing important roles with receptive language include the middle temporal, inferior temporal, fusiform, supramarginal, and angular gyri. The role of the insular cortex in the rapidity of automatized phonological processing is noteworthy for facilitating fluent reading (Shaywitz et al., 1995). There are emerging data as to gender differences and the functional organization of language (Frost et al., 1997). Similarly, the neural circuitry involved in complex visual object recognition and semantic memory has been mapped using fMRI (Ishai, Ungerleider, Martin, & Haxby, 2000; see Martin & Chao, 2001). It is interesting to note that their findings indicate that the cortical areas involved in recalling the names of objects are located near the representation of the physical attributes for the objects. This finding indicates a highly complex distributed network rather than isolated, modular areas of storage.

Executive Control and Memory

Another area extremely important in neuropsychology is memory processing. The supervisory attentional system or central executive that modulates the verbal and visual-spatial aspects of short-term memory are a major area of study. fMRI studies can quantitatively assess relationships between brain activation states and higher cognition. The role of the dorso-lateral prefrontal cortex (DLPFC) in the shifting, planning, and organizing of mental processes has been demonstrated by various experimental paradigms (Nystrom et al., 2000). The registration of novel information (i.e., anterograde memory processing) and subsequent transfer from short-term storage to long-term storage have been confirmed through fMRI studies showing activation of the bilateral posterior hippocampal formations, parahippocampal gyri, and fusiform gyri (C. E. Stern et al., 1996), whereas the anterior hippocampus may be preferentially involved memory encoding (see Schacter & Wagner, 1999). Similarly, others have identified other brain areas involved in memorial processes (primarily prefrontal and mesial temporal structures) and thus have started to show the complex brain circuitry involved in memory (see Buckner, Logan, Donaldson, & Wheeler, 2000; Cabeza & Nyberg, 2000; Fletcher & Henson, 2001).

Schizophrenia

Since the work of Andreasen and colleagues in the early 1990s, we have obtained objective, empirical evidence of structural anomalies associated with schizophrenia (Andreasen, Ehrhardt, et al., 1990; Andreasen et al., 1993; Andreasen et al., 1997). The dilatation of ventricular size in these patients was the earliest potential link between underlying neuropathological changes and psychiatric manifestations. Subsequent MRI studies (Chua & McKenna, 1995) replicated the findings of increased lateral and third ventricle enlargement in persons diagnosed with schizophrenia. Ventricular brain ratio (VBR) increases were seen most often with persons diagnosed with chronic schizophrenia who consequently had smaller frontal lobes, along with temporal lobe asymmetries and changes related to the size and surface area of the planum temporale and reduction in size and volume of the corpus callosum (Andreasen, Swayze, et al., 1990). Subcortical increases in gray matter in the basal ganglia were also reported (Hokama et al., 1995). Neuropsychological deficit patterns seem to be

linked to structural anomalies within the DLPFC, with the left hemisphere demonstrating more significant changes (Lawrie et al., 1997). PET studies over the last two decades have isolated functional metabolic changes through the use of radioactive isotopes such as 2-fluorodeoxyglucose (2-FDG 0^{15}). A diminution in glucose metabolism was seen in various regions of the frontal lobes of schizophrenic patients. This hypofrontality became a functional neuroradiological marker associated with this disease entity. Neuropsychological testing of these patients revealed dysexecutive functioning and anterograde memory impairment as associated neurobehavioral sequelae. These neuropsychological findings seem directly related to these metabolic lesions, which may be at the root of the poor reality testing—that is, delusional thinking and disorganized ability to connect cognition to emotions. Recent fMRI research is confirming prefrontal dysfunction on tasks of working memory (Perlstein, Carter, Noll, & Cohen, 2001). See Meyer-Lindenberg and Berman (2001) for a review prefrontal dysfunction in schizophrenia.

Affective Disorders

Structural and functional deviations were also seen on neuroimaging studies of affective disorders (unipolar and bipolar types; Videbech, 1997). The expanded width of the third ventricle and volume reductions of the basal ganglia were notable. Functional imaging with a number of radioisotopes demonstrated pathological changes associated with affective disorders. For depression, left (inferior) prefrontal region and anterior cingulate gyrus hypometabolism is a hallmark finding (see Bench, Friston, Brown, Frackowiak, & Dolan, 1993; Podell, Lovell, & Goldberg, 2001; and Mayberg, 2001, for reviews). The neuropsychological and neuroimaging data collectively demonstrated cognitive sequelae linked to metabolic changes within specific brain regions and their interconnecting neural networks. The bilateral inferior frontal gyri and right anterior cingulate gyrus seem to be implicated in the emotional aspects of behavior (George et al., 1993). Patients with elated and depressed moods demonstrated dysfunctional cognition on verbal fluency tasks. Associated metabolic changes were seen in the thalamus, cingulate gyrus, premotor and prefrontal cortices of the left hemisphere (see Mayberg, 2001).

In studies of generalized anxiety disorder (GAD), there were hypermetabolic changes in the frontal, temporal, and parietal corticies, and reductions were seen in the metabolic state of the basal ganglia. Relative to healthy controls, subjects with obsessive compulsive disorder (OCD) demonstrated metabolic increases in the head of the caudate nucleus and orbital gyri. SSRI treatments of OCD patients showed metabolic decreases in the entire cingulate gyrus (Baxter et al., 1992; Perani et al., 1995). Neurochemical changes were noted after behavioral interventions, psychopharmacological interventions, or both were undertaken. Posttreatment data revealed metabolic decreases in the entire cingulate gyrus that was associated with clinical improvement. Also revealed was the role of the amygdala in relation to anxiety-producing stimuli. Collectively, neuroimaging studies have linked limbic and paralimbic structures to the processing of emotional behaviors (George et al., 1993).

Dementia

In dementias, metabolic reductions were seen in both the anterior and posterior tertiary zones, as well as unimodal association areas within all cortices (Frackowiak, 1989; Smith et al., 1992). Dementias have also demonstrated hypometabolic changes in limbic, paralimbic, diencephalic, and periventricular regions (Mielke et al., 1996). Corresponding neuropsychological deficits are most prominent on measures of anterograde memory and executive functioning, with additional material-specific disturbances reported when discrete focal areas were implicated. Modulation within the cholinergic neurotransmitter system is often associated with amnestic changes. The right midfrontal gyrus seems to be linked to both working memory and general executive functioning in support of these activities (Furey et al., 1997). A review of numerous studies has revealed that although serotonergic and cholinergic neurotransmitter systems have been implicated in dementias—especially those of the Alzheimer's type—there are probably many additional neurotransmitter systems involved as well.

Transcranial Magnetic Stimulation

Unilateral repetitive transcranial magnetic stimulation (rTMS) is an experimental procedure currently under development that has great promise as a new breakthrough treatment for various psychiatric disorders. Several studies have demonstrated its efficacy in treating depression, mania, anxiety, and other psychiatric disorders (Klein et al., 1999; see George, Lisanby & Sackiem, 1999, for a review). rTMS works by placing a coil on the scalp over the prefrontal region, unilaterally, and passing a subthreshold electrical current (frequency ranging from 1–20 Hz). rTMS causes both neuronal excitation (fast rTMS) or inhibition (slow rTMS) depending upon frequency. It has the possibility of replacing electroconvulsive therapy because it may be able to effectively treat depression without the need for anesthesia, it does not produce a seizure, and it may not have any significant cognitive side effects (Koren et al., 2001). However, its potential application in neuropsychology is that it

can cause a temporary reversible lesion or selectively activate a very focal area of cortex. This capability allows for very well-controlled neuropsychological studies (using an A–B or A–B–A paradigm) in which very focal areas of cortex can be assessed in terms of excitation or as a lesion. What is yet to be determined is whether rTMS can incite a large enough area of cortex for meaningful research. For example, unilateral prefrontal rTMS is used in treating depression. This model can be applied to healthy volunteers and allow neuroscientists to selectively study unilateral prefrontal functions using either a temporary, reversible lesion (as in slow rTMS) or focal excitation (as in fast rTMS).

FUTURE DIRECTIONS

Neuropsychology has enjoyed a wide range of growth and development over the past several decades, particularly within the past several years. This growth and development has been fueled by technological advancements, such as more innovative and powerful neurodiagnostic equipment and tests such as fMRI, innovations in computerized and paper-and-pencil assessment techniques, and application of statistical procedures to improve assessment accuracy. Clinical neuropsychology has also grown by creating new clinical niches such as sports-related concussion assessment, as well as by improving already existing clinical specialties—for example, forensic clinical neuropsychology.

Other issues or factors are on the horizon and should continue to shape neuropsychology in the near future and may have a profound impact on the field. For example, we believe that there is a need for greater consistency within clinical neuropsychological assessments. The field needs to have more consistency not only in the tests used but also in the normative data being applied. We often see that the use of slightly different normative tables can drastically alter test results. Although having various normative tables for the same test is appropriate based upon varying demographic variables, often one can find the misuse of normative tables. For example, a large normative sample was developed out of the Mayo Clinic called the Mayo Older Adult Normative Study for older subjects (MOANS norms) for various commonly used neuropsychological tests such as Wechsler Memory Scale—Revised and the Mattis Dementia Rating Scale (Ivnik, Malec, Smith, Tangalos, & Petersen, 1996; Ivnik et al., 1992; Lucas et al., 1998). However, this normative sample tends to be highly educated (mean education of 13.1 years) and consists of disproportionately Caucasian suburbanites. Often we have seen clinicians apply these norms to urban African American populations. When the MOANs norms are compared to those of other recent studies

(Banks, Yochim, MacNeill, & Lichtenberg, 2000), one can clearly see the effects the demographic factors have on the test scores and how they can lead to a different interpretation. We would like to see better application of more demographically appropriate normative data.

Just as in the previously described problem, we would like to see a greater degree of fractionation of large normative samples to allow more accurate matching to the individual client. For example, the WMS-III is based on a large, census-matched normative sample. The normative data are broken down by age, but there is no way to take into account other variables (e.g., gender and education) that affect memory skills. (The same would apply to WAIS-III.) One would think that such a breakdown is a relatively easy thing for the publishers to do or allow others to do, but it has never been allowed.

Another interesting trend that we see in clinical neuropsychology is the incorporation of other disciplines into assessments. For example, in our clinics we often incorporate functional assessment techniques (such as the Independent Living Scales; Loeb, 1996) into our traditional neuropsychological assessment (see Baird, Podell, Lovell, & McGinty, 2001). This practice allows for a more comprehensive assessment that helps to address issues of functioning at home. It only improves the comprehensiveness of the neuropsychological assessment and better helps the patient and improves the role neuropsychology can have in the care of the patient.

Technological breakthroughs in neuroimaging have greatly improved our neuropsychological knowledge base. We believe that we have only seen the tip of the iceberg and that we will continue to see a rapid expansion of knowledge and understanding of brain-behavior relationships for years to come. Also, we believe that the rapid development of neuroimaging techniques has the potential to alter clinical neuropsychological assessment as we know it today. We foresee two probable changes. First, we believe that as neuroimaging techniques develop, we will start to see greater and greater assimilation of neuroimaging in daily clinical assessment. Such developments can already be seen in (for example) fMRI and MEG mapping of motor and sensory regions prior to neurosurgical intervention and—as mentioned previously—in Wada replacement techniques currently being developed. Second, if this trend is the future, then clinical neuropsychology assessment needs to undertake a paradigm shift in its conceptualization of assessment techniques and tools. This paradigm shift must have two components. First, it must change its entire conceptualization of how to develop tests and techniques; second, it must redesign how the tests are physically developed and administered. For example, current neuropsychological tests may not be entirely appropriate for use with fMRI; we are starting

to see this limitation somewhat already. fMRI studies of working memory have developed new tests to tap this cognitive construct. Also, neuropsychology must incorporate computers in testing more because paper-and-pencil testing does not lend itself to fMRI or other advanced neuroimaging techniques.

Innovations in clinical assessments have led to new clinical niches such as sports-related concussion assessment and our improved forensic assessment techniques. As the economy and health care continue to place pressure on traditional neuropsychological testing, our field will need to continue to be creative in countering the negative impact managed care has upon our clinical assessments. One of our fears is how this situation will affect training future neuropsychologists. We have already seen a trend toward shorter test protocols dictated by highly intrusive utilization management of the insurance companies. These shorter batteries can compromise clinical training (let alone quality of care) in that the trainees will not see the full complement of cognitive deficits with limited protocols. Although the field does need some adjustment, there is concern that training will become compromised as it is placed between the proverbial rock and a hard place wherein large institutions try to keep their training programs viable while balancing the need to cut costs (e.g., use shorter protocols) yet provide a diverse enough training experience. We also are concerned, as is all of health care, of the potential brain drain that managed care and the shrinking health care dollar have on attracting (or should we say steering away) talented young individuals to more lucrative professions.

The future of neuropsychology is still blossoming with many more exciting developments waiting to happen. However, as in all other health care fields, neuropsychology is also in the midst of historical changes from external forces (common to all industries), and it must be able to weather the storm if it wants to survive as a strong and viable clinical service and area of research growth.

REFERENCES

Alexander, M. P. (1995). Mild traumatic brain injury: Pathophysiology, natural history, and clinical management. *Neurology, 45,* 1253–1260.

Allen, L. M., Conder, R. L., Jr., Green, P., & Cox, D. R. (1998). *Computerized Assessment of response bias.* Durham, NC: Cognisyst.

Andreasen, N. C., Ehrhardt, J. C., Swayze, V. W., Alliger, R. J., Yuh, W. T., & Cohen, G. (1990). Magnetic resonance imaging of the brain in schizophrenia. The pathophysiologic significance of structural abnormalities. *Archives of General Psychiatry, 47,* 5–44.

Andreasen, N. C., Flaum, M., Swayze, V., II, O'Leary, D. S., Alliger, R., & Cohen, G. (1993). Intelligence and brain structure in normal individuals. *American Journal of Psychiatry, 150,* 130–134.

Andreasen, N. C., O'Leary, D. S., Flaum, M., Nopoulos, P., Watkins, G. L., & Boles Ponto. (1997). Hypofrontality in schizophrenia: Distributed dysfunctional circuits in neuroleptic-naive patients. *Lancet, 349,* 1730–1734.

Andreasen, N. C., Swayze, V. W., II, Flaum, M., Yates, W. R., Arndt, S., & McChesney, C. (1990). Ventricular enlargement in schizophrenia evaluated with computed tomographic scanning. Effects of gender, age, and stage of illness. *Archives of General Psychiatry, 47,* 1008–1015.

Atkinson, L. (1991). Three standard errors of measurement and the Wechsler Memory Scale—Revised. *Psychological Assessment, 3,* 136–138.

Aubry, M., Cantu, R., Duorak, J., Johnston, K., Kelly, J., Lovell, M. R., McCroy, P., Meeuwisse, W., & Schamosch, P. (2002). Summary agreement statement of the first International Conference on Concussion in Sport. *British Journal of Sports Medicine, 36,* 6–10.

Baird, A., Podell, K., Lovell, M., & McGinty, S. B. (2001). Complex real-world functioning and neuropsychological test performance in older adults. *Clinical Neuropsychologist, 15,* 369–379.

Baker, R., Donders, J., & Thompson, E. (2000). Assessment of incomplete effort with the California Verbal Learning Test. *Applied Neuropsychology, 7,* 111–114.

Banks, A. L., Yochim, B. P., MacNeill, S. E., & Lichtenberg, P. A. (2000). Expanded normative data for The Mattis Dementia Rating Scale for use with urban, elderly medical patients. *Clinical Neuropsychologist, 14,* 149–156.

Barbas, H., & Pandya, D. N. (1989). Architecture and intrinsic connections of the prefrontal cortex in the rhesus monkey. *Journal of Comparative Neurology, 286,* 353–357.

Barr, W. B., & McCrea, M. (2001). Sensitivity and specificity of standardized neurocognitive testing immediately following sports concussion. *Journal of the International Neuropsychological Society, 7,* 693–702.

Barth, J. T., Alves, W. M., Ryan, T. V., Macciocchi, S. N., Rimel, R. W., & Jane, J. A. (1989). Mild head injury in sports: Neuropsychological sequelae and recovery of function. In H. S. Levin, H. M., Eisenberg, & A. L. Benton (Eds.), *Mild head injury* (pp. 257–275). New York: Oxford University Press.

Baxter, L. R., Jr., Schwartz, J. M., Bergman, K. S., Szuba, M. P., Guze, B. H., & Mazziotta, J. C. (1992). Caudate glucose metabolic rate changes with both drug and behavior therapy for obsessive-compulsive disorder. *Archives of General Psychiatry, 49,* 681–689.

Bench, C. J., Friston, K. J., Brown, R. G., Frackowiak, R. S., & Dolan, R. J. (1993). Regional cerebral blood flow in depression measured by positron emission tomography: The relationship with clinical dimensions. *Psychological Medicine, 23,* 579–590.

Ben-Porath, Y. S., Graham, J. R., Hall, G. C. N., Hirschman, R. D., & Zaragoza, M. S. (1995). *Forensic application of the MMPI-2.* Thousand Oaks, CA: Sage.

Benton, A. (1987). Evolution of a clinical specialty. *Clinical Neuropsychologist, 1,* 5–8.

Benton, A. (1988). Neuropsychology: Past, present and future. In F. Boller & J. Grafman (Eds.), *Handbook of clinical neuropsychology* (Vol. 1, pp. 3–27). Amsterdam: Swets and Zeitlinger B.V.

Bigler, E. D., & Snyder, J. L. (1995). Neuropsychological outcome and quantitative neuroimaging in mild traumatic brain injury. *Archives of Clinical Neuropsychology, 10,* 159–174.

Binder, J. R., Swanson, S. J., Hammeke, T. A., Morris, G. L., Mueller, W. M., Fischer, W. M., Benbadis, S., Frost, J. A., Rao, S. M., & Haughton, V. M. (1996). Determination of language dominance using functional MRI: A comparison with the Wada test. *Neurology, 46,* 978–984.

Binder, L. M. (1992). Forced-choice testing provides evidence of malingering. *Archives of Physical Medicine and Rehabilitation, 73,* 377–380.

Binder, L. M. (1993). Assessment of malingering after mild head trauma with the Portland Digit Recognition Test. *Journal of Clinical and Experimental Neuropsychology, 15,* 170–182.

Binder, L. M. (1997). A review of mild head trauma: II. Clinical implications. *Journal of Clinical and Experimental Neuropsychology, 19*(3), 432–457.

Binder, L. M., & Pankrantz, L. (1987). Neuropsychological evidence of a factitious memory complaint. *Journal of Clinical and Experimental Neuropsychology, 9,* 167–171.

Binder, L. M., & Willis, S. C. (1991). Assessment of motivation after financially compensable minor head trauma. *Psychological Assessment, 3,* 175–181.

Bleiberg, J., Halpern, E. L., Reeves, D. L., & Daniel, J. C. (1998). Future directions for the neuropsychological assessment of sports concussion. *Journal of Head Trauma Rehabilitation, 13,* 36–44.

Bleiberg, J., Kane, R. L., Reeves, D. L., Garmoe, W. S., & Halpern, E. (2000). Factor analysis of computerized and traditional tests used in mild brain injury research. *Clinical Neuropsychologist, 14,* 287–294.

Bradshaw, J. L., & Mattingley, J. B. (1995). *Clinical neuropsychology: Behavioral and brain science.* San Diego, CA: Academic Press.

Brandt, J. (1988). Malingered amnesia. In R. Rogers (Ed.), *Clinical assessment of malingering and deception* (pp. 56–69). New York: Guilford Press.

Brockway, J. P. (2000). Two functional magnetic resonance imaging fMRI tasks that may replace the gold standard, Wada testing, for language lateralization while giving additional localization information. *Brain and Cognition, 43,* 57–59.

Brown, L., Sherbenou, R. J., & Johnson, S. K. (1982). *Test of Nonverbal Intelligence.* Austin, TX: ProEd.

Buckner, R. L., Logan, J., Donaldson, D. I., & Wheeler, M. E. (2000). Cognitive neuroscience of episodic memory encoding. *Acta Psychologica, 105,* 127–139.

Cabeza, R., & Nyberg, L. (2000). Neural bases of learning and memory: Functional neuroimaging evidence. *Current Opinions in Neurology, 13,* 415–421.

Cantu, R. C. (1998). Second-impact syndrome. *Clinical Sports Medicine, 17,* 37–44.

Chua, S. E., & McKenna, P. J. (1995). Schizophrenia: A brain disease? *British Journal of Psychiatry, 66,* 563–582.

Chelune, G. J., Naugle, R. I., Luders, H. S. J., Sedlak, J., & Awad, I. A. (1993). Individual change after epilepsy surgery: Practice effects and base-rate information. *Neuropsychology, 7,* 41–52.

Christensen, L., & Mendoza, J. L. (1986). A method of assessing change in a single subject: An alteration of the RC index. *Behavior Therapy, 17,* 305–308.

Collins, M., Grindel, S., Lovell, M., Dede, D., Moser, D., & Phalin, B. (1999). Relationship between concussion and neuropsychological performance in college football players. *Journal of the American Medical Association, 282,* 964–970.

Collins, M., & Hawn, K. L. (2002). The clinical management of sports concussion. *Current Sports Medicine Report, 1,* 12–22.

Damasio, H., Grabowski, T., Frank, R., Galaburda, A. M., & Damasio, A. R. (1994). The return of Phineas Gage: Clues about the brain from the skull of a famous patient. *Science, 264,* 1102–1105.

Davies, H. P., King, J. H., Klebe, K. J., Bajszer, G., Bloodworth, M. R., & Wallick, S. L. (1997). The detection of simulated malingering using a computerized priming test. *Archives of Clinical Neuropsychology, 12,* 145–153.

Detre, J. A., Maccotta, L., King, D., Alsop, D. C., Glosser, G., & D'Esposito, M. (1998). *Neurology, 50,* 926–932.

Dymek, M. P., Atchison, P., Harrell, L., & Marson, D. C. (2001). Competency to consent to medical treatment in cognitively impaired patients with Parkinson's disease. *Neurology, 9,* 17–24.

Earnst, K. S., Marson, D. C., & Harrell, L. E. (2000). Cognitive models of physicians' legal standard and personal judgments of competency in-patients with Alzheimer's disease. *Journal of American Geriatric Society, 48,* 1014–1016.

Echemendia, R. J., & Julian, L. J. (2001). Mild traumatic brain injury in sports: Neuropsychology's contribution to a developing field. *Neuropsychology Review, 11,* 69–88.

Ellwanger, J., Rosenfeld, J. P., & Sweet, J. J. (1997). The P300 event-related brain potential as an index of recognition response to autobiographical and recently learned information in closed head injury patients. *Clinical Neuropsychologist, 11,* 428–432.

Ellwanger, J., Rosenfeld, J. P., Sweet, J. J., & Bhatt, M. (1996). Detecting simulated amnesia for autobiographical and recently learned information using P300 event related potential. *International Journal of Psychophysiology, 23,* 9–23.

Ellwanger, J., Tenhulla, W. N., Rosenfeld, P., & Sweet, J. J. (1999). Identifying simulators of cognitive deficit through combined use of neuropsychological test performance and event-related potentials. *Journal of Clinical and Experimental Neuropsychology, 21,* 866–879.

Elwood, R. W. (1993). Clinical discriminations and neuropsychological tests: An appeal to Bayes' theorem. *Clinical Neuropsychologist, 7,* 224–233.

Fletcher, P. C., & Henson, R. N. (2001). Frontal lobes and human memory: Insights from functional neuroimaging. *Brain, 124,* 849–881.

Frackowiak, R. S. (1989). PET: Studies in dementia. *Psychiatry Research, 29,* 353–355.

Frederick, R. I. (1997). *Validity indicator profile manual.* Minnetonka, MN: NCS Assessments.

Frost, J. A., Springer, J. A., Binder, J. R., Hammeke, T. A., Bellgowan, P. S. F., & Rao. (1997). Sex does not determine functional lateralization of semantic processing: Evidence from fMRI. *Neuroimage, 5,* S564.

Furey, M. L., Pietrini, P., Haxby, J. V., Alexander, G. E., Lee, H. C., & VanMeter, J. (1997). Cholinergic stimulation alters performance and task-specific regional cerebral blood flow during working memory. *Proceedings from National Academy of Science, 94,* 6512–6516.

Gass, C. S. (1991). MMPI-2 interpretation and closed head injury: A correction factor. *Psychological Assessment, 3,* 27–31.

George, M. S., Ketter, T. A., Gill, D. S., Haxby, J. V., Ungerleider, L. G., & Herscovitch, P. (1993). Brain regions involved in recognizing facial emotion or identity: An oxygen-15 PET study. *Journal of Neuropsychiatry and Clinical Neuroscience, 5,* 384–394.

George, M. S., Lisanby, S. H., & Sackiem, H. A. (1999). Transcranial Magnetic Stimulation: Applications in neuropsychiatry. *Archives of General Psychiatry, 56,* 300–331.

Goldberg, E. (2001). *The executive brain: Frontal lobes and the civilized mind.* New York: Oxford University Press.

Goldberg, E., & Podell, K. (1999). Adaptive versus veridical decision making and the frontal lobes. *Journal of Consciousness and Cognition, 8,* 364–377.

Goldberg, E., & Podell, K. (2001). *The Cognitive Bias Test.* Melbourne, Australia: PsychPress.

Goldberg, E., Podell, K., Bilder, R., & Jaeger, J. (2000). *The Executive Control Battery.* Melbourne, Australia: PsychPress.

Goldberg, E., Podell, K., Harner, R., Lovell, M., & Riggio, S. (1994). Cognitive bias, functional cortical geometry, and the frontal lobes: Laterality, sex and handedness. *Journal of Cognitive Neuroscience, 6,* 276–296.

Grindel, S. H., Lovell, M. R., & Collins, M. W. (2001). The assessment of sports-related concussion: The evidence behind neuropsychological testing and management. *Clinical Journal of Sports Medicine, 11,* 134–143.

Gronwall, D. (1991). Minor head injury. *Neuropsychology, 5,* 253–265.

Guilmette, T. J., Hart, K. J., & Giuliano, A. J. (1993). Malingering detection: The use of a forced-choice method in identifying organic versus simulated memory impairment. *Clinical Neuropsychologist, 7,* 59–69.

Guskiewicz, K. M., Weaver, N. L., Padua, D. A., & Garrett, W. E. (2000). Epidemiology of concussion in collegiate and high school football players. *American Journal of Sports Medicine, 28,* 643–650.

Harlow, J. M. (1868). Recovery after severe injury to the head. *Publications of the Massachusetts Medical Society, 2,* 327–346.

Hinton-Bayre, A. D., Geffin, G. M., Geffen, L. G., McFarland, K. A., & Friss, P. (1999). Concussion in contact sports: Reliable change indices of impairment and recovery. *Journal of Clinical and Experimental Neuropsychology, 21,* 70–86.

Hirsch, J., Ruge, M. I., Kim, K. H., Correa, D. D., Victor, J. D., Relkin, N. R., Labar, D. R., Krol, G., Bilsky, M. H., Souweidane, M. M., DeAngelis, L. M., & Gutin, P. H. (2000). *Neurosurgery, 47,* 711–721.

Hiscock, M., & Hiscock, C. K. (1989). Refining the forced choice method for the detection of malingering. *Journal of Clinical and Experimental Neuropsychology, 11,* 967–974.

Hokama, H., Shenton, M. E., Nestor, P. G., Kikinis, R., Levitt, J. J., & Metcalf, D. (1995). Caudate, putamen, and globus pallidus volume in schizophrenia: A quantitative MRI study. *Psychiatry Research, 61,* 209–229.

Ishai, A., Ungerleider, L. G., Martin, A., & Haxby, J. V. (2000). The representation of objects in the human occipital and temporal cortex. *Journal of Cognitive Neuroscience, 12,* 35–51.

Iverson, G. L., & Binder, L. M. (2000). Detecting exaggeration and malingering in neuropsychological assessment. *Journal of Head Trauma Rehabilitation, 15,* 829–858.

Ivnik, R. J., Malec, J. F., Smith, G. E., Tangalos, E. G., & Petersen, R. C. (1996). Neuropsychological tests' norms above age 55: COWAT, BNT, MAE Token, WRAT-R, AMNART, Stroop, TMT, and JLO. *Clinical Neuropsychologist, 10,* 262–278.

Ivnik, R. J., Malec, J. F., Smith, G. E., Tangalos, E. G., Petersen, R. C., Kokmen, E., & Kurland, L. T. (1992). Mayo's older Americans studies: WMS-R norms for ages 56–94. *Clinical Neuropsychologist, 6,* 49–82.

Jacobson, N. S., & Truax, P. (1991). Clinical significance: A statistical approach to defining meaningful change in psychotherapy research. *Journal of Consulting and Clinical Psychology, 59,* 12–19.

Jacobson, N. S., Follette, W. C., & Revenstorf, D. (1984). Psychotherapy outcome research: Methods for reporting variability and evaluating clinical significance. *Behavior Therapy, 15,* 336–352.

Kaufman, A. S., & Kaufman, N. L. (1990). *Kaufman Brief Intelligence Test.* Circle Pines, MN: American Guidance Service.

Killgore, W. D., Glosser, G., Casasanto, D. J., French, J. A., Alsop, D. C., & Detre, J. A. (1999). Functional MRI and the Wada test provide complementary information for predicting postoperative seizure control. *Seizure, 8,* 450–455.

Klein, E., Kreinin, B., Chistyakov, A., Koren, D., Metz, L., & Marmur, S. (1999). Therapeutic efficacy of right prefrontal slow repetitive transcranial magnetic stimulation in major depression: A double-blind controlled study. *Archives of General Psychiatry, 56,* 315–320.

Koren, D., Shefer, O., Chistyakov, A., Kaplan, B., Feinsod, M., & Klein, E. (2001). Neuropsychological effects of prefrontal slow rTMS in normal volunteers: A double-blind sham-controlled study. *Journal of Clinical and Experimental Neuropsychology, 23,* 424–430.

Kraus, J. F., & McArthur, D. L. (1996). Epidemiologic aspects of brain injury. *Neurologic Clinics, 14,* 435–450.

Lawrie, S. M., Abukmeil, S. S., Chiswick, A., Egan, V., Santosh, C. G., & Best, J. J. (1997). Qualitative cerebral morphology in schizophrenia: A magnetic resonance imaging study and systematic literature review. *Schizophrenia Research, 25,* 155–166.

Lees-Haley, P., & Brown, R. (1993). Neuropsychological complaint base-rates of 170 personal injury claimants. *Archives of Clinical Neuropsychology, 8,* 203–209.

Lees-Haley, P., English, L., & Glen, W. (1991). A fake bad scale on the MMPI-2 for personal injury claimants. *Psychological Reports, 68,* 203–210.

Lees-Haley, P., Fox, D. D., & Courtney, J. C. (2001). A comparison of complaints by mild brain injury claimants and other claimants describing subjective experiences immediately following their injury. *Archives of Clinical Neuropsychology, 16,* 689–695.

Lehericy, S., Cohen, L., Bazin, B., Samson, S., Giacomini, E., Rougetet, R., Hertz-Pannier, L., LeBihan, D., Morsoult, C., & Boulec, M. (2000). Functional MR evaluation of temporal and frontal language dominance compared with the WADA test. *Neurology, 54,* 1625–1633.

Lezak, M. (1995). *Neuropsychological assessment* (3rd ed.). New York: Oxford University Press.

Loeb, P. A. (1996). *Independent Living Scales.* San Antonio, TX: Psychological Corporation.

Lovell, M. R., & Collins, M. W. (1998). Neuropsychological assessment of the college football player. *Journal of Head Trauma Rehabilitation, 13,* 9–26.

Lucas, J. A., Ivnik, R. J., Smith, G. E., Bohac, D. L., Tangalos, E. G., & Kokmen, E. (1998). Normative Data for the Mattis Dementia Rating Scale. *Journal of Clinical and Experimental Psychology, 20,* 536–547.

Luria, A. R. (1980). *Higher cortical functions in man* (2nd ed.). New York: Basic Books. (Original work published 1966)

Maassen, G. H. (2000). Principles of defining reliable change indices. *Journal of Clinical and Experimental Neuropsychology, 22,* 622–632.

Maroon, J. C., Lovell, M. R., Norwig, J., Podell, K., Powell, J. W., & Hartl, R. (2000). Cerebral concussion in athletes: Evaluation and neuropsychological testing. *Neurosurgery, 47,* 659–669.

Marson, D. C. (2001). Loss of competency in Alzheimer's disease: Conceptual and psychometric approaches. *International Journal of Law Psychiatry, 24*(2-3), 267–283.

Marson, D. C., Annis, S. M., McInturff, B., Bartolucci, A., & Harrell, L. E. (1999). Error behaviors associated with loss of competency in Alzheimer's disease. *Neurology, 53*, 1983–1992.

Marson, D. C., Chatterjee, A., Ingram, K. K., & Harrell, L. E. (1996). Toward a neurologic model of competency: Cognitive predictors of capacity to consent in Alzheimer's disease using three different legal standards. *Neurology, 46*, 666–672.

Marson, D. C., Cody, H. A., Ingram, K. K., & Harrell, L. E. (1995). Neuropsychologic predictors of competency in Alzheimer's disease using a rational reasons legal standard. *Archives of Neurology, 52*, 955–959.

Martin, A., & Chao, L. L. (2001). Semantic memory and the brain: Structure and processes. *Current Opinion in Neurobiology, 11*, 194–201.

Mayberg, H. S. (2001). Frontal lobe dysfunction in secondary depression. In S. P. Salloway, P. F. Malloy, & J. D. Duffy (Eds.), *The frontal lobes and neuropsychiatric illness* (pp. 167–186). Washington, DC: American Psychiatric Press.

Meehl, P. E., & Rosen, A. (1955). Antecedent probability and the efficiency of psychometric signs, patterns, or cutting scores. *Psychological Bulletin, 52*, 194–216.

Meyer-Lindenberg, A., & Berman, K. F. (2001). The frontal lobes and schizophrenia. In S. P. Salloway, P. F. Malloy, & J. D. Duffy (Eds.), *The frontal lobes and neuropsychiatric illness* (pp. 187–197). Washington, DC: American Psychiatric Press.

Mielke, R., Kessler, J., Szelies, B., Herholz, K., Wienhard, K., & Heiss, W. D. (1996). Vascular dementia: Perfusional and metabolic disturbances and effects of therapy. *Journal of Neural Transmission, Suppl 47*, 183–191.

Millis, S. R., Putnam, S. H., Adams, K. M., & Ricker, J. H. (1995). The California Verbal Learning Test in the detection of incomplete effort in neuropsychological testing. *Psychological Assessment, 7*, 463–471.

Mittenberg, W., & Strauman, S. (2000). Diagnosis of mild head injury and the postconcussion syndrome. *Journal of Head Trauma Rehabilitation, 15*, 783–791.

Morey, L. C. (1991). *Personality Assessment Inventory™*. Odessa, FL: Psychological Assessment Resources.

Morey, L. C. (1996). *An interpretive guide to the Personality Assessment Inventory (PAI)*. Odessa, FL: Psychological Assessment Resources.

Naglieri, J. A. (1999). *Essentials of CAS Assessment*. New York: Wiley.

Naglieri, J. A., & Bardos, A. N. (1997). *The General Ability Measure for Adults*. Minneapolis, MN: NCS Assessments.

Naglieri, J. A., & Das, J. P. (1997). *Das-Naglieri Cognitive Assessment System*. Odessa, FL: Psychological Assessment Resources.

Nicholson, R. A., Mouton, G. J., Bagby, R. M., Buis, T., Peterson, S. A., & Buigas, R. A. (1997). Utility of MMPI-2 indicators of

response distortion: Receiver operating characteristic analysis. *Psychological Assessment, 9*, 471–479.

Nies, K. J., & Sweet, J. J. (1994). Neuropsychological assessment and malingering: A critical review of past and present strategies. *Archives of Clinical Neuropsychology, 9*, 501–552.

Nystrom, L. E., Braver, T. S., Sabb, F. W., Delgado, M. R., Noll, D. C., & Cohen, J. D. (2000). Working memory for letters, shapes, and location: fMRI evidence against stimulus-based regional organization in human prefrontal cortex. *Neuroimage, 11*, 424–446.

Perani, D., Colombo, C., Bressi, S., Bonfanti, A., Grassi, F., & Scarone, S. (1995). [18F] FDG PET study in obsessive-compulsive disorder: A clinical/metabolic correlation study after treatment. *British Journal of Psychiatry, 166*, 244–250.

Perlstein, W. M., Carter, C. S., Noll, D. C., & Cohen, J. D. (2001). Relation of prefrontal cortex dysfunction to working memory and symptoms in schizophrenia. *American Journal of Psychiatry, 158*, 1105–1113.

Podell, K., Lovell, M., & Goldberg, E. (2001). Lateralization of frontal lobe functions. In S. P. Salloway, P. F. Malloy, & J. D. Duffy (Eds.), *The frontal lobes and neuropsychiatric illness* (pp. 83–100). Washington, DC: American Psychiatric Press.

Powell, J. W. (1999). Epidemiology of sports-related head injury. In J. E. Bailes, M. R. Lovell, & J. C. Maroon (Eds.), *Sports-related concussion* (pp. 75–90). St. Louis, MO: Quality Medical Publishing.

Powell, J. W., & Barber-Foss, K. (1999). Traumatic brain injury in high school athletes. *Journal of the American Medical Association, 282*, 958–963.

Prigatano, G. P., & Amin, K. (1993). Digit memory test: Unequivocal cerebral dysfunction and suspected malingering. *Journal of Clinical and Experimental Neuropsychology, 15*, 537–546.

The Psychological Corporation. (1997). *Wechsler Adult Intelligence Scale—III*. San Antonio, TX: Author.

The Psychological Corporation. (1997). *Wechsler Memory Scale—III*. San Antonio, TX: Author.

The Psychological Corporation. (1999). *Wechsler Abbreviated Scale of Intelligence*. San Antonio, TX: Author.

Reeves, D., Kane, R., & Winter, K. (1996). *ANAM V3.11a/96 User's Manual: Clinical and neurotoxicology subtests*. (Report No. NCRF-TR-96-01). San Diego, CA: National Recovery Foundation.

Reitan, R. M., & Wolfson, D. (1993). *The Halstead-Reitan Neuropsychological Test Battery* (2nd ed.). Tucson, AZ: Neuropsychology Press.

Resnick, P. J. (1988). Malingering of post-traumatic disorder. In R. Rogers (Ed.), *Clinical assessment of malingering and deception* (pp. 84–103). New York: Guilford Press.

Rose, F., Hall, S., & Szalda-Petree, A. (1995). Portland Digit Recognition Test—computerized: Measuring response latency improves the detection of malingering. *Clinical Neuropsychologist, 9*, 124–134.

Rosenfeld, J. P., & Ellwanger, J. W. (1999). Cognitive psychophysiology in detection of malingered cognitive deficits. In J. J. Sweet (Ed.), *Forensic neuropsychology: Fundamentals and practice* (pp. 287–312). Lisse, The Netherlands: Swets and Zeitlinger.

Rosenfeld, J. P., Ellwanger, J. W., & Sweet, J. J. (1995). Detecting simulated amnesia with event-related brain potentials. *International Journal of Psychophysiology, 19,* 1–11.

Ruff, R. M., & Richardson, A. M. (1999). Mild traumatic brain injury. In J. J. Sweet (Ed.), *Forensic neuropsychology: Fundamentals and practice* (pp. 313–338). Lisse, The Netherlands: Swets and Zeitlinger.

Schacter, D. L., & Wagner, A. D. (1999). Medical temporal lobe activation in fMRI and PET studies of episodic encoding and retrieval. *Hippocampus, 9,* 7–24.

Scott Killgore, W. D., & DellaPietra, L. (2000). Using the WMS-III to detect malingering: Empirical validation of the rarely missed index (RMI). *Journal of Clinical and Experimental Neuropsychology, 22,* 761–771.

Shaywitz, B. A., Shaywitz, S. E., Pugh, K. R., Constable, R. T., Skudlarski, P., & Fulbright, R. K. (1995). Sex differences in the functional organization of the brain for language. *Nature, 373,* 607–609.

Slick, D., Hopp, G., & Strauss, E. (1998). *Victoria Symptom Validity Test.* Odessa, FL: Psychological Assessment Resources.

Slick, D., Hopp, G., Strauss, E., Hunter, M., & Pinch, D. (1994). Detecting dissimulation: Profiles of simulated malingerers, traumatic brain injury patients and normal controls on a revised version of Hiscock and Hiscock's forced choice memory test. *Journal of Clinical and Experimental Neuropsychology, 16,* 472–481.

Smith, G. S., de Leon, M. J., George, A. E., Kluger, A., Volkow, N. D., & McRae, T. (1992). Topography of cross-sectional and longitudinal glucose metabolic deficits in Alzheimer's disease: Pathophysiologic implications. *Archive of Neurology, 49,* 1142–1150.

Spreen, O., & Strauss, E. (1998). *A compendium of neuropsychological tests: Administration, norms, and commentary* (2nd ed). New York: Oxford University Press.

Stern, C. E., Corkin, S., Gonzalez, R. G., Guimaraes, A. R., Baker, J. R., & Jennings, P. (1996). The hippocampal formation participates in novel picture encoding: Evidence from functional magnetic resonance imaging. *Proceedings of National Academy of Science, 93,* 8660–8665.

Stern, R. A., Javorsky, D. J., Singer, E. A., Singer-Harris, N. G., Somerville, J. A., & Duke, L. M. (1999). *The Boston Qualitative Scoring System for the Rey-Osterrieth Complex Figure.* Odessa, FL: Psychological Assessment Resources.

Storey, J. E., Rowland, J. T. J., Basic, D., & Conforti, D. A. (2001). A comparison of five clock scoring methods using ROC (receiver operating characteristics) curve analysis. *International Journal of Geriatric Psychiatry, 16,* 394–399.

Strauss, E., Hultsch, D. F., Hunter, M., Slick, D. J., Patry, B., & Levy-Bencheton, J. (1999). Using intraindividual variability to detect malingering in cognitive performance. *Clinical Neuropsychologist, 13,* 420–432.

Suhr, J. A., & Boyer, D. (1999). Use of The Wisconsin Card Sorting Test in the detection of malingering in student simulator and patient samples. *Journal of Clinical and Experimental Neuropsychology, 21,* 701–708.

Sweet, J. J. (1999). Malingering: Differential diagnosis. In J. J. Sweet (Ed.), *Forensic neuropsychology: Fundamentals and practice* (pp. 255–286). Lisse, The Netherlands: Swets and Zeitlinger.

Sweet, J. J., Wolfe, P., Sattlberger, E., Numan, B., Rosenfeld, J. P., & Clingerman, S. (2000). Further investigation of traumatic brain injury versus insufficient effort with the California Verbal Learning Test. *Archives of Clinical Neuropsychology, 15,* 105–113.

Tape, T. G. (2001). ROC Curves. In *Interpreting diagnostic tests.* Retrieved September 21, 2001, from http://gim.unmc.edu/dxtests/Default.htm

Tardif, H. P., Barry, R. J., Fox, A. M., & Johnstone, S. J. (2000). Detection of feigned recognition memory impairment using the old/new effect of the event-related potential. *International Journal of Psychophysiology, 36,* 1–9.

Temkin, N. R., Heaton, R. K., Grant, I., & Dikmen, S. (1999). Detecting significant change in neuropsychological test performance: A comparison of four models. *Journal of the International Neuropsychological Society, 5,* 357–369.

Tombaugh, T. N. (1996). *Test of memory malingering.* Toronto, Canada: Multi-Health Systems.

Trueblood, W., & Schmidt, M. (1993). Malingering and other validity considerations in the neuropsychological evaluation of mild head injury. *Journal of Clinical and Experimental Neuropsychology, 15,* 578–590.

Vickery, C. D., Berry, D. T. R., Hanlon-Inman, T., Harris, M. J., & Orey, S. A. (2001). Detection of inadequate effort on neuropsychological testing: A meta-analytic review of selected procedures. *Archives of Clinical Neuropsychology, 16*(1), 45–73.

Videbech, P. (1997). MRI findings in patients with affective disorder: A meta analysis. *Acta Psychologica Scandinavia, 96,* 157–168.

Warden, D. L., Bleiberg, J., Cameron, K. L., Ecklund, J., Walter, J. D., & Sparling, M. B. (2001). Persistent prolongation of reaction time in sports concussion. *Neurology, 57,* 524–526.

Warrington, E. K. (1984). *Recognition memory test: Manual.* Berkshire, UK: NFER-Nelson.

Youngjohn, J., Burrows, L., & Erdal, K. (1995). Brain damage or compensation neurosis? The controversial post-concussion syndrome. *Clinical Neuropsychologist, 9,* 112–123.

CHAPTER 20

Assessment of Interests

RODNEY L. LOWMAN AND ANDREW D. CARSON

Despite difficulties in reaching a consensus as to what interests are, how they develop, and how best to classify them, psychologists have created a number of assessment tools for measuring them, and the test-publishing industry has turned occupational interest inventories—the most common type of interest measure—into a flourishing business. Decades of research (yielding thousands of publications, making this necessarily a highly selective review) have established interests as their own major psychological domain, comparable in scope and importance to abilities and personality traits; assessment of interests has therefore become a mainstay of many psychologists and allied professionals. However, suggestions that group membership (e.g., age, sex, culture) may affect the validity of interpretations of interest measures for some purposes should inspire reasonable caution on the part of researchers and users alike.

In this chapter, we address issues related to the psychology and measurement of interests, as well as issues relating to future research directions. Specifically, this chapter begins with a discussion of a definition of interests, offering a working definition of the nature of interests. Many of the major interest-assessment measures, some of them among the longest-lived and most psychometrically sophisticated

measures in psychology, are then presented and briefly discussed. General findings and themes on the reliability and validity of interests are reviewed along with issues of group differences in their measurement. Interests are then placed in a broader context by looking at the relationships among interests and other domains, especially personality and ability. Finally, the chapter outlines some needed research that may help take interests to the next level of understanding and practical applications.

DEFINITIONS OF INTERESTS

Savickas (1999) and Crites (1969) each provided useful definitions of interests drawn from the major researchers in the field. They noted the impact of definitions of interests proffered by E. K. Strong Jr. Strong (1955) essentially accepted the Webster's dictionary definition, "a propensity to attend to and be stirred by a certain object," along with four attributes: *attention* and *feeling* for an object, *intensity* (preference for some activities over others), and *duration*. Savickas suggested that each of these attributes reflects an area of theoretical and research activity related to interests in the first third of this century. The formal definition of *interests* offered by Strong was

> activities for which we have liking or disliking and which we go toward or away from, or concerning which we at least continue or discontinue the status quo; furthermore, they may or may not be preferred to other interests and they may continue varying over time. Or an interest may be defined as a liking/disliking state of mind accompanying the doing of an activity, or the thought of performing the activity. (p. 138)

For Strong (1943), interests do not require consciousness or even thought; "they remind me of tropisms. We go toward liked activities, go away from disliked activities" (p. 7).

Lowman (in press) similarly defined *interests* as "relatively stable psychological characteristics of people [that] identify the personal evaluation (subjective attributions of 'goodness' or 'badness,' judged by degree of personal fit or misfit) attached to particular groups of occupational or leisure activity clusters." Within this definition, interests refer both to occupations that a person is likely to find appealing and satisfying, and to leisure interests and avocational interests that are likely to be enjoyable and to bring long-term satisfaction.

DEVELOPMENT OF INTERESTS

Several alternative—and not mutually exclusive—conceptualization of interests have been proposed. Although these approaches have never had the devoted enthusiasts that have attached to, say, approaches to psychotherapy, they still provide a useful categorizing and classifying approach.

Psychoanalytic theories of the development of personality strongly influenced Roe's (1957) account of the nature of interests, which stimulated several studies testing the relationship between quality of parent-child relationship and subsequent development of the child's vocational interests. However, empirical studies in general found little support for Roe's theory, suggesting that the environment—and especially the early parent-child relationship—may have relatively little lasting effect on the development of interests, seemingly disproving her theory. Roe (in Roe & Lunneborg, 1990) acknowledges as much. Freud's *psychosexual stage model* apparently also influenced Holland's original statement of his *theory of vocational choice* (1959). Bordin (1994) and Brown and Watkins (1994) reviewed modern *psychodynamic approaches* to interests and career issues.

The *social learning approach* to interests assumes that since they derive from appropriate reinforcements, parents and educators or interactions with one's environment may shape interests in preferred directions (Mitchell & Krumboltz, 1990). Theories with this basis assume, essentially, that people learn to become interested in what they are good at, and disinterested in what they are bad at, based on feedback from others. Holland's (1997a) current version of his *vocational personality theory* of the development of interests assumes that most interests are acquired through social learning experiences. Whatever biological factors may predispose to particular interests, environments, Holland contends, are composed of people with more similar interest patterns than not. These environments both attract others with similar patterns and influence the behavior of others by making those who stay in the environments more like the dominant interest patterns in the group (see L. Gottfredson, 1999; Walsh & Chartrand, 1994). Dawis's *theory of work adjustment* (1991) also posits the environment as consisting of reinforcers that attract and sustain particular types of people and behavior.

Genetic models assume that interests have considerable inheritability, suggesting a more fixed and determinative approach (see, e.g., McCall, Cavanaugh, Arvey, & Taubman, 1997; Moloney, Bouchard, & Segal, 1991). L. Gottfredson (1999) reviewed evidence from the as yet somewhat small behavior-genetic literature on psychological traits, including vocational interests. She concluded that there exists convincing evidence from twin and other studies that a sizable proportion of the variance in measured psychological traits, including interests, has a genetic component and that this proportion tends to increase with age (i.e., environmental effects decrease). In addition, shared family effects on the observed traits (i.e., effects of global factors shared across children in the family) tend to decrease with age, becoming much less a factor by adolescence. Thus, as represented by their measured characteristics such as abilities and interests, individuals essentially reach a period of maximum independence from the forces of family of origin and genes during their adolescent and early adult years, at the same time that secondary and higher education and the world of work would presumably serve to affect skills and motivations.

MEASUREMENT OF INTERESTS

Measurement Options

This review of interest theories suggests that theorists have developed somewhat incompatible accounts for the development of interests. Given this lack of consensus, it may appear surprising how much similarity exists among widely used measures of interests, which are almost always inventories consisting of statements about the strength of an individual's interest in particular activities or occupations. Although a variety of methods of assessing interests has developed over the past century, most of this diversity flourished only in the first decades and then vanished. Nevertheless, we can discuss different ways to measure interests (most with historical examples) and point to some ongoing efforts to diversify measurement methods.

The first and most important distinction is between interests as *observed behavior* versus *self-reported feelings or thoughts.* One may observe a person's behavior and infer his or her interests from it, on the assumption that people would not engage in behavior if they were not interested in it. Closely related to actually observing behavior would be to infer interests from behaviors recorded on behavioral checklists or biographical data forms, both of which often turn out to be strong predictors of job-related performance, and presumably therefore of fit to jobs. Crites (1999) noted that although observed behavior could provide indicators of interests, noninterest factors such as family and social pressures could affect them more than, say, expressed or inventoried interests. It is much more common to assess interests through self-reports of introspective states such as feelings or thoughts, such as through interest inventories.

The second important distinction is between measures of interests as *tests* versus *inventories.* On the assumption that people will learn more about that in which they are interested, tests can be constructed reflecting knowledge or skills across different occupational or leisure activity areas; individual differences in performance on these tests may reflect differences in practice or attentiveness associated with such activities, and therefore serve as indicators of underlying interests. Some vocabulary-based and knowledge-based interest inventories saw brief service in the middle of the last century, but apparently only briefly, and they were soon displaced by the growing popularity of inventory-based measures, in which an answer to an item on a questionnaire does not have an objectively correct answer. Super (1949, pp. 474–480) described and evaluated information tests (such as those on which Super worked during World War II), and the degree to which they might serve as indicators of interests. Crites (1999) concluded that although the idea of an interest test was intriguing, subsequent research has shown them lacking in criterion and predictive validity.

The third important distinction is between *expressed* versus *inferred interests.* Inferred interests have been assessed not only by inventories but also by tests and observed behavior. One way to assess a feeling or thought is to ask directly; the direct expression of that feeling or thought may involve different psychological processes than would a more indirect assessment of the same construct. Expressed interests may also

be more likely to tap not only an individual's current interests, but also the sort of interests he or she wishes to have.

Specific Measures of Interests

We shall discuss several popular or widely used measures of interests, including the Strong Vocational Interest Blank (Strong Interest Inventory), the Campbell Interest and Skill Survey, the Kuder Occupational Interest Survey, the Unisex Edition of the ACT Interest Inventory, the Self-Directed Search, the Vocational Preference Inventory, Johansson's measures, and the Interest-Finder Quiz. From consultations with colleagues, Savickas (1998) identified the first five as being widely used and included them in a special issue of the *Career Development Quarterly* dedicated to interpreting interest inventories. Our focus will be the design and types of scales within each inventory, other similarities and differences between the measures, and how the measures support joint interpretation with other constructs such as abilities and skills. Although we generally limit our discussion to paper-and-pencil versions, in many cases publishers have already adapted the measures for computerized administration, and increasingly administration via the Internet.

Strong Vocational Interest Blank (Strong Interest Inventory)

Strong began development of his Strong Vocational Interest Blank (SVIB) in the 1920s (see Donnay, 1997; Donnay & Borgen, 1996b). The current version is the Strong Interest Inventory, Fourth Edition (SII; Hansen, 2000; Harmon, Hansen, Borgen, & Hammer, 1994; see also Harmon & Borgen, 1995), which has several sets of scales formed from 317 items (most items contribute to several scales). The response format varies slightly across the sections of the SII, although in most cases the examinee responds to one of three levels of endorsement of an item (*essentially like, dislike,* and *indifferent*).

The original set of scales in the SVIB and still the most numerous set in the SII are the Occupational Scales. These scales offer separate norms for comparisons to women and men in particular occupations. The Occupational Scales include items from the SII that serve to distinguish members of the occupational norm group from members of a general population sample.

The next set of scales developed were the 25 Basic Interest Scales, homogenous scales that measure specialized interests in a presumably pure form. Next developed were the General Occupational Themes (GOTs), based on Holland's six types (Realistic, Investigative, Artistic, Social, Enterprising, and Convention), with explicit use made of their organization within Holland's hexagon in reporting results. (David Campbell and John Holland reportedly selected the original items to comprise the GOTs based primarily on how much they seemed to relate to the various personal orientations; thus, one could argue that the original themes were based mainly on rational rather than empirical scale construction methods. However, a different and more empirical basis underlies the GOTs of the current edition of the SII.) In addition, both the Occupational and Basic Interest scales are classified into best-corresponding Holland interest types for purposes of reporting results. Finally, a set of personality-related scales has been included across various editions of the SVIB; they are now grouped in the Personal Style Scales of the current SII, for which Lindley and Borgen (2000) have demonstrated predicted relations to the Big Five personality traits.

Because the Occupational Scales of the SVIB and SII tend to focus more on occupations requiring a college or professional education, some authors have argued that that the SVIB is relatively less useful for non–college bound students. Although it is true that the Occupational Scales are more representative of occupations requiring college or professional education, skilled interpretation of the SII may extend its reach to occupations in general. In particular, one may determine a three-letter Holland code from rank ordering scores on the GOTs and the other scales organized by Holland's types; one may then, using a crosswalk such as the *Dictionary of Holland Occupational Codes* (G. D. Gottfredson & Holland, 1996), match an SII profile to almost any occupation.

A more serious constraint in the general use of the SII may be its relatively high reading level. Although its manual claims a reading level at Grade 9, its effective reading level may be somewhat higher. Caution in the use of the SII with individuals in Grade 10 or lower is therefore suggested.

The SII's companion measure, the Skills Confidence Inventory (SCI; Betz, Borgen, & Harmon, 1996), assesses self-ratings of skills on dimensions corresponding to many facets of the SII. These dimensions include the Holland personal orientations assessed through the SII's GOTs.

Campbell Interest and Skill Survey

The Campbell Interest and Skill Survey (CISS; Campbell, 1994, 1995; Hansen & Neuman, 1999) is one of a family of career-assessment measures by Campbell and his colleagues, with companion instruments measuring leadership traits and related constructs of interest to organizations. The CISS consists of 200 interest and 120 skill items. An 11-page report provides scores on seven Orientation Scales (Influencing, Organizing, Helping, Creating, Analyzing, Producing, and Adventuring) that generally correspond to Holland's scales except for having two realistic analogues (Producing and

Adventuring); 29 Basic (interest and skill) Scales (clusters of occupations and skills, such as mathematics and science grouped with "write computer programs . . . perform lab research"); 60 Occupational Scales; and 2 Special Scales (Academic Focus and Extraversion, corresponding to the scales on the previous edition of the SII). This design clearly is similar to that used by the SII, with which it competes head-to-head in the market. Such similarity is hardly surprising, given that Campbell had directed development of the Strong for many years before moving on to develop the CISS.

Perhaps Campbell's most persuasive argument for use of the CISS instead of the SII appears to be that one may obtain an essentially identical set of scales despite the administration of many fewer (interest) items with the CISS (200, vs. 317 for the SII), which he argues is possible because of the use of a six-level Likert response format for items, compared to the SII's three-level response format. As with the corresponding scales on the SII, the Orientation and Basic scales on the CISS are homogenous, while the Occupational Scales are developed through use of occupational criterion groups. Another difference between the SII and the CISS is that where the SII's occupational norms were developed separately by gender, the CISS relies on combined-gender occupational groups, along with adjustments in development of the occupational norms to make up for sample differences in gender ratios. Occupational Scale scores are also reported somewhat differently than the corresponding scales on the SII, but still make use of comparisons of occupational group responses compared to a general reference-group sample (with the general reference sample including both genders). Another (minor) differences lies in Campbell's use of seven personal-orientation categories, compared to Holland's six, as we have already discussed. The reading level for the CISS (intended to be readable by the average person aged 15 or older) appears to be comparable to that of the SII; however, the CISS also offers definitions of occupations, perhaps easing the vocabulary burden, especially for individuals without much exposure to occupational information in their daily lives.

The CISS report provides recommendations for exploration of different occupational options: *pursue* (high interest, high skill), *develop* (high interest, low skill), *explore* (low interest, high skill), and *avoid* (low interest, low skill). Counselors may similarly compare interest inventory results on the SII (using the SCI for comparison), but such comparisons are not directly built into an automated report.

Kuder Occupational Interest Survey

Kuder (1939) began to develop his family of interest measures (e.g., Kuder, 1948, 1991; Kuder & Diamond, 1979) within a decade after the initial publication of the SVIB.

Today's versions include the Kuder Career Search (KCS; plus a related KCS with Person Match), Kuder General Interest Survey Form E, and the Kuder Occupational Interest Survey Form DD (KOIS; Diamond & Zytowski, 2000; Kuder, 1991). The KOIS, like the SII, includes criterion-based occupational scales, plus college-based major scales. The measure has 100 items, each formed of a triad of options; most and least preferred activities in each triad are chosen. Similarities between an examinee's responses to those typical of an occupation are calculated directly, without reference to differentiation from members of general population samples.

KOIS results are also reported for the examinee's norm group by gender across 10 vocational areas and those of satisfied workers in approximately 100 occupations. Although the 10 groups differ from Holland's six orientations, the scores and results can be interpreted in terms of those six orientations. The Kuder reportedly has a sixth-grade reading level, but typical use of the measure is with Grade 11 and above. Those in lower grades may find the reading level challenging.

Containing 60 triad-based items, the KCS is substantially shorter than the KOIS, and reportedly has a reading level that is truly closer to that of sixth-graders. It reports results into the same 10 Activity Preference Scales as used by the KOIS, along with six Career Cluster Scales (corresponding to Holland's six personal orientations), and Person-Matches corresponding to the 253 occupational classifications reported in the U.S. Department of Labor publications, extending the KCS's usefulness to include the full range of students, and not only those bound for college.

Unisex Edition of the ACT Interest Inventory

The Unisex Edition of the ACT (American College Test) Interest Inventory (or UNIACT) is one of the most widely used interest measures in the world, according to one of its authors (Swaney, 1995). The test is not marketed directly to counselors or examinees as a stand-alone measure but rather is available only through bundling with other ACT products, such as career-planning packages sold or licensed to schools, or the ACT college entrance examination.

Prediger and Swaney (1995) provide a thorough discussion of two forms of the UNIACT, each consisting of 90 activity-based items (as with the KOIS and KCS, only activities are used), 15 for each of the six Holland personal orientations, yielding the six Basic Interest Scales (Technical, Science, Arts, Social Service, Business Contact, and Business Operations, corresponding to the Holland orientations of Realistic, Investigative, Artistic, Social, Enterprising, and Conventional, respectively). The UNIACT also organizes its report according to a two-dimensional framework that incorporates the orientations measured by the Basic Interest

Scales. The first or these dimensions describes a Data-Ideas dimension (with Business Contact and Operations on the Data extreme, and Arts and Sciences on the Ideas extreme). The second delineates a People-Things dimension (with Social Service on the People extreme, and Technical on the Things extreme). The UNIACT report makes use of a coordinate system defined by these two bipolar dimensions to locate examinees, academic majors, and occupations within the same two-dimensional space, yielding the World-of-Work Map, a practical tool for inventory interpretation and counseling. Within this map, the UNIACT report clusters 23 job families within 12 regions. Interpretation of UNIACT results relies heavily on the spatial position of the examinee in relation to job families and regions. Perhaps the major difference between the UNIACT and the previously discussed measures is the decision to seek to eliminate gender-related differences in scale scores by retaining only items that showed no gender-related differences.

Self-Directed Search

Holland's Self-Directed Search (SDS; Holland, 1994; Holland, Fritzsche, & Powell, 1994) differs from the previously discussed interest inventories in several important respects. First, examinees can score and interpret it for themselves. Second, self-administration of the SDS encourages reliance on raw scores in lieu of scaled scores and comparisons to normative samples, which provides a simpler, if not always the most accurate, understanding for non–technically trained persons.

Spokane and Holland (1995) provide a review of the family of SDS measures, including Form R (Regular) for high school (or younger, for students with a minimum of sixth-grade reading ability) through adult; Form E (for adults and older adolescents with low (Grade 4 to 6) reading level; Form CP for higher-level individuals in organizations; a version for use with middle-school students; and versions in other languages. The sections of the SDS include Occupational Daydreams (examinee lists as many as eight occupations), Activities (six scales corresponding to each of the Holland vocational types, 11 items each), Competencies (six scales, 11 items each), Occupations (six scales, 14 items each), Self-Estimates (two sets of 6 ratings). In all sections except Occupational Daydreams, item response involves simply checking the item to endorse it; scores from each section except Occupational Daydreams contribute to summary scores for each of the six types, from which the examinee may determine his or her three-letter Holland code. Once the code is determined (say, Realistic-Investigative-Enterprising), one may use the code as the basis for exploring classifications of occupations, college majors, and leisure activities for corresponding (reasonable) matches to the code.

Holland was also the first author to seek to assess and integrate abilities and skills (via self-ratings) with interests within the same assessment system; in this way, the SDS anticipated the CISS, the SCI, and even the ability assessment systems into which ACT has embedded the UNIACT. In fact, the market success of the SDS probably spurred these changes in the other major measures.

Vocational Preference Inventory

Holland's original measure of personal orientations was the Vocational Preference Inventory (VPI; Holland, 1958, 1985), consisting of 160 occupations representing his six vocational personality types as well as five additional personality traits (Self-Control, Status, Masculinity-Femininity, Infrequency, and Acquiescence). Counselors can use (raw) scores from the six personality types to locate matching occupations, majors, or leisure activities in various resources. The measure offers the advantages of brevity and low cost, along with information about some additional personality-related traits, and—unlike with the SDS—the examinee does not know how particular items will contribute to various scales. However, the origin of the test's norms appears not to be clearly defined; at this point they need updating, and the validity evidence for the test could use newer studies, particularly establishing that the occupational titles in the test are still current and differentiating.

Johansson's Measures

Johansson has developed another family of interest inventories, two of which are especially appropriate for use with non-college-bound or nonprofessional populations. The earliest developed—the Interest Determination, Exploration, and Assessment System (IDEAS; Johansson, 1980)—essentially provides a replication of the SDS. It is a self-directing inventory yielding six Holland orientation scores and associated basic interest scales (all using combined gender norms) organized by orientation, appropriate for use by individuals not bound for college. The Career Assessment Inventory–Vocational Version (CAI-VV; Johansson, 1982) and the Career Assessment Inventory–Enhanced Version (CAI-EV; Johansson, 1986) are modeled closely on the SII, with each including criterion-based occupational scales, basic interest scales, and scales for each of Holland's personal orientations. The CAI-VV's design reflects intention for use with individuals not aiming for careers in the professions. The CAI-EV is intended to be more broadly applicable, through incorporation of more items and reporting that is more reflective of professional occupations. The manuals report the reading levels for the CAI-VV and CAI-EV to be

Grade 6 and Grade 8, respectively; however, as with the SII, KOIS, and similar measures, examinee unfamiliarity with some terms (especially occupational titles) suggests the need for caution in administration to younger students (see Vacc & Hinkle, 1994).

Interest-Finder Quiz

The Interest-Finder Quiz is part of the Armed Services Vocational Aptitude Battery (ASVAB) assessment offered for no cost through a majority of American high schools for purposes of military enlisted recruitment and selection (see Wall & Baker 1997). The Interest-Finder appears to be an adaptation of the SDS to be used in military recruitment, and to provide an interest inventory to complement the aptitude-oriented ASVAB. The measure includes six 40-item scales for each of Holland's personal orientations; each of the six scales includes three sections of items, based on activities (14 items), training (12 items), and occupations (14 items).

Other Inventories and Methods

Some other inventories of interest include the COPSystem (Knapp-Lee, 1995), the Harrington-O'Shea Career Decision-Making System (HOCDMS; Harrington & O'Shea, 2000), the Jackson Vocational Interest Survey (JVIS; Jackson, 1991), the Vocational Interest Inventory (VII; Lunneborg, 1981), and the Chronicle Career Quest (CCQ, Forms S and L; CGP Research Staff, 1992; see review by Livers, 1994). Of these measures, the COPSystem and HOCDMS probably are the most widely used. There are also several card sorts for measuring interests; Hartung (1999) discusses their rationale, history, and availability, including a review of eight interest card sorts of potential interest to users. Additionally, measures exist for classifying occupations rather than persons on interest-related factors (see, e.g., Gottfredson, 1986a).

Summary

Which measure of interests is preferable under what circumstances? No single measure of occupational interests can be declared universally superior for use in all circumstances and with all populations (Eby & Russell, 1998). The relative merits and limitations of each measure are counterbalanced by others. Some are preferable for certain age groups or reading levels, others for particular educational levels. The SVIB includes one of the most impressive normative bases and one that is regularly updated; the SDS lends itself to individual administration and scoring; the UNIACT attempts to minimize gender differences. All have value and all measures in one way or another incorporate Holland's factors. Still needed is more research examining the shared variance across these measures and whether it practically matters, in the measurement of interests, which measure was used. In the meantime, practitioners need carefully to choose measures of interests relevant for the particular assessment population and task at hand. Interpretation of interests should be done in the context of the client's understanding of self and in association with other variables (see Holland, 1996; Lowman & Carson, 2000).

RELIABILITY AND VALIDITY OF INTEREST MEASURES

In this section, we shall consider the reliability (focusing on short- and long-term stability) and validity of measures of interests. Determination of the validity of interests relates to the question of whether interests are empirically structured in a way consistent with espoused theory, whether they are differentiated from other relevant psychological concepts (such as attitudes, personality, or abilities), and whether they predict behaviorally relevant life and career choices. The first of these calls for factorial and internal-consistency studies, the second with the extent to which these constructs overlap with other relevant ones (such as personality and values; these matters will be discussed in a separate section), and the third to the relationship of interest constructs with relevant criterion measures. Fouad (1999) has provided a good survey of some of the validity issues and research findings. Because of their particular relevance for validity issues, we will also discuss in this section issues related to differences across groups (age, sex, and culture) on measures of interests.

Reliability of Interests

Short-Term Stability and Precision of Measurement

Most measures of interests demonstrate high to very high reliability when judged by standard reliability measures such as coefficient alphas (e.g., Blake, 1969; Campbell, 1995; Clark, 1961; Holland, 1985; Lowman & Schurman, 1982; Swaney, 1995). These measures are typically in the .80s to .90s (see Lowman, in press, for a summary of commonly reported reliabilities for the most common currently used measures of interests).

Long-Term Stability

Considering the long-term stability of interest measures (test-retest), both classical and more recent research finds adequate

to remarkable stability of interests (test-retest correlations typically in the .70s or higher over multiyear intervals; see Dawis, 1991), and this finding appears to hold independently of specific measurement instrument (see, e.g., Hansen & Johansson, 1972; Johansson & Campbell, 1971; Lau & Abrahams, 1971). Perhaps the most systematic longitudinal studies of the stability of interests to date have been those of Strong (1938a, 1938b, 1951, 1952), who persistently found the temporal stability of the interest patterns of men and women to be among the most stable of all psychological variables. More recently, Swanson (1999) discussed in detail issues concerning the stability of occupational interests and concludes that, although a small proportion of people do change their interests over the course of the life cycle, in general, interests are markedly stable.

Validity of Interests

Structure and Dimensionality of Interests

The structure of interests is a topic that has concerned researchers for some time (e.g., Cottle, 1950). In early studies, essentially atheoretical measures such as Strong's (1938b) were often examined factorially to determine their underlying structure. Thurstone (1931) extracted four factors in a study of the SVIB: science, business, people, and language. Strong's (1943) work in this area identified a similar set of dimensions, plus a things-versus-people dimension; Strong also bifurcated the business dimension into systems and contact. Roe (1954) proposed an eight-group model similar to Strong's. Holland's (1959) original theory proposed six interest-based personal orientations, which were later renamed *vocational personality types.*

Although a number of empirical efforts to measure and classify interests preceded his work, Holland's remains the dominant structural model of interests (e.g., Campbell & Borgen, 1999). Holland's contribution (Campbell & Borgen; Holland, 1959, 1997a), among others, was to add theory to empiricism to put factor results into a model that cuts across occupational types, work environments, and cultures.

Holland's (1997a; see also Spokane, 1996) six-factor model of interests consisted of the following factors with their now widely used labels:

1. *realistic* (preference for real-world activities involving the manipulation of things and enjoyment of the physical environment);

2. *investigative* (interest in science and intellectually relevant abstractions, and in a world of empirically based ideas; enjoyment of logic, order, and precision rather than subjectivity, elasticity, and fuzziness);

3. *artistic* (concern with the world of symbolic expression; a preference for subjectively experienced views; aesthetic idealism; a need for accurately understanding and communicating, often forcefully, subjectively experienced reality, even—or perhaps especially—when it runs counter to prevailing views of reality or of appropriate behavior, feelings, or conduct);

4. *social* (preference for continual involvement with people; liking to work with and through others and to better others and the human condition more generally);

5. *enterprising* (more aptly named *managerial,* a preference for working with others but from the perspective of managing or leading others; liking of prestige and extrinsic rewards; liking of upward mobility and control over others; liking activities involving persuasion and influence); and

6. *conventional* (preference for orderly and predictable activities involving repetitiveness, numbers, or data; liking of routine, predictability, and order; see, among others, Holland, 1997a).

Holland's model lends itself to complexity in that people do not have to be classified into one of six categories but rather, if the three most highly endorsed scales are considered, to one of 120 permutations of the three most highly endorsed interest patterns (see Gottfredson, 1999; Lowman, 1991). The factors are said to describe and to classify environments as well as individuals, and the question of the match between person and occupation or organization is at the heart of most contemporary career-assessment and counseling practice. There is considerable evidence for the existence of these factors in a variety of cultural measurements (e.g., Athanasou, O'Gorman, & Meyer, 1981; Day & Rounds, 1998).

We argue that Holland's theory has persisted for almost 50 years because (a) it is based on the empirically verified fact that preferences for a diversity of occupations can meaningfully be grouped into a small number of occupational clusters that have factorial integrity, and (b) the factors or scales (or types) have practical implications that can be readily grasped by end users, such as the general public or career counselors working with clients. Whatever the reasons, Holland's model continues to dominate the interest scene of both research and practice.

Holland's structural model of interests has been exhaustively studied (Holland, 1997a). Much of the research has been supportive of the idea of six factors and their general relationship with one another regardless of culture. Other reviews (e.g., Day & Rounds, 1998; Day, Rounds, & Swaney, 1998; Prediger & Vansickle, 1999; Rounds & Day, 1999;

Tracey & Rounds, 1993) challenge the criticality of the six factors and argue that the number of factors and their presumed relationship to one another are essentially arbitrary, and that they neither are limited to six nor necessarily assume the Holland circular (or hexagonal) structure. More recent studies have systematically begun to identify the underlying, or meta-, second-order factor structure of interests. It is the structural nature of the model that has generated the most successful challenge to Holland's models.

Although most (but not all) researchers would likely agree that there is still merit and especially practical utility in Holland's classical and persistent six-factor model of interests, there are exceptions. Campbell's (1995) CISS measure included seven measures of interests and juxtaposed the conventional and social (rather than conventional and enterprising) interests. Moreover, the structural models of interests also need to incorporate an underlying meta-structure that has increasingly been suggested by second-order-factor researchers. Most secondary factor structures generally reduce the six-factor solution to two overarching (perhaps more accurately, undergirding or foundational) dimensions: concern with data versus ideas, and concern with people versus things (see Einarsdottir & Rounds, 2000; Gati, 1991; Prediger, 1982, 1989; Rounds & Day, 1999; Tracey & Rounds, 1993). Einarsdottir and Rounds also claim to have identified a third structural factor, perhaps best labeled as *sex-role congruence.*

The practical implications for the underlying two-factor structure of interests remain to be demonstrated. Whether concern for things versus people and concern with ideas versus data is a sufficiently robust or detailed grouping from which individuals can make career decisions, and on which career assessors and counselors can provide guidance, remains to be demonstrated. The balance between scientific precision or parsimony and practical utility needs to be considered in evaluating the utility of such findings, since occupational choices are generally not experienced by individuals in abstract psychological or conceptual terms. People tend to think about occupational choices concretely: for example, "Should I go to medical school or law school?" Rounds and Day (1999) appropriately argue that the model of interests employed should match the counseling question. In this respect, the more detailed models clustering occupations into a larger number of psychologically meaningful dimensions may at this time be more pragmatically useful.

Criterion-Related Validity: School-Related Criteria

Some studies have demonstrated the ability of occupational interest test scores to predict well to school major, a common criterion measure. *Interest theory* suggests that persons with particular interests should prefer particular college majors in a manner generally consistent with the correspondence between persons in the adult work world and their college majors (e.g., persons with realistic-investigative interests would be predicted to choose both majors and careers in engineering or technology vs., say, art or history). Independent of the instrument used, these occupational interest variables predict well to groupings of like-minded students and to students' choice of college majors (see, among others, Betz & Taylor, 1982; Borgen & Helms, 1975; Fouad, 1999; Hansen & Neuman, 1999; Hansen & Swanson, 1983; Miller, Newell, Springer, & Wells, 1992; Naylor & Kidd, 1991; Silver & Barnette, 1970).

Criterion-Related Validity: Vocational Choices

The research results are generally positive but somewhat more mixed in supporting the validity of interest measures in predicting to real-world occupational and avocational (Super, 1940a) activity choices. In predicting to broadly categorized occupational choices years later, the interest measures on average are quite good in their predictive power (Donnay & Borgen, 1996b; Gottfredson & Holland, 1975; Lowman & Schurman, 1982; Lucy, 1976, Mount & Muchinsky, 1978a, 1978b; Spokane & Decker, 1999; Super, 1940b, 1949; Super & Crites, 1962; Upperman & Church, 1995). The more specific the predictive task, however, the less well the interest measures perform (DeFruyt & Mervielde, 1999; Fricko & Beehr, 1992; Upperman & Church; Zytowski & Hay, 1984).

Predicting to Work-Related Outcomes

Interest measures have generally had a better track record in predicting to career satisfaction (liking one's occupational choice) than to issues related to job satisfaction (liking one's specific job, including the specific work setting) or productivity (e.g., Dawis, 1991; Hogan & Blake, 1996; Schneider, Paul, White, & Holcombe, 1999). This is presumably because many other factors influence the degree to which someone is likely to be satisfied with or productive in a particular application of an occupation. Extrinsic factors, such a salary, satisfaction with coworkers, satisfaction with the quality of supervision, one's own history with a particular employer, and the context in which the employment occurs (e.g., in times of high unemployment or during relatively flush periods in which opportunities for job mobility abound) affect job satisfaction perhaps as much as goodness of career fit. On the other hand, recent research approaches addressing the *person-environment fit* (Spokane, 1994; Spokane, Meir, & Catalano, 2000) provide considerably more sophistication in

the definition of the job as it relates to interests theories (e.g., Maurer & Tarullie, 1997), so it is possible that over time more complex predictions of work-related outcomes can be made.

GROUP DIFFERENCES IN THE MEASUREMENT OF INTERESTS

Systematic group differences in interest patterns or interest test scores have been a cause of concern for some time because they may represent bias in a measure, perhaps leading to restriction in the sorts of occupations or other options considered. The fact that groups differ on items or scales does not necessarily indicate bias or invalidity, as observed score differences may reflect true group differences in interests. Groups have most often been compared through absolute levels of interests and by the ways in which interest scores correlate with one another (i.e., the structure of interests). Our focus will be on interest inventories and not other methods, such as card sorts. We shall briefly survey research on differences in interests across groups differing in age, sex and gender, and culture. We do not discuss differences across groups with different disabilities, except to refer interested readers to summaries of the topic (see Klein, Wheaton, & Wilson, 1997; Lowman, 1997), and to note that most manuals provide scant data about such groups (see Fouad & Spreda, 1995).

Age

In a thorough review of the literature on stability and change in interests across the life span, Swanson (1999) reports that there are few systematic, normative changes in interests over time, especially after age 30. She also notes that differences observed between groups of individuals at different ages are smaller than between occupational groups. Swanson further reports that one change reported across studies is that interests appear to become better defined over time.

Sex, Gender, and Sexual Orientation

It is useful to distinguish between *sex* and *gender differences,* the former related to an examinee's biological sex (male or female), and the latter related to the examinee's sense of gender-role identification (masculine or feminine) and behavior, which is (highly) correlated with biological gender. Gender is more difficult to assess than biological sex and generally requires specialized scales for assessment. Such measures can tap the degree to which a child has been socialized into, say, traditional masculine or feminine roles, or the degree to which an adolescent or adult has adopted androgynous characteristics in the course of education, peer socialization, or immersion in the popular culture. Of the extensive research on group differences in interests, almost all has been carried out in relation to biological sex, and almost none in relation to gender, although the masculinity-femininity scales included on some—and mostly older—interest inventories (such as the Vocational Preference Inventory; Holland, 1958, 1985) are essentially gender indicators in their own right. (Note that in the literature on sex differences in interests, authors generally use the word *gender* in lieu of *sex,* and often authors' discussions fail to distinguish the two concepts adequately.) Because of the paucity of recent research on gender-related group differences in interests, our remaining discussion will focus on sex differences; however, until research speaks to the issue, it remains a live possibility that it is primarily gender and not sex per se that accounts for observed sex differences in interests.

Sex-related differences in responses to interest inventory items have been reported since the earliest inventories. In most cases, such differences are more a matter of degree than of kind; in other words, although there may exist sex-related differences in mean level of endorsement of an item, there are usually some members of each sex who will respond on either extreme of endorsement. Typically, however, in broad general population samples, males more highly endorse realistic interests than do females, and females are more likely to endorse social and conventional interests.

One strategy to eliminate sex differences from a measure is to exclude from the final measure any inventory items that evince sex differences. The developers of the UNIACT (Swaney, 1995) followed this approach. Critics of this approach might argue that the resulting measure might not reflect the reality of possible interests on which the sexes, for whatever reason, really do differ. Fouad and Spreda (1995) report having found meaningful sex differences in endorsement of 25% of the items of the 1994 edition of the SII. They also reported that even in the UNIACT there were major sex differences in endorsement of some of the scales. Kuder and Zytowski (1991), using KOIS data, report that men and women in the same occupations have different interests. The conclusion after several decades of research is that the interests of men and women continue to differ at both the item and scale level (Fouad & Spreda). Hansen, Collins, Swanson, and Fouad (1993) also reported evidence, based on multidimensional scaling, that there are also sex differences in the structure of interests, but some have challenged those findings as being based on samples of inadequate size.

Authors of measures must also decide when to use same-sex or combined-sex samples when norming scales. The SII, KOIS, COPSystem, SDS, and JVIS are some measures that include scales making use of separate norm groups for men and women. The UNIACT and CISS are among the measures using only scales that make use of combined-sex norm groups. Again, critics of the practice of using combined-sex norm groups point to data suggesting that because men and women in occupations do appear to have different interest patterns, combined norm groups may mask real differences, although they may foster consideration and exploration of occupations that individuals might not otherwise have considered.

There is little published research on differences in interests based on sexual preference, consistent with Prince's (1997) claim that there has been little research on common assessment measures with gay, lesbian, and bisexual populations. Some authors (see Lowman, 1993a, p. 216; Rothenberg, 1990) have suggested that gay males are disproportionately represented in the arts (although there is no evidence that a majority of gay males are creatively talented). Chung and Harmon (1994) compared SDS scores of gay and heterosexual men; gay men scored relatively higher on artistic and social scales and lower on realistic and investigative ones. This research may suggest that, as with sex differences, interests likewise could vary with sexual orientation—although much wider and more representative samples would be needed to understand this issue more completely.

Culture

Culture is a diverse category; in reporting cultural differences in interests, we will focus mainly on ethnicity and race, although a more complete treatment would include language, nationality, religion, and other factors. Most authors of interest inventories have sought to study possible group differences related to race and ethnicity (see Lattimore & Borgen, 1999; Rounds & Day, 1998). However, such research generally does a poor job of making clear whether groups were selected on the biological construct *race,* versus the more socially determined construct *ethnicity.* Also, in most studies examinees are required to choose the single racial or ethnic category that best describes their background (e.g., Black, White). However, a growing proportion of the population has a mixed background in terms of race (a fuzzy concept to start with), and determining a single ethnic identification is a difficult if not impossible task for many individuals enculturated into more than one ethnic tradition. In addition, several authors concerned with career assessment and development also discuss the concept of *minority status* (see DeVaney & Hughey, 2000) in relation to race or ethnicity, but this likewise has become more problematic since some states no longer have a single racial or ethnic group that can claim a majority, and as nearly everyone is a member of a minority group in an increasingly global economy.

For many decades, interest inventories were normed mainly on samples of European descent. There had been relatively few studies of cultural differences in interests until recently. In an important review of the literature on the use of the SVIB and its later versions using Black samples, spanning the period from the 1920s to the 1980s, Carter and Swanson (1990) reported only eight studies (often with small or unrepresentative samples) that suggested that, compared to Whites, Black Americans had relatively higher interests in social and business occupations and relatively lower interests in scientific and technical ones. Over the past decade, a plethora of articles have appeared on the topic of *cultural assessment,* including a number directed at issues of interest patterns or structures in specific racial or ethnic groups (e.g., Leong & Leung, 1994).

Recently developed or renormed inventories generally seek to sample from diverse and representative ethnic and racial populations and then check to ensure that scale scores are approximately the same across groups. As with sex and gender, a number of studies have investigated whether the structure of interests—generally in reference to Holland's theory—remains the same across ethnic and racial groups (see Leong & Hartung, 2000). For example, using a sample of male and female Native American college students, Hansen and Haviland (2000) reported support for Holland's hexagonal model of interests using the GOTs from the 1985 edition of the SII, although the results for women slightly better fit the predicted hexagonal shape than did those for men. Fouad and Spreda (1995) summarize such research for the SII, KOIS, UNIACT, and SDS, generally finding great similarity across ethnic and racial groups, and at any rate more similarity than between the sexes. We would hasten to add that interests and occupational aspirations are not identical; people can be interested in one type of work but aspire to another that they believe is more realistic or achievable (L. S. Gottfredson, 1986b; L. S. Gottfredson & Lapan, 1997). Thus, there may still exist large differences between ethnic and racial groups in occupational aspirations, even when differences in interests are few.

COMPREHENSIVE ASSESSMENT OF INTERESTS WITH OTHER DOMAINS

The measurement of interests alone is generally insufficient from a research or practice perspective, because interests do not predict in a vacuum and they account for only one aspect of what goes into making choices affecting career, job, or life satisfaction. The senior author has been one of the most persistent advocates of the need to measure in multiple domains (Lowman, 1991, 1997). Real people do not consist of interests alone; they consist of various combinations of interests that, assuredly, interact with abilities and personality, among other trait variables, to determine occupational histories, best-fitting careers, and appropriateness for particular positions. The issues were well identified in a different context by Martindale (1999, p. 137):

> Creativity is a rare trait. This is presumably because it requires the simultaneous presence of a number of traits (e.g., intelligence, perseverance, unconventionality, the ability to think in a particular manner). None of these traits is especially rare. What is quite uncommon is to find them all present in the same person.

Increasingly, researchers are looking for the interaction of interests and other variables such as personality, ability, motivation, and life experiences (see, e.g., Lapan, Shaughnessy, & Boggs, 1996; Super, Savickas, & Super, 1996). Although there are some (and generally older) studies comparing interests and values (Sarbin & Berdie, 1940; Williams, 1972), we shall focus on the relations of interests to personality traits and abilities, for which robust literatures are now accruing.

Interest-Personality Relationships

There is considerable evidence (Hogan & Blake, 1996; Holland, 1997b; Ozone-Shinichi, 1998), some of it (e.g., Atkinson & Lunneborg, 1968) not new, that interests overlap substantially with personality characteristics and that these generally follow a predictable path at the aggregated level. Holland (1997b) argues that interest inventories actually are, in effect, personality measures. However, considerably more work is needed to determine the relationships other than at the aggregated basis. Most career counseling is done on an individual basis. Grouped overlaps address issues related to factors that tend to move in the same direction—for example, conscientiousness with conventional interest patterns. More data are needed determining the relationships between nonmatches—for example, strong conventional interest patterns and low scores on conscientiousness.

By far the most work has been done to date in exploring the relationships between occupational interests and personality (Holland, Johnston, & Asama, 1994). The usual research paradigm has been to administer paper-and-pencil measures of interests and paper-and-pencil measures of personality and to consider (a) whether there is common variance and (b) whether predicted relationships across domains (e.g., conventional interest patterns and conscientiousness) are correlated in a predictable manner. Generally, this research has found overlap between interest areas, typically using Holland's six-factor model, and corresponding personality variables predicted to covary with interests (e.g., artistic vocational interests with the personality variable of openness).

A more complicated question concerns the relationship of interests and what might be called *overarching personality variables*. Researchers (e.g., Betz & Borgen, 2000; Betz & Schifano, 2000; Donnay & Borgen, 1996a; Lapan et al., 1996) have demonstrated that self-efficacy can be a powerful additive, if not overarching, variable in determining whether people make appropriate use of their interest patterns, particularly when confronted with a culturally atypical career preference (e.g., women with realistic interests attracted to male-dominated fields).

Interest-Ability Relationships

Perhaps the least amount of systematic work to date has been done on measuring the overlap between interests and abilities, despite some early efforts to consider the question (e.g., Hartman & Dashiell, 1919; Wesley, Corey, & Stewart, 1950). A literature has begun to emerge in this important area (e.g., Ackerman, Kyllonen, & Roberts, 1999; Carson, 1996; L. S. Gottfredson, 1996; Lowman & Williams, 1987; Lowman, Williams, & Leeman, 1985; Randahl, 1991), but it remains limited. The measurement of abilities remains complex and hampers progress in this area. Some research, generally measuring abilities through self-ratings (Prediger, 1999a, 1999b; Tracey & Hopkins, 2001), has been reported, including a few detailed studies with comprehensive measures of abilities, but it is premature on the basis of this scanty record to draw many conclusions. So far, the interest and ability domains appear to be (a) separable; (b) interactive; and (c) similarly structured. The several studies (e.g., Prediger, 1999a, 1999b) that have addressed the topic from the perspective of self-ratings of both interests and abilities suffer from the absence of a convincing literature base establishing that self-rating abilities are equivalent to objectively rated ones (see Carson, 1998b; Lowman & Williams, 1987). Not surprisingly, generally more powerful results are shown in the relationship between self-ratings of abilities and interests, but this may partly be explained by common method variance because identical response formats are generally used. However, Lowman and Williams demonstrated that against the criteria of objective measures of ability, self-ratings are less than ideal.

Much more research work is needed to better understand how interests relate to abilities, and vice versa. An intriguing suggestion is that interests, if in large part essentially inherited and rather fixed characteristics of people, direct activity to specific, interest-related areas. Because ability (in contrast to interests) requires considerable practice to advance from raw talent to usable skills, it is likely that interests may direct where one's "ability capital" is invested (see Ericsson, 1996, p. 27). According to those in this theoretical group (which would include early psychologist Dewey; see Savickas, 1999, p. 32), the great importance of interests is that they drive practice, and practice determines skill acquisition.

The nature of abilities themselves is of course not without controversy. By most accounts, abilities are suffused with a general factor, often labeled g, or intelligence, and a series of primary abilities, p's, which are themselves correlated moderately with g (see Carroll, 1993). The question of whether to evaluate abilities only on the basis of g, or to include p's, is therefore not without controversy. Separate correlations of g and g-free specific abilities may be useful in sorting out interdomain relationships.

Interest-Ability-Personality Relationships

Very little research has been conducted examining the relationships of interests, abilities, and personality characteristics, measuring all three domains simultaneously (Carless, 1999; Carson, 1998a; Lowman, 1991; Lowman & Leeman, 1988). Perhaps the most relevant newer work is that of Ackerman and his colleagues (Ackerman & Heggestad, 1997). The Ackerman model addresses the three major domains so far shown to be important in determining career issues and job placement. However, his models need to be replicated using alternative measures of interests and abilities. Brown, Lent, and Gore (2000) found overlapping but separable information contributed from interests, self-rated abilities, and a personality measure.

In real life, of course, people are not simply one psychological variable or another. They have specific levels of abilities, specific types of generally quite stable interests, and personality structures that also have predictability. Theories that relate to all three domains (interests, abilities, and personality) simultaneously are few in number, and include Ackerman's (Ackerman & Heggestad, 1997; Ackerman et al., 1999) *process, personality, interests, and knowledge (PPIK) theory* and Lowman's (1991) *interdomain theory*.

NEEDED RESEARCH

By any reasonable standard, research in interests is dynamic and flourishing. Still, more work is needed to address several next-level issues. Looking ahead to the next research tasks, we can ask what is left to do and how such tasks should be prioritized. These tasks can be grouped into several categories: (a) psychobiology of interests; (b) specific versus general interest categories; (c) commonality and differences of alternative interest measures; (d) empirically based occupational and environmental codings; (e) the structure of interests; (f) interdomain relationships; and (g) additive value of measures related to interests.

Psychobiology of Interests

Although promising, the current research is inadequate for reliably differentiating the amount of variance that is more or less fixed genetically and the amount that can be influenced by environments. Preliminary studies suggest a sizable amount of heritability to interests, but this finding needs replication using alternative measures of interests. Certainly, a finding of high heritability would be expected, given the pronounced stability of interests across the life cycle and the marked efficiency with which people seem to self-select in right-fitting occupations. Nonetheless, among those with relatively fixed profiles, it matters which aspects of interests can change or are likely to change naturally, because there are career choice and satisfaction issues associated with that. Conversely, in cases in which interests appear to be unstable, to what extent is the profile, if highly genetic in origin, simply unknown to the person being counseled as opposed to something still in flux?

An approach integrating aspects of both the learning and genetic approaches might be to assume that there exist critical periods during which interests are modifiable based on environmental reinforcement, but after which they are more resistant to modification. Of course, psychoanalytic theories of interests placing special importance on the quality of parent–young child interaction represent a type of *critical-period theory*, but one may hypothesize critical periods for interests extending to much greater ages. One may also classify L. S. Gottfredson's (1996) theory of *circumscription and compromise* as a critical-period model of the development of interests, although her theory focuses mainly on the development of vocational aspirations and only secondarily on interests per se. Critical periods have been proposed for acquiring various cognitive abilities, such as acquisition of accent-free facility in learning a second language, or learning musical skills such as those associated with perfect pitch, although the concept of critical periods in ability acquisition is not without its critics. Carson (1995) proposed such a model of critical periods for the acquisition of interests, noting that several authors had reported that interests in physical sciences appeared to crystallize earlier than those in biological

ones (in the early teens and mid-teens, respectively), which crystallized still earlier than interests in the social sciences (by the early 20s). Perhaps there exist a number of potentially strong interests in any child, but without the actual exercise of related skills during a critical period the opportunity for crystallizing that interest would pass, and thereafter becoming exceedingly difficult to revive.

Specific Versus General Interests Categories

To date, studies have generally taken the easy approach to classifying people on interest patterns, using 1-point codes to establish criterion groups or doing simple correlations between interest and other variables. Such approaches ignore important within-category variance. Taking Holland's six-factor theory as a base, there are 120 possible combinations of three-interest-category codes. Few studies have yet examined the implications of this complexity of interests, or the personality or ability differences that may be associated with more complexly measured interest types. Presumably, there are significant differences between, say, enterprising-conventional and enterprising-realistic types. Research investigating the underlying structure of a few broad interests should be balanced by another line looking at a more complex and detailed (and narrower) classification of people. With modern computer technology and large sample sizes, we can now study all possible two- and three-letter interest combinations.

Commonality and Differences of Alternative Interest Measures

Commonalities and differences across interest measures need to be established more firmly (see, e.g., Zytowski, 1968). There is a paucity of research examining the degree of overlap between measures. Lowman and Abbott (1994) found an average correlation of only .75 between measures of interests given to the same respondents. This would imply that only about half the variance is accounted for when alternative instruments are used to classify people on interests. From a research perspective, this implies that the particular interest measure used may result in different classification outcomes. For the moment, researchers need to examine the extent to which their results are method bound, versus replicating to alternative measures of interests.

Empirically Based Coding of Occupations

Most of the literature on comparing persons' interests with chosen occupations rests on the average coding of job categories using measures such as contained in G. D. Gottfredson and Holland's (1996) *Dictionary of Holland Occupational Codes*. This compendium is based both on empirically validated ratings of occupational interest assignments and on those derived from a computer methodology that translated *The Dictionary of Occupational Titles* (U.S. Department of Labor, 1977) data into Holland interest codes. Only measures such as the SVIB (e.g., Hansen & Swanson, 1983) appear to use exclusively empirically derived criterion groups to establish the interest profiles of persons in occupations. However, even those measures inevitably include only a tiny fraction of possible occupations.

Since the match between individual characteristics and job characteristics is at the basis of much of the literature on career assessment and personnel selection, it matters as much whether jobs and occupations are correctly classified as it does that individual interest patterns are (see Gottfredson & Richards, 1999; Upperman & Church, 1995). Yet, the field has been surprisingly cavalier about accepting as valid far less than empirically well-established codings of occupations. Additionally, if mean interest profiles are taken as the criterion of what constitutes a particular occupation's code, complex research questions remain. Does not being matched with the average profile established empirically for an occupation result in lower job satisfaction or productivity levels? To what extent can employees be productive in an occupation yet not satisfied in it (as, e.g., what might be predicted for those having the requisite abilities for a profession but a lack of interest matching)? Finally, there appear to be complex relationships between occupations as classified on job-analytic methods and interest themes (Hyland & Muchinsky, 1991). These relationships need further exploration.

Interdomain Research

There is enough research now available to establish empirically that there are complex empirical relationships among, at the least, interests, abilities, and personality characteristics. The relevance of a multidomain model of career assessment was established some time ago (see Lowman, 1991; Lowman, Williams, & Leeman, 1985), but the specific empirical nature of interdomain relationships is not fully determined. Having established that interests and personality are highly related, more work is needed to determine ability-interest and ability-interest-personality relationships.

SUMMARY AND CONCLUSION

The measurement of interests is a prolific business enterprise and an area that has generated an impressive array of research findings. Interests appear to represent variables with profound

significance for predicting individuals' behavior, well-being, and occupational lives.

This chapter has reviewed definitions of interests and suggested an operational definition of the construct. The chapter notes that there is increasing evidence that there is a strong component of heritability to interests that may account for their unusually high test-retest reliability.

Several of the major contemporary measures of interests are discussed, including the Strong Vocational Interest Blank (Strong Interest Inventory), the Campbell Interest and Skill Survey, the Kuder Occupational Interest Survey, the Unisex Edition of the ACT Interest Inventory, the Self-Directed Search, the Vocational Preference Inventory, Johansson's measures, and the Interest-Finder Quiz.

The chapter briefly reviews a large and growing research literature addressing the validity and reliability of interests, concluding that they predict well to school and work choices. There is also both consensus and controversy regarding the existence of six interest factors (some say there are more, some fewer). It appears that there are underlying meta-factors that summarize the six Holland factors typically reported in the literature; however, there may be more practical utility to the six-factor model than to a two-dimensional one. The research literature is more scanty on the relationship among interests and other domains, such as abilities and personality variables. There is also little basis from which to determine the specific interest measures that work best for particular assessment tasks.

A number of research issues meriting attention in the next decade are also identified. These include (a) psychobiology of interests; (b) specific versus general interest categories; (c) commonality and differences of alternative interest measures; (d) empirically based occupational and environmental codings; (e) the structure of interests; (f) interdomain relationships; and (g) additive value of measures related to interests.

REFERENCES

Ackerman, P. L., & Heggestad, E. D. (1997). Intelligence, personality, and interests: Evidence for overlapping traits. *Psychological Bulletin, 121*, 219–245.

Ackerman, P. L., Kyllonen, P. C., & Roberts, R. D. (Eds.) (1999). *Learning and individual differences: Process, trait, and content determinants.* Washington, DC: American Psychological Association.

Athanasou, J. A., O'Gorman, J., & Meyer, E. (1981). Factorial validity of the vocational interest scales of the Holland Vocational Preference Inventory for Australian high school students. *Educational and Psychological Measurement, 41*, 523–527.

Atkinson, G., & Lunneborg, C. E. (1968). Comparison of oblique and orthogonal simple structure solutions for personality and interest factors. *Multivariate Behavioral Research, 3,* 21–35.

Betz, N. E., & Borgen, F. H. (2000). The future of career assessment: Integrating vocational interests with self-efficacy and personal styles. *Journal of Career Assessment, 8,* 329–338.

Betz, N. E., Borgen, F., & Harmon, L. (1996). *Skills Confidence Inventory applications and technical guide.* Palo Alto, CA: Consulting Psychologists Press.

Betz, N. E., & Schifano, R. S. (2000). Evaluation of an intervention to increase realistic self-efficacy and interests in college women. *Journal of Vocational Behavior, 56,* 35–52.

Betz, N. E., & Taylor, K. M. (1982). Concurrent validity of the Strong-Campbell Interest Inventory for graduate students in counseling. *Journal of Counseling Psychology, 29,* 626–635.

Blake, R. (1969). Comparative reliability of picture form and verbal form interest inventories. *Journal of Applied Psychology, 53,* 42–44.

Bordin, E. S. (1994). Intrinsic motivation and the active self: Convergence from a psychodynamic perspective. In M. L. Savickas & R. W. Lent (Eds.), *Convergence in career development theories: Implications for science and practice* (pp. 53–61). Palo Alto, CA: Davies-Black.

Borgen, F. H., & Helms, J. E. (1975). Validity generalization of the men's form of the Strong Vocational Interest Blank with academically able women. *Journal of Counseling Psychology, 22,* 210–216.

Brown, S. D., Lent, R. W., & Gore, P. A., Jr. (2000). Self-rated abilities and self-efficacy beliefs: Are they empirically distinct? *Journal of Career Assessment, 8,* 223–235.

Brown, S. D., & Watkins, C. E., Jr. (1994). Psychodynamic and personological perspectives on vocational behavior. In M. L. Savickas & R. W. Lent (Eds.), *Convergence in career development theories: Implications for science and practice* (pp. 197–206). Palo Alto, CA: Davies-Black.

Campbell, D. P. (1994). *Campbell Interest and Skill Survey manual.* Minneapolis, MN: National Computer Systems.

Campbell, D. P. (1995). The Campbell Interest and Skill Survey (CISS): A product of ninety years of psychometric evolution. *Journal of Career Assessment, 3,* 391–410.

Campbell, D. P., & Borgen, F. H. (1999). Holland's theory and the development of interest inventories. *Journal of Vocational Behavior, 55,* 86–101.

Carless, S. A. (1999). Career assessment: Holland's vocational interests, personality characteristics, and abilities. *Journal of Career Assessment, 7,* 125–144.

Carroll, J. B. (1993). *Human cognitive abilities: A survey of factor-analytic studies.* New York: Cambridge University Press.

Carson, A. D. (1995, August). The selection of interests. In A. D. Carson (Chair), *The nature of interests.* Symposium presented at the meeting of the American Psychological Association, New York, NY.

Carson, A. D. (1996). Aptitudes across Holland's types: Implications for school-based counsellors. *McGill Journal of Education, 31*(3), 319–332.

Carson, A. D. (1998a). The integration of interests, aptitudes, and personality traits: A test of Lowman's matrix. *Journal of Career Assessment, 6,* 83–105.

Carson, A. D. (1998b). The relation of self-reported abilities to aptitude test scores: A replication and extension. *Journal of Vocational Behavior, 53,* 353–371.

Carter, R. T., & Swanson, J. L. (1990). The validity of the Strong Interest Inventory for Black Americans: A review of the literature. *Journal of Vocational Behavior, 36,* 195–209.

Chung, Y. B, & Harmon, L. W. (1994). The career interests and aspirations of gay men: How sex-role orientation is related. *Journal of Vocational Behavior, 45,* 223–239.

Clark, K. E. (1961). *Vocational interests of nonprofessional men.* Minneapolis: University of Minnesota Press.

Cottle, W. C. (1950). A factorial study of the Multiphasic, Strong, Kuder, and Bell inventories using a population of adult males. *Psychometrika, 15,* 25–47.

Crites, J. O. (1969). *Vocational psychology: The study of vocational behavior and development.* New York: McGraw-Hill.

Crites, J. O. (1999). Operational definitions of vocational interests. In M. L. Savickas & A. R. Spokane (Eds.), *Vocational interests: Meaning, measurement, and counseling use* (pp. 163–170). Palo Alto, CA: Davies-Black.

Dawis, R. (1991). Vocational interests, values, and preferences. In M. D. Dunnette & Leaetta M. Hough (Eds.), *Handbook of industrial and organizational psychology* (pp. 833–871). Palo Alto, CA: Consulting Psychologists Press.

Day, S. X., & Rounds, J. (1998). Universality of vocational interest structure among racial and ethnic minorities. *American Psychologist, 53,* 728–736.

Day, S. X., Rounds, J., & Swaney, K. (1998). The structure of vocational interests for diverse racial-ethnic groups. *Psychological Science, 9,* 40–44.

DeFruyt, F., & Mervielde, I. (1999). RIASEC types and big five traits as predictors of employment status and nature of employment. *Personnel Psychology, 52,* 701–727.

DeVaney, S. B., & Hughey, A. W. (2000). Career development of ethnic minority students. In D. A. Luzzo (Ed.), *Career counseling of college students: An empirical guide to strategies that work* (pp. 233–252). Washington, DC: American Psychological Association.

Diamond, E. E., & Zytowski, D. G. (2000). The Kuder Occupational Interest Survey. In C. E. Watkins Jr. & V. L. Campbell (Eds.), *Testing and assessment in counseling practice: Contemporary topics in vocational psychology* (2nd ed., pp. 263–294). Mahwah, NJ: Erlbaum.

Donnay, D. A. C. (1997). E. K. Strong's legacy and beyond: Seventy years of the Strong Interest Inventory. *Career Development Quarterly, 46,* 2–22.

Donnay, D. A. C., & Borgen, F. H. (1996a). The incremental validity of vocational self-efficacy: An examination of interest, self-efficacy, and occupation. *Journal of Counseling Psychology, 46,* 432–447.

Donnay, D. A. C., & Borgen, F. H. (1996b). Validity, structure, and content of the 1994 Strong Interest Inventory, *Journal of Counseling Psychology, 43,* 275–291.

Eby, L. T., & Russell, J. E. A. (1998). A psychometric review of career assessment tools for use with diverse individuals. *Journal of Career Assessment, 6,* 269–310.

Einarsdottir, S., & Rounds, J. (2000). Application of three dimensions of vocational interests to the Strong Interest Inventory. *Journal of Vocational Behavior, 56,* 363–379.

Ericsson, K. A. (1996). The acquisition to expert performance: An introduction to some of the issues. In K. A. Ericsson (Ed.), *The road to excellence: The acquisition of expert performance in the arts and sciences, sports and games* (pp. 1–50). Mahwah, NJ: Erlbaum.

Fouad, N. A. (1999). Validity evidence for interest inventories. In M. L. Savickas & A. R. Spokane (Eds.), *Vocational interests: Meaning, measurement, and counseling use* (pp. 193–209). Palo Alto, CA: Davies-Black.

Fouad, N. A., & Spreda, A. L. (1995). Use of interest inventories with special populations: Women and minority groups. *Journal of Career Assessment, 3,* 453–468.

Fricko, M. A., & Beehr, T. A. (1992). A longitudinal investigation of interest congruence and gender concentration as predictors of job satisfaction. *Personnel Psychology, 45,* 99–117.

Gati, I. (1991). The structure of vocational interests. *Psychological Bulletin, 109,* 309–324.

Gottfredson, G. D. (1999). John L. Holland's contributions to vocational psychology: A review and evaluation. *Journal of Vocational Behavior, 55,* 15–40.

Gottfredson, G. D., & Holland, J. L. (1975). Vocational choices of men and women: A comparison of predictors from the Self-Directed Search. *Journal of Counseling Psychology, 22,* 28–34.

Gottfredson, G. D., & Holland, J. L. (1996). *Dictionary of Holland occupational codes* (3rd ed.). Odessa, FL: Psychological Assessment Resources.

Gottfredson, L. S. (1986a). Occupational Aptitude Patterns Map: Development and implications for a theory of job aptitude requirements [Monograph]. *Journal of Vocational Behavior, 29,* 254–291.

Gottfredson, L. S. (1986b). Special groups and the beneficial use of vocational interest inventories. In W. B. Walsh & S. H. Osipow (Eds.), *Advances in vocational psychology: Vol. 1. The assessment of interests* (pp. 127–198). Hillsdale, NJ: Erlbaum.

Gottfredson, L. S. (1996). Gottfredson's theory of circumscription and compromise. In D. Brown & L. Brooks (Eds.), *Career choice and development* (3rd ed., pp. 179–232). San Francisco: Jossey-Bass.

Gottfredson, L. S. (1999). The nature and nurture of vocational interests. In M. L. Savickas & A. R. Spokane (Eds.), *Vocational interests: Meaning, measurement, and counseling use* (pp. 57–85). Palo Alto, CA: Davies-Black.

Gottfredson, L. S., & Lapan, R. T. (1997). Assessing gender-based circumscription of occupational aspirations. *Journal of Career Assessment, 5,* 419–441.

Gottfredson, L. S., & Richards, J. M., Jr. (1999). The meaning and measurement of environments in Holland's theory. *Journal of Vocational Behavior, 55,* 57–73.

Hansen, J. C. (2000). Interpretation of the Strong Interest Inventory. In C. E. Watkins Jr. & V. L. Campbell (Eds.), *Testing and assessment in counseling practice: Contemporary topics in vocational psychology* (2nd ed., pp. 227–262). Mahwah, NJ: Erlbaum.

Hansen, J. C., Collins, R. C., Swanson, J. L., & Fouad, N. A. (1993). Gender differences in the structure of interests. *Journal of Vocational Behavior, 42,* 200–211.

Hansen, J. C., & Haviland, M. G. (2000). The interest structure of Native American college students. *Journal of Career Assessment, 8,* 159–165.

Hansen, J. C., & Johansson, C. B. (1972). The application of Holland's vocational model to the Strong Vocational Interest Blank for women. *Journal of Vocational Behavior, 2,* 479–493.

Hansen, J. C., & Neuman, J. L. (1999). Evidence of concurrent prediction of the Campbell Interest and Skill Survey (CISS) for college major selection. *Journal of Career Assessment, 7,* 239–247.

Hansen, J. C., & Swanson, J. L. (1983). Stability of interests and the predictive and concurrent validity of the 1981 Strong-Campbell Interest Inventory for college majors. *Journal of Counseling Psychology, 30,* 194–201.

Harmon, L. W., & Borgen, F. H. (1995). Advances in career assessment and the 1994 Strong Interest Inventory. *Journal of Career Assessment, 3,* 347–468.

Harmon, L. W., Hansen, J. C., Borgen, F. H., & Hammer, A. L. (1994). *Strong Interest Inventory: Applications and technical guide.* Palo Alto, CA: Consulting Psychologists Press.

Harrington, T., & O'Shea, A. (2000). *The Harrington-O'Shea Career Decision-Making System–Revised.* Circle Pines, MN: American Guidance Service.

Hartman, R., & Dashiell, J. F. (1919). An experiment to determine the relation of interests to abilities. *Psychological Bulletin, 16,* 259–262.

Hartung, P. J. (1999). Interest assessment using card sorts. In M. L. Savickas & A. R. Spokane (Eds.), *Vocational interests: Meaning, measurement, and counseling use* (pp. 235–252). Palo Alto, CA: Davies-Black.

Hogan, R., & Blake, R. J. (1996). Vocational interests: Matching self-concept with the work environment. In K. R. Murphy (Ed.), *Individual differences and behavior in organizations* (pp. 89–144). San Francisco: Jossey-Bass.

Holland, J. L. (1958). A personality inventory employing occupational titles. *Journal of Applied Psychology, 42,* 336–342.

Holland, J. L. (1959). A theory of vocational choice. *Journal of Counseling Psychology, 6,* 35–44.

Holland, J. L. (1985). *Vocational Preference Inventory manual.* Odessa, FL: Psychological Assessment Resources.

Holland, J. L. (1994). *The Self-Directed Search.* Odessa, FL: Psychological Assessment Resources.

Holland, J. L. (1996). Integrating career theory and practice: The current situation and some potential remedies. In M. L. Savickas & W. B. Walsh (Eds.), *Handbook of career counseling theory and practice* (pp. 1–12). Palo Alto, CA: Davies-Black.

Holland, J. L. (1997a). *Making vocational choices: A theory of vocational personalities and work environments* (3rd ed.). Odessa, FL: Psychological Assessment Resources.

Holland, J. L. (1997b). Why interest inventories are also personality inventories. In M. L. Savickas & A. R. Spokane (Eds.), *Vocational interests: Meaning, measurement, and counseling use* (pp. 87–101). Palo Alto, CA: Davies-Black.

Holland, J. L., Fritzsche, B. A., & Powell, A. B. (1994). *The Self-Directed Search technical manual.* Odessa, FL: Psychological Assessment Resources.

Holland, J. L., Johnston, J. A., & Asama, N. F. (1994). More evidence for the relationship between Holland's personality types and personality variables. *Journal of Career Assessment, 2,* 331–340.

Hyland, A. M., & Muchinsky, P. M. (1991). Assessment of the structural validity of Holland's model with job analysis (PAQ) information. *Journal of Applied Psychology, 76,* 75–80.

Jackson, D. N. (1991). *Manual for the Jackson Vocational Interest Survey.* Port Huron, MI: Research Psychologists Press.

Johansson, C. B. (1980). *Manual for IDEAS: Interest Determination, Exploration, and Assessment System.* Minneapolis, MN: National Computer Systems.

Johansson, C. B. (1982). *Manual for the Career Assessment Inventory* (2nd ed.). Minneapolis, MN: National Computer Systems.

Johansson, C. B. (1986). *Career Assessment Inventory: The enhanced version.* Minneapolis, MN: National Computer Systems.

Johansson, C. B., & Campbell, D. P. (1971). Stability of the Strong Vocational Interest Blank for men. *Journal of Applied Psychology, 55,* 34–37.

Klein, M. A., Wheaton, J. E., & Wilson, K. B. (1997). The career assessment of persons with disabilities: A review. *Journal of Career Assessment, 5,* 203–211.

Knapp-Lee, L. J. (1995). Use of the COPSystem in career assessment. *Journal of Career Assessment, 3,* 411–428.

Kuder, G. F. (1939). The stability of preference items. *Journal of Social Psychology, 10,* 41–50.

Kuder, G. F. (1948). *Kuder Preference Record–Personal.* Chicago: Science Research Associates.

Kuder, G. F. (1991). *Occupational Interest Survey, Form DD.* Monterey, CA: CTB McGraw-Hill.

Kuder, G. F., & Diamond, E. E. (1979). *Occupational Interest Survey: General manual* (3rd ed.). Chicago: Science Reseach Associates.

Kuder, G. F., & Zytowski, D. G. (1991). *Kuder DD/PC: User's guide.* Monterey, CA: CTB Macmillan/McGraw-Hill.

Lapan, R. T., Shaughnessy, P., & Boggs, K. (1996). Efficacy expectations and vocational interests as mediators between sex and choice of math/science college majors: A longitudinal study. *Journal of Vocational Behavior, 49,* 277–291.

Lattimore, R. R., & Borgen, F. H. (1999). Validity of the 1994 Strong Interest Inventory with racial and ethnic groups in the United States. *Journal of Counseling Psychology, 46,* 185–195.

Lau, A. W., & Abrahams, N. M. (1971). Stability of vocational interests within nonprofessional occupations. *Journal of Applied Psychology, 55,* 143–150.

Leong, F. T. L., & Hartung, P. J. (2000). Cross-cultural career assessment: Review and prospects for the new millennium. *Journal of Career Assessment, 8,* 391–401.

Leong, F. T. L., & Leung, S. A. (1994). Career assessment with Asian-Americans. *Journal of Career Assessment, 2,* 240–257.

Lindley, L. D., & Borgen, F. H. (2000). Personal Style Scales of the Strong Interest Inventory: Linking personality and interests. *Journal of Vocational Behavior, 57,* 22–41.

Livers, D. L. (1994). Review of the Chronicle Career Quest. In J. T. Kapes, M. M. Mastie, & E. A. Whitfield (Eds.), *A counselor's guide to career assessment instruments* (3rd ed., pp. 163–166). Alexandria, VA: National Career Development Association.

Lowman, R. L. (1991). *The clinical practice of career assessment: Interests, abilities, and personality.* Washington, DC: American Psychological Association.

Lowman, R. L. (1993a). *Counseling and psychotherapy of work dysfunctions.* Washington, DC: American Psychological Association.

Lowman, R. L. (1993b). The inter-domain model of career assessment and counseling. *Journal of Counseling and Development, 71,* 549–554.

Lowman, R. L. (1997). Career assessment and psychological impairment: Integrating inter-domain and work dysfunctions theory. *Journal of Career Assessment, 5,* 213–224.

Lowman, R. L. (in press). Assessment of interests. In R. Fernandez-Ballesteros (Ed.), *Encyclopedia of psychological assessment.* Thousand Oaks, CA: Sage.

Lowman, R. L., & Abbott, J. (1994, August). *Are alternative measures of vocational interest assessing identical constructs?.* Paper presented at the annual meeting of the American Psychological Association, Los Angeles.

Lowman, R. L., & Carson, A. D. (2000). Integrating assessment data into the delivery of career counseling services. In D. A. Luzzo (Ed.), *Career development of college students: Translating theory into practice* (pp. 121–136). Washington, DC: American Psychological Association.

Lowman, R. L., & Leeman, G. E. (1988). The dimensionality of social intelligence: Social interests, abilities, and needs. *Journal of Psychology, 122,* 279–290.

Lowman, R. L., & Schurman, S. J. (1982). Psychometric characteristics of a Vocational Preference Inventory short form. *Educational and Psychological Measurement, 42,* 601–613.

Lowman, R. L., & Williams, R. E. (1987). Validity of self-ratings of abilities and competencies. *Journal of Vocational Behavior, 31,* 1–13.

Lowman, R. L., Williams, R. E., & Leeman, G. E. (1985). The structure and relationship of college women's primary abilities and vocational interests. *Journal of Vocational Behavior, 27,* 298–315.

Lucy, W. T. (1976). An adult population reflects the stability of Holland's personality types over time. *Journal of College Student Personnel, 17,* 76–79.

Lunneborg, P. W. (1981). *The Vocational Interest Inventory manual.* Los Angeles: Western Psychological Services.

Martindale, C. (1999). Biological bases of creativity. In P. L. Ackerman, P. C. Kyllonen, & R. D. Roberts (Eds.), *Learning and individual differences: Process, trait, and content determinants* (pp. 137–152). Washington, DC: American Psychological Association.

Maurer, T. J., & Tarullie, B. A. (1997). Managerial work, job analysis, and Holland's RIASEC vocational environment dimensions. *Journal of Vocational Behavior, 50,* 365–381.

McCall, B. P., Cavanaugh, M. A., Arvey, R. D., & Taubman, P. (1997). Genetic influences on job and occupational switching. *Journal of Vocational Behavior, 50,* 60–77.

Miller, M. J., Newell, N. P., Springer, T. P., & Wells, D. (1992). Accuracy of the College Majors Finder for three majors. *Career Development Quarterly, 40,* 334–339.

Mitchell, L. K., & Krumboltz, J. D. (1990). Social learning approach to career decision making: Krumboltz's theory. In D. Brown & L. Brooks (Eds.), *Career choice and development: Applying contemporary theories to practice* (2nd ed., pp. 145–196). San Francisco: Jossey-Bass.

Moloney, D. P., Bouchard, T. J., Jr., & Segal, N. L. (1991). A genetic and environmental analysis of the vocational interests of monozygotic and dizygotic twins reared apart. *Journal of Vocational Behavior, 39,* 76–109.

Mount, M. K., & Muchinsky, P. M. (1978a). Concurrent validation of Holland's hexagonal model with occupational workers. *Journal of Vocational Behavior, 13,* 348–354.

Mount, M. K., & Muchinsky, P. M. (1978b). Person-environment congruence and employee job satisfaction: A test of Holland's theory. *Journal of Vocational Behavior, 13,* 84–100.

Naylor, F. D., & Kidd, G. J. (1991). The predictive validity of the Investigative scale of the Career Assessment Inventory. *Educational and Psychological Measurement, 51,* 217–226.

Ozone-Shinichi, J. (1998). The relationship between Holland's theory of vocational interest and the five factor model of personality (Doctoral dissertation). *Dissertation Abstracts International, 58*(7), 3962B.

Prediger, D. J. (1982). Dimensions underlying Holland's hexagon: Missing link between interests and occupations? *Journal of Vocational Behavior, 21,* 259–287.

Prediger, D. J. (1989). Extending Holland's hexagon: Procedures, counseling applications, and research. *Journal of Counseling & Development, 71,* 422–428.

Prediger, D. J. (1999a). Basic structure of work-relevant abilities. *Journal of Counseling Psychology, 46,* 173–184.

Prediger, D. J. (1999b). Integrating interests and abilities for career exploration: General considerations. In M. L. Savickas & A. R. Spokane (Eds.), *Vocational interests: Meaning, measurement, and counseling use* (pp. 295–325). Palo Alto, CA, Davies-Black.

Prediger, D. J., & Swaney, K. B. (1995). Using UNIACT in a comprehensive approach to assessment for career planning. *Journal of Career Assessment, 3,* 347–468.

Prediger, D. J., & Vansickle, T. R. (1999). Locating occupations on Holland's hexagon: Beyond RIASEC. *Journal of Vocational Behavior, 40,* 111–128.

Prince, J. P. (1997). Career assessment with lesbian, gay, and bisexual individuals. *Journal of Career Assessment, 5,* 225–238.

Rahdahl, G. J. (1991). A typological analysis of the relations between measured vocational interests and abilities. *Journal of Vocational Behavior, 38,* 333–350.

Roe, A. (1954). A new classification of occupations. *Journal of Counseling Psychology, 1,* 215–220.

Roe, A. (1957). Early determinants of vocational choice. *Journal of Counseling Psychology, 4,* 212–217.

Roe, A., & Lunneborg, P. W. (1990). Personality development and career choice. In D. Brown & L. Brooks (Eds.), *Career choice and development: Applying contemporary theories to practice* (2nd ed., pp. 68–101). San Francisco: Jossey-Bass.

Rothenberg, A. (1990). Creativity, mental health, and alcoholism. *Creativity Research Journal, 3,* 179–201.

Rounds, J., & Day, S. X. (1998). Universality of vocational interest structure among racial and ethnic minorities. *American Psychologist, 53,* 728–736.

Rounds, J., & Day, S. X. (1999). Describing, evaluating, and creating vocational interest structures. In M. L. Savickas & A. R. Spokane (Eds.), *Vocational interests: Meaning, measurement, and counseling use* (pp. 103–133). Palo Alto: Davies-Black.

Rounds, J., & Hesketh, B. (1994). Theory of work adjustment: Unifying principles and concepts. In M. L. Savickas & R. W. Lent (Eds.), *Convergence in career development theories: Implications for science and practice* (pp. 177–186). Palo Alto, CA: Davies-Black.

Sarbin, T. R., & Berdie, R. F. (1940). Relation of measured interests to the Allport-Vernon study of values. *Journal of Applied Psychology, 24,* 287–296.

Savickas, M. L. (1998). Interpreting interest inventories: A "case" example. *Career Development Quarterly, 46,* 307–310.

Savickas, M. L. (1999). The psychology of interests. In M. L. Savickas & A. R. Spokane (Eds.), *Vocational interests: Meaning, measurement, and counseling use* (pp. 19–56). Palo Alto, CA: Davies-Black.

Schneider, B., Paul, M. C., White, S. S., & Holcombe, K. M. (1999). Understanding high school student leaders, I: Predicting teacher ratings of leader behavior. *Leadership Quarterly, 10,* 609–636.

Silver, H. A., & Barnette, W. L. (1970). Predictive and concurrent validity of the Minnesota Vocational Interest Inventory for vocational high school boys. *Journal of Applied Psychology, 54,* 436–440.

Spokane, A. R. (1994). The resolution of incongruence and the dynamics of person-environment fit. In M. L. Savickas & R. W. Lent (Eds.), *Convergence in career development theories: Implications for science and practice* (pp. 119–137). Palo Alto, CA: Davies-Black.

Spokane, A. R. (1996). Holland's theory. In D. Brown & L. Brooks (Eds.), *Career choice and development* (3rd ed., pp. 33–74). San Francisco: Jossey-Bass.

Spokane, A. R., & Decker, A. R. (1999). Expressed and measured interests. In: M. L. Savickas & A. R. Spokane (Eds.), *Vocational interests: Meaning, measurement, and counseling use* (pp. 211–233). Palo Alto, CA: Davies-Black.

Spokane, A. R., & Holland, J. L. (1995). The Self-Directed Search: A family of self-guided career interventions. *Journal of Career Assessment, 3,* 347–468.

Spokane, A. R., Meir, E. I., & Catalano, M. (2000). Person-environment congruence and Holland's theory: A review and reconsideration. *Journal of Vocational Behavior, 57,* 137–187.

Strong, E. K. (1938a). Predictive value of the vocational interest test. *Journal of Educational Psychology, 26,* 331–349.

Strong, E. K. (1938b). *Vocational Interest Blank for men.* Palo Alto, CA: Stanford University Press.

Strong, E. K. (1943). *Vocational interests of men and women.* Palo Alto, CA: Stanford University Press.

Strong, E. K. (1951). Interest scores while in college of occupations engaged in 20 years later. *Educational and Psychological Measurement, 11,* 335–348.

Strong, E. K. (1952). Nineteen-year followup of engineer interests. *Journal of Applied Psychology, 36,* 65–74.

Strong, E. K. (1955). *Vocational interests 18 years after college.* Minneapolis: University of Minnesota Press.

Super, D. E. (1940a). *Avocational interest patterns: A study in the psychology of avocations.* Palo Alto, CA: Stanford University Press.

Super, D. E. (1940b). The measurement of interest in an occupation vs. patterns of interests similar to those of persons in that occupation. *Psychological Bulletin, 37,* 450–451.

Super, D. E. (1949). *Appraising vocational fitness by means of psychological tests.* New York: Harper and Brothers.

Super, D. E., & Crites, J. O. (1962). *Appraising vocational fitness by means of psychological tests* (rev. ed.). New York: Harper & Brothers.

Super, D. E., Savickas, M. L., & Super, C. M. (1996). The life-span, life-space approach to careers. In D. Brown & L. Brooks (Eds.), *Career choice and development* (3rd ed., pp. 121–178). San Francisco: Jossey-Bass.

Swaney, K. B. (1995). *Technical manual: Revised unisex edition of the ACT Interest Inventory (UNIACT).* Iowa City, IA: American College Testing Program.

Swanson, J. L. (1999). Stability and change in vocational interests. In M. L. Savickas & A. R. Spokane (Eds.), *Vocational interests: Meaning, measurement, and counseling use* (pp. 135–158). Palo Alto, CA: Consulting Psychologists Press.

Thurstone, L. L. (1931). A multiple factor study of vocational interests. *Personnel Journal, 10,* 198–205.

Tracey, T. J., & Rounds, J. B. (1993). Evaluating Holland's and Gati's vocational-interest models: A structural meta-analysis. *Psychological Bulletin, 113,* 229–246.

Tracey, T. J. G., & Hopkins, N. (2001). Correspondence of interests and abilities with occupational choice. *Journal of Counseling Psychology, 48,* 178–189.

Upperman, P. J., & Church, A. J. (1995). Investigating Holland's typological theory with Army occupational specialties. *Journal of Vocational Behavior, 47,* 61–75.

U.S. Department of Labor. (1977). *Dictionary of occupational titles.* Washington, DC: U.S. Employment Service.

Vacc, N. A., & Hinkle, J. S. (1994). Review of the Career Assessment Inventory—Enhanced Version and Career Assessment Inventory—Vocational Version. In J. T. Kapes, M. M. Mastie, & E. A. Whitfield (Eds.), *A counselor's guide to career assessment instruments* (3rd ed., pp. 145–150). Alexandria, VA: National Career Development Association.

Wall, J. E., & Baker, H. E. (1997). The Interest-Finder: Evidence of validity. *Journal of Career Assessment, 5,* 255–273.

Walsh, W. B., & Chartrand, J. M. (1994). Emerging directions of person-environment fit. In M. L. Savickas & R. W. Lent (Eds.), *Convergence in career development theories: Implications for science and practice* (pp. 187–195). Palo Alto, CA: Davies-Black.

Wesley, S. M., Corey, D. Q., & Stewart, B. M. (1950). The intra-individual relationship between interest and ability. *Journal of Applied Psychology, 34,* 193–197.

Williams, C. M. (1972). Occupational choice of male graduate students as related to values and personality: A test of Holland's theory. *Journal of Vocational Behavior, 2,* 29–46.

Zytowski, D. G. (1968). Relationships of equivalent scales on three interest inventories. *Personnel and Guidance Journal, 47,* 44–49.

Zytowski, D. G., & Hay, R. (1984). Do birds of a feather flock together? A test of the similarities within and the differences between five occupations. *Journal of Vocational Psychology, 24,* 242–248.

CHAPTER 21

Assessing Personality and Psychopathology With Interviews

ROBERT J. CRAIG

Interviews are the most basic and most frequently used method of psychological assessment and the most important means of data collection during a psychological evaluation (Watkins, Campbell, Nieberding, & Hallmark, 1995). They are endemic to the task performance of almost all psychologists—especially clinical and counseling psychologists. A computer search, using the key search words *clinical interview, assessment interview,* and *initial interview,* for the past 20 years yielded 1,260 citations, or 63 per year. Clearly interviewing continues to be an important process and one that continues to occupy clinicians and researchers alike.

This chapter discusses contemporary issues in assessing psychopathology and personality with interviews. We discuss types of interviews, how clients and clinicians approach an interview, and structured versus unstructured interviews. The structure of the interview is presented along with continuing concerns with official diagnostic systems. Issues that complicate the assessment process for personality disorders are discussed, including the base rate problem, the role of affective disorders, state versus trait assessment, the role of culture, reliability of psychiatric diagnosis, diagnostic overlap, and comorbidities. Current findings on the reliability of structured clinical interviews are presented. The chapter concludes with a discussion on computer-assisted diagnosis and suggestions for the future.

HISTORY OF INTERVIEWING

Diagnosing has a long history. In fact, conditions that we now label as depression and hysteria appear in both Sumerian and Egyptian literature as far back as 2400 B.C. (Wiens & Matarazzo, 1983). Initial attempts at formal psychiatric classification began in 1840 and grouped all disorders into two categories—idiotic and insane. In 1880, there were only seven psychiatric diagnoses in existence: dementia, dipsomania (alcoholism), epilepsy, mania, melancholia, monomania (depression), and paresis. There are now hundreds of diagnoses in *Diagnostic and Statistical Manual of Mental Disorders–Fourth Edition* (*DSM-IV;* American Psychiatric Association, 1994). Readers interested in the history of psychiatric diagnosis are referred to several excellent reviews of this elsewhere (Menninger, Mayman, & Pruyser, 1963, a 70-page history of psychiatric diagnosis from 2600 B.C. to 1963; Zilboorg, 1941) and to the several revisions of *DSM*.

The word *interview* was initially included in standard dictionaries in 1514 and designated a meeting of persons face-to-face for the purpose of formal conference on some point (Matarazzo, 1965). Initially assessment interviews were modeled on question-and-answer formats. The introduction of psychoanalysis allowed for a more open-ended, free-flowing format. During the 1940s and 1950s, researchers began to study interviews in terms of their content versus process, problem-solving versus expressive elements, degree of directedness within an interview, the amount of structure, and the activity of both the respondent and interviewer. Carl Rogers stimulated much research in the 1960s by emphasizing personal qualities of the clinician (e.g., warmth, accurate empathy, unconditional positive regard, genuineness). The 1970s introduced the idea of using structured diagnostic interviews, and advances in behavioral assessment resulted in more specificity and objectivity in interviews. Seminal behavioral assessment models include such approaches as the BASIC-ID model (behaviors, affect, sensation, imagery, cognition, interpersonal relations, and possible need for psychotherapeutic drugs). In the 1980s, the *DSM* revision provided improved reliability of diagnostic entities, and the 1990s afforded increasing appreciation of the role of culture, race, and ethnicity in the development of psychopathology. Managed health care also emphasized cost-setting measures and essentially required psychologists to rely on assessment interviews to the near exclusion of other assessment methods (e.g., psychodiagnostic testing; Groth-Marnatt, 1999).

Although assessment interviews have much in common with more social interactions such as group dynamics, dyadic considerations, and rules of etiquette and communication, they are fundamentally different. In assessment interviews, communication is generally both privileged (i.e., material discussed in the context of a professional relationship is not discoverable in legal evidentiary proceedings unless otherwise permitted in writing by the client) and confidential (material discussed in the context of a professional relationship cannot be disclosed and is protected from discovery by both professional ethics and laws). The demeanor of the clinician tends to be more professional, and the nature of the inquiry is often unidirectional and organized for the task at hand. There are limits on the nature of the interaction imposed by both law and ethics. The clinician's statements serve a larger purpose than mere mutual dialogue (Craig, 1989).

PURPOSE OF ASSESSMENT INTERVIEWS

Assessment interviews can be thought of as having four major functions: administration, treatment, research, and prevention (Wiens & Matarazzo, 1983). Sometimes, psychologists' interviews are for purposes of fulfilling certain agency requirements, such as determining eligibility for services. The treatment function of an interview might involve assigning differential diagnoses. For example, I was once asked to determine whether the patient had a delusional disorder or a borderline personality disorder. If the patient had a delusional disorder, the physician was going to treat the patient with medication, whereas if the patient had a borderline condition, the treatment would have been psychotherapy and no medication would be given. Assessment interviews are also conducted for research purposes. A salient example is the use of interviews for psychiatric epidemiological research or the use of structured psychiatric interviews to assess reliability and validity of clinical interviews. Finally, the prevention function follows the treatment and research function. If we have ways to reliably classify disorders, then we can include homogeneous groups of patients into research protocols. Findings from these studies then could serve a prevention function.

TYPES OF INTERVIEWS

We need to make a distinction between therapeutic versus assessment interviews. The former includes generic activities within a session designed to advance some treatment goal. The latter includes an array of activities in order to gain information that leads to the development of treatment goals and intervention plans or other decisions, such as personnel selection. An example of a therapeutic interview is Miller's (1991) *motivational interviewing.* Although this approach was developed for the purpose of changing addictive behavior, the principles are generic enough so that the technique could be applied to a number of assessment situations requiring behavior change.

This approach considers motivation a dynamic concept rather than inherently a personality trait. The behavior of the clinician is a salient determinant as to whether change will occur. Miller recommends that clinicians give *feedback,* emphasize that clients take *responsibility* for change, give clients *advice* and a *menu* of treatment choices and strategies, be *emphatic,* and promote *self-efficacy.* The acronym *FRAMES* is used here as a mnemonic device. The technique also requires that the clinician point out discrepancies in behavior, avoid arguments, roll with resistance, use reflective listening, emphasize personal choice, reframe, and continually support self-efficacy. Thus, motivational interviewing can be used as an assessment tool and as an intervention tool.

Several types of interviews have been delineated. They differ in purpose, focus, and duration. Listed in the following sections are several types of interviews that have been discussed in the literature. They are not necessarily mutually exclusive, and several of the formats listed in the following sections can be utilized within a single interview. For example, a clinician can begin with an orientation interview, transition into a screening interview, continue with an interview for etiology, and then conclude with an ending interview. On the other hand, there are settings and circumstances in which each of these types of interviews is conducted separately or perhaps to the exclusion of the others. There is no agreed-upon list of interview types and the list presented in this chapter is somewhat arbitrary, but it provides the reader with a reasonable array of the various kinds of interviews available for clinical use.

Case History Interviews

Sometimes additional or more elaborate and detailed sequencing of case history material is required in order to make final decisions. In this case a special interview is completed in which the focus is only on ascertaining the nature of the person's problems in historical sequence, with a possible focus on critical periods of development or events, antecedents and precipitants of behavior, and other matters of clinical interest. Case history interviews can be conducted with the respondent directly, the respondent's family, friends, or others.

Diagnostic Interviews

Here, the clinician attempts to categorize the behavior of the client into some formal diagnostic system. For psychopathology, there are two official diagnostic classification systems presently in widespread use. The first is the official classification system of the World Health Organization—*International Classification of Disease–Tenth Edition* (World Health Organization, 1992). The second is the *DSM* (American Psychiatric Association, 1980, 1987, 1994). For reimbursement purposes, insurance companies recognize both, but the *DSM* is more popular in the United States and is the more commonly used diagnostic system in psychiatric research, teaching, and clinical practice. The *DSM* is also becoming more popular internationally than *ICD-10* (Maser, Kaelber, & Weise, 1991). Although there have been calls for considering other classification systems (Dyce, 1994), *DSM* is the predominant diagnostic system in use today. For assessing personality, the issue is a bit more complicated. Most clinicians still use the personality disorder diagnostic categories contained in these two official diagnostic systems, but others prefer to assess people according to more theoretically derived personality classifications, such as Millon's (1991, 2000) bioevolutionary model, Cattell's (1989) factors, interpersonal models (Benjamin, 1996), the five-factor model (Costa & Widiger, 1997), or more biologically based systems (Cloninger, 2000).

Follow-Up Interviews

These are specific-focused interviews, which usually have a single purpose. Perhaps it is to review highlights of assessment results or to evaluate quality of services and patient satisfaction received from an HMO. Researchers may conduct a debriefing interview when the research involves deception.

Forensic Interviews

Psychologists may be called upon to contribute their expertise in legal matters that may be complicated by factors related to mental health. These factors include evaluations for dangerousness, competency to stand trial, various insanity pleas, behaviors that may be induced by substance abuse, or custody evaluations, to name a few. These interviews are typically far more investigative than many other types of interviews, often are of longer duration, and may occur over multiple sessions. Often the person being interviewed is not the client at all, but rather the court or perhaps private attorneys who retain these services on behalf of their clients. Forensic evaluations do not carry with them the same protection of privacy and confidentiality of material obtained in the evaluation as do most other mental health interviews.

Intake Interviews

These interviews are designed to obtain preliminary information about a prospective client and most typically occur within agencies; they may include a determination as to a person's eligibility in terms of the agency's mission. Intake interviews may also be used to acquire information to be presented at a case conference, to help clarify the kind of services available at the agency, to communicate agency rules and policies, or to consider whether the case needs to be referred elsewhere.

Interviewing for Etiology

This type of interview is designed to determine such matters as etiology and motivational attributions. The interviewer seeks to understand from a theoretical perspective why the person is behaving in a certain way. This kind of interview can be conducted from many theoretical frameworks, such as psychodynamic behavioral, cognitive-behavioral, family systems, and existential-humanistic perspectives. Also, within each of these defined frameworks are subcategories that also differ from each other. For example, an interview from an analytic perspective can proceed along the line of classical Freudian theory, object relations theory, or self psychology. An interview from a behavioral perspective can be conducted using Pavlovian (classical conditioning), Skinnerian (instrumental conditioning), or more cognitive-behavioral perspectives. The main point is that interviews for etiology are theory derived and theory driven.

Mental Status Exams

A special type of interview is the mental status exam, which is conducted to determine the kind and degree of mental impairment associated with a given clinical disorder. Mental status exams traditionally explore content areas such as reasoning, concentration, judgment, memory, speech, hearing, orientation, and sensorium. They are particularly relevant when evaluating for major psychiatric disorders, neurological involvement, or substance-induced disorders. These exams can be formal, wherein each content area is specifically addressed, or informal, wherein information is ascertained about these content areas while talking to the person about other issues. Table 21.1 presents content areas often addressed in a mental status exam.

Orientation Interviews

These interviews are designed to orient a person to some protocol. They may be used by clinical researchers, who are required to tell each prospective participant the basic procedures

TABLE 21.1   Common Content Areas in a Mental Status Exam

Appearance	Abnormal Physical Traits	Appropriate Age
	Attention to Grooming	Eye Contact
	Level of Consciousness	Position of Body
Attitude	Cooperative	Dysphoric
Mood (affect)	Alexithymic	Euthymic
	Anxious	Flat
	Apathetic	Hostile
	Appropriate	Manic
	Depressed	
Perception	Depersonalization	Hallucinations
	Derealization	Illusions
	Déjà vu	Superstitions
Orientation	Time	Place
	Person	Space and location
Thought processes		
Intellectual	Abstract thinking	Attention span
	Impairment in IQ	
Judgment	Intact	Impaired
Insight	Intact	Impaired
Associations	Connected	Directed
	Loose	
Memory	Immediate	Recent
	Remote	
Thought content	Blocking	Overinclusive thinking
	Clanging	Perseverations
	Compulsions	Phobias
	Concrete	Preoccupations
	Delusions	Ruminations
	Neologisms	Suicidal ideation
	Phobias	Violent thoughts
Speech and language	Articulation	Stream of speech
Movements	Automatic, spontaneous	Voluntary
	Compulsions	Tics
	Involuntary	

of the experiment, any risks associated with it, and the right to withdraw from the study at any point in time. The goal here is to obtain informed consent for the study. A clinician might use this type of interview to inform a new client about treatment options, program policies, rules, and expectations. A psychologist in private practice may use this procedure to orient the client to such matters as confidentiality, cancellation procedures, billing practices, insurance claims, and professional credentials. An industrial psychologist may begin executive assessments with this type of interview in order to prepare the interviewee for what lies ahead. Orientation interviews are particularly useful to help answer any questions the recipient may have and to help develop a client-interviewer contract for services, which may be either a formal document or an informal understanding between both parties.

Pre- and Posttesting Interviews

Modern methods of psychological assessment require interviews that initially explore with the client particular problem areas prior to more formal psychological assessment, and then a posttesting interview, wherein the psychologist reviews or highlights major findings or recommendations derived from the assessment, which may include psychological testing. These findings are also valuable in that hypotheses derived from the assessment can be later explored with the client in the posttesting interview.

Screening Interviews

These interviews are usually brief and designed to elicit information on a specific topic. They may include such areas as determining whether a client is eligible for services, whether the patient is acutely suicidal, whether the patient meets the criteria for a particular diagnosis, or whether the patient needs to be hospitalized as a danger to self or others. Screening interviews are very common in psychology and may in fact be the most frequent kind of clinical interview.

Specialized Interviews

Sometimes the clinician needs to conduct an interview for a special purpose, such as determining the ability to stand trial, determining legal insanity, assessing the need for psychiatric hospitalization, or making a specific diagnosis of a particular disorder. Many specialized clinical interviews have been published for these purposes.

TABLE 21.2 Content Areas of Assessment Interviews

History of Problem	Description of the Problem
	Onset (Intensity, Duration)
	Antecedents and Consequences
	Prior Treatment Episodes
Family background	Nuclear family constellation
	Cultural background
	Socioeconomic level
	Parents' occupations
	Medical history
	Family relationships
	Family atmosphere
Personal history	Developmental milestones
	School and work history
	Relationship with parents
	History of childhood abuse (physical, sexual)
	Current relationships
	Vocational problems
	Marital-partner history
	Emotional stability
	History of psychological treatment
	Legal problems
	Use of illicit substances
	Medical problems

Termination Interview

Very often, clinicians ending services to a client conclude with an interview designed to review treatment goals, progress, and future plans. Clinicians working in inpatient settings often have an ending interview to reinforce the need for continued outpatient follow-up services. Addiction specialists usually have a last session to review planned aftercare and to highlight patient risk factors for relapse. Industrial psychologists meet with a person to review highlights of assessment findings.

Table 21.2 presents topics frequently addressed in assessment interviews.

THE CLIENT'S APPROACH TO THE INTERVIEW

Interviews are influenced by a number of factors. First, is the client's visit voluntary or involuntary? Presumably a voluntary client has noticed that there is a problem, has made failed attempts to resolve it—perhaps through discussions with friends or clergy or through self-help methods—and then has sought professional assistance. The client may come with the expectation that the distress (often a particular symptom or cluster of symptoms) will be ameliorated through professional help. This fact tends to increase the truthfulness of client self-reports and promotes a therapeutic working alliance and a more goal-oriented approach within counseling.

When a third party has referred the client, the situation is quite different. There are many cases in which the client is receiving services at the insistence of someone else. Clients arrested for driving under the influence may be sent for an evaluation to a psychologist by a judge. A teenager showing oppositional and conduct-disordered behavior may be taken to a psychologist by his or her parents. A person who is addicted to drugs may come for help at the insistence of a spouse who threatened to leave the relationship unless he or she gets help. In each of these scenarios, the client may not feel the need for help and may actually resist it.

Second, the client's *purpose or motive* for the interview also affects its course and direction. Even if the patient seems to be self-referred, there may be hidden agendas that may compromise the purity of the interview. For example, a person may seek help for a problem with incestuous behavior, but the real motive may be to present a façade to the judge in order to escape more severe criminal sanctions and punishment. Another person may present asking for assistance with anxiety or depression, whereas the true motivation is to establish a record of psychological treatment pursuant to a worker's compensation claim for disability. A person with a drug addiction may seek inpatient treatment for detoxification but actually may be hiding out from the police. A psychiatric patient may allege delusions, hallucinations, and threats of suicide so that he or she is determined to be in need of inpatient care, whereas the true motivation may be to receive basic food and shelter during the severe cold weather. It is incumbent on the clinician, if possible, to ascertain the person's real motivation for assessment and treatment.

Third, client *expectations* can affect the quality of the assessment results. All clients come to the interview with expectations about the nature of the process, how the psychologist may approach the task, and what results the process will have. It is a good idea for psychologists, who will be in a subsequent professional relationship with the client, to clarify any misperceptions or misunderstandings about the interviewing process. In order to explore possible misconceptions, ask the person, "What do you think we are going to do here?" or "What do you expect to happen as a result of our meeting?"

Fourth, the client also has *perceptions of the psychologist,* which can affect the course and outcome of the interviewing process; analysts have referred to this as object relations. Here, the interviewer embodies all that is contained in a particular role, and all of the client's prior experiences and beliefs of people in this role are then projected onto the psychologist. The patient may view the relationship as parent-child, teacher-student, judged-accused, or lover-love object. These projections are transferences and tend to develop quickly in an ongoing relationship. Sometimes they are outside the awareness of the client. At other times they are at the surface and can contaminate the relationship with unreasonable expectations. In fact, a large body of research in social psychology has shown that humans tend to evaluate someone on the basis of their first impression, and all subsequent encounters with that person are evaluated in the light of those first impressions.

THE PSYCHOLOGIST'S APPROACH TO THE INTERVIEW

Psychologists approach an interview with certain preexisting values. The first of these values is *philosophical or theoretical orientation.* As clinical psychologists, we do not come to an interview with a blank slate; rather, we bring with us attitudes that may influence the areas of inquiry, the methods and techniques used in that inquiry, the words we use to subsequently describe the person, and the goals we set for clients. For example, a psychologist with an existential-humanistic theoretical orientation will conduct a very different interview from that of a psychologist who has a family systems orientation. Treatment goals developed from an assessment interview

with a behaviorist will look quite different from treatment goals from an analyst.

Just as the client has certain expectations and beliefs about the nature of the interview, the psychologist also comes to the interview with certain preexisting *beliefs and values* that may affect the course of the interview. First, some psychologists value a directed approach, whereas others value a nondirected approach. Some value humor, whereas others refrain from its use. One psychologist may value discussions about a client's manifest behavior, whereas another may value a focus on a person's inner mental life. Second, psychologists value certain kinds of material more than they do others, and they selectively respond to client material that is considered more important (e.g., more highly valued). Third, psychologists may have a set of assumptions about behavior change and may view the person in the light of those assumptions. There are certainly other areas that could be explicated, but the essential point here is that we all come to the interview with preconceived notions and then act according to these preexisting beliefs and assumptions.

Psychologists eventually try to *understand the client and problems* in the light of their theoretical orientation. Most arrive at a diagnosis or some formulation of the problem, but the nature of this description differs. Some may think of the client in terms of oedipal and preoedipal functioning. Others may think of the person in terms of a *homeostatic emotional system designed to maintain a dominant-submissive dyadic relationship against a triangulated third party.* Others may couch the problem as *lack of assertiveness because of a history of punishments during attempts at assertiveness.* Still others may see the person as primarily *dependent with borderline features.* All of these characterizations are a diagnosis of a sort, but by the end of the interview, the psychologist is likely to have a hypothesis upon which an intervention approach will be fashioned.

DIAGNOSTIC INTERVIEWING

Good interviewing consists of putting the client at ease, eliciting information, maintaining control, maintaining rapport, and bringing closure. Putting the client at ease consists of attending to privacy and confidentiality issues, reducing anxiety, avoiding interruptions, showing respect by using the client's preferred name, and arranging seating configurations that promote observation and interaction. Eliciting information is accomplished by asking open-ended questions, avoiding unnecessary interruptions, intervening at critical junctions of client elaborations, and clarifying any inconsistencies.

Controlling the interview does not mean assuming a completely directive interviewing stance; rather, it means that the psychologist has a purpose in mind for the interview itself and engages in behaviors that accomplish this purpose. The psychologist does not dominate the interview but rather guides it along a desired path. Skillfully disrupting client ramblings that are counterproductive, discouraging unnecessary material, and making smooth transitions from one stage of the interview to another can accomplish this goal. Rapport is maintained throughout by being nonjudgmental, displaying empathy, using language appropriate to the client, addressing salient client issues, and communicating a sense that the client's problems are understood and can be helped. Finally, the psychologist brings closure to the interview by informing the person about the next steps in the process.

STRUCTURE OF THE CLINICAL INTERVIEW

The interpersonal psychiatrist, Harry Stack Sullivan (1954), suggested a format for the clinical interview, conceiving it as a phase-sequenced process consisting of (a) the formal inception, (b) reconnaissance, (c) detailed inquiry, and (d) termination. This model remains viable even today (Craig, 1989).

In the *formal inception* (e.g., introduction) phase, the clinician learns what brought the client to the interview and explains to the patient what will transpire within the interview. Sometimes all that is necessary in this introductory phase is to tell the client *we're going to put our heads together and see if we can find ways to help you.* Next, tell the client what information you already know. If little or no information is available, it is acceptable to communicate that as well.

The *reconnaissance* (e.g., exploration) is the phase in which the clinician learns some basic information about the interviewee. The client will present what has come to be called the *presenting complaint.* Aside from demographics, the clinician also assesses for clinical syndromes and personality disorders during this part of the process. Sullivan (1954) believed this phase should not take longer than 20 min.

By assessing the syndrome, the clinicians convey that they understand the problem. Consider a patient who is new in town, is looking for a primary care provider to manage Type 2 diabetes and has narrowed down the search to two physicians. Doctor A takes a history, records the patient's present symptoms, reviews the most recent glucose levels, and gives the patient a prescription. Dr. B does the same thing but also inquires about the person's kidney function, examines the heart, eyes, and feet, and asks whether there is any numbness in the feet. In other words, Doctor B is telling the patient by

his or her actions that he or she knows about diabetes and its complications and assesses for them. Other things being equal, the patient will probably select Doctor B as the provider, feeling that he or she is more competent. Doctor A may be just as competent in managing diabetes but failed to communicate that to the patient through a systematic review of the disease. This same process is recommended in mental health interviews. Show the client that you understand the problem or syndrome by assessing its major symptoms, associated disorders, and comorbidities.

The third phase is called the *detailed inquiry* (e.g., hypothesis testing). Here the initial impression gained during the first two phases is further assessed, and the clinician interviews for an understanding of why the client is in the present situation and why the patient exhibits particular behaviors and coping styles. I term this phase "interviewing for etiology." Again, the clinician can frame the etiology within a preferred theoretical framework, citing such concepts as negative reinforcements, unbalanced family systems, or oral fixation. The crucial point is to develop a working hypothesis that will account for the behavior. At the end of this phase, the clinician should have a working hypothesis as to the source of the problem.

The final phase Sullivan called *termination,* but I prefer to call it *planning and intervention.* Here the clinician makes a summary statement (e.g., feedback) as to what has been learned in the session; this is not a mere repetition of what the interviewee has said but rather a clinical assessment from the interviewer's perspective. It can be framed in psychodynamic, behavioral, existential-humanistic, or family systems perspectives, but in any case, it tells the client that you understand the problem. It lays the groundwork for how the problem will be addressed. An important point in this phase is to communicate that you can help the client. You understand the problem and can address it so that you can give the client hope and an expectation of improvement. At this phase, basic procedural issues are also discussed. These issues include things such as frequency of visits, issues of confidentiality, fees, or emergency calls. I believe that if the clinician follows this format and satisfactorily addresses the items to be assessed in it, the probability that the client will return for therapeutic work is maximized.

INTERVIEWING TECHNIQUES

Regardless of one's theoretical position (for the most part), clinicians rely on a finite set of interviewing techniques that cut across interviewing systems.

Questioning

This interviewing technique is certainly the most often utilized. Clients rarely spontaneously reveal the kind of information necessary, and the interviewer must, perforce, ask questions to get more precise information. Questions may be either closed-ended or open-ended. In *closed-ended questions,* the interviewee is asked a specific question that has to be answered in a yes-no format. There is little opportunity for elaboration. An example of the closed-ended question is *Have you lost any weight within the past 30 days?* In contrast, an *open-ended question* allows for a full range of response and for client elaboration. An example would be *How does your spouse feel when you keep losing your job?* Both open-ended and closed-ended questions are necessary, but clinicians should try to avoid too many close-ended questions because they inhibit free-flowing communication.

Clarification

This technique is often necessary because the nature of a person's responses may remain obscure; this is usually done by using one of the other interviewing techniques (e.g., questioning, paraphrasing, restating) and is often appreciated by clients because it gives them a continued opportunity to tell their story.

Confrontation

This is a technique whereby the clinician points out the discrepancy between what is stated and what is observed. It has frequently been employed with substance abusers, who continue to deny or minimize their drinking and drug abuse. It is also used with persons with character disorder diagnoses to break down their defenses. When done in a nonhostile and factual manner, it can be helpful, but too often it is done in a destructive manner that increases client resistance. Neophyte interviewers often have a problem with this technique because they may not be prepared to deal with the client's response if this technique is mishandled. This technique probably should be minimized and rarely used because more recent evidence has called into question its utility (Miller, 1991).

Exploration

Some areas may require a review that is more in-depth than what is initially presented by the client. In this technique the clinician structures a more thorough inquiry into a given area. Most clients expect to be questioned about certain issues and may wonder why this was not done. Clinicians also should not be reluctant to explore areas that may be considered sensitive.

Humor

There is increasing recognition that humor does play a role in clinical interviews. It should not be overdone and should always be done to benefit the client. It can reduce anxiety, facilitate therapeutic movement, and enhance the flow of the session.

Interpretation

This technique has a long history in clinical psychology and emanates from the Freudian tradition, which considers much of human motivation outside of conscious awareness. It is probably the most difficult technique to use successfully because it requires a good knowledge of the client, personality, motivation, and dynamics. Interviewers in training should not employ this technique without first processing this technique with their supervisor. It is important to recognize that many clients will acquiesce to the authority of the clinician and agree with the interpretation when in fact it may be erroneous.

Reflection

Here the clinician skillfully and accurately restates what the client has just said to show that the feelings and statements have been understood.

Reframing

This technique is sometimes called cognitive restructuring. Attitudes, opinions, beliefs, or feelings are rephrased so that they correspond more to reality. Reframing can provide a client with a new perspective and may undercut negative self-statements that are often irrational and maladaptive. Reframing also suggests new ways of thinking and behaving.

Restatement

This technique is sometimes called paraphrasing. It differs from reflection primarily in purpose. Restatement is most often used to promote understanding and clarification, whereas reflection is used primarily as a therapeutic tool.

Silence

Sometimes no response is the best response. Silence can provide the client with an opportunity to process and understand

TABLE 21.3   Basic Interviewing Techniques

Technique	Patient Statement	Interview Response
Clarification	Sometimes my husband doesn't come home for days.	What do you think he's doing when this happens?
Confrontation	I no longer abuse my wife.	You hit her yesterday!
Exploration	In service I saw a guy get killed.	What were the conditions? Did you have any bad dreams about it?
Humor	Sometimes, doc, I act so crazy I think I got a split personality.	In that case, that will be $50.00 each.
Interpretation	I took my father's Valium and flushed them down the toilet.	If he were able to stand up to your mother, then you would not have to behave aggressively towards her.
Reflection	I'm not getting anywhere.	Your lack of progress frustrates you.
Reframing	My boyfriend left me for someone else.	Although it is upsetting now, it gives you the chance to meet someone else.
Restatement	I hear voices and get confused.	These strange things are disturbing you.
Self-disclosure	I just can't learn like the others. I get so upset with myself.	I am dyslexic too. It need not hold you up. You just have special needs.
Silence	Someday I'm going to tell her exactly how I feel.	(no response)
Questioning	As a youth I was in detention home.	What did you do to get in there?

what has just been said. It should be done to promote introspection or to allow clients to recompose themselves after an emotional episode. It needs to be done in such a way that the client understands that the clinician is using silence for a reason.

The basic techniques of interviewing and examples illustrating these techniques are presented in Table 21.3.

INTERVIEWING MODELS

The Medical Model

Many psychologists have argued that interviewing from the medical model is inappropriate. The medical model assumes that symptoms are developed due to external pathogens; heritable vulnerabilities that are biologically determined; or structural, anatomical, or physiological dysfunctions and abnormalities. These problems can only be corrected or ameliorated through surgery, medicine, or rehabilitation techniques. One can think of the medical model as having two broad functions. The first is to guide classification, diagnosis, and ultimately, treatment and prevention. The second major function is to control both socially and legally the health practices of society. Some psychologists would prefer that we adopt a *biopsychosocial* model, which admits the role of biological processes in the development of disorders but which also includes the role of psychological and social factors in their etiology, course, and treatment.

Behavioral Assessment

Many psychologists prefer a behavioral to a medical model of interviewing. Behavioral psychologists do not espouse the idea that health-related problems are rooted in biology. Rather, they believe that contingencies of reinforcement occurring in the context of certain environments are primarily responsible for problematic behaviors. They thus decry medical terminology and nosology in favor of such concepts as response patterns, positive and negative reinforcements, and antecedents and consequences. A behaviorally based interview might analyze the problem by taking a reinforcement history, looking for patterns of rewards and punishments following critical behaviors, and carefully defining and quantifying each targeted behavior for intervention. The chapter by O'Brien, McGrath, and Haynes in this volume discusses behavioral interviewing at greater length.

Interview Biases

Interviews are not without problems, and many sources of interviewer biases have been researched. These biases include factors such as positive and negative halo; reliance on first impressions; client attractiveness; theoretical biases (e.g., insisting that one theory can explain all forms of behavior); emphasizing trait, state, or situational determinants of behavior to the exclusion of the others; and conceptualizing behavior as a static rather than a dynamic process.

One problem with an assessment interview is the extent to which bias exists throughout the diagnostic process. One bias that has been particularly addressed is gender bias. There are other sources of bias as well, including biased constructs, biased criteria for making diagnoses, biased sampling populations to study the issue, biased application of the diagnostic criteria, and biased assessment instruments and gender biases in the methods used to assess diagnostic entities (see also Lindsay, Sankis, & Widiger, 2000). Hartung and Widiger (1998) have provided the most recent summary of prevalence rates of various diagnoses by gender, but these rates are not immune to systematic distortions, as mentioned previously. Biased representation within clinical settings, empirical studies, and biased diagnostic criteria sets can also skew the reported findings. However, these data presented by Hartung and Widiger (1998) are reasonable estimates of prevalence rates of psychiatric disorders by gender based on current research.

Brown (1990) proposed a model for integrating gender issues into the clinical interview. It includes preassessment activities, such as familiarizing oneself in the scholarship and research on gender and its relationship to clinical judgments; it also includes suggestions to attend to one's activities within the assessment process itself. These activities include inquiries that will help the clinician determine the meaning of gender membership for the client and the client's social and cultural environment, determine gender-role compliance or variation, notice how the client attends to the evaluator's gender, and guard against inappropriate gender stereotyping.

ASSESSING PSYCHOPATHOLOGY WITH CLINICAL INTERVIEWS

Structured Versus Unstructured Interviews

Interviews to assess for psychopathology vary considerably in how they are conducted. A basic dimension of interviews is their degree of structure. Structured interviews follow rigid rules. The clinician asks specific questions that follow an exact sequence and that include well-defined rules for recording and judging responses. This practice minimizes interview biases and unreliable judgments, hence providing more objective information. Although structured interviews generally have better psychometric properties than do unstructured ones, structured interviews may overlook idiosyncrasies that add to the richness of personality, artificially restraining the topics covered within the interview. They also may not create much rapport between client and clinician. Semistructured interviews are more flexible and provide guidelines rather than rules. There are neither prepared questions nor introductory probes. These types of interviews may elicit more information than would emerge from a structured interview because the

clinician is allowed more judgment in determining what specific questions to ask. The interviewer also may ascertain more detailed information about specific topics. In completely unstructured interviews, the clinician assesses and explores conditions believed to be present within the interviewee. These hypotheses are generated from the person's elaborations during the interview. In clinical practice, diagnoses are more often established using unstructured interviews, whereas in a research context diagnoses are more often established by using a structured or semistructured interview.

The introduction of criteria sets in *DSM-III* (American Psychiatric Association, 1980) ushered in renewed interest in the reliability of psychiatric diagnoses. Clinicians devoted a substantial amount of effort to improving diagnostic categories and to establishing psychiatric diagnoses. To respond to this challenge, clinical psychologists relied on their history of measuring individual differences in personality via structured inventories. Psychiatrists relied on their rich history of observation and interviews to establish a diagnosis, and they developed a spate of structured psychiatric interviews for an array of problems and disorders. This move was an attempt to reduce subjective clinical judgments. Table 21.4 presents a selected review of available structured psychiatric interviews for a variety of conditions. I provide a brief summary of the most frequently used structured diagnostic interviews. Although each of the structured instruments was designed for somewhat different purposes and was to be used with its companion diagnostic system, all have been revised and can now be used with *DSM-IV.*

The structured psychiatric interviews that have received the most attention are the Schedule of Affective Disorders and Schizophrenia (SADS; Endicott & Spitzer, 1978), the Diagnostic Interview Schedule (DIS; Robins, Helzer, Croughan, & Ratcliff, 1981), and the Structured Clinical Interview for *DSM* Disorders (SCID; Spitzer, Williams, Gibbon, & First, 1992).

The SADS is a standardized, semistructured diagnostic interview that was initially developed to make a differential diagnoses among 25 diagnostic categories in the Research Diagnostic Criteria, a precursor to *DSM-III*. The clinician uses a set of introductory probes and further questions to determine whether the responses meet the diagnostic criteria. The SADS has two main sections. In the first section, the interviewer ascertains a general overview of the client's condition by using detailed questions about current symptoms and their severity. Level of impairment is determined through the use of standard descriptions and is not left to clinical judgment. The second section covers the patient's history of mental disorders; questions are clustered within each diagnosis. It assesses psychopathology and functioning in the current episode, assessing mood, symptoms and impairment.

TABLE 21.4 A Selected Presentation of Structured Psychiatric Interviews

General interview schedules	
Schedule of Affective Disorders and Schizophrenia	Endicott & Spitzer, 1978.
Diagnostic Interview Schedule	Robins et al., 1981.
Structured Interview for *DSM* Disorders	Pfohl, Blum, & Zimmerman, 1983; Pfohl, Stangl, & Zimmerman, 1995.
Structured Clinical Interview for *DSM-III-R*	Spitzer, Williams, Gibbon, & First, 1992.
Axis I disorders	
Acute stress disorder	Bryant et al., 1998.
Anxiety	Spitzer & Williams, 1988.
Affective disorders and schizophrenia	Endicott & Spitzer, 1978.
Borderline personality disorder	Zanarini, Gunderson, et al., 1989.
Depression	Jamison & Scogin, 1992.
Depressive personality disorder	Gunderson, Phillips, Triebwasser, & Hirschfield, 1994.
Dissociative disorders	Steinberg, Cicchetti, Buchanan, & Hall, 1993.
Eating disorders	Cooper & Fairbairn, 1987.
Hypocondriasis Narcissism	Barsky et al., 1992. Gunderson, Ronningstam, & Bodkin, 1990.
Panic disorder	Williams, Spitzer, & Gibbon, 1992.
Personality disorders	Stangl Pfohl, Zimmerman, Bowers, & Corenthal, 1985.
	Selzer, Kernberg, Fibel, Cherbuliez, & Mortati, 1987.
	Zanarini, Frankenburg, Chauncey, & Gunderson, 1987; Zanarini, Frankenburg, Sickel, & Yong, 1995.
	Loranger et al., 1987, 1994.
	Widiger, Mangine, Corbitt, Ellis, & Thomas, 1995.
Posttraumatic stress disorder	Watson, Juba, Manifold, Kucala, & Anderson, 1991.
Psychopathy	Hare, 1991.
Miscellaneous	
Child abuse	Shapiro, 1991.
Suicide	Reynolds, 1990.
	Sommers-Flanagan & Sommers-Flanagan, 1995.
Symptoms	Andreasen, Flaum, & Arndt, 1992.

Current functioning is defined as level of function 1 week prior to the interview. The final results yield both current and lifetime diagnoses, and the interview requires 1–2 hours to administer. There are three versions of the SADS, including a lifetime version (SADS-L), a change version (SADS-C) that can be used to evaluate treatment effectiveness, and a children's version (K-SADS-P).

The DIS is a completely structured diagnostic interview designed to be used by lay interviewers. It was developed by National Institute of Mental Health to assess current and lifetime diagnoses in large-scale epidemiological surveys of psychopathology and psychiatric disorders, although it also has been used in clinical research studies. To administer the DIS, the interviewer reads the questions exactly as they are provided in the interview booklet. In general, there is no probing, although a separate probe flowchart can be used for organic diagnoses with psychiatric symptoms. Separate sections are provided for 32 specific diagnoses containing about 263 items. Current symptoms are assessed for four time periods: the past 2 weeks, the past month, the past 6 months, and the past year. Administration time is about 45–90 minutes. Much of the research with the DIS has compared DIS to psychiatric-clinician diagnosis established by traditional means. There are child and adolescent versions of the DIS, and both are available in a computerized DIS (C-DIS) program.

The SCID is a semistructured diagnostic interview designed to be used by clinical interviewers and was intended to have an administration time shorter than that of the SADS. It takes 60–90 minutes to administer and assesses problems within the past month (current) and lifetime. The interview begins with a patient's description of his or her problems. After the clinician has an overview of the client's difficulties, the more structured section begins, organized in a modular format depending on suspected diagnoses. The questions are open-ended. After each section, the interviewer scores the disorder for severity (*mild, moderate, severe*) within the past month, according to symptoms and functional impairment. The interview follows the hierarchical structure that appears in *DSM*. There are several versions of the SCID. One is designed for use with inpatients (SCID-P), one with outpatients (SCID-OP), and one with nonpatients (SCID-N). Subsequently, the SCID-II was developed to diagnose personality disorders. The SCID has been translated into several foreign languages. It is currently in use in Japan, Puerto Rico, and China and has become the most researched structured psychiatric interview.

Should you use a structured psychiatric interview? They can be useful to teach diagnostic interviewing for clinicians in training. They may be more valuable than are unstructured interviews in certain forensic applications. They can provide an automatic second opinion, and some may save valuable time for the professional because they can be administered by mental health paraprofessionals. However, for routine clinical practice, structured clinical interviews are cumbersome and time-consuming and seem more appropriate when methodological rigor is required for research diagnoses.

Psychometric properties, so often discussed in the context of assessing psychological tests, may also be applied to clinical interviews that assess psychopathology (Blashfield & Livesley, 1991). The purpose of these interview schedules was to improve the reliability of psychiatric diagnosis. Even so, serious problems in assessment reliability continue to exist; even when using structured interviews and response sets, both in the interviewer and patient can affect the outcome of the evaluation (Alterman et al., 1996).

One outcome of the development of structured clinical interviewing has been the inquiry of comorbidities of Axis I disorders associated with an Axis II disorders (and vice versa). For example, disorders that have been studied include *eating disorders* (Braun, Sunday, & Halmi, 1994; Brewerton et al., 1995), *psychotic disorders* (Cassano, Pini, Saettoni, Rucci, & Del'Osso, 1998), and *substance abuse* (Abbott, Weller, & Walker, 1994; Oldham et al., 1992). These findings are presented later in this chapter. It is incumbent on the interviewer to assess those disorders that may be associated with an Axis I or Axis II diagnosis.

Many factors interact and complicate the process of using interviews to assess psychopathology. These factors include (but are not limited to) definitional ambiguities, criterion unreliability, overlapping symptoms, contextual moderators, multidimensional attributes, population heterogeneity, and deficits in the instruments and processes (e.g. interviews) that we as clinicians use to assess psychopathology (Millon, 1991). Additionally, the diagnostic system we use (*DSM-IV*) is imperfect. Complaints about this system include conceptual obscurity, confusion, a questionable broadening of the range and scope of categories classified as mental disorder, use of a categorical rather than dimensional model, poor applicability to disorders in children, and issues the medicalization of psychiatric diagnosis (American Psychiatric Association, 1980).

ASSESSING PERSONALITY WITH CLINICAL INTERVIEWS

Personality Assessment Versus Assessing Personality Disorders

It is one thing to assess personality and quite another to assess personality characteristics. The latter is substantially easier because there are diagnostic criteria codified in official diagnostic classification systems (e.g., *DSM, ICD-10*), and to make the diagnosis one merely has to determine whether the client meets the criteria. Furthermore, there are both structured clinical interviews and psychometric tests available to supplement the clinical interview (Widiger & Frances, 1985b, 1987). Because there is no agreed-upon classification system for personality, the clinician typically looks for certain traits that are related to the referral or treatment issue.

Problems in Assessing Personality and Personality Disorders With Clinical Interviews

Many assessment difficulties complicate the diagnosis of personality disorders. Many issues have occupied the field of personality assessment (Zimmerman, 1994) and need to be considered by an individual clinician when interviewing for personality characteristics and personality disorders. First, the lines of demarcation between normal and pathological traits are porous and not well differentiated (Goldsmith, Jacobsberg, & Bell, 1989; Strack & Lorr, 1997). The normality-pathology continuum can be viewed from different theoretical positions, making it difficult for the clinician to determine whether the behavior observed in the interview is normative or aberrant. Second, official diagnostic classification systems have adopted a categorical system for personality disorders (Widiger, 1992). One criticism of this approach is that it artificially dichotomizes diagnostic decisions into present-absent categories when they are inherently continuous variables. From this perspective, personality disorders have no discrete demarcations that would provide a qualitative distinction between normal and abnormal levels (Widiger, 2000). In contrast, a dimensional approach assumes that traits and behaviors are continuously distributed in the population and that a particular individual may have various degrees of each trait or behavior being assessed. Dimensional systems are seen as more flexible, specific, and reliable and are able to provide more comprehensive information, whereas categorical systems lose too much information and can result in classification dilemmas when a client meets the criteria for multiple disorders (Widiger & Kelso, 1983). However, dimensional systems are too complex for practical purposes and may provide too much information. Determining the optimal point of demarcation between normal and abnormal would be difficult from a dimensional perspective.

Third, many have lamented that the *DSM* personality disorder section lacks a theoretical approach to the understanding and classification of personality disorders. Fourth, fixed decision rules—as contained in official diagnostic systems—decrease diagnostic efficiency when the cutoff points for diagnosis are not adjusted for local base rates (Widiger & Kelso, 1983). Fifth, affective disorders can influence the expression of traits and confound diagnostic impressions. For example, many patients with clinical depression appear to also have a dependent personality. However, when their depression abates, they no longer appear to be dependent. Patients with bipolar manic disorder may appear histrionic during the acute phase of the manic-depression but not when the affective disorder has stabilized. Affective disorders complicate the diagnosis of personality disorders. Sixth, is the

TABLE 21.5 Personality Disorders with Higher Prevalence Rates for Selected Axis I Syndromes

Clinical Syndrome	Personality Disorder
Anxiety disorders: General	Borderline
Panic disorders	Avoidant, dependent, obsessive-compulsive
Social phobia	Avoidant
Agoraphobia	Avoidant
Somatoform	Avoidant, paranoid
Depression: Dysthymia	Avoidant, borderline, histrionic
Major depression (episodic)	Borderline
Bipolar	Histrionic, obsessive-compulsive, borderline, paranoid
Eating disorders: Anorexia	Avoidant
Bulimia	Dependent, histrionic, borderline
Substance abuse (alcohol and drugs)	Antisocial, narcissistic

behavioral manifestation or expression seen in diagnostic interviews due to endemic personality traits, or is the manifestation situationally induced? Specific life circumstances can change behavior and confuse the diagnosis of personality disorders. Seventh, patients often meet the diagnostic criteria for more than one personality disorder, and the optimal number of diagnostic criteria needed for an individual diagnosis remains unclear.

One trend in the assessment literature has been to study the role of prevalence of personality disorders in Axis I syndromes. There is now recognition that personality disorders can influence the expression, course, and duration of Axis I disorders, as well as be a focus of treatment in their own right. Table 21.5 presents the personality disorders most often diagnosed for selected Axis I disorders. Clinicians who assess for specific Axis I disorders should evaluate for the presence of personality disorders commonly associated with those syndromes (Livesley, 2001; Millon & Davis, 1996).

One continuing concern is that although the reliability of personality disorder diagnoses has improved, their discriminant validity continues to be a problem. This means that there will continue to be high levels of comorbid personality disorder diagnosis within an individual patient (Blais & Norman, 1997).

Role of Culture

We are only beginning to appreciate the role of culture and how it affects behavior. *DSM-IV* has recognized many cultural manifestations that are viewed as common within the designated culture. However, while *DSM-IV* includes Axis I considerations in the Appendix, it has been slow to take into account the role of cultural considerations and applying them to the diagnostic criteria for Axis II disorders.

RELIABILITY OF CLINICAL INTERVIEWS AND PSYCHIATRIC DIAGNOSES

Most clinicians make a personality disorder diagnosis by listening to the person describe interpersonal interactions and by observing behavior in the interview itself (Westen, 1997). However, even with the introduction of criteria sets, personality disorder diagnoses generally obtain lower levels of reliability compared to Axis I disorders (Widiger & Frances, 1985a); this is because the clinician has to address the issues of boundary overlap, the possible influences of state, role, and situational factors on behavioral expression, the client's inability or unwillingness to report symptoms, and the difficulty of determining whether a trait is pervasive and maladaptive within the confines of a brief psychiatric interview (Gorton & Akhtar, 1990).

Prior to *DSM-III,* the mean interrater reliability (kappa) for the diagnosis of personality disorders was 0.32. *DSM-III* introduced criteria sets for the establishment of a diagnosis. *DSM-III* also included field trials of the reliability of the proposed diagnoses using over 450 clinicians involving over 800 patients, including adults, adolescents, and children. For personality disorders in adults, results indicated that the overall kappa coefficient of agreement on diagnosis was .66 after separate interviews. For Axis II personality disorders, the kappas were .61 for joint assessments and .54 for using a test-retest format (Spitzer, Williams, & Skodal, 1980). High kappas (.70 and above) reflect generally good agreement. With the introduction of criteria sets, the mean kappa for *DSM-III* personality disorders was 0.61 when the decision was *any personality disorder* but only a median 0.23 for individual disorders (Perry, 1992). Even so, Wiens and Matarazzo (1983) concluded that ". . . *DSM-III* is a remarkably reliable system for classifying disorders in Axis I and Axis II" (p. 320).

However, method variance contributes significantly to the observed results. Reliability estimates change depending on whether the reliability is based on unstructured interviews, semistructured interviews, or joint-interview raters compared to single-interview raters (Zimmerman, 1994), as well as long versus short test-retest intervals. Perry (1992) reported that the diagnostic agreement between a clinical interview and a self-report measure of personality disorders was not significantly comparable across methods. In fact, certain domains that are part of the clinical diagnostic picture of a personality disorder may not be reliably assessed by either structured clinical interviews or self-report measures because these domains pertain to implicit processes that may be outside the awareness of the client.

There has not been a comparable presentation on the reliability and validity of psychiatric interviewing and diagnosis since Matarazzo's work on these topics some time ago (Matarazzo, 1965, 1978; Wiens & Matarazzo, 1983); the focus of clinical interviewing research has changed from generic interviews, which were the focus of Mattarazo, to structured and focused interviews. It is not scientifically accurate to discuss the reliability of psychiatric diagnosis or to discuss the reliability of clinical interview because the reliability will change based on (a) diagnosis, (b) instrument used to assess reliability, and (c) the method used to determine reliability. Psychiatric research now addresses the reliability and validity (usually concurrent diagnoses) among these various structured and semistructured techniques.

There are three strategies to evaluate the reliability of structured psychiatric interviews. In the first strategy (test-retest methodology), two or more clinicians interview the same patient on two separate occasions and independently establish a diagnosis. In the second method, two raters interview the same patient simultaneously and the raters make independent judgments as to diagnosis. Often researchers using this method provide the raters with an audio or videotape of the interview. In the third method, two or more structured psychiatric interviews, self-report tests, or both are given to the same patient. In all methods, the extent of agreement between interviewers as to the presence or absence of a particular disorder is determined by using the kappa statistic. By consensus, kappa values greater than .70 are considered to reflect good agreement, values .50 to .70 reflect fair to good agreement, and values less than .50 reflect poor agreement. Values less than 0.00 reflect less than chance agreement between raters.

The Structured Clinical Interview for *DSM* diagnoses (SCID; First, Spitzer, Gibbon, & Williams, 1995a; Spitzer & Williams, 1984; Spitzer, Williams, Gibbon, & First, 1992) has been the diagnostic instrument most often used in psychiatric research, and researchers have considerable reliability data on this instrument. Our discussion on reliability of psychiatric diagnoses concentrates on research using this instrument.

The SCID and SCID-II were designed for use with experienced diagnosticians. It has different modules, including all Axis I and Axis II groups of disorders. SCID-I assesses 33 of the more commonly diagnosed *DSM-III-R* disorders. The structured format requires the interviewer to read the questions exactly as they are printed (in the first of three columns) and to determine the presence or absence of criteria, which appear in the second column. The third column contains three levels of certainty—*yes, no,* or *indeterminate*—as to whether the patient met the criteria. The structured clinical interview allows the clinician to probe and restate questions, challenge the response, and ask for clarification in order to determine whether a particular symptom is present. The use of opera-

tional criteria for a diagnosis has improved the selection of research participants, thereby improving participant homogeneity and reducing interviewer bias. But potential sources of bias, such as cultural bias, are present, which can influence the expression of psychiatric symptoms and psychopathology as well as the interpersonal nature of the diagnostic process between patient and interviewer (Lesser, 1997). However, these issues are extant in all structured clinical interviews as well. Prevalence rates of disorders may also vary based on which version of *DSM* (e.g., *DSM-II-R, DSM-IV*) is used as the criterion (Poling et al., 1999).

Segal, Hersen, and Van Hasselt (1994) have published the most recent literature review on the reliability of the SCID-I (Axis I) and SCID-II (Axis II) disorders. Their review found kappa values for the SCID-I ranging from −.03 to 1.00. It is interesting to note that both of these values were for the somatoform diagnosis in separate studies. The median kappa values for 33 different diagnoses reported in the literature was .78. Median kappa values for SCID-II reliability studies for Axis II disorders ranged from .43 (histrionic personality disorder) to 1.00 (dependent, self-defeating, and narcissistic personality disorders), with a median of .74.

Several additional reliability studies on SCID diagnosis have appeared since that review. Using test-retest methodology, 12-month reliability data for SCID-II diagnosis in 31 cocaine patients was .46 (Weiss, Najavits, Muenz, & Hufford, 1995). Kappa values ranged from .24 (obsessive-compulsive disorder) to .74 (histrionic personality disorder) with an overall kappa at .53 among 284 patients at multiple sites (First, Spitzer, Gibbon, & Williams, 1995b). Using a Dutch sample of 43 outpatients, six raters evaluated the same patient within 1–4 weeks of the initial interview. Kappa for one or more personality disorders was .53, suggesting only fair agreement (Dreessen & Arntz, 1998).

Research has found little agreement between SCID-II and the Minnesota Multiphasic Personality Inventory (MMPI) and Millon Clinical Multiaxial Inventory (MCMI-II) diagnoses (Butler, Gaulier, & Haller, 1991; Marlowe, Husband, Bonieskie, & Kirby, 1997). Although there were no apparent gender biases in assessing personality diagnoses between SCID-II and the Personality Diagnostic Questionnaire-Revised (Golomb, Fava, Abraham, & Rosenbaum, 1995; Hyler & Rieder, 1987), there is often low agreement between personality disorder diagnoses between these two assessment methods, with many false positives (Fossati et al., 1998). This same pattern of results appears between the SCID and the Personality Disorder Examination (Loranger, Susman, Oldham, & Russakoff, 1987)—low diagnostic agreement and many false positives (Lenzenweger, Loranger, Korfine, & Neff, 1997;

Modestin, Enri, & Oberson, 1998; O'Boyle & Self, 1990). Using two separate structured psychiatric interviews reveals different patterns of comorbidity of personality disorders (Oldham et al., 1992). Because the false negative rates between these instruments tends to be low, one possibility is to have a clinician question only those diagnostic elements endorsed in the self-report instrument (Jacobsberg, Perry, & Frances, 1995), but this has not been done to date.

In summary, *the present available data suggest that although structured psychiatric interviews are reliable, they show low to modest agreement* with each other in terms of individual diagnoses; this is true not only for the SCID but also for other major structured clinical interviews.

INCREMENTAL VALIDITY

Using a computer search that included the terms *incremental validity* and *clinical interviews* as well as *interviews,* we could find no references pertaining to research that addressed the question of whether adding an interview adds any other information than was attainable through other means (e.g., psychological tests, collateral information). Incremental validity studies are readily available for such entities as the addition of a particular test to a test battery (Weiner, 1999), the prediction of a specific behavior such as violence, (Douglas, Ogcuff, Nicholls, & Grant, 1999), or various constructs such as anxiety sensitivity (McWilliams & Asmund, 1999) or depression (Davis & Hays, 1997), but the criteria in these studies were all established using other self-report inventories rather than a clinical interview.

I did find studies that documented the fact that structured clinical interviews yield higher rates of various disorders than do unstructured interviews. For example, body dysmorphic disorder, which is relatively rare, was three times more likely to be diagnosed using a structured clinical interview (SCID) than with a routine clinical interview (Zimmerman & Mattia, 1998). Comparing comorbidities among 500 adult psychiatric patients assessed at intake with routine clinical interview and 500 patients assessed with the SCID, results showed that one third of the patients assessed with the structured diagnostic interview had three or more Axis I diagnoses, compared to only 10% of patients assessed with an unstructured clinical interview. In fact, 15 disorders were more frequently diagnosed with the SCID than with routine clinical assessment; they occurred across mood, anxiety, eating, somatoform, and impulse-control disorders (Zimmerman & Mattia, 1999a). Similarly, posttraumatic stress disorder (PTSD) is often overlooked in clinical practice when PTSD symptoms are not the

presenting complaint. However, PTSD was more frequently diagnosed using a structured clinical interview such as the SCID (Zimmerman & Mattia, 1999b). Also, these researchers found that without the benefit of the detailed information provided by structured interviews, clinicians rarely diagnose borderline personality disorder during routine intake evaluations (Zimmerman & Mattia, 1999c).

These studies attest to the fact that *structured clinical interviews diagnose more clinical disorders than do routine clinical interviews.* The need for incremental validity studies with clinical interviews is readily apparent. We especially need studies that compare clinical interviews to other assessment methods. Several studies have reported rates of diagnostic agreement between clinician-derived or structured clinical interviews compared to self-report measures, such as the MCMI, but they are reliability studies and not studies of incremental validity.

COMPUTER-ASSISTED DIAGNOSIS AND COMPUTER INTERVIEWS

In recent years the use of computers to interview patients has been attempted, mostly in research contexts. Its potential advantages include increased reliability of the information and an increased ability to obtain specific data about a patient. Critics complain that computer interviews are too impersonal and miss subtle aspects of a patient's problem. Perhaps the most promising use of computer interviewing is in highly focused evaluations of a particular problem, such as depression, substance abuse, or sexual disorders.

We can safely predict that computers and technological advances will eventually permeate future diagnostic studies. Indeed, researchers have already established that it is feasible to do diagnostic work via the computer (Keenan, 1994; Kobak et al., 1997; Neal, Fox, Carroll, Holden, & Barnes, 1997). Some research has shown that automated screening can record basic client information—particularly as it pertains to demographics and symptoms—even before clients see a clinician for the initial assessment and that clients view it as helpful to their treatment (Sloan, Eldridge, & Evenson, 1992).

Computerization of standardized clinician-administered structured diagnostic interviews has also been shown to have validity comparable to that obtained in face-to-face contexts (Levitan, Blouin, Navarro, & Hill, 1991; Lewis, 1994) and can also be reliably done via the telephone using structured formats (Ruskin et al., 1998). One study reported that outpatients in an acute psychiatric setting, who had been diagnosed by computer, generally liked answering questions on the computer (94%), understood the questions without difficulty (83%), and even felt more comfortable with the computerized interview than with a physician (60%). However, psychiatrists agreed with only 50% of the computer-generated diagnoses, and only 22% of psychiatrists believed that the computer generated any useful new diagnoses (Rosenman, Levings, & Korten, 1997).

Computer-based systems usually provide a list of probable diagnoses and do not include personality descriptions, in contrast to computer-derived psychological test interpretations (Butcher, Perry, & Atlis, 2000). Logic-tree systems are designed to establish the presence of traits or symptoms that are specified in the diagnostic criteria and thereby lead to a particular diagnosis. Examples of computerized systematized diagnostic interviews include the DTREE for *DSM-III-R* diagnoses (First, 1994), and the computerized version of the International Diagnostic Interview (CIDI-Auto; Peters & Andrews, 1995). However, research in this area has more commonly evaluated the computerized version of the Diagnostic Interview Schedule. This research has found that kappa coefficients for a variety of *DSM-III* diagnoses ranged from .49 to .68, suggesting fairly comparable agreement between clinician determined and computer-based psychiatric diagnoses (Butcher et al., 2000).

Research in the area has shown that computer-assisted diagnostic interviews yielded more disorder diagnoses than did routine clinical assessment procedures (Alhberg, Tuck, & Allgulander, 1996). Compared to computer-administered clinical interviews, clinician-administered interviews resulted in less self-disclosure—particularly of socially undesirable information (Locke & Gilbert, 1995). In fact, respondents seem more willing to reveal personal information to a computer than to a human being (Hofer, 1985) and tend to prefer a computer-administered interview to a clinician-conducted interview (Sweeny, McGrath, Leigh, & Costa, 2001). This is probably because they felt more judged when interviewed in person than when identical questions were administered from a computer. However, some evidence exists suggesting that computer diagnostic assessment, although it is reliable, shows poor concordance with SCID diagnoses, except for the diagnoses of antisocial and substance abuse (Ross, Swinson, Doumani, & Larkin, 1995; Ross, Swinson, Larkin, & Doumani, 1994).

Advances in technology are likely to find applications in the diagnostic process as well (Banyan & Stein, 1990). The future will certainly see more utilization of these types of sophisticated technologies. Technology, however, will not obviate the essential difficulties in the diagnostic process as described throughout this chapter—computer-assisted diagnostic formats are programmed to contain the same

problems and deficiencies inherent in a face-to-face diagnostic interview.

MISUSE OF THE INTERVIEW

Many clinicians have such faith in the clinical interview (and in their own skills) that interviews can be misused. One such current venue is that occasioned by managed care constraints that often preclude the use of other methods (e.g., psychological tests, collateral interviews) that would either add incremental validity in clinical practice or possibly confirm hypotheses gleaned from the interview itself. Psychologists need to guard against such practices and to advocate for the best possible psychological practice for a given problem.

WHAT NEEDS TO BE DONE?

Most problems in any classification system of personality disorders are endemically and systematically related to the issue of construct validity. One continuing problem in assessment is that it has been extremely difficult to find independent operationalizations of personality traits and personality disorder constructs that are consistent across assessment devices. Convergent validity between self-report measures and interview-based assessments range from poor to modest. Median correlations between structured psychiatric interviews range from .30 to .50; median correlations between self-report measures range from .39 to .68; and median correlations between questionnaires and structured interviews range from .08 to .42. Consistently moderate correlations between questionnaires have been reported for the diagnoses of borderline, dependent, passive-aggressive, and schizotypal personality disorders. Better convergent validity between questionnaires and clinical interviews has been found with diagnoses of borderline and avoidant personality disorders. For clinical interviews, consistently good convergence has been found for only avoidant personality disorder (Clark, Livesley, & Morey, 1997).

Although method variance and general measurement error may account for some of the findings, *the real problem is a lack of clear and explicit definitions of the diagnostic constructs and behavioral anchors* that explicate examples of specific items that define the disorder and aid the diagnostician (and researcher) to diagnose the disorder. For example, with a criteria set of eight items, of which five are need to make a diagnosis of borderline personality disorder, there are 95 different possible sets of symptoms that would qualify for this diagnosis (Widiger, Frances, Spitzer, & Williams, 1988).

Are there really 95 different types of borderline personality disorders? Obviously not! The criteria merely reflect our confusion on the diagnosis itself. This situation is clearly absurd and serves to illustrate the problems that accrue when the construct and defining criteria are obfuscating. Similarly, the problem of a patient's meeting two or more of the personality disorder diagnoses will continue to exist, due largely to definitional problems. A clinician can reduce this bias somewhat by carefully assessing all criterion symptoms and traits, but the problem in the criteria themselves remains.

Associated with the need for more conceptual clarity is *the need to reduce terminological confusion inherent in the criteria set.* For example, when does spontaneity become impulsivity? There is also a need for improved accuracy in clinician diagnosis. Evidence exists that trained interviewers are able to maintain high levels of interrater reliability, diagnostic accuracy, and interviewing skills, such that quality assurance procedures should be systematically presented in both research and clinical settings (Ventura, Liberman, Green, Shaner, & Mintz, 1998). For example, 18 clinical vignettes were sent to 15 therapists, along with *DSM* personality disorder criteria sets. Fourteen of the vignettes were based on *DSM* criteria and 14 were made up and suggested diagnoses of no personality disorder. Results showed and 82% rate of agreement in diagnosis. This type of procedure can be cost-effective to establish and to assess continuing competency in diagnosing personality disorders (Gude, Dammen, & Frilis, 1997).

Some have called for the explicit recognition of dimensional structures in official classification systems because such structures recognize the continuous nature of personality functioning (Widiger, 2000). Millon (2000) called for adoption of a coherent classification-guiding theory. However, it is unlikely that theorists would ever agree as to *the* parsimonious system to be adopted. Others suggested the use of prototype criteria sets to define pure cases (Oldham & Skodol, 2000; Westen & Shedler, 2000), but such prototypes might only rarely be observed in clinical practice, and hence such a system would live little practical utility, although Millon (2000) has persuasively argued otherwise. He has also called for the inclusion of personality disorder *subtypes* hierarchically subsumed under the major prototypes. Still others call for the inclusion of level of functioning (e.g., mild, moderate, severe), within the personality diagnostic system. Hunter (1998) suggested that personality disorder criteria be rewritten from the patient's perspective. This would have the effect of removing negative language and provide a simplified and more straightforward and objective means of assessment. Cloninger (2000) suggested that personality disorders be diagnosed in terms of four core features: (a) low affective stability, (b) low self-directedness, (c) low cooperativeness, and (d) low self-transcendence. Perhaps a blend of both the categorical and dimensional systems is preferable. The clinician could diagnose a personality disorder in a categorical system, reference personality (disorder) traits that are specific to the individual, and include a specifier that depicts level of functioning.

The aforementioned suggestions apply more to assessing personality disorders with interview. Karg and Wiens (1998) have recommended the following activities to improve clinical interviewing in general:

- *Prepare for the initial interview.* Get as much information beforehand as possible; be well-informed about the patient's problem area. This preparation will allow you to ask more meaningful questions. There may be important information learned from records or from other sources that warrant more detailed inquiry within the assessment interview. If this information is not available to you at the time of the interview, the opportunity for further inquiry may be lost.

- *Determine the purpose of the interview.* Have a clear understanding of what you want to accomplish. Have an interview structure in mind and follow it.

- *Clarify the purpose and parameters of the interview to the client.* If the client has a good understanding of what is trying to be accomplished, his or her willingness to provide you with meaningful information should increase.

- *Conceptualize the interview as a collaborative process.* Explain how the information will be used to help the client with his or her situation.

- *Truly hear what the interviewee has to say.* This may be accomplished by using *active listening* and by clarifying the major points of understanding with the interviewee during the interview.

- *Use structured interviews.* These interviews promote a systematic review of content areas and are more reliable.

- *Encourage the client to describe complaints in concrete behavioral terms.* This will help the psychologist to understand the client better and will provide examples of the potential problematic behavior in relevant context.

- *Complement the interview with other assessment methods, particularly psychological testing.* This may provide both convergent and incremental validity.

- Identify the antecedents and consequences of problem behaviors. This will provide more targeted interventions.

- *Differentiate between skill and motivation.* Some patients may have the desire to accomplish goals that are beyond their capacities, and vice versa.

- *Obtain base rates of behaviors.* This will provide a benchmark for later assessment of progress.
- *Avoid expectations and biases.* Self-monitor your own feelings, attitudes, beliefs, and countertransference to determine whether you are remaining objective.
- *Use a disconfirmation strategy.* Look for information that might disprove your hypothesis.
- *Counter the fundamental attribution error.* This occurs when the clinician attributes the cause of a problem to one set of factors, when it may be due to other sets of factors.
- *Combine testing with interviewing mechanistically.* This is because combining data from interview with data from other sources will be more accurate and valid than data from one source alone.
- *Delay reaching decisions while the interview is being conducted.* Don't rush to judgments or to conclusions.
- *Consider the alternatives.* Offering a menu of choices and possibilities should engender greater client acceptance of goals and interventions.
- *Provide a proper termination.* Suggest a course of action, a plan of intervention, recommended behavioral changes, and so on, that the person can take with them from the interview. It is pointless for the psychologist to conduct thorough assessments and evaluations without providing some feedback to the client.

The future will no doubt actively address, research, refine, and even eliminate some of these problems discussed in this chapter. We can look forward to improvements in diagnostic criteria, improved clarity in criteria sets, increased training so that clinicians can self-monitor and reduce any potential biases in diagnostic decision-making, and take the role of culture more into account in the evaluation of clients. I hope that these advances will lead to improvements in therapeutic interventions designed to ameliorate pathological conditions.

REFERENCES

Abbott, P. J., Weller, S. B., & Walker, R. (1994). Psychiatric disorders of opioid addicts entering treatment: Preliminary data. *Journal of Addictive Diseases, 13,* 1–11.

Alhberg, J., Tuck, J. R., & Allgulander, C. (1996). Pilot study of the adjunct utility of a computer-assisted Diagnostic Interview Schedule (C-DIS) in forensic psychiatric patients. *Bulletin of the American Academy of Psychiatry and the Law, 24,* 109–116.

Alterman, A. I., Snider, E. C., Cacciola, J. S., Brown, L. S., Zaballero, A., & Siddique, N. (1996). Evidence for response set

effects in structured research interviews. *Journal of Nervous and Mental Disease, 184,* 403–410.

American Psychiatric Association. (1980). *Diagnostic and statistical manual of mental disorders* (3rd ed.). Washington, DC: Author.

American Psychiatric Association. (1987). *Diagnostic and statistical manual of mental disorders* (3rd ed., rev.). Washington, DC: Author.

American Psychiatric Association. (1994). *Diagnostic and statistical manual of mental disorders* (4th ed.). Washington, DC: Author.

Andreasen, N., Flaum, M., & Arndt, S. (1992). The comprehensive assessment of symptoms and history (CASH). *Archives of General Psychiatry, 49,* 615–623.

Banyan, C. D., & Stein, D. M. (1990). Voice synthesis supplement to a computerized interview training program. *Teaching of Psychology, 17,* 260–263.

Barsky, A. J., Cleary, P. D., Wyshak, G., Spitzer, R. L., Williams, J. B., & Klerman, G. L. (1992). A structured diagnostic interview for hypocondriasis. *Journal of Nervous and Mental Disease, 180,* 20–27.

Benjamin, L. S. (1996). A clinician-friendly version of the Interpersonal Circumplex: Structured Analysis of Social Behavior. *Journal of Personality Assessment, 66,* 248–266.

Blais, M. A., & Norman, D. K. (1997). A psychometric evaluation of the *DSM-IV* personality disorder criteria. *Journal of Personality Disorders, 11,* 168–176.

Blashfield, R. K., & Livesley, W. J. (1991). Metaphorical analysis of psychiatric classification as a psychological test. *Journal of Abnormal Psychology, 100,* 262–270.

Braun, D. L., Sunday, S. R., & Halmi, K. A. (1994). Psychiatric comorbidity in patients with eating disorders. *Psychological Medicine, 24,* 859–867.

Brewerton, T. D., Lydiard, R. B., Herzog, D. B., Brotman, A. W., O'Neal, P. M., & Ballenger, J. C. (1995). Comorbidity of Axis I psychiatric disorders in bulimia nervosa. *Journal of Clinical Psychiatry, 56,* 77–80.

Brown, L. S. (1990). Taking account of gender in the clinical assessment interview. *Professional Psychology: Research and Practice, 21,* 12–17.

Bryant, R. A., Harvey, A. G., Dang, S. T., & Sackville, T. (1998). Assessing acute stress disorder: Psychometric properties of a structured clinical interview. *Psychological Assessment, 10,* 215–220.

Butcher, J. N., Perry, J. N., & Atlis, M. M. (2000). Validity and utility of computer-based test interpretation. *Psychological Assessment, 12,* 6–18.

Butler, S. F., Gaulier, B., & Haller, D. (1991). Assessment of Axis II personality disorders among female substance abusers. *Psychological Reports, 68,* 1344–1346.

Cassano, G. B., Pini, S., Saettoni, M., Rucci, P., & Del'Osso, L. (1998). Occurrence and clinical correlates of psychiatric comorbidity in patients with psychotic disorders. *Journal of Clinical Psychiatry, 59,* 60–68.

Cattell, H. B. (1989). *The 16PF: Personality in depth.* Champaign, IL: Institute for Personality and Ability Testing.

Clark, L. A., Livesley, W. J., & Morey, L. (1997). Special features: Personality disorder assessment: The challenge of construct validity. *Journal of Personality Disorders, 11,* 205–231.

Cloninger, C. R. (2000). A practical way to diagnose personality disorder: A proposal. *Journal of Personality Disorders, 14,* 99–108.

Cooper, Z., & Fairbairn, C. G. (1987). The eating disorder examination: A semi-structured interview for the assessment of the specific psychopathology of eating disorders. *International Journal of Eating Disorders, 6,* 1–8.

Costa, P. T., & Widiger, T. A. (Eds.). (1997). *Personality disorders and the five-factor model of personality.* Washington, DC: American Psychological Association.

Craig, R. C. (Ed.). (1989). *Clinical and diagnostic interviewing.* Northvale, NJ: Aronson.

Davis, S. E., & Hays, L. W. (1997). An examination of the clinical validity of the MCMI-III Depression Personality scale. *Journal of Clinical Psychology, 53,* 15–23.

Douglas, K. S., Ogcuff, J. R., Nicholls, T. L., & Grant, I. (1999). Assessing risk for violence among psychiatric patients: The HCR-20 Violence Risk Assessment Scheme: Screening version. *Journal of Consulting and Clinical Psychology, 67,* 917–930.

Dreessen, L., & Arntz, A. (1998). Short-interval test-retest interrater reliability of the Structured Clinical Interview for *DSM-III-R* personality disorders (SCID-II) in outpatients. *Journal of Personality Disorders, 12,* 138–148.

Dyce, J. A. (1994). Personality disorders: Alternatives to the official diagnostic system. *Journal of Personality Disorders, 8,* 78–88.

Endicott, J., & Spitzer, R. L. (1978). A diagnostic interview: The Schedule for Affective Disorders and Schizophrenia. *Archives of General Psychiatry, 35,* 837–844.

First, M. B. (1994). Computer-assisted assessment of *DSM-III-R* diagnosis. *Psychiatric Annals, 24,* 25–29.

First, M. B., Spitzer, R. L., Gibbon, M., & Williams, J. B. (1995a). The Structured Clinical Interview for *DSM-III-R* personality disorders (SCID-II): I. Description. *Journal of Personality Disorders, 9,* 83–91.

First, M. B., Spitzer, R. L., Gibbon, M., & Williams, J. B. (1995b). The structured clinical interview for DSM-III-R personality disorders (SCID-II): II. Multi-site test-retest reliability study. *Journal of Personality Disorders, 9,* 92–104.

Fossati, A., Maffei, C., Bagnato, M., Donati, D., Donini, M., Fiorelli, M., et al. (1998). Criterion validity of the Personality Diagnostic Questionnaire-R (PDQ-R) in a mixed psychiatric sample. *Journal of Personality Disorders, 12,* 172–178.

Goldsmith, S. J., Jacobsberg, L. B., & Bell, R. (1989). Personality disorder assessment. *Psychiatric Annals, 19,* 139–142.

Golomb, M., Fava, M., Abraham, M., & Rosenbaum, J. F. (1995). Gender differences in personality disorders. *American Journal of Psychiatry, 154,* 579–582.

Gorton, G., & Akhtar, S. (1990). The literature on personality disorders, 1985–1988: Trends, issues, and controversies. *Hospital and Community Psychiatry, 41,* 39–51.

Groth-Marnatt, G. (1999). *Handbook of psychological assessment* (3rd ed., pp. 67–98). New York: Wiley.

Gude, T., Dammen, T., & Frilis, S. (1997). Clinical vignettes in quality assurance: An instrument for evaluating therapists' diagnostic competence in personality disorders. *Nordic Journal of Psychiatry, 51,* 207–212.

Gunderson, J. G., Phillips, K. A., Triebwasser, J., & Hirschfeld, R. M. (1994). The diagnostic interview for depressive personality. *American Journal of Psychiatry, 151,* 1300–1304.

Gunderson, J. G., Ronningstam, E., & Bodkin, A. (1990). The diagnostic interview for narcissistic patients. *Archives of General Psychiatry, 47,* 676–680.

Hare, R. D. (1991). *The HARE PCL-R: Interview and information schedule.* Toronto, ON, Canada: Multi-Health Systems, Inc.

Hartung, C. M., & Widiger, T. A. (1998). Gender differences in the diagnosis of mental disorders: Conclusions and controversies of the *DSM-IV. Psychological Bulletin, 123,* 260–278.

Hofer, P. J. (1985). The challenge of competence and creativity for computerized psychological testing. *Journal of Consulting and Clinical Psychology, 53,* 826–838.

Hunter, E. E. (1998). An experiential-descriptive method for the diagnosis of personality disorders. *Journal of Clinical Psychology, 54,* 673–678.

Hyler, S. E., & Rieder, R. O. (1987). *Personality Diagnostic Questionnaire–Revised* (PDQ-R). New York: New York State Psychiatric Institute.

Jacobsberg, L., Perry, S., & Frances, A. (1995). Diagnostic agreement between the SCID-II screening questionnaire and the Personality Disorder Examination. *Journal of Personality Assessment, 65,* 428–433.

Jamison, C., & Scogin, F. (1992). Development of an interview-based geriatric depression rating scale. *International Journal of Aging and Human Development, 35,* 193–204.

Karg, R. S., & Wiens, A. N. (1998). Improving diagnostic and clinical interviewing. In G. Koocher, J. Norcross, & S. Hill III (Eds.), *Psychologist's desk reference* (pp. 11–14). New York: Oxford University Press.

Keenan, K. (1994). Psychological/Psychiatric Status Interview (PPSI). *Computers on Human Services, 10,* 107–115.

Kobak, K. A., Taylor, L. H., Dottl, S. L., Greist, J. H., Jefferson, J. W., Burroughs, D., et al. (1997). Computerized screening for psychiatric disorders in an outpatient community mental health clinic. *Psychiatric Services, 48,* 1048–1057.

Lenzenweger, M. F., Loranger, A. W., Korfine, L., & Neff, C. (1997). Detecting personality disorders in a nonclinical population: Application of a 2-stage for case identification. *Archives of General Psychiatry, 54,* 345–351.

Lesser, I. M. (1997). Cultural considerations using the Structured Clinical Interview for *DSM-III* for Mood and Anxiety Disorders assessment. *Journal of Psychopathology and Behavioral Assessment, 19,* 149–160.

Levitan, R. D., Blouin, A. G., Navarro, J. R., & Hill, J. (1991). Validity of the computerized DIS for diagnosing psychiatric patients. *Canadian Journal of Psychiatry, 36,* 728–731.

Lewis, G. (1994). Assessing psychiatric disorder with a human interviewer or a computer. *Journal of Epidemiology and Community Health, 48,* 207–210.

Lindsay, K. A., Sankis, L. M., & Widiger, T. A. (2000). Gender bias in self-report personality disorder inventories. *Journal of Personality Disorders, 14,* 218–232.

Livesley, W. J. (2001). *Handbook of personality disorders: Theory, research, and treatment.* New York: Guilford.

Locke, S. D., & Gilbert, B. O. (1995). Method of psychological assessment, self-disclosure, and experiential differences: A study of computer, questionnaire, and interview assessment formats. *Journal of Social Behavior and Personality, 10,* 255–263.

Loranger, A. W., Susman, V. L., Oldham, J. M., & Russakoff, L. M. (1987). The personality disorder examination: A preliminary report. *Journal of Personality Disorders, 1,* 1–13.

Loranger, A. W., Sartorius, N., Andreoli, A., Berger, P., Buchheim, P., Channabasavanna, S. M., et al. (1994). The International Personality Disorder Examination: The World Health Organization/Alcohol, Drug Abuse, and Mental Health Administration international pilot study of personality disorders. *Archives of General Psychiatry, 51,* 215–224.

Marlowe, D. B., Husband, S. D., Bonieskie, L. K. M., & Kirby, K. C. (1997). Structured interview versus self-report tests vantages for the assessment of personality pathology in cocaine dependence. *Journal of Personality Disorders, 11,* 177–190.

Maser, J. D., Kaelber, C., & Weise, R. E. (1991). International use and attitudes towards *DSM-III* and *DSM-III-R:* Growing consensus on psychiatric classification. *Journal of Abnormal Psychology, 100,* 271–279.

Matarazzo, J. D. (1965). The interview. In B. Wolman (Ed.), *Handbook of clinical psychology* (pp. 403–452). New York: McGraw-Hill.

Matarazzo, J. D. (1978). The interview: Its reliability and validity in psychiatric diagnosis. In B. Wolman (Ed.), *Clinical diagnosis of medical disorders* (pp. 47–96). New York: Plenum.

McWilliams, L. A., & Asmund, G. J. (1999). Alcohol consumption in university women: A second look at the role of anxiety sensitivity. *Depression and Anxiety, 10,* 125–128.

Menninger, K., Mayman, M., & Pruyser, P. (1963). *The vital balance: The life process in mental health and illness.* New York: Viking.

Miller, W. R. (1991). *Motivational interviewing: Preparing people to change addictive behavior.* New York: Guilford.

Millon, T. (1991). Classification in psychopathology: Rationale, alternatives, and standards. *Journal of Abnormal Psychology, 100,* 245–261.

Millon, T. (2000). Reflections on the future of *DSM* AXIS II. *Journal of Personality Disorders, 14,* 30–41.

Millon, T., & Davis, R. (1996). *Disorders of personality:* DSM-IV *and beyond.* New York: Wiley.

Modestin, J., Enri, T., & Oberson, B. (1998). A comparison of self-report and interview diagnoses of *DSM-III-R* personality disorders. *European Journal of Personality, 12,* 445–455.

Neal, L. A., Fox, C., Carroll, N., Holden, M., & Barnes, P. (1997). Development and validation of a computerized screening test for personality disorders in *DSM-III-R. Acta Psychiatrica Scandanavia, 95,* 351–356.

O'Boyle, M., & Self, D. (1990). A comparison of two interviews for *DSM-III-R* personality disorders. *Psychiatry Research, 32,* 85–92.

Oldham, J. M., & Skodol, A. E. (2000). Charting the future of AXIS II. *Journal of Personality Disorders, 14,* 17–29.

Oldham, J. M., Skodol, A. E., Kellman, H. D., Hyler, E., Doidge, N., Rosnick, L., et al. (1992). Comorbidity of Axis I and Axis II disorders. *American Journal of Psychiatry, 152,* 571–578.

Perry, J. C. (1992). Problems in the considerations in the valid assessment of personality disorders. *American Journal of Psychiatry, 149,* 1645–1653.

Peters, L., & Andrews, G. (1995). Procedural validity of the computerized version of the Composite International Diagnostic Interview (CIDI-Auto) in anxiety disorders. *Psychological Medicine, 25,* 1269–1280.

Pfohl, B., Blum, N., & Zimmerman, M. (1995). *Structured Interview for* DSM-IV *Personality SIDP-IV.* Iowa City: University of Iowa.

Pfohl, B., Stangl, D., & Zimmerman, M. (1983). *Structured Interview for* DSM-III-R *Personality SIDP-R.* Iowa City: University of Iowa College of Medicine.

Poling, J., Rounsaville, B. J., Ball, S., Tennen, H., Krantzler, H. R., & Triffleman, E. (1999). Rates of personality disorders in substance abusers: A comparison between *DSM-III-R* and *DSM-IV. Journal of Personality Disorders, 13,* 375–384.

Reynolds, W. M. (1990). Development of a semistructured clinical interview for suicide behaviors in adolescents. *Psychological Assessment, 2,* 382–390.

Robins, L. N., Helzer, J. E., Croughan, J., & Ratcliff, K. S. (1981). National Institute on Mental Health Diagnostic Interview Schedule. *Archives of General Psychiatry, 38,* 381–389.

Rosenman, S. J., Levings, C. T., & Korten, A. E. (1997). Clinical utility and patient acceptance of the computerized Composite International Diagnostic Interview. *Psychiatric Services, 48,* 815–820.

Ross, H. E., Swinson, R., Doumani, S., & Larkin, E. J. (1995). Diagnosing comorbidity in substance abusers: A comparison of the test-retest reliability of two interviews. *American Journal of Drug and Alcohol Abuse, 21,* 167–185.

Ross, H. E., Swinson, R., Larkin, E. J., & Doumani, S. (1994). Diagnosing comorbidity in substance abusers: Computer assessment and clinical validation. *Journal of Nervous and Mental Disease, 182,* 556–563.

Ruskin, P. E., Reed, S., Kumar, R., Kling, M. A., Siegel-Eliot, R., Rosen, M. R., et al. (1998). Reliability and acceptability of psychiatric diagnosis via telecommunication and audiovisual technology. *Psychiatric Services, 49,* 1086–1088.

Segal, D. L., Hersen, M., & Van Hasselt, V. B. (1994). Reliability of the Structured Clinical Interview for *DSM-III-R:* An evaluative review. *Comprehensive Psychiatry, 35,* 316–327.

Selzer, M. A., Kernberg, P., Fibel, B., Cherbuliez, T., & Mortati, S. (1987). The personality assessment interview. *Psychiatry, 50,* 142–153.

Shapiro, J. P. (1991). Interviewing children about psychological issues associated with sexual abuse. *Psychotherapy, 28,* 55–66.

Sloan, K. A., Eldridge, K., & Evenson, R. (1992). An automated screening schedule for mental health centers. *Computers in Human Services, 8,* 55–61.

Sommers-Flanagan, J., & Sommers-Flanagan, R. (1995). Intake interviewing with suicidal patients: A systematic approach. *Professional Psychology: Research and Practice, 26,* 41–47.

Spitzer, R., & Williams, J. B. (1984*). Structured clinical interview for* DSM-III *disorders.* New York: Biometrics Research Development, New York State Psychiatric Institute.

Spitzer, R. L., & Williams, J. B. (1988). Revised diagnostic criteria and a new structured interview for diagnosing anxiety disorders. *Journal of Psychiatric Research, 22*(Supp. 1), 55–85.

Spitzer, R., Williams, J. B., Gibbon, M., & First, M. B. (1992). *Structured Clinical Interview for* DSM-III-R *(SCID-II).* Washington, DC: American Psychiatric. Association.

Spitzer, R. L., Williams, J. B., & Skodol, A. E. (1980). *DSM-III:* The major achievements and an overview. *American Journal of Psychiatry, 137,* 151–164.

Stangl, D., Pfohl, B., Zimmerman, M., Bowers, W., & Corenthal, M. (1985). A structured interview for the *DSM-III* personality disorders: A preliminary report. *Archives of General Psychiatry, 42,* 591–596.

Steinberg, M., Cicchetti, D., Buchanan, J., & Hall, P. (1993). Clinical assessment of dissociative symptoms and disorders: The Structured Clinical Interview for *DSM-IV* Dissociative Disorders. *Dissociation: Progress-in-the-Dissociative-Disorders, 6,* 3–15.

Strack, S., & Lorr, M. (1997). Invited essay: The challenge of differentiating normal and disordered personality. *Journal of Personality Disorders, 11,* 105–122.

Sullivan, H. S. (1954). *The psychiatric interview.* New York: W. W. Norton.

Sweeney, M., McGrath, R. E., Leigh, E., & Costa, G. (2001, March). *Computer-assisted interviews: A meta-analysis of patient acceptance.* Paper presented at the annual meeting of the Society for Personality Assessment. Philadelphia.

Ventura, J., Liberman, R. P., Green, M. F., Shaner, A., & Mintz, J. (1998). Training and quality assurance with Structured Clinical Interview for *DSM-IV* (SCID-I/P). *Psychiatry Research, 79,* 163–173.

Watkins, C. E., Campbell, V. L., Nieberding, R., & Hallmark, R. (1995). Contemporary practice of psychological assessment by clinical psychologists. *Professional Psychology: Research and Practice, 26,* 54–60.

Watson, C. G., Juba, M. P., Manifold, V., Kucala, T., & Anderson, P. E. (1991). The PTSD interview: Rationale, description, reliability and concurrent validity of a *DSM-III*-based technique. *Journal of Clinical Psychology, 47,* 179–188.

Weiner, I. (1999). What the Rorschach can do for you: Incremental validity in clinical application. *Assessment, 6,* 327–340.

Weiss, R. D., Najavits, L. M., Muenz, L. R., & Hufford, C. (1995). 12-month test-retest reliability of the Structured Clinical Interview for *DSM-III-R* personality disorders in cocaine-dependent patients. *Comprehensive Psychiatry, 36,* 384–389.

Westen, D. (1997). Differences between clinical and research methods for assessing personality disorders: Implication for research and the evaluation of Axis II. *American Journal of Psychiatry, 154,* 895–903.

Westen, D., & Shedler, J. (2000). A prototype matching approach to diagnosing personality disorders: Toward *DSM-V. Journal of Personality Disorders, 14,* 109–126.

Widiger, T. A. (1992). Categorical versus dimensional classification: Implications from and for research. *Journal of Personality Disorders, 6,* 287–300.

Widiger, T. A. (2000). Personality disorders in the 21st century. *Journal of Personality Disorders, 14,* 3–16.

Widiger, T. A., & Frances, A. (1985a). Axis II personality disorders: Diagnostic and treatment issues. *Hospital and Community Psychiatry, 36,* 619–627.

Widiger, T. A., & Frances, A. (1985b). The *DSM-III* personality disorders: Perspectives from psychology. *Archives of General Psychiatry, 42,* 615–623.

Widiger, T. A., & Frances, A. (1987). Interviews and inventories for the measurement of personality disorders. *Clinical Psychology Review, 7,* 49–75.

Widiger, T. A., Frances, A., Spitzer, R. L., & Williams, J. B. (1988). The *DSM-III-R* personality disorders: An overview. *American Journal of Psychiatry, 145,* 786–795.

Widiger, T. A., & Kelso, K. (1983). Psychodiagnosis of Axis II. *Clinical Psychology Review, 3,* 491–510.

Widiger, T., Mangine, S., Corbitt, E. M., Ellis, C. G., & Thomas, G. V. (1995). *Personality Disorder Interview–IV: A semistructured interview for the assessment of personality disorders.* Odessa, FL: Psychological Assessment Resources.

Wiens, A. N., & Matarazzo, J. D. (1983). Diagnostic interviewing. In M. Hersen, A. Kazdin, & A. Bellak (Eds.), *The clinical psychology handbook* (pp. 309–328). New York: Pergamon.

Williams, J. B., Spitzer, R. L., & Gibbon, M. (1992). International reliability of a diagnostic intake procedure for panic disorder. *American Journal of Psychiatry, 149,* 560–562.

World Health Organization. (1992). *The ICD-10 classification of mental and behavioral disorders.* Geneva, Switzerland: Author.

Zanarini, M. C., Frankenburg, F. R., Chauncey, D. L., & Gunderson, J. G. (1987). The Diagnostic Interview for Personality Disorders: Inter-rater and test-retest reliability. *Comprehensive Psychiatry, 28,* 467–480.

Zanarini, M., Frankenburg, F. R., Sickel, A. E., & Yong, L. (1995). *Diagnostic Interview for* DSM-IV *Personality Disorders.* Cambridge, MA: Harvard University.

Zanarini, M., Gunderson, J., Frankenburg, F. R., & Chauncey, D. L. (1989). The revised Diagnostic Interview for Borderlines: Discriminating borderline personality disorders from other Axis II disorders. *Journal of Personality Disorders, 3,* 10–18.

Zilboorg, G. (1941). *A history of medical psychology.* New York: Norton.

Zimmerman, M. (1994). Diagnosing personality disorders: A review of issues and research methods. *Archives of General Psychiatry, 51,* 225–245.

Zimmerman, M., & Mattia, J. I. (1998). Body dysmorphic disorder in psychiatric outpatients: recognition, prevalence, comorbidity, demographic, and clinical correlates. *Comprehensive Psychiatry, 39,* 265–270.

Zimmerman, M., & Mattia, J. I. (1999a). Psychiatric diagnosis in clinical practice: Is comorbidity being missed? *Comprehensive Psychiatry, 40,* 182–191.

Zimmerman, M., & Mattia, J. I. (1999b). Is posttraumatic stress disorder underdiagnosed in routine clinical practice? *Journal of Nervous and Mental Disease, 187,* 420–428.

Zimmerman, M., & Mattia, J. I. (1999c). Differences between clinical and research practices in diagnosing borderline personality disorder. *American Journal of Psychiatry, 156,* 1570–1574.

CHAPTER 22

Assessment of Psychopathology With Behavioral Approaches

WILLIAM H. O'BRIEN, JENNIFER J. McGRATH, AND STEPHEN N. HAYNES

Imagine the following: You are intensely worried. You cannot sleep well, you feel fatigued, and you have a near-constant hollow feeling in the pit of your stomach. At the moment, you are convinced that you have cancer because a cough has persisted for several days. You've been touching your chest, taking test breaths in order to determine whether there is some abnormality in your lungs. Although you would like to schedule an appointment with your physician, you've avoided making the call because you feel certain that either the news will be grim or he will dismiss your concerns as irrational. In an effort to combat your worries about the cancer, you've been repeatedly telling yourself that you're probably fine, given your health habits and medical history. You also know that on many previous occasions, you developed intense worries about health, finances, and career that eventually turned out to be false alarms.

This pattern of repeatedly developing intense and irrational fears is creating a new and disturbing feeling of depressed mood as you realize that you have been consumed by worry about one thing or another for much of your adult life. Furthermore, between the major episodes of worry, there are only fleeting moments of relief. At times, you wonder whether you will ever escape from the worry. Your friends have noticed a change in your behavior, and you have become increasingly withdrawn. Work performance is declining, and

you are certain that you will be fired if you do not improve soon. You feel that you must act to seek professional help, and you have asked some close friends about therapists. No one has any strong recommendations, but you have learned of a few possible professionals. You scan the telephone book, eventually settle on a therapist, and after several rehearsals of what you will say, you pick up the phone.

Now, consider the following: If you were to contact a cognitive-behaviorally oriented therapist, what assessment methods would be used to evaluate your condition? What model of behavior problems would be used to guide the focus of assessment, and how would this model differ from ones generated by nonbehavioral therapists? What methods would be used to assess your difficulties? What sort of information would be yielded by these methods? How would the therapist evaluate the information, and how valid would his or her conclusions be? How would the information be used?

These and other important questions related to behavioral assessment are discussed in this chapter. Rather than emphasize applications of behavioral assessment to research questions and formal hypotheses testing, we concentrate on how behavioral assessment methods are operationalized and executed in typical clinical settings. The initial section of this chapter examines the conceptual foundations of behavioral assessment and how these foundations differ from other approaches to assessment. Then we present information about the extent to which behavioral assessment methods are being used by behavior therapists and in treatment-outcome studies. Specific procedures used in behavioral assessment are described next; here, our emphasis is on reviewing benefits and limitations of particular assessment strategies and data evaluation approaches. Finally, the ways in which assessment information can be organized and integrated into a comprehensive clinical model known as the functional analysis are presented.

CONCEPTUAL FOUNDATIONS OF BEHAVIORAL ASSESSMENT

Two fundamental assumptions underlie behavioral assessment and differentiate it from other theoretical approaches. One of these assumptions is *environmental determinism*. This assumption states that behavior is functional—it is emitted in response to changing environmental events (Grant & Evans, 1994; S. C. Hayes & Toarmino, 1999; O'Donahue, 1998; Pierce, 1999; Shapiro & Kratochwill, 1988). It is further assumed that learning principles provide a sound conceptual framework for understanding these behavior-environment relationships. Thus, in behavioral assessment, problem behaviors are interpreted as coherent responses to environmental events that precede, co-occur, or follow the behaviors' occurrence. The measurement of behavior without simultaneous evaluation of critical environmental events would be anathema.

A second key assumption of the behavioral paradigm is that behavior can be most effectively understood when assessment procedures adhere to an *empirical approach*. Thus, behavioral assessment methods are often designed to yield quantitative measures of minimally inferential and precisely defined behaviors, environmental events, and the relationships among them (Haynes & O'Brien, 2000). The empirical assumption underlies the tendency for behavior therapists to prefer the use of measurement procedures that rely on systematic observation (e.g., Barlow & Hersen, 1984; Cone, 1988; Goldfried & Kent, 1972). It also underlies the strong endorsement of empirical validation as the most appropriate means of evaluating the efficacy and effectiveness of interventions (Nathan & Gorman, 1998).

Emerging out of environmental determinism and empiricism are a number of corollary assumptions about behavior and the most effective ways to evaluate it. These additional assumptions characterize the evolution of thought in behavioral assessment and its openness to change, given emerging trends in learning theory, behavioral research, and psychometrics

(Haynes & O'Brien, 2000). The first of these corollary assumptions is an endorsement of the position that *hypothetico-deductive* methods of inquiry are the preferred strategy for identifying the causes and correlates of problem behavior. Using this method of scientific inquiry, a behavior therapist will often design an assessment strategy whereby client behavior is measured under different conditions so that one or more hypotheses about its function can be tested. Two excellent examples of this methodology are the functional analytic experimental procedures developed by Iwata and colleagues for the assessment and treatment of self-injurious behavior (Iwata et al., 1994) and the functional analytic psychotherapy approach developed by Kohlenberg for assessment and treatment of adult psychological disorders such as borderline spectrum behaviors (Kohlenberg & Tsai, 1991).

A second corollary assumption, *contextualism*, asserts that the cause-effect relationships between environmental events and behavior are often mediated by individual differences (e.g., Dougher, 2000; Evans, 1985; Hawkins, 1986; Russo & Budd, 1987). This assumption supports the expectation that behaviors can vary greatly according to the many unique interactions that can occur among individual characteristics and contextual events (Wahler & Fox, 1981). Thus, in contemporary behavioral assessment approaches, the therapist may be apt to measure individual difference variables (e.g., physiological activation patterns, self-statements) in order to evaluate how these variables may be interacting with environmental events.

A third corollary assumption is *behavioral plasticity* (O'Brien & Haynes, 1995). This assumption is represented in the behavioral assessment position that many problem behaviors that were historically viewed as untreatable (e.g., psychotic behavior, aggressive behavior among individuals with developmental disabilities, psychophysiological disorders) can be changed if the correct configuration of learning principles and environmental events is built into an intervention and applied consistently. This assumption supports persistence and optimism with difficult-to-treat problems. It may also underlie the willingness of behavior therapists to work with clients who are eschewed by nonbehavioral practitioners because they were historically deemed untreatable (e.g., persons with mental retardation, schizophrenia, autism, psychosis).

A fourth assumption, *multivariate multidimensionalism*, posits that problem behaviors and environmental events are often molar constructs that are comprised of many specific and qualitatively distinct modes of responding and dimensions by which they can be measured. Thus, there are many ways in which a single behavior, environmental event, or both can be operationalized. The multidimensional assumption is reflected in an endorsement of multimethod and multifaceted assessment strategies (Cone, 1988; Haynes, 2000; Morris, 1988).

Reciprocal causation is a fifth assumption that characterizes behavioral assessment. The essential position articulated in reciprocal causation is that situational events that influence a problem behavior can in turn be affected by that same behavior (Bandura, 1981). An example of reciprocal causation can be found in patterns of behavior observed among persons with headaches. Specifically, the headache patient may verbalize headache complaints, solicit behaviors from a spouse, and exhibit headache behaviors such as pained facial expressions. These pain behaviors may then evoke supportive or helping responses from a spouse (e.g., turning down the radio, darkening the room, providing medications, offering consolation). In turn, the supportive behavior provided by the spouse may act as a reinforcer and increase the likelihood that the pain behaviors will be expressed in the future. Hence, the pain behaviors may trigger reinforcing consequences, and the reinforcing consequences may then act as an important determinant of future pain behavior (O'Brien & Haynes, 1995).

A sixth assumption, *temporal variability,* is that relationships among causal events and problem behaviors often change over time (Haynes, 1992). Consequently, it is possible that the initiating cause of a problem behavior differs from the factors maintaining the behavior after it is established. Health promotion behaviors illustrate this point. Specifically, factors that promote the initiation of a preventive health regimen (e.g., cues, perceptions of susceptibility) may be quite different from factors that support the maintenance of the behavior (Prochaska, 1994).

The aforementioned conceptual foundations have a number of implications for therapists who use behavioral assessment techniques. First, it is imperative that persons who endorse a behavioral approach to assessment be familiar with learning principles and how these principles apply to behavior problems observed in clinical settings. Familiarity with learning principles in turn permit the behavior therapist to better understand complex and clinically relevant context-behavior processes that govern environmental determinism. For example, we have noted how virtually any graduate student or behavior therapist can describe classical conditioning as it applies to dogs salivating in response to a bell that was previously paired with meat powder or how Little Albert developed a rabbit phobia. These same persons, however, often have difficulty describing how anticipatory nausea and vomiting in cancer patients, cardiovascular hyperreactivity to stress, social phobia, and panic attacks may arise from classical conditioning. Similarly, most clinicians can describe how

operant conditioning may affect the behavior of rats and pigeons under various conditions of antecedent and consequential stimuli. However, they often have a limited capacity for applying these principles to important clinical phenomena such as client resistance to therapy directives, client transference, therapist countertransference, and how various therapy techniques (e.g., cognitive restructuring, graded exposure with response prevention) promote behavior change.

In addition to being well-versed in learning theory, behavior therapists must also learn to carefully operationalize constructs so that unambiguous measures of problem behavior can be either created or appropriately selected from the corpus of measures that have been developed by other researchers. This task requires a deliberate and scholarly approach to assessment as well as facility with research methods aimed at construct development and measurement (cf. Cook & Campbell, 1979; Kazdin, 1998). Finally, behavior therapists must know how to create and implement assessment methods that permit reasonable identification and measurement of complex relationships among behaviors and contextual variables.

Imagine once again that you are the client described in the beginning of the chapter. The assumptions guiding the behavior therapist's assessment would affect his or her model of the your problem behavior and the selection of assessment methods. Specifically, guided by the empirical and multivariate assumptions, the behavior therapist would be apt to use methods that promote the development of unambiguous measures of the problem behavior. Thus, he or she would work with you to develop clear descriptions of the key presenting problems (insomnia, fatigue, a feeling in the pit of the stomach, chronic worry, touching chest and taking test breaths, negative expectations about prognosis, use of reassuring self-statements). Furthermore, guided by environmental determinism and contextualism, the behavior therapist would encourage you to identify specific persons, places, times, and prior learning experiences that may account for variation in problem behavior (e.g., *do the various problem behaviors differ when you are alone relative to when you are with others, is your worry greater at work versus home,* etc.). Finally, guided by assumptions regarding reciprocal causation and temporal variability, the behavior therapist would allow for the possibility that the factors controlling your problem behaviors at the present time may be different from initiating factors. Thus, although it may be the case that your worries were initiated by a persistent cough, the maintenance of the worry may be related to a number of current causal factors such as your negative expectations about cancer prognosis and your efforts to allay worry by using checking behaviors (e.g., test breaths, chest touching) and avoidance (not obtaining a medical evaluation).

In the following sections, we review procedures used by behavioral assessors to operationalize, measure, and evaluate problem behavior and situational events. As part of the review, we highlight research findings and decisional processes that guide the enactment of these procedures. Prior to presenting this information, however, we summarize the current status of behavioral assessment in clinical settings and research applications.

CURRENT STATUS AND APPLICATIONS OF BEHAVIORAL ASSESSMENT

One indicator of the status and utility of an assessment method is the extent to which it is used among practitioners and researchers. Frequency of use among practitioners and researchers represents a combination of influences, including the training background of the practitioner, the treatment-utility of information provided by the method (i.e., the extent to which information can guide treatment formulation and implementation), and the extent to which the method conforms to the demands of a contemporary clinical settings. Frequency of use also represents the extent to which the method yields information that is reliable, valid, and sensitive to variation in contextual factors (e.g., treatment effects, variation in contextual factors, and experimental manipulations).

An examination of the behavioral assessment practices of behaviorally oriented clinicians was conducted to determine their status and utility among those who endorse a cognitive-behavioral perspective. Five hundred members of the Association for Advancement of Behavior Therapy (AABT) were surveyed (Mettee-Carter et al., 1999). The survey contained a number of items that were used in prior investigations of assessment practices (Elliott, Miltenberger, Kastar-Bundgaard, & Lumley, 1996; Swan & MacDonald, 1978). Several additional items were included so that we could learn about strategies used to evaluate assessment data and the accuracy of these data analytic techniques. The results of the survey regarding assessment practices are presented in this section. Survey results that pertain to the accuracy of data evaluation techniques are presented later in this chapter in the section addressing methods used to evaluate assessment data.

A total of 156 completed surveys were returned by respondents (31%). This response rate was comparable to that obtained by Elliott et al. (1996), who reported that 334 of 964 (35%) surveys were returned in their study. The majority of respondents (91%) held a PhD in psychology, with 4% reporting master's level training, 2% reporting attainment of a medical degree, and 1% reporting PsyD training. A large proportion of respondents reported that they were engaged in clinical practice in either a private setting (40%), medical center or medical school (16%), or hospital (9%). Thirty percent reported their primary employment setting was an academic department.

As would be expected, most respondents reported their primary orientation to assessment was cognitive-behavioral (73%). Less frequently endorsed orientations included applied behavior analysis (10%) and social learning (8%). Regardless of orientation, behavioral assessment was reported to be very important in treatment formulation (mean rating of importance = 5.93, $SD = 1.17$, on a Likert scale that ranged from 1 = *not at all important* to 7 = *extremely important*). Furthermore, they reported that they typically devoted four sessions to develop an adequate conceptualization of a client's problem behavior and the factors that control it.

The more commonly reported assessment methods used by behavior therapists in this study are summarized in Table 22.1. For comparison purposes, we included data reported by Elliot et al. (1996), who presented results separately for academic psychologists and practitioners. As is readily evident in Table 22.1, our data are quite similar to those reported by Elliott et al. Additionally, like Elliott et al., we observed that interviewing (with the client, a significant other, or another professional) is clearly the most commonly used assessment method. The administration of self-report inventories is the next most commonly used assessment method, followed by behavioral observation and self-monitoring. It is important to note that these latter two methods are more uniquely aligned with a behavioral orientation to assessment than are interviewing and questionnaire administration.

TABLE 22.1 Results of 1998 Survey Investigating Assessment Methods Used by Members of the Association for the Advancement of Behavior Therapy

Assessment Method	Percent of Clients Assessed with this Method	
	Current Study	Elliot et al. (1996)
Interview with client	92	93–94
Direct behavioral observation	55	52
Behavior rating scales and questionnaires	49	44–67
Self-monitoring	44	44–48
Interview with significant others	42	42–46
Interview other professionals	37	38–42
Mental status exam	32	27–36
Structured diagnostic interview	31	23–29
Personality inventory	16	15–20
Role play	15	19–25
Intellectual assessment	11	16–20
Analog functional analysis	10	10–16
Projective testing	3	3–5

TABLE 22.2   Assessment Methods Used in Treatment Outcome Studies Published in the Journal of Consulting and Clinical Psychology

Publication Year	Treatment Outcome Studies (N)	Self-Report Questionnaire (Percent)	Behavioral Observation (Percent)	Self-Monitoring (Percent)	Psychophysiological Assessment (Percent)	Projective Testing (Percent)
1968	9	33	56	33	0	0
1972	23	48	35	22	0	0
1976	34	50	44	9	18	4
1980	21	62	33	29	14	9
1984	37	51	16	32	16	0
1988	21	81	24	38	10	0
1992	21	81	33	14	9	0
1996	28	86	7	25	25	0
2000	42	98	17	17	33	0

In order to evaluate the extent to which the various assessment methods were associated with assessment orientation, we regressed values from an item that assessed self-reported degree of behavioral orientation (rated on a 7-point Likert scale) onto the 13 assessment method items. Results indicated that use of analog functional analysis ($\beta = .23$, $t = 2.8$, $p < .01$), interviewing with client ($\beta = -.22$, $t = -2.75$, $p < .01$), and projective testing ($\beta = -.18$, $t = 2.21$, $p < .05$) accounted for significant proportions of variance in the degree of behavioral orientation rating. The direction of association in this analysis indicated that persons who described themselves as more behaviorally oriented were more likely to use analog functional analysis as an assessment method and less likely to use interviewing and projective assessment methods.

In addition to the methods reported by therapists in surveys, another indicator of status and applicability of behavioral assessment is in clinical research. Haynes and O'Brien (2000) evaluated data on the types of assessment methods used in treatment outcome studies published in the *Journal of Clinical and Consulting Psychology* (*JCCP*) from 1968 through 1996. *JCCP* was chosen because it is a highly selective, nonspecialty journal that publishes state-of-the-art research in clinical psychology. Articles published in 2000 were added to these data; the results are summarized in Table 22.2.

Table 22.2 illustrates several important points about the relative status and applicability of behavioral assessment. First, it is apparent that self-report questionnaire administration has grown to be the dominant assessment method. Although it is not specifically reflected in the table, most of these questionnaires used in these treatment outcome studies assessed specific problem behaviors rather than broad personality constructs. Thus, their use is quite consistent with the behavioral approach to assessment, which supports the use of focused and carefully designed indicators of problem behavior. Second, the prototypical behavioral assessment methods—behavioral observation and self-monitoring—are

maintaining their status as useful measures for evaluating treatment outcomes, and psychophysiological measurement appears to be increasingly used.

Returning once again to your experiences as the hypothetical client with chronic worries, we would argue that in addition to encountering a behavior therapist who tends to endorse certain assumptions regarding behavior and who would seek careful operationalization of behavior and contexts, you would also be evaluated using a number of methods, including a clinical interview, questionnaire administration, self-monitoring, and direct observation. Alternatively, it is unlikely that you would undergo projective testing or complete a personality inventory.

GOALS AND APPLICATIONS OF BEHAVIORAL ASSESSMENT

The primary goal of behavioral assessment is to improve clinical decision making by obtaining reliable and valid information about the nature of problem behavior and the factors that control it (Haynes, 2000). This primary goal is realized through two broad classes of subordinate goals of behavioral assessment: (a) to objectively measure behavior and (b) to identify and evaluate relationships among problem behaviors and causal factors. In turn, when these subordinate goals are realized, the behavior therapist is better able to make valid decisions regarding treatment design, treatment selection, treatment outcome evaluation, treatment process evaluation, and identification of factors that mediate response to treatment (Haynes & O'Brien, 2000).

To attain the two subordinate goals, a behavior therapist must generate detailed operational definitions of problem behaviors and potential causal factors. After this step, strategies for collecting empirical data about relationships among problem behaviors and casual factors must be developed and enacted. Finally, after data collection, proper evaluation procedures must be used to quantify the magnitude of causal effects. In the following sections, the assessment processes and the decisions associated with these processes are reviewed.

Topographical Analysis: The Operationalization and Quantification of Target Behaviors and Contextual Variables

Target Behavior Operationalization and Quantification

In consonance with the empirical assumption, an important goal of behavioral assessment is to accurately characterize problem behaviors. To accomplish this goal, the behavior therapist must initially determine which behaviors emitted by the client are to be the focus of the assessment and subsequent intervention. These selected behaviors are commonly referred to as *target behaviors.*

After a target behavior has been identified, the behavior therapist must determine what constitutes the essential characteristics of the behavior. Operational definitions are used to capture the precise, unambiguous, and observable qualities of the target behavior. When developing an operational definition, the clinician often strives to maximize content validity (i.e., the extent to which the operational definition captures the essential elements of the target behavior), and—consistent with the multidimensional assumption—it is accepted that a client's problem behavior will need to be operationalized in a number of different ways.

In order to simplify the operationalization decisions, behavioral assessment writers have recommended that complex behaviors be partitioned into at least three inter-related modes of responding: verbal-cognitive behaviors, physiological-affective behaviors, and overt-motor behaviors (cf. Hollandsworth, 1986; Spiegler & Guevremont, 1998). The verbal-cognitive mode subsumes spoken words as well as cognitive experiences such as self-statements, images, irrational beliefs, attitudes, and the like. The physiological-affective mode subsumes physiological responses, physical sensations, and felt emotional states. Finally, the overt-motor mode subsumes observable responses that represent skeletal-nervous system activation and are typically under voluntary control.

The process of operationally defining a target behavior can be deceptively complex. For example, a client who reports that she is depressed may be presenting with myriad of cognitive, emotional, and overt-motor behaviors, including negative expectancies for the future, persistent thoughts of guilt and punishment, anhedonia, fatigue, sadness, social withdrawal, and slowed motor movements. However, another client who reports that he is depressed may present with a very different configuration of verbal-cognitive, physiological-affective, and overt-motor behaviors. It is important to note that these different modes of responding that are all subsumed within the construct of depression may be differentially responsive to intervention techniques. Thus, if the assessor measures a very restricted number of response modes (e.g., a measure only of feeling states), the validity of critical decisions about intervention design, intervention evaluation, and intervention process evaluation may be adversely affected.

After a target behavior has been operationalized in terms of modes, appropriate measurement dimensions must be selected. The most commonly used measurement dimensions used in clinical settings are frequency, duration, and intensity. Frequency refers to how often the behavior occurs across a given time frame (e.g., number per day, per hour, per minute). Duration provides information about the amount of time that elapses between behavior initiation and completion. Intensity provides information about the force or salience of the behavior in relation to other responses emitted by the client.

Although all of the aforementioned modes and dimensions of behavior can be operationalized and incorporated into an assessment, varying combinations will be evaluated in any given case. For example, Durand and Carr (1991) evaluated three children who were referred for assessment and treatment of self-injurious and disruptive behaviors. Their operationalization was limited to frequency counts of overt-motor responses. Similarly, Miller's (1991) topographical description of a veteran with posttraumatic stress disorder and an airplane phobia quantified self-reported anxiety, an affective-physiological response, using only a measure of intensity (i.e., subjective units of distress). In contrast, Levey, Aldaz, Watts, and Coyle (1991) generated a more comprehensive topographical description of a client with sleep onset and maintenance problems. Their topographical analysis emphasized the temporal characteristics (frequency and duration of nighttime awakenings, rate of change from an awake state to sleep, and interresponse time—the time that elapsed between awakenings) and variability (variation in sleep onset latencies) of overt-motor (e.g., physical activity), affective-physiological (e.g., subjective distress), and cognitive-verbal (i.e., uncontrollable presleep cognitions) target behaviors.

Contextual Variable Operationalization and Quantification

After operationally defining target behaviors, the behavior therapist needs to construct operational definitions of key contextual variables. Contextual variables are environmental events and characteristics of the person that surround the target behavior and exert nontrivial effects upon it. Contextual factors can be sorted into two broad modes: social-environmental factors and intrapersonal factors (O'Brien & Haynes, 1997). Social-environmental factors subsume interactions with other people or groups of people as well as the physical characteristics of an environment such as temperature, noise levels, lighting levels, food, and room design. Intrapersonal factors include verbal-cognitive, affective-physiological, and overt-motor behaviors that may exert significant effects on the target behavior.

The contextual factor measurement dimensions are similar to those used with target behaviors. Specifically, frequency, duration, and intensity of contextual factor occurrence are most often measured. For example, the intensity and duration of exposure to adult attention, demanding tasks, or both can be reliably measured and has been shown to have a significant impact on the frequency and magnitude of self-injurious behavior among some clients (Derby et al., 1992; Durand & Carr, 1991; Durand & Crimmins, 1988; Taylor & Carr, 1992a, 1992b). Similarly, the magnitude, frequency, and duration of exposure to hospital cues among chemotherapy patients with anticipatory nausea and vomiting have been shown to exert a significant impact on symptom severity (Burish, Carey, Krozely, & Greco, 1987; Carey & Burish, 1988).

In summary, careful operationalization of behavior and contextual variables is one of the primary goals of behavioral assessment. Target behaviors are typically partitioned into modes, and within each mode, several dimensions of measurement may be used. Similarly, contextual variables can be partitioned into types and dimensions. Applied to the hypothetical client with chronic worry regarding cancer, we can develop a preliminary topographical analysis. Specifically, negative expectations about prognosis, disturbing mental images, and reassuring self-statements would fall into the cognitive-verbal mode of responding. The affective-physiological mode would subsume feelings of fatigue, sleeplessness, sad mood, the sensation in the pit of your stomach, and specific physical symptoms associated with worry (e.g., increased heart rate, trembling, muscle tension, etc.). Finally, the overt-motor mode would include social withdrawal, checking behaviors, and avoidance behaviors. Each of the behaviors could also be measured along a number of different dimensions such as frequency, intensity (e.g., degree of belief in negative or reassuring self-statements, vividness of mental images, degree of heart rate elevation), duration, or any combination of these.

The contextual variables could also be identified and operationalized for this case. Specifically, the behavior therapist would seek to identify important social-environmental and interpersonal variables that may plausibly promote changes in target behavior occurrence. For example, what is the nature of current family and work environments, and have there been substantial changes in them (e.g., have increased stressors been experienced)? What sorts of social and situational contexts are associated with target behavior intensification and target behavior improvement?

Applications of the Topographical Analysis of Behavior and Contexts

The operationalization and quantification of target behavior and contextual factors can serve important functions in behavioral assessment. First, operational definitions can help the client and the behavior therapist think carefully and objectively about the nature of the target behaviors and the contexts within which they occur. This type of consideration can guard against oversimplified, biased, and nonscientific descriptions of target behaviors and settings. Second, operational definitions and quantification allow the clinician to evaluate the social significance of the target behavior or the stimulus characteristics of a particular context relative to relevant comparison groups or comparison contexts. Finally, operationalization of target behaviors is a critical step in determining whether behavioral criteria are met for establishing a psychiatric diagnosis using the *Diagnostic and Statistical Manual of Mental Disorders–Fourth Edition* (*DSM-IV*; American Psychiatric Association, 1994) or the ninth edition of the *International Classification of Diseases* (*ICD-9*; American Medical Association). This latter process of rendering a diagnosis is not without controversy in the behavioral assessment literature. However, it is the case that with the increasing development of effective diagnosis-specific treatment protocols, the rendering of a diagnosis can be a critical element of pretreatment assessment and intervention design. For example, the pattern of behaviors experienced by the hypothetical client with cancer worries would conform to a diagnosis of generalized anxiety disorder, and it would be reasonable to use the empirically supported treatment protocol for this disorder that was developed by Craske, Barlow, and O'Leary (1992).

Identification of Functional Relationships and the Functional Analysis of Behavior

After target behaviors and contextual factors have been identified and operationalized, the therapist will often wish to develop a model of the relationships among these variables. This model of causal variable-target behavior interrelationships is the functional analysis. As is apparent in the preceding discussion of target and causal variable operationalization, a wide range of variables will need to be incorporated into any reasonably complete functional analysis. As a result, behavior therapists must make important decisions regarding (a) how complex assessment data can be analyzed so that relationships among target behaviors and casual factors can be estimated, and (b) how the resultant information can be organized into a coherent model that in turn will guide treatment formulation and evaluation.

Defining the Functional Analysis

The term *functional analysis* has appeared in many research publications, and many behavioral assessment experts have argued that the functional analysis is the core research methodology in behaviorism (cf. Follette, Naugle, & Linnerooth, 2000; O'Neill, Horner, Albin, Storey, & Sprague, 1990; Sturmey, 1996). In terms of clinical utility, a number of authors have argued that an incorrect or incomplete functional analysis can produce ineffective behavioral interventions (e.g., Axelrod, 1987; Evans, 1985; S. L. Hayes, Nelson, & Jarret, 1987; Haynes & O'Brien, 1990, 2000; Iwata, Kahng, Wallace, & Lindberg, 2000; Nelson & Hayes, 1986).

Despite the fact that the functional analysis is considered to be a critical component of assessment, the term has been used to characterize a diverse set of clinical activities, including (a) the operationalization of target behavior (e.g., Bernstein, Borkovec, & Coles, 1986; Craighead, Kazdin, & Mahoney, 1981), (b) the operationalization of situational factors (Derby et al., 1992; Taylor & Carr, 1992a, 1992b), (c) single subject experimental procedures where hypothesized causal variables are systematically manipulated while measures of target behavior are collected (e.g., Peterson, Homer, & Wonderlich, 1982; Smith, Iwata, Vollmer, & Pace, 1992), (d) measurement of stimulus-response or response-response relationships (Hawkins, 1986), (e) assessment of motivational states (Kanfer & Phillips, 1970), and (f) an overall integration of operationalized target behaviors and controlling factors (Correa & Sutker, 1986; S. C. Hayes & Follette, 1992; Nelson, 1988). Because of the ambiguity surrounding the term, we proposed that the functional analysis be defined as "the identification of important, controllable, causal functional relationships applicable to a specified set of target behaviors for an individual client" (Haynes & O'Brien, 1990, p. 654).

This definition of functional analysis has several important characteristics. First, it is important to note that taken alone, a functional relationship only implies that the relationship between two variables can be adequately represented by a mathematical formula (Blalock, 1969; Haynes, 1992; James, Mulaik, & Brett, 1982). In behavioral assessment, the presence of a functional relationship is typically supported by the observation of covariation among variables. Some of these functional relationships represent a causal process,

whereas others do not. Because information about causality is most relevant to treatment design and evaluation, the functional analysis should be designed to assess *causal functional relationships.*

Many variables can exert causal effects on a particular target behavior. Consequently, the behavior therapist must decide which subset of causal functional relationships are most relevant for treatment design. Two criteria that are used to isolate this subset of relationships are the concept of shared variance and modifiability. Thus, our definition of the functional analysis specifies that there is a focus on identifying and evaluating *important* and *controllable* causal functional relationships.

Another important characteristic of the functional analysis is its idiographic emphasis—that is, it is postulated that enhanced understanding of target behavior and casual factor interactions will be found when the functional analysis emphasizes evaluation of *specific* target behaviors for an *individual* client. This idiographic emphasis is consistent with the behavioral principles of environmental determinism and contextualism.

Finally, it is important to note that the functional analysis is undefined in relation to methodology, types of variables to be quantified, and number of functional relationships to be evaluated. Given the complexity of causal models of problem behavior, it is important that behavior therapists employ diverse assessment methodologies that measure multiple modes and dimensions of behavior and contexts.

Reducing Complexity of Generating a Functional Analysis: The Role of Presuppositions

Given that there are at least three modes of responding and two broad modes of contextual variables, a single target behavior could have six combinations of interactions among target behavior modes and contextual factor modes (see Table 22.3). Furthermore, if we consider that there are many different relevant measurement dimensions (e.g., frequency, duration, intensity) for target behaviors and contextual factors, the number of possible interactions rapidly becomes unwieldy.

TABLE 22.3   Interactions Among Basic Target Behavior and Causal Factor Categories

Causal Variable Type	Mode of responding		
	Cognitive-Verbal	Affective-Physiological	Overt-Motor
Social-environmental			
Intrapersonal			

A behavior therapist cannot systematically assess all possible interactions among target behaviors and contextual factors and incorporate them into a functional analysis. Thus, he or she must decide which of the many interactions are most relevant for treatment design—that is, most important, controllable, and causal. These a priori clinical decisions are similar to presuppositions to the "causal field" described by Einhorn in his study of clinical decision making (1988, p. 57).

Causal presuppositions used by behavior therapists to reduce the complexity of assessment data have not been well evaluated, and as a result are not well understood (S. C. Hayes & Follette, 1992; Krasner, 1992). We have argued, however (cf. Haynes & O'Brien, 2000), that training and clinical experience exert a strong influence on the types of variables that are incorporated into a functional analysis. Suppose, for example, that you are once again the hypothetical client that we have discussed at various points in this chapter. If you selected a behavior therapist with a strong training history in cognitive therapy, he or she may presuppose that your worries and other target behaviors are caused by maladaptive thoughts that provoke autonomic activation. His or her topographical description and functional analyses may then tend to emphasize the measurement of verbal-cognitive modes of responding. Alternatively, a behavior therapist with training and experience in behavioral marital therapy may presuppose that dysfunctional communication patterns and consequent increases in daily stress are the most relevant causal variables in target behaviors. His or her topographical description and functional analysis may thus emphasize interpersonal-social interactions as key precipitants of marital distress.

A second factor that can influence presuppositions to the causal field among behavior therapists is research. For example, an extensive literature on the functional analysis of self-injurious behavior has provided evidence that four major classes of controlling variables often exert substantial causal influences on the target behavior. In addition, researchers in this area have published laboratory assessment protocols and functional analytic self-report inventories (e.g., Carr & Durand, 1985; Durand & Crimmins, 1988). Thus, a behavior therapist who is preparing to conduct an assessment of a client with self injurious behavior could use the published literature to partially guide decisions about which variables should be operationalized and incorporated into a functional analysis.

Although presuppositions to the causal field are necessary for simplifying what would otherwise be an impossibly complex assessment task, behavior therapists must guard against developing an excessively narrow or inflexible set of a priori assumptions because inadequate searches for causal

relationships and incorrect functional analyses are more likely to occur under these conditions. A few precautionary steps are thus advised. First, it is important that behavior therapists routinely evaluate the accuracy of their clinical predictions and diagnoses (Arkes, 1981; Garb, 1989, 1998). Second, behavior therapists should frequently discuss cases with colleagues and supervisors in order to obtain alternative viewpoints and to guard against biasing heuristics. Third, regular reading of the published literature is advised. Finally, behavior therapists should regularly evaluate hypotheses about the function of target behaviors (using single-subject evaluations or group designs) and attend conferences or workshops in which new information about target behaviors and causal factors can be acquired.

Identifying and Evaluating Causal Relationships

After topographical descriptions have been rendered and the causal field has been simplified, the behavior therapist must attempt to distinguish causal relationships out of a large family of functional relationships between target behaviors and contextual factors. This identification of causal relationships is important because many interventions are aimed at modifying the cause of a problem behavior. The critical indicator of a possible casual relationship is the presence of reliable covariation between a target behavior and contextual factor combined with temporal precedence (i.e., evidence that changes in the causal factor precede changes in the target behavior). To further differentiate causal relationships from noncausal relationships, the behavior therapist should be able to apply a logical explanation for the observed relationship and exclude plausible alternative explanations for the observed relationship (Cook & Campbell, 1979; Einhorn, 1988; Haynes, 1992).

Several behavioral assessment methods can be used to evaluate covariation among variables and to assist with the differentiation of causal relationships from noncausal relationships. Additionally, two predominant approaches to data evaluation are typically used; intuitive judgment and statistical testing. In the following section, methods used to collect assessment data and methods used to evaluate assessment data are reviewed.

BEHAVIORAL ASSESSMENT METHODS: SAMPLING, DATA COLLECTION, AND DATA EVALUATION TECHNIQUES

Given that target behaviors and causal factors have been adequately operationalized, the behavior therapist must then decide how to collect data on these variables and the relationships among them. These decisions are designed to address two interrelated assessment issues: (a) sampling—how and where the behavior and causal factors should be measured and (b) what specific techniques should be used to gather information. The overarching concern in these decisions is validity—simply put, the extent to which specific sampling strategies and assessment methods will yield information that accurately represents client behavior and the effects of causal variables in naturalistic contexts. The various strategies used to gather this information and the relative advantages and disadvantages of each are described in the following section.

Sampling

The constant change that characterizes behavior stems from variation in causal factors that are nested within specific contexts. Because we cannot observe variation in all behaviors and all causal factors within all contexts, sampling strategies must be used in any behavioral assessment. A major consideration in deciding upon a sampling system is degree of generalizability across situations and time. Specifically, we are often interested in gathering data that will allow us to validly infer how a client behaves in the natural environment (Paul, 1986a, 1986b). Thus, we must carefully consider *how* and *where* assessment data will be collected to maximize ecological validity. Issues related to behavior and casual factor sampling are described later in this chapter.

Event and Time Sampling

Target behaviors and causal events can be sampled in innumerable ways. An analysis of the behavioral assessment literature, however, indicates that there are five principal behavior sampling strategies most often used in applied settings. Each strategy has advantages and disadvantages as well as unique sources of error.

Event sampling refers to a procedure in which the occurrence of a target behavior or causal event is recorded whenever it is observed or detected. For example, when conducting a classroom observation, we might record each occurrence of an aggressive act emitted by a child (target behavior) and the nature (e.g., positive attention, negative attention, no discernible response) of teacher responses, peer responses, or both to the aggressive act (possible causal factor).

An estimate of frequency is most often calculated using event sampling procedures. Frequency estimates are simply the number of times the behavior occurs within a particular time interval (e.g., hours, days, or weeks). Event recording is most appropriate for target behaviors and causal events that have distinct onset and offset points.

Duration sampling is designed to sample the amount of time that elapses between the onset and offset of target

behaviors and causal factors. Returning to the aforementioned classroom observation example, we might be interested in not only how often aggressive actions occur, but also how long they persist after they have been initiated.

Interval sampling procedures involve partitioning time into discrete intervals lasting from several seconds to several hours. In partial-interval sampling, an entire interval is recorded as an occurrence if the target behavior is observed for *any* proportion of the interval. For example, if the child emits any aggressive act within a prespecified interval (e.g., during a 5-min observation period), the complete interval is recorded as an occurrence of the behavior. In whole-interval sampling, the target behavior must be emitted for the entire observation period before the interval is scored as an occurrence. Returning to the aggressive child example, we may decide to record an occurrence of target behavior only when the aggressive act continues across the entire 5-min observation period.

Partial- and whole-interval sampling strategies are recommended for target behaviors that have ambiguous onset and offset points. They are also well-suited for target behaviors that occur at such a high rate of frequency that observers could not reliably record each occurrence. One of the principle difficulties with interval sampling is misestimation of behavior frequency and duration. Specifically, unless the duration of a behavior exactly matches the duration of the interval and unless the behavior begins and ends at the same time as the observation interval, this sampling strategy will yield inaccurate estimates of behavior frequency and duration (Quera, 1990; Suen & Ary, 1989).

Real-time sampling involves measuring real time at the onset and offset of each target behavior occurrence, causal factor occurrence, or both. A principal advantage of real-time recording is that can simultaneously yield data about the frequency and duration of target behavior and causal factor occurrences. Like event and duration sampling, real-time sampling requires distinct onset and offset points.

Momentary time sampling is a sophisticated strategy that is most often used to gather data on several clients in a particular context such as a psychiatric unit or classroom. The procedure involves (a) conducting a brief observation (e.g., 20 s) of a client, (b) recording whether the target behavior or causal factor occurred during that brief moment of observation, and (c) repeating the first two steps for all clients being evaluated. In our classroom example, we might choose to observe a few normal students in order to gain a better understanding of the extent to which our client differs in terms of aggressive action. Thus, we would observe our client for a brief moment, then observe a comparison student for a brief interval, return to observing our client, and so on. In a sense, momentary time sampling is analogous to interval recording;

the primary difference is that several persons are being observed simultaneously for very brief periods of time.

Setting Sampling

Environmental determinism and the attendant assumption of contextualism require that the behavior therapist carefully select assessment settings, and—whenever possible—the assessment should occur in multiple situations. One dimension that can be used to gauge assessment location is the degree to which the locations represent the client's natural environment. At one end of the continuum is the naturalistic setting. Naturalistic contexts are settings where variation in target behaviors and causal factors occur as a function of naturally occurring and nonmanipulated contingencies. Assessment data collected in naturalistic settings are ecologically valid and more readily generalizable to criterion situations. One of the principal limitations of naturalistic assessment is that the inability to control target behavior or causal factor occurrences can preclude measurement of infrequent, clandestine, or subtle behaviors or stimuli.

At the other end of the continuum is the analog setting. In analog settings, the behavior therapist varies some aspect of one or more hypothesized causal factors while observational measures of the target behavior(s) are collected. A number of single-subject design strategies (e.g., ABAB, changing criterion, multiple baseline) can then be used to evaluate the direction and strength of the relationships between the causal factors and target behaviors. There are many different types of analog observation, including role playing, marital interaction assessments, behavioral approach tests, and functional analytic experiments.

In summary, sampling from natural settings allows for measurement of target behaviors and causal factors in criterion contexts. Thus, generalizability and ecological validity are enhanced. However, infrequent behaviors and an inability to control the occurrence of critical causal variables can introduce significant limitations with this sampling strategy. Assessment in analog settings allows for measurement of infrequent target behaviors because the assessor can introduce specific causal variables that may bring about the behaviors' occurrence. Because the analog setting is highly controlled, one cannot know how well the assessed behavior represents behavior in naturalistic contexts, which often contain multiple complex causal factors.

Assessment Methods

Our survey of behavior therapists indicated that the more commonly reported behavioral assessment methods were behavioral interviewing, rating scale and questionnaire administration, behavioral observation, and self-monitoring.

Furthermore, experimental functional analysis, although it is not a frequently reported assessment method, appeared to be the most reliable indicator of the degree to which a clinician identified him- or herself as behaviorally oriented. In the following section, these assessment methods are briefly described. More extensive descriptions of these individual assessment methods can be found in several recently published texts on behavioral assessment and therapy (e.g., Bellack & Hersen, 1998; Haynes & O'Brien, 2000; Shapiro & Kratochwill, 2000; Speigler & Guevremont, 1998) as well as specialty journals that publish articles on behavioral assessment and therapy methods (e.g., *Behavior Therapy, Cognitive and Behavioral Practice*).

Behavioral Assessment Interviewing

Behavioral interviewing differs from other forms of interviewing primarily in its structure and focus (e.g., Sarwer & Sayers, 1998). Structurally, behavioral interviewing tends to conform with the goals of behavioral assessment identified earlier in the chapter. Specifically, the assessor structures questions that prompt the client to provide information about the topography and function of target behaviors. Topographical questions direct the client to describe the mode and parameters of target behaviors, causal factor occurrences, or both. Functional questions direct the client to provide information about how target behaviors may be affected by possible causal factors.

Despite the fact that the interview is a very commonly used method, very little is known about its psychometric properties (Nezu & Nezu, 1989; Sarwer & Sayers, 1998). For example, Hay, Hay, Angle, and Nelson (1979) and Felton and Nelson (1984) presented behavior therapists with videotaped interviews of a confederate who was acting as a client. They subsequently measured the extent to which the therapists agreed on target behavior identification, causal factor identification, and treatment recommendations. Low to moderate levels of agreement were observed. These authors suggested that these results indicated that behavioral interviews do not appear to yield similar judgments about target behavior topography and function. However, these studies were limited because the therapists could only evaluate information that was provided in response another interviewer's questions. Thus, they could not follow up with clarifying questions or direct the client to provide greater details about various aspects of the client's target behavior. This methodological limitation creates the strong possibility that the observed agreement rates would be substantially different if interviewers were allowed to use their own questioning strategies and techniques. Further research is needed to improve our understanding of the psychometric properties of behavioral interviews.

Behavioral Observation

Systematic observations can be conducted by nonparticipant observers and participant observers. Because observation relies on visual recording, this method is restricted to the measurement of observable actions. Nonparticipant observers are trained observation technicians who record target behaviors and causal factors using any of the aforementioned sampling methods. Professional observers, research assistants, and volunteers have been used to collect observational data in treatment outcome studies (Cone, 1999). Because nonparticipant observers are essentially hired and trained to conduct observations, they are often able to collect data on complex behaviors, causal factors, and target behavior and casual event sequences. Although nonparticipant observation is a versatile assessment method, it is infrequently used in nonresearch clinical applications due to cost.

Participant observers are persons who have alternative responsibilities and share a relationship with the client. In most cases, participant observers are family members, coworkers, friends, or caregivers. Because participant observers are typically persons who are already involved in the client's life, they are able to conduct observations many settings. The major drawback associated with participant observation is limited focus and inaccuracy—that is, because participant observers have multiple responsibilities, only a small number of target behaviors and causal factors can be reliably and accurately observed (Cone, 1999).

Self-Monitoring

As the name implies, self-monitoring is an assessment method that relies on clients to systematically sample and record their own behavior. Because clients can access all three modes of responding (cognitive, affective, overt-motor) in multiple naturalistic contexts, self-monitoring has evolved into a popular and sophisticated assessment method (e.g., see the special section on self-monitoring in the December 1999 issue of *Psychological Assessment*). To maximize accuracy, target behaviors must be clearly defined so that clients consistently can record target behavior occurrence.

Self-monitoring has many advantages as an assessment method. As noted previously, clients can observe all modes of behaviors with self-monitoring. Additionally, private behaviors are more readily measured with self-monitoring. Finally, self-monitoring has a reactive effect that often promotes reductions in undesirable target behavior occurrence and increases in desired target behavior occurrence (Korotitsch & Nelson-Gray, 1999).

The principal limitations of self-monitoring are bias and reactivity. Specifically, a client may not accurately record target behavior occurrence due to a number of factors, including expectations for positive or negative consequences, lack of awareness of target behavior occurrence, the cuing function of self-monitoring behavior, and application of criteria for target behavior occurrence that are different from the therapist's. Additionally, noncompliance—and the resultant missing data—can be problematic with self-monitoring procedures (Bornstein, Hamilton, & Bornstein, 1986; Craske & Tsao, 1999). This risk for noncompliance can be reduced, however, by involving the client in the development of the self-monitoring system and providing consistent reinforcement for compliance through regular review and discussion of collected data.

Questionnaires

Questionnaires have several strengths. They are inexpensive, easily administered, and easily interpreted. Furthermore, there are a vast number of questionnaires that can be used to evaluate a wide array of target behaviors (e.g., see Hersen & Bellack, 1988, for a compilation of behavioral assessment inventories). Finally, questionnaires can be used for a number of behavioral assessment goals, including operationalization, identification of functional relationships, and treatment design.

The most significant problem with questionnaires is that they are often worded in a context-free manner. For example, many questionnaire items ask a client to rate agreement (e.g., *strongly agree, agree, disagree, strongly disagree*) with a contextuallynonbound statement about a target behavior (e.g., *I often feel angry*). Furthermore, many inventories sum distinct behaviors, thoughts, and affective states into a global score. This aggregation of behavioral information is, of course, contrary to the notion of operationalizing behavior into discrete and precise modes and dimensions. Taken together, the measurement limitations commonly found in questionnaires make it very difficult to abstract critical information about functional relationships. Therefore, many questionnaires are minimally helpful for intervention design. They can, however, be helpful in establishing the social significance of a target behavior and in tracking changes in target behaviors across time.

Summary of Assessment Methods

Different combinations of sampling and measurement strategies can be used to gather information about the topography and function of target behavior. Event, duration, and real-time sampling are most applicable to target behaviors that have distinct onset and offset points. Conversely, interval sampling is more suitable for high-frequency behavior and behaviors with ambiguous onset and offset points. Assessment locations can range from naturalistic settings to controlled analog settings. Analog settings allow for enhanced precision in target behavior measurement and the measurement of infrequently occurring behaviors. Alternatively, naturalistic settings allow for enhanced generalizability and evaluation of behavior in settings that present multiple and complex stimuli.

Behavioral interviewing, self-monitoring, and questionnaire administration can be used to assess all modes of target behaviors. In contrast, systematic observation is restricted to the measurement of overt-motor behavior. In addition to differences in capacity for measuring target behavior mode, each assessment method has advantages and disadvantages in its convenience, cost, and validity (for more complete reviews of the psychometric issues related to the various assessment methods, see Cone, 1999; Haynes & O'Brien, 2000; Skinner, Dittmer, & Howell, 2000).

The strengths and limitations of behavior sampling strategies, setting sampling strategies, and assessment methods must be considered in the design and implementation of a behavioral assessment. Because unique errors are associated with each method, it is prudent to use a multimethod assessment strategy. Furthermore, it is beneficial to collect target behavior data in multiple contexts.

Methods Used to Identify Causal Functional Relationships

The aforementioned assessment methods allow the behavior therapist to collect basic information about the topography of target behaviors and contextual factors. Additional information about functional relationships can be abstracted from data yielded by these methods when logical or quantitative decision-making strategies are applied. The more common strategies used to identify potential causal relationships are reviewed in the following sections.

Marker Variable Strategy

A marker variable is a conveniently obtained measure that is reliably associated with the strength of a causal functional relationship. Empirically validated marker variables can be derived from self-report inventories specifically designed to identify functional relationships, structured interviews, psychophysiological assessments, and role-playing exercises. The Motivational Assessment Scale for self-injurious behavior (Durand & Crimmins, 1988) and the School Refusal Assessment Scale (Kearney & Silverman, 1990) are two

examples of functional analytic questionnaires that have been shown to predict causal relationships in naturalistic settings. Similarly, Lauterbach (1990) developed a structured interviewing methodology that can assist with the identification of causal relationships between antecedent events and target behaviors. An example of an empirically validated psychophysiological marker variable is client response to the carbon dioxide inhalation challenge. In this case, it has been reliably shown that patients with panic disorder—relative to controls without the disorder—are significantly more likely to experience acute panic symptoms when they are asked to repeatedly inhale air with high concentrations of carbon dioxide (Barlow, 1988; Clark, Salkovskis, & Chalkley, 1985). Thus, the patient's responses to this test can be used as a marker for whether the complex biobehavioral relationships that characterize panic disorder are operational for a particular client. Finally, Kern (1991) developed a standardized-idiographic role-playing procedure in which setting-behavior relationships from recent social interactions are simulated and systematically evaluated for the purposes of identifying causal functional relationships.

Although the marker variable strategy can provide important information about the presence of causal functional relationships, only a few empirically validated marker variables have so far been identified in the behavioral literature. As a result, behavioral assessors have tended to rely on unvalidated marker variables, such as verbal reports obtained during behavioral interviews (e.g., a patient diagnosed with posttraumatic stress disorder may report that increased flashback frequency is caused by increased job stress), administration of traditional self-report inventories, and in-session observation of setting-behavior interactions (e.g., a patient with a social phobia shows increased sympathetic activation and topic avoidance when asked to describe feared situations), to identify causal functional relationships.

A major advantage of the marker variable strategy is ease of application. A behavior therapist can identify many potential causal functional relationships with a very limited investment of time and effort. For example, the number of markers of potential causal relationships that can be identified through a single behavioral interview can be extensive.

The most significant problem with using marker variables to infer the presence of causal functional relationships is related to generalizability. Specifically, the extent to which unvalidated marker variables such as patient reports, self-report inventory responses, laboratory evaluations, and in-session setting-behavior interactions correlate with actual causal relationships between contextual factors and target behavior is often unknown. Additionally, for those instances in which empirically validated marker variables are available, the magnitude of correlation between the marker variable and actual causal relationships can vary substantially for an individual client.

Behavioral Observation and Self-Monitoring of Context-Behavior Interactions

A second procedure commonly used by behavior therapists to obtain basic information on causal relationships is systematic observation of nonmanipulated context-behavior interactions. Most commonly, clients are instructed to self-monitor some dimension of a target behavior (e.g., frequency or magnitude) along with one or more contextual factors that are thought to be exerting a significant influence on the target behavior. Alternatively, direct observation of setting-behavior interactions can be conducted by trained observers or participant observers in naturalistic (e.g., the client's home, workplace) or analog (e.g., a therapist's office, laboratory) environments (Foster, Bell-Dolan, & Burge, 1988; Foster & Cone, 1986; Hartmann & Wood, 1990).

Self-monitoring and direct observation methods can yield data that support causal inferences (Gottman & Roy, 1990). However, these methods have two practical limitations. First, patients or observers must be adequately trained so that the target behaviors and controlling factors are accurately and reliably recorded. Second, as the number or complexity of the variables to be observed increases, accuracy and reliability often decrease (Foster et al., 1988; Hartmann & Wood, 1990; Paul, 1986a, 1986b). Taken together, these limitations suggest systematic observation methods are best suited for situations in which the target behavior and contextual variables are easily quantified and few in number.

Experimental Manipulation

The third method that can be used to identify casual relationships is experimental manipulation. Experimental manipulations involve systematically modifying contextual factors and observing consequent changes in target behavior topography. These manipulations can be conducted in naturalistic settings (e.g., Sasso et al., 1992), analog settings (e.g., Cowdery, Iwata, & Pace, 1990; Durand & Crimmins, 1988), psychophysiological laboratory settings (e.g., Vrana, Constantine, & Westman, 1992), and during assessment or therapy sessions (Kohlenberg & Tsai, 1987).

Experimental manipulation has received renewed interest in recent years because it can be an effective strategy for identifying specific stimulus conditions that may reinforce problematic behavior (Haynes & O'Brien, 2000). It can also be time efficient and can conform to the pragmatic requirements of outpatient settings while yielding information that facilitates effective intervention design. For example, Iwata and colleagues (Iwata et al., 1994) and Durand and colleagues (Durand, 1990; Durand & Crimmins, 1988) developed a standardized protocol for conducting experimental manipulations to identify the function of self-injurious behavior. In their protocols, clients with self-injurious behavior are evaluated under multiple controlled analog observation conditions so that the function of the behavior can be identified. One condition involves providing the client with social attention contingent upon the occurrence of self-injurious behavior (the client is ignored until the self-injurious behavior occurs, at which point, she receives social attention). A second condition involves providing tangible rewards (e.g., an edible reinforcer, a magazine) contingent upon the occurrence of self-injurious behavior. A third condition involves providing opportunities for negative reinforcement of self-injurious behavior (the client is exposed to an unpleasant task that would be terminated when the self-injurious behavior occurs). Finally, in the fourth condition, the client's level of self-injurious behavior is observed while he or she is socially isolated. It is presumed that rates of self-injurious behavior in this final context occur as a function of intrinsically reinforcing mechanisms such as opioid release, tension reduction, nociceptive feedback, or any combination of these.

Iwata et al. (1994) summarized data from 152 functional analyses using the aforementioned protocol. Based on visual data inspection procedures, they judged which of the four types of maintaining contexts were most closely associated with increased rates of self-injurious behavior. This information was then used to guide treatment design. Thus, if social attention or tangible reinforcement contexts were associated with higher rates of target behavior, the intervention would be designed so that attention and access to preferred materials were consistently provided when self-injurious behavior was not emitted by the client. Alternatively, if the client exhibited higher rates of self-injurious behavior during the negative reinforcement condition, the intervention would include procedures that provided negative reinforcement contingent upon nonperformance of self-injurious behavior (e.g., providing a break when a client was engaged in an unpleasant task, given that self-injurious behavior did not occur). Finally, if the client exhibited higher rates of self-injurious behavior during intrinsic reinforcement conditions, the intervention would provide alternative sources of self-stimulation, differential reinforcement of other behavior (sensory stimulation delivered contingent upon performance of non-self-injurious behaviors), or response interruption procedures.

Results from Iwata et al.'s (1994) study indicated that 80% of the treatments based on the results of functional analyses were successful (operationally defined as achieving self-injurious behavior rates that were at or below 10% of those observed during baseline). Alternatively, interventions not based on the functional analyses were described as having less adequate outcomes. Other researchers have supported these general findings (Carr, Robinson, & Palumbo, 1990; Derby et al., 1992).

Despite the potential treatment utility of experimental manipulations, several questions remain unanswered. First, the psychometric properties (e.g., reliability, validity) of analog observation are largely unexplored and—as a result—largely unknown. Second, an estimate of the incremental effect that analog observation has on treatment outcomes has not yet been adequately estimated. Finally, most demonstrations of the treatment utility of analog observation have been limited to a very restricted population of clients who were presenting with a restricted number of behavior problems. Thus, apparent treatment utility of this procedure for identifying the function of behavior may not adequately generalize to other patient populations, problem behaviors, and settings.

In summary, marker variables, behavioral observation of naturally occurring context-behavior interactions, and experimental manipulations can be used to identify potential causal functional relationships. The strength of causal inference associated with each method tends to vary inversely with clinical applicability. Experimental manipulations and behavioral observation of naturally occurring setting-behavior interactions yield data that support strong causal inferences. However, each method requires either a significant investment of time and effort, or only a few target behaviors and controlling factors can be evaluated. In contrast, the marker variable strategy typically supports only weak causal inferences, yet it is easily applied and can provide information on a broad range of potential causal relationships.

Methods Used to Estimate the Magnitude of Causal Functional Relationships

After a subset of hypothesized causal functional relationships have been identified using marker variables, observation, experimentation, or any combination of these techniques, the behavior therapist needs to estimate the magnitude of relationships. There are two primary methods available for accomplishing this task.

Intuitive Evaluation of Assessment Data

In an effort to determine the clinical activities of behavior therapists, part of a survey of AABT members (described earlier) requested that information be provided about how assessment data were typically evaluated. Results indicated that the respondents used subjective evaluation and visual examination of graphs to evaluate assessment data significantly more often than they used any statistical technique such as computing measures of central tendency, variance, or association.

Some have argued that intuitive data evaluation is an appropriate—if not preferred—method for evaluating behavioral assessment data. The primary strengths associated with this method are that (a) it requires only a modest investment of time and effort on the part of the behavioral clinician, (b) an intuitive approach is heuristic—it can promote hypothesis generation, and (c) intuitive approaches are well suited for evaluating complex patterns of data. An additional argument supporting intuitive evaluation is associated with clinical significance. Specifically, it has been argued that visual inspection is conservatively biased, and as a result, determinations of significant effects only will occur when the causal relationship is of moderate to high magnitude.

Matyas and Greenwood (1990) have challenged these supportive arguments by demonstrating that intuitive evaluation of data can sometimes lead to higher rates of Type I error when data are autocorrelated (i.e., correlation of the data with itself, lagged by a certain number of observations) and when there are trends in single-subject data. A similar finding was reported by O'Brien (1995). In his study, graduate students who had completed course work in behavioral therapy were provided with a contrived set of self-monitoring data presented on three target behaviors: headache frequency, intensity, and duration. The data set also contained information from three potentially relevant causal factors: hours of sleep, marital argument frequency, and stress levels. The data were constructed so that only a single causal factor was strongly correlated (i.e., $r > .60$) with a single target behavior (the remaining correlations between causal variables and target behaviors were of very low magnitude).

Students were instructed to (a) evaluate data as they typically would in a clinical setting, (b) estimate the magnitude of correlation between each causal factor and target behavior, and (c) select the most highly associated causal factor for each target behavior. Results indicated that the students predominantly used intuitive evaluation procedures to estimate correlations. Additionally, the students substantially underestimated the magnitude of the strong correlations and overestimated the magnitude of weak correlations. In essence, they demonstrated a central tendency bias, guessing that two variables were moderately correlated. Finally—and most important—the students only were able to correctly identify the most important causal variable for each target behavior about 50% of the time.

In our AABT survey, we further evaluated the potential limitations of intuitive data evaluation methods. Similar to the O'Brien (1995) study, we created a data set that contained three target behaviors and three potential causal variables in a three-by-three table. The correlation between each pair of target behaviors and casual factor was either low ($r = .1$), moderate ($r = .5$), or high ($r = .9$). Participants were then instructed to identify which of the three possible causal variables was most strongly associated with the target behavior. Results indicated that when the true correlation between the target behavior and casual factor was either low or moderate, the participants were able to correctly identify the causal variable at levels that were slightly better than chance (i.e., 55% and 54% correct identification, respectively). This finding replicated those reported by O'Brien (1995) when graduate students comprised the study sample. When the true correlation was high, the participants' performance rose to 72%. It is interesting to note that this improved performance was not consistent across tasks—that is, a correct identification of the causal variable in one pair of variables did not appear to be substantially associated with the likelihood of generating a correct answer on a different pair of variables.

Taken together, these results suggest that intuitive evaluation of behavioral assessment data is susceptible to misestimation of covariation, which (as noted earlier) is a foundation for causal inference. As Arkes (1981) has argued, when conducting an intuitive analysis of data similar to those described previously, many clinicians tend to overestimate the magnitude of functional relationships or infer an illusory correlation (Chapman & Chapman, 1969). One reason for this phenomenon is that confirmatory information or hits (i.e., instances in which the causal variable and hypothesized effect co-occur) are overemphasized in intuitive decision making relative to disconfirming information such as false-positive misses.

A number of other biases and limitations in human judgment as it relates to causal inference have been identified (cf. Einhorn, 1988; Elstein, 1988; Garb, 1998; Kanfer & Schefft, 1988; Kleinmuntz, 1990; also see the chapter by Weiner in this volume). A particularly troubling finding, however, is that a clinician's confidence in his or her judgments of covariation and causality increase with experience, but accuracy remains relatively unchanged (Arkes, 1981; Garb, 1989, 1998).

In summary, intuitive data evaluation approaches can be convenient and useful for hypothesis generation. Fundamental problems emerge, however, when behavior therapists intuitively estimate the magnitude of covariation between hypothesized contextual variables and target behaviors. This problem is compounded by the fact that multiple behaviors, multiple causes, and multiple interactions are encountered in a typical behavioral assessment. It is thus recommended that statistical tests be conducted whenever possible to evaluate the strength of hypothesized causal functional relationships.

Quantitative Evaluation of Assessment Data

One of the most clinically friendly methods for evaluating assessment data is the conditional probability analysis—a statistical method designed to evaluate the extent to which target behavior occurrence (or nonoccurrence) is conditional upon the occurrence (or nonoccurrence) of some other variable. Specifically, the behavior therapist evaluates differences in the overall probability that the target behavior will occur (i.e., base rate or unconditional probability) relative to the probability that the target behavior will occur, given that some causal factor has occurred (i.e., the conditional probability). If there is significant variation among unconditional and conditional probabilities, the behavior therapist concludes that the target behavior and causal factor are functionally related.

A broadly applicable and straightforward strategy for conducting a conditional probability analysis involves constructing a two-by-two table with target behavior occurrence (and nonoccurrence) denoting the columns and the causal factor presence (and absence) denoting the rows (see Table 22.4). To illustrate, we can return to our imagined client. The columns can be constructed so that they denote whether the client rated a particular day as consisting of high or low levels of checking. Let A = a clinically significant elevation in the frequency of checking for cancer tumors by touching your chest, B = level of perceived stress at work, and P = probability. A functional relationship tentatively would be inferred if the probability of experiencing heightened checking on a stressful day, $P(A/B)$, is greater than the base rate probability of checking, $P(A)$.

Conditional probability analyses have important strengths and limitations. First, only a modest number of data points can yield reliable estimates of association (Schlundt, 1985).

TABLE 22.4   A Two-by-Two Contingency Table for Context-Behavior Evaluation

		Target Behavior	
		Present	Absent
Causal factor	Present	A	B
	Absent	C	D

Note: Unconditional probability of target behavior occurrence: $A + C/A + B + C + D$. *Conditional probabilities:* Probability of target occurrence given causal variable presence: $A/A + B$, probability of target occurrence given causal variable absence: $C/C + D$, probability of target nonoccurrence given causal variable presence: $B/A + B$, and probability of target occurrence given causal variable presence: $D/C + D$.

Second, the statistical concepts underlying the methodology are easily understood. Third, many statistical packages can be used to conduct conditional probability analyses, or if none are available, the computations can be easily done by hand (e.g., Bush & Ciocco, 1992). Fourth—and most important— the procedure is easily incorporated into a clinical setting and clients can participate in the data evaluation process. Specifically, we have found that a two-by-two table that presents information about target behavior occurrence, given the presence or absence of causal variable occurrence, can be readily constructed and interpreted in a clinical session. A limitation, however, is that conditional probability analyses can evaluate the interactions among only a small number of variables. Furthermore, because it is a nonparametric technique, it can be used only when the controlling variables and target behaviors are measured using nominal or ordinal scales.

Analysis of variance (ANOVA), *t* tests, and regression are conventional statistical techniques that can be used to evaluate causal functional relationships when data are collected on two or more variables. For example, in a multiple-baseline design (e.g., AB, ABAB), the clinician can conduct *t* tests, ANOVA, or regression to determine whether the levels of target behavior occurrence differs as a function of contexts in which a causal factor is present (B) relative to contexts in which it is absent (A). The primary advantage of using *t* tests, ANOVA, and regression is that these procedures are well known to most behavior therapists who have received graduate training. The main disadvantage is that estimates of *t* and *F* are spuriously inflated when observational data are serially dependent (Kazdin, 1998; Suen & Ary, 1989). This inflation of *t* and *F* is not trivial. For example, Cook and Campbell (1979) noted that an autocorrelation of .7 can inflate a *t* value by as much as 265%. Thus, prior to using *t* tests, ANOVA, or regression, the clinician must determine whether data are substantially autocorrelated, and if they are, procedures must be used to reduce the level of autocorrelation (e.g., randomly select data from the series, partition out the variance attributable to autocorrelation).

Time series analyses involve taking repeated measures of the target behavior and one or more contextual factors across time. An estimate of the relationships among these variables is then calculated after the variance attributable to serial dependency is partitioned out (Gaynor, Baird, & Nelson-Gray, 1999; Matyas & Greenwood, 1996; Wei, 1990). When assessment data are measured with nominal or ordinal scales, lag sequential analysis can be used to evaluate functional relationships (Gottman & Roy, 1990). Alternatively with interval and ratio data, other time series methodologies such as autoregressive integrated moving averages (ARIMA) modeling and spectral analysis can be used (Cook & Campbell, 1979; McCleary & Hay, 1980; Wei, 1990).

Time series methods can provide very accurate information about the magnitude and reliability of causal functional relationships. They can also be used to examine the effects of controlling variables on target behaviors across different time lags. However, their applicability is limited because (a) a large number of data points is necessary for a proper analysis, and (b) most behavior therapists will be able to analyze relationships among a small number of variables. The first limitation can be reduced when the behavior therapist designs an assessment that yields a sufficient number of data points. The impact of the second limitation can be diminished if the behavior therapist carefully selects the most relevant target behaviors and causal factors using rational presuppositions and theory.

SUMMARY AND CONCLUSIONS

Behavioral assessment is a paradigm that is founded on a number of assumptions related to the nature of problem behavior and the ways that it should be measured. The overarching assumptions of empiricism and environmental determinism have been augmented by additional assumptions that arose from new developments in theory and research in the behavioral sciences. This broadening of assumptions occurred along with advancements in our understanding about the causes and correlates of target behavior. As a result, behavioral conceptualizations of target behavior have become increasingly complex, and contemporary behavior therapists must be able to identify and evaluate many potential functional relationships among target behaviors and contextual factors. Part of the ability to accomplish this task relies on a sound knowledge of (a) the different dimensions of topography that can be quantified, (b) the multiple ways that contextual variables and target behaviors can interact for a particular behavior disorder, and (c) one's own presuppositions and decisional strategies used to narrow causal fields.

In addition to conceptual foundations, familiarity with specific sampling and assessment methods and strategies for identifying functional relationships (e.g., the marker variable strategy, observation and self-monitoring of naturally occurring setting-behavior interactions, and experimental manipulation) are required to empirically identify causal functional relationships. Each method has strengths and limitations related to the strength of causal inference that can be derived from the collected data and the degree of clinical applicability.

After basic assessment data on hypothesized causal functional relationships have been collected, intuitive and statistical procedures can be used to evaluate the magnitude of association. Intuitive approaches are well suited for hypothesis formation. As a method for estimating the magnitude of covariation among variables, however, intuition is often inaccurate. Statistical approaches can provide unbiased information on the strength of functional relationships. Conditional probability analyses can be especially useful because they require only a modest amount of data, are easily understood, and are convenient to use. The principal limitation of statistical approaches is that they are limited to the evaluation of only a few variables; also, they appear to be incompatible with typical clinical settings, given their low reported use among behavior therapists.

All of the aforementioned assessment principles have been well developed in the behavioral assessment literature. However, our survey of behavior therapists suggests that many do not conduct assessments that are consistent with all of these principles. For example, most therapists appear to abide by behavioral assessment principles as these principles apply to the operationalization and quantification of target behaviors and contexts. However, few behavior therapists use quantitative decision aids to identify and evaluate the magnitude of context-behavior associations. Instead, they appear to rely predominantly on intuitive judgments of covariation and causation. Factors that may account for this mixed allegiance to behavioral assessment principles should be more thoroughly explored. Furthermore, in the coming years, research examining training procedures must be conducted that can be used to help clinicians learn and use quantitative decision-making procedures.

A final important question for future consideration is the treatment utility of behavioral assessment in light of the growing use of empirically supported protocols. Specifically, to what extent will individualized treatments that are based on an idiographic behavioral assessment outperform standardized treatment protocols that require less intensive pretreatment assessments such as diagnostic interviews? Failure to demonstrate significantly improved outcomes might create a diminished need for individualized behavioral assessment procedures. Alternatively, there may be a heightened need for behavioral assessment procedures that can help match interventions with client behavior problems and characteristics. In either case, there is a clear need to evaluate the treatment utility of behavioral assessment in relation to *both* idiographic treatment design and standardized treatment-client matching.

REFERENCES

American Psychiatric Association. (1994). *Diagnostic and statistical manual of mental disorders* (4th ed.). Washington, DC: American Psychiatric Association.

Arkes, H. R. (1981). Impediments to accurate clinical judgment and possible ways to minimize their impact. *Journal of Consulting and Clinical Psychology, 49,* 323–330.

Axelrod, S. (1987). Functional and structural analyses of behavior: Approaches leading to the reduced use of punishment procedures? *Research in Developmental Disabilities, 8,* 165–178.

Bandura, A. (1981). In search of pure unidirectional determinants. *Behavior Therapy, 12,* 30–40.

Barlow, D. H. (1988). *Anxiety and its disorders.* New York: Guilford Press.

Barlow, D. H., & Hersen, M. (1984). *Single case experimental designs: Strategies for studying behavior change* (2nd ed.). New York: Pergamon Press.

Bellack, A. S., & Hersen, M. (1998). *Behavioral assessment: A practical handbook* (4th ed.). Needham Heights, MA: Allyn and Bacon.

Bernstein, D. A., Borkovec, T. D., & Coles, M. G. H. (1986). Assessment of anxiety. In A. Ciminero, K. S. Calhoun, & H. E. Adams (Eds.), *Handbook of behavioral assessment* (2nd ed., pp. 353–403). New York: Wiley.

Bornstein, P. H., Hamilton, S. B., & Bornstein, M. T. (1986). Self-monitoring procedures. In A. R. Ciminero, C. S. Calhoun, & H. E. Adams (Eds.), *Handbook of behavioral assessment* (2nd ed., pp. 176–222). New York: Wiley.

Burish, T. G., Carey, M. P., Krozely, M. G., & Greco, M. G. (1987). Conditioned side effects induced by cancer chemotherapy: Prevention through behavioral treatment. *Journal of Consulting and Clinical Psychology, 55,* 42–48.

Bush, J. P., & Ciocco, J. E. (1992). Behavioral coding and sequential analysis: The portable computer system for observational use. *Behavioral Assessment, 14,* 191–197.

Carey, M. P., & Burish, T. G. (1988). Etiology and treatment of the psychological side effects associated with cancer chemotherapy. *Psychological Bulletin, 104,* 307–325.

Carr, E. G., & Durand, V. M. (1985). Reducing behavior problems through functional communication training. *Journal of Applied Behavior Analysis, 18,* 111–126.

Carr, E. G., Robinson, S., & Palumbo, L. R. (1990). The wrong issue: Aversive versus nonaversive treatment; The right issue: Functional versus nonfunctional treatment. In A. C. Repp & S. Nirbhay (Eds.), *Perspectives on the use of nonaversive and aversive interventions for persons with developmental disabilities* (pp. 361–379). Sycamore, IL: Sycamore.

Chapman, L. J., & Chapman, J. P. (1969). Illusory correlation as an obstacle to the use of valid psychodiagnostic signs. *Journal of Abnormal Psychology, 74,* 271–280.

Clark, D. M., Salkovskis, P. M., & Chalkley, A. J. (1985). Respiratory control as a treatment for panic attacks. *Journal of Behavior Therapy and Experimental Psychiatry, 16,* 23–30.

Cone, J. D. (1988). Psychometric considerations and multiple models of behavioral assessment. In A. S. Bellack & M. Hersen

(Eds.), *Behavioral assessment: A practical handbook* (3rd ed., pp. 42–66). Elmsford, NY: Pergamon Press.

Cone, J. D. (1999). Observational assessment: Measure development and research issues. In P. C. Kendall, J. N. Butcher, & G. N. Holmbeck (Eds.), *Handbook of research methods in clinical psychology* (2nd ed., pp. 183–223). New York: Wiley.

Cook, T. D., & Campbell, D. T. (1979). *Quasi-experimentation: Design and analysis issues for field settings.* Chicago: Rand McNally.

Correa, E. I., & Sutker, P. B. (1986). Assessment of alcohol and drug behaviors. In A. R. Ciminero, K. S. Calhoun, & H. E. Adams (Eds.), *Handbook of behavioral assessment* (2nd ed., pp. 446–495). New York: Wiley.

Cowdery, G. E., Iwata, B. A., & Pace, G. M. (1990). Effects and side effects of DRO as treatment for self-injurious behavior. *Journal of Applied Psychology, 23,* 497–506.

Craighead, W. E., Kazdin, A. E., & Mahoney, M. J. (1981). *Behavior modification: Principles, issues, and applications* (2nd ed.). Boston: Houghton Mifflin.

Craske, M. G., Barlow, D. H., & O'Leary, T. A. (1992). *Mastery of your anxiety and worry.* San Antonio, TX: The Psychological Corporation.

Craske, M. G., & Tsao, J. C. I. (1999). Self-monitoring with panic and anxiety disorders. *Psychological Assessment, 11,* 466–479.

Derby, K. M., Wacker, D. P., Sasso, G., Steege, M., Northrup, J., Cigrand, K., & Asmus, J. (1992). Brief functional analysis techniques to evaluate aberrant behavior in an outpatient setting: A summary of 79 cases. *Journal of Applied Behavior Analysis, 25,* 713–721.

Dougher, M. J. (2000). *Clinical behavior analysis.* Reno, NV: Context Press.

Durand, V. M. (1990). *Severe behavior problems: A functional communication training approach.* New York: Guilford Press.

Durand, M. V., & Carr, E. G. (1991). Functional communication training to reduce challenging behavior: Maintenance and application in new settings. *Journal of Applied Behavior Analysis, 24,* 251–264.

Durand, V. M., & Crimmins, D. (1988). Identifying the variables maintaining self-injurious behavior. *Journal of Autism and Developmental Disorders, 18,* 99–117.

Einhorn, H. J. (1988). Diagnosis and causality in clinical and statistical prediction. In D. C. Turk & P. Salovey (Eds.), *Reasoning, inference, and judgment in clinical psychology* (pp. 51–70). New York: Free Press.

Elliot, A. J., Miltenberger, R. G., Kaster-Bundgaard, J., & Lumley, V. (1996). A national survey of assessment and therapy techniques used by behavior therapists. *Cognitive and Behavior Practice, 3,* 107–125.

Elstein, A. S. (1988). Cognitive processes in clinical inference and decision making. In D. C. Turk & P. Salovey (Eds.), *Reasoning, inference, and judgment in clinical psychology* (pp. 17–50). New York: Free Press.

Evans, I. M. (1985). Building systems models as a strategy for target behavior selection in clinical assessment. *Behavioral Assessment, 7,* 21–32.

Felton, J. L., & Nelson, R. O. (1984). Inter-assessor agreement on hypothesized controlling variables and treatment proposals. *Behavioral Assessment, 6,* 199–208.

Follette, W., Naugle, A. E., & Linnerooth, P. J. (2000). Functional alternatives to traditional assessment and diagnosis. In M. J. Dougher (Ed.), *Clinical behavior analysis* (pp. 99–125). Reno, NV: Context Press.

Foster, S. L., Bell-Dolan, D. J., & Burge, D. A. (1988). Behavioral observation. In A. S. Bellack & M. Hersen (Eds.), *Behavioral assessment: A practical handbook* (3rd ed., pp. 119–160). Elmsford, NY: Pergamon Press.

Foster, S. L., & Cone, J. D. (1986). Design and use of direct observation systems. In A. R. Ciminero, C. S. Calhoun, & H. E. Adams (Eds.), *Handbook of behavioral assessment* (2nd ed., pp. 253–324). New York: Wiley.

Garb, H. N. (1989). Clinical judgment, clinical training, and professional experience. *Psychological Bulletin, 105,* 387–396.

Garb, H. N. (1998). *Studying the clinician: Judgment research and psychological assessment.* Washington, DC: American Psychological Association.

Gaynor, S. T., Baird, S. C., & Nelson-Gray, R. O. (1999). Application of time-series (single subject) designs in clinical psychology. In P. C. Kendall, J. N. Butcher, & G. N. Holmbeck (Eds.), *Handbook of research methods in clinical psychology* (2nd ed., pp. 297–329). New York: Guilford Press.

Goldfried, M. R., & Kent, R. N. (1972). Traditional versus behavioral assessment: A comparison of methodological and theoretical assumptions. *Psychological Bulletin, 77,* 409–420.

Gottman, J. M., & Roy, A. K. (1990). *Sequential analysis: A guide for behavioral researchers.* New York: Cambridge University Press.

Grant, L., & Evans, A. (1994). *Principles of behavior analysis.* New York: HarperCollins.

Hartmann, D. P., & Wood, D. D. (1990). Observational methods. In A. S. Bellack, M. Hersen, & A. E. Kazdin (Eds.), *International handbook of behavior modification and therapy* (2nd ed., pp. 107–138). New York: Plenum Press.

Hawkins, R. P. (1986). Selection of target behaviors. In R. O. Nelson & S. C. Hayes (Eds.), *Conceptual foundations of behavioral assessment* (pp. 331–383). New York: Guilford Press.

Hay, W. M., Hay, L. R., Angle, H. V., & Nelson, R. O. (1979). The reliability of problem identification in the behavioral interview. *Behavioral Assessment, 1,* 107–118.

Hayes, S. C., & Follette, W. C. (1992). Can functional analysis provide a substitute for syndromal classification? *Behavioral Assessment, 14,* 345–365.

Hayes, S. C., & Toarmino, D. (1999). The rise of clinical behavior analysis. *Psychologist, 12,* 505–509.

Hayes, S. L., Nelson, R. O., & Jarret, R. B. (1987). The treatment utility of assessment: A functional analytic approach to evaluate assessment quality. *American Psychologist, 42,* 963–974.

Haynes, S. N. (1992). *Models of causality in psychopathology: Toward dynamic, synthetic, and nonlinear models of behavior disorders.* New York: MacMillan.

Haynes, S. N. (2000). Behavioral assessment of adults. In G. Goldstein & M. Hersen (Eds.), *Handbook of psychological assessment* (3rd ed., pp. 453–502). New York: Pergamon/Elsevier.

Haynes, S. N., & O'Brien, W. H. (1990). Functional analysis in behavior therapy. *Clinical Psychology Review, 10,* 649–668.

Haynes, S. N., & O'Brien, W. H. (2000). Principles and practice of behavioral assessment. New York: Kluwer Academic/Plenum.

Hersen, M., & Bellack, A. S. (1988). *Dictionary of behavioral assessment techniques.* New York: Pergamon Press.

Hollandsworth, J. G. (1986). *Physiology and behavior therapy: Conceptual guidelines for the clinician.* New York: Plenum Press.

Iwata, B. A., Kahng, S. W., Wallace, M. D., & Lindberg, J. S. (2000). The functional analysis model of behavioral assessment. In J. Austin & J. Carr (Eds.), *Handbook of applied behavior analysis* (pp. 61–89). Reno, NV: Context Press.

Iwata, B. A., Pace, G. M., Dorsey, M. F., Zarcone, J. R., Vollmer, B., & Smith, J. (1994). The function of self injurious behavior: An experimental-epidemiological analysis. *Journal of Applied Behavior Analysis, 27,* 215–240.

James, L. R., Mulaik, S. A., & Brett, J. M. (1982). *Causal analysis: Assumptions, models, and data.* Beverly Hills: Sage.

Kanfer, F. H., & Phillips, J. (l970). *Learning foundations of behavior therapy.* New York: Wiley.

Kanfer, F. H., & Schefft, B. K. (1988). *Guiding the process of therapeutic change.* Champaign: Research Press.

Kazdin, A. E. (1998). *Research design in clinical psychology* (3rd ed.). Boston: Allyn and Bacon.

Kearney, C. A., & Silverman, W. K. (1990). A preliminary analysis of a functional model of assessment and treatment for school refusal behavior. *Behavior Modification, 14,* 340–366.

Kern, J. M. (1991). An evaluation of a novel role-playing methodology: The standardized idiographic approach. *Behavior Therapy, 22,* 13–29.

Kleinmuntz, B. (1990). Why we still use our heads instead of formulas: Toward an integrative approach. *Psychological Bulletin, 107,* 296–310.

Kohlenberg, R. J., & Tsai, M. (1987). Functional analytic psychotherapy. In N. Jacobson (Ed.), *Psychotherapists in clinical practice: Cognitive and behavioral perspectives* (pp. 388–443). New York: Guilford Press.

Kohlenberg, R. J., & Tsai, M. (1991). *Functional analytic psychotherapy: Creating intense and curative therapeutic relationships.* New York: Plenum Press.

Korotitsch, W. J., & Nelson-Gray, R. O. (1999). An overview of self-monitoring research in assessment and treatment. *Psychological Assessment, 11,* 415–425.

Krasner, L. (1992). The concepts of syndrome and functional analysis: Compatible or incompatible. *Behavioral Assessment, 14,* 307–321.

Lauterbach, W. (1990). Situation-response questions for identifying the function of problem behavior: The example of thumb sucking. *British Journal of Clinical Psychology, 29,* 51–57.

Levey, A. B., Aldaz, J. A., Watts, F. N., & Coyle, K. (1991). Articulatory suppression and the treatment of insomnia. *Behavior Research and Therapy, 29,* 85–89.

Matyas, T. A., & Greenwood, K. M. (1990). Visual analysis of single-case time series: Effects of variability, serial dependence, and magnitude of intervention effect. *Journal of Applied Behavior Analysis, 23,* 341–351.

Matyas, T. A., & Greenwood, K. M. (1996). Serial dependency in single-case time series. In R. D. Franklin, D. B. Allison, & B. S. Gorman (Eds.), *Design and analysis of single case research* (pp. 215–244). Mahwah, NJ: Erlbaum.

McCleary, R., & Hay, R. (1980). *Applied time series analysis for the social sciences.* Beverly Hills, CA: Sage.

Mettee-Carter, R., McGrath, J., Egan, M., Kulick, A., Maynard, C., O'Connell, M., Wryobeck, J., & O'Brien, W. (1999, November). *Estimation of functional relationships by AABT members: A comparison of tabular and graphic self-monitoring data.* Poster presented at the 33rd Annual Convention of the Association for the Advancement of Behavior Therapy, Toronto, Canada.

Miller, D. J. (1991). Simple phobia as a symptom of posttraumatic stress disorder in a former prisoner of war. *Behavior Modification, 15,* 25–260.

Morris, E. K. (1988). Contextualism: The world view of behavior analysis. *Journal of Experimental Child Psychology, 46,* 289–323.

Nathan, P. E., & Gorman, J. M. (Eds.). (1998). *A guide to treatments that work.* New York: Oxford University Press.

Nelson, R. O. (1988). Relationships between assessment and treatment within a behavioral perspective. *Journal of Psychopathology and Behavioral Assessment, 10,* 155–169.

Nelson, R. O., & Hayes, S. C. (1986). The nature of behavioral assessment. In R. O. Nelson & S. C. Hayes (Eds.), *Conceptual foundations of behavioral assessment* (pp. 3–41). New York: Guilford Press.

Nezu, A. M., & Nezu, C. M. (1989). *Clinical decision making in behavior therapy: A problem solving perspective.* Champaign, IL: Research Press.

O'Brien, W. H. (1995). Inaccuracies in the estimation of functional relationships using self-monitoring data. *Journal of Behavior Therapy and Experimental Psychiatry, 26,* 351–357.

O'Brien, W. H., & Haynes, S. N. (1995). A functional analytic approach to the assessment and treatment of a child with frequent migraine headaches. *Session: Psychotherapy in Practice, 1,* 65–80.

O'Brien, W. H., & Haynes, S. N. (1997). Functional analysis. In G. Buela-Casal (Ed.), *Handbook of psychological assessment* (pp. 493–521). Madrid, Spain: Sigma.

O'Donohue, W. (1998). *Learning and behavior therapy.* Needham Heights, MA: Allyn and Bacon.

O'Neill, R. E., Horner, R. H., Albin, R. W., Storey, K., & Sprague, J. R. (1990). *Functional analysis of problem behavior: A practical assessment guide.* Sycamore, IL: Sycamore.

Paul, G. L. (1986a). *Assessment in residential settings: Principles and methods to support cost-effective quality operations.* Champaign, IL: Research Press.

Paul, G. L. (1986b). *The time sample behavioral checklist: Observational assessment instrumentation for service and research.* Champaign, IL: Research Press.

Peterson, L., Homer, A. L., & Wonderlich, S. A. (1982). The integrity of independent variables in behavior analysis. *Journal of Applied Behavior Analysis, 15,* 477–492.

Prochaska, J. O. (1994). Strong and weak principles for progressing from precontemplation to action on the basis of twelve problem behaviors. *Health Psychology, 13,* 47–51.

Quera, V. (1990). A generalized technique to estimate frequency and duration in time sampling. *Behavioral Assessment, 12,* 409–424.

Russo, D. C., & Budd, K. S. (1987). Limitations of operant practice in the study of disease. *Behavior Modification, 11,* 264–285.

Sasso, G. M., Reimers, T. M., Cooper, L. J., Wacker, D., Berg, W., Steege, M., Kelly, L., & Allaire, A. (1992). Use of descriptive and experimental analysis to identify the functional properties of aberrant behavior in school settings. *Journal of Applied Behavior Analysis, 25,* 809–821.

Sarwer, D. B., & Sayers, S. L. (1998). Behavioral interviewing. In A. S. Bellack & M. Hersen (Eds.), *Behavioral assessment: A practical guidebook* (4th ed.). Needham Heights, MA: Allyn and Bacon.

Schlundt, D. G. (1985). An observational methodology for functional analysis. *Bulletin for the Society of Psychologists in Addictive Behaviors, 4,* 234–249.

Shapiro, E. S., & Kratochwill, T. R. (1988). *Behavioral assessment in schools: Theory, research, and clinical foundations* (2nd ed.). New York: Guilford Press.

Shapiro, E. S., & Kratochwill, T. R. (2000). *Behavioral assessment in schools: Theory, research, and clinical foundations* (2nd ed.). New York: Guilford.

Skinner, C. H., Dittmer, K. I., & Howell, L. A. (2000). Direct observation in school settings: Theoretical issues. In E. S. Shapiro & T. R. Kratochwill (Eds.), *Behavioral assessment in schools: Theory, research, and clinical foundations* (2nd ed., pp. 19–45). New York: Guilford Press.

Smith, R. G., Iwata, B. G., Vollmer, T. R., & Pace, G. M. (1992). On the relationship between self-injurious behavior and self-restraint. *Journal of Applied Behavior Analysis, 25,* 433–445.

Spiegler, M. D., & Guevremont, D. C. (1998). *Contemporary behavior therapy* (3rd ed.). Pacific Grove: Brookes/Cole.

Sturmey, P. (1996). *Functional analysis in clinical psychology.* New York: Wiley.

Suen, H. K., & Ary, D. (1989). *Analyzing quantitative behavioral data.* Hillsdale, NJ: Erlbaum.

Swan, G. E., & MacDonald, M. L. (1978). Behavior therapy in practice: A national survey of behavior therapists. *Behavior Therapy, 9,* 799–801.

Taylor, J. C., & Carr, E. G. (1992a). Severe problem behaviors related to social interaction: I. Attention seeking and social avoidance. *Behavior Modification, 16,* 305–335.

Taylor, J. C., & Carr, E. G. (1992b). Severe problem behaviors related to social interaction: II. A systems analysis. *Behavior Modification, 16,* 336–371.

Vrana, S. R., Constantine, J. A., & Westman, J. S. (1992). Startle reflex modification as an outcome measure in the treatment of phobia: Two case studies. *Behavioral Assessment, 14,* 279–291.

Wahler, R. G., & Fox, J. J. (1981). Setting events in applied behavior analysis: Toward a conceptual and methodological expansion. *Journal of Applied Behavior Analysis, 14,* 327–338.

Wei, W. S. (1990). *Time series Analysis: Univariate and multivariate methods.* Redwood City, CA: Addison-Wesley.

CHAPTER 23

Assessing Personality and Psychopathology with Projective Methods

DONALD J. VIGLIONE AND BRIDGET RIVERA

What are projective tests and what are their distinctive characteristics? How should we understand and interpret them? What do they add to assessment? The purpose of this chapter is to address these questions by providing the reader with a meaningful and comprehensive conceptual framework for understanding projective tests. This framework emphasizes a response process that includes both self-expressive and organizational components, that is, what the respondent says and how he or she structures the response. The framework's implications for projective testing and the contributions of projective testing to assessment are addressed. In the course of this discussion, we hope to correct some common misperceptions about projective tests and to establish a more informed approach to projective tests, projective testing, and assessment in general. Other related topics include implications of the model for interpretation, using projective tests as methods, controversies surrounding projective testing, response sets, response manipulation, and issues from a historical perspective.

It is clear that projective tests have value in the assessment process. This chapter addresses their value within a broad overview, incorporating projective tests and methods within a single domain. Encompassing all projective tests, as is the challenge of this chapter, necessitates this inclusive, global approach and precludes detailed, test-specific characterizations. In general, we have reserved our comments about specific tests to the Rorschach, Thematic Apperception Test (TAT), figure drawings, sentence completion tests, and the early memory tests. An evaluation of the specific strengths and weaknesses of these or any other individual projective measure awaits others' initiatives.

PROBLEMS WITH DEFINITIONS AND DISTINCTIONS

Anastasi and Urbina (1996) have characterized a *projective test* as a "relatively unstructured task, that is, a task that permits almost an unlimited variety of possible responses. In order to allow free play to the individual's fantasy, only brief, general instructions are provided" (p. 411). This global, descriptive definition identifies some important elements of projective tests. Ironically, however, this definition and others like it impede our understanding of the nature of projective tests when they are causally juxtaposed with so-called *objective tests*. Without pause, many American psychologists categorize tests according to the traditional projective-objective dichotomy. In thinking and communicating about assessment instruments, these psychologists treat the characteristics of each class of instrument as mutually exclusive or as polar opposites. For example, because objective tests are thought of as unbiased measures, projective tests, by default, are assumed to be subjective. As another example, because objective tests are seen as having standardized administration and scoring, projective tests are assumed to lack empirical rigor. There are a number of reasons that the projective-objective dichotomy leads to an oversimplified and biased understanding of projective tests. First, the projective-objective dichotomy often results in misleading reductionism. Instruments under the rubric of *projective* are assumed to be uniform in content, purpose, and methodology. For example, all projective instruments are often reduced and treated as equivalent to a classic exemplar such as the Rorschach. Reducing all projective instruments to the Rorschach ignores their incredible diversity. Not only do these tests target many different domains of functioning, but they also employ a great variety of methodologies for the purposes of inducing very different response processes. For example, early instruments included an indistinct speech interpretation, word association, cloud perception, hand-positioning perception, comic strip completion, and musical reverie tests (Anastasi & Urbina; Campbell, 1957; Frank, 1939/1962; Murray, 1938). Moreover, this great variety suggests that projective processes are ubiquitous and are involved in many real-life behaviors.

Second, the projective-objective dichotomy implies that there are characteristics unique to each class of test, but these supposed hallmarks are misleading. For example, test elements identified as projective, such as the flexible response format and ambiguous or incomplete stimuli, are employed by tests generally considered to be models of objectivity and quantification. Murstein (1963) notes from the flexible response format of some cognitive ability tests that "we learn a great deal about the person who, on the vocabulary subtests of the Wechsler Adult Scale of Intelligence, when asked to give the meaning of the word 'sentence,' proceeds to rattle off three or four definitions and is beginning to divulge the differences between the connotations and denotations of the word when he is stopped" (p. 3). E. Kaplan's (1991) approach to neuropsychological testing focuses on process, similar to the response-process approach in projective testing. Similarly, Meehl points out the projective element of stimulus ambiguity in self-report personality tests. In his *Basic Readings on the MMPI: A New Selection on Personality Measurement* (1945/1980), Meehl notes that many Minnesota Multiphasic

Personality Inventory (MMPI) items, such as "Once in a while I laugh at a dirty joke," contain ambiguities. At the most basic level, it is unclear whether "once in a while" refers to once a day, once a week, or once a month.

Third, the stereotypic juxtaposition of objective and projective testing lends a pejorative connotation to projective tests that suggests they lack objectivity. This is misleading. Many projective tests are quantified and standardized in terms of administration, and more should be. If we take the example of cognitive tests, the style or process of the response can be systematically observed, quantified, and standardized. This qualitative-to-quantitative test development strategy is exactly the same procedure used in sophisticated quantification of projective tests, as in the Rorschach Comprehensive System (Exner, 1993) and the Washington Sentence Completion Test (Loevinger & Wessler, 1970). Such approaches can result in psychometrically sound quantification and standardization. For example, Joy, Fein, Kaplan, and Freedman (2001) utilized this procedure to standardize observation of the Block Design subtest from the Wechsler scales. Other research summarized by Stricker and Gold (1999) and Weiner (1999) indicates that behavioral observation within projective tests can be used to elaborate previously developed hypotheses and to synthesize inferences about the respondent. These same authors also demonstrated these tactics in case examples.

Of course, quantification and reducing examiner bias, that is variability introduced by examiners, are important goals in improving psychological assessment. Nonetheless, reducing examiner variability is not the only goal of assessment and is not equivalent to validity and utility. Indeed, further research should address the extent to which the examiner's input is induced by the subject, as would be the case with reciprocal determinism, increasing the ecological validity of projective tests (Bandura, 1978; Viglione & Perry, 1991). Furthermore, one may speculate that overemphasis on eliminating examiner variability to achieve objectivity can increase test reliability at the expense of validity when it limits salient observations by the examiner.

Finally, projective and objective tests resemble each other in that they share the same goal: the description of personality, psychopathology, and problems in living. However, the dichotomy highlights the differences in method and overlooks fundamental differences in their approach to understanding personality. Later sections of this chapter will highlight some of these differences. As we shall see, the differences may be more in the philosophy of the psychologist using the tests rather than in the tests themselves.

The foregoing are only a few examples of the distortions involved in the unexamined use of the projective-objective dichotomy of tests. Furthermore, this familiar dichotomy damages the reputation of projective testing and misleads students. A more informed approach to projective testing is needed. Along those lines, we will juxtapose projective tests against self-report tests in the remainder of this chapter.

PROBLEMS WITH COMMON METAPHORS AND MODELS

Like the distinction between projective and objective tests, the common metaphors and models used to describe the projective response process can be grossly misleading. The two well-known metaphors of the projective response process are the blank screen and the X-ray machine. Each metaphor contains an implicit theoretical model of projective testing that shapes our understanding of the projective response process. In this section we critically examine both metaphors.

The Blank Screen Metaphor

The most common and stereotypic metaphor is that of the *blank screen*. In this metaphor, a projective test stimulus is portrayed as a blank screen or canvas upon which the respondent projects his or her inner world (Anastasi & Urbina, 1996). In the reductionistic application of this metaphor, response content is treated as a direct representation of the respondent's inner life. For example, when a respondent projects his or her aggression onto the stimuli, the response content contains aggressive themes as a result. The examiner then equates these aggressive themes with the personality trait of aggression. When taken to the extreme, the blank screen metaphor has had two consequences on our approach to projective tests: an overemphasis on response content and an underappreciation for the role of the projective test stimulus and the examination context. By *examination context* we mean the various situational factors as experienced by the respondent. These include the demands on the respondent given the circumstances of the evaluation, the implicit and explicit consequences of the examination, and the interaction between the examiner and respondent.

The blank screen metaphor suggests that the only necessary components to projective test stimuli are ambiguity and a lack of structure. These components are thought to facilitate response content, that is, the free expression of the respondent's internal world. The more ambiguous and unstructured the stimulus, the more it was presumed that the personality would be directly expressed in the response. Historically, this simplistic view has led to an emphasis on response content and to the interpretive viewpoint that the test was equivalent

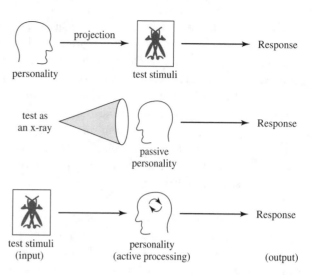

Figure 23.1   Panel A: The theoretical model of the response process as suggested by the blank screen metaphor; Panel B: The theoretical model of the response process as suggested by the X-ray metaphor; Panel C: The proposed problem-solving model of the response process.

to or symbolized an internal response or reality (Murstein, 1963). Aspects of test responses are often seen as symbolic of and equivalent to personality and constituted the basis for grand interpretations. Figure 23.1 presents a schematic for this and other models.

However, increasing the blankness (so to speak) of the screen by increasing the ambiguity of the stimuli does not necessarily produce more useful or valid information. Research into the relationship among amount of ambiguity, structure of pictorial stimuli, and test validity has not led to consistent findings (Murstein, 1961, 1963, 1965). For example, the blank TAT card produces relatively conventional responses that are less revealing of the individual than are the rest of the cards, all of which include a picture of either a person, a group of people, or some other scene. Moreover, eliminating the more recognizable and salient visual aspects of the Rorschach stimuli (what Exner, 1996, called the *critical bits*) does not lead to more productivity. In fact, the available research supports the view that the suggestive aspects of the stimulus, rather than the lack thereof, are what is important. Empirical data clearly demonstrate that the physical stimulus is crucial (Exner, 1974, 1980; Murstein, 1961; Peterson & Schilling, 1983).

What we know about Herman Rorschach's work in developing his test attests to the fact that it is not ambiguity or lack of structure that contributes to the test's usefulness. It appears that each stimulus plate was designed to contain visually recognizable forms, or critical bits, along with some arbitrary components (Exner, 1996, 2000). Rorschach may have included the arbitrary contours to interfere with the processing of these suggestive, recognizable forms. The plates were carefully chosen, drawn, and redrawn so that many versions existed before Rorschach finalized the designs. Anyone who has ever made inkblots has found that most products look simply like inkblots and are not suggestive of other forms or objects. Thus, it seems that the stimulus plates were intended to be provocative to respondents while also being just unclear enough to engage respondents' problem-solving skills. This inconsistency between the recognizable or suggestive components of the stimulus plates and the more arbitrary forms is critical because it constitutes a problem to be solved. In this sense, projective test stimuli have a clear purpose: to present the respondent with a problem-solving task. For example, a major part of the Rorschach projective task is to reconcile visual and logical inconsistencies among blot details and between the blot and the object (or objects) seen. It is the idiosyncratic ways in which respondents solve the problem, rather than merely the content they project onto a blank screen, that reveals useful and valid information. Thus, understanding projective stimuli as blank screens, rather than as problems to be solved, is a fundamental misconception about projective tests that can lead to inaccurate interpretations of test behaviors.

The X-Ray Metaphor

Another common metaphor is that of an *X-ray machine*. In this metaphor a projective test acts as an X-ray of the mind, so to speak, that allows the interpreter to observe directly the contents of the respondent's mind (see Figure 23.1). Both Frank (1939/1962) and Murray (1938) mentioned this image in their seminal work so that it has historical precedents. However, like the blank screen metaphor, the X-ray metaphor leads to a focus on response content and the way in which the content directly represents personality. More importantly, the X-ray metaphor diminishes the role of the respondent in the response process.

Examining Frank's (1939/1962) original work allows one to achieve a more adequate understanding of his purpose for using the X-ray metaphor. When Frank first used it, he compared learning about personality to the then-current technologies in medical and physical science that allowed one to study internal anatomical structures through noninvasive techniques. However, Frank included a critical distinction between projective tests and medical tools, a distinction that is typically excluded from today's common understanding of the X-ray metaphor. Frank noted that personality, unlike the target of an X-ray machine, is not a passive recipient of attention. In responding to projective test stimuli, personality does not simply cast a shadow of its nature onto a plate. Rather, Frank contended that *personality is an active organizing process.*

Despite having been written more than 60 years ago, Frank's ideas reveal a complex and informed perspective on personality, one that is especially relevant to understanding the nature of projective testing:

> Personality is approachable as a process or operation of an individual who organizes experience and reacts affectively to situations. This process is dynamic in the sense that the individual personality imposes upon the common public world of events (what we call nature), his meanings and significances, his organization and patterns, and he invests the situations thus structured with an affective meaning to which he responds idiomatically. (1939/1962, p. 34)

Frank went on to describe personality as a "dynamic organizing process." He contrasted this subjective, synthetic, dynamic process of personality to the objective, external, concrete reality of the world, including the host culture's shared conventional experiences. In Frank's view, the world of culture also influences the personality and its understanding of the external world but cannot account for personality processes and behavior.

Later in the same paper, Frank described projective techniques as essentially inducing the activity and processing of the personality:

> In similar fashion we may approach the personality and induce the individual to reveal his way of organizing experience by giving him a field (objects, materials, experiences) with relatively little structure and cultural patterning so that the personality can project upon that plastic field his way of seeing life, his meanings, significances, patterns, and especially his feelings. Thus, we elicit a projection of the individual personality's private world because he has to organize the field, interpret the material and react affectively to it. More specifically, a projection method for study of personality involves the presentation of a stimulus-situation designed or chosen because it will mean to the subject, not what the experimenter has arbitrarily decided it should mean (as in most psychological experiments using standardized stimuli in order to be "objective"), but rather whatever it must mean to the personality who gives it, or imposes it, his private, idiosyncratic meaning and organization. (1939/1962, p. 43)

These quotes make it clear that the respondent's organizational style and affect are critical to the projective testing process, and that the process involves more than simply adding content to a stimulus field. Moreover, unlike self-report tests, projective test stimuli give respondents an opportunity to express their organizational styles and affect. Thus, a projective test allows the examiner to observe personality in action with cognitive, affective, interpersonal, and meaning-making activities.

The Need for an Informed Conceptual Framework

This critical review of traditional metaphors and models for projective testing points to their serious shortcomings and oversimplifications. In contrast to a blank screen, projective stimuli are more like problem-solving tasks. In contrast to a passive personality that unknowingly projects itself onto a blank screen or that is examined with X-ray vision, personality in projective testing is seen as a much more active, organizing, and selective process. Perhaps the most accurate portrayal of projection is that the personality does not project light onto the blank screen of the test, but rather, the test projects itself through the active organizing process of the personality to the response. In other words, the individual's personal characteristics are observable in the refracted light—that is, the manner in which the person responds to the test. In sum, there is a need for a broader and more informed conceptual framework for understanding projective testing.

From comparisons between the overt stimuli and response, the interpreter infers the covert personality process. This input-processing-output sequence is the essence of our model for projective testing and is presented in the next section. Such a framework goes beyond projection and response content by embracing a problem-solving perspective.

THE BEHAVIORAL RESPONSE PROCESS MODEL

A *problem-solving model* leads us to approach personality as a processor of information. Rather than interpreting a response as a symbolic representation of personality, we interpret it in the context of the stimulus situation and used that interpretation to build a model of the respondent's processing and problem-solving styles. Rather than using a static conceptualization of *personality,* our understanding incorporates a model of personality as a problem-solving processor of life's ongoing challenges.

The projective test response can be seen as the development and formulation of a solution to a problem, the structure and content of which reveals something about the individual. Every projective test involves a task, which we can understand as a problem to be solved. For example, the TAT demands the creation of a story that reconciles the suggestive elements of the pictures with ambiguous and missing cues. As another example, the early memory test involves constructing, typically without a complete sense of certainty, a memory dating back to the beginning of one's life. The self-expressive quality and the adequacy of these solutions can be the object of the interpretive system (e.g., for the TAT, see Ronan, Colavito, & Hammontree, 1993).

The history of projective testing and misuses in current practice reveal that we have drifted from the focus on input-processing-output as first described by Frank (1939/1962). This drift has led to two gross oversimplifications of projective testing: (a) Projective test responses are inappropriately equated with personality, and (b) verbal and motor behaviors within projective test responses are thought to symbolize large patterns of life behavior. In contrast, an informed response process approach entails inferring a model of an individual's personality and behavior from projective test output based on a thorough understanding of the stimuli, task demands, and processing involved. The future of projective assessment depends on advancing this response process and problem-solving approach.

The *Standards for Educational and Psychological Tests* (American Educational Research Association, American Psychological Association [APA], & National Council on Measurement in Education, 1999) incorporate this interest in the response process. According to the standards, evidence based on examination of the response process, including eye movements and self-descriptions of the respondent's experience, should be used to validate tests inferences. Response process research is extremely valuable as a basis for clinical inference (e.g., Exner, Armbruster, & Mittman, 1978). The response characteristics of each commonly used projective test should be researched and delineated. Each projective test differs in its response process so that each test must be addressed and mastered separately, even if these tests share some common processes and principles.

Self-Expressive and Organizational Components

Within the response process in projective testing, two components have traditionally been identified: (a) a *content* or *self-expressive* component and (b) a *formal* or *organizational* component. Often these components are referred to as the *projective and problem-solving components* of projective tests, but these terms are subject to misinterpretation. This chapter refers to them as the *self-expressive and organizational components* of projective testing.

To oversimplify, the *self-expressive* component largely involves content features of the response—that is, what the subject says, writes, or draws and what associations the individual brings to the task. Self-expression occurs because projective stimuli provoke the imagination, acting as a stimulus to fantasy (Exner & Weiner, 1995; Goldfried, Sticker, & Weiner, 1971). Thus, respondents react to content suggestions in a task (a sentence stem, a picture, or a recognizable form or critical bit of a Rorschach plate) and rely on themselves to go beyond that content to access and express information from their own stores of images, experiences, feelings, and thoughts.

In contrast, the *organizational* component involves the formal or structural features of the response: how the individual answers the questions, solves the task, structures the response, and makes decisions. For example, the organizational component includes how the stimulus details are incorporated into TAT or Rorschach responses and whether the stimulus features are accurately perceived. Use of detail and the accuracy of the response are organizational features, which can be applied to almost all projective tests. Projective tests all pose problems to solve; the adequacy, style, and structure of the solutions to the problems are encompassed by the organizational component.

The common oversimplification in conceptualizing projective testing is to limit the scope of projective testing to the self-expressive component. Doing so leads one to interpret only response content themes. Even if the organizational component of a projective test is recognized, it is often conceptualized as separate from the content component.

We believe that separating the self-expressive and organizational components is another misconception that should be corrected. If one examines the projective test respondent's real-time processing while solving the task and developing a response, one observes that self-expressive and organizational aspects are simultaneous and interconnected. One solves the problem not only by organizing the input and the output, but also by selecting one's own self-expression to add to the response. From another perspective, including self-expression is not merely a projection of a trait, need, or perception. Thus, we are making an important distinction here: *Problem-solving within projective tests encompasses both content and formal, and both self-expressive and organizational, facets.* What are conventionally considered projective or content/self-expressive components are actually best understood as part of a single problem-solving process. Thus, the respondent's way of problem-solving may involve, for example, invoking dependent themes. A respondent's adding in certain thematic interpretations, motives, interests, or fantasies to projective test responses thus is part of the problem-solving component of these tests.

Moreover, there may be individual differences, both within an assessment and in one's everyday life, in terms of how much content is projected. Some people may project more personalized content than others. Others who express less personalized content might be characterized as stereotyped, overtly conventional (Schafer, 1954), or, alternatively, as efficient and economical (Exner, 1993). We will elaborate this problem-solving process as the centerpiece of this chapter. We

rely on information-processing and behavioral approaches in specifying its subcomponents.

The Projective Test Stimulus Situation

In our view, the projective-testing stimulus encompasses a complex of factors. The stimulus in a projective test is more than the concrete stimulus itself, that is, more than merely a picture, a sentence stem, a Rorschach plate, or an invitation to remember. Masling's (1960) work with the Rorschach and a variety of studies with the TAT (Murstein, 1961, 1963) reveal that situational, contextual, and interpersonal stimuli influence the response process. Extrapolating from these findings, we propose that the actual stimulus for a projective test is the entire situation, or what we call the *stimulus situation*. Rather than merely being concrete stimuli, the stimulus situation encompasses the interpersonal interaction with the examiner, what the respondent is asked to do with the stimulus, and contextual issues such as the reason for referral. For example, the TAT stimulus situation involves the fact that the respondent is being called on to tell a story to reveal something about him- or herself in front of another person, typically a stranger with some authority and power, about whom the respondent knows very little. Accordingly, when the stimulus is administered individually there is also a strong interpersonal component to the stimulus situation. Furthermore, this interpersonal component is implicit in paper-and-pencil projective tests. It is also present in self-report tests of personality, although it is often ignored.

A critical component of the stimulus situation is the respondent's awareness of the obvious potential for the response to reveal something of him- or herself. Reactions to the pressure to self-disclose are invoked by the stimulus situation. Accordingly, response sets, defensiveness, expression of social desirability, and response manipulation are fundamental to the response process. As will be addressed later, these are more than impediments or moderators of test validity.

Processing the Stimulus Situation

Taking all of these issues into consideration suggests that the respondent reacts to an overall situation, including both concrete and experiential components, as a *pattern* or *field*. Such patterning is a well-known fact in the study of human perception. The respondent organizes that field into *figure* and *ground*, responding more distinctly to the figural components of the stimulus situation. This figure-ground patterning exists not only within the processing of the concrete projective test stimulus, but also with the entire stimulus situation. Accurate interpretation depends on considering the concrete stimuli element in terms of, for example, Rorschach card pull, sentence-stem characteristics, and salient stimuli components for individual cards from storytelling tasks (Exner, 1996, 2000; Murstein, 1961, 1963; Watson, 1978). These prominent, recognizable aspects of the concrete stimulus elicit common or popular responses. Peterson and Schilling (1983) have written an informative, conceptual article that frames these issues for the Rorschach. Knowing the test and its input, processing, and output characteristics provide a context within which to understand the implications of responses for personality. Standardization data and empirical descriptions, the examiner's experience with the stimulus situation, recognition of the response pull for individual test stimuli, and knowledge of conventional and common responses all contribute to optimally valid interpretation.

The Free-Response Format

Freedom in the Stimulus Situation

Freedom and lack of direction are crucial characteristics of the projective test stimulus situation. The individualistic idiographic feature of the projective test response process starts with the individual differences in the perception of the stimulus situation (Colligan & Exner, 1985; Exner, 1980; Perry, Felger, & Braff, 1998). The individual can choose to attend to different components of the stimulus situation, focusing on, for example, a particular element of the physical stimulus, a demand within the task, or some interpersonal aspect related to the task. The individual may offer an overall gestalt, or may focus on a single element or on inconsistencies between stimulus subcomponents. Accordingly, self-regulation through stimulus control can be assessed through projective testing, in terms of what an individual attributes to a stimulus, when one identifies what the individual responds to in the stimulus situation.

Another important, related feature of the processing of the stimulus situation is decision making. For example, respondents must decide what to reveal or focus on within the story, image, early memory, or sentence completion item. Decision making also requires reconciling contradicting elements and completing unfinished information. The projective test stimulus situation does not provide much information to assist the respondent in evaluating the appropriateness and adequacy of a response. In contrast to ability tests, there are no obvious right answers. The lack of information in the stimulus situation interacts with the free-response format to impede attempts at self-evaluation of the appropriateness of the response. Thus, decision making and processing in the face of minimal external

guidance with concomitant insecurity is also a major component of the response process and projective test task. In other words, coping with insecurity and uncertainty without sufficient information about the adequacy of one's response is part of the response process.

Response Characteristics

With self-report tests, the *interpretive dimensions* (e.g., depression for Scale 2 of the MMPI) are predetermined. In contrast with projective tests, interpretive dimensions are implicit in the test behavior. The interpreter observes the respondent's behavioral patterns in order to construct the dimensions to be described. For example, implicit motives organize pictures into stories (McClelland, Koestner, & Weinberger, 1989), and the interpreter describes these dimensions within the interpretation. As noted earlier in this chapter, a crucial aspect of the projective test stimulus situation is the lack of information regarding the adequacy of the response. As suggested by Campbell, projective tests are "typically open-ended, free, unstructured, and have the virtue of allowing the respondent to project his own organization on the material" (1957, p. 208). In other words, it is the respondent who accounts for a great majority of the variation in the test responses in terms of their self-expressive and organizational components (Viglione & Perry, 1991). The fact that the response is wholly formed and created by the respondent has been referred to by Beck (1960) as the gold of the Rorschach.

Compared to self-report tests, the fixed test stimuli in self-report tests and limited response options themselves account for a much greater part of the variation among test responses or behaviors. Test developers predetermine structured test behaviors and, as a result, limit the freedom of response. In other words, there is much less variation in *true* versus *false* than there is in TAT responses or earlier memories. Historically, this fixed item and response format was typical of the personality and attitude measurement devices that dominated during the mental testing period from 1920 to 1935, and against which projective testers rebelled. On the other hand, free responses are not essential for a test to be projective because multiple-choice or rating-scale response formats have been used (Campbell, 1957). Nevertheless, the dominant projective tests in clinical practice use a free-response format. Multiple-choice and rating-scale formats have been primarily used for research on test validity and the response process (e.g., Exner et al., 1978).

Within the free-response format the respondent creates or organizes a response and expresses him- or herself through the content of the response. The response content is neither preselected nor prestructured by the test developer, but is an expression of the given individual in the context of the exam. In an article introducing a conceptual model for psychopathology and the Rorschach, Viglione and Perry (1991) couched this in terms of the limited environmental influence on Rorschach responses. This argument can be extended, in some degree, to all projective testing. As described in this article, projective test behaviors are largely influenced by the internal world rather than by the test environment and stimuli. The content, structure, and adequacy (and the evaluation of that adequacy) of the response come from the individual. The interpretive system accompanying the projective test is an aid in directly learning about the individual through analyzing the self-expressive and organizational aspects of these behavioral productions.

The free-response format maximizes the expression of individual variance. The population of possible answers is unbounded in free-response tasks, so that the response itself can capture much more individual variation than can an item in a self-report personality test. In this way projective tests maximize salience and relevance of the response to the individual, a characteristic that has been referred to as the *idiographic focus* of projective testing. Indeed, the complexity and variety of these responses have made it difficult to create comprehensive scoring systems. From a psychometric perspective, this complexity and variety may translate to less reliability and more interpreter bias but, nevertheless, more validity.

Interpretive Implications

What has been called *expressive style* is an example of the organizational component of a projective test response (Bellak, 1944). The free-response component of the projective test stimulus situation allows expressive style to emerge. It can be characterized by the following questions: "Does he talk very fast or stammer badly? Is he verbose or terse? Does he respond quickly or slowly . . ." (Murstein, 1963, p. 3). Expressive style is also captured in nonverbal ways, which are important to understanding an individual's functioning and interpersonal relationships. Does the respondent use space in drawing and sentence completion blanks neatly? Is the respondent overly concerned with wasting space and time, or sure to involve elaborated and elegant use of symbolic flair in his or her presentations? Indeed, the nonverbal mode of functioning and being in the world is accessed by the projective tests. In support of this importance of nonverbal functioning, neuropsychological research would suggest that aspects of interpersonal and emotional functioning are differentially related to visual-spatial, kinesthetic, and tactile modes in comparison to verbal modes. Future research might attempt to investigate the relative contributions of expressive style and nonverbal modes to validity and utility.

The multimodal characteristic of the projective test response greatly multiplies its informational value. For example, a behavioral observation of (a) tearfulness at a particular point in an early memory procedure, (b) a man's self-critical humor during a TAT response that describes stereotypic male behavior, (c) fits and starts in telling a story with sexual content, (d) a seemingly sadistic chuckle with "a pelt, it's road kill" Rorschach response, (e) rubbing a Rorschach plate to produce a response, or (f) a lack of positive, playful affect throughout an early memory testing are all critical empirical data subject to interpretation. Such test behaviors can lead to important hypotheses and allow one to synthesize various components of the test results by placing them in the context of the individual's life. These insights are not readily available or subject to systematic observation through other means in an assessment session. These are examples of the fundamental purpose of projective tests: to gather an otherwise unavailable sample of behavior to illuminate referral issues and questions emerging during the exam.

In addition, projective tests allow a rare opportunity to observe idiographic issues interacting with the instrumental dimension of behavior. Levy (1963) defined the *instrumental dimension of behavior* as the adequacy or effectiveness of the response in reaching some goal. In cognitive ability testing this dimension could be simplified to whether a response is right or wrong. Like respondents on ability, cognitive, or neuropsychological tests, projective test respondents perform a task. To varying degrees, all projective test responses can be evaluated along a number of instrumental dimensions including accuracy, synthesis, meaningfulness, relevance, consistency, conciseness, and communicability. For example, the instrumental dimension relates to the quality, organization, and understandability of a TAT story or early memory as explained to the examiner. In ability tests, we concern ourselves mostly with the adequacy of the respondent's outcome, answer, or product. In contrast, in projective tests we are concerned with not only the adequacy of the outcome, but also the process and behavior involved in producing the outcome. In our nomenclature, projective tests allow one to observe the interaction between the self-expressive and instrumental components of behavior—in other words, how adequate a response is in light of how one solves a problem. Extending this interaction, projective test behavior also allows the examiner to observe the impact of emotional and interpersonal pressures on the adequacy and approach to solving problems. This is a crucial contribution of projective tests to assessment, providing an interpretive link between findings from self-report tests and ability tests.

A Behavioral Approach to Validity

Behavioral Characteristics

Problem solving in projective testing entails a behavioral view of the response process. This behavioral approach is consistent with Anastasi and Urbina's definition of *psychological tests* as "essentially objective and standardized measure of a sample of behavior" (1996, p. 23). Psychological tests are undertaken when we cannot directly access behaviors important to assessment goals (Levy, 1963; Meehl, 1945/1980). In performance tests we induce and observe a sample of behavior that is similar to the behaviors of interest in real life. In this respect, projective tests are performance tests.

Projective tests are attempts to bring aspects of relevant behavior, associations, perceptions, organizations, and effective and interpersonal components into the consulting room to be observed. Such a tactic is eloquently describe by Levy (1963):

> We will be better able to predict this person's behavior in a given situation if we can bring a different frame of reference into play. We feel that in order to do this we will have to draw a different sample of behavior from that available to us now. Specifically, we want a sample of behavior that is amenable to description in our frame of reference, one that was designed with our particular language system in mind. (pp. 6–7)

Thus, projective tests induce a behavioral sample that we can observe and explore so as to synthesize a more valid picture of the life predicament of the respondent. From this behavioral perspective, a test response or behavior is not a chance event, but a behavior sample collected under controlled conditions, subject to behavioral laws.

In the earlier section on free-response format, we established that *variety* is a hallmark of projective test responses. They are also distinguished by their *richness*. The overall complexity of the stimulus situation elicits rich responses. Complex stimulus situations produce complex real-life, in vivo behaviors, which generalize to complex nontest behaviors in complete situations (Viglione, 1999). By design in projective tests, meaningful behavior is mediated by personality processes and invoked by the stimulus situation.

One might elucidate these ideas by contrasting projective and self-report testing. The test behavior involved in self-report personality tests differs greatly from projective test behavior in terms of richness and variety. Typically, self-report test behavior is merely an endorsement of *true* or *false,* or a rating of an opinion or sentiment along some dimension. The variety and richness of projective test responses allow the potential for generalizability to meaningful and salient real-life

behavior. In contrast, for example, within self-report testing there is no inherent similarity between (a) the act of responding *true* to aggressive risk items and (b) real-life aggressive risk.

Generalizability and Interpretation

In interpreting projective tests we observe test behavior and then generalize it to similar behavior in other situations. When considering a projective test as a behavioral problem-solving task, the question of validity; according to Foster and Cone (1995), is one of topographic similarity and functional equivalency. *Topographic similarity* refers to the degree to which the test behavior resembles the nontest behavior in concrete, physical, and descriptive terms. *Functional equivalence* refers to the degree to which the antecedents and consequences of a test behavior correspond to the antecedent and consequences of real-life behavior. Topographically, an aggressive attribution on a TAT response is similar to an aggressive attribution in real life.

To understand topographical similarity within projective tests, one must examine the behavior induced by projective test demands. Projective tests incorporate complex stimulus situations and induce rich and complex behaviors that vary greatly from person to person. Projective test behaviors, such as explaining what one sees and how one sees it (i.e., Rorschach; Viglione, 1999), creating a story to understand a suggestive interaction (TAT), recalling and explaining a personally salient memory (early memories), and interpreting or finishing a fragment of a sentence (sentence completion), are all topographically similar to important and familiar life tasks. They are all aspects of what one frequently does in real life—expressions of one's "way of seeing and feeling and reacting to life, i.e. personality" (Frank, 1939/1962). For example, it would not take much empirical support to justify the generalization of thought-disordered communication on the Rorschach or TAT to thought-disordered behavior in other contexts. The test behavior and target or in vivo behaviors are topographically and experientially quite similar and thus behaviorally equivalent. It is not surprising, then, that there is a great amount of empirical support for thought-disorder indices on the Rorschach (Acklin, 1999; Holzman et al., 1974; Kleiger, 1999; Perry & Braff, 1994; Perry, Geyer, & Braff, 1999; Perry, Viglione, & Braff, 1992; Viglione, 1999; Weiner, 1966).

Projective tests collect standardized samples of real-life behavior—the problem-solving of the personality operations in real life. This view of personality would incorporate thought organization and disorder as the problem-solving of the personality manifest in behavior. Moreover, the behavioral population of interest for projective tests is real-life behavior, just as the population for performance tests is the expression of abilities. On the other hand, more symbolic interpretations (e.g., using Rorschach color responses as a symbol of emotionality) lack topographical and experiential similarity. Accordingly, symbolic interpretations, as with self-report test findings, require much more empirical support.

In considering topographical similarity and generalizability, one must also consider the examination context and the stimulus situation. In this context, projective test activities, such as a child's ripping apart stimulus materials or an felon's expressing obvious pleasure in describing malevolent acts, are exceptional behaviors. Such behaviors that (a) oppose the social demands of the projective test interpersonal context and (b) possess obvious clinical implications may be understood as corresponding to salient nontest behaviors of interest. They are very low-probability events that are much more likely to spring from the individual rather than from situational factors. Thus, they are generalizable events, even if infrequent.

Experiential Interpretation

In projective testing we extend the behavioral notion of topographic similarity to incorporate *experiential* elements. These include subjective and covert problem-solving elements such as self-expressive and internal phenomena associated with the response process. Schachtel (1966) with the Rorschach, and Riethmiller and Handler (1997) with the figure drawing, demonstrated the value of this approach. For the Rorschach, it would mean asking what processes are involved in avoiding the complexity and contradictions of a blot so as to give simplistic, uninvolved answers. For the figure drawing, the *experience-near approach* would take into consideration not only the product (i.e., the drawing), but also the process of creating it. Experiential interpretation of a figure drawing might also require such questions as, "What experiences or covert processes might accompany drawing this frightening person? What would it be like to meet or have a conversation with this frightening person?" Answers to these questions are more likely to have nontest referents than are the nonexperiential, detail-oriented questions that have dominated some approaches to drawings (e.g., "How long are the arms? Are the hands represented? Did the respondent mention the head? Was shading involved?"). Answers to experience-near questions are the real behavioral patterns to be generalized from projective tests to real-life behavior. Given this stimulus situation, identifying experience-near components involves being in an interpersonal relationship with the respondent and empathizing with the respondent's

process and experience (Riethmiller & Handler). As research has demonstrated, this interpersonal component is a strength of projective tests given that it is an essential ingredient of the stimulus situation (Stricker & Healy, 1990).

Examining the three-dimensional *vista response* on the Rorschach might elucidate the experiential and contextual components of interpretation. These three-dimensional, shading responses might mean very different things in different contexts. From an experiential problem-solving perspective, the vista response involves a more precise way of dealing with the blots in which one experiences the self as stepping back and evaluating. Within the context of an inpatient's depression, such an activity might generalize to negative evaluation of the self, others, and the future that compromises adaptation. In the case of a passive but largely successful executive in a nonclinical examination, the vista response may be related to an analytic, evaluative ability to step back and gain perspective, and an ability to evaluate the self. Under stress, this capacity may be associated with self-criticism that, although painful, may lead to adjustments and improved functioning. In the context of an assessment of an incarcerated murderer, the vista responses may generalize to situationally induced self-criticism, possible guilt, or alternatively, an analytic approach to crime. Accordingly, test behaviors that are identical along overt, topographical parameters may correspond to different covert experience and in vivo behaviors. These distinctions, in turn, are based on the context of the exam and base-rate factors. Research on psychological assessment and on clinical judgment and decision theory has not addressed these ecologically valid interpretive inferences.

Functional Equivalence and Generalization

This interaction among interpretation, examination contexts, and topographical and experiential phenomena relates to functional equivalence and generalization. As noted earlier, *functional equivalence* refers to the degree to which the antecedents and consequences of a test behavior correspond to the antecedents and consequences of real-life behavior. The antecedents and consequences of test behaviors are encompassed by the projective stimulus situation. Projective stimulus situations or test environments vary to some extent from test to test and occasion to occasion. However, from the broadest and most inclusive point of view, projective tests involve new and unfamiliar situations in which one organizes incomplete, contradictory, and ambiguous material without any direct feedback from observers or authorities. They also involve little implicit feedback from the task about adequacy of performance within an interaction with another individual. Applying the principle of functional equivalence, we are safest when we generalize projective test behaviors to situations with similar characteristics. Thus, to some degree, interpretations may be context dependent rather than pervasive. Test interpretation may apply to situations with more individual control and less environmental control. More colloquially, these are situations in which the respondent has to make his or her own way and fend for him- or herself.

Functional equivalence helps us to interpret the contradictory information so often produced during assessment. Let us say that we observe evidence of depression and distortion of incoming information in a seemingly content, psychologically healthy individual. With such an individual, these data are likely to be related to circumscribed rather than pervasive problems. Functional equivalence and the projective test stimulus situation guide the interpretation and generalization of these test behaviors. With a healthy individual, one could safely attribute the depression and distortion to his or her occasional vulnerability to self-doubt, mistakes in judgment, or distress in new and unfamiliar situations. Alternatively, such negative information might be used to describe worst-case scenarios or self-defeating patterns or potentials. In the context of an exam with a psychiatric inpatient, these same data would suggest much more pervasive difficulties. Thus, the stimulus situation and functional equivalency guide the generalization and interpretation of projective test behaviors along a situation-specific (vs. pervasive) dimension. As interpretation becomes more specific, it should be confined to situations that more closely resemble the projective test stimulus situation.

Conclusion

In any event, the current approach to projective testing needs to adopt this experience-near perspective to identify problem-solving correlates of test behaviors. In addition, interpreters and researchers must recognize that these test behaviors have different implications in different situations. Technically, this approach can use differential base rates, conditional probabilities, statistical interactions, or moderator variables to investigate this phenomenon. Thus, the problem-solving approach to projective testing challenges the notion that test behaviors are always generalizable to personality at large. This may be true much of the time, but the nature of behavior and contextual factors influence the pervasiveness and situational specificity of generalizations. Current, dominant interpretations (e.g., those with the Rorschach Comprehensive System) often are based on research and formulations with clinically compromised individuals. Accordingly, many of these interpretations overemphasize the more pathological or problematic correlates of the test behavior. This fact probably contributes

to the error of overly negative interpretations of projective tests related to the neglect of base rates (Finn & Kamphuis, 1995; Murstein & Mathes, 1996; Viglione & Hilsenroth, in press).

INTERPRETIVE AND CONCEPTUAL ISSUES

This chapter highlights important characteristics of the projective stimulus situation and the integration of organizational and self-expressive components in the response process. In turn, these factors induce characteristic patterns and methods of interpretation. Projective test responses emphasize synthetic and individualistic approaches to interpretation (Rabin, 1981). In practice, those psychologists who are more inclined to emphasize the complexities of the individual are probably more inclined to use projective tests. The section on free-response format outlined the individual or idiographic component of projective test responses. This characteristic of the projective test data induces a similar focus on individual or idiographic approaches to interpretation.

Synthetic, Configurational Interpretation

As established in discussing the projective test stimulus situation and the response process, projective testing accesses multiple dimensions and allows one to elaborate on hypotheses derived earlier in the interpretive process. These factors induce the interpreter to adopt a synthetic or configurational approach in formulating interpretations (Stricker & Gold, 1999). Projective test data present connections and associations among various characteristics from different domains. In the TAT, for example, we can associate a cognitive slip or a problem-solving failure with the sexual or intimate themes stimulated by a particular card when such themes are mentioned in (but not meaningfully integrated into) a jumbled and unrealistic story. In terms used earlier in this chapter, projective test results bridge self-expressive, organizational, and response-set domains. One score or response parameter is analyzed in its relationship to another or in relationship to moderator variables and collateral, nontest variables. Temporal, spatial, and language factors—that is, when and how behaviors occur—allow interpreters to identify how various content and organizational aspects of an individual work together, how they interrelate, and how they may interact with different environmental conditions. Advocates of projective testing are not interested in isolated bits of behavior but study how it comes together in a whole person within a life predicament (Stricker & Gold; Viglione, 1999; Viglione & Perry, 1991; Weiner, 1999; Weiner, in press.) Projective test data assist us in putting the person in his or her life context and help us to understand the relationship between internal issues and the individual's biography and background. Murstein (1963) called this "configurational dominance" (p. 4). This synthetic or configurational approach can be attributed to Gestalt psychology, field theory, and psychodynamic influences on projective testing (Frank, 1939/1962).

Among the connections made possible by projective tests are those between personality factors and cognitive functions. Looking at projective tasks as problems to be solved allows the integration of nonintellectual with intellectual issues. From a configurational point of view, the relationships of abilities to affects, interests, motivations, and discriminative stimuli are addressed. A related advantage of projective tests is that they allow the examiner to make inferences about motivation. Other performance tests (i.e., ability tests) assume and attempt to induce optimal motivation. In real life, however, motivational variation is crucial to understanding personality and behavior.

We can conclude then that part of the utility of projective assessment—or in more concrete terms, its added value relative to self-report tests—is that it provides meaningful connections among different characteristics to enable an understanding of the whole person. Because the individual respondent produces the constructs and their interrelationships with the responses to the projective test in the free-response format, we know that the configurational information is relevant and possibly unique to the individual being assessed.

In synthesizing the picture of the individual from a projective-testing perspective, one constructs or builds an integrated picture of the person within a situation. Extrapolating from Kaufman's work on *Intelligent Testing with the WISC-R* (1979), each construction, each person's theory, is different in terms of concepts and relationships among concepts. Reflecting this uniqueness of each individual, projective testing can produce a different theory for each respondent. Along these lines, an important phenomenon is that projective testing often reveals remarkable aspects or concerns that become important hallmarks or organizing features in understanding an individual. Accordingly, assessment-report writers often excerpt quotes from sentence-completion responses or responses from other tests to communicate vividly the respondent's experience in the respondent's own words (Holaday, Smith, & Sherry, 2000). Invariably, this synthetic and constructive approach leads to discovering contradictions among test data. Resolving these contradictions often provides added insight into the individual. Recognition of contradictions (e.g., depressed but overly impressed with the self) is based on nomothetic notions. In other words, we see depression and self-importance as being contradictory

when we conceive of them as abstract concepts. Within a single individual, these characteristics need not be contradictory. We find that real people appear to possess both overly negative and overly positive views of the self. Positive views may ward off negative views. Positive views may arise in one situation but not another; among children, for example, positive views may arise in academic situations but not at home. It follows then that the inevitable contradictions among projective test data induce, if not necessitate, a dynamic view of individuals. This dynamic view entails opposing forces operating in the behavior, affect, motivation, and cognition in a way that reflects the opposing excitatory and inhibitory organization of the nervous system.

Psychological Testing, Not Psychological Tests

As suggested by the early leaders in assessment (Frank, 1939/1962; Meehl, 1945/1980), the difference between projective and so-called objective tests is not so much in the tests themselves but in the interpretive approach. This difference in approach is induced by the data—by their complexity and richness and their relevance to the individual. Projective tests induce an individualistic, synthetic and configurational, and constructive approach to interpretation that incorporates a view of the individual as embodying contradictions that might be explained dynamically. This approach also involves affects and interpersonal issues. In turn, those holding such a view of interpretation are probably more inclined to use projective tests. The interpreter is involved directly in the assessment administration process, because the individualistic and configurational issues are best known and explored by an active interpreter in a relationship with the respondent. In summary, one's preference for projective tests may largely reflect a philosophical approach to human nature so that it may be more appropriate to talk about projective testing rather than projective tests.

Self-Disclosure and Response Sets

"It would be very unsafe, unwise, and incorrect to assume that a patient either can or wants to present all aspects of his or her personality fully to the examiner" (W. G. Klopfer, 1981, p. 259). Indeed, this is a central problem that clinicians have struggled with in the practice of assessment over the years. Surveys on assessment practice have not explored the extent to which this unsafe assumption is made implicit in the interpretation of self-report personality tests. In the early part of the twentieth century, projective testing grew out of the practical need to access what the individual may be unwilling or unable to communicate directly (Frank, 1939/1962; Murray, 1938;

Murstein, 1961). This is the fundamental challenge or paradox in assessment: What is most important to know is often what the person is least willing or able to divulge. To uncover what the respondent may be unwilling or unable to divulge, projective tests go about the task of accessing behavior and problem solving indirectly. Task instructions (e.g., "Tell a story," "Explain what this might be," "Complete the sentence") distract the respondent from the interpretive goals of the examination. Projective tests are attempts to access the private world of the individual, to get to it more efficiently than through other means (Frank, 1939/1962; Viglione & Hilsenroth, in press; Viglione & Perry, 1991).

The reactions to pressures to self-disclose in an indirect stimulus situation are not captured neatly within individual scales on any test. Operating in every individual, idiosyncratically, is a conflict between pressures for self-disclosure versus those for self-protection. This conflict involves (a) a willingness and an ability to be self-revealing versus (b) rational and irrational concerns about negative consequence to self-disclosure, accompanied by (c) a motivation to create a favorable impression. Examination of the nuances of self-revealing behaviors and attitudes to testing in the context of the relationship with the examiner allows us to examine this *struggle over self-disclosure.*

The examiner's strict adherence to his or her own training and to test administration principles, along with careful observation of the respondent and of the respondent's own self-observations, are necessary to manage and observe the respondent's struggle over self-disclosure. For example, in constructing the Rorschach Comprehensive System and in its most recent modification, Exner has gone to great lengths to minimize and to systematize examiner and contextual influences (Exner, 1974, 1993; Exner et al., 2001). Moreover, being sensitive to and evaluating these influences can help one assess their impact on the test findings and inferences (Schafer, 1954). However, the influence of conflicts about self-disclosure and response sets cannot be eliminated. Projective tests offer an opportunity to observe, identify, and characterize these conflicts as a part of the ongoing interaction between the personality and the stimulus situation.

Interpretive Implications of the Pressure to Self-Disclose

The pressure to self-disclose within the projective test stimulus situation leads to a number of interpretive issues. Accordingly, studying and characterizing the response style of the individual is a crucial interpretive goal in all assessment. Response set is an important and complex moderator variable that should be scrutinized in each assessment through observation and analysis of all test data and collateral information. Test findings

should be interpreted differently as a function or response set so that the response set acts as a moderator variable for interpretive purposes and validity (Meyer, 1999).

More explicitly, within the interpretive process, results from projective testing can be characterized along the dimension of self-protection versus self-disclosure. Stereotypic, brief test protocols, or poorly or quickly executed productions with insufficient effort (e.g., in drawings) can be seen as attempts to suppress or resist pressure from the examiner to reveal the self. Thus, some test findings may have more to do with how the respondent protects him- or herself or suppresses, defends against, or avoids self-disclosure. Looking at these efforts as a moderator variable, such self-protective test protocols may lead to an underestimate of personality tendencies and weaknesses and to false-negative findings. From a behavioral perspective, this response set can be seen as an attempt to suppress or defend against self-disclosure. In such cases, the test findings do not survey the full array of personality processes and features, so that they may not reveal the personality as a whole. Moreover, these self-protective or suppressive response sets can result in inconsistencies among projective test data, self-report findings, and collateral information (Meyer, 1999).

On the other hand, longer, complex test responses may represent an effort to self-disclose or to express or engage fully in the examination. Such records survey the personality more fully. Alternatively, some overly long and involved test records may represent an effort to present the self in a positive light by demonstrating to the examiner one's talents and problem-solving skills (Viglione, 1996). Nevertheless, too much productivity on any projective test may be associated with overestimation of pathology and false-positive results (Meyer, 1993; Murstein & Mathes, 1996).

It has been well established that response sets vary along this *self-protection/self-disclosure* or *suppressive-expressive* continuum, and that this continuum acts as an important moderator variable in assessment interpretation. Self-report instruments such as the MMPI and the Personality Assessment Inventory (PAI) contain response-set measures such as validity scales and moderator variables. These scales are most useful in measuring the quantitative dimensions of response set. Projective test data are instrumental in individualizing and identifying nuances and complexities in that response set. For example, sentence-completion methods illuminate individual styles, worries, motives, and interests in presenting one's self in an overly positive or negative manner. In that sense, projective testing adds content to what we might learn from the validity scales of an MMPI.

Response sets have implications beyond the interpretation of a given test protocol. Attitudes toward self-disclosure/

544 Assessing Personality and Psychopathology with Projective Methods

self-protection are fundamental issues in any change process, be it within a clinical, forensic, or organizational setting. Accordingly, the respondent's engagement in testing has implications for motivation to self-disclose in response to interventions in the real world. Similar issues emerge in assessment of the risk of dangerousness. In these contexts, respondents' attitudes toward assessment may also resemble attitudes toward cooperation with management of their risk. Accordingly, these attitudes as a component of the response set are critical assessment targets, and need to be observed closely in assessments. Response set is important, not only as a mediator and discriminative stimulus for test validity, but as a target of assessment in and of itself.

Extreme response sets sometimes emerge as malingering and feigned presentations. For respondents to projective tests, adopting such a response set is quite challenging because of the complexity of the stimulus situation, the active role of the examiner, and the freedom allowed within the test responses. In general, malingering or faking successfully may be more difficult to achieve in projective testing than in self-report testing. A study by Shedler, Mayman, and Manis (1993) reveals that in self-report a substantial portion of respondents may incorporate this false-positive bias in their response styles so as to obscure these tests' sensitivity to problems. These data suggest that projective tests may more accurately describe these individuals' functioning. As for individual tests, research suggests that in some respects Rorschach is more resistant than self-report to response manipulation (Bornstein, Rossner, Hill, & Stepanian 1994; Viglione, 1999).

Nevertheless, the broad claim that the respondent has no control over the content of projective tests is a myth that does not withstand logical and empirical scrutiny. Accumulated research on faking and experimentally induced response sets suggests that a respondent can control content to some extent on many projective tests, including the Rorschach. For example, aggression and sexual content themes, but not dependent and many other themes, are routinely subject to considerable control (Exner, 1993; Viglione, 1999). On the TAT many themes are relatively easily controlled (Holmes, 1974; Murstein, 1961).

Test or Method?

Another long-standing controversy concerns whether projective instruments are actually tests or merely methods or techniques. A *psychological test* can be defined as a standardized administration with an interpretive system that is quantified and subjected to scientific validation. In contrast, a *method* is defined as a systematic way of collecting behavioral observations. Both a test and a method may produce valid interpretations. Within a method, the techniques and strategies of

interpretation, rather than quantities produced by scales, would be subject to scientific verification. An example of the use of a projective instrument as a method would be the recognition that completing the sentence stem "I was bothered by" with the written phrase "the way you looked at me when I was putting the blocks together" may have special interpretive significance for the interpretation of Block Design and interpersonal performances. Asking a respondent what he or she had in mind when endorsing "I have two personalities inside of me" would be an example of using a self-report test as a method. Thus, both self-report and projective instruments could be used as methods. In fact, one might argue that using either of them as a method enhances interpretation.

The Method Argument

These issues have been addressed in the literature. For example, Weiner (1994) published an article on the Rorschach that restimulated considerable controversy about its status as a test versus a method. He suggested that the Rorschach was foremost a method because the instrument is a means of collecting information about how people structure their experiences, express themselves, and interact affectively and interpersonally. It could not be reduced to a single quantification of any specific dimension (i.e., to a test). Similarly, B. Klopfer, Ainsworth, Klopfer, and Holt (1954) advocated for calling the test a *technique,* so that individualistic processing could be emphasized. From a more extreme, but current, viewpoint, Aronow, Reznikoff, and Moreland (1994) focus on response content and regard the Rorschach as a *structured interview*. Most practitioners do not score the TAT, and Little and Schneidman (1955) described it as a "sample of verbal behavior." Earlier, Tomkins (1947) had declared that the TAT was a systematic methodology for personality study—not a test itself. Finally, early memory, sentence, and drawing tasks are routinely used as methods without scoring to collect behavioral observations and personal productions.

Advocates and critics use the term "method" for different reasons. Some advocates of projective testing support the term *method* for these projective procedures. Beyond precision of language, they are concerned that essential qualitative and descriptive information will be excluded from consideration if this information is not captured in formal scoring. Critics of projective testing endorse the term *method,* claiming that the nonquantified components are not worthy of consideration. This extremist view excludes from consideration response nuances and connotations, test behaviors, and emotional expressions, as well as the interaction between examiner and the respondent. These characteristics constitute important empirical and objective observations. They are the essence of behavioral assessment and are not captured within the reductionistic view that only test quantities be considered. In cases in which they are relevant (i.e., related to other hypotheses firmly grounded in test-based inferences), these behavioral and empirical data derived from using projective instruments as methods must be included in the interpretive process.

Methods, Clinical Utility, and the N-*of-1 Problem in Assessment*

How does one fit a group or statistical concept, such as depression or aggressive risk, to an individual and describe its idiosyncratic experience and function within that individual? From a statistical viewpoint, if it is highly likely that a person is depressed based on a score, how do we confirm the presence of depression in the particular individual we are evaluating? These questions reflect the *N-of-1* problem in assessment—that is, the challenge of applying abstract, group-derived constructs and measurements to a single individual. Within individuals, constructs such as aggression or depression exist only in idiosyncratic forms. Accordingly, within a projective test protocol, idiosyncratic evidence of depression may serve to confirm and individualize a person's expression of depression. In this way, using projective instruments as a method helps address the *N*-of-1 problem in assessment by contextualizing and individualizing abstract concepts and group data.

This *N*-of-1 problem is often framed in terms of the distinction between nomothetic and idiographic science and knowledge (Murstein, 1963). *Nomothetic science* addresses laws and abstractions applicable across circumstances and individuals. Within psychology, it would be associated with group psychological principles, constructs, and data across individuals and situations. These abstractions may not actually exist in any individual case but are hypothetical constructs created for the purpose of explaining and summarizing relationships among groups of individuals. In contrast, *idiographic science* is concerned with understanding a particular event, such what led to a particular historical event or decision—in other words, how and why something happened. The aim of assessment, to characterize a unique individual within a life context, is an idiographic goal. Certainly, nomothetic science, methods, and comparisons are critical and necessary to address this goal, but not sufficient to achieve it fully. Idiographic and configurational information from a method perspective is necessary to address the uniqueness of each case. Thus, projective test data and observations are helpful in translating group, nomothetic, or actuarial data to the individual *N*-of-1 case.

In terms of clinical utility, using an instrument as a method offers considerable advantages over using instruments strictly as tests. Observations and inquiries can be adapted to address

any purpose. One cannot imagine all of the questions that will come up in an assessment. Thus, one method might replace many tests, offering considerable efficiency and cost savings. The superior status of tests in terms of the validity of a specific interpretation relies on stringent research validation of the test for that particular purpose. On the other hand, it is impossible to develop, research, and master a test for every purpose. Accordingly, projective methods, interviews, and observations are always necessary for a comprehensive assessment, lest we give up all idiographic assessment goals.

At the broadest level, research supporting the validity of a method addresses whether a projective procedure can produce valid and useful information when projective instruments are used in the standard ways. The research clearly supports the conclusion that the major projective instruments (inkblot perception and representation, storytelling, sentence completion, early recollection, and figure drawing) can yield valid and useful information. On the other hand, the limits of these methods and the limits of data they produce are not fully appreciated by some projective-test advocates. Further research needs to identify the types of inferences and generalizations that can be made about particular personality processes and from which types of data.

Conclusion and Recommendations for Tests and Methods

Projective instruments, like all psychological tests, can function both as methods and as tests. In both roles, they should be administered in a standardized fashion. When they are used as tests, one relies on quantification, measurement against comparison-group data, and preestablished criterion validity. These factors lead to a strong scientific foundation for the interpretation of tests. Because of the less sturdy support for inferences based only on using the instruments as methods, inferences derived from methods need additional support from other sources. Within a given assessment, this support can be accomplished in terms of addressing hypotheses that have derived initial support form data encountered earlier in the assessment process. For example, in established cases of depression, the TAT may yield important information about the idiographic experience of that depression and its interpersonal correlates. Early memories may provide subjective and experiential patterning associated with this depression. If we establish from a self-report test that the respondent is describing him- or herself in an overly positive and defensive fashion, an examination of sentence-completion results and observations about the examiner-respondent interaction may lead to important information about the character and motivation associated with that defensiveness. If new hypotheses emerge from method data, they must be supported by other data from other observations and findings, in a way that we would not require for an interpretation from an instrument used as a test. Thus, when these procedures are used as methods and not tests, they should generally be used as ancillary, or elaborative, procedures.

Rorschach Comprehensive System interpretation is a good example of using an instrument as both a test and a method. One first interprets structural quantitative data, then modifies these foundational interpretations with the Rorschach used as a method (i.e., through response verbalizations and behavioral observations). In this way, method findings are used to refine, elaborate, and qualify previously formulated general hypotheses.

Contribution to Assessment Relative to Self-Report Tests

One way to address the question of what projective testing contributes to assessment is to identify situations in which self-report tests do not yield clear and definitive findings. This approach is consistent with the current concerns about incremental validity. Many have noted that projective tests contribute most in contexts in which the person may be unwilling or unable to provide the sought-after information through more direct means (Bagby, Nicholson, Buis, & Radovanovic, 1999; Bathurst, Gottfried, & Gottfried, 1997; Bornstein, 1999; Viglione, 1999). Some might contend that, to some degree, no respondent is able to fully reveal critical information about the self in an efficient manner.

The traditional view, as first elaborated by Frank (1939/1962), is that projective testing goes beyond socially conventional meanings and roles. From this perspective, self-report items, typically a sentence or phrase, presume a conventional, widely shared understanding of their meaning. In these conventional contexts, individual behavior is best explained by situational phenomena as interpreted with shared cultural norms. Frank contrasted these conventional contexts to situations in which behavior is explained by the individual's unique ways of (a) ascribing meaning to the world and (b) organizing the world. In fact, one's unique ways of ascribing meaning to and organizing the world is the fundamental component of personality, according to Frank. Moreover, they correspond to the self-expressive and organizational components of projective tests addressed earlier in this chapter. Projective tests are designed to access these individualistic functions and thus reveal personality activity directly.

This linking of self-report tests to conventional contexts and projective tests to individualistic ones has led some to speculate about the relative contributions of these tests. For example, Hutt (1945) speculated that self-report tests may be valid only when the respondent is willing and able to self-rate on a known dimension. Meehl (1945/1980) disagreed by objecting that

although respondents may understand self-report test items differently, such differences are not relevant to validity. He claimed that the validity of a self-report test is not a function of a conventionally, socially prescribed understanding of the test items. Rather, it is a function of empirical relationships with external criteria. This *empirical keying approach* assumes that the content of the item really does not matter, only its empirical relationship with meaningful criteria.

Despite Meehl's (1945/1980) assertions, evidence suggests that what the item means to the respondent does make a difference in the validity of a self-report personality test. On the MMPI, it is well established that obvious items are more valid then subtle items (Graham, 2000; Greene, 2000; Gynther & Burkhart, 1983). In other words, when an item's content is semantically related to the scale on which it resides or the construct it measures, it works better. Also, the largely rationally derived content scales on the MMPI-2 rival the empirically keyed clinical scales in terms of validity (Graham; Greene), again suggesting that item content matters. The current test-development practice is to pick the item pool for content validity (i.e., what the item means to the respondent; American Educational Research Association et al., 1999; Anastasi & Urbina 1996; Morey, 1996). Again, the validity of these scales is partly based on an unequivocal meaning of the item to the respondent. As Frank (1939/1962) asserted theoretically and McClelland et al. (1989) and Bornstein et al. (1994) demonstrated with data, self-report personality tests reveal information about relevant but conventional, culturally prescribed dimensions.

The interpretive implication of all of these data is that self-report personality tests tell us the most about social role–related behavior, how one behaves in the role of a father or in the role of a rebellious adolescent in our society. These tests work best when the examinee translates individual items in conventional ways and when the examinee's response set reflects the host culture's norms. Psychometrically, this occurs when validity scales (e.g., L, F, and K with the MMPI) are near average values. Atypical, unconventional response sets, in terms of excessive defensiveness or exaggeration, reflect unconventional approaches to the tests; and atypical translation of test items, in turn, limits the validity of self-report personality tests (Meyer, 1999). Conversely, projective tests have the most to offer in understanding and predicting behavior outside prescribed social roles and demands across situation and time, as well as for issues that are idiographic, idiosyncratic, or implicit (see Bornstein, 1999; Shedler et al., 1993; Viglione, 1999). These would include environmental contexts or patterns of behavior that are structured by individual personality rather than by social roles and conventions.

PROJECTIVE TEST CONTROVERSY FROM A HISTORICAL PERSPECTIVE

This chapter attempts to clarify many misunderstandings about projective testing. These misunderstandings can also be seen in a historical perspective. Undeniably, historical developments have influenced our understanding of focal psychological constructs, even when we believe that these constructs are grounded in empirical science. For example, as a result of the Wechsler and Stanford-Binet scales, our implicit and conventional understanding of intelligence emphasizes the quantitative perspective at the expense of the conceptual and developmental aspects as articulated within the Piagetian approach. Self-report personality assessment has led us to simplify adult personality into an aggregate of traits demonstrated by subgroups of individuals. Response set or response manipulation has been reduced to quantitative notions about exaggeration and defensiveness (e.g., as defined through the *L*, *F*, and *K* scales on the MMPI). Thus, history and our experience have shaped our views, constructs, and what we consider to be science.

Emerging Clinical Needs versus Scientific Aspirations

Our current views of assessment and the relative values of projective and self-report tests of personality are shaped not only by metaphors and models, but by historical traditions as well. Misunderstandings about projective testing have shaped the ongoing and lengthy controversy about projective tests. It is surprising to learn that the current controversy about the utility of projective tests surrounding the use of these tests has existed since their introduction (Hirt, 1962; Murstein, 1965; Rabin, 1981). The popular academic-scientific position dating back to the 1920s is that projective tests are flawed. Periodically, this view has been a rallying cry of academic psychologists. In the 1920s and 1930s, American academic psychology focused on distinguishing psychology by making it a science with mathematical foundations much like those of physics. It is not surprising that it produced few concepts, facts, and methods applicable to clinical work. At that time, applied work in clinical psychology was largely diagnostic and descriptive in support of psychiatrists' work with individuals with mental disorders. These clinical and practical demands opposed the academic interests in developing the discipline and science of psychology.

The need for personnel selection in the military and evaluation and treatment of consequences of the two world wars further stimulated the practical needs of applied psychologists. More generally, clinicians thought that the individual was lost in the techniques of the so-called mental testers.

They wished to recognize the interaction between individual characteristics and "the total life situation which could lead to an adequate description of the person as a functioning human being" (Murstein, 1963, p. 4).

As it has been in the past, *projective testing* continues to be a rallying symbol for those wishing to move beyond the response manipulation in self-report tests so as to understand the individual. Thus, clinical and applied interest and questions that outstrip scientific and academic developments in the field have marked the whole history of assessment. As society changes, this pressure to address advanced and complex questions in everyday practice will certainly persist. Nonclinical psychologists who criticize projective tests may not fully understand the demand society justifiably places on our clinicians and the interpretive usefulness and validity of the behaviors collected and observed by using projective tests.

The Polarized and Moralistic Debate Continues

The controversy about the value of projective persists to this day. The result is that too much of the attention given to projective tests in the literature are polemical and editorial rather than scientific (APA, 1999; Dumont & Smith, 1996; Garb, 1998, 1999; Garb, Florio, & Grove, 1998, 1999; Garb, Wood, Nezworski, Grove, & Stejskal, 2001; Grove & Barden, 1999; Joiner & Schmidt, 1997; Wood & Lilienfeld, 1999; Wood, Lilienfeld, Garb, & Nezworski, 2000; Wood, Nezworski, & Stejskal, 1996, 1997). The end result is that projective and self-report tests are pitted against one another as adversaries. The most recent manifestation of this rivalry is the current application of incremental validity with the unqualified and simplistic assumption that projective tests should increment above self-report tests in regression equations (Hunsley & Bailey, 1999). This position grossly oversimplifies the clinical endeavor (Viglione & Hilsenroth, in press) while ignoring research demonstrating incremental validity for projective tests (e.g., for the Rorschach; Archer & Gordon, 1988; Archer & Krishnamurthy, 1997; Blais, Hilsenroth, Castlebury, Fowler, & Baity, 2001; Bornstein, Bowers, & Robinson, 1997; Cooper, Perry, & O'Connell, 1991; Holzman et al., 1974; Meyer, 2000a; O'Connell, Cooper, Perry, & Hoke, 1989; Perry & Braff, 1994; Perry & Viglione, 1991; Russ, 1980, 1981; Shapiro, Leifer, Martone, & Kassem, 1990; Skelton, Boik, & Madero, 1995; Viglione, 1999; Weiner, in press).

The very name *projective* is subject to these politics and polemics. The persistence of the nomenclature of *objective* for self-report tests, in juxtaposition with *projective,* further distorts the data and viewpoints of psychologists. This dichotomy implies that the virtues of objectivity and psychometric discipline are reserved for the self-report tests. Moreover, *projective* is associated with *subjective* and the cardinal sin of bias when it is juxtaposed against *objective*. Research demonstrations of the incremental validity of projective tests support the view that extra validity is accessed through involving the examiner in the interpretive processes with projective tests. This added validity is obtained even if there is more examiner variability or examiner unreliability with these procedures.

The most vexing problem in this debate is that the views are drenched in ethical and moralistic language, so that the polarized positions are experienced as moral imperatives. This moralism from the academic side has to do with claims of the righteousness of science and empirical foundations. On the other hand, there is some validity to the claim that clinicians using projective tests have historically shown a tendency to overpathologize (Murstein & Mathes, 1996; Viglione & Hilsenroth, in press).

The advocates of projective testing are not immune to similar criticisms. Murstein (1963) correctly pointed out that the seminal articles (e.g., Frank, 1939/1962; Rosenzweig, 1951) have a moralistic tone, with the hero being the idiographic clinician using projective testing to describe and understand the individual in all his or her complexity. The idea that clinical interpretation is an art was described by Levy (1963) as "a romanticism with which some are afflicted that seems to render its victims either insensitive or antagonistic to any attempt at rational analysis . . . [T]hey (proponents of projective testing) rely on 'moralism.' To criticize the 'mental testers,' they use epithets such as 'atomistic,' 'mechanistic,' and 'superficial' " (p. 3).

A. Kaplan (1964) has given a slightly different slant to these polemics in his description of seductive and reductive fallacies. Projective test advocates seduce themselves and others into believing there is always something else, subtle or otherwise, that can be gleaned from the data and applied to useful purposes. Kaplan refers to this belief as the *seductive fallacy*. On the other hand, projective tests critics embrace a *reductive fallacy,* which incorporates the view that science requires that test data incorporate a very limited number of key elements. Furthermore, this belief requires that automated techniques must be involved because clinicians cannot reliably identify these key elements.

As an example of this bias against projective tests, Masling (1997) questioned whether the data supporting the Rorschach would change the minds of the critics, given the persistent history of bias against projective tests. He attributes some of this rigidity, politicization, and bias to the fact that former students, emboldened by their teachers, have become critics of projective tests. Unfortunately, some students of psychology are socialized to believe in simplistic models, such as the blank screen, or in the supposedly unscientific foundation of projective techniques in order to continue the conflict (Viglione & Hilsenroth, in press). Weiner (1996) also observed that the critics had ignored 20 years of empirical support for the test. One can only conclude that these speculations were correct, as the recent debate about the Rorschach has demonstrated. Data and experience suggest that these critics continue to ignore the research supporting projective testing in general and the Rorschach in particular (e.g., Meyer, 1997a, 1997b, 2000a, 2000b; Meyer & Archer, in press; Riethmiller & Handler, 1997; Shedler et al., 1993; Stricker & Healy, 1990; Viglione, 1999; Viglione & Hilsenroth; Weiner, in press).

Recognition of Differences and a Resolution?

The rivalry and controversy about projective and objective personality tests may merely be a manifestation of the conflicts and misunderstandings between clinical and academic psychologists or between practice and science in psychology. A great deal of psychology's time, energy, and intellectual effort have been wasted within this war. Sadly, American psychology has not been able to resolve this dilemma, most likely because it is a basic philosophical and moral disagreement rather than a scientific one. American psychology perseveres under the goal of integration of science and practice, yet those who embrace this vision often hold very different perceptions of this integration. This science-versus-practice debate continues with little understanding or appreciation of the other's point of view, and with little hope for reconciliation and advancement of assessment psychology.

Our goal should be to diffuse this conflict and integrate the strengths of projective and self-report approaches to assessment. As Levy (1963) points out when he calls for systematic empirical and rational evaluations of clinical interpretation, "to this writer's way of thinking, rationality and human dignity are not antithetical to each other; nor are science and art for that matter" (p. 3). Each type of test has strengths and weakness. We are lucky that cognitive, projective, and self-report tests complement each other so well.

Meehl (1945/1980), an advocate of self-report personality testing and scientific psychology, asserted that "there is assuredly no reason for us to place self-report and unstructured types of instruments in battle order against one another, although it is admitted that when time is limited they come inevitably into a very real clinical 'competition' for use" (p. 302). He maintained that all personality tests can be see on a continuum and can be interpreted with the same principles. As described earlier in this chapter, he placed the difference between projective and self-report within the interpreters and their own philosophies rather than within the instruments.

Historically, advocates of projective and self-report personality testing have presented the arguments of the opposing side as being seriously flawed. This destructive rivalry could be replaced with reconciliation and is opposed by the argument that all tests incorporate so-called projective and objective features, as well as empirical characteristics. The basic premises, goals, and activities are different but potentially complementary (Masling, 1997; Meehl, 1945/1980). As Masling concludes his paper on projective testing,

> Psychology is fortunate to have available two such different means of assessing human behavior, each placing different emphasis on the importance of motive, rational thinking, fantasy, self-reflection, and defense. A wise discipline would value and embrace such differences rather than find fault and lack of respectability in either one. (p. 266)

Adopting some of the perspectives described in this chapter may assist in integrating projective and other approaches for more effective assessment. Most important among them may be adopting the response-process approach, including both problem-solving and behavioral components.

One challenge in writing this chapter has been to encompass the great diversity of projective tests under one umbrella. The extant research data and the response-process model itself would suggest that the next step would be to adapt the model to individual tests. This would include developing paradigms to address topographical and experiential similarity, functional equivalence, and personality as problem-solving in real life. The challenge in this research is to access the idiographic characteristics of the individual as validity criteria. This is not a simple manner and may require incorporating qualitative research with more traditional quantitative work. Research should also tackle the international and cross-cultural challenges, since projective testing has great potential in these applications. Every effort should be made to standardize administrations and coding of responses, with the Rorschach Comprehensive System as the model. It is unclear whether we can progress much further by lumping these tests together. Rather, the response process and generalization characteristics for each test can be researched and developed separately. Research in projective testing should address the interpretive process itself. Much more sophisticated clinical-judgment studies are needed to make them relevant to clinical practice (Karon, 2000; Levine, 1981; Viglione & Hilsenroth, in press). Such research should include investigations of these instruments as methods.

REFERENCES

Acklin, M. W. (1999). Behavioral science foundations of the Rorschach test: Research and clinical applications. *Assessment, 6,* 319–324.

American Educational Research Association, American Psychological Association, & National Council on Measurement in Education. (1999). *Standards for educational and psychological testing.* Washington, DC: American Educational Research Association.

American Psychological Association, Division 12, Presidential Task Force. (1999). Assessment for the twenty-first century: A model curriculum. *The Clinical Psychologist, 52,* 10–15.

Anastasi, A., & Urbina, S. (1996). *Psychological testing* (7th ed.). New York: Macmillan.

Archer, R. P., & Gordon, R. A. (1988). MMPI and Rorschach indices of schizophrenic and depressive diagnoses among adolescent inpatients. *Journal of Personality Assessment, 52,* 276–287.

Archer, R. P., & Krishnamurthy, R. (1997). MMPI-A and Rorschach indices related to depression and conduct disorder: An evaluation of the incremental validity hypotheses. *Journal of Personality Assessment, 69,* 517–533.

Aronow, E., Reznikoff, M., & Moreland, K. (1994). *The Rorschach technique: Perceptual basics, content interpretation, and applications.* Boston: Allyn and Bacon.

Bagby, R. M., Nicholson, R. A., Buis, T., & Radovanovic, H. (1999). Defensive responding on the MMPI-2 in family custody and access evaluations. *Psychological Assessment, 11,* 24–28.

Bandura, A. (1978). The self-system in reciprocal determinism. *American Psychologist, 33,* 344–358.

Bathurst, K., Gottfried, A. W., & Gottfried, A. E. (1997). Normative data for the MMPI-2 in child custody litigation. *Psychological Assessment, 7,* 419–423.

Beck, S. J. (1960). *The Rorschach experiment: Ventures in blind diagnosis.* New York: Grune and Stratton.

Bellak, L. (1944). The concept of projection: An experimental investigation and study of the concept. *Psychiatry, 7,* 353–370.

Blais, M. A., Hilsenroth, M. J., Castlebury, F., Fowler, J. C., & Baity, M. (2001). Predicting *DSM-IV* Cluster B personality disorder criteria from MMPI-2 and Rorschach data: A test of incremental validity. *Journal of Personality Assessment, 76,* 150–168.

Bornstein, R. F. (1999). Criterion validity of objective and projective dependency tests: A meta-analytic assessment of behavioral prediction. *Psychological Assessment, 11,* 48–57.

Bornstein, R. F., Bowers, K. S., & Robinson, K. J. (1997). Differential relationships of objective and projective dependency scores to self-reports of interpersonal life events in college student subjects. *Journal of Personality Assessment, 65,* 255–269.

Bornstein, R. F., Rossner, S. C., Hill, E. L., & Stepanian, M. L. (1994). Face validity and fakability of objective and projective measures of dependency. *Journal of Personality Assessment, 63,* 363–386.

Campbell, D. T. (1957). A typology of tests, projective and otherwise. *Journal of Consulting Psychology, 21,* 207–210.

Colligan, S. C., & Exner, J. E. (1985). Responses of schizophrenics and nonpatients to a tachistoscopic presentation of the Rorschach. The 11th International Rorschach Congress (1984, Barcelona, Spain). *Journal of Personality Assessment, 49,* 129–136.

Cooper, S. H., Perry, J. C., & O'Connell, M. (1991). The Rorschach Defense Scales: II. Longitudinal perspectives. *Journal of Personality Assessment, 56,* 191–201.

Dumont, F., & Smith, D. (1996). Projectives and their infirm research base. *Professional psychology: Research and Practice, 27,* 419–421.

Exner, J. E. (1974). *The Rorschach: A comprehensive system* (Vol. 1). New York: Wiley.

Exner, J. E. (1980). But it's only an inkblot. *Journal of Personality Assessment, 44,* 563–576.

Exner, J. E. (1993). *The Rorschach: A comprehensive system: Vol. 1. Basic foundations* (3rd ed.). New York: Wiley.

Exner, J. E. (1996). Critical bits and the Rorschach response process. *Journal of Personality Assessment, 67,* 464–477.

Exner, J. E. (2000, March). *Rorschach symposium.* Paper presented at the annual meeting of the Society for Personality Assessment, Albuquerque, NM.

Exner, J. E., Armbruster, G., & Mittman, B. (1978). The Rorschach response process. *Journal of Personality Assessment, 42,* 27–38.

Exner, J. E., Colligan, S. C., Hillman, L. B., Metts, A. S., Ritzler, B., Rogers, K. T., Sciara, A. D., & Viglione, D. J. (2001). *A Rorschach workbook for the Comprehensive System* (5th ed.). Asheville, NC: Rorschach Workshops.

Exner, J. E., & Weiner, I. B. (1995). *The Rorschach: A comprehensive system: Vol. 3. Assessment of children and adolescents* (2nd ed.). New York: Wiley.

Finn, S. E., & Kamphuis, J. H. (1995). What a clinician needs to know about base rates. In J. N. Butcher (Ed.), *Clinical personality assessment* (pp. 224–235). New York: Oxford University Press.

Foster, S. L., & Cone, J. D. (1995). Validity issues in clinical assessment. *Psychological Assessment, 7,* 248–260.

Frank, L. K. (1939/1962). Projective methods for the study of personality. In M. Hirt (Ed.), *Rorschach science* (pp. 31–52). New York: Free Press of Glencoe.

Garb, H. N. (1998). Recommendations for training in the use of the Thematic Apperception Test (TAT). *Professional Psychology: Research and Practice, 29,* 621–622.

Garb, H. N. (1999). Call for a moratorium on the use of the Rorschach Inkblot Test in clinical and forensic settings. *Assessment, 6,* 313–315.

Garb, H. N., Florio, C. M., & Grove, W. M. (1998). The validity of the Rorschach and the Minnesota Multiphasic Personality Inventory: Results from meta-analyses. *Psychological Science, 9,* 402–404.

Garb, H. N., Florio, C. M., & Grove, W. M. (1999). The Rorschach controversy: Reply to Parker, Hunsley, and Hanson. *Psychological Science, 10,* 293–294.

Garb, H. N., Wood, J. M., Nezworski, M. T., Grove, W. M., & Stejskal, W. J. (2001). Towards a resolution of the Rorschach controversy. *Psychological Assessment, 13*(4), 433–448.

Goldfried, M. R., Stricker, G., & Weiner, I. B. (1971). *Rorschach handbook of clinical and research applications.* Englewood Cliffs, NJ: Prentice-Hall.

Graham, J. R. (2000). *MMPI-2: Assessing personality and psychopathology* (3rd ed.). New York: Oxford University Press.

Greene, R. L. (2000). *The MMPI-2/MMPI: An interpretive manual.* Boston: Allyn and Bacon.

Grove, W. M., & Barden, R. C. (1999). Protecting the integrity of the legal system: The admissibility of testimony from mental health experts under Daubert/Kumho analyses. *Psychology, Public Policy, and Law, 5,* 224–242.

Gynther, M. D., & Burkhart, B. R. (1983). Are subtle MMPI items expendable? In J. N. Butcher & C. D. Spielberger (Eds.), *Advances in personality assessment* (Vol. 2, pp. 115–132). Hillsdale, NJ: Erlbaum.

Hirt, M. (1962). *Rorschach science: Readings in theory and method.* New York: Free Press of Glencoe.

Holaday, M., Smith, D. A., & Sherry, A. (2000). Sentence completion tests: A review of the literature and results of a survey of members of the society for personality assessment. *Journal of Personality Assessment, 74,* 371–383.

Holmes, D. S. (1974). The conscious control of thematic projection. *Journal of consulting and clinical psychology, 42,* 232–329.

Holzman, P. S., Proctor, L. R., Levy, D. L., Yasillo, N. J., Meltzer, H. Y., & Hurt, S. W. (1974). Eye-tracking dysfunctions in schizophrenic patients and their relatives. *Archives of General Psychiatry, 31,* 143–151.

Hunsley, J., & Bailey, J. M. (1999). The clinical utility of the Rorschach: Unfulfilled promises and an uncertain future. *Psychological Assessment, 11,* 266–277.

Hutt, M. L. (1945). The use of projective methods of personality measurement in army medical installations. *Journal of Clinical Psychology, 1,* 134–140.

Joiner, T. E., Jr., & Schmidt, K. (1997). Drawing conclusions—or not—from drawings. *Journal of Personality Assessment, 69,* 476–481.

Joy, S., Fein, D., Kaplan, E., & Freedman, M. (2001). Quantifying qualitative features of block design performance among healthy older adults. *Archives of Clinical Neuropsychology, 16,* 157–170.

Kaplan, A. (1964). *The conduct of inquiry.* San Francisco: Chandler.

Kaplan, E. (1991). A process approach to neuropsychological assessment. In T. Boll & B. K. Bryant (Eds.), *Clinical neuropsychology and brain function: Research, measurement, and practice* (pp. 125–168). Washington, DC: American Psychological Association.

Karon, B. P. (2000). The clinical interpretation of the Thematic Apperception Test, Rorschach, and other clinical data: A reexamination of statistical versus clinical prediction. *Professional Psychology: Research and Practice, 31,* 230–233.

Kaufman, A. S. (1979). *Intelligent testing with the WISC-R.* New York: Wiley.

Kleiger, J. H. (1999). *Disordered thinking and the Rorschach: Theory, research, and differential diagnosis.* Hillsdale, NJ: Analytic Press.

Klopfer, W. G. (1981). Integration of projective techniques in the clinical case study. In A. I. Rabin (Ed.), *Assessment with projective techniques: A concise introduction* (pp. 233–263). New York: Springer.

Klopfer, B., Ainsworth, M. D., Klopfer, W. G., & Holt, R. R. (1954). *Developments in the Rorschach technique: Vol. 1. Technique and theory.* Yonkers-on-Hudson, New York: World Book.

Levine, D. (1981). Why and when to test: The social context of psychological testing. In A. I. Rabin (Ed.), *Assessment with projective techniques: A concise introduction.* New York: Springer.

Levy, L. H. (1963). *Psychological interpretation.* New York: Holt, Rinehart, & Winston.

Little, K. B., & Shneidman, E. S. (1955). The validity of thematic projective technique interpretations. *Journal of Projective Techniques, 23,* 285–294.

Loevinger, J., & Wessler, R. (1970). *Measuring ego development: Construction and use of a sentence completion test* (Vol. 1). San Francisco: Jossey-Bass.

Masling, J. (1960). The influence of situational and interpersonal factors in projective testing. *Psychological Bulletin, 57,* 65–85.

Masling, J. M. (1997). On the nature and utility of projective and objective tests. *Journal of Personality Assessment, 69,* 254–270.

McClelland, D. C., Koestner, R., & Weinberger, J. (1989). How do self-attributed and implicit motives differ? *Psychological Review, 96,* 690–702.

Meehl, P. E. (1980). The dynamics of "structured" personality tests. In W. G. Dahlstrom and L. Dahlstrom (Eds.), *Basic readings on the MMPI: A new selection on personality measurement.* Minneapolis: University of Minnesota Press. (Original work published 1945)

Meyer, G. J. (1993). The impact of response frequency on the Rorschach constellation indices and on their validity with diagnostic and MMPI-2 criteria. *Journal of Personality Assessment, 60,* 153–180.

Meyer, G. J. (1997a). On the integration of personality assessment methods: The Rorschach and MMPI. *Journal of Personality Assessment, 68,* 297–330.

Meyer, G. J. (1997b). Thinking clearly about reliability: More critical corrections regarding the Rorschach Comprehensive System. *Psychological Assessment, 9,* 495–498.

Meyer, G. J. (1999). The convergent validity of MMPI and Rorschach scales: An extension using profile scores to define response-character styles on both methods and a re-examination of simple Rorschach response frequency. *Journal of Personality Assessment, 72,* 1–35.

Meyer, G. J. (2000a). Incremental validity of the Rorschach Prognostic Rating Scale over the MMPI Ego Strength Scale and IQ. *Journal of Personality Assessment, 74,* 356–370.

Meyer, G. J. (2000b). On the science of Rorschach research. *Journal of Personality Assessment, 75,* 46–81.

Meyer, G. J., & Archer, R. P. (in press). The hard science of Rorschach research: What do we know and where do we go? *Psychological Assessment, 13,* 486–502.

Morey, L. C. (1996). *An interpretive guide to the Personality Assessment Inventory (PAI).* Odessa, FL: Psychological Assessment Resources.

Murray, H. A. (1938). *Explorations in personality.* New York: Oxford University Press.

Murstein, B. I. (1961). Assumptions, adaptation-level, and projective techniques. *Perceptual and Motor Skills, 12,* 107–125.

Murstein, B. I. (1963). *Theory and research in projective techniques (emphasizing the TAT).* New York: Wiley.

Murstein, B. I. (1965). *Handbook of projective techniques.* New York: Basic Books.

Murstein, B. I., & Mathes, S. (1996). Projection on projective techniques = pathology: The problem that is not being addressed. *Journal of Personality Assessment, 66,* 337–349.

O'Connell, M., Cooper, S., Perry, C., & Hoke, L. (1989). The relationship between thought disorder and psychotic symptoms in borderline personality disorder. *Journal of Nervous and Mental Disease, 177,* 273–278.

Perry, W., & Braff, D. L. (1994). Information-processing deficits and thought disorder in schizophrenia. *American Journal of Psychiatry, 151,* 363–367.

Perry, W., Felger, T., & Braff, D. (1998). The relationship between skin conductance hyporesponsivity and perseverations in schizophrenia patients. *Biological Psychiatry, 44,* 459–465.

Perry, W., Geyer, M. A., & Braff, D. L. (1999). Sensorimotor gating and thought disturbance measured in close temporal proximity in schizophrenic patients. *Archives of General Psychiatry, 56,* 277–281.

Perry, W., & Viglione, D. J. (1991). The Ego Impairment Index as a predictor of outcome in melancholic depressed patients treated with tricyclic antidepressants. *Journal of Personality Assessment, 56,* 487–501.

Perry, W., Viglione, D., & Braff, D. L. (1992). The Ego Impairment Index and schizophrenia: A validation study. *Journal of Personality Assessment, 59,* 165–175.

Peterson, C. A., & Schilling, K. M. (1983). Card pull in projective testing. *Journal of Personality Assessment, 47,* 265–275.

Rabin, A. I. (1981). *Assessment with projective techniques: A concise introduction.* New York: Springer.

Reitan, R. R., & Wolfsan, D. (1985). *The Halstead-Reitan neuropsychological test battery: Theory and clinical interpretation.* Tucson, AZ: Neuropsychology Press.

Riethmiller, R. J., & Handler, L. (1997). The great figure drawing controversy: The integration of research and clinical practice. *Journal of Personality Assessment, 69,* 488–496.

Ronan, G. F., Colavito, V. A., & Hammontree, S. R. (1993). Personal problem-solving system for scoring TAT responses: Preliminary validity and reliability data. *Journal of Personality Assessment, 61,* 28–40.

Rosenzweig, S. (1951). Idiodynamics in personality theory with special reference to projective methods. *Psychological Review,* 21–223.

Russ, S. W. (1980). Primary process integration on the Rorschach and achievement in children. *Journal of Personality Assessment, 44,* 338–344.

Russ, S. W. (1981). Primary process integration on the Rorschach and achievement in children: A follow-up study. *Journal of Personality Assessment, 45,* 473–477.

Schachtel, E. G. (1966). *Experiential foundations of Rorschach's test.* New York: Basic Books.

Schafer, R. (1954). *Psychoanalytic interpretation in Rorschach testing.* New York: Grune and Stratton.

Shapiro, J. P., Leifer, M., Martone, M. W., & Kassem, L. (1990). Multimethod assessment of depression in sexually abused girls. *Journal of Personality Assessment, 55,* 234–248.

Shedler, J., Mayman, M., & Manis, M. (1993). The illusion of mental health. *American Psychologist,* 1117–1131.

Skelton, M. D., Boik, R. J., & Madero, J. N. (1995). Thought disorder on the WAIS-R relative to the Rorschach: Assessing identity disorder adolescents. *Journal of Personality Assessment, 65,* 533–549.

Stricker, G., & Gold, J. R. (1999). The Rorschach: Toward a nomothetically based, idiographically applicable configurational model. *Psychological Assessment, 11,* 240–250.

Stricker, G., & Healy, B. D. (1990). Projective assessment of object relations: A review of the empirical literature. *Psychological Assessment: A Journal of Consulting and Clinical Psychology, 2,* 219–230.

Tomkins, S. S. (1947). *The Thematic Apperception Test* (Rev. ed.). New York: Grune and Stratton.

Viglione, D. J. (1996). Data and issues to consider in reconciling self-report and the Rorschach. *Journal of Personality Assessment, 67,* 579–587.

Viglione, D. J. (1999). A review of recent research addressing the utility of the Rorschach. *Psychological Assessment, 11,* 251–265.

Viglione, D. J., & Hilsenroth, M. (in press). The Rorschach: Facts, fictions, and future. *Psychological Assessment, 13,* 452–471.

Viglione, D. J., & Perry, W. (1991). A general model for psychological assessment and psychopathology applied to depression. *British Journal of Projective Psychology, 36,* 1–16.

Watson, R. I. (1978). The Sentence Completion Method. In B. B. Wolman (Ed.), *Clinical diagnosis of mental disorders: A handbook* (pp. 255–280). New York: Plenum Press.

Weiner, I. B. (1966). *Psychodiagnosis in schizophrenia.* New York: Wiley.

Weiner, I. B. (1994). The Rorschach Inkblot Method (RIM) is not a test: Implications for theory and practice. *Journal of Personality Assessment, 62,* 498–504.

Weiner, I. B. (1996). Some observations on the validity of the Rorschach Inkblot Method. *Psychological Assessment, 8,* 206–213.

Weiner, I. B. (1999). What the Rorschach can do for you: Incremental validity in clinical applications. *Assessment, 6,* 327–338.

Weiner, I. B. (in press). Advancing the science of psychological assessment: The Rorschach Inkblot Method as exemplar. *Psychological Assessment, 13,* 423–432.

Wood, J. M., & Lilienfeld, S. O. (1999). The Rorschach Inkblot Test: A case of overstatement? *Assessment, 6,* 341–349.

Wood, J. M., Lilienfeld, S. O., Garb, H. N., & Nezworski, M. T. (2000). The Rorschach test in clinical diagnosis: A critical review with a backward look at Garfield (1947). *Journal of Clinical Psychology, 56,* 395–430.

Wood, J. M., Nezworski, M. T., & Stejskal, W. J. (1996). The Comprehensive System for the Rorschach: A critical examination. *Psychological Science, 7,* 3–10.

Wood, J. M., Nezworski, M. T., & Stejskal, W. J. (1997). The reliability of the Comprehensive System for the Rorschach: A Comment on Meyer (1997). *Psychological Assessment, 9,* 490–494.

CHAPTER 24

Assessing Personality and Psychopathology With Self-Report Inventories

YOSSEF S. BEN-PORATH

Self-report inventories (SRIs) have been a mainstay of assessment psychology for over seven decades. Researchers and clinicians use them frequently in a broad range of settings and applications. These assessment devices require that the test taker respond to a series of stimuli, the test items, by indicating whether, or to what extent, they describe some aspect of his or her functioning. The response format varies from a dichotomous "true" or "false" to a Likert scale indication of degree of agreement with the statement as a self-description. Some SRIs focus primarily on abnormal functioning or psychopathology, whereas others concentrate more on the normal personality range. Still others cover both normal and abnormal aspects of personality and psychopathology.

In addition to their relative emphasis on normal versus abnormal personality, self-report inventories differ in several notable ways. One important variable is their conceptual basis. Some SRIs are developed with guidance from a particular personality or psychopathology theory or model, whereas others are based more on the results of empirical analyses. In this context, Ben-Porath (1994) noted that personality test developers have pursued their efforts from two broad, non–mutually exclusive perspectives. One approach, the *clinical perspective,* is designed to produce clinically useful instruments that help detect psychopathology. Self-report inventory developers who follow this approach typically are clinically trained psychologists who focus on conducting applied research. On the other

hand, test developers working from the *normal personality perspective* typically have backgrounds in personality or developmental psychology and often seek to construct measures of normal-range personality constructs that can serve as tools in basic personality research.

The clinical perspective on self-report instrument development has its origins in the psychiatric medical model, in which psychopathology is viewed generally as typological in nature and measures are designed to identify membership in distinct diagnostic classes. In contrast, the normal personality perspective has its origins in the field of differential psychology. Its focus is on personality traits, and dimensional constructs are used to describe meaningful differences among individuals. As just noted, the two perspectives are not mutually exclusive. Tests developed from the clinical perspective have been found to be quite useful in personality research, and normal-range personality inventories are used in a variety of clinical applications. Self-report inventories can also be distinguished in terms of the approaches used to construct and interpret scores on their scales, the methods used to derive standard scores for these scales, and the availability and types of scales and techniques designed to monitor individuals' test-taking attitude and its impact on scale scores.

This chapter first describes the history and development of SRIs and summarizes early criticisms of this technique. Next, current issues in SRI interpretation are described and discussed. Finally, directions for future SRI research are outlined. This chapter's focus is on general issues related to SRI-based assessment of personality and psychopathology. Literature reviews relating to use of specific instruments have been provided by Craig (1999), Dorfman and Hersen (2001), Groth-Marnat (1997), Maruish, (1999), and Strack and Lorr (1994).

EARLY HISTORY

Ben-Porath and Butcher (1991) identified three primary personality assessment techniques and differentiated between them based on the means and sources used for data collection. *Behavioral observations* include methods in which personality is assessed by systematically recorded observations of an individual's behavior. Examples include Cattell's (1965, 1979) *T* (systematic experimentation) and *L* (behavioral observation) data. *Somatic examinations* consist of techniques that rely on some form of physical measurement as the basis for assessing psychological functioning. Examples include various psychophysiological measures (e.g., Keller, Hicks, & Miller, 2000). *Verbal examinations* rely on verbalizations (oral, written, or a combination of the two) produced by the individual being assessed or another person who presumably knows the assessment target. Self-report inventories, as defined earlier, are a subclass of the verbal examination techniques. Projective assessment techniques (e.g., the Rorschach and Thematic Apperception Test, or TAT) also fall under this definition and are reviewed by Viglione in his chapter in this volume.

Ben-Porath and Butcher (1991) traced the early origins of verbal examinations to an elaborate system of competitive examinations (described in detail by Dubois, 1970) used for over 3000 years to select personnel for the Chinese civil service. Candidates for government positions were tested (and retested every three years) to determine their suitability for these prestigious appointments. Examinees were required to write essays for hours at a time, over a period of several successive days. The essays were used (among other purposes) to gauge the candidates' character and fitness for office (DuBois, 1970).

In the modern era, Sir Francis Galton was the first to suggest and try out systematic procedures for measuring psychological variables based on verbalizations (as well as some novel approaches to behavioral observations). Influenced heavily by the writings of his cousin, Charles Darwin, Galton was interested in devising precise methods for measuring individual differences in mental traits he believed were the product of evolution. Laying the foundations for quantitative approaches to personality assessment, Galton wrote:

> We want lists of facts, every one of which may be separately verified, valued, and revalued, and the whole accurately summed. It is the statistics of each man's conduct in small everyday affairs, that will probably be found to give the simplest and most precise measure of his character. (Galton, 1884, p. 185)

Most of Galton's efforts to elicit such information through verbalizations focused on devising various associative tasks. The Dutch scholars Heymans and Wiersma (1906) were the first to devise a questionnaire for the task of personality assessment. They constructed a 90-item rating scale and asked some 3,000 physicians to use the scale to describe people with whom they were well acquainted. Based upon correlations they found among traits that were rated, Heymans and Wiersma, in essence, developed a crude, hierarchical, factor-analytically generated personality model. They proposed that individuals may be described in terms of their standing on eight lower-order traits: *Amorphous, Apathetic, Nervous, Sentimental, Sanguine, Phlegmatic, Choleric,* and *Impassioned.* These traits consisted, in turn, of various combinations of three higher-order traits labeled *Activity, Emotionality,* and *Primary versus Secondary Function.* This structure bears substantial similarity to Eysenck's three-factor (Extraversion, Neuroticism, Psychopathy) personality model (Eysenck & Eysenck, 1975).

Hoch and Amsden (1913) and Wells (1914) provided further elaboration on the Heymans and Wiersma (1906) model's utility for personality description and assessment by adding to it various psychopathology symptoms. Their work, in turn, laid the foundations for the first systematic effort to develop a self-report personality questionnaire, Woodworth's (1920) Personal Data Sheet. Woodworth developed the Personal Data Sheet to assist in identifying psychoneurotic individuals who were unfit for duty in the U.S. military during World War I. This need arose because of the large number of combat personnel who had developed shell shock during the conflict. The questionnaire was to be used as a screening instrument so that recruits who exceeded a certain threshold would be referred for follow-up examinations.

DuBois (1970) reported that Woodworth initially compiled hundreds of "neurotic" items from various sources as candidates for inclusion on his questionnaire. Candidate items were selected if their content was judged to be potentially relevant to identifying neurosis. Items were phrased in question form, and test takers were instructed to answer "yes" or "no" to indicate whether each item described them accurately. Woodworth conducted a series of empirical investigations and eliminated items answered "yes" by large numbers of normal individuals. The final questionnaire consisted of 116 items. All were keyed such that a "yes" response was an indication of psychoneurosis. Although the Personal Data Sheet was never used for the purposes for which it was constructed—the war had ended by the time it was completed—both its items and Woodworth's reliance (in part) on empirical analyses for its construction served as the cornerstones for most subsequent self-report personality inventories.

With the conclusion of World War I Woodworth abandoned his test development efforts and refocused his attention on experimental psychology. However, a number of researchers in the then-novel subdiscipline called personality psychology followed in his footsteps. Downey's (1923) Will-Temperament tests, Travis's (1925) Diagnostic Character Test, Heidbreder's (1926) Extraversion-Introversion test, Thurstone's (1930) Personality Schedule, and Allport's (1928) Ascendance-Submission measure were among the more prominent early successors to Woodworth's efforts. Over the next three decades, a substantial literature evaluating the SRI technique's merits accumulated. Two comprehensive reviews of this methodology reflected the normal personality and clinical perspectives on assessing personality and psychopathology by self-report. Both Allport (1937), adopting a normal personality perspective, and Ellis (1946), from the clinical perspective, noted SRIs' rapid proliferation, while expressing concern (for somewhat different reasons) about their scientific foundations.

Allport's (1937) Critique

Allport (1937), among the originators of the field of personality psychology, anticipated (correctly) that SRIs would enjoy widespread use in personality research and compared them (somewhat skeptically) with the then more established use of behavioral ratings as a source for quantitative personality data:

> Though less objective than behavioral scales, standardized questionnaires have the merit of sampling a much wider range of behavior, through the medium of the subject's report on his customary conduct or attitudes in a wide variety of situations. These paper and pencil tests are popular for a number of reasons. For one thing, they are fun to construct and fun to take. Students find them diverting, and teachers accordingly use them as agreeable classroom demonstrations. Furthermore, the scores on the tests can be manipulated in diverse ways, and when the quantitative yield of the coefficients and group differences is complete, everyone has a comforting assurance concerning the "scientific" status of personality. (p. 448)

In considering self-report personality questionnaires' merits, Allport (1937) identified several limitations that remain salient in current applications of this methodology. One was that "It is a fallacy to assume that all people have the same psychological reasons for their similar responses [to self-report items]" (p. 449). Allport answered this concern by quoting Binet: "Let the items be crude if only there be enough of them. . . . One hopes through sheer length of a series that the erroneous diagnoses will to a certain extent cancel one another, and that a trustworthy residual score will remain" (p. 449).

In describing a second major limitation of personality tests, Allport stated:

> Another severe criticism lies in the ability of the subject to fake the test if he chooses to do so. . . . Anyone by trying can (on paper) simulate introversion, conservatism, or even happiness. And if he thinks he has something to gain, he is quite likely to do so. . . . Even well intentioned subjects may fail insight or slip into systematic error or bias that vitiates the value of their answers. (p. 450)

Thus, Allport listed their transparent nature and susceptibility to intentional and unintentional manipulation among SRI's major limitations.

In reviewing the major SRIs of his time, Allport (1937) singled out the Bernreuter Personality Inventory (BPI; Bernreuter, 1933). The BPI consisted of 125 items (originating from several previous SRIs including the Personal Data Sheet) phrased as questions with a "yes" "no" or "?" (i.e., cannot say) response format. The items yielded scores on four common personality traits, labeled *Dominance, Self-Sufficiency, Introversion,* and *Neuroticism.* Each of the 125 items was scored on all four scales (although some were scored zero), according to empirically derived criteria. For example, if answered "?," the item "Do you often feel just miserable" was scored -3 on introversion, -1 on dominance, 0 on neuroticism, and 0 on self-sufficiency. Allport (1937) questioned the logic of this approach and recommended instead that items be scored on single scales only.

Finally, Allport (1937) grappled with the question of whether multiscaled SRIs should be designed to measure independent traits or constructs. Commenting on the then-budding practice of factor analyzing scores on multiscale SRIs to derive "independent factors," Allport noted:

> Unnecessary trouble springs from assuming, as some testers do, that *independent* factors are to be preferred to *inter-dependent* traits. What if certain scales do correlate with each other. . . . Each scale may still represent a well-conceived, measurable

common trait. . . . No harm is done by overlap; indeed, overlap is a reasonable expectation in view of that roughness of approximation which is the very nature of the entire procedure (also in view of the tendency of certain traits to cluster). Well-considered scales with some overlap are preferable to ill-conceived scales without overlap. To seek intelligible units is a better psychological goal than to seek independent units. (p. 329)

In summary, viewing SRIs from the normal personality perspective, Allport (1937) raised several important concerns regarding the early successors to Woodworth's Personal Data Sheet. Recognizing their simplicity of use and consequent appeal, Allport cautioned that SRIs, by necessity, distill human personality to common traits at the expense of a more complete, individually crafted personality description. He emphasized SRIs' tremendous vulnerability to intentional and unintentional distortion, viewing it as an inherent feature of this methodology. He criticized the BPI's method of scoring the same item on multiple scales, as well as early factor analysts' efforts to reduce multiscale instruments such as the BPI to a small number of independent factors. Allport (1937) offered this rather ambivalent concluding appraisal of the nascent area of personality assessment by self-report: "Historically considered the extension of mental measurements into the field of personality is without doubt one of the outstanding events in American psychology during the twentieth century. The movement is still in its accelerating phase, and the swift output of ingenious tests has quite outstripped progress in criticism and theory" (p. 455).

Ellis's (1946) Review of Personality Questionnaires

Ellis (1946), writing from the clinical perspective, offered a comprehensive appraisal of personality questionnaires near the midpoint of the twentieth century. He opened his critique with the following generalization:

While the reliabilities of personality questionnaires have been notoriously high, their validities have remained more questionable. Indeed some of the most widely known and used paper and pencil personality tests have been cavalierly marketed without any serious attempts on the part of their authors to validate them objectively . . . no real endeavors have been made to show that, when used according to their standard directions, these instruments will actually do the clinical jobs they are supposed to do: meaning, that they will adequately differentiate neurotics from non-neurotics, introverts from extroverts, dominant from submissive persons, and so on. (p. 385)

Ellis's (1946) opening comments reflected aptly the clinical perspective's focus on classifying individuals into dichotomous, typological categories. Ellis noted that several authors had preceded him in criticizing SRIs and outlined the following emerging points of concern:

- Most empirical SRI studies have focused on their reliability (which has been established), while ignoring matters of validity.
- SRIs do not provide a whole, organismic picture of human behavior. Although they may accurately portray a group of individuals, they are not useful in individual diagnosis.
- Some questionnaires (like the BPI) that purport to measure several distinct traits are, at best, measuring the same one under two or more names.
- Different individuals interpret the same SRI questions in different ways.
- Most subjects can easily falsify their answers to SRIs and frequently choose to do so.
- SRIs' "yes/?/no" response format may compromise the scales' validity.
- Lack of internal consistency may invalidate a questionnaire, but presence of internal consistency does not necessarily validate it.
- SRIs' vocabulary range may cause misunderstandings by respondents and thus adversely affect validity.
- Testing is an artificial procedure, which has little to do with real-life situations.
- Some personality questionnaires are validated against other questionnaires from which their items were largely taken, thus rendering their validation spurious.
- Even when a respondent does his best to answer questions truthfully, he may lack insight into his true behavior or may unconsciously be quite a different person from the picture of himself he draws on the test.
- Armchair (rather than empirical) construction and evaluation of test items is frequently used in personality questionnaires.
- Uncritical use of statistical procedures with many personality tests adds a spurious reality to data that were none too accurate in the first place.
- Many personality tests that claim to measure the same traits (e.g., introversion-extroversion) have very low intercorrelations with each other.
- There are no statistical shortcuts to the understanding of human nature; such as the ones many test users try to arrive at through involved factorial analyses.

Although generated from a notably different perspective, Ellis's (1946) concerns overlap substantially with Allport's

(1937) reservations. The two authors also shared consternation that, in spite of these glaring deficiencies, SRIs had become quite popular: "In spite of the many assaults that have been made against it, the paper and pencil personality test has got along splendidly as far as usage is concerned. For there can be little doubt that Americans have, to date, taken more of the Woodworth-Thurstone-Bernreuter type of questionnaires than all other kinds of personality tests combined" (Ellis, 1946, p. 388).

To explain their seemingly unfounded popularity, Ellis (1946) identified several advantages that their proponents claimed for SRIs:

- They are relatively easy to administer and score.
- Even if the respondent's self-description is not taken at face value, it may itself provide some clinically meaningful information.
- Although scale scores may be meaningless, examination of individual responses by experienced clinicians may provide valid clinical material.
- Statistical analyses had shown that the traits posited by questionnaires were not simply the product of chance factors.
- Normal and abnormal test takers tended to give different answers to SRI items.
- It does not matter if respondents answer untruthfully on personality questionnaires, since allowances are made for this in standardization or scoring of the tests.
- Traditional methods of validating questionnaires by outside criteria are themselves faulty and invalid; hence, validation by internal consistency alone is perfectly sound.

Having outlined the prevailing pros and cons for personality questionnaires (from a decidedly con-slanted perspective) Ellis (1946) proceeded to conduct a comprehensive, albeit crude, meta-analysis of the literature on personality tests' validity, differentiating between two methods for validating personality questionnaires. He dubbed one method *subjective* and described it rather derogatorily as consisting of "checking the test against itself: that is[,] seeing whether respondents answer its questions in a manner showing it to be internally consistent" (p. 390).

Ellis (1946) described the second method, labeled *objective personality test validation,* as

> checking a schedule, preferably item by item, against an outside clinical criterion. Thus, a questionnaire may be given to a group of normal individuals and to another group of subjects who have been diagnosed by competent outside observers as *neurotic,* or

maladjusted, or *psychotic, delinquent,* or *introverted.* Often, the clinically diagnosed group makes significantly higher *neurotic* scores than does the normal group, [so] the test under consideration is said to have been validated. (p. 390)

Ellis (1946) questioned whether the subjective method had any bearing on tests' validity, stating "Internal consistency of a questionnaire demonstrates, at best, that it is a reliable test of *something;* but that *something* may still have little or no relation to the clinical diagnosis for which the test presumably has been designed" (p. 391). He also found very limited utility in the objective methods of test validation, citing their sole reliance on questionable validity criteria. Nonetheless, he proceeded to review over 250 published objective validation studies classified into six types based on the method used to generate criterion validity data. Ellis sought to quantify his findings by keeping count of the number of positive, negative, and questionable findings (based on whether these were statistically significant) in each category of studies. Overall, he found positive results in 31 percent of the studies, questionable ones in 17 percent, and negative findings in 52 percent of the publications included in his survey. Ellis (1946) concluded, "Obviously, this is not a very good record for the validity of paper and pencil personality questionnaires" (p. 422).

In selecting studies for inclusion in his analysis, Ellis (1946) singled one instrument out for separate treatment and analysis, the then relatively unknown Minnesota Multiphasic Personality Inventory (MMPI; Hathaway & McKinley, 1943). Ellis explained that, unlike the more established instruments included in his review, which were administered anonymously by paper and pencil to groups of subjects, the MMPI was administered individually, simulating more accurately a clinical interview. Of the fifteen MMPI studies he reviewed, Ellis reported positive results in ten studies, questionable ones in three, and negative findings in two investigations.

Ellis's overall conclusions regarding SRIs' validity were quite negative:

> We may conclude, therefore, that judging from the validity studies on group-administered personality questionnaires thus far reported in the literature, there is at best one chance in two that these tests will validly discriminate between *groups* of adjusted and maladjusted individuals, and there is very little indication that they can be safely used to diagnose *individual* cases or to give valid estimations of the personality traits of *specific* respondents. The older, more conventional, and more widely used forms of these tests seem to be, for practical diagnostic purposes, hardly worth the paper on which they are printed. Among the newer questionnaires, the Minnesota Multiphasic schedule appears to be the most promising one—perhaps

because it gets away from group administration which has hitherto been synonymous with personality test-giving. More research in this direction is well warranted at the present time. (1946, p. 425)

Judged with the hindsight of 55 years, Ellis's critique appears rather naïve and inherently flawed. As has been shown, Ellis himself questioned the utility of the validation methods used in the studies he included in his analyses, noting (correctly) that many, if not most, relied on questionably valid criteria. Given this limitation, these studies could not adequately demonstrate SRIs' validity or invalidity. Although the tests he reviewed were indeed psychometrically inadequate, Ellis's effort to appraise them empirically was hampered significantly by limitations in the literature he reviewed. Moreover, his summary dismissal of internal consistency as having little or no bearing on validity was overstated.

Nonetheless, Ellis's review, published in the prestigious *Psychological Bulletin,* had a devastating effect on SRIs' position within the budding field of clinical psychology. Dahlstrom (1992) described the widespread skepticism with which all SRIs were perceived for the ensuing 10 years following this and several similar analyses. Indeed, use of tests (such as the BPI) singled out for their lack of validity waned dramatically in the years that followed. Ellis (1946) did, however, anticipate correctly that the MMPI might emerge as a viable alternative to the SRIs of the first half of the twentieth century.

Ellis (1953) revisited this issue seven years later, in an updated review of personality tests' validity. He concluded that there had been limited progress in developing valid personality SRIs and focused his criticism on the instruments' susceptibility to intentional and unintentional distortion. He was particularly concerned with the effects of unconscious defenses. Ellis (1953) again singled out the MMPI as an instrument whose authors had at least made an attempt to correct for these effects on its scale scores, but he expressed skepticism about such corrections' success. He also observed that the efforts involved in correcting and properly interpreting MMPI scores might better be otherwise invested, stating, "The clinical psychologist who cannot, in the time it now takes a trained worker to administer, score, and interpret a test like the MMPI according to the best recommendations of its authors, get much more pertinent, incisive, and depth-centered 'personality' material from a straightforward interview technique would hardly appear to be worth his salt" (p. 48).

Curiously, Ellis (1953) saw no need to subject the preferred "straightforward interview technique" to the type of scrutiny he applied handily to SRIs. That task would be left to Meehl (1956) in his seminal monograph comparing the validity of clinical and actuarial assessment techniques.

Summary of Early History

Self-report inventories emerged as an attractive but scientifically limited approach to personality assessment during the first half of the twentieth century. Representing the normal personality perspective, Allport (1937) criticized these instruments for being inherently narrow in scope and unnecessarily divorced from any personality theory. Ellis (1946), writing from the clinical perspective, concluded that there was little or no empirical evidence of their validity as diagnostic instruments. Both authors identified their susceptibility to intentional and unintentional distortion and the implicit assumption that test items have the same meaning to different individuals as major and inherent weakness of SRIs as personality and psychopathology measures.

CURRENT ISSUES IN SELF-REPORT INVENTORY INTERPRETATION

In spite of their shaky beginnings, SRIs emerged during the second half of the twentieth century as the most widely used and studied method for assessing personality and psychopathology. Modern SRI developers sought to address the limitations of their predecessors in a variety of ways. Various approaches to SRI scale construction are described next, followed by a review of current issues in SRI scale score interpretation. These include the roles of empirical data and item content in interpreting SRI scale scores, methods used to derive standard scores for SRI interpretation, and threats to the validity of individual SRI protocols.

Throughout this section, examples from the SRI literature are cited, and most of these involve either the MMPI or MMPI-2. Emphasis on the MMPI/MMPI-2 reflects this instrument's central role in the modern literature as the most widely studied (Butcher & Rouse, 1996) and used (Camara, Nathan, & Puente, 2000) SRI.

Approaches to SRI Scale Construction

Burisch (1984) described three primary, non–mutually exclusive approaches that have been used in SRI scale construction. The *external* approach involves using collateral (i.e., extratest) data to identify items for an SRI scale. Here, individuals are classified into known groups based on criteria that are independent of scale scores (e.g., psychiatric diagnoses) and items are chosen based on their empirical ability to differentiate among members of different groups. The method is sometimes also called *empirical keying.* Self-report inventory developers who view personality or psychopathology categorically and seek to develop empirical methods for classifying individuals into predetermined categories typically use the external scale construction method. Often, these categories correspond to diagnostic classes such as schizophrenia or major depression. As would be expected, scale developers who rely on this approach typically assume a clinical perspective on personality assessment.

Ellis (1946) highlighted a major limitation of the external approach in his critique of SRIs as measures of personality and psychopathology. That is, their validity is constrained by the criteria that are used in their development. Absent consensually agreed-upon criteria for classification (a situation not uncommon in psychological assessment, and what typically motivates efforts to develop a scale to begin with), test developers must rely upon imperfect or controversial external criteria for subject classification, item selection, and subsequent cross-validation. Consequently, scales developed with this method have generally not fared well as predictors of the class membership status that they were designed to predict. However, in some instances (e.g., the MMPI clinical scales), subsequent (to their development) empirical research has guided fruitful application of externally developed scales in ways other than those in which their developers intended originally that they be used, by identifying clinically meaningful correlates of these scales and the patterns of scores among them.

Scale developers who follow the *inductive* approach, according to Burisch (1984), assume that there exists a basic, probably universal personality structure, which they attempt both to discover and to measure. The approach is considered inductive because its adherents do not set out to measure a preconceived set of traits, but instead leave it up to empirical analyses to reveal important personality dimensions and the relations among them. In the process, an SRI is developed to measure the discovered personality structure. Scale developers who apply the inductive approach often adhere to a normal personality perspective on assessment. They typically rely on various forms of factor analysis, and the constructs they identify characteristically are dimensional. A leading example of an inductively derived SRI is Cattell's 16 Personality Factor Questionnaire (16PF; Cattell, Cattell, & Cattell, 1993). Inductive scale development often follows an iterative process of item writing, data collection, factor analysis, and item revision, followed by subsequent rounds of data collection, analysis, and item modification (e.g., Tellegen, 1982).

Finally, Burisch (1984) describes the *deductive* approach to personality scale construction as one in which developers start with a conceptually grounded personality model and rationally write or select items that are consonant with their conceptualization. Most early personality and psychopathology SRI developers followed this approach in developing the MMPI precursors so devastatingly criticized by Allport (1937) and

Ellis (1946). Consequently, deductive scale construction was viewed for many years as an inferior, less sophisticated form of SRI development. Burisch argued and demonstrated that these seemingly less sophisticated scale development techniques often yield measures that compare quite favorably with products of external and inductive scale construction.

The three approaches to scale construction are not mutually exclusive. Any combination of the three may be used in constructing an SRI scale, or different sets of scales within the same instrument. For example, the MMPI-2 (Butcher et al., 2001) contains three sets of scales, each initially based on a different one of the three approaches to scale construction—the clinical scales, originally (Hathaway, 1956; Hathaway & McKinley, 1940, 1942; McKinley & Hathaway, 1940, 1942, 1944) based on the external method; the Content Scales (Butcher, Graham, Williams, & Ben-Porath, 1990), constructed with a modified deductive approach; and the Personality Psychopathology Five (PSY-5; Harkness, McNulty, & Ben-Porath, 1995), the end product of an inductive research project (Harkness & McNulty, 1994).

Approaches to SRI Scale Score Interpretation

Two general approaches to SRI scale score interpretation can be identified based on their sources for interpretive conclusions. *Empirically grounded interpretations* rely on empirical data to form the basis for ascribing meaning to SRI scale scores. *Content-based interpretations* are guided by SRI scales' item content. Empirically grounded approaches have played a more central role in personality and psychopathology SRIs; however, more recently, content-based interpretation has gained increasing recognition and use. As will be discussed after the two approaches are described, they are not mutually exclusive.

Empirically Grounded Interpretation

Meehl (1945) outlined the basic logic of empirically grounded SRI scale interpretation in his classic article "The Dynamics of 'Structured' Personality Inventories." Responding to early SRI critics' contention that the instruments are inherently flawed because their interpretation is predicated on the assumption that test takers are motivated, and able, to respond accurately to their items, he stated:

> A "self-rating" constitutes an intrinsically interesting and significant bit of verbal behavior, the non-test correlates of which must be discovered by empirical means. Not only is this approach free from the restriction that the subject must be able to describe his own behavior accurately, but a careful study of structured personality tests built on this basis shows that such a restriction

would falsify the actual relationships that hold between what a man says and what he *is*. (p. 297)

Thus, according to Meehl, empirical interpretation is neither predicated nor dependent on what the test taker says (or thinks he or she is saying) in responding to SRI items, but rather on the empirical correlates of these statements (as summarized in SRI scale scores).

Two subclasses can be distinguished among the empirical approaches to SRI scale interpretation. Scales constructed with the external approach are expected, based on the method used in their construction, to differentiate empirically between members of the groups used in their development. This form of empirical interpretation, which may be termed *empirically keyed interpretation*, is predicated on the assumption that if members of different groups (e.g., a target group of depressed patients and a comparison sample of nonpatients) answer a set of items differently, individuals who answer these items similarly to target group members likely belong to that group (i.e., they are depressed). This turns out to be a problematic assumption that requires (and often fails to achieve) empirical verification. Consequently, empirically keyed interpretations, as defined here, are used infrequently in current SRI applications.

The second approach to empirical interpretation is predicated on post hoc statistical identification of variables that are correlated with SRI scale scores (i.e., their empirical correlates). The *empirical correlate interpretation* approach is independent of the method used to develop a scale and may be applied to measures constructed by any (one or combination) of the three methods just outlined. Unlike the empirically keyed approach, it requires no a priori assumptions regarding the implications of one scale construction technique or another. All that is required are relevant extratest data regarding individuals whose SRI scale scores are available. Statistical analyses are conducted to identify variables that are correlated empirically with SRI scale scores; these are their empirical correlates. For example, if a scale score is empirically correlated with extratest indicators of depressive symptoms, individuals who score higher than others on that scale can be described as more likely than others to display depressive symptomatology.

Empirical correlates can guide SRI scale interpretation at two inference levels. The example just given represents a simple, direct inference level. The empirical fact that a scale score is correlated with an extratest depression indicator is used to gauge the depression of an individual who produces a given score on that scale. The correlation between scale and external indicator represents its *criterion validity*, which in turn reflects the confidence level we should place in an interpretation based on this correlation.

Although the concept of interpreting scale scores based on their criterion validity represents a simple and direct inference level, the process of establishing and understanding SRIs' criterion validity is complex and challenging. As already noted, the absence of valid criteria often motivates scale development to begin with. In addition, as with any psychological variable, criterion measures themselves are always, to some extent, unreliable. Consequently, validity coefficients, the observed correlations between SRI scale scores and criteria, always underestimate the scales' criterion validity. If a criterion's reliability can be reasonably estimated, correction for attenuation due to unreliability is possible to derive a more accurate estimate of criterion validity. However, this is rarely done, and it does not address limitations in criterion validity coefficients imposed by the criterion measures' imperfect validity. Self-report inventory critics often point to rather low criterion validity coefficients as indications of these instruments' psychometric weakness, without giving adequate consideration to the limitations just noted.

A second, more complex, and less direct inference level in empirical interpretation of SRI scale scores involves reliance on their *construct validity*. Cronbach and Meehl (1955) indicated that

Construct validation is involved whenever a test is to be interpreted as a measure of some attribute or quality, which is not "operationally defined" . . . . When an investigator believes that no criterion available to him is fully valid, he perforce becomes interested in construct validity because this is the only way to avoid the "infinite frustration" of relating every criterion to some more ultimate standard . . . . Construct validity must be investigated whenever no criterion or universe of content is accepted as entirely adequate to define the quality to be measured. (p. 282)

Cronbach and Meehl (1955) described construct validation as an ongoing process of learning (through empirical research) about the nature of psychological constructs that underlie scale scores and using this knowledge to guide and refine their interpretation. They defined the seemingly paradoxical bootstraps effect, whereby a test may be constructed based on a fallible criterion and, through the process of construct validation, that same test winds up having greater validity than the criterion used in its construction. As an example, they cited the MMPI Pd scale, which was developed using an external scale construction approach with the intent that it be used to identify individuals with a psychopathic personality. Cronbach and Meehl (1955) noted that the scale turned out to have a limited degree of criterion validity for this task. However, as its empirical correlates became elucidated through subsequent research, a construct underlying Pd scores emerged that allowed MMPI interpreters to describe individuals who score high on this scale based on both a broad range of empirical correlates and a conceptual under-standing of the Pd construct. The latter allowed for further predictions about likely Pd correlates to be made and tested empirically. These tests, in turn, broadened or sharpened (depending on the research outcome) the scope of the Pd con-struct and its empirical correlates.

Knowledge of a scale's construct validity offers a rich, more comprehensive foundation for empirical interpretation than does criterion validity alone. It links the assessment process to theoretical conceptualizations and formulations in a manner described by Cronbach and Meehl (1955) as involving a construct's nomological network, "the interlocking system of laws which constitute a theory" (p. 290). Thus, empirical re-search can enhance our understanding of (and ability to inter-pret) psychological test results by placing them in the context of well-developed and appropriately tested theories.

Whether it is based on criterion or construct validity, or both, empirically grounded SRI interpretation can occur at two levels, focusing either on individual scale scores or on config-urations among them. *Configural interpretation* involves si-multaneous consideration of scores on more than one SRI scale. *Linear interpretation* involves separate, independent consideration and interpretation of each SRI scale score.

Much of the literature on this topic involves the MMPI. The move toward configural MMPI interpretation came on the heels of the test's failure to meet its developers' original goal, differential diagnosis of eight primary forms of psy-chopathology. Clinical experience, bolstered by findings from a series of studies (e.g., Black, 1953; Guthrie, 1952; Halbower, 1955; Hathaway & Meehl, 1951) led MMPI inter-preters to conclude that robust empirical correlates for the test were most likely to be found if individuals were classi-fied into types based on the pattern of scores they generated on the test's clinical scales. Based partly on this development, Meehl's (1954) treatise on clinical versus actuarial prediction advocated that researchers pursue a three-pronged task: First, they must identify meaningful classes within which individ-uals tend to cluster. These would replace the inadequate Kraepelinian nosology that served as the target for the MMPI clinical scales' original development. Next, investigators would need to devise reliable and valid ways of identifying to which class a given individual belongs. Finally, they would identify the empirical correlates of class membership.

In his subsequent call for a so-called cookbook-based interpretation, Meehl (1956) proposed that MMPI profiles could serve all three purposes. Patterns of scores (i.e., config-urations) on MMPI clinical scales could be used to identify clinically meaningful and distinct types of individuals; these scores could be used (based on a series of classification rules) to assign individuals to a specific profile type; and empirical research could be conducted to elucidate the correlates of

MMPI profile type group membership. Several investigators (most notably Marks and Seeman, 1963, and Gilberstadt and Duker, 1965) followed Meehl's call and produced such MMPI-based classification and interpretation systems.

Underlying configural scale score interpretation is the as-sumption that there is something about a combination of scores on SRI scales that is not captured by consideration of each scale score individually (i.e., a linear interpretation) and that the whole is somehow greater than (or at least different from) the sum of its parts. For example, there is something to be learned about an individual who generates his or her most deviant scores on MMPI scales 1 (Hypochondriasis) and 3 (Hysteria) that is not reflected in the individual's scores on these scales when they are considered separately. Statisti-cally, this amounts to the expectation of an interaction among scale scores in the prediction of relevant extratest data.

Surprisingly, the assumption that configural interpretation should be more valid than linear approaches has not been tested extensively. Goldberg (1965) conducted the most elab-orate examination of this question to date. He found that a linear combination of scores on individual MMPI scale scores was more effective than the configural set of classifi-cation rules developed by Meehl and Dahlstrom (1960) to differentiate between neurotic and psychotic test takers. The implicit assumption of an interaction among scales that make up the configuration has yet to be extensively tested.

Content-Based Interpretation

Content-based SRI interpretation involves reliance on item content to interpret scale scores. For example, if a scale's items contain a list of depressive symptoms, scores on that scale are interpreted to reflect the individual's self-reported depression. It is distinguished from deductive SRI scale construction in that the latter involves using item content for scale development, not necessarily interpretation. Indeed, scales constructed by any of the three primary approaches (ex-ternal, inductive, or deductive) can be interpreted based on their item content, and SRI measures constructed deductively can be interpreted with an empirically grounded approach.

Content-based SRI interpretation predates empirically grounded approaches and was the focus of many aspects of both Allport's (1937) and Ellis's (1946) early SRI critiques. Meehl's (1945) rationale for empirically grounded SRI scale score interpretation was a reaction to the criticism that content-based interpretation was predicated on the dubious assump-tions that test items have the same meaning to test takers that they do to scale developers and that all respondents understand items comparably and approach testing in a motivated and co-operative manner. Meehl (1945) agreed (essentially) that such assumptions were necessary for content-based interpretation and that they were unwarranted. His influential paper on this topic left content-based interpretation in ill repute among sophisticated SRI users for the next twenty years.

Content-based SRI interpretation began to make a comeback when Wiggins (1966) introduced a set of content scales developed with the MMPI item pool. Using a deductive scale development approach complemented by empirical refinement designed to maximize their internal consistency, Wiggins constructed a psychometrically sound set of 13 MMPI content scales and proposed that they be used to augment empirically grounded interpretation of the test's clinical scales. In laying out his rationale for developing a set of content scales for the MMPI, Wiggins commented:

> The viewpoint that a personality test protocol represents a communication between the subject and the tester (or the institution he represents) has much to commend it, not the least of which is the likelihood that this is the frame of reference adopted by the subject himself. (p. 2)

He went on to acknowledge that

> Obviously, the respondent has some control over what he chooses to communicate, and there are a variety of factors which may enter to distort the message . . . . Nevertheless, recognition of such sources of "noise" in the system should not lead us to overlook the fact that a message is still involved. (p. 25)

Wiggins was keenly aware of the inherent limits of SRI assessment in general, and content-based interpretation in particular. However, he argued that how an individual chooses to present him- or herself, whatever the reasoning or motivation, provides useful information that might augment what could be learned from empirically grounded interpretation alone. Wiggins (1966) advocated that although we need (and, indeed, should) not take it at face value, how a person chooses to present him- or herself is inherently informative and that it is incumbent upon SRI interpreters to make an effort to find out what it was that an individual sought to communicate in responding to an SRI's items. By developing internally consistent SRI scales, psychologists could provide a reliable means for communication between test takers and interpreters.

Empirically Grounded Versus Content-Based SRI Interpretation

Empirically grounded and content-based interpretations are not mutually exclusive. Often, scale scores intended for interpretation based on one approach can also be (and are) interpreted based on the other. For example, although the MMPI-2 clinical scales are interpreted primarily based on their empirical

correlates, the Harris-Lingoes subscales augment clinical scale interpretation by identifying content areas that may primarily be responsible for elevation on a given clinical scale. Conversely, although their interpretation is guided primarily by item content, the MMPI-2 Content Scales (Butcher et al., 1990) also are interpreted based on their empirical correlates.

A primary distinction between empirically grounded and content-based interpretation is that the latter (as SRI critics have long argued) is more susceptible to intentional and unintentional distortion. However, as is discussed later in detail, appropriate application of SRIs requires that test-taking attitude be measured and considered as part of the interpretation process. Because of its inherent susceptibility to distortion, content-based interpretation requires that an SRI be particularly effective in measuring and identifying misleading approaches and that its users apply tools designed to do so appropriately.

Generating Scores for SRI Interpretation: Standard Score Derivation

Depending upon their response format, SRI *raw scores* consist either of a count of the number of items answered in the keyed (true or false) direction or a sum of the respondent's Likert scale ratings on a scale's items. These scores have no intrinsic meaning. They are a function of arbitrary factors such as the number of items on a scale and the instrument's response format. Raw scores typically are transformed to some form of *standard score* that places an individual's SRI scale raw score in an interpretable context. Standard scores are typically generated by a comparison of an individual's raw score on a scale to that of a normative reference group(s) composed of the instrument's *standardization* or *normative sample*(s). Because of their critical role in SRI interpretation, it is important to understand how standard scores are derived as well as the factors that determine their adequacy.

The most common standard score used with SRIs is the *T* score, which expresses an individual's standing in reference to the standardization sample on a metric having a mean of 50 and a standard deviation of 10. This is typically accomplished through the following transformation:

$$T = \frac{RS - MRS}{SDRS} * 10 + 50,$$

where *T* is the individual's *T* score, *RS* is his or her raw score, *MRS* is the standardization sample's mean score, and *SDRS* is the sample's standard deviation on a given SRI scale. A *T* score of 50 corresponds to the mean level for the standardization sample. A *T* score equal to 60 indicates that the person's score falls one standard deviation above the normative mean. The choice of 50 and 10 for the standard scores' mean and standard deviation is arbitrary but has evolved as common practice in many (although not all) SRIs.

Standard scores provide information on where the respondent stands on the construct(s) measured by a SRI scale in comparison with a normative reference. A second important and common application of standard scores is to allow for comparisons across SRI scales. Given the arbitrary nature of SRI scale raw scores, it is not possible to compare an individual's raw scores on, for example, measures of anxiety and depression. Transformation of raw scores to standard scores allows the test interpreter to determine whether an individual shows greater deviation from the normative mean on one measure or another. Such information could be used to assist an assessor in differential diagnostic tasks or, more generally, to allow for configural test interpretation, which, as described earlier in this chapter, involves simultaneous consideration of multiple SRI scale scores.

The accuracy and utility of standard scores rest heavily on the nature and quality of the normative reference sample. To the extent that they aptly represent the target population, standard scores will provide an accurate gauge of the individual's standing on the construct(s) of interest and allow for comparison of an individual's standing across constructs and, more generally, facilitate configural SRI interpretation. Conversely, if the normative reference scores somehow misrepresent the target population, the resulting standard scores will hinder all of the tasks just mentioned. Several factors must be considered in determining whether a normative reference sample represents the target population appropriately. These involve various types and effects of normative sampling problems.

Types and Effects of Normative Sampling Problems

Identifying potential problems with standard scores can be accomplished by considering the general formula for transforming raw score to standard scores:

$$SS = \frac{RS - MRS}{SDRS} * NewSD + NewMean,$$

where SS is the individual's standard score, RS is his or her raw score, MRS is the standardization sample's mean score, $SDRS$ is the sample's standard deviation on a given SRI scale, $NewSD$ is the target standard deviation for the standard scores, and $NewMean$ is the target mean for these scores. As discussed earlier, the target mean and standard deviations are arbitrary, but common practice in SRI scale development is to use T scores that have a mean of 50 and a standard deviation of 10. An important consideration in evaluating standard scores'

adequacy is the extent to which the normative reference (or standardization) sample appropriately represents the population's mean and standard deviation on a given SRI scale.

Examination of the general transformation formula shows that if a normative sample's mean (MRS) is higher than the actual population mean, the resulting standard score will underestimate the individual's standing in reference to the normative population. Consider a hypothetical example in which T scores are used, the individual's raw score equals 10, the normative sample's mean equals 12, the actual population mean equals 8, and both the sample and population standard deviations equal 5. Applying the T score transformation formula provided earlier,

$$T = \frac{10 - 12}{5} * 10 + 50 = 46$$

we find that this normative sample yields a T score of 46, suggesting that the individual's raw score falls nearly half a standard deviation below the normative mean on this construct. However, had the sample mean reflected accurately the population mean, applying the T score transformation formula

$$T = \frac{10 - 8}{5} * 10 + 50 = 54$$

would have yielded a T score of 54, indicating that the individual's raw score falls nearly half a standard deviation above the population mean. Larger discrepancies between sample and population mean would, of course, result in even greater underestimates of the individual's relative standing on the construct(s) of interest. Conversely, to the extent that the sample mean underestimates the population mean, the resulting standard scores will overestimate the individual's relative position on a given scale.

A second factor that could result in systematic inaccuracies in standard scores is sampling error in the standard deviation. To the extent that the normative sample's standard deviation underestimates the population standard deviation, the resulting standard score will overestimate the individual's relative standing on the scale. As we apply again the T score transformation formula, consider an example in which the individual's raw score equals 10, the sample and population means both equal 8, and the sample standard deviation equals 2, but the population standard deviation actually equals 5. Applying the formula based on the sample data

$$T = \frac{10 - 8}{2} * 10 + 50 = 60$$

yields a T score of 60, indicating that the individual's score falls one standard deviation above the normative mean.

However, an accurate estimate of the population standard deviation

$$T = \frac{10 - 8}{5} * 10 + 50 = 54$$

would have produced a T score of 54, reflecting a score that falls just under half a standard deviation above the normative mean. Here, too, a larger discrepancy between the sample and population standard deviation results in an even greater overestimation of the individual's standing on the construct(s) of interest, and, conversely, an overestimation of the population's standard deviation would result in an underestimation of the individual's relative score on a given measure.

Causes of Normative Sample Inadequacies

In light of their importance in determining standard scores' adequacy, it is essential to identify (and thus try to avoid) reasons why standardization samples may inaccurately estimate a target population's mean or standard deviation on an SRI scale. Three general types of problems may generate inaccurate normative means and standard deviations: sampling problems, population changes, and application changes. Two types of sampling problems error may occur. The simplest among these is *random sampling error,* in which, as a result of random factors associated with the sampling process, the normative sample mean or standard deviation fails to represent accurately the relevant population statistics. This can be minimized effectively by collecting sufficiently large normative samples.

Systematic sampling errors occur when, due to specific sampling flaws, the sample mean or standard deviation reflects inaccurately the relevant population statistics. In such cases a normative sample fails to represent accurately one or more segments of the target population as a result of sampling bias. This will negatively affect the normative sample's adequacy if two conditions are met: (1) a sample fails to represent accurately a certain population segment, *and* (2) the inadequately represented population segment differs systematically (in its mean, its standard deviation, or both) from the remaining population on a particular SRI scale. For example, if as a consequence of the sampling method used younger adults are underrepresented in a normative sample that is designed to represent the entire adult population, and younger adults differ systematically from the remaining adult population on the scale being standardized, this could result in biased estimates of both the population mean and its standard deviation. This might occur with a scale designed to measure depression, a variable that tends to vary as a function of age.

If younger adults are represented inadequately in a normative sample (this could occur if the sampling process failed to incorporate college students and military personnel) used to develop standard scores on a depression scale, the normative sample would overestimate the population mean on the scale and underestimate its standard deviation, resulting in the effects discussed previously.

Note that in order for systematic sampling error to affect scale norms, both conditions just specified must be met. That is, a population segment must be misrepresented and this segment must differ systematically from the remaining population on the scale being standardized. If only the first condition is met, but the misrepresented segment does not differ systematically from the remaining population, this will not result in biased estimates of the population mean and standard deviation. Such a scenario occurred with the updated normative sample used to standardize the MMPI-2 (Butcher, Dahlstrom, Graham, Tellegen, & Kaemmer, 1989). Data included in the MMPI-2 manual indicated that the new normative sample differed substantially from the general adult population in education. Specifically, the normative sample significantly underrepresented individuals with lower levels of education and overrepresented people with higher levels of education in the general adult population. Some authors (e.g., Duckworth, 1991) expressed concern that this may introduce systematic bias in the updated norms. However, subsequent analyses demonstrated that this sampling bias had no significant impact on resulting test norms because education is not correlated substantially with MMPI scale scores (Schinka & LaLone, 1997).

Population changes are a second reason why normative samples may inadequately represent their target population. These occur when, over the course of time, the target population changes on the construct that a scale measures. For example, Anastasi (1985), in a review of longitudinal research on intelligence, found a trend for population-wide increases in intelligence over the first half of the twentieth century. These were the result primarily of increases in population education levels in general and literacy levels in particular. To account for these changes' effects on their norms, it has been necessary for intelligence test developers to periodically collect new normative data. To the extent that constructs measured by SRIs are affected similarly by population changes, it becomes necessary to update their normative databases as well. This was one of the considerations that led to the development of new norms for the MMPI (Butcher et al., 1989).

Application changes are a third reason why normative samples may misrepresent target populations. Two types of application changes can be distinguished. Changes in *administration practices* may affect normative data adequacy. For example, the original MMPI normative data were collected using the test's so-called Box Form. Each of the test's items was typed on a separate card and test takers were instructed to sort the cards (which were presented individually in a random order) into three boxes representing a "true," "false," or "cannot say" response. The instructions given to the original normative sample did not discourage the "cannot say" option. However, after the normative data were collected, an administration change was introduced and test takers were instructed to "be sure to put less than 10 cards behind the 'cannot say'." (Dahlstrom, Welsh, & Dahlstrom, 1972, p. 32). Later still, the Box Form was largely superseded by the MMPI Group Form, a booklet that presented the test's items in a fixed order and required that the test taker record his or her responses (true, false, or cannot say) on an answer sheet. Here, too, test takers were admonished to attempt to answer all of the test items.

To the extent that either of these changes in administration practices affected individuals' responses to the test items, this could have resulted in the original normative sample data's misrepresenting population statistics under the revised administration procedures. In fact, the updated MMPI-2 norms are significantly different from the original norms in both their means and standard deviations, and to some extent these shifts are a product of the administration changes just described. For example, as a result of the change in instructions regarding the "cannot say" option, the new normative sample members omitted far fewer items than did their original counterparts, which in turn probably contributed to the new sample's higher mean raw scores on many of the test's original scales. In other words, the original normative sample underestimated the target population's mean raw scores on the MMPI scales given the shift in administration procedure, contributing partly to the artificially elevated T scores generated by individuals and groups tested with the original MMPI when they were transformed to standard scores based on the original test norms.

A more recent change in SRI administration practices followed the introduction of computer technology. Although most SRI norms were collected using booklet forms, software is now available to administer most tests by computer. Such a change in administration practice could also, potentially, affect these instruments' norms' adequacy if the different administration format resulted in a systematic change in responses to SRI items. Reassuringly, a recent meta-analysis by Finger and Ones (1999) demonstrated that computerized test administration does not affect group means or standard deviations (and thus would have no negative impact on the test's norms) on MMPI/MMPI-2 scales. Butcher, in his chapter in this volume, provides further discussion of computer applications in psychological assessment.

A second type of application change that could potentially affect norms' adequacy involves *expansion of the target population.* When an SRI developed for use with a rather narrowly defined population is considered for application to a broader population, the possibility that its norms will no longer accurately reflect the expanded population's means and standard deviations on its scales needs to be considered. For example, the MMPI was developed originally for use at the University of Minnesota Hospital, and its normative sample, made up primarily of a group of Caucasian farmers and laborers with an average of eight years of education, represented fairly well this target population. As the test's use expanded to the broader U.S. population, concerns were raised (e.g., Gynther, 1972) about the MMPI norms' adequacy for interpreting scores generated by minorities, primarily African Americans, who were not included in the original normative sample.

The effects of expanding an SRI's population on its normative sample's adequacy depend upon the new population segment's performance on its scales. To the extent the new segment differs systematically from the original on a scale's mean or standard deviation, this would necessitate an expansion of the instrument's normative sample to reflect more accurately the expanded population's scale parameters. This was one of the primary considerations that led to the collection of new normative data for the MMPI and publication of the MMPI-2 (Butcher et al., 1989). Similarly, as the test's use has expanded beyond the United States to other countries, cultures, and languages, researchers throughout the world have collected new normative data for MMPI and later MMPI-2 application in an ever-increasing number of countries (c.f., Butcher, 1996; Butcher & Pancheri, 1976).

The effects of expanding an SRI's target population on normative data adequacy should not be confused with questions about an instrument's validity across population segments, although frequently these very separate concerns are confounded in the literature. Ensuring that various population segments are represented adequately in an SRI's normative sample is not sufficient to guarantee that the test is as valid an indicator of its target psychological constructs in the new segment as it was in the original. To the extent that an instrument's interpretation is predicated on an SRI's empirical correlates, its construct validity, or the combination of the two (as discussed earlier), its application to the expanded population is predicated on the assumption that these test attributes apply comparably to the new population segment.

General Population Versus Population Subsegment Norms

A final consideration in evaluating normative data adequacy is whether an SRI's standard scores are derived from general or more narrowly defined and specific normative samples. When a general population normative sample is used, the same set of standard scores is applied regardless of the assessment setting or the individual's membership in any specific population subsegments. Thus, for example, the MMPI-2 has just one set of standard scores generated based on a normative sample designed to represent the general U.S. population. The same set of standard scores is used regardless of where the test is applied.

A more recently developed SRI, the Personality Assessment Inventory (PAI; Morey, 1991) provides two sets of norms for its scales, based on a sample of community-dwelling adults and a clinical sample. Morey (1991) explains that clinical norms are designed to assist the interpreter in tasks such as diagnosis:

> For example, nearly all patients report depression at their initial evaluation; the question confronting the clinician considering a diagnosis of major depression is one of *relative* severity of symptomatology. That a patient's score on the PAI *DEP* [Depression] scale is elevated in comparison to the standardization sample is of value, but a comparison of the elevation relative to a clinical population may be more critical in formulating diagnostic hypotheses. (p. 11)

The ability to know how an individual compares with others known to have significant psychological problems may indeed contribute useful information to test interpretation. However, this particular approach to generating such information has a significant drawback. If, using Morey's example, nearly all members of a clinical reference sample report depression when their normative data are collected, then a typical patient experiencing significant problems with depression will produce a nondeviant score on the instrument's clinically referenced depression measure, thus obscuring depression's prominence in the presenting clinical picture.

A similar problem results when SRI scales are normed based on other narrowly defined, setting-specific population segments. For example, Roberts, Thompson, and Johnson (1999) developed several additional sets of PAI norms for use in assessing applicants for public safety positions. The additional reference samples were all made up of public safety job applicants. A feature common among individuals undergoing evaluations for possible employment in public safety positions is the tendency to deny or minimize any behavioral and emotional problems that they believe may cast them in a negative light and reduce the likelihood that they will be offered the position they seek. As a result, most individuals tested under these circumstances tend to score higher than the general population on defensive test-taking measures. Deviant scores on defensiveness scales alert the interpreter that the test

taker is probably minimizing or denying such problems. However, when compared with other individuals tested under similar circumstances, public safety position applicants produce nondeviant scores on defensiveness measures when they are in fact approaching the assessment with a defensive attitude. Here, too, narrowly defined norms may obscure an important feature (defensiveness) of a test taker.

Threats to SRI Protocol Validity

The impact of test-taking approaches on SRIs has long been the focus of heated debate. As reviewed earlier in this chapter, early SRI critics (e.g., Allport, 1937; Ellis, 1946) cited their vulnerability to intentional and unintentional distortion by the test taker as SRIs' primary, inherent limitation. The basic concern here is that, even if he or she is responding to a psychometrically sound SRI, an individual test taker may, for a variety of reasons, approach the assessment in a manner that compromises the instrument's ability to gauge accurately his or her standing on the construct(s) of interest. In such cases, a psychometrically valid test may yield invalid results.

Use of the term *validity* to refer to both a test's psychometric properties and an individual's test scores can be confusing. A distinction should be drawn between instrument validity and protocol validity. *Instrument validity* refers to a test's psychometric properties and is typically characterized in terms of content, criterion, and construct validity. *Protocol validity* refers to the results of an individual test administration. Use of the term *validity* to refer to these two very different aspects of SRI assessment is unfortunate, but sufficiently well grounded in practice that introduction of new terminology at this point is unlikely to succeed.

A need to distinguish between psychometric and protocol validity has been highlighted in a debate regarding the widely studied NEO Personality Inventory-Revised (NEO-PI-R). Responding to suggestions by Costa and McCrae (1992a; the NEO-PI-R developers) that practioners use this test in clinical assessment, Ben-Porath and Waller (1992) expressed the concern (among others) that the absence of protocol validity indicators on the NEO-PI-R may limit the instrument's clinical utility. Costa and McCrae (1992b) responded that validity scales were unnecessary, in part because evidence has shown that test scores may be psychometrically valid even in instances in which validity indicators showed evidence of limited protocol validity.

Most recently, Piedmont, McCrae, Riemann, and Angleitner (2000) sought to demonstrate this point by showing that scores on an SRI's validity scales (designed to assess protocol validity) were unrelated to the NEO-PI-R's psychometric validity. However, their analyses were based on data generated by research volunteers who completed the instruments anonymously. Thus, unlike respondents in most clinical assessment settings, these research volunteers had nothing at stake when responding to the NEO-PI-R. In contrast, as reviewed next, test takers in clinical settings may be motivated by various factors to present themselves in a particular manner. Moreover, psychometric validity in this and similar studies was established based on statistical analyses of group data, whereas protocol validity pertains to individual test results. If, for example, one of the participants in such a study marked his or her answer sheet randomly, without actually reading the SRI items, his or her resulting scale scores are completely invalid and uninterpretable, regardless of how others in the sample responded.

Consideration of protocol validity is one aspect of SRI-based assessment in which users are able to take an individualized perspective on a generally normative enterprise. Allport (1937) distinguished between idiographic (individualized) and nomothetic (generalized) approaches to personality research and assessment. Drawing an analogy to the diagnostic process in medicine, he noted that the two approaches are not mutually exclusive. Rather, a combined idiographic-nomothetic approach is likely to yield the optimal perspective on diagnosis and assessment. Consideration of protocol validity offers an important window into idiographic aspects of SRI-based assessment.

In sum, instrument validity is necessary but insufficient to guarantee protocol validity. Although it sets the upper limit on protocol validity, information regarding instrument validity does not address a critical question that is at issue in every clinical assessment: Is there anything about an individual's approach to a particular assessment that might compromise its user's ability to interpret an SRI's scores? To answer this question, users must be aware of various threats to protocol validity.

Types of Threats to Protocol Validity

Threats to SRI protocol validity need to be considered in each SRI application because of their potential to distort the resulting test scores. This information can be used in two important ways. First, knowledge of threats to protocol validity makes it possible for test users to attempt to prevent or minimize their occurrence. Second, it makes it possible to anticipate invalid responding's potential impact on the resulting test scores and, on the basis of this information, provide appropriate caveats in test interpretation. Such statements may range from a call for caution in assuming that an interpretation will likely reflect accurately the individual's standing on the construct(s) of interest to an unambiguous declaration that protocol validity has been compromised to a degree that

TABLE 24.1   Threats to Self-Report Inventory Protocol Validity

Non-content-based invalid responding
  Nonresponding
  Random responding
    Intentional random responding
    Unintentional random responding
  Fixed responding
Content-based invalid responding
  Overreporting
    Intentional overreporting
      Exaggeration versus fabrication
    Unintentional overreporting (negative emotionality)
  Underreporting
    Intentional underreporting
      Minimization versus denial
    Unintentional underreporting (social desirability)

makes it impossible to draw any valid inferences about the test taker from the resulting SRI scale scores.

Threats to protocol validity fall broadly into two categories that reflect test item content's role in the invalid responding. Important distinctions can be made within each of these categories as well. Table 24.1 provides a list of the various non-content- and content-based threats to protocol validity identified in this chapter.

Non-Content-Based Invalid Responding.   Non-content-based invalid responding occurs when the test taker's answers to an SRI are not based on an accurate reading, processing, and comprehension of the test items. Its deleterious effects on protocol validity are obvious: To the extent that a test taker's responses do not reflect his or her actual reactions to an SRI's items, then those responses cannot possibly gauge the individual's standing on the construct of interest. This invalidating test-taking approach can be divided further into three modes: nonresponding, random responding, and fixed responding.

Nonresponding occurs when the test taker fails to provide a usable response to an SRI item. Typically, this takes the form of failing to provide any response to an SRI item, but it may also occur if the test taker provides more than one response to an item. Nonresponding may occur for a variety of reasons. Test takers who are uncooperative or defensive may fail to respond to a large number of an SRI's items. Less insidious reasons why individuals may fail to respond appropriately to a SRI may include an inability to read or understand its items, cognitive functioning deficits that result in confusion or obsessiveness, or limits in the test taker's capacity for introspection and insight.

Nonresponding's effect on protocol validity depends, in part, on the SRI's response format. In tests that use a "true" "false" response format, a nonresponse is treated typically as a response in the nonkeyed direction. In SRIs with a Likert scale response format, a nonresponse typically receives the value zero. These ipso facto scores can by no means be assumed to provide a reasonable approximation of how the respondent would have answered had he or she chosen or been able to do so. Therefore, to the extent that nonresponding occurs in a given SRI protocol, this will distort the resulting test scores. For example, in a true/false response format a respondent's failure to respond appropriately to a large number of items will result in artificial deflation of his or her scores on the instrument's scales, which, if not identified and considered in scale score interpretation, may result in underestimation of the individual's standing on the constructs measured by the affected scales.

Random responding is a test-taking approach characterized by an *unsystematic* response pattern that is not based on an accurate reading, processing, and understanding of an SRI's items. It is not a dichotomous phenomenon, meaning that random responding may be present to varying degrees in a given test protocol. Two types of random responding can be distinguished. *Intentional random responding* occurs when the individual has the capacity to respond relevantly to an SRI's items but chooses instead to respond irrelevantly in an unsystematic manner. An uncooperative test taker who is unwilling to participate meaningfully in an assessment may engage in intentional random responding rather than becoming embroiled in a confrontation with the examiner over his or her refusal to participate. In this example, the test taker provides answers to an SRI's items without pausing to read and consider them. He or she may do this throughout the test protocol or at various points along the way in responding to an SRI's items.

Unintentional random responding occurs when the individual lacks the capacity to respond relevantly to an SRI's items, but, rather than refraining from giving any response to the items, he or she responds without having an accurate understanding of the test items. Often these individuals are not aware that they lack this capacity and have failed to understand and respond relevantly to an SRI's items.

Several factors may lead to unintentional random responding. *Reading difficulties* may compromise the test taker's ability to respond relevantly to an SRI's items. Most current SRIs require anywhere from a fourth- to a sixth-grade reading level for the test taker to be able to read, comprehend, and respond relevantly to the items. Regrettably, this is not synonymous with having completed four to six years of education. Some high school graduates cannot read at the fourth grade level. If the examiner has doubts about a test taker's reading ability, a standardized reading test should be administered to determine his or her reading level. For individuals who do not have the requisite reading skills, it may still be possible to administer the test if the problem is strictly one of literacy rather than

language comprehension. In such cases, an SRI's items can be administered orally, preferably using standard stimulus materials such as an audiotaped reading of the test items.

Comprehension deficits can also lead to random responding. In this case the individual may actually be able to read the test items but does not have the necessary language comprehension skills to process and understand them. This could be a product of low verbal abilities. In other instances, comprehension deficits may be found in those lacking familiarity with English language nuances, for example, among individuals for whom English is not their primary language.

Unintentional random responding can also result from *confusion* and *thought disorganization.* In some instances, these types of difficulties may have prompted the assessment and SRI administration. Whereas reading and comprehension difficulties tend to be relatively stable test-taker characteristics that will probably compromise protocol validity regardless of when an SRI is administered, confusion and thought disorganization are often (although not always) transitory conditions. If and when the individual's sensorium clears, she or he may be able to retake an SRI and provide valid responses to its items.

Finally, random responding may result from *response recording errors.* Many SRIs are administered by having the respondent read a set of items from a booklet and record the responses on a separate answer sheet. If the respondent marks his or her answer to an SRI's items in the wrong location on an answer sheet, he or she is essentially providing random responses. This could result from the test taker's missing just one item on the answer sheet or from an overall careless approach to response recording.

Fixed responding is a non-content-based invalidating test-taking approach characterized by a *systematic* response pattern that is not based on an accurate reading, processing, and understanding of an SRI's items. In contrast to random responding, here the test taker provides the same non-content- based responses to SRI items. If responding to a true/false format SRI, the test taker indiscriminately marks many of the test items either "true" or "false." Note that if the test taker provides both "true" and "false" responses indiscriminately, then he or she is engaging in random responding. In fixed responding the indiscriminant responses are predominantly either "true" or "false." In fixed responding on a Likert scale, the test taker marks items at the same level on the Likert rating scale without properly considering their content. Like nonresponding and random responding, fixed responding is a matter of degree rather than a dichotomous all-or-none phenomenon.

Unlike nonresponding and random responding, fixed responding has received a great deal of attention in the

SRI-based assessment literature. Jackson and Messick (1962) sparked this discussion when they proposed that much (if not all) of the variance in MMPI scale scores was attributable to two *response styles,* termed acquiescence and social desirability. *Acquiescence* was defined as a tendency to respond "true" to MMPI items without consideration of their content. This type of non-content-based responding is labeled fixed responding in this chapter.

A detailed examination of Jackson and Messick's arguments and the data they analyzed in its support is beyond the scope of this chapter. Essentially, Jackson and Messick factor analyzed MMPI scale scores in a broad range of samples and found recurrently that two factors accounted for much of the variance in these scores. They attributed variance on these factors to two response styles, acquiescence and social desirability, and cautioned that MMPI scale scores appear primarily to reflect individual differences on these nonsubstantive dimensions. They suggested that MMPI scales were particularly vulnerable to the effects of acquiescence and its counterpart, counteracquiescence (a tendency to respond "false" to self-report items without consideration of their content), because their scoring keys were unbalanced. That is, for some MMPI scales many, if not most, of the items were keyed "true," whereas on other scales most of the items were keyed "false."

In an extensive and sophisticated series of analyses, Block (1965) demonstrated that the two primary MMPI factors reflected substantive personality dimensions rather than stylistic response tendencies. With regard specifically to acquiescence, he showed that completely balanced MMPI scales (i.e., ones with equal numbers of "true" and "false" keyed items) yielded the same factor structure that Jackson and Messick (1962) attributed to the effect of response styles. He showed further that the so-called acquiescence factor was correlated with substantive aspects of personality functioning. Block (1965) labeled this factor *ego control* and demonstrated that its association with extratest data was unchanged as a function of whether it was measured with balanced or unbalanced scales.

It is important to note that Block's analyses did not indicate that acquiescence is never a problem in SRI-based assessment. In the relatively rare instances when they occur, acquiescence and counteracquiescence can indeed jeopardize protocol validity. In the most extreme case of acquiescence, if a respondent answers "true" to all of a scale's items without reference to their content, his or her score on that scale is obviously invalid. In addition, use of a Likert scale format does not obviate the potential effects of this response style, because with this format, as well, it is possible for test takers to provide a fixed response that is independent of item content.

Block's compelling demonstration notwithstanding, Jackson and Messick and their followers continued to advocate the response style position and argue that acquiescence represented a serious challenge to MMPI use and interpretation. Most recently, Helmes and Reddon (1993) revisited this issue and criticized the MMPI and MMPI-2 (among other things) for their continued susceptibility to the effects of acquiescence. These authors again identified the test's unbalanced scoring keys as a primary reason for its susceptibility to acquiescence. In constructing his own SRI, the Basic Personality Inventory (BPI), Jackson (1989) indeed adopted the balanced scoring key solution for its scales, each of which is made up of 20 items, half keyed "true" and the others keyed "false." However, balanced scoring keys actually provide no protection whatsoever against the protocol invalidating effects of fixed responding. Consider the hypothetical example just mentioned, in which a test taker responds "true" to all 20 BPI scale items without actually referring to their content. The only effect a balanced key might have in this instance might be to instill a false sense of security in the test interpreter that the scale is not susceptible to the protocol invalidating effects of acquiescence, when, in fact, it is.

In summary, although fixed responding does not pose as broad a threat to protocol validity as Jackson and Messick would argue, in cases in which a test taker uses this response style extensively, the resulting SRI scale scores will be invalid and uninterpretable. Constructing scales with balanced keys or Likert scale response formats does not make an SRI less susceptible to this threat to protocol validity. Self-report inventory users need to determine in each instance that a test is used whether, to what extent, and with what impact fixed responding may have compromised protocol validity. This requires that the SRIs include measures of fixed responding.

Content-Based Invalid Responding. Content-based invalid responding occurs when the test taker skews his or her answers to SRI items and, as a result, creates a misleading impression. This test-taking approach falls broadly into two classes that have been discussed under various labels in the literature. The first of these has been termed alternatively overreporting, faking bad, and malingering. The second type of content-based invalid responding has been labeled underreporting, faking good, and positive malingering. In this chapter, they will be discussed under the more neutral labels of over- and underreporting.

Overreporting occurs when, in responding to an SRI, a test taker describes him- or herself as having more serious difficulties, a greater number of them, or both than he or she actually has. Underlying this definition is the hypothetical notion that if a completely objective measure of psychological functioning was available, the overreporter's subjective self-report would indicate greater dysfunction than does the objective indicator. Two non–mutually exclusive types of overreporting can be distinguished. *Intentional overreporting* occurs when the individual knowingly skews his or her self-report. This test taker is typically motivated by some instrumental gain and thus fits the *DSM-IV* definition of *malingering* (APA, 2000). The label *faking bad* also carries with it a connotation of volitional distortion and similarly falls under the category of intentional overreporting.

It is important to note that intentional overreporting is not in itself an indication that psychopathology is absent. That is to say, if an individual intentionally overreports in responding to a SRI, that, in itself, does not indicate that he or she is actually free of bona fide psychological dysfunction. It is, in fact, possible for someone who has genuine psychological difficulties to amplify their extent or significance when responding to SRI items. On the other hand, some people who intentionally overreport in response to an SRI actually have no problems. The distinction here is between *exaggeration* and *fabrication* of difficulties. Both forms of intentional overreporting fall under the *DSM-IV* definition of malingering: "the intentional production of false or grossly exaggerated physical or psychological symptoms, motivated by external incentives such as avoiding military duty, avoiding work, obtaining financial compensation, evading criminal prosecution, or obtaining drugs" (APA, 2000, p. 739). In practice, distinguishing between exaggeration and fabrication in SRI protocol validity determination is quite challenging.

In *unintentional overreporting,* the test taker is unaware that she or he is deviating from a hypothetically objective self-description and describing her- or himself in an overly negative manner. Here, it is the test taker's self-concept that is skewed. Individuals who engage in this test-taking approach believe mistakenly that they are providing an accurate self-description when in fact they are overreporting their difficulties.

Tellegen (1985) has described a primary personality trait, *negative emotionality,* which predisposes individuals to perceive their environment as more threatening than it is in reality, and themselves as having greater subjective difficulty functioning than they actually have. Individuals high in negative emotionality do indeed experience psychological dysfunction; however, they overestimate, and as a result, overreport its extent and significance. As a consequence, they produce deviant scores on SRIs that confound genuine with unintentionally overreported dysfunction.

Demonstrating and evaluating the extent of the confound between genuine and unintentionally overreported psychological dysfunction is quite challenging because of the inherent difficulty in obtaining objective indicators of functioning. Just about any effort to derive an objective measure of psychological functioning relies, at least to some extent, on self-report or self-presentation. Structured diagnostic interviews and even informant reports are influenced by how an individual responds to specific interview questions (asked in person by an interviewer rather than impersonally by a questionnaire) or the impression a person creates on others who are asked to describe her or his psychological functioning.

Watson and Pennebaker (1989) provided a compelling illustration of this phenomenon by focusing on the role negative emotionality plays in assessing physical functioning. Unlike psychological functioning, in assessing physical health it is possible to obtain objective indicators of dysfunction that are independent of self-report. These investigators examined the relation between self-reported negative emotionality, self-reported health complaints, and objectively derived physical functioning indicators (e.g., fitness and lifestyle variables; frequency of illness; health-related visits or absences; objective evidence of risk, dysfunction, or pathology; and overall mortality). They found a consistent correlation between negative emotionality and self-reported health problems, but little or no correlation between self-reported negative emotionality and objective health indicators. The unintentional overreporting associated with negative emotionality accounted almost entirely for its relation with physical health complaints, leading the investigators to conclude that there was little or no association between this construct and actual physical health.

Negative emotionality's role in assessing mental health and personality functioning is more complex. People high in negative emotionality are genuinely psychologically distressed, and their difficulties are often manifested in multiple areas of psychological dysfunction. In diagnostic terms, this results in substantial levels of psychopathology comorbidity. Mineka, Watson, and Clark (1998) reported, for example, that anxiety and mood disorders have approximately a 50% rate of co-occurrence. Similar levels of comorbidity have been reported among other Axis I diagnostic categories, among Axis II diagnoses, and across Axis I and Axis II. Although diagnostic comorbidity is real, unintentional overreporting associated with negative emotionality probably inflates estimates of its extent. In SRI measures of personality and psychopathology, this inflation has the effect of yielding deviant scores on multiple scales. It also results in phenotypic correlations among SRI scales that overestimate the actual correlations among the latent constructs they are designed to measure. When correlations among SRI scales are factor analyzed, they yield typically one very strong general factor that represents both the genuine psychological sequela of negative emotionality (i.e., true phenotypic comorbidity) and the confounding effects of unintentional overreporting.

In summary, overreporting in response to SRI items results in scale scores that overestimate the extent or significance of psychological problems the respondent experiences. If overreporting is suspected, the test interpreter is confronted with the challenge of determining whether, and to what extent, it might involve intentional distortion versus manifestations of negative emotionality and, if it is intentional, whether it involves fabrication or exaggeration of problems. Moreover, these threats to protocol validity are not mutually exclusive, and the interpreter needs to consider the possibility that some or all may be manifested in a given protocol.

Underreporting occurs when in responding to an SRI a test taker describes him- or herself as having less serious difficulties, a smaller number of difficulties, or both than he or she actually has. To refer back to the hypothetical objective functioning indicator, in underreporting the individual's self-report reflects better functioning than would be indicated by an objective assessment. Here, too, a distinction may be drawn between intentional and unintentional underreporting. In *intentional underreporting,* the individual knowingly denies or minimizes the extent of his or her psychological difficulties or negative characteristics. As a result, the individual's SRI scale scores underestimate his or her level of dysfunction. Differentiation between *denial* and *minimization* is important but complex. The distinction here is between an individual who blatantly denies problems that she or he knows exist and one who may acknowledge some difficulties or negative characteristics but minimizes their impact or extent.

Unintentional underreporting occurs when the individual unknowingly denies or minimizes the extent of his or her psychological difficulties or negative characteristics. Here, too, objective and subjective indicators of psychological functioning would be at odds; however, in unintentional underreporting this discrepancy results from the individual's self-misperception rather than an intentional effort to produce misleading test results.

Much of the discussion of this topic in the assessment literature has appeared under the label *social desirability.* Edwards (1957) defined social desirability as "the tendency of subjects to attribute to themselves, in self-description, personality statements with socially desirable scale values and to reject those socially undesirable scale values" (p. vi). As was the case with acquiescence (discussed earlier), social desirability was proposed as a *response style,* "an organized disposition within individuals to respond in a consistent manner across a variety of substantive domains" (Wiggins, 1973). Edwards (1970) differentiated between social desirability and what he called "impression management," a deliberate

attempt to lie or dissimulate for ulterior motives, that is, intentional underreporting as defined in this chapter. Thus, as conceptualized by Edwards (1957, 1970), social desirability was a form of unintentional underreporting in response to SRI items.

Edwards (1957) argued that much of the variance in MMPI scale scores could be attributed to social desirability. He based this conclusion on research he did with an MMPI scale he constructed and labeled social desirability. The scale was made up of 39 items that 10 judges unanimously deemed to reflect highly desirable self-statements. Edwards (1957, 1970) reported that this scale was correlated highly with most MMPI scales in general, and the strong, omnipotent first factor that emerged from factor analyses of MMPI scale scores. He concluded that MMPI scale scores were thus hopelessly confounded with the social desirability response style and, therefore, could not be used to identify meaningful (rather than stylistic) individual differences.

As was the case with Jackson and Messick's (1962) argument regarding acquiescence (see the discussion of fixed responding), Block (1965) provided a definitive refutation of Edwards's (1957) social desirability critique. Block demonstrated that Edwards's social desirability scale was in fact a marker of a substantive personality dimension he termed *ego resiliency.* Following the earlier work of Wiggins (1959), Block developed an ego resiliency–free measure of social desirability and found much lower levels of overlap with substantive MMPI scale scores than Edwards reported for his social desirability scale. Moreover, Block demonstrated that both a social-desirability-independent ego resiliency scale he constructed and Edwards's social desirability scales were correlated with meaningful non-MMPI variables that reflected substantive individual differences.

Commenting on Edwards's (1957) claim that the MMPI scales were hopelessly confounded with social desirability, Block (1965) observed:

> Confounding is a blade that, if held too tightly, will cut its wielder. With the same logic advanced for social desirability as underlying MMPI scales, one can argue that the [first] factor of the MMPI represents a personality dimension that is vital to understanding the SD scale. Many of the MMPI scales have empirical origins and demonstrable validity in separating appropriate criterion groups. The high correlations found between these scales and the SD measure therefore plausibly suggest—not an artifact or naiveté in the construction of the earlier scales—but rather that the SD scale, wittingly or not, is an excellent measure of some important variable of personality. (pp. 69–70)

When we reflect on the methods Edwards (1957) used to construct his social desirability scale, the resulting confound is readily understood. Stated simply, psychopathology is undesirable. Ask a group of persons to identify SRI items that reflect undesirable characteristics, and, if they are included in the pool, participants will undoubtedly generate a list of items describing negative psychological characteristics. Edwards's assumption that individuals' responses to such items reflect a substantively meaningless response style proved subsequently to be unwarranted and was refuted by Block's (1965) analyses. Nonetheless, Edwards and some followers continued to raise these arguments. For example, relying (like Edwards) on scales that reflected desirability judgments, Jackson, Fraboni, and Helmes (1997) criticized the MMPI-2 Content Scales (Butcher et al., 1990) for being highly saturated with social desirability. As Edwards failed to do before them, these authors did not explain how scales that they concluded were highly saturated with irrelevant stylistic variance could account significantly for a wide range of extratest personality and psychopathology variables (Butcher et al., 1990).

Implications of Threats to Protocol Validity

The issues discussed and highlighted in this section illustrate the crucial role played by respondents' test-taking approaches in determining the interpretability of SRI scale scores. Allport (1937) and Ellis (1946) foresaw accurately that reliance on an individual's willingness and ability to generate an accurate self-portrayal when responding to test items was the among the greatest challenges facing SRI developers and users. Subsequent decades of research and practice have illuminated a host of threats to protocol validity (just described), all manifestations of the kinds of concerns identified early on by Allport and Ellis. Self-report inventory developers have responded to these threats in various ways, ranging from the development of *validity scales,* SRI measures designed to assess and, in some instances, correct for the effects of protocol invalidating test-taking approaches (e.g., the MMPI-2 validity scales; Butcher et al., 2001), to declaration and attempts to demonstrate that these threats do not really amount to much (Costa & McCrae, 1992a; Piedmont et al., 2000) and the consequent decision not to include validity scales on some instruments (e.g., the NEO-PI-R; Costa & McCrae, 1992c).

Commenting on the then-prevalent paucity of efforts by SRI developers to address threats to protocol validity, Meehl and Hathaway (1946) observed:

> It is almost as though we inventory-makers were afraid to say too much about the problem because we had no effective solution for it, but it was too obvious a fact to be ignored so it was met by a polite nod. Meanwhile the scores obtained are subjected to

varied "precise" statistical manipulations which impel the student of behavior to wonder whether it is not the aim of the personality testers to get as far away from any unsanitary contact with the organism as possible. Part of this trend no doubt reflects the lack of clinical experiences of some psychologists who concern themselves with personality testing . . . . (p. 526)

Acting on this concern, Hathaway and McKinley incorporated two validity scales, L and F, in their original MMPI development efforts. The MMPI was not the first SRI to make validity scales available to its users. Cady (1923) modified the Woodworth Psychoneurotic Inventory (derived from of the original Personal Data Sheet) to assess juvenile incorrigibility and incorporated negatively worded repeated items in the revised inventory to examine respondents' "reliability." Maller (1932) included items in his Character Sketches measure designed to assess respondents' "readiness to confide." Humm and Wadsworth (1935), developers of the Humm-Wadsworth Temperament Scales, incorporated scales designed to identify defensive responding to their SRI. Ruch (1942) developed an "honesty key" for theBPI, the most widely used SRI prior to the MMPI.

Hathaway and McKinley's inclusion of validity scales on the original MMPI was thus consistent with growing recognition among SRI developers of the need to incorporate formal means for assessing and attempting to correct for threats to protocol validity. In describing their efforts to develop and apply the MMPI K scale and K-correction, Meehl and Hathaway (1946) articulated the conceptual and empirical underpinnings of MMPI approaches to assessing threats to protocol validity. As MMPI use and research proliferated throughout the latter part of the twentieth century, Hathaway, McKinley, and Meehl's emphasis on assessing threats to protocol validity was continued through efforts to develop a variety of additional MMPI and MMPI-2 validity scales. Following in this tradition, most (but not all) modern SRIs include measures designed to provide information regarding threats to protocol validity.

FUTURE DIRECTIONS FOR SELF-REPORT INVENTORY RESEARCH

Self-report measures play a vital role in personality and psychopathology assessment. Self-report inventories are used commonly and routinely in various applied assessment tasks, and they have been the focus of thousands of empirical investigations. Considerable progress was made in developing this technology over the course of the twentieth century, and many of the concerns identified early on by Allport (1937) and Ellis (1946) have been addressed in modern self-report measures. Three primary aspects of SRI-based assessment were reviewed and analyzed in this chapter: approaches to SRI scale score interpretation, standard score derivation for SRIs, and threats to protocol validity. As discussed earlier, modern SRIs offer a variety of solutions to the challenges posed in each of these areas. However, this review has also pointed out needs for further research-based refinement in each of these aspects of SRI-based assessment. The final part of this chapter highlights needs and directions for further research in SRI-based approaches to assessing personality and psychopathology.

Approaches to SRI Scale Score Interpretation

Two primary approaches to SRI scale score interpretation, empirically grounded and content-based, were identified in this review. Not surprisingly, much of the research in this area has focused on empirically grounded SRI scale score interpretation. This is understandable because, by definition, empirically grounded interpretation is research-dependent. However, content-based interpretation can and should be subjected to rigorous empirical scrutiny. Specifically, research is needed to examine the validity of content-based SRI scale score interpretation. Such investigations should explore the content validity of content-based measures (i.e., the extent to which they adequately canvass the relevant content domain) and the criterion and ultimately construct validity of content-based interpretation. Moreover, as detailed earlier, content-based and empirically grounded approaches are not mutually exclusive, and research is needed to guide SRI users regarding optimal ways to combine them in scale score interpretation.

Several aspects of empirically grounded SRI scale score interpretation also require further elaboration. As reviewed previously, empirically keyed interpretation has garnered limited support in the SRI literature to date. It is unclear whether this is a product of limitations inherent in the external approach to SRI scale construction, in which case further efforts at developing empirically keyed interpretive approaches should be abandoned, or whether the problem rests more in deficiencies of previous efforts at external scale construction that attenuated the validity of their products. There has been no extensive effort at external scale construction since the original MMPI clinical scales were developed. Considerable progress has since been made in other approaches to diagnostic classification (e.g., development of structured diagnostic interviews) and in the methodologies and technology available to test constructors. It is possible (if not likely) that a comprehensive effort to develop SRI scales keyed to differentiate empirically between reliably (with the aid of structured diagnostic interviews) diagnosed classes of individuals will yield diagnostic

indicators that are more valid than the original MMPI clinical scales.

As noted previously, most empirically grounded SRI scale score interpretation has followed the empirical correlate approach. Much of the research in this area has focused on the direct, simple inference level afforded by knowledge of a scale score's criterion validity. Limited attention has been paid in this literature to an issue that receives prominent attention in the industrial/organizational (I/O) assessment literature, the question of *validity generalization:* Under what circumstances are empirical correlates identified in one setting likely to apply to others? Following the seminal work of I/O researchers Schmidt and Hunter (1977), I/O psychologists have developed various techniques to appraise validity generalization for their assessment instruments. In light of the particularly prominent role of criterion validity in SRI-based assessment of personality and psychopathology, similar research in this area is clearly needed.

Configural interpretation (examination of patterns among SRI scale scores; as distinguished from linear interpretation, which involves independent consideration of SRI scale scores) is another aspect of criterion-validity-based SRI application requiring further examination. As discussed earlier, the primary assumption underlying configural interpretation (that there is something about the pattern of scores on a set of SRI scales that is not captured when they are interpreted linearly) has seldom been tested empirically. Moreover, in the rare cases in which it has been tested, configural interpretation has not demonstrated incremental validity in reference to linear approaches. Configural approaches may improve upon linear interpretation either by enhancing the scales' convergent validity or by sharpening their discriminant validity. Research is needed to evaluate the extent to which configural interpretation adds (beyond linear interpretation) to either or both.

Finally, with respect to scale score interpretation, research has yet to mine adequately the prospects of construct validity. As a result, SRI users are unable to rely on construct validity adequately as an interpretive source. Most empirically grounded SRI scale score interpretation is guided by the simple, direct inference level afforded by criterion validity data. Concurrent with the move in psychiatry toward a descriptive, atheoretical nosology, research on clinical applications of SRIs has similarly focused narrowly on their scales' criterion validity. Cronbach and Meehl's (1955) admonition that psychological tests be used to identify and elucidate the nature of major constructs, and that the resulting enhancement in our understanding of these constructs guide our interpretation of test scores, has not been followed. We remain largely incapable of interpreting SRI scale scores in the context of theoretically grounded nomological networks.

A potential exception to this trend is the five-factor model (FFM) of personality, which focuses on five core personality traits: extraversion, agreeableness, conscientiousness, neuroticism, and openness/intellect. Although not without its critics (e.g., Block, 1995; Loevinger, 1994), this product of the normal personality assessment literature has generated an empirical literature base that can be used to elucidate a rich, theoretically grounded nomological network associated with its five core constructs (e.g., John & Srivastava, 1999). Unfortunately, efforts to date to apply this rich framework to clinical assessment tasks have met with limited success. These difficulties, however, appear largely to be a product of limitations in tests designed to measure the FFM (e.g., questions about the clinical utility of the NEO-PI-R related to its authors' decision not to measure potential threats to protocol validity; Costa & McCrae, 1992c). Alternative conceptualizations (e.g., Harkness and McNulty's PSY-5 model; 1994), developed from the clinical rather than normal personality perspective, may ultimately prove more fruitful. In any event, enhancing SRI interpreters' ability to rely on their construct validity should be a major goal of further research efforts in this area.

Standard Score Derivation for SRIs

Two primary needs for further research exist with respect to standard score derivation for SRIs. First, as reviewed earlier, various problems in normative sampling may result in over- or underestimation of an individual's standing on SRI-measured constructs. Current and future SRIs need to be scrutinized carefully to determine whether, and to what extent, the systematic sampling errors, population changes, and application changes described previously might compromise their normative samples' adequacy.

A second aspect of standard score derivation for SRIs that should be the focus of further research efforts relates to the advisability and feasibility of using special norms when applying SRIs to specific subpopulations or setting types. Some approaches to incorporating population subsegment information in SRI scale score interpretation involve developing separate norms for use in these applications (e.g., Roberts et al.'s approach to using the PAI in public safety personnel screening; 1999). However, as discussed earlier, use of so-called special norms may obscure features shared commonly by members of a population subsegment or by individuals tested under similar circumstances (e.g., defensiveness among individuals being screened for public safety positions or depression in people tested in clinical settings).

An alternative method for considering how an individual's SRI scale scores compare with those of population subsegments is to provide interpreters data on group members' means and standard deviations on the relevant scales. Such

data could be provided in professional publications or along with individual test scores generated through automated scoring services. For example, many automated scoring services currently include a graphic printout of the individual's standard scores on a profile sheet. Group mean profiles, along with their associated standard deviations or errors plotted as confidence intervals, could be added to these printouts. This would allow the test interpreter to learn how the individual's scores compare with both the general normative standard and with relevant comparison groups without obscuring the effects of group deviations from the mean.

Assessing Threats to Protocol Validity

Several types of threats to SRI protocol validity were identified in this chapter. Existing instruments vary in the extent to which they provide interpreters information regarding these threats' presence in a given protocol. Most SRIs provide means for assessing at least some of the categories of threats outlined in Table 24.1. The recently updated MMPI-2 (Butcher et al., 2001) contains scales designed to tap each of the types and subtypes of threats described earlier. Within the category of Non-Content-Based Invalid Responding, nonresponding is assessed by the Cannot Say scale; random responding by the Variable Response Inconsistency (VRIN) scale; and fixed responding is measured by the True Response Inconsistency (TRIN) scale. In the category of Content-Based Invalid Responding, overreporting is gauged by the infrequency scales F (Infrequency), Fb (Back Infrequency), and Fp (Infrequency psychopathology), and underreporting is assessed by the defensiveness indicators L (Lie), K (Defensiveness), and S (Superlative).

Existing validity scales fall short, however, in their ability to differentiate meaningfully among threats within these subtypes. For example, existing scales do not allow for differentiation among intentional versus unintentional random responding, intentional versus unintentional over- or underreporting, exaggeration versus fabrication, or minimization versus denial. Some of these distinctions may only be possible through consideration of extratest data; however, further research is needed to explore whether configural interpretation of existing validity scales or development of additional validity scales may allow SRI interpreters to more finely distinguish among the various threats and levels of threats to protocol validity.

CONCLUSION

This chapter provided an overview of the historical foundations and early criticisms of self-report measures, current issues and challenges in SRI interpretation, and needs for future research in this area. A great deal of progress has been made in developing this technology's conceptual and empirical foundations. Over the past 50 years, the challenges articulated early on by Allport (1937) and Ellis (1946) have been addressed (with varying degrees of success) by subsequent SRI developers and researchers. These efforts have been documented in an elaborate body of scholarly literature that, of course, goes well beyond the scope of this chapter. Other chapters in this volume cover additional aspects of this literature, in particular the chapters by Garb on clinical versus statistical prediction, Bracken and Wasserman on psychometric characteristics of assessment procedures, and Reynolds and Ramsey on cultural test bias. Chapters on assessment in various settings include reviews of more setting-specific aspects of the SRI literature. Overall, these chapters indicate that assessment of personality and psychopathology by self-report rests on solid foundations that leave this technology well positioned for future research and development efforts.

REFERENCES

Allport, G. W. (1928). A test for ascendance-submission. *Journal of Abnormal and Social Psychology, 23,* 118–136.

Allport, G. W. (1937). *Personality: A psychosocial interpretation.* New York: Henry Holt.

Anastasi, A. (1985). Some emerging trends in psychological measurement: A fifty year perspective. *Applied Psychological Measurement, 9,* 212–138.

Ben-Porath, Y. S. (1994). The MMPI and MMPI-2: Fifty years of differentiating normal and abnormal personality. In S. Strack & M. Lorr (Eds.), *Differentiating normal and abnormal personality.* (pp. 361–401) New York: Springer.

Ben-Porath, Y. S., & Butcher, J. N. (1991). The historical development of personality assessment. In C. E. Walker (Ed.), *Clinical psychology: Historical and research foundations* (pp. 121–156) New York: Plenum Press.

Ben-Porath, Y. S., & Waller, N. G. (1992). "Normal" personality inventories in clinical assessment: General requirements and potential for using the NEO Personality Inventory. *Psychological Assessment, 4,* 14–19.

Bernreuter, R. J. (1933). Theory and construction of the personality inventory. *Journal of Social Psychology, 4,* 387–405.

Black, J. D. (1953). The interpretation of MMPI profiles of college women. *Dissertation Abstracts, 13,* 870–871.

Block, J. (1965). *The challenge of response sets: Unconfounding meaning, acquiescence, and social desirability in the MMPI.* New York: Appleton-Century-Crofts.

Block, J. (1995). A contrarian view of the five factor approach to personality description. *Psychological Bulletin, 117,* 187–215.

Burisch, M. (1984). Approaches to personality inventory construction: A comparison of merits. *American Psychologist, 39,* 214–227.

Butcher, J. N. (1996). *International adaptations of the MMPI-2: Research and clinical applications.* Minneapolis: University of Minnesota Press.

Butcher, J. N., Dahlstrom, W. G., Graham, J. R., Tellegen, A., & Kaemmer, B. (1989). *The Minnesota Multiphasic Personality Inventory-2 (MMPI-2): Manual for administration and scoring.* Minneapolis: University of Minnesota Press.

Butcher, J. N., Graham, J. R., Ben-Porath, Y. S., Tellegen, A., Dahlstrom, W. G., & Kaemmer, B. (2001). *The Minnesota Multiphasic Personality Inventory-2 (MMPI-2): Manual for administration, scoring, and interpretation* (Revised ed.). Minneapolis: University of Minnesota Press.

Butcher, J. N., Graham, J. R., Williams, C. L., & Ben-Porath, Y. S. (1990). *Development and use of the MMPI-2 content scales.* Minneapolis: University of Minnesota Press.

Butcher, J. N., & Pancheri, P. (1976). *Handbook of cross-national MMPI research.* Minneapolis: University of Minnesota Press.

Butcher, J. N., & Rouse, S. V. (1996). Personality: Individual differences and clinical assessment. *Annual Review of Psychology, 47,* 87–111.

Cady, V. M. (1923). The estimation of juvenile incorrigibility. *Elementary School Journal, 33,* 1–140.

Camara, W. J., Nathan, J. S., & Puente, A. E. (2000). Psychological test usage implications in professional psychology. *Professional Psychology: Research and Practice, 31,* 141–154.

Cattell, R. B. (1965). *The scientific analysis of personality.* Baltimore: Penguin Books.

Cattell, R. B. (1979). *Personality and learning theory* (Vol. 1). New York: Springer.

Cattell, R. B., Cattell, A. K., & Cattell, H. E. (1993). *Sixteen Personality Factors Questionnaire, fifth edition.* Champaign, IL: Institute for Personality and Ability Testing.

Costa, P. T., & McCrae, R. R. (1992a). Normal personality assessment in clinical practice: The NEO Personality Inventory. *Psychological Assessment, 4,* 5–13.

Costa, P. T., & McCrae, R. R. (1992b). Normal personality inventories in clinical assessment: General requirements and the potential for using the NEO Personality Inventory. A reply. *Psychological Assessment, 4,* 20–22.

Costa, P. T., & McCrae, R. R. (1992c). *Revised NEO Personality Inventory (NEO-PI-R) and NEO Five Factor Inventory (NEO-FFI) professional manual.* Odessa, FL: Psychological Assessment Resources.

Craig, R. J. (1999). *Interpreting personality tests: A clinical manual for the MMPI-2, MCMI-III, CPI-R, and 16PF.* New York: Wiley.

Cronbach, L. J., & Meehl, P. E. (1955). Construct validity in psychological tests. *Psychological Bulletin, 52,* 281–302.

Dahlstrom, W. G. (1992). The growth in acceptance of the MMPI. *Professional Psychology: Research and Practice, 23,* 345–348.

Dahlstrom, W. G., Welsh, G. S., & Dahlstrom, L. E. (1972). *An MMPI handbook, Vol. 1: Clinical interpretation* (Revised ed.). Minneapolis: University of Minnesota Press.

Dorfman, W. I., & Hersen, M. (2001). *Understanding psychological assessment.* Dordecht, Netherlands: Kluwer Academic.

Downey, J. E. (1923). *The will-temperament and its testing.* New York: World Book.

Dubois, P. L. (1970). *A history of psychological testing.* Boston: Allyn and Bacon.

Duckworth, J. C. (1991). The Minnesota Multiphasic Personality Inventory-2: A review. *Journal of Counseling and Development, 69,* 564–567.

Edwards, A. L. (1957). *The social desirability variable in personality assessment and research.* New York: Dryden.

Edwards, A. L. (1970). *The measurement of personality traits by scales and inventories.* New York: Holt, Reinhart, and Winston.

Ellis, A. (1946). The validity of personality questionnaires. *Psychological Bulletin, 43,* 385–440.

Ellis, A. (1953). Recent research with personality inventories. *Journal of Consulting Psychology, 17,* 45–49.

Eysenck, J. J., & Eysenck, S. B. G. (1975). *Manual for the Eysenck Personality Questionnaire.* San Diego, CA: Educational and Industrial Testing Service.

Finger, M. S., & Ones, D. S. (1999). Psychometric equivalence of the computer and booklet forms of the MMPI: A meta-analysis. *Psychological Assessment, 11,* 58–66.

Galton, F. (1884). Measurement of character. *Fortnightly Review, 42,* 179–185.

Gilberstadt, H., & Duker, J. (1965). *A handbook for clinical and actuarial MMPI interpretation.* Philadelphia: W. B. Saunders.

Goldberg, L. R. (1965). Diagnosticians versus diagnostic signs: The diagnosis of psychosis versus neurosis from the MMPI. *Psychological Monographs, 79*(Whole No. 602).

Groth-Marnat, G. (1997). *Handbook of psychological assessment* (3rd ed.). New York: Wiley.

Guthrie, G. M. (1952). Common characteristics associated with frequent MMPI profile types. *Journal of Clinical Psychology, 8,* 141–145.

Gynther, M. D. (1972). White norms and black MMPIs: A prescription for discrimination? *Psychological Bulletin, 78,* 386–402.

Halbower, C. C. (1955). *A comparison of actuarial versus clinical prediction of classes discriminated by the MMPI.* Unpublished doctoral dissertation, Minneapolis, MN.

Harkness, A. R., & McNulty, J. L. (1994). The Personality-Psychopathology Five: Issues from the pages of a diagnostic manual instead of a dictionary. In S. Strack & M. Lorr (Eds.), *Differentiating normal and abnormal personality* (pp. 291–315). New York: Springer.

Harkness, A. R., McNulty, J. L., & Ben-Porath, Y. S. (1995). The Personality Psychopathology Five (PSY-5) Scales. *Psychological Assessment, 7,* 104–114.

Hathaway, S. R. (1956). Scales 5 (Masculinity-Femininity), 6 (Paranoia), and 8 (Schizophrenia). In G. S. Welsh & W. G. Dahlstrom (Eds.), *Basic readings on the MMPI in psychology and medicine* (pp. 104–111). Minneapolis: University of Minnesota Press.

Hathaway, S. R., & McKinley, J. C. (1940). A Multiphasic Personality Schedule (Minnesota): I. Construction of the schedule. *Journal of Psychology, 10,* 249–254.

Hathaway, S. R., & McKinley, J. C. (1942). A Multiphasic Personality Schedule (Minnesota): II. The measurement of symptomatic depression. *Journal of Psychology, 14,* 73–84.

Hathaway, S. R., & McKinley, J. C. (1943). *The Minnesota Multiphasic Personality Inventory.* Minneapolis: University of Minnesota Press.

Hathaway, S. R., & Meehl, P. E. (1951). The Minnesota Multiphasic Personality Inventory. In *Military clinical psychology* (Department of the Army Technical Manual TM 8:242; Department of the Air Force AFM 160-145). Washington, DC: Government Printing Office.

Heidbreder, E. (1926). Measuring introversion and extraversion. *Journal of Abnormal and Social Psychology, 21,* 120–134.

Helmes, E., & Reddon, J. R. (1993). A perspective on developments in assessing psychopathology: A critical review of the MMPI and MMPI-2. *Psychological Bulletin, 113,* 453–471.

Heymans, G., & Wiersma, E. (1906). Beitrage zur spezillen psychologie auf grund einer massenunterschung [Contribution of psychological specialists to personality analysis]. *Zeitschrift fur Psychologie, 43,* 81–127.

Hoch, A., & Amsden, G. S. (1913). A guide to the descriptive study of personality. *Review of Neurology and Psychiatry, 11,* 577–587.

Humm, D. G., & Wadsworth, G. W. (1935). The Humm-Wadsworth temperament scale. *American Journal of Psychiatry, 92,* 163–200.

Jackson, D. N. (1989). *Basic Personality Inventory manual.* Port Huron, MI: Sigma Assessment Systems.

Jackson, D. N., Fraboni, M., & Helmes, E. (1997). MMPI-2 content scales: How much content do they measure? *Assessment, 4,* 111–117.

Jackson, D. N., & Messick, S. (1962). Response styles on the MMPI: Comparison of clinical and normal samples. *Journal of Abnormal and Social Psychology, 65,* 285–299.

John, O. P., & Srivastava, S. (1999). The big five trait taxonomy: History, measurement, and theoretical perspectives. In L. A. Pervin & O. P. John (Eds.), *Handbook of personality: Theory and research* (pp. 102–138). New York: Guilford Press.

Keller, J., Hicks, B. D., & Miller, G. A. (2000). Psychophysiology in the study of psychopathology. In J. T. Cacioppo & L. G. Tassinary (Eds.), *Handbook of psychophysiology* (pp. 719–750). New York: Cambridge University Press.

Loevinger, J. (1994). Has psychology lost its conscience? *Journal of Personality Assessment, 62,* 2–8.

Maller, J. B. (1932). The measurement of conflict between honesty and group loyalty. *Journal of Educational Psychology, 23,* 187–191.

Marks, P. A., & Seeman, W. (1963). *The actuarial description of abnormal personality: An atlas for use with the MMPI.* Baltimore: Williams and Wilkins.

Maruish, M. E. (1999). *The use of psychological testing for treatment planning and outcomes assessment.* Mahwah, NJ: Erlbaum.

McKinley, J. C., & Hathaway, S. R. (1940). A Multiphasic Personality Schedule (Minnesota): II. A differential study of hypochondriasis. *Journal of Psychology, 10,* 255–268.

McKinley, J. C., & Hathaway, S. R. (1942). A Multiphasic Personality Schedule (Minnesota): IV. Psychasthenia. *Journal of Applied Psychology, 26,* 614–624.

McKinley, J. C., & Hathaway, S. R. (1944). A Multiphasic Personality Schedule (Minnesota): V. Hysteria, Hypomania, and Psychopathic Deviate. *Journal of Applied Psychology, 28,* 153–174.

Meehl, P. E. (1945). The dynamics of "structured" personality tests. *Journal of Clinical Psychology, 1,* 296–303.

Meehl, P. E. (1954). *Clinical versus statistical prediction: A theoretical analysis and review of the evidence.* Minneapolis: University of Minnesota Press.

Meehl, P. E. (1956). Wanted—A good cookbook. *American Psychologist, 11,* 263–272.

Meehl, P. E., & Dahlstrom, W. G. (1960). Objective configural rules for discriminating psychotic from neurotic MMPI profiles. *Journal of Consulting Psychology, 24,* 375–387.

Meehl, P. E., & Hathaway, S. R. (1946). The K factor as a suppressor variable in the MMPI. *Journal of Applied Psychology, 30,* 525–564.

Mineka, S., Watson, D., & Clark, L. A. (1998). Comorbidity of anxiety and unipolar mood disorders. *Annual Review of Psychology, 49,* 377–412.

Morey, L. C. (1991). *Personality Assessment Inventory: Professional manual.* Odessa, FL: Psychological Assessment Resources.

Piedmont, R. L., McCrae, R. R., Riemann, R., & Angleitner, A. (2000). On the invalidity of validity scales: Evidence from self-reports and observer ratings in volunteer samples. *Journal of Personality and Social Psychology, 78,* 582–593.

Roberts, M. D., Thompson, J. R., & Johnson, W. (1999). *The PAI Law enforcement, corrections, and public safety selection report: Manual for the professional report service.* Odessa, FL: Psychological Assessment Resources.

Ruch, F. L. (1942). A technique for detecting attempts to fake performance on a self-inventory type of personality test. In Q. McNemar & M. A. Merrill (Eds.), *Studies on personality* (pp. 61–85). New York: Saunders.

Schinka, J. A., & LaLone, L. (1997). MMPI-2 norms: Comparisons with a census-matched subsample. *Psychological Assessment, 9,* 307–311.

Schmidt, F. L., & Hunter, J. E. (1977). Development of a general solution to the problem of validity generalization. *Journal of Applied Psychology, 62,* 529–540.

Starck, S., & Lorr, M. (1994). *Differentiating normal and abnormal personality.* New York: Springer.

Tellegen, A. (1982). *Brief manual for the Multidimensional Personality Questionnaire.* Minneapolis, MN: Unpublished document.

Tellegen, A. (1985). Structure of mood and personality and their relevance to assessing anxiety, with an emphasis on self-report. In A. H. Tuma & J. D. Maser (Eds.), *Anxiety and the anxiety disorders* (pp. 681–706). Hillsdale, NJ: Erlbaum.

Thurstone, L. L. (1930). A neurotic inventory. *Journal of Social Psychology, 1,* 3–30.

Travis, R. C. (1925). The measurement of fundamental character traits by a new diagnostic test. *Journal of Abnormal and Social Psychology, 18,* 400–425.

Watson, D., & Pennebaker, J. W. (1989). Health complaints, stress, and distress: Exploring the central role of negative affectivity. *Psychological Review, 96,* 234–254.

Wells, F. L. (1914). The systematic observation of the personality—In its relation to the hygiene of the mind. *Psychological Review, 21,* 295–333.

Wiggins, J. S. (1959). Interrelations among MMPI measures of dissimulation under standard and social desirability instruction. *Journal of Consulting Psychology, 23,* 419–427.

Wiggins, J. S. (1966). Substantive dimensions of self-report in the MMPI item pool. *Psychological Monographs, 80*(22, Whole No. 630).

Wiggins, J. S. (1973). *Personality and prediction: Principles of personality assessment.* Reading, MA: Addison Wesley.

Woodworth, R. S. (1920). *Personal data sheet.* Chicago: Stoeling.

CHAPTER 25

Current Status and Future Directions of Assessment Psychology

JACK A. NAGLIERI AND JOHN R. GRAHAM

Assessment psychology is "concerned with methods of identifying similarities and differences among people in their personal characteristics and capacities" (see chapter by Weiner in this volume). This important branch of psychology has become so well researched and established that it can now be considered a subdiscipline within the field of psychology. Although psychological assessment has sometimes been equated with testing, assessment involves much more than administering tests. It involves the collection and integration of information, not only from psychological tests, but also from interviews, behavioral observations, collateral reports, and historical documents so that a more complete picture of a person is obtained.

BRIEF HISTORY

Assessment psychology can be dated to as early as 2200 B.C. when the Chinese emperor examined individuals to determine their fitness for public office (DuBois, 1970). In the late eighteenth and early nineteenth centuries, civil service tests, patterned after those of the Chinese, were introduced in Europe. In 1883 the United States endorsed the use of tests for the screening of applicants for Civil Service jobs (Graham & Lilly, 1984). At about the same time, Sir Francis Galton's work on the genetic transmission of characteristics required the development of measures to quantify the characteristics under study. The simple sensorimotor tasks that Galton developed were later introduced in the United States by James McKeen Cattell.

Alfred Binet and Theodore Simon, working in France, adapted some of these sensorimotor tasks and added others when they developed methods for assessing ability in school children. Their scales were modified for use in the United States by Lewis Terman and further adapted in part by the U.S. Army for evaluation of military personnel. David Wechsler's dissatisfaction with the Binet scales in his work with psychiatric patients led to the development of the first of the Wechsler intelligence scales. The availability of standardized methods for assessing intellectual ability provided American psychologists with unique skills that helped to establish their professional identity in clinical and educational settings.

Moreover, these tools to measure ability have had tremendous impact on our society and the practice of psychology.

CURRENT STATUS

The proportion of psychologists' time spent conducting psychological assessments has declined over time. In 1959 psychologists practicing in clinical settings spent 44% of their time conducting psychological assessments (Groth-Marnat, 1999), but by 1998 psychologists in similar clinical settings were spending only 16% of their time conducting psychological assessments (Phelps, Eisman, & Kohout, 1998). However, assessment is still a very important and viable specialty within psychology, especially among professionals working in educational and clinical settings. Earlier chapters in this volume elucidated some of the factors that have affected the use of assessment procedures. A recurring theme has been that economic factors, most currently represented by managed care programs, have had significant impact on assessment practices. Piotrowski, Belter, and Keller (1998) surveyed psychologists listed in the National Register of Health Service Providers in Psychology and found that 70% saw managed care as negatively affecting psychological assessment. Psychologists reported less reliance on procedures requiring much clinician time and more emphasis on briefer instruments. They also reported less emphasis on comprehensive assessments of general psychological functioning and more emphasis on techniques that were directly responsive to specific referral questions. Unfortunately, the validity of many of the specific and abbreviated procedures currently being used has not been adequately demonstrated.

Economic pressures have also forced psychologists to demonstrate that assessment activities contribute significantly to positive outcomes in a variety of settings (e.g., mental health, medical, business, education). Other chapters in this volume offer evidence concerning these contributions. For example, in his chapter in this volume Maruish presents some convincing arguments that assessment procedures can facilitate effective psychological interventions. An especially promising area is the development of standardized assessment procedures for documenting the effectiveness of treatment interventions. Likewise, the chapters in this volume by Sweet, Tovian, and Suchy and by Podell, DeFina, Barrett, McCullen, and Goldberg document the contributions of psychological assessment in relation to a variety of medical procedures including surgical interventions, organ transplantation, and physical conditions (e.g., neuropsychological dysfunction). Similarly, in his chapter in this volume Wasserman highlights

new advances in assessment of cognitive processing that have been shown to be relevant to academic interventions. An important role for assessment psychologists will be to further develop effective ways to assess patients' psychological coping and adjustment to their diseases and also to show relevance to treatment.

The Board of Professional Psychology of the American Psychological Association (APA) constituted the Psychological Assessment Work Group (PAWG) to examine the current status of psychological assessment and to make recommendations concerning its future. The work group documented the impact of managed care on psychological assessments (Eisman et al., 2000). Although many managed care companies argue that traditional psychological assessments do not add significantly enough to treatment to justify their cost and that less costly interviews are sufficient, the PAWG concluded that these views are not accurate and offered recommendations for rebutting them and preserving the stature of psychological assessment in the health care marketplace.

In a subsequent report, PAWG offered evidence from the research literature that some psychological assessment procedures are as valid as (and in some cases more valid than) medical procedures that are readily accepted by many as valid and necessary (Daw, 2001; Meyer et al., 2001). For example, the relationship between long-term verbal memory tests and differentiation of dementia from depression was of the same magnitude as the relationship between exercise echocardiography results and identification of coronary artery disease (effect size for both about .60). Neither the use of routine ultrasound examinations for predicting successful pregnancies nor the use of Minnesota Multiphasic Personality Inventory (MMPI) Ego Strength scale scores to predict subsequent psychotherapy outcome can be supported by empirical research findings (effect size for each less than .10). The report emphasized that both psychological and medical procedures have varying degrees of validity and that the validity and utility of each technique has to be demonstrated empirically. The PAWG concluded that "formal psychological assessment is a vital element in psychology's professional heritage and a central part of professional practice today" and that there is "very strong and positive evidence that already exists on the value of psychological testing and assessment" (Meyer et al., 2001, p. 155). It is the responsibility of assessment psychologists, individually and collectively, to use existing evidence to support assessment activities in a variety of settings and to generate additional evidence of the validity and efficiency of psychological assessment procedures in health care and other settings (e.g., business, forensic) where assessment is taking place.

ASSESSMENT SETTINGS

Child Mental Health

Lachar's chapter in this volume on assessment in child mental health settings illustrates the importance that psychological assessment services have in intake evaluation, treatment planning, and subsequent outcome review. His chapter especially illustrates the interplay of psychology and business, and particularly how delivery of services can be related to a variety of factors including annual institutional budgets from which resources are allocated and the extent to which associated expenses can be reimbursed. These realities of service delivery have considerable impact on children who receive mental health services because of emotional and behavioral adjustment problems.

Lachar describes how psychological assessment in child mental health settings focuses on the identification and quantification of symptoms and problems that should lead to the development of treatment strategies. There is a detailed discussion of the forms of psychological assessment that can be applied to answer specific diagnostic inquiries. This includes careful analysis of assessment instruments as well as topics such as qualifications of persons who conduct psychological assessment services, supervision issues, and certification and license considerations. Lachar recognizes that well-trained and well-supervised professionals are needed to mange the difficulties of making a diagnosis in an informational environment that can be complicated by problems such as co-morbidity and disparate reports from parents. Despite the challenges, psychological assessments ultimately play a pivotal role in the determination of the nature of the problem and the eventual effectiveness of the treatment. Because of the importance assessment plays in meeting the mental health needs of the client, Lachar notes that proper assessment should make use of multiple methods (e.g., behavioral rating scales, direct observation, interviews) by multiple informants (e.g., parents, teachers, the children themselves) of behavior in multiple settings (e.g., home, school). The ultimate success of treatment is, of course, related to the value of the methods used to obtain information and select treatments.

Importantly, Lachar's discussion of methods used by psychologists in this field, and especially the results of surveys of the assessment tools used in the child mental health arena, have shown that traditional tests of intelligence (e.g., Wechsler scales) and personality (e.g., MMPI; Rorschach; Thematic Apperception Test) remain standards in the profession. He also notes that recent surveys suggest the growing use of parent and teacher rating scales in a variety of areas (from rating scales of depression and attention deficit hyperactivity disorder to family adjustment scales). Additionally, Lachar notes the influence of managed care in reducing the use of some of the most labor-intensive psychological assessment procedures.

Lachar concludes that multidimensional multi-informant objective assessment makes a unique contribution to the assessment of youth adjustment, but more research is needed. He suggests that the validity of objective measures of youth adjustment should be more fully examined and especially the construct and actuarial validity of popular child and adolescent adjustment measures. Lachar stresses that validity will be best demonstrated when a measure contributes to the accuracy of routine decision-making that occurs in clinical practice (e.g., differential diagnosis or the selection of an optimal treatment plan). Further research is also needed on agreement among informants who have completed rating scales, in particular, the clinical implications of the results obtained from each informant rather than the magnitude of correlations. Additionally, researchers should examine incremental validity obtained from the use of a variety of objective assessment instruments. These and other issues presented by Lachar illustrate the important topics yet to be examined in this vibrant area of assessment psychology.

Adult Mental Health

In their chapter in this volume concerning assessment in adult mental health settings, Bagby, Wild, and Turner conclude that the main goals of assessment in such settings are providing an accurate description of the client's problems, determining what interpersonal and environmental factors precipitated and are sustaining the problems, and making predictions concerning outcome with or without intervention. Assessments are also useful in planning treatment programs, evaluating the effectiveness of treatment interventions, and guiding discharge and follow-up plans. Bagby et al. believe that assessments need to be comprehensive and that clients and patients are disadvantaged by trends toward abbreviated assessment instruments and procedures.

In inpatient settings, assessments often address questions of differential diagnosis. Although they discuss the limitations of the categorical approach to diagnosis underlying the *Diagnostic and Statistical Manual of Mental Disorders, fourth edition (DSM-IV)*, Bagby et al. believe that instruments that cover a broad array of symptoms (e.g., MMPI-2) are especially useful in addressing diagnostic questions.

Bagby et al. believe that assessments in adult mental health settings need to be evidence-based and multimodal. Psychologists conducting assessments should choose their tools and make their interpretations of the resulting data using the best available empirical evidence. They echo the opinion expressed by Garb (in his chapter in this volume) that judgments more closely tied to empirical data will be more accurate than those based on clinical experience and clinical impressions. They also believe that multiple data sources are necessary for reliable and valid inferences to be made about patients and clients. They prefer more structured interviews and more objective instruments, because in their judgment these approaches are more clearly supported by empirical evidence.

Geriatric

Edelstein noted in his chapter in this volume that the population of the United States is aging rapidly. Compared with the 1900 census data, the 75–84-year-old group is 16 times larger, and the 85 and older group is 33 times larger. Data suggest that approximately 80% of older adults suffer from some chronic health problem and about one fourth meet criteria for a diagnosable mental disorder. Thus, assessment of older adults will become more and more important over time.

Although there are many similarities in the assessment of younger and older adults, there also are some unique considerations when assessing older adults. Older adults may have deficits in vision, hearing, or cognitive processes that make completion of standard assessment procedures difficult or impossible. The presentation of major psychological disorders for older adults is often different from that for younger adults. For example, clinically depressed older adults are more likely than younger adults to present with somatic instead of psychological symptoms. All of these issues present significant challenges in assessing older adults that may best be met through the development of techniques and instruments tailored to the differing abilities and problems of the older adult.

Edelstein concludes that it is more important to assess the adaptive functioning of older adults than to describe clinical syndromes. Instruments and procedures for assessing the activities of daily living (ADLs; e.g., dressing, bathing) and instrumental activities of daily living (IADLs; e.g., meal preparation, money management) will become more important as the population continues to age. Also, because of an increasing awareness of the importance of social support (real and perceived) to the well-being of older adults, instruments and techniques for effective assessment of social support will become increasingly important.

Industrial/Organizational

In their chapter in this volume on assessment in industrial/ organizational settings, Klimoski and Zukin describe the important work psychologists have done to aid companies in their attempts to improve performance by better understanding how people think and behave. As is the case with other settings in which assessment is important, psychologists working in this field initially used tests developed by the U.S. military (also discussed by Wasserman in his chapter in this volume) to measure ability as well as for personnel selection, evaluation of social competence, and prediction of behaviors such as absenteeism. Many of the tests used in industrial/ organizational settings today were translated or adapted by former military officers who went into the private sector after military service (e.g., Otis and Wechsler). Although versions of these early methods are still in use today (e.g., Army Beta test), Klimoski and Zukin's chapter also provides information about the enlargement of the assessment batteries. This is especially important within the context of political considerations, including accommodation for disability and equal opportunities for employment, that must be taken into account in industrial decision-making processes.

Assessment in industrial/organizational settings, like assessment in educational settings (see Braden's chapter in this volume), has been influenced by the social context within which the measures and procedures are used. Not only have society's views of assessment issues shaped how assessment is conducted, but federal and state laws and regulations have also had a major impact on the field. In today's industrial/ organizational settings these considerations can be as important as psychometric issues such as reliability and validity, especially as they relate to problems such as job discrimination (fairness based on race, sex, ethnicity, age, or disability), equal opportunity, neutrality of decision-makers, and so on.

The role of psychologists as assessors within the industrial/ organizational setting has also been influenced by the demand for these valuable professionals. Business leaders have seen the advantages to industry provided by psychologists who can assist with selection, promotion, and career planning decisions so that the best people for specific jobs may be found. This has led psychologists to study and utilize a variety of instruments in addition to tests of intelligence and personality, to evaluate things like teamwork and interpersonal skills, specific knowledge and skills pertinent to the job, honesty and integrity, ability to learn, the five-factor structure of personality, and ratings of actual job performance.

Klimoski and Zukin discuss challenges facing the field of industrial/organizational psychology. These include research on determining the best prediction and criterion variables. Some researchers have argued that job performance itself is the best criterion, but definition of job performance can be difficult. Similarly, although researchers have found that factors such as ability and personality play an important role in overall job performance, many times the instruments selected were not developed for the purposes for which they are applied. For example, researchers have questioned the application of a test of personality like the MMPI in industrial/organizational settings because it was not developed for this purpose. How can a test like the MMPI be used to determine suitability for a particular job when it was developed to measure psychopathology, not personality factors associated with how well a person can perform a specific task? Another challenge facing industrial/organizational psychologists, and almost every other person in the assessment field, is the movement toward on-line testing, computer adaptive tests, and other advances that result from the use of the World Wide Web. These developments further illustrate the unique demands of those who work in the industrial/organizational field—an environment driven by the intersection of the science of testing, public opinion, and politics, and the culture of the business world.

Forensic

In their chapter in this volume, Ogloff and Douglas state that forensic psychology involves the application of the principles of psychology to legal questions and issues. Although psychologists have been involved in offering expert testimony in court since the early 1900s, It was not until 1962 that the U.S. District Court of Appeals for the District of Columbia in *Jenkins v. U.S.* clearly recognized psychologists as experts in court. In 2001 the Council of Representatives of the American Psychological Association voted to recognize forensic psychology as a specialty area in psychology.

Because the primary task of forensic psychologists as experts typically is to evaluate the extent to which individuals meet various legal standards and criteria (e.g., competency to stand trial, insanity), assessment is one of the most important tasks that forensic psychologists perform. Several factors have limited the contributions that psychologists have made in this area. Many psychologists, including some who practice forensic psychology on a regular basis, have not been trained in forensic psychological assessment. Although there are similarities between clinical and forensic assessments, there are also important differences. Ogloff and Douglas point out that forensic constructs and questions rarely map directly onto traditional psychological constructs. Thus, persons not adequately trained in forensic assessment will not be able to understand and specify the legal principles and standards relevant to a particular assessment issue. In addition, traditional assessment instruments (e.g., MMPI, Wechsler scales) were not developed within legal contexts and according to legal principles, so they are far less useful in forensic than in clinical evaluations.

Ogloff and Douglas believe that the role of psychologists in conducting assessments in the legal arena will continue to increase. However, several important changes are indicated if psychologists are to make significant contributions in forensic settings. First, formal forensic training programs need to be developed. Most psychologists currently conducting forensic evaluations have no formal training in forensic psychology. Second, formal procedures for credentialing and certifying forensic psychologists must be expanded. Currently, only nine states in the United States have certification procedures. Although the American Board of Forensic Psychology has procedures for establishing credentials for forensic psychological practice, relatively few psychologists undergo this voluntary evaluation process. Third, more research is needed to determine the extent to which traditional psychological assessment instruments and procedures can be used to address specific forensic constructs. Finally, psychologists should use their expertise in test construction and statistical methodologies to develop forensic psychological instruments designed specifically to address forensic questions and issues. Although Ogloff and Douglas state that "we have accomplished a great deal in a relatively short time in forensic psychology," there are significant issues associated with training and instrument development that remain to be addressed.

Medical

In their chapter in this volume, Sweet, Tovian, and Suchy state that assessment activities of psychologists in medical settings have become so commonplace that they are taken for granted. Recently trained physicians expect to have psychological assessment resources available in the settings where they practice. In general, psychological assessments in medical settings should contribute to a broader understanding of the patient. More specifically, assessments should document patients' response to disease and changes (both positive and negative) associated with medical procedures and treatments.

Traditional assessment procedures (e.g., MMPI-2, Rorschach) may contribute significantly to the understanding of patients' psychological status and personality characteristics, but the validity of traditional measures to do so must be demonstrated in medical settings. The issue of using general population norms versus norms for particular medical populations is a complex one that is dependent on the purpose for which the assessments are conducted. For example, if the referral question is whether or not a patient's emotional distress is severe enough to warrant intervention, general population norms are likely to provide the most useful information. However, if the referral question concerns a patient's adjustment to a specific illness at a particular stage in comparison to that of the typical patient, then illness-specific norms may be more appropriate.

In applied medical settings, the efficiency and cost effectiveness of assessment procedures are being increasingly emphasized. Psychologists must be in a position to demonstrate that psychological assessments contribute significantly to effective treatment programs for patients and that they do so in a cost-effective manner. Economic considerations have resulted in the development of many brief, narrow-band assessment instruments. Although such instruments can be quite valuable, matters of efficiency and cost-effectiveness often overshadow more traditional issues such as reliability and validity in evaluating them. There is likely to be a concomitant emphasis on actuarial judgments over clinical ones. Sweet, Tovian, and Suchy concluded in their chapter that both clinical and actuarial judgments make significant contributions in medical settings.

Correctional

In his chapter in this volume, Megargee points out that more than 5.7 million men and women in the United States are under some form of correctional supervision (i.e., jail, prison, probation, parole). The number of persons in jails and prisons has increased 667% since 1970. With such large numbers of persons to service with limited resources, assessment and classification in correctional settings are extremely important. In 1973 the National Advisory Commission on Criminal Justice Standards and Goals called for immediate implementation of comprehensive classification at all levels of the criminal justice system. In the case of *Palmigiano v. Garrahy* (1977), the courts agreed that accurate classification is essential to the operation of safe prisons.

In his chapter Megargee discusses in detail the purposes for which assessments are conducted in correctional settings and the instruments and procedures that have been used. There clearly has been a move away from using offense data for classification and toward consideration of individual needs, including psychological ones, of those assessed. Often instruments and procedures developed for use in other (e.g., mental health) settings have been employed in correctional settings. The validity of such applications has not often been studied, but available research indicates little support for the routine use of clinical instruments for correctional assessment. Many instruments and scales have been developed specifically for use in correctional settings, but the methodologies used have typically been inadequate and data concerning validity for the intended purposes lacking.

One of the most promising approaches to psychological assessment and classification in corrections settings has been

the MMPI–MMPI-2 system developed by Megargee and his colleagues (Megargee, Carbonell, Bohn, & Sliger, 2001). In a technique based on cluster analytic procedures, subtypes of inmates were identified using MMPI scores, and classification rules, which can be applied by computers, were developed to assign inmates to types. Megargee has demonstrated that his system is appropriate for local, state, and federal prison systems, with large proportions of inmates being classified in the various settings. External correlates, including institutional adjustment and postrelease behaviors, have been established for many of the Megargee types.

Megargee points out that there has been inadequate attention to the role of situational variables in predicting behaviors in correctional settings. Rather, many psychologists assume that personality variables, as assessed by traditional psychological tests, are the best predictors of such behaviors. While probably of great importance, the interaction of situational and personality variables also has been understudied.

Although the standards of the American Association of Correctional Psychologists and other organizations have recommended minimal qualifications for mental health workers providing services in correctional settings, there are few procedures for establishing that psychologists conducting assessments in correctional settings are adequately trained and competent to do so. Uniform standards and procedures for credentialing and certifying correctional psychologists are badly needed.

Educational

In the chapter in this volume on assessment psychology in educational settings, Braden begins by distinguishing psychological assessment in the schools from psychological assessment in other settings. He carefully describes how assessment in schools is conducted for screening and diagnostic purposes, for example, for the identification of children with special education needs. Other purposes of assessment in educational settings include the design of educational interventions as well as evaluation, selection, and certification functions. Braden also reviews more specific methods such as interviews and reviews of student records, observational systems, and response-to-intervention approaches. More specific checklists and self-report techniques, projective techniques, and standardized tests are also included.

Braden also provides a summary of methods used to assess academic achievement particularly because of the importance these tests play in identification of children's academic deficiencies and the role such tests play in psychoeducational diagnosis. The relationships between the use of these tests and educational accountability and standards-based educational reforms are also discussed. Braden's chapter concludes with the suggestion that assessment tools need to be in line with current scientific and technical advances and educational standards of learning. Additionally, assessments must be appropriate for diverse learners and have utility for instructional interventions.

TYPES OF ASSESSMENT

Cognitive/Intellectual

Wasserman's chapter in this volume provides a review of how the assessment of intelligence has had a long history in psychology and can be credited with being one of the most influential constructs in psychology and education. IQ tests have provided a structured method of evaluating ability that has been used in most settings within which psychologists work. Wasserman provides a discussion of how IQ tests have been used, but, more importantly, he also provides important historical facts on the origins of these tests as well as a discussion of their utility. Like the Reynolds and Ramsay chapter in this volume, which discusses the most controversial topic surrounding IQ tests (the question of bias), Wasserman's coverage of the more politically focused issues gives the reader a greater understanding of the complexities of this topic. Controversies notwithstanding, the contributions intelligence tests have made to our field are reflected in the many settings within which tests are used (schools, hospitals, clinics, industry, etc.) as well as the purposes for which they have been used (diagnosis of learning disorders, giftedness, mental retardation, attention deficits, etc.).

Wasserman emphasizes the importance of understanding the history behind conventional IQ tests, which goes back to the Army Mental Testing Program (Yoakum & Yerkes, 1920) so that instruments can be seen in perspective. He argues that the study of intelligence can be "characterized by the best and worst of science—scholarly debates and bitter rivalries, research breakthroughs and academic fraud, major assessment paradigm shifts, and the birth of a commercial industry that generates hundreds of millions of dollars in annual revenue." He makes the important suggestion that the study of intelligence has yet to claim status as a mature clinical science, despite some signs of progress.

Wasserman's view that the study of intelligence needs an evolutionary step is based on the recognition that this technology (like others in psychology) is dominated by tests created before 1930. He recognizes the tremendous advances in electronic scoring, analysis, and reporting of test results, but these advances are based on instruments that are close to 100 years

old (e.g., Wechsler and Binet scales). Wasserman suggests that if the past provides the best prediction of the future, then by about 2050 we may expect seventh-edition revisions of the Stanford-Binet, the Wechsler Intelligence Scale for Children (WISC), and the Wechsler Adult Intelligence Scale (WAIS). His discussion begs the question "Are these tests so valid that they should remain psychologists' primary tools in the twenty-first century?"

Wasserman argues that changes in fundamental assessment paradigms are needed so that psychological assessment results for a child referred for learning problems, for example, will (a) give information about how learning occurs, (b) describe the relevant impaired cognitive abilities or processes, (c) assess the degree to which the child's ability or process profile resembles that obtained by specific diagnostic groups (e.g., learning disability or attention deficit hyperactivity disorder), and (d) prescribe interventions that have demonstrated effectiveness for children with similar test score profiles. He concludes that "the combination of a well-developed theory, valid and reliable tests, a cognitive diagnostic nomenclature related to abilities and processes, and effective interventions linked to assessment may one day enable the field of intelligence assessment to become a mature applied clinical science."

Interests

The chapter on interests by Lowman and Carson begins with an important recognition of the fact that psychologists have not reached a consensual definition of what interests are, how they develop, and how best to classify them. As in the situation described by Wasserman in the intelligence testing chapter in this volume, although the field has not arrived at an accepted definition, the lack of consensus has not blocked the creation of a number of assessment tools for measuring interests, and the test publishing industry has evolved into a flourishing business. This has resulted in a situation in which the measures used to assess interests have defined the field, especially in the eyes of those professionals who use the inventories. Again, as in the situation in intelligence testing, Lowman and Carson see assessment of interests as an important field in psychology that is comparable in scope and importance to abilities and personality traits. The problems they discuss in the assessment of interests also parallel those found in the assessment of intelligence as it relates to issues of gender, age, race, and ethnic factors that may affect the validity of interpretations of interest measures.

The chapter on interests concludes with suggestions by Lowman and Carson for research on a number of important topics, including the heritability of interests. Although they suggest that high heritability would be expected because of the stability of interests across the life cycle and the efficiency with which people seem to self-select occupations that fit their characteristics, they note that further research is needed in this area. They also recognize the need to study the possibility of critical periods in the development of interests, especially to examine whether children have a number of potentially strong interests that become more stable with the development of related skills during a critical time period. Other areas of future research include further examination of the commonality and differences of alternative interest measures, empirically based coding of occupations, and the specific empirical nature of interdomain relationships. Finally, having established that interests and personality are highly related, they indicate that more work is needed to determine ability-interest and ability-interest-personality relationships. This area, like others in assessment psychology, is ripe with ample research opportunities.

Neuropsychology

The chapter on neuropsychological assessment in this volume by Podell, De Fina, Barrett, McCullen, and Goldberg is unique because neuropsychology has undergone considerably more advancement than many disciplines in psychology, especially in the assessment methods used. As the authors reflect on the history of the field, it becomes clear that most of neuropsychology is based on the large amount of clinical information obtained from studying World War II veterans who experienced brain damage. Psychologists used the understanding of the relationships between brain injury and performance deficits to help determine the likelihood and possible location of brain damage and associated cognitive impairments in a wide variety of clients since WWII. Recent advances in cutting-edge neuroimaging technology, such as functional magnetic resonance imaging (fMRI) and magnetoencephalography (MEG) enable today's neuropsychologists to study the brain's functioning more directly. These advances have allowed much greater evaluative ability than ever before and have revolutionized how neuropsychologists perform their job.

Despite the considerable advances these technologies have provided, economic factors have also had a substantial influence on the current and future status of neuropsychology. The current health care system has had a significant impact on the development of neuropsychology as a clinical discipline, as it has influenced others in the private practice arena. Reduction in funding opportunities has led to fewer graduate and postgraduate training programs, which reduction in turn reflects the reduced availability of well-paying jobs in neuropsychology. The shrinking health care dollar has also caused neuropsychologists to reexamine how they administer services and to consider alternative employment opportunities such as forensic and sports neuropsychology. In the latter setting, for example, neuropsychologists have found a new and important role in helping teams assess and manage sports-related concussions. They have been helpful in evaluating the effect of a concussion and using this information to help the team trainer and physicians determine when an athlete is able to return to play. This opportunity is, of course, an expansion of the field that reflects changes in health care delivery more than advancements in technology. These economic stressors along with new technologies have transformed neuropsychology into a more diverse and scientific subspecialty of psychology.

Podell et al. illustrate how the subspecialty of neuropsychology has evolved and reinvented itself as the technology and demands of the profession have changed. Although this field is still wedded to many traditional instruments and methods (e.g., Wechsler scales), it has experienced a widening through the inclusion of assessment tools that have made some rather significant impacts in advancing neuropsychology, for example, in the areas of computerized assessment and the development of novel assessment techniques. Computerized testing techniques, such as the Automated Neuropsychological Assessment Metrics and the Immediate Post-Concussion Assessment and Cognitive Testing approaches, allow for effective evaluation of a variety of factors (e.g., working memory, reaction time, concussion symptomatology). Novel assessment techniques have included those that blend neuropsychology with educational psychology as well as combining complex theoretical models of cognition to measure critical cognitive abilities such as attention and executive control (Cognitive Assessment System; Naglieri & Das, 1997), which is also discussed in the chapter in this volume by Wasserman. These new methods, combined with traditional tests, new neuroimaging techniques, and the changing economic situations, have facilitated the advancement of the discipline of neuropsychology in important ways. Not only is neuropsychology in an important transition period, as are all other health-care related fields, but it is also in the midst of historical changes from external forces, and it must be able to withstand new challenges to survive as a strong and viable clinical service.

Personality and Psychopathology

The assessment of personality and psychopathology has long been a part of psychology, and the techniques and methods used in assessment have been quite varied. Projective approaches (see the Viglione and Rivera chapter in this volume) have involved human figure drawings, responses to inkblots, and stories about ambiguous pictures. Self-report measures (also see the Ben-Porath chapter in this volume) have been constructed to assess normal personality (e.g., California Psychological Inventory) and psychopathology (e.g., MMPI-2). As Craig notes in his chapter in this volume, interviews of various kinds have been widely used for years by psychologists and members of other professions.

Much has been said and written about the assumptions underlying the various assessment approaches and their relative advantages and disadvantages in assessing personality and psychopathology. Virtually every technique for assessing personality and psychopathology has been criticized by some and defended by others, and examples abound. Criticisms that the MMPI clinical scales measure only acquiescence or social desirability response sets (Edwards, 1957, 1964; Messick & Jackson, 1961) were rebutted by Block (1965) and others. More recently, the validity of many Rorschach Comprehensive System scores and indexes and the adequacy of its norms have been called into question (Lilienfeld, Wood, & Garb, 2000; Shaffer, Erdberg, & Haroian, 1999) and subsequently defended by Bornstein (2001), Meyer (2000), Meyer and Archer (2001), and Weiner (2000, 2001). Unfortunately, the controversies surrounding assessment of personality and psychopathology have not led to constructive conclusions about validity or subsequent changes or modifications in the way the assessment techniques are used. Despite the criticisms, assessment of personality and psychopathology remains a hallmark of assessment psychology.

Interviews

Interviewing is the oldest and most widely used assessment method, with almost every psychological evaluation including some kind of interview data. Unstructured clinical interviews are more commonly used than structured interviews in applied clinical settings. Structured diagnostic interviews, such as the Structured Clinical Interview for *DSM-IV* Axis I Disorders (SCID) or Diagnostic Interview Schedule (DIS), are widely used in research studies. In his chapter in this volume, Craig points out that structured interviews generally lead to more reliable inferences and judgments than unstructured interviews. However, he also acknowledges that diagnoses resulting from one structured interview do not necessarily agree with those resulting from other structured interviews.

Craig concludes that relatively little information exists about the validity of interviewing as an assessment method, largely because interview-based data typically are used as criterion measures against which other methods are evaluated.

This is especially true with structured diagnostic interviews, which often are seen as the gold standard. Craig maintains that a basic problem that limits the reliability and validity of interview-based judgments is the lack of clear and explicit definitions and criteria for determining the presence and extent of specific personality characteristics and symptoms of psychopathology.

Craig points out that there is an increasing use of computer-assisted interviewing, and some of the structured diagnostic interviews were designed specifically for computerized use. Computerized interviews utilize less professional time and therefore are more cost-effective. It is interesting to note that most people have a positive reaction to the computerized interview format and are more likely to acknowledge problems and symptoms in a computerized interview than in a clinician-conducted interview. Computerized interviews generally lead to more reliable inferences or judgments about patients than do clinician-conducted interviews. In addition, they are likely to reduce sources of error associated with interviewer biases.

Behavioral Approaches

The behavioral assessment chapter in this volume by O'Brien, McGrath, and Haynes describes an approach that is founded on assumptions of empiricism and environmental determinism that arose from new developments in theory and research in the behavioral sciences. The authors recognize that cognitive-behavioral conceptualizations of behavior have become increasingly complex due to advances in research and a broadening of assumptions. A typical assessment, therefore, requires that the behaviorally oriented researchers and clinicians recognize the increasing complexities of human behavior in order to decipher the functional relationships among target behaviors and contextual factors. O'Brien and his coauthors also discuss the need for familiarity with new sampling and assessment methods combined with strategies for identifying functional relationships to empirically identify the root causes of behaviors. The authors note that each method has strengths and limitations that influence the degree of clinical utility.

O'Brien et al. indicate that intuitive and statistical procedures can be used to evaluate hypothesized causal functional relationships, but intuitive evaluation is often inaccurate (also see Garb's chapter in this volume). They urge the use of statistical approaches that can provide better information on the strength of functional relationships, and they suggest that practitioners use conditional probability analyses because they require only a modest amount of data, are easily understood, and are convenient to use. They note, however, that this approach is limited to the evaluation of only a few variables and appears to be incompatible with typical clinical settings.

O'Brien and his coauthors suggest a number of avenues for future research, including the examination of the treatment utility of behavioral assessment. They suggest that it will be especially important to examine the extent to which individualized treatments based on behavioral assessment outperform other treatment protocols. They strongly urge researchers to determine the treatment utility of behavioral assessment in relation to idiographic treatment design and standardized treatment-client matching. Their chapter, like others in this volume, illustrates the evolution of behavioral methods and the increasing recognition of the complexities of human performance.

Projective Approaches

Projective techniques have long been a part of psychological assessments, although recent surveys suggest that their popularity in most settings has been declining somewhat (e.g., Camara, Nathan, & Puente, 2000). In fact, the Rorschach inkblots are almost synonymous with psychology in the minds of many laypersons. As Viglione and Barker discuss in their chapter in this volume, various approaches to the interpretation of projective data have been developed and employed. In most settings, content analysis, in which responses are seen as a reflection of a person's unconscious, has given way to more empirically based approaches (e.g., Exner's Comprehensive System). Although these more empirical approaches have become quite popular, critics have raised questions about the reliability and validity of interpretations based on the scoring systems and about the norms used to generate interpretive statements.

Lilienfeld et al. (2000) reviewed literature concerning the validity of inferences based on three major projective techniques (human figure drawings; Thematic Apperception Test, or TAT; Rorschach). They concluded that there is no consistent empirical support for the relationship between specific drawing characteristics and either personality or psychopathology. Although they found some support for using global scoring methods to distinguish psychopathological individuals from nonclinical persons, they point out that the effects of artistic ability have not been taken into account adequately and that there are no consistent research findings suggesting that human figure drawings possess incremental validity above and beyond that associated with demographic information and with other psychometric data.

Lilienfeld et al. (2000) concluded that there is modest support for the construct validity of several TAT scoring schemes, particularly those assessing need for achievement and object relations. However, survey data have suggested that few clinicians who use the TAT use any of these scoring schemes, relying instead on subjective, content-based interpretations, which tend to lead to the overpathologizing of respondents (e.g., Pinkerman, Haynes, & Keiser, 1993; Wade & Baker, 1977).

Although many clinicians believe that Exner's Comprehensive System (CS) for the Rorschach has improved its validity, Lilienfeld et al. (2000) concluded that the scientific status of the CS is less than convincing. They maintained that the norms used for some Rorschach variables lead to misclassification of many normal individuals as psychopathological, that the interrater and test-retest reliabilities of many of the CS variables are weak or unknown, and that there is at best limited support for the validity of most CS variables and indexes. They cite research supporting the use of some Rorschach variables for the identification of schizophrenia, borderline personality disorder, and perhaps schizotypal personality disorder and bipolar disorder. Other Rorschach variables seem to be correlated with thought disturbance, psychotherapy prognosis, and dependency. Lilienfeld et al. (2000) concluded that most of the variables for which there is empirical support are not part of the CS and are not routinely scored or interpreted by Rorschach users. However, Weiner (1996) described what he maintained to be four demonstrably valid uses of the Rorschach, and all involve indexes included in the CS.

Supporters of the Rorschach and other projective techniques have responded to the criticisms of Lilienfeld et al. by pointing out methodological deficiencies in many of the studies reviewed (e.g., use of untrained examiners, unrepresentative samples) and suggesting that the review is not objective and scientific (Meyer, 2000; Weiner, 2000, 2001). They also point out that the review of individual Rorschach variables does not do justice to the complex and interactive ways in which variables are conceptualized in the CS. Exner (2002) reported some preliminary data for a contemporary normative sample involving representative sampling and use of trained examiners. He concluded that these data support the appropriateness of the original CS norms.

The issues being debated by critics and supporters of projective techniques are quite complex and not readily resolved. It is beyond the scope of this chapter to reach conclusions about these issues. However, it seems clear to us that we need less emotional approaches to the issues and methodologically sophisticated research studies designed to address specific issues.

In their chapter in this volume, Viglione and Barker suggest that the debate about the relative validity of objective and projective approaches to assessment may reflect differences between psychologists in academic and applied settings. They see academic psychologists as needing to promote their scientific status and doing so by attacking projective techniques. They see psychologists in clinical settings as being rather uncritical in their acceptance of the validity and usefulness of a wide variety of assessment and therapeutic techniques. Viglione and Barker see the continuing debate as philosophical and moral, not scientific. They emphasize that each assessment approach has its strengths and weaknesses and that we all should be trying to determine how they could be combined to achieve a better understanding of those we evaluate. In their chapter Viglione and Barker describe an approach to Rorschach interpretation that views a projective test as involving a new and unfamiliar situation in which one organizes incomplete, contradictory, and ambiguous material without any direct feedback from observers or authorities. How respondents complete this problem-solving task should have implications for how they deal with many important tasks in their real lives. Of course, relationships between problem-solving in responding to projective test stimuli and problem-solving in real-life situations need to be demonstrated empirically.

Self-Report Approaches

Self-report approaches in psychological assessment typically involve asking respondents to indicate whether—and sometimes to what extent—particular symptoms, behaviors, and personality descriptors are characteristic of them. Survey data indicate that self-report inventories generally, and the MMP-2 specifically, are the most widely used methods of psychological assessment in the United States (Camara et al., 2000).

In his chapter in this volume Ben-Porath traces the use of self-report measures over more than seven decades, pointing out the major strengths and weakness of this assessment approach. Self-report inventories have been developed to assess various dimensions of psychopathology as well as normal personality functioning. Early scales were constructed using empirical procedures and gave little attention to the content of items. More contemporary scales (e.g., MMPI-2 content scales) have emphasized the selection of items based on the relevance of their content to the constructs being assessed. Ben-Porath indicates that it is important to demonstrate the content validity (i.e., the extent to which items adequately cover the relevant content domain for the constructs being assessed) and the empirical and eventually the construct validity of these content-based scales.

In his chapter Ben-Porath discusses criticisms of self-report inventories (especially the MMPI/MMPI-2) by those

convinced that their scales measure only response sets such as social desirability and acquiescence (e.g., Edwards, 1964; Messick & Jackson, 1961) and the rebuttals by those who demonstrated empirically that the scales account for valid variance even when the effects of these response sets are removed (e.g., Block, 1965). It is extremely difficult to determine to what extent the manner in which respondents approach self-report inventories represents error variance as opposed to valid variance in the constructs being assessed.

One advantage of some self-report inventories (e.g., MMPI-2, Personality Assessment Inventory) is that they include scales and indexes for assessing tendencies of respondents to over- or underreport problems and symptoms to create the impression of being more adjusted or maladjusted that they really are. Much evidence has accumulated, for example, suggesting that the validity scales of the MMPI-2 can detect malingering and defensiveness even when respondents have been given information about the disorders to be feigned or denied and the validity scales designed to detect their invalid responding.

Self-report inventories lend themselves readily to computer administration, scoring, and interpretation. In his chapter in this volume Butcher describes ways in which computer technology contributes to psychological assessment. Ben-Porath stresses the need to demonstrate that norms based on standard administration of tests are applicable to computer-administered versions, and Butcher emphasizes the importance of determining empirically the validity of computer-generated inferences and statements. Many self-report inventories, including the MMPI and MMPI-2, have come to be used in settings quite different from those in which the instruments were developed and normed. As Ben-Porath stresses in his chapter, future research should focus on determining the extent to which empirical correlates of scales established in one setting are equally valid in other settings.

CONCLUDING ISSUES IN ASSESSMENT PSYCHOLOGY

Assessment psychology is an important and viable specialty within the discipline of psychology and in many instances is at a defining point in its development. Many of the methods of assessment in use today were developed during the early part of the twentieth century, and the field is now in need of redefinition. The considerable base of knowledge that has defined the field as a subdiscipline in psychology is both an advantage and a limitation. The vast amount of research and knowledge in the field provides considerable advantage because we have been able to better detect and understand various attributes of people and how these attributes relate to a variety of factors such as job performance, academic achievement, personality, job performance, social interactions, and so forth. The accumulation of information creates a base of knowledge that has been used by researchers and clinicians alike as the foundation of their efforts. Although this provides a comfortable footing for practice, it is not without limitations.

The current state of the art in assessment psychology raises a variety of important issues. For example, procedures are being used in settings different from those in which they were developed and normed. The MMPI was developed for diagnosis in inpatient psychiatric settings, but it is used now in personnel selection, medical settings, correctional settings, and so on. The adequacy of the original norms and the validity of inferences in these broader settings must be demonstrated empirically. This raises questions about the comparison of performance in a unique setting to the performance in settings existing in the original normative group. The limitation on generalizability of interpretive inferences in these other settings warrants greater attention. Similarly, conventional IQ tests were originally developed to sort people on the basis of overall general ability, but now the tests are used for many types of diagnostic purposes (learning disabilities, attention deficit disorders, etc.) for which the tests were not intended and that research has not supported (see Wasserman's chapter in this volume).

Another of the more thorny issues in assessment psychology involves the debate on clinical versus actuarial (statistical) decision making. The debate continues between those who advocate practices supported by clinical experience and those who stress the need for empirically supported decision-making. This issue cuts across many dimensions of assessment psychology and involves most tests and methods. For example, research on clinical judgment (see Garb's chapter in this volume) alerts practitioners that they need to know the empirical support for the methods they use and that they should *not* use an instrument or treatment method merely because it seems to work. Similarly, interpretations of subtest or subscale scores obtained from tests of personality and intelligence, for example, that have not been empirically validated should not be made. This tendency is especially evident in the practice of intelligence test subtest analysis. The limitations of assessment psychology have not gone unnoticed by those who pay for this information, especially the insurance industry.

The influences of managed care companies and the resulting reduction in reimbursements for evaluation and treatment pose a considerable challenge to assessment psychology. Clinicians have seen how managed care has encouraged brief, symptom-focused measures and the need to demonstrate that assessment contributes to successful outcomes in efficient, cost-effective ways. One new effort in assessment psychology that fits some of these needs is the application of computer technology, which can reduce costs by utilizing less expensive methods of administration, scoring, and interpretation of assessment instruments. Another new technology is adaptive testing, which, like others, requires considerable empirical justification, but represents an important evolution in the field of assessment psychology.

Perhaps the most serious impediment to the future advancement of assessment psychology is the conservative nature of the industry and of many in the profession, which has led to the overreliance on conventional practices. Apparent in many of the chapters in this volume, with some notable exceptions (e.g., neuropsychology), is a strong reliance on traditional instrumentation. Clinicians tend to use what they learned in their training programs and are resistant to change. For example, despite that fact that the Wechsler scales represent a technology developed in the early 1900s, the instrument continues to be widely used in a variety of settings. Moreover, training of new graduate students is inadequate, is limited to traditional instruments, and emphasizes tests over a problem-solving approach that views tests and other evaluative methods as part of an overall assessment process (see the chapter by Handler and Clemence in this volume). The future development of assessment psychology will determine whether the field can evolve into the mature science described by Wasserman in his chapter in this volume on assessment of intelligence. The field has excellent potential, which is perhaps most apparent in its emergence as a viable specialty within the discipline of psychology. Division 12 (Clinical Psychology) of the American Psychological Association recently approved an assessment psychology section, and the American Board of Assessment Psychology continues to evaluate credentials of assessment psychologists and to advocate for assessment as an important part of the science and practice of psychology. Despite these successes, there are important challenges ahead for assessment psychology.

Changes in the way graduate students are educated must occur if assessment psychology is to evolve into a mature science. There has been far too much emphasis on traditional instruments and approaches. For example the MMPI-2, Wechsler scales, TAT, and Rorschach are still the most widely taught and used assessment instruments, and not enough training has occurred on innovative approaches. Some examples of more innovative approaches include the five-factor model of personality and resulting instruments (PSY-5 scales for MMPI-2; Harkness, McNulty, & Ben-Porath, 1995), neuroimaging techniques in neuropsychology (functional Magnetic Resonance Imaging), and cognitive processing approaches to intelligence (e.g., Cognitive Assessment System; Naglieri & Das, 1997). These new efforts require attention in training programs, and these programs need to focus more on the purposes for which the assessments are conducted than on the tests themselves. Additionally, there is a dire need to demonstrate more clearly the link between assessment and intervention, especially as it relates to cognitive measures and educational interventions as well as personality measures and treatment planning (e.g., therapeutic assessment work by Finn and colleagues (Finn, 1996). Finally, credentialing and certification of assessment psychologists that includes uniform standards and compulsory evaluation of those conducting assessments should be mandated. The future advancement of assessment psychology will also be related to how well disputes in the field can be resolved. Although there is very strong and positive evidence on the value of psychological testing and assessment and much research has been accumulated, virtually every approach and technique has been criticized by some and defended by others. Some of the controversies (for example, the dispute over projective tests) have led to conclusions that a particular method should not be used. Rather than arguing against use of a method, we believe that the worth of any assessment technique must be determined empirically through systematic research. An important focus of this type of research is to demonstrate that inferences based on the technique are related to *specific* uses that occur in *specific* applications of the *specific* instrument. For example, is the form quality of responses by adults to inkblots related to disturbed thinking? Are scores on the Depression content scale of the MMPI-2 related to symptoms of clinical depression? Can results for a particular type of projective test (e.g., Draw-A-Person) be used for general identification of emotional problems rather than the specific diagnosis of children? In other words, for what purposes (and in what circumstances) are various scales and measures valid?

Some argue that advancement in assessment psychology is limited because the issues involved are so complex. Others suggest that researchers advocating any method or instrument (e.g., behavioral vs. projective; MMPI-2 vs. Rorschach) are not very objective. Still others contend that we can expect only limited advances in assessment psychology as long as we continue to use and study instruments and approaches that are many decades old. Additionally, some argue that instruments and procedures developed for use in one setting have been employed in other settings without adequate examination of the validity of such applications. We believe that all of these factors contribute to limited advancements in assessment psychology. It seems that what is needed are comprehensive and innovative studies conducted by reasonably impartial assessment researchers.

Our position is that the validity and usefulness of any psychological instrument must be established empirically for the specific purposes and in the specific settings in which the instruments are to be used. This is equally true for interviews, tests of cognitive processes, interest and achievement tests, objective approaches, and projective techniques. As Weiner emphasizes in the opening chapter to this volume, and as others have echoed in subsequent chapters, the most valid and useful psychological assessments are likely to result when data from various sources and instruments are integrated to address important questions and problems.

FUTURE OF ASSESSMENT PSYCHOLOGY

Assessment psychology is alive and well and taking place in many different settings. Although considerable work is needed to demonstrate the validity and cost-effectiveness of assessment, much evidence already exists that psychologists can use to promote assessment. Although managed care may be seen as a threat to assessment psychology, it also provides opportunities and stimulus to help the profession grow into a more mature science (see Maruish's chapter in this volume). Only time will tell if the next 100 years of assessment psychology will be more of the same or if innovative approaches will develop and be embraced. However, it is clear that although traditional instruments and methods have allowed assessment psychology to develop into a viable subdiscipline of psychology, they cannot sustain the field for another 100 years because so many of the goals of assessment have changed. The assessment needs of today and tomorrow are not the same as those present when traditional tests and methods were developed in the early 1900s. Assessment psychology must meet these new demands to continue its evolution into a mature science and a strong subdiscipline of psychology.

REFERENCES

Block, J. (1965). *The challenge of response sets: Unconfounding meaning, acquiescence, and social desirability in the MMPI.* New York: Appleton-Century-Crofts.

Bornstein, R. F. (2001). Clinical utility of the Rorschach Inkblot Method: Reframing the debate. *Journal of Personality Assessment, 77,* 48–70.

Camara, W. J., Nathan, J. S., & Puente, A. E. (2000). Psychological test usage: Implications in professional psychology. *Professional Psychology: Research and Practice, 31,* 141–154.

Daw, J. (2001). Psychological assessments shown to be as valid as medical tests. *APA Monitor, 32*(7), 46–47.

DuBois, P. H. (1970). *A history of psychological testing.* Boston: Allyn & Bacon.

Edwards. A. L. (1957*). The social desirability variable in personality assessment and research.* New York: Dryden.

Edwards, A. L. (1964). Social desirability and performance on the MMPI. *Psychometrika, 29,* 295–308.

Eisman, E. J., Dies, R. R., Finn, S. E., Eyde, L. D., Kay, G. G., Kubiszyn, T. W., et al. (2000). Problems and limitations in using psychological assessment in the contemporary health care delivery system. *Professional Psychology: Research and Practice, 31,* 131–140.

Exner, J. E., Jr. (2002). A new nonpatient sample for the Rorschach Comprehensive System: A progress report. *Journal of Personality Assessment, 78,* 391–404.

Finn, S. E. (1996). *Manual for using the MMPI-2 as a therapeutic intervention.* Minneapolis: University of Minnesota Press.

Graham, J. R., & Lilly, R. S. (1984). *Psychological testing.* Englewood Cliffs, NJ: Prentice-Hall.

Groth-Marnat, G. (1999). Financial efficacy of clinical assessment: Rational guidelines and issues for future research. *Journal of Clinical Psychology, 55,* 813–824.

Harkness, A. R., McNulty, J. L., & Ben-Porath, Y. S. (1995). The personality psychopathology five (PSY-5): Constructs and MMPI-2 scales. *Psychological Assessment, 7,* 104–114.

Lilienfeld, S. O., Wood, J. M., & Garb, H. N. (2000). The scientific status of projective techniques. *Psychological Science in the Public Interest, 1,* 27–66.

Megargee, E. I., Carbonell, J. L., Bohn, M. J., & Sliger, G. L. (2001). *Classifying criminal offenders with the MMPI-2: The Megargee system.* Minneapolis: University of Minnesota Press.

Messick, S., & Jackson, D. N. (1961). Acquiescence and the factorial interpretation of the MMPI. *Psychological Bulletin, 58,* 299–304.

Meyer, G. J. (2000). On the science of Rorschach research. *Journal of Personality Assessment, 75,* 46–81.

Meyer, G. J., & Archer, R. P. (2001). The hard science of Rorschach research: What do we know and where do we go? *Psychological Assessment, 13,* 486–502.

Meyer, G. J., Finn, S. E., Eyde, L. D., Kay, G. G., Moreland, K. L., Dies, R. R., et al. (2001). Psychological testing and psychological assessment: A review of evidence and issues. *American Psychologist, 56,* 128–165.

Naglieri, J. A., & Das, J. P. (1997). *Cognitive Assessment System.* Itasca, IL: Riverside.

Palmigiano v. Garrahy, 443 F. Supp. 956 (D.R.I. 1977).

Phelps, R., Eisman, E. J., & Kohout, J. (1998). Psychological practice and managed care: Results of the CAPP practitioner survey. *Professional Psychology: Research and Practice, 29,* 31–36.

Pinkerman, J. E., Haynes, J. P., & Keiser, T. (1993). Characteristics of psychological practice in juvenile court clinics. *American Journal of Forensic Psychology, 11,* 3–12.

Piotrowski, C., Belter, R. W., & Keller, J. W. (1998). The impact of "managed care" on the practice of psychological testing: Preliminary findings. *Journal of Personality Assessment, 70,* 441–447.

Shaffer, T. W., Erdberg, P., & Haroian, J. (1999). Current nonpatient data for he Rorschach, WAIS, and MMPI-2. *Journal of Personality Assessment, 73,* 305–316.

Wade, T. C., & Baker, T. B. (1977). Opinion and use of psychological tests. *American Psychologist, 32,* 874–882.

Weiner, I. B. (1996). Some observations on the validity of the Rorschach Inkblot method. *Psychological Assessment, 8,* 206–213.

Weiner, I. B. (2000). Making Rorschach interpretation as good as it can be. *Journal of Personality Assessment, 74,* 164–174.

Weiner, I. B. (2001). Considerations in collecting Rorschach reference data. *Journal of Personality Assessment, 77,* 122–127.

Yoakum, C. S., & Yerkes, R. M. (1920). *Army mental tests.* New York: Holt.

Author Index

Subject Index

16 Personality Factor Questionnaire (16PF), 328, 559
  computerized assessment and, 148, 149–150
  I/O settings and, assessment in, 328

Abuse:
  sexual, 173
  substance, 226, 308–309, 498
Academic Competence Evaluation Scale (ACES), 268, 283–284
Academic Intervention Monitoring System (AIMS), 268, 283–284
Acculturation, 105–106
Activities of daily living (ADLs):
  geriatric settings and, assessment in, 401, 582
  instrumental (IADLs), 404, 582
Actuarial prediction. *See* Prediction, actuarial
Adolescent Behavior Checklist, 268
Adolescent Psychopathology Scale (APS), 252–253, 268
Adult Internal Management System (AIMS): correctional system,
    assessment in, 376–377
Affective disorders, 458–459. *See also specific types*
African Americans:
  correctional system, assessment in, 374
  Kaufman Assessment Battery for Children (K-ABC) and, 424
  neuropsychological functioning and, 459
  older adults, assessment of, 391
  teaching personality assessment and, 195
  test bias and, 73–74, 77–79, 80–83, 85–86
Age, interest assessment and, 475
Age Discrimination in Employment Act of 1967 (ADEA), 325
Ageism. *See under* Geriatric settings, assessment in
Agitation, in older adults, 396
AIDS. *See* HIV/AIDS
Alaska Natives, 195
Alcohol Use Inventory, 224
Alzheimer's disease, 6, 293, 298–299
  early detection, 150
  hearing loss and, 393
  intellectual functioning and, assessment of, 435
  neuropsychological functioning and, 459
American Academy of Forensic Psychology, 345, 346
American Association for Correctional Psychologists (AACP), 366,
    368, 369, 370, 584
American Association on Mental Retardation (AAMR), 434
American Board of Professional Psychology (ABPP), 32, 33
American College Test (ACT). *See* Unisex Edition of the ACT Interest
    Inventory (UNIACT)
American College Testing Program, 176
American Correctional Association (ACA), 366
American Educational Research Association, 155
American Guidance Service (AGS), 423
American Personnel and Guidance Association, 68
American Psychiatric Association, 366
American Psychological Association (APA), 580

Committee for the Advancement of Professional Practice (CAPP), 132
Committee on Professional Standards, 142
computerized psychological assessment and, 155
correctional settings, assessment in, 366, 375
cross-cultural psychology and, 95, 104
ethics and, 166, 168, 169, 170, 172, 177–178
forensic assessments and, 345, 346–348, 349
involvement in medical education, 293
lawsuits against managed health care companies, 294
Psychological Assessment Work Group, 6
sampling and, 48
teaching personality assessment and, 188–189, 196, 198–199,
    200, 204
test bias and, 68, 79
therapeutic assessment and, 121
treatment and, assessment in, 132
American Psychologist, 176
American Psychology Law Society, 345, 358
American Public Health Association, 366
American Sign Language (ASL), 263, 283
Americans with Disabilities Act (ADA), 169, 263, 318, 325, 335, 338
Analysis of variance (ANOVA), 80, 85, 525
Anchor items, 111
Anorexia, 21. *See also* Bulimia; Eating disorders
Anoxia, 395
Antidepressants, 237
Antisocial personality disorder, 21
Anxiety:
  mental health settings and, assessment in
    adults, 226
    children, 236, 238, 255
  in older adults, 394, 395
  surgical interventions and, 304
APA Monitor, 176
"Appropriate Use of High Stakes Testing in Our Nation's
    Schools," 177
Aptitude by treatment interactions (ATI), 53–54
Area transformations, 50
Arizona Social Support Interview Schedule, 404
Armed Services Vocational Aptitude Battery (ASVAB), 472
Army Alpha, 105
Army Beta, 105
Army General Classification, 318
Army Mental Testing Program, 585
Arrhythmias, 395
Artificial intelligence. *See* Intelligence, artificial
Ascendance-Submission measure, 555
Asian Americans:
  cross-cultural psychology and, 95
  older adults, assessment of, 391
  teaching personality assessment and, 195
  test bias and, 74, 78

Heart failure, 395
Hecaen, Henry, 444
Heuristics:
    availability, 36
    cognitive, 35
Higher Cortical Functions in Man, 444
High-stakes tests, 55, 177–178, 265
Hindsight bias. *See* Bias, hindsight
Hispanic Americans:
    cross-cultural psychology and, 95, 102, 103
    Kaufman Assessment Battery for Children (K-ABC) and, 424
    older adults, assessment of, 391
    teaching personality assessment and, 195
    test bias and, 86, 87
    See also Mexican Americans
HIV/AIDS, 293, 310
Hoffman-La Roche Laboratories, 142–143
Hogan Personality Inventory (HPI), 323, 330–331
Hogan Personnel Selection Series, 331
Holland Vocational Preference Inventory (VPI), 8, 327, 332
Holt Primary Process Scale, 194, 203
Hopi, 391
Hostility and Paranoid Ideation Scales, 308
Human Resources Development Report (HRDR), 149–150
Humor, as interviewing technique, 494
Huntington's disease, 150
Hypertension, 31, 395
Hypothetical construct, 69
Hypothetico-deductive methods, 510
Hypoxia, 395

Idiographic focus, 538
Idiographic science. *See* Science, nomothetic/idiographic
If-then statements, 27
Illinois Test of Psycholinguistic Ability (ITPA), 436
Illusions, in older adults, 396
Illusory correlation, 33–34
Immediate Post-Concussion Assessment and Cognitive Testing (ImPACT), 451–452, 586
Impressions, environmental, 20–21
Inception, formal, 493
Independent Living Scales, 460
Individual dimensionality, 320
Individualized education plan (IEP), 166–167
Individuals with Disabilities Education Act (IDEA), 169, 263, 435
Individual training needs, 319
Industrial/organizational settings, assessment in:
    approaches, 321
    assessment data and organizational decisions, 322–323
    attributes measured, 320–321
    focus, 327–330
    major issues
        business care, 333–336
        social policy, 338–339
        technical issues, 336–338
    marketplace and business care, 321–322
    overview, 317–319, 582–583
    purposes, 319–320, 325–327
    self-report inventories and, 573
    technical parameters, 323–325
    tools, 330–333

Inferred Abilities and Influences Chart, 427
Influence, examiner's, 8
Injury cases, personal, 17
Inquiry, detailed, 493
Insanity, 4
Insomnia, in older adults, 396
Instructional Environment Scale-II (TIES-II), 267
Intake interview, 377–378
Intellectual functioning:
    diagnostic classification and, 433–435
    intervention and, 435–438
    major intelligence tests, descriptions of, 418–433
    overview, 417–418, 438, 585
Intelligence:
    artificial, 143, 204
    crystallized, 423
    fluid, 423
    interpersonal, 204
    intrapersonal, 204
    practical, 204
Intelligent Testing with the WISC-R, 542
Interactive voice response (IVR) systems, 136, 311
Interdomain theory, 478
Interest Determination, Exploration, and Assessment System (IDEAS), 472, 480
Interest-Finder Quiz, 469, 472, 480
Interests, assessment of:
    definitions, 467–468
    development, 468
    group differences, 475–477
    interest-ability-personality relationships, 478
    interest-ability relationships, 478
    interest-personality relationships, 477–478
    measurement, 468–473
    overview, 467, 480, 585–586
    reliability of, 473
    research areas, needed, 478–480
    validity of, 473–475
Interest theory, 475
Internalizing disorders, 237–238, 254–255
International Classification of Diseases (ICD), 295
    ICD-9, 515
    ICD-10, 123, 217, 435, 489
"International Conference on Test Adaptation: Adapting Tests for Use in Multiple Languages and Cultures," 106
International Diagnostic Interview (CIDI-Auto), computerized version of, 502
International Neuropsychological Society, 444
International Test Commission, 103, 106, 169
Internet. *See under* Computer technology, psychological assessment of
Interpretations:
    idiographic, 15–16
    as interviewing technique, 494
    nomothetic, 15–16
Interrater comparisons, 246–247
Intervening variable, 69
Interventions, surgical, 304–305
Interviewing, 218–219, 220, 223, 224, 226–227, 231
    behavioral assessment, 519
    case history, 489
    client's approach, 491–492